Frommer's

Cruises

& Ports of Call

From U.S. & Canadian Home Ports to the Caribbean, Alaska, Hawaii & More

2008

by Heidi Sarna & Matt Hannafin

Here's what the critics say about Frommer's:

"Amazingly easy to use. Very portable, very complete."

—*Booklist*

"Detailed, accurate, and easy-to-read information for all price ranges."

—*Glamour Magazine*

"Strategies for getting the best price, including when to book. Ship ratings, cabin evaluation."

—*Newark Star Ledger*

". . . is one of the most thorough, easy-to-navigate references that has stats, reviews and realties of both ships and ports."

—*Pittsburgh Post Gazette*

Wiley Publishing, Inc.

Published by:

Wiley Publishing, Inc.

111 River St.

Hoboken, NJ 07030-5774

ISBN: 978-0-470-13735-2

Editor: Naomi Kraus
with Leslie Shen and Anuja Madar
Production Editors: Heather Wilcox, Lindsay Conner
Cartographer: Guy Ruggiero
Photo Editor: Richard Fox
Anniversary Logo Design: Richard Pacifico
Production by Wiley Indianapolis Composition Services

For information on our other products and services or to obtain technical support, please contact our Customer Care Department within the U.S. at 800/762-2974, outside the U.S. at 317/572-3993 or fax 317/572-4002.

Wiley also publishes its books in a variety of electronic formats. Some content that appears in print may not be available in electronic formats.

Manufactured in the United States of America

5 4 3 2 1

Contents

Part 1: Planning, Booking & Preparing for Your Cruise

1 Choosing Your Ideal Cruise   19

2 Booking Your Cruise & Getting the Best Price   38

3 Things to Know Before You Go 62

4 The Cruise Experience 73

Part 2: The Cruise Lines & Their Ships

5 The Ratings & How to Read Them 95

6 The Mainstream Lines 110

7 The Ultraluxury Lines 269

8 Small Ships, Sailing Ships & Adventure Cruises 323

Part 3: The Ports

9 The Ports of Embarkation 403

10 The Caribbean, The Bahamas & the Panama Canal 517

11 Alaska & British Columbia   609

12 The Mexican Riviera & Baja   636

13 Bermuda   652

14 Hawaii   658

15 New England & Eastern Canada   674

16 U.S. River Cruise Routes   690

Index   702

List of Maps

About the Authors

Heidi Sarna is a freelance writer who has sailed the oceans blue for more than a decade, often with her young twin sons and lucky husband in tow. Coauthor of *Frommer's European Cruises & Ports of Call* and a contributor to several other guidebooks, she also writes regular travel columns for Frommers.com. She's written for many magazines, newspapers, and websites, including *Forbes Traveler,* the *International Herald Tribune, Condé Nast Traveler, Gourmet, Parenting, Brides, Modern Bride,* the *Boston Herald,* and *Travel Weekly.*

Matt Hannafin is a freelance writer, editor, and musician based in Portland, Oregon. Coauthor of *Frommer's European Cruises & Ports of Call,* he also contributes to dozens of books, newspapers, magazines, and websites, including Frommers.com, *Gourmet, Modern Bride,* the *Boston Herald, Travel Weekly, Porthole,* and *Avid Cruiser.* In 2007 he was a major contributor to the book *1,000 Places to See in the U.S.A. & Canada Before You Die,* writing nearly a quarter of the entries. His editing clients include U.N. agencies, book publishers, and major consultancy firms, and his musical activities range from teaching Persian classical percussion to performances of contemporary free improvisation.

Acknowledgments

A select group of travel writers and experts contributed to this book. **Mike Driscoll,** editor of the probing industry newsletter *Cruise Week,* provided insights into current booking trends. Merchant Marine officer and travel writer **Ben Lyons** wrote our new review of American Cruise Lines and helped out on a few other lines too. Our editor, **Naomi Kraus,** kept our Orlando coverage up to date. Big thanks go out to Frommer's authors **Lesley Abravanel, Mary Herczog, Marie Morris, Bill Goodwin, Matthew Poole, Mary K. Tilghman, Leslie Brokaw, Lauren McCutcheon,** and **Mark Hiss,** who helped out with our ports of embarkation coverage. We also appreciate the efforts **Felisa Mahabal** and Steamship Historical Society of America director **Steve Swanson** put into updating our Caribbean coverage. For their work in previous editions of this book, big thanks go to writer/biologist **Dr. Christina Colon,** SeaTrade Cruise Review U.S. editor **Anne Kalosh,** cruise expert **Art Sbarsky,** travel journalist **Marilyn Green,** ship authority and author **Ted Scull,** writer/travelers **Ken Lindley** and **Darlene Simidian,** and passenger ship expert **Alan Zamchick.**

Lastly, Matt would like to thank his wife, **Rebecca,** who thinks writing about cruises is a really strange way to make a living (or at least part of one). Ain't that the truth. Heidi thanks her best shipmates, twin sons **Kavi and Tejas,** for being such good sailors at the ripe old age of five (15 cruises and counting), and salutes hubby **Arun** for going along with the crazy cruising life all these years.

An Invitation to the Reader

In researching this book, we discovered many wonderful places—hotels, restaurants, shops, and more. We're sure you'll find others. Please tell us about them, so we can share the information with your fellow travelers in upcoming editions. If you were disappointed with a recommendation, we'd love to know that, too. Please write to:

Frommer's Cruises & Ports of Call 2008
Wiley Publishing, Inc. • 111 River St. • Hoboken, NJ 07030-5774

An Additional Note

Please be advised that travel information is subject to change at any time—and this is especially true of prices. We therefore suggest that you write or call ahead for confirmation when making your travel plans. The authors, editors, and publisher cannot be held responsible for the experiences of readers while traveling. Your safety is important to us, however, so we encourage you to stay alert and be aware of your surroundings. Keep a close eye on cameras, purses, and wallets, all favorite targets of thieves and pickpockets.

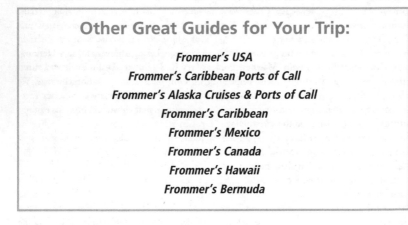

Other Great Guides for Your Trip:

Frommer's USA

Frommer's Caribbean Ports of Call

Frommer's Alaska Cruises & Ports of Call

Frommer's Caribbean

Frommer's Mexico

Frommer's Canada

Frommer's Hawaii

Frommer's Bermuda

Frommers.com

Now that you have this guidebook to help you plan a great trip, visit our website at **www.frommers.com** for additional travel information on more than 3,600 destinations. We update features regularly to give you instant access to the most current trip-planning information available. At Frommers.com, you'll find scoops on the best airfares, lodging rates, and car rental bargains. You can even book your travel online through our reliable travel booking partners. Other popular features include:

- Online updates of our most popular guidebooks
- Vacation sweepstakes and contest giveaways
- Newsletters highlighting the hottest travel trends
- Online travel message boards with featured travel discussions

Cruising 2008: Big Boats, Big Business

If you've picked up this book, it's unlikely we have to talk you into a cruise—that idea's probably already in your head. And anyway, it's not our job to try to talk you into anything. We know some people just love traveling by ship and others just hate it. We also know that some people just *assume* they'd hate it, without having the full story.

Because, y'know, it's a pretty big story, and new chapters are being added every year. Time was, the cruise biz was a pretty homogenous cow, attracting mostly older folks plus a smattering of honeymooners and party-makers. They're all still there, but today so is everyone else: young families, young professionals, young couples in Harley shirts, baggy-jeans teens, middle-aged gym rats, multigenerational family groups, Democrats, Republicans, Rastafarians, and a corps of Canadians, Brits, and other "others" to help us all get along.

In a certain sense, it's an old-fashioned kind of vacation, a shout back to the old European Grand Tours, with travelers hitting a region's high points in quick succession—bam, bam, bam—then getting back aboard ship to socialize with people who were strangers until circumstance pushed them together. In another sense, though, cruising is a thoroughly modern Millie, where the newest ships are packed with every possible widget to win over prospective travelers and turn them into repeat customers. We'll be honest, though. It's not this stuff that grabs us—not the three-story theaters or sushi bars, not the rock-climbing walls or the hot rock massages or the surfing simulators, either. It's simply being at sea on a ship. It's the teak decks, white steel railings, thick mooring lines, and that distant rumble of the engines way down in the hull. It's the feeling that you've untethered yourself from the world, as you stand on deck at night, lean over the rail, and watch the waves break around your ship's bow as it heads to the next port of call. The sea: It's a powerful thing.

CRUISING TODAY: NEW SHIPS, MORE PAX

Between 2000 and 2007, the major lines launched some 80 new cruise ships, and that's not even counting foreign and small-ship cruise lines. Fortunately for the industry, they've been able to persuade more and more passengers (or "pax" in agent-speak) to come aboard to fill all those ships: Just over 3.6 million North Americans took a cruise in 1990. By 2005 that number was up to nearly 10 million and in 2007 it was expected to top 10.6 million, with many cruising from the growing number of home ports around the country.

The industry keeps on building new ships, though not quite at the pace of a few years back. Six major new vessels launched in 2007: Carnival's *Freedom,* NCL's *Norwegian Gem,* Princess's *Emerald Princess,* Royal Caribbean's *Liberty of the Seas,* Cunard's *Queen Victoria,* and Costa's *Costa Serena.* Additionally, the year saw the introduction of three slightly older, refurbished ships—Princess's *Royal Princess* and Azamara's *Journey* and *Quest,* all three midsize vessels originally built for Renaissance Cruises.

At press time, 2008 was shaping up to be a five-megaship year, with the new 86,000-ton, 2,044-passenger *Eurodam* scheduled for HAL; the 118,000-ton, 2,850-passenger *Solstice* scheduled for Celebrity; the 160,000-ton, 3,634-passenger *Independence of the Seas* coming for Royal Caribbean; the 112,000-ton, 3,006-passenger *Splendor* coming for Carnival; and the 133,500-ton, 3,300-passenger *Fantasia* and 89,000-ton, 2,550-passenger *Poesia* on deck for MSC.

With bookings up and the need to fill more new ships decreasing, the ridiculously low prices we were seeing just a few years ago have leveled off. You still won't pay brochure rates (see below), but $400 weeklong cruises are nowhere near as commonplace as they were.

THE REAL SCOOP ON CRUISE PRICES

Cruise pricing is really . . . well, dumb. Beyond the fuzzy math that often makes the new ships the cheapest to book, you also have the problem of brochure prices. Check out Brochure X, which lists a weeklong sailing at $1,900 per person for a standard outside cabin. Now click over to your favorite travel agency's website and you'll probably see that same cruise going for $699. What gives?

Just like new-car prices, cruise line brochure prices are notoriously inflated—in fact, some lines are talking about dropping them from brochures altogether. In the meantime, you should basically just ignore brochure rates. Everything, and we mean everything, is discounted. Other guidebooks and articles print those inflated brochure prices anyway, leaving it up to you to take a guess at what the real price may be. We don't. Instead, we've partnered with the agency **Just Cruisin' Plus** to provide you with the **actual prices** consumers were paying for cruises aboard all the ships reviewed in this book. Each review shows you approximately how much you can expect to pay for an inside cabin (one without windows), an outside cabin (with windows or a balcony), and a small suite, and in chapter 2 we provide a chart that shows how these prices compare with the published brochure rates, and with those of all the other ships in the book.

AND NOW, COMING TO A PORT NEAR YOU . . .

For the past 6 years, the big trend in the cruise world is putting ships where people can get to them. It seems like an obvious idea, but for decades the cruise lines only nibbled around its edges, homeporting most of their ships in Miami, Fort Lauderdale, Los Angeles, and a few other cities, and forcing people to fly to a port before their vacation could get underway. Today, ships are sailing regularly from more than two dozen **U.S. and Canadian home ports,** so unless you live in North Dakota, there's a good chance you can drive to your ship—saving yourself both time and money. While you're doing that, you may just want to stick around and see the sights, 'cause some of those port cities are pretty interesting, whether you're sailing to the **Caribbean** from New York, Charleston, Galveston, or New Orleans; to **Alaska** from Seattle, San Francisco, or Vancouver; to **Bermuda** from Baltimore, Boston, or Philly; to the **Mexican Riviera** from Los Angeles or San Diego; to **Hawaii** from Ensenada or right from Honolulu; or to **New England** from Norfolk or Montreal. When you add in small ships sailing from places such as Portland, Oregon; Warren, Rhode Island; and Memphis, Tennessee, you realize there's a whole lot of country out there to explore. In chapter 9, "The Ports of Embarkation," we discuss the high points of all the major cruise home ports, giving you the lowdown on what to see if you're going to be there only for a day or two pre- or post-cruise. Chapters 10 through 16 give you the scoop on all the major ports of call in all the so-called "homeland cruising" regions, with info on sights and attractions to see on your own as well as recommendations for the best shore excursions.

FINDING A SHIP IS EASY, BUT WILL YOU CLICK?

Comparing cruise ships and lines is like scanning an online dating site: "Attractive young cruise ship with nice body and good personality seeks friend for dating, possible relationship." The ship looks good, but we all know how photos can lie. Ditto for the descriptions.

Just like in dating, there are ships that you'll get along with and ships that you

won't. It's all a matter of personality. Your dream ship is probably out there, somewhere—you just need to figure out what you want. If those huge Vegas-style floating resorts you see advertised on TV aren't your cup of tea, there are also quiet, refined ships where you're left to do your own thing, with outstanding service staff standing by in case you need anything, anything at all. Other ships are more like intimate B&Bs, where the vibe is casual, the cabins are cozy, and the focus is all on history, culture, and the outdoors. A few are honest-to-God sailing ships that offer nostalgic adventure.

Chances are there's a ship out there with your name on it, and as your cruise matchmakers, we're here to help you wade through the different options and experiences and meet the cruise of your dreams. To do this, we've divided the cruise lines into three main categories— **mainstream lines** (chapter 6), **ultraluxury lines** (chapter 7), and **small ships, sailing ships, and adventure cruises** (chapter 8)—and developed a rating system that judges them only against other ships in the same category: megaship against megaship, luxe against luxe, small ship against small ship.

SAFETY AT SEA: MORE SECURITY, FEWER GERMS

For better or worse, we're currently living in a security-obsessed world. People have to show ID to get into office buildings, and take off their shoes to go through airport X-rays, so you'd better believe security measures are in place on cruise ships, too.

All the major cruise lines have their own **dedicated onboard security forces** who monitor people coming aboard (passengers, crew, delivery people, and contractors) and keep an eye out during the cruise, and we're not just talking the kind of rent-a-cops you see at your local convenience store. Some lines have even hired Gurkhas, the famed Nepalese fighters, as onboard security personnel and ex–Navy SEALs as top-level security consultants, and have trained deck officers in how to react to takeover attempts. Other security measures are also in place, but the cruise lines prefer to keep them under their hats.

On a day-to-day basis, passengers will mostly notice ship security when boarding, both initially and at the ports of call. Most cruise lines photograph passengers digitally at embarkation and then match their pictures to their faces every time they get back aboard thereafter. Digital pass-cards also allow them to tell instantly who's aboard at any given time. Other security processes include screening and X-raying of all hand-carried and checked bags, the use of sniffer dogs in port, and maintenance of a security zone around cruise ships while they're in port. Back-office changes include a rule that ships must submit a complete list of passengers and crew to the Coast Guard 96 hours before arriving at a U.S. port. Internationally, regulations issued by the International Maritime Organization (IMO) in 2004 require all ports around the world to operate within a consistent framework to address security issues.

Many of these systems were already in place at most cruise lines and ports, so passengers generally don't notice much difference. Exception: It may take you longer to get through the check-in process in the terminal.

The other major cruise safety issue that occasionally hits the news is **norovirus** (aka Norwalk-like virus), a stomach bug that causes nausea, vomiting, and diarrhea. An extremely common bug that hits some 23 million Americans a year (mostly on land), it's also extremely contagious. According to the Centers for Disease Control (CDC), people infected with norovirus can pass the bug on from the moment they begin feeling ill to between 3 days and 2 weeks after they recover—meaning the cruise ship outbreaks that seem to occur on a regular basis are probably the result of contagious passengers bringing the infection aboard, rather than of unsanitary practices on the ships themselves. Face it, cruise ships are a lot like kindergarten: When one kid shows up sick, everybody gets sick.

In any case, don't worry too much. It's no fun to have your vacation spoiled by illness, but norovirus causes no long-term health effects for most people. Persons unable to replace liquids quickly enough—generally the very young, the elderly, and people with weakened immune systems—may become dehydrated and require special medical attention, but that's about the worst of it. More good news: Outbreaks have been on the downswing since they were first reported. Cruise lines are keeping a close eye on boarding passengers for signs of illness, and have further stepped up their already vigilant sanitation routines to reduce the chance of transmission. A small outbreak on one of our cruises in 2006 was contained immediately after the first sick passengers were identified, and did not spread any further among passengers and crew.

The Best of Cruising

People are always asking us about our favorite ships, and we always say, "Well, what do you like to do when you're *not* on a ship?" In this section we've broken out different kinds of cruises, interests, and destinations to help you find one that best matches what you're looking for. You'll find complete information on each pick in part 2, "The Cruise Lines & Their Ships," and part 3, "The Ports."

1 Our Favorite Mainstream Ships

Mainstream ships are the big boys of the industry, carrying the most passengers and providing the most diverse cruise experiences to suit many different tastes, from party-hearty to arty-farty.

- **Celebrity's Millennium class and Century class:** *Millennium, Infinity, Summit,* and *Constellation* offer elegant decor, incredible spas, great service, edgy art collections, and the best alternative restaurants at sea. Class, charm, personality—what's not to like? Celebrity's older Century-class ships (*Century, Galaxy,* and *Mercury*) aren't too far behind, either. See p. 143 and 147.
- **NCL's** *Jewel, Pearl,* **and** *Jade:* NCL's best ships yet, this nearly identical trio combines an incredible number of dining choices, great entertainment, an always-casual vibe, and decor that's just plain fun. They have the best beer-and-whiskey bars at sea, too, with a selection that's light-years ahead of the competition.
- **Royal Caribbean's Radiance class:** The most elegant vessels Royal Caribbean has produced to date, *Radiance, Brilliance, Serenade,* and *Jewel of the Seas* combine a sleek, seagoing exterior; a nautically themed interior; and acres of windows.
- **Princess's Diamond class and Coral class:** Princess's huge but cozy *Diamond* and *Sapphire Princess* are its most beautiful ships to date, combining gorgeous exterior lines with wood-heavy, old-world lounges and a great covered promenade that lets you stand right in the ship's prow. The smaller *Coral Princess* and *Island Princess* are big winners, too, with similar decor and a smaller size that lets them traverse the Panama Canal. See p. 236 and 240.

2 Best Luxury Cruises

Here's the very best for the cruiser who's used to traveling deluxe and who doesn't mind paying for the privilege. These ships have the best cuisine, accommodations, and service at sea.

- **Silversea** *Shadow, Whisper,* **and** *Wind:* Silversea is the best of the highbrow small-ship luxury lines, with its exquisite cuisine, roomy suites, over-the-top service, and niceties that include complimentary free-flowing champagne. See p. 315.
- **Crystal** *Symphony* **and** *Serenity:* Carrying 940 to 1,080 passengers, these are the best midsize ships out there, big enough to offer lots of dining, entertainment, and fitness options, and small enough to bathe passengers in luxury. See p. 270.

- **SeaDream Yacht Club** *SeaDream I and II:* What's not to love? These cool 110-passenger yachts are elegant but casual, and carry along jet skis, mountain bikes, and kayaks for jaunts around such ports as St. Barts and Jost Van Dyke. See p. 307.

- **Regent Seven Seas** *Navigator* **and** *Voyager:* Not only are cabins aboard these midsize 490- and 700-passenger, all-suite ships roomy, but their huge bathrooms are fabulous. To top it off, food and service on both are among the very best at sea. See p. 291.

- **Cunard** *Queen Mary 2: QM2* has her very own niche in the luxe market—and in the cruise market as a whole, for that matter. While too enormous to offer the kind of intimate luxury you'll get with Silversea, Seabourn, and SeaDream, she is able to give you a pretty close idea of what life aboard the great old ocean liners was like, and that's pretty luxe all by itself. See p. 281.

3 The Most Romantic Cruises

Of course, all cruises are pretty romantic when you consider the props they have to work with: the undulating sea all around, moonlit nights on deck, cozy dining and cocktailing, cozy cabins. Here are the best lines for getting you in the mood.

- **Star Clippers:** With the wind in your hair and sails fluttering overhead, the top decks of the tall-masted *Royal Clipper* and *Star Clipper* provide a most romantic setting. Below decks, the comfy cabins, lounge, and dining room make these ships the most comfortable adventure on the sea. See p. 372.

- **Cunard:** Like real royalty, *Queen Mary 2* was born with certain duties attendant to her station, and one of the biggest of those duties is to embody the romance of transatlantic travel and bring it into the new century. Take a stroll around that promenade deck, dine in that fabulous dining room, and thrill to be out in the middle of the ocean on nearly a billion dollars' worth of Atlantic thoroughbred. See p. 281.

- **SeaDream Yacht Club** *SeaDream I and II:* With comfy Balinese daybeds

lining the teak decks, champagne flowing freely, and toys like MP3 players and high-powered binoculars at your fingertips, these 110-passenger playboy yachts spell romance for the spoiled sailing set. See p. 307.

- **Windstar Cruises:** Windstar's tall-masted *Wind Surf* and *Wind Spirit* offer a truly unique cruise experience, giving passengers the delicious illusion of adventure and the ever-pleasant reality of great cuisine, service, and itineraries. See p. 390.

- **Sea Cloud Cruises:** Really, when it comes right down to it, what setting is more movie-star romantic than a zillionaire's sailing yacht? That's what you get with *Sea Cloud,* once owned by Edward F. Hutton and Marjorie Merriweather Post, with some cabins retaining their original grandeur. See p. 370.

- **Windjammer Barefoot Cruises:** They may not be everybody's idea of romantic, but if you and your significant other have always dreamed of chucking it all and taking off on a Harley, these are the ships for you: rum-swigging, T-shirt-wearing, ultra-free, and quirky as hell. See p. 379.

4 Best Cruises for Families with Kids

The kids are boss, or so you'd think the way cruise lines are catering to families these days. All the lines included here offer supervised activities for three to five age groups between ages 2 or 3 and 17, plus well-stocked playrooms, group and/or private babysitting, wading pools, kids' menus, and cabins that can accommodate three to five. See "Cruises for Families," in chapter 1, and the cruise line reviews in chapters 6 through 8 for more info.

- **Disney Cruise Line:** This family magnet offers the most sophisticated, flexible, and well-thought-out kids' program in the cruise world, bar none. Huge play areas, family-friendly cabins (the majority have two bathrooms—a sink and toilet in one and a shower/tub combo and a sink in the other), baby nursery, and the ubiquitous Mickey all spell success. Plus, the 3- and 4-night Bahamas cruises aboard the *Disney Wonder* are marketed in tandem with stays at Walt Disney World, so you can have your ocean voyage and your Cinderella Castle too. See p. 158.

- **Royal Caribbean:** The huge Voyager-class ships are truly theme parks at sea, with features such as onboard rock-climbing walls, ice-skating rinks, in-line skate rinks, miniature golf, burger-joint diners, and Disney-esque Main Streets running down their centers, with parades and other entertainment throughout the day. The new *Freedom* and *Liberty of the Seas* go them one better, adding a top-deck water park and surfing simulator. All this is in addition to bigger-than-normal kids' playrooms, teen centers, wading pools, and video game rooms, plus regulation-size basketball, paddle ball, and volleyball courts. The Radiance-class ships are also a great family choice, and even the line's older ships have impressively roomy kids' facilities. See p. 245.

- **Carnival Cruise Lines:** While Carnival's let-the-good-times-roll attitude appeals to adults, the line also does a particularly fine job with kids. Several hundred per cruise is pretty normal, with as many as 800 to 1,000 on Christmas and New Year's cruises. You'll find the biggest and brightest playrooms in the fleet on the Conquest-class vessels, with computer stations, a climbing maze, a video wall showing movies and cartoons, arts and crafts, and oodles of toys and games, plus great water slides out on the main pool deck. Carnival's Destiny- and Spirit-class ships are pretty great, too. See p. 112.

- **Princess Cruises:** The Grand-, Diamond-, and Coral-class ships each have a spacious children's playroom, a sizable piece of fenced-in outside deck for toddlers, and another for older kids, with a wading pool. Teen centers have computers, video games, and a sound system, and the ones on the Grand-class ships even have teen hot tubs and private sunbathing decks. See p. 225.

- **Norwegian Cruise Line:** The kids' facilities on *Norwegian Dawn, Star,* and *Spirit* are fantastic, with a huge, brightly colored crafts/play area, a TV corner full of beanbag chairs, an enormous ball-jump/play-gym, a teen center, and a huge outdoor play/pool area. Parents will appreciate the many restaurant options on board, while kids can dine in tiny chairs at a kid-size buffet of their own. *Norwegian Jewel, Pearl, Jade,* and *Pride of America* have good indoor playrooms, but their tiny outdoor play areas are a disappointment. See p. 199.

- **Cunard:** Though you'd hardly expect it from such a seriously prestigious line, the *QM2* has a great program and facilities for kids, starting at age 1. Aside from Disney, no other line offers such extensive care for children so young. There's even a special daily children's teatime that's perfect as an early dinner, and the children's programming is free of charge until midnight daily.

5 Best Cruises for Pure Relaxation

Sometimes it's all about doing absolutely nothing, but some ships are better at letting you do nothing (in style and comfort) than others.

- **SeaDream Yacht Club:** SeaDream's two intimate, 110-passenger yachts deliver an upscale yet very casual experience without regimentation. Cabin beds are fitted with fine Frette linens, but the best snooze on board is to be had in one of the 18 queen-size, Bali-style sun beds that line each vessel's top deck. Each features an extrathick mattress, teak bed tables, and sea views, and is ensconced in its own raised, semipartitioned "bedroom." Reading lights are provided at night, and some guests just end up sleeping out here. See p. 307.

- **Oceania Cruises:** Aboard Oceania's midsize, classically styled ships, the dress code is "country club casual" at all times; you can show up for dinner whenever you like; activities and entertainment are small scale and personal; itineraries visit many quiet, refined ports; and the cabin beds are some of the best at sea. For the ultimate experience, you can rent a private on-deck cabana with retractable shade roof, plush daybed built for two, and a dedicated attendant to bring food and drink, spritz you with cold water, and order up massages. Step aboard, take a deep breath, and *relax.* See p. 219.

- **Celebrity Cruises:** If your idea of relaxation involves regular massages; lolling around in ornate steam rooms, mud baths, and hydrotherapy pools; and then letting your limbs tingle in gorgeous solariums, Celebrity's Millennium-class ships are tops. Afterward, have a long, relaxed dinner at the ships' amazing alternative restaurants, then decide what kind of pillow you want: The line's "ConciergeClass" suites feature a whole menu of different varieties, plus tension-absorbing mattresses and comfy duvets. See p. 136.

- **American Safari Cruises:** Every October and November, luxury small-ship line American Safari offers a series of 3- and 4-night California Wine Country cruises aboard its 22-passenger yacht *Safari Spirit.* Days are spent on private tours of various vineyards and estates, with wine tastings, art tours, gourmet lunches, and even a massage by a local therapist included in the rates. In the late afternoon you can take out a kayak and explore the rivers on your own, then come back and soak in the top-deck hot tub. See p. 334.

- **Star Clippers:** You won't find better ships for the Caribbean, really, than Star Clippers' two tall-masted modern clipper ships, with acres of sail shining in the sun and you down below them in a deck chair, listening to sailors working the winches, heading for the next small yachting port. No megaship bustle here. See p. 372.

6 Best Dining Experiences

Here's where you'll find the finest restaurants afloat, with food rivaling what you'd find in the world's major cities.

- **Silversea Cruises:** Hit it on a sunset departure from port and the windowed, candlelit La Terrazza restaurant becomes a window to the passing scenery and a home for some of the best Italian cuisine at sea, created by chef Marco Betti. Excellent wines accompany dinner and are included in the cruise rates. A second alternative venue offers a new twist on cruise dining, offering menus that pair food with wine rather than the other way 'round. (Though those wines'll cost ya.) See p. 315.

- **Crystal Cruises:** While all the food you'll get on these ships is first-class, their reservations-only Asian specialty restaurants are the best at sea, especially *Serenity's* Silk Road restaurant, overseen by Master Chef Nobuyuki "Nobu" Matsuhisa. The accouterments help set the tone, too—chopsticks, sake served in tiny sake cups and decanters, and sushi served on thick blocky square glass platters. An Asian-themed buffet lunch, offered at least once per cruise, gives passengers an awesome spread, from jumbo shrimp to chicken and beef satays to stir-fry dishes. See p. 271.

- **Regent Seven Seas Cruises:** The award-winning chefs aboard all the line's ships produce artful culinary presentations that compare favorably to those of New York's or San Francisco's top restaurants, and the waiters are some of the industry's best. See p. 293.

- **Seabourn Cruise Lines:** There's nothing quite like dining at the outdoor restaurant called "2," which serves five- to six-course tasting menus for only about 50 guests a night. With the ship's wake shushing just below, it's a rare opportunity to dine with the sea breezes and starry night sky surrounding you. See p. 301.

- **Celebrity Cruise Line:** It doesn't get much better than the alternative restaurants on the Millennium-class ships, all of them designed to mimic dining experiences aboard the golden-age ocean liners of yesteryear. *Millennium's* Olympic restaurant boasts the actual gilded French walnut wood paneling used aboard White Star Line's *Olympic,* sister ship to *Titanic;* while sister ships *Infinity, Summit,* and *Constellation* have restaurants themed around artifacts from the SS *United States, Normandie,* and *Ile de France.* A highly trained staff dotes on diners with table-side cooking, musicians play elegant period pieces, and the entire decadent experience takes about 3 hours. See p. 139.

- **Oceania Cruises:** Oceania's dining experience is near the top in the mainstream category, with menus created by renowned chef Jacques Pepin and passengers able to choose between four different restaurants, all of them excellent. Service is doting and fine-tuned, even at the casual semi-buffet dinner option, offered on an outdoor terrace that's elegant and totally romantic at sunset. See p. 220.

- **Norwegian Cruise Lines:** NCL gets onto this list by sheer weight of numbers. Get this: The line's megaships each offer between 8 and 10 different dining options, including multiple main dining rooms, multiple specialty restaurants, teppanyaki rooms, and casual options. While the fare in the main dining rooms is totally average, it's quite good in some of the alternative venues, including the sushi bar and the elegant French/Continental Le Bistro. See p. 202.

7 Best Cruises for the Party Set

Whether you're traveling solo or with your significant other, these ships can keep you in a party mood all day and night.

- **Windjammer Barefoot Cruises:** If you have an informal attitude, these cruises are a great bet, extremely dress-down and very, very, very casual. It's amazing what a little wind, waves, stars, and moonlight can do for your social skills—and the free rum punch, cheap beers, and visits to legendary Caribbean beach bars don't hurt, either. There are even a handful of rowdy singles-only cruises annually—erotic tart-eating contest, anyone? See p. 379.

- **Carnival Cruise Lines:** Lots of men and women in their 20s, 30s, and 40s seek out Carnival's "fun ships" for their nutso decor and around-the-clock excitement. The Pool Deck is always bustling (especially on the short 3- and 4-nighters), with music playing so loudly you'll have to go back to your cabin to think, and the discos and nightspots hop until the early morning hours. See p. 112.

- **Royal Caribbean:** This line draws a good cross section of men and women from all walks of life. As with Carnival, a decent number of passengers are singles in their 20s, 30s, and 40s, especially on the short 3- and 4-night weekend cruises. For an exciting Saturday-night-out-on-the-town barhopping kind of thing, the Voyager- and Freedom-class ships feature a unique multideck, boulevard-like indoor promenade lined with bars, restaurants, shops, and entertainment outlets. See p. 245.

- **Norwegian Cruise Line:** Everything's fun and casual on NCL's ships, and *Jewel, Pearl, Gem,* and *Jade* have the best beer-and-whiskey bars at sea, hands down. An added plus: The ships all have casual dress codes and open-seating dining at their 8 or 10 restaurants, creating more mingling opportunities. See p. 199.

8 Best Beaches

All warm-water cruises offer easy access to beaches, either close to the dock or, more likely, via a short taxi ride. These are some of the best in the various regions.

- **In the Eastern and Southern Caribbean:** So many . . . Palm Beach, Aruba; the Gold Coast beaches (Paynes Bay, Brandon's Beach, Paradise Beach, Brighton Beach), Barbados; Cane Garden Bay, Tortola, British Virgin Islands; Dickenson Bay, Antigua; Grand Anse Beach, Grenada; Diamond Beach, Martinique; Pinney's Beach, Nevis; St-Jean Beach and Grand Cul-de-Sac, St. Barts; Cupecoy Beach and Orient Beach, Sint Maarten/St. Martin; Pigeon Point Beach, Tobago; Trunk Bay, St. John; and Paradise Beach, Nassau, Bahamas. All are within a taxi ride of the cruise piers. See chapter 10.

- **In the Western Caribbean:** Grand Cayman's Seven Mile Beach is a stretch of pristine sand easily accessible via a short taxi ride from Georgetown. Meanwhile, Jamaica's own Seven Mile Beach is located in Negril, which is closer to Montego Bay than to Ocho Rios. See chapter 10.

- **On the Mexican Riviera:** For those in search of a back-to-basics beach, the best and most beautiful is Playa La Ropa, close to Zihuatanejo. Next door, the wide beach at Playa Las Gatas is pocked with restaurants and snorkeling sites. At Puerto Vallarta, spectacularly wide Banderas Bay offers 26 miles of beaches, including popular Playa Los Muertos, full of *palapa* restaurants, beach volleyball, and parasailing. Acapulco is all about beaches, of which the best include Caleta, Caletilla, and the beach on Roqueta Island. Ditto for Cabo San Lucas, with its famous Lovers Beach at Land's End, where the Pacific meets the Sea of Cortez. See chapter 12.

- **In Hawaii:** Hawaii *is* beaches, hundreds of 'em. But because you'll be arriving by ship and only have limited time, you have to concentrate on ones that aren't too far off. Among the best that are accessible by taxi are Ala Moana Beach Park and Waikiki Beach on Oahu, the former a lot like L.A.'s casual Venice Beach, the latter a bit like Miami's vibrant South Beach. A bit farther afield, Lanikai Beach is just too gorgeous to be real. On the Big Island, Hapuna Beach regularly wins kudos as the state's most beautiful beach, and it's not too far from where you come ashore in Kailua-Kona. You'll have a longer taxi ride on Maui to visit Kapalua Beach, the island's prize stretch. On Kauai, try Poipu Beach, with stretches of sand as well as a grassy lawn graced by coconut trees. We once saw a Hawaiian monk seal here sunning himself on the sand, with police tape around him like he was a crime scene. See chapter 14.

9 Best Small-Ship Adventure Cruises

Among the small-ship lines, some offer great opportunities for real adventure, whether you're talking about getting out into the wilderness, interacting with wind and wildlife, or just sailing to places you never imagined you'd go.

- **Lindblad Expeditions (Alaska and Baja):** Lindblad is the most adventure- and learning-oriented of the small-ship lines, offering itineraries that stay far away from the big ports, concentrating instead on wilderness, wildlife, and history. Your time is spent learning about the outdoors from high-caliber expedition leaders and guest scientists, some of them aboard as part of Lindblad's alliance with the National Geographic Society. Try them in Alaska or in Mexico's Sea of Cortez for whale-watching and exploring starkly beautiful uninhabited islands. See p. 345.

- **Cruise West (Alaska/Russia):** Want a real expedition? Cruise West's *Spirit of Oceanus* offers 2-week cruises that sail from mainland Alaska, through the Aleutian Islands, and then across the Bering Sea to Russia's severe Chukchi Peninsula, visiting coastal towns and wilderness areas. See p. 335.

- **The Maine Windjammers (Maine Coast):** You get a fairly relaxing adventure on these owner-operated vessels, but it's an adventure nonetheless because these are real sailing ships, relying on the coastal winds for propulsion. If you like, you're welcome to learn the ropes of sailing while aboard, as you sail to small islands around Penobscot Bay. See p. 349.

10 Best History & Learning Cruises

And then there are ships that are oriented toward learning about the region through which you're sailing, or that are parts of history themselves.

- **Majestic America Line (Mississippi River):** The wooden, 174-passenger *Delta Queen* was built in 1926 and is one of the great links to the

Mississippi's stern-wheeler past. Cruises are a celebration of Americana, with lots of history and river lore, meals that feature Cajun and southern cooking, and a music program heavy on Dixieland jazz and swing. Special theme cruises focus on the Civil War and antebellum home visits. See p. 359.

- **American Canadian Caribbean (Erie Canal/Finger Lakes):** Designed to be able to sail in puddles, it seems, ACCL's ships can navigate through the narrow, shallow waters of the old northeast canal system, with much time spent in the region's rivers and lakes, plus visits to historic sites such as Fort Ticonderoga, Cooperstown and the Baseball Hall of Fame, West Point, and the old Erie Canal. You don't get expert lecturers the way you do on many other small-ship lines, but they don't sail here. See p. 326.

- **Imperial Majesty (Bahamas):** This one's a bit of a ringer. The itinerary visits nowhere you'd normally call historic, but *Regal Empress,* the line's one ship, is historic in and of itself. Built in 1953, it's one of the only real old ocean liners still operating in the American market. By 2010, Coast Guard regulations will make it almost impossible for old vessels like this to sail, so if you want to see what

ocean ships were like in the mid–20th century, *Regal Empress* is one of your last options. And it's cheap, too! See p. 187.

- **The Maine Windjammers (Maine Coast):** On the Maine coast, more than a dozen owner-operator schooners offer 3- to 6-night cruises throughout the summer. Several of them date back to the 19th century, including the 22-passenger *Lewis R. French* and *Stephen Taber* (both launched in 1871), while boats like the 26-passenger *American Eagle* and 20-passenger *Timberwind* date to the 1930s. Cruises let you become familiar with old-style sailing ships and learn something about handling the sails, all while tooling around the bays and coves of the gorgeous Maine coast. See p. 349.

- **Cruise West, Lindblad, and American Safari Cruises (Columbia/Snake rivers):** Follow in the steps of Lewis and Clark through the rivers of the Pacific Northwest, transiting locks and dams, visiting Indian petroglyphs, and experiencing one of the most beautiful river landscapes in the U.S. Some cruises also offer recreational activities such as kayaking, while others visit vineyards in Washington's wine country. See p. 335, 345, and 334.

11 Best Cruises for Sports Nuts & Gym Rats

Many cruise ships today are a far cry from the days when no one did anything more active than play shuffleboard and take a walk around the deck. In fact, we've heard of people who actually *lost* weight on their cruise by taking advantage of all the active options available. Here are some of the best.

- **Best Cruises for Onboard Sports:** Royal Caribbean wins hands down. Its five Voyager-class ships offer huge

gyms, full-size basketball courts, rock-climbing walls, miniature golf courses, in-line skating tracks, and ice-skating rinks. Their larger sisters, *Freedom of the Seas* and *Liberty of the Seas,* go them one better by adding a surfing simulator. See p. 248.

- **Best Onboard Gyms:** Once relegated to dank little rooms, onboard gyms now hold pride of place, usually occupying spacious digs on one of the top decks and boasting wraparound windows, aerobics rooms, and as many exercise machines, free weights, and spinning bikes as most large dry-land gyms. The best are aboard Royal Caribbean's *Freedom* and *Liberty of the Seas* (a huge, 12,000-sq.-ft. space that includes a Pilates studio and a full-size boxing ring, with boxing training available throughout the cruise). The ones on Royal's Voyager-class ships are pretty spiffy too, as are those aboard Carnival's Destiny-class ships and Holland America Vista-class ships and *Rotterdam, Amsterdam, Volendam,* and *Zaandam.* See p. 252, p. 129, and p. 175.

- **Best Golf Cruises:** While practically all the major cruise lines offer golf excursions and some level of golf instruction (usually at an outdoor driving net), several lines go the extra mile. Carnival, Holland America, Celebrity, Princess, and ultraluxe line Silversea all feature programs created by Florida's Elite Golf Cruises that offer comprehensive golf-cruise vacations. In addition to onboard instruction, high-tech computer simulators allow virtual play that mimics some three dozen of the world's top courses, with software that analyzes your swing to give a perfect real-time simulation. In port, the programs bundle priority tee times, early debarkation, transportation, golf pro escort, cart rental, and greens fees into one excursion cost. See p. 112, 167, 136, 225, and 315.

- **Best Snorkeling and Scuba Cruises:** Virtually any warm-water cruise you take will offer snorkeling on shore excursions, and certified scuba divers can often arrange their own trips. In the Caribbean, islands with particularly good waters for snorkeling and diving include Bonaire, Grand Cayman, Cozumel (especially at the Chankanaab National Park), Curaçao, and the U.S. Virgin Islands (at Buck Island Reef). In Central America, the waters off Belize (especially its famous Blue Hole) and Honduras's Roatan Island offer great waters, and Hawaii is known as one of the best dive destinations in the world. See chapters 10 and 14 for more information on these destinations.

12 Best Ships for Spa-Goers

One company, Steiner Leisure, runs the vast bulk of cruise ship spas, but facilities vary.

- **Cunard:** *QM2*'s two-story, 20,000-square-foot spa was designed and is operated by Canyon Ranch, one of the most famous spas in North America. Done up in a vaguely Art Deco and nautical motif, the place looks as good as it feels. More than 50 therapists dole out the latest treatments, and you can finish off your spa time with a dip in the ultrarelaxing aquatherapy pool. See p. 281.

- **Celebrity Cruises:** Celebrity's Millennium-class and Century-class ships are at the top of the mainstream spa heap. Their huge and exceedingly attractive AquaSpas manage to combine a huge repertoire of the latest wraps, packs, soaks, and massages with striking aesthetics inspired by Japanese gardens and bathhouses and Moorish and Turkish spas. Facilities include saunas, mud baths, massage rooms, Turkish baths, and thalassotherapy pools (a sort of giant New Age hot tub). See p. 136.

- **Royal Caribbean:** The two-level spa complexes aboard the line's Voyager-class and Freedom-class ships are among the largest and best equipped out there. A peaceful waiting area has New Age tropical bird-song music piped in overhead. Ahhhh, relaxation—until you get your bill. The Radiance-class ships have huge exotically themed solariums and 13 treatment rooms, including a special steam-room complex featuring heated, tiled chaise longues and special showers simulating tropical rain and fog. See p. 245.

- **Regent Seven Seas:** Regent's spas are some of the few not run by the ubiquitous Steiner. Instead, the French spa company Carita imports staffs and hairdressers from Parisian salons, and offers company specialties such as the Rénovateur exfoliating process as well as such cruise spa standards as hydrotherapy; reflexology; aromatherapy; body wraps; facials; manicures/pedicures; and antistress, therapeutic, and hot-rock massage. See p. 291.

- **Windstar Cruises:** The intimate, 308-passenger *Wind Surf* has extensive spa facilities for a ship its size, with prebookable spa packages combining six or more treatments tailored to both men and women. See p. 391.

13 Best Shopping Ports

Folks who lament our consumer culture should look into the small-ship lines in chapter 8, where shopping hardly ever rears its head. If, however, you think vacationing means an opportunity to indulge your plastic gland, the following ports will give you the fix you crave.

- **In the Caribbean:** Most ports in the Caribbean have a sprawling market or complexes near the cruise ship docks that blend seamlessly with the shopping streets beyond. If a ship is coming to an island, people there will be ready to sell you stuff. The biggest shopping ports are Charlotte Amalie, St. Thomas; Nassau and Freeport, Bahamas; Christiansted, St. Croix; San Juan, Puerto Rico; Georgetown, Grand Cayman; Philipsburg and Marigot, St. Martin; and Oranjestad, Aruba. Expect jewelry, perfume, cosmetics, clothing, liquor, arts and crafts, and souvenirs, with about an equal mix of chain stores and locally owned shops. At some smaller ports, such as Dominica, you'll still find good indigenous Caribbean arts (that island's Caribe Indian baskets are gorgeous), but on the whole the "island crafts" you'll find are pretty lame and/or made in Hong Kong. The American islands (Puerto Rico and the U.S. Virgins) allow you to bring home more cheap booze duty-free (see chapter 3). See chapter 10.

- **In Alaska:** If you've cruised in the Caribbean, you'll have a bit of déjà vu when you step off your ship in Skagway, Juneau, or Ketchikan and see chain stores such as Little Switzerland. Mixed in among the jewelry and perfume, though, you'll also have the opportunity to see art created by the vibrant Alaska Native cultures of Southeast, the Tlingit, Haida, and Tsimshian. Paintings, sculpture, carved masks, and ornate ceremonial rattles are frequently gorgeous, but also frequently very, very expensive. Ketchikan and Skagway are a bit too shopping-frantic for our tastes. We prefer Juneau and the much-less-busy Sitka. See chapter 11.

- **On the Mexican Riviera:** The best shopping bet among the Mexican Riviera ports is **Puerto Vallarta,** which combines typical tourist shopping with opportunities for buying real works of art. Dozens of galleries are dedicated to Mexican modern art, while the city's proximity to the High Sierras means it's also a center for gorgeous Huichol Indian art. Among the other ports usually included on Riviera itineraries, Cabo San Lucas is a veritable shopping mall, though distinctive only if you're in the market for tequila and T-shirts. See chapter 12.

• **In Hawaii:** For those who like to do some serious window-shopping, head to Kalakaua Avenue at Oahu's Waikiki Beach. Here you can find everything from Coach bags to board shorts, all on a bustling strip complete with statues, reflecting pools, street performers, and, at dusk, flaming tiki torches and alfresco dining. It's Beverly Hills meets Greenwich Village. Lahaina, Maui, has a lovely historic district that offers great beachfront shopping on Front Street. By the courthouse, artists congregate under a big banyan tree, creating a sort of open-air gallery. See chapter 14.

• **In New England and Canada:** You won't have time to go New England antiquing in the traditional get-in-the-car-and-drive way, but New England/Canada itineraries offer some good shopping ports. Newport, Rhode Island's downtown is full of cutesy boutiques and shops selling nautically themed merchandise, the latter of which you'll also find a lot of along the hilly streets of New Bedford, Massachusetts. In Boston, head for historic Fanueil Hall and the adjacent Quincy Market, or to Newbury Street if you've got money to burn— it's Boston's version of New York's Fifth Avenue. If you're sailing from New York, you can just *go* to Fifth Avenue, with pricey shops stacked end-to-end from 42nd Street to 57th, or head downtown to SoHo or Chelsea for art. From Portland, Maine, the L.L.Bean outlet is within striking distance at nearby Freeport, a town that's almost nothing but outlets. See chapter 15.

Part 1

Planning, Booking & Preparing for Your Cruise

With advice on choosing and booking your ideal cruise and tips on getting ready for the cruise experience.

1

Choosing Your Ideal Cruise

Forget the "overfed, newlywed, nearly dead" stereotype. Today's cruises are tailored for your tastes, whether you're a senior, a traveling family, a swinging single, a wheelchair user, or a swinging, wheelchair-using granddad. You can sail on a floating country club to little yachting islands; bop around Hawaii in the first new U.S.-flagged cruise ships in generations; take an expedition from Alaska over to the Russian Far East; take the *Queen Mary 2* across the pond to England; sail a 100-year-old schooner off the Maine coast or a floating B&B down the Mississippi; travel among the reefs and indigenous cultures of Central America; or spend a week in the Caribbean on board a big white megaship. There are also active adventure cruises, cruises geared to fine food and wine, cruises with a cultural or historic bent, and, of course, the classic fun-in-the-sun relaxation escape. In this chapter, we'll introduce you to the lot of them.

1 Homeland Cruise Regions in Brief

Whether because of convenience or an aversion to flying (that is, the cost of flying or the fear of it), the idea of cruising from a port within driving distance holds a lot of appeal for a lot of folks. And anytime a lot of folks want to do something, you can be sure the cruise lines will be right there, ready to hand them an umbrella drink. Today, you can cruise to the Caribbean from Miami or from New York, New Orleans, Houston, Norfolk, and about 10 other ports. You can visit Bermuda on ships that depart from Boston, New York, Philadelphia, and Baltimore. Alaska, Mexico, and Hawaii are now accessible from half a dozen embarkation ports along the West Coast. With all of these choices, there's a good chance you can drive right up to the gangway. In the chapters that follow, we cover all regions to which you can cruise from 17 U.S. and 2 Canadian home ports. Below is a snapshot of those regions to get you started.

CARIBBEAN/BAHAMAS/CENTRAL AMERICA

When most of us think of a cruise, we think of the islands. We imagine pulling up in our big white ship to a patch of sand and palm-tree paradise, a steel band serenading us as we stroll down the gangway in our shorts and flip-flops and step into the warm sun. Well, the good news is that this image is a pretty darn accurate depiction of many ports in the Caribbean, The Bahamas, and Central America. Sure, some are jam-packed with other cruise ships and passengers, and many are pretty weak in the palm-tree department; but you're guaranteed nearly **constant sunshine** and plenty of beaches. On some you'll find lush **rainforests, volcanic peaks, Maya ruins,** winding **mountain roads,** and beautiful **tropical flowers.** And all of them have **great beaches** and that laid-back don't-hurry-me island pace.

Most Caribbean cruises are a week long, though you'll also find sailings as short as 5 nights and as long as 14 nights. Cruises to The Bahamas (which are actually outside the Caribbean basin) are usually 3 or 4 nights, though many Caribbean routes also include a stop in Nassau or one of the cruise lines' private Bahamian islands. Stops at Cozumel, Playa del Carmen, and other spots along Mexico's Yucatán Peninsula are common, as increasingly are visits to Central American ports such as Belize City, Belize, and Roatan, Honduras. You'll find itineraries usually stick to one region of the Caribbean, either **eastern** (typically calling on some combination of the U.S. Virgin Islands, Puerto Rico, St. Martin, and The Bahamas), **western** (usually Grand Cayman, Jamaica, Key West, Cozumel or one of the other Mexican ports, and sometime Belize or Honduras), or **southern** (less defined, but often departing from San Juan and including Aruba, Curaçao, Barbados, St. Lucia, Antigua, and Grenada). Small-ship cruises frequently visit the less-developed islands, mostly in the eastern and southern Caribbean, including the beautiful British Virgin Islands and ports such as St. Barts, Dominica, Nevis, and the tiny islands of the Grenadines. **Season:** Year-round, with the greatest number of ships cruising here between October and April.

THE PANAMA CANAL

Imagine the particularly 19th-century kind of hubris it took to say, "Let's dig a huge canal all the way across a country, linking two oceans." Imagine, too, the thousands of workers who pulled it off. Both those things are much on the mind of people today as they sail through the Panama Canal, one of the greatest engineering achievements of all time. There's a lot of history here, as well as a lot of rich Central American culture to explore on port days surrounding your transit. Many ships offer only two Panama Canal cruises annually, when repositioning between their summer season in Alaska and the fall/winter season in the Caribbean, but these days many cruise lines are including **partial Canal crossings** as part of extended western Caribbean itineraries from Florida, sailing through the Canal's locks westbound to Gatun Lake, docking for a day of excursions, and then sailing back out in the evening. The big draw of these itineraries is the pure kick of sailing through the Canal, whose walls pinch today's megaships so tight that there might not be more than a few feet on either side. The Canal's width and the length of its locks are so much on shipbuilders' minds that they coined the term *panamax* to describe the largest ships that are able to transit its length. Those measurements will soon be changing, though, since in 2006 Panama voters approved the digging of a new, 60 percent wider channel that will parallel the existing canal along its narrowest sections, allowing transit by larger ships. **Season:** Roughly November through April.

ALASKA & BRITISH COLUMBIA

Alaska is America's frontier, a land of mountain, forest, and tundra just remote enough and harsh enough that it remains mythic, even if some of its "frontier" towns do have a Starbucks. The main draws here are all things grand: huge glaciers flowing down from the mountains, enormous humpback whales leaping from the sea, eagles soaring overhead, and forests that seem to go on forever. Alaska Native culture figures in too, with the Tlingit, Haida, and Tsimshian tribes all holding a considerable place in everyday life, from the arts to the business world. Most cruises concentrate on the **Southeast Alaska panhandle** (the ancestral home of those three tribes), which stretches from Ketchikan in the south to Yakutat in the north, with British Columbia to the east and the vast reaches of interior Alaska and Canada's Yukon Territory to the north. Typical cruises sail either round-trip from Seattle or Vancouver, British Columbia, or north- or southbound between Vancouver and one of Anchorage's two major port towns, Seward and Whittier. Both options concentrate on ports and natural areas along the Southeast's **Inside Passage,** the intricate web of waterways that link the region's thousands of forested islands. Highlights of most itineraries include glaciers (those in famous Glacier Bay or several others), the old prospector town of Skagway, state capital Juneau, and boardwalked Ketchikan in the south. Cruises between Vancouver and Anchorage may also visit natural areas along the **Gulf of Alaska,** such as College Fjord and Hubbard Glacier. Small-ship cruises frequently visit much smaller towns and wilderness areas on the Inside Passage. Some avoid civilization almost entirely, and a few particularly expeditionary (and expensive) cruises sail far west and north, past the Aleutian Islands, and cross the Bering Sea into the Russian Far East. **Season:** Roughly mid-May through mid-September, although some smaller ships start up in late April.

THE MEXICAN RIVIERA & BAJA

The so-called Mexican Riviera is the West Coast's version of the Caribbean—a string of sunny ports within proximate sailing distance of San Diego, L.A., and San Francisco. The first stop geographically is Cabo San Lucas, a party-oriented town at the southern tip of the Baja Peninsula, with the Pacific Ocean on one side and the Sea of Cortez on the other. Think beaches, beer, and bikinis, with thatched palapa bars providing some regional character. From there, cruises head southeast to such ports as Puerto Vallarta, Mazatlán, Acapulco, Ixtapa, and Manzanillo, a stretch famed for white-sand beaches, watersports, deep-sea fishing, and golf, with some history thrown in for good measure. Hernán Cortés blew through the region in the 1520s looking for treasure, and in the 1950s and 1960s Hollywood did the same, mining the area both for locations and for off-camera relaxation. Small-ship lines also offer **Baja/Sea of Cortez** cruises that concentrate on the peninsula's small towns, natural areas, and remarkable whale-watching. These cruises typically sail from Cabo or the state capital, La Paz. **Season:** The heaviest traffic is October through April, though ships sail year-round—especially short 3- and 4-night cruises that stop in Cabo or Ensenada, just south of the U.S./Mexico border. Small ships typically cruise Baja in the winter months.

BERMUDA

Perhaps the one place in the world where you'll have a chance to see hundreds of British men's knees, Bermuda is a beautiful island chain known for its powdery pink sand beaches, created by pulverized shells and coral over the eons; golf courses; and sane and friendly manner. The locals really do wear brightly colored Bermuda shorts with jackets, ties, and knee-highs, but don't feel obligated to join them. **Hamilton** and **St. George's** are Bermuda's two main port towns, though the largest ships will dock on the west end at the **Royal Naval Dockyard.** Ships pull alongside piers at all three places, and it takes just minutes to walk into town. There's plenty to do, too, from shopping in Hamilton for English wool and Irish linens to checking out the many historical sites, which range from the 300-year-old St. Peter's Church to the impressive nautical exhibits at the Dockyard's Maritime Museum. Most people, though, are headed for Bermuda's many dreamy beaches, which are easily accessible by taxi or motor scooter. To keep things from getting too chaotic, Bermuda limits the number of ships allowed to call there, so there are generally just six doing 7-night cruises from New York, Boston, Philadelphia, Baltimore, and occasionally Norfolk. **Season:** Late April through early October.

HAWAII

If a place can simultaneously be the number-one honeymoon destination in America *and* one of the few places to which the Brady Bunch schlepped Alice and the kids, it must have something going for it, right? Hawaii is gorgeous, with an almost embarrassing richness of stunning beaches, hula girls, and hunky Polynesian men, and the weather really is perfect all the time, putting both locals and visitors in a friendly and mellow mood. Learn to surf, go to a luau, snooze on the sand, enjoy the local coffee, or check out the native Hawaiian culture, which the locals are fiercely proud of. The past survives alongside the modern world in a vibrant arts scene, which includes traditional Polynesian dance and music, as well as painting, sculpture, and crafts. And the diverse landscape of the islands includes fuming volcanoes, crashing surf, serene beaches, lush jungles, and abundant orchids and other tropical flowers. Pearl Harbor is another important attraction.

For the foreseeable future, Norwegian Cruise Line rules the roost in Hawaii, with four ships doing year-round cruises round-trip from Honolulu. Other lines typically visit the islands in April, May, September, and October, on their way between seasons in Alaska and the Caribbean. The four main calls are to **Oahu,** with the famous Waikiki beach; **Maui,** home of the historical town of Lahaina; **Kauai,** the most natural and undeveloped of the four; and the **Big Island,** where the state's famous volcanoes reside, including Mauna Kea and the still-active Kilauea. **Season:** Year-round; the islands are about the same latitude as Jamaica.

EASTERN CANADA/NEW ENGLAND

Humpback, finback, and minke whales, lobster pots, Victorian mansions, and lighthouses on windswept bluffs are just a taste of what a journey along the coast of New England and Canada has in store for cruise passengers. America and Canada were born in these parts, so you'll be in for lots of **historical sites** along the way, from Boston's Paul Revere House to Halifax, where *Titanic* victims were brought (and many buried) after the ship's tragic sinking nearly 100 years ago. Itineraries may include passing through **Nantucket Sound,** around **Cape Cod,** and into the **Bay of Fundy** or **Gulf of St. Lawrence.** Some ships traverse the St. Lawrence Seaway or the smaller Saguenay River. The classic time to cruise here is in autumn, when a brilliant sea of **fall foliage** blankets the region, but as the route becomes more and more popular, cruise lines are scheduling 4- to 12-night trips in spring and summer, too. Big 2,000-passenger-plus ships cruise here, as well as much smaller vessels carrying 100 passengers or less. Most sail to or from New York, Boston, and Montréal. **Season:** Most ships cruise here in September and October, with a few lines also offering late spring and summer sailings.

U.S. RIVER CRUISES

So who needs the ocean? If your interests run toward history, nature, and U.S. culture, a river cruise is a fantastic option. Small ships sail throughout the year, navigating the historic **Mississippi River** system to cities and towns of the South; sailing through the **California Wine Country** for tastings, tours, and meals at noted vineyards; following Lewis and Clark down the Pacific Northwest's **Columbia and Snake rivers;** and even offering cruises on the **Erie Canal** and the rivers of New England, timed to take in the region's fall foliage. Some of these ships (such as the American Canadian Caribbean Line vessels) are tiny and basic, carrying fewer than 100 passengers and designed to sail in very shallow, narrow waterways. Others (such as the Majestic

America Line ships) are vintage or re-created stern-wheelers that evoke classic 19th-century river travel. **Season:** Throughout the year in different regions. (See small-ship reviews in chapter 8 for itineraries.)

2 Itineraries: The Long & the Short of It

Now that you've decided where you want to go, you have to examine the available itineraries. Do you just want to get away for a few days, or are a few weeks more your style? Do you want an itinerary that visits somewhere different every day, or are you looking forward to just relaxing on the ship? And, if you're flying or driving a long way to the cruise's home port, do you want to spend a few days seeing that part of the country either before or after your cruise? Options are what you have; choices are what you need to make.

LONG CRUISE OR SHORT?

The vast majority of cruises are **7 nights** long and depart on a Saturday or Sunday, whether we're talking Caribbean, Alaska, Hawaii, or Mexico. Many of us like the weeklong vacation concept, but if you're looking to spend less money or you're a first-time cruiser interested in testing the waters, there are also 2-, 3-, 4-, and 5-night cruises to choose from. Many of the **3- and 4-night cruises** sail from Florida to The Bahamas, or from California to Baja, Mexico. You can also find a lot of **4- and 5-night cruises** to the Caribbean and the Bahamas, as well as to New England/Canada in the summer and fall. Naturally, these depart on different days of the week, with some time to sail over the weekend.

On one hand, shorter cruises make sense if you're not sure you'll like the cruise experience. On the other, short cruises tend to be the rowdiest cruises, geared to people who want to pack as much party into as short a time as possible. This is especially true of the 3-night weekend cruises offered by Carnival and Royal Caribbean. There's also the fact that cruise lines tend to put their oldest, most beaten-up ships on short-cruise schedules, saving their new ships for their bread-and-butter weeklong itineraries.

Longer cruises, ranging from **9, 10, and 12 nights** to multiweek voyages, give you the chance to really get away and settle into the community aboard your ship. Longer cruises tend to be relaxed and steady, and are popular with older folks who have the time and money to travel. You'll find a few longer sailings in Alaska, the Caribbean, and New England/Canada, and also many long **repositioning cruises,** offered when ships leave one cruise region and sail to another (for instance, heading from Alaska to the Caribbean in stages). These are often deeply discounted and sometimes visit unusual ports, but they often also spend more days at sea than they do in port.

DAYS AT SEA VS. DAYS IN PORT

When evaluating an itinerary, take a look at its day-by-day schedule. A few ships will visit a different port every day, but it's much more typical for them to spend 1 or 2 days at sea— either because they have to sail a long way between ports, or just to give passengers a chance to rest (and spend some money on board while they're at it). Many cruises these days—especially ones that sail from more northerly home ports to Caribbean destinations—are spending up to 3 days at sea on a 7-night itinerary and 4 days on an 8-night itinerary. That's not a bad thing if your main vacation goal is to decompress, but if your goal is to see a lot of different ports, this is not an ideal situation. Ditto if you think you'll get that "are we there yet?" feeling between ports.

CRUISETOURS & ADD-ONS

Cruise lines offer a variety of options for extending your vacation on land, either before or after your cruise. These range from simple 1- and 2-night add-on **hotel packages** to longer resort stays and full-blown land tours of a week or longer. The latter, known as **cruisetours,** are offered mostly in Alaska, where Holland America, Princess, Royal Caribbean, and Celebrity have an elaborate hotel and transportation infrastructure. Many parts of inland Alaska can be accessed this way, including Denali National Park, Fairbanks, Wrangell–St. Elias National Park, and the Kenai Peninsula. If you've a mind to, you can even go all the way to the oil fields of the North Slope of Prudhoe Bay, hundreds of miles north of the Arctic Circle. Many tours also head east into Canada, spending time in the starkly beautiful Yukon Territory or heading to Banff, Lake Louise, and Jasper National Park in the Canadian Rockies.

Caribbean-bound ships originating in Florida often offer extensions to Orlando's theme parks. Disney, naturally, is tops in this regard, offering seamless 1-week land/sea vacations, with 3 days in the park and 4 aboard *Disney Wonder,* or vice versa. Other regions offer their own specialties: Small-ship cruises in Baja, for example, typically offer an extension to the amazing Copper Canyon, larger than the U.S. Grand Canyon.

3 Different Boats for Different Folks

Different cruise lines offer different kinds of experiences, but judging physical factors such as the size and age of the ship are also part of choosing your ideal cruise. What kind of ship floats your boat?

MEGASHIPS (1,800–3,600 PASSENGERS)

For the past dozen years, the so-called "megaships" have dominated the market, carrying upward of 1,800 passengers and offering an onboard experience any city dweller will recognize: food and drink available at any hour, entertainment districts filled with neon and twinkling lights, monumental architecture, big crowds, and a definite buzz. You often won't see the same faces twice from day to day, and, in fact, if you don't plan specific times and places to meet up with your spouse, lover, or friend, you may roam the decks for hours looking for them. (Some passengers even bring a set of walkie-talkies to stay in touch—annoying to the rest of us, maybe, but it keeps them happy.) The megas have as many as 15 passenger decks full of shops, restaurants, bars, and lounges, plus cabins of all shapes and sizes. Most have a grand multistory atrium lobby, three or four swimming pools and hot tubs, theaters, a pizzeria, a specialty coffee shop, and one or more reservations-only restaurants. Mammoth spas and gyms boast dozens of exercise machines and treatment rooms, and vast children's areas include splash pools, playrooms, computer rooms, and video arcades. Countless activities are offered all day long, including wine tastings, fashion shows, dance lessons, art auctions, aerobics classes, bingo, bridge, lectures, cooking demonstrations, pool games, computer classes, and trivia contests. And at night you have a choice of piano bars, discos, martini and champagne bars, sports bars, casinos, theaters, and big glitzy showrooms.

But even the megas aren't all alike. **Carnival**'s and **Costa**'s ships are the most theme-park-like, with their over-the-top decor and ambience. **Royal Caribbean**'s and **NCL**'s megas are more like Times Square hotels, blending a lot of flash with some elegant areas. **Princess** goes for a sort of Pottery Barn design sense and fun but not-too-daring activities and shows; **Holland America** and **Disney** blend tradition with some bright, modern spaces; and **Celebrity** is all about chic modernity.

As a general rule, these ships are so large that they're limited as to where they can go. Ships in the 100,000-ton range are currently too big to fit through the Panama Canal, and so operate from the same coast year-round—West Coast ships doing Mexico itineraries in winter and Alaska in summer, say; East Coast ships either staying in the Caribbean year-round or spending the summers sailing in Europe or New England/Canada. (Note that this will change by 2014, when the canal's planned expansion is complete.) Some ports also lack docking facilities to accommodate these huge ships, meaning you either won't visit them at all or you'll have to be tendered ashore in shuttle boats.

MIDSIZE SHIPS (600–1,800 PASSENGERS)

For a while it looked as if midsize vessels were going the way of the dodo, but the past few years have seen a small resurgence in their fortunes, with a number of older but still not *old*-old midsize ships continuing to soldier on.

The term *midsize* is, of course, relative. Measuring in at between 20,000 and 60,000 gross tons, most of these ships are still larger than some of the great old ocean liners. *Titanic,* for instance, was only 46,000 tons. They're plenty big and spacious enough to provide a diverse cruise experience, though you won't find the range of activities and attractions you do on the megaships. Consider that a good thing: For some people, a more toned-down, lower-key cruise is just what the doctor ordered. Most of **Holland America**'s fleet fits the midsize description, aside from its mega-size Vista-class ships. Ditto for **MSC Cruises,** which operates four 58,600-ton, 1,590-passenger vessels, at least one of which spends winter in the Caribbean. **Oceania** and **Azamara** both operate even smaller vessels, carrying about 700 passengers apiece in a country-club-type setting. **NCL** also still offers a couple of midsizers, though they're the oldest ships in its fleet and are already on the chopping block. (All will leave the fleet by 2009.)

Among the true ultraluxury lines, midsize is about as big as it gets, excluding Cunard's megaliners. **Crystal** and **Regent Seven Seas** both operate ships in the 50,000-ton range, carrying 700 to 940 passengers—a telling figure when you consider that MSC and NCL's similarly sized ships pack in twice as many passengers. Along with high-toned service, cuisine, and amenities, personal space is a major difference between the mainstream and luxe lines.

SMALL SHIPS (12–450 PASSENGERS)

If the thought of sailing with thousands of other people makes you want to jump overboard, a smaller ship may be more up your alley. Small ships are ideal for those who crave a calm, intimate experience where conversation is king. As in a small town, you'll quickly get to know your neighbors, since you'll see the same faces at meals and on deck throughout the week.

The small ships in this book can be broken down into four groups: sailing ships, coastal and river cruisers, expedition ships, and small luxury ships.

Sailing ships, obviously, have sails. But what's not necessarily obvious is how much—or how little—those sails are used to actually propel the ship. On Maine's coast, the 14 independently owned schooners of the **Maine Windjammer Association** are honest-to-God sail-powered vessels, most without engines of any kind. If the wind stops blowing, their only option is to let down their motorized yawl boat and push the ship until it catches a blow. The ships of **Windjammer Barefoot Cruises, Star Clippers,** and **Windstar,** on the other hand, usually operate under wind power for a part of each cruise, but they have engines to do most of the pushing. All these

SHIP SIZE COMPARISONS

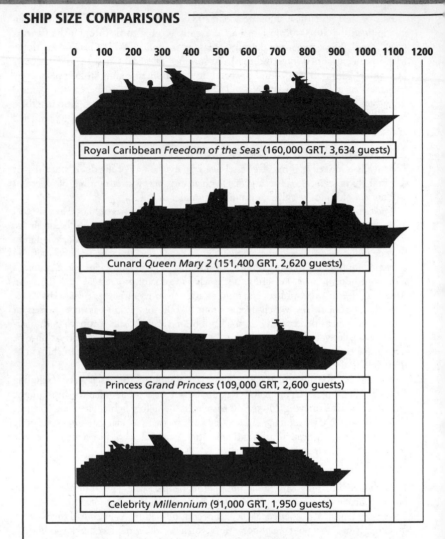

| 0 | 100 | 200 | 300 | 400 | 500 | 600 | 700 | 800 | 900 | 1000 | 1100 | 1200 |

Royal Caribbean *Freedom of the Seas* (160,000 GRT, 3,634 guests)

Cunard *Queen Mary 2* (151,400 GRT, 2,620 guests)

Princess *Grand Princess* (109,000 GRT, 2,600 guests)

Celebrity *Millennium* (91,000 GRT, 1,950 guests)

Ships in this chart represent the range of sizes in the current cruise market. See reviews in chapters 6 through 8 for sizes of ships not shown here, then compare. Note that GRT = gross register tons, the standard measure of vessel size. Rather than representing weight, it indicates the amount of interior, revenue-producing space on a vessel. One GRT = 100 cubic feet of enclosed, revenue-generating space.

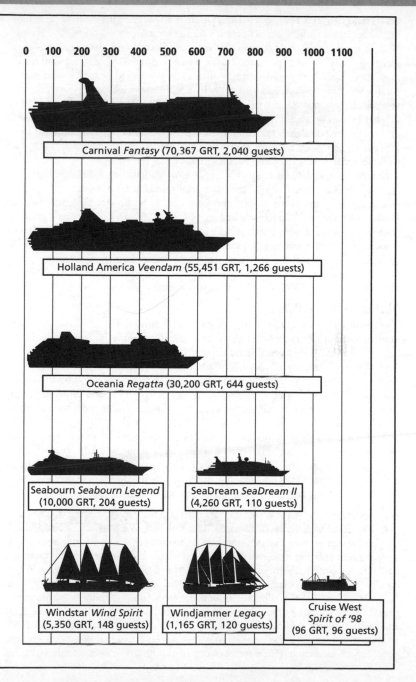

0   100   200   300   400   500   600   700   800   900   1000 1100

Carnival *Fantasy* (70,367 GRT, 2,040 guests)

Holland America *Veendam* (55,451 GRT, 1,266 guests)

Oceania *Regatta* (30,200 GRT, 644 guests)

Seabourn *Seabourn Legend* (10,000 GRT, 204 guests)

SeaDream *SeaDream II* (4,260 GRT, 110 guests)

Windstar *Wind Spirit* (5,350 GRT, 148 guests)

Windjammer *Legacy* (1,165 GRT, 120 guests)

Cruise West *Spirit of '98* (96 GRT, 96 guests)

vessels tend to attract as many passengers in their 30s as in their 70s, all of them look-ing for something a little different from a regular cruise.

Most of the other small ships in this book are **coastal and river cruisers**—small vessels designed to sail in protected coastal waters and rivers. Very casual (and for the most part relatively plain), these ships offer a cruise oriented heavily toward nature, wildlife watching, culture, and history, with onboard naturalists to help interpret what you see. In addition to coastal cruisers, **Cruise West** and **Lindblad** also operate tougher expedition ships able to sail in the open ocean. Rounding out the small-ship options are the nostalgic Mark Twain–style stern-wheelers of **Majestic America Line,** which turn the clock back on trips along the Mississippi, the Pacific Northwest's Columbia and Snake rivers, and Alaska's Inside Passage.

See "Active Travel & Adventure Cruises," below, and chapter 8, "Small Ships, Sail-ing Ships & Adventure Cruises," for more details on all these options.

The **small luxury ships** of high-end lines such as **Seabourn, Silversea,** and **Sea Dream** offer a refined, ultraelegant ambience. Cabins are spacious, service is gracious, gourmet meals are served on fine china, and guests dress to impress. These ships offer few activities besides watersports, putting more emphasis on quiet relaxation and visits to high-end ports such as St. Barts. **American Safari Cruises** operates truly tiny 12- and 22-passenger yachts. Service-oriented like the luxe ships, they also offer an adventure-travel vibe, with lots of built-in active excursions.

OLD SHIP OR NEW?

The age of a ship used to be a bigger topic than it is now. The 2000 edition of this book included no fewer than 12 really old vessels, 10 of which have been sold off, laid up, or scrapped. Aside from Cunard's classic *QE2* (now sailing primarily from Eng-land), the small luxury yacht *Sea Cloud,* and most of the Maine Windjammer Associ-ation fleet, the only truly antique ship remaining in this book for 2008 is Imperial Majesty's old and endearing *Regal Empress,* a liner built in 1955 and still going strong (if a little worn around the edges). She's probably the last chance you'll have to sail on a mid-century liner.

The majority of ships in this book, by contrast, have been built in the past 17 years, though a few date from the late 1980s. Those older ships are generally a bit dated, though some cruise lines are doing a lot of work to bring them up-to-date. Royal Caribbean, for instance, is updating the interiors of their older ships so they look more like their new ones, and retrofitting some of the same activities options.

4 Cruises for Families

There's a reason so many families with kids go on cruises: It's easy (or at least as easy as traveling with kids ever is), convenient, safe, fun for the kids, and relaxing for mom and dad. Cruise lines have been going to great lengths to please parents and kids alike, as families become an ever larger and more influential segment of the cruising public. In fact, since 2000, Royal Caribbean, among the most family-friendly lines, has seen a more than 50% increase in the number of kids under 3 cruising with their parents. Same story with Carnival, which now carries 300% more children under 18 than in 1995. During school holidays, there can be so many kids on board that playrooms get jam-packed. Both toddlers and teens are taken care of too: Royal Caribbean, for instance, has

Family Cruising Tips

Here are some suggestions for better sailing and smoother seas on your family cruise.

- **Reserve a crib.** If you'd like a crib brought into your cabin, request one when booking your cruise.
- **Bring baby food and diapers.** If your infant is still on jar food, you'll have to bring your own. You can store milk and snacks in your cabin's minifridges/minibar, which comes standard on most new ships. (Ships more than 5 or 10 years old may offer them only in suites.) If yours is pre-stocked with beer and peanuts, you can ask your steward to clear it out.
- **Keep a tote with you on embarkation day.** Fill it with diapers, baby food, a change of clothes, bathing suits, or anything you'll need for the afternoon. After boarding a big ship, it may take a few hours for your luggage to be delivered to your cabin.
- **Pack some basic first-aid supplies, and even a thermometer.** Cruise lines have limited supplies of these items, and charge for them, too. If an accident should happen on board, virtually every ship (except the smallest ones) has its own infirmary staffed by doctors or nurses. Keep in mind that first aid can usually be summoned more readily aboard ship than in port.
- **Warn younger children about the danger of falling overboard,** and make sure they know not to play on the railings.
- **Make sure your kids know their cabin number** and what deck it's on. The endless corridors and doors on the megaships often look exactly alike, though some are color-coded.
- **Prepare kids for TV letdown.** Though many ships today receive satellite TV programming, you won't get the range of options you have at home.

daily play groups for parents and toddlers (6 months–3 years), while elaborate teen facilities are all the rage across the industry. Lines know teens are their future business, and they do their best to keep teenagers entertained and out of mischief.

The megaships cater most to families and attract the largest numbers of them, with playrooms, video arcades, and complimentary **supervised activities** usually provided for children ages 2 or 3 to 17 (generally, young children must be potty-trained to participate), and programs broken down into several age categories. Some lines set a minimum age for children to sail aboard (usually 6–12 months), but Disney offers a supervised nursery for ages 3 months and up (it wouldn't surprise us if this became a trend). See the individual cruise line reviews for details.

Disney offers the most family-friendly ships at sea today, followed by **Royal Caribbean,** whose ships (especially the Freedom-, Voyager-, and Radiance-class ships) have huge play areas. The **Carnival** ships do a pretty good job, too, especially the Conquest class (kids as young as 4 months are included in the group babysitting program), as do the **Norwegian, Princess,** and **Celebrity** megaships. Even lines traditionally geared to older folks are getting in on the kid craze. Holland America has renovated all of its ships' kids' facilities over the past few years, and the kids' facilities and programs on Cunard's *QM2* are the best-kept secrets at sea.

See the section "Best Cruises for Families with Kids," on p. 7, for more info.

BABYSITTING   After the complimentary daylong roster of supervised activities wraps up somewhere between about 7 and 10pm, most mainstream lines offer slumber-party-style **group babysitting** in the playroom. Services are usually from about 10pm until about 1 to 3am and are for ages 3 to 12, costing about $4 to $6 per hour per child. Some lines do accommodate younger kids, with toys, cribs, and nap areas geared to infants and toddlers: Disney's nurseries take children as young as 3 months and Carnival includes kids as young as 4 months. The counselors will even change diapers. **Private in-cabin babysitting** by a crewmember is also offered by Celebrity, MSC, Royal Caribbean, and most high-end lines at a steeper $8 to $10 per hour (and sometimes a few bucks more for additional siblings). Using a private babysitter every night isn't cheap, but Heidi's gone this route when her boys were babies and swears by it—how else to dine and have a cocktail or two in peace after a long kid-centric day? Try to get them tucked in and asleep before the sitter arrives so they won't have to deal with a new face just before bedtime.

FAMILY-FRIENDLY CABINS   Worried about spending a whole week with the family in a cramped little box? Depending on your budget, you may not have to.

On the low end, a family of four can share a cabin that has bunk-style third and fourth berths, which fold out of the walls just above the regular beds. A few lines, such as Carnival and NCL, will even accommodate a fifth person on a rollaway bed on certain ships, if space permits, and a baby crib can be brought in if requested in advance. There's no two ways about it, though: A standard cabin with four people in it will be cramped, and with one bathroom . . . well, you can imagine. However, when you consider how little time you'll spend in the cabin, it's doable, and many families take this option. The incentive is price: Whether children or adults, the rates for third and fourth persons sharing a cabin with two full-fare (or even heavily discounted) passengers are usually about half of the lowest regular rates. Norwegian Cruise Line allows children under 2 to sail free with two full-fare passengers (though you must pay port charges and government taxes for the kids, which run about $100–$200 per person). Crystal has offered free passage for all children under 12 for summer sailings in Alaska. *Note:* Because prices are based on double adult occupancy of cabins, single parents sailing with children usually have to pay adult prices for their kids, though deals for single parents are offered every once in a while.

Disney's *Magic* and *Wonder* boast the family-friendliest cabins at sea: The majority of the ships' 875 cabins are equipped with two bathrooms and a sitting area with a sofa bed, plus there's a tub and a minifridge. (While minifridges or minibars are fairly standard these days, tubs are a rarity unless you're splurging on a suite.) They're almost as big as most ships' minisuites and comfortably sleep families of three or four—but, of course, Disney's rates are generally higher than those of their mainstream competition. The ships' bona fide suites accommodate families of five to seven. In general, whatever line you choose, families who can afford it should **consider booking a suite or junior suite.** Many have a pullout couch in the living room (or, better yet, two separate bedrooms) and can accommodate up to three or four children.

If you have older kids, it may just be cheaper to book **connecting cabins**—two separate standard cabins with interconnecting doors. Almost every ship reviewed in this book offers connecting cabins, with the exception of most small ships and a small handful of midsize and megaships.

TAKING THE KIDS ON SMALL SHIPS   Most small-ship cruises are not kid-friendly, but if your children are at least 10 or 12, some of the sailing ships (for example, Windjammer's *Legacy* and *Polynesia* and Star Clippers' *Royal Clipper*) can be loads of fun and educational to boot. You won't find a kids' playroom or even many other kids on board, but since these cruises usually visit a port every day, you'll be aboard ship only in the evenings anyway. If your child is inquisitive and well behaved, he or she may be able to talk with the crew and learn how a sailing ship operates.

5 Cruises for Honeymooners & Anniversary Couples

Practically all cruises have what it takes to make your honeymoon or anniversary memorable: moonlight and stars, the undulating sea all around, dimly lit restaurants, and the pure romance of travel. Of course, different ships are romantic to different kinds of people. The megaships offer a big, flashy experience, like a trip to Vegas without the dry heat. The ultraluxury lines are more like a trip to Paris, with gourmet cuisine, fine wine, perfect service, and the finest bed linens. And some of the small-ship lines are like staying at a Vermont B&B—though others are more like a Motel 6 with a view. Beyond the ships themselves are the ports of call, offering experiences that are variously exotic, charming, exciting, and sybaritic.

HONEYMOON & ANNIVERSARY PACKAGES

Besides their inherent romantic qualities, cruises are a good honeymoon choice for the practical reason that many depart on Sundays, so couples that marry on Saturday can leave the next day. Some lines offer honeymooner freebies such as a special cake in the dining room one night, or an invitation to a private cocktail party. Couples celebrating anniversaries are often invited as well. To get your share of freebies, be sure to tell your travel agent or the cruise line reservation agent that you'll be celebrating on the cruise. Beyond the freebies, the mainstream cruise lines aren't shy about selling a variety of **honeymoon/anniversary packages.** You'll get a pamphlet describing the available packages when you receive your cruise tickets in the mail. NCL's $79 Honeymoon Package is about average for its price range, and includes champagne and strawberries at embarkation, a dinner for two with complimentary wine at the ship's specialty restaurant, an invitation to a cocktail party, a keepsake photo, and canapés in your cabin 1 evening. Their $229 Deluxe Package adds breakfast in bed 1 day and two 25-minute massages at the spa. All the mainstream lines offer similar deals, with packages in the $300 to $500 range generally piling on more spa treatments, champagne, shore excursions, canapés, chocolate-covered strawberries, and the like. These packages must be ordered before the cruise.

Ultraluxe lines such as Silversea, Seabourn, Regent Seven Seas, SeaDream, and Crystal are less involved in these kinds of promotions, but that's because free champagne and canapés, whirlpool bathtubs, and five-course dinners served in your cabin are all a matter of course with these lines.

VOW-RENEWAL & "ROMANCE" PACKAGES

Some lines offer vow-renewal packages for couples who'd like to celebrate their marriage all over again, or packages that simply add romance to a vacation. On Holland America, for example, couples can renew their vows at a special group ceremony at

Getting Married on Board or in Port

If you'd like to have your marriage and honeymoon all in one, you can legally get hitched on many cruises, either aboard ship or at one of your ports of call.

Practically all the mainstream lines offer wedding packages, with Carnival, Princess, and Royal Caribbean being the romance leaders, followed by NCL, Celebrity, Disney, Holland America, and Costa. In almost all cases a local justice of the peace, notary, or minister must officiate; so even if you choose to hold your ceremony aboard ship, it will have to take place while the ship is in port, not at sea. Princess's Grand-, Diamond-, and Coral-class ships have **wedding chapels** on board, as do Royal Caribbean's Freedom- and Voyager-class ships, Carnival's Spirit-class ships, and NCL's *Norwegian Sun, Star, Dawn, Jewel, Pearl, Gem, Jade,* and *Pride of America.* Other ships hold ceremonies in lounges that are decorated for the occasion.

If you want nonsailing family and friends to attend, you can hold the ceremony and reception at your port of embarkation, before the ship leaves. Guests will be on a special list with port security, and they'll have to bring the requisite ID to board. Ceremonies can also be arranged at various ports of call. On Caribbean routes, you can tie the knot in ports such as Aruba, Barbados, Grand Cayman, St. Thomas, Sint Maarten, San Juan (Puerto Rico), Ocho Rios and Montego Bay (Jamaica), Cozumel (Mexico), Nassau (The Bahamas), and Key West (Florida). Other options include Bermuda and the Alaskan ports of Juneau and Ketchikan. If you've always wanted to be married on a beach or by a tropical waterfall, this is the way to go. In Alaska, you can even arrange to be married on the ice of Juneau's Mendenhall Glacier courtesy of **Temsco** (✆ **877/789-9501;** www.temscoair.com), which also handles glacier helicopter tours for the cruise lines. If contemplating marriage in a port of call, remember that your cruise itinerary limits how far afield you can go, since ships generally stay in port only a limited number of hours.

Wedding packages generally start around $850 for intimate shipboard ceremonies for the bride and groom only. That price usually includes the services of an officiant (though you can bring your own if you prefer), a bouquet and boutonniere, champagne and keepsake glasses, a wedding cake, and the services of a photographer but not the photos themselves—

sea, catered with drinks and cold hors d'oeuvres; the $149 package includes a floral arrangement in your cabin, a photo and photo album, a certificate presented by the captain, and dinner for two at the Pinnacle alternative restaurant. Princess offers souped-up vow-renewal packages for $205 and $485 per couple. The former includes the ceremony, an orchid bouquet and boutonniere, a bottle of champagne and souvenir champagne glasses, a framed formal portrait of the ceremony, a commemorative certificate signed by the captain, and a framed photo of the ceremony; the latter adds a champagne breakfast in bed, two terry-cloth robes, a visit to the spa for half-hour those will cost extra, should you choose to buy them. Adding a reception for eight guests will bring the price up. The basic wedding/reception package offered by Carnival goes for $1,125. Prices go up from there based on the complexity and size of your reception (from a simple open bar and hors d'oeuvres to a formal meal in the ship's restaurant) and by port. Additional guests can be accommodated for an additional per-person charge. Ceremonies can also be performed off-ship in port, at higher prices.

THE LEGAL DETAILS No matter where you choose to wed, you must arrange for a marriage license from the U.S. or foreign port far in advance of your cruise. Policies vary from country to country, so you'll save a lot of headaches by having the cruise line help you with the details. Carnival and Princess have actual wedding departments to help you with these matters; other lines handle wedding planning through their guest-relations office or refer you to a wedding consultant with whom they work. Be sure to check with these departments before booking your cruise to be sure wedding space is available on the date you have in mind.

HAVING THE CAPTAIN OFFICIATE Princess Cruises is currently the only line where the captain himself does the honors, performing six or seven civil ceremonies a week. Adorned with fresh flower arrangements and stained glass, the charming wedding chapels on the line's Grand-, Diamond-, and Coral-class ships seat about three dozen. Assistant pursers in dress-blue uniforms are available to escort a bride down the short aisle. Three different ceremony packages are offered, starting at $1,800 per couple (plus $450 for licensing fees). Depending on which you choose, they can include photography, video, music, and salon treatments for the bride. You can also arrange onboard receptions that can be custom-tailored with a variety of options—hors d'oeuvres, champagne, wedding cake, and so on. Friends and relatives who aren't sailing can even monitor the wedding courtesy of the ships' chapel Web cams, which broadcast an updated photo every minute or so. (Look at the very bottom of the Princess website home page for "Bridge Cams." Pick a ship, then click on "Wedding Chapel" from the drop-down menu.) Don't wait till the last minute if you're considering Princess for your wedding, as there's often a waiting list.

massages or facials, canapés or petits fours in your stateroom every evening, and a personalized invitation from the captain to visit the bridge while in port. These are fairly representative of what's offered by the other mainstream lines.

6 Cruises for Gay Men & Lesbians

A number of specialized travel agencies offer cruises for gay men and/or lesbians, either chartering a full ship outright or reserving blocks of cabins with cruise lines that are known to be particularly gay-friendly. Full-charters typically bring aboard their own entertainers (as well as the ship's usual entertainment staff) and program many of their own activities. Hosted group trips typically have cocktail parties for group members and specially programmed activities on board and in port.

- **Atlantis Events Inc.,** 9200 Sunset Blvd., Suite 500, West Hollywood, CA 90069 (© **800/628-5268** or 310/859-8800; www.atlantisevents.com), offers all-gay charters with lines such as Celebrity, Royal Caribbean, and NCL. In addition to the lines' own entertainment, Atlantis brings aboard its own featured performers. Past guests have included Patti LuPone, Cybill Shepherd, and Chaka Khan.
- **Friends of Dorothy Travel,** 1177 California St., Suite B, San Francisco, CA 94108-2231 (© **800/640-4918** or 415/864-1600; www.fodtravel.com), offers many full-gay charters with lines such as Celebrity, NCL, and the ultraluxe Sea-Dream Yachts, as well as hosted tours on *Queen Mary 2* and other ships.
- **Olivia Cruises and Resorts,** 434 Brannan St., San Francisco, CA 94107 (© **800/ 631-6277** or 415/962-5700; www.olivia.com), offers full-ship charters targeted specifically to the lesbian community, mostly aboard Holland America's ships. Guest performers in recent years have included k. d. lang, the Indigo Girls, Wynonna Judd, Shawn Colvin, and Melissa Etheridge.
- **Pied Piper Travel,** 330 W. 42nd St., Suite 1804, New York, NY 10036 (© **800/ 874-7312** or 212/239-2412; www.piedpipertravel.com), offers hosted gay cruises that include various onboard parties and activities and arranged visits with the gay community at the various ports of call.
- **R Family Vacations,** 5 Washington Ave., Nyack, NY 10960 (© **866/732-6822;** www.rfamilyvacations.com), was founded by Rosie O'Donnell's partner, Kelli O'Donnell, along with gay travel veteran Gregg Kaminsky. Trips are targeted to the gay and lesbian family market.
- **RSVP Vacations,** 2535 25th Ave. S., Minneapolis, MN 55406 (© **800/328-7787** or 612/729-1113; www.rsvpvacations.com), offers full-ship charters on lines such as Holland America and Star Clippers. All sailings are targeted to both gay men and lesbians, and bring aboard their own guest performers. RSVP works through more than 10,000 different travel agencies; locate one by calling the 800 number or checking the website above.

7 Active Travel & Adventure Cruises

It's true: Cruises *can* be active and adventurous, whether you want to really get off the beaten track on an expeditionary small ship or just keep your heart rate elevated a few hours a day on a megaship.

ADVENTURE & EXPEDITIONARY CRUISES

A few years ago we met this great Australian couple in Alaska. They'd wanted to see the state for years, and wanted to really get into its forests and see its wildlife, but they didn't have time to do a 3-week wilderness trek. Their solution? They booked a small-ship cruise that split its sailing week between exploring wilderness areas and visiting tiny fishing towns. It was a perfect choice for them.

These types of ships offer few of the usual activity options, but that's by design: Their focus is on what's outside the vessel, not inside. Most offer itineraries that mix visits to large and small ports with days spent steering through natural areas in search of wildlife. However, some are more active than others. Lindblad Expeditions, for instance, builds activities such as hiking, kayaking, and exploring by inflatable launch into its adventure itineraries. On Star Clippers' sailing ships, those inflatable launches might be used to take passengers water-skiing or on banana-boat rides. See "Different Boats for Different Folks," earlier in this chapter, for more on the different kinds of small-ship experiences.

KEEPING ACTIVE ON THE MAINSTREAM & LUXE SHIPS

Ships started becoming more active around the dawn of the 1990s, and today it's unheard of for a new megaship to launch without a huge gym, jogging tracks, and sports decks that may have basketball courts, golf nets, and marquee activities such as rock-climbing walls, bungee trampolines, or surfing simulators (the latter three associated with Royal Caribbean). A handful of smaller and mostly high-end ships concentrate on watersports, with retractable or floating watersports platforms to allow easy swimming, water-skiing, and windsurfing right from the ship. See "Keeping Fit: Gyms, Spas & Sports," in chapter 4, for an overview, and the "Pool, Fitness, Spa & Sports Facilities" section of each ship review in part 2 for a rundown on which ship has what.

ACTIVE SHORE EXCURSIONS

On shore, the cruise lines are offering more and more active excursions. No need to sit on a bus for 3 hours if you'd rather be feeling the burn. Along with snorkeling and diving, options such as biking, hiking, kayaking, horseback riding, zipline canopy tours, and river rafting are offered in many ports from the Caribbean to Alaska and beyond. For more details, see the port reviews in part 3.

8 Cruises for the Young & Old

"So which are the ships for young people?" We get this question all the time, and the answer is, there aren't any. That is, there aren't any that attract *only* young people, just like there aren't many hotels or resorts that do. Most ships are a mixed bag of ages, with couples in their 40s, 50s, and 60-plus making up the majority, along with a growing percentage of younger couples, often with kids. Destination plays into the balance, with the Caribbean and Mexican Riviera attracting a sizable young crowd as well as lots of retirees. Alaska, Europe, New England/Canada, and Asia itineraries, on the other hand, draw mostly an older, 50-plus crowd (though you will see families with young kids in Alaska and Europe during the summer). That said, here are some general guidelines about ships and the ages of the people you'll find on them.

The **youngest crowds,** in the 20s-to-40s range, are typically found on 2-, 3-, and 4-night warm-weather cruises (and next on the 7-night cruises) offered by mainstream lines such as Carnival, Royal Caribbean, and NCL. Young-at-heart types, who may be 54 or 72 but wear bikinis and short-shorts and drink piña coladas for lunch, will also be attracted to those lines, as well as to smaller fun-loving lines such as Windjammer and Star Clippers.

The **oldest folks,** upward of 60, will be the vast majority on luxury lines such as Seabourn, Silversea, Cunard, and Regent. Mainstream line Holland America has also traditionally attracted a mature crowd, though they're trying hard to broaden their demographic, particularly on their newer megaships. Among the small-ship lines, you'll find a generally older crowd aboard American Canadian Caribbean, American Cruise Lines, Cruise West, INTRAV, Majestic America, and RiverBarge Excursions.

9 Cruises for People with Disabilities & Health Issues

Though most of the cruise industry's ships are foreign-flagged and are not required to comply with the **Americans with Disabilities Act,** the newest ships have all been built with accessibility in mind, and some older ships have been retrofitted to offer access. Most ships that can accommodate wheelchair-bound passengers require that they be accompanied by a fully mobile companion. The ship reviews in chapters 6 through 8 include information about access and facilities in the "Cabins" sections, but be sure to discuss your needs fully with your travel agent prior to booking.

See the "Onboard Medical Care" box on p. 37 for information on medical facilities aboard ship.

ACCESSIBLE CABINS & PUBLIC ROOMS   Most ships have a handful of cabins specifically designed for travelers with disabilities, with extrawide doorways, large bathrooms with grab bars and roll-in showers, closets with pull-down racks, and furniture built to a lower height. The "Ships at a Glance" chart on p. 98 identifies ships with accessible cabins, and the "Cabins" section in each of the ship reviews in chapters 6 through 8 indicates how many. The vast majority of the ships reviewed in the **mainstream** and **luxury** categories (chapters 6 and 7) have accessible cabins, but of the **adventure ships** in chapter 8, only the four American Cruise Lines ships, Cruise West's *Spirit of '98* and *Spirit of Oceanus,* and some of the Majestic America ships are fully or partially wheelchair-friendly.

Most public rooms on newer vessels have ramps, and some also have lifts to help passengers with disabilities into the pools. A few older ships still have small sills or lips in cabin and bathroom doorways that may rise as high as 6 to 8 inches (and were originally created to contain water). Those that do may be able to install temporary ramps to accommodate wheelchair users. This must be arranged in advance.

ELEVATORS   Most shipboard elevators (particularly aboard today's megaships) are wide enough to accommodate wheelchairs, but make sure before booking. Due to the size of the megaships (where it can sometimes be a long way from place to place), cabins designed for wheelchair users are intentionally located near elevators. If you don't use a wheelchair but have trouble walking, you'll want to choose a cabin close to an elevator to avoid a long hike. The vast majority of small vessels and sailing ships do not have elevators.

TENDERING INTO PORT   If your ship is too large to dock or if a port's docks are already reserved by other vessels, your ship may anchor offshore and shuttle passengers to land via small boats known as *tenders.* Some tenders are large and stable and others are not, but the choppiness of the water can be a factor when boarding either way. If you use a wheelchair or have trouble walking, it may be difficult or impossible to get aboard. For liability reasons, many lines forbid wheelchairs to be carried onto tenders, meaning you may have to forgo a trip ashore and stay on board when in these ports. An exception to this is Holland America, which has a wheelchair-to-tender transport system aboard all of their ships except *Prinsendam.* The system works by locking a wheelchair on a lift, which transports it safely between the gangway and the tender.

Check with your travel agent to find out if itineraries you're interested in allow your ship to dock at a pier. Note that weather conditions and heavy traffic may occasionally affect the way your ship reaches a port.

TRAVEL-AGENT SPECIALISTS   A handful of experienced travel agencies specialize in booking cruises and tours for travelers with disabilities. **Accessible Journeys,**

Onboard Medical Care

The vast majority of ships have a nurse and sometimes a doctor aboard to provide medical services for a fee. Most of their cases involve seasickness, sunburn, and the like, but they may also be required to stabilize a patient with a more serious ailment until he or she can be brought to a hospital at the next port of call (or, in extreme cases, be evacuated by helicopter). If they're very unlucky, the medical staff may also have to deal with an outbreak of **norovirus,** the flulike gastrointestinal bug that strikes a ship every once in a while, making a big media splash. More common than the common cold, the virus causes vomiting, stomach cramps, diarrhea, and general nausea for a few days, and is brought on by simple contagion: One infected passenger comes aboard, leaves his germs on a handrail, and all of a sudden everyone's sick—just like kindergarten. Outbreaks are relatively rare but make for really bad media, so cruise lines have stepped up their already vigilant sanitation routines to further reduce the chance of transmission.

All large ships have **staffed infirmaries,** but if you have special needs, check with the line to see exactly what medical services are provided. The quality of ships' staffs and facilities can definitely vary. Generally, big ships have the best-equipped facilities and largest staff since they're dealing with such a huge number of passengers and crew. In 2003, the author of an extensive *New York Times* article concluded that **Holland America** and **Princess** had the best onboard medical facilities, as well as the most generous pay packages for their doctors. Princess's Grand- and Coral-class ships, for instance, carry at least one and sometimes two doctors as well as two to five nurses, and are linked via a live video and camera system with U.S.-based medical centers. All Holland America ships can consult 24 hours a day (via phone or e-mail) with the University of Texas Medical Branch at Galveston, and their Vista-class ships have a teleradiology system that allows X-rays to be transmitted to a shore-side medical facility. (Princess's *Sea Princess* and Carnival's Spirit- and Conquest-class ships also have this system.) HAL's *Amsterdam* has the capability to do live television telemedicine conferencing and transmit X-rays to shore-side medical facilities. Note that shipboard doctors are not necessarily certified in the United States, and aren't always experts in important areas such as cardiology.

Small ships (those discussed in chapter 8) generally don't carry onboard medical staff since they sail close to shore and can evacuate sick passengers quickly. Usually, some crewmembers have nursing or first-aid experience. Small ships always carry doctors when sailing more far-flung international itineraries.

35 W. Sellers Ave., Ridley Park, PA 19078 (© **800/846-4537** or 610/521-0339; www.disabilitytravel.com), organizes both group and individual cruises on accessible ships, with accessible airport transfers and shore excursions, as well as an escort on group tours. **Flying Wheels Travel,** 143 W. Bridge St., Owatonna, MN 55060 (© **507/451-5005;** www.flyingwheelstravel.com), is another option.

2

Booking Your Cruise & Getting the Best Price

The only thing consistent about cruise pricing is its unpredictability. When the overall economy and conditions within the industry and the travel agent community shift, it all affects cruise rates. Though there's no magic secret to getting the best price on your cruise, we can help you hedge your bets and map out the best savings strategy. In this chapter we've laid out the best booking strategies for 2008, along with other money-saving suggestions and booking tips.

1 The Caribbean: A Bargain Hunter's Dream

The old tenet of supply and demand still determines cruise rates: When the lines have more ships than they can fill, prices are low. They're higher when people are clamoring to cruise. That means, depending on when you cruise and which ship and cabin you choose, there can be a wide variance in price: Expect to pay anywhere from $400 to $4,000 a person for a week in the Caribbean, with the average somewhere around $799 for a standard cabin. With so much new supply on the market in the Caribbean, bargain hunters are in luck. With the exception of the summer months, when lots of families are traveling, Caribbean cruise pricing has been soft of late, so booking at the last minute (up until a few weeks before sailing) can often land you the lowest rates. Of course, to reap the deals, it'll help if you're flexible with the cabin category you get and even the ship.

For the other destinations covered in this book, it's not as easy to generalize. "Pricing differs from market to market," says Mike Driscoll, editor of industry bible *Cruise Week.* He says you can't count on the same discounting on Alaska cruises, for instance, as you'll find in the Caribbean. Especially for cruisetour packages and more unique itineraries, it's advisable to book at least 90 days ahead and sometimes even 4 to 6 months early, because typically less price cutting is done. Again, if you're ultraflexible about when you can travel and which ship you take, you may find a last-minute deal. Just don't count on it.

As for the actual booking process, cruise lines still tend to do what they've been doing for years, relying on traditional **travel agents** and **websites** to sell their product, rather than retaining huge in-house reservations departments.

Generally, travel agents have less leeway in discounting than they used to, as the cruise lines have taken more control of their pricing. This means you're less likely than in the past to find rates being dramatically different from travel agent to travel agent.

For tips on using both online and brick-and-mortar agencies to the best advantage, see "Agents & the Web: Finding the Best Deals," later in this chapter.

2 The Prices in This Guide

Just like the airbrushed models dancing and lounging all over the cruise lines' brochures, the prices printed in those brochures aren't real, varying from just a little more than people really pay to wildly inflated. Apparently, even the cruise lines are ignoring them these days: We've heard from a reliable industry insider that many lines are planning to phase them out altogether. In any case, remember that **you'll always pay less,** except aboard some of the specialized small-ship lines.

Many cruise guides and magazines print these brochure rates despite knowing how useless they are in the real world, but we've come up with a new approach, working with Nashville, Tennessee–based **Just Cruisin' Plus** (© **800/888-0922;** www.just cruisinplus.com) to present a sample of the **actual prices** people are paying for cruises aboard all the ships in this book. The brochure rate for a 7-night eastern Caribbean cruise aboard Holland America's beautiful *Noordam* is $2,639 for a low-end outside cabin. In reality, however, during our sampling period (Nov 2007 cruises, priced in mid-Apr) customers were able to get that same cabin for $899. In the ship-review chapters, we've listed these realistic prices for every ship, and in the "Price Comparisons: Discounted Rates vs. Brochure Rates" table in this chapter, we've shown how the brochure prices for every ship stack up against what consumers actually pay. The table gives prices for the lowest-priced **inside cabins** (ones without windows) and lowest-priced **outside cabins** (with windows) aboard each ship, and the ship reviews in chapters 6 through 8 also provide sample discount prices for the cheapest **suites.** Remember that cruise ships generally have many different categories of cabins within the basic divisions of inside, outside, and suite, all priced differently. The rates we've listed represent the *lowest-priced* (which usually equates to smallest) in each division. If you're interested in booking a roomier, fancier cabin or suite, the price will be higher, with rates for high-end inside cabins being close to those for low-end outsides, and rates for high-end outsides being close to those for low-end suites.

Remember that rates are always subject to the basic principles of supply-and-demand, so those listed here are meant as a guide only and are in no way etched in stone—the price you pay may be higher or lower, depending on when you book, when you choose to travel, whether any special discounts are being offered by the lines, and a slew of other factors. All rates are cruise-only, per person, based on double occupancy, and, unless otherwise noted, include **port charges** (the per-passenger fee each island charges the cruise line for entry). Government fees and taxes are additional.

3 The Cost: What's Included & What's Not

Overall, a cruise is superconvenient and adds up to a pretty good deal when you consider that your main vacation ingredients—accommodations; meals and most snacks; stops at ports of call; a packed schedule of activities; use of gyms, pools, and other facilities; and shows, cabaret, jazz performances, and more—are covered in the cruise price. Just don't think it's *all* free. To beef up their bottom lines as much as possible, cruise lines are pushing a slew of **added-cost onboard extras.** You can always just say no, but if you're like most of us, you'll have an "oh, what the heck" attitude once you step across that gangway. So, when figuring out your budget, be sure to figure in the additional costs you'll incur for shore excursions (which can run from $25 up to $500, with many being in the neighborhood of $75 a pop), bar drinks and specialty coffees,

Price Comparisons: Discounted Rates vs. Brochure Rates

Cruise Line	Ship	Itinerary (region / number of nights)	Lowest-Priced Inside Cabin (discounted / brochure)	Lowest-Priced Outside Cabin (discounted / brochure)	Lowest-Priced Suite (discounted / brochure)
American Cruise Line	American Eagle	Florida Rivers / 7	N/A	$2,560 / $2,560	N/A
	American Glory	Antebellum South / 7	N/A	$2,560 / $2,560	N/A
	American Spirit	Antebellum	N/A	$2,560 / $2,560	N/A
	American Star	Antebellum	N/A	$2,560 / $2,560	N/A
Azamara*	Celebrity Journey	S. America / 18	$3,269	$3,449	$5,649
	Celebrity Quest	Panama Canal / 14	$1,869	$2,099	$3,299
Carnival	Carnival Conquest	W. Caribbean / 7	$459 / $1,669	$579 / $1,919	$1,329 / $2,619
	Carnival Destiny	S. Caribbean / 7	$459 / $1,669	$569 / $1,919	$1,259 / $2,619
	Carnival Freedom	W. Caribbean / 7	$469 / $1,669	$569 / $1,919	$1,319 / $2,819
	Carnival Glory	W. Caribbean / 7	$449 / $1,669	$549 / $1,919	$1,299 / $2619
	Carnival Legend	W. Caribbean / 7	$469 / $1,669	$569 / $1,969	$1,269 / $2,619
	Carnival Liberty	E. Caribbean / 8	$629 / $1,819	$769 / $2,019	$1,519 / $2,819
	Carnival Miracle	W. Caribbean / 8	$559 / $1,819	$779 / $2,039	$1,479 / $2,769
	Carnival Pride	Mex. Riviera / 7	$549 / $1,669	$679 / $1,969	$1,369 / $2,619
	Carnival Spirit	Mex. Riviera / 8	$579 / $1,819	$709 / $2,119	$1,379 / $2,769
	Carnival Splendor	not yet available	not yet available	not yet available	not yet available
	Carnival Triumph	E. Caribbean / 7	$429 / $1,510	$529 / $1,760	$1,249 / $2,460
	Carnival Valor	E. Caribbean / 7	$429 / $1,669	$529 / $1,919	$1,279 / $2,819
	Carnival Victory	W. Caribbean / 7	$429 / $1,669	$529 / $1,919	$1,279 / $2,619
	Celebration	Bahamas / 5	$229 / $999	$299 / $1,149	$999 / $1,749
	Ecstasy	W. Caribbean / 5	$269 / $999	$349 / $1,149	$799 / $1,649
	Elation	Mex. Riviera / 4	$249 / $999	$339 / $1,089	$729 / $1,549
	Fantasy	W. Caribbean / 5	$259 / $999	$329 / $1,179	$979 / $1,749
	Fascination	Bahamas / 3	$189 / $699	$239 / $789	$629 / $1,149
	Holiday	W. Caribbean / 5	$229 / $999	$299 / $1,149	$999 / $1,749
	Imagination	E. Caribbean / 5	$289 / $999	$359 / $1,149	$809 / $1,549
	Inspiration	W. Caribbean / 5	$259 / $999	$359 / $1,149	$779 / $1,549
	Paradise	Mex. Riviera / 4	$209 / $849	$259 / $979	$689 / $1,379
	Sensation	Bahamas / 4	$199 / $849	$249 / $979	$699 / $1,379
Celebrity*	Century	W. Caribbean / 4	$359	$459	$859
	Constellation	S. Caribbean / 10	$1,049	$1,229	$2,749
	Galaxy	S. Caribbean / 10	$819	$949	$2,699

Price Comparisons: Discounted Rates vs. Brochure Rates

Cruise Line	Ship	Itinerary (region / number of nights)	Lowest-Priced Inside Cabin (discounted / brochure)	Lowest-Priced Outside Cabin (discounted / brochure)	Lowest-Priced Suite (discounted / brochure)
	Infinity	S. America / 13	$1,449	$1,649	$3,999
	Mercury	Alaska / 7	$799	$899	$1,599
	Millennium	E. Caribbean / 7	$729	$849	$1,999
	Solstice	not yet available	not yet available	not yet available	not yet available
	Summit	Panama Canal / 14	$1,299	$1,649	$3,949
Costa	Costa Fortuna	E. Caribbean / 7	$529 / $1,079	$629 / $1,279	$1,599 / $2,099
	Costa Mediterranea	W. Caribbean / 7	$499 / $1,049	$599 / $1,279	$1,599 / $2,099
Cruise West	Pacific Explorer	Costa Rica & Panama / 7	N/A	$3,249 / $3,249	N/A
	Spirit of Alaska	Columbia & Snake rivers / 10	$3,242 / $3,549	$4,097 / $4,499	N/A
	Spirit of Columbia	Alaska / 10	$3,242 / $3,549	$4,097 / $4,499	N/A
	Spirit of Discovery	NW Coastal / 7	N/A	$2,799 / $2,799	N/A
	Spirit of Endeavour	NW Coastal-Canada / 7	N/A	$2,699 / $2,699	N/A
	Spirit of Glacier Bay	not yet available	not yet available	not yet available	not yet available
	Spirit of '98	Alaska / 8	N/A	$6,549 / $6,549	$4,097 / $4,499
	Spirit of Oceanus	Alaska / 12	N/A	$6,477 / $7,499	$9,199 / $9,399
	Spirit of Yorktown	Sea of Cortez / 8	N/A	$4,599 / $4,599	N/A
Crystal	Crystal Serenity	S. Caribbean / 10	N/A	$3,295 / $6,440	$7,204 / $10,325
	Crystal Symphony	W. Caribbean / 7	N/A	$2,244 / $4,320	$5,169 / $7,580
Cunard	Queen Mary 2	S. Caribbean / 10	$1498 / $2284	$1,698 / $2,641	$2,999 / $3,789
Disney	Disney Magic	E. Caribbean / 7	$799 / $1899	$1,249 / $2,799	$2,999 / $4,499
	Disney Wonder	Bahamas / 4	$499 / $999	$839 / $1,599	$1,549 / $2,449
Holland America	Amsterdam	S. Caribbean / 10	$849 / $1569	$949 / $2,179	$1,789 / $3,079
	Maasdam	S. Caribbean / 10	$849 / $1,869	$949 / $2,449	$1,699 / $3,259
	Noordam	S. Caribbean / 11	$899 / $2,389	$999 / $2,639	$1,849 / $4,409
	Oosterdam	Mex. Riviera / 7	$499 / $1,199	$649 / $1,439	$1,249 / $2,559
	Ryndam	Mex. Riviera / 10	$874 / $1,959	$999 / $2,099	$1,674 / $3,279
	Statendam	Alaska / 7	$949 / $1,549	$1,149 / $1,999	$1,699 / $2,699
	Veendam	W. Caribbean / 7	$599 / $1,259	$649 / $1,469	$1,224 / $2,339
	Volendam	Panama Canal / 10	$949 / $2,239	$1,049 / $2,589	$2,149 / $4,059
	Westerdam	E. Caribbean / 7	$599 / $1,259	$699 / $1,469	$1,274 / $2,729
	Zaandam	Hawaii / 15	$1,799 / $2,959	$1,999 / $3,159	$3,199 / $5,319
	Zuiderdam	E. Caribbean / 7	$599 / $1,259	$699 / $1,469	$1,274 / $2,729
Imperial Majesty	Regal Empress	Bahamas / 2	$139 / $139	$199 / $199	$299 / $299

Price Comparisons: Discounted Rates vs. Brochure Rates

Cruise Line	Ship	Itinerary (region / number of nights)	Lowest-Priced Inside Cabin (discounted / brochure)	Lowest-Priced Outside Cabin (discounted / brochure)	Lowest-Priced Suite (discounted / brochure)
Lindblad Expeditions	Sea Bird	Sea of Cortez / 8	N/A	$3,390 / $3,390	N/A
	Sea Lion	Sea of Cortez / 8	N/A	$3,680 / $3,680	N/A
	Sea Voyager	Costa Rica / 8	N/A	$3,970 / $3,970	N/A
Majestic America	American Queen	Mississippi / 7	$1,497 / $1,698	$2,367 / $2,698	$3,332 / $3,808
	Columbia Queen	Pacific Northwest / 7	$2,079 / $2,599	$2,719 / $3,399	$3,599 / $4,499
	Contessa	Alaska / 7	N/A	$2,697 / $3,595	$4,196 / $5,595
	Delta Queen	Mississippi / 7	N/A	$1,748 / $2,689	$2,599 / $3,999
	Empress of the North	Pacific Northwest / 7	$1,105 / $1,248	$1,366 / $1,548	$3,280 / $3,748
	Mississippi Queen	Mississippi / 7	$1,169 / $2,339	$1,449 / $2,899	$2,114 / $4,299
	Queen of the West	Pacific Northwest / 7	$1,148 / $1,148	$1,348 / $1,348	$3,048 / $3,048
MSC Cruises	Lirica	W. Caribbean / 7	$479 / $985	$629 / $1,285	$1,199 / $2,425
	Opera	S. Caribbean / 11			
Norwegian	Norwegian Dawn	E. Caribbean / 7	$529 / $1,599	$629 / $1,799	$1,179 / $2,399
	Norwegian Gem	Transatlantic / 9	$699 / $929	$849 / $1,149	$1,199 / $1,599
	Norwegian Jewel	W. Caribbean / 5	$299 / $1,099	$399 / $1,349	$699 / $1,699
	Norwegian Majesty	W. Caribbean / 7	$449 / $1,099	$519 / $1,299	$1,399 / $1,899
	Norwegian Pearl	W. Caribbean / 5	$299 / $1,079	$399 / $1,349	$699 / $1,699
	Norwegian Spirit	W. Caribbean / 7	$519 / $1,199	$599 / $1,399	$2,499 / $3,299
	Norwegian Star	Mex. Riviera / 8	$599 / $1,599	$799 / $1,799	$1,249 / $2,499
	Norwegian Sun	W. Caribbean / 7	$549 / $1,599	$649 / $1,899	$1,149 / $2,599
	Pride of Aloha	Hawaii / 7	$999 / $3,199	$1,149 / $3,399	$3,599 / $7,999
	Pride of America	Hawaii / 7	$849 / $2,799	$949 / $3,049	$2,299 / $6,799
Oceania	Regatta	Panama Canal / 16	$2,549 / $5,598	$2,949 / $6,398	$4,749 / $9,998
Princess	Caribbean Princess	E. Caribbean / 7	$599 / $1,099	$699 / $1,299	$1,049 / $1,649
	Coral Princess	Panama Canal / 10	$1,199 / $1,999	$1,199 / $2,224	$1,769 / $2,569
	Crown Princess	S. Caribbean / 7	$599 / $1,099	$699 / $1,299	$1,049 / $1,649
	Dawn Princess	Mex. Riviera / 7	$499 / $1,029	$599 / $1,279	$1,499 / $1,699
	Diamond Princess	Hawaii / 15	$1,699 / $3,070	$1,898 / $3,385	$2,795 / $3,945
	Emerald Princess	S. Caribbean / 10	$899 / $1,699	$1,055 / $1,959	$1,655 / $2,599
	Golden Princess	Mex. Riviera / 7	$549 / $1,059	$599 / $1,309	$999 / $1,689
	Grand Princess	W. Caribbean / 7	$599 / $1,099	$655 / $1,319	$1,049 / $1,649
	Island Princess	Panama Canal / 11	$1,299 / $2,099	$1,299 / $2,324	$1,869 / $2,669
	Sapphire Princess	Alaska / 7	$799 / $1,399	$1,019 / $1,619	$1,507 / $2,174
	Sea Princess	S. Caribbean / 14	$1,319 / $2,449	$1,649 / $2,749	$2,049 / $3,149

Price Comparisons: Discounted Rates vs. Brochure Rates

Cruise Line	Ship	Itinerary (region / number of nights)	Lowest-Priced Inside Cabin (discounted / brochure)	Lowest-Priced Outside Cabin (discounted / brochure)	Lowest-Priced Suite (discounted / brochure)
	Star Princess	Transatlantic / 17	$1,599 / $3,500	$1,698 / $3,920	$2,999 / $4,865
	Sun Princess	Alaska / 7	$799 / $1,399	$1,549 / $2,174	$1,899 / $2,724
Regent Seven Seas	Seven Seas Mariner	Caribbean / 11	N/A	$3,598 / $7,195	$4,948 / $9,895
	Seven Seas Navigator	W. Caribbean / 7	N/A	$2,740 / $5,240	$3,140 / $6,040
	Seven Seas Voyager	Caribbean / 11	N/A	$3,598 / $7,195	$4,948 / $9,895
Royal Caribbean*	Adventure of the Seas	S. Caribbean / 7	$669	$799	$1,449
	Brilliance of the Seas	Panama Canal / 10	$1,349	$1,549	$2,499
	Empress of the Seas	S. Caribbean / 11	$949	$1,049	$1,899
	Enchantment of the Seas	W. Caribbean / 5	$349	$429	$799
	Explorer of the Seas	S. Caribbean / 12	$1,299	$1,449	$2,389
	Freedom of the Seas	E. Caribbean / 7	$799	$1,349	$1,699
	Grandeur of the Seas	W. Caribbean / 5	$379	$449	$789
	Jewel of the Seas	W. Caribbean / 6	$399	$499	$1,199
	Legend of the Seas	S. Caribbean / 7	$749	$949	$1,499
	Liberty of the Seas	E. Caribbean / 7	$849	$899	$1,649
	Majesty of the Seas	Bahamas / 4	$269	$309	$679
	Mariner of the Seas	E. Caribbean / 7	$659	$698	$1,299
	Monarch of the Seas	Mex. Riviera / 4	$249	$279	$579
	Navigator of the Seas	W. Caribbean / 5	$429	$559	$899
	Radiance of the Seas	E. Caribbean / 8	$899	$948	$2,099
	Rhapsody of the Seas	Far East / 12	$1,699	$2,199	$3,999
	Serenade of the Seas	S. Caribbean / 7	$599	$699	$1,299
	Sovereign of the Seas	Bahamas / 4	$269	$309	$679
	Splendour of the Seas	W. Caribbean / 4	$519	$609	$889

Price Comparisons: Discounted Rates vs. Brochure Rates~

Cruise Line	Ship	Itinerary (region / number of nights)	Lowest-Priced Inside Cabin (discounted / brochure)	Lowest-Priced Outside Cabin (discounted / brochure)	Lowest-Priced Suite (discounted / brochure)
	Vision of the Seas	Mex. Riviera / 7	$559	$649	$1,249
	Voyager of the Seas	W. Caribbean / 7	$719	$799	$1,499
Seabourn	Seabourn Legend	Panama Canal / 14	N/A	$5,995 / $8,325	$8,397 / $13,995
	Seabourn Pride	S. Caribbean / 7	N/A	$2,987 / $4,595	$4,937 / $7,595
SeaDream	SeaDream I	S. Caribbean / 7	N/A	$3,112 / $5,313	$8,252 / $12,663
	SeaDream II	S. Caribbean / 5	N/A	$2,494 / $4,195	$6,534 / $10,045
Silversea	Silver Shadow	Panama Canal / 15	N/A	$6,371 / $8,520	$7,946 / $10,520
	Silver Wind	S. Caribbean / 10	N/A	$4,545 / $5,645	$5,666 / $7,045
Star Clippers	Royal Clipper	S. Caribbean / 7	$1,940 / $1,940	$2,040 / $2,040	$3,960 / $3,960
Windjammer	Legacy	Costa Rica / Panama / 8	N/A	$1,355 / $1,355	$1,755 / $1,755
	Mandalay	E. Caribbean / 6	$1,300 / $1,300	$1,500 / $1,500	$1,800 / $1,800
	Polynesia	E. Caribbean / 6	$1,200 / $1,200	$1,700 / $1,700	$1,800 / $1,800
	Yankee Clipper	S. Caribbean / 6	$1,300 / $1,300	$1,500 / $1,500	$1,800 / $1,800
Windstar	Wind Spirit	S. Caribbean / 7	N/A	$1,849 / $2,699	$2,849 / $3,987
	Wind Star	Central Amer. / 7	N/A	$1,949 / $2,899	$3,049 / $4,257
	Wind Surf	S. Caribbean / 7	N/A	$1,749 / $2,599	$2,949 / $4,109

* These lines no longer offer brochure rates.

** All rates were supplied by Nashville-based Just Cruisin' Plus (© 800/888-0922; www.justcruisinplus.com) at press time in April 2007 and are subject to change and based on availability. All fares include port charges.

spa treatments ($25–$500, plus tip, though $100–$150 is above average for a 50-minute massage), souvenirs, and even fresh flowers and fancy cakes if your self-restraint is really low. **Gratuities** are also typically charged to guests' accounts at the end of the cruise; the cruise lines pay their service staff minimal salaries on the assumption that they'll make most of their pay in tips. Generally, you can expect to tip about $70 per person during a weeklong cruise. (For more on tipping, see chapter 3, "Things to Know Before You Go.") If you're the gambling type, you're a prime candidate for increasing your ship's revenue stream, whether your game is craps or bingo, scratch-off cards or Caribbean stud poker.

Some of the most luxurious and expensive lines—Silversea, Seabourn, Regent Seven Seas, and SeaDream Yacht Club—come closest to being truly all-inclusive by including all alcoholic beverages and gratuities in their cruise rates. Aside from these aberrations, though, you can expect to shell out at least another $250 to $500 per person for an average 7-night cruise, and easily double that if, for instance, you have a bottle of wine with dinner every night, a couple of cocktails after, go on three $90 shore excursions, hit the ship's $30-per-person alternative restaurants a few times, try your luck at bingo, and buy some trinkets in the onboard shops or at the ports of call. Of course, just as at a hotel, you'll also pay extra for items such as ship-to-shore phone calls and e-mails, massages, manicures, facials, haircuts, fancy coffees, and medical treatments in the ship's infirmary. If you're not cruising from a port you can drive to, then you'll have to figure in **airfare to the ship,** which is rarely included in cruise prices.

4 Money-Saving Strategies

From early-booking discounts and last-minute deals to sharing cabins and senior and frequent-cruiser discounts, there are a lot of ways to save money on your cruise.

As they have for years, cruise lines continue to offer **early-booking discounts,** and some are better than others (generally, they're better for Alaska cruises than Caribbean, for example). "Generally speaking, when it comes to the major cruise lines, the farther away your cruise goes from North America, the farther out (that is, the earlier) you should book it," says travel guru Driscoll. That means you often get the best rates and availability for cruises to Alaska (especially Alaska cruisetour packages, and to all Europe and Asia cruises, for that matter) if you book at least 4 to 6 months early. Price aside, when booking early you naturally have much more assurance of getting exactly what you want in terms of cruise line, ship, and everything else.

If you're in the habit of traveling at the last minute, you can still snag good deals for Caribbean cruises this way, especially during **slow periods** such as September, October, and nonholiday weeks in November and December. The main thing you may sacrifice when booking late is a measure of choice: You'll have to take the ship, itinerary, and cabin category that's available, whether it's the one that you wanted or not. Getting airfare at the last minute may be tough, too. Plus, most last-minute deals are completely nonrefundable; if you book a week before the cruise, for example, the full fare is due upfront and you get zip back if you change your mind a few days later.

You'll find **last-minute deals** advertised online and in the travel section of a handful of Sunday newspapers, namely the *Miami Herald, Los Angeles Times, Chicago Tribune,* and *New York Times.* But the best route is checking with a travel agent that specializes in cruises, and getting on their e-mail blast list to be alerted about special promotions and discounts. See "Agents & the Web: Finding the Best Deals," later in this chapter.

From time to time some cruise lines offer discounts to **seniors** (usually defined as anyone 55 years or older); so don't keep your age a secret, and always ask your travel agent about these discounts when you're booking. For discounts in general, the best organization to belong to is **AARP,** 601 E St. NW, Washington, DC 20049 (© **888/687-2277;** www.aarp.org), the biggest outfit in the United States for people 50 and over.

If you've cruised with a particular cruise line before, you're considered a valued **repeat passenger,** and will usually be rewarded with 5% to 10% discounts (sometimes higher) on future cruises. Depending on how many times you've sailed, you may also get cabin upgrades, invitations to private cocktail parties, priority check-in at the terminal, casino vouchers, logo souvenirs, a special newsletter, and a bottle of wine or a fruit basket in your cabin on embarkation days. The catch to all of this is that repeat-passenger discounts often cannot be combined with other pricing deals, particularly in the case of the mainstream lines.

If you're a serious repeater, though, the generous booty you get on the small upscale ships can add up to something substantial. After you sail a total of 140 days with Seabourn, for instance, you're entitled to a free 14-day cruise, while Silversea passengers

Average Cost of Onboard Extras

Just so you're not shocked when your shipboard account is settled at the end of your trip, here are some average prices for onboard extras.

Laundry	$1–$6 per item
Self-service laundry	$1–$2 per load
Pressing	$1–$4 per item
5×7-inch photo from ship photographer	$7–$10
Scotch and soda at an onboard bar	$3.95–$6
Bottle of beer (domestic/imported)	$3.50/$6
Bottle of wine to accompany dinner	$20–$300
Glass of wine	$5–$10
Bottle of Evian water (.5 liter/1.5 liters)	$1.50/$3.50
Can of Coca-Cola	$1.50–$2
Ship-to-shore phone call or fax	$4–$15 per minute
Cellphone calls at sea	$1.70 per minute
Sending e-mails	50¢–$1 per minute
50-minute massage	$109–$139
Sunscreen, 6-ounce bottle	$10
Disposable camera	$15–$20

get a free 7-night cruise after sailing 350 days and a free 14-night cruise after 500 days. Some of the small adventure-oriented lines offer similar deals. ACCL, for instance, gives passengers an 11th cruise free after their 10th paid cruise of at least 12 nights.

Some cruise lines offer reduced **group rates** to folks booking at least eight or more cabins, but this is really based on supply and demand. If a ship is selling well, group deals may not be available, but if it isn't, lines have a lot more incentive to wheel and deal. Carnival even guarantees that if individual fares fall below what a group has already paid, group members get the difference back in the form of a shipboard credit. Groups may be family reunions and the like, but travel agents may also create their own "groups" whose members don't even know they're part of one. Quick explanation: The travel agent reserves a block of cabins on a given ship and the cruise line in turn gives them a discounted group rate that agents can pass on to their clients. The cruise line benefits because they're potentially selling a lot of cabins through agency X, and the agent benefits because they can offer their clients a good price. So, always ask your travel agent if you can be piggybacked onto some group space.

Very small groups—three or four people max in most cases—can share one cabin if it's equipped with **third or fourth berths** (sofa beds or bunk-style berths that pull down from the ceiling or wall). This route isn't recommended for anyone who suffers from claustrophobia. Disney, Carnival, and NCL go one better by offering standard cabins geared to families that can accommodate five people—Disney's even have 1½ bathrooms. The rates for third, fourth, and fifth passengers in a cabin, whether adults or children, are typically 30% to 60% or more off the normal adult fare. You can also look into **sharing a suite.** Many can accommodate five to seven people, and some are almost outlandishly roomy.

If cruising solo, you'll be charge something called the **single supplement,** which entails a charge that adds 50% to 100% to the standard per-person cruise fare—a consequence of cruise lines basing their revenue expectations on two people sharing every cabin. Some lines quietly forego or reduce this kind of supplemental charge if a ship isn't filling up as a particular departure date approaches, but there's no way to predict this kind of thing. A few lines (HAL and Windjammer barefoot) offer a **cabin-share service** that matches you with a same-gender roommate. If the cruise line can't find a roommate for you, you'll probably get the cabin at the regular double occupancy rate anyway. Very few ships offer cabins specifically designed for solo passengers anymore.

5 Agents & the Web: Finding the Best Deals

Today, practically everybody has a website, and the difference between so-called **Web-based cruise sellers** and more **traditional travel agencies** is that the former rely on their sites for actual bookings, while the latter use theirs as glorified advertising space to promote their offerings, doing all actual business in person or over the phone. With a few exceptions, the cruise lines also have **direct-booking engines** on their own sites, but we don't recommend using them. Why? Because agents and Web-based sellers may have negotiated group rates with the lines, be part of a consortium with whom a line is doing an upgrade promotion, or have other deals going that enable them to offer you lower rates. Though it may sound peculiar, the cruise lines actually prefer that you book through third parties because having agents and websites do the grunt work allows the lines to maintain small reservations staffs and, simultaneously, maintain goodwill in a system that works—something they have to consider because the vast majority of cruises are booked through agencies of one type or another. Typically, mainstream cruise lines report that about 70% to 80% of their bookings come from more traditional travel agencies (for the luxury lines, about 98% use travel agents). "The more you pay, the more likely you are to need or want a travel agent," says Driscoll.

WHICH OFFERS BETTER PRICES?

As far as cruise prices go, there's no absolutely quantifiable difference between the real-live travel agents (whether your hometown brick-and-mortar mom-and-pop agency or a big anonymous mega-agency) and Internet-based cruise sellers. For some years now, the major lines starting doing something they had talked about for years, offering all agencies large or small the same rates—a major coup for small agencies struggling to keep up with the Expedias of the world. Carnival, Norwegian, Royal Caribbean, Crystal, and Celebrity, for example, have declared in one way or another that they would offer all agencies the same rates, and further, that they would have no dealings with any agency that publicly (via print or website advertising) doled out rebates to clients—that is, gave their customers additional discounts by sacrificing some of their own commissions. The lines believe rebating and cutthroat discounting among agencies cheapens the cruise product; lines want travel agents to emphasize the benefits of cruise vacations, not just the fact that one agent is offering a cheaper price than another. Don't think there aren't any loopholes; there are. Customers and agents can privately wheel and deal, plus it's not uncommon for some agencies to now offer customers gift cards, bottles of wine, or other incentives in lieu of reduced rates.

Be Savvy & Beware of Scams

With the number of offers a potential cruise buyer sees, it can be difficult to know if an agency is or isn't reliable, legit, or, for that matter, stable. It pays to be on your guard against fly-by-night operators and agents who may lead you astray.

- **Get a referral.** A recommendation from a trusted friend or colleague (or from this guidebook) is one of the best ways to hook up with a reputable agent.
- **Use the cruise lines' agent lists.** Many cruise line websites include agency locator lists, naming agencies around the country with whom they do business. These are by no means comprehensive lists of all good or bad agencies, but an agent's presence on these lists is usually another good sign of experience.
- **Beware of snap recommendations.** If an agent suggests a cruise line without asking you a single question first about your tastes, beware. Because agents work on commissions from the lines, some may try to shanghai you into cruising with a company that pays them the highest rates, even though that line may not be right for you.
- **Always use a credit card to pay for your cruise.** It gives you more protection in the event the agency or cruise line fails. When your credit card statement arrives, make sure the payment was made to the cruise line, not the travel agency. If you find that payment was actually made to the agency, it's a big red flag that something's wrong. If you insist on paying by check, you'll be making it out to the agency, so it may be wise to ask if the agency has default protection. Many do. (**Note:** The only exception to this is when an agency is running a charter cruise—for example, a music cruise with special entertainment.)
- **Always follow the cruise line's payment schedule.** Never agree to a different schedule the travel agency comes up with. The lines' terms are always clearly printed in their brochures and usually require an initial deposit, with the balance due no later than 75 to 45 days before departure. If you're booking 2 months or less before departure, full payment is usually required at the time of booking.
- **Keep on top of your booking.** If you ever fail to receive a document or ticket on the date it's been promised, inquire about it immediately. If you're told that your cruise reservation was canceled because of overbooking and that you must pay extra for a confirmed and rescheduled sailing, demand a full refund and/or contact your credit card company to stop payment.

WHICH PROVIDES BETTER SERVICE?

Since pricing is closer to being equitable across all types of cruise agencies than ever before, it's really service that distinguishes one agency from another. Most websites give you only a menu of ships and itineraries to select from, plus a basic search capability that takes into account only destination, price, length of trip, and date, without consideration of the type of cruise experience each line offers. That's fine if you know exactly what you want, and are comfortable on the computer. If, on the other hand, you have limited experience with cruising and with booking on the Web, it may be better to see a traditional agent, who can help you wade through the choices and answer your questions. For instance, a good agent can tell you which cabins have their views obstructed by lifeboats; which are near loud areas such as discos and the engine room; which ships and itineraries you should avoid if you're not looking for a party vibe; and, in general, what the major differences are between cabin categories. A lot of this kind of detailed information won't be found on the Web—you need to hear it from a person. To be better prepared before you call an agent, it's a good idea to do some research on the Web first.

Keep in mind, though, that you need to find an agent who really knows the business—and this applies to every type of agent: those who work out of their home or an agency office, those who work for large conglomerates and deal mostly over the phone, and those who staff toll-free numbers associated with Web-based sellers. Some are little more than order-takers: They may not know much more than pricing, and may never even have been on a cruise themselves. This system works okay for selling air travel, where the big question is coach or first class, case closed; but a lot more variables are associated with booking a cruise. An experienced cruise agent—someone who's sailed on or inspected a variety of ships and booked many customers aboard in the past—will be able to tell you about special promotions (such as cabin upgrades), act as an intermediary should any problems arise with your booking, order special extras such as a bottle of champagne in your cabin when you arrive, and in general make your planning easy.

So how do you know if an agent is any good? The best way, of course, is to use one who has been referred to you by a reliable friend or acquaintance. This is particularly valuable these days, when agents are being pressed to squeeze more profit from every sale, making them less likely to take the time to discuss options. When you're searching for a good agent, it doesn't hurt if an agent is an **Accredited Cruise Counselor (ACC), Master Cruise Counselor (MCC),** or **Elite Cruise Counselor (ECC),** designations doled out by the Cruise Lines International Association (CLIA), an industry trade organization, after agents take classes and inspect a number of ships. Many of the cruise lines' websites list **preferred agencies** (generally broken down or searchable by city or state), as does the CLIA site **(www.cruising.org).** Many of the most reliable agencies are also members of **agent groups,** such as Virtuoso, Signature Travel Network, and Vacation.com. In the sections below, we list some of the best agencies and also evaluate the major cruise-selling websites.

6 Recommended Agencies & Websites

Of the approximately 20,000 U.S. travel agencies (including home-based, the largest growing segment), 15% (or about 3,000 agencies) sell 90% of all cruise travel in North America; about 10% to 15% of those are considered cruise-only. Agencies come in all shapes and sizes, from small neighborhood stores to huge chain operations. Like banking, telecommunications, and media, the travel industry has been rife with consolidation over the past decade, so even that mom-and-pop travel agency on Main Street may turn out to be an affiliate of a larger agency. When it comes to home-based agents, they may or may not be affiliated with a national group such as CruiseOne or

SeaMaster Cruises. It's better if they are so they have access to more resources and competitive rates. Use a home-based agent only if she's been doing this for a long time.

Even though you'll get similarly low rates from both traditional and Web-based agencies these days, we can't stress enough that service counts for something, too. There's value in using a travel agent you've worked with in the past or one who comes highly recommended by someone you trust. A good agent will be there for you if problems arise.

TRADITIONAL AGENCIES SPECIALIZING IN MAINSTREAM CRUISES

To give you an idea of where to begin, here's a sampling (by no means comprehensive) of both cruise-only and full-service agencies that have solid reputations selling cruises with mainstream lines such as Princess, Carnival, Royal Caribbean, Celebrity, Holland America, and Norwegian. A few are affiliated with the big chains; most are not. While all have websites to promote current deals, the agencies listed primarily operate from a combination of walk-in business and toll-free telephone-based business.

- **America's Vacation Center,** 520 W. Valley Park Way, Suite A, Escondido, CA 92025 (℅ **800/646-4319;** www.americasvacationcenter.com)
- **The Cruise Company,** 10760 Q St., Omaha, NE 68127 (℅ **800/289-5505** or 402/339-6800; www.thecruisecompany.com)
- **Cruise Holidays,** 7000 NW Prairie View Rd., Kansas City, MO 64151 (℅ **800/869-6806** or 816/741-7417; www.cruiseholidayskc.com)
- **Cruises Only,** 10 Harbor Park Dr., Port Washington, NY 11050 (℅ **800/278-4737;** www.cruisesonly.com), part of World Travel Holdings, the largest cruise retailer in the world
- **Cruise Value Center,** 6 Edgeboro Rd., Suite 400, East Brunswick, NJ 08816 (℅ **800/231-7447** or 732/257-4545; www.cruisevalue.com)
- **Just Cruisin' Plus,** 5640 Nolensville Rd., Nashville, TN 37211 (℅ **800/888-0922** or 615/833-0922; www.justcruisinplus.com)
- **Vacations To Go,** 1502 Augusta Dr., Suite 415, Houston, TX 77057 (℅ **800/338-4962** or 713/974-2121; www.vacationstogo.com)

Another way to find a reputable travel agency in your town is by contacting one of a handful of **agency groups** or **consortiums,** which screen their members. The following groups, whose members specialize in mainstream cruises, all maintain websites that allow you to search for local agencies with your zip code or city: **TravelSavers** (℅ **800/366-9895;** www.travelsavers.com) is a group of more than 1,000 agencies; **Cruise Ship Centers** (℅ **800/707-7327;** www.cruiseshipcenters.com) has about 80 locations in Canada; and **Vacation.com** (℅ **800/843-0733;** www.vacation.com) is the largest group in the U.S., with some 6,000 members. **Carlson Wagonlit Travel** (www.carlsontravel.com) and **Cruise Holidays** (www.cruiseholidays.com) are both large, reputable chains, and their websites allow you to find a local branch near you.

TRADITIONAL AGENCIES SPECIALIZING IN LUXURY CRUISES

This sampling of reputable agencies, both cruise-only and full-service, specializes in selling ultraluxury cruises such as Cunard, Seabourn, Silversea, Crystal, Radisson Seven Seas, and SeaDream Yacht Club.

- **All Cruise Travel,** 1213 Lincoln Ave., Suite 205, San Jose, CA 95125 (℅ **800/227-8473** or 408/295-1200; www.allcruisetravel.com)

- **Concierge Cruises & Tours,** 13470 N. Sunset Mesa Dr., Marana, AZ 85653 (© **800/940-8385** or 520/572-6377)
- **Cruise Professionals,** 130 Dundas St. E., Suite 103, Mississauga, Ontario L5A 3V8, Canada (© **800/265-3838** or 905/275-3030; www.cruiseprofessionals.com)
- **Strictly Vacations,** 108 W. Mission St., Santa Barbara, CA 93101 (© **800/447-2364;** www.strictlyvacations.com; expert on Windstar)

If you're looking for a top-of-the-line cruise, definitely use an agency that's a member of one of the following agency groups whose members specialize in luxury cruises. Agency members can pass on lots of great extras to clients, from cabin upgrades to private cocktail parties. Members are ultraknowledgeable and it's not unusual for someone from the agency to sail on board the cruise to assist clients. All maintain websites that allow you to search for local agencies with your zip code or city. **Virtuoso** (© **866/401-7974;** www.virtuoso.com) is a consortium of more than 300 member agencies nationwide, including some on the list above. To find an agency in your area, call their toll-free number, or e-mail **travel@virtuoso.com**. Another group is **Signature Travel Network** (© **800/339-0868;** www.signaturetravelnetwork.com), with about 200 member agencies across the country. Call to find an agency in your area, or e-mail **info@signaturetravelnetwork.com**.

WEB-BASED AGENCIES SPECIALIZING IN MAINSTREAM CRUISES

The following sites are reputable Web-based cruise specialists (though, again, not a comprehensive list). All allow searches by destination, date of travel, length of cruise, and price range, as well as cruise line or ship if you know exactly what you want. All allow you to book online for at least some if not most lines. In many cases, though, this does not involve a live connection with the cruise line's reservations database, so you'll have to wait up to 24 hours for a confirmation via e-mail, fax, or phone call. Sometimes you can research your cruise online, but have to call a toll-free number when you're ready to get down to business. Keep in mind, these websites are constant works in progress, adding new features all the time.

- **Cruise411.com** (www.cruise411.com; © **800/553-7090**)
- **Expedia** (www.expedia.com; © **888/249-3978**)
- **Icruise.com** (www.icruise.com; © **888/427-8473**)
- **Travelocity** (www.travelocity.com; © **877/815-5446**)

7 Choosing Your Cabin

When it comes right down to it, choosing a cabin is really a question of money. From a windowless lower-deck cabin with upper and lower bunks to a 1,400-square-foot suite with a butler and mile-long private veranda, cruise ships can offer a dozen or more stateroom categories that differ by size, location in the ship, amenities, and, of course, price. To see what we mean, go to the Cruises Only website (**www.cruises only.com**) for 360-degree tours and photos of most ships.

It's traditionally been a rule of thumb that the higher up you are and the more light that gets into your cabin, the more you pay; the lower you go into the bowels of the ship, the cheaper the fare. On some of the more modern ships, however, that old rule doesn't always ring true. On ships launched recently by Carnival, for instance, designers have scattered their most desirable suites on midlevel decks as well as top decks, thereby diminishing the prestige of an upper-deck cabin. For the most part, though, and especially on small ships, where most cabins are virtually identical, cabins on higher decks are still generally more expensive, and outside cabins (with windows or balconies) are more expensive than inside cabins (those without). Outside cabins whose windows are obstructed by lifeboats will be cheaper than ones with good views.

EVALUATING CABIN SIZE

Inch for inch, cruise ship cabins are smaller than hotel rooms. Of course, having a private balcony attached to your cabin, as many do, makes your living space that much bigger.

A roomy **standard cabin** is about 170 to 190 square feet, although some of the smallest are about 85 to 100 square feet. Disney has some of the more spacious standard cabins at sea, at 226 square feet. Celebrity's standards are spacious enough at around 170 to 175 square feet, with those on its Millennium-class ships sometimes as big as 191 square feet. Carnival's and Holland America's are about 185 square feet or more. By way of comparison, equivalent standard cabins on a good number of ships in the Norwegian and Royal Caribbean lines are quite a bit smaller—try 120 to 160 square feet—and can be cramped. Cabins on the small-ship lines such as Windjammer, Clipper, and ACCL can be very snug—on the order of 70 to 100 square feet.

All the standard cabins on the high-end lines are roomy—in fact, many of the high-end ships are "suite only." For example, on Silversea's *Silver Shadow* and *Silver Whisper,* cabins are 287 square feet, plus a 58-square-foot balcony. Across the board, from mainstream to luxe, **suites and penthouses** are obviously the most spacious, measuring from about 250 square feet to more than 1,400 square feet, plus private verandas.

Most cruise lines publish schematic drawings in their brochures, with square footage and, in some cases, measurements of length and width, which should give you some idea of what to expect. (We also include square footage ranges for inside cabins, outside cabins, and suites in the cruise ship descriptions in chapters 6–8.) Consider measuring off the dimensions on your bedroom floor and imagining your temporary oceangoing home, being sure to block out part of that space for the bathroom and closet. As a rough guideline, within a cabin of around 100 square feet, about a third of the floor space is gobbled up by those functional necessities.

Now, while you may be thinking, "Gee, that's really not a lot of space," remember that, like a bedroom in a large house, your cabin will, in all likelihood, be a place you use only for sleeping, showering, and changing clothes.

THE SCOOP ON INSIDE CABINS VS. OUTSIDE CABINS

Whether you really plan to spend time in your cabin is a question that should be taken into account when deciding whether to book an inside cabin or an outside cabin (that is, one without windows or one with windows or a balcony). If you plan to get up bright and early, hit the buffet breakfast, and not stop till the cows come home, you can probably get away with booking an inside cabin and save yourself a bundle. Inside cabins are generally neither as bad nor as claustrophobic as they sound. Many, in fact—such as those aboard most of the Carnival and Celebrity fleets—are the same size as the outside cabins, and most cruise lines design and decorate them to provide an illusion of light and space.

If, on the other hand, you want to lounge around and take it easy in your cabin, maybe ordering breakfast from room service and eating while the sun streams in—or,

MODEL CABIN LAYOUTS

Typical Outside Cabins
- Twin beds (can usually be pushed together)
- Some have sofa bed or bunk for third passenger
- Shower (tubs are rare)
- TV and music
- Window or porthole, or veranda

Outside Cabin   Outside Cabin with Veranda

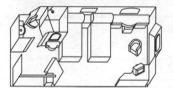

Typical Suites
- King, queen, or double beds
- Sitting areas (often with sofa beds)
- Large bathrooms, usually with tub, sometimes with Jacuzzi
- Refrigerators, sometimes stocked
- TVs w/VCR and stereo
- Large closets
- Large veranda

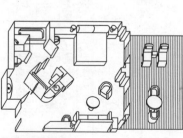

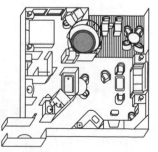

Suite with Veranda   Grand Suite with Veranda

Thanks to Princess Cruises for all photos and diagrams.

READING A SHIPíS DECK PLAN

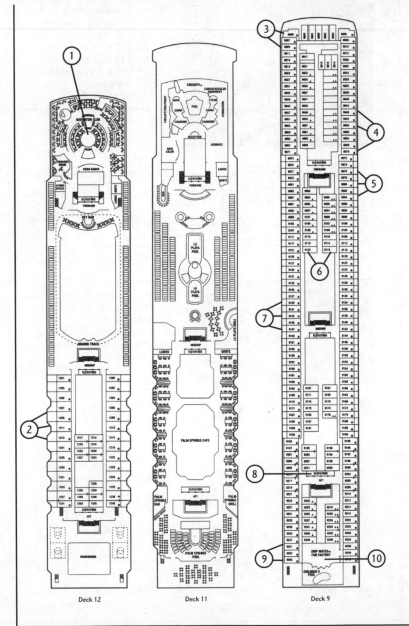

Deck 12   Deck 11   Deck 9

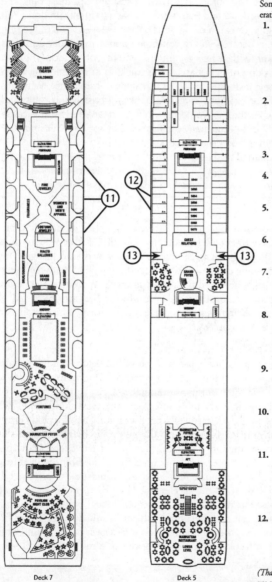

Deck 7

Deck 5

Some cabin choice considerations:

1. **Note the position of the ship's disco** and other loud public areas, and try not to book a cabin that's too close or underneath. This disco is far from any cabins—a big plus.

2. **Cabins on upper decks** can be affected by the motion of the sea. If you're abnormally susceptible to seasickness, keep this in mind.

3. **Ditto for cabins in the bow.**

4. **Outside cabins without verandas** appear as solid blocks of space.

5. **Outside cabins with verandas** are shown with a line dividing the two spaces.

6. **Inside cabins** (without windows) can be a real money-saver.

7. **Cabins amidships** are the least affected by the motion of the sea, especially if they're on a lower deck.

8. **Cabins that adjoin elevator shaftways** might be noisy. (Though proximity makes it easier to get around the ship.)

9. **Cabins in the stern** can be affected by the motion of the sea, and tend to be subject to engine vibration.

10. **Cabins near children's facilities** may not be the quietest places, at least during the day.

11. **Check that lifeboats** don't block the view from your cabin. The ones in this example adjoin public rooms, and so are out of sight.

12. **Cabins for people with disabilities** are ideally located near elevators and close to the ship's entrances (#13).

(Thanks to Celebrity Cruises for use of the Mercury's deck plan.)

Smoking at Sea . . . or Not

All ships covered in this book prohibit smoking in all restaurants, theaters, and such places as shops and the library. If you want to light up, most bars and lounges have smoking sections, and you're free to have a cig out on deck. You can also have a butt in your cabin or on your balcony. Now, if you're looking for a nonsmoking cabin because you're concerned about the lingering smells from a previous smoker, with a few exceptions, you're out of luck. The vast majority of cruise lines do not designate cabins smoking or nonsmoking (with the exception of Disney: It designates all of its cabins nonsmoking). Why? It's impossible to control (for example, someone books a nonsmoking cabin and then smokes anyway). Further, it would be a big fat headache for the cruise lines' inventory department—how many cabins should be set aside for smokers? Do they sit empty if not enough smokers book the cruise?

Luckily, cabins are cleaned well between cruises, if necessary by shampooing the rug or using air purifiers. Matt, a fairly smoke-sensitive nonsmoker, can't recall ever walking into a cabin and smelling residual smoke.

---

better yet, eating out *in* the sun, on your private veranda—then an outside cabin is definitely a worthwhile investment. Remember, though, that if it's a view of the sea you want, be sure when booking that your window or balcony doesn't just give you a good view of a lifeboat or some other obstruction (and remember, there are likely to be balconies on the deck right above your balcony, so they're more like porches than actual verandas). Some cruise line brochures tell you which cabins are obstructed, and a good travel agent or a cruise line's reservation agent can tell you which cabins on a particular ship might have this problem.

OTHER CABIN MATTERS TO CONSIDER

Unless you're booking at the last minute (a few weeks or less before sailing), as part of a group, or in a cabin-share or cabin-guarantee program (which means you agree to a price, and find out your exact cabin at the last minute), you can work with your agent to pick an exact cabin. If possible, try to go into your talks with some idea of what kind of cabin category you'd like, or at least with a list of must-haves or must-avoids. Need a **bathtub** rather than just a shower? That narrows your choices on most ships. Want **connecting cabins** so you and your kids, friends, or relatives can share space? Most ships have 'em, but they sometimes book up early, as do cabins with **third or fourth berths** (usually pull-down bunks or a sofa bed). Almost all ships have cabin TVs these days, but a few don't. Want an **elevator** close by to make it easy to get between decks? Is the view out the cabin's windows obstructed by lifeboats or other ship equipment? Most important, **keep cabin position in mind if you suffer from seasickness.** A midships location on a middle deck is best because it's a kind of ful-crum point, the area least affected by the vessel's rocking and rolling in rough seas.

8 Booking Your Air Travel

Except during special promotions, airfare is rarely included in cruise rates for Caribbean, Alaska, Mexico, and New England/Canada cruises, though it often is on Europe and Asia itineraries. So if you can't drive to your port of embarkation and need to fly to get to Miami, New York, San Juan, New Orleans, or one of the other 20-plus home ports, you'll have to either purchase airfare on your own through an agent or online, or buy it as a package with your cruise. The latter is often referred to as an **air add-on** or **air/sea package.** You can usually find information on these programs in the back of cruise line brochures and on their websites, along with prices on flights from more than 100 U.S. and Canadian cities to the port of embarkation. Here are the pros and cons to booking your airfare through the cruise line.

- **Pros:** When you book through the cruise line, they'll know your airline schedule and, in the event of delayed flights and other unavoidable snafus, will do what they can to make sure you get to the ship. For instance, during the fierce hurricane season in fall 2004 and 2005, those who had booked the cruise lines' air package were given priority when it came to rebooking. People who book their air transportation and transfers separately are on their own.
- **Cons:** Odds are it will be more expensive to book through the cruise line than on your own. In the past, cruise lines offered more competitive fares, but the airlines aren't giving them the bulk discounts they used to, meaning prices have gone up. Consequently, fewer passengers are now booking the lines' air packages. Also, if you book through the lines, you probably won't be able to use any frequent-flier miles you've accumulated, and the air add-on could require a circuitous routing—with indirect legs and layovers—before you finally arrive at your port of embarkation. Sources tell us only about 10% of passengers book airfare through the cruise lines.

If you choose to arrange your own air transportation, make absolutely sure that airfare is not included as part of your cruise contract. It rarely is with the exception of Europe and Asia cruises, but if it is, you're often granted a deduction (usually around $250 per person) off the cruise fare. If you purchase your own airfare, you can buy **bus transfers from the airport to the ship** through the cruise line (if you buy the cruise line airfare, transfers are often included in the price), but it's often cheaper to take a taxi, as is the case in Miami and Fort Lauderdale.

9 Prebooking Your Dinner Table & Arranging Special Diets

In addition to choosing your cabin when booking your cruise, on most ships you can also choose an **early or late seating** for dinner in the main restaurant (the buffet restaurants most ships have are always open seating), and sometimes even put in a request for the size table you're interested in (tables for 2, 4, 8, 10, and so on). Assignments for breakfast and lunch are rarely required, as dining rooms operate with open seating during these meals. At night, though, early seatings allow you to get first dibs on shipboard nightlife (or, conversely, promptly hit the sack), while late seatings allow you to linger a little longer over your meal. In the past few years, more lines—especially Norwegian and, to a slightly lesser extent, Princess—have junked this traditional early-late paradigm (in at least some of their restaurants) in favor of **open-seating dining** in which you simply show up when hunger pangs strike. For a more detailed discussion, see "Onboard Dining Options," on p. 84.

If you follow a **special diet**—whether vegetarian, low-salt, low-fat, heart-healthy, kosher, halal, or any other, or if you have certain food allergies—make this known to your travel agent when you book, or at least 30 or more days before the cruise, and make sure your diet can be accommodated at all three meals (sometimes special meal plans will cover only breakfast and dinner). The vast majority of ships offer vegetarian meals and health-conscious choices as part of their daily menus these days (Crystal even offers kosher food as part of its daily offerings), but it can't hurt to arrange things ahead of time. A cruise is not the place to go on an involuntary starvation diet.

10 Booking Pre- & Post-Cruise Hotel Stays

Cruise lines often offer hotel stays in the cities of embarkation and debarkation, and because most of these cities are tourist attractions in their own right, you may want to spend some time in New York, Oahu, or Vancouver before you sail, or drive to Disney World from Port Canaveral. The cruise lines' package deals usually include hotel stays and transportation from the hotel to the ship (before the cruise) or from the docks to the hotel (after the cruise). Inquire with your travel agent, and compare what the line is offering with what you may be able to arrange independently. Nowadays, you may be able to get a hotel stay much cheaper on your own.

11 Cancellations & Insurance

Given today's unpredictable geopolitical situation and instances of extreme weather conditions, cancellation protection and insurance are more important than ever, and ever-changing cruise line policies and procedures mean that it pays to stay informed.

What should you do if the cruise you've booked is canceled before it departs? A cruise could be canceled because of shipyard delays (if you've booked an inaugural cruise), or because of the outbreak of an infectious disease, mechanical breakdowns (such as nonfunctioning air-conditioning or an engine fire), the cruise line going out of business, an act of war, or an impending hurricane.

"Insurance was sure a big help to those who bought it for cruises during the 2004 and 2005 hurricane season, but for 2006 it was a waste of money because there weren't any hurricanes," says *Cruise Week* editor Mike Driscoll.

That said, in today's competitive market, cruise lines have been making extraordinary efforts to appease disappointed passengers, whether they bought insurance or not. Typically, a line will reschedule the canceled cruise and offer passengers big discounts on future cruises—after all, they don't want the bad press they'd get if they cheated hundreds or thousands of people. There are, however, no set rules on how a line will compensate you, over and above a refund, in the event of a cancellation.

Now, if the shoe's on the other foot and you need to cancel your own cruise, you'll generally get a refund—most lines give you every cent back if you cancel at least 2 to 3 months before your departure date, although details vary from line to line. If you cancel closer to departure, you'll usually get a partial refund up until about 15 to 30 days before the cruise.

"You buy insurance if you're concerned about medical issues or work commitments possibly preventing you from taking a cruise at the last minute," adds Driscoll. For all of these reasons—worries about travel, worries about cruise lines canceling or going belly up, sudden illness or other emergencies, missed flights that cause you to miss the ship, or even if you just change your mind—you may want to think about purchasing **travel insurance.**

If you're *just* worried about missing the ship, go a day early and spend your money on a hotel and nice dinner instead. If you're worried about medical problems occurring during your trip, on the other hand, travel insurance may be more vital. Except for the small coastal cruisers described in chapter 8, most cruise ships have an infirmary staffed by a doctor and a nurse or two; but in the event of a dire illness, the ship's medical staff can only do so much. Therefore, you may want a policy that covers **emergency medical evacuation** and, if your regular insurance doesn't cover it, the potential cost of major medical treatment while away from home.

There are policies sold through the cruise lines (with details varying from line to line) and others sold independently. Both sources have pros and cons.

CRUISE LINE POLICIES VS. THIRD-PARTY INSURERS

A good travel agent can tell you about policies sold through the cruise lines and ones sold independently of the lines. No matter which you choose, it's absolutely crucial to read the fine print because terms vary from policy to policy.

Both kinds typically reimburse you in some way when your trip is affected by unexpected events (such as canceled flights, plane crashes, dockworkers' strikes, or the illness or death of a loved one, as late as the day before or day of departure), but not by "acts of God," such as hurricanes and earthquakes (the exception being if your home is made uninhabitable, putting you in no mood to continue with your cruise plans). Both also typically cover **cancellation of the cruise** for medical reasons (yours or a family member's); **medical emergencies** during the cruise, including evacuation from the ship; lost or damaged luggage; and a cruise missed due to airline delays (though some only cover delays over 3 hr.). Neither kind of policy will reimburse you if your travel agent goes bankrupt, so using a travel agent you're very familiar with or who has been recommended to you is the safest precaution you can take. (And, of course, *always use a credit card,* never a check. If a corrupt travel agent cashes it, or a decent one just goes out of business, then you could get screwed.) Most cancellation policies also do not cover cancellations due to work requirements.

THIRD-PARTY COVERAGE   Even though agents get a commission for selling both cruise line policies and independent policies, most agents and industry insiders believe that non-cruise line policies are the best bet because some, such as Access America (see below), will issue insurance to those with **preexisting medical conditions** if the condition is stable when you purchase the insurance (a doctor would have to verify this if you ever made a claim) and if you purchase the policy within 14 days of your initial deposit on the cruise. They also offer **supplier-default coverage** that kicks in if a cruise line goes bankrupt, which a handful did between 2000 and 2003.

Still, you shouldn't be afraid to book a cruise. A well-connected travel agent should see the writing on the wall months before a cruise line fails—commissions will slow or stop being paid, phone calls won't be returned, and industry trade publications will report on any problems. The less customer-service-driven cruise sellers may not stop pushing a troubled cruise line, however, and may continue selling these lines up to the very last minute.

According to the Fair Credit Billing Act, if you paid by credit card (and again, you should *always* pay with a credit card), you'll generally get your money back if you dispute the charge within 60 days of the date the charge first appears. If you paid in full 4 months before the cruise, you'll likely be out of luck going the credit-reimbursement route and may have to resort to litigation. Also, while many lines post a multimillion-dollar bond with the Federal Maritime Commission, creating a fund from which they can reimburse creditors should they fail financially, it's no guarantee you'll get all or any of your money back. Technically, the bond covers cruise payments for all passengers embarking from U.S. ports, but because the line would have banks or other vendors to pay off first, you'd likely get only pennies on the dollar, if that. Still, it's better that a cruise line have a bond than not—and if you learn that a line is having trouble making bond payments, it may be a sign of serious financial woes.

Policies are available from reputable insurers such as **Access America,** Box 71533, Richmond, VA 23286 (✆ **866/807-3982;** www.accessamerica.com), and **Travel Guard International,** 1145 Clark St., Stevens Point, WI 54481 (✆ **800/826-4919;** www.travelguard.com), whose websites maintain lists of the lines they cover (or no longer cover); these are helpful in figuring out which lines may be considered financially shaky.

CRUISE LINE COVERAGE   Cruise lines offer their own policies, many of them administered by New York–based **BerkelyCare** (✆ **800/797-4514**). If you opt for this type of policy out of sheer convenience (the cost is added right onto your cruise fare), keep in mind they do not cover you in the event of a cruise line bankruptcy (though using a credit card can save you here; see above) or for cancellation of your cruise due to a preexisting medical condition, which is usually defined as an unstable condition existing within 60 days of your buying the insurance. Some lines' policies will issue a cruise credit for the penalty amount if a medical claim is deemed preexisting, and issue you cash if you cancel for a covered reason. Generally, the cancellation penalty imposed by the cruise line would be 100% of the cruise fare, for example, if you cancel a few days before the cruise (assuming you've paid in full), or it could be just $300 if you cancel right after making the initial cruise deposit. Be sure the coverage offered is truly an insurance policy. In some cases, the coverage is really a cancellation waiver that provides a credit for a future cruise under limited conditions.

Sounds like the third-party policies win hands down, right? Well, to make it just a little more complicated, a handful of cruise line policies are actually better in some areas than outside policies. For example, **Princess Cruises** has an insurance policy that allows you to cancel for all the reasons that an outside policy would (illness, injury) and get cash reimbursement, or they will let you cancel for any reason whatsoever (from fear of flying to a bad hair day) up until the day of departure and have 75% to 90% of the normal penalty for canceling your cruise applied toward a future trip. **Norwegian, Celebrity,** and **Royal Caribbean** offer similar "any reason" policies, which provide a cruise credit for up to 75%. For an extra $100 above their standard insurance fee (or $250 if purchased alone), high-end **Silversea** allows you to cancel cruises for any reason 1 to 14 days before sailing and get a credit for 100% of the penalty amount (including airfare, if booked through Silversea), applicable toward any cruise within the following 12 months. Many other lines offer similar cancellation plans. The cruise lines using the BerkelyCare policies (see above) also reimburse passengers for days missed on a cruise—say, if you missed your flight and had to join up with the cruise 2 days later—covering hotel costs during the missed days and transportation to the ship (though typically only to a max of $500). Keep in mind, cruise line policies do change, so before purchasing insurance be sure you understand exactly what you're getting.

12 Putting Down a Deposit & Reviewing Tickets

If you're booking several months or more ahead of time, then you have to leave a deposit to secure the booking; if you're booking last minute, the full fare will be due when you make the reservation. Depending on the policy of the line you selected, the amount will either be fixed at a predetermined amount or represent a percentage of the ticket's total cost. The length of time cruise lines will hold a cabin without a deposit is getting shorter by the minute. It seems pretty clear, in this age of near-obsessive "shopping around," that the cruise lines are doing their part to discourage it. It used to be a cruise could be held for a week before you had to plunk down cash; most lines have now shortened this window to 1 to 3 days (exceptions include exotic itineraries that aren't ultracompetitive). Carnival, for instance, now requires a deposit within 24 hours.

The balance of the cruise price is due anywhere from about 60 to 90 days before you depart; holiday cruises may require final payments earlier, perhaps 90 days before departure; and for some long cruises, it may be 120 days or more before you depart. The payment schedule for deposits on groups is often more liberal. Booking at the last minute usually requires payment in full at the time of booking.

Credit card payments are made directly to the cruise line, but payments by check are made out to the agency, which then passes payment on to the cruise line. As we've said repeatedly, it's preferable to pay by credit card, for the added protection it offers.

"Except in certain circumstances, if the travel agency asks, prefers, or insists on running your credit card through the agency processing terminal, it is a *major* red flag that most often should send you running from the building," says Charlie Funk, co-owner of Just Cruisin' Plus in Nashville. The only exception to this is when an agency is doing a charter or group with special entertainment or features, and the cruise is offered only through the agency.

Carefully review your ticket, invoice, itinerary, and/or vouchers to confirm that they accurately reflect the departure date, ship, and cabin category you booked. The printout usually lists a specific cabin number; if it doesn't, it designates a cabin category. Your exact cabin location may sometimes not be assigned to you until you board ship.

If you need to cancel your cruise after putting down a deposit, you'll get all or most of your money back, depending on how close you are to departure. With Royal Caribbean, for instance, customers get a 100% refund if they cancel more than 70 days ahead. Less than 30 days from the cruise, the refund drops to 50%, and within the last week it's your loss. Note that some travel agencies charge an administrative fee for cancellation regardless of if the cruise line does or does not. More service-oriented agencies tend not to charge these fees in most cases. Always ask *before* handing over your credit card number.

3

Things to Know Before You Go

You've bought your ticket and you're getting ready to cruise. Here are a few details you need to consider before you set sail.

1 Passports & Visas

For decades, U.S.-based cruise ships operated under rules that permitted U.S. citizens to travel to Canada, Mexico, and the Caribbean without need of a passport, but that's all changing. In January 2007, the first phase of the **Western Hemisphere Travel Initiative** began, requiring U.S. citizens to possess a valid passport to reenter the U.S. after traveling in Canada, Mexico, Central and South America, the Caribbean, and Bermuda. The first phase covers only people traveling by air, but, by the time you read this, those regulations will have been extended to include cruise travel and people crossing the border by car, bus, train, and foot.

If you don't currently have a passport or you need to replace an expired one, the **U.S. State Department website** (http://travel.state.gov) provides information. You can also inquire at your local passport acceptance facility, or call the **National Passport Information Center** (© 877/487-2778). Fees for new passports are $97 adults, $82 children under 16. Renewals cost $67. If you're leaving within a few weeks, you can pay an additional $60 fee to have your passport expedited for delivery within 2 weeks.

As you would before any trip abroad, make two photocopies of your documents and ID before leaving home. Take one set with you as a backup (keeping it in a different piece of luggage from the one holding your originals) and keep one at home.

After accepting your passport to board ship at the beginning of your cruise, the cruise line might hang onto it for the duration of your cruise, thus allowing the line to facilitate clearance procedures quickly at each port. Don't worry, this is normal. Your documents will be returned to you after the ship has departed the last foreign port of call, en route back to your home port.

Non-U.S./Canadian citizens departing from and/or returning to the U.S./Canada should check with their travel agent or cruise line to determine required paperwork. Generally, you'll need a valid passport, alien-registration card as applicable, and any visas required by the ports of call.

Vaccinations Required?

Travel to the Caribbean, Mexico, and Central America does not generally warrant inoculations against tropical diseases, though the Centers for Disease Control (CDC) occasionally recommends prescription antimalarial drugs if conditions in certain destinations warrant. CDC recommendations and warnings can be viewed at **www.cdc.gov/travel/destinat.htm**.

2 Money Matters

Know how they say cruises are all-inclusive vacations? They're lying. True, the bulk of your vacation expense is covered in your fare, but there are plenty of extras. We've detailed the specifics in "The Cost: What's Included & What's Not," in chapter 2. In this section, we'll examine the way monetary transactions are handled on board and in port.

ONBOARD CHARGE CARDS

Cruise ships operate on a cashless basis. Basically, this means you have a running tab and simply sign for what you buy on board during your cruise—bar drinks, meals at specialty restaurants, spa treatments, shore excursions, gift-shop purchases, and so on—then pay up at the end. Very convenient, yes—and also very, very easy to forget your limits and spend more than you intended to.

Shortly before or after embarkation, a purser or check-in clerk will take an imprint of your credit card and issue you an **onboard charge card,** which, on most ships, also serves as your room key and as your cruise ID, which you swipe through a scanner every time you leave or return to the ship. Some ships issue separate cards for these functions, or a card and an old-fashioned room key. Some adventure lines that carry 100 or fewer passengers just ask for your cabin number for onboard purchases.

On the last night of your cruise, an **itemized account** of all you've charged will be slipped beneath your cabin door. If you agree with the charges, they'll automatically be billed to your credit card. If you'd rather pay in cash or if you dispute any charge, you'll need to stop by the office of the ship's cashier or purser. There may be a long line, so don't go if you don't have to.

BRINGING CASH ASHORE

The cashless system works just fine on board, but remember, you'll need cash in port. Many people get so used to not carrying their wallets aboard ship that they get off in port and find themselves without any money in their pockets—a minor annoyance if your ship is docked and it just means trudging back aboard for cash, but a major annoyance if it's anchored offshore and you have to spend an hour ferrying back and forth by tender.

Credit cards are accepted at most port shops, but we recommend having some cash, ideally in small denominations, to cover the cost of taxi rides, tips for tour leaders, or purchases you make from craft markets and street vendors. Information on local currency is included in chapters 9 through 16, but for the most part you don't have to worry about exchanging money at all. In the Caribbean, the U.S. dollar is the legal currency of the U.S. Virgin Islands, Puerto Rico, and (oddly enough) the British Virgin Islands, but vendors on islands that have their own currency almost always accept dollars too. Mexican, Central American, and Canadian ports are similarly dollar-friendly, and Alaska and Hawaii are, of course, states.

If you're running low on cash, **ATMs** are easy to find in nearly every cruise port covered in this guide, often right at the cruise terminal. Remember that you'll get local currency from machines where the dollar isn't the legal tender, so don't withdraw more than you need. Many megaships also have ATMs (usually near the casino, surprise, surprise), but you can expect to be charged a hefty fee for using them—up to $5 in addition to what your bank charges you.

Many lines will cash **traveler's checks** at the purser's desk, and sometimes **personal checks** of up to about $200 to $250 (but sometimes only when accompanied by an American Express card, for guarantee). You can also often get a **cash advance** through your Visa, MasterCard, or Discover card.

Except aboard some of the ultraluxury lines, **gratuities for the crew** are not normally included in the cruise rates, though many lines these days are either automatically adding a suggested gratuity to your end-of-cruise bill or offering passengers the option of charging gratuities. Where this is not the case, you should reserve some cash so that you won't feel like Scrooge at the end of your cruise. See "Tipping, Customs & Other End-of-Cruise Concerns," later in this chapter, for more on this subject. Information on how each line deals with gratuities is included in the "Service" section of each line review in chapters 6 through 8.

3 Keeping in Touch While at Sea

Some people take a cruise to get away from it all, but others are communication addicts. For them, today's mainstream and luxury vessels (and some small ships) offer a spectrum of ways to keep in touch.

CELLPHONES & SAT PHONES

Over the past 3 years, more and more cruise ships have been wired with technology that enables cellphone users to make and receive calls aboard ship, even when far out at sea. **Costa Cruises** was the first to introduce it, in late 2003 (with service going fleetwide in 2006), and now **Royal Caribbean, Celebrity, Carnival, Disney,** and **Oceania** offer service fleetwide. **Norwegian Cruise Line** offers it on all ships except *Norwegian Majesty.* Its Hawaii ships don't need any special hookups, since they sail close enough to the islands to allow service through shore-side towers. At press time, **Holland America** offers service aboard *Volendam* only, but has plans to extend service fleetwide, possibly by the time this book hits the shelves. **MSC Cruises** offers service aboard *Lirica, Opera, Musica,* and *Orchestra.* Among the luxury lines, cell service is available aboard **Silversea, Crystal,** and **Regent Seven Seas. Windstar** is currently the only small/sailing-ship line to offer any cellular connectivity, aboard its 308-passenger *Wind Surf* only.

Holdouts against the cellphone tide include Cunard, Princess, Seabourn, SeaDream, and almost all the small-ship lines.

The service is turned on once a ship sails beyond the range of shore-side towers, typically at about 12 miles. Calls are billed through your regular carrier according to its usual roaming rates, which can vary depending on your provider and sometimes on where in the world you're calling from. Rates typically range between $2 and $3 per minute, with some going as high as $5. That ain't cheap, but it's nowhere near the average $8 or $9 per minute (and sometimes up to $15 a minute) cruise lines typically charge for **in-cabin satellite-phone service.** Text messages from cellphones and e-mails sent from PDAs are more affordable, sometimes costing only a few cents, making them a great idea for couples and families trying to find each other aboard very large megaships.

In addition to cell service and in-cabin SAT phones, each ship has a central phone number, fax number, and e-mail address, which you'll sometimes find in the cruise line's brochure and usually in the documents you'll get with your tickets. Distribute these to family members or friends in case they have to contact you in an emergency. It also can't hurt to leave behind the numbers of the cruise line's headquarters and/or reservations department, both of whom will be able to put people in touch with you.

INTERNET & E-MAIL AT SEA

Aside from some of the small, adventure-oriented ships in chapter 8, pretty much every cruise ship has computers from which passengers can send and receive e-mail and browse the Internet. In many cases, their computer centers are decked out with state-of-the-art flatscreen monitors, plush chairs, coffee bars, and Web cams. They're often open around the clock, and many offer basic classes for computer novices.

E-mail access is usually available through the Web via your Earthlink, AOL, Hotmail, Yahoo!, or other personal account, with charges calculated on a per-minute basis (usually 50¢–$1) or in prepurchased blocks (say, $40 for a 3- or 4-night cruise or $90 for a 7-night cruise). A few ships still offer e-mail through temporary accounts you set up once aboard ship, with rates averaging roughly $1 to $4 per message.

Many ships built over the past several years have been wired with **dataports** in all, most, or some cabins and suites, allowing passengers who travel with laptops to log on in privacy. The cost for these services tends to be higher than access in the Internet centers. **Wireless Internet (Wi-Fi)** is also offered aboard Azamara, Carnival, Celebrity, Crystal, Cunard (*QM2* only), Disney, Holland America, Lindblad Expeditions, MSC, NCL, Oceania, Princess, Regent, Royal Caribbean, Seabourn, Silversea, and Windstar, usually in designated areas such as the atrium and some public rooms. A few ships—the small luxury ships of Seabourn and Silversea, and the huge *Carnival Valor*—offer wireless access everywhere on board. To take advantage of this service, you must have a wireless card for your laptop, rent a card, or rent a laptop, then purchase minutes either on an as-used basis or in packages.

KEEPING ON TOP OF THE NEWS

Most ships have CNN and sometimes other news stations as part of their regular TV lineup. Some ships also maintain the old tradition of reprinting headline news stories pulled off the wire and slipping them under passengers' doors each morning.

4 Packing for the Different Cruise Climates

One of the great things about cruising is that even though you'll be visiting several countries (or at least several ports) on a typical weeklong itinerary, you won't be living out of your suitcase: You just check into your cabin on day 1, put your clothes in the closet, and settle in. The destinations come to you. But what exactly do you need to pack? Evening wear aboard ship is pretty much the same wherever you go, but your destination definitely affects what you'll need during the day.

SHIPBOARD DRESS CODES (OR LACK THEREOF)

Ever since Norwegian Cruise Line started the casual trend back at the turn of the 20th century, cruise lines have been toning down or turning off their dress codes. During the day, no matter what the itinerary, you'll find T-shirts, polo shirts, and shorts or khakis predominating, plus casual dresses for women and sweat shirts or light sweaters to compensate for the air-conditioning. The vibe is about the same on the luxury lines, though those polos and khakis probably sport better labels. On the megaships, retractable glass roofs mean the pool scene keeps going strong whether you're in the sunny Caribbean or icy Alaska. So, pack that **bathing suit,** as well as a cover-up and

Tuxedo Rentals

Despite the casual trend, there's usually a contingent of folks on board who like to get all decked out. If you don't own a tux or don't want to bother lugging one along, you can often arrange a rental through the cruise line or your travel agent for about $75 to $120 (the higher prices for packages with shirts and both black tux jacket and white dinner jacket). Shoes can be rented for an additional $10 to $12. In some cases, a rental offer arrives with your cruise tickets; if not, a call to your travel agent or the cruise line can facilitate a rental. If you choose this option, your suit will be waiting in your cabin when you arrive.

sandals if you want to go right from your deck chair to one of the restaurants or public rooms. If you plan on hitting the gym, don't forget sneakers and your **workout clothes.**

Evenings aboard ship used to be a lot more complicated, requiring passengers to pack for more situations than today's cruises demand. On most lines these days, **formal nights** have either melted away entirely or slid closer to what used to be considered semiformal. When Oceania Cruises started up in 2003, its dress code was set as "country club casual" every single night, on every voyage. NCL has also pretty much ditched formal nights completely, though its "optional formal" captain's cocktail night accommodates those who choose to dress up. Disney Cruise Line has toned formality down to the point where a sports jacket is considered dressy enough. Most other mainstream lines still have 2 traditional formal nights during any 7-night itinerary—usually the second and second-to-last nights of the cruise, the former for the captain's cocktail party. For these, imagine what you'd wear to a nice wedding: Men are encouraged to wear tuxedos or dark suits; women dress in cocktail dresses, sequined jackets, gowns, or other fancy attire. If you just hate dressing up, women can get away with a blouse and skirt or pants—and, of course, jewelry, scarves, and other accessories can dress up an otherwise nondescript outfit. (Most cabins have personal safes where you can keep your good jewelry when you're not wearing it.) Men can get away with a blue blazer and tie if they choose to. **Casual nights** (sometimes called "smart casual" or something similar) make up the rest of the week, though some lines still cling to an old distinction between full casual (decent pants and collared shirts for men, and maybe a sports jacket; dresses, skirts, or pantsuits for women) and informal or semiformal (suits or sports jackets; stylish dresses or pantsuits). Suggested dress for the evening is usually printed in the ship's daily schedule. Cruise lines also typically describe their dress codes in their brochures and on their websites.

Most of the **ultraluxury lines** maintain the same ratio of formal, semiformal, and casual nights, with passengers tending to dress on the high end of all those categories. Tuxedos are very common. That said, even the luxe lines are relaxing their dress standards. Seabourn doesn't request ties for men anymore except on formal nights, and Windstar and SeaDream have a casual "no jackets required" policy every day, though dinners usually see some men in sports jackets and women in nice dresses.

Aboard all the **small-ship lines** covered in this book, it's very rare to see anything dressier than a sports jacket at any time, and those usually appear only for the captain's dinner. Most of these lines are 100% casual 100% of the time, with passengers sometimes changing into clean shirts, trousers, and dresses at dinner.

DRESSING FOR YOUR DESTINATION

The cruise destinations covered in this book divide fairly easily into warm-weather regions (Caribbean, Central America, Mexican Riviera, Hawaii, and Bermuda) and the cooler northern regions of Alaska and its milder neighbor on the other side of the continent, New England/Canada.

Average Temperatures in the Cruise Regions*

Destination	Jan	Feb	Mar	Apr	May	June	July	Aug	Sept	Oct	Nov	Dec
Eastern Caribbean	70/83	70/84	71/85	73/86	74/87	76/87	76/88	76/89	76/89	75/88	74/86	72/84
Western Caribbean	65/82	66/84	72/86	73/90	75/90	75/90	75/90	75/91	75/90	73/86	72/84	70/82
Southern Caribbean	73/82	73/82	73/84	75/88	76/88	76/88	77/88	77/88	77/88	76/87	77/84	74/83
Panama Canal/ Central America	76/84	76/84	76/85	77/86	76/87	75/86	75/85	75/85	75/87	74/86	74/84	75/84
Southeast Alaska	19/29	23/34	27/39	32/47	39/55	45/61	48/64	47/63	43/56	37/47	27/37	23/32
Mexican Riviera	72/87	72/87	72/87	72/87	76/89	77/89	77/89	77/89	77/88	77/88	75/88	73/88
Bermuda	61/69	60/68	60/69	63/71	68/75	73/81	77/85	78/86	76/84	72/80	67/75	63/70
Hawaii	65/78	65/78	66/78	68/79	70/81	72/83	73/84	74/85	73/85	72/83	70/81	67/79
Canada/New England*	19/30	19/30	25/40	34/48	41/57	50/66	57/73	57/73	54/68	45/57	36/48	25/37

* Temperatures are in degrees Fahrenheit, representing average lows and highs. Canada/New England temperatures represent Halifax, Nova Scotia. Temperatures farther south along the coast will be on the high side of the temperature range. **Note:** Humidity can make summer temperatures in warm-weather destinations seem hotter, while Alaska's damp climate can make its summer temperatures seem colder.

WARM-WEATHER ITINERARIES

In the **Caribbean,** the temperature stays within a fairly narrow range year-round, averaging between 75°F and 85°F (24°C–29°C), though in summer the combination of sun and humidity can get very intense, especially at midafternoon. Trade winds help cool things off on many of the islands, as may rainfall, which differs island to island— Aruba, for instance, is very dry, while it seems to rain briefly every other time we're in Nassau. Winter is generally the driest season throughout the region; but even then it can be wet in mountainous areas, and afternoon showers often give the shores a good soaking, sometimes just for a few minutes, sometimes for hours. Temperatures on Mexico's Yucatán Peninsula and in **Central America** can feel much hotter, especially on shore excursions to the humid interior. Hurricane season lasts officially from June 1 to November 30, traditionally the low cruise season.

The **Mexican Riviera** is traditionally sunny, with average daytime temperatures in the mid-80s. Showers are brief and usually occur at night, when the temperature drops by about 10 degrees. Humidity is moderate during the November to April dry season and higher from May to October.

Hawaii is, of course, paradise. Along the coast, daytime temperatures are usually between the mid-70s and mid-80s, while the mountains can be quite a bit cooler, with summer daytime temperatures in the 60s. On the leeward side of the islands, away from the wind, temperatures occasionally get into the low 90s, while the high slopes of Mauna Kea, the state's highest volcanic peak, are regularly covered with snow in the winter.

Bermuda, too, enjoys a wonderfully temperate climate due to the proximity of the Gulf Stream, which flows between the island and North America. There's no rainy season and no typical month of excess rain. Showers may be heavy at times, but the skies clear quickly. During the April-to-October cruise season, temperatures stay in the mid-70s to mid-80s, and even in summer the temperature rarely rises above 85°F (29°C), with a breeze cooling things down at night.

WHAT TO PACK   No matter which warm-weather region you'll be visiting, casual daytime wear aboard ship means shorts, T-shirts or polos, sundresses, and bathing suits. The same dress code works in port too, but in many places it's best to cover that skimpy bikini top if straying from the beach area. Bring a good pair of **walking shoes** or sandals if you intend to do more than lie on the beach, and **aqua-socks** might also be a good idea if you plan to snorkel, take inflatable launches to shore, or participate in watersports. They're also very good for shore excursions that traverse wet, rocky terrain, such as Jamaica's Dunn's River Falls trip. They're cheap to buy, but if you forget, many cruise lines rent them for excursions for about $5 a pair. A folding umbrella or lightweight raincoat or poncho is a good idea for destinations that experience regular tropical showers.

Last, remember to pack sunglasses, a hat, and **sunscreen.** All are available aboard ship and in the ports, but sunscreen in particular will be a lot cheaper at your local market than in a gift shop. You might also consider bringing a **plastic water bottle** that you can refill aboard ship, rather than buying overpriced bottled water in port.

ALASKA ITINERARIES

While Southeast Alaska, where most cruises sail, has more temperate year-round weather than the rest of the state, summers here are still unpredictable. In May, when the cruise season gets going, we've experienced icy rain at the waterline and hiked in new snow at the top of Juneau's Mount Roberts—but we've also seen a lot of beautiful, crisp, sunny days. June is the driest of the true summer months, July the warmest (and also the busiest), and August the month where you'll usually experience the most rain. Rainy weather usually continues into September, though we've sailed here as the season wrapped up and had sunny days all week long. Some towns are rainier than others no matter what time you sail—Ketchikan, for instance, gets about 150 inches of precipitation annually, more than three times Juneau's total. In general, daytime summer temperatures are usually in the 50s and 60s, though the damp climate can make it seem colder (as can wind, proximity to glaciers, and excursions to higher elevations). Some days can also be nicely warm, getting up into the 70s or occasionally into the 80s. The all-time high temperature in Juneau was 90°F (32°C) in July 1975—a rarity.

This far south you won't experience the famed Midnight Sun, though days still seem to go on forever. In June, Juneau gets about 18 hours of sunlight—sometimes at 10pm there's still enough to read by. Farther north, in Anchorage, Denali, and Fairbanks, the sun dips below the horizon for only a little more than 4 hours on some June days. Summer temperatures here are roughly comparable to those in the Southeast.

WHAT TO PACK   The rule for Alaska is layering. In addition to some lightweight clothing to wear aboard ship (including a bathing suit, as most megaships have covered pool areas), you'll want to bring some variation of the following items for daytime use:

- A lightweight, waterproof jacket
- Two sweaters or fleece pullovers, or substitute a warm vest for one
- Two to four pairs of pants or jeans

- Two pairs of walking shoes (preferably waterproof)
- A warm hat and gloves
- Long underwear if you're on a May/September shoulder-season cruise
- A folding umbrella

Despite the cool temperatures and sometimes overcast conditions, you'll still want to pack **sunglasses and sunscreen,** especially if you'll be doing a lot of active shore excursions or spending a lot of time on deck whale-watching. That's also the reason you'll want to bring **binoculars** and/or a good **camera,** preferably with a telephoto or zoom lens and with lots of digital memory or film. Regarding binoculars, many of the small-ship adventure lines have enough aboard for all passengers, but it can't hurt to bring your own if you have them. Because whales, eagles, and bears aren't the only wildlife in Alaska, you'll also do well to pack some **mosquito repellant.** Bugs aren't as big a problem in Southeast as in the more central parts of the state, but if you get into the forest on shore excursions, they can still get annoying.

EASTERN CANADA/NEW ENGLAND ITINERARIES

Temperatures on summer Canada/New England cruises are usually very pleasant, averaging in the 60s and 70s. Temperatures in Nova Scotia will be on the low end of that scale, often dipping into the 50s at night, while you can expect hot temperatures if you're sailing from New York, where summer days are often in the 80s or 90s. Temperatures in Boston are usually in the 70s in summer. On September/October fall-foliage cruises, expect temperatures in Canada to range from the low 40s to the low 60s. Rain-wise, the situation is unpredictable. We've experienced bright, crisp, sunny days followed by a full 24-hour socker of a storm. Fog is also common, especially on New Brunswick's Fundy Coast and the Atlantic Coast of Nova Scotia.

WHAT TO PACK   A lighter version of layering is called for here, with a long-sleeve shirt or light sweater over your T-shirts, polos, and dresses. Pack a combination of shorts and long casual pants as well, plus good walking shoes and a light jacket for use in the evenings. Fall cruises call for a bit heavier clothing, but you'll rarely experience bone-chilling cold on these cruises. As always, remember your sunblock, sunglasses, hat, and folding umbrella.

SUNDRIES

Except on the small ships, most vessels have a **laundry service** on board and some dry cleaning, too, with about a 24-hour turnaround time; a price list will be in your cabin. Cleaning services tend not to be cheap—$1 or $1.50 per pair of socks, $2.50 to $3 for a T-shirt, and $9 to dry-clean a suit—so if you plan to pack light and wear the same outfit several times, consider the self-service laundry rooms aboard some ships (Carnival, Crystal, Princess, and Holland America, among others). The small-ship lines often provide no laundry service at all.

Like hotel rooms, most cabins (especially those aboard the newest and the most high-end ships) come with **toiletries** such as soap, shampoo, conditioner, and lotion, although you still may want to bring your own products—the ones provided often seem watered down. If you forget something, all but a few of the smallest ships in this book have at least one shop on board, selling razor blades, toothbrushes, sunscreen, film, and other sundries, usually at inflated prices.

Most cabins also have **hair dryers** (the "Cabins & Rates" charts in chapters 6–8 tell you which have them and which don't); but they tend to be weak, so don't expect miracles—if you have a lot of hair, bring your own. All ships reviewed in this book run on **110 AC current** (both 110 and 220 on many), so North Americans won't need an adapter.

You don't need to pack a **beach towel,** as they're almost always supplied on board (again, except aboard some small-ship lines). If you insist on big and fluffy, however, you might want to pack your own. Bird-watchers and whale-watchers will want their **binoculars** and manuals, golfers their clubs unless they intend to rent, and snorkelers their gear (which can also be rented, usually through the cruise lines).

If you like to read but don't want to lug hefty novels on board, most ships of all sizes have libraries stocked with books and magazines. Some are more extensive than others. Most ships also stock paperback bestsellers in their shops.

5 Tipping, Customs & Other End-of-Cruise Concerns

We know you don't want to hear about the end of your cruise before you've even gone, but it's best to be prepared. Here's a discussion of a few matters you'll have to take care of before heading home.

TIPPING

Most cruise lines pay their service staff low base wages with the understanding that the bulk of their income will come from tips. Each line has clear guidelines for gratuities, which are usually printed in their brochures and on their website, on your cruise documents, and in the daily schedule toward the end of your trip. The traditional way of tipping was to simply hand your waiter, assistant waiter, and cabin steward cash in a little envelope, but these days many lines (Carnival, Costa, NCL, Oceania, Holland America, and Princess, to be exact) add an **automatic gratuity** (sometimes called a "service charge") to a passenger's onboard account—generally between $8.50 and $12 per person, per day total, with the amount adjustable up or down if you request it at the purser's desk before the end of the cruise. Other lines, such as Royal Caribbean and Disney, often give you the option of paying cash directly to staff or adding the gratuities onto your account. Some small-ship lines pool the tips and divide them equitably among all crew. Ultraluxury lines Silversea, Seabourn, SeaDream, and Regent include tips in the cruise rates. Windstar promotes its "tipping not required" policy, but "required" is the operative word: Tipping really is expected.

Among lines that don't add an automatic charge, **suggested tipping amounts** vary slightly with the line and its degree of luxury, from about $8 to $14 total per passenger, per day, and half that for children. As a rule of thumb, each passenger (not each couple) should expect to tip at least $3.50 per day for his cabin steward, $3.50 for his dining room waiter, and about $2 for his assistant waiter, and sometimes 75¢ for his headwaiter. Some lines suggest you tip the maitre d' about $5 per person for the week and slip another couple bucks to the chief housekeeper, but it's your choice. If you've never even met these people, don't bother. Guests staying in suites with butler service should also send $3.50 per day his way. A 15% gratuity is usually included on every **bar bill** to cover gratuities to bartenders and wine stewards. The captain and other professional officers definitely do not get tips. That'd be like tipping your doctor.

On lines that follow traditional person-to-person gratuity policies, tip your waiter and assistant waiter during the cruise's final dinner, and leave your cabin steward his or her tip on the final night or morning, just before you disembark. Tip **spa personnel** immediately after they work on you, but note that on some ships the spa will automatically add a tip to your account unless you indicate otherwise, so inquire before adding one yourself.

DISEMBARKING

It's a good idea to begin packing before dinner on your final night aboard. Be sure to fill out the **luggage tags** given to you and attach them securely to each piece. Most ships ask that you leave your luggage outside your cabin door by midnight or so, after which service staff will pick it up and spirit it away. Two points here: (1) First-time cruisers always worry about leaving their bags out in public, but we've never heard an instance of anything being stolen; (2) because ship's personnel have to get thousands of pieces of luggage into bins and off the ship, don't expect your luggage to be treated gently. Rather than packing bottles of duty-free liquor and other breakables, carry them off the ship yourself.

Once you debark, you'll find your bags waiting for you in the terminal, organized by the colored or numbered tags you attached. Attendants are standing by to help you should your bag not be where it's supposed to be.

Ships normally arrive in port on the final day between 6 and 8am, and need at least 90 minutes to unload baggage and complete docking formalities. Debarkation rarely begins much before 9am, and sometimes it may be 10am before you're allowed to leave the ship, usually via debarkation numbers assigned based on flight times. (Not surprisingly, suite passengers get expedited debarkation.) Have breakfast. Have coffee. Have patience.

In the cruise ship terminal, claim your luggage and then pass through Customs before exiting. This normally entails handing the officer your filled-out declaration form as you breeze past, without even coming to a full stop. There are generally porters available in the terminals (to whom it's traditional to pay about $2 per bag carried), but you may have to haul your luggage through Customs before you can get to them.

U.S. CUSTOMS

Except for some small-ship itineraries in Alaska and U.S. rivers, and NCL's cruises in Hawaii, all the other ships in this book will visit at least one foreign port on their itinerary, meaning you'll have to go through Customs and be subject to duty-free purchase allowances when you return. We've found clearing Customs at U.S. cruise ports usually painless and speedy, with officials rarely asking for anything more than your filled-out declaration form as they nod you through. Better safe than sorry, though. Keep receipts for all purchases you make abroad. And, if you're carrying a particularly new-looking camera or expensive jewelry (and are a particularly nervous type), you may want to consider carrying proof that you purchased them before your trip. Similarly, if you use any medication containing controlled substances or requiring injection, carry an original prescription or note from your doctor.

The standard personal duty-free allowance for U.S. citizens is $800, an amount that applies to **Mexico, Canada,** and most of the **Caribbean** islands. There are also limits on the amount of alcoholic beverages (usually 1 liter), cigarettes (1 carton), cigars (100 total, and no Cubans), and other tobacco products you may include in your personal duty-free exemption. If returning directly from the **U.S. Virgin Islands,** you may bring in $1,600 worth of merchandise duty-free, including 5 liters of alcohol, of which at least 1 liter should be a product of those islands.

As you may be visiting both foreign and U.S.-territory ports, things get more complicated: If, for instance, your cruise stops in the U.S. Virgin Islands and The Bahamas, your total limit is $1,600, of which no more than $800 can be from The Bahamas. Note that you must declare on your Customs form all gifts received during your cruise.

Joint Customs declarations are possible for family members traveling together. For instance, for a husband and wife with two children, the total duty-free exemption from most destinations would be $3,200.

Note that most meat or meat products, fruit, plants, vegetables, or plant-derived products will be seized by U.S. Customs agents unless they're accompanied by an import license from a U.S. government agency. The same import rules apply even if you are returning from Puerto Rico, Hawaii, and the U.S. Virgin Islands.

For more specifics, visit the **U.S. Customs Service** website at **www.customs.gov**. Canadian citizens should look at the **Canada Border Services Agency** site (**www. cbsa.gc.ca**), and citizens of the U.K. should visit the **U.K. Customs and Excise** site (**www.hmce.gov.uk**).

4

The Cruise Experience

Cruise ships evolved from ocean liners, which were once the only way of getting from point A to point B, assuming there was an ocean in between. This was often no easy matter, entailing a real journey of several weeks, often in harsh weather. Competition quickly came down to two elements over which the shipping lines had some control: speed ("Get me off this damn ship as fast as possible") and comfort ("Don't rush on my account, I'm having a great time"). While the former was great for businessmen in a rush, the latter had more intriguing possibilities, and it wasn't long before ship owners began offering pleasure cruises around scenic parts of the world, lavishing their passengers with shipboard comforts between ports of call. And thus the cruise industry was born.

Today, though the cruise experience varies from ship to ship, the common denominator is choice, with nonstop entertainment and activities, multiple dining options, and opportunities to be as sociable or private as you want to be. On most of the big ships, you can run from an aerobics class to ballroom dancing, then to a computer class or informal lecture, then to a wine tasting session or goofy poolside contest—all before lunch. On warm-weather itineraries, you can choose to do nothing more than sunbathe in a quiet corner of the deck all day, and in Alaska you can camp out on deck with your binoculars, scanning for whales. It's your choice. In the pages that follow, we'll give you a taste of cruise life.

1 Checking In, Boarding & Settling into Your Cabin

It's cruise day. If you've flown to your city of embarkation, uniformed attendants will be waiting at baggage claim, holding signs bearing your cruise line's or ship's name and ready to direct you to buses bound for the terminal. You've probably already paid for these **transfers** when you bought your ticket. If not, you can arrange them now, or take a taxi to the ship. If you've driven to the port, it's just a matter of parking and trundling your luggage into the terminal. If it's still morning or early afternoon, don't feel rushed. Remember, another shipload of passengers is just getting off, and cabins still need to be cleaned, supplies loaded, and paperwork and Customs documents completed before you can board. Even if your ship has been berthed since 6am, new passengers are often not allowed on board until about 1pm, though lines are increasingly offering preboarding—which means you can get on at 11am or noon, have lunch, and start checking out the ship, though your cabin probably won't be ready till early afternoon. See chapter 9, "The Ports of Embarkation," for more information on flying, driving, and parking.

A Brief History of Cruising

It wasn't until the late 19th century that British shipping companies realized they could make money not just by transporting travelers, cargo, mail, and immigrants from point A to point B, but also by selling a luxurious experience at sea. Most historians agree that the first cruise ship was Peninsular & Oriental Steam Navigation Company's *Ceylon,* which in 1881 was converted to a lavish cruising yacht for carrying wealthy, adventurous guests on world cruises. A few years later, in 1887, North of Scotland, Orkney & Shetland Steam Navigation's *St. Sunniva* was launched as the first steamer built expressly for cruising.

The Germans joined the cruise trade in 1891 when the Hamburg-America Line sent its *Augusta Victoria* on a Mediterranean cruise, and during the early 1900s, more and more players entered the picture, spending warmer seasons crossing the Atlantic and Pacific and offering pleasure cruises the rest of the year. During these boom years, competition became fierce between famous shipping lines such as **Cunard,** White Star, Hamburg-America, French Line, North German Lloyd, **Holland America,** Red Star Line, and others, which all sought to attract customers by building the largest, fastest, or most luxurious new vessels, with extravagant appointments you'd never find on a modern cruise ship—stained-glass ceilings, frescoes, ornate wooden stairways, and even plaster walls. (Oddly, onboard activities and entertainment were relatively sparse amid all the grandeur. Besides lavish social dinners, about the only pastimes were reading, walking around the deck, and sitting for musical recitals.) These same ships, with their first-class ballrooms, smoking lounges, and suites decorated with the finest chandeliers, oriental rugs, and artwork, also carried immigrants in inexpensive, bare-bones steerage accommodations, with second-class cabins available between these two polar extremes. This multiclass system survived until the late 1960s, and even today you can see vestiges of it in the *QM2*'s dining rooms, which are assigned to passengers depending on the level of cabin they book.

Soon after Cunard launched its popular 2,165-passenger *Mauretania* and *Lusitania* in 1906, the White Star Line's J. Bruce Ismay envisioned a trio of the largest and most luxurious passenger vessels ever built, designed to appeal to rich American industrialists. The first of these sisters, the 2,584-passenger, 46,000-ton *Olympic,* was in service by 1911, introduced with such fanfare that the 1912 launch of the second sister, *Titanic,* was not nearly as anticipated. Still, that ship soon became the most famous of all time, through the most tragic of circumstances. Vestiges of Ismay's dream ships survive today on Celebrity Cruise's *Millennium,* whose alternative restaurant is decorated with original carved wall panels from the *Olympic,* salvaged before the ship was scrapped in 1935.

The Brits and Germans continued building bigger and bigger ships up until **World War I,** when almost all vessels were requisitioned to carry soldiers, supplies, and weaponry. Many grand ships were lost in the conflict, including Cunard's *Lusitania* and the third of Ismay's trio, launched in 1914 as the *Britannic* and sunk by a mine in 1916.

After World War I, the popularity of cruising increased tremendously, and more ships were routed to the Caribbean and the Mediterranean for long, expensive cruises—Cunard's *Mauretania* and its new running mate *Aquitania* were both yanked off the Atlantic for a millionaire's romp through the Med, carrying as few as 200 pampered passengers in the lap of luxury. As they headed to warmer climes, many ships' traditional black hulls were painted white to help them stay cool in those pre-air-conditioning days. This became a tradition itself, to the point where in the 1960s and 1970s nearly all ships sailing in the Caribbean and western Mexico were painted a dazzling white.

By the 1930s, shipboard activities and amenities were becoming much more sophisticated, with morning concerts, quoits, shuffleboard, bridge, Ping-Pong, motion pictures, and the first "swimming baths" (that is, pools) appearing on board, though these were often no more than burlap or canvas slung over wooden supports and filled with water. The first permanent outdoor pools appeared in the 1920s, and in the 1930s, the large outdoor pool on the *Rex* actually included a patch of sand to evoke Venice's Lido beach. When the great French liner *Normandie* made its maiden voyage in 1935, its first-class dining room boasted the cruising world's first air-conditioning system.

World War II saw the great liners again called into service. Cunard's *Queen Elizabeth* and *Queen Mary* and Holland America's *Nieuw Amsterdam* completed distinguished wartime service and sailed on into the postwar years, but many great liners never made it back to civilian life. *Normandie,* probably the greatest and most beautiful liner of all time, burned and cap-sized in New York while being converted into a troopship.

Shipboard travel boomed in the 1950s, and for the first time, pleasure cruising became accessible to the growing middle class, with onboard life enhanced by pool games, bingo, art classes, dance lessons, singles' parties, and midnight buffets—all of which you'll still find on ships today. By the 1960s, however, jet planes had replaced ships as the public's transportation of choice, and the boom was over. Increasingly expensive to maintain, many of the great 1950s liners were sent to the scrap yards.

The industry seemed doomed, but in the early 1960s, Norwegian cargo and tanker ship operator Knut Kloster teamed up with Israeli shipping and air-freight man Ted Arison to form **Norwegian Cruise Line,** the first major cruise operation to sail from Miami. It was a tremendous success. **Royal Caribbean Cruise Line** was formed in January 1969 to capitalize on the newly exploding Caribbean cruise market, and in 1971 Ted Arison split from NCL and started **Carnival Cruise Lines.** On the west coast, **Princess Cruises** was up and running by the mid-sixties, but hit the big time in 1977 when two of its ships began starring in the network TV series *The Love Boat,* which introduced millions to the cruise concept.

When you arrive at the port, you'll find an army of **porters** to help transport your luggage into the terminal (at a cost of about $2 per bag) and another army of cruise line employees waiting to direct you to the check-in desks. Once you're inside, your tagged luggage will be taken from you, scanned, and delivered to your cabin, sometimes arriving not long after you check in but more often showing up a few hours later. For this reason, it's a good idea to pack a small **essentials bag** you can carry on board with you, containing a change of clothes and maybe a swimsuit, plus a pair of sunglasses and any toiletries, medications, or other essentials you may need immediately.

Once in the terminal, you'll hand over your cruise tickets, show your **passport** (see "Passports & Visas," in chapter 3, for information), and give an imprint of your credit card to establish your **onboard account** (see "Money Matters," in chapter 3, for more on this). Depending upon when you arrive and how large the crowd is, you may find yourself waiting in line for an hour or more, but usually it's less.

For security reasons, cruise lines do not allow unofficial **visitors** aboard ship, so if friends or relatives brought you to the pier, you'll have to say your goodbyes on land.

Once on board, you may be guided to your **cabin** (you don't need to tip the person who leads you, though we usually give a couple bucks if he's carried our bags), but in many cases you'll have to find it on your own. Your **cabin steward** will probably stop by shortly to introduce him- or herself, inquire if the configuration of beds is appropriate (that is, whether you want separate twin beds or a pushed-together double), and give you his or her extension so you can call if you need anything. If your steward doesn't put in an appearance, feel free to call housekeeping to request anything you need. The brochures and **daily programs** in your cabin will answer many questions you may have about the day's activities, the recommended dress for dinner that night, and the ship's safety procedures. There may also be a **deck plan** that will help you find your way around. If not, you can pick one up at the guest services desk— signs near the staircases and elevators should be able to guide you there.

With a few notable exceptions, cruise ships have **direct-dial telephones** in cabins, along with instructions on how to use them and a directory of phone numbers for the departments or services on board. You can call anywhere in the world from most cabins' phones via satellite, but you'll break the bank to do it, with charges ranging from around $3 to about $15 a minute, with $8 or $9 being about average. It's cheaper to call home from your **cellphone** (if your ship is appropriately wired) or from a public telephone in port, or to send **e-mail** from the Internet center. (See "Keeping in Touch While at Sea," in chapter 3, for more info.)

All ships reviewed in this book have North American–style **electrical outlets** (twin flat prongs, 110 AC current), and some have outlets for both European current (220 AC) and North American. Keep in mind, there's often only one outlet for your curling iron or hair dryer, and it's usually above the desk or dresser, rather than in the bathroom.

Most ships also have **in-cabin safes** for storing your valuables, usually operated via a self-set combination. On ships that don't offer them, you can usually check valuable items at the purser's desk.

A **lifeboat safety drill** will be held either just before or after sailing. It's required by the Coast Guard, and attendance is mandatory. Check to make sure your cabin has enough life preservers for everyone in your party, since you'll have to wear them to the drill. (Hope you look good in orange.) If you need extra—or for that matter, if you need additional blankets or pillows—let your steward know ASAP.

2 Exploring the Ports of Call: Shore Excursions vs. Going It on Your Own

How you spend your time in port can make the difference between a great cruise experience and a big fat disappointment. The ports covered in this guide vary greatly, from quiet **undeveloped islands** such as Jost Van Dyke in the Caribbean, where yours will likely be the only ship in sight, to **super bustling towns** such as Charlotte Amalie on St. Thomas and Ketchikan in Alaska, both of them jampacked with ships and souvenir shops. Due to factors such as accessibility of local transportation, condition of roads, terrain, and the amount of time your ship is in port (which can range from 4 or 5 hr. to 10 hr. or more), some ports are easy to **explore independently,** others less so. In the port chapters that come later in this guide, we'll advise you which ports of call are good bets for solo explorations (and whether you should go it on foot or by taxi, motor scooter, ferry, or otherwise) and where you should sign up for an **organized shore excursion.**

When it comes to going on your own, one downside is that you'll be forgoing the kind of narrative you get from a guide, and may miss out on some of the historical and cultural nuances of a particular attraction. On the other hand, you may find your own little nuances, things that an organized tour skips over as being too minor to bother with. Touring alone allows you to avoid groups and crowds, and hopefully connect with the destination in a more personal way. When going the solo route, though, be sure you know exactly when your ship departs for the next port—the captain won't wait forever if you're late, leaving you on your own to get to the next port of call.

Sometimes a port's real attractions may be miles (sometimes a lot of miles) from where your ship is docked—a common enough occurrence in Hawaii, Alaska, and Mexico's Yucatán Peninsula, among other places. In such cases, touring on your own could be an inefficient use of your time, entailing lots of hassles and planning, and possibly costing more. Here, the shore excursions offered by the cruise lines are a good way to go. Under each port review we'll run through a sampling of both the best excursions and the best sights and activities you can see and do on your own.

Shore excursions run the gamut, from snoresville bus tours and catamaran booze cruises to more stimulating options such as snorkeling, jungle walks, whale-watching, and glacier helicopter treks. For those who like a little sweat in their port visit, there are more **physically challenging options** than ever, such as kayaking, horseback riding, mountain biking, ziplining, dog sledding, and river rafting. There's a decent selection of tours in all of the regions covered in this guide (generally at least 10–20 per port), with the greatest number offered in Alaska, Hawaii, and the Caribbean. Keep in mind that **shore-excursion prices** vary from line to line, even for the exact same tour. Also note that some cruise lines may not offer all these tours, while others may offer even more. Keep in mind there are often, but not always, lower kids' prices for the shore excursions. Note also that the excursions can often fill up fast, especially on the megaships, so don't dawdle in signing up. When you receive your cruise documents and/or confirmation numbers, or at the latest when you board the ship, you'll get a listing of the excursions offered for your itinerary. To get a jump on things, most lines list their shore excursions on their website, and Carnival, Celebrity, Costa, Crystal, Disney, Holland America, NCL, Princess, Regent Seven Seas, Royal Caribbean, and Silversea all allow you to **prebook or prereserve them,** either online or through some other system. It's a good option if you have your heart set on a particular site. If you change your mind once on board, cruise line policies vary, with some allowing you to switch to another tour or get an onboard credit for the amount, as long as you cancel out at least 24 hours in advance. Read the fine print before signing up.

If a tour offered by your ship is booked up, you can try to book it independently once you get to port. The popular Atlantis submarine tour, for example—offered at Grand Cayman, Nassau, and St. Thomas, among others—usually has an office/agent in the cruise terminals or nearby. In Juneau, it's easy to walk over to the Mt. Roberts Tramway and buy a ticket yourself for the hull up the mountainside.

Other options include contacting an outside company, such as **Port Promotions** (**www.portpromotions.com**), at least a few weeks before your cruise. This tour company will arrange many of the same tours the lines do, often for a few bucks less, and also put together custom tours tailored to your group's needs. Port Promotions currently offers tours in the Caribbean, Alaska, Hawaii, and Europe.

3 A Typical Day at Sea: Onboard Activities

Most of the mainstream lines and the larger luxury ships offer an extensive schedule of activities throughout each day, especially during days at sea, when the ship isn't visiting a port. To keep track of the games, contests, lessons, and classes, ships print a **daily program,** which is placed in your cabin the previous evening, usually while you're at dinner. A cruise director and his or her staff are in charge of the festivities and do their best to make sure passengers are having a good time. As a general rule, the smaller the ship, the fewer the activities: Midsize ships like Oceania's *Regatta* and *Insignia* are intentionally low-key (as are most of the ultraluxury ships), while most of the small adventure lines shun organized activities unless they involve the nature, culture, and history of their destinations.

ONBOARD LEARNING OPPORTUNITIES

For years, lists of shipboard classes read as if they'd been lifted straight out of the Eisenhower-era home-entertainment playbook: napkin folding, vegetable carving, scarf tying, mixology, and the like. Old habits die hard, so you'll still find these kinds of things aboard many ships; but in recent years the cruise lines have finally started catching up to the modern world. Today, most mega- and midsize ships also offer **informal lectures** on subjects such as personal investing, health and nutrition, the arts (and crafts), handwriting analysis, and computers (word processing, digital photography, website design, and so on). Don't expect to gain valuable life skills or credits toward your college degree—these are mostly hour-long sessions, and tend to be pretty basic—but they make a nice addition to the day.

Many lines also feature **cooking demonstrations** and **wine-tasting seminars,** the former often resembling the kind you see on TV, complete with model kitchen and video monitors for an up-close view of the preparations. Wine tastings are usually conducted by the ship's sommeliers, though some lines bring aboard guest experts. There's usually a $5 to $15 charge for wine tastings. Participants may be offered special prices on ordering wine in the restaurants and will be introduced to some of what's offered for sale in the dining rooms.

Dance classes (most frequently salsa, country, and ballroom) are usually held several times a week, taught by one of the onboard entertainers. Staff from the gym, spa, and beauty salon offer frequent seminars on **health, beauty, and fitness,** with topics including skin and hair care, detox for weight loss, and wrinkle reductions. These seminars are free, but they have an ulterior motive: getting you to sign up for not-so-cheap spa treatments or buy expensive beauty products. Just remember: *You don't have to buy anything.*

In general, the ultraluxury lines have more refined and interesting enrichment programs. **Crystal**'s Creative Learning Institute (CLI), for example, offers classes targeted toward enhancing quality of life, and was developed in association with organizations and schools such as the Society of Wine Educators, Berlitz, Yamaha, and The Cleveland Clinic. Offered year-round on every cruise, the program is divided into five "centers," including wine and food, arts and entertainment (from fashion design to language instruction), business and technology, "lifestyle" (including interior design and book clubs), and "wellness" (ranging from CPR instruction to tai chi). The wine and food seminars offered include Cocktail Making, Wine Appreciation, Chocolate, Spa Cuisine, and Beer Essentials. Aboard *Queen Mary 2*'s transatlantic crossings, **Cunard** is offering a similar program developed in association with Oxford University and featuring talks on history, global politics and cultural trends, theater, science, music, literature, and more.

ONBOARD GAMES

Vacations promote mental health by allowing people to do things they wouldn't ever do at home—for instance, participate in **wacky poolside contests** on days at sea. Almost all the mainstream lines continue this tradition, in which passengers compete to see who can do the best belly-flop, who has the hairiest back, or who can stuff the most Ping-Pong balls into their bathing suits. Sometimes passengers are teamed up for relay races that require members to pass bagels to one another with their teeth. Classic party lines like Costa offer frantic games like the **"Election of the Ideal Couple,"** where said couple is judged based on their ability to burst balloons with their butts. Even normally staid cruise lines let their hair down sometimes. At its weekly deck parties, Holland America sometimes features a team **water-bottle relay** in which one person chugs a bottle of water, and, as the line's printed instructions advise, "puts it in their swimsuit." The other team members each get a sponge, which they use to fill that bottle with ice water from a bucket on the other side of the deck. Other HAL cruises might have a **shipbuilding contest,** with groups of passengers constructing vessels from junk they find around the ship, then sending them for sea trials in one of the hot tubs. Small-ship lines such as Cruise West even get in on this kind of action, with passengers using tabletop items to construct sculptures at one dinner a week. The winner gets a bottle of wine.

Game shows, such as the **Newlywed/Not-So-Newlywed Game,** are always popular. Volunteer yourself or just listen to fellow passengers blurt out the truth about their personal lives—just like on *Oprah.* **Disney** and **Carnival** often stage very realistic game-show-type games, with buzzers, contestant podiums, digital scorekeeping, and prizes.

If you're a performer at heart, volunteer for the weekly **passenger talent show** held aboard many ships. Among the more bizarre displays we've seen: an elderly lady aboard *Norwegian Sun,* wearing red hot pants and heels and lip-synching Shirley Temple's "On the Good Ship Lollipop." Or, head to the nightclub and wiggle your way into the

hula-hoop or twist competitions. Gaming fans can sign up for **trivia quizzes,** do puzzles, or join **chess, checkers, bridge,** and **backgammon tournaments.**

SHIPBOARD CASINOS & GAMES OF CHANCE

Almost every cruise ship has a **casino,** the biggest and flashiest of which are aboard the Carnival, Royal Caribbean, Costa, Celebrity, and Princess megaships, which offer literally hundreds of slot machines and dozens of roulette, blackjack, poker, and craps tables. Luxury lines such as Regent and Seabourn have scaled-down versions. Stakes aboard most ships are relatively low, with maximum bets rarely exceeding $200. Average minimum bets at blackjack and poker tables are generally $5 or $10; the minimum at roulette is typically 50¢ or $1.

Most ships also have a **card room,** which is usually filled with serious bridge or poker players, and is occasionally supervised by a full-time instructor. Most ships furnish cards for free, although some charge $1 or so per deck. Another time-honored shipboard tradition is **horse racing,** a very goofy activity in which toy horses mounted on poles are moved around a track by hand, based on rolls of the dice. Passengers bet on the outcome, and the end of the cruise features an "owners cup" race and best-dressed-horse show.

Ships are free to offer gambling in international waters, but local laws almost always require onboard casinos to close down whenever a ship is in port. Big gamblers should keep this in mind when cruising to Bermuda, where ships stay in port for 3 whole days, with no gambling whatsoever during that period. Also, Hawaii law prohibits casino gambling on ships sailing round-trip from the state, so there are no casinos on NCL's *Pride of America* and *Pride of Aloha.* In Alaska, where ships sail mostly in the protected waters of the Inside Passage, a dispensation allows shipboard casinos to stay open except when ships are within 3 miles of a port.

Children are not permitted to enter onboard casinos; the minimum age is generally 18 or 21.

Disney's two ships lack casinos due to Disney's essentially puritan nature. Most of the small ships in chapter 8 lack casinos because their passengers are too busy looking for whales.

ART AUCTIONS

You'll find shipboard art auctions either a fun way to buy pictures for your living room or an incredibly annoying and blatantly tacky way for the cruise lines to make more money by selling a lot of marginally interesting or just plain awful originals and some good but fantastically overpriced lithographs and animation cels to unsuspecting passengers—not that we're taking sides, of course. They're big business on mainstream and ultraluxury lines, held three or four times a week for an hour or two at a time. From a stage or in one of the ship's lounges, the auctioneer (a salesman for an outside company that arranges the shows) briefly discusses a selection of the hundreds of works displayed around the auction space, sometimes paintings by well-knowns such as Peter Max and Erté; lithographs by greats such as Dalí, Picasso, and Miró; animation cels, often by Disney; and many pieces by artists you've never heard of. The art, framed or unframed, is duty-free to U.S. citizens and is packed and mailed home to the winner. The one big plus about these auctions? **Free champagne,** and they'll keep bringing it to you whether you bid or not. Just look interested.

4 Keeping Fit: Gyms, Spas & Sports

Since the early 1990s, cruise lines have been making their spa and fitness areas bigger and more high-tech, moving them out of windowless corners of bottom decks and into prime top-deck positions with great views from floor-to-ceiling windows. The best of them—aboard the Celebrity, Royal Caribbean, Princess, Carnival, Norwegian, and Holland America ships—probably beat out your gym at home, with dozens of state-of-the-art workout machines, large aerobics rooms, spinning and Pilates classes, and spa treatments that run from the basic to the bizarre. Sports areas are also getting super-sized on some ships, and options you'd never have imagined possible on a ship just a few years ago, from spinning bikes to BOSU balls, are becoming almost commonplace.

GYMS: AN ANTIDOTE TO THE MIDNIGHT BUFFET

The well-equipped **fitness centers** on the megaships may feature 20 or more treadmills and just as many stationary bikes (many with virtual reality screens), step machines, upper- and lower-body machines, free weights, and aerobics rooms. Expect great gym facilities on Royal Caribbean's Freedom-, Radiance- and Voyager-class ships; Carnival's Conquest, Spirit, and Destiny classes; Princess's Grand and Coral class; all of NCL's modern megaships; Holland America's Vista-class ships; and Celebrity's Millennium class. Working out on your own is free, as are many basic aerobics and stretching classes, but if you want to take a trendier class such as boxing, spinning, Pilates, yoga, or tai chi, it'll usually cost you $10 or more per class. **Personal training sessions** are usually also available for around $75 a pop. Royal Caribbean's new *Freedom of the Seas,* currently the biggest cruise ship on earth with an absolutely gigantic gym, boasts everything from a full-size Everlast boxing ring to lots of trendy classes, machines, and training accouterments.

Gyms on the few older ships remaining in the American cruise market are generally smaller and more spartan, but you'll find at least a couple of treadmills, a stationary bike or step machine, and some free weights on all but the smallest, most adventure-oriented cruise lines. On ships with limited or no gym facilities, aerobics and stretching classes may be held out on deck or in a lounge.

ONBOARD SPORTS OPTIONS

If you're into sports, the megaships pack the most punch, with jogging tracks; outdoor volleyball, basketball, and paddle-tennis courts; plus several pools for water polo, volleyball, aqua aerobics, and swimming. The most mega of the megas—Royal Caribbean's enormous Freedom- and Voyager-class ships—pack a bona fide ice-skating rink, an outdoor rock-climbing wall, an in-line skating track (on the Voyager ships), a surfing simulator (on the Freedoms), a full-size basketball court, miniature golf, and lots more. In addition to rock climbing, Royal's *Enchantment of the Seas* has a set of bungee trampolines, while the line's Radiance-class ships have gyro-balanced pool tables.

GOLF

In old movies, you always see the stars whacking golf balls off the backs of ships. You can't do that anymore—the environment, you know—but today's ships are catering to golfers in other ways, and more than ever before. While practically all the major cruise lines offer some level of golf instruction or excursions, several go the extra mile. For instance, **Carnival** (www.carnivalgolf.com), **Holland America** (www.hollandamerica golf.com), **Celebrity** (www.celebritycruisesgolf.com), **Princess** (www.princessgolf. com), and **Silversea** (www.silverseagolf.com) all feature programs on all or some of their ships created by Florida's **Elite Golf Cruises** (www.elitegolfcruises.com), which offer comprehensive onboard golf academies with various combinations of instruction, guided golf excursions in almost every port of call, and pro-shop-style extras.

These lines feature an onboard golf pro who schedules private, couple, or group **lessons.** The lessons typically include having your stroke analyzed via V1 digital video coaching, which uses a split screen to compare your stroke side-by-side with that of various golf legends—which could either be totally demoralizing or totally inspiring, depending on your frame of mind. A 1-hour private lesson is usually about $80. Many ships have driving nets or putting greens that are free for guests to use, and on sea days, demonstrations, clinics, and onboard putting contests are often held.

Many lines' ships, including Royal Caribbean, Princess, Celebrity, and SeaDream Yacht Club, have **computerized golf simulators** that allow virtual play that mimics some three dozen of the world's top courses, including Scotland's St. Andrews, North Carolina's Pinehurst, and California's Pebble Beach. The system analyzes every nuance of a golfer's swing to give a perfect real-time simulation of the shot on a 10×12-foot screen. The hitting mat even simulates different fairway conditions, from light rough to sand. Minicompetitions are held on most sea days for all levels of players, from beginners to serious competitors. Prices for the simulators range from $25 to $50 per person, per session. For those not so serious, **Royal Caribbean** has miniature golf courses on their Freedom-, Radiance- and Voyager-class ships (with minigolf also available on *Splendour* and *Legend of the Seas*), as does **Princess** on many of its ships including the *Grand, Golden, Star, Coral, Island, Diamond, Sapphire, Caribbean,* and *Crown Princess.*

In port, just about every line out there offers **golf excursions,** which bundle early debarkation, transportation, priority tee times, golf pro escort, cart rental, and greens fees into one excursion cost, with clubs and golf shoes available for demo, rental, or purchase if you don't want to lug your own. Some of the best courses in the world are included in the packages. **Norwegian Cruise Line,** for example, has gone big into golfing on its new Hawaii cruises, offering excursion packages at several courses each day, including Puakea, Poipu Bay, Princeville, and Kaua'i Lagoons (Kauai); Mauna Lani Resort, Hapuna, and Big Island Country Club (Hawaii); Makena, Wailea, and The Dunes at Maui Lani (Maui); and Ko'olau Golf Club (Oahu). Excursions run from $95 to $335 per person, or are available at a package price. A wide variety of Callaway clubs are available for rent on board, and the onboard pro shop offers balls, hats, visors, gloves, shirts, and more.

SPORTS FOR COUCH POTATOES

No need for all you sports-loving couch potatoes to be deprived. Almost every megaship has a **dedicated sports bar** with large-screen televisions broadcasting ESPN and whatever live games are available that day. Even those that don't have sports bars might outfit a public area or bar with televisions for viewing during popular sporting events such as the Super Bowl. If you want to watch the game from the comfort of your cabin, no problem: **ESPN** is available on cabin TVs on most of the mainstream and ultraluxe lines.

ONBOARD SPAS: TAKING RELAXATION ONE STEP FURTHER

If your idea of a heavenly vacation is stripping down to a towel and having someone rub mystery oil over your body, choose a cruise ship with a well-stocked spa—it won't be hard. For the past 15 years, spas have been big business on cruise ships, and have gotten progressively more amazing as the years have gone by. Most are perched on top decks and boast views from as many as 20 or so treatment rooms, where you can choose from dozens of massages, mud packs, facials, and even teeth whitening, acupuncture, and other esoteric treatments.

If you've taken a few cruises and noticed that the spas on different lines look suspiciously alike, that's because almost all of them (as well as the ships' hair salons) are staffed and operated by the London-based firm **Steiner Leisure.** NCL, Oceania, and Silversea's spas are operated by a company called **Mandara,** but (surprise) it's owned by Steiner, too. Companies bucking the Steiner hegemony include Regent Seven Seas (whose spas are run by **Carita**), Cunard (whose *QM2* spa is run by **Canyon Ranch**), and SeaDream and Star Clipper, both of which have in-house spa operations.

The young, mostly female Steiner employees are professional and charming for the most part, but we've found their abilities to be inconsistent, with some definitely more talented than others. Overall, **massages** are a pretty safe bet, whether you choose a standard neck massage, a full-body shiatsu massage, or a deep-tissue sports massage (which can verge on painful but gives you the most bang, wallop, and burn for your buck). The highest profile massage today is the **hot stone massage,** in which the therapist rubs you down with heated river rocks and oil—think soothing rather than invigorating.

We've found other treatments to often be disappointing and not worth the money unless you live in a place where access to unusual spa and beauty treatments is limited. For the same 50 bucks you spend on a pedicure aboard ship, you could get two much better ones in New York, but if you live in, say, rural North Dakota? Well, it's your vacation, so live it up.

A word about some of the more exotic and expensive treatments, such as electrode facials and **Ionithermie** slimming/detox, which allegedly stimulates cells, releases toxins, and contributes directly to weight loss: Whenever we've asked for details, it's clear most spa staffers don't have a clue about them beyond the descriptions they've memorized. We suspect—and this is just our opinion, mind you—that that's because they're a load of hooey.

Here's a sampling of treatments and their standard Steiner rates:

- 25-minute Swedish massage: $60 to $75
- 50-minute full-body massage: $90 to $130
- 75-minute hot stone massage: $140 to $190
- 50-minute facial: $90 to $130
- Manicure: $25 to $45
- Pedicure: $40 to $65
- 40-minute teeth whitening session: about $200

Note that rates for identical treatments can vary by as much as $20 or $30 from ship to ship. Treatments are charged to your onboard account. Usually they do not include a **gratuity,** but on a few lines Steiner does add them directly to your bill. Before you sign, ask your therapist or the desk attendant whether a tip is included, and write one in if not. Of course, if you were unhappy with your treatment, you're not required to tip at all.

It's almost guaranteed that at the end of your session, just as you're coming out of a semiconscious trance, your Steiner or Mandara therapist will give you an itemized list of expensive **creams, exfoliants, moisturizers, toners,** and **masks** that will help you get the spa effect at home—all for just a couple of hundred bucks. In fact, on a recent *Norwegian Dawn* cruise, Heidi's massage therapist spent a whopping 15 minutes telling her how Gwyneth Paltrow and the other stars swore by the $124 Elemis face cream she was pushing. Enough already. The products are often very good, but the sales pitch is just a little too shameless. So, remember our mantra: *You can say no*—unless, of course, you're in a spending mood. See "Best Ships for Spa-Goers," in the "Best of Cruising" chapter, to see which ships have the best facilities.

Tip: Make your spa appointments on the first day out to snag the best times.

5 Programs for Kids & Teens

With the cruise lines falling all over themselves to cater to kids these days, amenities and services for children rival those offered for adults. The cruise execs know that if the kiddos are happy, mom and dad will be too (and will hopefully want to book more cruises). Dedicated playrooms, camplike counselors, computers, state-of-the-art video arcades, pools, and new teen centers have most kids so gaga for cruising, you'll have to drag them away kicking and screaming at the end of the week. Even if your kids are too young to join the programming (which typically starts at age 2 or 3), there are more options than ever. In this age of play dates, it's no surprise that a line, Royal Caribbean, has introduced daily 45-minute **play groups** for infants, toddlers, and parents.

The youngest kids frolic in toy- and game-stocked **playrooms,** listen to stories, go on treasure hunts, and do arts and crafts; older kids keep busy with **computer games,** lip-sync competitions, pool games, volleyball, and now many more educational activities focused on art, science, music, and exercise. There's usually a TV showing movies throughout the day, and, for the younger ones, there might be ball bins and plastic jungle gyms to crawl around in. Many megaships have shallow kiddie pools for diaper-trained young'uns, sometimes sequestered on an isolated patch of deck.

The newest ships of the mainstream lines invite hard-to-please **teens** to hang out in their very own space, complete with a dance floor, bar (nonalcoholic of course), video wall for movie watching, video arcade, and sometimes private Internet area. The best facilities are on the *Carnival Freedom, Liberty, Valor, Glory,* and *Conquest; Disney Wonder* and *Magic;* Royal Caribbean's Freedom, Voyager, and Radiance classes; *Norwegian Dawn, Star,* and *Spirit;* and the *Grand, Golden, Star,* and *Caribbean Princess.*

See "Cruises for Families," in chapter 1, for more details, including information on **babysitting.**

6 Onboard Dining Options

Perhaps nothing has changed the cruise experience as much as the evolution of dining. When we started covering ships a decade ago, pretty much every ship offered traditional five-course, assigned-seating dinners in formal dining rooms, plus an optional buffet for breakfast and lunch. Now it's a free-for-all, with numerous **casual dining options** that allow passengers not only to dress down but also to dine with complete flexibility, choosing when, with whom, and where they want to eat, with several different restaurant options. In mid-2000, **Norwegian Cruise Line** got the ball rolling with its Freestyle Cruising arrangement, which allows passengers to dine anytime between 5:30pm and midnight in any of several venues, with the last seating at 10pm. **Oceania Cruises's** much smaller ships operate on essentially the same system, and both **Princess** and **Holland America** offer passengers the option of choosing flexible or traditional dining.

Formal or casual aside, the bottom line is that cruise lines are willing to feed you till you pop, and these days are offering more and more cuisine options, too. On the megaships, you can get elegant **multicourse meals** served in grand two- and three-story dining rooms; make reservations at an intimate specialty restaurant for Asian, Italian, French, Tex-Mex, Pacific Northwest, or Creole cuisine; drop in at the ship's buffet restaurant or cafe for an ultracasual meal; take in some **24-hour** pizza or other late-night option; grab a **snack** (ice cream, cookies, pastries, or specialty coffees); and maybe have some **sushi** to top it all off. Carnival offers pizza, Caesar salad, and garlic rolls 24 hours a day, and many lines now deliver pizza to your cabin; Disney has a burger and hot dog counter by the pool; and Royal Caribbean's Freedom- and Voyager-class ships have entire 1950s-style diners out on deck. The midsize ships generally have fewer choices, though Oceania's vessels, which carry only 684 passengers apiece, have four different venues at dinner, including Italian and steakhouse specialty restaurants and an alfresco restaurant serving Spanish dishes. The ultraluxe lines are offering alternatives, too.

All but the most cost-conscious cruise lines will attempt to satisfy reasonable culinary requests, so if you follow a **special diet,** inform your line as early as possible, preferably when booking your cruise, and make sure they'll be able to satisfy your request at all three meals. **Vegetarian dishes** and a selection of **healthier, lighter meals** (usually called "spa cuisine" or "light and healthy options") are available as a matter of course on just about every ship at breakfast, lunch, and dinner. And the latest trend? Trans-fat-free cooking. Some of the small-ship lines need advance notice for any special requests. Most large ships will provide kosher and halal meals if requested in advance, but expect them to be prepackaged. You'll get better choices at **Chosen Voyage** (© **800/990-0890;** www.chosenvoyage.com), a division of INTRAV (parent company of Clipper Cruise Line) that offers full-kosher trips along with onboard and shore programs themed on Jewish history and culture.

TRADITIONAL DINING

Though casual and specialty dining are all the rage, most ships still continue to offer formal, **traditional dinners** in at least one restaurant, generally from about 6:30 to 10pm. Ships carrying fewer than 400 passengers generally have one **open-seating dinner,** where guests can stroll in when they want and sit with whomever they choose. Those carrying more than 400 passengers typically have two **assigned seatings** in one or more main dining rooms. Princess offers a combination of both, with one or more restaurants on each ship offering open restaurant-style seating and another offering traditional early and late seating. Disney puts a unique twist on things by offering two seatings in three main themed dining rooms that passengers and their servers rotate through over the course of the cruise.

Most ships still require you to reserve either the early or late seating (sometimes called first and second seating) when booking your cruise. Elderly passengers and families with children tend to choose the **early seating** (served at around 6 or 6:30pm), though you have to be ready to leave the table once the dishes are cleared. If you choose **late seating** (served around 8 or 8:30pm), you won't have to rush through pre-dinner showering and dressing after an active day in port, and the meal tends to be more leisurely, allowing you to linger over coffee and after-dinner drinks.

If you get assigned to the first seating and you want the second, or vice versa (or you get no assignment at all), see the maitre d' staff, which will probably have a table set up in the dining room during embarkation for this purpose. Most can accommodate your wishes, if not on the first night of sailing, then on the second. Ditto if you find that you don't get along with your assigned tablemates. Most of the time you'll be seated at a table with 4 to 10 people. If you want privacy, you can request a table for two, but unless you're sailing aboard one of the smaller, more upscale ships, don't get your hopes up, as couples' tables are usually few and far between.

Seven-night cruises offering traditional dining generally have 2 **formal nights** per week, when the dress code in the main dining room may call for dark suits or tuxedos for men and cocktail dresses or fancy pantsuits for women. Other nights in the main dining rooms will probably be designated informal and/or casual. Ten- to 14-night cruises usually have 3 formal nights. (See "Packing for the Different Cruise Climates," in chapter 3, for more information.) If you want to skip formality altogether, most ships offer casual dining in the buffet restaurant every evening and/or other casual alternative options (see below).

Though some ships still offer early and late seatings for breakfast and lunch (served around 7 and 8:30am and noon and 1:30pm, respectively), most ships are now offering open-seating setups within certain hours.

Smoking is prohibited in virtually all ships' dining rooms.

SPECIALTY DINING

Variety + intimacy = specialty dining. Over the past several years, all the mainstream lines and most of the luxe lines have retooled their ships' layouts to make room for a greater number of small, alternative dining venues, where 100 or so guests can sample various international cuisines with sometimes elaborate presentations. Of course, you often have to pay for the treat, with most specialty restaurants charging between $10 and $30 per person, per meal. Frankly, sometimes the food isn't any better than in the main dining rooms (especially in Holland America's, Carnival's, and Costa's specialty restaurants), but the venues are at least quieter and more intimate. The best, without a doubt, are on the Celebrity, Crystal, Silversea, and Regent ships. NCL also gets special mention for having so many of them—six on the line's newest ships, plus casual choices. Here's what's available at each of the lines:

Specialty Dining: Who's Got What

Cruise Line & Ships	Type of Specialty Restaurants	Per-Person Charge
Carnival		
Spirit and Conquest classes	Steakhouse/Seafood	$30
Celebrity		
Millennium class	Continental	$30
Costa		
Costa Magica, Costa Mediterranea	Italian	$23
Crystal		
Crystal Serenity	Asian, Sushi, Italian	"suggested" $6 tip
Cunard		
Queen Mary 2	Mediterranean	$30
	Chef's Galley	$35
	Italian, Asian, Carvery	no extra charge
Disney		
Disney Magic, Disney Wonder	Italian	$10
Holland America		
Fleetwide	Pacific Northwest	$20
Norwegia		
Pearl, Dawn, Star, Spirit, Jewel, Jade	Steakhouse	$20
	French/Continental	$15
	Pan-Asian	$10
	Sushi	$15, all you can eat
	Teppanyaki	$20
	Tapas/Tex-Mex, Italian	no extra charge
Majesty, Dream	French/Continental	$15
Pride of Aloha	Pan-Asian, Italian	$10
	French/Continental	$10
Pride of America	Pan-Asian	$10
	Italian	no extra charge
	French/Continental	$15
	Steakhouse	$20
	Sushi	$15, all you can eat
	Teppanyaki	$20
Sun	Italian	$10
	French/Continental	$15
	Steakhouse	$20
	Sushi	$15, all you can eat
	Teppanyaki	$20
	Tapas/Tex-Mex	no extra charge

Cruise Line & Ships	Type of Specialty Restaurants	Per-Person Charge
Oceania		
Regatta, Insignia, Nautica	Italian, Steakhouse	no extra charge
Princess		
Caribbean	Italian Trattoria	$20
	Steakhouse	$15
	Caribbean	no extra charge
Crown, Emerald	Italian Trattoria	$20
	Steakhouse	$25
Diamond, Sapphire	Italian Trattoria	$20
	Steakhouse	$15
Golden, Grand, Star	Italian Trattoria	$20
	Steakhouse	$15
Coral, Island Princess	Italian Trattoria	$20
	New Orleans-style	$15
Sun class	Steakhouse	$15
	Sit-down pizzeria	no extra charge
Regent		
Seven Seas Mariner	French, Mediterranean, Indochinese	no extra charge
Seven Seas Voyager	French, Mediterranean, Indochinese	no extra charge
Navigator	Italian	no extra charge
Royal Caribbean		
Freedom class	Italian, Steakhouse	$20
Radiance class	Italian, Steakhouse	$20
Voyager class	Italian	$20
Mariner, Navigator, Enchantment	Steakhouse	$20
Seabourn		
Legend, Pride	Asian, Mediterranean, Steakhouse, Tasting Menus*	no extra charge
Silversea		
Shadow, Whisper, Wind	Italian	no extra charge
	Regional with wine pairings	$150

Seabourn hosts varying theme nights in one restaurant aboard each ship.

CASUAL DINING

If you'd rather skip the formality and hubbub of the main dining room, all but the tiniest ships serve breakfast, lunch, and dinner in a **casual, buffet-style restaurant.** Usually located on the Lido Deck, with indoor and outdoor poolside seating, these restaurants serve a spread of both hot and cold items. On the megaships, a grill may be nearby where, at lunchtime, you can get burgers, hot dogs, and often chicken and veggie burgers; sometimes you can find specialty stations offering taco fixings, deli sandwiches, or Chinese food, too. On most ships, breakfast and lunch buffets are generally served for a 3- to 4-hour period, so guests can stroll in and out whenever they want; but many of the mainstream lines also keep portions of their Lido cafes open almost round-the-clock. Most lines serve nightly buffet-style dinners here as well, with some offering a combination of sit-down service and buffet.

BETWEEN-MEAL SNACKING

"Between-meal snacking" is the cruise industry's middle name. Almost all the mega- and midsize ships have complimentary **pizzerias** (24 hr. daily on Carnival's ships) and **self-serve frozen yogurt and ice-cream machines,** as well as cafes or coffee shops where you can grab a snack, sandwich, or specialty coffee (the latter at an extra charge). The upscale lines and some of the mainstreamers (such as Celebrity, Princess, Oceania, and Holland America) offer **afternoon tea service,** serving finger sandwiches, pastries, and cookies along with tea and coffee. Carnival and several others do their own, less fancy versions. Most of the small-ship lines serve **pre-dinner snacks and hors d'oeuvres** on deck or in the main lounge or bar area.

The **midnight buffet,** a staple of cruising back in the '80s and '90s, has been scaled back in recent years, in part because so many casual dining options are available for late-night snacking. Today, you'll usually find it offered in all its overwhelming extravagance only once or twice a week on most lines, with heaps of elaborately decorated fruits, vegetables, pastries, cold cuts, pasta, and sometimes shrimp and other treats. Sometimes the nighttime feast will be focused on a culinary theme, such as Tex-Mex, Caribbean, or chocolate. Sometimes smaller **snack stations** will be set up instead, or servers will cruise the ships with trays of hors d'oeuvres—which keeps drinkers where the cruise lines want them: at the bar, running up their tabs.

If you'd rather not leave your cabin, most ships offer **24-hour room service** from menus that vary from limited to lush. Passengers on luxury ships (and suite guests on all ships) can usually have the same meals being served in the dining room delivered to their rooms course by course.

7 Onboard Entertainment

Entertainment is a big part of the cruise experience on almost all ships, but especially on the megaships of Carnival, Royal Caribbean, Celebrity, Costa, Princess, NCL, and Holland America, which all offer an extensive variety throughout the day. Afternoons, you can dance on deck with the **live dance band,** which we'll bet 10-to-1 will be jamming calypso music or tunes by Bob Marley and Jimmy Buffett. Or put on your waltzing shoes and head inside to one of the lounges for some **swing dancing.** Lines such as Holland America, Crystal, NCL, Oceania, and Royal Caribbean often feature a 1940s-style big band playing dance tunes. Some of the most pleasant concerts we've seen at sea were aboard the Royal Caribbean Voyager ships. On one, a trio was so inspiring that two passengers joined in, belting out Italian opera songs like real pros. At another, the ship's big band set up just outside the pub, among the crowd, and played a relaxed set of standards.

Pre-dinner entertainment starts to heat up around 5pm, and continues all night to accommodate passengers dining early and late. Head to the **piano bar** for a cocktail or do some pre-dinner dancing to some small-group jazz.

Usually twice or three times in any weeklong cruise, there's apt to be **Vegas-style musical revues** performed early and late in the main show lounge, with a flamboyant troupe of anywhere from 6 to 16 feather-boa-and-sequin-clad male and female dancers sliding, kicking, and lip-synching as a soloist or two belt out show tunes and pop faves. Expect a lot of Andrew Lloyd Webber; "YMCA"; at least one tune each from *Grease, Footloose,* and *A Chorus Line;* and maybe a few Richard Rodgers tunes. A live orchestra accompanies most of these productions, though not all. While the quality of shows industry-wide is inconsistent, opinion here at Casa Frommer's is divided on the whole revue format, with Heidi enjoying the medleys "if the singing's good—which, granted, it isn't always," and Matt thinking most of them are "all flash and no substance." Two lines we can agree on, though, are Disney and NCL. Disney offers absolutely the best shows at sea, with characters and stories based on its parent company's classic films. Recent shows on NCL are also standouts, with strong soloists and really original staging, choreography, and choice of material.

Nights when the shows aren't scheduled may feature a **magic show** complete with sawing in half a scantily clad assistant and pulling rabbits from a hat; **acrobatic acts** and **aerialists** (always a big hit); **headline soloists,** some of them quite good (such as singer Jane L. Powell, a perennial NCL favorite whose amazing range takes her from Louis Armstrong to Bette Midler); or **guest comedians or specialty acts,** such as Costa's regular operatic recitals, Oceania's pianists, and Royal Caribbean's a cappella singing groups. **Comedians** frequently perform in the main theater or a second performance space, sometimes doing PG- and R-rated material at an early show and then running the X up the mast at an adults-only midnight performance. Raising the humor bar, Norwegian Cruise Line offers hysterical shows by the famed Second City improv comedy group on *Norwegian Dawn, Norwegian Spirit, Norwegian Star, Norwegian Jewel, Norwegian Pearl,* and *Norwegian Gem.*

The **disco** gets going on most ships around 9 or 10pm and works it until 2 or 3am, sometimes later. Occasionally a live band plays until about midnight, when a DJ takes over until the wee hours, spinning tunes from the 1970s through to today; sometimes there's only a DJ. A **karaoke session** may also be thrown in for an hour or two in the afternoon or evening.

An alternative to the disco or the main show may be a pianist or jazz trio in one of the ship's romantic nightspots, or a **themed party,** sometimes on deck. For a quiet evening, many lines show **recent-release movies,** in a theater, a dedicated cinema, or up on deck on a giant LED screen.

To prove not all innovative entertainment has to be big, Celebrity features **strolling vocal quartets** that roam around the ships in the evening, performing wherever people are gathered. On Royal Caribbean's Voyager- and Freedom-class ships, a troupe of **clowns** performs impromptu juggling, acrobatic, and comedy routines in various public areas. At different points of the cruise they also give juggling lessons and provide a little talk on clown history and technique. Big thumbs up! Along similar lines, on a *Carnival Valor* cruise, a couple of entertainers on high stilts did a dance routine on the pool deck.

Ships carrying 100 to 400 passengers have fewer entertainment options and a more mellow evening ambience overall. The high-end lines may feature a quartet or pianist performing before dinner and maybe a small-scale song-and-dance revue afterward, plus dancing in a quiet lounge. The small adventure-oriented ships may at most have a solo performer before and after dinner, or **local musicians and/or dancers** aboard for an afternoon or evening.

8 Shopping Opportunities on Ship & Shore

Even the smallest ships have at least a small shop on board selling T-shirts, sweatshirts, and baseball caps bearing the cruise line logo. The big new megaships, though, are like minimalls, offering as many as 10 different stores selling items from toiletries and sundries to high-end china. In case you're in need, you'll usually find **formal wear** such as sequined dresses and jackets, silk dresses and scarves, purses, satin shoes, cummerbunds, ties, and tuxedo shirts, as well as perfume, cosmetics, and jewelry (costume and the real stuff).

A few ships have **name-brand stores,** or sections of stores. Many of Carnival's ships, for instance, have Fossil boutiques on board, while Cunard's *QM2* has a Harrods shop offering lots of those cute stuffed bears, green totes, and biscuits. The high-end lines, such as Silversea, Crystal, and Regent, have boutiques selling fine jewelry, bags, and accessories.

All merchandise sold on board while a ship is at sea is **tax-free** (though you must declare them at Customs when returning to the U.S.); to maintain that tax-free status, the shops are closed whenever a ship is in port. Prices can vary, though; and just like at a resort, items such as disposable cameras, sunscreen, candy, and snack foods will cost substantially more than you'd pay at home. On the other hand, by midcruise there are often decent sales on things like T-shirts, tote bags, jewelry, and booze.

See "Best Shopping Ports," in the "Best of Cruising" chapter, for the best shopping islands.

Before each port of call, the cruise director or shore-excursion manager gives a **port talk** about that place's attractions and shopping. Now, it's no secret that many cruise lines have mutually beneficial deals with certain shops in every port (generally of the touristy chain variety), so on the big, mass-market ships especially, the vast majority of the port info disseminated will be about shopping. Better bring along your own guidebook (this one!) if you want information on history or culture. The lines often recommend a list of shops in town where they say the merchandise is guaranteed, and if the stone falls out of the new ring you bought at one of them once you get home, the cruise lines say they'll try to help you get a replacement. Don't hold your breath, though; the whole thing is a bit ambiguous. If you're not an expert on jewelry or whatever else you want to buy, it may be safer to shop at these stores; however, you won't get much of a taste for the local culture in one of them. Browsing at outdoor markets and in smaller craft shops is a better way to get an idea of the port's real flavor.

Part 2

The Cruise Lines & Their Ships

Detailed, in-depth reviews of all the cruise lines sailing from U.S. and Canadian home ports and a few Caribbean islands, with discussions of the type of experience they offer and the lowdown on all their ships.

5

The Ratings & How to Read Them

The following three chapters are the heart and soul of this book, our expert reviews and ratings of the cruise lines operating in the American market. This chapter is your instruction manual, with hints on how to use the reviews to compare the lines and find the one that's right for you.

1 Cruise Line Categories

To make your selection easier (and to make sure you're not comparing apples and oranges), we've divided the cruise lines into three distinct categories, given each category a chapter of its own, and rated each line only in comparison with the other lines in its category (see more about this in "How to Read the Ratings," below). The categories are as follows:

THE MAINSTREAM LINES (chapter 6)   This category includes the most prominent players in the industry, the jack-of-all-trades lines with the biggest ships, carrying the most passengers and providing the most diverse cruise experiences to suit many different tastes, from party-hearty to elegant and refined. With all the competition in the industry today, these lines tend to offer good prices, too. Mixed in among these lines you'll find a few oddballs such as budget line Imperial Majesty.

THE ULTRALUXURY LINES (chapter 7)   These are the Dom Perignon of cruises, offering elegant, refined, and doting service, extraordinary dining, spacious cabins, and high-toned entertainment aboard intimate, finely appointed small and midsize vessels—and at a high price.

SMALL SHIPS, SAILING SHIPS & ADVENTURE CRUISES (chapter 8)   If you don't like crowds; want an experience that revolves around nature, history, or culture; want to visit out-of-the-way ports; or prefer quiet conversation to a large ship's roster of activities, these small, casual ships may be your cup of tea.

2 Reading the Reviews & Ratings

Each cruise line's review begins with **The Line in a Nutshell** (a quick word about the line in general) and **The Experience,** which is just what it says: a short summation of the kind of cruise experience you can expect to have aboard that line, followed by a few major **pros and cons.** The **Ratings Table** judges the individual elements of the line's cruise experience compared with the other lines in the same category (see below for ratings details). The text that follows fleshes out these summations, providing all the details you need to get a feel for what kind of vacation the cruise line will give you.

The individual **ship reviews** give you details on each vessel's accommodations, facilities, amenities, comfort level, upkeep, and vital statistics—size, passenger capacity, year launched and most recently refurbished, number of cabins, number of crew, and so on—to help you compare. Size is described in terms of **gross register tonnage (GRT)**, which is a measure not of actual weight but of the interior space (or volume) used to produce revenue on a ship: 1 GRT equals 100 cubic feet of enclosed, revenue-generating space. By dividing the GRTs by the number of passengers aboard, we arrive at the **passenger/space ratio,** which gives you some idea of how much elbowroom you'll have on each ship. To compare the amount of personalized service you can expect, we have the **passenger/crew ratio,** which tells you approximately how many passengers each crewmember is expected to serve—though this doesn't literally mean a waiter for every two or three passengers, since "crew" includes everyone from officers to deckhands to shop clerks.

Note that when several vessels are members of a class—built on the same design, with usually only minor variations in decor and attractions—we've grouped the ships together into one **class review.**

HOW TO READ THE RATINGS

To make things easier on everyone, we've developed a simple ratings system based on the classic customer-satisfaction survey, rating both the cruise line as a whole and the individual ships as poor, fair, good, excellent, or outstanding on a number of important qualities. The **cruise line ratings** cover all the elements that are usually consistent from ship to ship within the line (overall enjoyability of the experience, dining, activities, children's program, entertainment, service, and value), while the **individual ship ratings** cover those things that vary from vessel to vessel—quality and size of the cabins and public spaces, comfort, appearance and upkeep, decor, number and quality of dining options, gyms/spas (or, for the small-adventure lines that don't have gyms and spas, "Adventure & Fitness Options"), and children's facilities—plus a rating for the overall enjoyment of the onboard experience. To provide an **overall score,** we've given each ship an overall star rating (for example, ★★★½) based on the combined total of our poor-to-outstanding ratings, translated into a 1-to-5 scale:

1	=	Poor	4	=	Excellent
2	=	Fair	5	=	Outstanding
3	=	Good			

In instances where the category doesn't apply to a particular ship (for example, none of the adventure ships has children's facilities), we've simply noted "not applicable" (N/A) and absented the category from the total combined score, as these unavailable amenities would be considered a deficiency only if you plan to travel with kids.

Now for a bit of philosophy: The cruise biz today offers a profusion of experiences so different that comparing all lines and ships by the same set of criteria would be like comparing a Park Avenue apartment to an A-frame in Aspen. That's why, to rate the cruise lines and their ships, we've used a sliding scale, rating lines and ships on a curve that compares them only with others in their category—mainstream with mainstream, luxe with luxe, adventure with adventure. Once you've determined what kind of experience is right for you, you can look for the best ships in that category based on your particular needs. For example, if you see in the "Small Ships, Sailing Ships & Adventure Cruises" chapter that Windstar achieves an "outstanding" rating for dining, that means that among the lines in that category/chapter, Windstar has the best cuisine. It may not be up to the level of, say, the ultraluxurious Silversea (it's not), but if you're looking for a sailing-ship cruise that also has terrific food, this line would be a great bet.

3 Evaluating & Comparing the Listed Cruise Prices

As we explain in detail in chapter 2, the cruise lines' brochure prices are almost always wildly inflated—they're the "sticker prices" cruise line execs would love to get in an ideal world. In reality, passengers typically pay anywhere from 10% to 50% less. Instead of publishing these inflated brochure rates, then, we've worked with Nashville's **Just Cruisin' Plus** (© **800/888-0922;** www.justcruisinplus.com) to provide you with samples of the **actual prices** customers were paying at press time. Other travel agencies and online sites will generally offer similar rates. Each ship review includes per diem prices (the total cruise price divided by the number of days) for the following three basic types of accommodations:

- Lowest-priced inside (without windows) cabin
- Lowest-priced outside (with windows) cabin
- Lowest-priced suite

Remember that cruise ships generally have several categories of cabins within each of these three basic divisions, all priced differently, and that the prices we've listed represent the *lowest* categories for inside and outside cabins and suites. Remember, too, that because this book covers cruises in several different regions, the prices we've listed are not applicable to all sailings—cruises in Alaska and Hawaii, for instance, are almost always more expensive than comparable cruises in the Caribbean. These prices are meant as a guide only and are in no way etched in stone—the price you pay may be higher or even lower, depending on when you choose to travel, when you book, what specials the lines are offering, and a slew of other factors. Prices listed include **port charges** (the per-passenger fee ports charge for ships to dock) but do not include taxes.

See chapter 2, "Booking Your Cruise & Getting the Best Price," for more details on pricing and to compare our discount prices with the cruise lines' published brochure rates (in the "Price Comparisons: Discounted Rates vs. Brochure Rates" table). Seeing how much you'll probably save can be a real eye-opener.

A NOTE ON ITINERARIES

Our fleet itinerary tables give you an idea of which ships sail which regions, and when. See the cruise lines' websites or a travel agent for full details on each itinerary. Note that we have not listed itineraries outside the geographical range of this book.

Ships at a Glance

Cruise Line	Ship	Frommer's Star Rating	Year Built
ACCL (sm. ship): A family-owned New England line operating tiny, no-frills ships that travel to offbeat places, carrying casual, down-to-earth, older passengers.	**Grande Caribe**	★★★	1997
	Grande Mariner	★★★	1998
American Cruise Lines (sm. ship): Part cruise, part Rotary Club meeting, part historical tour, this Connecticut-based line offers a comfortable, reserved, and hassle-free cruise experience.	**American Eagle**	★★★½	2000
	American Glory	★★★½	2002
	American Spirit	★★★½	2005
	American Star	★★★½	2007
American Safari Cruises (sm. ship): The most luxurious of the small-ship soft-adventure lines.	**Safari Escape**	★★★★	1983
	Safari Quest	★★★★	1992
	Safari Spirit	★★★★	1981
Azamara (mainstream): Comfy exploration, country-club comfort.	**Azamara Quest**	★★★★	2000
Carnival (mainstream): When you're hankering for an utterly unpretentious and totally laid-back cruise, Carnival's colorful, jumbo-size resort ships deliver plenty of bang for the buck. If you like the flash of Vegas and a serious party vibe, you'll love Carnival's brand of flamboyant fun.	**Carnival Conquest**	★★★★½	2002
	Carnival Destiny	★★★★½	1996
	Carnival Freedom	★★★★½	2007
	Carnival Glory	★★★★½	2003
	Carnival Legend	★★★★	2002
	Carnival Liberty	★★★★½	2005
	Carnival Miracle	★★★★	2004
	Carnival Pride	★★★★	2001
	Carnival Spirit	★★★★	2001
	Carnival Splendor	not yet in service	2008
	Carnival Triumph	★★★★½	1999
	Carnival Valor	★★★★½	2004
	Carnival Victory	★★★★½	2000
	Celebration	★★★	1987
	Ecstasy	★★★½	1991
	Elation	★★★½	1998

Gross Tonnage	Passenger Capacity (Double Occupancy)	Passenger/Space Ratio	Passenger/Crew Ratio	Wheelchair Access	Sailing Regions	Full Review on Page
99*	100	N/A*	5.5 to 1	no	New England, U.S. East Coast/Intracoastal Waterway	326
99*	100	N/A*	5.5 to 1	no	New England, Great Lakes, U.S. East Coast/Intracoastal Waterway, Caribbean, Bahamas	326
86*	49	N/A*	2.7 to 1	yes	U.S. East Coast/Intracoastal Waterway	332
86*	49	N/A*	2.7 to 1	yes	New England, U.S. East Coast/Intracoastal Waterway, Florida	332
97*	100	N/A*	3.8 to 1	yes	New England, U.S. East Coast/Intracoastal Waterway	332
97*	100	N/A*	3.8 to 1	yes	New England, U.S. East Coast/Intracoastal Waterway, Florida	332
N/A*	12	N/A*	2 to 1	no	Alaska	334
99*	22	N/A*	2 to 1	no	Alaska, Baja/Sea of Cortez	334
N/A*	12	N/A*	1.7 to 1	no	Alaska, Pacific Northwest Rivers	334
30,277	710	42.6	1.8 to 1	yes	Caribbean, Panama Canal	111
110,000	2,974	37	2.5 to 1	yes	Caribbean	122
101,353	2,642	38.4	2.6 to 1	yes	Caribbean	129
110,000	2,974	37	2.5 to 1	yes	Caribbean	122
110,000	2,974	37	2.5 to 1	yes	Caribbean	122
88,500	2,124	41.7	2.3 to 1	yes	Caribbean	126
110,000	2,974	37	2.5 to 1	yes	Caribbean	122
88,500	2,124	41.7	2.3 to 1	yes	Caribbean	126
88,500	2,124	41.7	2.3 to 1	yes	Mexican Riviera	126
88,500	2,124	41.7	2.3 to 1	yes	Mexican Riviera, Alaska	126
112,000	3,006	37.3	2.6 to 1	yes	Caribbean	121
102,000	2,758	37	2.6 to 1	yes	Caribbean	129
110,000	2,974	37	2.5 to 1	yes	Caribbean	122
102,000	2,758	37	2.6 to 1	yes	Caribbean, Bahamas, New England/Canada	129
47,262	1,486	31.8	2.2 to 1	yes	Caribbean	135
70,367	2,040	34.5	2.2 to 1	yes	Caribbean	132
70,367	2,040	34.5	2.2 to 1	yes	Baja, Mexico	132

Ships at a Glance (continued)

Cruise Line	Ship	Frommer's Star Rating	Year Built
Carnival (continued)	Fantasy	★★★½	1990
	Fascination	★★★½	1994
	Holiday	★★★	1985
	Imagination	★★★½	1995
	Inspiration	★★★½	1996
	Paradise	★★★½	1998
	Sensation	★★★½	1993
Celebrity (mainstream): Celebrity offers an elegant and refined cruise experience, yet one that's fun, active, and doesn't cost a bundle. Each ship is spacious, glamorous, and comfortable, mixing sleekly modern and Art Deco styles and throwing in cutting-edge art collections to boot.	Century	★★★★½	1995
	Constellation	★★★★★	2002
	Galaxy	★★★★½	1996
	Infinity	★★★★★	2001
	Mercury	★★★★½	1997
	Millennium	★★★★★	2000
	Summit	★★★★★	2001
Costa (mainstream): Fun, festive, international megaships.	Costa Fortuna	★★★★	2003
	Costa Mediterranea	★★★½	2003
Cruise West (sm. ship): Family-owned Cruise West is the preeminent small-ship line in Alaska, and over the past decade it's branched out to include trips in warmer destinations, too. Most of its itineraries are port-to-port and geared to older, well-traveled, intellectually curious passengers.	Pacific Explorer	★★★½	1995
	Spirit of Alaska	★★★½	1980
	Spirit of Columbia	★★★½	1979
	Spirit of Discovery	★★★½	1976
	Spirit of Endeavour	★★★½	1983
	Spirit of Glacier Bay	★★★	1984
	Spirit of '98	★★★★	1984
	Spirit of Oceanus	★★★★★	1991
	Spirit of Yorktown	★★★	1988
Crystal (luxury): Fine-tuned and fashionable, with pampering service, scrumptious cuisine, and ships large enough to offer generous fitness and entertainment facilities.	Crystal Serenity	★★★★½	2003
	Crystal Symphony	★★★★½	1995

Gross Tonnage	Passenger Capacity (Double Occupancy)	Passenger/Space Ratio	Passenger/Crew Ratio	Wheelchair Access	Sailing Regions	Full Review on Page
70,367	2,040	34.5	2.2 to 1	yes	Caribbean	132
70,367	2,040	34.5	2.2 to 1	yes	Caribbean	132
46,052	1,452	31.7	2.2 to 1	yes	Caribbean	135
70,367	2,040	34.5	2.2 to 1	yes	Caribbean	132
70,367	2,040	34.5	2.2 to 1	yes	Caribbean	132
70,367	2,040	34.5	2.2 to 1	yes	California/Baja	132
70,367	2,040	34.5	2.2 to 1	yes	Caribbean	132
70,606	1,750	40.3	2 to 1	yes	Caribbean	147
91,000	1,950	46.7	2 to 1	yes	Caribbean, Bermuda, New England/Canada	143
77,713	1,896	41	2 to 1	yes	Caribbean	147
91,000	1,950	46.7	2 to 1	yes	Panama Canal, Alaska, Caribbean	143
77,713	1,896	41	2 to 1	yes	Hawaii, Alaska, British Columbia, Panama Canal	147
91,000	1,950	46.7	2 to 1	yes	Caribbean, Panama Canal, Alaska, Hawaii	143
91,000	1,950	46.7	2 to 1	yes	Caribbean, Panama Canal	143
105,000	2,720	38.6	2.5 to 1	yes	Caribbean, Bermuda	154
85,000	2,112	40.2	2.3 to 1	yes	Caribbean	156
1,716	100	17.2	3 to 1	no	Costa Rica/Panama	336
97*	78	N/A	3.7 to 1	no	Alaska	344
97*	78	N/A	3.7 to 1	no	Alaska	344
94*	84	N/A	4 to 1	no	Alaska, Pacific Northwest Rivers	344
99*	102	N/A	3.6 to 1	no	Alaska, British Columbia	342
1,471	100	14.7	3.2 to 1	no	Alaska	342
96*	96	N/A	4.2 to 1	partial	Alaska, Pacific Northwest Rivers	340
4,500	114	39.5	2 to 1	no	Alaska	339
2,354	138	17	3.5 to 1	no	Alaska, Baja/Sea of Cortez, California Wine Country	342
68,000	1,080	63	1.7 to 1	yes	Caribbean, Panama Canal	276
51,044	940	52.5	1.7 to 1	yes	Panama Canal, Mexican Riviera, New England/Canada, Caribbean/Bermuda	278

Ships at a Glance (continued)

Cruise Line	Ship	Frommer's Star Rating	Year Built
Cunard (luxury): A legendary line with a nearly legendary new vessel—the largest ocean liner in the world.	Queen Mary 2	★★★★★	2004
Disney (mainstream): Family ships where both kids and adults are catered to equally, and with style.	Disney Magic	★★★★½	1998
	Disney Wonder	★★★★½	1999
Holland America (mainstream): Holland America has been in business since 1873, and has managed to hang on to more of its seafaring history and tradition than any line today except Cunard. It offers a moderately priced, classic, and casual yet refined cruise experience.	Amsterdam	★★★★	2000
	Maasdam	★★★★	1993
	Noordam	★★★★	2006
	Oosterdam	★★★★	2003
	Ryndam	★★★★	1994
	Statendam	★★★★	1993
	Veendam	★★★★	1996
	Volendam	★★★★½	1999
	Westerdam	★★★★	2004
	Zaandam	★★★★½	2000
	Zuiderdam	★★★★	2002
Imperial Majesty (mainstream): Vintage fun.	Regal Empress	★★	1953
Lindblad Expeditions (sm. ship): One of the most adventure-oriented small-ship lines, concentrating on wilderness and wildlife.	Sea Bird	★★★½	1982
	Sea Lion	★★★½	1981
Majestic America Line (sm. ship): Real live stern-wheel steamboats plying the Mississippi River system, the Pacific Northwest, and Alaska.	American Queen	★★★★	1995
	Columbia Queen	★★★★	2000
	Contessa	★★★½	1986
	Delta Queen	★★★★	1927
	Empress of the North	★★★★	2003
	Mississippi Queen	★★★★	1976
	Queen of the West	★★★★	1995
MSC Cruises (mainstream): Italian line offers midsize ships and gadget-free fun.	Lirica	★★★½	2003

Gross Tonnage	Passenger Capacity (Double Occupancy)	Passenger/Space Ratio	Passenger/Crew Ratio	Wheelchair Access	Sailing Regions	Full Review on Page
150,000	2,620	54.3	2.1 to 1	yes	Caribbean, Bahamas, New England/Canada, transatlantic	288
83,000	1,754	47.3	1.8 to 1	yes	Caribbean, Mexican Riviera Panama Canal	164
83,000	1,754	47.3	1.8 to 1	yes	Bahamas	164
61,000	1,380	43.8	2.1 to 1	yes	Alaska, Panama Canal	178
55,451	1,266	43.8	2.1 to 1	yes	Caribbean, Panama Canal, New England/Canada, U.S. East Coast/Canada	184
85,000	1,848	46	2.3 to 1	yes	Caribbean	175
85,000	1,848	46	2.3 to 1	yes	Mexican Riviera, Alaska	175
55,451	1,266	43.8	2.1 to 1	yes	Mexican Riviera	184
55,451	1,266	43.8	2.1 to 1	yes	Alaska, Panama Canal, Caribbean	184
55,451	1,266	43.8	2.1 to 1	yes	Caribbean, Panama Canal, Alaska	184
63,000	1,440	43.7	2.2 to 1	yes	Panama Canal, Alaska	181
85,000	1,848	46	2.3 to 1	yes	Caribbean, Bahamas, Panama Canal, Alaska	175
63,000	1,440	43.7	2.2 to 1	yes	Alaska	181
85,000	1,848	46	2.3 to 1	yes	Caribbean, Panama Canal	175
21,909	875	25	2.4 to 1	partial	Bahamas	190
100*	70	N/A	3.2 to 1	no	Baja/Sea of Cortez, Alaska	348
100*	70	N/A	3.2 to 1	no	Baja/Sea of Cortez, Alaska	348
3,707	436	8.5	2.6 to 1	yes	Mississippi/Ohio/ Cumberland Rivers	364
1,599	150	10.7	2.6 to 1	yes	Pacific Northwest Rivers	364
98*	49	N/A	2.7 to 1	no	Baja/Sea of Cortez, Alaska	368
3,360	174	19.3	2.1 to 1	no	Mississippi/Ohio/ Cumberland Rivers	362
3,388	235	14.4	2.8 to 1	yes	Pacific Northwest Rivers, Alaska	364
3,364	414	8.1	2.6 to 1	yes	Mississippi/Ohio/ Cumberland Rivers	364
1,308	136	9.6	2.3 to 1	yes	Pacific Northwest Rivers	364
58,600	1,586	36.9	2.1 to 1	yes	Caribbean	197

Ships at a Glance (continued)

Cruise Line	Ship	Frommer's Star Rating	Year Built
Norwegian (mainstream): NCL may be the most mainstream of the mainstream lines these days—and we mean that in a good way, hewing to the center with always-casual dining (and lots of it); bright, cheerful decor; and fun innovations like gourmet beer bars and onboard bowling alleys. Its newest ships are real standouts, and it's the go-to line for Hawaii cruises.	Norwegian Dawn	★★★★½	2002
	Norwegian Dream	★★★	1992
	Norwegian Gem	not yet in service	2007
	Norwegian Jade	★★★★★	2006
	Norwegian Jewel	★★★★★	2005
	Norwegian Majesty	★★★	1992
	Norwegian Pearl	★★★★★	2006
	Norwegian Spirit	★★★★½	1999
	Norwegian Star	★★★★½	2002
	Norwegian Sun	★★★★	2001
	Pride of Aloha	★★★★	1999
	Pride of America	★★★★	2005
Oceania (mainstream): Casual premium.	Regatta	★★★★	1998
Princess (mainstream): With a fleet of mostly large and extralarge megaships, including some of the biggest at sea, L.A.-based Princess offers a quality mainstream cruise experience with a nice balance of tradition and innovation, relaxation and excitement, casualness and glamour.	Caribbean Princess	★★★★½	2004
	Coral Princess	★★★★½	2003
	Crown Princess	★★★★½	2006
	Dawn Princess	★★★★	1995
	Diamond Princess	★★★★★	2004
	Emerald Princess	★★★★½	2007
	Golden Princess	★★★★½	2001
	Grand Princess	★★★★½	1998
	Island Princess	★★★★½	2003
	Sapphire Princess	★★★★★	2004
	Sea Princess	★★★★	1998
	Star Princess	★★★★½	2002
	Tahitian Princess	★★★★	1999

Gross Tonnage	Passenger Capacity (Double Occupancy)	Passenger/Space Ratio	Passenger/Crew Ratio	Wheelchair Access	Sailing Regions	Full Review on Page
92,250	2,224	41.5	2 to 1	yes	Caribbean, Bermuda, New England/Canada	206
50,760	1,748	29	2.8 to 1	yes	Bermuda, New England/Canada	217
93,000	2,380	39	2 to 1	yes	Caribbean, Bahamas/Florida	206
92,100	2,466	37.3	2.4 to 1	yes	U.S. East Coast	207
93,502	2,376	39.4	2 to 1	yes	Caribbean, New England/Canada	206
38,000	1,462	26	2.7 to 1	yes	Caribbean, New England/Canada	217
93,530	2,394	39	2 to 1	yes	Caribbean, Alaska	206
76,800	1,960	39.2	2 to 1	yes	Caribbean, Bahamas/Florida, New England/Canada	206
92,250	2,224	41.5	2 to 1	yes	Mexican Riviera, U.S. Pacific Coast	206
78,509	1,936	40.6	2 to 1	yes	Alaska, Caribbean, Mexican Riviera	214
77,104	2,002	38.5	2 to 1	yes	Hawaii	210
81,000	2,146	37.7	2.1 to 1	yes	Hawaii	210
30,200	684	44.2	1.8 to 1	yes	Caribbean, Panama Canal	223
116,000	2,600	37.4	2.4 to 1	yes	Caribbean, New England/Canada, Bermuda	233
91,627	1,970	46.5	2 to 1	yes	Panama Canal, U.S. Pacific Coast, Alaska	240
113,000	3,080	36.7	2.6 to 1	yes	Caribbean	233
77,000	1,950	39.5	2.2 to 1	yes	Mexican Riviera, U.S. Pacific Coast, Alaska	243
113,000	2,670	42.3	2.4 to 1	yes	Hawaii, U.S. Pacific Coast, Alaska	236
113,000	3,080	36.7	2.6 to 1	yes	Caribbean	233
109,000	2,600	41.9	2.4 to 1	yes	Mexican Riviera, U.S. Pacific Coast, Alaska	233
109,000	2,600	41.9	2.4 to 1	yes	Caribbean	233
91,627	1,970	46.5	2 to 1	yes	Panama Canal, U.S. Pacific Coast, Alaska	240
113,000	2,670	42.3	2.4 to 1	yes	U.S. Pacific Coast, Alaska	236
77,000	1,950	39.5	2.2 to 1	yes	Caribbean, New England/Canada	243
109,000	2,600	41.9	2.4 to 1	yes	Mexican Riviera, Alaska	233
30,277	670	45.2	1.8 to 1	yes	Alaska	230

Ships at a Glance (continued)

Cruise Line	Ship	Frommer's Star Rating	Year Built
Regent Seven Seas (luxury): Formerly known as Radisson Seven Seas, this line carries passengers in style and extreme comfort. Its brand of cruising is casually elegant and subtle, and its cuisine is near the top.	Seven Seas Mariner	★★★★½	2001
	Seven Seas Navigator	★★★★	1999
	Seven Seas Voyager	★★★★½	2003
RiverBarge (sm. ship): Slow river trips.	River Explorer	★★★½	1998
Royal Caribbean (mainstream): Royal Caribbean offers some of the best-looking, best-designed, most activity-packed, and just plain fun megaships in the biz. Along with NCL, they're also out in the forefront of innovation, always challenging the status quo regarding what can and can't be done aboard ships.	Adventure of the Seas	★★★★½	2001
	Brilliance of the Seas	★★★★½	2002
	Enchantment of the Seas	★★★½	1997
	Explorer of the Seas	★★★★½	2000
	Freedom of the Seas	★★★★½	2006
	Grandeur of the Seas	★★★½	1996
	Independence of the Seas	★★★★½	2008
	Jewel of the Seas	★★★★½	2004
	Legend of the Seas	★★★½	1995
	Liberty of the Seas	★★★★½	2007
	Majesty of the Seas	★★★	1992
	Mariner of the Seas	★★★★½	2003
	Monarch of the Seas	★★★	1991
	Navigator of the Seas	★★★★½	2003
	Radiance of the Seas	★★★★½	2001
	Rhapsody of the Seas	★★★½	1997
	Serenade of the Seas	★★★★½	2003
	Sovereign of the Seas	★★★	1988
	Splendour of the Seas	★★★½	1996
	Vision of the Seas	★★★½	1998
	Voyager of the Seas	★★★★½	1999
Seabourn (luxury): Seabourn's ships are floating pleasure palaces, giving passengers doting service and some of the finest cuisine at sea.	Seabourn Legend	★★★★	1992
	Seabourn Pride	★★★★	1988

Gross Tonnage	Passenger Capacity (Double Occupancy)	Passenger/Space Ratio	Passenger/Crew Ratio	Wheelchair Access	Sailing Regions	Full Review on Page
50,000	700	71.4	1.6 to 1	yes	Caribbean, Bermuda, Panama Canal, U.S. West Coast, Alaska	296
33,000	490	67.3	1.5 to 1	yes	Caribbean, Bermuda	298
46,000	700	65.7	1.6 to 1	yes	Caribbean	296
8,884	198	44.9	4.3 to 1	yes	Missippi/Ohio/Cumberland Rivers, Intracoastal Waterway	369
142,000	3,114	45.6	2.7 to 1	yes	Caribbean	256
90,090	2,100	42.9	2.5 to 1	yes	Caribbean, Panama Canal	259
80,700	2,252	35.8	2.7 to 1	yes	Caribbean	263
142,000	3,114	45.6	2.7 to 1	yes	Caribbean, Bermuda, New England/Canada	256
160,000	3,634	44	2.7 to 1	yes	Caribbean	252
74,137	1,950	38	2.5 to 1	yes	Caribbean, Bermuda, New England/Canada	263
160,000	3,634	44	2.7 to 1	yes	Caribbean	245
90,090	2,100	42.9	2.5 to 1	yes	Caribbean, New England/ Canada, Panama Canal/ Caribbean	259
74,137	1,804	41.1	2.5 to 1	yes	Caribbean	263
160,000	3,634	44	2.7 to 1	yes	Caribbean	252
73,941	2,390	30.9	2.9 to 1	yes	Bahamas	266
142,000	3,114	45.6	2.7 to 1	yes	Caribbean	256
73,941	2,390	30.9	2.9 to 1	yes	Baja, Mexico	266
142,000	3,114	45.6	2.7 to 1	yes	Caribbean	256
90,090	2,100	42.9	2.5 to 1	yes	Caribbean, Panama Canal, Hawaii, Alaska	259
78,491	2,000	39.2	2.5 to 1	yes	Alaska, Hawaii	263
90,090	2,100	42.9	2.5 to 1	yes	Caribbean, Panama Canal, Alaska, Hawaii	259
73,192	2,292	31.9	2.7 to 1	yes	Bahamas	266
69,130	1,804	38.3	2.5 to 1	yes	South America	263
69,130	2,000	34.6	2.5 to 1	yes	Mexican Riviera	263
142,000	3,114	45.6	2.7 to 1	yes	Caribbean	256
10,000	208	48.1	1.5 to 1	yes	Caribbean, Panama Canal	305
10,000	208	48.1	1.5 to 1	yes	Caribbean	305

Ships at a Glance (continued)

Cruise Line	Ship	Frommer's Star Rating	Year Built
Sea Cloud Cruises (sailing ships): Classic luxe.	Sea Cloud	★★★★★	1931
	Sea Cloud II	★★★★★	2001
SeaDream (luxury): An upscale yet casual line without the traditional regimentation.	SeaDream I	★★★★½	1984
	SeaDream II	★★★★½	1985
Silversea (luxury): Silversea caters to guests who won't settle for anything but the best, with free-flowing champagne and exceptional service.	Silver Cloud	★★★★★	1994
	Silver Shadow	★★★★★	2000
	Silver Wind	★★★★★	1994
Star Clippers (sailing ships): Classic clipper ships with all the amenities.	Royal Clipper	★★★★	2000
Windjammer (sailing ships): Ultracasual and delightfully carefree, this eclectic fleet of cozy, rebuilt sailing ships (powered by both sails and engines) lures passengers into a fantasy world of pirates-and-rum-punch adventure.	Legacy	★★★½	1959
	Mandalay	★★	1923
	Polynesia	★★	1938
	Yankee Clipper	★★	1927
Windstar (sailing ships): The no-jackets-required policy aboard Windstar sums up the line's casually elegant attitude. The ships feel like private yachts—they're down-to-earth, yet service and cuisine are first-class.	Wind Spirit	★★★½	1988
	Wind Star	★★★½	1986
	Wind Surf	★★★★	1990

* Tonnage figures for small ships are often calculated differently than those of larger ships, making comparisons and passenger/space figures difficult to gauge.

Gross Tonnage	Passenger Capacity (Double Occupancy)	Passenger/Space Ratio	Passenger/Crew Ratio	Wheelchair Access	Sailing Regions	Full Review on Page
2,532	64	39.6	1 to 1	no	Caribbean	370
3,849	94	40.9	1.6 to 1	no	Caribbean	370
4,260	100	38.7	1.2 to 1	no	Caribbean	312
4,260	110	38.7	1.2 to 1	no	Caribbean	312
16,800	296	56.8	1.4 to 1	yes	Caribbean	321
28,258	388	72.8	1.3 to 1	yes	Caribbean, Panama Canal, Alaska, Mexican Riviera	319
16,927	296	57.2	1.4 to 1	yes	Caribbean	321
5,000	227	22	2.2 to 1	no	Caribbean	377
1,165	120	9.7	2.8 to 1	no	Caribbean	385
420	72	5.8	2.6 to 1	no	Caribbean	388
430	126	3.4	2.8 to 1	no	Caribbean	388
327	64	5.1	2.2 to 1	no	Caribbean	388
5,350	148	36.1	1.6 to 1	no	Caribbean	398
5,350	148	36.1	1.6 to 1	no	Caribbean, Panama Canal	398
14,745	308	47.9	1.9 to 1	no	Caribbean	395

6

The Mainstream Lines

These are the cruise lines you know—the ones that get on TV, jump up and down, and say, "*This* will be the vacation you've been looking for!" Maybe yes, maybe no. That depends on you.

Today's mainstream ships are part theme park, part shopping mall, part gym, and part faux downtown entertainment and dining district, all packaged in a sleek hull with an oceanview resort perched on top. The biggest are *really* big: 14 stories tall, 1,000 feet long, with cabin space for between 2,000 and 4,000-plus passengers and a couple thousand crew. Most of the mainstream lines (but particularly the "Big Four"—Carnival, Royal Caribbean, Princess, and Norwegian) have spent the past 10 years pumping billions into ever-newer, bigger, and fancier ships, and the intense competition means they're constantly trying to outdo each other with entertainments and activities. The newer the ship, the more whoopee you can expect: ice-skating rinks, bowling alleys, water parks, on-deck movie theaters, pottery studios, surfing machines, giant spas, rock-climbing walls, full-size basketball courts, and virtual-reality golf, plus classics like hot tubs, theaters, water slides, and bars, bars, bars. The action is just outside your cabin door, though if you crave some downtime, there's always your private balcony or some quiet lounge that's deserted while everybody else is at the pool.

On days at sea, you can choose from a dizzying number of things to do, from dancing lessons, bingo, and game-show contests to lectures on finance and nutrition, classes on photography and website design, and wine tastings. Mixers encourage singles to mingle and grandmothers to pull out the grandkid pictures, while contests at the pool encourage passengers to toss away all restraint as they try and stuff the most Ping-Pong balls down their bathing suits or swim across with a bagel in their mouths. Overall the atmosphere is very social and active, especially on warm-weather cruises in the Caribbean, Bahamas, Bermuda, and Mexico, which tend to draw the youngest mix of fun-loving, like-to-party passengers (lots of 20s, 30s, and 40s). Itineraries in Alaska and New England tend to appeal more to a mellower crowd mostly in their 40s, 50s, and up.

The more elegant and refined of the lines are commonly referred to as **premium,** a notch up in the sophistication department from others that are described as **mass-market.** Quality-wise, they're all more similar than they are different, especially in regard to dining and entertainment. Ditto for lines such as Oceania and MSC, whose fleets of midsize ships are almost throwbacks to the days before supersizing. For even more of a throwback there's Imperial Majesty, with its one midsize antique ocean liner. Though these lines' ships are tiny compared with the Carnivals and Royal Caribbeans of the world, they're in this chapter because they offer well-rounded cruises for a fairly diverse mix of passengers.

Frommer's Ratings at a Glance: The Mainstream Lines

1 = poor   **2** = fair   **3** = good   **4** = excellent   **5** = outstanding

Cruise Line	Enjoyment Factor	Dining	Activities	Children's Program	Entertainment	Service	Worth the Money
Carnival	4	3	3	4	3	3	4
Celebrity	5	4	4	3	3	5	5
Costa	3	2	4	2	3	2	3
Disney	4	3	3	5	5	3	4
Holland America	4	4	3	2	4	5	5
Imperial Majesty	3	3	2	1	2	3	3
MSC Cruises	3	3	2	3	3	2	4
Norwegian	5	4	4	4	4	4	5
Oceania	4	4	2	N/A	3	4	4
Princess	4	4	4	4	4	4	4
Royal Caribbean	5	4	5	4	4	4	5

Note: Cruise lines have been graded on a curve that compares them only with the other mainstream lines. See "How to Read the Ratings," in chapter 5, for a detailed explanation of the ratings methodology.

DRESS CODES   For the most part, just about anything goes. Norwegian Cruise Line was the first to completely do away with "mandatory" formal nights earlier this decade, and many of the other mainstream lines have followed. Aside from Oceania and Imperial Majesty (which are all casual, all the time), the rest of the lines in this chapter still have one or two formal (or "formal optional") nights a week, with the remaining nights designated as semiformal and casual. Most ships also have at least one casual dining venue open every night in case you just can't face dressing up. (See chapter 3 for more on dress codes.)

1 Mini-Review: Azamara Cruises

1050 Caribbean Way, Miami, FL 33132. (877/999-9553. www.azamaracruises.com.

THE LINE IN A NUTSHELL   When Renaissance Cruises folded in 2001, its beautiful fleet of eight identical and almost-brand-new midsize ships was disbursed to the four winds. Oceania got two (and later three), Princess got two (and later three), and two ended up operated by Spain's Pullmantur S.A., that country's largest cruise line. In late 2006, **Celebrity**'s parent company Royal Caribbean purchased Pullmantur and soon after pulled the old switcheroo, sending Celebrity's old *Zenith* to Spain and claiming the two ex-Renaissance ships in her place. Rather than fold them into its regular fleet, though, Celebrity opted to create an entirely new cruise line around them, dedicated to longer, more exotic itineraries, taking in ports not frequented by the vast majority of mainstream ships. And thus was born Azamara Cruises.

THE EXPERIENCE   The idea behind Azamara is pretty much the same idea that animates all the other former Renaissance vessels, whoever they sail for: smaller, more

Azamara Fleet Itineraries

Ship	Itineraries
Azamara Quest	**Caribbean:** 14-night eastern & southern (Jan–Mar), round-trip from Miami. **Panama Canal:** 14-night westbound (Jan, Mar) and eastbound (Feb, Mar), between Miami, FL, and Acapulco, Mexico.

intimate ships sailing longer itineraries, visiting out-of-the-ordinary ports, and offering a casual yet country-clubbish experience, with extraspecial service. That's not to call Azamara a copycat, though. Fact is, there are only so many different kinds of cruise experiences you can offer, and this is the kind that these ships were made for. In an age dominated by bigger and bigger megaships, we welcome the return of mid-size vessels with open arms, and are happy that another mainstream line is putting the resources into keeping this kind of cruise option alive.

Physically, *Azamara Journey* ★★★★ and *Azamara Quest* ★★★★ retain Renaissance's beautiful boutique-hotel aesthetic while also incorporating some signature Celebrity rooms and experiences. For dining, they offer a choice between a lovely open-seating main dining room (dine when you like, with whom you like, within a set window), two smaller **specialty restaurants** (Prime C, serving steaks and seafood, and Aqualina, serving Mediterranean cuisine), and a buffet. Public rooms include the top-deck Looking Glass observation lounge, with floor-to-ceilings windows all around; a theater seating 300-plus; a small casino; a martini bar; and several rooms added by Celebrity when they took over the ships in 2007, including the Michael's Club jazz/piano bar, a spa with an outdoor relaxation room, an Acupuncture at Sea program, and a sushi cafe. Cabins are generally spacious, and all come with butler service, new European bedding and soft goods, flatscreen televisions, and new veranda-decking and furniture. Ninety-three percent of staterooms offer ocean views, and 68% have private verandas.

Enrichment programs offer lectures on topics such as the sailing region, art, culture, photography, cooking, and wine. Entertainment features the usual raft of musical revues, pianists, and dance bands, while gym and spa offerings include sunset yoga classes, Pilates, and Elemis-branded wellness treatments.

At press time, per diems for these ships were starting from about $140 per day, though prices were higher on some itineraries. For 2008, only *Azamara Quest* will be sailing in the regions covered in this book.

2 Carnival Cruise Lines

3655 NW 87th Ave., Miami, FL 33178-2428. ✆ **800/227-6482** or 305/599-2200. Fax 305/405-4855. www.carnival.com.

THE LINE IN A NUTSHELL   When you're hankering for an utterly unpretentious and totally laid-back cruise, Carnival's colorful, jumbo-size resort ships deliver plenty of bang for the buck. If you like the flash of Vegas and a serious party vibe, you'll love Carnival's brand of flamboyant fun. **Sails to:** Caribbean, Mexican Riviera, Alaska, Canada/New England, Hawaii (plus Europe, transatlantic).

THE EXPERIENCE   The everyman cruise, Carnival's got the most recognized name in the biz and serves up a very casual, down-to-earth, middle-American

Caribbean vacation. Food and service are pretty decent considering the huge numbers served, and Carnival gets points for trying to offer a higher-quality vacation than in years past. Enhancements include partnering with Michelin three-star chef Georges Blanc to create a series of signature dishes for the dining rooms, switching from plastic to china in the buffet restaurants, and stocking cabins with thicker towels, duvet blankets, and more TV channels. The fleet has even gone wireless, offering Wi-Fi access throughout each ship.

On many ships in the fleet you'll find a sushi bar, supper club, wine bar, coffee bar, and great amenities for children. Like the frat boy who graduated to a button-down shirt and an office job, Carnival has definitely moved up and on to some extent. But like that reformed frat boy who still likes to meet his old pals for happy hour every week, Carnival hasn't lost touch with its past. Sure, the line's decor, like its clientele, has mellowed to some degree since its riotous, party-hearty beginnings, but each ship is still an exciting, bordering-on-nutty collage of textures, shapes, and images. Where else but on these floating play lands would you find a giant octopus-like chandelier with lights that change color, bar stools designed to look like baseball bats, or real oyster-shell wallpaper? The outrageousness of the decor is part of the fun. Evolved yes, dull no.

"We are who we are; we're still the Fun Ships," Dickinson reminds us.

Pros

- **Fun, theme-park ambience:** The fanciful, sometimes wacko, decor on these vessels is unmatched.
- **Large standard cabins:** At 185 square feet or larger, Carnival's standard inside and outside cabins are among the roomiest in the mainstream category.
- **Melting pot at sea:** You name 'em, they'll be on a Carnival cruise, from rowdy, pierced 20-something singles and honeymooners to *Leave It to Beaver* families with young kids to grandparents along for the show.
- **An insomniac's delight:** When passengers on most ships are calling it a night, Carnival's guests are just getting busy with diversions such as midnight adult comedy shows, raging discos, and 24-hour pizza parlors.

Cons

- **You're never alone:** Not in the hot tubs, on shore excursions, in the pool, while sunbathing, at the gym, at the frozen-yogurt machine . . .
- **No enrichment:** Activities are pretty much confined to fun and games on the pool deck; no guest speakers and classes like most other mainstream lines offer.

CARNIVAL: BIG LINE, BIG FUN

Carnival has enjoyed an extended run as big cheese of the cruise world. The assets of its parent company, Carnival Corporation, are enormous and growing: In addition to its own fleet of 21 ships, Carnival Corp. holds full ownership of Cunard, Seabourn, Costa, Windstar, and Holland America Line—all told, the company has a stake in 12 cruise brands in North America, Europe, and Australia. And, in April 2003, Carnival beat out Royal Caribbean to acquire P&O Princess, adding yet another major cruise brand to its cruise dynasty. When all is said and done, Carnival Corp. will operate a combined fleet of 82 ships, with another 19 scheduled for delivery through fall 2009.

The origins of the Miami-based company were as precarious as they were accidental. Company patriarch Ted Arison, a somewhat reclusive billionaire who passed away

Compared with the other mainstream lines, here's how Carnival rates:

	Poor	Fair	Good	Excellent	Outstanding
Enjoyment Factor				✓	
Dining			✓		
Activities			✓		
Children's Program				✓	
Entertainment			✓		
Service			✓		
Worth the Money				✓	

in 1999, had sold an airfreight business in New York in 1966 and intended to retire to his native Israel to enjoy the fruits of his labor—after a few more little ventures. After he negotiated terms for chartering a ship, he assembled a group of paying passengers, then discovered that the ship's owner could no longer guarantee the vessel's availability. According to latter-day legend, a deal was hastily struck whereby Arison's passengers would be carried aboard a laid-up ship owned by Knut Kloster, a prominent Norwegian shipping magnate. The ship was brought to Miami from Europe, and the combination of Arison's marketing skill and Kloster's hardware created an all-new entity that, in 1966, became the corporate forerunner of Norwegian Cruise Line.

After a bitter parting of ways with Kloster, Carnival got its start in 1972 when Arison bought *Empress of Canada,* known for its formal and somewhat stuffy administration, and reconfigured it into Carnival's first ship, the anything-but-stuffy *Mardi Gras.* After a shaky start—the brightly painted ship, carrying hundreds of travel agents, ran aground just off the coast of Miami on its first cruise—Arison managed to pick up the pieces and create a company that, under the guidance of astute and tough-as-nails company president Bob Dickinson and chairman Micky Arison (Ted's son), eventually evolved into the most influential trendsetter in the cruise ship industry. The rest is history, as they say.

Today, Carnival's fleet includes 21 ships, most of which cruise the Caribbean and The Bahamas year-round. The 110,000-ton 2,974-passenger *Carnival Freedom,* sister to *Liberty, Valor, Conquest,* and *Glory,* is the newest, having just debuted in March 2007. In spring 2008, a new class of ship will debut. Based on the Conquest ships, the 112,000-ton, 3,006-passenger *Carnival Splendor* will sport some new features, including a water park and the line's largest and most elaborate spa and kids' facilities to date. In fall of 2009 and summer of 2011, a pair of 130,000-ton ships named the *Carnival Dream* and *Carnival Magic,* respectively, will be introduced as Carnival's largest vessels so far.

PASSENGER PROFILE

In the old days, Carnival was basically a floating college frat house: Heidi sailed in 1996 when more than 500 graduating high-school seniors practically took over (and ruined) a cruise on *Celebration.* She still gets nightmares. Guidelines implemented in early 1997 put a stop to all of that, mandating that no one under 21 can sail unless sharing a cabin with an adult over 25, with exceptions made for married couples and young people traveling with their parents in separate cabins. So, while you'll still find teen groups on board (especially Mar–June), things are not what they were.

A Carnival cruise is a huge melting pot—couples, singles, and families; young, old, and lots in between. I've met doctors on Carnival cruises as well as truck drivers. And no matter what their profession, you'll see people wearing everything from Ralph Lauren shirts and Gucci sunglasses to Harley-Davidson tank tops and eyebrow studs. Carnival estimates about 30% of passengers are under age 35, another 40% are between 35 and 55, and 30% are over age 55. At least half of all passengers are first-time cruisers. Although it's one of the best lines to choose if you're single, Carnival's ships certainly aren't overrun by singles—families and couples are definitely in the majority. The line's 3-, 4-, and 5-night cruises tend to attract the most families with kids and the highest number of 20- and 30-something single friends traveling together in groups.

Regardless of their age, passengers tend to be young at heart, ready to party, and keyed up for nonstop fun and games. Many have visited the casinos of Las Vegas and Atlantic City and the resorts of Cancún and Jamaica, and are no strangers to soaking in sardine-can hot tubs, sunbathing, hitting the piña coladas and beer before lunch, and dancing late into the night.

The typical Carnival passenger likes to dress casual, even at dinner, with sweat suits, jeans, and T-shirts just as prevalent as Dockers, sundresses, and Hush Puppies on all but formal nights—and even on formal nights, it's not uncommon for some passengers to run back to their cabins to change out of their dressier duds and put on shorts or jeans before heading out to the discos and bars. Tuxedos are in the minority here. A few don't even bother with dressing up at all, even on formal nights. A hotel director on the *Carnival Liberty* recently told Heidi about the restaurant dress codes. "We're very flexible on this," he said, adding that they draw the line only at bathing suits, and T-shirts or hats with "bad words." Otherwise, just about anything goes.

DINING

Like most lines these days, Carnival offers a raft of dining options. Though not to the degree of flexibility that NCL, and to a lesser extent Princess, offers, Carnival's newest Spirit- and Conquest-class ships offer about as many dining venues as you'll really need.

TRADITIONAL   In its two-story "formal" dining rooms (and take *formal* with a grain of salt—some Carnival passengers don't seem to know anything but T-shirts and jeans), Carnival's food quality and presentation, plus its wine selection, are much improved from its early days, and for the most part on par with Royal Caribbean, Princess, and NCL. You'll find more exotic options such as chicken satay with peanut sauce and Indian-themed meals that include lamb chops, basmati rice, lentils *(dal),* and potatoes *(aloo);* as well as all-American favorites such as lobster and prime rib, plus pasta dishes, grilled salmon, and Thanksgiving-style turkey served with all the trimmings. Unfortunately, the preparation is uneven (as is true on many of the mainstream

---

Carnival's Vacation Guarantee

Unhappy with your Carnival cruise? Dissatisfied guests may disembark at their first non-U.S. port of call and, subject to some restrictions, get a refund for the unused portion of their cruise and reimbursement for coach-class airfare back to their ship's home port. To qualify, passengers must inform the ship's purser before their first port of call.

lines); one night your entree is great, the other it's blah. On a recent *Liberty* cruise, what was consistently good night after night was the line's new signature Georges Blanc dishes, which were featured on the dinner menus in the main restaurants and included delicious grilled jumbo shrimp in beurre blanc and free-range spring chicken with a creamy foie gras sauce. A couple of years back, Carnival entered a partnership with French master chef Georges Blanc, whose six restaurants in France have earned the coveted three stars from Michelin. There are some 50 healthier **"Spa Carnival"** dishes (which include calorie, fat, sodium, and cholesterol stats), and **vegetarian** options are also on each menu.

Despite the hectic pace and ambience, dining service is usually friendly and somewhat classier than in earlier years, if not always the most efficient. The staff still presents dessert-time song-and-dance routines, at times quite elaborate, and passengers seem to love it. Sophistication goes only so far, however: Carnival still has its waiters handle all wine service, rather than employing sommeliers; and on a recent *Liberty* cruise, Heidi was unpleasantly surprised to find the lights turned up abruptly at 9:30pm each evening in the dining room, just 1 to 1½ hours after the late dinner seatings started. It was clearly a very inelegant way to encourage any stragglers to finish their coffee and dessert ASAP and hit the road so the staff could clean up and close the dining room for the night.

In a nod to a more flexible system in its formal restaurants, Carnival offers **four different seatings** on most ships rather than the traditional two. However, because you can choose only to dine early (5:45 and 6:15pm) or late (8 and 8:30pm), with the line selecting your exact time, it's hardly more flexible (though it's better for the galley staff, who have a more spaced window to prepare meals). The Spirit-class ships retain the traditional two seatings.

SPECIALTY   *Carnival Spirit,* which debuted in spring 2001, was the line's first to have a reservations-only restaurant, a two-level venue serving steaks and other dishes for a $30-per-person cover charge (plus tip and not including wine). Subsequent Spirit-class and Conquest-class ships—and all future Carnival ships—have this intimate alternative venue. Here, service is more gracious, and dedicated sommeliers are on hand to take your wine order. Menus are leather-bound, and elegant table settings feature beautiful Versace show plates and Rosenthal, Fortessa, and Revol china. Tables for two and four are available, and a musician or two serenades diners with soft ballads. There's even a dance floor. Like in a traditional steakhouse, the menu includes starters, salads, and side dishes such as creamed spinach and mashed potatoes. The steaks range from New York strip to porterhouse and filet mignon, and other options include grilled lamb chops, and a fish and chicken dish. The experience is intentionally designed to be slow and lingering, so don't go if you're looking for a fast meal. The food and service are the most doting you'll find on Carnival.

CASUAL   At the opposite end of the alternative-dining spectrum, guests aboard all Carnival ships can opt to have any meal in the buffet-style Lido restaurants at no extra charge. For an unstructured and casual dinner, walk in anytime between about 6 and 9:30pm for serve-yourself entrees such as chicken, pasta, stir-fry, and carved meats. At lunch, buffets in the Lido feature the usual suspects—salads, meats, cheeses, pastas, grilled burgers, and chicken filets, and several hot choices such as fish and chips, roast turkey, and stir-fry. The lunchtime buffets also feature specialty stations, serving up things such as pasta or Chinese food or a Cajun fish dish. All ships have a deli station for sandwiches; a pizza station open 24 hours, where you can also get a Caesar salad; and an outlet for grilled chicken sandwiches, burgers, hot dogs, and fries—just be prepared for a loooooooong line at lunchtime, as the Carnival crowd loves burgers and fries. In general, the various buffet sections can get backed up at times as passengers wait for bins to be restocked and servers scramble to fill them. Though the food is unmemorable, upgrades to tableware are not: Kudos to Carnival for bringing in colorful ceramic sugar bowls, salt and pepper shakers, and dinnerware in place of the old white plastic stuff.

SNACKS & EXTRAS   But wait, there's more: Carnival ships give you 24-hour pizza (anywhere from 500–800 pies are flipped a day!), calzones that are surprisingly tasty, Caesar salad with or without chicken, and self-serve soft ice cream and frozen yogurt, as well as a complimentary **sushi bar** in the promenade on the newest ships (on older ships, sushi is served in the Lido buffet restaurants at lunch or dinner), and a deli on some vessels. There are nightly **midnight buffets** in the Lido restaurants, with a gala, pull-out-all-the-stops buffet once per cruise. The newest ships also have specialty (read: not free) coffee and pastry bars, some with milkshakes and banana splits, too.

All ships offer **24-hour room service,** with a new limited menu including such items as a focaccia sandwich with grilled zucchini, fresh mozzarella, and portobello mushrooms, plus the standard tuna salad, cookies, fruit, and so on. Kids can select from **children's menus.** Kids and adults can buy the Funship Fountain Card for unlimited fountain sodas throughout the cruise; a nifty plastic cup with a lid is usually part of the deal.

ACTIVITIES

Carnival's all about lounging by the pool, drink in hand (or bucket of beers at foot), and soaking up the sun and some loud music or whatever **goofy contests** may be taking place. On sea days, you can get a hoot out of watching (or joining, if you're not the wallflower type) the men's hairy chest contest or similar tomfoolery, participate in a trivia contest, or sign up for some group dancing lessons. A blaring band will play a few sets by the pool, and on the line's newest ships (so far, the *Liberty* and *Freedom*), a **giant video screen** smack-dab in the center of the pool area broadcasts movies, concerts, and various shipboard activities at eardrum-shattering decibels (and do we mean loud—don't expect to have a conversation without shouting). On all but the line's oldest ships, it's a little quieter up on the second tier of the Sun Deck, and each ship has a quieter pool and sunbathing area at the stern, sans loudspeakers. Spirit-class vessels have a second midships pool separated from the main action by a bar and solid dividers that keep most of the noise out and provide a more serene lounging space; one of the four pools on the Conquest-class ships is quieter and covered by a retractable glass roof.

Slot machines begin clanging by 8 or 9 in the morning in the **casinos** when the ships are at sea (tables open at 11am), and servers start tempting passengers with trays of fruity theme cocktails long before the lunch hour. Expect to hear the ubiquitous art auctioneer shouting into a microphone about some Peter Max masterpiece. There are **line-dancing and ballroom classes,** trivia contests, facial and hairdo demonstrations (intended to entice passengers to sign up for expensive treatments), singles and newlywed parties, game shows, shuffleboard, bingo, art auctions, and movies. Overall, though, there's not as much variety of activities as aboard lines such as Norwegian, Holland America, and Celebrity (read: absolutely no enrichment lectures on history or other cerebral topics).

Handy Hot Line

Carnival offers a 24-hour hot line for help with unexpected snafus or emergencies. Call ✆ **877/885-4856** toll-free, or 305/406-4779.

You can spend some time in the roomy gyms on the Fantasy-, Destiny-, Spirit-, and Conquest-class ships (and take the handful of **free aerobics classes** or the ones they charge $10 for, such as Pilates, yoga, and spinning) or playing volleyball on the top deck, or treat yourself to one of dozens of relaxing (and expensive) treatments in the Steiner-managed **spas.** All ships have covered and lighted golf driving nets, with **golf pros** sailing on board to give lessons with video analysis starting at $25 for a 15-minute session and $80 for an hour. Pros also accompany guests on golf excursions on shore, and clubs, golf shoes, balls, gloves, and other paraphernalia are available for rent.

If you want to escape it all and find a truly quiet nook for a while, retire to the subdued libraries/card/game rooms and 24-hour **Internet centers** on each ship; you'll find Wi-Fi service fleetwide as well. You can also now use your cellphone while at sea or in port.

CHILDREN'S PROGRAM

Carnival is right up there with the best ships for families—the line estimates that about 575,000 kids will sail aboard its ships in 2007. Some 600 to 800 children per cruise is pretty normal, and there can be in the neighborhood of 1,000 on holiday cruises and during the summer months, when it'll be difficult to find a kid-free hot tub. On Carnival's post-1990 ships, the **child facilities** are fairly extensive, with the Conquest-class, Spirit-class, and Destiny-class ships, as well as *Elation* and *Paradise*, offering the biggest and brightest playrooms in the fleet, with arts and crafts, oodles of toys and games, video screens and televisions showing movies and cartoons, and computer stations loaded with the latest educational and entertainment software. The facilities on the line's older ships—including the oldest, *Celebration* and *Holiday*—are no competition.

The **Camp Carnival program** offers complimentary supervised kids' activities on sea days nearly nonstop from 9am to 10pm, and on port days, from 8am, or earlier, if there are shore excursions departing earlier for ages 2 through 14 in four age groups: toddlers 2 to 5, juniors 6 to 8, intermediates 9 to 11, and teens 12 to 14. Ten to 16 counselors (all of whom are trained in CPR and first aid) organize the fun and games on each ship, which include face painting, computer games, puzzles, fun with Play-Doh, picture bingo, pirate hat making, and pizza parties for toddlers. For juniors, there's PlayStation 2, computer games, ice-cream parties, story time and library visits, T-shirt coloring, and swimming. For intermediates, there are scavenger hunts, trivia and bingo, Ping-Pong, video-game competitions, arts and crafts, computer games, dance classes, and talent shows. Across all age groups, activities with a somewhat educational bent may include art projects with papier-mâché, oil paintings, and watercolors; music appreciation, which gets kids acquainted with different musical instruments; science projects where kids can make their own ice cream and create minihelicopters; and a fitness program that encourages today's couch-potato computer-head kids to actually get up and run around. Club 02 teen centers are geared to 12- to 14-year-olds (the cruise director's department schedules activities for the 15- to

17-year-old set), and are quite elaborate on the newest ships. Besides karaoke parties, computer games, scavenger hunts, talent shows, card and trivia games, and Ping-Pong, teens can watch movies there and go to dance parties. Most ships are also equipped with iMacs, but there is no Internet center specifically for teens like some ships offer. Of course, teens can also hang out in the video arcades—the newest ships have virtual-reality games and air-hockey tables. For something more refined, Carnival now offers a collection of spa treatments geared to teens.

The entire fleet has children's wading pools, though they're very basic compared to what you'll find on some of the Royal Caribbean, Celebrity, NCL, and Princess ships, and for bigger kids there's a great signature snaking slide at the main pool of each ship. A new activity is the "Water Wars" water-balloon attraction that's based on a diversion offered in amusement parks around the world. It basically boils down to teams flinging water balloons at each other with catapults.

Parents wanting a kid-free evening can make use of the supervised children's activities, offered from 7 to 10pm nightly free of charge, after which time group **slumber-party-style babysitting** kicks in for ages 4 months through age 11 till 3am in the playroom, at $6 per hour for the first child, $4 per hour for each additional child. No private babysitting is available. Infants between 4 and 23 months can also be cared for on port days between 8am and noon, but it's considered babysitting and the hourly fee mentioned above will apply. On sea days between noon and 2pm, you can also drop off children under 2 at the rate above, or parents may use the playroom with their babies for these 2 hours at no charge. And, yes, counselors will change diapers (though parents are asked to provide them along with wipes)! Parents with kids age 8 and under checked into the children's program get free use of beepers on most ships, in case their kids need to contact them. A handful of strollers are available for rent fleetwide for $25 for 7- and 8-night cruises (less for shorter cruises), and a limited number of bouncy seats, travel swings, and Game Boys are for rent.

Mom and Dad can get an earlier start on their kid-free evening, when the counselors supervise **kids' mealtime** in the Lido restaurant between about 6 and 7pm in a special section reserved for kids; it's offered nightly except the first night of the cruise, and, on cruises 5 nights or longer, it's also not offered on the last night. The children's dining room menu, printed on the back of a fun coloring/activity book (crayons are provided), features the usual favorites—hot dogs, hamburgers, french fries, chicken nuggets, pepperoni pizza, peanut-butter-and-jelly sandwiches, banana splits, Jell-O, and a daily special.

Cribs are available if you request them when making your reservations. When you first board, head for the kids' playroom to get a schedule for the week and to sign up your child for the program. Children must be at least 4 months old to sail on board.

ENTERTAINMENT

Aboard its newer megaships, Carnival has spent millions on stage sets, choreography, and sound equipment. The theaters on the Conquest-class, Spirit-class, and Destiny-class ships are spectacular three-deck extravaganzas, and the casinos are so large you'll think you've died and gone to Vegas; but even aboard its smaller, older ships, Carnival consistently offers some of the most lavish entertainment extravaganzas afloat.

Carnival megaships each carry about 8 to 16 flamboyantly costumed dancers (fewer on *Celebration* and *Holiday*) for twice- or thrice-weekly **Vegas-style musicals.** One or two live soloists carry the musical part of the show, while dancers lip-sync the chorus. An 8- to 10-piece orchestra of traditional and digital instruments deftly accompanies

Carnival Fleet Itineraries

Ship	Itineraries
Carnival Conquest	**Caribbean:** 7-night western, round-trip from Galveston, TX (year-round).
Carnival Destiny	**Caribbean:** 7-night southern, round-trip from San Juan, PR (year-round).
Carnival Freedom	**Caribbean:** Alternating 7-night eastern and western, round-trip from Miami (Jan–Apr). Alternating 6- & 8-night western, round-trip from Ft. Lauderdale (Nov–Dec).
Carnival Glory	**Caribbean:** Alternating 7-night eastern and western, round-trip from Port Canaveral, FL (year-round).
Carnival Legend	**Caribbean:** 7-night western, round-trip from Tampa, FL (year-round).
Carnival Liberty	**Caribbean:** 6- & 8-night western, round-trip from Fort Lauderdale, FL (Jan–May). Alternating 7-night eastern and western, round-trip from Miami, FL (May–Dec).
Carnival Miracle	**Caribbean:** Alternating 8-night eastern and western, round-trip from Tampa, FL (Jan–Apr). 8-night eastern, round-trip from New York, NY (Apr–Oct). Alternating 8-night eastern and western, round-trip from Fort Lauderdale, FL (Oct–Dec).
Carnival Pride	**Mexican Riviera:** 7 nights, round-trip from Long Beach, CA (year-round).
Carnival Spirit	**Mexican Riviera:** 8 nights, round-trip from San Diego, CA (Jan–Mar and Oct–Dec). **Alaska:** 7-night Gulf of Alaska, north- or southbound between Vancouver, BC, and Anchorage/Whittier, AK (May–Sept).
Carnival Triumph	**Caribbean:** Alternating 7-night eastern and western, round-trip from Miami (year-round).
Carnival Valor	**Caribbean:** Alternating 7-night eastern and western, round-trip from Miami (year-round).
Carnival Victory	**Caribbean:** Alternating 7-night eastern and western, round-trip from Miami (Jan–Apr & Oct–Dec). **Bahamas:** 6 nights, round-trip from Norfolk, VA (June & Oct). **New England/Canada:** 4, 5 & 7 nights, round-trip from New York, NY (May–Sept).
Celebration	**Caribbean:** 4- & 5-night Bahamas/Key West, round-trip from Jacksonville, FL (year-round).
Ecstasy	**Caribbean:** 4- & 5-night western, round-trip from Galveston, TX (year-round).
Elation	**Baja, Mexico:** 4 & 5 nights, round-trip from San Diego, CA (year-round).
Fantasy	**Caribbean:** 4- & 5-night western, round-trip from New Orleans, LA (year-round).
Fascination	**Caribbean:** Alternating 3-night Bahamas and 4-night western Caribbean, round-trip from Miami, FL (year-round).
Holiday	**Caribbean:** 4- & 5-night western, round-trip from Mobile, AL (year-round).
Imagination	**Caribbean:** 4- & 5-night western, round-trip from Miami, FL (year-round).
Inspiration	**Caribbean:** 4- & 5-night western, round-trip from Tampa, FL (year-round).
Paradise	**California/Baja:** 3-night Ensenada & 4-night Ensenada/Catalina Island, round-trip from Long Beach, CA (year-round).
Sensation	**Caribbean:** 3- & 4-night Bahamas, round-trip from Port Canaveral, FL (year-round).

the acts each night, sometimes enhanced by synchronized recorded music. You'll also find comedians, jugglers, acrobats, rock-'n'-roll bands, country-and-western bands, classical string trios, pianists, and Dorsey- or Glenn Miller–style big bands, all performing during the same cruise, and sometimes on the same night. Special entertainment may include a local mariachi band when a ship's in port late in Cozumel.

Besides the main theater, most entertainment happens somewhere along the indoor Main Street–like promenade (except on the Spirit-class ships, which are more spread out). Many are called the "Something-or-other Boulevard" or "Something-or-other Way." This area stretches along one entire side of each ship and is lined with just about the entire repertoire of the ship's nightclubs, bars, lounges, patisseries, disco, and casino. One bar on all the Fantasy-, Destiny-, Spirit-, and Conquest-class ships welcomes cigar smoking, and fleetwide, cigars are sold at the pool bar and during midnight buffets.

By day, entertainment includes an ultraloud Caribbean-style calypso or steel-drum band performing Bob Marley tunes and other pop songs on a deck poolside, and a pianist, guitarist, or string trio playing in the atria of the line's newest ships. The *Liberty* and *Freedom* sport a giant video screen up on the pool deck (and we wouldn't be surprised if other ships in the fleet get retrofitted with 'em soon) that tends to monopolize much of the day by loudly (and I mean loudly) broadcasting concerts, movies, and shipboard activities. Personally, we don't like 'em. Sure, a couple of movies in the late afternoon and evening are nice, but who needs the thing screeching away all day long?

SERVICE

All in all, a Carnival ship is a well-oiled machine, and you'll certainly get what you need—but not much more. When you board, for instance, you're welcomed by polite and well-meaning staff at the gangway, given a diagram of the ship's layout, and then pointed in the right direction to find your cabin on your own, carry-on luggage in tow. Chalk it all up to the size of the line's ships. It's a fact of life that service aboard all megaliners is simply not as attentive as that aboard smaller vessels—with thousands of guests to help, your dining-room waiter and cabin steward have a lot of work ahead of them and have little time for chitchat. Lines can get long at the breakfast and lunch buffets and, at certain times, at the pizza counter, though there always seem to be plenty of drink servers roaming the pool decks, looking to score drink orders.

Service certainly doesn't benefit from Carnival's **automatic tipping policy.** Like most of the major lines these days, gratuities for the crew are automatically added to your account at the end of your cruise to the tune of $10 per person per day fleetwide, and they're divvied up among the staff automatically. You can adjust the amount—or

---

Preview: *Carnival Splendor*

Expected to enter service in June 2008, the 112,000-ton, 3,006-passenger *Carnival Splendor* will represent an all new design for Carnival. Highlights will include an enormous 17,800-square-foot spa spread across two forward decks and featuring an elaborate thermal suite, Carnival's first thalassotherapy pool, and a variety of health and beauty treatment rooms. Encircling the spa's upper level will be a winter garden with a ceremonial tea house. A 5,500-square-foot children's playroom—the largest in the Carnival fleet—will be located midships and include a newly designed water play area. In the ship's stern, a new sports deck will feature arena-style seating for games and other events. On tap elsewhere: five restaurants (including a supper club), 22 bars (including a wine bar, sports bar, and jazz bar), and a sushi bar. *Splendor* will sail her initial season in Europe, then move to Florida in November 2008 to commence a season of weeklong Eastern Caribbean sailings from Ft. Lauderdale.

eliminate it completely and hand out cash in envelopes—by visiting the purser's desk. On Carnival and the other lines with automatic tipping policies, we've found waiters and cabin stewards don't seem as eager to please as they did when the tip carrot was hanging directly over them. On our recent *Liberty* cruise, for example, our cabin steward never introduced himself like they did in the old days and the relationship was very impersonal (a trend that will only increase as ships get even bigger).

There is a **laundry service** aboard each ship for washing and pressing only (with per-piece charges), as well as a handful of **self-service laundry rooms** with irons and coin-operated washers and dryers. There's a pleasant-smelling liquid soap and shampoo dispenser in cabin bathrooms fleetwide, plus a small basket of trial-size toiletries (refilled only upon request).

The Conquest Class: Carnival Conquest • Carnival Glory • Carnival Valor • Carnival Liberty • Carnival Freedom

Carnival Conquest *(photo: Carnival Cruise Lines)*

The Verdict

The best of the Carnival bunch to be sure, the Conquest class offers the fleet's largest children's and teen's facilities, a giant video screen on the pool deck, and plenty of bars and lounges—all packaged in a pastiche of both pleasing and jarring colors and design themes.

Specifications

Size (in tons)	110,000	Year Launched	
Passengers (double occ.)	2,974	*Conquest*	2002
Passenger/Space Ratio	37	*Glory*	2003
Total Cabins/Veranda Cabins	1,487/556	*Valor*	2004
Crew	1,160	*Liberty*	2005
Passenger/Crew Ratio	2.5 to 1	*Freedom*	2007
		Last Refurbishment/Upgrade	N/A

Frommer's Ratings (Scale of 1–5)   ★★★★½

Cabin Comfort & Amenities	4.5	Dining Options	4
Appearance & Upkeep	5	Gym, Spa & Sports Facilities	5
Public Comfort/Space	4.5	Children's Facilities	4.5
Decor	4	Enjoyment Factor	4

These five 110,000-ton 2,974-passenger sisters are Carnival's largest vessels. The $500-million Conquest-class ships closely resemble the Destiny series, though they stretch about 60 feet longer and add Spirit-class features such as supper clubs. If all berths are occupied, each Conquest liner can carry an eyebrow-raising 3,700-plus passengers (that's not counting the more than 1,000 crew). These mondo megas boast more than 20 bars and lounges, Carnival's largest children's facilities, and an entire, separate zone dedicated to teens. Each has a state-of-the-art "teleradiology" system that enables the ship's doctors to digitally transmit X-rays and other patient information to medical facilities on shore for consultation on a broad range of medical situations.

Cabins & Rates

Cabins	Per Diems From	Sq. Ft.	Fridge	Hair Dryer	Sitting Area	TV
Inside	$64	185	yes	yes	no	yes
Outside	$81	185–220	yes	yes	yes	yes
Suite	$186	275–345	yes	yes	yes	yes

CABINS Standard outside cabins measure a roomy 220 square feet. These categories (6A and 6B) take up most of the Riviera and Main decks. Of the ship's outside cabins, 60% (556 of 917) offer balconies. The standard balcony cabins (categories 8A–8E) measure a still-ample 185 square feet plus a 35-square-foot balcony. For those who simply must have a bigger balcony, a little extra dough buys an "extended balcony" (60 sq. ft.) or "wraparound large balcony." There are only a handful of these category-9A accommodations, and they're tucked all the way aft on the Upper, Empress, and Verandah decks. The 42 suites are a full 275 square feet plus a 65-square-foot balcony, and bigger still are the 10 Penthouse Suites at 345 square feet plus an 85-square-foot balcony. Most of the suites are sandwiched in the middle of the ship on Deck 7 and between two other accommodations decks, eliminating the danger of noisy public rooms above or below. Specially designed family staterooms, at a comfortable but not roomy 230 square feet, are located one deck below the children's facilities, and a couple of them can be connected to the room next door. In lieu of a private veranda, these family staterooms feature floor-to-ceiling windows for ocean views.

All categories of cabins come with a TV, safe, hand-held hair dryer (not the wall-mounted, wimpy variety), stocked minifridge (items consumed are charged to your onboard account), desk/dresser, chair and stool, and bathroom with shower and a handy makeup/shaving mirror. But the best part about Carnival's cabins these days is the beds. Called the Carnival Comfort Bed sleep system, they're darn comfortable. Mattresses, duvets, linens, and pillows are superthick and ultracomfy. The towels and bathrobes in each cabin are pretty luxurious too.

There are 28 cabins for passengers with disabilities.

PUBLIC AREAS The Conquest ships are bright and playful—a sort of Mardi Gras feel instead of the dark and glittery Las Vegas look sported by some of the older ships in the fleet. Architect Joe Farcus was inspired by the great Impressionist and post-Impressionist artists—not only their paintings, but also their color palette—so *Conquest* bursts with sunny yellows and oranges, and vivid blues and greens. Maybe Farcus is running a little low on inspiration these days, as the *Glory's* theme also revolves around "color," with public rooms bearing names such as the White Heat Dance Club, the Amber Palace (show lounge), and On The Green (golf-themed sports bar). On the *Valor,* a liberally applied "heroism" theme connects everything from the Bronx Bar Yankee-themed sports bar with white leather bar stools and banquettes designed to look like baseballs, to the One Small Step disco, a tribute to Neil Armstrong's walk on the moon a la weird little volcano-like craters that stand several feet tall and glow with LED lighting. On the *Liberty,* "artisans and their crafts" is how Farcus describes the motif. In some places it works better than others. The Paparazzi wine bar is a cool place that's all about photography. A huge 3-D collage of photographs of celebrities covers the walls, while images of cameras make up the ceiling and bar front. The floral laminate walls overlaid with wrought-iron-like curlicues in *Liberty's* atrium, stair landings, and elevators, on the other hand, may be a little much.

The general arrangement of public areas on these ships closely resembles that of the Destiny class, with a pair of two-story main dining rooms (one midships, one aft), a three-deck-high showroom in the bow, and a secondary lounge in the stern.

As on the Destiny ships, passengers step across the gangway and into the base of a soaring, nine-deck-high atrium, dressed to the nines in each ship's respective theme. On the *Conquest,* for example, it's a mural collage of works by masters such as Claude Monet, Paul Gauguin, and Edgar Degas, with backlit flowers of Murano glass popping up from the granite-topped atrium bar. On the *Liberty,* a giant octopus-like black wrought-style chandelier is the focal point, and its many "arms" support light bulbs that continually change color. Each vessel sports 22 bars and lounges, many of these rooms clustered on the Atlantic and Promenade decks.

The 1,400-seat Show Lounge stages Carnival's big production shows. On the *Valor,* it's called Ivanhoe and it comes complete with knights in shining armor a la Sir Walter Scott's classic tale. There's also a secondary entertainment venue for dance bands and late-night comedians, as well as a piano bar, wine bar (the best place for people-watching, as its open to the main promenade), and another live-music venue where combos belt out oldies, country, and requests.

Nobody does disco better than Carnival. You can groove on an enormous floor (on the *Conquest,* it's a jungle ambience straight from the exotic paintings of Henri Rousseau; on the *Valor,* it's all about the moon; and on *Liberty,* the theme is tattoos), or just perch with a drink on funky bar stools (lotus-shaped on the *Conquest,* and hand-shaped on the *Liberty,* for example). One deck down is the ships' most elegant lounge, done in wood paneling and dark, rich colors. The Internet cafe is tucked away off a back corner of the room; it's a real quiet retreat, if you can find it.

The casinos sprawl across 8,500 square feet, packing in almost 300 slot machines and about two dozen gaming tables. To one side is the sports bar; on the *Liberty,* the theme of boxing is worked into the furniture and decor.

These ships boast by far the biggest children's facilities in the fleet: At 4,200 square feet, Children's World and the separate teen center offer more than triple the space for kids and teens available on Destiny-class ships. Children's World sits atop the spa (instead of sharing the same deck, as on the Destiny vessels) and holds an arts-and-crafts station, video wall, computer lab, PlayStation 2 game units, and lots of fun toys for younger children, from play kitchens to push toys, mini sliding boards, farm sets, and more. The enclosed adjacent deck offers a dipping pool that's oddly industrial looking when compared to the kids' pools on many NCL, Celebrity, Disney, and Royal Caribbean ships. The ships' nod to teenagers is a big one. Teen facilities on earlier ships were, at most, a room, but here's a space so large it forms its own secondary promenade, branching off the main one. The teen area has a soda bar and separate dance floor flowing into a huge video games area with air-hockey tables that is open to all passengers.

DINING OPTIONS   Each ship has a pair of two-story main restaurants, styled in keeping with each ship's theme. On the *Conquest,* a monumental sunflower marking the entrance to the Monet Restaurant is by the Murano glass artist Luciano Vistosi, while the artwork in the Renoir Restaurant is inspired by the cafe scene in the painting *Lunch at the Restaurant Fournaise.* On the *Valor,* the Washington and Lincoln dining rooms won't win any design awards; described by the line as "contemporary colonial," what oddly dominates the decor are bright peach colored walls . . . hmmm. As Heidi's husband is fond of saying, "You can't eat ambience." Well, then bring out the lobster. You'll see broiled tail on the menu once a cruise, and there are six desserts nightly. Low-fat, low-carb, low-salt Spa Carnival Fare, vegetarian dishes, and children's selections are available.

The Conquest-class ships borrow the by-reservation supper club from the Spirit-class ships. The venue serves USDA prime-aged steaks, fish, and other deluxe items for a $30-per-person cover charge. On the Spirit ships, the club sits under a glass portion of the ship's funnel for a more dramatic setting, but the Conquest ships' room has low ceilings and a more intimate feel. The best food and most refined service on board are here, where dinner is meant to stretch over several hours and several bottles of wine (for which there's an extra charge).

Breakfast, lunch, and dinner are served in the two-story restaurant on the Lido Deck, where you'll also find a 24-hour pizza counter (the mushroom and goat cheese pies are scrumptious). Separate buffet lines (more than on the Destiny ships, to alleviate crowding) are devoted to Asian and American dishes, deli sandwiches, salads, and desserts. A new concept (on the upper level) is Sur Mer: Carnival modestly describes this as a fish and chips shop, but the choices include such goodies as calamari, lobster salad, and bouillabaisse. There's no charge here or for the stand-up sushi bar down on the main promenade, but the pastries, cakes, and specialty coffees at the patisserie cost a couple of bucks each.

There's also 24-hour room service with new menus that include items such as a chicken fajita with greens and guacamole in a jalapeño and tomato wrap, plus the standard tuna salad, cookies, fruit, and so on.

POOL, FITNESS, SPA & SPORTS FACILITIES   The ships' four swimming pools include the main pool, with its two huge hot tubs and a stage for live (and realllly loud) music. If you don't love reggae and calypso, don't go here. This space is where all the action (and noise) of pool games plus the occasional outbreak of line dancing occurs. (Anyone for the Electric Slide?) Carnival's trademark twisty slide shoots into a pool one deck up. The aft pool, covered by a retractable glass dome, usually provides a more restful setting, although the pizzeria and burger grill are here (along with two more oversize hot tubs). The fourth pool is a really basic one for kiddies outside the playroom.

The ships' 12,000-square-foot health club and salon, with neat his-and-hers ocean-view steam and sauna rooms, perches high on Deck 11. Though the decor is a real yawner—it's as though Farcus simply forgot about the waiting area and locker room— you'll find today's latest treatments available, from hot stone massages to hair and scalp massages. The spa is run by Steiner, the company that controls most cruise ship spas, so expect a hard sell for products after your treatment. One more pet peeve: You won't find a hair dryer, Q-tips, cotton balls, or any other amenities in the locker room—it's unabashedly no frills. On the fitness side, you'll find the nontrendy aerobics classes offered for free (such as stretching and step), and the cool stuff everyone wants to do, such as Pilates and spinning, going for $10 a class. There's a hot tub that sits in a glass-enclosed space jutting into the fitness room.

The jogging track loops above an open deck so that no cabins underneath get pounded.

The Spirit Class: Carnival Spirit • Carnival Pride • Carnival Legend • Carnival Miracle

The Verdict

Bright and fun with multistory dining and entertainment venues and a reservations-only restaurant, the Spirit ships offer everything you'll need, but packaged in a more sane size than the larger Destiny- and Conquest-class ships.

Carnival Spirit *(photo: Gero Mylius, Indav Ltd.)*

Specifications

Size (in tons)	88,500	Year Launched	
Passengers (double occ.)	2,124	*Spirit*	2001
Passenger/Space Ratio	41.7	*Pride*	2001
Total Cabins/Veranda Cabins	1,062/682	*Legend*	2002
Crew	930	*Miracle*	2004
Passenger/Crew Ratio	2.3 to 1	Last Refurbishment/Upgrade	N/A

Frommer's Ratings (Scale of 1–5)   ★★★★

Cabin Comfort & Amenities	5	Dining Options	4
Appearance & Upkeep	4	Gym, Spa & Sports Facilities	4
Public Comfort/Space	4	Children's Facilities	4
Decor	4	Enjoyment Factor	4

When the $375-million Carnival *Spirit* debuted in April 2001, she ushered in a new class for the fun-ship line. Bigger than Carnival's eight Fantasy-class ships and smaller than its three Destiny-class vessels, the 2,124-passenger, 88,500-ton, 960-foot *Spirit, Pride, Legend,* and *Miracle* update Carnival's rubber-stamp style with a handful of innovations and more elegance, placing them closer to the newest Royal Caribbean and Princess vessels than to Carnival's earlier Fun Ships. The Spirit ships eliminate the cluster of nightclubs in favor of stretching the music venues from bow to stern on Decks 2 and 3, and there's an appealing supper club, which the subsequent Conquest class has also adopted. A state-of-the-art "teleradiology" system enables the ship's doctors to digitally transmit X-rays and other patient information to medical facilities on shore for consultation on a broad range of medical situations.

Interestingly, the Spirit-class ships bear more than a little resemblance to Costa's 6-year-old *Costa Atlantica* and newer sister *Mediterranea:* Their hull and superstructure were built from identical plans, and Carnival design guru Joe Farcus did the decor for them all.

Cabins & Rates

Cabins	Per Diems From	Sq. Ft.	Fridge	Hair Dryer	Sitting Area	TV
Inside	$78	185	yes	yes	some	yes
Outside	$89	185	yes	yes	yes	yes
Suite	$196	275–300	yes	yes	yes	yes

CABINS The Spirit-class ships have verandas on more than 60% of their cabins, though most are pretty small, with a wood-tone plastic chair, a small table, and a deck chair. (Cabins with larger balconies are amidships and aft on Decks 6, 7, and 8.) Their 213 inside cabins and outsides without balconies are a roomy 185 square feet (standard outsides with balconies are the same size plus a 40-sq.-ft. balcony). Of the 44 category-11 suites, most measure 275 square feet, plus an 85-square-foot balcony, while 10 located at the stern of Decks 4 through 8 measure 245 square feet, plus a jumbo wraparound 220-square-foot balcony. The six category-12 suites measure 300 square feet, plus a 115-square-foot balcony. On Deck 4, all category-5A cabins have lifeboats obstructing the view, though they do have sliding-glass doors that allow you to lean out into the fresh air.

In a subtle departure from the minimalist, somewhat cold cabin decor of the rest of Carnival's older ships, the *Spirit's* cabins are warmer and more sophisticated, with toasted-caramel wood-tone furniture and mango- and coral-hued upholstery, drapes, and bedspreads. The pointy lighting fixtures are more stylish but don't throw a lot of light on the desk mirror. Also, there are none of those great little reading lights over the beds like the rest of the fleet offers, just lamps on the night tables.

All cabins, even the least expensive inside ones, have a decent amount of storage space in both closets and drawers (with small leather handles that some people find difficult to grab hold of), plus a safe, TV, desk and stool, chair, well-designed bathroom with a shower stall that is a tad larger than that on other ships, and glass shelves on either side of the large mirror to stash your toiletries. Just about all cabins have a small sitting area with a sofa and coffee table (some insides have only a chair and table), and all have a real hair dryer (stored in the desk/vanity drawer). Like the rest of the fleet, all beds are outfitted with new extrathick and comfy mattresses, duvets, linens, and pillows, and you'll enjoy the thick and fluffy towels and bathrobes too.

There are 16 cabins for passengers with disabilities.

PUBLIC AREAS Carnival designer Joe Farcus works his whimsy once again aboard the Spirit-class ships, blending marble, wood-veneer walls, tile mosaic work, buttery leathers, rich fabrics, copper and bronze, Art Nouveau and Art Deco themes, and all manner of glass lighting fixtures. Though a relatively subdued bronze color scheme defines many public areas, these ships still are glitzy and blinding in the same fun Vegas way as the rest of the Carnival fleet.

A string trio or pianist performs throughout the day at the lower-level lobby bar that anchors each ship's spectacular, jaw-dropping, nine-deck atrium, even more of a central hub than aboard earlier Carnival ships owing to its placement amidships. Just about all the indoor action is on Decks 2 and 3, where you'll find the piano bar (on *Spirit*, it's a neat Oriental-style spot with carved rosewood detailing, paper-lantern lighting fixtures, a red lacquer piano, and rich Chinese silk walls; on *Legend*, it's an understated tribute to Billie Holiday in stainless steel), large sports bar, disco, jazz nightclub (where karaoke and other contests are held), cafe (where you can purchase specialty coffees and pastries), combination library and Internet center (with a ridiculously spare book collection), elegant string of shops, modern-style wedding chapel, and a sprawling photo gallery. The low-ceilinged lounge tucked into the bow on Deck 1, at the end of a corridor of cabins, is so well hidden it's often empty.

The three-level showrooms are something to see; on *Spirit*, Farcus had Verdi's Egypt-themed opera *Aida* in mind when he covered it head to toe in brightly painted gold-and-blue King Tut–style sarcophagi and hieroglyphics (on the *Legend*, it's a flashy Mediterranean-style movie palace). Sightlines are severely limited from parts of the Deck 2 and Deck 3 level, so arrive early if you want a decent view. The disco is a two-story barrel-shaped place with a giant video wall; on *Spirit*, the funky spot has a Jackson Pollock–inspired splatter-painted design. On the *Miracle*, the disco was made to look like a Gothic castle in ruins with faux stone walls.

The ships' broad outdoor promenade is wonderfully nostalgic (almost), but unfortunately does not wrap around the entire ship; near the bow you are channeled through a door and the promenade suddenly (and oddly) becomes enclosed and narrower, turning into a cute but kind of odd jungle-themed area lined with comfy chairs and small tables with views through jumbo-size portholes. The kids' playroom and a video arcade are tucked away in the far forward reaches of the bow on Decks 4 and 5. Playrooms are divided into three sections connected via tunnels and offer sand art, a candy-making machine, a computer lab with a handful of iMacs and PlayStations, and other diversions. They're of decent size, but nowhere near the size and scope of what you'll find on the Conquest-class fleetmates or on Royal Caribbean's Freedom-, Voyager-, and Radiance-class ships and Disney's *Magic* and *Wonder*. The video arcade is huge, with 30-plus machines, including air hockey and foosball.

DINING OPTIONS   Unlike most of the fleet, the Spirit ships have one sprawling, two-story, 1,300-seat formal dining room (offering the traditional early and late seating). They're pleasant places to dine, especially if you can snag an intimate booth or a table along the glass railing on the second level, with views of the scene below. The Spirit ships were the first in the Carnival fleet to also offer an alternative reservations-only restaurant for more intimate and elegant dining from a menu of mostly steaks and seafood, for a cover charge of $30 per person. The newer Conquest class also has them. Main drawback on the Spirit class: Rowdy crowd noise sometimes filters up from the atrium bar below. In the huge, well-laid-out indoor/outdoor casual buffet restaurant, menu items range from standard American to French, Italian, and Asian; sushi is offered in the buffet restaurant at lunch. The food is fine, but don't expect anything resembling gourmet.

As aboard the rest of the fleet, 24-hour pizza and Caesar salad are offered from a counter in the buffet restaurant. You can get a tasty deli sandwich from the New York Deli all day long, and self-serve frozen yogurt and soft ice cream are also on hand.

POOL, FITNESS, SPA & SPORTS FACILITIES   The Spirit-class spas are the only ones in the fleet to have any decor to speak of; the rest have had a bland, institutional look, as though Farcus forgot to design them. The *Spirit*, for instance, sports a Greek-inspired motif of white fluted columns and images of Greek gods on the walls. The multilevel gyms are based loosely on a Greek amphitheater, and though they're more than adequate, with dozens of machines, they're a bit more cramped than the huge spaces on the Conquest- and Destiny-class ships.

In general, there are lots of places for sunbathing across the three topmost decks, including the area around the two main pools amidships on the Lido Deck, as well as around a third pool on the aft end of this deck. All told, there are four hot tubs (including one in the gym), plus a jogging track, combination volleyball/basketball court, and shuffleboard. A fun, snaking water slide for kids and adults is sequestered high up and aft on a top deck, and adjacent is a small, sort of forlorn, fenced-in kids' wading pool. With no shade up on this part of the ship, don't forget to put sunscreen on your kids' delicate skin—and your own, for that matter.

The Destiny Class: Carnival Destiny • Carnival Triumph • Carnival Victory

The Verdict

These three behemoths capture the classic Carnival whimsy, though with a somewhat mellower color scheme than the line's older ships—but let's not split hairs, they're still bright.

Carnival Destiny *(photo: Carnival Cruise Lines)*

Specifications

Size (in tons)		Destiny	1,321/480
Destiny	101,353	Triumph/Victory	1,379/508
Triumph/Victory	102,000	Crew	1,000
Passengers (double occ.)		Passenger/Crew Ratio	2.6 to 1
Destiny	2,642	Year Launched	
Triumph/Victory	2,758	Destiny	1996
Passenger/Space Ratio		Triumph	1999
Destiny	38.4	Victory	2000
Triumph/Victory	37	Last Refurbishment/Upgrade	
Total Cabins/Veranda Cabins		Destiny	2005

Frommer's Ratings (Scale of 1–5)   ★★★★½

Cabin Comfort & Amenities	5	Dining Options	3.5
Appearance & Upkeep	4	Gym, Spa & Sports Facilities	5
Public Comfort/Space	4.5	Children's Facilities	4
Decor	4	Enjoyment Factor	4.5

Taller than the Statue of Liberty, these 13-deck ships cost $400 million to $440 million apiece and carry 2,642 passengers based on double occupancy and 3,400-and-change with every additional berth filled (and some cruises do indeed carry a full load). All three are nearly identical, though *Triumph* and *Victory* are a tad larger than *Destiny* (having an additional deck at top) and are reconfigured in a few minor ways. *Destiny* was the first cruise ship ever built to exceed 100,000 tons, and her sheer size and spaciousness inspired the cruise industry to build more in this league. In late 2005, the *Destiny* received a healthy multi-million-dollar face-lift that took 3 weeks and included the addition of a new teen club, renovated lido buffet restaurant, vamped-up children's pool, redesigned casino, and spruced-up suites.

Cabins & Rates

Cabins	Per Diems From	Sq. Ft.	Fridge	Hair Dryer	Sitting Area	TV
Inside	$61	185	no	yes	no	yes
Outside	$76	185–220	no	yes	yes	yes
Suite	$183	275–345	yes	yes	yes	yes

CABINS   The Destiny-class sisters, along with the new Conquest-class ships, have the line's biggest standard outside cabins, with the category-6A and -6B cabins (which take up most of the Riviera and Main decks) measuring 220 square feet (and that's not including the balcony); the rest of the fleet's standard outsides measure 185 square feet—still very roomy. If that's not enough, more than 60% of the *Destiny* sisters' outside cabins (480–508 of them) have sitting areas and private balconies. That's compared to a paltry 54 private verandas out of 618 outside cabins on Carnival's Fantasy-class ships.

There are two categories of suites: Veranda Suites measuring 275 square feet, plus a 65-square-foot balcony; and Penthouse Suites, where you can live like a king with 345 square feet, plus an 85-square-foot balcony. Both are located on Deck 7, smack-dab in the middle of the ship, and on *Destiny,* both kinds of suites were upgraded in late 2005 with updated bathrooms, carpeting, and wall coverings. Specially designed family staterooms, at a comfortable but not roomy 230 square feet, are located convenient to children's facilities, and many of them can be connected to the stateroom next door. In lieu of a private veranda, these family-friendly staterooms feature floor-to-ceiling windows for ocean views. All standard cabins have a TV, safe, hair dryer, desk, dresser, chair and stool, bathroom with shower, and Carnival's great new bedding system, featuring extrathick mattresses, duvets, linens, and pillows, along with fluffy towels and bathrobes.

A total of 25 cabins on *Destiny,* 27 on *Triumph,* and 30 on *Victory* are wheelchair accessible.

PUBLIC AREAS   At the time these ships were designed, Carnival interior designer Joe Farcus never had so much public space to play with, and he took full advantage. The ships are dominated by staggering nine-deck atria with casual bars on the ground level, and the three-deck-high showrooms are a sight—*Destiny*'s was the first of this magnitude on any cruise ship, and subsequent models tread a fine line between outrageous and relatively tasteful: for example, *Triumph*'s wacko chandelier, which looks like DNA strands made from crystal golf balls, topped with little Alice-in-Wonderland candleholders. The ships' mondo casinos span some 9,000 square feet and feature more than 300 slot machines and about two dozen gaming tables. The *Destiny*'s casino was refurbished in late 2005, along with just about all the other public rooms on that ship.

Many of the ships' 12-plus bars and entertainment venues are located along the bustling main drag of the Promenade Deck. The Sports Bar on each ship boasts multiple TV monitors projecting different sporting events. Each ship has a wine bar, a cappuccino cafe, and a piano bar, which aboard *Triumph* is a bizarre New Orleans–themed place called the Big Easy, sporting thousands of real oyster shells covering its walls (collected from New Orleans's famous Acme Oyster House—only on Carnival!). Each also has a sprawling disco with a wild decor: On *Victory,* an Arctic motif features black faux-fur bar stools, while *Triumph*'s decor is a little more reserved, with goofy little Barney-purple chairs, and glass panels and tubes filled with bubbling water throughout. One deck below is an elegant lounge for a drink or a cigar: On *Triumph,* it's a clubby place called the Oxford Bar, with dark-wood paneling, leather furniture, and gilded picture frames (too bad you can hear the disco music pounding above late at night). The ships' Internet centers are adjacent to this lounge.

Each ship has several shopping boutiques, a spacious beauty salon, a library, a card room, and a fairly large children's playroom and video arcade. In late 2005, a teen club was added to the *Destiny,* and it comes decked out with a dance floor, high-tech sound/light system, three large-screen plasma TVs, music listening stations, video game pods, and soft-drink bar.

DINING OPTIONS   Each ship has a pair of two-level dining rooms with ocean views from both the main floor and the mezzanine level, as well as a two-story indoor/outdoor casual buffet restaurant (which was recently refurbished on the *Destiny*) that includes two specialty food stations that make Asian stir-fry and deli-style sandwiches to order; sushi is also served in the buffet restaurant at lunch. There's also a grill section for burgers, fries, and kielbasa-size hot dogs, a salad bar, and a dessert island. Specialty coffee bars and patisseries sell gourmet goodies for a few bucks a pop.

POOL, FITNESS, SPA & SPORTS FACILITIES   Along with the Conquest-class ships, the Destiny-class facilities are the most generous among the Carnival vessels, with four pools (including a kids' wading pool); seven hot tubs; and a 214-foot, two-deck-high, corkscrew-shaped water slide.

The tiered, arena-style decks of the sprawling midships Lido pool area provide optimal viewing of the band and stage, pool games, and all the hubbub that happens in this frenetically busy part of the ship. Along with two hot tubs, *Destiny* has swim-up bars at two of its main pools; *Triumph* and *Victory* eliminated the swim-up bars in exchange for more deck space, larger pools, and the addition of a wading area a few inches deep surrounding the pools. Unfortunately, this area can be very difficult to get across, due to a lack of obvious "corridors" through all the deck chairs. The aft pool area on all three ships features two hot tubs and a retractable roof that covers all, enabling deck activities and entertainment to continue even in rainy weather. On *Triumph* and *Victory,* the big stage adjacent to the Main Continent pool is even bigger than the one on *Destiny,* and it has been reconfigured to provide more space for guests at deck parties, and to make the pool deck more open and visually appealing. Another modification is the placement of a small performance stage aft on the Lido Deck near the New World pool.

Even though the ships' huge gyms aren't as large as those on Royal Caribbean's Voyager class, Carnival's are much roomier and actually feel bigger. The two-deck-high spa and fitness centers feature more than 30 state-of-the-art exercise machines, including virtual-reality stationary bikes. There are men's and women's saunas and steam rooms, and a pair of hot tubs. Spas offer all the latest treatments (at the latest high prices), but as on all Carnival ships (except for the newer Spirit class), they're surprisingly drab, and the only place to wait for your masseuse is on a cold, high-school-locker-room bench, wrapped in a towel—no robes are provided (unless, supposedly, you ask for one). So much for ambience. There are separate aerobics rooms (though they're smaller than they used to be, as half the space was snapped up to create a teen room a few years back).

The well-stocked 1,300-square-foot indoor/outdoor children's play center has its own pool and is nicely sequestered on a top deck, out of the fray of the main pool deck areas. The ships also have virtual-reality video arcades that promise hours of fun.

The Fantasy Class: Fantasy • Ecstasy • Sensation • Fascination • Imagination • Inspiration • Elation • Paradise

The Verdict

These time-tested favorites are the line's original megas, and their whimsical decor and endless entertainment and activities spell excitement from the get-go, though they do feel outdated compared to Carnival's newer classes.

Fantasy *(photo: Carnival Cruise Lines)*

Specifications

Size (in tons)	70,367	*Inspiration*	1996
Passengers (double occ.)	2,040	*Paradise*	1998
Passenger/Space Ratio	34.5	*Elation*	1998
Total Cabins/Veranda Cabins	1,020/54	Last Refurbishment/Upgrade	
Crew	920	*Fantasy*	2007
Passenger/Crew Ratio	2.2 to 1	*Sensation*	2008
Year Launched		*Ecstasy*	2007
Fantasy	1990	*Inspiration*	2007
Ecstasy	1991	*Imagination*	2007
Sensation	1993	*Fascination*	2007
Fascination	1994	*Elation*	2008
Imagination	1995	*Paradise*	2008

Frommer's Ratings (Scale of 1–5)   ★★★½

Cabin Comfort & Amenities	4	Dining Options	3
Appearance & Upkeep	4	Gym, Spa & Sports Facilities	3.5
Public Comfort/Space	4	Children's Facilities	4
Decor	3.5	Enjoyment Factor	4

These Fun Ships and their risqué names offer a successful combination of hands-on fun and a glamorous, fantasyland decor, with acres of teak decking plus all the diversions, distractions, and entertainment options for which Carnival is famous. They really are fun! (Or are they cheesy? It's such a fine line.) Each was built on the same cookie-cutter design at Finland's Kvaerner Masa shipyard (at a cost of $225 million–$300 million each . . . a bargain compared to the $500-million price tag of a new ship today), and they are nearly identical in size, profile, and onboard amenities, with different decorative themes. These ships have been run hard and they look a bit worn out compared to their newer fleetmates; but you won't notice a thing after a couple of Carnival Fun Ship drink specials!

From the first ship of the series *(Fantasy)* to the last *(Paradise)*, the ships' decor evolved toward a relatively mellow state (note, *relatively*). *Fantasy* features a Roman-themed entertainment promenade inspired (loosely, of course) by the ancient city of Pompeii, with a faux-stone floor, terra-cotta urns, Doric columns, and electric torches—but where's the flowing lava? In late 2003, the ship underwent a major refurbishment, which included a brand-new atrium bar (like the ones on the *Elation* and all newer ships), completely overhauled cabins, a redesigned promenade, and new carpeting and wall coverings throughout much of the other areas.

Ecstasy follows a city-at-sea theme, with no shortage of neon-metallic skyscraper imagery. *Fascination* is big on flashy fantasy, with a retina-shattering chrome atrium and a heavy Broadway and Hollywood theme, while *Sensation* avoids obvious razzle-dazzle in favor of artwork enhanced with ultraviolet lighting, sound, and color. Aboard *Imagination,* miles of fiber-optic cable make the mythical and classical artwork glow in ways the Greek, Roman, and Assyrian designers of the originals never would have imagined. *Inspiration* was reportedly inspired by artists such as Toulouse-Lautrec and Fabergé, and architects such as Frank Lloyd Wright—though in a . . . brighter style. You'll find a Greek mythology theme on the *Elation* that's all about Carnival-style "classic" columns, flutes, and harps, while the *Paradise* pays tribute to classic ocean liners. The newest of the Fantasy-class ships—the *Paradise* and the *Elation*—sport a few improvements over their sisters, including an expanded kids' playroom and the hublike atrium bar. The *Sensation* added an atrium bar a few years back. By the way, the *Paradise,* touted as the line's only completely nonsmoking ship when she debuted in 1998, changed its policies in late 2004; you can now light up in designated areas, just like on the rest of the fleet.

The Fantasy-class ships are in the midst of a multi-million-dollar face-lift that has added, or will soon add, an expanded children's water park, the creation of the Serenity adults-only deck area, flat-screen televisions in staterooms, new atrium lobby bar and new coffee bar, and a 9-hole miniature golf course.

Cabins & Rates

Cabins	Per Diems From	Sq. Ft.	Fridge	Hair Dryer	Sitting Area	TV
Inside	$58	185	no	no	no	yes
Outside	$72	185	no	no	no	yes
Suite	$162	330	yes	no	yes	yes

CABINS   Accommodations range from lower-deck inside cabins with upper and lower berths to large suites with verandas, king-size beds, sitting areas, and balconies. Standard cabins are roomy (at least 185 sq. ft.) and minimalist in design, with stained-oak trim accents and conventional, monochromatic colors such as salmon red—subdued compared to the flamboyance of the public areas. The cabins are not big on personality but are functional and well laid out. There are 26 demisuites and 28 suites, all with private verandas. The 28 330-square-foot suites each have a whirlpool tub and shower, an L-shaped sofa that converts into a foldaway bed, a safe, a minibar, a walk-in closet, and sliding-glass doors leading to a 70-square-foot private balcony, and are positioned midway between stern and bow, on a middle deck subject to the least tossing and rocking during rough weather.

All cabins, even the least expensive inside ones, have enough storage space to accommodate a reasonably diverse wardrobe, and feature a safe, TV, desk and stool, chair, reading lights for each bed, and bathroom with a roomy shower and generous-size mirrored cabinet to store your toiletries. All cabins have Carnival's great new extrathick mattresses, duvets, linens, and pillows, along with fluffy towels and bathrobes. In early 2006, all of the *Ecstasy's* cabins were completely refurbished, and the suites on the *Sensation* were remodeled. By year-end 2007, cabins and suites on the *Imagination* and *Inspiration* were slated to be upgraded as well.

About 20 cabins on each ship are suitable for passengers with disabilities.

DINING OPTIONS   In addition to a pair of big one-story dining rooms with windows, there's a large indoor/outdoor casual buffet restaurant (which was recently spruced up on the *Ecstasy*). You'll also find specialty coffee bars and patisseries on *Sensation, Elation, Ecstasy, Paradise, Imagination,* and *Inspiration* selling gourmet goodies for a couple of bucks a pop. There's a complimentary sushi bar serving fresh, tasty sushi in late afternoons on all but the *Sensation,* with sake available for an extra charge.

PUBLIC AREAS   Each ship boasts the same configuration of decks, public lounges, and entertainment venues, including a six-story atrium flanked by glass-sided elevators, casinos, new Internet centers, and at least eight bars, plus several (usually packed) hot tubs. The cluster of disappointing shops on each ship is surprisingly cramped and won't be winning any design awards; it's much better on the newer ships.

In early 2006, the *Ecstasy* and *Sensation* both got new 9-hole miniature golf courses and new children's play areas. The same upgrades were planned for the *Imagination* and *Inspiration* by late 2007.

POOL, FITNESS, SPA & SPORTS FACILITIES   Although totally blah in the decor department, the 12,000-square-foot spas and fitness areas are well enough equipped. Each has a roomy, mirrored aerobics room and a large, windowed gym with more than a dozen workout machines plus free weights. Each has men's and women's locker rooms and massage rooms (both areas surprisingly drab and institutional feeling), as well as a sauna and steam room, whirlpools, and three swimming pools, one of which has a spiraling water slide. The spa area on the *Sensation* was renovated in early 2006. The Sun Deck of each ship offers an unobstructed ⅛-mile jogging track covered with a rubberized surface. Both the spas and the gyms aboard the *Imagination* and *Inspiration* were to be updated by year-end 2007.

Holiday • Celebration

The Verdict

Fun Ships, yes, but these older Carnival vessels are outdated and frumpy compared to their slick, glamorous newer sisters. To compensate, Carnival has been basing them at offbeat home ports, such as Mobile (Alabama) and Jacksonville (Florida).

Celebration *(photo: Carnival Cruise Lines)*

Specifications

Size (in tons)		*Holiday*	726/10
Celebration	47,262	Crew	
Holiday	46,052	*Celebration*	670
Passengers (double occ.)		*Holiday*	660
Celebration	1,486	Passenger/Crew Ratio	2.2 to 1
Holiday	1,452	Year Launched	
Passenger/Space Ratio		*Holiday*	1985
Celebration	31.8	*Celebration*	1987
Holiday	31.7	Last Refurbishment/Upgrade	
Total Cabins/Veranda Cabins		*Holiday*	2006
Celebration	743/10	*Celebration*	1999

Frommer's Ratings (Scale of 1–5)   ★★★

Cabin Comfort & Amenities	3	Dining Options	3
Appearance & Upkeep	3	Gym, Spa & Sports Facilities	2
Public Comfort/Space	3	Children's Facilities	3
Decor	3	Enjoyment Factor	4

Take them for what they are: near relics. Museum pieces, really. Refreshing if today's new megaships are too big for your liking, and nostalgic if you can appreciate the design ideals of the disco era. The decor encompasses all the colors of the rainbow, with healthy doses of chrome, brass, and mirrors a la the late 1970s/early 1980s—Tony Manero would go gaga. These medium-size, nearly identical ships were built some 20 years ago for about $100 million to $170 million apiece. Sure, they can't compare with their new post-1990 sisters in the style and amenities departments, but they're often priced less and you can enjoy that wild-and-crazy brand of Carnival fun if your expectations are reasonably low.

There's no atrium, and the pool deck of each ship can get crowded and cramped at high noon. Refurbishments over the years have improved the ships and kept them somewhat up-to-date, though they remain in a completely different league than their fleetmates.

The *Holiday* was one of three Carnival ships chartered to the U.S. government and used for housing in the aftermath of Hurricane Katrina. Before returning to the fleet in spring 2006, the ship got a much-needed face-lift. A brand-new miniature golf course was added to the ship, and there were enhancements made to the gym, dining rooms, and lobby area to give the ship a fresher look.

Cabins & Rates

Cabins	Per Diems From	Sq. Ft.	Fridge	Hair Dryer	Sitting Area	TV
Inside	$46	186	no	no	no	yes
Outside	$60	186	no	no	no	yes
Suite	$200	374	yes	no	yes	yes

CABINS Like the standard cabins in the entire Carnival fleet, they're big. Done in blond-wood tones with pinky-red accenting, they're clean and uncluttered—though nothing to write home about—and are all virtually identical. Beds can be configured as twins or doubles, and each cabin has piped-in stereo music as well as a wall-mounted TV. The medium-size bathrooms have showers.

At 374 square feet, the 10 suites on the Verandah Deck of each ship are as large and comfortable as those offered aboard vessels charging a lot more. Each has a whirlpool tub and shower, an L-shaped sofa that converts into a foldaway bed, a safe, a minibar, a walk-in closet, and sliding-glass doors leading to an 87-square-foot private balcony. As in the rest of the fleet, you'll find ultracomfy bedding, robes, and towels.

Just over a dozen cabins are wheelchair accessible. There are no connecting cabins.

PUBLIC AREAS You may need to keep your sunglasses on even when you're inside: Public areas explode with color in that original outrageous (even scary) Carnival way. We're talking healthy doses of fuchsia, black, red, chrome, brass, glass, and neon. On *Celebration*, there's a bar designed like the inside of a trolley car, and the Red Hot Piano Bar is just that—all red. On *Holiday* one bar features an authentic British bus from 1934. In all, each ship has seven bars, six entertainment lounges, a casino, a disco, a library, an Internet center, and a video arcade. There are also a children's playroom, a beauty salon, and shops. Elevators interconnect all eight decks.

DINING OPTIONS Two main one-story dining rooms and one casual indoor/outdoor buffet restaurant serve breakfast, lunch, and dinner. Both have a pizzeria and a complimentary sushi bar open in late afternoons, with sake available for an extra charge.

POOL, FITNESS, SPA & SPORTS FACILITIES Even though the gyms and spas were remodeled and expanded in 1998 and 1999, you can tell fitness just wasn't a big priority when these ships were built—they're tiny and drab, with a sauna for men and women and a small hair salon. Each ship has two hot tubs and three pools, including a small wading pool for children and a pool with a snaking water slide.

3 Celebrity Cruises

1050 Caribbean Way, Miami, FL 33132. ℂ **800/437-3111** or 305/539-6000. Fax 800/722-5329. www.celebrity.com.

THE LINE IN A NUTSHELL You can have it all with Celebrity: If you like elegance without stuffiness, fun without bad taste, and pampering without a high price, Celebrity delivers. **Sails to:** Caribbean, Panama Canal, Alaska, Mexican Riviera, Bermuda, Hawaii, Canada/New England (plus Europe, transatlantic, South America, Asia, South Pacific).

THE EXPERIENCE   Celebrity juices up the mainstream cruise experience with a touch of refinement and a dash of class, all while keeping things fun, active, and within the price range of Joe and Sally Cruiser. Each ship is spacious, glamorous, and comfortable, mixing sleekly modern and Art Deco styles and throwing in cutting-edge art collections to boot.

An exceedingly polite and professional staff contributes greatly to the elegant mood. Dining-wise, the dashing alternative restaurants on the line's Millennium-class ships outclass all other mainstream ship restaurants for both quality of food and gorgeous decor.

Like all the big-ship lines, Celebrity offers lots for its passengers to do, though its focus stays mainly on mellower pursuits such as bridge, spelling bees, darts challenges, and expert-led seminars on such topics as wildlife, astronomy, photography, personal investing, and history. The AquaSpas on the line's megaships are among the most attractive at sea, decor shipwide is the most original, and the art collections are the most compelling you'll find on any ships at sea.

Pros

- **Best mainstream alternative restaurants at sea:** The Millennium-class ships offer remarkable service, food, and wine in their classy alternative venues, whose elegant decor incorporates artifacts from cherished old ocean liners like the *Olympic, Normandie,* and SS *United States.*
- **Spectacular spas:** Beautiful and well equipped, the spas on the Millennium- and Century-class ships are some of the best at sea.
- **Contemporary Art:** The Century-class ships feature outstanding collections of contemporary art, thanks to the line's art-savvy original owners. On *Mercury* alone, you'll see works by world-class names like Richard Serra, Andy Goldsworthy, Richard Long, Robert Rauschenberg, and an entire wall created for the ship by Sol LeWitt. Free handheld-audio art tours are available on all seven of the line's megaships.

Cons

- **Mechanical problems on Millennium-class ships:** When Celebrity introduced its four Millennium-class ships between 2000 and 2002, little did they know that their much-vaunted Mermaid Pod propulsion system—in which propellers are mounted on swiveling pods attached to the ship's hull—would turn into the headache they have, with worn bearings requiring the line to cancel a few sailings pretty much every year. Affected passengers are compensated very well, receiving full refunds, a certificate applicable toward a future cruise, and/or onboard credit, depending on the extent to which their trip was affected.
- **Nickel-and-diming:** Though almost all cruise lines now supplement their income by offering extra-charge alternative restaurants, fancy coffee drinks, specialty ice creams, and the like, Celebrity's high-toned image means the line's passengers get more ticked off by this kind of nickel-and-diming. For instance, passengers we polled on one recent Caribbean cruise were uniformly outraged by the $30 bingo charge.

CELEBRITY: MEGA CHIC

Celebrity's roots go back to the powerful Greek shipping family Chandris, whose patriarch John D. Chandris founded a cargo shipping company in 1915. The family

Compared with the other mainstream lines, here's how Celebrity rates:

	Poor	Fair	Good	Excellent	Outstanding
Enjoyment Factor					✓
Dining			✓		
Activities			✓		
Children's Program		✓			
Entertainment		✓			
Service				✓	
Worth the Money				✓	

expanded into the cruise business in the late 1960s and by 1976 had the largest passenger-cruise fleet in the world. In the late 1970s, they introduced the down-market Chandris-Fantasy Cruises, which served a mostly European clientele. In 1989, the Chandris family dissolved Fantasy and created Celebrity Cruises, building beautiful, innovative ships that were immediately recognizable by their crisp navy-blue-and-white hulls and their rakishly angled funnels decorated with a giant X—which was really the Greek letter *chi*, for Chandris.

The company's rise to prominence was so rapid and so successful that in 1997 it was courted and acquired by the larger and wealthier Royal Caribbean Cruises, Ltd., which now operates Celebrity as a sister line to Royal Caribbean International. With their distinctive profiles and striking contemporary decor, they're some of the most distinctive and stylish ships out there, but Celebrity nevertheless has been having a hard time distinguishing itself in the marketplace since it became part of RCCL. Perhaps some new developments, though, will help give the line attention it deserves. In 2006, Celebrity announced construction of four new 118,000-ton, 2,850-passenger ships, the *Celebrity Solstice* (slated to debut in fall 2008), *Celebrity Equinox* (due in summer 2009), *Celebrity Eclipse* (due in 2010), and an as-yet-unnamed sister due in fall 2011. It also acquired two smaller, 30,277-ton, 710-passenger vessels originally built for defunct Renaissance cruises. Now dubbed *Azamara Journey* and *Azamara Quest*, they're sailing for Celebrity's new exploratory sub-brand **Azamara Cruises** (p. 111).

Zenith, one of the first new ships built for Celebrity (back in 1992), was retired from the fleet in 2007 and now sails for Spain's Pullmantur Cruises, another Royal Caribbean subsidiary.

PASSENGER PROFILE

Celebrity tries to focus on middle- to upper-middle-income cruisers and even wealthy patrons who want a great megaship experience (especially while nestled in one of the line's amazing Penthouse Suites), but its generally low prices—more or less comparable to those of Carnival and Royal Caribbean—ensure the demographic stays democratically wider. Clients who choose their cruise based on more than just price like Celebrity because it offers a well-balanced cruise, with lots of activities and a glamorous, exciting atmosphere that's both refined and fun.

Most passengers are couples in their 40s and up, though you'll see passengers of all ages, with a decent number of honeymooners and couples celebrating anniversaries, as well as families with children in summer and during the holidays.

DINING

TRADITIONAL Though Celebrity started out with a rep for truly exceptional cuisine, today the dishes served in its main dining rooms are really on par with mainstream peers Princess, Royal Caribbean, NCL, and Holland America. **Dining service,** however, remains excellent. Dinner menus are likely to feature entrees such as veal shank cooked in an aromatic tomato velouté with orange zest, served with risotto; broiled sliced tenderloin with béarnaise and Madeira sauces; and boneless chicken breast with bananas and ham, coated with coconut flakes and served with curry peanut sauce. At every meal, Celebrity also offers lighter "spa" fare whose calorie, fat, cholesterol, and sodium breakdowns are listed on the back of the menu. Vegetarians, meanwhile, can enjoy one of the few dedicated **vegetarian menus** offered in the cruise biz. It's available upon request and changes every night, with multiple appetizer and entree options. Celebrity offers a good wine list that includes a line of proprietary wines called **Celebrity Cruises Cellarmaster Selection,** available on board and also online, at **www.celebrityvineyards.com.**

SPECIALTY Cuisine, service, and ambience really shine at the Millennium-class ships' intimate alternative restaurants, each of which carries a $30-per-person cover charge and seats just over 100 passengers. Presentation is paramount: Decor is centered around artifacts from the historic passenger vessels that give the restaurants their names; there often seems to be more waitstaff than diners; Caesar salads and zabaglione are prepared table-side; maitre d's carve passengers' meat dishes with the finesse of a concert pianist; and a selection of excellent French cheeses arrives at the end of the meal.

Menus feature at least one menu item inspired by a dish served aboard the venue's namesake—for instance, the original Waldorf Pudding recipe from the White Star Liner *Olympic,* served in *Millennium*'s Edwardian-style Olympic restaurant. Appetizers include such items as creamy lobster broth, tartare of salmon garnished with quail eggs, and goat cheese soufflé with tomato coulis, followed by entrees such as sea bass brushed with tapenade, scampi flambéed in Armagnac, and rack of lamb coated with mushroom duxelles and wrapped in a puff pastry. For dessert, you can't go wrong with a chocolate soufflé or a plate of bite-size desserts. You can order a la carte or opt for a set multicourse tasting menu, with an optional $28 slate of wine pairings. Wines are also available by the glass or bottle.

CASUAL Breakfast and lunch in the buffet restaurants are on par with those of lines such as Royal Caribbean and Princess, and include such features as a **made-to-order pasta bar** and a **pizza station** serving very tasty pies. On most nights, the buffet space is transformed into the **Casual Dining Boulevard,** with waiters serving entrees such as pasta, gourmet pizzas, and chicken between about 6 and 9:30pm. Reservations are recommended, though if there's space, walk-ins are accepted, too. During dinnertime, Celebrity also offers a **sushi bar** in one section of the buffet restaurant, serving both appetizer-size portions and full meals.

Light breakfast eaters or those looking for a pre- or postbreakfast snack will want to grab an incredibly good croissant from **Cova Café.** They're free, but you'll have to pony up a few bucks for an accompanying latte or cappuccino. Each Millennium-class ship also has an **Aqua Spa Cafe** in a corner of the thalassotherapy pool area where you can get low-cal treats for lunch or dinner from noon to 8pm, including raw veggie platters, poached salmon with asparagus tips, vegetarian sushi, and pretty salads with tuna or chicken. Spa breakfasts offer items such as bagels and lox, fresh fruit, cereal, and boiled eggs. For the opposite of spa cuisine, outdoor grills on all ships offer burgers and the like.

SNACKS & EXTRAS   The line offers **afternoon tea** at least once per cruise fleetwide, with white-gloved waiters serving tea, finger sandwiches, scones, and desserts from rolling carts. Several nights per cruise, roving waiters present a late-night culinary soiree known as **Gourmet Bites,** serving upscale canapés and hors d'oeuvres in the ship's public lounges between midnight and 1am. There's also a traditional **midnight buffet** on 1 night, and occasional themed lunches (Asian, Italian, Tex-Mex, tropical smorgasbord) in the buffet restaurant.

The line's room service allows passengers to order off a limited menu 24 hours a day and also from the lunch and dinner menus during set meal hours. You can even get tasty **pizza** delivered right to your cabin between 3 and 7pm and 10pm and 1am daily, in a box and pouch just like the ones used by your local pizzeria.

ACTIVITIES

Celebrity offers lots of options for those who want to stay active, but it also caters to those who want to veg.

Celebrity's **spas** are some of the best in the business, beautifully appointed and offering a nice raft of treatments, from the exotic to the everyday-but-it-still-feels-good. If you're looking for the latter, though, make it a point to ask: Often (as on its website), Celebrity tends to list its fancy, high-priced treatments but not its standard massages, facials, and pedicures. If you're the "try something new type," the line offers its **Acupuncture at Sea program** fleetwide on all cruises, with professionals offering acupuncture and medicinal herbal treatments for pain management, smoking cessation, weight loss, stress management, and other ailments. Free talks on acupuncture and other holistic health treatments are also offered at various times throughout the cruise. In the gyms, various aerobic-type classes are available throughout the day. Basic classes are free, while the cool ones, such as **Pilates and yoga,** cost extra and can be booked only at a package price at the start of the cruise.

Other activities include wine tastings (for a fee), horse racing, bingo, bridge, art auctions, trivia games, game shows, arts and crafts, cooking demos, computer classes (from Web page design to the basics of Excel), and ballroom and line-dancing lessons. Up to four featured speakers/performers also sail on every cruise, offering **complimentary enrichment lectures.** Speakers may include naturalists (on Alaska, Hawaii, and South America sailings), caricature artists (on weeklong Caribbean and Bermuda sailings), chefs from well-regarded restaurants, and wine experts who offer onboard seminars and pre-dinner tastings. From time to time actors, politicians, and journalists also sail aboard and hold talks. Recent speakers included former NBC News chief economics correspondent Irving R. Levine, maritime historian and author John Maxtone Graham, and actors Dick Van Patten and Rita Moreno.

During the day, a live pop band plays on the pool deck for a couple of hours, and you can expect a pool game or two, such as a pillow fight, volleyball match, or "King of the Ship" contest.

All the ships have a well-equipped Internet center as well as Wi-Fi capability in various public areas, and the Millennium-class ships and *Century* also offer Internet access in every cabin and suite for guests who bring their laptops. Interactive cabin TVs allow guests to order room service from on-screen menus, select the evening's wine in advance of dinner, play casino-style games, browse in "virtual" shops, and order pay-per-view movies, including some adult titles.

CHILDREN'S PROGRAM

Celebrity pampers kids as well as adults, especially during the summer months and holidays when its Caribbean- and Bermuda-bound ships typically carry 400-plus children. Each ship has a dedicated youth staff of six or more supervising playroom activities practically all day long, and private and group babysitting is available in the evenings. The Millennium class's indoor/outdoor kids' facilities are by far the best in the fleet, with features like ball bins, slides, jungle gyms, and wading pools (the latter also available on *Galaxy* and *Mercury*).

During kid-intensive seasons, **supervised activities** are geared toward four age groups for ages 3 to 17. Kids ages 3 to 6, dubbed "Ship Mates," can enjoy treasure hunts, clown parties, T-shirt painting, dancing, movies, ship tours, and ice-cream-sundae-making parties. "Cadets," ages 7 to 9, have T-shirt painting, scavenger hunts, board games, arts and crafts, ship tours, and computer games. Your 10- to 12-year-old may want to join the "Ensign" activities, such as karaoke, computer games, board games, trivia contests, arts and crafts, movies, and pizza parties. In summer, these three age groups put on summer-stock theater presentations, with Ship Mates and Cadets singing, dancing, and acting, and Ensigns directing and producing. There are also masquerade parties where Ship Mates and Cadets make their own masks and then parade around the ship, and Junior Olympics where the whole family is encouraged to cheer on the kids who compete in relay races, diving, and basketball free throws. Various activities and tours give kids a behind-the-scenes look at the ship's entertainment, food and beverage, and hotel departments.

Toddlers under age 3 can participate in activities and use the playroom if accompanied by a parent.

For **teens** ages 13 to 17 (subdivided into two groups, 13–15 and 16–17), the Century-class and Millennium-class ships have attractive teen discos/hangout rooms, plus activities like talent shows, karaoke, pool games, and trivia contests.

Group babysitting in the playroom ($6 per child, per hour) is available for ages 3 to 12 between noon and 2pm on port days, and every evening from 10pm to 1am for children ages 3 to 12. Kids can dine with the counselors most nights between 5 and 7pm (free on sea days; $6 per child, per hour, on port days). On the last night of the cruise, a complimentary **Parents' Night Out party** is offered between 5pm and 1am, and includes pizza and fun activities for kids while their parents step out. Female

---

Preview: *Celebrity Solstice*

Celebrity hasn't launched a new vessel in 6 years, but that'll change this fall when the line introduces the 118,000-ton, 2,850-passenger *Celebrity Solstice*, its largest vessel ever. Though few details of the ship's amenities had yet been announced at press time, we do know that she'll boast a tremendous number of outside cabins (more than 90% of the total, with more than 85% of those having balconies) and that the average standard cabin will be quite roomy at some 215 square feet.

The vessel is currently under construction at Germany's Meyer Werft shipyard, which was responsible for Celebrity's first five newbuilds—*Horizon, Zenith, Century, Galaxy,* and *Mercury*. A sister ship to *Solstice* named **Celebrity Equinox** is slated to debut in summer 2009, followed by **Celebrity Eclipse** in 2010 and a fourth, still-unnamed sister for fall 2011.

Celebrity Fleet Itineraries

Ship	Itineraries
Century	**Caribbean:** 2-, 4- & 5-night western, round-trip from Miami, FL (Jan–Apr & Dec).
Constellation	**Caribbean:** Alternating 10-night eastern and 11-night western, round-trip from Ft. Lauderdale (Jan–Mar & Nov–Dec). **Bermuda/Caribbean:** 11 nights, Bayonne, NJ, to Ft. Lauderdale, FL (Oct). **New England/Canada:** 10 & 11 nights, round-trip from Bayonne, NJ (Sept–Oct).
Galaxy	**Caribbean:** 10- & 11-night eastern/southern, round-trip from San Juan, PR (Jan–Mar & Dec).
Infinity	**Panama Canal:** 15-night westbound (Apr) and 16-night eastbound (Oct), between Ft. Lauderdale, FL, and San Francisco, CA. **Alaska:** 7-night Inside Passage, round-trip from Seattle, WA (May–Sept). **Alaska/British Columbia:** 11 nights, San Francisco, CA, to Vancouver, BC (Apr). **Alaska/British Columbia/Pacific Northwest:** 14 nights, Vancouver, BC, to San Francisco, CA (Sept). **Caribbean:** 4-night western, round-trip from Ft. Lauderdale, FL (Dec).
Mercury	**Hawaii:** 12 nights, Honolulu, HI, to Ensenada, Mexico (Mar). **U.S. Pacific Coast:** 7 & 8 nights, round-trip from San Francisco, CA (Mar–Apr). **Alaska:** 7-night Inside Passage, round-trip from Vancouver, BC (May–Sept). **Alaska/U.S. Pacific Coast:** 14 nights, San Francisco, CA, to Vancouver, BC (Apr). **British Columbia:** 3 & 4 nights, round-trip from Seattle (Sept–Oct). **U.S. Pacific Coast:** 9 nights, Vancouver, BC, to San Diego, CA (Oct). **Hawaii:** 15 nights, round-trip from San Diego, CA (Oct–Dec). **Panama Canal:** 14-night eastbound (Nov) and westbound (Dec) between San Diego, CA, and Ft. Lauderdale, FL.
Millennium	**Caribbean:** 7-night eastern, round-trip from Ft. Lauderdale (Jan–Apr). **Panama Canal:** 15 nights, Ft. Lauderdale, FL, to San Francisco, CA (Apr). **Alaska:** 7-night Gulf of Alaska, north- or southbound between Vancouver, BC, and Seward/Anchorage, AK (May–Sept). **Alaska/U.S. Pacific Coast:** 14-night round-trip from San Francisco, CA (May), northbound from San Francisco to Vancouver, BC (May), or southbound from Vancouver to San Diego, CA (Sept). **British Columbia:** 3 nights, round-trip from Vancouver, BC (Sept). **Hawaii:** 11 nights, Ensenada, Mexico, to Honolulu, HI (Oct).
Summit	**Panama Canal:** 14 nights, Los Angeles, CA, to San Juan, PR (Jan). **Caribbean:** 7-night southern, round-trip from San Juan, PR (Jan–Mar & Dec).

crewmembers offer evening **private in-cabin babysitting** on a limited basis, for $8 per hour for up to two children. Kids must be at least 6 months old, and the service must be requested 24 hours in advance.

There is no **minimum age** for sailing.

ENTERTAINMENT

Celebrity offers all the popular cruise favorites, such as magicians, comedians, cabaret acts, **passenger talent shows,** and Broadway-style musical revues. Overall quality of music and comedy acts is good, but on our last sailing the musical revues were poor. For something a little different, the line offers some nice, understated entertainment touches such as **harpists** and **string quartets** performing in various lounges.

All the ships also have cozy lounges and bars where you can retreat for a romantic nightcap and some music, from laid-back jazz to music from the big-band era, spiced with interpretations of contemporary hits. There are also the elegant and plush **Michael's Club** piano lounges for cordials and some quiet conversation. Each ship has late-night disco dancing, usually until about 3am. You'll also find karaoke and recent-release movies in the ship theaters and cinemas.

Each ship has a rather spacious **casino,** and while they may not be as Vegasy as the ones on Carnival, they're bustling enough to put gamblers in the mood.

SERVICE

Service is Celebrity's strongest suit, with staff uniformly polite, attentive, cheerful, knowledgeable, and professional. Stewards wear white gloves at embarkation as they escort passengers to their cabins. Waiters have a poised, upscale-hotel air about them, and their manner does much to create an elegant mood. There are very professional sommeliers in the dining room, and waiters are on hand in the Lido breakfast and lunch buffet restaurants to carry passengers' trays from the buffet line to a table of their choice. If you occupy a suite, you'll get a **tuxedo-clad personal butler** who serves afternoon tea, complimentary cappuccino and espresso, and complimentary pre-dinner hors d'oeuvres. If you ask, he'll also handle your laundry, shine your shoes, make sewing repairs, deliver messages, and even serve a full five-course dinner en suite or help you organize a cocktail party. (You foot the bill for food and drinks, of course.) Other hedonistic treats bestowed upon suite guests include a bottle of champagne on arrival, personalized stationery, terry robes, oversize bath towels, priority check-in and debarkation, express luggage delivery at embarkation, and so on. **ConciergeClass staterooms**—a middle zone between regular cabins and suites—offer some of the same perks but without the high price of actual suites (and no butler, sorry).

When it comes to **tipping,** Celebrity passengers can dispense gratuities personally, in cash, at the end of the cruise, or choose to add them to their onboard accounts at a rate of $11 per person, per day.

Laundry and dry-cleaning services are available fleetwide for a nominal fee, but there are no self-service laundry facilities.

The Millennium Class: Millennium • Infinity • Summit • Constellation

The Verdict

Among the classiest big ships at sea, the Millennium ships offer all the leisure, sports, and entertainment options of a megaship and an atmosphere that combines old-world elegance and modern casual style.

Millennium *(photo: Celebrity Cruises)*

Specifications

Size (in tons)	91,000	Year Launched	
Passengers (double occ.)	1,950	*Millennium*	2000
Passenger/Space Ratio	46.7	*Infinity*	2001
Total Cabins/Veranda Cabins	975/590	*Summit*	2001
Crew	999	*Constellation*	2002
Passenger/Crew Ratio	2 to 1	Last Refurbishment/Upgrade	N/A

Frommer's Ratings (Scale of 1–5) ★★★★★

Cabin Comfort & Amenities	5	Dining Options	5
Appearance & Upkeep	5	Gym, Spa & Sports Facilities	5
Public Comfort/Space	5	Children's Facilities	4
Decor	5	Enjoyment Factor	5

In creating its third generation of newbuilds, Celebrity took the best ideas from the wonderful *Century, Galaxy,* and *Mercury* and ratcheted them up in terms of both scale and number: bigger ships, bigger spas and theaters, more veranda cabins, more dining options, more shopping, more lounges, and more sports and exercise facilities, plus more of the same great service, cuisine, and high-style onboard art for which the company was already known. If there's one downside to these vessels, it's their innovative Mermaid Pod propulsion systems, whose propellers are mounted on swiveling pods attached to the ship's hull, offering greater maneuverability. Great idea, but apparently not without glitches: In the past 2 years alone, Celebrity has had to cancel five cruises and send the ships to dry dock to replace worn bearings, a circumstance that's cost the line in both revenue and passenger goodwill. There's nothing unsafe about them, mind you; it's just annoying and expensive. Passengers on cancelled sailings generally receive refunds and vouchers that can be applied to a future cruise.

Cabins & Rates

Cabins	Per Diems From	Sq. Ft.	Fridge	Hair Dryer	Sitting Area	TV
Inside	$105	170	yes	yes	yes	yes
Outside	$123	170–191	yes	yes	yes	yes
Suite	$275	251–1,432	yes	yes	yes	yes

CABINS Improving upon Celebrity's already-respectable cabins, the Millennium-class ships push the bar up yet another notch, with their elegant striped, floral, or patterned fabrics in shades such as butterscotch and pinkish terra cotta, along with Art Deco–style lighting fixtures and marble desktops. Standard inside and outside cabins are a roomy 170 square feet and come with a small sitting area, stocked minifridge, TV, safe, ample storage space, cotton robes, and shampoo dispensers built right into the shower. Only thing missing? Individual reading lights above the beds, though there are table lamps on the nightstands.

Premium and Deluxe staterooms have slightly larger sitting areas and approximately 40-square-foot verandas. The 12 simply titled "Large" oceanview staterooms in the stern measure in at a very large 271 square feet and have two entertainment centers with TVs/VCRs, a partitioned sitting area with two convertible sofa beds, and very, very, very large 242-square-foot verandas facing the ships' wake.

Passengers booking the ConciergeClass staterooms on Sky Deck get a bunch of cushy extras, from a bottle of champagne to a choice of pillow, upgraded bedding, oversize towels, double-thick Frette bathrobes, priority for just about everything (dining, shore excursions, luggage delivery, embarkation, and disembarkation), and cushioned chairs and high-powered binoculars on their 41-square-foot balconies. Unfortunately, many of those balconies (as well as those attached to several Deluxe Ocean View cabins at Sky Deck midships) catch a little shadow from the overhanging deck above. *Hint:* Several Concierge Class cabins on Sky Deck (9038 and 9043) and Panorama Deck (8045 and 8046) offer extralarge verandas at no extra cost. Ask your travel agent.

Suites on the Millennium ships offer 24-hour butler service and come in four levels, from the 251-square-foot Sky Suites with balconies to the eight 467-square-foot Celebrity Suites (with dining area, separate bedroom, two TV/VCR combos, and whirlpool bathtub, but no verandas) and the 538-square-foot Royal Suites (also with a separate living/dining room, two TV/VCR combos, a standing shower and whirlpool bathtub, and a huge 195-sq.-ft. veranda with whirlpool tub). At the top of the food chain, the massive Penthouse Suites measure 1,432 square feet and offer herringbone wood floors, a marble foyer, a computer station, a Yamaha piano, and a simply amazing bathroom with ocean views and a full-size hot tub. And did we mention a 1,098-square-foot veranda that wraps around the stern of the ship and features a whirlpool tub and full bar? The only downside is you sometimes feel the vibrations of the engines a few decks below. If these suites have a Park Avenue feel, it's no wonder— the designer, Birch Coffey, also does apartments for New York's elite.

Passengers requiring use of a wheelchair have a choice of 26 cabins, from Sky Suites to balcony cabins to inside staterooms.

PUBLIC AREAS   There's simply nothing else at sea like the Grand Foyer atrium, the stunning hub of all four ships. Each rectangular, three-deck area features a translucent, inner-illuminated onyx staircase that glows beneath your feet, plus giant silk flower arrangements and topiaries, oceanview elevators, and an attractive Internet center.

In each ship's bow is the elegant three-deck theater whose warm glow is provided by faux torches spaced all around. Seating on all three levels is unobstructed except in the far reaches of the balconies. You'll also find elegant martini, champagne, and caviar bars, as well as brighter, busier lounges for live music. For the real dancing, head up to the stunning observation lounge/disco on Sunrise Deck. Other rooms include a two-deck library; a large casino; an oceanview florist/conservatory (created with the help of Paris-based floral designer Emilio Robba and filled mostly with silk flowers and trees, some of which are for sale); and the huge, high-tech conference center and cinema. Celebrity's signature Michael's Club is a quiet, dignified piano bar, replete with fake fireplace and comfy leather club chairs. Little-used during the day, it's a great place to snuggle up with a good book, while at night it's an excellent place for an after-dinner drink.

The ships' Emporium Shops have a nice variety of high-end name brands as well as cheap (and fun) souvenir stuff.

For kids, the Shipmates Fun Factory has both indoor and outdoor soft-surface jungle gyms, a wading pool, a ball bin, a computer room, a movie room, an arts-and-crafts area, a video arcade, a teen center, and more.

DINING OPTIONS   The main dining rooms are beautiful two-level spaces with huge stern-facing windows, oversize round windows to port and starboard, and a dramatic central double staircase. *Summit's* dining room boasts a 7-foot Art Deco bronze of the goddess Athena that once overlooked the grand staircase on the legendary SS *Normandie* ocean liner. (She'd resided for years near the pool at Miami's Fontainebleau Hotel before Celebrity bought her and returned her to sea.)

The real *pièce de résistance* on these ships, however, is their alternative, reservations-only restaurants, which offer dining experiences unmatched on any other ship today.

Millennium's is the Edwardian-style Olympic restaurant, whose decor features several dozen hand-carved French walnut wall panels made by Palestinian craftsmen for the A La Carte restaurant on *Titanic*'s sister ship *Olympic,* which sailed from 1911 to 1935. *Infinity*'s SS United States restaurant features etched-glass panels from the 1950s liner of the same name, which still holds the transatlantic speed record for a liner. (Though mothballed since the 1970s, the *United States* is now owned by NCL, which is studying the feasibility of returning her to service.) *Summit*'s Normandie restaurant features original gold-lacquered panels from the smoking room of the legendary *Normandie,* while the *Constellation*'s Ocean Liners restaurant has artifacts from a variety of luxury liners, including sets of original red-and-black lacquered panels from the 1920s *Ile de France,* which add a whimsical Parisian air. Dining here is a 2- to 3-hour commitment, with some 100 guests served by a gracious staff of more than 20, including 8 dedicated chefs, 6 waiters, 5 maitre d's, and 4 sommeliers. Cuisine is a combination of Continental specialties mixed with original recipes from the ships the restaurants are named after (such as the Long Island duckling featured on the original SS *United States*), and includes the first use of table-side flambé cooking at sea. Waiters remove domed silver dish covers with a flourish, exceptional cheeses are offered post-meal, and a pianist or a piano/violin duo performs period music. Diners can order a multicourse tasting menu for $30 or order a la carte. A menu of suggested wine pairings is available for $28.

The huge buffet restaurant on each ship is open for breakfast, lunch, and dinner, offering regular buffet selections plus pizza, pasta, and ice-cream specialty stations. Depending on how busy the restaurant is, waiters may carry passengers' trays to their tables and fetch coffee. For snacks, visit the appealing Cova Café, a bustling, Italian-style joint with rich fabrics, cozy banquettes, and wood-frame chairs, serving exceptionally good freshly baked pastries (complimentary) and specialty coffees (for an extra charge).

POOL, FITNESS, SPA & SPORTS FACILITIES   The spas on the Millennium-class ships are gorgeous and sprawling, their 25,000 square feet taken up with hydrotherapy treatment rooms; New Agey "Persian Garden" steam suites whose nooks offer showers that simulate a tropical rainforest, heated tiled couches, and the aromas of chamomile, eucalyptus, mint; and large, bubbling thalassotherapy pools with soothing pressure jets in a solarium-like setting under a glass roof. The pool is free to all adult guests, and you can stretch out the experience by grabbing a casual breakfast or lunch at the AquaSpa Cafe, set back by the seaview windows.

The spa itself offers all the usual treatments, plus a series of special multihour spa packages that combine several Eastern-influenced treatments that employ coconut- and frangipani-scented oils, seaweed-infused pastes, and other exoticisms to induce bliss—at about $200 to $400 per package.

Next door to the spa there's a very large gym with dozens of the latest machines and free weights, and a large aerobics floor.

Up top, the Sports Deck has facilities for basketball, volleyball, quoits, and paddle tennis. Just below, on the Sunrise Deck, are a jogging track and a golf simulator. Below that is the well-laid-out pool deck, where you'll find two pools, four hot tubs, a couple of bars, and a sunning area. Head up to the balcony level above the pool, at both the bow and the stern, for quieter sunbathing spots.

The Century Class: Century • Galaxy • Mercury

The Verdict

Though now a decade old, Celebrity's Century-class ships remain three of the most attractive and appealing megaships at sea: down-to-earth yet exciting, elegant yet casual.

Mercury *(photo: Matt Hannafin)*

Specifications

Size (in tons)		Crew	
Century	70,606	*Century*	843
Galaxy/Mercury	77,713	*Galaxy/Mercury*	900
Passengers (double occ.)		Passenger/Crew Ratio	2 to 1
Century	1,750	Year Launched	
Galaxy/Mercury	1,896	*Century*	1995
Passenger/Space Ratio	41	*Galaxy*	1996
Total Cabins/Veranda Cabins		*Mercury*	1997
Century	875/61	Last Refurbishment/Upgrade	
Galaxy/Mercury	948/220	*Century*	2006
		Mercury	2007

Frommer's Ratings (Scale of 1–5)

★★★★½

Cabin Comfort & Amenities	5	Dining Options	4
Appearance & Upkeep	4	Gym, Spa & Sports Facilities	5
Public Comfort/Space	5	Children's Facilities	4
Decor	5	Enjoyment Factor	5

These are the ships that ushered Celebrity into the megaship world and also sealed the line's rep for offering elegant, gorgeously designed vessels with a truly modern flair. It's difficult to say what's most striking: The elegant spas and their 15,000-gallon thalassotherapy pools? The distinguished Michael's Club piano lounges with their leather wingbacks and velvet couches? The two-story old-world dining rooms set back in the stern, with grand floor-to-ceiling windows allowing diners to spy the ship's wake glowing under moonlight? An absolutely intriguing modern-art collection unmatched in the industry? Take your pick—you won't go wrong.

Galaxy and *Mercury* are truer sisters, with a chic and sophisticated decor of warm wood tones, rich textures, deep-toned fabrics, buttery soft leathers, and futuristic-looking applications of glass and marble. The oldest of the three vessels, *Century,* was long the odd ship out with its more glitzy mid-'90s decor, but in late 2006 she underwent a $55-million refurbishment that spruced up her dated interiors and added many of the features associated with the line's more modern Millennium-class vessels. For instance, you'll now find a 76-seat sushi bar, a Cova Café, a "Persian Garden" steam suite, a 54-seat Spa Cafe, an outdoor Sunset Bar, 314 verandas added to existing staterooms, 14 new suites, an expanded number of Concierge-Class staterooms, and a new 66-seat specialty restaurant called Murano. In spring 2007 *Mercury* also got a big upgrade, which added new verandas to 14 cabins in the stern (offering wonderful views of the ship's wake), a new shopping "boulevard" with several upscale shops, new bedding in all cabins, and all new equipment in the gym. We sailed immediately after her upgrade and are happy to report that she's as lovely now as when we were first aboard her 10 years ago, during her inaugural season.

Cabins & Rates

Cabins	Per Diems From	Sq. Ft.	Fridge	Hair Dryer	Sitting Area	TV
Inside	$90	170–175	yes	yes	no	yes
Outside	$115	170–175	yes	yes	some	yes
Suite	$215	246–1,433	yes	yes	yes	yes

CABINS Simple yet pleasing decor is cheerful and based on light-colored furniture and muted color themes. Standard inside and outside cabins are larger than the norm (although not as large as Carnival's 185-footers), and suites, which come in four categories, are particularly spacious, with marble vanity/desk tops, Art Deco–style sconces, and rich inlaid wood floors. Some, such as the Penthouse Suite, offer more living space (1,219 sq. ft., expandable to 1,433 sq. ft. on special request) than you find in many private homes, plus such wonderful touches as a private whirlpool bath on the veranda. Royal Suites run about half that size (plus 100-ft. balconies) but offer touches such as French doors between the bedroom and seating area, both bathtub and shower in the bathroom, and TVs in each room. *Galaxy* and *Mercury's* 246-square-foot Sky Suites offer verandas that, at 179 square feet, are among the biggest aboard any ship—bigger, in fact, than those in the more expensive Penthouse and Royal suites on these ships (you may want to keep your robe on, though, as people on the deck above can see down onto part of the Sky Suite verandas). All suite bathrooms have bathtubs with whirlpools and magnified makeup mirrors. Like the Millennium-class ships, the Century-class ships also offer ConciergeClass staterooms, which are located mostly on the Sky and Penthouse decks. Though a tad less cushy and amenities-filled than regular suites, they offer a lot of extras without the full-suite price.

All cabins are outfitted with built-in vanities/desks, stocked minifridges (accounts are billed for any snacks or drinks consumed), hair dryers, cotton robes, and safes. Closets and drawer space are roomy and well designed, as are the bathrooms. Cabin TVs are wired with an interactive system that allows guests to order room service from on-screen menus, select wine for dinner, play casino-style games, or go shopping.

Note that the sternmost cabins on Vista Deck are right next to the children's center—a consideration if you want to spend lots of quiet time inside.

Eight cabins aboard each ship (one inside and seven outside) were specifically designed for passengers with disabilities.

PUBLIC AREAS All three ships are designed so well that it's never hard to find a quiet retreat when you want to feel secluded but don't want to be confined in your cabin.

Each vessel boasts a cozy Michael's Club piano bar, decorated like the parlor of a London men's club. They're great spots for a fine cognac or a good single-malt Scotch while enjoying soft music. On *Century* and *Galaxy,* Michael's Club piano bar maintains its wood-paneled clubbiness somewhat better than aboard the *Mercury,* where it wraps around the main atrium and lets onto a very uncozy view of the shopping below. Still, you can't beat the high-backed, buttery-leather chairs and dark ambience.

For those who don't find that clubby ambience appealing, the Cova Café offers an alternative, with specialized upscale java at extra cost. There's also the popular Rendez-Vous Square, arranged so that even large groups can achieve a level of privacy and couples can find a nook of their own. Champagne bars appear aboard *Galaxy* and *Mercury.* In the latter, it's combined with a martini bar in a gorgeous, two-level space defined by rounded wooden walls, champagne-bubble carpeting and glass panels, and a two-story Sol LeWitt mural created specifically for the ship. Various other bars, both indoor and outdoor, are tucked into nooks and crannies throughout all three ships.

The multistoried, glass-walled nightclubs/discos are spacious and cleanly, modernly elegant, designed with lots of cozy nooks for romantic conversation over champagne. Each of the three ships has double-decker theaters with unobstructed views from almost every seat (though avoid those at the cocktail tables at the back of the rear balcony boxes, unless you have a really long neck).

The ships have held up remarkably well in their 10-plus years at sea, both in practical and aesthetic terms. On our 2007 sailing aboard *Mercury,* we noticed little wear and tear beyond a few dents in the cabin corridors (courtesy of luggage carts), a missing tile or two in the spa pools, and an occasional tarnishing of metalwork. The ship's decor, meanwhile, has a timeless quality that looks more modern than what you find on a lot of much more recent newbuilds.

DINING OPTIONS   The two-story formal dining rooms on all three ships are truly stunning spaces reminiscent of the grand liners of yesteryear, with wide, dramatic staircases joining the two levels and floor-to-ceiling walls of glass facing astern to a view of the ship's wake. If you lean toward the dramatic, don a gown or tux and slink down the stairs nice and slow like a 1930s Hollywood starlet. There aren't many places you can do that these days.

Century, which got a major renovation in 2006, now offers a dinner alternative at the Murano restaurant, named for the Venetian island famous for its glass blowing and decorated with Murano chandeliers. The restaurant's decor also includes a floor designed to resemble medieval European paving stones; a hand-painted mural themed on travel and adventure; and glass-fronted, polished nickel wine armoires displaying backlit bottles. Elaborate, multicourse meals follow the style of Celebrity's Millennium-class specialty restaurants, with their table-side cooking, carving, and flambé.

Each ship also has an indoor/outdoor buffet restaurant open for breakfast, lunch, and dinner, as well as pizza and ice-cream stations.

POOL, FITNESS, SPA & SPORTS FACILITIES   Pool decks aboard these vessels feature a pair of good-size swimming areas rimmed with teak benches for sunning and relaxation. Even when the ships are full, these areas don't seem particularly crowded. Aboard *Galaxy* and *Mercury,* retractable domes cover one of the swimming pools during inclement weather.

The ships' excellent 10,000-square-foot AquaSpa and fitness facilities are as aesthetically pleasing as they are functional. The gym wraps around the starboard side of an upper forward deck like a hook, the large spa straddles the middle, and a very modern and elegant beauty salon faces the ocean on the port side. On *Galaxy* and *Mercury,* the focal point of the spas is a 115,000-gallon thalassotherapy pool, a bubbling cauldron of warm, soothing seawater. After a relaxing 15- or 20-minute dip, choose a massage, a facial, or something more exotic, such as a Rasul treatment (a mudpack and steam bath for couples), an herbal steam bath, or a variety of water-based treatments involving baths, jet massages, and soft whirling showers. A day pass to the thalassotherapy pool is $20, a weeklong pass is $99, and you get use of the pool free if you book any spa package. There are also saunas and a steam room, including *Mercury*'s impressive Turkish hammam, with its uniformly heated surfaces and beautiful tile work.

The gyms are generously sized, with aerobics classes in a separate room. Standard classes are free, but trendy ones like Pilates and spinning are $10 a pop. There is also an outdoor jogging track on an upper deck, a golf simulator, and one deck that's specifically designed for sports.

4 Costa Cruises

200 S. Park Rd., Suite 200, Hollywood, FL 33021-8541. ℂ 800/462-6782 or 954/266-5600. Fax 954/266-2100. www.costacruises.com.

THE LINE IN A NUTSHELL   Imagine a Carnival megaship hijacked by an Italian circus troupe: That's Costa. The words of the day are fun, festive, and international, with big, bright new megaships providing the venue. Expect a really good time, but don't set your sights too high for cuisine. **Sails to:** Caribbean (plus Europe and Asia).

THE EXPERIENCE   For years, Costa has played up its Italian heritage as the main factor that distinguishes it from Carnival, Royal Caribbean, and the rest—even though the line is part of the Carnival Corporation empire, and many members of the service staff are as Italian as Chico Marx. Still, there's an Italianate essence here, with more pasta dishes on the menu than on any other line; more classical Italian music among the entertainment offerings; Italian-flavored activities facilitated by a young, mostly Italian, and ridiculously attractive "animation staff"; and a huge number of Italian Americans among the passengers. The interiors of the line's newest ships are by Carnival's designer-in-chief Joe Farcus, who took inspiration from Italy's traditions of painting and architecture but still stuck close to his signature "more is more" style—think Venice a la Vegas.

Pros

- **Italian flavor:** Entertainment, activities, and cuisine are presented with an Italian carnival flair.
- **Very active, very fun:** There are a lot of activities, and Costa passengers love to participate, creating a festive and social environment morning to night.

Cons

- **Average dining:** While the pizza is excellent and some of the pasta dishes work well, overall the cuisine only gets a "C" compared with the other big mainstream lines.

COSTA: CONTINENTAL FLAVOR IN THE CARIBBEAN

Costa's origins are as Italian as could be. In 1860, Giacomo Costa established an olive-oil refinery and packaging plant in Genoa. After his death, his sons bought a ship called *Ravenna* to transport raw materials and finished products from Sardinia through Genoa to the rest of Europe, thereby marking the founding of Costa Line in 1924. Between 1997 and 2000, Carnival Corporation bought up shares in Costa until it became sole owner. Today Costa's Italianness is as much a marketing tool as anything else, but it must be working: The line's presence in Europe is huge—and it's even got a foothold in the Far East too—and in the past 4 years it's introduced five new megaships: *Costa Mediterranea* and *Costa Fortuna* in 2003, *Costa Magica* in 2004, *Costa Concordia* in 2006, and *Costa Serena* set to debut in Europe in spring 2007, with an as-yet-unnamed sister in summer 2009.

Compared with the other mainstream lines, here's how Costa rates:

	Poor	Fair	Good	Excellent	Outstanding
Enjoyment Factor			✓		
Dining		✓			
Activities				✓	
Children's Program		✓			
Entertainment			✓		
Service		✓			
Worth the Money			✓		

PASSENGER PROFILE

Most of Costa's ships sail in Europe, where they sail with 80% to 85% Europeans. In contrast, the 2,112-passenger *Costa Mediterranea* and 2,720-passenger *Costa Fortuna* are marketed to Americans for winter Caribbean sailings, attracting passengers of all ages who want lots of fun and action, and like the idea of "Cruising Italian Style," as the line's ad slogan goes. Italian Americans are heavily represented aboard every Caribbean cruise, and in general Costa passengers are big on participation, the goofier the better: Witness, for instance, the number of passengers wearing togas on Roman Bacchanal Toga Night. And we've never seen as many guests crowding the dance floor, participating in contests, or having a go at boccie or mask painting as aboard Costa's ships.

In the Caribbean, Costa appeals to retirees and young couples alike, although there are more passengers over 50 than under. Typically you won't see more than 40 or 50 kids on any one cruise except during holidays such as Christmas and spring break, when there may be as many as 500 children on board. About 80% of passengers are from North America, with the remainder mostly from Europe and South America. Because of the international mix, public announcements, lifeboat drills, and some entertainment are given in both English and Italian. The cruise director is often American or British during Caribbean sailings, but much of the activities staff is composed of multilingual Italians.

DINING

In general, file Costa's cuisine under "average," though there are exceptions. Pastas are totally authentic and are often very good, the pizza is fantastic, and on a recent cruise the roast turkey with trimmings and the Caribbean lobster tail in tarragon sauce went over big. Most guests at our table ordered two each of the latter.

TRADITIONAL Each dinner menu features five courses from a different region of Italy—Liguria one night, Sicily the next, and so on—plus several alternatives for each course, including the traditional pasta course. Most of the pastas, from fettuccine to spaghetti and raviolis, are shipped in direct from Italy. Many of these dishes are heavy on the cream and so are richer than some Americans are used to, but they're definitely the dining highlight. If you feel like a change from the pasta course, try one of the interesting risottos—the crabmeat-and-champagne selection on our last cruise was fantastic. Otherwise, expect cruise staples such as poached salmon, lobster tail, grilled lamb chops, roast duck, and beef tenderloin, plus always-available classic selections such as Caesar salad and baked or grilled fish or chicken. **Vegetarian options** are available at each meal, and **Health and Wellness menu** selections are listed with their calorie, fat, and carbohydrate breakdowns. On the second formal night, flaming baked Alaska is paraded through the dining room and complimentary champagne is poured. Other desserts include tiramisu, gelato, zabaglione (meringue pie), and a tasty chocolate soufflé.

SPECIALTY Each ship features a reservations-only alternative restaurant ($23 per person) offering Mediterranean dishes such as rigatoni served with lobster and tomatoes, or grilled lamb chops. A Tuscan steakhouse menu is also available. The ambience is considerably quieter and more romantic than in the main dining room, with pleasant piano music and a small dance floor if you feel like a waltz between courses. *Magica*'s Vincenza Club Restaurant is outstanding, with an adventurous menu by restaurateurs Zefferino and a romantic ambience, all Versace china, dark woods, and Italy-inspired art. If you order wine, you're in for a show, with a steward decanting your bottle using a steady hand and a candle.

CASUAL Each ship offers a large buffet restaurant with multiple serving areas. Breakfast is a standard mix of eggs, meats, fruits, cereals, and cheeses. At lunch, several of the stations will serve standard dishes while others will be given over to a different national or regional cuisine (Spanish, Greek, Asian, and so forth). Casual dining is also available nightly till 9:30pm. The line's **fresh-baked pizza** (offered in one section of the buffet noon–2am) looks a little weird, but trust us, it's fantastic—one of the highlights of the food on board. On our last *Mediterranea* cruise, a Costa staffer quipped that because it was real Italian pizza (very thin, without excess cheese and sauce), you can eat as much as you like and not get fat. We *believe* him. Out on deck there's a **grill** serving burgers and hot dogs, as well as a **taco bar** at lunch. If you're looking for another afternoon snack, head over to the ice-cream station in the buffet area, which offers daily specials such as fresh banana or coconut, along with traditional flavors.

SNACKS & EXTRAS Most cruise lines have scrapped their **midnight buffets,** but Costa still offers them nightly, often focusing on a theme taken from that evening's activity. On Mediterranean Night, the buffet offers pastry, fruits, desserts, pastas, and savories from Spain, Greece, France, and Turkey. On another night, the guests head below to the ship's massive galley for the buffet. Look for the polenta with mushroom sauce there—on our last cruise it was excellent. **Room service** is available 24 hours a day. Suite guests can order full meals delivered; all others can choose from various sandwiches, appetizers, and a full bar menu.

ACTIVITIES

More than anything else, Costa is known for its lineup of exuberant and often Italian-inspired activities, and passengers on these ships love to participate. Three nights per 7-night cruise are given over to Italian and Mediterranean themes. **Festa Italiana** turns the ship into an Italian street festival where guests are encouraged to wear the colors of the Italian flag and participate in boccie, tarantella dance lessons, pizza-dough tossing, Venetian-mask-making, and Italian karaoke. **Serata Tropical** is a deck party with a Mediterranean twist, where guests can enjoy ethnic dancing and ice-carving demonstrations amid the typical Caribbean deck party trimmings. **Mediterranean Night** transforms various parts of the ship to represent France, Turkey, Greece, and Spain, with appropriate skits, activities, singing, and games. The highlight of many cruises is **Roman Bacchanal Toga Night,** when at least some of the guests don bedsheets, with many repeat passengers bringing their own custom models and toga

Costa Fleet Itineraries

Ship	Itineraries
Costa Fortuna	**Caribbean:** Alternating 7-night eastern & western, round-trip from Ft. Lauderdale, FL (Jan–Apr). **Bermuda:** 7 nights, round-trip from Ft. Lauderdale, FL (Apr).
Costa Mediterranea	**Caribbean:** Alternating 7-night eastern & western, round-trip from Ft. Lauderdale, FL (Jan–Apr).

accouterments. (The line provides bedsheets and tying instructions for those who don't like to plan ahead.) The evening ends with the hysterical Roman Bacchanal show, which is half slapstick vaudeville and half passenger talent show. After each act, "Julius Caesar" (and the audience) decides whether to send the performers to the buffet or throw them to the lions. It's a hoot.

During the day, activities include **Italian language and cooking classes,** as well as traditional cruise staples such as jackpot bingo, dance classes, art auctions, horse racing, bridge, arts and crafts, Ping-Pong, and fun poolside competitions in which teams have to put on Roman-style costumes or don silly hats. Each ship also has a combo library and Internet center, as well as a large card room. **Enrichment lectures** focus on topics such as personal finance, romance, and health. **Aerobics and stretch classes** are usually held on the covered pool area's dance floor, which also secs live steel-drum music throughout the rest of the day. Luckily, there's lots of deck space across several levels for sunbathing, so you can escape the noise if you want to. In the stern, a fun all-ages water slide operates a couple of hours per day.

A **Catholic Mass** is held almost every day in each ship's small chapel.

CHILDREN'S PROGRAM

Costa's kids' programs aren't nearly as extensive as those on Disney or Royal Caribbean (or Carnival's Conquest-class and Spirit-class ships), but then, there are usually far fewer children on board. At least two full-time youth counselors sail aboard each ship, with additional staff whenever more than a dozen or so kids are on the passenger list. Both ships offer **supervised activities** for kids 3 to 18, divided into two age groups unless enough children are aboard to divide them into three (3–6, 7–12, and 13–18 years) or four (3–6, 7–10, 11–14, and 15–18). The **Costa Kids Club,** for ages 3 to 12, includes such activities as Nintendo, galley tours, arts and crafts, scavenger hunts, Italian-language lessons, bingo, board games, face painting, movies, kids' karaoke, and pizza and ice-cream-sundae parties. The ships each have a pleasant children's playroom and a teen disco. If there are enough teens on board, the **Costa Teens Club** for ages 13 to 18 offers foosball and darts competitions, karaoke, and other activities.

When ships are at sea in the Caribbean, supervised Kids Club hours are typically from 9am to noon, 3 to 6pm, and 9 to 11:30pm. The program also operates during port days, but on a more limited basis.

On Gala nights there's a great complimentary **Parents' Night Out program** from 6 to 11:30pm during which kids 3 and older (they must be out of diapers) are entertained and given a special buffet or pizza party while Mom and Dad get a night out alone. All other times, **group babysitting** for ages 3 and up is available every night from 9 to 11:30pm at no cost, and from 11:30pm to 1:30am if you make arrangements in advance. No private, in-cabin babysitting is available.

Children must be at least 3 months old to sail with Costa; under-2s sail free.

ENTERTAINMENT

Although the passengers are mostly American and the location is the Caribbean, expect most entertainment to be Italian, with concerts, operatic soloists, puppet or marionette shows, mimes, acrobats, and cabaret—no language skills required. On a recent cruise, one of the shows had a unicycle-riding, ball-balancing, flame-juggling, plate-spinning entertainer—the kind you used to see on *The Ed Sullivan Show.* Other featured performers included an operatic tenor singing a program of high-note crowd pleasers and a classical pianist performing Beethoven and Gershwin. The line's production shows mostly follow the typical song-and-dance revue formula, with both good elements (creative costumes and choreography, for instance) and bad (the male soloist on one *Mediterranea* cruise was the worst we've ever seen on a ship). Participatory shows are much more fun overall, and more in tune with what Costa passengers seem to want. The "Election of the Ideal Couple," and a *Newlywed Game* takeoff, for instance, both clip along at a frantic pace, with the cruise staff helping and hindering as appropriate to get the most laughs. Who knew the criterion for being an ideal couple was the ability to burst a balloon with your butt?

Both ships have glitzy casinos as well as hopping discos, which often get going only after 1am.

SERVICE

In past years our main complaint about Costa was its service, which on particularly bad nights resembled a Three Stooges skit. But things have gotten better. While it's still not the Four Seasons, our last cruises showed marked improvement, with waiters seeming better trained and more polished, cabin stewards more attentive and helpful, and everyone more accommodating and friendly.

There are no self-service laundry facilities on any of the Costa ships.

Costa Fortuna

The Verdict

Fortuna continues Costa's trend toward heavily decorated, Carnival-like interiors, but with a lighter, almost feminine feel and a "grand Italian ocean liners of the past" theme.

Costa Fortuna *(photo: Costa Cruises)*

Specifications

Size (in tons)	105,000	Crew	1,068
Passengers (double occ.)	2,720	Passenger/Crew Ratio	2.5 to 1
Passenger/Space Ratio	38.6	Year Launched	2003
Total Cabins/Veranda Cabins	1,358/522	Last Refurbishment/Upgrade	N/A

Frommer's Ratings (Scale of 1–5)   ★★★★

Cabin Comfort & Amenities	4	Dining Options	4
Appearance & Upkeep	4	Gym, Spa & Sports Facilities	5
Public Comfort/Space	4	Children's Facilities	3
Decor	4	Enjoyment Factor	4

Costa Fortuna, along with sister ship *Costa Magica* (which currently sticks to the Mediterranean and South America), was both Costa's and Italy's largest ship before the debut of the Europe-based *Costa Concordia* in summer 2006. Elegant with an old-world touch, *Fortuna*'s public rooms and restaurants are rich with detail, including memorabilia from legendary and historic Italian liners, including vintage posters and ship models. As on most Costa ships, *Fortuna*'s disco is very lively, and many public rooms stay crowded long after the last show has finished.

Cabins & Rates

Cabins	Per Diems From	Sq. Ft.	Fridge	Hair Dryer	Sitting Area	TV
Inside	$76	160	yes	yes	no	yes
Outside	$90	160	yes	yes	yes	yes
Suite	$228	275–345	yes	yes	yes	yes

CABINS   Standard cabins tend toward elegant, with soft, warm colors and magic-themed prints by Augusto Vignali. Of the 1,358 cabins, 456 have balconies, as do the 64 suites. Inside cabins are very well designed, with two closet areas, a fairly generous amount of drawer space, twin or queen bed configuration, and showers. Outside staterooms with verandas are the same size, with an additional 65 square feet of private balcony, including lounge chairs and a small table. Suites range from 275 square feet with 65-square-foot balconies to 345 square feet with 85 square feet of private veranda. All staterooms have minibars, hair dryers, and safes, and suites have whirlpool baths. Some of the furnishings, especially lamps, are unusual and charming.

Twenty-seven staterooms are wheelchair accessible.

PUBLIC AREAS   Inspired by grand Italian oceans liners of a bygone era, there's a wonderful display featuring 26 models of past and present Costa ships showcased from the ceiling of the main atrium. The restaurants and public lounge are named after famed liners, like Rex and Cristoforo Colombo. Old map replicas as well as murals of 1930s and 1940s ship scenes are found throughout the ship along with copies of vintage ship posters and ads. The line's classic "C" initial logo is imprinted in the wood of the sprawling dance floor and featured elsewhere around the ship, lending a nostalgic touch to the otherwise modern ship.

DINING OPTIONS   Although Costa's food has been uneven, the choices aboard the *Fortuna* show great improvement, and the Tavernetta Club Conte Grande restaurant is outstanding. The menu by restaurateur Zefferino has items that may be too exotic for some, but more conservative tastes have plenty of steaks, seafood, fowl, and vegetables to choose from, along with outrageously good desserts and wines. The ambience is romantic, with Versace china and gold napkins standing out against rich, dark woods and shining gold ware, with friezes from Palladio's villas reproduced around a giant skylight. The two main restaurants, Costa Michelangelo and Raffaello, feature striking memorabilia from the great Italian ocean liners of the past. At the entrance to the Michelangelo, for example, is a 19-foot scale model of the famed transatlantic liner of the same name. Copies of vintage ship posters and ads from the 1920s and 1930s are also displayed in the two restaurants. Rounding out the dining options is the Cristoforo Colombo buffet restaurant, with a seating capacity of 926 guests.

POOL, FITNESS, SPA & SPORTS FACILITIES   The 4,600-square-foot Saturnia Spa is exceptionally spacious, and a huge wall of glass extends the space even more. The multilevel gym is similarly beautiful and well equipped with Pilates balls, free weights, and yoga mats. The Technogym equipment can be programmed to parameters set for you by one of the ship's personal trainers, with a digital key that will repeat the program every time you use it. Spinning bikes, treadmills, yoga classes, and health seminars supplement the range of skincare treatments, facials, wraps, and massages at the spa. A Turkish bath and sauna are also available.

The main pool area is built like an amphitheater and is clearly a place to see and be seen. The aft lido pool is covered by a removable glass roof, and on our cruise the pool and hot tubs were in use in the evenings as well as daytime. A third pool area is dedicated to children and their families.

Costa Mediterranea

The Verdict

Is it a carnival or is it Carnivale? Decorated in a Europe-meets-Vegas style, with spacious public rooms and an almost futuristic-looking atrium-top specialty restaurant, *Mediterranea* is eye candy for the ADD set.

Costa Mediterranea *(photo: Costa Cruises)*

Specifications

Size (in tons)	85,000	Crew	920
Passengers (double occ.)	2,112	Passenger/Crew Ratio	2.3 to 1
Passenger/Space Ratio	40.2	Year Launched	2003
Total Cabins/Veranda Cabins	1,056/678	Last Refurbishment/Upgrade	N/A

Frommer's Ratings (Scale of 1–5)   ★★★½

Cabin Comfort & Amenities	4	Dining Options	3
Appearance & Upkeep	4	Gym, Spa & Sports Facilities	4
Public Comfort/Space	4	Children's Facilities	3
Decor	4	Enjoyment Factor	4

Along with European-based sister ship *Costa Atlantica*, *Mediterranea* ushered in the future for Costa, being a kind of European version of the "Fun Ships" operated by sister company Carnival. In fact, they're almost identical, built along the same lines as Carnival's Spirit-class ships and with interiors designed by Carnival's designer-in-chief, Joe Farcus. Build megaship, add tomato sauce, and stir. At nearly 1,000 feet long, *Mediterranea* cuts a sleek profile, and her bright yellow, barrel-like smokestack, emblazoned with a big blue COSTA C, distinguishes her from her Carnival cousins.

Despite the obvious success of the Spirit-class design (six Carnival and Costa ships are based on it, and Holland America has adapted it for its Vista-class vessels), we're not completely in love with it. The main public decks have a zigzagging layout that lacks the easy flow of some competitors, and some areas in the bow are downright bizarre: For instance, the wide outdoor promenade on Deck 3 ducks indoors as it goes forward, becoming a long, strange, marble-floored lounge. Is it a place to sit? Is it a place to walk? No one seems to know, so it gets hardly any use. But maybe that's a plus, making its little marble tables, wicker chairs, and small couches decent places to escape the crowds.

Cabins & Rates

Cabins	Per Diems From	Sq. Ft.	Fridge	Hair Dryer	Sitting Area	TV
Inside	$71	160	yes	yes	no	yes
Outside	$90	210	yes	yes	yes	yes
Suite	$228	360–650	yes	yes	yes	yes

CABINS   All cabins feature caramel-color wood tones and warm autumn-hued fabrics that create a pleasant environment, and well over half of the cabins have private balconies. Each has a stocked, pay-as-you-go minifridge, hair dryer, personal safe, and more than adequate storage space, and all outside cabins have sitting areas with couches. The views from all category-4 cabins on Deck 4 are completely obstructed by lifeboats, and the category-6 balcony cabins directly above, on Deck 5, are partially obstructed as well. Bathrooms have good storage space.

The 32 Panorama suites on Deck 5 and 6 measure 272 square feet, and have a 90-square-foot balcony with attractive granite coffee tables, wooden chairs, and desks. Suites have large couches that can double as a bed, two separate floor-to-ceiling closets, lots of drawer space, and large bathrooms with bathtubs, marble counters, and double sinks. Adjacent is a dressing room with a vanity table, drawers, and a closet. The Grand Suites are the largest accommodations aboard. Six are located amidships on Deck 7 and measure 372 square feet, plus 118-square-foot balconies; the other eight are aft on Decks 4, 6, 7, and 8 and measure 367 square feet, plus 282-square-foot balconies.

Eight cabins are wheelchair accessible.

PUBLIC AREAS   Interiors on the *Mediterranea* are inspired by noble 17th- and 18th-century Italian *palazzi,* and are heavy on dance and theater imagery—in fact, they're heavy on just about everything. From her carpets to her decorated ceilings, hardly any surface aboard *isn't* decorated somehow. When you first lay eyes on her *Alice in Wonderland*–like fantasyland atrium, for instance, it's a bit jarring, all bright colors, glowing light panels, textured and sculpted metal surfaces, Roman-style ceiling murals, and fiber-optic squid swarming up eight decks. Soon, though, you'll grow attached to the buttery-soft red leather chairs (including several pairs of pleasantly absurd ones with towering tall backs) and huge framed black-and-white photographs of dancers that fill the space, with its dramatic central bar and more intimate wings spreading out port and starboard. Just astern, another bar/lounge leads to the two-story dining room.

The ship's disco is a darkish, two-story, cavelike space with video-screen walls, fog machines, and translucent dance floors. The three-level theater has velvety high-backed seating and very high-tech and elaborate stages. Downstairs, on the lowest passenger deck, a smaller show lounge used for late-night comedy acts, karaoke, and cocktail parties is decorated with an underwater motif, but don't worry, you're still above the waterline. There's also a big glitzy casino with a festive Vegas-style mood, several large lounges that feature musical entertainment in the evenings, a smallish but pleasant library/Internet center, and a roomy, elegant card room. A kids' playroom, teen center, large video arcade, and Catholic chapel (one of these things is not like the others . . .) are all squirreled away in the bow on Decks 4 and 5.

DINING OPTIONS   Aside from an elegant two-story dining room, there's a two-story alternative, reservations-only restaurant high up on Deck 10, charging guests $23 per person for the privilege of dining (suite guests can go free of charge once per cruise). Its atmosphere is its best feature, with dim lights, candlelight, fresh flowers, soft live music, and lots of space between tables. On our last cruise the *Corzetti al pesto* (pasta with basil sauce) was very good, while the sea bass and flounder entrees were not great. The roasted rack of lamb was presented with a bit more care than in the main restaurant, and the chocolate parfait sabayon was a decadent and elegant finish. For a quieter and more romantic mood, the alternative restaurant is a nice change of pace, but don't linger past 10pm if you don't want cigar smoke to spoil your elegant dinner: That's when the restaurant's second story becomes a cigar lounge.

For casual breakfast, lunch, and (6 nights a week) dinner, head to the sprawling indoor/outdoor buffet restaurant. Soft ice cream and pizza made with herbs and fresh mozzarella are served from stations here. Look up when you get to the very end of the restaurant, before heading out to the stern pool area: There's a huge, amazing Murano glass chandelier up there that you'd never notice unless you craned your head on purpose.

POOL, FITNESS, SPA & SPORTS FACILITIES   *Mediterranea*'s gym is a pleasant tiered affair with machines on many different levels and a large hot tub in the center. The spa offers your typical menu of treatments, including 50-minute massages, facials, and reflexology treatments. There are three pools on Deck 9, two of them in the loud, active main pool area and another in the stern. Above the latter is a neat water slide for all ages. Other sports and relaxation amenities include four hot tubs, a golf driving net, and a combo volleyball, basketball, and tennis court. If you explore, you'll find lots of deck space for sunbathing and hiding away with a deck chair and a page turner.

5 Disney Cruise Line

P.O. Box 10210, Lake Buena Vista, FL 32830. ℭ **800/951-3532** or 888/325-2500. Fax 407/566-3541. www.disney cruise.com.

THE LINE IN A NUTSHELL   Disney's king of the hill when it comes to family fun. Though Royal Caribbean, Carnival, Celebrity, NCL, and Princess all devote significant attention to kids, it took Disney to create vessels where both kids and adults are really catered to equally, and with style and elegance. If you love Disney, you'll love these two floating theme parks. **Sails to:** Caribbean, The Bahamas, Mexican Riviera (plus Europe).

THE EXPERIENCE   Both classic and ultramodern, the line's two ships are like no others in the industry, designed to evoke the grand transatlantic liners but also boasting a handful of truly innovative features, including extralarge cabins for families, several restaurants through which passengers rotate on every cruise, fantastic Disney-inspired entertainment, separate adult pools and lounges, and the biggest kids' facilities at sea. In many ways, the experience is more Disney than it is cruise (for instance, there's no casino); but, on the other hand, the ships are surprisingly elegant and well laid out, with the Disney-isms sprinkled around subtly, like fairy dust, amid the Art Deco and Art Nouveau design motifs. Head to toe, inside and out, they're a class act.

Disney's is nothing if not organized, so its 3- and 4-night cruises aboard *Disney Wonder* are designed to be combined with a Disney theme park and hotel package to create a weeklong land/sea vacation. You can also book these shorter cruises (as well as *Disney Magic's* weeklong cruises) separately.

Pros

- **Kids' program:** In both the size of the facilities and the range of activities, it's the most extensive at sea.
- **Entertainment:** The line's family-oriented musicals are some of the best onboard entertainment today.
- **Family-style cabins:** All have sofa beds to sleep families of at least three, and the majority have 1½ bathrooms.
- **Innovative dining:** No other ships have diners rotating among three different but equally appealing sit-down restaurants.

Cons

- **Limited adult entertainment:** There's no casino or library, and adult nightclubs tend to be quiet after busy family days.
- **Small gyms:** Considering the ships' large size, their gyms are tiny.
- **Packed pools:** Though there are three pools, they're packed like sardine cans on sunny days, especially the kids' pools.
- **Expensive:** Compared to peers Royal Caribbean, Celebrity, Carnival, and Princess, Disney cruises tend to run a few hundred dollars more. Why? There are only two ships and lots of Disney lovers to fill them.

DISNEY: THE OLD MOUSE & THE SEA

For at least half a century now, Disney has been in the business of merging modern-day expectations and cutting-edge technology with a nostalgic sense of American culture: for childhood innocence, for the frontier, for an idealized turn-of-the-20th-century past, for our mythic heroes. And whether you're a fan or a critic, it's indisputable that at this point the company itself has become a part of our culture. There are probably few people alive—and certainly few Americans—who could fail to recognize Disney's more high-profile creations: Mickey, Donald Duck, Sleeping Beauty, "When You Wish Upon a Star." They've become part of our national identity. And that's why *Disney Magic* and *Disney Wonder* work so well. In nearly every aspect of the onboard experience, they have what most other ships lack: a cultural frame of reference that's recognized by almost everyone.

Though 7-night cruise itineraries are available, many Disney passengers purchase their cruises as part of 7-night seamless land/sea packages that combine 3- or 4-night cruises with 4- or 3-night pre-cruise park stays. Disney buses shuttle passengers between Orlando and the ship—about an hour's drive, during which an orientation video imparts some info about the cruise experience. At Disney's swank cruise terminal at Port Canaveral, check-in is usually made easier and faster because guests who have come from the resorts already have their all-purpose, computerized Key to the World cards, which identify them at boarding, get them into their cabins, and serve

Compared with the other mainstream lines, here's how Disney rates:

	Poor	Fair	Good	Excellent	Outstanding
Enjoyment Factor				✓	
Dining			✓		
Activities			✓		
Children's Program					✓
Entertainment					✓
Service			✓		
Worth the Money				✓	

as their onboard charge cards. (If you're doing just the cruise, you get your Key to the World card when you arrive at the terminal.) You don't have to worry about your luggage, either: It's picked up at the resort and delivered to your cabin soon after you board.

At press time, Disney has announced construction of a pair of **new 122,000-ton ships,** scheduled to debut in 2011 and 2012.

PASSENGER PROFILE

Disney's ships attract a wide mix of passengers, from honeymooners to seniors, but naturally a large percentage is made up of young American families with children (with a smallish number of foreign passengers as well). Because of this, the overall age demographic tends to be younger than that aboard many of the other mainstream ships, with many passengers in their 30s and early to mid-40s. The bulk of the line's passengers are first-time cruisers, and because the line attracts so many families (sometimes large ones), more than half of its bookings are for multiple cabins.

DINING

While Disney's food is average cruise fare, its dining concept sets it apart from the big-ship crowd.

TRADITIONAL   The neat catch with Disney's version of set dining is that there are three restaurants that passengers (and their servers) rotate among for dinner over the course of the cruise. On one night, passengers dine on dishes such as roasted duck, garlic-roasted beef tenderloin in a green peppercorn sauce, or herb-crusted Atlantic cod in *Magic*'s elegant 1930s-era **Lumiere's** restaurant or *Wonder*'s equally elegant nautical-themed **Triton's.** On another night, they enjoy the likes of potato-crusted grouper, baby back pork ribs, or mixed grill in the tropical **Parrot Cay** restaurant. And on the third, they nosh on maple-glazed salmon, pan-fried veal chop, or roasted chicken breast with smashed potatoes at **Animator's Palate,** a bustling eatery with a gimmick: It's a sort of living animation cel, its walls decorated with black-and-white sketches of Disney characters that over the course of the meal gradually become filled in with color. Video screens add to the illusion, and the waiters even disappear at some point to change from black-and-white to full-color vests. It's kinda corny, but fun.

Each restaurant has an early and a late seating, and similar groups are scheduled to rotate together as much as possible (for example, families with young children, adults alone, and families with teens). **Vegetarian options** are offered at all meals, and kosher, halal, low-salt, low-fat, and other **special diets** can be accommodated if you request them when you book your cruise, or soon thereafter; once you're aboard, a chef and head server will meet with you to determine your exact needs. Kids' menus start with appetizers such as fruit cocktail and chicken soup before heading on to such familiar entree items as meatloaf, ravioli, pizza, hot dogs, hamburger, Jell-O, and mac-and-cheese. The wine list is fair, and includes bottles by Silverado Vineyards, owned by members of the Disney family.

Magic's 7-night itineraries have 1 formal night and 1 semiformal night. The rest of the evenings are casual (no jackets or ties necessary for men). *Wonder,* with its shorter itineraries, is casual throughout the cruise, though (on both ships) sports jackets are recommended for men dining in Palo and Lumiere's/Triton's. Overall, on Heidi's last 3-night *Wonder* cruise, many went ultracasual: You could always count on a number of people in shorts and flip-flops at dinner (except for Palo).

SPECIALTY   Both ships also have a romantic adults-only restaurant called **Palo,** serving Italian specialties such as tortellini stuffed with crabmeat, grilled salmon with risotto, and excellent gourmet pizzas, such as one topped with barbecued chicken, black olives, and spinach. A decent selection of Italian wines is available, and the dessert menu includes a fine chocolate soufflé and a weird-but-tasty dessert pizza. The restaurant itself is horseshoe-shaped and perched way up on Deck 10 to offer a 270-degree view. Service is attentive but not overly formal, and you don't have to dress up, though a jacket for men may be nice. Reservations are essential, and should be made immediately after you board, as the docket fills up fast ($10 per-person cover charge).

CASUAL   Breakfast and lunch are served in several restaurants, both sit-down and buffet. Casual dinners are served on nights 2 though 6 in Topsiders *(Magic)* and Beach Blanket *(Wonder),* the indoor/outdoor buffet. This poorly designed and cramped buffet venue is the one dining outlet on the ships that just doesn't work—Heidi found that trying to squeeze through the throngs with kids and trays in tow during busy breakfast and lunch times practically qualified as a circus trick.

SNACKS & EXTRAS   A boon for families with fussy kids, Pluto's Dog House, on the main pool deck, is always bustling because of its complimentary chicken tenders, fries, burgers, nachos, bratwurst, and other quick snacks served from lunch through the dinner hour. Nearby, Goofy's Galley serves up wraps, fresh fruit, and ice cream with lots of toppings, and there's brick oven pizza at Pinocchio's Pizzeria. More highbrow options include champagne brunch (for $10 per person) on 4- and 7-night cruises and an afternoon tea on the *Magic*'s 7-night itineraries ($5 per person). On 7-night cruises, themed dining ops include breakfast with the Disney characters (for picture taking and posting) and afternoon iced tea and cookies with Peter Pan's pal Wendy. The 7-night itineraries offer the "Pirates in the Caribbean" dinner and deck party (the shorter cruises do only the deck party). It starts as a themed dinner in the restaurants, with waiters and passengers in pirate garb, and entree choices such as Black Beard's jumbo crab cakes, then moves up on deck for a party with music and lots of special effects, from black lighting to pirates rappelling from the funnel.

If you, or your kids, are soda junkies, Disney is the only mainstream line that dispenses the stuff for free! You can pour yourself a fountain soda (and then another and another) from a poolside station 24-7 on both ships, which can add up to a substantial savings for you by the end of the cruise. There's also the Cove Café, serving gourmet coffees (at an extra cost) and light fare for adults (for free!).

The **24-hour room service** menu includes kid favorites such as pizza and cookies.

Disney Fleet Itineraries

Ship	Itineraries
Disney Magic	**Caribbean:** 7-night eastern (Jan–Apr) and alternating 7-night eastern & western (Sept–Dec), round-trip from Port Canaveral, FL. **Mexican Riviera:** 7 nights, round-trip from Los Angeles, CA (May–Aug). **Panama Canal:** 15-night westbound (May) and eastbound (Aug), between Port Canaveral, FL, and Los Angeles, CA.
Disney Wonder	**Bahamas:** Alternating 3 & 4 nights, round-trip from Port Canaveral, FL (year-round).

ACTIVITIES

Unlike on pretty much every other cruise ship, there's no casino of any kind on board, not even a card room. These are family ships. Activities on both vessels include basketball, Ping-Pong, and shuffleboard tournaments; sports trivia contests; weight-loss, health, and beauty seminars; bingo, Pictionary, and other games; wine tastings; and singles mixers (though these family-focused ships aren't great choices for singles). Each ship also has a spa and a gym (surprisingly small on the *Wonder*). There are enrichment activities on all itineraries—though more on the longer 7-night routes—including galley tours, backstage theater tours, informal lectures on nautical themes and Disney history as well as current Disney productions, animation and drawing classes, Q & As with the captain, and home entertaining and cooking demos. All these activities are complimentary except wine tasting, which costs a hefty $12 per person. There are also dance classes, movies, and that cruise stalwart the Not-So-Newlywed Game, which Disney calls "Match Your Mate." All itineraries offer a captain's cocktail party with complimentary drinks once per cruise, where the master of the ship (and a bunch of Disney characters) makes an appearance. Sports fanatics can watch "the game" in the Diversions sports pub.

CHILDREN'S PROGRAM

Not surprisingly, with potentially hundreds of kids on any given sailing (1,000 is typical), Disney's kids' facilities are the most extensive at sea, with at least 50 counselors supervising the fun for five age groups between 9am and midnight daily. Nearly half a deck (comprising two huge play spaces and a nursery) is dedicated to kids. The **Oceaneer Club,** for ages 3 to 7 (with separate activities for ages 3–4 and 5–7), is a kid-proportioned playroom themed on Captain Hook. Kids can climb and crawl on the bridge, ropes, and rails of a giant pirate ship, as well as on jumbo-size animals, barrels, and a sliding board; get dressed up from a trunk full of costumes; dance with Snow White and listen to stories by other Disney characters; or play in the kiddie computer room on PlayStations. The interactive **Oceaneer Lab** offers kids ages 8 to 12 a chance to work on computers, learn fun science with microscopes, build from an enormous vat of K'nex (they're like fancy Legos), do arts and crafts, hear how animation works, and direct their own TV commercial. Activities are arranged for two groups, ages 8 to 9 and 10 to 12, and both rooms are open till at least midnight, and till 1am on certain days.

The new kids space on the *Magic* is called **Ocean Quest.** Built where three conference rooms had been on Deck 2, the hangout space geared to the 'tweens 10 to 14 features a replica of the ship's bridge, with real live footage of the real thing upstairs. Kids can sit in a traditional captain's chair and play a simulation game where they can pretend to steer the ship in and out of port. A computer simulator like this was recently added to the Oceaneer Lab on the *Wonder.* Both ships also have computer and video games, arts and crafts, and movies. Overall, new activities are being introduced all the time to keep the program fresh (some 11 in 2006, for example) for the 8-to-17 set. There's also a video arcade, though it's really cramped compared to most on Royal Caribbean, Princess, and the newest Carnival ships. Kids can eat lunch and dinner with counselors in the Topsider and Beach Blanket buffet restaurants, or one of the other dining outlets, all but the first evening of the cruise.

For teens (13–17), there's a teen hangout called **The Stack** on the *Magic* and **Aloft** on the *Wonder.* Three times the size of the old Common Grounds teen room and more isolated from mom and dad, the teen centers, each with a different design motif, have two separate rooms, one with video screens for movies and the other a teen disco with a teens-only Internet center. Dance parties, karaoke, trivia games, improv comedy lessons, and workshops on photography are offered for teens on all cruises. There are even more options on 7-night sailings, including learning how to DJ!

Neither ship offers private babysitting services. Instead, the **Flounder's Reef Nursery** for kids ages 3 months to 3 years operates from 6pm to midnight daily, and also for a few hours during the morning and afternoon (hours vary according to the day's port schedule). No other line offers such extensive care for babies. Stocked with toys and decorated with *Little Mermaid*–themed bubble murals and lighting that gives an "under the sea" look, the area also has one-way portholes that allow parents to check on their kids without the little ones seeing them. The space has cribs and counselors do change diapers (though you should bring your own). The price is $6 per child per hour, and $5 for each additional child in a family (with a 2-hr. minimum). Parents get a tuned beeper when they first check into the nursery, or the kids' program, so that counselors can contact them anywhere on the ship if their child needs them.

When the ship calls on **Castaway Cay,** Disney's private island in The Bahamas, kids can head for Scuttle's Cove, a veritable paradise for the 12-and-under set. There are barrels to crawl through, a giant whale-dig site to explore, and more; kids' counselors are on hand to supervise the fun if mom and dad want to head to Serenity Bay, the adults-only beach. For families who want to play together, there are bike rentals and lots more. For details, see section 1, "The Cruise Lines' Private Islands," in chapter 10.

ENTERTAINMENT

Disney's fresh, family-oriented entertainment is some of the very best at sea. On both ships, performances by Broadway-caliber entertainers in the nostalgic Walt Disney Theatre include *Disney Dreams,* a sweet musical medley of Disney classics, taking the audience from *Peter Pan* to *The Lion King;* and the *Golden Mickeys,* a tribute to Disney films through the years that combines song and dance, animated film, and special effects. On *Wonder,* there's also a staging of *Hercules, A Muse-ical Comedy,* a salute to the popular Disney film that's part story, part song, and part stand-up comedy. The *Magic* also offers three other shows: *Twice Charmed: An Original Twist on the Cinderella Story; All Aboard: Let the Magic Begin Variety Show;* and the *Remember the Magic* show. On both ships, the stage design allows for lots of magic, with actors flying above the boards and disappearing in and out of trap doors, but the most refreshing thing about these shows is that they have story lines—rare almost to the point of extinction in the cruise world, which mostly presents musical revues.

Family game shows (including a trivia contest called "Mickey Mania" and another, *"Who Wants to Be a Mouseketeer,"* in the spirit of the millionaire quiz show) and karaoke take place in the **Studio Sea family nightclub.** Adults (18 and older) can take advantage of the **adults-only entertainment area** in the forward part of Deck 3, with its three themed nightclubs: one quiet, with piano music or soft jazz (with the kids safely tucked away in the Flounder's Reef nursery, Heidi and her husband enjoyed a great evening listening to a pianist tickle the ivories in the romantic Cadillac Lounge on the *Wonder*); the second a dance club; and the third, Diversions, a combination pub and sports bar. Another nightspot is the **Promenade Lounge,** where live music is featured daily. The **Buena Vista Theater** shows movies day and evening.

SERVICE

Just as at the parks, Disney staff hail from some 60 countries, including the United States. Service in the dining rooms is efficient and precise, but leans toward friendly rather than formal. The crew keeps the ship exceptionally clean and well maintained. Overall, things run very smoothly.

Though the ships typically sail full and are bustling, the crew seems to remain perpetually good-natured and smiley. When Heidi was last on *Wonder,* everyone from the young crewmember doling out nonstop trays of chicken tenders at Pluto's Dog House to the gals working at the nursery and the ultrasmooth maitre d's at the restaurants seemed to really like their job. The "happy to serve" mentality trickles right on up to the officer level too: The captain personally autographs guests' scrapbooks, photographs, and mementos in a public area at least once per cruise, while top officers participate in the beloved Disney "pin-trading" sessions. So, what makes everyone work so dang hard? Hotel Director Mike Mahendran told Heidi that performance expectations are high, but that it certainly doesn't hurt that crew members earn 10% to 30% more than the industry standard, and enjoy other perks that foster productivity.

It's no great surprise that travel agents tell us many guests rate service among the top features of a Disney Cruise.

Services include **laundry** and **dry cleaning** (the ships also have self-service laundry rooms) and 1-hour photo processing. Tips can be charged to your onboard account, which most passengers opt for, or you can give them out in the traditional method: cash.

Disney Magic • Disney Wonder

The Verdict

The only ships on the planet that successfully re-create the grandeur of the classic transatlantic liners, albeit in a modern, Disneyfied way.

Disney Magic *(photo: Disney Cruise Line)*

Specifications

Size (in tons)	83,000	Year Launched	
Passengers (double occ.)	1,754*	*Magic*	1998
Passenger/Space Ratio	47.3	*Wonder*	1999
Total Cabins/Veranda Cabins	877/378	Last Refurbishment/Upgrade	
Crew	950	*Magic*	2005
Passenger/Crew Ratio	1.8 to 1	*Wonder*	2006

* Note: *With children's berths filled, capacity can go as high as 3,325.*

Frommer's Ratings (Scale of 1–5)   ★★★★½

Cabin Comfort & Amenities	5	Dining Options	4.5
Appearance & Upkeep	5	Gym, Spa & Sports Facilities	3
Public Comfort/Space	4	Children's Facilities	5
Decor	5	Enjoyment Factor	5

These long, proud-looking ships carry 1,754 passengers at the rate of two per cabin, but because Disney is a family company and its ships were built expressly to carry three, four, and five people in virtually every cabin, the ship could theoretically carry a whopping 3,325 passengers. Although numbers rarely reach that high, Hotel Director Mike Mahendran told Heidi they rarely carry fewer than 2,500 passengers. Though service is a high point of a Disney cruise and the ships are well laid out, these high numbers mean certain areas of the ship will feel crowded at times, namely the kids' pool area, the buffet restaurants, and the photo gallery and shops after dinner. Overall, though, the ships are well laid out and frequently updated and upgraded, most recently the *Wonder* in 2006 and the *Magic* in 2005.

Cabins & Rates

Cabins	Per Diems From	Sq. Ft.	Fridge	Hair Dryer	Sitting Area	TV
Inside	$117	184–214	yes	yes	yes	yes
Outside	$193	226–268	yes	yes	yes	yes
Suite	$407	259–1,029	yes	yes	yes	yes

CABINS   The Disney ships offer the family-friendliest cabins at sea, with standard accommodations equivalent to the suites or demisuites on most ships—they're about 25% larger than the industry standard. All of the 877 cabins have at least a sitting area with a sofa bed to sleep families of three (or four if you put two small children on the sofa bed, as Heidi did when her boys were just under 2 years old). Some cabins also have one or two pull-down bunks to sleep families of four or five. Nearly half have private verandas. One-bedroom suites have private verandas and sleep four or five comfortably; two-bedroom suites sleep seven. Outside cabins that don't have verandas have jumbo-size porthole windows.

The decor is virtually identical from cabin to cabin, combining modern design with nostalgic ocean-liner elements such as a steamer-trunk armoire for kids, globe- and telescope-shaped lamps, map designs on the bedspreads, and a framed black-and-white 1930s shot of Mr. and Mrs. Walt Disney aboard the fabled ocean liner *Rex*. Warm wood tones predominate, with Art Deco touches in the metal and glass fittings and light fixtures. The majority of cabins have two bathrooms—a sink and toilet in one and a shower/tub combo and a sink in the other (both of them compact, though with ample shelf space). This is something you won't find in any other standard cabin industry-wide, and it's a great boon for families. All cabins have a minifridge (empty), hair dryer, safe, TV, tub/shower combo, sitting area, and lots of storage space.

One-bedroom suites are done up with wood veneer in a definite Deco mood. Sliding frosted-glass French doors divide the living room from the bedroom, which has a large-screen TV, queen-size bed (which can be split to make two twins), chair and ottoman, dressing room, makeup table, and whirlpool tub in the bathroom. A second guest bathroom is located off the living room, which also has a bar and a queen-size sofa bed. The veranda extends the length of both rooms. Two-bedroom and Royal suites are also available.

Sixteen cabins are fitted for wheelchair users.

PUBLIC AREAS   Both ships have several theaters and lounges, including an adults-only area with three separate venues: a piano/jazz lounge, disco, and sports-pub-cum-karaoke bar. There's also a family-oriented entertainment lounge called Studio Sea for game shows, karaoke, and dancing; the Promenade Lounge for classic pop music in the evenings; and a 24-hour Internet cafe with eight flatscreen stations. The Cove Café is a comfy place for gourmet coffees (for a price) or cocktails in a relaxed setting with books, magazines, Internet stations, Wi-Fi access, and TVs. A 270-seat cinema shows mostly recent-release Disney movies; both ships have a new jumbo 336-square-foot screen attached to the forward funnel outside on Deck 9 that shows classic Disney animated films. The children's facilities, as you'd expect, are the largest of any ship at sea (see "Children's Program," above, for details).

Throughout, both ships have some of the best artwork at sea, owing to Disney's vast archive of animation cels, production sketches, costume studies, and inspirational artwork, featuring characters we've all grown up with. Other art—notably the "Disney Cruise Line Seaworthy Facts" near the photo shop and A-to-Z of seagoing terms near the theater—was created specifically for the ships and gets a big, big thumbs up. Canned music pumped into the public areas and corridors tends toward big-band music and crooner tunes or surf-type pop.

DINING OPTIONS   Disney's unique rotation dining setup has guests sampling three different restaurants at dinner over the course of their cruise, with an adults-only specialty restaurant also available, by reservation only (see "Dining," earlier in this review). At breakfast and lunch, the buffet-style spread in *Magic*'s Topsider and *Wonder*'s Beach Blanket restaurants offers deli meats, cheeses, and rice and vegetable dishes, as well as a carving station, a salad bar, and a dessert table with yummy chocolate chip cookies. Though the culinary offerings are fine, the layout and tiny size of the place are not. During the morning rush, for example, it's tough to squeeze through the place, let alone with kids and a tray full of breakfast. Be prepared to dine elsewhere if the place is packed.

Options for afternoon noshing poolside include Pinocchio's Pizzeria; Pluto's Dog House for hot dogs, hamburgers, chicken tenders, fries, and more; and an ice-cream bar (which also includes a generous selection of toppings). There's 24-hour room service from a limited menu, but no midnight buffet unless you count the spread offered at the evening deck party held once per cruise and the dessert buffet offered once on 7-night itineraries. Instead, hors d'oeuvres are served to passengers in and around the bars at about midnight.

POOL, FITNESS, SPA & SPORTS FACILITIES   The pool deck of each ship has three pools: Mickey's Kids' Pool, shaped like the mouse's big-eared head, with a great big white-gloved Mickey hand holding up a snaking yellow slide (this pool can get crooooww-ded!); Goofy's Family Pool, where adults and children can mingle; and the Quiet Cove Adult Pool, with whirlpools, gurgling waterfalls, teak deck and lounge chairs with plush cushions, a poolside bar, and a coffee spot called Cove Café. On sunny days, the kids' pool will feel like a sardine can—watch those canon balls! A consolation prize for families with young children, adjacent is a splash pool with circulating water for diaper-wearing babies and toddlers. It's the only one at sea as the lines' official party line is no diaper-wearing children (and that includes pull-ups and swim diapers) are allowed in any pool, wading or adult, for hygiene reasons. On *Wonder*, there's a new larger toddler pool that now sports interactive fountains and splash zones.

Just beyond the adult pool area at the stern is a spa and gym, which is newly refurbished and expanded to twice its size on both ships. The Steiner-managed Vista Spa & Salon is impressive, with attractive tiled treatment rooms and a thermal suite with a sauna, steam room, misting shower, and heated contoured tile chaise longues. Among the many treatments is a selection geared to teens. Both ships' spas have been remodeled and three spa villas were added. Each one is an indoor treatment suite that's connected to a private outdoor veranda with a personal hot tub, an open-air shower, and a chaise longue. Sounds great, yes, but renting one isn't cheap! They can be reserved for one person or couples. A 50-minute massage for one in a spa villa, for example, is $199 and it includes 55 more minutes in the villas to enjoy tea, a soak in the hot tub, and what Disney calls a "foot bathing ceremony." (The couples' version of this villa treatment is $449 per couple and includes a pair of 50-min. massages and 70 min. to loll about the villa afterward.) Both ships have an outdoor Sports Deck with basketball and paddle tennis. There are also shuffleboard and Ping-Pong, and joggers and walkers can circuit the Promenade Deck, which is generally unobstructed (though the forward, enclosed section may be closed off when the ship is arriving and departing port because it's adjacent to the anchor mechanisms).

6 Holland America Line

300 Elliott Ave. W., Seattle, WA 98119. ℂ **877/724-5425** or 206/281-3535. Fax 800/628-4855. www.holland america.com.

THE LINE IN A NUTSHELL   Holland America has been in business since 1873, and has managed to hang on to more of its seafaring history and tradition than any line today except Cunard. It offers a moderately priced, classic, and casual yet refined cruise experience. **Sails to:** Caribbean, Panama Canal, Alaska, Mexico, Hawaii, Canada/New England (plus Asia, Australia/New Zealand, Europe, South America, and Africa).

THE EXPERIENCE   Holland America is a classy operation, offering all-around appealing cruises with a touch of old-world elegance and such cushy amenities as plush bedding and flat-panel TVs with DVD players in all cabins. Though the line has been retooling itself to attract younger passengers and families, it still caters mostly to older folks, and so generally offers a more sedate and stately experience than other mainstream lines, plus excellent service for the money. Its fleet, which until a few years ago consisted of midsize, classically styled ships, is in the process of being supersized, and the new Vista-class megaships are a mite bolder in their color palette, that's for sure. New or old, the vessels are all well maintained and have excellent (and remarkably similar) layouts that ease passenger movement. More so on the pre-Vista-class ships, throughout the public areas of the fleet you'll see flowers that testify to Holland's place in the floral trade, Indonesian touches that evoke the country's relationship with its former colony, and seafaring memorabilia that often harks back to Holland America's own history.

Pros

- **Great service:** HAL's primarily Indonesian and Filipino staff is exceptionally gracious and friendly.
- **Traditional classic ambience:** The Vista-class ships are pushing the HAL envelope, but overall the line's ships are classy, with impressive art collections and a touch of traditional ocean-liner ambience.
- **Chocolate!** The once-per-cruise dessert extravaganzas and the occasional spreads of sweets guarantee you'll gain a few pounds.

Cons

- **Sleepy nightlife:** While there are always a few stalwarts and a couple of busyish nights, these aren't party ships. If you're big on late-night dancing and barhopping, you may find yourself partying mostly with the entertainment staff.
- **Fairly homogenous passenger profile:** Although younger faces are starting to pepper the mix (especially on 7-night cruises to warm-weather destinations), most HAL passengers still tend to be low-key, fairly sedentary 55-plus North American couples.

HOLLAND AMERICA: GOING DUTCH

One of the most famous shipping companies in the world, Holland America Line was founded in 1873 as the Nederlandsch-Amerikaansche StoomvAart Maatschappij (Netherlands-American Steamship Company). Its first ocean liner, the original *Rotterdam,* took her maiden, 15-day voyage from the Netherlands to New York City in 1872. By the early 1900s, the company had been renamed Holland America and was one of the major lines transporting immigrants from Europe to the United States, as well as providing passenger/cargo service between Holland and the Dutch East Indies via the Suez Canal. During World War II, the company's headquarters moved from Nazi-occupied Holland to Dutch-owned Curaçao, then the site of a strategic oil refinery, and after the war the company forged strong links with North American interests. The line continued regular transatlantic crossings up until 1971, and then turned to offering cruises full time. In 1989, it was acquired by Carnival Corporation, which improved the line's entertainment and cuisine while maintaining its overall character and sense of history. Today, most of HAL's vessels are named for other classic vessels in the line's history—*Rotterdam,* for example, is the sixth HAL ship to bear that name—and striking paintings of classic HAL ships by maritime artist Stephen Card appear in the stairways on every ship.

Compared with the other mainstream lines, here's how HAL rates:

	Poor	Fair	Good	Excellent	Outstanding
Enjoyment Factor				✓	
Dining				✓	
Activities			✓		
Children's Program		✓			
Entertainment				✓	
Service					✓
Worth the Money					✓

In addition to introducing its first three megaships in the past few years, by late 2006 HAL had completed a fleetwide $225-million upgrade program it calls "Signature of Excellence." All staterooms now have flat-panel plasma TVs and DVD players, extrafluffy towels, and terry-cloth bathrobes, plus new massage shower heads, lighted magnifying makeup mirrors, and salon-quality hair dryers. There's more: You'll find plush triple-sheeted mattresses and 100% Egyptian cotton bed linens in all cabins. Suites have new duvets, fully stocked minibars, and personalized stationery, and all suite guests have access to a one-touch 24-hour concierge service and exclusive concierge lounge. In addition to an expanded lecture series, each ship now sports a really cool demonstration kitchen where a Culinary Arts program offers interactive programs about food and wine. Fleetwide, there's a combination lounge, library, coffee shop, and Internet cafe called the "Explorations Café," and pretty dramatically upgraded facilities for kids. Spa facilities have been enhanced to match the Greenhouse Spas introduced on the line's Vista-class megaships, with new treatments, expanded fitness and treatment facilities, a thermal suite (a kind of New Age steam room), and a hydrotherapy pool (a souped-up hot tub).

Though Holland America offers cruises in every major region covered in this book, it's particularly strong in Alaska. In 1971, it acquired Westours, a pioneering tourism company founded by the late Chuck West (who also created small-ship line Cruise West), and over the years it's acquired more and more Alaska properties, including trains, river cruisers, and hotels. The line operates one of the most extensive land-tour operations in the state, so many passengers opt to combine their cruise with a visit to Denali and Kenai Fjords national parks, Fairbanks, and/or Canada's Yukon Territory and Kluane National Park.

Holland America is building a new pair of 2,044-passenger, 86,000-ton ships, called the **Signature class,** that are due in summer 2008 and spring 2010. Both ships are being built by Italy's Fincantieri shipyards.

PASSENGER PROFILE

For years, HAL was known for catering to an almost exclusively older crowd, with most passengers in their 70s on up. Today, following intense efforts to attract younger passengers, about 40% of the line's guests are under age 55 (with the average age being 57), with a few young families peppering the mix, especially in summers and during holiday weeks. While the average age skews a bit lower on the newer Vista-class ships, HAL just isn't Carnival or Disney, and its older ships especially were designed with older folks in mind. On cruises longer than a week, there's no shortage of canes, walkers, and wheelchairs.

Passengers tend to be amiable, low-key, better educated than their equivalents aboard sister line Carnival, and much more amenable to dressing up—you'll see lots of tuxedos and evening gowns on formal nights. Though you'll see some people walking laps on the Promenade Deck, others taking advantage of the ships' gyms, and some taking athletic or semiadventurous shore excursions, these aren't terribly active cruises, and passengers overall tend to be sedentary. HAL has a very high repeat-passenger rate, so many of the people you'll see aboard will have sailed with the line before.

Parties for solo travelers (only 30–40 of whom tend to be on any particular cruise) encourage mixing, and you can ask to be seated with other solo passengers at dinner. On cruises of 10 nights or longer, gentlemen hosts sail aboard to provide company for single women, joining them at dinner as well as serving as dance partners.

DINING

Much improved over the years, Holland America's cuisine is fine, but hardly memorable. On a recent cruise, meals in the main restaurant were hit-and-miss, ranging from so-so to pretty good.

TRADITIONAL In the line's lovely formal restaurants, appetizers may include prawns in spicy wasabi cocktail sauce, duck pâté, deep-fried hazelnut brie, and escargot; the soup-and-salad course always includes several options, from a plain house salad and minestrone to a chilled raspberry bisque and spicy two-bean soup; and main courses are heavy on **traditional favorites** such as broiled lobster tail, grilled salmon, beef tenderloin, roast turkey, seared tuna steak, grilled pork chop, and filet mignon. Those wanting something less substantial can opt for lighter dishes such as grilled fish or chicken, and fresh fruit medley. A few entrees on most dinner menus are marked as signature dishes recommended by Master Chef Rudi Solamin, and include the likes of a salmon tartare with avocado appetizer and, as a main course, chicken *cordon bleu*. Some vegetarian entrees are available on the main menu, but you can also ask for a **full vegetarian menu,** with half a dozen entrees and an equal number of appetizers, soups, and salads. (Don't miss the tofu stroganoff and celery-and-stilton soup if they're offered—yum.) Children can enjoy tried-and-true staples such as pizza, hot dogs, burgers with fries, chicken fingers, and tacos, plus chef's specials such as pasta and fish and chips. The **wine list** comprises about 70% U.S. vintages, with the rest from Europe, Chile, and Australia.

During the first half of 2008, Holland America will introduce a new **As You Wish Dining** program similar to Princess's Personal Choice program. At booking, passengers will be asked to choose either traditional early or late seating dining (at the same table nightly, served on one level of the ship's main restaurant) or a completely flexible schedule (offered from 5:15 to 9pm nightly on the restaurant's other level). Guests opting for flexible dining can make reservations during the day or just show up whenever they like. By late January, the program will be in place aboard *Noordam, Ryndam, Volendam, Statendam, Oosterdam,* and *Rotterdam,* followed by *Zaandam* and *Westerdam* (Feb), *Zuiderdam* (Mar), *Veendam* and *Maasdam* (Apr), and *Amsterdam* and *Prinsendam* (May).

SPECIALTY Aboard every vessel, the intimate Pinnacle Grill restaurant offers a menu of mostly steaks, chops, and fish. Options many include such dishes as Dungeness crab cakes, pan-seared rosemary chicken with cranberry chutney, wild mushroom ravioli with pesto cream sauce, or lamb rack chops with drizzled mint sauce, plus premium beef cuts. All entrees are complemented with regional wines from Chateau Ste. Michelle, Canoe Ridge, Willamette Valley Vineyards, and others. The cover charge is $20 per person for dinner and $10 for lunch. On a recent *Statendam* outing, the service was top rate and the food exceeded our expectations. Don't miss the opportunity to dine here at least once per cruise. Make reservations as early as possible when you come aboard. In addition to dinners, alternative restaurants may be open for lunch on sea days.

CASUAL As has become industry standard, **casual dining** is available each night in the ships' buffet-style Lido restaurants, which also serve breakfast and lunch. They're some of the best-laid-out buffets at sea, with separate stations for salads, desserts, drinks, and so on, keeping lines and crowding to a minimum. Diners here are offered open seating from about 6 to 8pm. Tables are set with linens and a pianist may provide background music; but service is buffet style, with waiters on hand to serve beverages. The set menu features the basics: Caesar salad, shrimp cocktail, or fresh-fruit-cup appetizer; French onion soup; freshly baked dinner rolls; and entree choices, which may include salmon, sirloin steak, roast chicken, and lasagna, served with a vegetable of the day and a baked potato or rice pilaf. Most main dishes are similar to what you'll find in the main restaurant that evening. At lunch, the buffet restaurants offer pasta, salads, stir-fry, burgers, and, usually, an ethnic option, like an Indian shrimp curry, sushi, or Dutch crepes. Pizza and ice-cream stations are open till late afternoon. Out on the Lido Deck, by the pool, a **grill** serves hamburgers, hot dogs, veggie and turkey burgers, and a special of the day, such as knackwurst or spicy Italian sausage, between about 11:30am and 6pm. A **taco bar** nearby offers all the fixings for tacos or nachos, and it's generally open about the same hours. Once a week, the Lido also hosts a **barbecue buffet dinner.**

SNACKS & EXTRAS   Once per cruise, a special Royal Dutch High Tea features teatime snacks and music provided by the ships' string trio, making it one of the most truly "high" among the generally disappointing high teas offered on mainstream lines. On other days, a more standard **afternoon tea** has white-gloved waiters passing around teeny sandwiches, scones, and cookies in the dining room or one of the main lounges. We're told a new Indonesian Tea and Coffee Ceremony will also be offered once a cruise and feature such goodies as spring rolls, sweet rice balls, and coconut. Pizza, soft ice cream, and frozen yogurt round out the afternoon offerings.

Free hot canapés are served in some of the bars/lounges during the cocktail hour, and free iced tea and lemonade are served on deck, one of many thoughtful touches provided at frequent intervals by the well-trained staff. The new **Explorations Café** has a coffee bar that serves a premium Starbucks blend, for a charge.

Each evening around midnight, a spread of snacks is available in the Lido restaurant, and at least once during each cruise the dessert chefs get to go wild in a midnight **Dessert Extravaganza.** Cakes are decorated with humorous themes, marzipan animals guard towering chocolate castles, and trays are heavy with chocolate-covered strawberries, truffles, cream puffs, and other sinful things.

Room service is available 24 hours a day and is typically efficient and gracious. A plus, the breakfast options include eggs and meats, not just pastries and cereals like most mainstream ships offer. You can also order room service on the final morning of the cruise, another rarity.

ACTIVITIES

Though varied and fun, HAL's onboard activities tend to be low-key. You can take ballroom dance lessons; take an informal class in photography; play bingo or bridge; sit in on a trivia game or Pictionary tournament; participate in Ping-Pong, golf-putting, basketball free-throw, or volleyball tournaments; take a gaming lesson in the casino or an aerobics class at the gym; take a self-guided iPod tour of the ship's art collection or a backstage theater tour; go high-toned at a wine tasting; or go low-toned at the goofy games poolside or in a lounge. During one frisky relay-race-like team game called Seaquest on a recent 14-night cruise, a group of mostly senior passengers enthusiastically slipped off their bras and dropped their drawers in the name of friendly competition—the team that deposited more undergarments on the show lounge stage won. The place was a sea of geriatric goofballs tottering around in their boxer shorts or (yikes!) briefs, crumbled trousers in hand. It was a riot. Talk about young at heart.

Some cruises also feature model shipbuilding contests in which you can use only junk you can find around the ship, with seaworthiness tested in one of the ship's hot tubs. Each ship has a great **Explorations Café**, which is a combo Internet center, coffee bar, and library set in a well-traveled part of each ship. Comfy lounge chairs come equipped with music stations and headphones. Generous shelves of books, DVDs, and games line the walls, and a magazine stand holds current issues of popular magazines plus the latest edition of various newspapers, when the ship can get them. If you're a crossword buff you can tackle the *New York Times*' crossword puzzles embedded under glass in the room's cafe tables (wax pencils are provided). Explorations also functions as the Internet cafe, but passengers toting their Wi-Fi–enabled laptops can take advantage of wireless hot spots here and throughout the ship. Another of the fleet's newer offerings is the **Culinary Arts** center, which includes free cooking demos, usually twice per 7-day cruise (go early to get a front-row seat, or sit in the back and watch the food preparation on the flat-panel TVs around the room), and more intimate, hands-on cooking classes (available for a charge). The center is also used for other demos, such as flower arranging.

On 7-night Alaska cruises, Native artists demonstrate traditional arts such as ivory and soapstone carving, basket weaving, and mask making as part of the line's **Artists in Residence Program,** created under the auspices of Anchorage's Alaska Native Heritage Center. Another program offered during visits to Glacier Bay brings a member of the Huna tribe aboard to talk about the land, which the Huna have called home for centuries. In Hawaii and Mexico, cultural dancers perform for passengers.

CHILDREN'S PROGRAM

Holland America isn't Disney—and they don't claim to be—but they're trying harder to cater to families with children. The biggest change to the Club HAL program a few years back is the lowering of the age minimum from 5 years down to 3. If there are more than about 30 kids aboard, activities are programmed for three age brackets (3–7, 8–12, and 13–17), and there's always at least one counselor on board every sailing, and more when demand warrants. You'll find the most children on cruises during summers and holiday weeks. At these times, there may be as many as 300 to 400 kids aboard the Vista-class ships, especially in the Caribbean, though around 100 to 200 is typical overall. When there are fewer than 20 or 30 kids, a two-tiered Club HAL program is offered—children 3 to 12 in one group, teens in another—on a limited basis, generally about 6 hours on sea days and even fewer hours on port days. On cruises with more children, activities are offered for three or more age groupings and for much longer hours. Typically, each evening kids receive a program detailing the next day's activities, which may include arts and crafts, cooking classes, youth sports tournaments, movies and videos, scavenger hunts, PlayStations, disco for teens, storytelling for younger kids, miniature golf, charades, bingo, Ping-Pong, and pizza, icecream, and pajama parties. The playrooms typically operate on a limited schedule on port days, and in the Caribbean the line offers kids' activities on its private beach, Half Moon Cay (see section 1, "The Cruise Lines' Private Islands," in chapter 10). All the ships have dedicated playrooms with separate teen centers with video screens and a dance floor; the Statendam-class ships even have a totally cool outdoor space sequestered away on a top deck for teens called the Oasis, a beachlike setting complete with a waterfall, hammocks, and chaise longues. Otherwise, the playrooms are bright and cheerful, though they lack the ball jumps, padded climbing and crawling areas, and fanciful decor that make kids' facilities aboard Disney, Royal Caribbean, Princess, NCL, and Celebrity so compelling.

Group babysitting in the playroom is offered between 10pm and midnight for $5 per hour for ages 3 to 12. In-cabin babysitting is also offered, assuming a crewmember is available. The cost is $8 an hour for the first child (minimum age 12 weeks), and $5 per hour for additional kids. Inquire at the guest services desk.

Children must be 12 weeks or older to sail aboard.

Holland America Fleet Itineraries

Ship	Itineraries
Amsterdam	**Panama Canal:** 22 nights, New York, NY, to Seattle, WA (Apr). Shorter segments bookable from Ft. Lauderdale, with debarkation in Los Angeles, CA, and Vancouver, BC. **Alaska:** 7-night Inside Passage, round-trip from Seattle, WA (May–Sept).
Eurodam	**New England/Canada:** 10 nights, north- or southbound between Quebec City, QC, and New York, NY (Sept). **U.S. East Coast/Canada:** 14 nights, Quebec City, QC, to Ft. Lauderdale, FL (Oct). **Bahamas:** 3 nights, round-trip from Ft. Lauderdale, FL (Oct). **Caribbean:** 7-night eastern, round-trip from Ft. Lauderdale (Oct–Dec).
Maasdam	**Caribbean:** 10-night southern, round-trip from Ft. Lauderdale, FL (Jan–Apr & Oct–Dec). **Panama Canal:** 15-night eastbound and westbound between San Diego, CA, and Ft. Lauderdale, FL (Jan–Feb). **New England/Canada:** 7 nights, north- or southbound between Boston, MA, and Montreal, QC (May–June & Aug–Sept). **U.S. East Coast/Canada:** 13 nights, Fort Lauderdale, FL, to Montreal, QC (May). 10 nights, Montreal, QC, to Ft. Lauderdale, FL (Oct).
Noordam	**Caribbean:** 10- & 11-night southern/eastern, round-trip from New York, NY (Jan–Mar & Oct–Dec).
Oosterdam	**Mexican Riviera:** 7 nights, round-trip from San Diego, CA (Jan–Apr & Nov–Dec). **Alaska:** 7-night Inside Passage, round-trip from Seattle, WA (May–Sept).
Ryndam	**Mexican Riviera:** 7 nights (Oct), 10 nights (Feb–Apr & Oct–Dec), 11 nights (Sept), 12 nights (Apr), and 14 nights (Dec), round-trip from San Diego, CA.
Statendam	**Alaska:** 7-night Inside Passage, round-trip from Vancouver, BC (May–Sept). **Panama Canal:** 16-night eastbound, San Diego, CA, to Ft. Lauderdale, FL (Oct). **Caribbean:** 7- & 14-night southern, round-trip from Ft. Lauderdale, FL (Dec).
Veendam	**Caribbean:** 7-night western (Jan–Apr & Nov–Dec) & 14-night southern (Jan–Mar & Nov), round-trip from Tampa, FL. **Panama Canal:** 19 nights, Tampa, FL, to San Diego, CA (Apr). **Panama Canal/South America/Caribbean:** 36 nights, Vancouver, BC, to Tampa (Sept). **Alaska:** 7-night Inside Passage, round-trip from Vancouver, BC (May–Sept). 7-night Gulf of Alaska, north- or southbound between Vancouver and Seward/Anchorage, AK (May–Sept).
Volendam	**Panama Canal:** 10 nights, round-trip from Ft. Lauderdale, FL (Jan–Apr). 19-night westbound, Ft. Lauderdale to Vancouver, BC (Apr). **Alaska:** 7-night Gulf of Alaska, north- or southbound between Vancouver and Seward/Anchorage, AK (May–Sept).
Westerdam	**Caribbean:** Alternating 7-night eastern, western and southern, round-trip from Ft. Lauderdale, FL (Jan–Mar & Oct–Dec). **Bahamas:** 3 nights, round-trip from Ft. Lauderdale, FL (Apr). **Panama Canal:** 19-night westbound (April) and 18-night eastbound (Sept), between Ft. Lauderdale, FL, and Seattle, WA. **Alaska:** 7-night Inside Passage, round-trip from Seattle, WA (May–Sept).
Zaandam	**Alaska:** 7-night Gulf of Alaska, north- or southbound between Vancouver and Seward/Anchorage, AK (May–Sept).
Zuiderdam	**Caribbean:** 7-night eastern, round-trip from Ft. Lauderdale, FL (Jan–Mar). **Panama Canal:** 10-night, round-trip from Ft. Lauderdale, FL (Nov–Dec).

ENTERTAINMENT

Don't expect HAL's shows to knock your socks off, but hey, at least they're trying. Each ship features small-scale **Vegas-style shows,** with live music (except on the Vista-class ships, where, we're told, there isn't enough space for a live orchestra in the main show lounges—ain't that the pits?), laser lights, and lots of glimmer and shimmer. Overall, though, you'll find better quality entertainment from the soloists, trios, and quartets playing jazz, pop, and light-classical standards.

Recent-release movies are shown an average of twice a day in an onboard cinema, with free popcorn available for the full movie effect. There's also a **crew talent show** once a week, in which crewmembers (Indonesians one week, Filipinos the next) present songs and dances from their home countries. **Passenger-participation shows** are a different animal, with the crowd-pleasing *American Idol*–style contest called "Superstar" featuring passenger crooners being critiqued by a staff of judges (who are definitely nicer than Simon).

Aboard each ship, one of the lounges becomes a disco in the evening, with a small live band generally playing before dinner and a DJ taking over for after-dinner dancing. The new Vista-class ships have the line's first dedicated discos, and on the other ships, the Crow's Nest lounges have been redecorated for a more disco-y feel.

SERVICE

Holland America is one of the few cruise lines that maintains a real training school (a land-based school in Indonesia known in HAL circles as "ms Nieuw Jakarta") for the selection and training of staffers, resulting in service that's efficient, attentive, and genteel. The soft-spoken, primarily Indonesian and Filipino staffers smile more often than not and will frequently remember your name after only one introduction, though they struggle occasionally with their English. (Be cool about it: Remember, you probably can't speak even a word of Bahasa Indonesia or Tagalog.) During lunch, a uniformed employee may hold open the door of a buffet, and at dinnertime, stewards who look like vintage hotel pages walk through the public rooms ringing a chime to formally announce the dinner seatings.

Like many other lines these days, HAL now automatically adds **gratuities** to passengers' shipboard accounts, at the rate of $10 per day, adjustable up or down at your discretion. A 15% service charge is automatically added to bar bills and dining room wine accounts.

Only the Vista-class ships (and the *Prinsendam*) come with minifridges standard in cabins. On the other vessels, they can be rented for $2 a day (inquire before your cruise if you're interested). All cabins have complimentary fruit baskets on embarkation day. A new early-boarding program allows guests to get aboard in the port of embarkation as early as 11:30am, when some lounges and facilities will be open for their use, although cabins generally won't be ready until 1pm.

Onboard services on every ship in the fleet include **laundry** and **dry cleaning.** Each ship—except the new Vista-class ships, oddly enough—also maintains several **self-service laundry rooms** with irons.

Preview: HAL's New *Eurodam*

In addition to the ships reviewed in this chapter, Holland America will be setting its newest ship, the 2,044-passenger, 86,000-ton *Eurodam,* on itineraries to the Caribbean, the Bahamas, and New England/Canada following her summer 2008 launch. The ship will be the largest ever for Holland America, slightly edging out the 1,848-passenger, 85,000-ton *Zuiderdam, Oosterdam, Westerdam,* and *Noordam.* She'll boast a new 144-seat Pan-Asian restaurant, a new Italian specialty restaurant, an expanded Greenhouse Spa and Salon with thermal suites and a hydro-pool, and the largest gym ever built for HAL.

The Vista Class: Zuiderdam • Oosterdam • Westerdam • Noordam

Zuiderdam *(photo: Holland America Line)*

The Verdict

Holland America's first foray into megasize ships married traditional HAL style with a partying Caribbean feel; by the time the *Westerdam* was launched, and the kinks were worked out, the relationship was working.

Specifications

Size (in tons)	85,000	*Oosterdam*	2003
Passengers (double occ.)	1,848	*Westerdam*	2004
Passenger/Space Ratio	46	*Noordam*	2006
Total Cabins/Veranda Cabins	924/623	Last Refurbishment/Upgrade	
Crew	800	*Zuiderdam*	2005
Passenger/Crew Ratio	2.3 to 1	*Oosterdam*	2006
Year Launched		*Westerdam*	2006
Zuiderdam	2002	*Noordam*	N/A

Frommer's Ratings (Scale of 1–5)   ★★★★

Cabin Comfort & Amenities	4.5	Dining Options	4
Appearance & Upkeep	4	Gym, Spa & Sports Facilities	4.5
Public Comfort/Space	4	Children's Facilities	3
Decor	3.5	Enjoyment Factor	4

Built on a similar design as Carnival's Spirit-class ships, *Zuiderdam* (named for the southern point of the Dutch compass, and with a first syllable that rhymes with "eye"), *Oosterdam* (eastern, and with a first syllable like the letter *O*), *Westerdam*, and *Noordam* (northern compass point) are Holland America's biggest ships to date, though their 85,000-ton, 1,848-passenger size doesn't put them anywhere in the running among today's true behemoths, and relatively speaking, they're downright cozy. Still, the line hopes they'll help it finally shed its image as your grandmother's cruise line and compete better for the all-important baby boomer and family cruise dollars. Can't fault them for that, but let's just say hipness isn't something you can grow overnight. *Zuiderdam,* the first of the series, came off totally unnatural, like a 60-something banker trading in his Mercedes and suits for a red Corvette and tight black jeans. Its peculiar style—mixing ultrabright Carnival-esque colors, stark W Hotel modernism, and the traditional style for which HAL was previously known—was toned down some for sister ship *Oosterdam*, introduced in 2003. By the time the *Westerdam* came on the scene, the new look was refined, though there still are ultrabright pockets, such as the lemon-yellow and grape leather furniture in the piano bar. The fourth and final sister, *Noordam* (which replaced the previous *Noordam*, which left the fleet in Nov 2004), seems to do it just right, mixing classic wine reds, dark blues, and earth tones, with just a hint of zany, seen in the silver framed benches in the elevator landings and in the Pinnacle Grill and Pinnacle Bar. Overall, this class is a winner, especially the *Westerdam* and *Noordam*. In the spirit of learning from their mistakes, HAL has gone back and tweaked parts of the *Zuiderdam*, replacing some of the loudest carpeting with darker shades, for example, and even removing some of the more jarring "art" pieces. The giant red lips are gone and so is the ice-block sculpture in the disco, which was replaced with a more benign wall of video screens. All four sisters are extraordinarily spacious, with large standard cabins, truly glamorous two-level dining rooms, and distinctive specialty restaurants.

Cabins & Rates

Cabins	Per Diems From	Sq. Ft.	Fridge	Hair Dryer	Sitting Area	TV
Inside	$82	185	yes	yes	no	yes
Outside	$91	194–200	yes	yes	yes	yes
Suite	$168	298–1,000	yes	yes	yes	yes

CABINS Cabins in all categories are comfortable and, as aboard every HAL ship, are among the industry's largest, with a simple decor of light woods, clean lines, and subtly floral bedding. Overall, more than two-thirds of them have verandas, with the deluxe veranda suites and staterooms in the stern notable for their deep balconies, nearly twice the size of those to port and starboard. You get a romantic view of the ship's wake, too, but because the decks are tiered back here, residents of the cabins above you can see right down. Keep your clothes on.

Standard outside and veranda cabins all have a small sitting area and a tub in the bathroom—a relatively rare thing in standard cabins these days. Closet space in all categories is more than adequate for 7-night cruises, with nicely designed fold-down shelves and tie rack. Each has a flatscreen TV and DVD player, makeup mirror, real hair dryer, massage shower head, bathrobes, and extrathick super-comfortable bedding. Dataports allow passengers to access e-mail and the Internet from every cabin via their own laptops.

Suites run from the comfortably spacious Superior Veranda Suites (with wide verandas, large sofa bed, walk-in closet, separate shower and bathroom, and extra windows) to the Penthouse Veranda Suites—extremely large multiroom apartments with a flowing layout, pantry, palatial bathrooms with oversize whirlpool baths, and ridiculously large private verandas with a second, outdoor whirlpool. Their decor is reminiscent of 1930s moderne style. Guests in every suite category have use of a concierge lounge whose staff will take care of shore-excursion reservations and any matters about which you'd normally have to wait in line at the front desk. The lounge is stocked with reading material, coffee, and juice, and a continental breakfast is served daily.

Twenty-eight cabins are wheelchair accessible.

PUBLIC AREAS Public rooms on the Vista-class ships run the gamut from the traditional to the modern, and from the lovely to the weird (again, we're talking mostly the *Zuiderdam* and *Oosterdam*) when wacky color schemes go the way of blinding oranges, red, and purples. The more traditional spaces, done mostly in blues, teals, burgundys, and deep metallics, include the signature Explorer's Lounge, a venue for quiet musical performances and high tea. The top-of-the-ship Crow's Nest lounge, an observation lounge during the day and nightclub/disco at night, offers wide-open views, comfortable leather recliners toward the bow (a perfect reading perch during days at sea), and even a few rococo thrones on the starboard side, good for "wish you were here" cruise photos. The rear port corner of the Crow's Nest is the most truly elegant lounge area aboard, with high-style, striking, and comfortable furniture; it's also one of the ships' Wi-Fi hot zones.

Lower Promenade Deck is the hub of indoor activity on these ships. In the bow, the three-deck Vista Lounge is the venue for large-scale production shows, while the Queen's Lounge/Culinary Arts Center at midships hosts chef demos by day and comedians and other cabaret-style acts in the evening. Between the two there's a piano bar and a casino, the latter really flashy on all but the *Noordam*. You'll also find HAL's first-ever dedicated discos, but they're uninspired at best (and, on *Zuiderdam,* just butt-ugly). Our favorite room, the Sports Bar, looks as little like the standard rah-rah sports-hero-and-pennants sports bar as you can imagine, with comfortable free-form leather seating and table lamps. *Très* chic. Only the multiple TVs give away the place's true identity.

One deck up, the traditional Ocean Bar wraps around the understated three-deck atrium—whose focal point on all ships is a Waterford crystal chandelier—with bay windows to port and starboard looking out onto the promenade and the room's namesake. Moving forward, you pass through the drab shopping arcade, whose displays spill right into the central corridor courtesy of retractable walls, forcing you to browse as you walk from stem to stern. A lot of lines are doing this and it's a pretty crass sales pitch; it gets a big thumbs-down from us. Once you get through, you come to Explorations Café, the ships' hub, and a combination specialty coffee shop, Internet center, and library, with HAL's signature inlaid marble tables.

Other public rooms include the Main Deck's Atrium Bar, a very comfortable small-scale nook vaguely reminiscent of a 1930s nightclub; the wicker-furnitured outdoor Lido Bar on the Lido Deck (which unfortunately lacks the charm of similar spaces on the line's older ships); and the KidZone and WaveRunner children/teen centers, which are a bit bare, though roomy and sunny. Art in the public areas of the ships includes maritime artwork by Stephen Card, replica 18th-century Dutch engravings, ship models, and on the *Zuiderdam,* some nice humorous paintings by Hans Leijerzapf, commedia dell'arte statues, and jazz sketches and paintings by Wil van der Laar. *Oosterdam*'s Java Corner has several sketches of landmark Frank Lloyd Wright designs.

Oceanview elevators at port and starboard midships are a little boxy, closing off some of the intended inspiring views. Much better views are to be had from outdoor areas forward on Decks 5, 6, and 7, and from an area just forward of the gym, above the bridge. You can even check a ship's compass here.

DINING OPTIONS   The main Vista Dining Room is a two-deck affair, decorated traditionally but with nice touches of modernism, for instance in the *Zuiderdam*'s black, high-backed wooden chairs, which are very sharp. On the *Noordam,* the elegant space is a throwback with wine-red fabrics, darkish woods, and a cozy living-room-like feeling. It's a lovely dining room. The ship's alternative Pacific Northwest restaurant, the 130-seat Pinnacle Grill, wraps partially around the three-deck atrium—ask for a table by the windows or in the aft corner for the coziest experience. The design is appealing, with marble floors, bright white linens, gorgeous Bulgari place settings, and ornate, organically sculpted chairs by Gilbert Libirge, who also created the ships' beautiful, batik-patterned elevator doors.

Diners wanting something more casual can opt for the well-laid-out and attractive Lido buffet restaurant; the outdoor Grill for burgers, dogs, and the like; or, on all but the *Noordam,* the Windstar Café, serving specialty coffees (for a price), snacks, and light meals in a tall-ship atmosphere.

POOL, FITNESS, SPA & SPORTS FACILITIES Gyms are well equipped with a full complement of cardio equipment and weight machines arranged in tiers around the cardio floor; the space is attached to another room where you'll find chaise longues and a large dipping pool. There's also a basketball/volleyball court on the Sports Deck. The Greenhouse Spa is fully 50% larger than any other in the HAL fleet, and besides offering the usual massage, mud, and exotic treatments, it has a couple of HAL firsts: a thermal suite (a series of saunas and other heat-therapy rooms) and a hydrotherapy pool, which uses heated seawater and high-pressure jets to alleviate muscle tension. Oddly, there's no compelling design motif like you'd find in other signature spas. Around the pool, extraheavy wooden lounge chairs are thick-padded and nap-worthy. The pool area doesn't quite work on *Zuiderdam,* where the colors are jarring and the materials cheap looking, but as in many other areas, *Oosterdam*'s, *Westerdam*'s, and *Noordam*'s are a vast improvement, very pleasant all around.

Outdoors, the wraparound Promenade Deck is lined with classy wooden deck chairs—a nice touch of classic ocean-liner style—and is popular with walkers and joggers. The main pool deck is the hub of outdoor activity on sea days, with hot tubs, music, and pool games, and can be covered with a sliding roof in inclement weather. The hallmarks of the pool area on both ships are giant bronze animal statues—from a polar bear, to a penguin and dolphin. Another pool, in the stern on Lido Deck, is a lovely spot for sunbathing and open views of the sea.

Rotterdam • Amsterdam

The Verdict

Modern throwbacks to the glory days of transatlantic travel without the stuffiness or class separation, these attractive, gloriously midsize sisters offer great features, from classic art to rich mahogany woodwork and elegant yet understated public rooms.

Amsterdam *(photo: Holland America Line)*

Specifications

Size (in tons)		Crew	
Rotterdam	56,652	*Rotterdam*	593
Amsterdam	61,000	*Amsterdam*	647
Passengers (double occ.)		Passenger/Crew Ratio	
Rotterdam	1,316	*Rotterdam*	2.2 to 1
Amsterdam	1,380	*Amsterdam*	2.1 to 1
Passenger/Space Ratio		Year Launched	
Rotterdam	43	*Rotterdam*	1997
Amsterdam	44.2	*Amsterdam*	2000
Total Cabins/Veranda Cabins		Last Refurbishment/Upgrade	
Rotterdam	658/161	*Rotterdam*	2005
Amsterdam	690/172	*Amsterdam*	2005

Frommer's Ratings (Scale of 1–5)

★★★★½

Cabin Comfort & Amenities	4.5	Dining Options	4
Appearance & Upkeep	4	Gym, Spa & Sports Facilities	4.5
Public Comfort/Space	5	Children's Facilities	3
Decor	5	Enjoyment Factor	4.5

With 3 years separating them, near-twins *Rotterdam* and *Amsterdam* combine classic elegance with contemporary amenities and provide a very comfortable cruise, especially on itineraries of 10 nights and longer. Carrying just over 1,300 passengers double occupancy, they're a breath of fresh air in the sea of super-megaships that ply the oceans these days. *Rotterdam,* the sixth HAL ship to bear that name, is popular with passengers who previously sailed aboard the legendary *Rotterdam V,* which was sold in 1997. At press time, it appears that *Rotterdam* will not be sailing from any U.S. ports in 2008.

Like the rest of the fleet, the ships were upgraded to feature HAL's Signature of Excellence enhancements, including the Explorations Café Internet center and coffee shop, beefed-up kids' facilities, a culinary-arts demonstration kitchen, and upgraded cabin amenities.

Cabins & Rates

Cabins	Per Diems From	Sq. Ft.	Fridge	Hair Dryer	Sitting Area	TV
Inside	$182	no	yes	yes	yes	
Outside	$197	no	yes	yes	yes	
Suite	$225–937	yes	yes	yes	yes	

CABINS Unlike the beige color schemes of the older Statendam-class ships, the decor here is livelier, with corals, mangoes, blues, and whites brightening things up. The standard cabins are among the most spacious at sea and offer enough hanging and drawer space for 10-night-plus cruises. Bathrooms are generous as well, with bathtubs in all but the standard inside cabins (and, on *Amsterdam,* in a handful of outsides as well). Each cabin has a sitting area, a desk, a safe, two lower beds convertible to a queen, and great reading lights above each bed, in addition to the line's new amenities: flat-panel plasma TVs and DVD players, terry-cloth bathrobes, massage shower heads, lighted magnifying makeup mirrors, and salon-quality hair dryers. Beds now have plush, amazingly comfy triple-sheeted mattresses and 100% Egyptian cotton bed linens.

Veranda Suites are 225 square feet and have a 59-square-foot private veranda; Deluxe Veranda Suites measure 374 square feet and have a 189-square-foot veranda and a dressing room. Both have sitting areas, whirlpool tubs, and stocked minibars, and are kept stocked with fresh fruit. Penthouse Suites measure 937 square feet and have a 189-square-foot veranda, living room, dining room, guest bathroom, and an oversize whirlpool tub. All suite guests have use of a concierge lounge whose staff will take care of shore-excursion reservations and any matters about which you'd normally have to wait in line at the front desk. The lounge is stocked with reading material, and a continental breakfast is served daily.

Twenty-one cabins are wheelchair accessible.

PUBLIC AREAS Both ships have great, easy-to-navigate layouts that allow passengers to move easily among public rooms. Most of the inside public areas are concentrated on two decks; ditto for the pools, sunning areas, spa, sports facilities, and buffet restaurant, which are all on the Lido and Sports decks.

Overall, the ships give you the feeling of an elegant old hotel, with dark red and blue upholstery and leathers, damask fabrics, mahogany tones, and gold accents. Artwork is everywhere, from the stairwells to the walkways on the Promenade and Upper Promenade decks. Aboard *Amsterdam,* the theme is Dutch and nautical; aboard *Rotterdam* it's Continental and Asian. In *Amsterdam*'s atrium, a clock tower combines an astrolabe, a world clock, a planetary clock, and an astrological clock. You can't miss it; it's been wedged into the space with barely an inch to spare. *Rotterdam*'s passengers are greeted in the atrium by a large reproduction Flemish clock.

The new Explorations Café is a main hub on the ships and the place to check your e-mail or surf the Web while enjoying a cappuccino.

The Ocean Bar serves complimentary hot hors d'oeuvres before dinner nightly, and passengers pack into the bar to listen and dance to a lively trio. More elegant is the Explorer's Lounge, whose string ensemble performs a classical repertoire. Nearby is the open-sided piano bar, featuring a red lacquered baby grand piano on the *Amsterdam.*

The Crow's Nest observation lounge/disco gets fairly little use during the day unless there's a special event being held (such as line-dance classes), but it's a popular spot for pre-dinner cocktails and after-dinner dancing. Near the room's entrance on *Amsterdam* you'll see the *Four Seasons* sculptures originally created for the old *Nieuw Amsterdam* in 1938, and purchased back by the line from a private collector. On *Rotterdam,* a highlight of the Crow's Nest is the life-size terra-cotta human and horse figures, copies of ancient statues discovered in Xian, China.

The *Amsterdam*'s main showroom, perhaps the brightest of the rooms, is done in red and gold and is more a nightclub than a theater. Sit on the banquettes for the best sightlines, as alternating rows of individual chairs sit lower and don't permit most passengers to see over the heads of those in front of them. The balcony offers decent sightlines.

Other public rooms include a large casino, library, card room, and the Wajang Theater for movie viewing and also the spot where HAL's Culinary Arts demonstration kitchen resides.

DINING OPTIONS Aboard both ships, the attractive two-level formal dining rooms have floor-to-ceiling windows and an elegant, nostalgic feel, and never seem crowded. The Pinnacle Grill seats fewer than 100 diners and offers romantic, intimate Pacific Northwest cuisine in an elegant setting. The only downside here: no windows. And be careful of those funky chairs; they tip forward if you lean too far toward your soup. Aboard *Amsterdam,* make a point of looking at the paintings, all of which have a joke hidden somewhere on the canvas—look for the RCA "his master's voice" dog on the Italian rooftop, and for Marilyn Monroe by the lily pond.

As in the rest of the fleet, a casual buffet-style breakfast, lunch, and dinner are offered in the Lido restaurant, a bright, cheerful place done in corals and blues. It's a well-laid-out space, with separate salad, drink, deli, dessert, and stir-fry stations. There's a taco bar poolside at lunchtime, and pizza is available in the afternoon.

POOL, FITNESS, SPA & SPORTS FACILITIES *Amsterdam* and *Rotterdam* have spacious, well-equipped gyms with a very large separate aerobics area, floor-to-ceiling ocean views, plenty of elbowroom, and a nice spa. There's a pair of swimming pools: one amidships on the Lido Deck, with a retractable glass roof and a pair of hot tubs, and another smaller, less trafficked and thus more relaxing one in the stern, letting on to open views of the ship's wake. Both ships have great wraparound Promenade decks lined with wooden deck chairs, a quiet and nostalgic spot for reading, snoozing, or—especially on *Amsterdam's* Alaska itineraries and *Rotterdam's* Europe cruises—scoping the scenery.

There's a combo volleyball and tennis court on the Sports Deck, and Ping-Pong tables are on the Lower Promenade in the sheltered bow.

Volendam • Zaandam

The Verdict

These handsome ships represent a successful marriage of HAL's usual elegance and gentility with a well-done dose of classy modern pizzazz. And they're an ideal size too: big enough to offer lots of amenities and small enough to be much more intimate than today's jumbo megaships.

Volendam *(photo: Holland America Line)*

Specifications

Size (in tons)	63,000	Year Launched	
Passengers (double occ.)	1,440	*Volendam*	1999
Passenger/Space Ratio	43.7	*Zaandam*	2000
Total Cabins/Veranda Cabins	720/197	Last Refurbishment/Upgrade	
Crew	647	*Volendam*	2005
Passenger/Crew Ratio	2.2 to 1	*Zaandam*	2005

Frommer's Ratings (Scale of 1–5)   ★★★★½

Cabin Comfort & Amenities	4.5	Dining Options	4
Appearance & Upkeep	4	Gym, Spa & Sports Facilities	4.5
Public Comfort/Space	5	Children's Facilities	3
Decor	5	Enjoyment Factor	4.5

Introduced at the turn of this century, *Volendam* and *Zaandam* marked Holland America's first steps into a more diverse, mainstream future, offering an experience designed to attract the vital 40-something boomers while still keeping the line's core older passengers happy. The ships have alternative restaurants, Internet centers, and huge gyms that many lines attracting younger crowds can't match, but their overall vibe is more traditional than Carnival, Princess, and Royal Caribbean—and, for that matter, than the line's newer and much more glitzy Vista-class vessels. These are classy, classic ships, but with just a touch of funk to keep things from seeming too old-fashioned—note the autographed Bill Clinton saxophone and Iggy Pop guitar in *Zaandam's* elegant Sea View Lounge.

These ships, along with the rest of the HAL fleet, were upgraded with the line's Signature of Excellence enhancements, including the Explorations Café Internet center, beefed-up kids' facilities, a Culinary Arts demonstration kitchen, and upgraded cabin amenities.

Cabins & Rates

Cabins	Per Diems From	Sq. Ft.	Fridge	Hair Dryer	Sitting Area	TV
Inside	$110	186	no	yes	yes	yes
Outside	$120	196	no	yes	yes	yes
Suite	$214	284–1,126	yes	yes	yes	yes

CABINS   In a word: roomy. These standard cabins are among the largest in the industry, and with a much more modern, daring look than on the line's older ships. Fabrics are done in salmon red, burgundy, gold, and bronze, and the walls in a striped pale-gold fabric, hung with gilt-framed prints. Bathrooms are roomy and well designed, with adequate storage shelves and counter space. All outside cabins have shower/tub combos (short tubs, but tubs nonetheless), while inside cabins have only showers. Cabin drawer space is plentiful, and closets are roomy, with great shelves that fold down if you want to adjust the configuration of space. There's a storage drawer under each bed.

All cabins have sitting areas, plus Holland America's Signature of Excellence enhancements, from flat-panel TVs and DVD players, to terry-cloth bathrobes, massage shower heads, lighted magnifying makeup mirrors, and salon-quality hair dryers. Beds are supercomfy with plush new triple-sheeted mattresses and 100% Egyptian cotton bed linens.

On the Verandah and Navigation decks, 197 suites and minisuites have balconies, including the single gorgeous Penthouse Suite, which measures 1,126 square feet, including veranda, and is adorned with one-of-a-kind pieces such as 19th-century Portuguese porcelain vases and Louis XVI marble table lamps.

Twenty-one cabins are wheelchair accessible.

PUBLIC AREAS   *Volendam*'s public areas are floral-themed; *Zaandam*'s sport musical motifs. Aboard *Volendam,* each aft staircase landing has a still-life painting of flowers, and a spot outside the library has a collection of elaborate delft tulip vases (ironically, with fake silk tulips). You could even call the gorgeous graduated colors in the show lounge seating florally themed, with colors from magenta to marigold creating a virtual garden in bloom. *Zaandam*'s theme is exemplified by one of the more bizarre and inspired atrium decorations we know of—a huge, mostly ornamental baroque pipe organ decorated with figures of musicians and dancers—as well as by numerous musical instruments scattered around the ship in display cases, from a classic Ornette Coleman–style plastic Grafton sax in the Sea View Lounge to the elaborate Mozart harpsichord display (with busts and a candelabra) outside the card room. The display of electric guitars in the atrium stair tower, signed by Queen, Eric Clapton, the Rolling Stones, says something about HAL's drive to attract younger passengers—even if "younger" means 50-somethings.

In general, as aboard almost the entire HAL fleet, public areas are very easy to navigate. Corridors are broad, and there's little chance of getting lost or disoriented. Surfaces and fabrics overall are an attractive medley of subtle textures and materials, from tapestry walls and ceilings to velveteen chairs, marble tabletops, and smoky glass. *Volendam* even has a red-lacquer piano and suede walls woven to resemble rattan. *Zaandam's* pianos are all funky: The one in the piano bar is painted to look as though it's made of scrap lumber and rusty nails; the one in the Lido restaurant is downright psychedelic.

The main hub of the ship for many is the Explorations Café, a combination Internet center and coffee bar, with plenty of comfy seating and magazines to read.

The warm and almost glowingly cozy Explorer's Lounge is another favorite area, along with the nearby Sea View Lounge and the adjacent piano bar, with its round, pill-like leather bar stools and plush sofas. On busy nights, the Ocean Bar can get crowded by the bar, but there's usually plenty of space across the room or near the dance floor, where a live jazz band plays danceable music before and after dinner.

The ever-popular Crow's Nest nightclub has been redesigned and now has features such as banquettes in bright, modern colors and translucent white floor-to-ceiling curtains that function both as decor and movable enclosures for private events. Cocktail mixology classes and other events are offered here during the day; after dinner, it becomes the ships' disco and nightclub. The Culinary Arts demo kitchen shares space with the Wajang Theater, and is the venue for at least two cooking demonstrations per cruise that are hosted by well-regarded chefs. As on other HAL vessels, the ships' main showrooms are two-story affairs with movable clusters of single seats and banquettes on the ground level in front of the stage so passengers can get comfortable.

Both vessels have impressive art and antiques sprinkled throughout their public areas. The booty on *Volendam* includes an authentic Renaissance fountain outside the casino (the ship's most pricey piece), an inlaid marble table in the library (a HAL signature), and a small earthenware mask dating from 1200 B.C. that's kept in a display case near the Explorer's Lounge. On *Zaandam,* an area outside the library features reproductions of Egyptian jewelry and a huge repro Egyptian statue fragment.

DINING OPTIONS   The two-story main dining rooms are truly glamorous, framed with floor-to-ceiling windows and punctuated by dramatic staircases. A classical trio serenades guests from a perch on the top level. Just outside the second level of the dining room is a place women won't want to miss: a wonderful powder room with ocean views and lots of elbowroom for primping, with vanity tables and stools in one room and the toilets and sinks adjacent. Both ships also feature HAL's fleetwide Pacific Northwest specialty restaurant, the intimate Pinnacle Grill (see "Dining," on p. 170).

The Lido buffet restaurants are attractive and efficiently constructed, with separate stations for salads, desserts, and beverages, cutting down on the chance of monstrously long lines. A sandwich station serves its creations on delicious fresh-baked breads.

POOL, FITNESS, SPA & SPORTS FACILITIES   The gyms on these ships are attractive and roomy, with floor-to-ceiling windows surrounding dozens of state-of-the-art machines. The ship's spa was recently upgraded and you won't be disappointed with the offerings.

Three pools are on the Lido Deck: a small and quiet aft pool (behind the Lido buffet restaurant) and the main pool and wading pool, located under a retractable glass roof in a sprawling area that includes the pleasant, cafelike Dolphin Bar, with rattan chairs and shade umbrellas. There are more isolated areas for sunbathing above the aft pool on a patch of the Sports Deck and in little slivers of open space aft on most of the cabin decks. The Sports Deck also has a pair of practice tennis courts, as well as shuffleboard. Joggers can use the uninterrupted Lower Promenade Deck to get their workout.

The Statendam Class: Statendam • Maasdam • Ryndam • Veendam

The Verdict

These ships are well made and designed, and certainly hold their own in this age of gigantic circuslike megas. Public areas are functional and appealing, with just a dash of glitz and plenty of classic European and Indonesian art.

Veendam *(photo: Holland America Line)*

Specifications

Size (in tons)	55,451	*Maasdam*	1993
Passengers (double occ.)	1,266	*Ryndam*	1994
Passenger/Space Ratio	43.8	*Veendam*	1996
Total Cabins/Veranda Cabins	633/149	Last Refurbishment/Upgrade	
Crew	602	*Statendam*	2005
Passenger/Crew Ratio	2.1 to 1	*Maasdam*	2006
Year Launched		*Ryndam*	2004
Statendam	1993	*Veendam*	2004

Frommer's Ratings (Scale of 1–5)   ★★★★

Cabin Comfort & Amenities	4	Dining Options	4
Appearance & Upkeep	4	Gym, Spa & Sports Facilities	4
Public Comfort/Space	5	Children's Facilities	3
Decor	4	Enjoyment Factor	4.5

Refreshingly intimate, agile, and handsome looking, these four vessels are, like all the HAL ships, extremely well laid out and easy to navigate. Holland America's 55,451-ton Statendam-class ships are cozy at one-third the size of the today's biggest megas and, relatively speaking, are classics at ages running from 12 to 15. Decor is a subdued scheme of earthy tones and traditional art works. Touches of marble, teak, polished brass, and multi-million-dollar collections of art and maritime artifacts lend a classic ambience, and many decorative themes emphasize the Netherlands' seafaring traditions. The onboard mood is low-key (though things get dressy at night), the cabins are large and comfortable, and there are dozens of comfortable nooks all over the ships in which you can curl up and relax. And, there's hardly anything more appealing about a ship than a sleek hull with a dark paint job, tiered aft decks, and a long sweeping foredeck—these are covered in teak, offering passengers a great place to view the passing scenery.

The S-ships were recently upgraded and now feature HAL's Signature of Excellence enhancements, most notably an Explorations Café Internet center, improved kids' facilities, a Culinary Arts demonstration kitchen, and upgraded cabin amenities.

Cabins & Rates

Cabins	Per Diems From	Sq. Ft.	Fridge	Hair Dryer	Sitting Area	TV
Inside	$85	186	no	yes	yes	yes
Outside	$95	197	no	yes	yes	yes
Suite	$170	284–1,126	yes	yes	yes	yes

CABINS   Cabins are roomy, unfussy, and comfortable, with light-grained furniture and fabrics in safe shades of blue, beige, and burgundy. Show curtains separate the sleeping area from the sitting area. White-gloved stewards add a hospitable touch. All cabins have twin beds that can be converted to a queen and, in some cases, a king, all with plush triple-sheeted mattresses and 100% Egyptian cotton bed linens—the most comfortable cruise ship beds Heidi has ever slept on. About 200 cabins can accommodate a third and fourth passenger on a foldaway sofa bed and/or an upper berth. Closets and storage space are larger than the norm, and bathrooms are well designed and well lit, with bathtubs in all but the lowest category. All cabins have personal safes and music channels, plus flat-panel TVs and DVD players (great if you have kids—bring those cartoons from home!), terry-cloth bathrobes, massage shower heads, lighted magnifying makeup mirrors, and salon-quality hair dryers.

Outside cabins have picture windows and views of the sea, though those on the Lower Promenade Deck have pedestrian walkways (and, occasionally, pedestrians) between you and the ocean. Special reflective glass prevents outsiders from spying in during daylight hours. To guarantee privacy at nighttime, you have to close the curtains. No cabin views are blocked by dangling lifeboats or other equipment.

Minisuites are larger than those aboard some of the most expensive lines, such as SeaDream. Full suites are 563 square feet, and the Penthouse Suite sprawls across a full 1,126 square feet. Suite passengers have the choice of three pillow types. Six cabins are outfitted for passengers with disabilities, and public areas are also wheelchair friendly, with spacious corridors, wide elevators, and wheelchair-accessible public toilets.

PUBLIC AREAS   For the most part, public areas are subdued, consciously tasteful, and soothing. The Sky Deck offers an almost 360-degree panorama where the only drawback is the roaring wind. One deck below, almost equivalent views are available from the ever-popular Crow's Nest nightclub, which has been redesigned in a fresh, new way. Highlights include a subtly glowing bar; banquettes in bright, modern colors; and translucent white floor-to-ceiling curtains that function as both decor and movable enclosures for private events. Cocktail mixology classes and other events are offered here during the day; after dinner, it becomes the ships' disco and nightclub where theme parties and dancing take place. The ships' small, three-story atria are pleasant enough and refreshingly unglitzy, housing the passenger-services and shore-excursions desks as well as officers' offices.

The ships' two-story showrooms are modern and stylish, but overdone. On the *Statendam,* for instance, muted gold columns blend elegantly with lovely tile mosaic work in shades of blue and green. Unlike aboard most ships, which have rows of theater-like seats or couches, the lower levels are configured with cozy groupings of cushy banquettes and chairs that can be moved. The balcony, however, has bench seating, with low backs that make it impossible to lean back without slouching.

The trendiest spot is the Explorations Café, a well-stocked library and Internet center with a coffee bar and ocean views. A buzzing hub of activity, there are 12 computer stations and several plug points for those going wireless with laptops. Five leather chaise longues partnered with CD players and headphone stations face the sea through floor-to-ceiling windows, while other clusters of couches and chairs are set among the generous shelves of periodicals and books, which include everything from travel to fiction, science, history, gardening, and reference titles. A magazine rack holds current issues of popular magazines and newspapers, when the ship can get them. If you're a crossword buff, you can tackle the *Times'* puzzles embedded under glass in the room's cafe tables (wax pencils are provided).

There's a dark and cozy piano bar, where requests are taken, or head to the elegant Explorer's Lounge, a popular venue for high tea in the afternoon and for light classical and parlor music after dinner. A live band plays for dancers before dinner in the very popular Ocean Bar, and the nice-size casinos are spacious though not as pleasingly designed as aboard the line's newer ships. A small movie theater shows films a few times a day, and this space also houses the new Culinary Arts demonstration kitchen—the movie screen descends in front of the kitchen during showtimes.

For children, the youngest play in a bright but smallish room decorated like a giant paint box, and preteens have a karaoke machine and video games. Lucky teens, however, get the Oasis, a top-deck sun deck with a wading pool with waterfall, teak deck chairs, hammocks, colorful Astroturf, and lamps designed as metal palm trees, all enclosed by a bamboo fence. This would be a great space for group events on sailings with few kids aboard.

DINING OPTIONS   These ships have elegant, two-story main dining rooms at the stern, with dual staircases swooping down to the lower level for grand entrances and a music balcony at the top where a duo or trio serenades diners. Ceilings are glamorous with their lotus-flower glass fixtures, and two smaller attached dining rooms are available for groups. HAL's specialty restaurant, the Pinnacle Grill (see "Dining," on p. 170), has a classy, more modern feel to it.

The casual indoor/outdoor buffet restaurant is well laid out, with separate stations for salads, desserts, and drinks, which helps keep lines to a minimum. The restaurant serves breakfast, lunch, and dinner daily, and its pizza and ice-cream stations are open until just before dinner. An outdoor grill on the Lido Deck serves burgers and other sandwich items throughout the afternoon, and a nearby station allows you to make your own tacos or nachos at lunch.

POOL, FITNESS, SPA & SPORTS FACILITIES   Each ship has a sprawling expanse of teak-covered aft deck surrounding a swimming pool. One deck above and centrally located is a second swimming pool, plus a wading pool, hot tubs, and a spacious deck—all under a sliding glass roof to allow use in Alaska, or in inclement weather elsewhere. Imaginative, colorful tile designs and a dolphin sculpture add spice, and the attractive Dolphin Bar, with umbrellas and wicker chairs, is the perfect spot for a drink and snack in the late afternoon after a shore excursion.

The Sports Deck of each ship has combo basketball/tennis/volleyball courts, and the lovely Lower Promenade Deck offers an unobstructed circuit of the ship for walking, jogging, or just lounging in the snazzy, traditional-looking wooden deck chairs. The ships' windowed Ocean Spa gyms offer a couple of dozen exercise machines, a large aerobics area, steam rooms, and saunas. The redesigned Greenhouse Spas are an improvement, each including thermal suites with a hydrotherapy whirlpool and heated tile loungers.

The Forward Observation Deck, a huge expanse of open teak deck, is accessible only via two stairways hidden away in the forward (covered) portion of the Promenade Deck, and so gets little use. But don't miss going there. There's no deck furniture here, but standing in the very bow as the ship plows through the ocean is a wonderful, wonderful experience.

7 Imperial Majesty Cruise Line

4161 NW 5th St., Suite 200, Plantation, FL 33317-2158. ℃ 800/394-3865 or 954/453-4625. Fax 954/453-4626. www.imperialmajesty.com.

THE LINE IN A NUTSHELL   Imperial Majesty offers nothing but 2-night round-trips between Fort Lauderdale and Nassau, year-round. The one big reason to sail? The line's ship, the 1953-vintage *Regal Empress*, is probably the last chance you'll ever get to sail on a real, old-fashioned ocean liner. They don't make 'em like this anymore. **Sails to:** Nassau, Bahamas.

THE EXPERIENCE   If you want to get a glimpse of what ocean travel was like in the 1950s, plunk down a couple of hundred bucks and take a quick ride aboard *Regal Empress*. Today, the 55-year-old vessel is more over-the-hill vaudeville trouper than glamorous star, but she's one of the very few working ships where you can see the kind of woody interiors and chunky steelwork that characterized the great old liners. She's a real ship-ship, totally unlike today's hotel-like megaships. Former owners Regal Cruises (see below) kept her in good shape, initiating several well-planned refurbishments that ripped out bad, glitzy '80s additions and reemphasized the classic elements of her decor. Let's not be dishonest, though: The *Empress* shows her age, and for every classic element there's a worn one to balance it, like scuffed cabin walls, stained or sagging ceiling tiles, and a "been at sea too long" smell in some areas. Quirks and all, though, the *Regal Empress* is an absolute classic—and with international maritime regulations threatening retirement for vessels like this by 2010, time is running out.

Pros
- **She's a time machine:** Lots of old wooden wall paneling survives, providing a window back to the old *An Affair to Remember* days.
- **Classic nautical lines:** The ship's long, bowed hull and tiered aft decks cut a snazzy, classic profile in this age of boxy look-alike megaships.
- **It's cheap:** Cruises in high season start at $218 per person, and in the off season rates can get as low as $129. The best suite on the ship usually goes for under $500 per person.

Cons
- **Wear and tear:** On a vessel like this, "shipshape" means keeping her running and safe, not shiny and new. The crew does a great job keeping her clean, but 55 years of hard use show through in innumerable scrapes, scratches, scuffs, and bruises.
- **Feels crowded:** For her size, this ship carries a lot of passengers, and because there aren't too many public rooms, things can get crowded. That said, maybe crowds are a plus on a 40-hour good-time cruise.

REGAL EMPRESS: OLD, CHEAP & CHARMING
Imperial Majesty Cruise Line has been around since 1999, first operating the steamship *OceanBreeze*, then, following the bankruptcy of Regal Cruises, taking over

the *Regal Empress*—which, due to her age, was in serious danger of being sold for scrap. Big thanks go out to former Imperial Majesty president Arthur Pollack for the reprieve, because ships like this are rare birds in the 21st century, and getting rarer every day. In 2010, *Empress*'s kind of woody interiors and mazelike layout will be prohibited by international safety-at-sea regulations, and it's an open question as to whether the line will invest the funds needed to bring her into compliance. Since she started life as the Greek Line vessel *Olympia,* there's also been talk of turning the old girl into a museum of Greek maritime history, permanently moored in either Greece or New England. Stay tuned.

PASSENGER PROFILE

At any given time, about 50% of passengers book the ship as part of land-sea package deals, often sold via telemarketers. The other 50% are generally south Florida locals and vacationers looking to add a quick Bahamas hop to their Florida vacation. A fair number are first-timers sampling the cruise experience before committing to a longer voyage, and a few are ocean-liner fans aboard for a dose of the real thing.

DINING

The dining experience on *Regal Empress* is surprisingly pleasant, with meals served either inside at the formal restaurant or at the indoor/outdoor buffet, which is also the venue for a daily midnight buffet themed on Italian, Latin, and other dishes.

TRADITIONAL There are two seatings for each meal in the *Empress*'s attractive, wood-paneled Caribbean dining room, which retains much of its original ocean-liner charm with etched glass, ornate wall sconces, oil paintings, and an original mural of New York. The cuisine, while not gourmet in any way, is decent and served professionally by a fleet of waiters and assistants. Main courses tend to be classic cruise fare: prime rib, catch of the day, chicken *cordon bleu,* and veal scaloppine, with appetizers such as shrimp cocktail, prosciutto with melon, and spinach and feta strudel. Soups and salads (including good gazpacho and Greek salad) round out the courses, and there's always one **vegetarian option** such as spinach quiche or linguine Toscana. Desserts include a perfectly acceptable napoleon, cheesecake, and mousse, plus an assortment of ice creams and (predictably, but still charming) a baked Alaska paraded around the room with some flair by the waitstaff.

Compared with the other mainstream lines, here's how Imperial Majesty rates:

	Poor	Fair	Good	Excellent	Outstanding
Enjoyment Factor			✓		
Dining			✓		
Activities		✓			
Children's Program	✓				
Entertainment		✓			
Service			✓		
Worth the Money			✓		

Imperial Majesty Fleet Itineraries

Ship	Itineraries
Regal Empress	**Bahamas:** 2 nights, round-trip from Ft. Lauderdale, FL (year-round).

CASUAL   The buffet adjoins the stern pool area and serves lunch on embarkation day and breakfast on day two and disembarkation day. Breakfast offers a good selection of fruits, meats, eggs, omelets, and pastries. Lunches include the usual salads, cheese, fruit, cold cuts, and meats, plus good pasta. On the opposite side of the stern bar, an open-air grill serves burgers, hot dogs, and pizzas.

ACTIVITIES

As you're aboard for only 2 nights, the range of activities is limited to bingo, gambling, dancing, drinking, and karaoke—and on night 2 all guests are invited to a complimentary champagne reception with the captain. At port in Nassau, the line offers several extra-cost shore excursions to Cable Beach, including simple beach runs, parasailing, snorkeling, glass-bottom boat tours, and stingray swims.

CHILDREN'S PROGRAM

Just behind the pool deck there's a small, very drab **children's room** where a youth counselor supervises activities for kids 3 and up for a few hours each evening. Expect coloring contests, movies, arts and crafts, and pizza parties, plus a Kids' Disco Party in the ship's regular adult disco on night 2. There are also seven video game machines bunched together in the rear section of the enclosed promenade, aft. No babysitting is available.

ENTERTAINMENT

Let's start by saying we're suckers for this kind of budget entertainment. Limited facilities, no sets, a punishing schedule—how can you not root for them? In the not-very-grand **Grand Lounge,** a seven-member song-and-dance troupe and three-piece "orchestra" (all from Romania when we were aboard) gives its all on the small, low-ceilinged stage, with rapid costume changes and big smiles to keep things lively. Elsewhere, the completely charming **Commodore Lounge** has a pianist from 8:30pm till after midnight, and the **Mermaid Lounge** next door has live dance music and karaoke throughout the evening. Down one of the ship's many mysterious stairways, the drab **Mirage disco** thumps until late night, while a trio performs on the pool deck.

SERVICE

Service is better than you might expect from such an inexpensive line. The dining staff is professional and experienced, cabin stewards and ship maintenance staff are top-notch (they have to be, as the old ship requires constant care), and the friendly bartenders at the Pool Bar have their job down pat. As booze sales are a big part of the line's revenue, stewards are constantly roving the public areas asking if you need a drink, but it never gets to the point of annoyance. Room service is not available, nor is laundry service.

Regal Empress

The Verdict

However worn around the edges, this indomitable old war horse retains some charming vestiges of old ocean-liner days.

Regal Empress *(photo: Matt Hannafin)*

Specifications

Size (in tons)	21,909	Crew	370
Passengers (double occ.)	875	Passenger/Crew Ratio	2.4 to 1
Passenger/Space Ratio	25	Year Launched	1953
Total Cabins/Veranda Cabins	457/10	Last Refurbishment/Upgrade	1997

Frommer's Ratings (Scale of 1–5) ⭑⭑

Cabin Comfort & Amenities	2	Dining Options	2.5
Appearance & Upkeep	3	Gym, Spa & Sports Facilities	1
Public Comfort/Space	2	Children's Facilities	1
Decor	2.5	Enjoyment Factor	3

Now 55 years young, *Regal Empress* is the oldest cruise ship in the U.S. market. Built in Scotland in 1953 as a two-class Greek Line ocean liner called the *Olympia,* the ship made her debut sailing from Glasgow and Liverpool to New York. In 1970, long after air travel killed the transatlantic trade, she switched to cruising, but by 1974 ended up mothballed at a pier in Piraeus, Greece, where she languished until 1983. In 1984, after a major refitting, she sailed as the *Caribe I* ("The Happy Ship") for now-defunct Commodore Cruise Lines. She was sold to Regal in 1993, then to Imperial Majesty 10 years later. Today, the *Empress* is a hodgepodge of old and new, with some of her original ocean-liner decor existing side by side with cheap lounge furnishings. On one sailing after her last major renovation, we heard a passenger say of the interior, "It's not dull, but it could use a little more glitter." We disagree. In fact, for us it's the lack of glitter that really makes the *Empress* worthwhile—the rich wood paneling that covers the main stair landings, the dining room, and the purser's lobby; the sunken seating clusters port and starboard in the cozy Commodore Lounge (our favorite spot for cocktails and conversation); and the little-used but delightfully old-fashioned enclosed promenade.

The ship's layout is also peculiarly charming, owing to years of alterations and also to the fact that she was originally built as a two-class ocean liner, carrying 138 first-class passengers and 1,169 tourist-class, with her layout configured to keep the two mostly separate. Today, with the areas merged for use by everyone, the *Regal Empress* is full of odd little stairways leading from deck to deck, doors that go where you wouldn't think they would, and corridors that twist and turn like an English hedge maze. It's like an old house: quirky and unique, and as different as can be from the open design of most modern ships.

Cabins & Rates

Cabins	Per Diems From	Sq. Ft.	Fridge	Hair Dryer	Sitting Area	TV
Inside	$139	80–106	no	no	no	yes
Outside	$199	116–120	no	no	no	yes
Suite	$299	216–408	yes	yes	yes	yes

CABINS   Because cruises are only 40 hours long, it doesn't really matter what cabin you book, but you sure do have a lot of choices: *Empress*'s 457 cabins vary widely in size, location, and configuration, with the smallest measuring a cramped 80 square feet and the largest suites a spacious 410 square feet. The majority are about 100 to 120 square feet, including many inside cabins without views. Cabins look their age for the most part, with drab walls and sparse furnishings, though bright matching drapes and bedspreads cheer things up a bit. Ceilings are low in the cabins as well as in the corridors outside. Closet space is more than adequate as all you need is an overnight bag for these trips. All cabins have televisions and telephones. Bathrooms are generally small and cramped.

Suites E and F and minisuites U90 and U91 on the Upper Deck are the most distinctive cabins aboard, with their woody interiors and odd-though-appealing shapes. In late 1997, 10 suites were reconfigured to include large private verandas. A few also have very bizarre, unattractive enclosed balconies (actually forward sections of the enclosed promenade, now partitioned off) with hot tubs. Unless you just can't live without a Jacuzzi, we'd give 'em a pass.

Sixty-seven cabins can be configured for four through bunk bed arrangements. Others are configured for single passengers. Two cabins are accessible to wheelchairs, but overall this ship is not a good option for people with limited mobility.

PUBLIC AREAS   The chunky, caramel-colored wood Pool Bar is the hub of outdoor action and is a total classic. Inside, the Grand Lounge is used for stage performances and bingo. One deck down, the smoky casino is either cheesy looking or retro-cool, depending on your perspective. The disco, however, is just plain drab. Up on Sun Deck, the Mermaid Lounge nightclub is a pleasant space with a large dance floor and glass-brick, brass-railed bar. A bit of trivia: This lounge used to be the first-class swimming pool, back in the old days. You can still see the mechanism that was used to retract its glass ceiling.

For us, the best room on the ship (and one of our favorite rooms on any ship, period) is the Commodore Lounge, a clubby, intimate bar with sunken seating areas to port and starboard. A pianist performs here in the evenings. For quiet lounging, we also recommend the enclosed promenade decks to port and starboard. Essential in the old days for north Atlantic crossings (where winter cold and winds made outdoor promenades uncomfortable), indoor promenades are now a thing of the past—even the new *Queen Mary 2*, the first real ocean liner built in decades, doesn't have one. *Empress* sports rich teak decking, potted trees and plants, and a smattering of couches and small tables for two. This is probably the only chance you'll ever get to experience this aspect of old ship life.

A small card room, a kids' playroom, and a three-screen Internet center are located behind the Pool Bar. The ship's wood-paneled library, a lovely old vestige of her ocean-liner days, is usually closed to guests but is available to groups for business meetings.

DINING OPTIONS See "Dining," above.

POOL, FITNESS, SPA & SPORTS FACILITIES The ship's tiered aft decks are very attractive in that classic liner kind of way, with one small pool and two hot tubs surrounded by deck chairs and tables. For a private moment alone with the sea, take the stairs down from here (or exit the rear starboard-side doors of the Grand Lounge) and walk to the very stern. It's a spot many passengers never explore. Ditto for the forward observation deck just below the bridge, accessible via a stairway on the enclosed promenade.

There's no gym, but a tiny massage room and beauty salon are located on the Upper Deck, near the passenger services desk.

8 MSC Cruises

6750 N. Andrews Ave., Fort Lauderdale, FL 33309. ℂ **800/666-9333**. www.msccruises.com.

THE LINE IN A NUTSHELL MSC is attempting the kind of change NCL has accomplished over the past 5 years, transforming itself from a catch-as-catch-can company offering cheap cruises on older ships into (it hopes) a true player in the American market. With six new mid- and mega-size vessels built in the past decade, and more on the way, they sure have the hardware, but they're still lacking in the finesse department. One American passenger we met aboard *Lirica* in the Caribbean noted, "MSC is still in rehearsal." Indeed, this is what cruising was like 30 years ago, more a venue for socializing and low-key activities than a something-for-everyone theme park. For some passengers, that lack of novelty has its own appeal. Still, except for its Italian menu items and European-style entertainment, there is little that makes MSC stand out from the competition. Unless the line makes dramatic enhancements, its appeal to North Americans may continue to be limited. **Sails to:** Caribbean (plus Europe, South America).

THE EXPERIENCE Based in Italy, where it was born as an adjunct of Mediterranean Shipping Company (the world's second-largest container-shipping operation), MSC's all about "Italian style," but defining that style is a problem—especially on Caribbean itineraries, where the line attempts to Americanize the cruise experience and has internationalized its crews. The result winds up neither fish nor fowl: not Italian enough, not American enough. If Italian-style means laid-back, MSC succeeds—though that's just one way of interpreting the staff and crew's laissez-faire attitude. This is not a line that holds its passengers' hands. In fact, how good a time you have is mostly up to you. That approach runs counter to the usual pampering style most cruise lines practice, but whether that suits you fine or leaves you less than satisfied depends on your personal taste. On the downside, the line has a way to go to compete with its mainstream rivals, particularly in its dining and menu options, presentation, and service. On the upside, there are few announcements to disturb the serenity of a drink or conversation in any number of cozy bars, or to intrude on the sanctity of passenger cabins.

The ships that the line typically positions in the U.S., the identical, midsize *Lirica* and *Opera,* were launched in 2003 and 2004 and are almost a throwback to an earlier era of cruising, carrying "only" 1,590 passengers and with almost none of the pop-culture themes and flashiness of most modern ships. The newer megaships, *Musica* and *Orchestra,* put a bit more muscle into the flash department, but the onboard ambience still conveys a time when cruising relied less on gadgets and gimmicks and more on old-fashioned entertainment and socializing. Let's just say you won't be overwhelmed by the ships' printed program of daily activities.

Pros

- **Human-size ships:** Small enough to be homey and big enough that they don't get boring, *Lirica* and *Opera* are surprisingly spacious despite being pipsqueaks compared to the competition's megaships. They're also immaculately maintained.
- **Fun (if limited) activities:** As at Costa, the European entertainment staff knows how to get people in the mood for fun.
- **Italian cuisine:** MSC's distinctive regional dishes and pastas may be among the best at sea. Pizza, in particular, wins high praise.
- **Unusual entertainment touches:** While production shows can lapse into the usual song-and-dance, the circus-style contortionists, acrobats, stilt performers, and even operatic singers add a nice touch.
- **Low prices:** Despite some negatives, this is still a line on which you can get a good bang for your buck. If price is a big concern and your expectations aren't super-high, you won't be disappointed.

Cons

- **Lackadaisical service:** Staff can be surprisingly inattentive, provoking one passenger we met to comment, "You get the feeling that everyone has something more important to do than focus on you." In the dining room, waiters were reluctant to accommodate off-the-menu requests, undermining the "sophisticated" atmosphere the line's promotions promise.
- **Small cabins & showers:** Standard inside and outside cabins are only 140 square feet, and 247-square-foot suites would pass for junior suites aboard most vessels. Showers in cabin bathrooms are among the smallest in the cruise business.
- **No alternative dining:** In the evening, the only alternative to the two dining rooms is the late-night (11:30pm) buffet on the pool deck or pizza served until 8pm.
- **Insufficient gym facilities:** The filled-to-capacity gyms on *Lirica* and *Opera* are small and inadequately equipped for a contingent of nearly 1,600 passengers.
- **Uninformed shore excursion staff:** Independent travelers will need to rely on guidebooks (this one!) and other advance research for advice on how to spend a day ashore in the Caribbean. The excursion staff was clueless about anything other than their own offerings and, even there, were often uninformed. The line clearly expects you to do your own homework.

MSC: ITALIAN LINE GOES INTERNATIONAL

The cruise wing of Mediterranean Shipping Company, one of the world's largest container-shipping operations, MSC came into being in 1990, concentrating on the European market. In 1998 it bought the Big Red Boat *Atlantic* from defunct Premier Cruises and began offering 11-night Caribbean cruises for both Europeans and Americans. And that, essentially, was the line's story for the next 5 years. In 2003, the company built its first new ship, the midsize *Lirica,* and then in 2004 things started to change fast. In April that year, MSC purchased Festival Cruises' ship *European Vision*

Compared with the other mainstream lines, here's how MSC rates:

	Poor	Fair	Good	Excellent	Outstanding
Enjoyment Factor			✓		
Dining			✓		
Activities		✓			
Children's Program			✓		
Entertainment			✓		
Service		✓			
Worth the Money				✓	

after that company's financial meltdown; in May it hired former Celebrity president Richard Sasso to head its North America division; in June it launched the new 58,000-ton *Opera;* and in August it bought *European Vision*'s sister ship, *European Stars. Vision* and *Stars* (renamed *Armonia* and *Sinfonia*) are almost identical to MSC's *Lirica* and *Opera,* all of them having been built by France's Alstom Marine, which was also responsible for *Queen Mary 2.* The twin 89,000-ton megaships *Musica* and *Orchestra* followed in 2006 and 2007; a third 89,000-ton ship *(Poesia)* and two 133,500-ton, 3,300-passenger supermegas *(Fantasia* and *Splendida)* are scheduled to debut in March 2008, June 2008, and March 2009, respectively.

PASSENGER PROFILE

The typical age range is mid-40s and up, and while MSC's Mediterranean itineraries tend to carry 85% European and 15% "other" (including North Americans), Caribbean itineraries are exactly reversed, with Americans dominating. Also, while European itineraries tend to carry a lot of kids, those in the Caribbean don't except at holidays. To accommodate the cultural mix, announcements in the Caribbean are made in English and Italian (in that order) and possibly German and French as well, depending on the passenger complement.

DINING

In keeping with the line's intention of offering an old-fashioned cruise experience, dining service is generally traditional, with a touch of European sensibility. Dining service needs major work (see "Service," below).

The tug of war between Italian, American, and "other" traditions plays itself out in both positive and negative ways. On the positive (and surprising) side, MSC is the only line on which we've noticed a kosher category on the wine list—and the only line we've been on where poppy-seed bagels are a staple on the buffet. On every other line, it's plain bagels, period. On the negative, or at least annoying side, you have to specially request coffee in the dining room after meals (only Americans do this, several Italian staff members told us), and you'll probably be asked to order your dessert selection at the same time you make your full meal request.

TRADITIONAL Two formal dining rooms serve traditional breakfast, lunch, and dinner in two fixed seatings, with an emphasis on Italian cuisine. Six-course lunches include appetizers such as smoked salmon tartare, tomatoes stuffed with tuna mousse, and barbecued chicken wings; a soup of the day; a choice of salads; pasta selections such as ravioli, risotto with pears and Bel Paese cheese, and traditional spaghetti; and main courses that might include pan-roasted chicken breast in a Riesling wine sauce, sliced sirloin, Caribbean red snapper filet, frittata with zucchini and Swiss cheese, or a plain old turkey sandwich. A selection of vegetables, cheeses, and desserts rounds out the offerings, along with a special **vegetarian menu,** burgers and dogs from the grill, and **healthy-choice options.**

Expect about the same for dinner, with appetizers such as lamb-and-mushroom quiche, avocado boat with seafood salad, and crispy fried spring rolls; a salad of the day; three soup selections, such as Trieste-style red bean soup, oxtail broth with sherry, and chilled orange and tomato cream soup; pasta selections such as risotto with artichokes and fresh mint leaves, and pappardelle pasta with white veal ragout; and main courses such as rock Cornish hen with mushrooms and crispy bacon, prime rib, grilled mahimahi filet, and vegetable couscous with raisins and cashews. As at lunch, dinner also offers a vegetarian menu, a healthy menu, and a selection of cheeses and desserts (including sugar-free desserts), plus a bread of the day. The daily **Italian regional specialties** tend to be the highlight of the menus, winning nearly unqualified approval from every passenger nationality on board. An "always available" list rounds out the offerings with steak, chicken, salmon filets, Caesar salad, baked potato, and corn on the cob.

SPECIALTY   None.

CASUAL   A buffet restaurant serves all three meals, with dinner available from 6 to 8pm. Buffet offerings overall are never quite eye-popping and can quickly become repetitious.

SNACKS & EXTRAS   In true Italian style, every bar on the ship also is a **coffee bar,** so passengers can enjoy an espresso or macchiato anytime, anywhere. Pizza, burgers, and other items are available from the pool-deck grill during the day. From late afternoon until around 8pm, the grill serves really excellent **pizza** and Italian specialty snacks. Inside, the ship offers one of the few daily **midnight buffets** left in the industry, though it tends to be more sparse than special. At the other end of the spectrum, waiters on Captain's Night proffer an assortment of pleasant **free drinks**—not just punch and cheap champagne but the kind of mixed drinks once ubiquitous aboard gracious ocean liners, such as Manhattans, whiskey sours, and martinis.

Room service is available 24 hours a day from a very limited menu.

ACTIVITIES

Activities on MSC tend toward cruise traditions, many of them with a European sense of fun. Outside, expect a round of **goofy pool games,** including water polo, treasure hunts, and various team games, plus foosball, darts, and **golf tournaments,** the latter on a putting green that wraps around the top deck. Goofiness continues in the evenings, with the kind of participatory games for which Italian ships are known. Leave your self-consciousness at home. Flamenco and tango **dance lessons** might be held in one of the lounges. Other classes include Italian language, basic computer use, and cooking, and the spa and salon staffs put on the usual raft of **beauty demonstrations.** Next door, the gyms offer stretching and standard aerobics classes, plus Pilates and yoga at an added charge ($14 per class, or five for $55). Other activities include cards and bingo, gambling in the **casinos,** arts and crafts, and various meet-and-greet events such as singles and honeymooners cocktail parties.

MSC Fleet Itineraries

Ship	Itineraries
Lirica	**Caribbean:** 7- & 10-night eastern and Western, round-trip from Fort Lauderdale, FL (Jan–Mar).

In the Caribbean, MSC offers numerous **theme cruises** throughout the season, generally centered around baseball and music (from classical to big band), with such activities as question-and-answer sessions, storytelling sessions, clinics, and trivia games.

CHILDREN'S PROGRAM

Each ship has a cute (if smallish) children's center, while other kid-centric activities around the ship might include "baby disco" and balloon-tying shows. In the Caribbean, private in-cabin babysitting can be arranged through the main desk for $15 an hour.

ENTERTAINMENT

Evening entertainment is centered around the extrawide stage of each ship's main theater. On our most recent cruise the usual Vegas song-and-dance routines caused yawns, but several shows drew on European circus traditions, featuring contortionists, acrobats, and stilt performers. It's that European influence—also evident at **audience-participation shows** and in the lively disco—that distinguishes MSC's entertainment from the American cruise lines. Other shows in the lineup may include a Spanish show with flamenco and modern dancers, an Italian-style show featuring an operatic tenor, a classic concert, or a magic show. Quieter options around the ship include **daytime films** in the main theater and music in the jazz bar and piano bar.

SERVICE

Service is the number-one downside that MSC must address if it wants to reach a wider audience. While the line touts its Italian officers and crew—a distinction that appeals to passengers who fondly recall the Golden Age of ocean travel—MSC has in fact blurred its Italianness by recruiting service staff from Indonesia and other Asian nations. As on other lines, the Asian crew distinguishes itself with its attention and eagerness, but in many instances the international crew mix has resulted in a Tower-of-Babel language barrier, even among crew.

An MSC Megaship Hits the Caribbean for 2008–09

For those who like to plan ahead, here's a heads-up: In winter 2008–09, MSC Cruises will be positioning a megaship in the Caribbean for the first time. The 2,550-passenger, 89,600-ton *Orchestra* will sail mostly 7-night alternating round-trip eastern and western Caribbean itineraries from Ft. Lauderdale. The second megaship built by MSC, *Orchestra* was launched in 2007 and features contemporary European styling and all the usual megaship amenities, plus pleasant oddities like a beautifully tiled Turkish bath, a thalassotherapy pool, a Chinese restaurant, and a wine-tasting bar.

Real problems seem to stem more from the line's Italian staff, whose surprising inattentiveness—especially in the dining rooms—is a major deviation from the sophisticated ambience the line's advertising promises. On our most recent cruise (aboard *Lirica*), a request for egg whites at lunch in the main restaurant was received by the waiter with an insistent, "Only what's on the menu."

Tipping is done on an automatic basis, with $12 per person, per day added to your onboard account. While this amount is adjustable up or down at your request, the line doesn't volunteer that this option is available. You have to ask.

Laundry service is also available, though there are no self-serve laundries.

Lirica • Opera

The Verdict

Straightforward midsize vessels. Rather than hitting guests over the head with self-consciously "fun" decor, they just present a venue in which passengers and staff can create their own good times.

Opera *(photo: MSC)*

Specifications

Size (in tons)		Crew	
Lirica	58,600	*Lirica*	760
Opera	58,600	*Opera*	800
Passengers (double occ.)		Passenger/Crew Ratio	
Lirica	1,586	*Lirica*	2.1 to 1
Opera	1,756	*Opera*	2.2 to 1
Passenger/Space Ratio		Year Launched	
Lirica	36.9	*Lirica*	2003
Opera	33.5	*Opera*	2004
Total Cabins/Veranda Cabins		Last Refurbishment/Upgrade	
Lirica	795/132	*Lirica*	N/A
Opera	878/200	*Opera*	N/A

Frommer's Ratings (Scale of 1–5)   ★★★½

Cabin Comfort & Amenities	3.5	Dining Options	3
Appearance & Upkeep	4	Gym, Spa & Sports Facilities	3.5
Public Comfort/Space	4	Children's Facilities	3
Decor	3	Enjoyment Factor	4

Opera and *Lirica* almost seem like a different species from today's brand of enormoships, lacking any kind of overt gimmicks— no planetariums, no rock-climbing walls, no "decorate every surface" design schemes. What they are are ships on which people can get together to talk, loll in the pool, throw away their inhibitions, and relax, without having their senses overwhelmed. Whether that's a good thing or not depends on your point of view.

Another aspect of *Lirica* and *Opera*'s old-fashionedness? Their moderate size, which is on a par with Holland America's well-loved Statendam-class ships. Long and low, both vessels seem a lot larger than they really are, with a surprising amount of space both in their public rooms and out on the pool deck. For this, credit their small cabins.

Cabins & Rates

Cabins	Per Diems From	Sq. Ft.	Fridge	Hair Dryer	Sitting Area	TV
Inside	$68	140	yes	yes	no	yes
Outside	$90	140	yes	yes	no	yes
Suite	$171	236–247	yes	yes	yes	yes

CABINS   Cabins come in only four varieties: standard 140-square-foot inside cabins, 140-square-foot oceanview and balcony cabins, and suites that would pass for junior suites aboard most vessels. Though not palatial, staterooms are pleasantly and unfussily decorated, with simple light wood trim and upholstery patterns, good lighting and storage, and niceties such as a writing/makeup desk and minibar. Balcony cabins seem roomier than they are thanks to strategically placed mirrors and extremely wide balcony doors. Bathrooms, on the other hand, are stuck with some of the smallest shower stalls in the industry—the only serious design flaw noted on board, and one they probably can't do much about. Suites have larger tub/shower combos.

Four cabins on *Lirica* and five on *Opera* are wheelchair accessible.

PUBLIC AREAS   Decor on MSC is as far a cry from Carnival's over-the-top themed decor as it is from the more chic decor of Celebrity. Somewhere between plain and restrained, *Opera* and *Lirica*'s public areas are done up in blonde woods, floral and geometric carpets, functional solid-colored chairs and banquettes, and a smattering of marble and brass. Fully mirrored walls—and lots of them—dominate most public spaces, brightening the areas, creating a soothing quality, and making the ships seem twice their size.

Ship layout is simple and easy to navigate. Most public rooms are on two adjoining decks, starting with the main forward theater. Avoid seats in the back corners, which offer lousy sightlines even when other passengers don't stand at the rail in front of them, completely blocking the view. Heading aft there are a coffee bar wrapped around the small, comfortable atrium; a lounge for music, karaoke, and other entertainment; several shops; a casino; an intimate piano bar; several nook lounges and seating areas; and an internet cafe. (Wi-Fi access is also available in several hot spots.) One deck down, just below the theater, is a bar/lounge that's your best bet for a quiet evening drink, as it's off the main evening traffic routes. A room that doubles as a card room and library adjoins, but the selection of books is nearly nonexistent. Bring your own. Atop the ship is a disco/observation lounge with several dance floors and a generally hopping vibe.

Kids get a playroom tucked weirdly into the same complex as the spa, gym, and beauty salon, in the bow on the pool deck. On *Opera,* the room has a Buffalo Bill Wild West theme, with a puffy, cushioned cacti, Western wall paintings, and signs pointing to Monument Valley, the Colorado River (a wide blue line meandering across the floor), and Fort Laramie, a large play structure. On *Lirica,* it's done in a tropical pirate theme, with plastic palm trees, bright wall paintings of pirate ships and treasure maps, and a variety of small slides, crafts tables, and a cushiony play area. Counselors are on hand to organize activities, but remember (as a memorable sign said when we were aboard), IT'S NOT POSSIBLE ENTRY IN THE MINI-CLUB IF IS NOT PRESENT ONE ANIMATOR!

DINING OPTIONS   Each ship's two restaurants are downright old-fashioned, eschewing the multiple levels, grand staircases, columns, and chandeliers common aboard most megaships in favor of a simple one-story approach. Decor is restrained to the point of being irrelevant—just warmly colored walls and carpets, a smattering of ceiling and fixture lights, and lots of people dining at tables that are maybe just a little too close together.

A standard buffet restaurant occupies the stern of the pool deck, with an additional outdoor seating area separated off from the main pool. An outdoor grill serves pizza, burgers, pork cutlets, and the like. Pizza and Italian specialty snacks are also served indoors from late afternoon until around 8pm.

POOL, FITNESS, SPA & SPORTS FACILITIES   The main recreation deck has two pools and two hot tubs that are central to the vitality of the vessel during the day, with row upon row of sun worshippers napping or reading. Like many other spaces on board, it's almost a throwback to early 1990s ship design—just a plain-vanilla pool deck without showy frills—but it does boast one neat feature not seen on other lines: Every lounge chair has its own sun canopy. A jogging track wraps around the deck above.

Gyms are tiny and inadequately equipped for the number of people on board. On our last cruise, three outdated treadmills were in such constant demand that passengers were asked to reserve time on them—a frequent point of contention when other passengers inadvertently cut the line. A bike machine, about a dozen weight machines, free weights, and a small aerobics floor complete the picture. Spa treatment rooms encircle the space, with a pre- or post-treatment "relaxation room" off to one side. Up on the top deck, a golf putting green encircles the stern.

9 Norwegian Cruise Line

7665 Corporate Center Dr., Miami, FL 33126. © 866/234-0292 or 305/436-4000. Fax 305/436-4126. www.ncl.com.

THE LINE IN A NUTSHELL   NCL may be the most mainstream of the mainstream lines these days—and we mean that in a good way. At a time when even Carnival is pushing the quote/unquote "luxury" elements of its onboard program, NCL hews to the center, with always-casual dining (and lots of it); bright, cheerful decor; and such fun innovations as gourmet beer bars and onboard bowling alleys. Its newest ships are real standouts, giving Royal Caribbean and Princess a run for their money, and it's the go-to line for Hawaii cruises, completely dominating that market. Nutshell? NCL's the kind of cruise line you want to sit down and have a beer with. **Sails to:** Caribbean, Panama Canal, Alaska, Mexican Riviera, Bermuda, Hawaii, Canada/New England (plus South America, Europe).

THE EXPERIENCE   Back in the mid- to late '90s, NCL operated a mixed-bag fleet of older ships whose onboard vibe was only a couple steps above budget. What a difference a few years makes. Today it's one of the top players in the industry, with innovative itineraries (especially in Hawaii), a fleet composed almost entirely of new megaships, a casual onboard atmosphere, top-drawer entertainment, and a staggering number of dining choices. The line was the first to dump the old system of formal/informal/casual nights, going totally casual in 2000 and starting a trend across the industry. The new program also did away with fixed dining times and seating assignments, leaving passengers free to choose when and where they want to dine among a variety of venues. Traditional tipping also went away, replaced by a system where gratuities are added directly to passenger accounts. Busy, busy, busy they've been, and it shows. This is one fun cruise line.

Pros

- **Hawaii, Hawaii, Hawaii:** If you want to sail the islands, NCL's U.S.-flagged sub-brand, NCL America, offers the only cruises that never leave state waters.
- **Flexible dining:** NCL's "Freestyle Cruising" policy lets you dine when and where you want, dressed "however."
- **Restaurants galore:** With between 6 and 10 places to have dinner, you won't know where to turn.
- **Above-average entertainment:** In addition to above-average Vegas-style shows and musical groups, NCL also offers comedy shows by the Second City comedy troupe aboard *Norwegian Dawn, Jewel, Sprit,* and *Pearl.*

Cons

- **Small cabins:** Though with each new ship they seem to get a little bigger, at about 110 to 165 square feet, standard inside and outside cabins are a tighter squeeze than those of most of the competition.
- **Below-average older ships (for now):** At least until 2009, NCL is still saddled with two old ships that represent "the old NCL."

NCL: SAY ALOHA TO INNOVATION

Talk about pulling yourself up by your bootstraps. Norwegian was one of the pioneers of the North American cruise market, beginning in 1966 as an alliance between Norwegian ship owner Knut Kloster and Israeli marketing genius Ted Arison, who later started Carnival Cruises. After these auspicious beginnings, it spent many years relegated to the industry's back seat behind biggies Carnival and Royal Caribbean, but beginning in 1997 (and especially since its purchase by Asian line Star Cruises in 2000), it began a sequence of moves that transformed it into a true leader and innovator.

Latest move after going casual and giving Hawaii a big fat aloha? Going modern. As part of an ongoing upgrade, Star Cruises has formally acquired all of the midsize ships in the NCL fleet and will be taking possession gradually over the coming years. This will leave NCL with a totally up-to-date fleet, including 10 new ships launched between 1999 and 2007. Two huge, 150,000-ton, 4,200-passenger super-megaships are also on order with French shipbuilder Aker Yards S.A., due to debut in 2009 and 2010. The company also has an option for a third sister ship, which would be delivered in 2011.

The one caveat to all that modernity? The old **SS** *United States.* In April 2003, NCL announced that it had purchased the legendary American liner, which was built in 1952 to be the fastest, safest ship at sea. It still holds the record for transatlantic passage by an ocean liner, but has been laid up since 1969. NCL's plans are vague at best.

Compared with the other mainstream lines, here's how NCL rates:

	Poor	Fair	Good	Excellent	Outstanding
Enjoyment Factor					✓
Dining				✓	
Activities				✓	
Children's Program				✓	
Entertainment				✓	
Service				✓	
Worth the Money					✓

Why NCL Owns Hawaii

The way NCL talks up its Hawaii itineraries, you'd think they were something special, huh? Well, they are, and to explain why, here's a bit of history.

The **Passenger Vessel Services Act,** which became U.S. law in 1886, forbids passenger ships from operating itineraries entirely within U.S. waters (for instance, sailing from New York to Miami with stops in Baltimore and Charleston) unless they're built in the United States, owned by a U.S. entity, registered and flagged in the U.S., and manned by a U.S. crew. The law was originally designed to protect U.S. shipping interests from foreign competition, but in modern times—with U.S. cruise lines commonly building, flagging, and manning their vessels overseas—its effect has been that vessels sailing to U.S. ports have had to visit a foreign port too as part of their itineraries. This makes Hawaiian itineraries particularly difficult, requiring that they either depart from foreign mainland ports (such as Ensenada, Mexico) or sail from the islands themselves but make a multiday detour to a foreign port in the middle of an otherwise all-Hawaii itinerary.

Enter NCL. In late 2002, the company acquired the unfinished hulls of two ships whose construction had been started in the U.S. by now-bankrupt American Classic Voyages under the name "Project America." Intense lobbying in Congress led to a deal in which NCL was able to have these hulls built out at a German shipyard yet still sail under the U.S. flag. As part of the fine print, NCL was also able to reflag the foreign-built *Norwegian Sky,* renaming it *Pride of Aloha* and relaunching it under the company's new U.S.-flag brand, NCL America, in July 2004. By July 2006 the two Project America ships had been reborn as *Pride of America* and *Pride of Hawai'i* and NCL had itself the only cruise operation in the business manned by U.S. officers and crew, sailing round-trip from Honolulu, and concentrating exclusively on the Hawaiian islands. They may have moved too fast—market problems in 2007 forced the line to pull *Hawai'i* from Hawaii, rename her *Norwegian Jade,* and send her to Europe—but the bottom line is still that NCL has no real competition in Hawaii. If you want to sail there, odds are it'll be on one of their vessels. Aloha!

Some speculate that the line purchased *United States* (as well as the old, 1951-built SS *Independence,* which spent years sailing for defunct American Hawaii Cruises) to prevent competitors from purchasing and refurbishing them as competition to NCL America's Hawaii operation. Or maybe they really *do* intend to relaunch them someday. Stay tuned.

PASSENGER PROFILE

In general, NCL passengers are younger, more price-conscious, and more active than those aboard lines such as HAL, Celebrity, and Princess. Typical NCL passengers are couples ages 25 to 60, and include a fair number of honeymooners and families with kids during summers and holidays. Kids under age 2 travel free (though they're still charged taxes and fees). The atmosphere aboard all NCL vessels is informal and well suited to casual types, party makers, and first-time cruisers.

DINING

All the restaurants on all NCL ships follow an open-seating policy each and every evening, allowing you to dine whenever you like within the 5:30 to 10pm window, sit with whomever you want (rather than having a table preassigned), and dress however you like: Management says anything goes except jeans, shorts, and tank tops, but we've seen those in the restaurants, too. This flexible setup really works for families, groups, and anyone else who doesn't want to be tied down to fixed timings and tables, and who hates the idea of having to chat up the same bunch of dinner companions all week. If you end up sitting with people you like, you can always make plans to dine with them again.

The night of the captain's cocktail party is officially an **"optional formal" night,** meaning you can wear a suit, tie, or fancy dress if you like, but no one will complain if you don't. That said, we were surprised on a recent cruise at just how many people did dress up.

TRADITIONAL The main dining rooms, like the rest of the ships' eating venues, operate with open seating and casual dress codes, so the only really "traditional" thing about them is their size and a touch of traditional ocean-liner elegance. For cuisine, you can usually count on such choices as grilled swordfish with lemon-caper sauce, salmon or poached sea bass, beef Wellington, broiled lobster tail, chicken Parmesan, fettuccine Alfredo, or perhaps a Jamaican jerk pork roast, Wiener schnitzel, or roast prime rib. The wine lists appeal to standard mid-American tastes, and prices aren't offensively high.

A **light choice** (prepared with recipes from NCL partner *Cooking Light* magazine) and a **vegetarian entree** are available at lunch and dinner. **Children's menus** feature the popular standards (burgers, hot dogs, grilled cheese sandwiches and french fries, spaghetti and meatballs, ice-cream sundaes, and so on) plus unexpected dishes like vegetable crudités and cheese dip.

SPECIALTY In addition to one or two main dining rooms, all the modern NCL ships have between six and eight alternative specialty restaurants serving food that's on a par with all but the very best of the competition. (The older *Majesty* and *Dream* have two specialty restaurants apiece.) Each ship has a French/Continental restaurant called **Le Bistro,** and the line's modern ships also offer choices such as Pan-Asian, Italian, Japanese, Pacific Rim, and Tex-Mex tapas (see ship reviews for which ship has what). The food in Le Bistro is better than that in the main dining rooms, and includes items such as a yummy Caesar salad made right at your table and a marvelously decadent chocolate fondue served with fresh fruit (both by request only). Tables are sometimes available for walk-ins, but make your reservations as early as possible to be on the safe side.

Most of the specialty restaurants carry a cover charge, which ranges from $10 to $20 per person. Even with a reservations system, it inevitably happens that you'll sometimes have to wait for a table, but NCL's working on that too. Six of its ships (*Spirit, Jewel, Pearl, Gem, Pride of America, Pride of Aloha,* and *Norwegian Jade,* the latter sailing in Europe this year) now feature large **computerized billboard screens** placed outside restaurants and in various public areas. Each displays a listing of every restaurant on board (with photos and a description of the cuisine), along with the restaurant's status (open/closed), how busy it is at that moment, how close it is to filling up, and how long a wait there will be if it *is* filled up. For those who don't like to plan too far ahead, it's a great boon: You can head out for the evening and just decide where to dine on the fly. Maitre d's at every restaurant can take reservations at any of the other restaurants too, so if one looks like it's filling up you won't have to sprint to catch that last table—just amble to the nearest restaurant and have them call ahead for you. The system will eventually be rolled out to *Norwegian Sun, Norwegian Star, and Norwegian Dawn,* though no date has yet been set. It'll also eventually be available fleetwide through a new interactive TV system that's in the works.

CASUAL   In addition to the numerous sit-down venues highlighted above (all of them casual in their own way), all NCL ships also have a standard Lido buffet restaurant with indoor/outdoor seating, open for breakfast, lunch, and dinner. The newer the ship, the better designed this outlet is, serving stir-fries and theme offerings such as an all-vegetarian Indian buffet in addition to popular standards like burgers. See ship reviews for more details.

SNACKS & EXTRAS   Snacking ops include pizza and ice cream offered throughout the day from the buffet restaurant, a coffee bar serving specialty java and other beverages, and 24-hour room service for pizza, sandwiches, and other munchies. Food is also available 24 hours a day at the Blue Lagoon restaurant aboard *Norwegian Star, Dawn, Spirit, Jewel, Pearl,* and *Gem;* at the sports bar on *Norwegian Sun;* and at the Cadillac Diner on *Pride of America.* One night a week (on all but the Hawaii ships), you can also drool over the popular **Chocoholic Extravaganza** buffet, offering everything from tortes to brownies.

ACTIVITIES

Especially aboard the line's newer, larger ships, you can take cha-cha lessons; watch a cooking demo; play bingo, shuffleboard, or basketball; attend an art auction or spa or beauty demonstration; and, on some cruises, sit in on enrichment lectures about classic ocean liners, nutrition, personal investing, or other topics. There are snorkeling demonstrations in the pool, makeovers, talent shows, wine tastings (for $15 per person), and trivia contests, plus your classic cruise ship "silly poolside games." In Hawaii, *Pride of Aloha* and *Pride of America* offer many activities themed on **Hawaiian arts and culture,** while *Norwegian Pearl* has the modern cruise world's first full-size, four-lane, 10-pin onboard **bowling alley.**

Internet cafes offer e-mail and Internet access fleetwide. For those wanting flexibility in their Web surfing, a Wi-Fi wireless system lets you log on from various places on all the line's ships using your own or a rented laptop and an NCL network card. You can also use your **cellphone** through an onboard relay system (see chapter 3 for details). In Hawaii the ships sail close enough to shore that signals get picked up by regular land towers.

Gyms fleetwide are open 24 hours and offer stretching, step, aerobics, and other traditional classes at no extra charge. Spinning, kickboxing, Pilates, yoga, and other trendy choices cost an extra $10. All ships except *Norwegian Majesty* have golf driving cages where guests can practice their putting and swinging at their leisure. In port, NCL's **Dive-In program** offers at least one snorkeling and one scuba excursion at almost every Caribbean port, escorted by the ship's certified instructors. In Hawaii, the line offers a comprehensive program of **golf excursions** to some of the islands' best courses, including Puakea, Poipu Bay, Princeville, and Kaua'i Lagoons (Kauai); Mauna Lani Resort, Hapuna, and Big Island Country Club (Hawaii); Makena, Wailea, and The Dunes at Maui Lani (Maui); and Ko'olau Golf Club (Oahu). The Hawaii ships also have an onboard pro shop.

NCL Fleet Itineraries

Ship	Itineraries
Norwegian Dawn	**Caribbean:** 7-night southern, round-trip from Miami (Jan–Mar). 13 nights, New York to Miami, FL (Nov). **Bermuda:** 7 nights, round-trip from New York, NY (Apr–Oct). **New England/Canada:** 7 nights, round-trip from New York, NY (Aug–Sept).
Norwegian Dream	**Bermuda:** 7 nights, round-trip from Boston, MA (May–Oct). **New England/Canada:** 7 nights, round-trip from Boston, MA (Aug–Sept).
Norwegian Gem	**Caribbean:** 10- & 11-night southern, round-trip from New York, NY (Jan–Feb). **Nowhere:** 1 night, round-trip from New York, NY (Jan). **Bahamas/Florida:** 7 nights, round-trip from New York, NY (Feb–Apr & Nov–Dec).
Norwegian Jade	**Weekender:** 2 nights, round-trip from New York, NY (Dec).
Norwegian Jewel	**Caribbean:** 5-night western (Jan–Mar & Nov–Dec), 9-night southern (Jan–Apr & Nov), and 14-night southern (Jan–Apr), round-trip from Miami, FL. **New England/Canada:** 10 nights, round-trip from New York, NY (Sept–Oct).
Norwegian Majesty	**Caribbean:** 7 nights, round-trip from Charleston, SC (Jan–Apr & Nov–Dec). **New England/Canada:** 7 nights, round-trip from Philadelphia, PA (Oct).
Norwegian Pearl	**Caribbean:** 5-night western (Jan–Mar & Oct–Dec), 9-night southern (Jan–Apr & Oct–Dec), and 14-night southern (Jan–Apr & Oct–Dec), round-trip from Miami, FL. **Alaska:** 7-night Inside Passage, round-trip from Seattle, WA (May–Sept).
Norwegian Spirit	**Caribbean:** 7-night western, round-trip from New Orleans, LA (Jan–Mar). 8-night eastern, round-trip from New York, NY (Apr–June & Aug).14-night western, New Orleans to New York (Mar). **Bahamas/Florida:** 6 nights, round-trip from New York, NY (Apr–Aug). **New England/Canada:** 6 nights, round-trip from New York, NY (Sept–Oct). **Nowhere:** 1 night, round-trip from New York, NY (Sept–Oct).
Norwegian Star	**Mexican Riviera:** 8 nights, round-trip from Los Angeles, CA (Jan–Apr). **U.S. Pacific Coast:** 3 nights, Los Angeles, CA, to Vancouver, BC (Apr) and Vancouver to Los Angeles (Sept). 5 nights, Seattle, WA, to Vancouver (Sept).
Norwegian Sun	**Alaska:** 7-night Inside Passage, round-trip from Vancouver, BC (May–Sept). **Caribbean:** 7-night western, round-trip from Miami, FL (Jan–Apr). **Mexican Riviera:** 11 nights, round-trip from San Francisco, CA (Oct). **Nowhere:** 1 night, round-trip from Miami, FL (Apr) & round-trip from Vancouver, BC (May).
Pride of Aloha	**Hawaii:** 10 and 11 nights (Jan–Apr) and 7 nights (May–Dec); round-trip from Honolulu.
Pride of America	**Hawaii:** 7 nights, round-trip from Honolulu (year-round).

CHILDREN'S PROGRAM

NCL's Kids Crew program offers year-round **supervised activities** for children ages 2 to 17, divided into four age groups: Junior Sailors, ages 2 to 5; First Mates, ages 6 to 9; Navigators, ages 10 to 12; and teens, ages 13 to 17. Activities include sports competitions, dances, face painting, treasure hunts, magic shows, arts and crafts, cooking classes, T-shirt painting, and the "Officer Snook Water Pollution Program," which uses games, crafts, storytelling, coloring books, a simulated beach cleanup, and other activities to educate young people about the affects of marine pollution and ways to prevent it. **Family events** such as family pizza-making parties and family scavenger hunts are also on the schedule, with kids getting their own daily program detailing the day's events.

All the modern NCL ships offer huge kids' facilities that include a separate teen center and a wading pool, as well as a large, well-stocked playroom. Those on *Dawn, Star,* and *Spirit* are especially wonderful, with a huge combo climbing maze and ball bin indoors and a kids' pool and hot tub area outside with a fun theme—dinosaurs on *Dawn,* rockets on *Star,* and pirates on *Spirit. Jewel* and *Pride of America* have a much smaller kids' pool. On sea days, youth programs are offered 9am to noon, 2 to 5pm, and then 7 to 10pm; on port days the complimentary hours are from 7 to 10pm. Port program times can also be adjusted to accommodate parents on shore excursions.

Once per cruise the ships offer a **Mom and Dad's Night Out,** when kids dine with counselors. Otherwise, **group babysitting** for kids age 2 to 12 is offered nightly between 10pm and 1am (and 9am–5pm on port days) for $5 per child per hour, plus $3 an hour for each additional sibling. Counselors do not do diapers; parents are given beepers so they can be alerted when it's time for the dirty work. Private babysitting is not available.

Unlimited soda packages are $16 for kids under age 17 on 7-night cruises, and a "Teen Passport" coupon book is available for teens—for $30 they get up to 20 nonalcoholic drinks such as Virgin Daiquiris.

ENTERTAINMENT

NCL offers some of the best entertainment of all the mainstream lines, including (aboard *Dawn, Jewel, Sprit, Pearl,* and *Gem*) sketch comedy shows by members of the famed **Second City comedy troupe,** which has launched the careers of such legends as Bill Murray, John Belushi, and Gilda Radner. **Production shows** are way above average too, with talented performers and good choreography, costumes, and set design. A show called *Tubez,* offered aboard *Pearl* in 2007, was one of the few truly contemporary shows we've ever seen at sea, with a mix of older and recent pop hits, hip-hop-inflected choreography and ballet, a rapper as the lead male vocalist, and even bizarro elements like BMX bicycle acrobatics. Bollywood- and South Beach–inspired shows in recent years have also been standouts. Ditto for most of the other performers, including the musicians and comedians who play the ships' lounge circuit. On the Hawaii ships, 1 night a week is devoted to **Polynesian music and dance,** while another features an extra-charge production of the off-Broadway hit *Tony n' Tina's Wedding.*

For closet entertainers, the line puts on **Star Seeker,** its version of the *American Idol* talent program, giving adults and kids the chance to prove themselves onstage. Videos of the winners are sent to NCL's shore-side entertainment department for consideration as a one-time entertainer aboard a future free NCL cruise.

Compulsive gamblers should avoid the three Hawaii-based ships as Hawaiian law prohibits all gambling onboard.

SERVICE

Fleetwide, cabin service, room service, and bar service tend to be speedy and efficient. Dining service is a mixed bag: On recent cruises service in the main dining room and Pan-Asian restaurants was accommodating but less than stellar, while service in the Le Bistro, Il Adagio, and Cagney's Steakhouse alternative restaurants was very sharp and attentive.

NCL got a lot of flack about poor service when it first spun its U.S.-flagged operation in Hawaii back in 2004, owing to its all-American crew's complete lack of shipboard experience. Intensive training over the succeeding months and years improved the situation markedly. On the plus side, crewmembers are almost uniformly friendly and helpful, and passengers love the fact there are no English-as-a-second-language problems to deal with. On the downside, some staff on our two NCL Hawaii trips have been just a little bit too . . . American (read: casual and blasé). What are you gonna do? We are who we are.

Fleetwide, tipping is done automatically, with a $10-per-day **service charge** added to each passenger's onboard account ($5 for kids 3–12). Though officially nonrefundable, the charge can be adjusted if you've experienced serious problems that the customer-service staff was unable to remedy.

NCL ships offer **laundry** and **dry-cleaning service.** *Norwegian Dawn, Jewel, Pearl,* and *Gem* all have self-service launderettes and ironing facilities for guests, and all ships have ironing boards and irons available from housekeeping upon request.

Norwegian Spirit • Star • Dawn • Jewel • Pearl • Gem (preview)

The Verdict

Really original megaships don't come along too often these days, but these babies are it, with a mix of classy and fun spaces, a lively atmosphere, awesome kids' facilities, and more restaurant options than you'll likely have time to sample.

Norwegian Pearl *(photo: NCL)*

Specifications

Size (in tons)		Total Cabins/Veranda Cabins	
Spirit	75,338	*Spirit*	980/390
Star	91,000	*Star*	1,120/515
Dawn	92,250	*Dawn*	1,112/509
Jewel	93,502	*Jewel, Pearl, Gem*	1,188/510
Pearl	93,530	Crew	
Gem	93,000	*Spirit*	965
Passengers (double occ.)		*Star*	1,100
Spirit	1,966	*Dawn*	1,126
Star	2,240	*Jewel, Pearl, Gem*	1,150
Dawn	2,224	Passenger/Crew Ratio	2 to 1
Jewel	2,376	Year Launched	
Pearl	2,394	*Spirit*	1999
Gem	2,380	*Star*	2001
Passenger/Space Ratio		*Dawn*	2002
Spirit	39.2	*Jewel*	2005
Star	41.5	*Pearl*	2006
Dawn	41.5	*Gem*	2007
Jewel	39.4	Last Refurbishment/Upgrade	
Pearl, Gem	39	*Spirit*	2004

Frommer's Ratings (Scale of 1–5) ★★★★½–★★★★★*

Cabin Comfort & Amenities	4	Dining Options	5
Appearance & Upkeep	5	Gym, Spa & Sports Facilities	4
Public Comfort/Space	5	Children's Facilities	5
Decor	4.5	Enjoyment Factor	4.5

* More fully realized than their sister ships, Norwegian Jewel, Pearl, and Gem earn a five-star rating.

Talk about innovation: These ships get straight A's. Want dining choice? How about 8 to 10 different restaurants apiece, from fancy steakhouses and teppanyaki restaurants to casual Tex-Mex and burger joints. Want something other than the generic Caribbean theme so prevalent on many ships? The ships mix it up with touches of Latin Miami, Indonesia, and urban lounge. Want high style? Check out *Spirit's* Maharini's Lounge, *Dawn's* and *Star's* Gatsby's Champagne Bar, and *Jewel, Pearl,* and *Gem's* "Bar Central" on Deck 6. Want fun? How about Pearl's Bliss Ultra Lounge and Nightclub, which juxtaposes bordello-like, velvet-draped seating nooks (with beds, even!) and a four-lane, 10-pin onboard bowling alley. Want the biggest suites aboard any ship, anywhere? The ships' Garden Villas spread out up to a mind-blowing 5,350 square feet and feature private gardens, multiple bedrooms with extravagant bathrooms, separate living rooms, full kitchens, and private butler service. Zowie! Zowie, too, on their price: $26,000 a week for up to six guests. Normal cabins, on the other hand, come at normal prices. The ships' children's centers are a knockout, so large and completely kid-centric that we wished we were 5 again. Ditto for our reaction to the buffet restaurant's Kids' Café, a miniaturized version of the adult cafe, accurate down to tiny chairs and a miniature buffet counter. It's the cutest thing going.

Overall, these ships are nearly identical in layout, though *Norwegian Spirit,* which came to NCL from the Star Cruises fleet, is slightly smaller and has a slightly different (though no less attractive) layout. At press time, few details were yet available about *Norwegian Gem,* which is due to debut in October 2007, just after this book prints.

Norwegian Jade, a seventh sister to this class of vessels, began her life as NCL America's *Pride of Hawai'i,* but was pulled from the Hawaiian market in 2008 and sent to sail in Europe, with an international crew. She won't touch these shores again until December 2008, when she does a series of short cruises from New York.

Cabins & Rates

Cabins	Per Diems From	Sq. Ft.	Fridge	Hair Dryer	Sitting Area	TV
Inside	$75	142	yes	yes	yes	yes
Outside	$100	158–205	yes	yes	yes	yes
Suite	$156	229–5,350	yes	yes	yes	yes

CABINS   Standard cabins, though not overly large compared to some in the industry (particularly those of Carnival's and Holland America's ships), are larger than elsewhere in the NCL fleet. Decor is a mix, with stylish elements (such as cherrywood wall paneling and snazzy rounded lights), kitschy elements (such as bright island-colored carpeting), and cheap touches (such as some spindly chairs and end tables, and wall-mounted soap dispensers in the bathrooms). Each comes with a small TV and minifridge, a tea/coffeemaker, a private safe, and cool, retro-looking hair dryers. Closet and drawer space are more than ample for weeklong sailings, and bathrooms in all categories are well designed, with large sinks whose faucets swing out of the way, a magnifying mirror inset in the regular mirror, adequate though not exceptional counter/shelf space, and (in all but inside cabins) separate shower and toilet compartments. Balconies in standard cabins accommodate two metal pool chairs and a small table, but aren't terribly roomy.

Minisuites provide about 60 more feet of floor space than standard cabins, with a large foldout couch, a curtain between the bed and the sitting area, and a bathtub, while the so-called "Romance Suites" really are, with 288 square feet of space, stereo with CD/DVD library, bathroom with separate shower and tub, and nice wooden deck chairs on the balcony. Penthouse Suites offer the same, plus gorgeous bathrooms with a whirlpool tub and tiled, seaview shower stall; a larger balcony; and a walk-in closet. Some suites offer a separate kids' room and bathroom. Those facing the bow on Decks 9 and 10 have large windows and deep balconies, but safety requirements mandate that instead of a nice glass door, the balconies are accessed via an honest-to-God steel bulkhead that's marked, "For your own safety, open only when the vessel is in port."

The ships' Owner's Suites are huge, with two balconies, living and dining areas, powder room, guest bathroom, and 750 square feet of space. Compared to the two Garden Villas up on Deck 14, however, these suites are peasant's quarters. The Garden Villas are, in a word, HUGE, the biggest at sea today, with three bedrooms, enormous living rooms, private Italian gardens with hot tub, panoramic views all around, private butler service, grand pianos, and totally extravagant seaview bathrooms with whirlpool tubs. They're priced beyond the range of . . . well, pretty much everybody. *Norwegian Jewel, Pearl,* and the yet-to-be-launched *Gem* have an intermediate level of smaller Courtyard Villas on the same top-of-the-ship deck as the Garden Villa. They offer spacious suite accommodations coupled with access to a villa-guests-only courtyard, a private sun deck, and a staffed concierge lounge. The courtyard is a stunner, with a small private swimming pool, hot tub, and several plush, shaded sun beds. Suites (which due to safety regulations open to a hallway around the courtyard rather than right into it) are also knockouts, with a separate bedroom and living/dining room; a huge, gorgeously appointed bathroom with oceanview whirlpool tub and shower; large private balcony; and floor space that ranges from 440 to 572 square feet. The larger Courtyard Penthouses also offer a separate children's room with foldout couch bed and second bathroom. Prices tend to hover in the $4,400-to-$5,400 range for weeklong itineraries.

Four cabins are wheelchair accessible aboard *Spirit,* 20 on *Star,* 24 on *Dawn,* and 27 on *Jewel* and *Pearl.*

PUBLIC AREAS   You'll be in a party mood from the moment you step aboard into the ships' large, broad, skylit atrium lobbies. Public areas throughout are fanciful and extremely spacious, done in a mix of bright, Caribbean- and Miami-themed decor and high-style Art Deco, with lots of nooks and some downright wonderful lounges and bars mixed in among all the restaurant choices.

On the main entertainment deck, a multideck theater has a thousand seats sloping down to a large stage. There's also a nightclub for smaller-scale cabaret entertainment and dancing. Deck 12 features a complex of "sit-down" rooms, including a comfortable cinema with traditional theater seats, a library, a card room, a reading room, a "lifestyles" room (used for classes, private functions, and so on), several meeting rooms, and a small wedding chapel. Forward of these is an observation lounge/disco with some fanciful *Alice in Wonderland* seating. Up top, on Deck 13, there's a nice bar/lounge with piano entertainment in the evening. *Dawn, Spirit,* and *Star* offer a British-themed pub with piano entertainment, a big-screen TV for sports, and tasty fish and chips; and *Spirit* and *Star* also feature a covered outdoor Bier Garten stocked with German pilsner, hefeweizen, and wheat beers. *Jewel, Pearl,* and *Gem* instead have three themed bars clustered together in a "Bar Central" arrangement on Deck 6. Their beer and whiskey bars are the best at sea, with 46 beers and 63 whiskies to choose from. Next door are a martini/cocktail bar and a champagne/wine bar.

Aboard *Spirit,* a renovation in 2005 resulted in a new room called Maharini's, which combines Bollywood Indian themes with a kind of fashion-world ambience, its mood-lit nooks separated by thick velvet curtains and outfitted with large, comfortable daybeds strewn with pillows. Stylish! A similar room on *Pearl* takes things in a different direction with the addition of four 10-pin bowling lanes, gaining NCL points for retro-chic credibility.

Other rooms include a spacious casino, an Internet center, several shops, and a coffee bar.

For kids, these ships have some of the better facilities at sea, with a huge, brightly colored crafts/play area, a big-screen TV room stuffed full of beanbag chairs, a huge ball jump/crawling maze play-gym, and a computer room. Outside, the pool areas on *Dawn, Star,* and *Spirit* are fantastic. On the *Dawn,* it's right out of *The Flintstones,* with giant polka-dotted dinosaurs hovering around faux rock walls, slides, a paddling pool, and even a kids' Jacuzzi. The *Star's* has a space-age rocket theme. *Norwegian Jewel, Pearl,* and *Gem* have much smaller outdoor play areas. There are video arcades and teen centers on all six ships, with computers, a dance floor equipped with a sound/video system, and a soda bar.

DINING OPTIONS   These ships are all about their restaurants, with between 8 and 10 options on each—two or three main formal restaurants plus a buffet, at least one casual diner/cafe, and several alternative specialty restaurants, serving Italian, steakhouse, French/Continental, and Asian cuisine. The Asian restaurants include three separate experiences, with a main restaurant as well as a separate sushi and sake bar, and an intimate Japanese teppanyaki room where meals are prepared from the center of the table as guests look on. The high-end French/Continental restaurant, Le Bistro, serves classic and nouvelle cuisine in an atmosphere of floral tapestry upholstery and fine place settings. On *Dawn,* Le Bistro is adorned with original Impressionist paintings by Matisse and Monet, while *Pearl* has paintings by van Gogh and Renoir, all lent from the private collection of Tan Sri Lim Kok Thay, chairman and CEO of NCL's parent company, Star Cruises. All the ships but *Spirit* also have a casual Tex-Mex/tapas eatery. *Star* has a restaurant serving Pacific Rim cuisine. Specialty restaurants cost between $10 and $20 per person.

Out on deck, each ship has a casual grill serving up burgers, dogs, and fries during the day.

POOL, FITNESS, SPA & SPORTS FACILITIES   Main pool areas have the feel of a resort, ringed by flower-shaped "streetlamps," terraces of deck chairs leading down to the central pool and hot tubs, and (on *Star, Jewel, Pearl,* and *Gem*) a large corkscrew water slide. A huge bar, running almost the width of the ship, serves ice cream on one side, drinks on the other. Nice space, but the real plaudits go to the spa, especially on *Dawn,* where you'll find a large lap pool, hot tub, jet-massage pool, and sunny windowed seating areas furnished with wooden deck chairs, the latter harking back to the classic indoor pools on the transatlantic liners. *Spirit* also has an "Aqua Swim" room with two stationary lap pools. Spas are generally stylish, with the one aboard *Dawn* taking the prize with its sunlit entranceway that rises three decks high and is decorated with plants and Maya reliefs, with a juice bar on the side. *Jewel* and *Pearl* have two of the better onboard gyms of recent years—large and extremely well appointed, with dozens of fitness machines and a large aerobics/spinning room. Contrastingly, *Dawn's* gym and *Jewel's* spa are sort of blah—large and well-enough appointed, but nothing to write home about.

Outside there's an extralong jogging track, a sports court for basketball and volleyball, golf-driving nets, and facilities for shuffleboard and deck chess, plus acres of open deck space for sunning. *Dawn* and *Star* offer a nice spot on the tiered Sun Deck, where a lone hot tub looks out over the bow. *Spirit,* on the other hand, has a beautiful tiered, amphitheater-like stern looking down to a pirate-themed kids' pool.

NCL America: Pride of Aloha • Pride of America

The Verdict

Sailing from Honolulu, concentrating solely on the islands, and with Hawaii themes playing a major part in the onboard atmosphere, these vessels are literally in a class by themselves.

Pride of Aloha *(photo: NCL)*

Specifications

Size (in tons)		*Pride of America*	1,073/665
Pride of Aloha	77,104	Crew	1,000
Pride of America	81,000	Passenger/Crew Ratio	
Passengers (double occ.)		*Pride of Aloha*	2 to 1
Pride of Aloha	2,002	*Pride of America*	2.1 to 1
Pride of America	2,146	Year Launched	
Passenger/Space Ratio		*Pride of Aloha*	1999
Pride of Aloha	38.5	*Pride of America*	2005
Pride of America	37.7	Last Refurbishment/Upgrade	
Total Cabins/Veranda Cabins		*Pride of Aloha*	2004
Pride of Aloha	1,001/257	*Pride of America*	N/A

Frommer's Ratings (Scale of 1–5)   ★★★★

Cabin Comfort & Amenities	4	Dining Options	5
Appearance & Upkeep	4	Gym, Spa & Sports Facilities	4
Public Comfort/Space	4	Children's Facilities	4
Decor	4	Enjoyment Factor	5

By virtue of some complicated legal maneuvers and a lot of persistence (see "Why NCL Owns Hawaii," earlier in this review, for an explanation), NCL effectively has a lock on the Hawaii cruise market, at least for the foreseeable future. So what are the big draws on these cruises?

- **All Hawaii, all the time:** Because *Aloha* and *America* are U.S.-flagged and U.S.-crewed, they're in compliance with U.S. cabotage laws, which forbid foreign-flagged vessels from sailing itineraries composed only of U.S. ports. And because Hawaii's islands are all relatively close together, these ships' itineraries can include a port every single day.

- **All-American crew:** American crews are as rare as dodo birds on today's ships, but on the *Pride*s practically everybody's American, save a handful of foreign passengers.

- **Overnights in port:** Most cruise itineraries have passengers reboarding by 6pm so the ship can sail to its next port, but NCL's itineraries include overnight stays in Kauai and Maui, giving you an opportunity to sample nightlife ashore and get a better feel for both of these beautiful islands.

- **Enough shore excursions to choke a horse:** NCL offers nearly 150 excursion options in port, allowing you to create a Hawaii itinerary to suit your preferences, from easy bus tours to adventurous excursions to golf outings at some of the islands' best courses. For more information on shore excursions in Hawaii, see chapter 14.

On the downside, these are busy, noisy ships—especially in summer and during holidays, when many families with kids sail. Things can get tight out on deck and in lines for buffets and early dinners at the restaurants, and sometimes to get on and off ship in port. Also, because these cruises put so much emphasis on the port experience, with many excursions starting in early morning and taking up most of the day, passengers tend to come back to the ship, eat an early dinner, and crash from exhaustion, so if you want a cruise with lots of onboard activities and a heavy nightlife, this isn't the one for you. Lastly, although prices for the cruises themselves are relatively low, expect lots of **extra costs,** from the $10-a-day automatic gratuity to expensive drinks, pricey Internet access, and the bundle you're bound to spend on shore excursions or renting cars in port. (Because most of the islands' real attractions aren't near the port facilities, you have to take an excursion or rent a car if you're going to see anything worth seeing.)

Cabins & Rates

Cabins	Per Diems From	Sq. Ft.	Fridge	Hair Dryer	Sitting Area	TV
Inside	$131	121–147	yes	yes	yes	yes
Outside	$151	149–243	yes	yes	yes	yes
Suite	$405	321–4,390	yes	yes	yes	yes

CABINS   Cabins on the *Pride* vessels are pretty, most with wood-grain walls, and carpets, upholstery, and bedspreads done in vibrant, Hawaiian-accented pinks, blues, oranges, purples, and greens; but spacious they're mostly not. Continuing a long-standing NCL tradition, the vast majority of standard outsides and insides measure about 40 square feet smaller than Carnival's standards. Storage space is fairly limited.

All have a small sitting area or desk, a minifridge, a hair dryer, TVs, and (on *Pride of America*) coffee- and tea-making equipment and a dataport to accommodate laptop users. Bathrooms are adequately sized. Balcony cabins come in particularly handy on the run between Kona and Hilo, letting you watch the lava flowing from Kilauea Volcano without changing out of your pajamas. The captain turns the ship 360 degrees at the optimum viewing point, so cabins on both sides get a view. The majority of *Pride of America*'s outsides have balconies, including cabins located almost all the way forward (some to port and starboard, some facing front with recessed balconies).

Six cabins on *Aloha* and 23 on *America* are equipped for wheelchairs. The ships offer laundry and dry-cleaning service but do not have self-serve launderettes.

PUBLIC AREAS   *Pride of Aloha* boasts a decor that draws on the beauty of Hawaii's tropical landscape—a welcome change from the cruise world's ubiquitous Caribbean imagery. You'll find references to Hawaiian culture and history throughout, from orchids to outrigger canoes, beaches, fish, waterfalls, and colonial plantations. *Aloha* offers nearly a dozen bars, including a surfing-themed sports bar, two large poolside bars, a coffee bar, an Internet cafe, a library, and the dark and cozy Captain Cook's Bar and Churchill's Cigar Club, the latter a dimly lit nook with oversize soft leather furniture and an out-of-the-way location. It's the most appealing place on the ship for a quiet drink, though tolerance for smoke is required. Up on Deck 12, the Plantation Club lounge is a pleasant getaway, with quiet piano or guitar music, cozy tables, and a decor of palms and black-and-white photos of old Hawaii. One deck down in the bow, the Outrigger Lounge is a very woody observation lounge/disco, with rattan chairs, tropical foliage, outrigger canoes, and carpeting that suggests the ocean. Hawaiian dance and crafts classes are held here throughout the week. Most other recreation venues are on decks 5, 6, and 7, including the centerpiece Kumu Cultural Center, a museum of Hawaiian culture with displays on Hawaiian woodworking, boat building and navigation, music, history, and classic Hawaii travel kitsch. A large video screen shows movies on culture, marine life, and other topics throughout the day. On the same deck, a pro shop serves as a focal point for NCL America's extensive golf program. On Deck 6, the Blue Hawaii show lounge hosts karaoke, dancing, and other small-scale entertainments amid pop-culture Hawaiian decor. In the stern, the two-story Stardust Lounge theater is the venue for large-scale revues. For kids, a huge children's area includes a sprawling playroom with cathedral-high ceilings, a teen center with a large movie screen and a pair of foosball games, and a video arcade. A children's wading pool is located outdoors on Deck 12.

Pride of America's decor matches her name, with public rooms throughout decorated to celebrate aspects of American culture and geography. Giant photographs of the Grand Canyon, Monument Valley, Mount Rainier, the Golden Gate Bridge, the Chicago skyline, and other sites adorn her stair towers, and U.S. themes dominate the decor of many of the restaurants (see below). *America,* the ship—that is, the old United States Line's vessel SS *America*—is the motif of the SS *America* Library, which holds memorabilia and artifacts from the vessel as well as a scale model built specifically for the room. Despite her year-round Hawaiian itineraries, *America* actually employs relatively little Hawaiian imagery beyond some art, some carpeting and upholstery, and the small Hawaiian cultural display in the atrium. If you like, you can enjoy Hawaii's own Kona Beer on tap in the (hmmm . . .) Gold Rush Saloon, with its prospector decor. For a more elegant drinking experience, head to the Napa Wine Bar, whose decor of stone-pattern walls, box-shaped light fixtures, and light woods and upholsteries straddles the line between Napa Valley casual and hip 1950s lounge. In a nice touch, a door opens to outdoor seating on the Promenade Deck. Nearby, Pink's Champagne and Cigar Bar spans the width of the ship, with bright Hawaii-patterned carpeting and a contrastingly 19th-century-casino-style chandelier hovering above its piano-bar piano. Way up on Deck 13, the small, intimate, and beautifully designed Lanai Bar & Lounge is located next to one of the largest dedicated meeting spaces at sea, with auditoriums and facilities for up to 550 participants. For kids, the Rascal's Kids Club offers an elaborate indoor jungle gym, a movie room full of beanbag chairs, computer terminals, a large play space, and a protected outdoor splash pool with tube slide. Next door, the teen center is designed like an adult lounge, with a "bar," dance floor, and games.

Because of Hawaiian law, there's no casino or any other gambling on either of the *Pride* ships. If you've got a jones, head to the card room, where you might find a secret game of Texas Hold 'Em in progress. The password is *swordfish*.

DINING OPTIONS   Above all else, NCL excels in the restaurant department. For breakfast, lunch, and dinner, each *Pride* ship has two main dining rooms whose almost-elegant decor belies their often casually dressed customers. For dinner, you can also choose from several extra-charge alternative restaurants, which offer superior service, presentation, and cuisine.

Aboard *Pride of Aloha,* the Royal Palm Bistro, high atop the ship opposite the Plantation nightclub, serves French/Mediterranean cuisine in a pseudocolonial Hawaiian decor. On Deck 11, Pacific Heights serves Pan-Pacific cuisine, including local fish, steak, Asian dishes, and (hmm . . .) pizza, which you can get free late into the night. Most interesting of the three is the Kahili Restaurant, a long, narrow space stretched along the starboard side of Deck 5. Serving Italian cuisine in a setting of elegant burl-wood paneling, cozy booths, and window-side tables for two, the restaurant is a little hard to find, located at the bottom of a stairway from Deck 6. The per-person charge is $10 for Kahili, the Royal Palm Bistro, and Pacific Heights. Reservations are required for dinner in all of the specialty restaurants, though you can sometimes get a table as a walk-in. For casual dining there's a large but poorly organized indoor/outdoor casual buffet restaurant on the pool deck serving all three meals plus snacks in between. If you arrive and find a huge line, slip outside to the covered Lanai Deck in the stern, where there are additional lines that get much less use.

Pride of America's two main restaurants are the Skyline Restaurant, with its Art Deco decor and skyscraper motifs, and the mucho Americano Liberty Restaurant, with its greeting statues of George Washington and Abe Lincoln, its stars-and-ribbons carpeting, its soaring-eagle-motif glass ceiling and glass Mount Rushmore, and its bunting-style curtains that give it the look of an old-time political rally. Passengers can also choose from several intimate, extra-cost options: the Lazy J Texas Steakhouse, where waiters serve in cowboy hats; Jefferson's Bistro, an elegant venue modeled after the president's home and serving French cuisine; the Little Italy Italian restaurant; and East Meets West, a Pan-Asian restaurant with attached sushi/sashimi bar and teppan-yaki room. Alternative, reservations-only restaurants carry a charge of $10 to $20 per person. For late-night cravings, the Cadillac Diner serves burgers, shakes, and other diner fare 24 hours, with additional seating outside on the promenade deck. On Deck 11, the Aloha Cafe buffet is designed with multiple serving islands both inside and out, rather than a few long central lines.

Because of these ships' emphasis on port calls, restaurants tend to be busiest early, with long lines often forming right at 5:30pm. The later you dine, the less the wait and the better the service, as the staff won't be as rushed. *Tip:* It's easier to get reservations at alternative restaurants for the first couple of nights and on luau night in Maui, when most passengers stay ashore.

POOL, FITNESS, SPA & SPORTS FACILITIES   The well-stocked oceanview gyms on these ships are open 24 hours a day, and the adjacent aerobics room has floor-to-ceiling windows and a great selection of stretching, step, and other traditional classes at no extra charge, and spinning, kickboxing, and other trendy choices for which they'll squeeze an extra $10 a pop out of ya. Nearby, the spa and beauty salon offer ocean views as well, plus (on *Pride of America* only) a small outdoor "Oasis Pool." Out on deck, *Pride of Aloha* has a pair of pools with a cluster of four hot tubs between them; one deck up is a combo basketball/volleyball court, a pair of golf driving nets, and shuffleboard. There's also a kids' wading pool and some cute mini-chaise-longues located far forward on the Sports Deck, where there's also a fifth hot tub. *Pride of America*'s pool deck, her central outdoor space, is a bit underwhelming, perhaps an admission that whatever the line came up with, it couldn't compete with Hawaii's beaches. Look to the deck above, however, for a couple of fun toys: a trampoline with bungee harness to keep you from flying over the side, and a "spaceball challenger" gyroscope in which passengers, suitably strapped in, can revolve 360 degrees in any direction, like astronauts in outer space.

Wraparound promenade decks on both ships offer a great stroll.

Norwegian Sun

The Verdict

If you like your ships big but intimate, *Sun* has a cozier feel than the newer ships above, yet still features multiple restaurants and lots of cabins with balconies.

Norwegian Sun *(photo: Matt Hannafin)*

Specifications

Size (in tons)	78,509	Crew	968
Passengers (double occ.)	1,936	Passenger/Crew Ratio	2 to 1
Passenger/Space Ratio	40.6	Year Launched	2001
Total Cabins/Veranda Cabins	1,001/432	Last Refurbishment/Upgrade	N/A

Frommer's Ratings (Scale of 1–5)   ★★★★

Cabin Comfort & Amenities	4	Dining Options	4.5
Appearance & Upkeep	4	Gym, Spa & Sports Facilities	4
Public Comfort/Space	4	Children's Facilities	3.5
Decor	4	Enjoyment Factor	4

Norwegian Sun was the second megaship built for NCL's modern era (after *Norwegian Sky*, since renamed *Pride of Aloha*), and blazed the trail that all the later ships followed, with 9 restaurants, 12 bars, and everything else designed with casual cruising in mind.

Cabins & Rates

Cabins	Per Diems From	Sq. Ft.	Fridge	Hair Dryer	Sitting Area	TV
Inside	$78	118–191	yes	yes	yes	yes
Outside	$93	154–173	yes	yes	yes	yes
Suite	$164	264–570	yes	yes	yes	yes

CABINS *Sun* is heavy on suites and minisuites, the latter of which measure a roomy 264 to 301 square feet (plus 68- to 86-sq.-ft. balconies) and have walk-in closets, sitting areas, and bathtubs. Twenty 355- to 570-square-foot Penthouse and Owner's suites (with 119- to 258-sq.-ft. balconies) include the services of a butler and concierge who will get you on the first tender in ports, make dinner reservations, and generally try to please your every whim. The pair of penthouses also has a separate living room and dining area.

Among the regular balcony cabins, categories BA, BB, and BC (which take up most of decks 8–10) are laid out awkwardly, with the twin beds and the closet-dresser unit positioned too close together. A person dragging a suitcase or pushing a stroller has to twist up like a pretzel to squeeze by. Other than that, the decor is pleasant with caramel wood veneers, attractive gilt-framed artwork, and navy, gold, and Kelly green fabrics and carpeting. Storage space is plentiful, so much so that on a recent cruise we couldn't even manage to fill up all the shelves. The bathrooms have a pair of shelves above the counter and a really useful one in the shower, though otherwise the skinny shower stalls are a tight squeeze for all but Kate Moss types. Cabins at the forward end of Deck 6 have large portholes that look out on the ship's wraparound Promenade Deck (which is popular with walkers and runners, so you'll probably want to have your curtains closed most of the time unless you like being peeped on).

Every cabin has a small sitting area, a minifridge (not stocked), a hair dryer, TV, desk and chair, and a coffee-/teamaker. Bathrooms are equipped with shampoo and liquid-soap dispensers attached right to the wall. Suites are stocked with robes for use during the cruise.

Twenty cabins are equipped for wheelchairs.

PUBLIC AREAS *Sun* is bright and, well, sun-filled due to an abundance of floor-to-ceiling windows. Surrounding the understated three-level atrium on several levels are a bar, clusters of chairs creating relaxing pockets, and an area where a pianist performs. The color scheme is a pleasing, unjarring pastiche of mostly cool blues, sages, deep reds, and soft golds blended with marble, burled-wood veneers, and brass and chrome detailing. There are nearly a dozen bars, including a sports bar, a wine bar, a nightclub/disco centrally located amidships, two large poolside bars, a coffee bar, an Internet cafe, and a dark and cozy cigar club. As on *Pride of Aloha*, the latter is one of the nicest nooks on the ship, with soft ballads coming from the adjacent piano bar and oversized soft leather furniture to sink into—just as long as you're not coughing from the smoke.

In addition to the so-so main theater there's also an attractive observation lounge wrapped in windows high atop the ship, with live music at night. The casino is large and flashy enough, though not over the top. The layout of the shops is attractive, with a wide streetlike corridor cutting between the main boutiques and a long jewelry counter. As the passage is the only way to get between the casino and show lounge, you're forced to browse whether you want to or not.

For kids, the ship's huge children's area includes a sprawling playroom with cathedral-high ceilings, a teen center with a large movie screen and a pair of foosball games, a video arcade, and a wading pool.

DINING OPTIONS   Breakfast, lunch, and dinner are served in two main dining rooms with many tables for two and four. At dinner you can also choose from six alternative restaurants, including Le Bistro, an elegant space with lots of windows and several comfy round booths with cushy pillows as well as regular tables ($15 cover charge). There's also the Il Adagio Italian restaurant, a long, skinny space between the two main restaurants, where the lighting is low and the views are good from both the raised round booths along the wall and the tables for two at the windows ($10 cover charge). Caesar salads are prepared from scratch table side, and the warm chocolate hazelnut cake is to die for.

Sun's sushi bar ($15 cover) serves expertly prepared, fresh-tasting maki and California rolls, while the adjacent teppanyaki venue ($20 cover) does lunch and dinner just like Benihana, with the theatrical cutting and flinging of shrimp, chicken, beef, and whatever else you order from the a la carte menu. Nearby is a no-charge Tex-Mex/tapas restaurant with tile mosaic and terra-cotta pottery, serving an odd assortment of finger food along with sangria and a selection of Mexican beer. At dinnertime, live Spanish music is featured; at lunch the mood is more casual. Pacific Heights is a health-oriented dinner venue where calories, fat, protein, and other similar stats are listed on the menu. On the opposite end of the spectrum there's the East Meets West Steakhouse, where $20 per person will buy you some mighty slabs of meat.

The casual buffet restaurant is large but poorly organized, and is often backed up at mealtimes. Open 24 hours, it serves snacks (including pizza and jumbo, really yummy homemade cookies) between meals. Pizza is also available from room service 24 hours a day.

POOL, FITNESS, SPA & SPORTS FACILITIES   *Sun's* well-stocked oceanview gym is open 24 hours a day, and the adjacent aerobics room has floor-to-ceiling windows and a great selection of no-charge traditional classes (including stretch classes and step classes), as well as spinning, kickboxing, and other trendy choices that carry a $10 charge. At the nearby spa, you can wait for your treatment in a serene sitting area that has a wall of glass facing the hypnotic sea. Heidi got the best shiatsu massage of her life here, so good she signed up for a second.

Out on deck is a pair of pools with a cluster of four hot tubs between them. One deck up are the combo basketball/volleyball court, a pair of golf driving nets, and shuffleboard. The kids' wading pool and some cute mini-chaise-longues are conveniently tucked along the starboard side of the Sports Deck.

Norwegian Majesty • Norwegian Dream

The Verdict

Old workhorses soon going to pasture, *Majesty* and *Dream* still get the job done with good food and enough entertainment and activity options to keep everyone occupied.

Norwegian Majesty *(photo: NCL)*

Specifications

Size (in tons)		Crew	
Majesty	38,000	*Majesty*	620
Dream	50,764	*Dream*	614
Passengers (double occ.)		Passenger/Crew Ratio	
Majesty	1,462	*Majesty*	2.7 to 1
Dream	1,748	*Dream*	2.8 to 1
Passenger/Space Ratio		Year Launched	
Majesty	26	*Majesty*	1992
Dream	29	*Dream*	1992
Total Cabins/Veranda Cabins		Last Refurbishment/Upgrade	
Majesty	730/0	*Majesty*	1999
Dream	874/0	*Dream*	2001

Frommer's Ratings (Scale of 1–5)

★★★

Cabin Comfort & Amenities	3	Dining Options	3
Appearance & Upkeep	3.5	Gym, Spa & Sports Facilities	3
Public Comfort/Space	3	Children's Facilities	3
Decor	3	Enjoyment Factor	3

Meet the old NCL—and then wave goodbye, because in a year or so these ships will be gone, put out to pasture (read: sold to the Asian market) as part of NCL's long-term modernization program. It was to be expected. In people years 16 is nothing, but in ship years it's time to buy a walker and an ear trumpet. Thus, the 1992 vintage *Norwegian Majesty* and *Norwegian Dream* are veritable antiques, a reminder of just how long ago and far away the early '90s really were.

Cabins & Rates

Cabins	Per Diems From	Sq. Ft.	Fridge	Hair Dryer	Sitting Area	TV
Inside	$64	130–150	no	some	no	yes
Outside	$74	160–176	no	some	some	yes
Suite	$200	270–385	yes	yes	yes	yes

CABINS *Norwegian Majesty's* cabins were designed with short 3- and 4-night cruises in mind; today, with the vessel sailing mostly 7-night Bermuda and Caribbean itineraries, those small cabins can seem particularly small. Most Superior Oceanview Staterooms are adequate at 145 square feet, but in lower inside and outside categories (which make up a good portion of the total cabins) it gets even tighter at a ridiculous 108 square feet. Some cabins on the Norway and Viking decks have views that are obstructed by lifeboats. On the Promenade Deck, cabin windows look out onto the promenade, meaning you may open your curtain in the morning and see a jogger's head bob by. The suites (18 of them) are more than adequate, with bathtubs and tile bathrooms, sitting areas, and enough room to move. The best nonsuite accommodations are the category C rooms on the Majesty Deck, especially the ones in the bow that have windows offering sweeping vistas of the sea ahead. All cabins have hair dryers, safes, and televisions, and cabins far forward and far aft have minifridges. Seven cabins are equipped for passengers with disabilities.

Some 80% of *Norwegian Dream*'s cabins are outsides, most with sitting areas and picture windows. In general, cabin decor is pleasant and breezy, with wood accents and pastels evocative of the West Indies. Storage space is minimal: Two people can just barely manage, and when a third or fourth person shares a cabin, it can get truly cramped. Bathrooms are also small, though overall standard cabins are larger than *Majesty*'s, measuring 160 to 176 square feet. Clustered on the Sun Deck, the top-of-the-line Owner's Suites are 271 square feet plus a 65-square-foot balcony and include a living room with convertible double-bed sofa, separate bedroom, minifridge, stereo with CD library, DVD player, and bathroom with tub and shower. Lifeboats block the views of the category F and G cabins at midships on the Norway Deck. Thirteen cabins are wheelchair accessible.

PUBLIC AREAS Aside from Deck 7's Frame 52 Disco, the rest of *Majesty*'s nightlife is on Decks 5 and 6, including the Rendezvous Lounge piano bar and Royal Fireworks dance lounge. The Palace Theater could be described as intimate; it could also be described as claustrophobic, with support columns all around and a low ceiling that prevents performers from getting too energetic. The Polo Club, just outside the theater, usually features a pianist/vocalist. On the opposite end of the long, narrow room is the dark, moody Monte Carlo Casino, a decent place for you and your money to part ways. The Royal Observatory Lounge, tucked away in the bow, offers great views and live entertainment nightly, including karaoke. A coffee bar sits next door to the Le Bistro alternative restaurant. Shops are forward from the lobby, and there's also a card room, a small video arcade, a library, a children's playroom, and a meeting room.

Aboard *Dream*, Lucky's Bar and Dazzles Nightclub see the most late-night action, with many folks also spending lots of time at the Sports Bar & Grill, a real bar-bar for real guy-guys decorated with sports memorabilia and giant-screen TVs. On the International Deck, the library is small and feels like an afterthought. The Observatory Lounge on the Sports Deck, a sequestered oceanview spot behind the gym and spa, has dancing in the evenings. A basketball/volleyball court is just overhead, creating its own kind of thump-thump. A small children's playroom is located on Sun Deck and a dark, Vegas-style adult playroom (aka casino) is on Star Deck.

DINING OPTIONS Both *Majesty* and *Dream* offer two main dining rooms. On *Dream*, the most appealing is Terraces, a cozy, three-level restaurant with a 1930s supper-club feel and floor-to-ceiling windows facing the stern. Aboard both ships, the small, intimate Le Bistro serves French cuisine at $15 per person, while Italian trattoria-style dinners are served at the Royal Observatory on *Majesty* and the Sun Terrace on *Dream* (no charge). Majesty offers a standard (if smallish) buffet restaurant in the bow, but *Dream* does without, instead offering a casual breakfast buffet at its Four Seasons main restaurant and sit-down breakfasts and lunches at its Sun Terrace and Terraces dining rooms. *Dream*'s small, indoor/outdoor Sports Bar & Grill also serves casual meals: continental-style breakfast; burgers, hot dogs, and salad at lunch; dishes like chili con carne and stir-fry spicy chicken for dinner; and snacks throughout the day. Its outdoor Pizzeria adjacent to the main swimming pool offers a limited breakfast buffet, plus pizza, pasta, and a salad bar at lunch. Aboard *Majesty*, the sternside Piazza San Marco grill serves pizza, hot dogs, and burgers.

POOL, FITNESS, SPA & SPORTS FACILITIES   Gyms on both ships are small and basic, with several weight stations and cardiovascular stations, while the small spa offers the typical range of treatments. Joggers can work out on the wraparound Promenade Deck. Each ship has two pools, with a swim-up bar at the larger one on *Dream*.

10 Oceania Cruises

8300 NW 33rd St., Suite 308, Miami, FL 33122. ℂ **800/531-5619** or 305/514-2300. www.oceaniacruises.com.

THE LINE IN A NUTSHELL   Oceania is the phoenix that rose from the ashes after Renaissance Cruises went belly-up in September 2001. Headed by former Renaissance and Crystal Cruises executives, the line owns three of Renaissance's ships and mimics some attributes of much pricier lines, with excellent service and cuisine and a quiet, refined onboard feel. **Sails to:** Caribbean (plus Europe, South America, Asia).

THE EXPERIENCE   Oceania is positioned as an "upper premium" line intended to fill the gap—in terms of both ship size and level of luxury—between big-ship premium lines such as Celebrity and real luxe lines such as Radisson. It's going for a kind of floating country club feel, with a low-key ambience, few organized activities, low-key entertainment, a casually sporty dress code, an emphasis on cabin comfort, and long itineraries that favor smaller, less-visited ports like St. Kitts and St. Barts. Despite such luxe-travel touches, the line's prices are competitive with—and often even lower than—those of the other premium lines.

Pros

- **Excellent cuisine:** In both the main dining room and specialty restaurants, Oceania is near the top among mainstream lines.
- **Excellent, personal service:** The ships' international crews are extremely friendly and eager to please.
- **Intimate size:** Oceania's ships carry only 684 passengers apiece, making for a much more human-scale feel than you get aboard a megaship.
- **Nonsmoking policy:** On these ships, smoking is permitted only in two small areas of the pool deck and nightclub. (Of course, this is a "con" for smokers.)

Cons

- **Few outside decks:** There's only a pool deck, a sun deck, and the deserted promenade/boat deck, which is never used because it has no deck chairs or other furniture. Aside from the many private cabin balconies, you'd have a hard time finding a quiet little outdoor nook.
- **Few activities:** By design, Oceania generally leaves passengers to their own devices. This is a "con" only if you need constant stimulation.

Compared with the other mainstream lines, here's how Oceania rates:

	Poor	Fair	Good	Excellent	Outstanding
Enjoyment Factor				✓	
Dining				✓	
Activities		✓			
Children's Program	N/A*				
Entertainment			✓		
Service				✓	
Worth the Money				✓	

* Oceania offers no children's program.

OCEANIA: CLASS ACT, COZY SHIPS

Remember Renaissance Cruises? Founded in 1988, it made news in the '90s by building a large fleet of identical medium-size ships and going direct to consumers rather than working with travel agents. Both of these were fairly revolutionary moves back then, and, as often happens with revolutions, this one didn't work out too well. Already in bad financial shape when 9/11 hit, the line was forced into bankruptcy when the resultant travel downturn came. Left high and dry, its eight ships were put up for auction to the highest bidder. Oceania, founded by former Renaissance CEO Frank Del Rio and former Crystal president Joseph Watters, started up in 2003 with two of them (the former *R1* and *R2*, renamed *Regatta* and *Insignia*) and added a third, *Nautica*, in late 2005. The remaining Renaissance vessels are now owned by Princess (*Pacific Princess, Tahitian Princess*, and *Royal Princess*) and Celebrity (*Celebrity Journey* and *Celebrity Quest*). At press time, Oceania had just announced plans for two new 1,260-passenger, 65,000-ton ships, to be built at Italy's Fincantiari shipyards and delivered to the line in 2010 and 2011.

Oceania's itineraries are world-ranging, with one ship generally positioned in the Caribbean for the winter and the others sailing to Europe, South America, Africa, India, Southeast Asia, and China.

PASSENGER PROFILE

Due partially to the length of these cruises (mostly 10, 12, and 14 days, going up to 26) and partially to the low-key onboard atmosphere, Oceania tends to attract older passengers who prefer to entertain themselves, reading in the library and enjoying the destination-heavy itineraries. Most are Americans, with many from the West Coast and many "returning," having sailed previously with Oceania or with Renaissance back in the old days. A sprinkling of younger couples usually find themselves on board as well, though children are rare enough to be surprising. Whatever their age, passengers tend to be drawn by the line's 100% casual dress code and ambience.

Because of Oceania's stringent **no-smoking rules,** most passengers are nonsmokers. Aside from one corner of the pool deck and one corner of the Horizons nightclub, smoking is not permitted anywhere on board—even in your cabin or private balcony.

DINING

Oceania's dining experience is one of its strongest suits, with menus created by renowned chef Jacques Pepin (one-time personal chef to Charles de Gaulle and, more recently, one of America's best-known chefs and food writers). Passengers are able to choose among four different restaurants for dinner: the main Grand Dining Room, the Mediterranean-style Toscana restaurant, the Polo Grill steakhouse, and the "Tapas on the Terrace" casual outdoor option. All four venues work on an open-seating basis (dine when you want, with whom you want), with meals usually served in a 3-hour window from 6:30 to 9:30pm.

TRADITIONAL The **Grand Dining Room,** the main restaurant aboard each ship, features French-inspired Continental cuisine in five courses, with a string quartet providing music at dinner. Appetizers might include grilled marinated prawns, frog-leg mousse, and crushed new potatoes with chives and Malossol caviar, while soups might be as traditional as beef oxtail consommé or as unusual as Moroccan harira chicken soup. There are always several salads and a pasta of the day, and entrees are elaborate, well-presented versions of the big faves (lobster tail butterfly, beef Wellington, steamed Alaskan king crab legs), plus some uncommon dishes: sautéed sea bream filet and pheasant breast ballotine stuffed with morel mushrooms. There's always a tasty **vegetarian option,** plus an alternative selection of basics: grilled sirloin, broiled chicken, salmon filet, and the like.

SPECIALTY As an alternative, passengers can make a reservation at the ships' specialty restaurants, the Italian **Toscana** or the **Polo Grill** steakhouse. Toscana is sinfully overwhelming, serving half a dozen antipasti and an equal number of pasta dishes, soups, salads, and main courses such as medallions of filet mignon topped with sautéed artichoke and smoked mozzarella; swordfish steak sautéed in garlic, parsley, Tuscan olives, capers, and orvieto wine; and braised double-cut lamb chops in a sundried tomato, olive, and roasted garlic sauce. Desserts include the remarkable if weird-sounding chocolate lasagna. Polo Grill serves chops, seafood, and cuts of slow-aged beef, with all the substantial trimmings: seafood appetizers, soups such as New England clam chowder and lobster bisque, straight-up salads such as Caesar and iceberg wedge with blue cheese and crumbled bacon, and side dishes such as a baked potato, wild mushroom ragout, and creamed spinach. Passengers can make reservations for either restaurant during breakfast or lunch hours at the Terrace Cafe. There's no extra charge, but there's an initial two-reservation limit to ensure that all guests get a chance. If you'd like to dine here more than twice, add your name to the waiting list and you'll be contacted if there's space (which there usually is).

CASUAL On the casual side, the **Terrace Cafe** is a standard cruise ship buffet serving a range of sides, salads, and main courses. An attached pizzeria serves very tasty thin-crust pies. At lunch the pool deck's grill is also fired up, serving burgers, hot dogs, and specialty sandwiches. In the evening, the outdoor portion of the Terrace is transformed into **Tapas on the Terrace,** a romantic option with regional Spanish and Mediterranean specialties, other ethnic dishes, and home-style favorites served from a buffet. Waiters are on hand to serve drinks and generally be charming.

SNACKS & EXTRAS **High tea** is served daily at 4pm in the Horizons Lounge, with a good spread of pastries, tea sandwiches, and scones. **Room service** is available 24 hours. Guests in Owners, Vista, and Penthouse suites can have full meals served course by course in their rooms.

ACTIVITIES

By design, activities are not a high priority for Oceania. Expect **enrichment lectures** themed around the region being visited, fitness and computer classes, informal health

Oceania Fleet Itineraries

Ship	Itineraries
Regatta	**Caribbean:** 10- & 12-night eastern and 14-night western, round-trip from Miami, FL (Jan–Mar). **Panama Canal:** 16-night west- & eastbound, between Miami and Los Angeles, CA (Jan).

and beauty seminars by the spa and salon staff, and a handful of old cruise standards: bingo, shuffleboard, and the like. For people who are self-motivated and/or prefer to spend their time aboard reading on deck or in one of the library's overstuffed leather armchairs, this is ideal. If you like a lot of organized activities, though, this is not the line for you.

All of Oceania's ships have smallish, 19th-century-style casinos that see a fair amount of action. Internet access is available in Deck 9's Oceania@Sea Internet center and at two terminals in the library. The ships' full-service spas are run by Mandara, a subsidiary of Steiner Leisure, which operates almost every spa at sea.

CHILDREN'S PROGRAM

There are no special facilities on these ships, and the line typically carries very few children.

ENTERTAINMENT

The good news: You won't be assailed by steel-drum bands doing bad Bob Marley covers. Instead, you'll get a 12-piece jazz band on deck in the afternoon and in the club at night; pianists performing Cole Porter, Hoagy Carmichael, and other standards at the martini bar before dinner; and an occasional string quartet.

The bad news: That's the high point of the onboard entertainment. Each night, the main show lounge presents a comedian, solo musician, folkloric act, or other headliner, but the shows don't have the breadth you'll find on larger vessels. Of course, there also aren't any big, bad Vegas-style song-and-dance revues, for which we whisper a prayer of thanks.

Other entertainment options include the occasional karaoke session or a movie presented out on deck.

SERVICE

The staff in the restaurants are crack troops, delivering each course promptly but without any sense that they're hurrying passengers through their meals. Service balances precision with friendliness, skewing close to the kind of understated professionalism you see on the real luxury lines. The relatively small number of passengers aboard also means service is more personal than you find aboard the megaships. In the bars, staff tend to remember your drink order by the second day, and cabin stewardesses greet their passengers by name in the corridors. Like many other lines, Oceania adds an **automatic gratuity** to your shipboard account ($12 per person, per day, which may be adjusted up or down at your discretion). For guests occupying Owner's, Vista, and Penthouse suites, there's an additional $3.50-per-day gratuity added for butler service.

There's a **self-service laundry** and ironing room on Deck 7, in addition to standard laundry, dry cleaning, and pressing service offered by the ship's laundry.

Regatta

The Verdict

With her smallish size, understated decor, and serene atmosphere, this mostly non-smoking ship is more like a quiet boutique hotel than a cruise vessel, providing a comfortable, laid-back, yet stylish way to experience the Caribbean.

Regatta *(photo: Oceania)*

Specifications

Size (in tons)	30,200	Crew	400
Passengers (double occ.)	684	Passenger/Crew Ratio	1.7 to 1
Passenger/Space Ratio	44.2	Year Launched	1998
Total Cabins/Veranda Cabins	343/232	Last Refurbishment/Upgrade	2005

Frommer's Ratings (Scale of 1–5)   ★★★★

Cabin Comfort & Amenities	4	Dining Options	4
Appearance & Upkeep	4	Gym, Spa & Sports Facilities	4
Public Comfort/Space	4.5	Children's Facilities	N/A
Decor	4	Enjoyment Factor	4

Imagine an old-style Ritz-Carlton hotel in the shape of a cruise ship and you've pretty much got the idea. Like all of the former Renaissance vessels, *Regatta* is comfortable and spacious, decorated mostly in warm, dark woods and rich fabrics. She's traditional and sedate, with an emphasis on intimate spaces rather than the kind of grand, splashy ones you'll find on most megaships. Of course, her small size means there'd be no *room* for grand spaces, even if they'd been wanted: Carrying only 684 passengers, *Regatta*'s intimacy is one of her main selling points. The atmosphere is relaxed and clubby, with no formal nights that demand tuxedos and gowns.

Regatta has two identical sister ships, *Insignia* and *Nautica,* which sail in Europe, South America, and Asia.

Cabins & Rates

Cabins	Per Diems From	Sq. Ft.	Fridge	Hair Dryer	Sitting Area	TV
Inside	$159	160	no	yes	yes	yes
Outside	$184	160–216*	no	yes	yes	yes
Suite	$297	322–962*	yes	yes	yes	yes

* *Including veranda.*

CABINS   Staterooms aboard *Regatta* are straightforward, no-nonsense spaces with a hint of modern European city hotel: plain off-white walls, dark-wood trim and furniture, and rich carpeting. The highlight of each, though, is its "Tranquility Bed," an oasis of 350-thread-count Egyptian cotton sheets and duvet covers, down duvets and pillows, custom-designed extrathick mattresses, and a mound of throw pillows to prop you up during the late-late show. Spacious balconies have teak decking for a classic nautical look, and all cabins have televisions, safes, vanities with mirrors, hair dryers, phones, full-length mirrors, and French-milled toiletries. Closet space is a little skimpy considering the lengthy itineraries these ships sail, but drawer space scattered around the cabin, and space under the beds, make up for this a bit. Overall cabin size is in the 165-square-foot range—not tiny, but not exceptionally large, either. There are also some bizarre little quirks. Light switches, for instance, can be mystifying: There doesn't seem to be any way to turn off the bedside lights until you discover the tiny, almost hidden buttons up near their shades. There are also switches for the overheads right in the headboard, which makes it very easy to switch them on accidentally in your sleep.

Suites include minibars, bathtubs, and a small area with a cocktail table for intimate in-room dining. Ten Owner's Suites measure 786 to 982 square feet and are located at the ship's bow and stern, featuring wraparound balconies, queen-size beds, whirlpool bathtubs, minibars, living rooms, and guest bathrooms. Owners Suites, Vista Suites, and Penthouse Suites feature butler service. Concierge-class staterooms (in between regular cabins and suites) add some warm-and-fuzzy to the amenities: a welcome bottle of champagne, DVD player, personalized stationary, cashmere throw blanket, complimentary tote bag, priority embarkation, dedicated check-in desk and priority luggage delivery, priority restaurant reservations, complimentary shoeshine service, and additional bathroom amenities like massaging shower heads, luxury toiletries, and a hand-held hair dryer.

Three cabins are wheelchair accessible.

PUBLIC AREAS   Overall, *Regatta*'s an elegant yet homey ship, with dark-wood paneling, fluted columns, ornate faux-iron railings, gilt-framed classical paintings, Oriental-style carpets, frilly moldings, marble and brass accents, and deep-hued upholstery, all contributing to a kind of "English inn at sea" look. In the bow, the spacious, woody Horizons lounge has floor-to-ceiling windows and brass telescopes on three sides and is used for dancing in the evenings and for various activities during the day. The 345-seat show lounge offers cabaret and variety acts, musical recitals, magic shows, and comedy; and the smallish but comfortable casino offers blackjack, poker tables, roulette, and slots. The attached Martini Bar has a ridiculously long martini list (some 30 recipes and an equal number of vodka choices) and is a very relaxing space in the pre-dinner hours, when a pianist plays standards. A jazz band performs here in the evenings.

Another notable space is the comfortable library, decorated in a traditional English style with warm red upholstery, mahogany paneling, *trompe l'oeil* garden skylight, and marble faux fireplace.

DINING OPTIONS   The main dining room is an elegant single-level space surrounded on three sides by windows. It's spacious and understated, with simple wood-veneer wall panels, wall sconces, and teal carpeting. Tables seating between two and eight are available, though the smaller arrangements go fast. Just outside the maitre d' station is a cozy bar area where you can have a pre-dinner cocktail while waiting for your dinner companions. The ship's two specialty restaurants, the Polo Grill and Toscana, are both located in the stern on Deck 10, and are decorated to match their cuisine: woody, old-Hollywood decor in Polo and a bright white Mediterranean feel with Roman urns and reliefs in Toscana. The restaurants serve 96 and 90 guests, respectively. On Deck 9, the Terrace serves buffet breakfast, lunch, and dinner, the latter out under the stars, with drink service, Spanish cuisine, and candles flickering in lovely hurricane lamps. It's a very romantic spot if you can time your meal to the sunset.

POOL, FITNESS, SPA & SPORTS FACILITIES   The attractive teak pool deck, dotted with canvas umbrellas, offers a pair of hot tubs plus a slew of deck chairs and large day beds for sunbathing. The Patio, a shaded outdoor lounge located in the aft port corner of the pool deck, is furnished with thickly cushioned sofas, chairs, and day beds. Drapes and general ambience add a hint of partition from the pool goings-on (not to mention shade), but you still feel like you're in the action. For more privacy, passengers can rent one of eight private cabanas on Deck 11, each with privacy partitions and white drapes that can be drawn or left open, plus great sea views, a retractable shade roof, and a plush day bed built for two. They're available for rent either daily ($50 on port days, $100 on sea days) or for the entirety of your cruise, and come with the services of a dedicated attendant who provides food and beverage service, chilled towels, and water spritzes. Guests can even arrange to get massages and other spa treatments in their cabana.

A small jogging track wraps around the pool one deck above the pool deck, while the fully equipped spa on Deck 9 offers a variety of treatments, including aromatherapy massages, hot-stone treatments, and various wraps and facials. Just forward of the spa there's an outdoor hydrotherapy whirlpool overlooking the bow. A decent-size oceanview gym and beauty salon are attached.

11 Princess Cruises

24305 Town Center Dr., Santa Clarita, CA 91355. © 800/PRINCESS or 661/753-0000. Fax 661/259-3108. www.princess.com.

THE LINE IN A NUTSHELL   With a fleet of mostly large and extralarge megaships, L.A.-based Princess offers a quality mainstream cruise experience with a nice balance of tradition and innovation, relaxation and excitement, casualness and glamour. **Sails to:** Caribbean, Alaska, Mexican Riviera, Hawaii, Canada/New England, Panama Canal (plus Europe, South America, Asia, South Pacific, Antarctica, and transatlantic).

THE EXPERIENCE   If you were to put Royal Caribbean, NCL, and Holland America in a blender and mix them together, then add a pinch of both British maritime tradition and California style, you'd come up with Princess. Dining, entertainment, and activities are geared to a wide cross section of cruisers: The more traditional minded can spend some time in the library, join a bridge tournament, enjoy a traditional dinner in a grand dining room, and then take in a show. Those seeking something different can spin a pottery wheel or work toward their PADI scuba certification, and then dine in an intimate Italian or steakhouse restaurant and take in a set of small-group jazz afterward. The line's largest vessels are some of the biggest at sea, yet still manage to offer intimate spaces for quiet time.

Pros

- **Lots of dining choices and flexibility:** Each ship offers two or three main dining rooms plus an intimate alternative restaurant or two and a 24-hour buffet. The line's "Personal Choice" program allows you to dine at a fixed time and place or wing it as you go along.
- **Excellent lounge entertainment:** Princess books top-quality entertainers for its piano lounges and smaller showrooms.
- **On top of trends:** From a wide range of enrichment classes to wireless Internet access fleetwide and online spa reservations (for a few ships), Princess doesn't rest on its laurels.

Cons

- **Pottery Barn decor:** More of a qualifier than a con: Princess's ships are very pleasant, yes, but the sea of beiges and blues is so safe that it can be a bit of a yawn. Artwork in public areas and cabins tends toward bland.
- **Small gyms:** For such large vessels, the gyms are surprisingly small and can even feel cramped.

PRINCESS: SMART CASUAL

The Princess story goes back to 1962, when company founder Stanley McDonald chartered a vessel called the *Yarmouth* for use as a floating hotel at the Seattle World's Fair. In 1965, he officially started Princess Cruises, naming the company after another chartered vessel, the *Princess Patricia,* which offered cruises between Los Angeles, Alaska, and Mexico's Pacific coast. In 1974, Princess was snapped up by British shipping giant P&O, and later that decade got a big boost by having its ships featured in the TV series *The Love Boat.* To this day, Gavin "Captain Stubing" MacLeod acts as occasional pitchman for the line, though the original *Pacific Princess* and *Island Princess,* the twin 640-passenger vessels used in the series, finally left the fleet in 1999 and 2002. (Their names have since been assigned to new vessels.) In April 2003, P&O/Princess was purchased by Carnival Corporation, the 500-pound gorilla of the cruise world.

Although its ships sail to nearly every destination covered in this book, Princess is particularly strong in **Alaska,** where it's been locked in competition with Holland America for decades. Through its affiliate, Princess Tours, it offers more than 20 different cruisetour itineraries in conjunction with its Gulf of Alaska and Inside Passage voyages, visiting Denali National Park, Fairbanks, the Kenai Peninsula, Wrangell–St. Elias National Park, Canada's Yukon Territory, and distant Prudhoe Bay on Alaska's north coast. Guests on these land tours stay in five Princess-owned wilderness lodges and travel via motorcoach and the line's domed train cars. Since 2004, Princess has also had an increased presence in the **Caribbean.**

New for 2008 are the 3,080-passenger *Emerald Princess* (sister ship to 2006's *Crown Princess*) and the intimate, 710-passenger *Royal Princess. Royal Princess* was built for Renaissance Cruises before its 2001 collapse and brings to three the number of ex-Renaissance vessels now in the Princess fleet, along with *Pacific Princess* and *Tahitian Princess.* In November 2008, Princess will introduce *Ruby Princess,* a third sister to *Crown* and *Emerald.*

Compared with the other mainstream lines, here's how Princess rates:

	Poor	Fair	Good	Excellent	Outstanding
Enjoyment Factor				✓	
Dining				✓	
Activities				✓	
Children's Program				✓	
Entertainment				✓	
Service				✓	
Worth the Money				✓	

Still the Love Boat

Ever the romantic, Princess has things covered from proposal through "I do." On *Crown, Emerald, Caribbean, Grand,* and *Sea Princess,* prospective fiancés can propose to their future mates via video on the ship's giant movie screens. Called **Engagement Under the Stars,** the $695 package includes the creation of a personalized proposal video with the ship's videographer as well as champagne and chocolates, an engagement portrait session, candid photos of the proposal, an in-room breakfast, dinner for two at one of the ship's specialty restaurants, a couple's massage in the Lotus Spa, and other extras. Meanwhile, *Coral, Island, Diamond,* and *Sapphire Princess* and the six Grand-class ships are all outfitted with **wedding chapels.** *Grand* was the first cruise ship to have one, and now a string of other ships have followed suit, including Royal Caribbean's Voyager class; Carnival's Spirit class; NCL's *Norwegian Sun, Star, Dawn, Jewel, Pearl,* and *Gem;* and others. Princess's ships, though, remain the only ones where the captain conducts the ceremonies.

Romantics sailing aboard any Princess ship can have **dinner under the stars** served by a dedicated waiter on their private balcony, at a table set with a tablecloth, hurricane candle lamp, and champagne. While the waiter is setting everything up, you and your significant other can have a complimentary cocktail in one of the ship's bars. The whole thing costs $50 per person. You can also order breakfast served on the balcony for $25 per couple.

PASSENGER PROFILE

The majority of Princess's passengers are in their 50s, 60s, and older, though more and more 30- and 40-somethings (and their families) are sailing these days, particularly during summer school holidays. Overall, Princess passengers are less boisterous than those aboard Carnival and not quite as staid as those aboard Holland America. Its ships all have extensive kids' facilities and activities, making them suitable for families, while their balance of formal and informal makes them a good bet for a romantic vacation too, with opportunities for doing your own thing mixed in among more traditional cruise experiences.

DINING

All Princess ships sailing from the U.S. and Canada offer a wide variety of dining options, though their cuisine generally doesn't quite live up to the number and attractiveness of their restaurants. Most dishes sit squarely in the "average to tasty" range, approximately on par with what's served aboard Royal Caribbean and NCL.

TRADITIONAL   Princess's Personal Choice Dining program allows passengers two options: dining at a set time with set dining companions in one of the ship's two or three main restaurants, or just showing up anytime during a 4½-hour window and being seated by the maitre d'. If you're not sure which option you'll prefer once you're on board, sign up for traditional, as it's easier to switch to anytime dining than it is to go the other way round. Passengers choosing the flexible option but wishing to be served by the same waiter nightly can usually be seated in his or her section if they make a special request.

Whether you choose traditional or flexible dining, your menu in the main dining room will be the same, offering several appetizers, soup and salad, and a choice of five to eight dinner entrees that may include prime rib, lobster, king crab legs, turkey and trimmings, mahimahi filet with dill butter sauce, rack of lamb with Dijon sauce, Cornish hen, sautéed frogs' legs, or duck a l'orange. There are always **healthy choices** and **vegetarian options,** too, plus staples such as broiled Atlantic salmon, grilled chicken, and grilled sirloin steak.

Unlike the no-dress-code dress code that's part of NCL's "Freestyle" dining plan, Princess maintains the tradition of holding 2 formal nights per week, with the other nights designated smart casual, which is defined as "an open-neck shirt and slacks for gentlemen and a dress, skirt and blouse, or trouser suit outfit for ladies." Men, however, should take our advice and pack at least a jacket. Otherwise, you may be down in the gift shop buying one after you realize everyone on the ship except you decided to dress for dinner. We speak from experience on this one.

All of the restaurants offers a **kids' menu,** which includes goodies such as burgers, hot dogs, fish sticks, chicken fingers, and, of course, PB&J sandwiches; this menu is also offered in the Horizon Court during its sit-down Bistro hours 11pm to 4am nightly.

SPECIALTY   All Princess ships that sail from the U.S. feature alternative restaurants: an Italian trattoria and steakhouse on the Grand- and Diamond-class ships, trattoria and New Orleans–style restaurants on *Coral* and *Island Princess,* and a steakhouse and free sit-down pizzeria on the Sun-class ships.

Sabatini's Trattoria ($20 per person) is a traditional Italian restaurant with an airy decor, an open kitchen, balloon-back chairs, and Italian scenes in faux tilework. Dinners here are eight-course extravaganzas emphasizing seafood, with all dishes brought automatically—you just select your main course.

The Sterling Steakhouse ($15 per person) offers a dark and woody ambience. Passengers can choose their favorite cut of beef—rib-eye, New York strip, porterhouse, and filet mignon—and have it cooked to order, with starters such as chili, blooming onion, jalapeño poppers, and fresh Caesar salad, plus the usual sides of baked potato or fries, sautéed mushrooms, creamed spinach, and corn on the cob.

Crown and *Emerald Princess* also offers a steak and seafood restaurant called the Crown Grill ($25 per person).

Reservations are recommended for all alternative restaurants as seating is limited. See the individual ship reviews for more details.

CASUAL   Fleetwide, passengers can choose casual dining at breakfast, lunch, and dinner in the 24-hour, buffet-style Horizon Court restaurant. At breakfast, you'll find the usual: fresh fruit, cold cuts, cereal, steam-table scrambled eggs, cooked-to-order fried eggs, meats, and fish. At lunch, you'll find several salads, fruits, hot and cold dishes, roasts, vegetarian choices, and sometimes sushi. Evenings (until 10pm), the space serves a casual buffet dinner that usually has the same dishes as in the main dining room. From 11pm to 4am every night it serves a late-night menu of pastas, seafood, poultry, and red meats, along with a chef's special of the day. The food here is as good as you'll find in the main dining rooms, and the atmosphere is strictly casual. *Crown* and *Emerald Princess* offer two casual dining venues in the piazza-style atrium: an International Café serving a rotating menu throughout the day, and a wine and seafood bar (a la carte pricing at both).

SNACKS & EXTRAS Poolside grills serve burgers, hot dogs, and pizza; a patisserie offers coffee and pastries; and an ice-cream bar serves Princess's house brand for a charge. There's also 24-hour room service available in the cabins.

ACTIVITIES

Like the other big mainstream lines, Princess offers onboard activities designed to appeal to a wide range of ages and tastes. For active types, all the ships offer traditional shipboard sports such as Ping-Pong and shuffleboard; more athletic activities such as aerobics classes and water volleyball; and virtual-reality golf simulators. The Grand-, Coral-, and Diamond-class ships all offer basketball/volleyball courts and 9-hole miniature-golf courses, and the latter are also available on the Sun-class ships.

For something more cerebral, the line's **ScholarShip@Sea** enrichment program offers classes in cooking, computer skills (such as basic Web design, Photoshop, and Excel), finance, photography, scrapbooking, and even ceramics. Large-group seminars are free, while small-group and individual classes carry a charge of around $20 to $25 per person. Charges for paint-your-own ceramics are calculated based on the piece you create.

Sit-down activities include bingo, cards, trivia games, dance lessons, and recent-release **big-screen movies** (shown on giant outdoor LCD screens on the *Caribbean, Grand, Sea, Crown,* and *Emerald Princess*). Activities designed to part you from your cash include art auctions and beauty and spa demonstrations. Others designed to part you from your dignity include belly-flop contests, the perennial Newlywed/Not-so-Newlywed game, an *American Idol*–style "Princess Idol" competition, and a reality-TV style makeover show called "If They Could Sea Me Now." On *Crown Princess,* **The Bee at Sea** is a spelling bee with rounds for both adults and kids, with the winners receiving a dictionary signed by the ship's captain.

In the Caribbean, guests can earn PADI scuba diving certification while on board (contact the **PADI New Waves Dive Line** at ℭ **888/919-9819,** or check out **www. newwaves.com**). In Alaska, rangers, naturalists, and guest lecturers present talks and slide shows on such topics as the Iditarod sled-dog race, the wildlife and ecology of Glacier Bay and the Tongass National Forest, oceanography and marine life, glaciers, Native Alaskan cultures, and Alaskan history.

All Princess ships offer well-stocked libraries, 24-hour Internet centers, and wireless Internet hot zones for laptop users (wireless cards are available if you don't have one).

CHILDREN'S PROGRAM

Princess offers great facilities and amenities for kids and their parents, but it's not a line that's completely gung-ho about *only* catering to families—and therein lies a big advantage: Princess ships aren't overrun with children. In fact, a Princess reservations agent has told us that they cap the total number of kids under 18 at about 14% to 15% of a ship's capacity. On one cruise Heidi took her young sons aboard *Caribbean Princess* (maximum occupancy 3,782), which maxed out at about 600 children—20% to 50% less than the biggest ships at Carnival, Disney, and Royal Caribbean routinely see.

Princess's "Princess Kids" program offers activities year-round for three age groups: **Princess Pelicans** (ages 3–7), **Shockwaves** (ages 8–12), and **Remix** (ages 13–17), supervised by a counseling staff whose size varies depending upon the number of children aboard. Each ship has a spacious indoor/outdoor **children's playroom** with a splash pool, an arts-and-crafts corner, game tables, and computers or game consoles, plus a **teen center** with computers, video games, a dance floor, and a music system. The two-story playrooms on *Golden* and *Grand* have a large fenced-in outside deck dedicated to kids only and featuring a teen section with a hot tub and private sunbathing area. The rest of the Grand-class ships have a great fenced-in outdoor play space for toddlers, and the *Coral, Island, Diamond,* and *Sapphire Princess* have a small swimming pool for adults adjacent to the outdoor kids' deck, allowing parents to relax while their kids play.

Traditional kids' activities include arts and crafts, scavenger hunts, game tournaments, spelling bees, movies and videos, coloring contests, pizza and ice-cream parties, karaoke, dancing, tours of the galley or behind the scenes at the theater, hula parties (complete with grass skirts!), and teen versions of *The Dating Game*.

Learning activities may include **environmental education programs** developed by the California Science Center that teach about oceans and marine life through printed materials and specially created films. The kids' equivalent of an onboard guest lecturers program is also offered occasionally, allowing children to go stargazing with an astronomer, learn drawing skills from an animator, and so on.

Children must be at least 6 months of age to sail. When kids are registered in the youth program, their parents are given pagers so that they can be contacted if their children need them. Parents may also rent walkie-talkies through the purser's desk if they want two-way communication with their kids. Two **parent "date nights"** let adults have a calm evening while kids dine with counselors in a separate restaurant. Teens have their own group night in one of the main dining rooms, complete with photographs and an after-dinner show. Younger kids can then be taken straight to group babysitting in the children's center (available nightly 10pm–1am for kids 3–12; $5 per hour, per child). Princess does not offer private in-cabin babysitting.

Tahitian Princess in the Frozen North

For summer 2008, Princess will be sailing one of its three midsize vessels, the 670-passenger *Tahitian Princess,* on 14-night Gulf of Alaska cruises that take in all the usual ports along the Inside Passage (Ketchikan, Skagway, and Juneau), plus the lovely "Outside Passage" port of Sitka, Glacier Bay National Park, the Canadian port of Victoria, Valdez and Seward (on Prince William Sound), and even the island of Kodiak, known for its population of huge brown bears. It's one of the best Alaska itineraries going this season.

Tahitian Princess was originally built for Renaissance Cruises, whose 2001 bankruptcy supplied Princess, Oceania, and Azamara/Celebrity with eight lovely, hardly used, nearly identical midsize vessels perfect for longer, more intimate, and exploratory cruises. For an idea of what the ship is like, read the "Cabins" and "Public Areas" sections in the review of Oceania's *Regatta,* a twin to *Tahitian Princess* save for some branding details (such as Princess's two specialty restaurants, Sabatini's Italian restaurant and the Sterling Steakhouse).

Princess Fleet Itineraries

Ship	Itineraries
Caribbean Princess	**Caribbean:** 7-night eastern, round-trip from Ft. Lauderdale, FL (Jan–Apr). 9-night eastern, round-trip from New York, NY (May–Aug). **New England/Canada:** 7 nights, round-trip from New York, NY (Aug–Oct). **Bermuda/Caribbean:** 7 nights, New York to San Juan, PR (Oct).
Coral Princess	**Panama Canal:** 10 nights, round-trip from Ft. Lauderdale, FL (Jan–Apr). 15 nights, Ft. Lauderdale to San Francisco, CA (Apr). **U.S. Pacific Coast:** 2 nights, San Francisco, CA, to Vancouver, BC (May). **Alaska:** 7-night Gulf of Alaska, north- or southbound between Vancouver, BC, and Whittier/Anchorage, AK (May–Sept).
Crown Princess	**Caribbean:** 7- & 14-night southern, round-trip from San Juan, PR (Jan–Apr).
Dawn Princess	**Mexican Riviera:** 7 nights, round-trip from San Diego, CA (Jan–Apr). **U.S. Pacific Coast:** 2 nights, San Diego, CA, to Vancouver, BC (May). **Alaska:** 10-night Inside Passage, round-trip from San Francisco, CA (May–Sept).
Diamond Princess	**Hawaii:** 15 nights, round-trip from Los Angeles, CA (Jan–Apr). **U.S. Pacific Coast:** 3 nights, Los Angeles, CA, to Vancouver, BC (May). **Alaska:** 7-night Gulf of Alaska, north- or southbound between Vancouver, BC, and Whittier/Anchorage, AK (May–Sept).
Emerald Princes	**Caribbean:** 10-night southern (Feb–Apr) & 10-night eastern (Jan–Mar), round-trip from Ft. Lauderdale.
Golden Princess	**Mexican Riviera:** 7 nights, round-trip from Los Angeles, CA (Jan–Apr). **U.S. Pacific Coast:** 6 nights, Los Angeles, CA, to Vancouver, BC (May). **Alaska:** 7-night Inside Passage, round-trip from Seattle, WA (May–Sept).
Grand Princess	**Caribbean:** 7-night western, round-trip from Ft. Lauderdale (Jan–Apr).
Island Princess	**Panama Canal:** 10-night east- or westbound between Acapulco, Mexico, and San Juan, PR (Jan). 11-night eastbound, Acapulco to Ft. Lauderdale, FL (Jan). 15-night east- or westbound between Los Angeles, CA, and Ft. Lauderdale, FL (Feb–Apr). 19-night round-trip from Los Angeles, CA (Apr). **U.S. Pacific Coast:** 3-night, Los Angeles, CA, to Vancouver, BC (May). **Alaska:** 7-night Gulf of Alaska, north- or southbound between Vancouver, BC, and Whittier/Anchorage, AK (May–Sept).
Sapphire Princess	**U.S. Pacific Coast:** 3 nights, Los Angeles, CA, to Vancouver, BC (May). **Alaska:** 7-night Gulf of Alaska, north- or southbound between Vancouver, BC, and Whittier/Anchorage, AK (May–Sept).
Sea Princess	**Caribbean:** 14-night eastern/southern/western, round-trip from Barbados or Montego Bay, Jamaica (Jan–Mar). **New England/Canada:** 10-night, north- or southbound between New York, NY, and Quebec City, QC (Sept–Oct).
Star Princess	**Mexican Riviera/U.S. Pacific Coast:** 8 nights, Acapulco, Mexico, to Seattle, WA (Apr). **Alaska:** 7-night Inside Passage, round-trip from Seattle, WA (May–Sept).
Tahitian Princess	**Alaska:** 14-night round-trip from Vancouver, BC (May–Sept).

On days in port, Princess offers children's center activities straight through from 8am to 5pm (on sea days the center closes for lunch), allowing parents to explore the port while their kids do their own thing. On Princess's private Bahamas beach,

Princess Cays, kids can be checked in at a play area supervised by the shipboard youth staff (for details on Princess Cays see section 1, "The Cruise Lines' Private Islands," in chapter 10). In Alaska, kids ages 6 to 12 and teens ages 13 to 17 can participate in the **Junior Ranger and Teen Explorer program,** a joint effort between Princess and the National Parks Service that uses interactive projects to teach kids about Glacier Bay's natural and cultural history.

ENTERTAINMENT

Princess has some of the best entertainment at sea, with variety acts on the ships' main stages ranging from Vegas-style song-and-dance revues and cabaret singers to ventriloquists, acrobats, aerialists, stand-up comics, and musical soloists. The Sun-class ships offer entertainment in two showrooms, while the Grand-, Diamond-, and Coral-class vessels offer three shows nightly in their main theater and two smaller venues, plus quieter music in a few lounges, including the popular piano bars. At several other venues, including the Wheelhouse Lounge and the atrium, you'll find pianists, guitarists, or string quartets providing live background music, and out by the pool a deck band plays at various times during the day. For those who would rather participate, there are regular karaoke nights and a **passenger talent show.** The ships' **casinos** are among the most comfortable at sea, very large and well laid out.

SERVICE

Overall, service is efficient and passengers rarely have to wait in lines, even in the busy Horizon Court buffet restaurants. As is true generally of staff aboard all the mainstream lines, you can expect them to be friendly, efficient, and happy to help, though probably not of the level you'll find aboard the luxe lines or at fine hotels. Cabin steward service is the most consistent, with dining service only slightly behind. Suite guests get extra service goodies, including complimentary Internet access, dry cleaning, laundry, and shoe polishing; complimentary corsage and boutonniere on formal nights; en suite afternoon tea; expedited embarkation and debarkation; and other perks.

Through the line's **Captain's Circle loyalty program,** cruisers who have sailed with Princess before are issued specially colored onboard keycards and cabin-door nameplates (gold after taking 1 to 5 cruises, platinum after 5, and elite after 15) so that staffers will know to be extra helpful. Platinum Captain's Circle members also get expedited embarkation and credit toward free Internet access, while Elite members receive free laundry and dry-cleaning services, a complimentary wine-tasting class, 10% off in the onboard gift shops, and more.

Gratuities for all service personnel are automatically added to passengers' shipboard accounts at the rate of $10 per person per day, as is the case now on most lines. You can make adjustments (up or down) by visiting or calling the purser's desk at any time. Passengers who wish to tip more traditionally—dispensing cash in person—can also make arrangements for this through the desk.

All of the Princess vessels offer laundry services, and also have **self-service laundromats.**

The Grand Class: Grand Princess • Golden Princess • Star Princess • Caribbean Princess • Crown Princess • Emerald Princess (preview)

Grand Princess *(photo: Princess Cruises)*

The Verdict

These huge, well-accoutered vessels are very easy to navigate, never feel as crowded as you'd expect, and are amazingly intimate for their size.

Specifications

Size (in tons)		Crew	
Grand/Golden/Star	109,000	*Grand/Golden/Star*	1,100
Caribbean/Crown/Emerald	113,000	*Caribbean/Crown/Emerald*	1,200
Passengers (double occ.)		Passenger/Crew Ratio	
Grand/Golden/Star	2,600	*Grand/Golden/Star*	2.4 to 1
Caribbean	3,100	*Caribbean/Crown/Emerald*	2.6 to 1
Crown/Emerald	3,080	Year Launched	
Passenger/Space Ratio		*Grand*	1998
Grand/Golden/Star	41.9	*Golden*	2001
Caribbean/Crown/Emerald	36.7	*Star*	2002
Total Cabins/Veranda Cabins		*Caribbean*	2004
Grand/Golden/Star	1,300/710	*Crown*	2006
Caribbean	1,557/881	*Emerald*	2007
Crown/Emerald	1,538/1,102	Last Refurbishment/Upgrade	N/A

Frommer's Ratings (Scale of 1–5)   ★★★★½

Cabin Comfort & Amenities	5	Dining Options	4
Appearance & Upkeep	4.5	Gym, Spa & Sports Facilities	5
Public Comfort/Space	5	Children's Facilities	4
Decor	4	Enjoyment Factor	4.5

Princess's signature vessels, the Grand-class ships were so ahead of their time when they debuted in 1998 (when *Grand Princess* was briefly the largest passenger ship in the world) that the design of even recent sisters like *Crown* and *Emerald Princess* isn't significantly changed. They look like nothing else at sea, with their 18 decks soaring up to space-age discos hovering in the air at their very stern, stretching from port to starboard. Though the vessels give an impression of immensity from the outside, inside they're extremely well laid out, very easy to navigate, and surprisingly cozy. In fact, their public areas never feel as crowded as you'd think they would with almost 4,000 people aboard, including passengers and crew. The cozy carries over to public rooms like the clubby and dimly lit Explorer's and Wheelhouse lounges, whose traditional accents recall a grander era of sea travel. In the elegant three-story atriums, classical string quartets perform on formal nights and during embarkation.

Caribbean Princess, Crown Princess, and *Emerald Princess* are slightly larger versions of the original Grand-class concept, with a similar layout but one extra deck, plus a cafe serving Caribbean dishes. *Crown* and *Emerald* also include an international cafe, a wine and seafood bar, and a steak and seafood house, plus a "piazza-style" atrium with a street-cafe vibe.

Cabins & Rates

Cabins	Per Diems From	Sq. Ft.	Fridge	Hair Dryer	Sitting Area	TV
Inside	$86	160	yes	yes	no	yes
Outside	$100	165–232	yes	yes	no	yes
Suite	$150	323–1,314•	yes	yes	yes	yes

* Includes veranda.

CABINS   Though cabins on these vessels are divided into some 35 categories, there are actually fewer than 10 configurations. For the most part, the category differences reflect location—such as amidships versus aft. Cabins are richly decorated in light hues and earth tones, and all have safes, hair dryers, minifridges, and TVs. Storage is adequate and offers more closet shelves than drawer space. Cabin balconies are tiered so they get more sunlight, but this also means your neighbors above can look down at you. Be discreet.

A standard outside cabin without a balcony, such as categories F and FF, ranges from 165 to 210 square feet, while insides, such as category JJ, measure 160 square feet. Balcony cabins range from 165 to 257 square feet, including the balcony. At 324 square feet, including the balcony, the 180 minisuites on each vessel are smaller than the 32 minisuites on the Sun-class ships, but are ultracomfortable and offer a roomy sitting area with a full-size pullout couch, two televisions, minifridge, large bathroom with full tub and shower, generous closet and drawer space, and terry robes. When Heidi sailed with her young sons on the *Caribbean Princess,* she had two cribs set up in the living area and there was still plenty of space for playing. Storage was so plentiful that, even with the kids' copious gear, she didn't fill it all.

Two Grand Suites measure 782 square feet and feature all the above amenities plus a bathroom with large whirlpool tub and multidirectional shower plus a separate toilet compartment. There are two 607-square-foot family suites that can sleep up to eight, with two bathrooms. Minibars in the suites are stocked once on a complimentary basis with soda, bottled water, beer, and liquor. Suite guests are also on the receiving end of a slew of perks highlighted in the "Service" section above.

Lifeboats partially or completely obstruct the views from most cabins on Emerald Deck. More than 600 cabins can accommodate a third passenger in an upper berth. Each ship has 28 wheelchair-accessible cabins.

PUBLIC AREAS   Even sailing with a full load of passengers (as many as 3,100 on *Grand, Golden,* and *Star* if all additional berths in every cabin are filled, and almost 3,800 on *Caribbean, Crown,* and *Emerald*), you'll wonder where everyone is. These are huge ships with a not-so-huge feeling. Because of their smart layout, six dining venues, expansive outdoor deck space, multiple sports facilities, four pools, and nine hot tubs, passengers are dispersed rather than concentrated into one or two main areas.

Coupled with this smart layout is Princess's pleasing-if-plain contemporary decor. Public areas are done up in tasteful caramel-colored wood tones and color schemes of warm blue, teal, and rust, with some brassy details and touches of marble.

While the decor is soothing, the entertainment is pretty hot. Gamblers will love each ship's sprawling casino. Three main entertainment venues include a well-equipped two-story theater for big Vegas-style musical revues; a second one-level show lounge for smaller-scale entertainment such as hypnotists and singers; and the travel-themed Explorer's Club, decorated with vaguely Islamic tile motifs, African and Asian art pieces, primitivist exotic paintings, and a dark, woody atmosphere. It's a venue for bands, comedians, or karaoke nightly. There's also the clubby, old-world Wheelhouse Lounge, offering laid-back pre- and post-dinner dancing and jazz in an elegant setting, as well as a woody sports bar and a wine bar selling caviar by the ounce and wine, champagne, and iced vodka by the glass.

Skywalkers multilevel disco/observation lounge, sequestered 150 feet above the ship's stern like a high-tech treehouse, is a unique spot offering floor-to-ceiling windows with two impressive views: forward for a look over the ship itself, or back toward the sea and the giant vessel's very impressive wake. It's well positioned away from any cabins (so the noise won't keep anyone up) and is our favorite disco at sea. Check out the view at sunset.

For kids, the indoor/outdoor Fun Zone kids' play area has tons of games, toys, computers, and—the jewel for Heidi, a mother of toddlers—an outdoor, fenced-in play area equipped with a fleet of tricycles and minibasketball setup. Nearly always deserted (we're told there are rarely more than 10 children under 3 on any given cruise), it's an awesome place to let your little ones run free while you sit on the sidelines and relax. A kiddie pool is located nearby. A separate teen center has several computers, plus video games, a dance floor, and a sound system. On the *Grand* and *Golden*, there's also a teens-only sunbathing area with deck chairs and a hot tub, as well as a cavernous and truly amazing arcade, with virtual reality hang gliding, downhill skiing, fly-fishing, motorcycle riding, and more.

Each ship also has a library, a small writing room, a card room, a large Internet center, and an attractive wedding chapel where the captain himself performs about six or seven bona fide, legal marriages every cruise.

DINING OPTIONS Each ship has three pleasant, one-story main dining rooms, laid out on slightly tiered levels. By way of some strategically placed waist-high dividers, they feel cozy, although the ceilings are a tad on the low side. The 24-hour Horizon Court casual restaurant offers buffet-style breakfasts and lunches and is designed to feel much cozier than it actually is. With clusters of buffet stations serving stir-fry, beef, turkey, pork, and lots of fruit, salads, cheeses, and more, lines are kept to a minimum and you're hardly aware of the space's enormity. On *Grand, Golden, Star,* and *Caribbean Princess,* this restaurant turns into a sit-down bistro from 11pm to 4am, with the same dinner menu each night. If you like the idea of New York strip sirloin at midnight, this is the place to go.

For a more intimate yet still casual meal, there are two alternative, reservations-required restaurants. Sabatini's specializes in Italian cuisine, featuring an eight-course menu emphasizing seafood. Service is first-rate and the food is decent. The second venue is the Sterling Steakhouse, where you can choose your favorite cut of beef and have it cooked to order. *Caribbean, Crown,* and *Emerald Princess* also offer the Café Caribe, a themed buffet carved out of the Horizon Court, serving Caribbean specialties such as jerk chicken, grilled Caribbean rock lobster, whole roast suckling pig, Guiana pepper pots and curries, and paella-style prawns. Musicians play Caribbean music, and passengers can order their meal cooked to taste at the cafe's open kitchen. There's no cover charge here. On *Crown* and *Emerald*, the International Cafe serves food 24 hours a day—pastries in the morning; tapas, panini, and the like later; and cookies 'round the clock (with some items at extra charge).

POOL, FITNESS, SPA & SPORTS FACILITIES   The Grand-class ships have around 1¾ acres of open deck space, so it's not hard to find a quiet place to soak in the sun. On *Grand, Golden,* and *Star,* our favorite spot on a hot, humid day is portside aft on the deck overlooking the swimming pool, where the tail fin vent blows cool air. It's like having an outdoor air-conditioner. *Crown* and *Emerald* offer a different kind of wonderful at a space called The Sanctuary. Three-quarters canopied and dotted with lounge chairs, trees, and private cabanas, it's a perfect onboard chill-out space, staffed with "serenity stewards" tasked with making sure things stay quiet. Light meals, massages, and beverages are available. Admission carries a $15 fee for half-day use, a measure intended to limit use to those who really want some peace and quiet.

The ships have four great swimming pools. On *Grand, Golden,* and *Star,* one has a retractable roof for inclement weather. Another aft, under the disco, feels miles from the rest of the ship, while outside the spa a resistance pool allows you to swim steadily against a current. The fourth pool is for kids. Other recreational offerings include a Sports Deck with a jogging track and (aboard *Crown, Emerald, Caribbean,* and *Grand Princess*) a 300-square-foot outdoor LED movie screen for watching movies under the stars. You can reserve deck chairs for evening feature films, and, yes, there's popcorn (free) and Raisinettes (for a price). It's great fun, and the sound is awesome.

Spa, gym, and beauty-parlor facilities are located in a large, almost separate part of each ship, surrounding the lap pool and its tiered, amphitheater-style wooden benches. As is the case fleetwide with Princess, the oceanview gym is surprisingly small for ships of this size, although there's an unusually large aerobics floor. The spa is located under the Sports Deck. Hope there's no basketball game going on during your shiatsu appointment.

The Diamond Class: Diamond Princess • Sapphire Princess

The Verdict

Diamond and *Sapphire* are two of the best megaships ever, with beautiful proportions, airy outdoor spaces, and clubby, intimate public areas.

Diamond Princess *(photo: Princess Cruises)*

Specifications

Size (in tons)	116,000	Crew	1,100
Passengers (double occ.)	2,670	Passenger/Crew Ratio	2.4 to 1
Passenger/Space Ratio	42.3	Year Launched	2004
Total Cabins/Veranda Cabins	1,337/748	Last Refurbishment/Upgrade	N/A

Frommer's Ratings (Scale of 1–5)

★★★★½

Cabin Comfort & Amenities	4.5	Dining Options	4
Appearance & Upkeep	5	Gym, Spa & Sports Facilities	4.5
Public Comfort/Space	5	Children's Facilities	5
Decor	4.5	Enjoyment Factor	5

Built by Mitsubishi Heavy Industries in Nagasaki, Japan, these two vessels are Princess's biggest and best ever, but they're also poster children for the line's philosophy of offering "big ship choice with small ship feel." Outside, they're an appealing update of the Grand class's groundbreaking design, but more sleek, graceful, and streamlined. On board, expect some of the same features that make the Coral- and Grand-class ships such winners: comfortable cabins (tons of 'em with balconies), woody lounges with hints of seagoing history, understated central atrium lobbies, relaxing indoor/outdoor "Conservatory" pool areas, large Asian-themed spas, and—a personal favorite of ours—covered Promenade decks that wrap around the bow, just below the open top deck. When we sailed, we walked up to this perch late one moonless night and made a discovery: Standing right in the bow, with the whistling wind drowning out the ship's hum and no light coming from above, behind, or to the sides, the starry sky and dark sea merge and you feel as if you're all alone, flying into outer space. Second star to the right, and straight on till morning . . .

Cabins & Rates

Cabins	Per Diems From	Sq. Ft.	Fridge	Hair Dryer	Sitting Area	TV
Inside	$114	168	yes	yes	no	yes
Outside	$146	183–275	yes	yes	no	yes
Suite	$215	354–1,329•	yes	yes	yes	yes

* Includes veranda.

CABINS   Though cabins on *Diamond* and *Sapphire* are a bit bigger than those on the Coral- and Grand-class ships, they still stick close to the Princess family look, with upholstery and walls done in easy-on-the-eyes earth tones and off-whites, all trimmed in butterscotch wood. All have safes, hair dryers, minifridges, and TVs broadcasting one of the widest selections of channels at sea. Standard inside and outside cabins are smaller than those aboard the newer Holland America and Carnival ships, but are still comfortable and stylish, and more than 70% of outside cabins have verandas. Balconies are tiered, ensuring direct sunlight for those on Decks 8 and 9 (where most of the popular minisuites are located), but also ensuring voyeurism, since folks standing on the balconies above can look right down on you. Standard cabin bathrooms have smallish shower stalls and adequate counter space.

Minisuites provide substantially more space without jumping into the cost stratosphere. All have those big, less-than-private balconies and offer sizable sitting areas with sofa beds and two televisions, one facing the sitting area and the other the bed (cheaper and less bothersome, the line told us, than installing a lazy Susan to let one TV swivel). They're ideal for families with children. Bathrooms have bathtubs and more counter space than in standard cabins. Storage space in both standard outsides and minisuites is more than adequate, with a large shelved closet and open-sided clothes rack facing a small dressing alcove by the bathroom door. Sixteen full suites have curtained-off sitting and sleeping areas, very large balconies, complimentary stocked minibar, robes, whirlpool tubs and separate showers in the bathroom, and a walk-in closet. Suite guests are also on the receiving end of numerous perks highlighted in the "Service" section, above.

Twenty-seven cabins on each ship are wheelchair accessible.

PUBLIC AREAS These ships are huge—a fact you'll learn the first time you have to walk from one end to the other to retrieve something you forgot in your cabin. On the other hand, when you're sitting in one of their cozy lounges or bars, you might well think you're on a 40,000-ton ship rather than one three times that size. It's an appealing combination, giving passengers a large ship's range of options in a more personal, human-scaled package. You don't feel like you're lost in the crowd.

Most public rooms on these ships are on Decks 6 and 7. Toward the bow, the two-deck Princess Theater is the main show space, with tiers of upholstered theater seats (with little cocktail tables that fold out of their armrests, airline-style) and a pair of opera boxes to either side of the large stage. It's a very minimalist room, and a very appealing one, putting the emphasis on the stage rather than distracting with fanciful decor. Just outside the entrance is the clubby Churchill's, a classically decorated cigar bar with TVs for sports. You'll also find a multipurpose entertainment lounge called Club Fusion, used principally for games (think bingo and "Princess Idol" talent shows) and evening music. Down a spiral staircase in the back of the room, you'll find one of our favorite spaces, the very small, cozy Wake View Bar, a classy nook full of dark wood, leather chairs, and paintings depicting turn-of-the-20th-century tobacconists. TVs are tuned to sports (though the sound is often off), and six portholes overlook the namesake wake. Few people seem to venture down here, so let's keep it to ourselves, okay?

At midships are two of Princess's signature lounge spaces: the English-adventurer-themed Explorer's Lounge and the ocean-liner-themed Wheelhouse Bar, the former a secondary show lounge for comedians, impressionists, and other small-scale entertainment; the latter the prime space aboard for elegant music, with a jazz combo playing in the evenings. Decor matches the name for both rooms, with Egyptian art, jungle-pattern carpeting, clubby furniture, and faux Moorish screens in Explorer's, and leather couches, dark wood, brass candlestick sconces, and paintings of old P&O liners in Wheelhouse. There's dancing here, but the "I love the nightlife, I like to boogie" crowd is more likely to be up in the top-deck disco, the highest point of the ship, with a balcony looking back over the stern if you want to head out for air or romance. (Or a smoke.)

Explorer's jungle theme carries over into the ships' casinos, with their tree-trunk pillars and leafy ceilings. Next door, the three-story atrium is admirably restrained, with lots of creamy marble and wood, understated grillwork art fronting the atrium elevators, and musicians performing throughout the day. Opening off the space are the relaxing library, the charmingly old-fashioned writing room, several shops, a coffee bar, and Crooners, a Rat Pack–themed bar serving 56 different martini recipes in two sizes: the standard "Sinatra" and the supersize (and misspelled) "Deano." Clusters of low-slung wicker-frame chairs along the windows give a '50s-rumpus-room effect. Very slinky.

On Deck 7, the ships' Internet Cafes are notable not only for being large and exceedingly stylish (among the most attractive at sea), but also for being cafes in more than just name: A bar toward the back of the room dispenses gourmet coffee for a few bucks, along with free croissants and sweet rolls. Passengers who bring their laptops can connect wirelessly here, as well as in the atrium. Four computer terminals are also located in the atrium's library, and computer classes are generally held in the wedding chapel, just across from the Wheelhouse Bar.

For kids, *Diamond*'s and *Sapphire*'s Fun Zone centers are divided into four separate and sizable rooms, segregating kids by age. Younger tots get a climbing maze, flower-backed chairs, toys, computers, and a great, cushiony amphitheater for watching movies. Teens get a sort of Austin Powers–looking room, brightly colored and looking much like a normal adult bar. "That was on purpose," one Princess exec told us. "What teen wants to be treated like a kid?"

DINING OPTIONS   Passengers opting for traditional dining take their meals in the 518-seat International Dining Room with its simple but elegant wood-panel walls and classical paintings, or in the smaller Vivaldi Restaurant, with its 18th-century European decor. Passengers on the anytime-dining program can dine in any of four smaller restaurants, all serving the same menus.

Guests wanting to gorge long and hard should make a reservation at Sabatini's, the extra-cost Italian trattoria, which serves eight-course, 2½-hour meals. Meat lovers can also make a reservation at the Sterling Steakhouse. For ultracasual dining, head to the Horizon Court buffet.

POOL, FITNESS, SPA & SPORTS FACILITIES   Like most megaships, *Diamond* and *Sapphire* have two pools at midships: a partying main pool out in the sun and a secondary "Conservatory" space with a large pool, two hot tubs, a balcony (which does double duty as sunning space and as a venue for the line's pottery-making classes), and a retractable roof for bad weather. Our favorite outdoor spaces are in the stern, where four decks descend in curved, horseshoelike tiers, creating a multilevel resort with two pools, two hot tubs, two bars, and a magnificent view of the ship's wake.

Another pool, this one an adults-only resistance pool for swimming laps in place, is set in a cleft just outside the large, well-appointed spa, totally minimal in its elegant Asian theme, with a great suite of steam rooms and stone lounging chairs for guests to use before or after their treatment. Next door, the gym is one of the few sour notes on board—well stocked (and with little TVs on all the aerobics machines), but still inadequately small considering the number of people aboard—as is true on most Princess ships. When we sailed, it got crowded often. A large aerobics studio is attached, offering spinning, yoga, and other aerobics and fitness classes ($10 for most of them).

Out on Deck 16, at the top of a very quietly marked stairway and almost completely shielded from wind and view, is a small miniature-golf course. More serious golfers can play illusory courses at a virtual-reality center farther forward, near a nicely designed, covered, and netted sports court suitable for basketball and volleyball.

The Coral Class: Coral Princess • Island Princess

The Verdict

Beautiful, spacious, and at the same time surprisingly intimate, *Coral* and *Island* offer beautiful looks inside and out, a nice range of entertainment options and venues, and great onboard learning experiences.

Coral Princess *(photo: Matt Hannafin)*

Specifications

Size (in tons)	91,627	Crew	981
Passengers (double occ.)	1,970	Passenger/Crew Ratio	2 to 1
Passenger/Space Ratio	46.5	Year Launched	2003
Total Cabins/Veranda Cabins	987/727	Last Refurbishment/Upgrade	N/A

Frommer's Ratings (Scale of 1–5)   ★★★★½

Cabin Comfort & Amenities	4.5	Dining Options	4
Appearance & Upkeep	5	Gym, Spa & Sports Facilities	4
Public Comfort/Space	5	Children's Facilities	4
Decor	4.5	Enjoyment Factor	4.5

Coral Princess and *Island Princess* are some of the loveliest cruise vessels out there, further refining Princess's vision of mega-size ships with an intimate feel. Outside, there are balconies on some 83% of their outside cabins, but their tiered design is a vast improvement over the typical megaship "wall of balconies" look, contributing to a clean and flowing profile. Up top, the ships' futuristic-looking but purely decorative jet-engine funnels give you the impression the ships are going to fly right out of the water and into orbit.

Built to juuuuuussst be able to squeeze through the Panama Canal (with approximately 2 ft. of space on each side), these ships are extremely spacious and well laid out, and never feel crowded even when full. Though they're a fifth larger than the line's Sun-class ships, they carry only 20 more passengers apiece based on double occupancy, meaning more room for you. Understated interiors are both classic and modern, with Internet centers and Times Square–style news tickers right around the corner from woody, almost Edwardian lounges. Our favorite spaces: the clubby Wheelhouse Bar for a before-dinner drink; the bar at the New Orleans–themed Bayou Restaurant for jazz until around midnight; the peaceful, Balinese-style solarium, where your book will have to be damn good to keep you from dozing off; and the Universe Lounge for everything from cooking classes and lectures to full-blown production performances.

Cabins & Rates

Cabins	Per Diems From	Sq. Ft.	Fridge	Hair Dryer	Sitting Area	TV
Inside	$118	160	yes	yes	no	yes
Outside	$118	168–232	yes	yes	no	yes
Suite	$170	323–591*	yes	yes	yes	yes

* Includes veranda.

CABINS   Decor sticks to Princess's fleetwide standard, with upholstery and walls done in easy-on-the-eyes earth tones and off-whites, all trimmed in butterscotch wood. All have safes, hair dryers, minifridges, and TVs. Inside and standard outside cabins are serviceable, but don't expect much room to stretch out—at 160 and 168 square feet respectively, they're on the low end of average in the mainstream category, much larger than on Princess's Sun-class ships and some ships in the Costa and NCL fleets but nowhere near the 185 to 195 square feet you get with the newer Carnival, Holland America, and Disney ships. Most private balconies are set up in descending tiers—a positive for soaking up the sun, a negative for total privacy. Standard cabin bathrooms have smallish shower stalls and adequate counter space.

Minisuites provide substantially more space without jumping into the cost stratosphere, and have larger balconies and sizable sitting areas with sofa beds and two televisions, one facing the sitting area and the other the bed—an odd touch since there's no partition, but what the hell. Bathrooms have bathtubs and more counter space than in standard cabins. Storage space in both standard outsides and minisuites is more than adequate, with a large shelved closet and open-sided clothes rack facing a small dressing alcove by the bathroom door. Sixteen full suites have curtained-off sitting and sleeping areas, very large balconies, complimentary stocked minibars, robes, whirlpool tubs and separate showers in the bathroom, and a walk-in closet. Suite guests get additional perks highlighted in the "Service" section above.

Twenty cabins on each ship are wheelchair accessible.

PUBLIC AREAS   Layout is one of the areas in which these vessels really shine, with decks and public areas arranged so it's always easy to find your way around. Most indoor public spaces are on Decks 6 and 7, starting with the large Princess Theater in the bow. Unlike the ornately decorated two- and three-deck theaters on many new ships, this is a classic sloping one-level space, decorated with no theme whatsoever. You get a good view from every one of the comfortable theater seats, which have little flip-up tables in their arms to hold drinks or, when the room is used for lectures or other enrichment activities, your notebook. Farther aft, the Explorer's Lounge is a smaller-scale show lounge for comedians, karaoke, game shows, and dancing, decorated to evoke the romantic European explorers of the 19th century, with vaguely Islamic tile motifs, African and Asian art pieces, primitivist exotic paintings on the walls, and a dark, woody atmosphere. Important sports events are broadcast here on multiple large screens. In the very stern, the Universe Lounge is an innovative multipurpose space, hosting TV-style cooking demonstrations (with a full kitchen onstage), computer classes (with hookups for 50 computers around the room), lectures, and full-blown production performances on three low interconnected stages, which revolve and rise and segment and contort and do more things than you think a stage could—it's a regular three-ring circus. Shows are tailored to utilize all these options, with much of the action taking place at ground level for a true floor-show feel.

Some standout bars and lounges include the maritime-themed Wheelhouse Bar, an intimate spot decorated in classic dark woods, with heavy leather and corduroy armchairs and love seats, faux marble pillars, domed ceiling lights, and small end-table lamps. In the evening, a small band performs smooth jazz and pop numbers for dancing, and some afternoons the ships' string quartets perform classical repertoire. At one entrance to the lounge, a small museum displays memorabilia from P&O history, including (on *Coral*) an original brass bell from the SS *Oronsay*, children's dolls from the SS *Orsova* and SS *Strathnaver,* postcards sent from the legendary SS *Canberra,* and so on. Nearby, the low-key four-deck atrium is surrounded by the ships' shops, the Internet center and news ticker, and several other rooms. Churchill's cigar lounge is a cozy room with big windows, a humidor under a portrait of the room's namesake, and armchairs and sofas seating just 10 people. Crooner's is a Rat Pack–themed piano bar with a Vegas/martini vibe. A real live crooner performs at the piano each evening.

One level down, the ship's library and card room are both exceptionally large and comfortable, though the layout—with entrances both from the atrium and from the midships elevators/stair tower—means that people often use the rooms as a passageway, adding more bustle than we'd like in a library. Themed casinos (London on *Coral,* Paris on *Island*) and a wedding chapel round out the adult public room offerings, while at the stern on Deck 12, there's the bright and very kid-scaled Fun Zone and Pelican's Playhouse children's center and smallish Off Limits teen center, with computers and a dance floor. Outside are a children's play area and the small Pelican Pool. The ships' bright pottery studio is hidden away back here as well, giving it the feel of a playroom for grown-ups.

DINING OPTIONS   To accommodate Princess's Personal Choice concept, two similar dining rooms—the Provence and the Bordeaux—are dedicated to traditional fixed-seating dining and to Anytime Personal Choice dining, respectively. Both single-level rooms are understated and spacious, with lots of elbowroom (except, that is, in the unusually narrow arm chairs at some tables).

There are two specialty restaurants aboard: the traditional Italian Sabatini's Trattoria for eight-course extravaganzas and the Bayou Cafe and Steakhouse ($15 per person), a New Orleans–themed restaurant with a subdued, woody ambience, faux brick walls, lantern lighting, and primitivist New Orleans murals on the walls. Dinners here include barbecued alligator ribs appetizers and main courses like seafood gumbo, fried catfish, grilled jumbo prawns, and chicken-and-chorizo jambalaya. Steak lovers can also be sated with varieties from New York Strip to porterhouse. A jazz trio plays during dinner, then continues on till midnight for patrons of the attached bar. Tables are sprinkled with Mardi Gras beads for extra atmosphere.

The ships' 24-hour Horizon Court buffet restaurants are comfortable enough, though the circular layout of the food stations—and no clear path through them—often leads to light chaos. Overlooking the main pool, the Grill serves burgers, dogs, and the like in the afternoon, with very good pizza available one deck down (just forward of the pool) and extracost ice cream and fresh juices available afterward at the solarium's ice-cream bar and juice bar. Inside, at the bottom of the atrium, La Patisserie is a pleasant lounge/cafe serving regular coffee free and specialty coffees at extra cost, with cookies and sweets free for the taking. As the room is almost at sea level, it's a great spot from which to watch the waves go by, and it's worth spending at least a minute here as your ship goes through the Panama Canal: The Canal walls are literally only a couple of feet away. It's a startlingly weird experience.

POOL, FITNESS, SPA & SPORTS FACILITIES   The ships' main pool areas are spacious but surprisingly plain, with a main pool and three large hot tubs surrounded by sunning areas. A steel-drum duo performs on a tiny, low-key stage at one end during the day. Moving toward the stern, the solarium (aka the Lotus Pool) is a much more interesting area, decorated with a Balinese motif that gives a sense of tranquillity—though if there are lots of kids aboard, that tranquillity probably won't last. The stylish wooden deck chairs here (and more traditional "Royal Teak" ones on the wrap-around Promenade Deck) are much classier than the white plastic loungers around the main pool. A sliding-glass roof protects the area during inclement weather. Up on the Sports Deck there's a wading pool for adults.

Fitness facilities include a surprisingly small though reasonably equipped gym, plus a relatively large separate aerobics room. Up on the top decks there's a basketball/volleyball court, a computerized golf simulator, and a 9-hole miniature-golf course. Though the latter is in the open air, you have to enter through a windowless wooden door that makes it look permanently closed. It's not; just go on in.

In the stern on Deck 14, the Balinese-themed Lotus Spa offers the usual massage, mud, and beauty treatments, plus a thermal suite (a unisex room offering various heat treatments) and a lovely seaview salon. For what it's worth—because the spa is run by Steiner (the company that runs almost all cruise ship spas) and personnel change regularly—we had one of our best cruise ship massages on *Coral Princess,* an almost painful deep-tissue sports massage that left us feeling completely loose and refreshed.

The Sun Class: Sun Princess • Dawn Princess • Sea Princess

The Verdict

These relaxed, pretty ships are pleasant and comfortable, great for families and for grown-ups who like to enjoy the good life without too much flash.

Sun Princess *(photo: Princess Cruises)*

Specifications

Size (in tons)	77,000	Year Launched	
Passengers (double occ.)	1,950	*Sun Princess*	1995
Passenger/Space Ratio	39.5	*Dawn Princess*	1997
Total Cabins/Veranda Cabins	975/410	*Sea Princess*	1998
Crew	900	Last Refurbishment/Upgrade	N/A
Passenger/Crew Ratio	2.2 to 1		

Frommer's Ratings (Scale of 1–5)   ★★★★

Cabin Comfort & Amenities	4	Dining Options	4
Appearance & Upkeep	4	Gym, Spa & Sports Facilities	4
Public Comfort/Space	5	Children's Facilities	4
Decor	5	Enjoyment Factor	4

Here's the scoop on *Sea Princess, Dawn Princess,* and *Sun Princess:* They're just like all the other Princess ships, only less so. Being among the line's oldest vessels (dating from the mid- to late '90s), they're the ones that led the way toward the design Princess has used ever since. They're pretty vessels, with a decor that mixes classic and modern, using materials such as varnished hardwoods, marble, etched glass, granite, and textured fabrics. The look doesn't sock you between the eyes with its daring; in fact, it's a bit plain Jane: comfortable, quiet, and (so far) aging gracefully. Light color schemes predominate, with lots of beiges, and their layout is very easy to navigate. By the end of the first day you'll know where everything is.

For 2008, *Sun Princess* will be sailing primarily in Australia and the South Pacific.

Cabins & Rates

Cabins	Per Diems From	Sq. Ft.	Fridge	Hair Dryer	Sitting Area	TV
Inside	$94	135–148	yes	yes	no	yes
Outside	$118	147–160	yes	yes	no	yes
Suite	$146	365–678*	yes	yes	yes	yes

* Includes veranda.

CABINS　Though cabins on these vessels are divided into some 28 categories, there are actually fewer than 10 configurations—for the most part, the category differences reflect location (amidships versus aft, and so on), and thus price. More than 400 cabins on each vessel boast private balconies, though they're small at about 3×8½ feet. And that leads to our main point: The staterooms on these ships are cramped. Standard outside cabins, such as categories BC and BD, are 178 square feet *including* their balconies, while Carnival's standards, by comparison, are nearly 186 square feet without balconies. On these ships, what little balcony space you gain is deducted from your room.

Each ship's six suites sprawl out over 678 square feet of space and include robes to use while aboard and minibars stocked once on a complimentary basis with soda, bottled water, beer, and liquor. Suite guests also get a slew of perks highlighted in the "Service" section above. The 32 minisuites on each ship are really nice, with a separate bedroom area divided from the sitting area by a curtain. Each has a pullout sofa, a chair and desk, a minifridge, two TVs, a walk-in closet, and a whirlpool tub and shower in a separate room from the toilet and sink.

All cabins have minifridges, safes, TVs, and hair dryers, and 300 will accommodate third passengers in upper berths. Nineteen cabins on each vessel are wheelchair accessible.

PUBLIC AREAS　These ships have a decidedly unglitzy decor that relies on lavish amounts of wood, glass, marble, and collections of original paintings, statues, and lithographs. The one-story showrooms offer good lighting and sound and unobstructed views from every seat, and several spaces in the back are reserved for wheelchair users. The smaller Vista Lounge also presents entertainment, with good sightlines and comfortable cabaret-style seating. The elegant, nautical-motif Wheelhouse Bar is done in warm, dark-wood tones and features small bands, sometimes with a vocalist; it's the perfect spot for pre- or post-dinner drinks.

There's a dark and sensuous disco; a bright, spacious casino; a wine bar selling caviar by the ounce and wine, champagne, and iced vodka by the glass; and lots of little lounges for an intimate rendezvous.

DINING OPTIONS In these ships' two dining rooms there are no dramatic, sweeping staircases for making an entrance; instead, the rooms feel intimate, broken up by dividers topped with frosted glass. Each ship also has two alternative dining venues. The sit-down pizzeria (no extra charge) on Dolphin Deck is open approximately 11am to 2:30pm and 7pm to 1am for casual and quiet dining, with tables seating two, four, and six. Sorry, no takeout or delivery. The Sterling Steakhouse is set out of the wind just outside the Horizon Court, overlooking the main pool, and is open from 6 to 10pm. On Alaska sailings, the steakhouse option is moved inside to one side of the 24-hour Horizon Court buffet restaurant, which also offers an ultracasual option for all meals, including sit-down bistro-style dinners from 11pm to 4am.

POOL, FITNESS, SPA & SPORTS FACILITIES The pool decks on these ships are well laid out, with three adult pools (one of them in the stern), one kids' wading pool, and hot tubs scattered around the Riviera Deck, along with a 300-square-foot LED movie screen for showing feature films, sports events, and other entertainment. Three spacious decks are open for sunbathing.

The ships' gyms are appealing, and though they're on the small side for vessels of this size, they're actually roomier than the ones on the much larger Grand-class ships. Aerobics, stretching, and meditation classes are available in the conversely spacious aerobics room, and the nearby spas offer the usual massages, mud treatments, and facials. The teak Promenade Deck provides space for joggers, walkers, and shuffleboard players, and a computerized golf center called Princess Links simulates the trickiest holes at some of the world's best golf courses.

12 Royal Caribbean International

1050 Caribbean Way, Miami, FL 33132. ℂ **800/327-6700** or 305/539-6000. Fax 800/722-5329. www.royalcaribbean.com.

THE LINE IN A NUTSHELL Royal Caribbean's ships are good-looking, activity-packed floating resorts, and the line is among the most innovative in the cruise biz, always adding something that's never been seen at sea before. Surfing, rock climbing, ice-skating, boxing . . . what's next? **Sails to:** Caribbean, Panama Canal, Alaska, Mexican Riviera, Bermuda, Hawaii, Canada/New England (plus Europe, transatlantic, Australia/New Zealand).

THE EXPERIENCE Royal Caribbean prides itself on being ultrainnovative and cutting edge, pushing the envelope with each new class of ship they build. If there's something that's never been done at sea before, Royal Caribbean will figure out how to offer it. The latest ships, *Freedom of the Seas* and *Liberty of the Seas,* not only have the rock-climbing walls and ice-skating rink inherited from the Voyager class before them, but a surfing simulator, a full-size boxing ring, and the world's first onboard water park. Cruises on these fun, active, and glamorous (but not too over-the-top-glitzy) megaships offer a great experience for a wide range of people, whether your idea of a good time is riding a wave or relaxing in the Solarium pool. There are huge children's centers for the kids and elegant jazz clubs, kick-back sports bars, and flashy entertainment for adults. Decor-wise, these ships are a shade or two toned down from the Carnival brood: Rather than trying to overwhelm the senses, many of their public areas are understated and classy. The Radiance-class vessels are the line's most elegant to date, with a sophistication that's up near the level of Royal Caribbean's sister line, Celebrity Cruises.

Pros

- **Activity central:** With rock-climbing walls, surfing machines, water parks, basketball courts, miniature golf, ice-skating, and bungee trampolines among the many diversions, these ships are tops in the adrenaline department.
- **Pretty public areas:** Lounges, restaurants, and outdoor pool decks are well designed, spacious, glamorous, and just plain inviting.
- **Great solariums:** Solariums on the Vision-, Voyager-, Freedom-, and especially the Radiance-class ships are oh-so-relaxing oases designed around a theme (Venice, Africa, and so forth), a pool, and a pair of enormous whirlpool tubs.

Cons

- **Small cabins on the older ships:** At just about 120 to 160 square feet, most cabins aboard the line's pre-1999 vessels are downright tiny.

ROYAL CARIBBEAN: BIG HIP SHIPS

Royal Caribbean was the first company to launch a fleet specializing exclusively in Caribbean ports of call—hence the company name. In the late 1980s it expanded its horizons beyond the Caribbean (hence the "international") and now offers cruises in every major cruising region. It's the line that launched the megaship trend (with 1988's 73,192-ton *Sovereign of the Seas*), as well as the mega-megaship trend (with 1999's 3,114-passenger *Voyager of the Seas*) and the super-duper-megaship trend (with the 3,634-passenger *Freedom of the Seas* in 2006), but beyond sheer size its ships have been innovative, challenging any traditional notions of cruise ship activities. *Voyager* launched the idea of ice-skating rinks, interior boulevards, and rock-climbing walls. Now with five Voyager-class vessels and the even larger Freedom-class ships in the water, these features almost seem standard. Who would have thought?

In 1997, Royal Caribbean acquired the smaller and more high-end Celebrity Cruises, which it continues to operate as a separate brand. For the past several years the two lines have been making incursions into Princess and Holland America's dominance of the **Alaska cruisetour** market. For 2008, they're offering more than 25 options, including some to Whistler and the Canadian Rockies, plus train service between Anchorage and its distant cruise port in Seward, with 360-degree views available from glass-domed viewing cars.

Compared with the other mainstream lines, here's how RCI rates:

	Poor	Fair	Good	Excellent	Outstanding
Enjoyment Factor					✓
Dining				✓	
Activities					✓
Children's Program				✓	
Entertainment				✓	
Service				✓	
Worth the Money					✓

At press time, Royal Caribbean had just announced that its 1990-vintage *Empress of the Seas* would be transferred to Madrid-based subsidiary Pullmantur Cruises in March 2008, to serve the European market. Adios, *Empress*.

PASSENGER PROFILE

You'll find all walks of life on a Royal Caribbean cruise: passengers in their 20s through 60s and older, mostly couples (including a good number of honeymooners), some singles traveling with friends, and also lots and lots of families. Overall, passengers are energetic, social, and looking for a good time, no matter what their age. While the majority of passengers come from somewhere in North America, the huge Voyager- and Freedom-class ships in particular attract a lot of foreigners, including many Asians and Latin Americans.

Over the past several years the line has been making a push for younger, hipper, more active passengers via an ad campaign that portrays the ships as a combination of hyperactive urban health club, chic restaurant district, and adventure-travel magic potion—which of course is a bit of a stretch. They're active, yes, but don't expect the Shackleton expedition. RCI's shorter 3- and 4-night cruises tend to attract a more party-oriented crowd, as is the case with most short cruises.

DINING

Royal Caribbean's cuisine falls in the "pretty tasty" to "impressively good" range. Unlike NCL, Oceania, and Princess, which have adopted looser, "walk-in" dining programs, Royal Caribbean sticks to offering early- and late-seating dinners in traditional main dining rooms, with guests assigned a set dinner table. Just as with all the other mainstream lines, there are also many casual and specialty dining options.

TRADITIONAL   Dinners are offered in two seatings in the main dining rooms, with typical entrees including poached Alaskan salmon, oven-roasted crispy duck served with a rhubarb sauce, sirloin steak marinated with Italian herbs and served over a chunky tomato stew, and shrimp scampi. At lunch and dinner, there's always a **light and healthy option** such as herb-crusted baked cod with steamed red-skinned potatoes and vegetables; or a pasta tossed with smoked turkey, portobello mushrooms, and red-pepper pesto; as well as a **vegetarian option** such as vegetable strudel served in a puff pastry with black-bean salsa.

SPECIALTY   Unlike lines such as NCL, Royal Caribbean hasn't gone overboard with alternative, extra-charge specialty restaurants. Instead, it's integrated some new dining options into the casual and snacking categories. The Voyager-class ships each have one intimate, reservations-only Italian restaurant called Portofino, while the Radiance- and Freedom-class ships and *Mariner* and *Navigator of the Seas* have Portofino and the Chops Grill steakhouse. They're all attractive and intimate getaways, and food and service are the best on board, justifying the $20-per-person cover charge. Specialty restaurants are being installed on the line's older ships as they're renovated.

CASUAL   Fleetwide, an open-seating casual dinner option is offered every night from 6:30 to 9:30pm in the buffet-style Windjammer Cafe. Meals follow the general theme of dinners in the main restaurants (Italian, Caribbean, and so on), and the room is made a bit more inviting through dimmed lighting and the addition of tablecloths. Long open hours mean this option rarely gets crowded. You can also eat breakfast and lunch in the Windjammer—and most passengers do. Aboard *Freedom, Liberty,*

Mariner, Navigator, and *Monarch of the Seas,* the buffet area has an Asian specialty buffet called Jade, serving sushi and a variety of traditional and modern dishes. Aboard *Sovereign* and *Majesty of the Seas,* an expanded buffet called the Windjammer Marketplace has a variety of themed islands for different regional cuisine, including Asian, Mediterranean, and Latin, plus a carving station, pasta station, and soup and salad bar.

RCI's Freedom- and Voyager-class ships and the older *Sovereign* and *Majesty* also have one of the most distinctive casual-dining options at sea: an honest-to-God **Johnny Rockets diner** with red vinyl booths and chrome accents, serving burgers, milkshakes, and other diner staples. There's a nominal $4-per-person service charge, and sodas and shakes are a la carte; but that doesn't stop lines from forming here during prime lunch and dinner times.

SNACKS & EXTRAS   Freedom- and Voyager-class ships have an extensive coffee shop on the indoor promenade (serving a variety of pastries, sandwiches, and pizza) plus several self-serve soft ice-cream stations, nacho-and-hot-dog-type snacks in the sports bars, and a multistation buffet restaurant. The line's other ships have similar options, with decent pizza served afternoons and late night for those suffering from post-partying munchies, and ice cream and toppings available throughout the day from a station in the Windjammer. The Radiance-class ships and *Sovereign* and *Majesty* all have Latte'tudes coffee shops serving gourmet java, cookies, and other baked goods. *Freedom, Liberty, Mariner, Navigator,* and *Sovereign* also have a **Ben & Jerry's** ice-cream shop. All ships offer three midnight buffets per week, with "Midnight Treats" hors d'oeuvres served late on the other days.

A fairly extensive **kids' menu** (which is fun in and of itself, with word and picture games and pictures to color in, crayons included) features the usual options: burgers, hot dogs, fries, fish sticks, burritos, oven-fried lemon chicken, spaghetti and meatballs, and pizza, plus lots of desserts.

Room service is available 24 hours a day from a fairly routine, limited menu. During normal lunch and dinner hours, however, a cabin steward can bring many items served in the restaurant to your cabin.

ACTIVITIES

It's safe to say Royal Caribbean's ships offer the greatest variety of activities and sports facilities at sea. Fleetwide, you'll find **rock-climbing walls** (with multiple climbing tracks and training available) plus lots of typical cruise fare: spa and beauty demonstrations, art auctions, wine tastings, salsa and ballroom dance lessons, bingo, oddball crafts/hospitality classes (such as napkin folding), "horse race" gambling, and outrageous poolside games such as the men's sexy legs contest, designed to draw big laughs. Sports facilities vary by ship: There are **ice-skating rinks** and in-line skating tracks on the Freedom- and Voyager-class ships; combo basketball/volleyball courts on the Radiance-, Freedom-, Voyager-, and Vision-class ships; and miniature-golf courses on the Freedom, Radiance, and Voyager classes as well as *Splendour* and *Legend of the Seas.* If shopping can be considered an activity, Royal Caribbean has an impressive selection of boutiques clustered around the each ship's atrium.

For those whose goal is to not gain 5 pounds at the buffet, **gyms** are well equipped fleetwide, with specialized fitness classes such as yoga and cardio-kickboxing available for $10 per person. **Onboard spas** offer the usual range of massages, facials, and other

Royal Caribbean Fleet Itineraries

Ship	Inside
Adventure	**Caribbean:** 7-night southern, from San Juan, PR (year-round).
Brilliance	**Caribbean:** 9-night round-trip from Miami, FL (Jan). **Panama Canal:** 10 & 11 nights, round-trip from Miami, FL (Jan–Apr).
Enchantment	**Caribbean:** 4- & 5-night western, round-trip from Ft. Lauderdale (year-round).
Explorer	**Caribbean:** 9-night eastern & 12-night eastern/southern, round-trip from Bayonne, NJ (Jan–Mar & Nov–Dec). **Bermuda:** 5 nights, round-trip from Bayonne, NJ (Apr–Oct). **Bermuda/Caribbean:** 9 nights, round-trip from Bayonne, NJ (Apr, June–Aug & Oct). **New England/Canada:** 9 nights, round-trip from Bayonne, NJ (July–Oct).
Freedom	**Caribbean:** Alternating 7-night eastern & western, round-trip from Miami, FL (year-round).
Grandeur	**Caribbean:** 4- & 5-night, round-trip from Tampa, FL (Jan–Mar & Nov–Dec). 7 nights, Tampa to San Juan, PR (Apr). 9-night eastern, round-trip from Baltimore, MD (May, Oct) and from Norfolk, VA (June–Aug). 11-night eastern, Baltimore to Tampa, FL (Oct). **Caribbean/Bermuda:** 7 nights, San Juan, PR, to Baltimore, MD (Apr). **Bermuda:** 5 nights, round-trip from Baltimore, MD (Apr–June & Sept–Oct), and from Norfolk, VA (July–Aug). **New England/Canada:** 8 & 9 nights, round-trip from Norfolk, VA (June–Sept), and round-trip from Baltimore, MD (Sept–Oct).
Independence	**Caribbean:** Alternating 6-night western & 8-night eastern, round-trip from Ft. Lauderdale, FL (Nov–Dec).
Jewel	**Caribbean:** Alternating 6-night western & 8-night eastern, round-trip from Ft. Lauderdale, FL (Jan–Mar). 10-night, Boston, MA, to Miami, FL (Oct). **New England/Canada:** 5 & 9 nights, round-trip from Boston, MA (Sept–Oct). **Panama Canal/Caribbean:** 10 & 11 nights, round-trip from Miami, FL (Nov–Dec).
Legend	**Caribbean:** 7-night southern, round-trip from Santo Domingo, Dominican Republic (Jan–Mar & Dec).
Liberty	**Caribbean:** Alternating 7-night eastern & western, round-trip from Miami, FL (year-round).
Majesty	**Bahamas:** Alternating 3 & 4 nights, round-trip from Miami, FL (year-round).
Mariner	**Caribbean:** Alternating 7-night eastern & western, round-trip from Port Canaveral, FL (year-round).
Monarch	**Baja Mexico:** Alternating 3 & 4 nights, round-trip from Los Angeles, CA (year-round).
Navigator	**Caribbean:** Alternating 4- & 5-night western, round-trip from Ft. Lauderdale, FL (Jan–Apr & Nov–Dec).
Radiance	**Caribbean:** Alternating 6-night western & 8-night eastern, round-trip from Ft. Lauderdale, FL (Jan–Mar). **Panama Canal:** 14 nights, Ft. Lauderdale to San Diego, CA (Apr). 15 nights, San Diego to Ft. Lauderdale (Oct). **Hawaii:** 14 nights, Ensenada, Mexico, to Honolulu, Hawaii (May). 13 nights, Honolulu to Vancouver, BC (May). 15 nights, round-trip from San Diego, CA (Sept–Oct). **Alaska:** 7-night Gulf of Alaska, north- or southbound between Vancouver, BC, and Seward/Anchorage, AK (May–Sept). **Alaska/U.S. Pacific Coast:** 14 nights, Vancouver, BC, to San Diego, CA (Sept).
Rhapsody	**Alaska:** 7-night Inside Passage, round-trip from Seattle, WA (May–Sept). **Hawaii:** 12 nights, Vancouver, BC, to Honolulu, HI (Sept).
Serenade	**Caribbean:** 7-night southern, round-trip from San Juan, PR (Jan–Apr & Nov–Dec). **Panama Canal:** 14 nights, San Juan, PR, to San Francisco, CA (Apr) & San Diego to San Juan (Oct). **Alaska/U.S. Pacific Coast:** 14 nights, San Francisco, CA, to Vancouver, BC (May). 13 nights, Vancouver to San Diego, CA (Sept). **Alaska:** 7-night Inside Passage, round-trip from Vancouver, BC (May–Sept). **Hawaii:** 15 nights, round-trip from San Diego (Oct).

Royal Caribbean Fleet Itineraries *(continued)*

Ship	Inside
Sovereign	**Bahamas:** 3 & 4 nights, round-trip from Port Canaveral, FL (year-round).
Vision	**Mexican Riviera:** 7 nights, round-trip from Los Angeles, CA (year-round).
Voyager	**Caribbean:** 7-night western, round-trip from Galveston, TX (Jan–Apr & Dec).

beauty treatments, but here's a piece of advice: If you want a treatment, sign up immediately after boarding, as these are big ships and a lot of people will be competing with you for desirable time slots. If you're flexible, you can often find more openings and special discounts on port days and off times. During a rainy stay in Halifax, Heidi signed up for a 50-minute combo back massage and minifacial that was discounted to $89 from $120, not including the tip.

CHILDREN'S PROGRAM

Year-round and fleetwide, Royal Caribbean offers its **Adventure Ocean** supervised kids' programs for children ages 3 to 17, divided into Aquanauts (ages 3–5), Explorers (ages 6–8), Voyagers (ages 9–11), Navigators (ages 12–14), and older teens (ages 15–17). All youth staff have college degrees in education, recreation, or a related field. Each ship has a large children's playroom and facilities for teens, with complimentary supervised activities offered on sea and port days. In general, the scope of the kids' facilities on the Freedom-, Voyager-, and Radiance-class ships far exceeds that of the rest of the fleet, with huge playrooms, and a large, sequestered outdoor deck with ship-shaped play equipment. The *Freedom of the Seas* offers an amazing **water park** on a top deck that makes the lawn sprinklers we grew up with seem downright prehistoric. Radiance-class ships and *Voyager, Adventure,* and *Explorer* also have a water slide and a kids' pool. Activities fleetwide include movies, talent shows, karaoke, pizza and ice-cream parties, bingo, scavenger hunts, game shows, volleyball, face painting, and beach parties. **Internet access** is available to Adventure Ocean kids at half price (25¢ vs. 50¢ for adults).

Three programs mix learning with play. The **Adventure Science** program teaches and entertains kids with fun yet educational scientific experiments, while **Adventure Art,** offered in partnership with Crayola, focuses on art projects made with the company's crayons, modeling clay, glitter, glue, markers, and paint. There are also activities geared to the whole family, including Mom and Dad. For younger kids (ages 6 months–3 years), RCI has partnered with Fisher-Price on a program of **supervised play dates** in which babies (6–18 months) and toddlers (18 months–3 years) are invited to daily 45-minute play sessions with their parents. Offered on all but embarkation day, the interactive dates incorporate music, storytelling, and a variety of Fisher-Price toys to explore physical development, problem-solving skills, cause and effect, and other lessons. In ship cabins, Fisher-Price TV offers programming for kids.

For teens, each ship has a **teen center,** a disco, and a video arcade. *Freedom, Mariner, Navigator, Monarch,* and *Sovereign of the Seas* have three teen-only areas, including a dedicated teen sun deck.

Slumber-party-style **group babysitting** for children 3 and up is available in the kids' playroom nightly between 10pm and 1am. The hourly charge is $5 per child (kids must be at least 3 years old and potty-trained). Private, in-cabin babysitting for kids 6 months and up is available from off-duty crewmembers 8am to 2am, and must be booked at least 24 hours in advance through the purser's desk. The cost: $8 per hour for up to two siblings; $10 per hour for a maximum of three. The 4 hours of adult time to enjoy dinner, drinks, and entertainment: priceless.

Alternatively, the **Adventure Ocean dinner program** is a kind of "get out of parenting free" card for adults, inviting kids to dine with youth staff in the Windjammer Cafe, the Solarium, or Johnny Rockets diner (depending on the ship) from 6 to 7pm, then take part in an activities session till 10pm. This is offered on 3 nights of a 7-night cruise and once or twice on shorter cruises. A complete child's menu is offered.

There is no minimum age for kids to sail with Royal Caribbean.

ENTERTAINMENT

RCI doesn't scrimp in the entertainment department, with music and comedy acts, some of the best Vegas-style shows at sea, passenger talent shows, karaoke, sock hops, and occasional **"name" groups and soloists,** such as the Platters, the Drifters, the Coasters, John Davidson, and Marty Allen. Other names may not be as familiar, but can be pretty amazing, such as the Knudsen Brothers (aka "Six"), a six-member family a cappella group that mixes great harmonies, human-beat-box rhythms, and a lot of comedy about its male-pattern baldness. The newer the ship, the larger and more sophisticated the stage, sound, and lighting equipment, with some boasting a wall of video monitors to augment live performances.

Aside from its showrooms and huge glitzy casinos, Royal Caribbean is big on signature spaces, with each ship offering the nautical, woodsy **Schooner Bar** as well as the **Viking Crown Lounge,** an observation-cum-nightclub set high on a top deck and boasting panoramic views of the sea and ship in all directions. The Latin-themed **Bolero's bar** (aboard *Freedom, Liberty, Navigator, Mariner, Monarch, Sovereign,* and *Majesty*) serves a mean mojito and has Latin music into the night. Atrium bars also feature live music, often classical trios. One evening on a recent cruise, two very talented passengers spontaneously began singing as the atrium trio played, attracting a huge crowd. Suddenly the 3,000-passenger ship felt like an intimate cabaret lounge.

SERVICE

In general, dining, bar, and cabin service is surprisingly good considering the sheer volume of passengers with which crewmembers must deal. At meals on a recent cruise we found that even when staff was rushed our water glasses were always filled, wine orders were delivered promptly, and our servers always found time for a little friendly chitchat as they skated around their tables. Other times we found ourselves greeted with a smile by a crewman polishing the brass, and had busboys in the buffet restaurant going out of their way to bring coffee and water, even though the room is officially self-service. These folks work long, hard days, though, and on ships this size (and especially on those operating quick-turnaround 3- and 4-night cruises) you'll probably run into some crewmembers who look like they need a vacation.

Laundry and **dry-cleaning services** are available on all the ships, but none have self-service laundromats.

The Freedom Class:
Freedom of the Seas •
Liberty of the Seas

Freedom of the Seas *(photo: RCCL)*

The Verdict

Supersized versions of the already-supersized Voyager-class ships, *Freedom* and *Liberty* offer everything those ships do and more, though they come very close to being too big (and too commercial) for their own good.

Specifications

Size (in tons)	160,000	Passenger/Crew Ratio	2.7 to 1
Passengers (double occ.)	3,634	Year Launched	
Passenger/Space Ratio	44	*Freedom*	2006
Total Cabins/Veranda Cabins	1,815/844	*Liberty*	2007
Crew	1,360	Last Refurbishment/Upgrade	N/A

Frommer's Ratings (Scale of 1–5)   ★★★★½

Cabin Comfort & Amenities	4	Dining Options	4.5
Appearance & Upkeep	5	Gym, Spa & Sports Facilities	5
Public Comfort/Space	4.5	Children's Facilities	5
Decor	4	Enjoyment Factor	5

Freedom and *Liberty of the Seas* are currently the largest passenger ships in the world, besting Cunard's *Queen Mary 2* by 9,000 gross register tons and 1,000-plus passengers. So are they great? Are they marvelous? Are they everything the biggest passenger ships in the world should be? Well, it kind of depends on what your definition of "great" is and whether you think size really matters. For us, frankly, it doesn't matter very much. What matters is what a cruise line and its designers *do* with all that space. Some massive ships feel crowded and uncomfortable, while others are so well designed you wonder where all the people are. For cruise lines, it's all about balance: maximizing the number of cabins (and thus revenue) while also making sure passengers don't feel lost in the crowd. For passengers, it's about deciding how many bells and whistles you want in a ship, and how many other humans you're willing to travel with. *Freedom* and *Liberty of the Seas* push the line on that balance.

The ships are, at essence, just larger versions of Royal Caribbean's popular, 142,000-ton, 3,114-passenger *Voyager*-class ships (see review following), which introduced the line's now-brandwide "active vacation" image with their rock-climbing walls, ice-skating rinks, and full-size basketball courts. Extremely well-designed, the Voyager vessels disperse their large complement of passengers among many interesting public areas—including their four-story, boulevard-like interior Royal Promenades, which run more than a football field's length down their center and are lined with bars, shops, and entertainment lounges. These promenades, with their strollable, urban feel, make the Voyager vessels a great compromise for couples who can't decide between a tropical cruise and a city vacation. They really do feel like "cities at sea."

Freedom and *Liberty*, carrying at least 500 more passengers (and more if all berths are full), offer a nearly identical layout and ambience to the Voyager ships, but stretched out and with a few new eye-catching activities and entertainment features. But those extras come with a price: *Freedom*'s Royal Promenade, for instance, is more dominated by shops and corporate co-branding arrangements (a Ben & Jerry's ice-cream parlor, a sportswear shop with a dedicated New Balance section, and so on), giving it a feel that's as much mall as theme park. When crowds are low—say, during the early dinner seating, or late at night—it can still be a lot of fun to sit at the "sidewalk" cafe or bar and catch a drink, but when things are hopping, you'd be forgiven for thinking your car was parked outside, in lot D.

Overall, *Freedom* and *Liberty* offer the same big, active, city-vacation feel that's the Voyager ships' stock in trade, and that ain't a bad thing. Additionally, they include an amped-up top-deck experience, with a great kids' water park and a surfing simulator. If you're the type that's already attracted to the Voyagers, there's no real reason to stay away. On the other hand, unless you're a surfing or water park fan, there's little reason to specifically seek out *Freedom* or *Liberty* instead of the Voyagers, which in a way is good: With six ships to choose from, you can pick your trip based on the destination, which is what you should be doing anyway.

Cabins & Rates

Cabins	Per Diems From	Sq. Ft.	Fridge	Hair Dryer	Sitting Area	TV
Inside	$114	152	yes	yes	no	yes
Outside	$193	161–189	yes	yes	some	yes
Suite	$243	287–1,406	yes	yes	yes	yes

CABINS Standard outside cabins are a livable if not overlarge 161 square feet, though standard insides seem small at 152 square feet. All cabins come with Internet dataports, minifridges, safes, TVs, pleasant pastel color schemes, and regular hair dryers. Bathrooms are on the cramped side, with little storage space, few amenities (soap and shampoo only), and only a thin sliver of counter. The cylindrical shower stalls, though definitely tight for large-size people, have RCI's standard sliding doors that keep the water and warmth in.

Of the 1,815 cabins, 1,084 have ocean views and 844 have verandas. Suites range from the affordable junior suites (with sitting area and balcony) to a handful of family suites (with two bedrooms, two bathrooms, and a living area with sofa bed) up to the huge Presidential Suite with its four bedrooms, four bathrooms, and 810-square-foot balcony.

For those who want an "urban" experience, the 168 atrium cabins on the second, third, and fourth levels of the four-story Royal Promenade have windows facing the action below, with curtains and soundproofing to keep most of the light and noise out, when you want downtime.

Thirty-two cabins are wheelchair accessible.

PUBLIC AREAS *Freedom* and *Liberty* have more than 3 miles of public corridors apiece, and it can feel like a real hike if your cabin's on one end of the ship and you have to get to the other. Running 445 feet down the center of Deck 5 is the bustling, four-story Royal Promenade, designed to resemble Memphis's Beale Street or New Orleans's Bourbon Street. Like those famous thoroughfares, it's lined with shops, bars, and cafes, and features evening musical performances by the ships' various musical groups, including their big bands. Other promenade attractions include a Ben & Jerry's ice-cream parlor, a coffee bar, a casual pizza and snacks restaurant, an English-style pub with evening entertainment, a champagne bar, a wine bar that offers tastings (see description in the Voyager-class review), a small bookstore, several shops, and, for our money, the best thing on the whole strip: a men's barber shop offering old-timey professional shaves spiced with a helping of New Age spa frippery. The half-hour Express Shave includes hot towels, deep-cleansing exfoliation, a super-close shave, and did we mention hot towels? Niiiice. Only downside? They use safety razors instead of straight. Wimps.

Down on decks 3 and 4, the two-level disco is entered though a theme-parky "secret passage." There's also a huge multistory theater, a casino with more than 300 slot machines, a Latin-themed bar with live music, and the nautically themed Schooner Bar. One deck down, excellent ice shows as well as game shows and fashion shows are held throughout each cruise at the "Center Ice" ice rink, which has a sliding floor to cover the ice during nonskate events. Other public rooms include a library, an Internet center, a sprawling kids' area with huge oceanview playroom, a living-room-style teen center, a jumbo arcade, a top-deck jazz club and cocktail lounge, a card room, and a wedding chapel.

DINING OPTIONS *Freedom* and *Liberty*'s three-level main dining rooms are, like those on RCI's Voyager-class ships, among the most stunning and classy aboard any of today's megaships, with a design that follows a generally classical theme. Each level—linked by a large open area and grand staircase at its center—is considered a separate restaurant, though service and menus are consistent throughout. A pianist or piano trio entertains from a platform in the aft end of the room and a huge crystal chandelier hangs overhead, both setting an elegant mood.

Two alternative restaurants occupy spots immediately to port and starboard at the entrance to the buffet restaurant: Portofino, serving Italian meals in a cozy setting, and Chops Grille, a woody room for manly steaks. Both entail an additional $20-per-person charge. Out in the buffet, a section called Jade serves Japanese, Chinese, Indian, and Thai dishes.

Another casual option for lunch, dinner, and late-night snacks is the popular Johnny Rockets, a 1950s-style diner set out on deck and offering burgers, shakes, fries, and the like, with veggie burgers to satisfy non-meat-eaters. There's a nominal $4-per-person service charge and sodas and shakes are a la carte.

POOL, FITNESS, SPA & SPORTS FACILITIES Sticking with their active image, Royal Caribbean has outfitted *Freedom* and *Liberty* with several features sure to entertain both actual athletes and weekend warriors, as well as their active kids. The biggest hoo-ha is each ship's FlowRider surfing simulator—similar to swim-in-place lap pools with their recycling currents, except that this one features a stream that flows up an inclined, wedge-shaped surface 40 feet long and 32 feet wide. At the bottom are powerful jets that pump 30,000 gallons per minute up the slope, creating a wavelike flow on which boarders can ride—at least in theory. Located in the stern of each ship's sports court, spanning decks 12 and 13, the ride is adjoined by bleachers for gawkers and fans, creating a bonding atmosphere where those who aren't inclined to flow can wager on those who are. We had our money on the kid with the puka beads and board shorts, who did manage to get to his knees before falling off and being swept up and BAM! into the padded back bumper—just like everybody else. It's sports as a metaphor for life: Eventually, you fall down and get swept away by the currents, only here you can get back in line and try again. Participants must sign up for free group sessions and go through a quick introduction, after which they and the other members of their group take turns riding the wave, in either traditional stand-up surfing or less-balance-demanding body-boarding style. A soft, flexible surface absorbs the impact when you fall. Which you will.

A free-standing "surf shack" bar near the FlowRider offers drinks. Also nearby are Royal Caribbean's signature rock-climbing wall (the biggest one at sea, naturally), a miniature-golf course, a golf simulator, a jogging track, and a full-size basketball court.

In the ship's gym, an honest-to-God 20×20-foot boxing ring takes the place of the large hot tub that greets guests on the Voyager ships. The ring is part of what the line bills as the largest fitness center at sea, offering an enormous number of aerobics and weight machines plus workouts that are rare even in shore-side gyms. Options include "Fight Klub" boxing training (one-on-one training sessions using speed bags, jump ropes, heavy bags, and padded punching mitts), personal training with Pilates instructors, onboard yoga and a class on the beach at Labadee (Royal Caribbean's private resort in Haiti), "Boot Camp X-Treme Training," and linked treadmill workouts. Stretch and fitness tips are located at intervals along the onboard running track, and a program of mapped running/jogging routes is available in the ports of call.

On deck, the kid-friendly H2O Zone Water Park takes up almost half the pool deck, with water canons, jets, buckets, and sprays hidden among colorful cartoon statues, some controlled by motion sensors, others by the kids themselves. The area also includes two wading pools (one geared to toddlers) and two hot tubs, a great place for mom and dad to soak while the kiddos are having a ball. Farther forward, the main pool area offers two pools (one traditional, one "sports") and two large hot tubs at port and starboard, extending 12 feet over the edge of the ship and some 112 feet above the sea. Extremely popular, they get socially crowded—but, of course, with hot tubs that's a good thing.

While crowds tend to disperse around the ships' public areas, on sunny days things can get very crowded out on the main pool and sports decks. Guests seeking something more peaceful can sometimes find it in the adjacent, adults-only Solarium, where a second swimming pool is bisected by a little bridge.

The Voyager Class: Voyager of the Seas • Explorer of the Seas • Adventure of the Seas • Navigator of the Seas • Mariner of the Seas

Explorer of the Seas *(photo: Matt Hannafin)*

The Verdict

Sports club meets Vegas meets theme park meets cruise ship, these enormous vessels are real winners if you like your vacations larger than life. As we overheard one little boy say to his father, "This doesn't look like a ship, daddy. It looks like a city!"

Specifications

Size (in tons)	142,000	Year Launched	
Passengers (double occ.)	3,114	*Voyager*	1999
Passenger/Space Ratio	45.6	*Explorer*	2000
Total Cabins/Veranda Cabins	1,557/757	*Adventure*	2001
Crew	1,176	*Navigator*	2002
Passenger/Crew Ratio	2.7 to 1	*Mariner*	2003
		Last Refurbishment/Upgrade	N/A

Frommer's Ratings (Scale of 1–5)   ★★★★½

Cabin Comfort & Amenities	4	Dining Options	4.5
Appearance & Upkeep	4	Gym, Spa & Sports Facilities	5
Public Comfort/Space	5	Children's Facilities	5
Decor	4	Enjoyment Factor	5

Truly groundbreaking when they were first launched, the Voyager-class ships are still among the largest and most activity-rich passenger ships at sea, boasting a full-size ice-skating rink; an outdoor in-line skating track; a 1950s-style diner sitting right out on deck; a 9-hole miniature-golf course and golf simulator; regulation-size basketball, paddleball, and volleyball courts; huge two-level gyms and spas; and the rock-climbing walls that have become one of Royal Caribbean's most distinguishing features. And did we mention they also have monumentally gorgeous three-story dining rooms, florist shops, and a "peek-a-boo" bridge on Deck 11 that allows guests to watch the crew steering the ship?

What really sets these ships apart from any other passenger ship, though, are the four-story, boulevard-like Royal Promenades that run more than a football field's length down their center, lined with bars, shops, and entertainment lounges and anchored at each end by huge twin atria. The promenade is a great place to people-watch, and weirdly enough, you can watch from your cabin if you want to: Three decks of inside cabins have views from bay windows of the "street scene" below.

The strollable feel of these promenades leads to our major conclusion: These vessels are a perfect compromise for couples who can't decide between a tropical cruise and a city vacation. They may, in fact, be the first ships to really live up to the old "city at sea" cliché. There are enough people aboard to warrant the comparison too: Each ship carries 3,114 guests at double occupancy, but because many staterooms have third and fourth berths, total capacity for each vessel can reach as high as 3,838. Remarkably, though, the ships rarely feel crowded. On our last three sailings we found many public rooms nearly empty during the day and didn't have to wait in line much at all the entire week, even though more than 3,200 passengers were aboard. As we heard one woman comment to her companion, "I know there are 3,000 people on this ship, but where are they all?" Kudos go to the crew for efficiency, and also to Royal Caribbean for a design that features enough appealing public areas to diffuse crowds comfortably, plus a layout that encourages traffic to flow in several different directions. This keeps crowding down and also means you don't tend to find yourself in the same spots day after day—it's entirely possible to be aboard for 6 days, turn a corner, and find yourself in a room you've never seen before.

Cabins & Rates

Cabins	Per Diems From	Sq. Ft.	Fridge	Hair Dryer	Sitting Area	TV
Inside	$103	160	yes	yes	no	yes
Outside	$114	161–328	yes	yes	some	yes
Suite	$214	277–1,325	yes	yes	yes	yes

CABINS   Though not huge (at 160 sq. ft. for insides and 173 for standard ocean views, including balcony), Voyager-class cabins are comfortable, offering Internet dataports, minifridges, safes, TVs, pleasant pastel color schemes, and hair dryers. Bathrooms are on the cramped side, with little storage space, few amenities (soap and shampoo only), and only a thin sliver of counter. The cylindrical shower stalls, though definitely tight for large-size people, have good sliding doors that keep the water and warmth in.

Of the 1,557 cabins, 939 have ocean views and 757 have verandas. There's a single huge Penthouse Suite, 10 Owner's Suites, and 4 Royal Family Suites that accommodate a total of eight people with two bedrooms plus a living room with sofa bed and a pair of bathrooms. Smaller and cheaper family cabins sleep six, some on sofa beds. For voyeurs, the 138 atrium cabins on the second, third, and fourth levels of the four-story Royal Promenade have windows facing the action below, with curtains and soundproofing to keep most of the light and noise out when you want downtime.

Twenty-six cabins are wheelchair accessible.

PUBLIC AREAS   Each ship has about 3 miles of public corridors, and it can feel like a real hike if your cabin's on one end of the ship and you have to get to the other. Running down the center of each is the bustling, four-story Royal Promenade, which is lined with shops, bars, and cafes, and is the center of onboard life. Other promenade attractions include an elegant champagne bar; a comfy English/Irish bar with "sidewalk" seating; a self-serve soft ice-cream station with lots of toppings; shops; and a bright cafe that serves pizza, cookies, pastries, and coffee 24 hours a day. *Voyager, Explorer,* and *Adventure* also have a large sports bar that gets big, raucous crowds when games are broadcast (and puts out free hot dogs and nachos to keep them there), and an arcade stocked with classic 1980s video games. On *Navigator* and *Mariner,* those were scrapped in favor of Vintages Wine Bar, created in collaboration with the Mondavi, Beringer Blass, and Niebaum-Coppola wineries. Full of wood and leather, with terra-cotta floors, attractive vineyard-themed lithographs, and a 600-bottle "cellar," the bars showcase more than 60 vintages. Prices are reasonable and guests can taste any variety before ordering. Classes in wine appreciation are held here throughout the week, and passengers can also stage their own tastings by ordering any of 13 special "wine flight" tasting menus, with selections grouped by taste profile, varietal, or region—for example, Merlots, Australian wines, and so on.

In total, there are some 30 places aboard each ship to grab a drink, including the Viking Crown complex on the top deck, with its elegant jazz club and golf-themed 19th Hole bar; the dark, romantic, nautically themed Schooner Bar; and the clubby cigar bar, tucked away behind a dark door and hosting blackjack games on formal evenings. Aboard each ship, the futuristic or Gothic-dungeon-themed disco is entered though a theme-parky "secret passage," while the huge three-story showrooms occupy the opposite end of the kitsch spectrum: beautifully designed, with simple, elegant color schemes and truly lovely stage curtains—the one on *Adventure* decorated with peacock designs, the one on *Explorer* depicting a chorus of women standing under golden boughs amid a rain of leaves. Excellent ice shows as well as game shows and fashion shows are held throughout each cruise at the "Studio B" ice rink, which has a sliding floor to cover the ice during nonskate events. Open skating for passengers is scheduled throughout the week.

Each ship has a two-story library-cum-computer-room with about 18 computer stations and Web cams that allow you to send your picture as an electronic postcard. There are also sprawling kids' areas with huge oceanview playrooms, teen discos, and jumbo arcades. Families with science-minded kids will appreciate *Explorer*'s pair of working $1.5-million laboratories, where scientists from the University of Miami's Rosenstiel School of Marine & Atmospheric Science conduct research on wind patterns, water chemistry, UV and solar radiation, and air pollution via sensors attached to the ship's mast and hull. Over the course of each cruise, these scientists present talks on their research and show off their labs to passengers on free organized tours.

The best spots for chilling out with a book during days at sea include the seaview Seven of Hearts card room and Cloud Nine Lounge on Deck 14. Those really wanting to get away from people can retreat up the curving stairway to Deck 15's Skylight Chapel, which gets almost no traffic and is even free of piped-in music. (Though it also lacks windows.)

DINING OPTIONS The three-level main dining rooms on these ships are among the most stunning and classy aboard any of today's megaships, with designs that follow a general European theme. Each level—linked by a large open area and grand staircase at its center—is considered a separate restaurant, though service and menus are consistent throughout. A pianist or piano trio entertains from a platform in the aft end of the room and a huge crystal chandelier hangs overhead, both setting an elegant mood.

For a dining alternative, the oceanview Portofino restaurant serves Italian meals in a cozy setting (and at an additional $20-per-person charge), but be sure to reserve a table as soon as you get aboard, as they book up fast.

The pleasant, spacious Island Grill and Windjammer casual buffet restaurants are joined into one large space but have separate lines and stations to keep things moving. On *Navigator* and *Mariner,* this area also incorporates the Asian-themed Jade buffet. There's no outdoor seating per se, but the ship's main pool area is on the same deck, just outside the restaurants' entrances.

Another casual option for lunch, dinner, and late-night snacks is the popular Johnny Rockets, a 1950s-style diner set out on deck and offering burgers, shakes, fries, and the like, with veggie burgers to satisfy non-meat-eaters. The international wait-staff is cute enough in their '50s-style soda-jerk clothes, but we could do without the cutesy lip-sync-and-dance routines to songs such as "YMCA" and "Respect." There's a $4-per-person service charge and sodas and shakes are a la carte.

POOL, FITNESS, SPA & SPORTS FACILITIES   Each ship has a large, well-equipped oceanview gym, though the arrangement of machines and the many pillars throughout can make them feel tight when full. Each has a large indoor whirlpool and a huge aerobics studio (among the biggest on any ship), and their two-level spa complexes are among the largest and best accoutered at sea, with peaceful waiting areas where New Agey tropical-birdsong music induces total relaxation—until you get your bill. (Steiner, the company that manages spas aboard most cruise ships, keeps rates steep in all of 'em.)

While crowds tend to disperse around the ships' public areas, on sunny days things can get tight out on the main pool decks, where deck chairs are squeezed into every level of the multistoried, amphitheater-like decks. The vibe can be electric (or at least loud) when the pool band starts playing. Guests seeking something more peaceful can usually find it in the adjacent Solarium, with a second swimming pool and two enormous whirlpool tubs under a sliding roof. Behind the Johnny Rockets diner, *Voyager, Adventure,* and *Explorer* have a kids' pool area with a water slide, wading pool, hot tub for adults, and dozens of adorable half-size deck chairs for the kids. On *Navigator* and *Mariner* the area is reserved for teens, with deck chairs for sunbathing and an outdoor dance floor with sound and light systems. Deck 13 is the hub of sports action, with the much-touted rock-climbing wall, skating track, miniature-golf course, and basketball court. Appointments must be made to use the more popular options (especially the wall), but this is a good thing as it cuts down on lines.

The Radiance Class: Radiance of the Seas • Brilliance of the Seas • Serenade of the Seas • Jewel of the Seas

The Verdict

Royal Caribbean's most elegant vessels combine classic nautical profiles and interior decor with a lot of the fun and games of RCI's Voyager class, including rock climbing and miniature golf.

Radiance of the Seas *(photo: RCCL)*

Specifications

Size (in tons)	90,090	Year Launched	
Passengers (double occ.)	2,100	*Radiance*	2001
Passenger/Space Ratio	42.9	*Brilliance*	2002
Total Cabins/Veranda Cabins	1,050/577	*Serenade*	2003
Crew	857	*Jewel*	2004
Passenger/Crew Ratio	2.5 to 1	Last Refurbishment/Upgrade	N/A

Frommer's Ratings (Scale of 1–5)

★★★★½

Cabin Comfort & Amenities	4	Dining Options	4.5
Appearance & Upkeep	5	Gym, Spa & Sports Facilities	5
Public Comfort/Space	5	Children's Facilities	4
Decor	5	Enjoyment Factor	5

These ships are just plain handsome, with some of the adventure features of their larger Voyager- and Freedom-class siblings but a sleeker seagoing profile outside, a more nautical look and feel inside, and acres of windows to bring the two together. When you first board, you'll see one of Royal Caribbean's typical wiry modern art sculptures filling the bright, nine-story atrium, but venture a little farther and you'll see that the ships have a much more traditional interior, with dark-wood paneling, caramel-brown leathers, and deep sea-blue fabrics and carpeting. Some 110,000 square feet of glass cover about half of their sleek exteriors, offering wide-open views from the Viking Crown Lounge, Singapore Sling's piano bar, Crown & Anchor Lounge, Sky Bar, Windjammer Cafe, Champagne Bar, and even the atrium, which is an uninterrupted wall of glass from Decks 5 through 10 portside, and has four banks of glass elevators. All this transparency comes in handy in scenic destinations such as Alaska.

A bit of trivia: The giant "GTV" painted toward the rear of each vessel means "gas turbine vessel," a reference to the ships' environmentally friendly gas turbine engines, which run cleaner than standard diesels and are virtually vibration free. The "GTV" is a relatively new nautical appellation that takes its place beside the old SS (steamship) and the more recent MV (motor vessel, for example, diesel).

Cabins & Rates

Cabins	Per Diems From	Sq. Ft.	Fridge	Hair Dryer	Sitting Area	TV
Inside	$86	165	yes	yes	yes	yes
Outside	$100	170	yes	yes	yes	yes
Suite	$186	293–1,001	yes	yes	yes	yes

CABINS Cabins are fairly spacious, with the smallest insides measuring 165 square feet and some 75% of outside staterooms measuring at least 180 square feet, some with 40-square-foot verandas. The rest have jumbo-size portholes. Decor is appealing, done in attractive navy blues and copper tones. All cabins have minifridges, hair dryers, interactive televisions (for buying shore excursions, checking your onboard account, and looking up stock quotes), small sitting areas with minicouches, lots of drawer space, roomy closets, bedside reading lights, and TVs. Vanity/desks have pullout trays to accommodate laptops, plus modem jacks to connect them to the Internet. Bathrooms are small, with Royal Caribbean's typical hold-your-breath-and-step-in shower stalls, but they do have lots of storage space.

All but a handful of suites are located on Deck 10. The best, the Royal Suite, measures 1,001 square feet and offers a separate bedroom, living room with baby grand piano, dining table, bar, entertainment center, and 215-square-foot balcony. Six Owner's Suites are about half that size, with 57-square-foot balconies, a separate living room, a bar, and a walk-in closet; and the 35 Grand Suites one step below at 358 to 384 square feet, with sitting areas and 106-square-foot balconies. Three 586-square-foot Royal Family Suites have 140-square-foot balconies and two bathrooms and can accommodate six people in two separate bedrooms (one with third and fourth berths) and another two on a pullout couch in the living room. Suite guests are treated to complimentary in-cabin butler service in addition to cabin stewards, and there's also a Concierge Club on Deck 10 where suite guests can request services and grab a newspaper.

One snag on the balcony front: On each ship, Cabin Decks 7 through 10 are narrower than those on the rest of the ship, resulting in cabin balconies on Deck 10 (many of them suites) being shaded by the overhang of the deck above. Meanwhile, cabin balconies on the aft and forward ends of Deck 7, being indented, look out onto the top of Deck 6 instead of directly out onto the sea. Balconies on cabins 7652 to 7670 and 7152 to 7170, also aft on Deck 7, are not completely private because the dividers between them don't go all the way to the edge of the space. Keep your clothes on; your neighbors can look right over at you.

Fifteen cabins can accommodate wheelchair users.

PUBLIC AREAS Our favorite space aboard is the cluster of five intimate, wood-and-leather lounges on Deck 6, which recall the decor of classic yachts, university clubs, and cigar lounges. Expect low lighting, inlaid wood flooring, cozy couches, and Oriental-style area rugs. The best of these rooms is the romantic piano bar and lounge that stretches across each ship's stern, with a bank of floor-to-ceiling windows. For amazing views, don't miss having a cocktail here on a moonlit night. Adjacent is a lovely Colonial-style Billiard Club boasting herringbone wood floors, redwood veneer paneling, and a pair of ultra-high-tech gyroscopic pool tables. No excuse for missing shots: The tables compensate for the ship's movements, staying remarkably level.

The main theaters are refreshingly different from most in the cruise biz, with a cool ambience, warm wood tones, and seating in deep sea-blues and greens. Artful hand-made curtains, indirect lighting, and fiber optics all come together to create a quiet, ethereal look. But guys, watch those protruding armrests: It's very easy to snag your pants pockets on them.

Other public areas include the attractive Casino Royale, with more than 200 slot machines and dozens of gaming tables; a baseball-themed sports bar with interactive games on the bar top; the nautically themed Schooner Bar; a 24-hour Internet center; specialty-coffee bar with several Internet stations; a small library; a conference-center complex with a small movie theater; and, high up on Deck 13, Royal Caribbean's signature Viking Crown Lounge, which is divided between a quiet lounge and a large disco with a rotating bar. Even the ships' high-style public bathrooms are impressive, with their marble floors and counters and funky portholelike mirrors.

The huge kids' area on Deck 12 includes a sprawling playroom divided into several areas, with a video arcade and an outdoor pool with water slide. Teens have their own nightclub, with a DJ booth, music videos, and a soda bar.

DINING OPTIONS   The two-story main dining rooms on all four ships are glamorous and elegant, like something out of a 1930s movie set. Four willowy silk-covered columns dominate the vaulted main floor, and a wide double staircase connects the two decks dramatically—all that's missing are Cary Grant and Katharine Hepburn. On *Serenade,* painter Frank Troia's huge, Impressionist *Gala Suite* amplifies the mood, depicting formally dressed couples dancing amid floating globes of light.

The nautically decorated Windjammer Cafe takes self-serve buffet dining to new levels, with 11 food stations (9 inside and 2 outside) set up as islands to keep the lines down and the crowds diffused. It really works. If you prefer taking your meals while reclining, there's a small strip of cozy tables with oversize rattan chairs and thick cushions between the indoor and outdoor seating areas.

The cozy 90-seat Chops Grille is an oceanview venue with dark woods, rich upholsteries, and high-backed booths that bring home the meat-and-potatoes mood. You can watch your steak being cooked in the open kitchen. Adjacent is the 130-seat Portofino, an oceanview Italian restaurant. Expect more refined and gracious service than in the main dining room, plus a more leisurely pace (and, of course, a $20 cover charge). Up on the Sport Deck, the Seaview Cafe is a casual lunch and dinner venue with checkered floors, rattan chairs, and lots of light, serving quick meals such as fish and chips, popcorn shrimp, and burgers.

A counter in the Solarium serves freshly made pizza by the slice, and a coffee shop offers cappuccino and pastries.

POOL, FITNESS, SPA & SPORTS FACILITIES   The Radiance vessels offer tons of recreation outlets and acres of space to flop on a deck chair and sunbathe. At the main pool, passengers pack in like sardines on sunny days at sea, and deck chairs can be scarce during the prime hours before and after lunch—par for the cruise ship course. On *Radiance,* the pool deck is presided over by a 12-foot-high cedar totem pole carved for the ship by Alaska Native artist Nathan Jackson of Ketchikan.

Much more relaxing are the ships' large, lush Solariums, with their exotic eastern motifs. Tropical foliage and waterfalls impart an Asian-spa mood, and stone reliefs, regional woodcarvings, and statues drive home the mood. The area's adjacent (and popular) pizza counter adds a little pandemonium to the otherwise serene scene (as can kids, if they happen to find the place), but overall this is a great spot to settle in for a lazy afternoon at sea. The padded wooden chaise longues are heavenly. The adjacent spa has 13 treatment rooms and a special steam-room complex with heated tiled lounges and showers that simulate tropical rain and fog.

The Sports Deck has a 9-hole miniature-golf course and golf simulators, a jogging track, a rock-climbing wall attached to the funnel, and a combo basketball, volleyball, and paddle-tennis court. The sprawling oceanview gym has a huge aerobics floor and dozens of exercise machines, including sea-facing treadmills and elliptical stair-steppers.

The Vision Class: Legend of the Seas • Enchantment of the Seas • Grandeur of the Seas • Rhapsody of the Seas • Splendour of the Seas • Vision of the Seas

The Verdict

These ships are glitzy and exciting without going overboard, though they're on the frumpy side compared to the newer, snazzier Radiance, Voyager, and Freedom ships.

Rhapsody of the Seas *(photo: RCCL)*

Specifications

Size (in tons)			
		Grandeur	975/212
Legend/Splendour	69,130	*Enchantment*	1,126/248
Grandeur	74,140	*Rhapsody/Vision*	1,000/229
Enchantment	80,700	Crew	
Rhapsody/Vision	78,491	*Legend/Splendour*	720
Passengers (double occ.)		*Grandeur*	760
Legend/Splendour	1,804	*Enchantment*	840
Grandeur	1,950	*Rhapsody/Vision*	765
Enchantment	2,252	Passenger/Crew Ratio	
Rhapsody/Vision	2,000	*Enchantment*	2.5 to 1
Passenger/Space Ratio			2.7 to 1
Legend/Splendour	41.1/38.3	Year Launched	
Grandeur	38	*Legend*	1995
Enchantment	35.8	*Splendour/Grandeur*	1996
Rhapsody/Vision	39.2/34.6	*Enchantment/Rhapsody*	1997
Total Cabins/Veranda Cabins		*Vision*	1998
Legend/Splendour	902/231	Last Refurbishment/Upgrade	
		Enchantment	2005

Frommer's Ratings (Scale of 1–5)   ★★★½

Cabin Comfort & Amenities	3	Dining Options	3
Appearance & Upkeep	4	Gym, Spa & Sports Facilities	4
Public Comfort/Space	4	Children's Facilities	4
Decor	3.5	Enjoyment Factor	4

It's a funny thing with cruise ships. One year they're the newest, hottest, biggest thing on water, and just a few cycles around the sun later you look at them and think, "How quaint. How '90s." They may be just fine, and still offer a great cruise experience, but things have changed so fast in the cruise biz that even the best ships from the late 20th century can seem dated. That's sort of the story with RCI's Vision-class vessels, which offer an open, light-filled feel and many of the same amenities as aboard the line's newer, larger ships. They're just not the new kid on the block anymore.

All the ships have been kept up-to-date (they were even retrofitted with rock-climbing walls after those proved so popular on the Voyager ships), but *Enchantment of the Seas* is by far the most modernized of the bunch. In mid-2005, RCI revisited a trend common in the mid-'90s, literally sawing the ship in half like a magician's assistant, inserting a new 73-foot midsection, and then welding it all back together. As a result, *Enchantment* offers a lot more than her Vision-class sisters. On the much-enlarged pool deck there's an additional stage and midships bar for adults and an "interactive splash deck" with water jets kids can control to spray each other or create their own water ballet. Additions to the nearby Sports Deck include four bungee trampolines where guests can bounce up to 35 feet above the deck, doing somersaults in midair. Disabled passengers aren't left out, with new accessibility features including pool and Jacuzzi lifts, access to the Splash Deck, a lift to the bungee trampoline area, and improved thresholds and ramps throughout the vessel. Below-deck changes include the addition of a Latin-themed bar, an expanded casino, a larger shopping area, and a new coffee bar serving Seattle's Best coffee and Ben & Jerry's ice cream—features currently available aboard RCI's newer vessels. No word yet on whether *Enchantment's* sister ships will get a similar refurbishment anytime soon.

Splendour is spending 2008 sailing in Europe and South America.

Cabins & Rates

Cabins	Per Diems From	Sq. Ft.	Fridge	Hair Dryer	Sitting Area	TV
Inside	$80	138–174	no	no	yes	yes
Outside	$93	154–237	some	no	yes	yes
Suite	$178	241–1,140	yes	no	yes	yes

CABINS   To be polite, cabins are "compact"—larger than on the line's Sovereign-class ships but smaller than those on the Voyager- and Radiance-class ships and on many competitors' vessels. For big, check out the 1,140-square-foot Royal Suites, which feature a baby grand piano and huge marble bathroom with double sinks, a big whirlpool bathtub, and a glass-enclosed shower for two. For something in between, check the roomy 190-square-foot category-D1 cabins, with private verandas, minifridges, small sitting areas with pullout couches, and tons of storage space. All told, about a quarter of each ship's cabins have private verandas, about a third can accommodate third and fourth passengers, and all have safes, TVs, and an impressive amount of storage space. Bathrooms are not the largest you'll ever see, with shower stalls that are a tight squeeze for anyone thicker than a supermodel. Expect a decor of pastel and beige with varnished wood trim—not adventurous, but not hideous either.

Each vessel has between 14 and 17 staterooms equipped for wheelchair users.

PUBLIC AREAS   Throughout each vessel, warm woods and brass, gurgling fountains, green foliage, glass, crystal, and buttery leathers highlight the public areas, whose ambience ranges from classic to glitzy. The bright, wide open, and easy-to-navigate Promenade and Mariner decks are home to most public rooms, their corridors converging at a seven-story atrium where glass elevators take passengers from Deck 4 all the way up to the stunning, glass-walled Viking Crown Lounge on Deck 11. Full musical revues are staged in glittery, two-story showrooms, where columns obstruct views from some balcony seats. The ship's casinos are Vegas-style flashy, with hundreds of gambling stations so densely packed that it's sometimes difficult to move and always difficult to hear. Other nice spots include the Schooner piano bar (a great place for a pre-dinner drink or late-night unwinding, with a nautical wood-and-rope decor) and the Champagne Terrace at the foot of the atrium, where you can sip a glass of fine wine or bubbly while swaying to the dance band.

In contrast to its showcase spaces, each ship also contains many hideaway refuges, including an array of cocktail bars, a library, and card rooms. Hundreds of potted plants and more than 3,000 original artworks aboard each ship add humanity and warmth, though some of that art is, as we said above, "so '90s."

For kids there's a playroom stocked with toys, books, and games, while the nearby teen center goes the video-game route.

DINING OPTIONS   The large dining rooms aboard these vessels span two decks connected with a very grand staircase and flanked with 20-foot walls of glass. The rooms are of their era, with lots of stainless steel, mirrors, dramatic chandeliers, and a bit of banquet-hall feel. There's also a large indoor/outdoor buffet restaurant serving breakfast, lunch, and dinner.

POOL, FITNESS, SPA & SPORTS FACILITIES   The Steiner-managed spas on these ships offer a wide selection of treatments as well as the standard steam rooms and saunas. Adjacent Solariums offer a pool, lounge chairs, floor-to-ceiling windows, and a retractable glass ceiling for inclement weather. Designed after Roman, Egyptian, or Moorish models, these bright, spacious areas are a peaceful place to lounge before or after a spa treatment, or any time at all. Gyms are surprisingly small and cramped considering the ships' size.

Each ship has a higher-than-expected amount of open deck space. The outdoor pool on the Sun Deck has the usual blaring rah-rah music during the day, along with silly contests of the belly-flop variety. A rock-climbing wall, jogging track, shuffleboard, and Ping-Pong round out the on-deck options.

The Sovereign Class: Sovereign of the Seas • Monarch of the Seas • Majesty of the Seas

Sovereign of the Seas *(photo: RCCL)*

The Verdict

These three ships started Royal Caribbean's trip into megaship land. They aren't spring chickens, but they are a bargain, sailing inexpensive 3- and 4-night cruises on the East and West coasts.

Specifications

Size (in tons)		*Sovereign*	840
Sovereign	73,192	*Monarch/Majesty*	825
Monarch/Majesty	73,941	Passenger/Crew Ratio	
Passengers (double occ.)		*Sovereign*	2.7 to 1
Sovereign	2,292	*Monarch/Majesty*	2.9 to 1
Monarch/Majesty	2,390	Year Launched	
Passenger/Space Ratio		*Sovereign*	1988
Sovereign	31.9	*Monarch*	1991
Monarch/Majesty	30.9	*Majesty*	1992
Total Cabins/Veranda Cabins		Last Refurbishment/Upgrade	
Sovereign	1,138/62	*Sovereign*	2004
Monarch/Majesty	1,177/62	*Monarch*	2003
Crew		*Majesty*	2007

Frommer's Ratings (Scale of 1–5)   ★★★*

Cabin Comfort & Amenities	3	Dining Options	3
Appearance & Upkeep	4	Gym, Spa & Sports Facilities	3
Public Comfort/Space	3	Children's Facilities	4
Decor	3.5	Enjoyment Factor	3.5

* *Ratings based on* Monarch *and* Sovereign. Majesty *has not yet been refurbished to the same standards.*

When she was launched in 1988, *Sovereign of the Seas* was the largest passenger vessel built in half a century, and caused such a sensation that Royal Caribbean quickly followed her up with the slightly larger *Monarch* and *Majesty of the Seas*. Times change, though, and today these once-giant ships are less than half the size of their largest fleetmates. A decade and a half of hard use gave them their share of bumps and bruises, but in 2003 Royal Caribbean began a major makeover program designed to hammer out the dents and bring them into the 21st century. *Monarch of the Seas* went under the knife first, with *Sovereign* following in November 2004 and *Majesty* in January 2007.

Cabins & Rates

Cabins	Per Diems From	Sq. Ft.	Fridge	Hair Dryer	Sitting Area	TV
Inside	$67	120	no	no	no	yes
Outside	$77	120–157	some	no	some	yes
Suite	$170	264–670	yes	no	yes	yes

CABINS   Standard staterooms are very snug at only 120 square feet, bathrooms are similarly cramped, and closet space is limited—but then, how much space do you need on the kind of short itineraries these ships offer? More than 100 cabins have upper and lower berths to accommodate four, albeit very tightly. Overall, cabin decor is spartan and uninspired, with pastel fabrics and blond woods, and like other ships of their generation, relatively few have balconies. All cabins have TVs, plus personal safes on *Majesty* and *Monarch* (on *Sovereign,* they're only in cabin categories R, A, B, C, and D; for everyone else, there are lockboxes at the purser's desk). Soundproofing in these cabins isn't the greatest; in some you can hear every word your neighbors say.

Four to six cabins on each ship can accommodate wheelchair users.

PUBLIC AREAS   A dramatic five-story atrium is the focal point of each ship, separating the public areas (which are mostly clustered in the stern) from the cabins forward, an arrangement that minimizes bleed-through noise and also gives the impression that these ships are smaller than they are. Shops, the ship's salon, the Internet center, the library, several information desks, and a champagne bar are all clustered around the atrium at various levels. Elsewhere, you'll find a sprawling casino, a cinema, the popular Schooner piano bar, and (as on all pre-*Voyager* RCI ships) the Viking Crown Lounge, perched on the topmost deck some 150 feet above sea level and letting on to amazing panoramic views. It's a great place for a pre-dinner drink and after-dinner dancing. Down on Decks 5 and 7, the two-story main show lounge is roomy and well planned, with lots of cocktail-table-and-chair clusters for two and a huge stage.

As part of their 2003/2004/2007 makeovers, all three ships were fitted with a Boleros Latin Lounge, featuring Latin music, a dueling-piano-players act, and drinks from Brazil, Cuba, and Central America. The ships' children's centers were also expanded and three teen-only hangouts added: the Living Room coffee bar, a disco called "Fuel," and a private outdoor sun deck with dance floor.

DINING OPTIONS   Each ship offers a pair of one-story dining rooms, plus a large indoor/outdoor buffet restaurant on Deck 11 serving breakfast, lunch, and dinner. *Monarch's* buffet also offers an Asian option, and *Sovereign's* and *Majesty's* feature multiple self-service islands offering regional dishes from Asia, Latin America, the Mediterranean, the U.S., and elsewhere, plus a cooked-to-order pasta station, a carving station, a deli, and a soup-and-salad bar. You can also nosh at a dedicated pizzeria or grab a specialty coffee or Ben & Jerry's ice cream from the Latte'tudes coffee shop. *Sovereign* and *Majesty* also feature a '50s-style Johnny Rockets diner serving burgers and shakes.

POOL, FITNESS, SPA & SPORTS FACILITIES   The deck layout and two good-size swimming pools seem plenty spacious when they're empty, but the number of passengers who typically sail these short itineraries almost guarantees that they'll fill up, becoming a wall-to-wall carpet of people. That said, there are many patches of more isolated deck space all over each ship, from the quiet slices on the tiered aft decks to two levels of far-forward deck space.

The Sports Deck, up high in the stern, has Ping-Pong tables and a basketball court. The half-moon-shaped gym on Deck 10 is fairly spacious, with a wall of windows facing aft. Treadmills, stationary bikes, step machines, and free weights line the perimeter of the room, facing the sea, and the inner part of the room serves as the aerobics space. A smallish spa is adjacent.

All three ships sport rock-climbing walls, a feature that's become one of Royal Caribbean's signature offerings.

7

The Ultraluxury Lines

On these ritzy ships, guests don't line up for a cone of frozen yogurt or a slice of pepperoni pizza en route to St. Thomas or Nassau. Instead, they sip a '98 Bordeaux with their *filet de boeuf* in truffle sauce while sailing to St. Barts. They order jumbo shrimp from the room-service menu and take indulgent baths in ritzy marble bathrooms. There are no midnight buffets, dancing waiters, belly-flop contests, or many of the other typical cruise ship trappings, but instead doting service, spacious suites with walk-in closets, and an overall feeling of calmness and elegance. Delicious French, Italian, and Asian cuisine often rivals that of respected shore-side restaurants, and even if it's not quite what you find at a three-star Michelin restaurant, it's pretty darn good and absolutely the best you'll find at sea, served in high style by gracious waiters who know their jobs. A full dinner can even be served to you in your cabin, if you like.

Ships in the luxury class come in three basic flavors: the enormous, 2,620-passenger *Queen Mary 2* and Crystal's pair of 1,000-passenger vessels; the midsize vessels of Regent Seven Seas (formerly Radisson Seven Seas) and Silversea, which carry between 300 and 700 guests; and the small boutique ships of Seabourn and SeaDream, which serve only 110 to 208 passengers at a time. Whatever their size, they all cater to discerning travelers who don't blink at paying top dollar to be pampered. Service is very personal, and staff will get to know your likes and dislikes early on. The onboard atmosphere is much like a private club, with guests trading traveling tales and meeting for drinks or dinner.

Entertainment and organized activities are more dignified than on other ships, and are more limited as guests tend to amuse themselves, enjoying cocktails and conversation in a piano bar, listening to singers or musicians, and maybe watching small-scale Broadway-inspired song-and-dance reviews.

While the high-end lines discount at times, they'll still cost two or three times as much as your typical mainstream cruise. Expect to pay at least $2,000 per person for a week in the Caribbean, and easily more if you opt for a large suite or choose to cruise during the busiest times of the year. Many extras are often included in the cruise rates. For instance, Silversea, Seabourn, Regent, and SeaDream include unlimited wine, liquor, and beverages, along with gratuities, a stocked minibar, and a complimentary shore excursion on most cruises (with the exception of Regent). Crystal includes all soft drinks in its rates. Many of these lines also include other free perks the mainstream lines don't, from Godiva chocolates on your pillow on formal nights (Silversea) to cotton logo pj's (SeaDream), a CD of classic jazz (Seabourn), luggage tags and document portfolio (Seabourn offers Tumi versions), and high-end bathroom amenities from names such as Bulgari, Bronnely, Molton Brown, and Acqua di Parma.

Frommer's Ratings at a Glance: The Ultraluxury Lines

1 = poor   2 = fair   3 = good   4 = excellent   5 = outstanding

Cruise Line	Enjoyment Factor	Dining	Activities	Children's Program	Entertainment	Service	Worth the Money
Crystal	5	5	5	3	4	4	5
Cunard	5	4	5	5	4	4	5
Regent Seven Seas	5	4	3	2	3	5	5
Seabourn	5	5	2	N/A*	2	4	4
SeaDream	5	4	4	N/A*	3	5	5
Silversea	5	5	3	N/A*	2	5	4

Note: Cruise lines have been graded on a curve that compares them only with the other lines in the ultraluxury category. See "How to Read the Ratings," in chapter 5, for a detailed explanation of the ratings methodology.

*Lines with N/A rating for children's programs have no program.

Most people attracted to these types of cruises are sophisticated, wealthy, relatively social, and used to the finer things in life. Most are well traveled though not necessarily adventurous, and tend to stick to five-star experiences. These ships are not geared to children, although aboard lines such as Crystal and especially Cunard you might see 100 or more during holidays or school vacation months. Babysitting can often be arranged privately with an off-duty crewmember.

DRESS CODES   With the exception of casual SeaDream, these are the most formal cruises out there: For the main dining rooms, you need to bring the tux or a dark suit and the sequined gown or cocktail dress for the two or three formal nights scheduled each week. Informal nights call for jackets (skip the tie if you want to; things are getting more casual even on the fancy ships) and smart dresses, skirts, or pantsuits for women. Sports jackets or nice shirts for men and casual dresses or pantsuits for women are the norm on casual nights. That said, like the rest of the industry, even the high-end lines are relaxing their dress codes, heading closer to SeaDream, which espouses a casual "no jackets required" policy during the entire cruise. All the ultraluxe lines now have casual dining venues, so if you just want to throw on a sundress (or polo shirt and chinos) and be done with it, you'll be fine.

1 Crystal Cruises

2049 Century Park E., Suite 1400, Los Angeles, CA 90067. © 888/799-4625 or 310/785-9300. Fax 310/785-0011. www.crystalcruises.com.

THE LINE IN A NUTSHELL   Stylish and upbeat, Crystal offers top-shelf service and cuisine on ships large enough to offer lots of outdoor deck space, generous fitness facilities, tons of activities, multiple restaurants, and more than half a dozen bars and entertainment venues. **Sails to:** Caribbean, Panama Canal, Mexican Riviera, Hawaii, Canada/New England (plus Europe, Africa, Asia, Australia/New Zealand, South Pacific, South America, transatlantic, and world cruise).

THE EXPERIENCE   Aside from Cunard's *Queen Mary 2*, Crystal has the only truly upscale large ships in the industry. Carrying 940 to 1,080 passengers, they aren't huge, but they're big enough to offer much more than their high-end peers. You won't feel hemmed in and you likely won't be twiddling your thumbs from lack of stimulation. Service is excellent and the line's Asian cuisine is tops. Unlike Seabourn's small ships, which tend to be more calm and staid, Crystal's sociable California ethic and large passenger capacity tend to keep things mingly, chatty, and more active. No question, these vessels have a vitality and energy the smaller Seabourn and Silversea ships definitely do not.

Pros

- **Four or five restaurants:** In addition to the formal dining room, there are two or three alternative restaurants (including, on *Serenity*, two with cuisine by famed chef Nobu Matsuhisa), plus a poolside grill, an indoor cafe, and a casual restaurant that puts on great theme luncheon buffets.
- **Best Asian food at sea:** The ships' reservations-only Asian restaurants serve up utterly delicious Japanese food, including sushi. At least once per cruise, an Asian-theme buffet lunch offers an awesome spread.
- **Fitness choices:** There's a nice-size gym, paddle-tennis courts, shuffleboard, Ping-Pong, a jogging circuit, golf-driving nets, and a putting green.
- **Enrichment programs:** No other line has as many, with four or five impressive lecturers as well as complimentary computer training classes on every cruise, plus dozens of theme sailings focused on food and wine, art, film, jazz music, wellness, and other subjects.

Cons

- **Least all-inclusive of the luxe lines:** Only nonalcoholic drinks are included in the rates, not tips, booze, and so on.
- **Cabin size:** Accommodations (especially on *Symphony*) are smaller than those aboard Silversea, Seabourn, and Regent.

CRYSTAL: SPARKLING & SPACIOUS

Established in 1990, Crystal Cruises has established its own unique place in the high-stakes, superupscale cruise market. Its ships are the largest true luxury vessels aside from Cunard's *QE2* and *QM2*, and while not quite as generous in the stateroom department (cabins are smaller than those on Regent, Silversea, Seabourn, and Sea-Dream) and the freebies department (Crystal doesn't include complimentary champagne, liquor, and wine in the rates, though cruise fares tend to be less expensive than the lines that do), they provide a truly refined cruise for discerning guests who appreciate really good service and top-notch cuisine. No doubt about it, Crystal is one of our favorite lines.

The line is the North American spinoff of Japan's largest container shipping enterprise, Nippon Yusen Kaisha (NYK). Despite these origins, a passenger aboard Crystal could conceivably spend an entire week at sea and not even be aware that the ship is Japanese owned and funded. More than anything else, Crystal is international, with a strong emphasis on European service. The Japanese exposure is subtler, and you'll feel it in the excellent Asian cuisine and tasty sake served in the alternative restaurants and at the Asian-theme buffets. A Japanese activities director is on board to attend to the handful of Japanese passengers you'll see on many cruises.

Compared with the other ultraluxury lines, here's how Crystal rates:

	Poor	Fair	Good	Excellent	Outstanding
Enjoyment Factor					✓
Dining					✓
Activities					✓
Children's Program			✓		
Entertainment				✓	
Service				✓	
Worth the Money					✓

In late 2005, the line's oldest ship, the 1990-built *Harmony*, left the Crystal fleet to take up service with parent company NYK's Asian cruise division. In announcing the move, Crystal also hinted at future construction of a replacement vessel, though no details are yet available.

PASSENGER PROFILE

Like other high-end lines, Crystal draws a lot of repeat passengers. On many cruises more than 50% hail from affluent regions of California, and many are Crystal fans who have sailed with the line numerous times. There's commonly a small contingent of passengers (about 15% of the mix) from the United Kingdom, Australia, Japan, Hong Kong, Mexico, Europe, South America, and other places. Most passengers are well-heeled couples over 55. A good number of passengers step up to Crystal from lines such as Princess and Holland America.

Many Crystal passengers place great emphasis on the social scene before, during, and after mealtimes, and many enjoy dressing up (sometimes way up) for dinner. You'll see no shortage of diamonds and gold Rolexes, and it's obvious that women on board have devoted much care and attention to their wardrobes and accessories. The onboard jewelry and clothing boutiques also do a brisk business, and guests forking over $50,000 for a diamond-encrusted watch isn't uncommon. On formal nights—2 or 3 of which occur during every 10- or 11-day cruise—the majority of men wear tuxes and many women wear floor-length gowns, although your classic black cocktail dress is just fine. As on all ships, dress codes are much more relaxed during the day.

Though not a kid-centric line compared to the mainstream lines, in the high end, Crystal is the most accommodating for families with kids. Each ship has a dedicated playroom and teen club, and supervised activities for ages 3 and up are offered when demand warrants it. During holidays and the summer holiday months of July and August, 100 or so kids on board is not that unusual.

DINING

Service by the team of ultraprofessional, gracious, European waiters is excellent. In the main dining room—and to a somewhat lesser degree in the alternative restaurants—table settings are lavish and include heavy leaded crystal, Frette linens, and Villeroy & Boch as well as Wedgwood china. Even in the Lido restaurant, waiters are at hand to serve you your salad from the buffet line, prepare your coffee, and then carry your tray to wherever it is you want to sit.

TRADITIONAL Dinner is served in two seatings in the main dining rooms; lunches and breakfasts are open seating. Cuisine selections include dishes such as coq au vin (braised chicken in burgundy red-wine sauce with glazed onions and mushrooms over a bed of linguine), Black Angus beef tenderloin with burgundy wine gravy, oven-baked quail with porcini mushroom and bread stuffing, or seared sea scallops served with a light lobster beurre blanc over a bed of risotto. At lunch and dinner, there's a **light, low-cholesterol selection** such as grilled fresh halibut served with steamed vegetables and herbed potatoes, as well as an entree salad—for example, a mixed salad with grilled herb-marinated chicken breast, lamb, or filet mignon. **Vegetarian selections,** such as spinach and ricotta cannelloni or a brochette of Mediterranean vegetables are also featured, as are **kosher foods** and **low-carb choices.** Sugar-free, gluten-free, and low-fat options are now part of all menus too, even at buffets. Virtually any special diet can be accommodated.

In a kind of homage to the California wine industry, Crystal offers one of the most sophisticated inventories of **California wines** on the high seas, as well as a reserve list of two dozen or so rare wines and an extensive selection of French wines. In 2004, the line also created its own proprietary label called **C Wines,** six chardonnays, cabernet sauvignons, and merlots made in limited production with grapes from the Napa and Sonoma valleys, Arroyo Seco, and the Santa Lucia Highlands. All are available on board by the glass or the bottle.

SPECIALTY The line's Asian venues are among the best at sea. *Symphony's* Jade Garden showcases the Asian cuisine of Wolfgang Puck's acclaimed Santa Monica restaurant, Chinois on Main. Even better, master chef **Nobuyuki "Nobu" Matsuhisa,** known for his restaurants in New York, Miami, L.A., London, Paris, and other cities, partnered with Crystal to create menus for *Serenity's* Sushi Bar and its Pan-Asian restaurant Silk Road. Dishes feature Nobu's eclectic blends of Japanese cuisine with Peruvian and European influences. In the Sushi Bar, sample the salmon tartare with sevruga caviar or the yellowtail sashimi with jalapeño; in Silk Road, choices include lobster with truffle yuzu sauce and chicken with teriyaki balsamic. While Nobu himself makes occasional appearances on *Serenity,* chef Toshiaki Tamba, personally trained by Nobu, oversees the restaurants.

Aboard both ships, famed restaurateur Piero Selvaggio showcases the cuisine of his award-winning Santa Monica and Las Vegas Valentino restaurants at the Italian **Valentino at Prego.** Reservations are required for each of the specialty restaurants, and a $7 gratuity is suggested.

CASUAL Excellent **themed luncheon buffets**—Asian, Mediterranean, Western barbecue, or South American/Cuban, for instance—are generously spread out at lunchtime by the pool, and an extraspecial **gala buffet** is put on once per cruise in the lobby/atrium. No expense or effort is spared to produce elaborate food fests, with heaps of jumbo shrimp, homemade sushi, Greek salads, shish kabobs, beef satay, stir-fry dishes, gourmet cheeses, and more.

While you can have breakfast in the Lido restaurant, the Bistro serves a late continental breakfast from 9:30 to 11:30am and is open between 11:30am and 6pm for complimentary grazing at the buffet-style spread of cheeses, cold cuts, fruit, cookies, and pastries. Nonalcoholic specialty drinks, such as hazelnut latte and fruit shakes, are complimentary here. On a recent Symphony cruise, the Bistro was hopping and a real social hub and people-watching spot.

For something casual poolside, the Trident Grill serves casual lunches daily between 11:30am and 6pm for those who'd like something simple and easy poolside (beef, chicken, and salmon burgers; wraps and tuna melts; pizza, hot dogs, and fries; fruit; and a special of the day). You can place your order at the counter and either have a seat at the adjacent tables or head back to your deck chair and let a waiter bring you your lunch. You don't even have to change out of your bathing suit. It also operates several evenings per cruise between 6 and 9pm, offering an open-air ambience and serving dishes such as grilled shrimp, Cobb salad, and gourmet pizza.

SNACKS & EXTRAS   For **afternoon tea,** it's the ultrachic Palm Court on one of the uppermost decks. A sprawling space with floor-to-ceiling windows and pale-blue and white furniture in leather and rattan, the area gives off a light, ethereal ambience. Pre-dinner and midnight hot and cold canapés in the lounges include the likes of delicious foie gras, caviar, and marinated salmon.

There is, of course, **24-hour room service,** as well as complimentary unlimited nonalcoholic drinks everywhere aboard, from cappuccino to soda and bottled water.

ACTIVITIES

Crystal offers an interesting selection of activities, most of which are part of the ships' Creative Learning Institute. The extensive program features an array of expert speakers, plus alliances with well-known organizations, schools, and brands—Yamaha, Berlitz, Barnes&Noble.com, The Cleveland Clinic, and the Tai Chi Cultural Center to name a few—to provide an even greater oomph to the classes. You can count on several **enrichment lectures** throughout each cruise, such as a historian presenting a slide show and speaking about the Panama Canal and how it was built, a former ambassador speaking about regional politics, or a scientist talking about conservation. Most speakers are not celebrities, but well-known personalities do occasionally show up. Recent guests have included political commentators James Carville and Mary Matalin, songwriter Neil Sedaka, business consultant Ken Blanchard, former press secretary Marlin Fitzwater, medical expert Dr. Art Ulene, biographer Chris Ogden, and publisher Steve Forbes.

In addition to each cruise's guest lecturers, some of Crystal's sailings feature **theme programs** with activities built around them. More than a dozen annual Wine & Food Festival cruises feature a respected wine expert who conducts at least two complimentary tastings, plus guest chefs conducting cooking demonstrations for guests and then presenting the results of those lessons at dinner. There are also music-theme cruises from time to time, featuring big bands, ballroom dance, jazz singers, and film and theater. Other cruises have experts conducting seminars on finance issues, language, and art appreciation, the latter with speakers from the famous auction house Sotheby's.

Guest teachers teach swing, rumba, and merengue dance lessons on some cruises. Group lessons are complimentary, and private lessons can sometimes be arranged with the instructors for about $50 per hour per couple. Other activities include bridge and paddle-tennis competitions; game-show-style contests; trivia games; midafternoon dance music with the resident dance trio or quartet; interesting arts and crafts such as glass etching; and even guest fashion shows. Commonly, a **golf expert** sails on board, too, conducting complimentary group golf lessons by the driving nets several times per cruise (again, private lessons can be arranged; prices start at $50 per hour). A variety of free aerobics classes is also offered in the fitness center, including Pilates and yoga (private personal trainers are available for a fee).

Crystal Fleet Itineraries

Ship	Itineraries
Crystal Symphony	**Panama Canal:** 16 nights, Los Angeles, CA, to Miami, FL (Jan). 11 nights, west- or eastbound between Miami and Caldera, Costa Rica (Jan–Feb). 14 nights, Miami to Los Angeles (Feb). 13 nights, Miami to Los Angeles (Nov). **Mexican Riviera:** 7 nights, round-trip from Los Angeles (Feb & Nov–Dec). **New England/Canada:** 11 nights, north- or southbound between New York, NY, and Montréal, QC (Sept–Oct). **Caribbean/Bermuda:** 12 nights, New York to Miami (Oct).
Crystal Serenity	**Panama Canal:** 15 nights, Miami, FL, to Los Angeles, CA (Jan). 11 nights, east- or westbound between Miami and Caldera, Costa Rica (Dec). **Caribbean:** 14-night eastern/southern, round-trip from Miami (Dec).

The line's **Computer University @ Sea** offers some complimentary courses on all cruises, with topics such as basic computing, understanding the Internet, website design, and creating spreadsheets using Excel. Private lessons are also available for $50 an hour. Internet centers have about 30 workstations apiece, featuring Dell PCs; though oddly enough, you must buy Internet time in 2-hour $50 installments—not convenient if you just need a few minutes to do some e-mailing toward the end of the cruise. There are now Wi-Fi hot spots for passengers who want to work on their own laptops, and onboard cellphone service via a satellite link, at prices in the same range as your provider's regular roaming charges.

CHILDREN'S PROGRAM

Crystal is a sophisticated cruise line that focuses its attention on adults, but more than any other line in the luxury end of the market, it also does its part to cater to the little people. Each ship has a bright **children's playroom,** primarily used during holiday and summer cruises (mostly in Europe), when some 100 kids may be aboard. Both ships also have another room with PlayStations, computers, and arcade machines for older kids and teens, with counselors on hand to supervise activities such as scavenger hunts, arts and crafts, karaoke, and games that take place during several hours in the morning and in the afternoon, for three age groups between 3 and 17. There are kiddy books and videos in the library for guests to take back to their staterooms, and a children's menu in the main dining room, as well as kid favorites at the poolside Trident Grill.

For children as young as 6 months, **in-cabin babysitting** can be arranged privately through the concierge at an hourly rate of $7.50 for one child, $10 for two kids, and $13 for three kids. Cribs, highchairs, and booster seats are available, and as for food, if you notify the line ahead of time, they'll special-order jars of baby food, at no charge. Or the chef will puree organic food for your baby. Note that children 11 and under pay 50% of the lowest adult fare when accompanied by two full-fare guests.

The minimum age for sailing is 6 months.

ENTERTAINMENT

Onboard entertainment is good (and plentiful), but it's certainly not the high point of the cruise. Shows in the horseshoe-shaped, rather plain Galaxy Lounge encompass everything from classical concertos by accomplished pianists to comedy. A troupe of spangle-covered, lip-syncing dancers and a pair of lead singers perform Vegas-style shows, and from time to time there's a featured celebrity entertainer aboard, such as the Tommy Dorsey Orchestra, Maureen McGovern, Tommy Tune, or Marvin Hamlisch.

After dinner each night, a second large, attractive lounge is the venue for **ballroom-style dancing** to a live band, with a clutch of gentleman hosts aboard each sailing to provide dance (and dinner) partners for single ladies. Both ships have roomy **casinos** and rooms for dancing, in either *Serenity*'s dedicated disco or *Symphony*'s Starlight lounge. A pianist in the dark, paneled, and romantic Avenue Saloon—our favorite room on board—plays standards, show tunes, and pop hits before and after dinner. On both ships you can also enjoy cigars (from Monte Cristo to Davidoff) in the Connoisseurs Club, recent-release movies several times a day in the theater (which also serves as a venue for lectures and religious services), and a varied and full menu of movies on the in-cabin TVs.

SERVICE

The hallmark of a high-end cruise such as Crystal is its service, so the line's staff is better trained and more attentive than that aboard most other cruise lines. Dining room and restaurant staffs hail from Italy, Portugal, and other European countries, and have trained in the grand restaurants of Europe and North America, while the stewardess who tidies your stateroom is likely to be from Scandinavia, Hungary, or elsewhere in the E.U. Everyone, from the dining/bar staff to those staffing the information and concierge desks in the lobby, is endlessly good-natured and very helpful. Guests in Penthouse Suites are treated to the services of male butlers. As far as tipping goes, most passengers charge gratuities to their onboard accounts, though you can pay in cash if you wish.

All guests get complimentary unlimited nonalcoholic drinks everywhere aboard, from cappuccino to soda and bottled water.

In addition to laundry and dry-cleaning services, complimentary **self-serve laundry rooms** are available.

Crystal Serenity

The Verdict

Crystal Serenity is Crystal's best ship yet, offering an ultraelegant cruise with a huge array of onboard choices, from dining to activities and public spaces.

Crystal Serenity *(photo: Crystal Cruises)*

Specifications

Size (in tons)	68,000	Crew	655
Passengers (double occ.)	1,080	Passenger/Crew Ratio	1.6 to 1
Passenger/Space Ratio	63	Year Launched	2003
Total Cabins/Veranda Cabins	540/460	Last Refurbishment/Upgrade	N/A

Frommer's Ratings (Scale of 1–5)   ★★★★½

Cabin Comfort & Amenities	4.5	Dining Options	5
Appearance & Upkeep	5	Gym, Spa & Sports Facilities	5
Public Comfort/Space	4.5	Children's Facilities	3.5
Decor	4	Enjoyment Factor	5

The largest truly ultraluxe vessel afloat, *Serenity* is 38% bigger than the older *Symphony* but carries only 15% more guests. It's one of the most spacious ships out there, from the beautifully designed public rooms to an expansive pool deck. There's simply no crowding at any time. In every way, this ship's a star.

Cabins & Rates

Cabins	Per Diems From	Sq. Ft.	Fridge	Hair Dryer	Sitting Area	TV
Outside	$330	202–226	yes	yes	yes	yes
Suite	$720	403–1,345*	yes	yes	yes	yes

* Including veranda.

CABINS   Standard staterooms on this ship are about the same size as those on *Symphony,* though the bathrooms and balconies are larger. The majority of standard cabins (categories A and B) are 202 square feet, not including balconies; cabin size is not Crystal's strong suit when compared to the line's luxury peers. There are 100 suites in three different categories, with the largest running 1,345 square feet.

Most of the standard cabins, called "Deluxe Staterooms," have a veranda, while 80 rooms have a large picture window. All feature a seating area, complimentary soft drinks and water, TV and DVD, small refrigerator, computer dataport, Egyptian cotton sheets and feather bed toppers, and a pillow menu. Choose from "regular" king- and standard-size pillows or four specialty options, which include round, foam-filled neck pillows for neck or lumbar support. Besides all of this, Penthouse Staterooms toss in butler service and complimentary beer, while the Penthouse Suites also throw in complimentary liquor and wine setup upon embarkation, a flatscreen TV, a separate bedroom area with a vanity, a Jacuzzi tub, a bidet, and a walk-in closet. If you're going straight to the top, the ship's Crystal Penthouses are incredibly spacious abodes, with a separate living room, a dining area, a CD player, three TVs (one in the bathroom if that floats your boat!), a cordless phone, a library, a pantry, and, believe it or not, a small gym.

Decor-wise, wood accents and furniture in the staterooms are on the medium to dark side, creating an elegant atmosphere offsetting the more colorful curtains, wall coverings, upholstery, and bedcovers. The feel is soothing. As aboard *Symphony,* the bathrooms are nicely laid out but still on the small side for a ship of such a high quality. You'll find plenty of drawer and closet space for a cruise of up to about 2 weeks.

Only a handful of cabins have a third berth available, and none offers four berths. Eight rooms are designated as wheelchair accessible.

PUBLIC AREAS   Public rooms on the *Serenity* are all so appealing that it's difficult to pick a favorite. The ship has a quiet, elegant atmosphere throughout, so much so that you won't even find glitz in the casino. Color schemes throughout are muted and calming, with lots of blues, greens, reds, golds, and grays. As aboard *Symphony,* one of the most popular lounges is dark and cozy Avenue Saloon, with its wonderful round bar and plenty of table seating. The two show lounges, Galaxy Lounge and Stardust Club, offer great sightlines and comfy seating, both theater- and table-style.

The ship has a good library that's well stocked with books, DVDs, and CDs that can be checked out only when the librarian is on duty. Two large rooms are dedicated to the line's learning programs: one for computer instruction and the other for classes offered in partnership with well-known institutions, such as piano instruction by Yamaha, language immersion by Berlitz, art classes conducted by the Parsons School of Design, and wellness programs run by the Cleveland Clinic and the Tai Chi Cultural Center.

DINING OPTIONS   Fine dining has been a trademark of Crystal's since the line began sailing in 1990, and the *Serenity* carries on the tradition with its two impressive alternative open-seating specialty restaurants, both of which require reservations (and a suggested $6 cover charge). In Prego, the surroundings really make you feel you're in a fine Italian restaurant ashore, with meat, pasta, and fish dishes offered a la carte or through a tasting menu with items selected by Piero Selvaggio, proprietor of the Valentino restaurants in Santa Monica and Las Vegas. On the Asian side of things, famed chef Nobu Matsuhisa oversees the menus in Silk Road, an ultrastylish space designed in a sea of ethereal mints and whites, with seating available at tables or at the sushi bar. Just forward of Silk Road, the Vintage Room is an intimate boardroom-style wine cellar that hosts special wine- and champagne-themed dinners and other events. In the ship's formal restaurant, the Crystal Dining Room, there are two seatings each evening at assigned tables. The lovely decor is a rich blend of dark woods with blue and mauve chairs. The latest dining option on board is Tastes, a casual venue serving breakfast, lunch, and dinner under a retractable roof near the Neptune Pool. It has a completely separate menu from the other dining areas and is a great dinner alternative when you don't feel like dressing up.

Other dining outlets include the Bistro Café, open for a variety of snacks and beverages all day long; the poolside Trident Grill; and the Lido Café, which serves buffet-style breakfast and lunch, with some made-to-order specialties such as omelets and pastas.

The 24-hour room-service menu is quite extensive. During dining hours, guests can also order from the Crystal Dining Room menu for in-cabin delivery.

POOL, FITNESS, SPA & SPORTS FACILITIES   There are two reasonably sized pools, one of which features a sliding glass roof. Indoors, the stunning Crystal Spa was designed according to feng shui principles, putting you right into relaxation mode. The complex includes a quiet room with very comfortable seating and great aft-facing views for those relaxing moments before or after a spa treatment. The changing rooms are stocked with lotions, shampoos, hair dryers, clocks, and bottles of water, while the steam rooms boast large picture windows for great views while you roast. A wide range of treatments includes a handful geared to men, such as a pro-collagen shave, frangipani hair conditioning, and aroma stone therapy massage. There's also a spacious beauty salon and a gym with separate weight room, aerobics studio, two full-size paddle-tennis courts, table tennis, golf driving nets, and a putting green.

Crystal Symphony

The Verdict

A gracious, floating pleasure palace, small enough to feel intimate and personal, yet large enough for a whole range of entertainment, dining, and fitness diversions.

Crystal Symphony *(photo: Crystal Cruises)*

Specifications

Size (in tons)	51,044	Crew	545
Passengers (double occ.)	940	Passenger/Crew Ratio	1.7 to 1
Passenger/Space Ratio	52.5	Year Launched	1995
Total Cabins/Veranda Cabins	480/276	Last Refurbishment/Upgrade	2006

Frommer's Ratings (Scale of 1–5)

★★★★½

Cabin Comfort & Amenities	4	Dining Options	5
Appearance & Upkeep	4	Gym, Spa & Sports Facilities	5
Public Comfort/Space	4.5	Children's Facilities	3
Decor	4	Enjoyment Factor	5

Plush, streamlined, extravagantly comfortable, and pleasingly midsize, *Symphony* competes with the high-end Silversea, Regent, and Seabourn vessels, although she's almost five times as large as Seabourn's, with a broader choice of onboard diversions. In late 2006 she had a major overhaul, to the tune of $23 million bucks, resulting in a more contemporary look—goodbye brass, chrome, and prissy pastels! Cabins and bathrooms were refurbished, along with entertainment lounges, the casino, boutiques, and more.

Cabins & Rates

Cabins	Per Diems From	Sq. Ft.	Fridge	Hair Dryer	Sitting Area	TV
Outside	$321	198–215	yes	yes	yes	yes
Suite	$738	287–782	yes	yes	yes	yes

CABINS   Though the majority of *Symphony*'s cabins are smaller than those aboard competing luxe lines Silversea, Regent, and Seabourn, they're still quite comfortable and were completely redone in late 2006. Cabins, which start at 198 square feet (plus 48-sq.-ft. verandas on many) now all feature stylish touches like Murano glass bedside lamps, Rubelli fabrics, and leather headboards. Each has a 20-inch LCD flatscreen TV, VCR, LED reading lights, sitting area, stocked minibar (snacks and alcoholic beverages consumed are charged to your onboard account except in the Penthouse Suites on Deck 10, where they're complimentary), hair dryer, and safe. Bathrooms, which have both shower and bathtub (a short little one in the lower category cabins), were hugely improved and now have a pair of oval glass sinks atop granite countertops. Egyptian cotton sheets, feather bed toppers, and a pillow menu make sleeping a dream, though when it comes to closets, they're smaller and tighter than you'd expect on ships of this caliber.

Deck 10 holds the ship's spectacular, attractively styled penthouses, the best of which measure more than 750 square feet, plus nearly 200-square-foot balconies, with full-fledged oceanview Jacuzzis in their living rooms, dark-wood furniture, and sofas upholstered in silk and satin, plus Oriental rugs and entertainment centers with 35-inch flatscreen TVs, and DVD and CD players. They also enjoy the services of a doting butler in addition to two stewardesses. The other two categories are about 287 and 396 square feet, plus 72- to 98-square-foot balconies.

Cabins without verandas have large rectangular windows. The category E cabins located amidships on Decks 7 and 8 have views obstructed by lifeboats. There are no inside cabins.

Five cabins are wheelchair accessible.

PUBLIC AREAS   Throughout the ship you'll find marble, glass, and hardwood paneling mingling with flowers and potted plants. The ship's recent face-lift has given the ship an even more open feel on the main entertainment deck, 6. The three large shops are among the most elegant at sea, and really are styled like ritzy Fifth Avenue or Rodeo Drive boutiques. The adjacent Bistro coffee and snack cafe is open to the atrium and is the place to see and be seen; it's the ship's social heart. Have an herbal tea, an ice coffee, or a decaf whatever; there's a lot of choice and the place is hopping. The egg custards at breakfast are to die for.

Aside from the several bar/entertainment lounges, a roaming staff wanders the public areas throughout the day and much of the night, offering to bring drinks to wherever you happen to be sitting. The dark Avenue Saloon, where polished mahogany, well-maintained leather upholstery, and a live pianist draw passengers in, is one of the prime before- and after-dinner cocktail spots and our personal favorite, by far. There are also two large entertainment lounges, including a completely re-created venue called the Starlite Club that's used for lectures by day and dancing by night (though if you're there for a lecture, avoid seating in the back of the room; the noise from passersby looking at mug shots in the adjacent photo gallery is a distraction). The hub has a dramatic round bar and walls of sparkling Swarovski crystals. You'll find a large theater for movies and slide lectures, and a hushed library outfitted with comfortably upholstered chairs and a worthy collection of books, periodicals, and videos. The revamped Casino now features a dramatic black-and-silver color scheme, while next door a new nightclub, called Luxe, attracts attention with its polished aluminum Phillipe Stark bar stools and glass Bizzaza mosaics. The cozy little spot is the venue for karaoke a couple of times per cruise.

If learning is more your speed, there's a 25-seat classroom and an adjacent Internet center, both with brand-new Dell computers. The Connoisseur's Club cigar lounge (Monte Cristo, anyone?) is attractive with wood tones and dark leather furniture.

For young kids, *Symphony* has a cute playroom with a tiered movie-viewing nook; for teens there's a teen center/video arcade.

DINING OPTIONS   Designed with curved walls and low, vaulted ceilings, the ship's main dining room is elegant and spacious, with dark wall paneling. Tables are not too close together, and there are well over 20 tables for two, mostly along the side or near the oceanview windows.

The ship's two themed, reservations-only alternative restaurants—the Italian Prego and the Pan-Asian Jade Garden—are right up there with the best at sea. The Vintage Room, an intimate boardroom-style wine cellar, was added during the ship's 2004 refit to host special wine and champagne theme dinners and other events.

A casual indoor/outdoor buffet restaurant is open for breakfast and lunch, and the poolside Trident Grill serves ultracasual lunch as well as dinners several evenings per cruise. The newly redecorated Bistro Café is going for an earthy European ambience and it's open from 9:30am to 6pm for continental breakfast, snacks, specialty coffees, and more.

POOL, FITNESS, SPA & SPORTS FACILITIES   *Symphony* offers a lot of outdoor activities and spacious areas in which to do them. There are two outdoor swimming pools separated by a bar, ice-cream counter, and sandwich grill, as well as two hot tubs. One of the pools is refreshingly oversize, stretching almost 40 feet across one of the sun decks; the other can be covered with a retractable glass roof. The gym and aerobics area are positioned for a view over the sea, with plenty of space for the line's complimentary yoga, Pilates, and aerobics classes (and personal training sessions too, for a fee). The Steiner-managed spa and beauty salon is accessorized with a quiet ocean-view waiting room to create an atmosphere of peace and relaxation. On deck, there's a pair of golf driving nets, a putting green, a large paddle-tennis court, Ping-Pong tables, and a broad, uninterrupted teak Promenade Deck for walkers and joggers. The ship's gorgeous and generous tiered afterdecks provide quiet places for an afternoon spent dozing in a deck chair.

2 Cunard

24303 Town Center Dr., Suite 200, Valencia, CA 91355-0908. © 800/7-CUNARD. www.cunard.com.

THE LINE IN A NUTSHELL The most venerable line in the cruise industry, Cunard is a classic, offering a link to the golden age of passenger ships. **Sails to:** Caribbean, New England/Canada, transatlantic (plus Europe, Africa, South America, world cruise).

THE EXPERIENCE The Cunard of today is not the Cunard of yesterday, but then again, it is. Formed in 1840 by Sir Samuel Cunard, the line provided the first regular steamship service between Europe and North America, and was one of the dominant players during the great years of steamship travel, which lasted roughly from 1905 to the mid-1960s. In 1969, long after it was clear that jet travel had replaced the liners, the company made what some considered a foolhardy move, launching *Queen Elizabeth 2* and setting her on a mixed schedule, half crossing, half cruising. Through sheer persistence, the ship proved the critics wrong, and even today, she is still going strong, even if the company has endured some rough times.

Today *QE2* is about to be retired from the Cunard fleet, relinquishing her transatlantic routes to the massive *Queen Mary 2*, the first true ocean liner built in more than 30 years. The 148,528-ton *QM2* is as modern as passenger ships get, and was bigger than them all until Royal Caribbean's 160,000-ton *Freedom of the Seas* came along (though *QM2* remains the *longest* passenger ship by 20 ft.). But she's also an homage to all that went before, designed with oversize grandeur, old-world formality, and even a dose of blatant class structure: Some restaurants and outdoor decks are set aside specifically for suite guests only, if you please. As she's the only Cunarder currently serving the North American market, all details in this review refer to her alone.

Pros

- **Classic ambience:** Despite a few chintzy touches, the ship really does live up to its billing as the grandest afloat, with some rooms that could have come right out of a 1940s liner.
- **S-p-a-c-e:** This ship is absolutely enormous, from her hangar-size ballroom to the cavernously high ceilings of many public areas.
- **Special Experiences:** The bustling ballroom on formal evenings, dozing in one of the hundreds of teak deck chairs on the Promenade, or slicing through Atlantic swells at 28 knots are intangible though immensely pleasurable experiences.
- **Pure prestige:** There used to be ships that everyone in the world knew—"Oh, you're sailing on the *Queen Mary,*" they'd say. "That's the ship Marlene Dietrich took on her last crossing." *QM2* is the only ship launched in more than a quarter century with that kind of broad public cachet.

Cons

- **Not *quite* luxe:** Despite her grandeur, *QM2* carries too many passengers to provide the kind of intimacy and personal feel you get on the other luxe lines—especially those operating small ships (Silversea, SeaDream, and Seabourn), but also on relatively large vessels such as *Crystal Serenity.*
- **Occasional off notes:** If you're going to design a huge corridor of showy Art Deco wall panels, don't make those panels out of plastic. And what's with the jarring white pillars in the atrium and the virtual market of cheap trinkets set up some afternoons in the main passageway?

CUNARD: GETTING THERE IS HALF THE FUN

Once upon a time, Cunard ruled the waves. Its ships—first *Mauretania* and *Lusitania,* later *Queen Mary* and *Queen Elizabeth*—were the fastest and most reliable at sea. Then somebody invented the jet airliner and the whole passenger-shipping business went to hell. Numbers dropped. Ships went cruising for their bread. Cunard stuck to its guns, though, keeping *QE2* on the Atlantic until sheer doggedness gave it a certain cachet as the last of the old breed. Fleetmates came and went, including the little *Sea Goddess* yachts (now with SeaDream) and a number of midsize ships acquired from other lines, but *QE2* soldiered on and managed to carry the company, and its reputation, through some rough times.

An almost 3-decade-long period of corporate troubles and shuffling ownership ended in April 1998, when Carnival Corporation acquired Cunard from the Norwegian company Kvaerner Group. To some it seemed a comedown for the venerable line, but Commodore Ronald Warwick and other Cunard employees saw it as an unqualified boon. "To my mind," Warwick told a group of journalists, "Carnival Corporation were the white knights that saved us from demise, and when the planning of the *Queen Mary 2* was announced, I experienced a feeling of pleasure and relief. They'd delivered a message to the world and to those of us on the 'shop floor' that they were determined to build on the maritime heritage for which our company has been famous."

Today Cunard is again very famous indeed after all the media attention that accompanied *QM2*'s launch, but it's hardly the old British brand that its advertising might lead you to believe. In late 2004, for instance, the company was swallowed whole by Carnival Corp. subsidiary Princess Cruises. Its operations and staff were absorbed into Princess's at the latter's suburban Los Angeles headquarters, which meant crew members and officers would be rotated between the two lines—a move considered blasphemous by many hard-core Cunard fans (but frankly, something that the average passenger won't realize or mind if they do). It remains to be seen whether Cunard will

Compared with the other ultraluxury lines, here's how Cunard rates:

	Poor	Fair	Good	Excellent	Outstanding
Enjoyment Factor					✓
Dining			✓		
Activities					✓
Children's Program					✓
Entertainment				✓	
Service				✓	
Worth the Money					✓

maintain an independent identity under the Princess umbrella or, like Celebrity Cruises when it was swallowed by Royal Caribbean in 1997, enter a period of identity crisis and uncertain market image.

QM2 is currently the only Cunard ship spending substantial time in North American waters. Cunard has a new liner named *Queen Victoria* set to debut in late 2007, sailing primarily European voyages. *QE2*, the ship that kept Cunard alive for 3 decades, is retiring in November 2008, and will spend the rest of eternity serving as a hotel, retail, and entertainment destination at the **Palm Jumeirah** resort in Dubai.

PASSENGER PROFILE

In general, Cunard attracts a well-traveled crowd of passengers mostly in their 50s and up, many of them repeaters who appreciate the line's old-timey virtues and are more the 4-o'clock-tea crowd than the hot-tub-and-umbrella-drink set. That said, the hoopla surrounding the launch of *QM2* is attracting a much wider demographic, especially on summer Atlantic crossings when families travel together and maybe about 50% of passengers might be from the U.S. British passengers make up the next largest percentage, and usually several hundred passengers hail from various other nations, making Cunard one of the few truly international cruises.

DINING

TRADITIONAL   Cunard is the last bastion of the old steamship tradition of segregating passengers according to class, though for the most part the practice is limited to dining hours. What this means is that passengers are assigned to one of the three reserved-seating restaurants according to the level of cabin accommodation they've booked: Suite passengers dine in the 206-seat **Queen's Grill;** junior-suite passengers dine in the 180-seat **Princess Grill;** and everyone else dines in the three-deck, 1,351-passenger **Brittania Restaurant**—decor-wise, the most beautiful of the three and a fitting heir to the grand restaurants of the past. The two Grills are always single seating at an assigned table, while the Britannia has early and late seatings for dinner and open seating for breakfast and lunch.

To make matters a bit more confusing, this spring Cunard introduced the Britannia Club, an intimate section of the Britannia seating around 100 passengers who are booked in the deluxe balcony cabins. Thanks to its single-seating dining, and more table-side preparation and enhanced menu options, those dining here won't have to pay the significant fare hike to dine in the Grills while still having a more personalized and leisurely dining experience. *QM2*'s cuisine sticks close to tradition, with entrees that might include pheasant with southern haggis and port-wine sauce, roasted prime rib, grilled lobster with garden pea risotto, and scallion wild-rice crepes with mushroom filling and red-pepper sauce. On a recent cruise, the food and service were very good, on par roughly with what you might experience in the main dining rooms of the Celebrity ships. The Grill restaurants also offer the option of requesting whatever dish comes into your head—if they have the ingredients aboard, someone in the galley will whip it up for you (caviar is available on request). Otherwise, it's the intimacy and cachet of the Grill restaurants that sets them apart more than the food does, as many of the same dishes are offered in the Britannia as well. The location on the promenade deck near the casual dining venue makes the experience less exclusive than the Grills on *QE2*. At all three restaurants, **special diets** can be accommodated, and vegetarian and health-conscious Canyon Ranch Spa dishes are available as a matter of course.

Cunard Fleet Itineraries

Ship	Itineraries
Queen Mary 2	**Caribbean:** 10-night eastern/southern (Jan–Apr) and 13-night western (Feb & May), round-trip from New York, NY. 8-night eastern, New York to Ft. Lauderdale, FL (Nov). 10-night southern (Nov–Dec) and15-night eastern/southern/western, round-trip from Ft. Lauderdale. **Bahamas:** 4 days, round-trip from New York, NY (Feb–Mar & Oct). **New England/Canada:** 5-, 6- & 7-night, round-trip from New York, NY (May, July, Sept).

SPECIALTY In the stern on Deck 8, *QM2*'s **Todd English restaurant** is a small 156-seat Mediterranean venue that echoes the original *Queen Mary*'s Verandah Grill, one of that ship's most legendary spaces. Created by celebrity chef Todd English, the restaurant serves elaborate and often very rich lunches ($20 per person) and dinners ($30 per person), with some truly amazing desserts. On Heidi's recent *QM2* crossing, she enjoyed her best meal in Todd English.

One deck down, adjacent to the King's Court, the contemporary **Chef's Galley** serves only two dozen guests (no cover charge), who get to watch the chef prepare their meal via an open galley and several large monitor screens. Just don't expect to be dazzled by the decor—it's minimalist.

CASUAL Almost a third of Deck 7 is given over to the **King's Court,** a large buffet restaurant that stretches out for nearly half a deck along both sides of the ship. The somewhat overwhelming cluster of food stations, which some passengers find quite frustrating to navigate, runs down the center of the area, with many small, cozy areas along the sides; there is no outdoor seating. At night, the space is partitioned off into three separate casual restaurants: **The Carvery,** serving carved beef, pork, lamb, and poultry, along with gourmet English favorites; **La Piazza,** serving pizza, pasta, and other Italian specialties 24 hours; and **Lotus,** a Pan-Asian restaurant blending Chinese, Japanese, Thai, and Indian influences. All are free, but reservations are recommended at dinner.

SNACKS & EXTRAS On Deck 2, the oversized Golden Lion Pub serves English pub grub, while waaaaay up on Deck 12 you can get standard burgers and dogs at the outdoor Boardwalk Café, weather permitting. Traditional **afternoon tea,** usually accompanied by a string quartet, is served in the Queen's Room, the ship's most classic, traditional space. The selection of some 23 teas includes Darjeeling, Jasmine, and Japanese Green Tea. The elegant room harks back to the dramatic ballrooms of yesteryear, with a high arched ceiling and crystal chandeliers. **Room service** is available 24 hours a day.

ACTIVITIES

As you would expect, Cunard offers a more distinguished variety of activities than most other big ships, especially their "Fun Ship" Carnival cousins. Rather than woohoo good times, Cunard concentrates on learning experiences and the arts, with a healthy dollop of pampering to keep things light.

Central to the onboard experience is the onboard lecture program, where instructors, celebrities, and other learned authors and superaccomplished authorities present talks on literature, political history, marine science, ocean-liner history, music and culture of the 1960s, modern art, Shakespeare on film, architectural history, cooking, computer applications, languages, and many other topics. On crossings, there are so many worthwhile lectures you may find yourself sitting in the theatre all morning. *QM2* has even managed to attract a handful of stars, with Uma Thurman, Rod Stewart, Lenny Kravitz, Richard Dreyfuss, John Cleese, and others having sailed, and some lectured, in the past 2 years.

Passengers who prefer book learning can take advantage of the largest and by the far the most impressive **library** at sea, a huge, beautifully designed space that actually looks like a library, unlike the typical rooms-with-a-few-bookshelves on most megaships. Next door, a **bookshop** sells volumes on passenger-ship history, as well as Cunard memorabilia. Other shops, clustered around *QM2*'s atrium, sell everything from high-end Hermes to low-end souvenirs and jewelry, some of it sold in a rather undignified way from long tables set up in the public corridors. Continuing the marine-history topic, the ship's **Maritime Quest** (MQ—get it?) history trail offers a museum-quality timeline set up in various places throughout the ship, with an audio tour available to tie it all together.

A visit to *QM2*'s attractive **Canyon Ranch**–designed and –operated spa is another popular activity. The pleasant decor combines nautical undertones with a modern minimalist motif to create a most relaxing space that includes a thermal suite, a beauty salon with wonderful ocean views, and more than 20 treatment rooms clustered around a coed thalassotherapy pool and hot tub reserved for spa-goers. The only seagoing Canyon Ranch spa, it's a refreshing break from the Steiner-run spas on most ships and it offers some truly different therapies—for example, the Ashiatus massage incorporates the therapist's feet—and far less of Steiner's pushiness to sell skin-care products. The *QM2*'s gym, which wraps around the bow on Deck 7, is surprisingly small and uninspired for a ship this large and well conceived, but it does what it needs to do and offers treadmills and stationary bikes with flatscreen TV monitors. Classes include Pilates and yoga.

Aside from all these interesting options, you'll find a number of less-cerebral pursuits as well, from wine tasting to art auctions to scarf-tying seminars.

CHILDREN'S PROGRAM

The *QM2* is more than high tea and stiffer upper lips. Finger paints and cartoons are just as much a part of the ship's offerings as ballroom dancing and quoits. Though you might not expect it from a grand liner that (one imagines) is filled with sophisticated seniors, *QM2* offers great digs for kids. The kids' complex, called **The Zone,** is open to kids ages 1 and up—an extraordinarily young minimum age shared only by Disney's ships. (Most ships with kids' programming welcome kids 3 and up, a few ages 2 and up.) Facilities are divided by age. The 1-to-6 set occupies half of a bright and cheery and roomy area with lots of toys, arts and crafts, a play gym and ball pit, and big-screen TVs (and the staff do change diapers). There's also a separate **nursery** with 10 crib/toddler-bed combos for napping tots (no other line has a separate room for sleepers). Bring a stroller if your kids are young: Remember the *QM2* is the longest passenger ship in the world, so getting from one end of a deck to the other is a hike.

Just beyond the oceanview space is a play gym outside on the stern of Deck 6, along with a wading pool, a regular pool, and a water-spray fountain for kids (of all ages) to run through. Officially it's called the "family deck," though anyone who doesn't mind screeching children can lounge there. The other half of the play area is reserved for kids 7 to 17, with the 7-to-12 crowd usually occupying a play area with beanbag chairs, lots of board games, TVs, and a number of Xbox video-game systems. **Activities for teens**—including ship tours, movies and production shows in the theaters, and pizza parties—are usually held elsewhere.

The kids' program is staffed by several British nannies, who have completed a 2-year program in the discipline back in England, plus a handful of other activities counselors, many of whom have backgrounds as schoolteachers. The best part? Aside from 2 hours at lunchtime and an hour or two in the afternoon, The Zone offers complimentary supervised activities and care from 9am to midnight, so you can dine with the adults and know that your offspring are being well cared for (on other lines, you must generally pay an hourly fee after 10pm). You can take your kids to eat earlier in the King's Court buffet restaurant in a special section of the restaurant, the Chef's Galley, that's reserved for a **children's tea** daily from 5 to 6pm (of course, it's not really tea that's served, but the standard kiddy favorites of pasta, chicken fingers, and the like).

Though *QM2*'s kids program is awesome, there are rarely more than 250 kids aboard and usually fewer (compared to the 800–1,200 kids and teens typically aboard similar-size ships). This is a plus: Fewer kids means more attention and space for the ones who are there. Keep in mind, though, if a sailing is particularly full, the counselors reserve the right to limit participation and will ask parents to choose either the morning or the afternoon session; everyone can be accommodated evenings. In contrast, other major lines have "don't turn away" policies, so you're guaranteed that your child will be accommodated, even if the playrooms are jampacked because of it (as they usually are during the early evening hours).

On top of everything else, there's an impressive medical center on the *QM2* as well, which came in handy when Heidi's son got an ear infection on a crossing. No question: top-rate facilities.

ENTERTAINMENT

Entertainment aboard *QM2* runs the gamut from plays featuring graduates of Britain's Royal Academy of Dramatic Arts (RADA) to some pretty run-of-the-mill song-and-dance revues. The former perform generally from April to November as part of a partnership between Cunard and the school, with RADA graduates and students also offering a variety of readings and workshops, including acting classes. Besides theater, *QM2*'s lounges feature a wide variety of music, from string quartets and harpists in the Winter Garden conservatory to jazz in the Chart Room to high-toned dance music in the gorgeous Queen's Ballroom (with gentleman hosts on hand to partner with single ladies) and low-toned in the G32 disco. On Deck 2, the large, beautifully appointed Empire Casino is more Monte Carlo than Vegas, with refined art and furnishings rather than the usual clangorous arcade vibe.

Whereas most ships have one theater, *QM2*'s lecture program is so busy there are two. As the secondary theater, Illuminations is smaller than the Royal Court Theater, but is probably the most used room on the ship. It serves triple duty as a lecture hall, a movie theater, and also the world's only oceangoing planetarium that shows 3-D films, some of them created in conjunction with noted institutions such as the American Museum of Natural History and the Smithsonian's National Air and Space Museum.

Preview: *Queen Victoria*

Queens don't birth easy. Way back in December 2001, Cunard and parent company Carnival Corporation announced construction of a new, 1,968-passenger vessel, to be built on a hull design identical to Holland America's Vista-class ships. In April 2003 the line dubbed the not-yet-begun vessel *Queen Victoria*, but just 1 year later the new vessel, already well under construction, was stripped of her title and transferred to Carnival's recently acquired P&O brand, where she later launched as *Arcadia*. What had happened? Well, *QM2* had. Seems the fanfare that greeted the new ship, and her status as the first real ocean liner built in 30 years, convinced Carnival Corp. that any new Cunard vessel needed to be a little more special than your standard boilerplate megaship. So things were rethought, and in place of the defrocked vessel, Cunard ordered a new vessel with a greater family resemblance to *QE2* and *QM2*.

Now scheduled to debut on December 10, 2007, the new *Queen Victoria* has traditional Cunard style, with the line's classic black-and-red hull livery on the outside and grand public spaces on the inside. At 90,000 gross tons, she'll be the second-largest Cunarder ever, after *QM2*, and though still based to some degree on the HAL Vista-class design, *Queen Victoria*'s hull has reportedly been lengthened and strengthened to improve the vessel's sea-keeping abilities.

Inside, expect spaces that preserve elements of the old ocean-liner days, including a two-story, wood-paneled library with a spiral staircase and some 6,000 books; a classically styled ballroom with a 1,000-square-foot dance floor; and a colonial-esque Winter Garden with tropical foliage, a fountain, wicker furniture, and a retractable glass roof. Like *QM2*, *Victoria* will also retain her class structure. Fixing the problem of her bigger sister, the Grills on the *QV* will be set apart on the top of the ship in an exclusive setting, including an alfresco courtyard for dining and a private lounge overlooking the ship.

Queen Victoria will debut with two European sailings, followed by her first world cruise. Further routes had not been announced at press time.

Up on Deck 12, the Boardwalk Café doubles at night as a venue for **outdoor movie screenings** when weather permits. See the ship review below for a discussion of *QM2*'s other theaters and lounges.

SERVICE

With their classy uniforms and cordial, gracious efficiency, *QM2*'s crew exhibits a polished sort of British demeanor—even when they're actually from the Philippines. That said, the sheer size of the vessel and large number of passengers mean they must do their share of rushing around and keeping up, as aboard all the other huge cruise ships today.

Queen Mary 2

The Verdict

Faster than a speeding bullet, more powerful than a locomotive, *QM2* is literally in a class by herself: a modern reinterpretation of the golden age luxury liner, bigger than anything that's gone before and built to sail hard seas well into the 21st century.

Queen Mary 2 *(photo: Cunard)*

Specifications

Size (in tons)	148, 528	Crew	1,253
Passengers (double occ.)	2,592	Passenger/Crew Ratio	2.1 to 1
Passenger/Space Ratio	54.3	Year Launched	2003
Total Cabins/Veranda Cabins	1,296/783	Last Major Refurbishment	2005

Frommer's Ratings (Scale of 1–5)   ★★★★★

Cabin Comfort & Amenities	5	Dining Options	4.5
Ship Cleanliness & Maintenance	5	Gym, Spa & Sports Facilities	4.5
Public Comfort/Space	5	Children's Facilities	5
Decor	4.5	Enjoyment Factor	5

Before her launch, we often heard *QM2* referred to by industry types as "Micky's White Elephant"—Micky being Micky Arison, chairman of Carnival Corporation, the criticism referring to the fact that *QM2*'s design and construction sucked up about a billion dollars and 5 years of labor, a record expenditure to match her record-breaking size.

But that was before her launch. That was before the Queen of England did the honors at her naming ceremony. That was before the fireworks and traffic jams that attended her first arrival into every port, and amazingly enough, still continue to this day in many ports. And it was definitely before the media glommed onto her as the first really newsworthy ship to be launched since . . . well, since *QE2*, probably. And when you control about half the cruise industry, as Carnival Corp. does, that kind of publicity is priceless.

When all is said and done, *QM2* deserves all the hype. She's a really remarkable ship: classic yet contemporary, refined yet fun, huge yet homey, and grand, grand, grand. The longest passenger ship at sea (when Royal Caribbean's *Freedom of the Seas* was launched in spring 2006, it snatched the title as biggest in terms of tonnage), she's also the only real ocean liner built since her older sister hit the water in 1969—and that, perhaps, needs some explanation. What is it exactly that makes an ocean liner different?

In a word, "more"—of everything. "We had a working definition that built on the idea of 'enhancement,'" Stephen Payne, *QM2*'s designer, told us just before the ship debuted. "The ship had to have enhanced strength and sea-keeping characteristics to withstand continuous exposure to North Atlantic conditions; enhanced speed to maintain her schedule [because unlike a cruise ship, a transatlantic liner has no ports that can be skipped to make up time lost to harsh seas]; enhanced passenger facilities to keep her passengers happy for 5 days at sea; and enhanced endurance to allow her great range between refueling." All of these mandates created the ship you see today. The need for speed meant her hull had to be more knife-prowed than a normal cruise ship's. The need for strength meant her steel plating had to be uncommonly thick and her skeleton unusually dense and super-reinforced. The need to battle high waves meant her superstructure had to be set much farther back on her hull than is common on today's cruise ships. The list goes on and on. In a sense, you could almost say that it was the sea itself that designed *QM2*. They were made for each other.

Inside, *QM2* was laid out in such a way that even after a weeklong crossing you might still be finding new places to explore on board. And it's very unlikely you'll feel hemmed in or claustrophobic, as Heidi feared before she made her first crossing. She never once felt antsy in the spacious and gracious ship, and in fact, sort of wished the crossing was a few days longer! Our favorite rooms? The Queen's Room ballroom on formal night; the classic Chart Room for drinks before dinner; the forward-facing Commodore Club with its clubby atmosphere; and the forward observation deck on Deck 11, just below the bridge—probably the best spot aboard when sailing out of New York Harbor. Throughout, artwork functions both as decoration and as mood enhancement, with iconography that recalls the ocean liner's golden age. The most evocative art of all, though, may be a sound: Way up on *QM2*'s funnel, on the starboard side, is one of the original Tyfon steam whistles from the first *Queen Mary*—the same whistle that sounded when the *Mary* made her first crossing in 1936, now on permanent loan from the city of Long Beach, California. Mounted beside an identical replica, it has a low bass "A" note that literally shakes the rafters, and if that doesn't put a smile on your face, nothing will.

Cabins & Rates

Cabins	Per Diems From	Sq. Ft.	Fridge	Hair Dryer	Sitting Area	TV
Inside	$150	155-161	yes	yes	no	yes
Outside	$170	194–269*	yes	yes	yes	yes
Suite	$300	381–2,249*	yes	yes	yes	yes

* *Including veranda.*

CABINS　All of *QM2*'s cabins, from the smallest inside to the largest outside, are decorated in a smooth, contemporary style, with light-blond woods, simple lines, and a clean, uncluttered look. They range from roomy 194-square-foot outside cabins with portholes, minifridges, and large showers, to the truly over-the-top duplex Grand Suites. Each of the latter is 1,500 to 2,200 square feet and has views of the stern through two-story walls of glass. Heidi's living proof that a family of four can do fine in a standard cabin without a balcony (there are no standard balcony cabins that accommodate families of four), but if you've got a larger budget, the junior suites are ideal. They're almost twice as big as a standard and have a huge bathroom with tub, walk-in closet, sitting area, and oversize balcony. Even standard inside and outside cabins, though by no means huge, have a simple elegance and a nice helping of amenities, including terry robes and slippers, fridge, safe, dataport, and interactive TV with e-mail capability. The vast majority of cabins are outsides with balconies, but in order to ensure they stay dry in even the roughest seas, many of them are recessed back into the hull with steel bulkheads that block ocean views when seated. All suites and junior suites feature Frette linens, flatscreen TVs with Xbox game systems, personalized stationery, pre-dinner canapés, concierge service, a bottle of champagne on embarkation, and use of the Queens Grill Lounge. Queens Grill Suites get fully stocked bars and other niceties, such as use of a large private deck overlooking the stern.

There are 30 wheelchair-accessible cabins total in various cabin grades.

PUBLIC AREAS   Because *QM2* was designed for comfortable sailing in rough seas, most of her public areas are clustered unusually low, down on Decks 2 and 3. At midships, the relatively restrained (and a bit too white) Grand Lobby atrium lets onto two central promenades, decorated with huge Art Deco wall panels. Some are stunning and recall decorated glass panels from the opulent liner *Normandie,* while others are a bit chintzy (they look like they're plastic) and miss the mark.

Getting beyond that one flaw, Deck 2's promenade leads down to the elegant Empire Casino and the too-big-to-be-cozy Golden Lion pub. Up one deck, the very attractive Veuve Clicquot Champagne Bar (serving a variety of champagnes, as well as caviar and foie gras) is decorated with slightly abstracted images of mid-20th-century movie stars and leads into one of the most beautiful rooms on board, The Chart Room, a high-ceilinged space with green-glass Deco maps on one wall, 1940s-style furnishings, and the feel of a great ocean liner. You expect David Niven to come strolling through any minute. By day, both of these rooms are popular hangouts for book readers, letter writers, and daydreamers. Across, on the ship's port side, Sir Samuel's Wine Bar now serves coffee, sandwiches, and cakes in the morning and afternoon. Forward, the Royal Court Theater is a two-deck grand showroom and the principal theatrical venue on board, seconded by the striking Illuminations planetarium farther forward (see "Entertainment," above).

In the stern on Deck 3, the Queen's Room ballroom perfectly captures the essence of Cunard style, running the full width of the ship and boasting a high, arched ceiling, the largest ballroom dance floor at sea, crystal chandeliers, and a truly royal quality. The G32 nightclub, almost hidden behind silver doors at the head of the Queen's Room, is decorated in industrial style to match its name—"G32" was the number by which *QM2*'s hull was known at the shipyard, before Cunard decided what she'd be called.

Other notable spaces include the Winter Garden on Deck 7, a light, airy space designed to provide an outdoor garden feel on long transatlantic crossings that somehow misses the mark; and the Commodore Club bar/observation lounge on Deck 9, with its wonderful white-leather chairs, dramatic bow views, and attached Churchill's cigar room. There's also a card room hidden away on Deck 11, just behind the observation deck, as well as the remarkable library and bookshop forward on Deck 8 (see "Activities," earlier in this chapter).

DINING OPTIONS   Decor-wise, the Queens Grill and Princess Grill restaurants that serve suite passengers exclusively are the very models of restrained good taste, with a series of elegant blown-glass vases as their one bold touch. The Britannia Restaurant, on the other hand, is a large dramatic space, intended to recall *Queen Mary*'s magnificent first-class restaurant and featuring a vaulted, Tiffany-style glass ceiling, a curved balcony that echoes the shape of the *Mary*'s famous bridge, candlelit tables, soaring pillars, and the largest art tapestry at sea, depicting a liner against the New York skyline. Although it's large, the space is exceedingly glamorous, and designed to feel grand but not overwhelming. The new Britannia Club area has liter-ally been carved out of a corner of the restaurant, but misses out on the full dramatic height of the room. All guests can dine in the cozy and elegant Todd English restau-rant for a $30 cover charge. King's Court is the ship's casual buffet option, and it becomes several separate (complimentary) specialty dinner restaurants each evening.

See "Dining," earlier in this chapter, for more details on the ship's dining experience.

POOL, FITNESS, SPA & SPORTS FACILITIES   The Canyon Ranch Spa is a two-story complex occupying some 20,000 square feet. At the center of its treatment rooms is a coed 15×30-foot aqua-therapy pool whose relaxation gizmos include airbed recliner lounges, neck fountains, a deluge waterfall, an air tub, and body-massage jet benches. There's a hot tub adjacent, and nearby is a thermal suite composed of aro-matic steam rooms and an herbal sauna. A salon occupies the top level of the com-plex, offering tremendous views from its lofty perch. The gym, one deck down, is sort of drab and chopped up, but is perfectly well equipped to make people sweat, with free weights and the latest digitally enhanced climbers, steppers, runners, and rowers.

A more classic exercise is a walk or jog around the wide outdoor Promenade Deck, which encircles the loooooooonggg ship on Deck 7 and offers beautiful sea views; three times around equals 1 mile. For some shoulder work, there's a pair of golf simulators adjacent to the covered pool solarium on Deck 12. Other dips include a splash pool and hot tubs way up on Deck 13, and several in the tiered stern, including a wading pool, family pool, and play fountain on Deck 6, outside of the children's playrooms. Rounding out the sports options are Ping-Pong, basketball, quoits, a paddle-tennis court, and, of course, shuffleboard—this is a transatlantic liner, after all.

3 Regent Seven Seas Cruises

1000 Corporate Dr., Suite 500, Fort Lauderdale, FL 33334. ✆ **877/505-5370.** Fax 402/501-5599. www.rssc.com.

THE LINE IN A NUTSHELL   Operating a fleet of stylish and extremely comfort-able midsize vessels, Regent—which changed its name from Radisson in 2006—offers a casually elegant and subtle luxury cruise experience. Its service is as good as it gets, and its cuisine is near the top. **Sails to:** Caribbean, Alaska (plus Europe, South America, Antarctica, South Pacific, Australia/New Zealand, world cruise).

THE EXPERIENCE   If you insist on luxury but like to keep it subtle, Regent might be your cruise line of choice. Its ships are spacious and understated, with a relaxed onboard vibe that tends to be less stuffy than Seabourn and Silversea. As aboard all the luxury ships (with the exception of the huge *QM2*), entertainment and activities are relatively low-key, with passengers left to enjoy their vacations at their own pace. Dress tends toward casual, though tuxedos and gowns aren't uncommon on formal evenings. Service is friendly and absolutely spot-on, and cuisine is some of the best at sea, in both the formal dining rooms and the alternative restaurants. Even if what tickles your fancy isn't on the menu, the chef will prepare it for you. Passengers tend to be unpre-tentiously wealthy. When we've sailed, our social circle at dinner has included an Atlantic City nightclub owner, retired executives, a graphic artist, a theatrical casting director, and a woman who owned a string of Taco Bell franchises—all of them aboard to enjoy a quiet, relaxed vacation.

Pros

- **Great dining:** Cuisine is superb, and the main dining room and alternative restaurants operate on an open-seating basis, the latter by reservation.
- **Frequent sales:** Regent frequently offers free air and other deals, making its rates attractive to mainstream cruisers looking to move up to the luxe world.
- **Lots of private verandas:** The all-suite *Seven Seas Navigator* has them in 90% of hers, and the all-suite *Mariner* and *Voyager* have them in every single stateroom.
- **Amazing bathrooms on *Navigator* and *Voyager*:** Bigger and better than those on Seabourn and Crystal, cabin bathrooms all have separate shower stalls and full-size bathtubs long enough for normal-size humans.

Cons

- **Not-quite-private balconies:** Walls separating the balconies aboard *Voyager* and *Navigator* don't extend to the edge of the ship's rail, making it possible to lean out and see what your neighbors are up to.

REGENT: NEW NAME, SAME LOW-KEY ELEGANCE

The word of the day is *rebranding,* and this is how it happened: See, the Carlson Companies owned a cruise line, Radisson Seven Seas, which got its start in the early '90s and has been growing steadily ever since. Carlson also owns a group of upscale hotels called Regent International, with properties in Asia, Europe, and North America. In March 2006, after hinting about it for years, Carlson announced that it was combining the two operations, with the cruise line adopting the hotel chain's name and becoming **Regent Seven Seas Cruises.** Though no grand strategic changes are planned for the cruise line, it has implemented a series of onboard upgrades that include improvements to amenities, decor, and technology, and training for all crew in something called "The Tao of Regent."

Regent currently operates a four-ship fleet, including three that sail regularly from U.S. ports: *Seven Seas Navigator, Seven Seas Mariner,* and *Seven Seas Voyager.* The 320-passenger *Paul Gauguin* spends the year doing 7- to 14-night cruises in French Polynesia. Additionally, Regent charters the expedition ship *Explorer II* each January and February for a series of Antarctic cruises. While many luxury ships hopscotch from cruise region to cruise region, never staying long in any one place, Regent's ships sometimes spend full seasons in the Caribbean, the Mediterranean, and Alaska.

PASSENGER PROFILE

RSSC appeals primarily to well-traveled and well-heeled passengers in their 50s and 60s, but younger passengers, honeymooners, and older passengers pepper the mix as

Compared with the other ultraluxury lines, here's how Regent rates:

	Poor	Fair	Good	Excellent	Outstanding
Enjoyment Factor					✓
Dining				✓	
Activities			✓		
Children's Program		✓			
Entertainment			✓		
Service					✓
Worth the Money					✓

Regent Fleet Itineraries

Ship	Itineraries
Mariner	**Caribbean:** 7-night eastern (Mar), 10-night western (Mar), and 11-night eastern (Apr), all round-trip from Ft. Lauderdale, FL. **Bermuda & U.S. East Coast:** 12-night, round-trip from Ft. Lauderdale, FL (Apr). **Panama Canal:** 16-night, Ft. Lauderdale, FL, to San Francisco, CA (Apr). 16-night, Los Angeles, CA, to Ft. Lauderdale (Dec). **U.S. West Coast/Alaska:** 11-night, San Francisco, CA, to Vancouver, BC (May). **Alaska:** 7-night Gulf of Alaska, north- or southbound between Vancouver, BC, and Seward/Anchorage, AK (May–Aug).
Navigator	**Caribbean:** 11-night eastern (Jan–Feb & Dec), 7-night western (Jan & Mar), 10-night western (Jan–Mar), 14-night eastern/southern (Mar), 11-night western (Dec), all round-trip from Ft. Lauderdale, FL. **Bermuda & U.S. East Coast:** 11-night, round-trip from Ft. Lauderdale, FL (Apr).
Voyager	**Caribbean:** 7- & 10-night western, 10-night eastern, and 11-night southern (Dec), all round-trip from Ft. Lauderdale, FL.

well. Many passengers are frequent cruisers who have also sailed on Silversea, Seabourn, and Crystal, or are taking a step up from Holland America, Celebrity, or one of the other mainstream lines. Though they have sophisticated tastes and can do without a lot of inane shipboard activities, they also appreciate the line's less formal ambience. On our recent cruises, casual nights in the formal dining room saw some passengers dressed in polo shirts and jackets and others in nice T-shirts with khakis and sneakers. You're also likely to find some women in full makeup, coifed hairdos, and coordinated jewelry, shoes, and handbags, and many men sporting gold Rolexes. A kids' program on summer sailings and some holiday sailings attract some **families,** but the limited number of third berths in cabins tends to keep those numbers down.

DINING

Superb menus are designed for a sophisticated palate, and the overall cuisine is some of the best in the cruise industry. Each ship has an extensive wine list, with vintages from Germany, Italy, and Chile.

TRADITIONAL   In the main restaurants, elaborate and elegant meals are served in open seatings by a staff of mostly Europeans. Caesar salads are tossed to order; appetizers may include baked escargots in garlic-herb butter, beef carpaccio, and an eggplant-tomato-mozzarella roll; and main entrees include such enticing dishes as grilled venison medallions and mushroom fricassee, Chinese tangerine shrimp, and grilled grouper filet with pink grapefruit. Each dinner menu also offers a **vegetarian option** such as a forest mushroom quiche, and a **light and healthy choice** such as broiled whole Dover sole. When you've had enough of fancy, several standards called **simplicity dishes** are also available daily: pasta with tomato sauce, filet mignon, grilled chicken breast, or salmon filet. **Special diets** (kosher, halal, low-fat, low-salt, and so on) can be accommodated at all meals, but for very stringent regimes, such as glatt kosher, you must make arrangements before your cruise.

Breakfasts include made-to-order omelets, as well as a typical selection of hot and cold breakfast foods. Lunch entrees include soups, salads, sandwiches, and entrees like

Indian lamb patties with mint-coriander-lentil chutney, pan-seared chicken breast, and a fisherman's platter of friend jumbo prawns, scallops, and filets.

SPECIALTY   *Seven Seas Navigator* has only one alternative choice: Portofino, an indoor/outdoor Italian restaurant serving dishes like Genoese minestrone soup, risotto primavera, spaghetti alla Bolognese, and sliced beef steak on wild rice with a balsamic vinegar sauce. *Mariner* and *Voyager* each have three alternate choices. The 110-seat Signatures restaurants are directed by chefs from Paris's famed **Le Cordon Bleu** cooking school, while their Latitudes restaurants serve **Indochine cuisine,** with such dishes as Cambodian wafu salad; steamed fresh halibut in a Matsutake mushroom broth with gingered vegetables; and a spiced rack of lamb accompanied by aromatic Jasmine rice, wok-seared snow peas, and fresh sprouts in peanut jus. La Veranda serves Mediterranean and North African dishes in a casual setting. All alternative venues are intimate spaces with tables for two or four. Make reservations early in the cruise to guarantee yourself a table. Booked passengers can make specialty-dining reservations online before their cruise.

CASUAL   All three vessels have casual buffet restaurants, plus a poolside sandwich grill staffed by waiters.

SNACKS & EXTRAS   Hot hors d'oeuvres are served in the lounges before dinner, and if you take advantage of the 24-hour room service, a steward will come in and lay out a white tablecloth along with silverware and china, whether you've ordered a full-course dinner, a personal pizza, or just a plate of fruit. Specialty coffees, soft drinks, and mineral water are complimentary at all times, and **high tea** is served each afternoon.

ACTIVITIES

Days not spent exploring the ports are basically unstructured, with a few activities thrown in for those who aren't pursuing their own relaxation. During the day, there may be ballroom dance classes, wine tastings, art auctions, bingo, computer classes, bridge (with instructors sailing on all cruises), and **lectures** by visiting writers, anthropologists, naturalists, and retired diplomats, often speaking on a topic relevant to the region you're sailing—for example, Colonial America on New England/Canada cruises, Incan culture on South America cruises, and so on.

On many cruises, the line's **Circle of Interest** program lets guests book packages of onboard lectures, workshops, and specially created shore excursions, all themed on such topics as art, nature, antiques, photography, performing arts, food and wine, or archaeology. On **Le Cordon Bleu cooking cruises,** for instance, chefs trained in the Le Cordon Bleu cooking method offer three onboard workshops, a special chef's dinner, and a market visit in port to see how the chef chooses the best local ingredients. Participation costs $395 per person. On **Art Experience** cruises, Regent teams with noted museums to offer art-related shore excursions and onboard lectures.

Active passengers can work out in the ships' gyms, run on the tracks, or whack some balls into a golf net, then take a massage at the ships' spas, run by the French company **Carita of Paris.** Staffed by Carita-trained therapists and hairdressers imported from Parisian salons, the spas offer company specialties such as their Rénovateur exfoliating process, as well as cruise spa standards such as hydrotherapy, reflexology, aromatherapy, body wraps, facials, manicure/pedicures, and antistress, therapeutic, and hot-rock massage.

CHILDREN'S PROGRAM

These ships are geared to mature adults, but summer sailings and select holiday cruises offer a **Club Mariner** kids program in which counselors supervise activities such as games, craft projects, and movies for three age groups (5–9, 10–13, and 14–17). For younger kids, counselors lead games, crafts projects, movies, and "food fun," while teens help the counselor select the activities they prefer. On non-summer/holiday cruises, an ad-hoc kids program is put together if enough kids are aboard to warrant it. Minimum age for children to sail aboard is 1 year, and the line reserves the right to limit the number of children under age 3 on any one sailing. **Babysitting** may be available for $25 an hour if a female crewmember is willing to perform the service outside of her regular-duty hours.

ENTERTAINMENT

As on most luxe ships, entertainment is low-key and modest, with most passengers content to spend their evenings exploring the cocktail circuit, visiting the casino, singing along in the piano bar, or dancing to the ships' elegant musical groups. All three ships offer **musical revues** in their show lounges, and though they're certainly not a high point of the cruises, they add a nice option to the evenings. Recent shows have included *Thoroughly Modern Broadway*, a mix of musical theater numbers from the 1960s through 1980s; the Beatles tribute *Here, There and Everywhere; Beyond Imagination*, which mixes opera and classical song with sea songs, folk tunes, and pseudoclassical modern hits; *On a Classical Note*, with music by Mozart, Verdi, Rossini, Puccini, Gilbert and Sullivan, and Bizet; and *Oh What a Night*, with hits by The Four Seasons, Billy Joel, Simon and Garfunkel, Ray Charles, Neil Diamond, and others.

Occasional sailings offer **themed entertainment**—small-group and big-band jazz, for instance, or performances by a chamber group. Check with the line or your travel agent for a schedule of upcoming theme cruises.

SERVICE

Service by the mostly European and Filipino staff is a major plus. You rarely if ever hear the word *no,* and because the crew-to-passenger ratio is quite high, you rarely have to wait for someone else to get served first. Stewardesses care for your cabin ably and unobtrusively, **room service** is speedy and efficient, and restaurant waitstaff are supremely gracious and professional, with an intimate knowledge of the menu. Bar staff will often remember your drink order after the first day.

The ships all have complimentary **self-serve laundries** in addition to standard laundry and dry-cleaning services. **Cellphone service** is available (with passengers charged a roaming fee by their carrier), and **Wi-Fi hot spots** on each ship allow laptop users to connect to the Web without visiting the Internet center.

Gratuities are included in the cruise rates, but many passengers end up leaving more anyway at the end of their trip.

Seven Seas Mariner •
Seven Seas Voyager

The Verdict

The 700-passenger, all-suite *Mariner* and *Voyager* are Regent's largest ships, boasting balconies on every single stateroom, plus extra helpings of pampering.

Seven Seas Mariner *(photo: Regent)*

Specifications

Size (in tons)		Crew	447
Mariner	50,000	Passenger/Crew Ratio	1.6 to 1
Voyager	46,000	Year Launched	
Passengers (double occ.)	700	*Mariner*	2001
Passenger/Space Ratio		*Voyager*	2003
Mariner	71.4	Last Refurbishment/Upgrade	
Voyager	65.7	*Mariner*	2007
Total Cabins/Veranda Cabins	350/350	*Voyager*	2007

Frommer's Ratings (Scale of 1–5)   ★★★★½

Cabin Comfort & Amenities	5	Dining Options	4
Appearance & Upkeep	5	Gym, Spa & Sports Facilities	3.5
Public Comfort/Space	5	Children's Facilities	N/A
Decor	4.5	Enjoyment Factor	4.5

Introduced in 2001, the all-suite *Seven Seas Mariner* was designed to be exceedingly spacious, and was the first vessel built by any line to offer a private balcony on every single stateroom. Sister ship *Seven Seas Voyager,* which entered service 2 years later, continued this theme and offers improvements in some areas where we found *Mariner* lacking, particularly public-room warmth and bathroom layout. In addition, *Voyager* was designed with an efficient one-corridor approach, making for extremely smooth traffic flow in the public areas.

Cabins & Rates

Cabins	Per Diems From	Sq. Ft.	Fridge	Hair Dryer	Sitting Area	TV
Suite	$327	252–1,204*	yes	yes	yes	yes

* These measurements for Seven Seas Mariner only. Suites on Voyager are slightly larger at 306 to 1,216 square feet.

CABINS   Deluxe Suites represent the vast majority of the available accommodations aboard *Mariner* and *Voyager.* On *Mariner,* they measure 252 square feet, plus a 49-square-foot balcony; on *Voyager,* they've been enlarged to 306 square feet, with a 50-square-foot balcony. Even beyond size, *Voyager*'s standard accommodations are superior, with a warmer feel and more over-the-top marble bathrooms, each with separate shower/bathtub facilities. Conversely, *Mariner*'s top-end suites are somewhat larger than *Voyager*'s, from the forward-facing, 1,204-square-foot Master Suites (with two balconies, including one enormous 721-sq.-ft. expanse) down to the 359-square-foot Horizon Suites, located in the stern and opening onto expansive views of the ship's wake from their oversized balconies. (*Voyager*'s Master Suites have only one balcony, measuring a comparatively tiny 183 sq. ft.)

All staterooms are designed with blond woods and rich fabrics and feature king-size beds convertible to twins, cotton bathrobes, hair dryer, flatscreen TV with DVD player (with movies available from the ships' DVD libraries), stocked refrigerator, safe, and large walk-in closet. In 2006 and 2007, all suites received new upholstery, mattresses, bed linens and duvets, towels, and bathroom amenities, plus slippers and bathrobes for guest use while aboard. Balconies overall are a little less than private—walls separating them do not extend to the edge of the ship's rail, making it possible to lean out and see what your neighbor is up to. Top-level accommodations, from Penthouses up to Master Suites, come with butler service and iPods with Bose speakers.

Six suites on *Mariner* and four on *Voyager* are wheelchair friendly.

PUBLIC AREAS   Both ships have beautifully laid-out two-deck theaters with terrific sightlines from virtually every seat, plus an Observation Lounge sitting high up on the top deck and featuring a semicircular bar, plush chairs and sofas, and a 180-degree view of the sea. It's a particularly attractive room at night. Lower down, each ship also boasts a well-stocked library, a cigar lounge, a card and conference room (popular with bridge players), and a computer center. A very nice feature here is that guests are charged only for transmission time, meaning you can compose a document in Word or another program free of charge, then open your e-mail and paste it in, and incur a cost only while you're in active e-mail mode. Wi-Fi hot spots also let laptop users surf from several public areas, and cellphone access is also available via a satellite system. *Mariner* also has a dedicated disco, but who needs a disco on a luxe ship (except maybe the officers who hang out there)? On *Voyager*, the Voyager Lounge serves as the disco at night and (as aboard *Mariner*) as a piano lounge before dinner.

DINING OPTIONS   *Mariner* and *Voyager* each have four restaurants, with the main dining room, the Compass Rose, serving all three meals in single open seatings. Casual breakfasts and lunches are available in the indoor/outdoor La Veranda Restaurant, up near the top of the ship on Deck 11.

Two reservations-only (but no-charge) restaurants are open for dinner only. Signatures features world-ranging cuisine prepared in classic French style by chefs trained at Paris's famous Le Cordon Bleu School. Latitudes offers an Indochine menu (see "Dining," above). On *Voyager*, Latitudes has an open galley, allowing guests to watch as items are prepared. On a 2006 cruise, one example of the galley's creativity was the different varieties of chicken soup served in the two restaurants: "cappuccino style" in Signatures, with stuffed wild mushroom profiteroles, and Hanoi-style in Latitudes, with Asian noodles. Both used the same base, but the effect was utterly different, and delicious.

In the evening, half of La Veranda is turned into an excellent candlelit, white-table-cloth Mediterranean Bistro with a combination of waiter and self-service dining. Grilled food is available poolside, and room service runs 24 hours—guests can even have the Compass Rose dinner menu served course by course in their suites during dinner hours.

POOL, FITNESS, SPA & SPORTS FACILITIES   Each ship's one pool and three hot tubs are located on Deck 11. Deck chairs are set up around the roomy pool area, as well as on the forward half of the deck above, where you'll also find a paddle-tennis court, golf driving nets, shuffleboard courts, and an uninterrupted jogging track. Sunbathing doesn't seem to be the biggest priority for Regent guests, so deck chairs are usually readily available, even on sea days in warm cruising areas.

Each ship's Carita spa is located in an attractive but rather small space. A similarly smallish oceanview gym and separate aerobics area are located in the same area, as well as a beauty salon.

Seven Seas Navigator

The Verdict

Warm and appealing, the 490-passenger *Navigator* is an ideal size for an ultraluxe cruise: small enough to be intimate and large enough to offer plenty of elbowroom, more than a few entertainment outlets, and some of the best cabin bathrooms at sea.

Seven Seas Navigator *(photo: Regent)*

Specifications

Size (in tons)	33,000	Crew	324
Passengers (double occ.)	490	Passenger/Crew Ratio	1.5 to 1
Passenger/Space Ratio	67.3	Year Launched	1999
Total Cabins/Veranda Cabins	245/215	Last Refurbishment/Upgrade	2007

Frommer's Ratings (Scale of 1–5)   ✦★★★

Cabin Comfort & Amenities	5	Dining Options	4
Appearance & Upkeep	4	Gym, Spa & Sports Facilities	4
Public Comfort/Space	4	Children's Facilities	N/A
Decor	4	Enjoyment Factor	4.5

Navigator has well-laid-out cabins and public rooms, and if you've been on the Silversea ships, you'll notice a similar layout (especially in the Star Lounge and Galileo Lounge), as the interiors were all designed by the same architects and built at the same yard, Italy's Mariotti. While *Navigator*'s interior is very attractive, outside she looks a little bit top-heavy, a consequence of her odd provenance: Her hull was originally built to be a Russian spy ship. When Regent purchased the uncompleted vessel, they redesigned her superstructure with additional decks.

Cabins & Rates

Cabins	Per Diems From	Sq. Ft.	Fridge	Hair Dryer	Sitting Area	TV
Suite	$391	301–1,067	yes	yes	yes	yes

CABINS *Navigator* is an all-suite, all-outside-cabin ship, so there's not a bad room in the house. Each elegant suite is done up in shades of deep gold, beige, and burnt orange, with caramel-toned wood furniture and a swath of butterscotch suede just above the beds. Nearly 90% of them have private balconies, with only suites on the two lowest passenger decks having bay windows instead. Of these, the only ones with obstructed views are those on the port side of Deck 6 looking out onto the promenade. The standard suites are a roomy 301 square feet; the 18 top suites range from 448 to 1,067 square feet, plus 47- to 200-square-foot balconies. Every suite has a sitting area with couch, terry robes, pair of chairs, desk, vanity table and stool (with an outlet above for a hair dryer or curling iron), flatscreen TV with DVD player (and movies available from an onboard library), minibar stocked with two complimentary bottles of wine or spirits, private safe, and wide walk-in closet with a tall built-in dresser. The marble bathrooms that come standard in all suites are absolutely huge, with a separate shower stall, a long tub, and lots of counter space. Along with those on *Seven Seas Voyager* and Silversea's *Silver Whisper,* they're the best bathrooms at sea today. In 2006 and 2007, all suites received new upholstery, mattresses, bed linens and duvets, towels, and bathroom amenities, plus slippers and bathrobes for guest use while aboard. Top-level accommodations, from Penthouses up to Master Suites, come with butler service and iPods with Bose speakers.

Four suites are wheelchair accessible.

PUBLIC AREAS   Full of autumn hues and deep blues, *Navigator*'s attractive decor is a marriage of classic and modern design, with contemporary wooden furniture, chairs upholstered in buttery leather, walls covered in suede, and touches of stainless steel, along with silk brocade draperies, dark-wood paneling, burled veneer, and marble. The ship has lots of intimate spaces, so you'll never feel overwhelmed the way you sometimes do on larger ships.

Most of the public rooms are on Decks 6 and 7, just aft of the three-story atrium and main elevator bank (whose exposed wiring and mechanics could have been better disguised). The well-stocked library has 10 computers with e-mail and Internet access, while Wi-Fi hot spots let laptop users surf from several public areas. The cozy Navigator Lounge, paneled in mahogany and cherrywood, is a popular place for pre-dinner cocktails, which means it can get tight in there during rush hour. Next door is the Connoisseur Club cigar lounge, a somewhat cold and often underutilized wood-paneled room with umber leather chairs. Down the hall is the roomier Stars Lounge, with a long, curved, black-granite bar and clusters of oversize ocean-blue armchairs around a small dance floor. A live music duo croons pop numbers here nightly. The attractive dark-paneled casino with its striking mural is bound to attract your eye, even if you don't gamble.

Galileo's Lounge, surrounded by windows on three sides, is our favorite spot in the evening, when a pianist is on hand and the golden room glows magically under soft light. On warm nights the doors to the outside deck are thrown open and dancers spill out from the small dance floor, creating a truly romantic, dreamy scene. By day, Galileo's is a quiet venue for continental breakfast, high tea, seminars, and meetings, and is also a perfect perch from which to view the seascape.

The stage of the twinkling two-story Seven Seas Lounge is large enough for the kind of sizable, Vegas-style song-and-dance revues typical of much larger ships—a rarity in the luxe market. While sightlines are good from the tiered rows of banquettes on the first level, views from the sides of the balcony are severely obstructed.

The cheerful windowed Vista observation lounge is used for meetings and is another great scenery-viewing spot. It opens directly out to a huge patch of forward deck space just over the bridge.

DINING OPTIONS There are two restaurants, the formal Compass Rose dining room and the more casual Portofino Grill, which serves buffet-style breakfast and lunch and is transformed every evening into a very cozy, dimly lit, reservations-only restaurant specializing in Tuscan cuisine with southern Italian accents. Many tables for two are available, and wine tastings are done just before dinner. Its menus are inspired by Chef Angelo Elia of Fort Lauderdale's Casa D'Angelo Ristorante, though its overall dinner experience was inherited from the popular Don Vito's restaurant on the line's dear, departed *Radisson Diamond,* with its singing Italian waiters and fun, participatory vibe. The Compass Rose, a pleasant, wide-open room done in warm caramel-colored woods, offers a single open seating at all meals. There's also a casual grill on the pool deck for burgers, grilled-chicken sandwiches, fries, and salads at lunchtime, as well as a Coffee Corner on Deck 6, with complimentary deluxe coffees available (from a machine) 24 hours a day.

POOL, FITNESS, SPA & SPORTS FACILITIES The oceanview gym is bright and roomy for a ship of this size, and a separate aerobics room offers impressively grueling classes, such as circuit training and step. A pair of golf nets and two Ping-Pong tables are available for guest use, but they're situated high on Deck 12 in an ash-plagued nook just behind the smokestacks, and are accessible only by a hard-to-find set of interior crew stairs. The whole area looks like an afterthought. At the pool area, a wide set of stairs joins a balcony of deck chairs to a large pool and pair of hot tubs on the deck below. Adjacent to the gym is *Navigator*'s six-room Carita spa.

4 Seabourn Cruise Line

6100 Blue Lagoon Dr., Suite 400, Miami, FL 33126. ✆ **800/929-9391** or 305/463-3070. www.seabourn.com.

THE LINE IN A NUTSHELL Genteel and refined, these small megayachts are intimate, quiet, and very comfortable, lavishing guests with plenty of personal attention and very fine cuisine. **Sails to:** Caribbean (plus Europe, Asia, South Pacific, and South America).

THE EXPERIENCE Strictly upper-crust Seabourn caters to guests who are well mannered and prefer their fellow vacationers to be the same. Generally, they aren't into pool games and deck parties, preferring a good book and cocktail chatter, or a taste of the line's special complimentary goodies, such as free minimassages on deck and soothing Eucalyptus-oil baths drawn in suites upon request.

Due to the ships' small size, guests mingle easily and enjoy mellow pursuits such as trivia games and presentations by guest lecturers. With 157 crewmembers to just 208 guests (a higher ratio than on almost any other line), service is very personal. Staff members greet you by name from the moment you check in, and your wish is their command.

Pros

- **Top-shelf service:** Staff seems to know what you need before you ask.
- **Totally all-inclusive:** Unlimited wines and spirits are included, as are gratuities.
- **Excellent dining:** Even the breakfast buffets are exceptional, and having dinner on the outside decks of the Veranda Café, with the churning wake shushing just below you, is divine.
- **Remote ports of call:** These small ships are able to visit less-touristed Caribbean ports that larger ships can't.

Cons

- **Limited activities and nightlife:** There's not a whole lot going on, but most guests like it that way.
- **Aging vessels:** When compared to the newer ships of its competitors, Seabourn's 15- to 19-year-old *Legend* and *Pride* lack luster and suffer from a poorly configured pool deck.
- **Shallow drafts mean rocky seas:** Rough seas in the Caribbean are relatively rare, but not unheard of. Because the ships are small, they can get tossed around a lot more (and in less-rough waters) than larger vessels.

SEABOURN: THE CAVIAR OF CRUISE SHIPS

Seabourn was established in 1987, when luxury-cruise patriarch Warren Titus and Norwegian shipping mogul Atle Brynestad commissioned a trio of ultraupscale 10,000-ton vessels from a north German shipyard. They sold out to industry giant Carnival Corporation in 1991 and eventually transferred the ships' registries from Oslo to The Bahamas, somewhat diluting the link to the line's Norwegian roots. That said, the ships' captains are still Norwegian; the ships' decor is very Scandinavian, with its cool, almost icy pastels; and you may still find your suite minibar stocked with bottles of Norwegian Ringnes Pilsener.

Today "The Yachts of Seabourn" (as the line officially calls itself) operates some of the smallest vessels in the luxury market, and focuses on the strengths that go along with that: doting, personalized service; fine food and wine; and the ability to venture into exotic harbors where megaships can't go. Over the past few years it's introduced such niceties as free Tumi luggage tags, complimentary minimassages on deck, one complimentary shore excursion per cruise, Molton Brown toiletries in suite bathrooms, and bow-to-stern Wi-Fi Internet access for guests with laptops.

In late 2006, Seabourn announced that it had signed a letter of intent for the construction of **two new ships,** each measuring 32,000 gross register tons and accommodating 450 guests—more than double the size of Seabourn's three current sister ships. The vessels will be built by T. Mariotti S.p.A. of Genoa, Italy, and be equipped with two bow thrusters to enhance maneuverability, two stabilizers, and advanced wastewater treatment technology to lessen their environmental impact. The first vessel, named *Seabourn Odyssey,* is scheduled to enter service in mid-2009. Its twin sister will follow in 2010.

PASSENGER PROFILE

Seabourn's guests are well-traveled, mature adults mostly in their 50s, 60s, and 70s and used to the five-star treatment. Many are former CEOs, lawyers, investment bankers, real-estate tycoons, and entrepreneurs and have net worths in the millions. The majority of passengers are couples, and there's always a handful of singles as well, usually widows or widowers. Though most passengers are American, British, German, Swiss, and Australian, guests sometimes spice up the mix. As for families with children, they're the exception rather than the rule, and only occasionally appear during the holidays and summers. These ships do not cater to kids at all, and Seabourn passengers prefer it that way.

DINING

Seabourn's cuisine is very, very good and remains one of the line's strong points.

TRADITIONAL   Fleetwide, dining is offered in a single open seating in the main dining rooms, allowing guests to dine whenever they choose and with whomever they

Compared with the other ultraluxury lines, here's how Seabourn rates:

	Poor	Fair	Good	Excellent	Outstanding
Enjoyment Factor					✓
Dining					✓
Activities		✓			
Children's Program	N/A*				
Entertainment		✓			
Service				✓	
Worth the Money				✓	

* Seabourn has no children's program.

want, between about 7 and 10pm. Dinner service is high-style, with waiters dramatically lifting silver lids off dishes in unison and almost running at a trot through the elaborate, six-course European service. Service is attentive and unobtrusive, and the waitstaff is programmed to please. Celebrity restaurateur **Charlie Palmer,** of New York's Aureole fame, is behind the ships' menus, and the ships' chefs are trained in Palmer's shore-side restaurants.

Appetizers may include such dishes as citrus-marinated fluke, iced Russian Malossol caviar, sautéed escalope of foie gras, and eggplant relish and hummus. Five entrees change nightly, and may include such dishes as pink-roasted rack of veal, rosemary-grilled double-cut lamb chops, roast prime rib, pan-fried sea bass, whole pan-fried Dover sole, scallops wrapped in smoked bacon, and of course lobster. **Vegetarian entrees** might include toasted angel-hair pasta with black trumpet mushrooms and barigoule of artichoke with white beans, thyme roasted tomatoes, and saffron potato dice. A number of **classics** are also always on the menu (with options like baked filet of salmon, grilled New York sirloin, filet mignon, and Caesar salad), as are a number of **lighter-choice** options. If nothing on the menu appeals to you, just ask for something you'd prefer and the galley will do its best to whip it up. Decadent **desserts** include the likes of three-chocolate crème brûlée and hot Grand Marnier soufflé, plus ice creams, sorbets, frozen yogurt, and a selection of international cheeses.

Formal nights (two per weeklong cruise) are very formal, with virtually every male wearing a tuxedo and ladies dressed in sequins and gowns. On other nights, things have relaxed somewhat as Seabourn focuses on attracting a younger crowd (younger as in 40- and 50-somethings), so ties are not required. Regardless, passengers always look very pulled together.

Complimentary wines (about 18 on any given cruise, including champagne) are served not only at lunch and dinner, but basically any time and place you want them. Ditto for spirits and soft drinks. An extensive list of extra-cost vintages is also available. For those with exceedingly refined palates, Seabourn introduced a special collection of wines called **Vintage Seabourn.** For $195, guests can choose three bottles from a list of six premium whites and six premium reds (or choose six bottles for $390).

SPECIALTY Every evening per cruise, including on formal nights, the Veranda Café (see "Casual") is transformed into a new venue called **Restaurant 2,** featuring multicourse tasting menus for as many as 50 guests a night (reservations are suggested). A pair of chefs prepares an array of small plates typically served two to a course during the five- to six-course meals. Expect such dishes as artichoke salad, cured and roasted duck breast, lemongrass seafood presse, crisp sea bass, and barbecue-glazed short ribs. Your meal might end with something like a "sweet coffee sandwich" with sea salt caramel ice cream and hazelnut foam. The ambience is more casual here than at The Restaurant, with a "jackets but no ties" rule for men followed on formal nights.

An outdoor dining alternative is scheduled a couple of nights per cruise, weather permitting, at the **Sky Bar** on Deck 8, which serves freshly grilled seafood and sizzling steak dinners to about 40 guests, by reservation only.

Neither of these alternative dining options entails an extra charge.

CASUAL   The indoor/outdoor Veranda Café offers a combination buffet and table-service menu at breakfast and lunch. At breakfast, omelets are made to your specifications, and there's also an impressive fresh-fruit selection as well as the usual breakfast spread. At lunch, you'll find salads, sandwich makings, fresh pasta, and maybe jumbo shrimp, smoked salmon, and smoked oysters, plus hot sliced roast beef, duck, and ham on the carving board.

One night on each warm-weather itinerary includes a **festive buffet dinner** served by the pool, and **silver-service beach barbecues**—complete with china and linen, and, of course, champagne and caviar in the surf—are also a big hit in remote ports such as Virgin Gorda, Jost Van Dyke, tiny Mayreau in the Grenadines, and Hunting Caye in Belize.

SNACKS & EXTRAS   Daily afternoon **tea service** includes a slew of exotic teas, freshly loose-brewed to order. **Room service** is available 24 hours a day on all ships. During normal lunch or dinner hours, your private multicourse meal can mirror the dining room service, right down to the silver, crystal, and porcelain. Don't expect the same level of service dining you get in the restaurants (courses may arrive together, for instance), but do expect a very cushy, lazy way of "ordering in" one night. Outside of mealtimes, the room-service menu is more limited, though you can order treats such as jumbo shrimp and caviar along with the more humdrum burgers, salads, sandwiches, pizza, pastas, ice cream, and cookies. In-cabin breakfasts are popular, and you can have your eggs prepared any way you like them.

ACTIVITIES

The Seabourn ships are sociable because of their small size, but organized activities are typically limited to things like trivia contests, galley tours, computer classes, **wine tastings,** bridge tournaments, exercise classes, and makeover demonstrations. The lack of in-your-face, rah-rah activities is what most passengers like about Seabourn, though each ship does have a cruise director to organize things. Public announcements are few, and, for the most part, passengers are left alone to enjoy conversation and pursue their own personal peace.

Each of the ships has a retractable **watersports marina** that unfolds from its stern (weather and sea conditions permitting), allowing passengers direct access to the sea for water-skiing, windsurfing, sailing, snorkeling, banana-boat riding, kayaking, and swimming. Many cruises feature a **guest lecturer** or two discussing upcoming ports as well as other random topics. Noted chefs, scientists, historians, authors, or statesmen may be aboard, or maybe a wine connoisseur, composer, anthropologist, TV director, or professor, presenting lectures and mingling with guests.

Seabourn Fleet Itineraries

Ship	Itineraries
Seabourn Pride	**Caribbean:** 11-night eastern, Ft. Lauderdale, FL, to Barbados (Nov). 7-night eastern, Barbados to Ft. Lauderdale (Dec). 7-night southern, round-trip from Barbados (Nov–Dec). 14-night eastern/southern, round-trip from Ft. Lauderdale (Dec).
Seabourn Legend	**Caribbean/Panama Canal:** 14-night, east- or westbound between Ft. Lauderdale and Caldera, Costa Rica (Jan–Feb & Nov–Dec). **Caribbean:** 11-night eastern, Ft Lauderdale, FL, to St. Thomas (Feb). 7-night eastern, round-trip from St. Thomas (Feb–Mar). 14-night holiday, round-trip from Ft. Lauderdale (Dec).

Each ship has a small business center with computers for e-mail and Internet access. Internet Wi-Fi connections are also available everywhere aboard for people who bring their own laptops. **Recent-release movies** are available for viewing in cabins, and movies are sometimes shown out on deck as well, with popcorn. All suites have flatscreen TVs, DVD players, and Bose Wave CD players, and each ship has a library of music and books-on-disc.

CHILDREN'S PROGRAM
These ships are not geared to children, but you may occasionally see a young and very bored child aboard—bored because the line offers no special programs, menus, or playrooms. In a pinch, you may be able to arrange for an available crewmember to provide babysitting service. Minimum age for sailing is 1 year.

ENTERTAINMENT
Due to the ships' small size, there are no elaborate, splashy production shows such as you sometimes find on the larger ships of Silversea, Regent, and Crystal. Instead, two roomy entertainment lounges serve as venues for cabaret singers, jazz groups, instrumental soloists, or maybe a comedian or puppeteer. In an effort to loosen things up a bit, the line is also offering things like a 1950s/1960s rock-'n'-roll show, in which a cast member might try to get guests to dance a few numbers. Comedians-cum-pianists are also popular. On one cruise, a hilarious Steve Allen–style performer delighted the audience with his wisecracking and musical talents.

Before dinner, a pianist plays and sings for cocktailers in The Club; adjacent is the small, rather drab casino with a handful of card tables and slots. You'll also find a pianist playing in the observation lounge on Deck 8, where passengers enjoy cocktails, a little dancing, and quiet conversation.

SERVICE
Seabourn's staff is among its most valuable assets, offering service that's friendly, courteous, eager to please, discreet, and highly competent. Most of the staff are European, and most have gained experience at the grand hotels of Europe. The cabin staff is all female. All **gratuities** are included in the rates.

If you don't want to deal with lugging your luggage to the airport (or your car), Seabourn offers a service that will **ship your bags** directly to the ship and back.

Wi-Fi Internet access for guests with laptops is available everywhere on the ship. **Laundry** and **dry cleaning** are available, and there are also complimentary self-service laundry rooms.

Seabourn Pride •
Seabourn Legend

The Verdict

These smallish megayachts are in a class by themselves, representing almost a throwback to a more intimate and refined, less frenetic, and definitely less glitzy style of cruising.

Seabourn Legend *(photo: Seabourn Cruise Line)*

Specifications

Size (in tons)	10,000	Passenger/Crew Ratio	1.5 to 1
Passengers (double occ.)	208	Year Launched	
Passenger/Space Ratio	48.1	*Pride*	1988
Total Cabins/Veranda Cabins	100/6	*Legend*	1992
Crew	157	Last Refurbishment/Upgrade	2000

Frommer's Ratings (Scale of 1–5)   ★★★★

Cabin Comfort & Amenities	4	Dining Options	3.5
Appearance & Upkeep	4	Gym, Spa & Sports Facilities	3
Public Comfort/Space	5	Children's Facilities	N/A
Decor	3	Enjoyment Factor	4

Want posh and private? Then grab your Louis Vuitton valise and come aboard these sleek, attractive ships for a cruise to some of the smaller Caribbean ports or up the East Coast for fall foliage. The vessels hold just 208 passengers each, so you'll never feel lost in the crowd. In fact, you'll practically feel like you own the place. Choose to be as social or as private as you wish, with no rowdiness or loud music and no one exhorting you to get involved. While you're aboard, the ship is your floating boutique hotel or your private yacht. You make the call.

Cabins & Rates

Cabins	Per Diems From	Sq. Ft.	Fridge	Hair Dryer	Sitting Area	TV
Suite	$428	277–575	yes	yes	yes	yes

CABINS Just about everything in Seabourn's standard 277-square-foot suites has the feel of an upscale Scandinavian hotel, offering ocean views, ice-blue or champagne color schemes, lots of bleached oak or birch-wood trim, and mirrors and spot lighting to keep things bright. While only the top six Owner's Suites have proper balconies, 36 regular suites on Decks 5 and 6 have French balconies with sliding doors and a few inches of decking—not nearly enough to fit a chair, but they do allow sunlight to pour into the cabin, and offer a great view up and down the length of the ship. You can sit on the sofa or in a chair and read while sunning yourself out of the wind and out of view. You can also sleep with the doors wide open, going to sleep with the sounds and smells of the ocean—unless, of course, the officers on the bridge decide to lock the doors: If seas get even a little choppy or the wind picks up, a flick of a switch locks your door automatically and there's not a darn thing you can do about it. (Remember, these ships are small, so you're not that far above the waterline. They like to avoid waves and sea spray messing up their lovely decor.)

The best features of the suites are their bathrooms and walk-in closets, with plenty of hanging space for Seabourn's extended cruises. Drawer space, on the other hand, is minimal. White marble bathrooms usually include both a tub and a shower (though 10–14 suites on each ship have only showers), and lots of shelf, counter, and cabinet space. Those on *Seabourn Pride* have twin sinks; those on *Legend* have single sinks. Molton Brown bath products plus designer soaps by Chanel, Bijan, Hermès, and Bronnley are provided for guests along with a world atlas, terry bathrobes, slippers, and umbrellas to use on board.

The coffee table in the sitting area can be pulled up to become a dining table, and the complimentary minibar is stocked upon arrival with two bottles of liquor or wine of your choice (a request form comes with your cruise documents) and a chilled bottle of champagne. Unlimited bottled water, beer, and soft drinks are restocked throughout the cruise. Ice is replenished twice daily (more often on request), and bar setups are in each room. There's a desk, hair dryer, safe, radio/CD player (music and book CDs are available for borrowing), and flatscreen TVs and DVD players. Fresh fruit and a flower complete the suite scene.

The two Classic Suites measure 400 square feet, and two pairs of Owner's Suites are 530 and 575 square feet and have verandas, dining areas, and guest powder rooms. Their dark-wood furnishings make the overall feeling more like a hotel room than a ship's suite, but, as is true of any cabins positioned near the bow of relatively small ships, they can be somewhat uncomfortable during rough seas. Owner's Suites 05 and 06 have obstructed views.

Connecting suites are available. Some are marketed as 554-square-foot Double Suites, and that's exactly what they are: two 277-square-foot suites, with one converted to a lounge. There are four wheelchair-accessible suites.

PUBLIC AREAS   Step onto most ships today and you'll oooh and ahhh at the decor. Not so here, where the minimalist Scandinavian design ethic is in play. For the most part, public rooms are spare and almost ordinary looking. Art and ornamentation are conspicuous by their absence, with the exception of the small lobby area in front of the purser's desk on Deck 5, where attractive murals of ship scenes liven up the curved walls.

The forward-facing observation lounge on Sky Deck is the most attractive public room, a quiet venue all day long for reading or cards, the spot for afternoon tea (during which a pianist provides background music), and a good place for a drink before meals. A chart and compass on the wall outside will help you pinpoint the ship's current position, and a computerized wall map lets you track future cruises.

The Club piano bar in the stern offers great views during daylight hours, is packed before dinner, and sometimes offers after-dinner entertainment such as a Name That Tune game or a cabaret show. Hors d'oeuvres are served here both before and after dinner. A tiny, cramped casino is adjacent, with a couple of blackjack tables, a roulette wheel, and about 10 slots. The downstairs show lounge is a dark, tiered, all-purpose space for lectures, the captain's cocktail party, and featured entertainers such as singers, comedians, and pianists.

One of the best places for a romantic, moonlit moment is the isolated patch of deck far forward in the bow on Deck 5, where a lone hot tub also resides.

DINING OPTIONS   The formal Restaurant, located on the lowest deck, is a large, low-ceilinged room with elegant candlelit tables. It's open for breakfast, lunch, and dinner, and officers, cruise staff, and sometimes guest lecturers host tables at dinnertime. If you're not in the mood for the formal dining room, the Veranda Café serves a combination buffet and full-service breakfast and lunch. Come evening, the cafe becomes the casual specialty Restaurant 2, serving multicourse tasting menus by reservation only.

Along with burgers, chicken, hot dogs, and grilled items, a special of the day—maybe pizza with pineapple topping, or fresh ingredients for tacos—is also available at the pleasant Sky Bar, overlooking the Lido Deck, for those who don't want to change out of their swimsuits. On sunny days, themed lunches are also often set up here, and at night it offers a steak-and-seafood menu by reservation.

POOL, FITNESS, SPA & SPORTS FACILITIES   The outdoor pool, which gets little use, is awkwardly situated in a shadowy location aft of the open Deck 7, between the twin engine uptakes and flanked by lifeboats hanging from both sides. A pair of whirlpools is better located just forward of the pool. A third hot tub is perched far forward on Deck 5. It's wonderfully isolated and a perfect spot (as is the whole patch of deck here) from which to watch a port come into sight or fade away.

A retractable, wood-planked watersports marina opens out from the stern of each ship so that passengers can hop into sea kayaks or go windsurfing, water-skiing, or snorkeling right from the vessel. An attached steel mesh net creates a protected saltwater pool when the marina is in use.

Located forward of the Lido Deck, the gym and Steiner-managed spa are surprisingly roomy for ships this small, and were renovated recently with modern equipment. Yoga and Pilates as well as more traditional aerobics classes are offered in a lounge or on deck, and you'll also find two saunas, massage rooms, and a beauty salon.

5 SeaDream Yacht Club

2601 S. Bayshore Dr., Penthouse 1B, Coconut Grove, FL 33133. ℂ 800/707-4911 or 305/631-6100. Fax 305/631-6110. www.seadreamyachtclub.com.

THE LINE IN A NUTSHELL   Intimate cruise-ships-turned-yachting-vessels, SeaDream's two small ships deliver an upscale yet casual experience without the regimentation of traditional cruise itineraries and activities. **Also sails to:** Europe and South America.

THE EXPERIENCE   SeaDream was created for independent-minded travelers craving high-end service and food sans formality and rigid schedules. Step aboard one of these 100-passenger yachts and you're boarding a floating club of mostly like-minded travelers who cringe at the thought of sailing en masse to the St. Thomases of the world. It's an intimate group that wants to feel like it's inhabiting an exclusive and remote seaside hamlet on some hard-to-reach, difficult-to-spell island, where the food is good, the spa is well equipped, and the drinks are flowing. On a SeaDream cruise, everything is included in the cruise fare and you'll never be pestered to pay for drinks or tip the crew. There also aren't art auctions, roving photographers, or "special" restaurants vying for your money, but instead cool adult toys such as WaveRunners, appealing Caribbean ports off the megaship drag, and pampering service that includes complimentary orders of jumbo shrimp served to you in the hot tub (or wherever) whenever the desire strikes. The line's flexible itineraries and fluid daily schedules should appeal to landlubbers used to exclusive resort vacations.

Pros

- **Truly all-inclusive:** Unlimited wines and spirits as well as tips are included in the rates.
- **Cool tech stuff:** These ships were built in the mid-1980s, but they've been outfitted for the 21st century. Every cabin is equipped with a flatscreen TV, Internet access, and CD and DVD players; and jet skis, MP3 players, and Segway Human Transporters are available for passenger use.
- **Late-night departures from key ports:** Instead of leaving port around cocktail hour—just when things begin to get interesting—the ships will stay late or even overnight in places such as St. Barts to allow passengers a night of carousing on terra firma.
- **Flexible itineraries:** Captains have the authority to duck inclement weather by visiting a different port or to extend a stay off an island because of perfect snorkeling conditions.

Cons

- **Rough seas:** While the intimacy of these ships can be a selling point, their size can be a detriment: They bob like buoys in even mildly rough waters, and the diesel engines sometimes produce a shimmying sensation.
- **Limited entertainment:** A piano player and a sidekick are the sum total of the ship's entertainment. Mostly it's socializing with other passengers over cocktails at the Top of Yacht bar (who's complaining?).

SEADREAM: YOUR YACHT AWAITS

In fall 2001, Norwegian entrepreneur Atle Brynestad, who founded Seabourn in 1987 and chaired the company for a decade, bought out Carnival Corporation's stake in Seabourn's *Sea Goddess I* and *Sea Goddess II,* then worked with former Seabourn and Cunard president and CEO Larry Pimentel to form the SeaDream Yacht Club, reintroducing the ships as twin yachts. *SeaDream II* was redesigned and refitted at a Bremerhaven, Germany, shipyard and was unveiled in Miami in February 2002. Her sister ship debuted 2 months later, following her own refurbishment.

The mantra from management is that these vessels are not cruise ships. They are yachts and have been painstakingly renovated to invoke the ambience of your best

Compared with the other ultraluxury lines, here's how SeaDream rates:

	Poor	Fair	Good	Excellent	Outstanding
Enjoyment Factor					✓
Dining			✓		
Activities			✓		
Children's Program	N/A*				
Entertainment		✓			
Service					✓
Worth the Money					✓

* Seabourn has no children's program.

friend's private vessel, on the theory (as president and CEO Pimentel told us once) that "cruising is about what happens inside the vessel; yachting is about what happens outside." Toward this end, deck space has been expanded and refurbished with such touches as queen-size sun beds. The Main Salon is cozy, with fabrics and art hand-picked by Linn Brynestad, the owner's spouse. The dress code steers clear of the traditional tux-and-sequins dress-up night by favoring "yacht casual" wear. Some men wear jackets, but never ties. Itineraries are designed so that ships stay overnight once or twice a week, because, as Pimentel explained, "There's no sense in leaving a port at 5 if it doesn't start really happening till 11." Plus, because SeaDream's ports of call tend to be the less-commercialized ones that are generally off the megaship main drag, you'll rarely be meandering around a port town with thousands of others (thank goodness). If the ships are anchoring offshore, their size generally enables them to get close enough so that the tender ride between ship and shore is short. And given how few passengers the ships carry, you'll never have to queue up to be shuttled back and forth—it's practically on demand.

With many crewmembers having migrated to SeaDream from the *Goddess* days, meticulous attention to detail and personalized service are still the ships' greatest assets.

PASSENGER PROFILE

Most passengers are in their 40s and 50s, with the line reporting an average age of 46. About 70% are American (with British, Canadians, and other Europeans making up most of the remainder), and are not veteran cruisers. They're the kind who have refined tastes and want top-notch service and gourmet food, but are secure enough to dispense with a stuffy atmosphere. On a recent sailing aboard the *SeaDream I* in the Caribbean, the mix included a fun-loving, middle-aged doctor and his wife from Texas; a 30-something couple-next-door from Pennsylvania that ran a successful baking business and liked to swig beer from the bottle; a retired travel executive who was clearly used to the good life; a restaurant owner; and a group of well-dressed, hard-drinking friends celebrating a 40th birthday. Many passengers have chartered their own small yachts for a vacation or actually own one. Passengers were friendly and mingled easily, and by day three, alliances had been made and clusters of new friends were enjoying drinks by the pool and dining together in the open-seating restaurants.

The SeaDream yacht experience is most similar to a cruise with Windstar, whose intimate motorized sailing ships offer casually elegant yachty jaunts for mostly 40- and 50-somethings to similarly great places in the Caribbean and Europe—though not with SeaDream's all-inclusive price tag. The SeaDream experience is less highbrow and way more playful than Seabourn, whose three 208-passenger ships attract an older, more sober clientele.

A big chunk of the line's business comes from full charters of the ships, often by large (rich) families. Smaller groups can sometimes take advantage of a deal that offers one free cabin for every four booked, up to a maximum of 25 cabins. Groups of 50 are a significant presence on ships this size, so when booking, inquire whether there will be any large groups aboard, to avoid the "in crowd/out crowd" vibe.

DINING

TRADITIONAL   Dining is a high point of the SeaDream experience; it's roughly on a par with Windstar's cuisine, and just under Silversea and Seabourn. Daily five-course dinners in the Dining Salon include five entrees that change nightly, with a **healthy selection** always among them. Expect delicious dishes such as a hot and tangy prawn and fruit salad; sautéed sea scallops with cauliflower crème, herb lettuce and potato crisps; and yellowfin tuna steak on roast zucchini and tomato compote. You'll also find a **vegetarian option** and a la carte items such as linguine with pesto and rosemary-marinated lamb chops. The kitchen will prepare **special requests** provided the ingredients are on board. **Local specialties,** such as fresh fish from markets in various ports, are likely to be incorporated into the menu. Open-seating dining is offered from 7:30 to 9:30pm, and table arrangements include everything from the nine-seat captain's table to cozier places for two (though during the evening rush, it's not easy to snag one). Generally, you'll be seated with other guests unless you don't want to, and by the second or third day of the cruise, many passengers prefer to sit at larger tables with new friends.

There are no formal evenings. Jackets are not required; some men wear them, but many just stick to collared shirts. On our recent cruise, passengers' interpretation of the **informal dress code** ranged from a classic navy blue sport jacket to Bermuda shorts and a T-shirt—the latter frowned upon by the ship's manager, but generally overlooked. It's not easy to tell someone who paid several thousand dollars for his cruise to go back to his cabin to change clothes.

Guests can venture "out" for dinner by requesting a spot in advance at one of several private alcoves on Deck 6, or even on the bridge. These special dining ops may not be advertised heavily on board—you'll have to ask for them.

CASUAL   The partially covered, open-sided Topside Restaurant on Deck 5 serves breakfast and lunch daily, with guests choosing from a buffet or menu.

SNACKS & EXTRAS   Room service is available 24 hours a day for those who don't want to pause their DVD player. You'll also find minisandwiches, wraps, pastries, and other snacks throughout the day in the Topside Restaurant's buffet area or at the pool. One afternoon on a recent cruise, waiters circulated by the pool at happy hour with trays of bloody marys and homemade minipizzas. For a real treat, you can ask for a generous (and complimentary) jumbo shrimp cocktail whenever the mood strikes; on our last cruise, the craving struck while we were soaking in the hot tub. Caviar is available, though it's no longer complimentary (except on special occasions); a 1-ounce portion goes for $32.

Dining highlights from the old *Sea Goddess* cruises are carried over here, including lavish **beach barbecues,** called the Caviar and Champagne Splash, on Jost Van Dyke and Virgin Gorda (see "Activities," below, for more details). A buffet lunch, served on tables with linen and china, includes grilled shrimp and chicken, pork ribs, and plenty of side dishes.

The line's **open-bar policy** means that unlimited alcoholic beverages are served throughout the vessels, though cabin minifridges are stocked only with complimentary beer and soft drinks. If you want wine and spirits for your minifridge, you'll have to pay. Advance requests for favorite libations are encouraged. Each ship's wine cellar includes some 3,500 bottles, of which an excellent selection is complimentary.

ACTIVITIES

If hanging out can be considered an activity, you can do it well on a SeaDream cruise. Who can complain about summoning a waiter from the hot tub for a jumbo shrimp cocktail and a piña colada? As Larry Pimentel, SeaDream's co-owner, chairman, and CEO, is fond of saying, "Yachting is about the outdoors, cruising is about the indoors." The ship's main social hubs are not the indoor entertainment lounge or library, but out

SeaDream Fleet Itineraries

Ship	Itineraries
SeaDream I	**Caribbean:** 7-night eastern, round-trip from San Juan, PR (Jan, Mar–Apr & Dec); round-trip from St. Thomas (Feb); St. Thomas to San Juan (Feb & Dec); round-trip from Antigua (Nov); Antigua to San Juan (Dec); San Juan to St. Thomas (Dec).
SeaDream II	**Caribbean:** 7-night eastern, round-trip from San Juan, PR (Jan, Mar–Apr & Dec); San Juan to St. Thomas (Jan–Feb); St. Thomas to San Juan (Jan–Feb); Barbados to Antigua (Mar); round-trip from Antigua (Mar); Antigua to San Juan (Mar); San Juan to Barbados (Apr); Miami, FL, to San Juan (Nov).

on deck at the Top of the Yacht Bar, pool deck, and sunbathing areas, where there are chaise longues, a pair of hammocks, and the line's much-touted ultrafirm **Balinese sun beds** (p. 314). Upon request, you can even sleep on them under the stars with duvets and pillows. There's also a **golf simulator** up top, and below, a **retractable marina for watersports** and swimming that operates a couple of hours a day in ports where the ship anchors, which is virtually everywhere in the Caribbean, but fewer ports in Europe. Cabins have DVD players and you can borrow a portable **MP3 player** from the reception desk (there are about 25, and they're preprogrammed with a wide selection of music).

The ships carry along **mountain bikes** for use in port and even **Segway Human Transporters,** those two-wheeled, upright scooters that can be used (at a cost of $49 for 45 min.) when the ship ties up at a dock, which isn't often in the Caribbean.

For those who consider a **massage** a beloved pastime—like we do—the ship's well-equipped spa and gym are very impressive for ships so small. Staffs of eight Thai women run the spas, which feature traditional therapies such as Swedish massage, along with Asian ones. Heidi sampled an excellent Thai massage during which the therapist used her arms and legs, as well as hands, to execute a variety of stretching moves. The adjacent oceanview gym offers up-to-date equipment and daily classes such as tai chi and yoga.

One of the week's highlights is an ultrapopular holdover from the *Sea Goddess* days, the lavish **Champagne and Caviar Splash beach party** thrown on Jost Van Dyke or Virgin Gorda. Guests are tendered ashore by zodiacs to a quiet beach, where chaise longues are set up on the sand and a rustic pavilion offers a buffet lunch. The main event that gets the cameras clicking is when the manager and his assistants wade into the surf with their uniforms on and serve champagne and caviar from a floating surfboard. Appealing to the inner frat boy in all of us, passengers of all types just loved the whole ritual on a recent cruise. The entire ship was happily treading through the water to partake of a glass (or two or three) of bubbly and a dollop of caviar, reveling in the frivolity of it. A nice buffet lunch is served on long tables (with linens and china). The ship also offered a pair of kayaks and snorkeling equipment, though few people had the energy to bother. Nearby, a local vendor was renting paddle boats, windsurfers, and other watercraft.

CHILDREN'S ACTIVITIES

Though the only actual restriction is that children under age 1 are prohibited, these ships are by no means kid-friendly. There are no babysitting services or child-related activities. Teens, though, may enjoy these cruises' emphasis on watersports and unstructured activities. Keep in mind, the standard Yacht Club staterooms can accommodate only three people; the third person/child sleeps on the couch (which doesn't pull out) and generally pays half of the full per-person rate. If you've got a larger family, you'll have to spring for two staterooms. The rate for a child up to age 12 is $100 per day and $200 per day for children over 12; in both cases it is assumed that they'll be sharing a stateroom with two adults.

ENTERTAINMENT

Evening entertainment is mostly of the socializing-over-drinks variety—and that's how passengers seem to like it. This isn't generally a musical-loving cabaret crowd. On a recent cruise, a **pianist** played after dinner in the Main Salon lounge, while a **guitarist** serenaded diners at the entrance to the restaurant and sometimes afterward up on deck at the Top of the Yacht bar, the liveliest spot to hang out before and after dinner on our most recent sailing. Occasionally, **local bands** are brought on for the night, and there is a **tiny casino** area with two poker tables and a handful of slots. Weather permitting, on 1 night per cruise a large **movie** screen is set up on deck so that passengers can watch a flick under the stars (with popcorn, of course).

SERVICE

Given the small number of guests and large number of crew, everyone is quick to satisfy whims and commit your name to memory. Make sure that your first drink is your favorite; you may find fresh ones reappearing automatically throughout the evening. The dining room waitstaff is courteous and knowledgeable, though a bit harried; even though dining is open seating, most passengers tend to dine about the same time each evening. As aboard the Silversea ships, cabin bathrooms are stocked with Bulgari amenities and guests all get a complimentary set of frumpy (but comfortable) SeaDream pj's. **Laundry, dry cleaning,** and **pressing** are available, but there is no self-service laundry.

SeaDream I • SeaDream II

The Verdict

The service, cuisine, and intimacy of the old *Sea Goddess* ships in an even better package, with flexible itineraries and a laid-back atmosphere designed to pry landlubbers from their resorts and out to sea.

SeaDream II *(photo: SeaDream Yacht Club)*

Specifications

Size (in tons)	4,260	Passenger/Crew Ratio	1.2 to 1
Passengers (double occ.)	110	Year Launched	
Passenger/Space Ratio	38.7	*SeaDream I*	1984
Total Cabins/Veranda Cabins	55/0	*SeaDream II*	1985
Crew	89	Last Refurbishment/Upgrade	2007/2008

Frommer's Ratings (Scale of 1–5)   ★★★★½

Cabin Comfort & Amenities	5	Dining Options	3.5
Appearance & Upkeep	4	Gym, Spa & Sports Facilities	4
Public Comfort/Space	4.5	Children's Facilities	N/A
Decor	4	Enjoyment Factor	5

Care for a chronology? The year is 1984, and Sea Goddess Cruises begins offering luxury small-ship cruises for very affluent travelers. Unfortunately, not enough affluent travelers are interested, and within 2 years the line sells out to Cunard, which takes over operation of its two vessels and retains a similar approach, featuring impeccable service and cuisine. In 1998, Carnival Corporation purchases Cunard and transfers the *Sea Goddess* ships to its Seabourn division, which operates similar-size luxury vessels. Then, in August 2001, Carnival sells the ships to Atle Brynestad, founder of Seabourn Cruises. Brynestad then brings aboard former Seabourn and Cunard president and CEO Larry Pimentel as co-owner, chairman, and CEO of the new line, and hires a raft of other ex-Cunard executives to fill the company's top spots.

Man, the business world is complicated. But because this line is geared to affluent travelers, we thought you might be interested. Now let's get to the details.

Cabins & Rates

Cabins	Per Diems From	Sq. Ft.	Fridge	Hair Dryer	Sitting Area	TV
Suite	$499	195–450	yes	yes	yes	yes

CABINS All of the 54 one-room, 195-square-foot, oceanview suites are virtually identical, with the bedroom area positioned alongside the cabin's large window (or portholes in the case of Deck 2 suites) and the sitting area inside, the exact opposite of most ship cabin layouts. During a May 2007 dry dock, the suites on *SeaDream I* were refreshed with new furniture upholstery, curtains, and bedspreads (*SeaDream II* will get the same treatment in 2008). The standard cabins are a bit bigger than Windstar's, and about 100 square feet smaller than those of Seabourn, Silversea, and Radisson. None have balconies. Soundproofing between cabins is good and engine noise minimal, as all cabins are located forward and amidships.

Built in the mid-1980s, these ships have a lot more real wood incorporated into the cabins than you'll see on today's newer ships that sport veneers and synthetics at every turn. Wood cabinetry and moldings are complemented by blue and white fabrics to create an appealing nautical look with a modern twist. Each suite has a small sitting area with a couch (that can accommodate a third adult or a child) and an entertainment center that includes a flatscreen TV with CD/DVD player (and wired for Internet access). On her last cruise, Heidi was impressed by the amount of storage space (she never used it all), and the stash of large bottles of water. A minifridge is stocked with sodas and beer (though booze from any of the bars and restaurants is included in the rates, oddly enough, if you want liquor for your minibar you'll have to pay for it). Bathrooms are compact, as you would expect on ships of this size, but feature huge marble showers with glass doors and a generous supply of Bulgari toiletries. Each cabin comes with a hair dryer and extrathick bathrobes, and all guests get a set of personalized cotton pajamas with the SeaDream logo to take home. Unlike Silversea and

Seabourn, the 24-hour room-service menu is limited to salads and sandwiches, and you cannot order from the restaurant menus.

There are 16 staterooms that are connectable to form eight 390-square-foot Commodore Club Staterooms. The gorgeous 450-square-foot Owner's Suite has a bedroom, living room, dining area, main bathroom with bathtub and separate oceanview shower, and guest bathroom.

These ships are not recommended for passengers requiring the use of a wheelchair: Doorways leading to staterooms are not wide enough, many thresholds in public areas are several inches tall, and tenders that shuttle passengers from ship to shore in many ports cannot accommodate wheelchairs. Though there are elevators, they don't reach all decks.

PUBLIC AREAS The SeaDream yachts retain much of *Sea Goddess*'s former sophisticated decor, and a recent face-lift spruced things up even more with new carpeting and other touch ups (in spring 2007 for *SeaDream I* and a year later for *SeaDream II*). Stained wood floors, Oriental carpets, and striking exotic floral arrangements delight the eye. The Main Salon and its small but popular alcove bar is the venue for the weekly captain's cocktail party, plus other group events. One deck above is the Piano Bar, and next door are the ship's small casino, a gift shop, and an attractive library furnished with comfy chairs and stocked with offerings ranging from military history to Oprah Book Club favorites.

By far, the favorite place to socialize is the Top of the Yacht Bar amidships on Deck 6, which has been designed with teak decking, rattan furniture, and contrasting blue-striped cushions. The bar area is partially covered and offers alcove seating. On this deck you'll also find a flotilla of queen-size sun beds for reading, sunbathing, or napping; they're slightly elevated at the stern of the ship to allow for uninterrupted ocean viewing. For those who might want to sleep on deck one night, management will allow it and outfit beds with blankets. There's a large collection of original artwork by exclusively Scandinavian artists, located throughout the ship and commissioned or otherwise chosen by Linn Brynestad.

DINING OPTIONS Dinners are served indoors in the simple but elegant Dining Salon on Deck 2. On 1 or 2 nights during the trip, a festive dinner is served in the open-sided, teak-floored Topside Restaurant on Deck 5, and some special meals are served on the beach during port calls. (See "Dining," above, for details.)

POOL, FITNESS, SPA & SPORTS FACILITIES Because yachting is all about being outdoors, there are great open spaces on the SeaDream ships. Stake an early claim to a sun bed because they're prime real estate. Eight of them are aftward on Deck 6, and more are forward, near the golf simulator. Aft on Deck 3 is the attractive pool area, with comfortable lounge chairs and umbrellas, tables, a bar, and, not too far away, a hot tub. It's the place where social passengers gather when the ship departs a port to enjoy the view. A covered deck above has more chairs.

Toward the bow on Deck 4 are the beauty salon and an impressively well-designed and -equipped spa and gym, with four treadmills with flatscreen TVs, an elliptical machine, two stationary bikes, and free weights (and lowish ceilings if you're on the tall side). Classes include aerobics, yoga, and tai chi. The uninterrupted ocean views add a calming diversion while you're burning calories. The teak-lined spa, the Asian Spa and Wellness Center, has three treatment rooms and features the usual decadent (and pricey) suspects, including wraps, facials, and massages, plus more exotic options such as hot lava rock massages, a spice and yogurt scrub, and a cucumber and aloe wrap. You can prebook treatments online at www.seadreamspa.com.

6 Silversea Cruises

110 E. Broward Blvd., Fort Lauderdale, FL 33301. ℭ **800/722-9955.** Fax 954/522-4499. www.silversea.com.

THE LINE IN A NUTSHELL It doesn't get better than Silversea if you're looking for a total luxury experience at sea. From exquisite service and cuisine to such niceties as free-flowing Pommery Brut Royal champagne and Acqua di Parma and Bulgari bath products in the marble cabin bathrooms, these handsome ships offer the best of everything. **Sails to:** Caribbean (plus Europe, Asia, South America, Australia/New Zealand, Africa, transatlantic, world cruise).

THE EXPERIENCE Fine-tuned and genteel, a Silversea cruise caters to guests who are used to the good life, and nothing seems to have been overlooked. The food and service are the best at sea, and the ships' Italian-style decor is warm and inviting. Tables are set with Christofle silver and Schott-Zwiesel crystal. These are dignified vessels for a dignified crowd that likes to dress for dinner, compare travel dossiers, and plan their next big trip. If you want the VIP treatment 24-7, this is your cruise line.

Pros

- **Doting service:** Gracious and ultraprofessional, the Silversea crew knows how to please well-traveled guests with high expectations.
- **Truly all-inclusive:** An impressive selection of wines and spirits is included in the rates, as are gratuities.
- **Excellent cuisine:** Rivaling the best restaurants ashore, cuisine is as exquisite as it gets at sea. Each ship has two alternative venues for dinner, buffets are bountiful, and the room-service menu includes jumbo shrimp and other delish treats.
- **Large staterooms and great bathrooms:** Most of the line's suites are larger than Seabourn's and Crystal's, and the huge marble bathrooms are the best at sea (along with those on Regent's *Seven Seas Navigator* and *Voyager*).

Cons

- **Stuffy crowd:** Of course, not every guest fits that bill, but expect a good portion of the crowd on any cruise to be . . . reserved.

SILVERSEA: THE CROWN JEWELS

Silversea Cruises was conceived in the early 1990s by the Lefebvre family of Italy, former owners of Sitmar Cruises, a legendary Italian line that was merged into P&O/Princess in the late '80s. Created to cater to discerning travelers looking for a superluxurious cruise experience, the line's four ships were built and outfitted at shipyards in Italy and no expense was spared in their design.

The new line joined Seabourn right at the top of the heap when it introduced the 296-passenger *Silver Cloud* and *Silver Wind* in 1994 and 1995—and in fact, features such as stateroom balconies and a two-level show lounge actually gave them the edge. With the introduction of the larger, even more impressive *Silver Shadow* and *Silver Whisper* in 2000 and 2001, that bar was raised even higher, with larger staterooms and huge marble bathrooms, dimly lit and romantic cigar lounges, and more entertainment lounges—all in all, the absolute height of style, paired with itineraries that spanned the globe. A concerted effort has been made to play up the line's Italian connections. The

Compared with the other ultraluxury lines, here's how Silversea rates:

	Poor	Fair	Good	Excellent	Outstanding
Enjoyment Factor					✓
Dining					✓
Activities			✓		
Children's Program	N/A*				
Entertainment		✓			
Service					✓
Worth the Money				✓	

* *Silversea has no children's program.*

specialty Italian restaurants are under the guidance of Marco Betti, owner of Florence's award-winning Antica Posta restaurant; Italian-made bath amenities come from Acqua di Parma and Bulgari; high-end Italian clothes and accessories are in the boutiques; and bronze statues and reliefs from Italian sculptor Francesco Messina are on loan from a private collection.

PASSENGER PROFILE

While Silversea's typical passenger mix is 48-plus, shorter cruises and Caribbean sailings often skew the mix a tad younger, adding at least a handful of 30- and 40-something couples to the pot. Still, the cruise director on a recent *Silver Whisper* cruise told us a 30-something honeymoon couple on the previous sailing had cut out halfway through because the crowd and vibe were older and more sedate than they had expected. Typically, about 70% of passengers are American and they're well traveled, well heeled, well dressed, well accessorized, and well into their 50s, 60s, and 70s. Most guests are couples, though singles and small groups of friends traveling together are usually part of the scene, too. Many have cruised with Silversea before; in fact, every single person Heidi met on a recent cruise had sailed with the line at least once, if not many times.

DINING

Foodies should consider Silversea for the food alone. The cuisine is well prepared and presented, and creative chefs continually come up with a wide variety of dishes. Many ingredients are imported from Italy (the pasta, cheese, and Parma ham, for instance) and much of the baked goods—including the excellent focaccia and flat breads—are made right on board. Each ship has a formal open-seating venue and two more casual options. There are plenty of tables for two in all restaurants, though in the main dining room you may have to wait.

TRADITIONAL   While the cuisine in the elegant main dining room (straightforwardly called "The Restaurant") is not quite as impressive as that of the more intimate and casual La Terrazza, it still offers delicious meals, with entrees such as a duet of king prawn and halibut with wild rice cakes, crispy roasted duck, and a penne pasta with spicy tomato, olive, caper, and anchovy sauce. The wine list is excellent, and a pair of complimentary wines is suggested at each meal from more than 40 choices; if you'd like something other than the featured ones, ask and ye shall find. You can also choose one of the wines not included on the complimentary list—a $745 1990 Château Margaux, anyone?

Silversea Fleet Itineraries

Ship	Itineraries
Silver Cloud	**Caribbean:** 7-night eastern/southern, round-trip from Barbados (Nov).
Silver Shadow	**Caribbean:** 10-night eastern, round-trip from Ft. Lauderdale, FL (May). 9-night eastern/southern, east- or westbound between Ft. Lauderdale and Barbados (Dec). 14-night eastern/southern/western, round-trip from Ft. Lauderdale (Dec). **Panama Canal:** 15-night, Ft. Lauderdale, FL, to Los Angeles, CA (May). **Alaska:** 9-night Inside Passage, round-trip from Vancouver, BC (June–Aug). 10-night Inside Passage, north- or south bound between San Francisco, CA, and Vancouver, BC (June–July); southbound between Seward/Anchorage and Vancouver (Aug). 12-night Inside Passage, Los Angeles to Vancouver (May); round-trip from San Francisco (July); Vancouver to Los Angeles (Sept). **Mexican Riviera:** 9 nights, round-trip from Los Angeles (Nov).
Silver Wind	**Caribbean:** 7- & 8-night eastern/southern, Barbados to San Juan, PR, and round-trip from San Juan (Mar–Apr).

SPECIALTY   Two specialty restaurants serve dinner on each ship, both by reservation. Open most evenings for dinner, **La Terrazza** is an intimate venue offering Italian cuisine created by chef Marco Betti, owner of the award-winning Antica Posta restaurants in Florence, Italy, and Atlanta, Georgia. Start with a plate of antipasto—fresh Parmigiano prosciutto, olives, sun-dried tomatoes, and marinated eggplant—before moving on to delicious dishes such as a mushroom tartlet or buffalo mozzarella with fresh tomato and basil; gnocchi filled with Gorgonzola; and a juicy pork loin. Featured desserts, such as a delicious millefoglie, are paired with a tray of Italian-made biscotti.

The second alternative venue offers a new twist on cruise dining, offering menus that pair food with wine—and not the other way around. Developed in consultation with master sommeliers trained in the member boutique lodgings and restaurants of Relais & Châteaux–Relais Gourmands, the wine menus reflect regions of the world known for their rich viticultural heritage, including France, Italy, northern California, South Africa, Australia, and New Zealand. Sommeliers describe the origin and craft of each vintage, then offer dishes created especially to bring out the wine's full richness. Guests enjoy a different wine with each course, with the extra charge for dinner varying in accordance with the wines presented. On a recent cruise it was $150 per person, and frequented mostly by European passengers.

CASUAL   Burgers, sandwiches, and salads are served poolside at lunchtime, in addition to service in The Restaurant and the buffet-style Terrace Cafe (which is transformed into La Terrazza in the evenings). Once per cruise, passengers are also invited into the galley for the traditional **galley brunch,** which features more than 100 delectable dishes, from stone crab claws to pickled herring, Hungarian goulash, rabbit a la Provençal, and German bratwurst. A red carpet is rolled out, literally, through the galley, and the chef is on hand to chat with guests about the feast.

SNACKS & EXTRAS   The line's **24-hour room-service menu** includes such mouthwatering choices as jumbo shrimp cocktail, a snack-sized portion of crabmeat served with lime mayonnaise and guacamole, and delicious thin-crust gourmet pizzas. Plus, if you'd rather dine in one evening, you can order off The Restaurant's menu (during its dinnertime operating hours) and have your meal served course by course on a table set with linens and china in your suite. There's an elegant white-gloved tea service in one of the lounges on most days.

ACTIVITIES

Aside from trivia games, card tournaments, stretch and aerobics classes, and bridge tours, Silversea tries to focus on more cerebral pursuits. **Wine-tasting seminars** are excellent, and the line's enrichment lectures are varied and interesting; at least one guest speaker is featured on every sailing, ranging from explorers and adventurers to authors and journalists. **Culinary theme cruises,** offered in partnership with Relais & Châteaux, are hosted by Relais Gourmands chefs and feature demos and tastings.

Other pursuits include language classes, **golf instruction** and driving nets, and computer classes. *Silver Shadow* also offers special golf cruises that feature PGA golf pros, golfing excursions, and the latest video-teaching technology.

Lighter activities include a dip in the pool or two hot tubs; shopping in the boutiques (which include an H Stern, where you'll find high-end gold, diamond, and gemstone pieces); and surfing in the Internet center. Passengers who travel with their laptops can take advantage of Wi-Fi hot spots on board. **Onboard cellphone service** is also now an option. Overall, though, these ships are low-key (don't expect music on the pool deck, for instance) and guests are left to their own devices when it comes to keeping busy—just the way most guests like it. Reading, dozing, and sipping cool drinks seem to keep most happily occupied.

The ships' Balinese-inspired **Mandara spa** beckons with its flower-strewn copper foot bowls, warm massage stones, and other Asian-inspired treatments. To avoid waiting in line on the first day of the cruise to make your appointments, you can now book your treatments via the line's website up to 48 hours before your cruise. You can also prebook **shore excursions** online up to the week before sailing.

CHILDREN'S PROGRAM

These ships are not geared to children, though every so often one or two are aboard. Babysitting may be arranged with an available crewmember (no guarantee); otherwise, no activities or services are offered specifically for children. The minimum age for sailing is 12 months.

ENTERTAINMENT

For evening entertainment, the ships each have a small casino; a combo entertaining in the nightclub adjacent to the show lounge; a pianist in another lounge; and dozens of in-cabin movies, including oldies and current films. At press time, the small-scale song-and-dance revues that had been offered in the two-level show lounges were being phased out, with the line trying a three-person magic act in its place. On other nights, performers include singers, instrumentalists, and jugglers. Cruise Director Steve Lewis told Heidi on a recent cruise that they were trying to experiment with different types of entertainment, as some guests weren't crazy about the glitzy production shows. Popular **theme cruises** from time to time feature classical musicians, guest chefs, and renowned wine experts conducting demonstrations and talks. The pace is calm, and that's the way most Silversea guests like it; most are perfectly content to spend their after-dinner hours with cocktails and conversation. Occasionally, depending on the crowd, the Panorama Lounge (on *Whisper*) or The Bar (on either ship) attracts a contingent of revelers who dance and drink into the wee hours.

SERVICE

Certified by the Guild of Professional English Butlers, the top suites include the services of a butler who will unpack your bags, draw your bath, make spa or dinner reservations, put together an in-suite cocktail party for you and the maharajah, or arrange a private car at the next port—as long as you cough up the bucks to stay in one of the ships' Grand, Royal, Rossellini, or Owner's suites.

Even if you're not in a top suite, though, the gracious staff knows how to please. Staff members are friendly and remember your name, but are never obtrusive or pushy. Waitstaff and stewards are as discreet as the guests are, and chances are you'll never hear the word *no*. The room-service menu is extensive and at dinnertime you can also order from The Restaurant's menu and have it served in your suite course by course. Unlimited wines, champagne, spirits, and soft drinks are included in the rates, as are gratuities. Hot and cold canapés are served in the lounges before dinner, and Godiva chocolates are left on suite pillows on formal evenings. For an extra charge ($100–$150 per person), you can take advantage of flexible embarkation and debarkation, getting into your suite as early as 10:30am on embarkation day and debarking as late as 5pm on the last day.

Laundry and **dry cleaning** are available. There are also **self-service laundry** rooms.

Silver Shadow

The Verdict

This is the most handsome, well-run ship you can find in the ultraluxe market—absolutely as good as it gets for fine cuisine, service, and suites.

Silver Shadow *(photo: Silversea Cruises)*

Specifications

Size (in tons)	28,258	Crew	295
Passengers (double occ.)	382	Passenger/Crew Ratio	1.3 to 1
Passenger/Space Ratio	72.8	Year Launched	2000
Total Cabins/Veranda Cabins	194/157	Last Refurbishment/Upgrade	2007

Frommer's Ratings (Scale of 1–5)

★★★★★

Cabin Comfort & Amenities	5	Dining Options	5
Appearance & Upkeep	5	Gym, Spa & Sports Facilities	4
Public Comfort/Space	5	Children's Facilities	N/A
Decor	5	Enjoyment Factor	5

With *Silver Shadow* and her sister ship, *Silver Whisper* (which is sailing in Europe and Asia for '08), Silversea set the bar very high for the rest of the ultraluxe lines. They're small enough to be intimate, but large enough to offer a classy two-story show lounge, dark and romantic cigar lounge, three dining venues, an impressive spa and gym, and some really great suites, in addition to the fine service and cuisine offered fleetwide.

Cabins & Rates

Cabins	Per Diems From	Sq. Ft.	Fridge	Hair Dryer	Sitting Area	TV
Suite	$425	287–1,435*	yes	yes	yes	yes

* Includes balconies.

CABINS The suites aboard *Silver Shadow* leave nothing to be desired. With a chilled bottle of Pommery Brut Royal at your side, just settle down in the comfy sitting area and bask in the ambient luxury. Private balconies are attached to three-quarters of the plush staterooms, which measure a roomy 287 square feet or more. They're done up in an ultrapleasant color scheme focused on rich blues and soft golds, along with coppery-brown wood tones. Each suite has a walk-in closet, minibar, DVD player, sitting area, lighted dressing table with hair dryer, writing desk, and wonderful marble-covered bathrooms stocked with Acqua di Palma or Bulgari toiletries (the stewardess comes around at the beginning of the cruise to ask your preference). The separate shower stall and long bathtub, along with double sinks, make these among the best loos at sea; only Regent's *Seven Seas Navigator* and *Voyager* have bathrooms this good. All beds have feather-down pillows and duvets, and Egyptian cotton linens. The largest of the four two-bedroom Grand Suites are really something else, measuring 1,435 square feet with three bathrooms, a pair of walk-in closets, an entertainment center, two verandas, and a living room and dining area. By year-end 2007, all suites are slated to get new flatscreen televisions and plusher mattresses and bedding.

PUBLIC AREAS The low-key main lobby area, where the purser's desk resides, branches out into a pair of attractive four-deck-high staircases, with shiplike railings, and corridors done in a mix of Wedgwood blue and golden peach fabrics and carpeting, along with warm caramel wood tones. The impressive two-story show lounge has tiered seating and lots of cozy clusters of chairs, while The Bar, just outside the show lounge's first level, can be a social hub, with a long bar, dance floor, and plenty of seating. The Observation Lounge, high on Deck 10 overlooking the bow, is a great place to relax, read, and watch the scenery unfold through floor-to-ceiling windows. You'll find a radar screen, astronomical maps, binoculars, and reference books, and, during the day, a self-service coffee, tea, and juice bar. On Deck 8 at the stern, the windowed Panorama Lounge also affords great sea views and lots of comfortable seating. By day, enjoy a continental breakfast or high tea here, while by night the venue becomes an intimate nightspot, with a pianist serenading dancers. The Humidor cigar lounge is a dark, cozy, and plush spot for cocktails—even nonsmokers can't help but be drawn to the ambience, while cigar lovers should enjoy the walk-in humidor. There's also a small casino and attached bar, a card room with felt-topped tables, a boutique, and a pool bar.

DINING OPTIONS In The Restaurant, the main dining room, a live trio plays romantic oldies on some nights, and guests are invited to take a spin around the small dance floor. There are plenty of tables for two, though during popular times you may have a short wait. Breakfast, lunch, and dinner are served here in high style, while a more casual buffet-style breakfast and lunch are offered in the indoor/outdoor La Terrazza. Service is doting even in the casual venue, with waiters rushing to carry plates to your table, serve drinks, and clear things off just moments after you finish. A special pasta dish is made to order by a chef for guests who do lunch in La Terrazza. Come evenings, it serves a wonderful Italian menu; reservations are required. A third venue offers special wine-pairing menus (see "Dining," above) in an intimate setting on Deck 7 next to the Terrace Cafe.

POOL, FITNESS, SPA & SPORTS FACILITIES A combination of old-style wooden deck chairs and plastic chaise longues padded with royal blue cushions line the open decks. Unfortunately, jolting grass-green AstroTurf covers the entirety of decks 9 and 10 (they could have at least chosen a teak-colored synthetic flooring). There are plenty of places to retire with a good book or for an afternoon snooze, either near the pool and hot tubs on Deck 8 (which is teak, by the way) or at the stern on that deck. There's also a golf driving cage and shuffleboard.

The spa, gym, and hair salon occupy much of Deck 10, and are spacious for a ship of this size. There's a separate workout room with exercise machines, plus a separate aerobics room. The spa features a pleasant subtle Asian decor, but you'll hardly notice once you're under the spell of the masseuse.

Silver Cloud • Silver Wind

The Verdict

Big enough to offer a two-story show lounge and several other entertainment outlets, and cozy enough that you'll feel like you practically have the vessel to yourself, *Silver Cloud* and *Silver Wind* are absolute dreams.

Silver Wind *(photo: Silversea Cruises)*

Specifications

Size (in tons)	16,800	Year Launched	
Passengers (double occ.)	296	*Cloud*	1994
Passenger/Space Ratio	56.8/57.2	*Wind*	1995
Total Cabins/Veranda Cabins	148/110	Last Refurbishment/Update	
Crew	210	*Cloud*	2007
Passenger/Crew Ratio	1.4 to 1	*Wind*	2003

Frommer's Ratings (Scale of 1–5)   ★★★★★

Cabin Comfort & Amenities	4	Dining Options	4
Appearance & Upkeep	4	Gym & Spa Facilities	4
Public Comfort/Space	4	Children's Facilities	N/A
Decor	4	Enjoyment Factor	5

Both super-intimate and large enough to have multiple entertainment venues, two restaurants, and lots of outdoor deck space, sister ships *Silver Cloud* and *Silver Wind* were built in the mid-1990s, just in time to get in on must-have ship fashions such as balconies.

Cabins & Rates

Cabins	Per Diems From	Sq. Ft.	Fridge	Hair Dryer	Sitting Area	TV
Suite	$455	240–1,314*	yes	yes	yes	yes

* Includes balconies.

CABINS   Like her fleetmates, *Silver Wind* is an all-suite ship, with balconies on more than three-quarters of the staterooms. All 148 suites have sitting areas, roomy walk-in closets, bathtubs, vanities, TVs and DVD players, stocked minibars, and

Acqua di Palma or Bulgari toiletries; while the top of the lot, the Grand Suites, have two bedrooms, two living rooms, three televisions, two bathrooms, and a full-size Jacuzzi tub. Color schemes revolve around creamy beige fabrics and golden brown wood. Swirled peachy-gray marble covers bathrooms from head to toe, and though indulgent enough, the bathrooms don't hold a flame to the larger, simply decadent loos on newer fleetmate *Silver Shadow*. Goose-down pillows ensure a good night's rest.

PUBLIC AREAS Public areas inside and out are spacious and open. High tea is served by day in the windowed Panorama Lounge, which at night hosts piano entertainment. Magic and other acts are performed in the attractive two-story show lounge, and, on most nights, a dance band plays oldies or a DJ spins in the intimate and dimly lit adjacent bar. There's a small casino, too, plus boutiques where you can spend your winnings, including a fine jewelry shop with the requisite gold and diamond-studded watches. An observation lounge is positioned on the far-forward part of a top deck and is oddly not attached to the ship's interior, so you must go out on deck to enter.

DINING OPTIONS The formal, open-seating dining venue, called The Restaurant, is delicately decorated in pale pink and gold, and elegant candlelit tables are set with heavy crystal glasses, chunky Christofle silverware, and doily-covered silver show plates. The indoor/outdoor La Terrazza cafe, where buffet-style breakfast and lunch are served, is transformed into a nightly venue for more casual evening dining, featuring a scrumptious Italian menu created under the guidance of chef Marco Betti.

POOL, FITNESS & SPA FACILITIES There is a pool and two hot tubs. The oceanview gym is compact, but adequate for a ship of this size, though tall folks should beware of the low ceiling when considering a go on the treadmill. The small spa offers a variety of massages and facials.

8

Small Ships, Sailing Ships & Adventure Cruises

Aside from the fact that they both sail in water, mainstream cruise ships and the small ships in this chapter have hardly anything in common. Whereas big ships allow you to see a region while immersed in a resortlike onboard atmosphere, small ships allow you to see it from the waterline, without distraction from anything that's not an inherent part of the locale—no glitzy interiors, no big shows or loud music, no casinos, no spas, and no crowds either, as the majority of these ships carry fewer than 100 passengers. Whether sailing through Alaska's coastal wilderness, along the Erie Canal or the Mississippi River, between tiny islands in the Caribbean or the Sea of Cortez, or from vineyard to vineyard in California's wine country, you're a part of your destination from the minute you wake up until the minute you fall asleep, and for the most part you're left alone to form your own opinions.

Of the lines reviewed in this chapter, most operate small, motorized **coastal and river cruisers** that are like floating B&Bs, with a main public lounge, a dining room, and little else besides cabins and open decks. A few of these lines also operate slightly larger ships with deep drafts that are suitable for longer open-sea cruises. Four of the lines we review—Star Clippers, Windstar, Windjammer Barefoot Cruises, and the independently owned schooners of the Maine Windjammer Association—operate honest-to-God **sailing ships,** the former two with a yachtlike vibe, the latter more like summer camps for adults.

Beyond these physical distinctions, the experience provided by all these lines breaks down into two main subcategories.

1. **Soft-adventure cruises** are more or less the anticruise, dispensing with the whole "spend a few hours in port, see the sights, do some shopping" tropism. Instead, these ships often stick entirely to wilderness areas, only occasionally making a port call, and then usually at tiny, out-of-the-way towns. The primary focus is on outdoor activities such as hiking, kayaking, tide-pooling, and snorkeling, with inflatable landing craft bringing passengers from ship to shore. Resident naturalists are usually on hand to explain what you're seeing. Lines that provide this kind of experience include Lindblad Expeditions, the Maine Windjammer Association, and (on a few of their vessels) Cruise West.

2. **Port-to-port cruises** tend to follow the cruise model a little more closely, interspersing days in port with days spent visiting great natural sites. Because of their shallow draft, though (the amount of ship below the waterline), these vessels aren't limited to big, deep-water ports, but can also visit small, out-of-the-way towns and villages. On board, the vibe is a less intense version of what you'll find on the soft-adventure lines, with passengers typically interested in bird-watching, botany,

marine life, and history. Lines providing this kind of trip include American Canadian Caribbean, American Cruise Lines, Majestic America Line, RiverBarge Excursions, and Star Clippers. American Safari Cruises straddles the adventure/port divide, offering a luxe trip that also includes a lot of time out in the wild.

Several lines are in categories of their own. **Windjammer Barefoot Cruises** operates a fleet of clunky, charming old sailing ships, primarily in the Caribbean and Central America. While its ships sail the same kind of itineraries as the other port-to-port lines, there's not as much focus on outdoor or enrichment-type activities—just the occasional casual hike, snorkeling session, or beach volleyball game. The line's passengers are mostly out to have a good time—and what's wrong with that? **Windstar** is more like a standard premium or pseudo-luxe cruise experience, visiting a mix of large and small ports most days.

There are also a handful of ships that sail what might be called **expedition cruises,** though for the most part these operate in Antarctica and other regions not covered in this book. Cruise West, though, has one vessel that sails from Alaska across the Bering Sea into the Russian Far East, taking in the Aleutian Islands and some little-visited parts of coastal Alaska in the process.

LOOK BEFORE YOU LEAP   The small-ship experience is not for everyone. Here are a few things to keep in mind:

- **For the most part, don't expect luxury:** With a handful of exceptions, most of the ships in this chapter are pretty basic. Food is usually good but not gourmet, and there's usually no room service. Cabins are generally very small and many lack amenities such as TVs or telephones.
- **If you're not a self-starter, stay away:** With the possible exception of Windjammer Barefoot, these ships aren't for people who need constant stimulation. On board, you're on your own to entertain yourself. Rather than the usual cruise song-and-dance, entertainment usually takes the form of informal lectures; occasional video presentations on wildlife, history, and culture; and maybe a crew talent show. And that's it.
- **Weak stomach? Think before you book:** As there are no stabilizers on most of these smaller ships, the ride can be bumpy in rough seas.
- **Check your bank balance, too:** You might think that because small ships lack the amenities of the megaships, their cruises would be cheaper—but you'd be dead wrong. With only a few exceptions (such as Windjammer Barefoot Cruises and the Maine Windjammers), you'll find weeklong trips starting from around $1,600 per person and going up, up, up. On the other hand, the onboard costs of these trips

---

The Scoop on Small-Ship Tonnage

When reading the reviews in this chapter, bear in mind that small-ship lines often measure their ships' **gross register tonnage** or GRTs (a measure of internal space, not actual weight) differently than the large lines. There's not even a definite standard within the small-ship market, so to compare ship sizes it's best to just look at the number of passengers aboard. Also note that where GRTs measures are nonstandard, **passenger/space measurements** are impossible or meaningless.

Frommer's Ratings at a Glance: The Ultraluxury Lines

1 = poor   2 = fair   3 = good   4 = excellent   5 = outstanding

Cruise Line	Enjoyment Factor	Dining	Activities	Children's Program	Entertainment	Service	Worth the Money
American Cruise Line	4	5	2	N/A	3	4	4
Cruise West	4	3	4	N/A	2	4	4
Lindblad Expeditions	5	4	5	N/A	2	4	4
Maine Windjammers•	5	3	3	N/A	2	3	5
Majestic America Line	5	4	4	3	5	4	4
Star Clippers	5	4	4	N/A	3	4	5
Windjammer Barefoot Cruises	4	3	3	3	3	3	5
Windstar	5	4	2	N/A	2	5	4

Note: Cruise lines have been graded on a curve that compares them only with the other lines in the Soft-Adventure and Sailing Ships category. See chapter 5 for the ratings methodology. Few of the lines and vessels in this chapter offer a children's program. Lines we've covered in mini-reviews have not been rated.

* Because the Maine schooners are all owner-operated, programs vary significantly. These ratings should be taken only as a general indication of fleetwide quality.

(that is, everything not covered by your cruise fare) tend to be less. Whereas megaship passengers may drop hundreds or even thousands on shore excursions, spa treatments, and all the other extras offered on ship and shore, small-ship passengers don't have to. Aside from alcohol, there's almost nothing aboard on which to spend money, even if you want to. More important, some lines include **shore excursions** in the base fare. On the more adventure-oriented ships, *all* off-ship activities may be included, so if you refrain from running up a bar tab, you could get through the week without ever dipping into your wallet, at least 'til it's time to tip the crew.

- **Most of these ships don't carry a doctor or nurse:** Because they mostly sail close to land, it's easy to get sick passengers to medical care ashore. Ships that do sail more far-flung itineraries carry medical staff.
- **Most aren't good for kids:** Of the ships in this chapter, only a few (aboard some Windjammer Barefoot and Majestic America vessels) ever have children's programs. A few others schedule some family-oriented sailings in high season, but most of these ships are so adult oriented that kids would be as out of place as Martians.
- **Most small ships are not appropriate for people with serious mobility problems:** Of the ships reviewed here, only the four American Cruise Lines ships, Cruise West's *Spirit of '98* and *Spirit of Oceanus,* and some of the Majestic America ships are fully or partially wheelchair friendly.

A NOTE ON LINE/SHIP RATINGS   Because the small-ship experience is so completely different from the megaship experience, we've had to adjust our ratings. For instance, because all but a tiny fraction of these ships have just one dining room for all meals, we can't judge them by the same standard we use for ships with 5 or 10 different restaurants. So, we've set the default **Dining Options** rating for these ships at

3, or "good," with points deducted if a restaurant is particularly uncomfortable and points added for any options above and beyond. Similarly, we've changed the "Gym & Spa Facilities" rating to **Adventure & Fitness Options** to reflect the fact that on small ships the focus is what's outside, not inside. Options covered in this category might include kayaks, trips by inflatable launch, bow-landing capability, an A-1 ice rating (allowing Arctic and Antarctic sailing), and frequent hiking, tide-pooling, and/or snorkeling trips.

DRESS CODES The word is *casual*. Depending on the region sailed, polo shirts, khakis or shorts, and a fleece pullover and Gore-Tex shell will pretty much take care of you all week. On Windjammer you could show up to dinner in your bathing suit and not feel out of place. On warm-weather cruises, consider bringing a pair of aqua-socks or rubber sandals, as you may be going ashore in rubber landing crafts and have to step out into the surf.

1 Mini-Review: American Canadian Caribbean Line

461 Water St., Warren, RI 02885. 🕿 800/556-7450 or 401/247-0955. Fax 401/247-2350. www.accl-smallships.com.

THE LINE IN A NUTSHELL A family-owned New England line, ACCL operates tiny, no-frills ships that attract a well-traveled, extremely casual, and down-to-earth older crowd. It's a "what you see is what you get" experience: friendly, homespun, and visiting places few other ships go. **Sails to:** U.S./Canada river/coastal cruises, Intracoastal Waterway, Caribbean, Central America.

THE EXPERIENCE ACCL began in 1966 when late Rhode Island shipbuilder Luther Blount realized there was a demand for small-ship sailing on the rivers, canals, and coast of New England and Canada. Over the years, his company's vessels have gone well beyond their regional home. Today, many of ACCL's almost universally older passengers (average age around 72) have sailed with the line before, and appreciate its casualness, its lack of glitz and gimmicks, its early-to-bed lifestyle, and its "just us folks" features such as a BYOB policy. (A real money saver for passengers, who can stock up in port and keep their bottles in the bar area, labeled with their cabin number. Tonic and soda are free.)

Built in 1997 and 1998, the line's two vessels—the 100-passenger twins *Grande Caribe* 🟊🟊🟊 and *Grande Mariner* 🟊🟊🟊—are as basic as cruise ships come, with tiny, spartan cabins; no-fuss decor; miniscule head-style cabin bathrooms; and only two public rooms (a lounge and a dining room). But no one expects luxury on these cruises. Instead, ACCL cruises are all about the real life of the regions it visits, with most activities oriented toward exploring ports and natural areas. Some 85% to 90% of cruises sail in domestic waters, concentrating on visits to historically rich Colonial ports and plant- and wildlife-rich natural areas. Innovative exploratory features aboard built into both ships help them go where few others can: a shallow draft and retractable wheelhouse that allow them to sail through shallow canals and under low bridges, bow ramps that allow them to pull right up to pristine dockless beaches, and a platform in the stern for swimming and launching the ships' glass-bottom boats.

Onboard activities and entertainment are usually limited to occasional informal lectures, a few printed quizzes, cooking demonstrations, card playing, and movies from the ship's video collection. Meals are well prepared and all-American, but limited and not terribly inspiring. The daily menu, with selections for all three meals, is posted

ACCL Fleet Itineraries

Ship	Itineraries
Grande Caribe	**Colonial America:** 11 nights, north- or southbound between Philadelphia, PA, and Alexandria, VA (Apr–May). **U.S. East Coast/Intracoastal Waterway:** 12 & 14 nights, south- or northbound between Philadelphia, PA, and Jacksonville, FL (May) and southbound between Warren, RI, and Jacksonville, FL (Nov). **Cape Cod & New England Islands:** 5 nights, round-trip from Warren, RI (June–Sept). **New England:** 5 nights, north- or southbound between Warren, RI, and Portland, ME (July–Aug). **Maine Coast:** 7 nights, round-trip from Portland, ME (July–Aug). **Erie Canal/Saguenay River:** 12 nights, round-trip from Warren, RI (Sept). **Northeast Fall Foliage:** 12 nights, round-trip from Warren, RI (Sept–Oct).
Grande Mariner	**Caribbean:** 11-night Virgin Islands, round-trip from St. Thomas (Jan–Mar). 11-night eastern/southern, north- or southbound between Antigua and St. Maarten (Jan–Feb). **Bahamas:** 11 nights, round-trip from Nassau (Mar). **U.S. Antebellum South:** 7 nights, north- or southbound between Jacksonville, FL, and Charleston, SC (Mar–Apr). **U.S. East Coast/Intracoastal Waterway:** 14 nights, Jacksonville, FL, to Warren, RI (Apr). **Great American Waterways:** 15 nights, east- or southbound between Chicago, IL, and Warren, RI (May–July & Sept). **Lake Michigan:** 6 nights, round-trip from Chicago, IL (June–Aug). **Erie Canal/Saguenay River:** 12 nights, round-trip from Warren, RI (Sept). **Northeast Fall Foliage:** 12 nights, round-trip from Warren, RI (Oct).

every morning on the blackboard in the dining room. There's only one entree per meal, so anyone wanting an alternative must notify the kitchen before 10am. Owing to the average passenger age, ACCL cooks try to keep things low in salt and fat. Service by the staff of young Americans (many from ACCL's home state of Rhode Island) is casual and friendly.

These ships won't appeal to the vast majority of young couples, singles, honeymooners, and families. Children under age 14 are prohibited, and the line offers no children's facilities or activities, nor any particularly active activities. Very tall people should also stay away, as ceilings on all ACCL ships are set at not much more than 6 feet 4 inches.

ACCL is one of the less expensive of the small-ship lines, with per diems usually starting around $215.

2 American Cruise Lines

741 Boston Post Rd., Suite 200, Guilford, CT 06437. ✆ 800/814-6880. www.americancruiselines.com.

THE LINE IN A NUTSHELL   Part cruise, part Rotary Club meeting, part historical tour, Connecticut-based American Cruise Lines operates four U.S.-flagged vessels with unusually large cabins, a congenial ambience, and an emphasis on American history and culture. Life on board is comfortable, reserved, and so hassle free many passengers don't even lock their cabin doors. If you want to bring a guest on board for dinner one night when in port, simply tell the cruise director. If you decide not to go on a shore excursion you signed up for, don't worry: If you don't show up, you don't get billed. **Sails to:** U.S. coastal cruises from Maine to Florida.

THE EXPERIENCE   Take some great East Coast destinations, throw in some very comfortable small ships, add a few enrichment lectures and complimentary cocktails and a boatload of uniformly older passengers, and you end up with American Cruise Lines. Operating exclusively along the eastern seaboard, the company's four ships are designed to poke into the smallest and most scenic ports, docking among sailboats at marinas or within a few blocks of museums, shops, and historic districts. Itineraries are port intensive, with the ship underway for only a few hours in the morning or afternoon, usually putting into the evening's port before dinnertime and spending the night at dock.

Not quite fancy enough to be considered luxury and not quite adventurous enough to be an expedition company, the company falls into a pleasant niche that succeeds in large part because its ships are far younger and roomier than the competition's, boasting the largest cabins in the small-ship market, many of them with balconies. This appeals to its passengers, who want the comforts of a shrunken cruise ship and will gladly pay for the extra space and slightly better service. A young crew tries hard and usually succeeds in the latter department, and their generational informality helps ensure that the experience never becomes too stuffy. Guest lecturers provide some enrichment, helping passengers learn about their destination, and chefs from the Culinary Institute of America provide good regional selections.

Pros

- **America the beautiful:** From Florida's Okeechobee Swamp to Maine's rocky coast, American Cruise Lines' ships sail wonderful coastal itineraries off-limits to larger, foreign-flagged ships, and spend every night in port.
- **Roomy rooms with a view:** Cabins are the largest by far in the small-ship category, and almost half of them feature balconies—a first for this type of coastal ship, and an exclusive to ACL. No other small-ship line offers them.
- **Have a drink:** The company tries for an upscale feel, and complimentary drinks go a long way in making the cruise seem a bit more luxurious than it really is.
- **Hassle? Not here:** American Cruise Lines works hard to keep things straightforward, relaxed, and sensible, even to the point of letting passengers invite friends on board for dinner. Everything that seems like it should be simple on other companies but isn't, is here.

Cons

- **A bit too staid:** In the end, the ships can be just a little too quiet, lacking the quirky charm of ACCL or the ever-so-slightly more active feel of Cruise West.
- **Limited activities:** While the ships are comfortable, there isn't much choice in activities—not even any nature hikes.

Compared with the other small-ship lines, here's how ACL rates:

	Poor	Fair	Good	Excellent	Outstanding
Enjoyment Factor				✓	
Dining					✓
Activities		✓			
Children's Program	N/A				
Entertainment			✓		
Service				✓	
Worth the Money				✓	

AMERICAN CRUISE LINES: HASSLE-FREE AMERICANA

If only every company got a second chance. Originally formed in the late 1970s, American Cruise Lines operated more or less successfully until being sold to a new owner, and by the late 1980s the company that had helped to pioneer coastal small-ship cruising had gone bankrupt. Jump forward to 2000, and the same original owner decides to do it again. Rather than reinventing the wheel, he uses the same name, the same basic ship design, similar itineraries, and even the same logo. This time around the formula seems to be working well and the company has grown quickly. Since its reincarnation, it's launched four ships built right in its own shipyard on the Chesapeake Bay.

Continuing with its expansion plans, ACL recently announced the formation of a sister company, **Pearl Seas Cruises** (© **800/983-7462;** www.pearlseascruises.com), whose first ship will sail foreign itineraries to the Caribbean, Nova Scotia, Newfoundland, and the St. Lawrence River beginning in 2008. Built in Canada and registered in the Marshall Islands, she'll be slightly larger and more luxurious than the ACL vessels, will more closely compete with the rest of the foreign-flagged small ships in this chapter, and will feature amenities missing on the ACL ships, including a spa.

PASSENGER PROFILE

Make no mistake about it: American Cruise Line passengers are older, and then some. The company's low-impact, cozy American style of cruising suits them perfectly, and the fact that each ACL ship has an elevator linking all the decks is one of the biggest draws. Hailing from all over the country, they generally appreciate changing for cocktail hour, with about half the men wearing a jacket or tie. They are also the types who readily wear the provided name tags for the entire week and don't mind visiting four historic homes in one cruise.

In port, slightly less than half tend to explore town independently, combing antiques shops for the perfect find or simply strolling along Main Street. Well educated and usually well heeled, they are eager to learn about the region and enthusiastically attend the nightly lecture. With diverse cruising backgrounds (from luxe Seabourn to mainstream Princess), they do not necessarily expect five-star service but they do want comfy, spacious cabins along with the conveniences and camaraderie of a small ship. A very high percentage consists of repeaters, who collect the line's various itineraries like game pieces.

DINING

Located on the lowest deck all the way at the stern, the pleasant but uninspiring dining room is surrounded on three sides by windows that afford a good view of the passing scenery. Since all the tables seat six, you end up meeting someone new every night, and it doesn't take long before you've dined with everyone on board.

The usually straightforward, unfancy meals can be surprisingly good, though quality can vary depending on the individual chef. Seafood frequently appears on the menu, with local specialties like Maryland crab cakes on Chesapeake Bay cruises or lobster in Maine being welcome additions, and seasonal flavors such as butternut squash or apple pie adding some spice. In order to minimize waste, waiters tell you at breakfast what's for lunch and dinner, and you choose what you're going to have to eat

ACL Fleet Itineraries

Ship	Itineraries
American Eagle	**U.S. East Coast/Intracoastal Waterway:** 14 nights, north- or southbound between Baltimore, MD, and Jacksonville, FL (Nov). 7-night mid-Atlantic inland passage, north- or southbound between Baltimore, MD, and Charleston, SC (May, June). **Chesapeake Bay:** 6 & 7 nights, round-trip from Baltimore, MD (June–Nov).
American Glory	**U.S. Antebellum South:** 7 nights, north- or southbound between Jacksonville, FL, and Charleston, SC (Apr–May & Nov–Dec). **U.S. East Coast/Intracoastal Waterway:** 10 & 14 nights, north- or southbound between Baltimore, MD, and Jacksonville, FL (Apr–May & Nov). 7-night mid-Atlantic inland passage, north- or southbound between Charleston, SC, and Baltimore, MD (May). **Chesapeake Bay:** 6 & 7 nights, round-trip from Baltimore, MD (May–June & Nov). **Hudson River Fall Foliage:** 6 & 7 nights, round-trip from New York, NY (Sept–Oct). **Great Rivers of Florida:** 7 nights, round-trip from Jacksonville, FL (Feb–Mar & Dec). **New England Islands:** 6 & 7 nights, round-trip from Providence, RI (June–Sept). **New England:** 10 nights, north- or southbound between Providence, RI, and Bangor, ME (July–Aug). **Maine Coast:** 6 & 7 nights, round-trip from Bangor, ME (Aug–Sept).
American Spirit	**U.S. Antebellum South:** 7 nights, north- or southbound between Jacksonville, FL, and Charleston, SC (Mar–May & Nov–Dec). **U.S. East Coast/Intracoastal Waterway:** 14 nights, north- or southbound between Baltimore, MD, and Jacksonville, FL (May, Nov). 7-night mid-Atlantic inland passage, north- or southbound between Charleston, SC, and Baltimore, MD (May, Nov). **Chesapeake Bay:** 6 & 7 nights, round-trip from Baltimore, MD (May–June & Nov). **Hudson River Fall Foliage:** 6 & 7 nights, round-trip from New York, NY (Oct). **Great Rivers of Florida:** 7 nights, round-trip from Jacksonville, FL (Nov–Dec). **New England Islands:** 6 & 7 nights, round-trip from Providence, RI (June–Sept).
American Star	**U.S. Antebellum South:** 7 nights, north- or southbound between Jacksonville, FL, and Charleston, SC (Apr–May & Nov–Dec). **U.S. East Coast/Intracoastal Waterway:** 14 nights, north- or southbound between Baltimore, MD, and Jacksonville, FL (May, Nov). 7-night mid-Atlantic inland passage, north- or southbound between Charleston, SC, and Baltimore, MD (May, Nov). **Chesapeake Bay:** 6 & 7 nights, round-trip from Baltimore, MD (May, Oct). **Hudson River Fall Foliage:** 6 & 7 nights, round-trip from New York, NY (Oct). **Great Rivers of Florida:** 7 nights, round-trip from Jacksonville, FL (Nov–Dec). **New England Islands:** 6 & 7 nights, round-trip from Providence, RI (June). **Maine Coast:** 6 & 7 nights, round-trip from Bangor, ME (June–Sept).

for the rest of the day—although at the last minute plenty change their mind, or can't remember what they ordered. Surprisingly there are only two entrees available, but three appetizers.

Lunch options might include a ham sandwich on a baguette with apples and melted brie or pork loin with goat cheese and onion. While there is no official vegetarian choice, tasty salads often appear on the menu, and special requests can always be accommodated if you let the line know in advance.

SNACKS & EXTRAS While the fresh-baked cookies that appear at 10am are a welcome delight and a favorite conversation topic, the real highlight of everyone's day is the 5:30pm cocktail hour. Almost without exception, everyone tidies up and gathers in the main lounge for complimentary drinks and chatting. By 9pm, just as the lecture is finishing, trays of **root beer floats and ice-cream sundaes** appear. It doesn't matter that it's only 2 hours after dinner, and it's amazing how passengers in their 70s and 80s seem to drop a few decades when sipping ice cream through a straw.

The ship does not offer room service.

ACTIVITIES

Forget art auctions or poolside games; you won't even find such low-impact activities as dance lessons aboard these sedate ships. In the main lounge, passengers might be quietly playing a board game or reading, while in the two smaller lounges you're sure to find at least one game of bridge. Most passengers seem content to just sit quietly on deck or chat. **Guest lecturers** speak most evenings, and spend days pointing out passing sights. One night might also find a local musician brought on board for a concert, or bingo slotted in place of the nightly lecture. Besides an occasional documentary shown in the lounge, a tour of the ship's bridge, or a once-per-week teatime, there really aren't any other organized activities, although some summer itineraries may feature **kite flying** one afternoon from the stern. In port, about half the passengers choose the reasonably priced **shore excursions,** which are usually bus tours to museums, areas of natural beauty, or historic homes. Unusual or active excursions simply aren't offered, which is just fine for this crowd.

CHILDREN'S PROGRAM

This is a cruise line for older adults, so children are extremely rare. In summer, a very few families may sail on the New England itineraries, but the ships offer no kids program or activities.

ENTERTAINMENT

Entertainment is limited to the nightly lectures, the occasional entertainer brought on board for an evening to sing regional ballads, and a TV with satellite reception in the corner of the main lounge, tuned to football. Otherwise, that's it. This is a line for self-starters.

SERVICE

Because of the Passenger Vessel Services Act (which requires ships to be U.S. flagged and U.S. staffed if they want to sail all-U.S. itineraries; see p. 201), ACL's crews are all fresh-faced, college-age American kids. They aren't about to make shipping, or even waiting, their career, but they decided to try an unusual job for a summer while getting a chance to see part of their country. Mostly enthusiastic and genuine, they try hard and are eager to please, even if the finer points of service don't come naturally. Don't expect to find fine polished service or even a particularly formal atmosphere: Being addressed by your waiter as "Sweetie" every once in a while only adds to the charm. A more senior maitre d' keeps a watchful eye over the restaurant operations and keeps his relatively inexperienced crew on the right track.

Tipping can be charged to your onboard account, with a relatively steep recommended amount of $125 per person, per week.

American Eagle • Glory • Spirit • Star

The Verdict

Simple but comfortable, these ships were built to nestle into small coves and ports along the East Coast, and their large cabins, numerous balconies, and multiple lounges have really raised the standard for the U.S. coastal fleet.

American Spirit *(photo: ACL)*

Specifications

Size (in tons)		Crew	
Eagle/Glory	86*	*Eagle/Glory*	18
Spirit/Star	97*	*Spirit/Star*	26
Passengers (double occ.)		Passenger/Crew Ratio	
Eagle/Glory	49	*Eagle/Glory*	2.7 to 1
Spirit/Star	100	*Spirit/Star*	3.8 to 1
Passenger/Space Ratio		Year Launched	
Eagle/Glory	N/A*	*American Eagle*	2000
Spirit/Star	N/A*	*American Glory*	2002
Total Cabins/Veranda Cabins		*American Spirit*	2005
Eagle	28/6	*American Star*	2007
Glory	27/14	Last Major Refurbishment	N/A
Spirit/Star	48/27		

* See note on p. 324 regarding small-ship tonnage and passenger/space measurements.

Frommer's Ratings (Scale of 1–5)   ★★★½

Cabin Comfort & Amenities	5	Dining Options	3
Appearance & Upkeep	4	Adventure & Fitness Options	2
Public Comfort/Space	4	Children's Facilities	N/A
Decor	3	Enjoyment Factor	4

American Cruise Lines' four vessels were all built at the line's own shipyard in Salisbury, Maryland, and while they're a bit boxy on the outside, they're refreshingly large and comfortable within, with a simple and pleasant (if a bit dull) decor. Numerous floor-to-ceiling windows surround the main lounge, and everywhere you go there are large windows for viewing the passing scenery. Except for their size (the still-small *Spirit* and *Star* are twice as large as the tiny *Eagle* and *Glory*), the ships are virtually identical, right down to the carpet patterns and furniture. Many passengers find the greater intimacy of the smaller ships a plus, equating fewer passengers with smaller tour groups when in port. Others find that the larger complement of *Spirit* and *Star* means twice as many possibilities for striking up a friendship.

The ship's shallow drafts allow passage up small rivers straight into the heart of town, where port facilities might look like they were designed for a kayak rather than a cruise ship—in one port, we actually sent the ship's mooring lines to a tree in a park rather than to the usual iron bollards. This attitude of keeping things simple extends on board as well. Forget electronic ID cards to get you on or off the ship; here, the crew just recognizes everyone. Rather than waiting for scheduled sailing times, the ships often just sail when everyone is back aboard. A small boat hung from the stern can be used to tender passengers ashore in the very rare ports where the ship doesn't dock. It's also occasionally used for bird-watching excursions.

Because the itineraries always hug the coast, there are rarely any waves or motion to speak of, so these cruises are popular with those who suffer from seasickness. On the occasional exposed sea passages, however, even the smallest waves make these unstabilized ships bounce around.

Cabins & Rates

Cabins	Per Diems From	Sq. Ft.	Fridge	Hair Dryer	Sitting Area	TV
Outside	$366	225	no	yes	no	yes

CABINS   If there is one thing that really differentiates American Cruise Lines from other coastal competitors, it's their cabins. Rather than the closet-sized boxes usually found on similarly sized American ships, these cabins average 225 square feet—bigger than standard megaships cabins, and nearly twice the size offered by main regional competitor American Canadian Caribbean. Cabins are comfortable, clean, and pleasant—not to mention bright, thanks to large picture windows that actually slide open or the narrow but serviceable balconies (you get one or the other)—but like the public areas, their decor isn't exactly stylish. Each comes with a large writing desk, decent storage, bedside tables, and a satellite TV that gets about 20 channels. Bathrooms are very roomy, with excellent water pressure. Cabins on the older *Eagle* and *Glory* are a touch smaller than those on the newer ships, especially on the forward end of the lowest deck, where the curvature of the bow reduces square footage.

Each ship has several cabins for solo passengers (a real rarity these days) as well as at least one that's wheelchair accessible. Each ship also has an elevator, giving wheelchair-using passengers access to the entire ship.

PUBLIC AREAS   Three public lounges (one large enough for everyone aboard, the other two smaller, cabin-sized reading rooms) and plenty of open deck space provide passengers plenty of elbowroom. All are decorated in the same simple, muted colors and functional, unpretentious furniture, all of it attractive without being exciting. The main lounge is located forward, directly underneath the bridge, and has tall windows on three sides that provide great views. As the venue for the nightly cocktail hour and the evening lecture, it is the ship's social hub and a good spot for board games or chatting during the day. Just forward of the lounge is a small deck with a few chairs and tables, allowing you to imbibe outdoors while watching the sunset.

An important component of the ship's spacious feel is the two smaller, cabin-sized lounges located by the central stairwell. These allow smaller groups the opportunity to mingle before dinner or play bridge at any time without being bothered by others.

The very top of each ship is covered in an AstroTurf-like material and sports awnings, plastic-webbed sun lounges, and tables and chairs. On warm, sunny days, this deck is a great spot for reading and chatting, with attractive shorelines and small communities often within view.

DINING OPTIONS   Each ship's single dining room is located on the lowest deck all the way at the stern, with windows on three sides. Breakfast usually runs from 7:30am to 9am, preceded by early-risers' coffee and muffins, which are set out in the main lounge at 6:30am. Lunch is timed to start shortly after the shore excursion returns, usually around 12:30pm. Dinner is served at 6:30pm, following the cocktail hour.

ADVENTURE & FITNESS OPTIONS   Exercise equipment is limited to a single exercise bike and a StairMaster. Most passengers get their exercise by going ashore independently and walking the towns.

3 Mini-Review: American Safari Cruises

19221 36th Ave. W., Suite 208, Lynnwood, WA 98036. *©* **888/862-8881.** Fax 425/776-8889. www.amsafari.com.

THE LINE IN A NUTSHELL   American Safari Cruises offers one of the most luxurious and yet adventurous experiences in the small-ship market—and also one of the most expensive. **Sails to:** Alaska and British Columbia, Sea of Cortez/Baja, U.S./Canada coastal/river cruises.

THE EXPERIENCE   Unlike the competition's mostly basic vessels, American Safari's three ships—12-passenger *Safari Spirit* ✦✦✦✦ and *Safari Escape* ✦✦✦✦ and the 22-passenger *Safari Quest* ✦✦✦✦—are honest-to-God yachts bathing passengers in plush comfort, with homey lounges, hot tubs, and large cabins. Everything except gratuities is included in the pricey base price, including alcoholic beverages and shore excursions. The always-casual onboard vibe is in keeping with mostly middle-aged passengers who tend to be wealthy granola types looking to bond with nature without sacrificing luxury. Some days are spent kayaking in the wilderness (kayaks and inflatable launches are carried on board) and others visiting small ports of call, sometimes overnighting there for a taste of the local nightlife. Expedition leaders accompany passengers on off-vessel exploration, and in Alaska, you might take out a Zodiac boat or kayak to investigate shoreline black bears or river otters, or to navigate fjords packed with ice floes and lolling seals. Expeditions include trips to boardwalked cannery towns, Tlingit villages, and tiny villages.

Cabins are comfortable and have TV/DVDs. *Spirit* has the largest cabins and is considered the most luxurious of the fleet. Best accommodations are the Admiral's Cabins, which have large picture windows, a small sitting area, plus other features such as a cedar-lined sauna or small step-out balcony with sliding glass door (two cabins have balconies on *Spirit* and four on *Quest*). The main lounge is the social center of each ship, a place for guests to relax, listen to an informal lecture by the ship's naturalist, play a game of cards or Scrabble, or watch a movie from the ship's library on the big-screen TV. There's a hot tub up on deck and a couple of fitness machines for those who want to work out. For dining, all meals are served family-style on a burnished mahogany table in a casual room on *Spirit* and *Escape,* and at a cluster of round tables on *Quest,* usually when the ship is at anchor.

American Safari is one of the most expensive of the small-ship lines, with per diems starting at upward of $500.

American Safari Cruises Fleet Itineraries

Ship	Itineraries
Safari Escape	**Alaska:** 8-night Inside Passage, north- or southbound between Prince Rupert, BC, and Juneau, AK (May–Sept). 14 nights, north- or southbound between Seattle, WA, and Juneau, AK (Apr & Sept).
Safari Quest	**Alaska:** 7-night Inside Passage, north- or southbound between Sitka and Juneau, AK (May–Aug). 14 nights, Juneau, AK, to Seattle, WA (Sept). **Baja/Sea of Cortez:** 7 nights (Jan–Mar & Nov–Dec) and 9 nights (Apr), round-trip from Loreto, Mexico.
Safari Spirit	**Alaska:** 7-night Inside Passage, north- or southbound between Petersburg and Juneau, AK (May–Aug). 14 nights, north- or southbound between Seattle, WA, and Juneau, AK (May & Sept). **Columbia & Snake Rivers/Pacific Northwest:** 8 nights, east- or westbound between Astoria, OR, and Lewiston, ID (Sept–Nov).

4 Cruise West

2301 5th Ave., Suite 401, Seattle, WA 98121. (✆ 800/426-7702 or 206/441-8687. Fax 206/441-4757. www.cruise west.com.

THE LINE IN A NUTSHELL   Family-owned Cruise West has been the preemi-nent small-ship line in Alaska for decades, but over the past 10 years it's also branched out to Central America, Mexico, the California wine country, Asia, the U.S. East Coast and Great Lakes, and the Caribbean. Most of its itineraries are port-to-port and geared to older, well-traveled, intellectually curious passengers. There are also a hand-ful of more expeditionary sailings on the deep-water *Spirit of Oceanus.* **Sails to:** Alaska, Central America/Caribbean, Sea of Cortez/Baja, U.S./Canada river/coastal cruises (plus South Pacific, Asia).

THE EXPERIENCE   Like all small ships, Cruise West's nine vessels can navigate tight waterways, visit tiny ports, and scoot up close to shore for wildlife watching. The majority of their cruises are casual, relaxed, port-to-port trips in which passengers watch nature from the deck rather than trekking out into it. On most cruises, a quick excursion by inflatable launch is as active as it gets. At sea, the lack of organized activ-ities leaves you free to scan for wildlife, peruse the natural sights, talk to the other guests, or read. In port—whether one of the large, popular ports or a less visited one—the line offers a good slate of shore excursions oriented mostly to nature and history.

Cruise West also offers some more outdoors-oriented and exploratory cruises. Its flagship, the 114-passenger *Spirit of Oceanus,* sails 13- and 24-night Bering Sea/Russ-ian Far East expedition cruises that are among the most far-ranging in the small-ship category, taking in Siberian native communities and incredibly remote islands off the Alaskan coast. Closer to home, "Wilderness Inside Passage" trips concentrate on Alaska's outdoors, with most days spent either in wilderness areas or visiting tiny towns such as Elfin Cove, population 32.

Pros

- **The staff:** The line's friendly, enthusiastic staffs are a big plus, making guests feel right at home.
- **Comfort and old-fashioned style:** Two of the line's ships—the oceangoing *Spirit of Oceanus* and the *Spirit of '98,* a re-creation of a late-19th-century coastal steamer—offer snazzier surroundings than most of their small-ship competitors.

Cons

- **Limited adventure:** Most Cruise West trips are geared to older passengers, so don't book if you're looking for a serious adventure cruise.

CRUISE WEST: ALASKA'S SMALL-SHIP LEADER & THEN SOME

Cruise West is the legacy of Chuck West, a man who arrived in Alaska after serving as a pilot in World War II, liked what he saw, and decided to share it with others. After offering the first flightseeing tours above the Arctic Circle, he went on to found Alaska's first hotel chain and first motorcoach sightseeing line; then in the mid-1980s he started experimenting with cruises, and the rest is history. Chuck West died in October 2005 (R.I.P., Mr. Alaska), but his company—now the largest small-ship line in America—is still run by his son Dick, and it's still growing: In January 2006, Cruise West acquired INTRAV's two U.S.-flagged coastal ships, *Nantucket Clipper* and *Yorktown Clipper* (now renamed *Spirit of Glacier Bay* and *Spirit of Yorktown*), from now-defunct Clipper Cruise Line, allowing it to expand its reach to the U.S. East Coast, the Great Lakes, and the Caribbean.

PASSENGER PROFILE

Passengers with Cruise West tend to be in the higher end of the 50-to-75 age demographic, financially stable, well educated, and intellectually curious. Many have sailed with the mainstream lines but came to Cruise West because they wanted to visit Alaska's ports and see its natural wonders in a relaxed, dress-down atmosphere. When we sailed last, our fellow passengers included two vacationing State Department employees, several teachers, a retired bank president, and a magazine art director. On another cruise, the passenger list included a group of 30-odd Yale alumni, including one 80-something lady from New Haven who was set on doing every active shore excursion she could—hiking, kayaking, the lot. Ditto for a 40-ish couple from Pennsylvania we met in 2003, who, in between activities, had a list of local experiences they were bent on sampling, including one delicacy known as halibut cheeks.

DINING

Breakfast, lunch, and dinner are served at set times at one unassigned seating. An early riser's buffet is set out in the lounge before the set breakfast time, but if you're a late riser you'll miss breakfast entirely, as no room service is available. At all meals the fare is home-style American—not overly fancy, but varied enough. Chefs make a point of stocking up on fresh seafood while in port. **Vegetarian options** aren't particularly notable, but are offered at every meal, as are **heart-healthy entrees** and staple favorites

Compared with the other small-ship lines, here's how Cruise West rates:

	Poor	Fair	Good	Excellent	Outstanding
Enjoyment Factor				✓	
Dining			✓		
Activities				✓	
Children's Program	N/A				
Entertainment		✓			
Service				✓	
Worth the Money				✓	

Cruise West Fleet Itineraries

Ship	Itineraries
Pacific Explorer	**Costa Rica/Panama:** 9 nights, between Colón and Los Sueños (Jan–Apr & Nov–Dec).
Spirit of Alaska	**Alaska:** 8-night wilderness Inside Passage, round-trip from Juneau, AK (June–Aug). 10 nights, north- or southbound between Seattle, WA, and Juneau (May & Sept).
Spirit of Columbia	**Alaska:** 3- & 4-night Prince William Sound, round-trip from Whittier/Anchorage (May–Aug). 10 nights, north- or southbound between Seattle, WA, and Juneau (May & Sept).
Spirit of Discovery	**Columbia & Snake Rivers:** 7 nights, round-trip from Portland, OR (Apr & Sept–Oct). **Alaska:** 8-night wilderness Inside Passage, round-trip from Juneau, AK (June–Aug). 10 nights, north- or southbound between Seattle, WA, and Juneau (May & Sept).
Spirit of Endeavour	**British Columbia:** 7 night, round-trip from Seattle, WA (Sept). **Alaska:** 8-night Inside Passage, north- or southbound between Ketchikan and Juneau (May–Sept). 10 nights, north- or southbound between Seattle, WA, and Juneau (May & Sept).
Spirit of Glacier Bay	**Alaska:** 3- & 4-night Inside Passage/Glacier Bay, round-trip from Juneau, AK (May–Aug). 10 nights, north- or southbound between Seattle, WA, and Juneau (May & Sept).
Spirit of '98	**Alaska:** 8-night Inside Passage, north- or southbound between Ketchikan and Juneau (May–Sept). 10 nights, north- or southbound between Seattle, WA, and Juneau (May & Sept). **Columbia & Snake Rivers:** 7 nights, round-trip from Portland, OR (Apr & Sept–Oct).
Spirit of Oceanus	**South Pacific:** 16 nights, between Guam and Fiji (Jan & Mar). 12 nights, between Fiji and Papeete, Tahiti (Jan–Feb). 11 nights, round-trip from Papeete, Tahiti (Feb). **Japan:** 11 nights (Apr–May & October), round-trip from Kobe. **Alaska:** 12-night coastal odyssey, north- or southbound between Vancouver, BC, and Whittier/Anchorage, AK (May & Sept). 24-night Inside Passage/Gulf of Alaska/Alaska west coast, north- or southbound between Vancouver, BC, and Nome, with connecting flight to Anchorage (May & Sept). **Alaska/Siberia:** 13-night Bering Sea, Whittier/Anchorage to Nome, AK (May–Sept). **Japan/Kuril Islands:** 20-night Ring of Fire, from Anchorage, AK, to Tokyo (Sept).
Spirit of Yorktown	**Baja/Sea of Cortez:** 7 nights, round-trip from Cabo San Lucas (Jan–Mar & Dec). **Alaska:** 8-night Inside Passage, north- or southbound between Ketchikan and Juneau (May–Sept). 10 nights, north- or southbound between Seattle, WA, and Juneau (May & Sept). **California Wine Country:** 3 & 4 nights, round-trip from San Francisco, CA (Sept–Oct).

such as steak, chicken, and fish. With advance notice, the galley can accommodate other special diets (kosher, low-salt, low-fat). Aboard all ships, a buffet-style lunch and/or dinner may be served on the top deck in good weather. *Spirit of Oceanus* has an outdoor buffet restaurant that serves breakfast and lunch daily.

SNACKS & EXTRAS   A late-afternoon snack is provided every day to tide passengers over until dinner, and the chef will occasionally whip up a batch of cookies. Pretzels, nuts, and other crunchy snack foods are usually left out in the lounge/bar, where there's also a 24-hour coffee/tea/cocoa station.

ACTIVITIES

As with most small ships, Cruise West vessels don't offer much in the way of onboard diversions. What activities there are may include **post-dinner discussions** of the port or region to be visited the next day, **afternoon talks** by expert guests while at sea, and perhaps a tour of the bridge or galley. Onboard fitness options are limited to walking around the open decks (except aboard *Oceanus,* which has a small gym). Along with a full slate of extra-cost excursions, one **complimentary shore excursion** is offered at each port. Sometimes they're very worthwhile—as at the Alaska Native town of Met-lakatla, where passengers are treated to a wonderful performance by a Native music and dance troupe, or on the California wine country cruises, which include luncheons and tours at various wineries. Other times, though, they're just short bus trips.

Occasionally, expedition leaders will take passengers for a spin in the ships' inflatable **Zodiac boats,** getting close in to shore. **Kayaking** is also available on some itineraries.

At least one and sometimes two **"expedition leader" naturalists** accompany each trip to answer passengers' questions about flora, fauna, geology, and history, and other experts are brought aboard at various ports to add to the experience. On Columbia and Snake river itineraries, for instance, a Nez Perce poet and storyteller comes aboard to talk about the region's Native peoples. *Spirit of Oceanus*'s longer itineraries sail with several historians, naturalists, and cultural experts, who provide numerous in-depth lectures throughout the cruise.

CHILDREN'S PROGRAM

No children's program is available.

ENTERTAINMENT

As is standard on small-ship lines, entertainment is almost nonexistent, and what you do get will be catch-as-catch-can. One evening the crew might put on a **talent show** featuring skits, music, magic, and whatever else they can drum up. Passengers sometimes get involved. Another evening, during dinner, passengers might be set the task of creating art from whatever's on their tables, with the winning table getting a bottle of wine for their effort. Some cruises also bring local musicians and dancers aboard to perform. *Pacific Explorer, Spirit of Endeavor, Spirit of '98,* and *Spirit of Oceanus* have TV/VCRs in their cabins and a shelf of videos in the lounge for passengers to take at will. *Spirit of Oceanus, Spirit of '98, Spirit of Glacier Bay,* and *Spirit of Yorktown* all have pianos in their lounges for passenger use.

SERVICE

The line strives for a family feeling, employing young, energetic crews composed mostly of American college students. Crewmembers do double and triple duty, waiting tables at breakfast, making beds and cleaning cabins, polishing the handrails, and unloading baggage at the end of the trip. They may not be consummate pros, but they do go out of their way to learn your name and offer personal service. Passengers tend to find them adorable. Crews aboard *Spirit of Oceanus* and *Pacific Explorer* are international. Laundry service is available only on *Spirit of Oceanus* and *Pacific Explorer.*

Spirit of Oceanus

The Verdict

Spirit of Oceanus is one of the most luxurious small ships in the market, an ocean cruiser able to sail far-flung itineraries in style and comfort. Her cabins are downright huge.

Spirit of Oceanus *(photo: Cruise West)*

Specifications

Size (in tons)	4,500	Crew	59
Passengers (double occ.)	114	Passenger/Crew Ratio	2 to 1
Passenger/Space Ratio	39.5	Year Launched	1991
Total Cabins/Veranda Cabins	57/12	Last Refurbishment/Upgrade	2001

Frommer's Ratings (Scale of 1–5)   ★★★★★

Cabin Comfort & Amenities	5	Dining Options	5
Appearance & Upkeep	4	Adventure & Fitness Options	5
Public Comfort/Space	5	Children's Facilities	N/A
Decor	5	Enjoyment Factor	5

The name says it all. Unlike all the other Cruise West ships, *Spirit of Oceanus* was built for sailing in open (rather than coastal) waters, allowing the line to offer more wide-ranging itineraries. The ship was launched in 1991 as *Renaissance V,* one of the original vessels of now-defunct Renaissance Cruises. She sailed briefly for Star Cruises before Cruise West bought and refurbished her in 2001. Today, she's the line's largest and most luxurious ship, with more public rooms, a small gym, an elevator, and even a hot tub on the top deck. Her decor is more private yacht than cruise ship, with corridors and cabins paneled in a glossy wood-look studded with gleaming brass work, and her cabins are absolutely massive. Her incredible 12- and 13-night Alaska Bering Sea/Russian Far East cruises (among the very best cruises we've ever taken) make the average Inside Passage cruise seem like a trip on the Circle Line. At the opposite pole of those Siberian outings, winters see the vessel sailing to the South Pacific and Japan.

Cabins & Rates

Cabins	Per Diems From	Sq. Ft.	Fridge	Hair Dryer	Sitting Area	TV
Outside	$540	215–250	yes	yes	yes	yes
Suite	$767	277–353	yes	yes	yes	yes

CABINS All 57 staterooms are outsides with picture windows or (in a few cases) large portholes, and range in size from 215 to 353 square feet, which ranks them among the largest in the small-ship world. Each has a couch, TV/VCR, minifridge, marble-topped vanity, walk-in closet or wardrobe, and comfortably sized bathroom. Decor is a far cry from the usual off-white walls and modular furnishings of most small ships. Instead, walls are paneled in dark, polished wood tones, with rich carpeting helping to create a yachtlike look. Twelve staterooms on Sun and Sports decks have private teak balconies, but the cabins themselves are actually smaller than those without balconies—what you gain in outside, you lose in inside.

Spirit of Oceanus is one of the few small ships with an elevator—a boon to folks with mobility problems—but no cabins are designed specifically for wheelchair users.

PUBLIC AREAS   Public rooms include the main Oceanus Lounge—the venue for frequent lectures and slide presentations by the ship's large staff of naturalists and historians—and the smaller Oceanus Club, a combo bar and reading room with a baby grand that gets infrequent use. Corner nooks in the Club are stocked with games, a small book and video library, and the ship's one public computer (for e-mailing only). On Alaska/Bering Sea trips, passengers go off-vessel most days via inflatable Zodiac landing boats, with rubber boots provided by the line. (Bring rain gear, though, as trips ashore are often wet.) Destination-specific activities are also built into the trip price on South Pacific and Japan itineraries.

DINING   All meals are served in single open seatings in the pleasantly decorated Pacifica Restaurant. Passengers can also take breakfast and lunch at the partially covered outdoor buffet on Sun Deck—a very pleasant perch in most weather, offering great views.

ADVENTURE & FITNESS OPTIONS   There's a small gym with free weights, a step machine, an exercise bike, and two treadmills. A hot tub is located outside, just behind the Bistro buffet. Several inflatable launches allow frequent off-vessel exploration.

Spirit of '98

The Verdict

Built as a replica of a 19th-century coastal steamer, *Spirit of '98* is one of the most distinctive small ships you'll ever see.

Spirit of '98 *(photo: Cruise West)*

Specifications

Size (in tons)	96*	Crew	23
Passengers (double occ.)	96	Passenger/Crew Ratio	4.2 to 1
Passenger/Space Ratio	N/A*	Year Launched	1984
Total Cabins/Veranda Cabins	49/0	Last Refurbishment/Upgrade	1995

* See note on p. 324 regarding small-ship tonnage and passenger/space measurements.

Frommer's Ratings (Scale of 1–5)   ✮✮✮✮

Cabin Comfort & Amenities	4	Dining Options	4
Appearance & Upkeep	4	Adventure & Fitness Options	2
Public Comfort/Space	4	Children's Facilities	N/A
Decor	4	Enjoyment Factor	5

The *Spirit of '98* is a time machine. Built in 1984 as a replica of a 19th-century steamship and extensively refurbished in 1995, it carries its Victorian flavor so well that some of the people we've met on board think the ship really is a hundred years old. If you want to get a look at her, rent Kevin Costner's movie *Wyatt Earp*, whose ending was filmed on board.

Cabins & Rates

Cabins	Per Diems From	Sq. Ft.	Fridge	Hair Dryer	Sitting Area	TV
Outside	$410	81–228	some	no	some	yes
Suite	$819	550	yes	no	yes	yes

CABINS   Cabins are comfortable and of decent size, continue the Victorian motif (except in their bathrooms), and feature TV/VCR combos. Deluxe cabins have a minifridge, a seating area, and a trundle bed to accommodate a third passenger. One Owner's Suite provides a spacious living room with meeting area, large bathroom with whirlpool tub, king-size bed, stocked bar with refrigerator, TV/VCR, stereo, and enough windows to take in all of Alaska at one sitting.

Cabin 309, located on the upper deck, is fully wheelchair accessible, and there's an elevator connecting most passenger decks, though it doesn't get up to the Sun Deck. Two cabins are for solo passengers.

PUBLIC AREAS   The Grand Salon is the ship's bar/lounge, with a suitably plinky-sounding player piano, a 24-hour tea/coffee station, and a small library and video shelf. The room continues the ship's 19th-century design theme with decorative ceiling tiles, balloon-back chairs, ruffled draperies, and plenty of polished woodwork and brass. Just aft of the dining room, a small bar called Soapy's Parlour (after legendary Skagway con man Soapy Smith) is used only at mealtimes, making it a good, quiet reading spot at other times. Out in the air, passengers congregate in the large bow area, on the open top deck (where staff will sometimes set up a bar on nice days), and at the railing in front of the bridge, which is open except when the ship is passing through rough water.

DINING OPTIONS   The Klondike Dining Room is beautifully decorated and large enough to seat all guests in booths and at round center tables.

ADVENTURE & FITNESS OPTIONS   The Upper Deck circles the ship, allowing walking for exercise. Inflatable launches allow off-vessel exploration.

In Central America with the *Pacific Explorer*

In addition to the ships profiled here, Cruise West also operates the 100-passenger *Pacific Explorer*. Launched in 1995 as the *Temptress Explorer* of Costa Rica's Temptress Adventures Cruises, the vessel was taken over by Cruise West in 1998 and now offers 7- and 9-night Costa Rica and Panama cruises, with prices starting around $4,650. *Pacific Explorer* cruises tend to be more active than most other Cruise West itineraries, with guided hikes, kayaking, and snorkeling excursions built into the rates.

Spirit of Yorktown • Spirit of Glacier Bay • Spirit of Endeavour

The Verdict

Low on frills and style but high on coziness and comfort, these ships all make a nice home base for a week of coastal cruising.

Spirit of Endeavor *(photo: Matt Hannafin)*

Specifications

Size (in tons)		Crew	
Glacier Bay	1,471	*Glacier Bay*	32
Yorktown	2,354	*Yorktown*	40
Endeavour	1,471	*Endeavour*	28
Passengers (double occ.)		Passenger/Crew Ratio	
Glacier Bay	102	*Glacier Bay*	3.2 to 1
Yorktown	138	*Yorktown*	3.5 to 1
Endeavour	102	*Endeavour*	3.6 to 1
Passenger/Space Ratio		Year Launched	
Glacier Bay/Endeavour	14.7	*Endeavour*	1983
Yorktown	17	*Glacier Bay*	1984
Total Cabins/Veranda Cabins		*Yorktown*	1988
Glacier Bay	51/0	Last Refurbishment/Upgrade	
Yorktown	69/0	*Glacier Bay/Yorktown*	2007
Endeavour	51/0	*Endeavour*	1999

Frommer's Ratings (Scale of 1–5)   ★★★½

Cabin Comfort & Amenities	3	Dining Options	3
Appearance & Upkeep	4	Adventure & Fitness Options	2
Public Comfort/Space	3	Children's Facilities	N/A
Decor	3	Enjoyment Factor	5

The impression we keep coming back to when discussing these ships is that someone took a Holland America or Princess vessel and shrunk it to one-fiftieth its normal size. Though not boasting the many bright public rooms of those large vessels, the four-deck *Spirit of Yorktown, Spirit of Glacier Bay,* and *Spirit of Endeavour* offer similar clean styling, with cozy cabins and lounges.

Spirit of Endeavour formerly sailed as the *Newport Clipper* of INTRAV/Clipper Cruise Line, so it was natural that in early 2006, when Clipper decided to sell its two remaining coastal ships (a first step on the way to its eventual dissolution), Cruise

West would bite. *Spirit of Glacier Bay* (the former *Nantucket Clipper*) is nearly identical to *Spirit of Endeavour,* while the former *Yorktown Clipper* is a slightly larger version of the same design, with more cabins.

Cabins & Rates

Cabins	Per Diems From	Sq. Ft.	Fridge	Hair Dryer	Sitting Area	TV
Outside	$385	93–204	some	some	no	some

CABINS Although generally smallish, cabins are pleasantly styled, with blond-wood writing desks, chairs, and bed frames; "better than a bare wall"–style paintings; and a goodly amount of closet space, plus additional storage under the beds. Beds are either permanently fixed into an L position (better for tall people) or set parallel to one another and abutted by wall and headboard. Some cabins have twin beds that can be pushed together to make a double, and some contain upper berths to accommodate a third person. Each ship has three or four extralarge cabins measuring 163 to 204 square feet. Cabin bathrooms are compact, with toilets wedged between the shower and sink area. Bathrooms have showers but no tubs.

All cabins have picture windows except for a handful of forward cabins on the Main Deck, which have portholes. All cabins on each ship's Promenade/Upper Deck and a handful at the stern on the Lounge Deck open onto the outdoors rather than onto an interior corridor. No leaving the doors open for fresh air, though: They open out.

There are no cabins suitable for travelers with disabilities, and no elevators between decks.

PUBLIC AREAS Each ship has four decks and only two indoor public areas: the dining room and the Observation Lounge. The pleasant lounge has big windows, a bar, a small library, a piano (on *Yorktown* and *Glacier Bay*), and enough space to comfortably seat everyone on board for lectures and meetings. It's the main hub of onboard activity.

DINING OPTIONS Each ship has a single large dining room down by the waterline, with windows on both sides. This was the spot from which we sighted our first bear on our last trip, midway through our main course. The captain obligingly made a U-turn, cut his engines, and let the ship drift within easy view for almost 30 minutes. Dessert was served after.

Snacks are offered in the lounge throughout the day, along with coffee, tea, and other drinks.

ADVENTURE & FITNESS OPTIONS The only onboard fitness options are walking or jogging around the deck. When anchored in calm, warm waters, you can sometimes go swimming and snorkeling right from the ship, courtesy of a small platform that's lowered into the water. Inflatable launches allow off-vessel exploration.

Spirit of Discovery • Spirit of Columbia • Spirit of Alaska

Spirit of Alaska *(photo: Cruise West)*

The Verdict

Utilitarian small ships that have been in service since the '70s, these three offer Cruise West's same intimate cruise experience, but the word of the day is *spartan*.

Specifications

Size (in tons)		Passenger/Crew Ratio	
Discovery	94*	*Discovery*	4 to 1
Columbia/Alaska	97*	*Columbia/Alaska*	3.7 to 1
Passengers (double occ.)		Year Launched	
Discovery	84	*Discovery*	1976
Columbia/Alaska	78	*Columbia*	1979
Passenger/Space Ratio	N/A*	*Alaska*	1980
Total Cabins/Veranda Cabins		Last Refurbishment/Upgrade	
Discovery	43/0	*Discovery*	1992
Columbia/Alaska	39/0	*Columbia/Alaska*	1995
Crew	21		

* See note on p. 324 regarding small-ship tonnage and passenger/space measurements.

Frommer's Ratings (Scale of 1–5)

★★★½

Cabin Comfort & Amenities	3	Dining Options	3
Appearance & Upkeep	4	Adventure & Fitness Options	2
Public Comfort/Space	3	Children's Facilities	N/A
Decor	3	Enjoyment Factor	5

Though of slightly dissimilar sizes and passenger capacities, these four vessels are extremely similar, all offering the friendly Cruise West experience, though in a somewhat plainer package than their fleetmates. Though they're older ships, all have been kept in good condition. *Alaska* and *Columbia* were originally built by Captain Luther Blount for his American Canadian Caribbean Line, and therefore share a problem common to all Blount vessels: They're not good choices for very tall people, as ceilings throughout are set at little more than 6 feet 4 inches, and many beds are too short for those 6 feet 2 inches or taller. On the other hand, both have Blount's patented bow ramp, which, in combination with their shallow draft, allows the ships to basically beach themselves, disembarking passengers right onto shore in wild areas without ports.

Cabins & Rates

Cabins	Per Diems From	Sq. Ft.	Fridge	Hair Dryer	Sitting Area	TV
Inside	$324	80	no	no	no	no
Outside	$410	95–128	some	no	some	some

CABINS Cabins aboard all three ships are very snug (smaller than those aboard their fleetmates) but comfortable, with light, B&B-ish decor and lower twin or double beds. (Aboard the *Discovery,* one category has upper and lower bunks, and deluxe cabins have queen-size beds.) Storage space is ample, and most Bridge and Lounge Deck cabins feature picture windows. None of the cabins accommodates wheelchairs.

PUBLIC AREAS All three ships have a lounge with a bar, a 24-hour tea/coffee station, and a book and video library. Lounges are a little too small to accommodate all passengers comfortably when the ships are full.

DINING OPTIONS A single dining room serves all meals.

ADVENTURE & FITNESS OPTIONS Inflatable launches allow off-vessel exploration.

5 Lindblad Expeditions

96 Morton St., New York, NY 10014. ℭ **800/397-3348** or 212/765-7740. Fax 212/265-3770. www.expeditions.com.

THE LINE IN A NUTSHELL Lindblad Expeditions is the most adventure- and learning-oriented of the small-ship lines, offering itineraries that stay far away from the big ports, concentrating instead on wilderness and wildlife. **Sails to:** Alaska, Columbia and Snake rivers, Sea of Cortez/Baja, Central America (plus Europe, Arctic Norway, Antarctica, South America, Galapagos).

THE EXPERIENCE Operating cruises worldwide for nearly 3 decades, Lindblad has a more international, professional feel than any of its small-ship competitors, its cruises designed for intellectually curious travelers who want a casual, jeans-and-fleece experience that's educational as well as relaxing. Your time is spent learning about the outdoors from high-caliber expedition leaders and guest scientists, many of them aboard as part of Lindblad's alliance with the **National Geographic Society.** Days are spent observing the world around you, either from the ship or on frequent kayaking, motor-launch, and hiking excursions, which are included in the cruise price. Flexibility and spontaneity are key, with the captain able to alter his route at any time to follow a pod of whales or school of dolphins. Depending on weather and sea conditions, there are usually two or three excursions every day.

Pros

- **Great expedition feeling:** Lindblad's programs offer innovative, flexible itineraries, outstanding lecturers/guides, and a friendly, accommodating staff.
- **Alliance with National Geographic:** Beyond providing top-notch lecturers aboard ship, Lindblad's relationship with the Geographic Society means its ships are actively engaged in scientific research, with passengers right in the thick of things.
- **Built-in shore excursions:** Lindblad programs its shore excursions as an integral part of its cruises, with all excursion costs included in the cruise fare. And they'd better be, because these trips are . . .

Cons

- **Very expensive:** Lindblad's fares are among the highest in the small-ship market.

LINDBLAD: LEARNING CRUISES FOR THE WELL-HEELED

In 1984, Sven-Olof Lindblad, son of adventure-travel pioneer Lars-Eric Lindblad, followed in his father's footsteps by forming Lindblad Expeditions. From the beginning, the line has specialized in providing environmentally sensitive adventure/educational cruises to remote places in the world, with visits to a few large ports thrown in for good measure. In 2004, the company's commitment to true exploration rose to a new level when it formed an alliance with the National Geographic Society, whose scientists, photographers, and film crews now sail aboard Lindblad's ships to provide guests with an enhanced experience and to conduct actual research. The line's most adventure-oriented vessel, the *National Geographic Endeavour*, has been outfitted with advanced research equipment, while NGS explorer-in-residence Sylvia Earle and her advisory group help develop research, conservation, and educational initiatives for the fleet.

The line's two Alaska ships, the identical, 70-passenger *Sea Bird* and *Sea Lion*, are more jeeps than sports cars, with small cabins and basic public areas. In addition to Alaska, these ships also sail Washington and Oregon's Columbia and Snake rivers and Mexico's Baja Peninsula. Another vessel, the 64-passenger *Sea Voyager*, is based in Central America and Baja year-round, while *National Geographic Explorer* sails many of the line's most exploratory sailings, occasionally making a voyage through the Caribbean en route between other regions. In the Galapagos, Lindblad operates two vessels year-round, the 48-passenger *Islander* and the 80-passenger *Polaris*.

PASSENGER PROFILE

Lindblad tends to attract well-traveled and well-educated professionals who are looking for an active, casual, up-close experience with their destinations. They're the granola crowd with money. Most are in the 55-plus age range though there are sometimes younger couples and occasionally families. Most tend to be interested in wildlife (particularly whale- and bird-watching) and in the culture and history of the region they're visiting.

DINING

Lindblad's cuisine often reflects the culture and tastes of the sailing region, with many ingredients bought fresh at ports along the way. Dinners are served in single open seatings, and may include regional dishes as well as such entrees as filet mignon, glazed shallots with red-wine sauce and giant scallops, and pasta primavera with spinach

Compared with the other small-ship lines, here's how Lindblad rates:

	Poor	Fair	Good	Excellent	Outstanding
Enjoyment Factor					✓
Dining				✓	
Activities					✓
Children's Program	N/A				
Entertainment		✓			
Service				✓	
Worth the Money				✓	

Lindblad Expeditions Fleet Itineraries

Ship	Itineraries
Sea Lion	**Baja/Sea of Cortez:** 7 & 8 nights, round-trip from La Paz, Mexico (Jan–Mar). 14 nights, round-trip from San Carlos, Mexico (Mar). 7 nights, round-trip from Loreto, Mexico (Apr). **Alaska:** 11-night Inside Passage, Seattle, WA, to Juneau, AK (Apr). 7-night Inside Passage, round-trip from Juneau, AK (May–Aug).
Sea Bird	**Baja/Sea of Cortez:** 7 & 8 nights, round-trip from La Paz, Mexico (Jan–Mar). 14 nights, round-trip from San Carlos, Mexico (Mar). 7 nights, round-trip from Loreto, Mexico (Apr). **Alaska:** 11-night Inside Passage, Seattle, WA, to Juneau, AK (Apr). 7-night Inside Passage, round-trip from Juneau, AK (May–Aug).**Sea Voyager Panama Canal/Costa Rica:** 7 nights, round-trip from Colón, Panama (Jan–Mar). 10 nights, east- or westbound between Herradura, Costa Rica, and Colón, Panama (Jan–Mar). **Baja/Sea of Cortez:** 7 nights, round-trip from Loreto, Mexico (May–July).

fettuccine. Lecturers and other staff members dine with passengers. **Vegetarian options** are available at every meal, and other special diets (low-fat, low-salt, kosher, and so forth) can be accommodated with advance notice. Weather permitting, *Sea Bird* and *Sea Lion* offer **deck barbecues,** as well as **beach barbecues** in Mexico's Sea of Cortez, featuring such local dishes as grilled local seafood, handmade tortillas, tomatillo salsa, and a selection of Baja wines such as Monte Xanic and Santo Tomas. Guests eat their fish tortillas by tiki torch light, then sip their wine by a shore-side bonfire, soaking in some of that fabled "sense of place." A similar beach barbecue is offered during *Sea Voyager*'s stops at Costa Rica's Osa Peninsula.

SNACKS & EXTRAS Appetizers served in the late afternoon include items such as fruit and cheese platters, and baked brie with pecans and brown sugar.

ACTIVITIES

During the day, most activity takes place off the ship, aboard Zodiac boats and/or on land excursions. While on board, passengers entertain themselves with the usual small-ship activities: wildlife watching, reading, and conversation. Four to five **naturalists,** one historian, and an undersea specialist sail with each cruise (the most carried by any of the small-ship lines), presenting lectures and slide shows throughout each cruise and also leading guest exploration on shore. Many voyages also feature guest scientists, photographers, and lecturers from the **National Geographic Society.**

CHILDREN'S PROGRAM

Though Lindblad is primarily an adult line, all Alaska and Costa Rica/Nicaragua trips (plus Galapagos sailings) have staff that has been trained in childhood and environmental education.

ENTERTAINMENT

Each evening the onboard naturalists lead discussions recapping the day's events, and, after dinner, documentary and feature films are occasionally screened in the main lounge. In some regions, local musicians may come aboard to entertain. Books on nature and wildlife are available from each ship's small library.

Lindblad Central America & Caribbean Cruises

In addition to the ships profiled here, Lindblad also operates the 64-passenger *Sea Voyager,* which sailed as the Temptress Adventures vessel *Temptress Voyager* before being acquired and refurbished by Lindblad in 2001. The vessel sails from Central American home ports most of the year, visiting Costa Rica and Panama and putting the emphasis on the region's jungle and marine life. Panama cruises also incorporate the history of the Canal. In spring the vessel sails Baja's Sea of Cortez. Prices start around $3,900 per person for weeklong Central America sailings.

Lindblad also occasionally charters Sea Cloud Cruises' *Sea Cloud II* for Caribbean sailings.

SERVICE

Dining room staff and room stewards are affable and efficient, and seem to enjoy their work. As on other small ships, there's no room service unless you're ill and unable to make it to the dining room, and no laundry service.

Sea Lion • Sea Bird

The Verdict

Fairly utilitarian expedition vessels, *Sea Bird* and *Sea Lion* are designed to get you out into the wilderness, with naturalists aboard to teach you something about it too.

Sea Bird *(photo: Lindblad Expeditions)*

Specifications

Size (in tons)	100*	Passenger/Crew Ratio	3.2 to 1
Passengers (double occ.)	70	Year Launched	
Passenger/Space Ratio	N/A*	*Sea Lion*	1981
Total Cabins/Veranda Cabins	36/0	*Sea Bird*	1982
Crew	22	Last Refurbishment/Upgrade	N/A

* See note on p. 324 regarding small-ship tonnage and passenger/space measurements.

Frommer's Ratings (Scale of 1–5) ★★★½

Cabin Comfort & Amenities	3	Dining Options	3
Appearance & Upkeep	4	Adventure & Fitness Options	4
Public Comfort/Space	3	Children's Facilities	N/A
Decor	3	Enjoyment Factor	5

The shallow-draft *Sea Lion* and *Sea Bird* are identical twins, right down to their decor schemes and furniture. Unfancy, with just two public rooms and utilitarian cabins, they're very similar to several other small ships in this chapter, including the ACCL ships and Cruise West's *Spirit of Alaska*. As a matter of fact, *Spirit of Alaska* and the two Lindblad ships all sailed at one time for the now-defunct Exploration Cruise Lines.

Cabins & Rates

Cabins	Per Diems From	Sq. Ft.	Fridge	Hair Dryer	Sitting Area	TV
Outside	$424	95–110	no	no	some	no

CABINS   Postage-stamp cabins are tight and functional rather than fancy. No cabins are large enough to accommodate more than two, and each features twin or double beds, an adequate closet and drawers under the bed for extra storage, and a sink and mirror in the main room. Behind a folding door lies a tiny bathroom with a head-style shower (toilet opposite the shower nozzle). All cabins have picture windows that open except the lowest-priced cabins, which have small "portlights" that provide light but no view. Top-level cabins have a seating area. No cabins are wheelchair accessible.

PUBLIC AREAS   Public space is limited to an observation lounge that serves as the nerve center for activities, plus open areas on the Sun Deck and in the bow. In the lounge, you'll find a bar and a library of atlases and books on the culture, geology, history, plants, and wildlife of the sailing region.

DINING OPTIONS   A single dining room serves all meals.

ADVENTURE & FITNESS OPTIONS   Each cruise involves frequent hikes in wilderness areas, accessed via Zodiac landing craft. You can also walk around the Upper Deck for exercise.

6 The Maine Windjammers

See individual ship reviews for contact information.

THE LINE IN A NUTSHELL   Actually, it's not a line. Unlike every other review in this book, this one discusses a collection of owner-operated vessels—classic schooners that in some cases date back as far back as 1871—all offering sail-powered summer trips along the gorgeous mid-Maine coast. It's the most natural cruise you'll ever take. **Sails to:** Mid-Maine coast.

THE EXPERIENCE   Let's take a poll: How many of you harried, PDA-toting, 21st-century types dream of going quietly off-line for a while, back to some kind of ideal summertime memory—you in a sailboat on the open water, cozy bunks and kerosene lamps at night, stars in the sky, and quiet all around? Aboard Maine's fleet of old-time schooners, that's exactly what you get, on mostly 3- to 6-night cruises that run from about $395 to $930. With no engines on most vessels, little electricity, and only the most basic accommodations, these ships offer their passengers a reminder that days don't all have to be rushed and multitasked. Days are filled with sailing and walks around quaint Maine towns, and evenings are pure serenity.

Pros

- **Off-the-grid experience:** You can hardly get more away than this, and with the ships relying almost exclusively on sail power (and policing what goes over the side very rigidly), it's an environmentally friendly way to cruise, too.
- **Relaxation in the pure sense of the word:** Passengers on these ships have no obligations and nothing to distract them from just sitting back and enjoying. The experience is casual all the way, and you and the crew will bond in no time.
- **Classic ships:** Some of the association's member vessels date from as far back as 1871, and fully half the fleet has been named to the National Register of Historic Places.
- **Gorgeous scenery:** The Penobscot Bay region is one of the most picturesque sailing grounds anywhere, made all the more gorgeous by other schooners off in the distance. It's a perfect match of vessel and venue, picking up where New England's great 19th-century whaling ships and cargo schooners left off.

Cons

- **Rustic accommodations:** Cabins are almost universally tiny, most with only rudimentary furniture and lighting. This is actually a plus for many passengers, who come seeking just that kind of experience.
- **Few private facilities:** Only nine cabins in the whole fleet have private toilets (known as "heads" in the Windjammer world). Generally, ships have two or more shared toilets and showers.
- **Few activities:** Again, it's why a lot of people sign up, but if you need a lot of organized stimulation, look elsewhere.

MAINE WINDJAMMIN': A CURE FOR THE 50-HOUR WORKWEEK

It all began in the 1930s, decades after steamships had supplanted the schooners and other sail craft that had been the mainstay of commerce and transportation for centuries. In Maine, formerly one of the top boatbuilding regions of the country, the boats that had escaped the scrap yard were in danger of simply rotting away from despair and disuse. In 1936, though, Maine artist Frank Swift began offering pleasure cruises on one of the old vessels, confident that people would be glad to escape the

Compared with the other small-ship lines, here's how the schooners rate:

	Poor	Fair	Good	Excellent	Outstanding
Enjoyment Factor					✓
Dining			✓*		
Activities			✓*		
Children's Program	N/A*				
Entertainment		✓*			
Service			✓*		
Worth the Money					✓*

* Because the Maine schooners are all owner-operated, programs vary significantly. These ratings should be taken as only a general indication of fleetwide quality. Ratings for "activities" and "entertainment" should be read in the spirit of these cruises, which are entirely outdoors oriented, with few organized activities. There's also very little of what you'd traditionally call "service." If you want a drink, you bring it aboard yourself, and there's no cabin service unless something goes drastically wrong. Meals are often prepared by the same people who trim the sails. There are no real children's programs aboard any of these ships.

bustle of modern life for a few days of relaxation and simple pleasures. As Swift later recalled of his first trip, "We had only three lady passengers from Boston. The next time, I believe, we took off without any passengers." But Swift didn't give up, and soon his trips were in such demand that over the next 3 decades he not only grew his fleet but also lured other captains into the business. By 1977, there were so many schooners operating in coastal Maine that several decided to pool their advertising and marketing dollars and form the **Maine Windjammer Association** (© **800/807-WIND**; www.sailmainecoast.com). Today the association includes 12 member vessels, all of which are included in this review. You can request information for all member ships from the association and get basic info through their website, but bookings must be made directly with the captain of each schooner. Phone numbers and Web addresses for each are listed below. Two of the other schooners discussed here—the *Timberwind* and *J & E Riggin*—are former association members who have now teamed up as **Maine Adventure Sails** (© **877/300-3377**; www.maineadventuresails.com).

PASSENGER PROFILE

The Maine windjammers attract passengers in their 30s and passengers in their 90s, and everything in between. Many are returnees who sail a particular schooner every year, often coordinating with friends they've met on previous trips. Some are sailors themselves who enjoy helping out or taking a turn at the wheel. Most folks know the kind of experience they're signing on for, but first-timers often aren't quite prepared for just how rustic it can be. Bob Tassi, owner/captain of the schooner *Timberwind*, told us that, "initially, a lot of passengers experience some sense of shock, especially if they're not sailors and don't understand what a boat is. You can see it in the eyes of people who get on the boat Sunday night and they're very anxious about the accommodations, and claustrophobia, and only two toilets, but then suddenly by Wednesday they almost transform. Where they were checking their messages and looking at cellphones, all of a sudden that stuff gets put away, and something gets inside of them. Very few go away unhappy."

DINING

Meals on all the schooners are prepared on wood stoves in rustic galleys and served out on deck, picnic-style. In inclement weather, all passengers pack into the galley for meals. Expect traditional **New England staples** such as fresh seafood, chowder, roasts, Irish soda bread, and homemade ice cream. The cooks can accommodate vegetarian and some other special diets, but be sure to mention your needs when you book. Dinner is served soon after the ship drops anchor for the night, and chances are that other schooners will be anchored not far away. You'll hear their passengers off across the water, singing folk songs or saluting you with blasts from their tiny brass signal cannons. A few passengers or crew may even brave the frigid Maine water and swim over for a visit.

All the ships are **BYOB**, with coolers and ice provided if you've got beer to keep chilled. During the day, snacks are usually available in the galley. Once per cruise, most of the ships debark passengers onto a quiet, rocky beach for a traditional **lobster bake**, sometimes with champagne.

Maine Windjammer Fleet Itineraries

Ship	Itineraries
Entire fleet	**2- to 6-night Maine coastal cruises:** The whole fleet sails from Rockland, Rockport, and Camden, ME, late May through mid-Oct.

ACTIVITIES

An exact opposite of the typical cruise experience, the Maine schooners sail during the day and anchor in protected coves every night. In the evenings or mornings they'll often run a small boat to shore to allow passengers to explore small **fishing towns** and uninhabited islands. You can also see the sights at your port of embarkation because all the schooners encourage guests to arrive a day before sailing and spend the night on board, at the dock.

Most guests participate in the work of sailing: hauling the sails, raising the centerboard, or hand-cranking the anchor from the bay's floor (the latter not for sissies). Otherwise, days aboard are totally unstructured, leaving guests free to talk ship with the captain, take a turn at the wheel, climb the rigging for a watchman's view, or just read or stare out over the water, looking for seals, porpoises, puffins, and the occasional whale. An easy intimacy develops fast, and because the mid-Maine coast is a cruising paradise, passengers can expect to encounter any number of other schooners, sloops, and other sail craft. Often, two or more ships will take each other on in an impromptu race.

CHILDREN'S PROGRAM

Many of the Maine windjammers have restrictions on young children sailing aboard (see individual reviews below). Others accept kids as young as 5, but there are no formal programs to keep them entertained. On one of our recent trips, a Texas couple was aboard with their 6-year-old daughter, who spent the week playing with the captain's young son. The schooner became a whole world to explore, the week an opportunity to use the imagination most kids cede to TV and video games.

ENTERTAINMENT

None to speak of, though many of the schooner captains and crew are musicians who may break out their instruments in the evening. Guests who play are encouraged to bring acoustic instruments.

SERVICE

Don't expect much. Crew aboard these ships are *really* crew—the folks who haul the sails and swab the decks. In their spare time they do the dishes, clean the shared restrooms, and mend what needs mending. The first mate might also be the cook (and, often, the spouse of the captain). For the most part, you're on your own.

American Eagle

Launched in 1930, *American Eagle* was a fishing schooner for 53 years before being refurbished for passenger sailing. She's an immaculately maintained vessel, with a sleek profile and gleaming, polished woodwork. Named a National Historic Landmark in 1991, she's the only schooner in the area certified to sail internationally, enabling her to make an annual cruise to Canada.

Ambience: Quiet. There's often a cribbage game in the galley, and in the evening Captain John Foss reads Maine stories and poems appropriate to the day's sights. Guests spend an hour a day on shore, minimum. **Cabins:** Cabins have hot and cold running water, reading lights, and some heat in the spring and fall. **Bathrooms/Showers:** Two shared heads below deck, each with a wash sink. One shower in the midships compartment. **Size:** 92 ft. **Passengers:** 26 (min. age 12). **Contact:** Captain John Foss, P.O. Box 482, Rockland, ME 04841. ℂ **207/594-8007;** www.schooneramericaneagle.com.

Angelique

Launched in 1980 for passenger sailing, she's the only nonschooner in the fleet, rigged instead as a gaff topsail ketch with dark-red sails that really make her stand out.

Ambience: Quiet, with no organized activities. There's music if someone brings aboard an instrument and isn't shy. (There's also a piano in the deckhouse salon.) Guests can go ashore both morning and evening if time allows. **Cabins:** Cabins have upper and lower bunks or double beds. All have running water and reading lights. **Bathrooms/Showers:** Three shared heads below deck, and three showers. **Size:** 95 ft. **Passengers:** 29 (min. age 12). **Contact:** Yankee Packet Company, P.O. Box 736, Camden, ME 04843. ℂ **800/282-9989;** www.sailangelique.com.

Grace Bailey

Launched in 1882, *Grace Bailey* came to Maine for cargo work in 1910. Designated a National Historic Landmark in 1990, she's won and placed multiple times in the Windjammer Association's annual Great Schooner Race.

Ambience: Quiet, with no predetermined activities. There's music if any musicians are aboard (there's a piano in the after-cabin lounge). Guests can often go ashore in the mornings, with hiking time also available during the lobster bake on longer sailings. **Cabins:** Rustic cabins with upper and lower bunks, a water basin, and battery-powered lights. **Bathrooms/Showers:** Three shared heads below deck. One hot/cold freshwater shower. **Size:** 80 ft. **Passengers:** 29 (min. age 16, but younger teens can be accommodated with supervision). **Contact:** Maine Windjammer Cruises, P.O. Box 617, Camden, ME 04843. ℂ **800/736-7981;** www.mainewindjammercruises.com.

Heritage

Built by her captains on a 19th-century model, *Heritage* was launched in 1983 for the windjammer trade and is an exceptionally spiffy vessel, with clean lines and a lovely profile.

Ambience: Flexible to whatever the group on board is interested in: singing, storytelling, games, and/or quiet. Guests are able to go ashore several times a week, as time permits. **Cabins:** Cabins have hot and cold running water and 12-volt cellphone charging outlets. Two cabins have private heads—talk about luxury! **Bathrooms/Showers:** Three shared heads. One hot/cold freshwater shower. **Size:** 95 ft. **Passengers:** 30 (min. age 12, but returning guests may bring younger children). **Contact:** Schooner Heritage, P.O. Box 482, Rockland, ME 04841. ℂ **800/648-4544;** www.schoonerheritage.com.

Isaac H. Evans

Launched in 1886, the *Evans* spent 85 years working Delaware Bay as an oyster schooner before switching to passenger sailing in Maine. Named to the National Register, she's currently the only Maine schooner exclusively owned and operated by a woman.

Ambience: Varies, with games, music, and activities programmed if passengers want them. Guests are able to go ashore at least once per day, sometimes twice. Some sailings are themed on photography, hiking, knitting, and so on. **Cabins:** Cabins have hot and cold running water, electric reading lights, windows for light and ventilation, and more than the average number of extras (soap, lotion, shampoo, and so on). Six cabins have double beds; the rest have upper and lower berths. **Bathrooms/Showers:** Two shared heads. One enclosed shower whose water is heated by the galley's wood stove. **Size:** 65 ft. **Passengers:** 22 (min. age 6, though younger children are sometimes okay). **Contact:** Captain Brenda Walker, P.O. Box 791, Rockland, ME 04841. ℂ **877/238-1325;** www.midcoast.com/~evans.

J & E Riggin

Launched in 1927, *Riggin* worked as an oyster dredger before being rebuilt for passenger sailing in 1977. Known for her speed, she won the first and only oyster schooner race ever held on the Delaware Bay, and has won the Great Schooner Race several times. She was named a National Historic Landmark in 1991.

Ambience: Days are quiet, while nights usually see music, games, and storytelling. Guests can usually go ashore in the mornings for an hour or two. Co-captain Anne Mahle is known for her cooking, and has published a cookbook of the dishes served on board. **Cabins:** All cabins have quilts, reading lights, a porthole, and a sink with cold running water and handmade soap. **Bathrooms/Showers:** Two shared heads and one hot/cold shower, all on deck. **Size:** 89 ft. **Passengers:** 24 (min. age 12, but summer family cruises take kids as young as 6). **Contact:** Captain Jon Finger and Anne Mahle, 136 Holmes St., Rockland, ME 04841. ℂ **800/869-0604;** www.riggin.com.

Lewis R. French

Built in Maine in 1871, the *French* is the oldest schooner in the fleet (along with *Stephen Taber*) and the only Maine-built 19th-century schooner still in existence. She operated as a cargo schooner until 1971, after which she was converted for passengers and named to the National Register.

Ambience: There are no planned events, leaving guests to make their own atmosphere. Guests can go ashore almost every day for 1 or 2 hours. Smoking is not allowed on board. Nor are cellphones, TVs, or loud radios. **Cabins:** Cabins have cold running water and a window for ventilation. **Bathrooms/Showers:** Two shared heads and one hot/cold freshwater shower, all on deck. **Size:** 64 ft. **Passengers:** 22 (min. age 16). **Contact:** Captain Garth Wells, P.O. Box 992, Camden, ME 04843. ℂ **800/469-4635;** www.schoonerfrench.com.

Mary Day

Launched in 1962, *Mary Day* was the first schooner built specifically as a windjammer and the first coastal schooner built in Maine since 1930.

Ambience: Games and music are encouraged aboard *Mary Day*, with Captain Barry King often playing guitar. Guests are able to go ashore every day for an hour or more, and the weekly lobster bake allows for 3 hours ashore on a remote beach. **Cabins:** Cabins have cold running water, reading lights, skylights and windows, and unusually high headroom (9 ft. in most). **Bathrooms/Showers:** Two heads and two hot/cold showers, all on deck. **Size:** 90 ft. **Passengers:** 30 (min. age 15). **Contact:** Schooner Mary Day, P.O. Box 798, Camden, ME 04843. *©* **800/992-2218;** www.schoonermaryday.com.

Mercantile

Launched in 1916, *Mercantile* hauled cargo before windjammer pioneer Frank Swift converted her for passengers in 1942. She was named a National Historic Landmark in 1990.

Ambience: Onboard experience is tailored to the passengers aboard, with music and games offered if anyone's interested. When possible, guests can go ashore in the mornings, and on longer sailings extra hiking time is available during the lobster bake. **Cabins:** Rustic cabins with bunks, a water basin, and battery-powered lights. **Bathrooms/Showers:** Two heads below deck and a third in the galley/dining area. One hot/cold freshwater shower. **Size:** 78 ft. **Passengers:** 29 (min. age 16, but younger teens can be accommodated). **Contact:** Maine Windjammer Cruises, P.O. Box 617, Camden, ME 04843. *©* **800/736-7981;** www.mainewindjammercruises.com.

Mistress

The smallest ship in the windjammer fleet, *Mistress* was launched in 1960 as a blend of traditional schooner and private yacht. A local blacksmith did all her ironwork, and much of her hardware was secured from an old-time ship's chandlery in Nova Scotia.

Ambience: Onboard experience is tailored to the passengers, with music, games, and time ashore offered based on interest. Lobster bakes are included on 4- and 5-day cruises, with time for hiking. **Cabins:** Each of her three private cabins has its own head, sink, and private companionway from the deck. Two have double beds; the third has upper and lower bunks. **Bathrooms/Showers:** Three private heads. One sun shower for impromptu wash-ups during warm weather, plus stops at friendly B&Bs and inns, where passengers may use the showers. **Size:** 46 ft. **Passengers:** 6 (min. age 16 unless booking whole boat). **Contact:** Maine Windjammer Cruises, P.O. Box 617, Camden, ME 04843. *©* **800/736-7981;** www.mainewindjammercruises.com.

Nathaniel Bowditch

Built in East Boothbay, Maine, and launched in 1922 as a private racing yacht, *Bowditch* won class honors in the Bermuda Cup in the 1920s and during WWII was used by the Coast Guard for submarine surveillance. She fished the North Atlantic in the postwar years and was rebuilt for the passenger trade in the early 1970s.

Ambience: Music is encouraged, and games and puzzles are kept in the galley for passenger use. Guests are able to go ashore most days. Quiet time is encouraged after 8pm. **Cabins:** Rustic cabins with either double or single beds, barrel water, and reading lights. Some cabins have skylights. **Bathrooms/Showers:** Three shared heads below deck. One hot/cold shower on deck, with a privacy curtain set up while the ship is at anchor. **Size:** 82 ft. **Passengers:** 24 (min. age 14, but designated family sailings accept kids as young as 5). **Contact:** Captain Owen & Cathie Dorr, 4 Gay Street Place, Rockland, ME 04841. ℂ **800/288-4098**; www.windjammervacation.com.

Stephen Taber

Like the *Lewis R. French, Stephen Taber* was built way back in 1871, and is the oldest sailing vessel in continuous service in the U.S. She hauled lumber, stone, and produce up and down the eastern seaboard for a full century, and is now listed on the National Register.

Ambience: The *Taber* is known as a fun vessel, and a day's sail often ends with music and stories. Guests are able to go ashore once or twice daily, weather permitting. Operated by the same family for over a quarter century, the *Taber* is known for her food (former captain Ellen Barnes, mother of the current captain, has published many of their recipes in the cookbook *A Taste of the Taber*) and draws a huge number of repeat passengers—upward of 70% on most sailings. **Cabins:** Cabins have running water, lights, windows, and enough headroom to stand and dress. **Bathrooms/Showers:** Two shared heads and one hot-water shower, all on deck. **Size:** 68 ft. **Passengers:** 22 (min. age 14). **Contact:** Captain Noah Barnes, Windjammer Wharf, P.O. Box 1050, Rockland, ME 04841. ℂ **800/999-7352**; www.mainewindjammers.com.

Timberwind

Built in Portland, Maine, in 1931, *Timberwind* spent the first 38 years of her life stationed 18 miles off Portland Head, taking pilots to meet large ships and navigate them in. She was converted for passenger sailing in 1969, designated a National Historic Landmark in 1992, and today is one of the most rustic vessels in the fleet, offering a real back-in-time experience.

Ambience: Quiet, with days spent sailing and guests able to go ashore most days for 1 to 3 hours. Music lovers might be particularly interested in this vessel because her owner, Captain Bob Tassi, was a Nashville studio engineer before chucking it all to become a schooner man. Evenings frequently find him on guitar, and a framed portrait of Frank Sinatra adds an incongruous grace note to the rustic galley. **Cabins:** Tiny varnished-wood cabins have small electric lights, barrel water, and an enamel wash basin. Beds are either bunks or doubles. **Bathrooms/Showers:** Two shared heads below deck. One on-deck shower with privacy curtain. **Length:** 70 ft. **Passengers:** 20 (min. age 5). **Contact:** Schooner Timberwind, P.O. Box 247, Rockport, ME 04856. © 800/759-9250; www.schoonertimberwind.com.

Victory Chimes

Launched in 1900, *Victory Chimes* is the largest U.S.-flagged commercial sailing vessel and the only classic three-masted schooner still operating. Because of her size, her onboard feel is less cozy than the other vessels in the fleet—more ship than sailboat. Her image adorns the back of the Maine State Quarter, minted in 2003.

Ambience: There are no scheduled activities, though music and games often break out. Guests can go ashore in the morning and evening every day for 1 to 2 hours. **Cabins:** Cabins have bunk beds, portholes, 110-volt outlets, reading lights, and sinks with hot and cold running water. Most have upper and lower berths. There are also three single cabins, one cabin with twin beds, one that sleeps four, and four cabins with double beds and private toilets. **Bathrooms/Showers:** Three shared heads (two on deck, one below). Two showers. **Size:** 132 ft. **Passengers:** 40 (min. age 10). **Contact:** Victory Chimes, P.O. Box 1401, Rockland, ME 07841. © 800/745-5651; www.victorychimes.com.

7 Majestic America Line

2101 4th Ave., Suite 1150, Seattle, WA 98121. ℭ 800/434-1232. Fax 206/340-0975. www.majesticamericaline.com.

THE LINE IN A NUTSHELL   A new line formed from the 2006 merger of Delta Queen Steamboat Company and American West Steamboats, Majestic America offers journeys on America's rivers and coasts aboard a fleet of old-timey paddle-wheel riverboats and one sleek coastal cruiser.

THE EXPERIENCE   If you want to sail the Mississippi, chances are real good that you'll do so with Majestic America Line, which practically owns the franchise (with only one full-time competitor, RiverBarge Excursions). Plying the Mississippi River system from New Orleans to as far north as St. Paul and as far east as Pittsburgh, the line offers a good old-fashioned cruise that's more Mark Twain than Las Vegas, full of history and river lore, Cajun and Southern cooking, and a music program heavy on Dixieland jazz and swing. The vessels themselves are virtual museum pieces, whether an actual antique like the 1927-built *Delta Queen,* or a re-created one like *Mississippi Queen* (launched in 1976) or *American Queen* (1995). Heading west, the line offers similar experiences on the Pacific Northwest's Columbia and Snake rivers aboard *Queen of the West* (1995), *Columbia Queen* (2000), and *Empress of the North* (2003), and in Alaska's Inside Passage aboard *Empress* and the 49-passenger catamaran *Contessa.*

All around, Majestic America's vessels offer more lavish surroundings and better food and service than you'll find on most other small ships, and its boats have an intimacy and personality that bigger cruise ships lack. Throw in a healthy dose of the American history and culture and you have a totally unique and memorable cruise. **Sails to:** U.S. river cruises.

Pros

- **Old-fashioned fun:** From flying kites on the stern to playing the boisterous steam calliope, life on board is old-timey and carefree.
- **America, America . . . :** These all-American ships are awash in American nostalgia, with an authentic flavor you won't find on other cruises. Visits to small, charming ports in the South, the Pacific Northwest, and Alaska drive home the point.
- **History:** The *Delta Queen* is a National Historic Landmark, and just being on the river is enough to make Mark Twain come alive.

Cons

- **Limited Activities:** While the historical program is great and the live music is first-rate, don't expect cruise ship activities like gambling, yoga, or late-night partying. That's not what these ships are about.

MAJESTIC AMERICA: BIG WHEELS KEEP ON TURNIN'

This is the line to sail with if you want to cruise like Mark Twain. All six of the line's paddle-wheelers offer a time-travel option that re-creates what it was like to sail America's rivers back in the old days. The small, wooden *Delta Queen* was actually there. Built in 1927, she's a direct link to steamboat days, and even has National Historic Landmark status. The larger *Mississippi Queen, American Queen, Queen of the West, Empress of the North,* and *Columbia Queen* (the latter most recently operated by Great American River Journeys) are modern vessels built between 1976 and 2003,

Compared with the other small-ship lines, here's how Majestic America rates:

	Poor	Fair	Good	Excellent	Outstanding
Enjoyment Factor					✓
Dining				✓	
Activities				✓	
Children's Program			✓		
Entertainment					✓
Service				✓	
Worth the Money				✓	

and offer a combination of old-style decor and a few cruise ship amenities. Rounding out the fleet is the 49-passenger *Contessa,* a small, speedy catamaran that formerly sailed for Glacier Bay Cruiseline. She's the only non-stern-wheeler in the fleet, and more closely resembles one of the Cruise West vessels in her onboard vibe.

Empress of the North hit the news in mid-2007 after she struck a rock in Alaska's Icy Strait, began taking on water, and was forced to evacuate all her passengers to a rescue fleet of fishing boats, Coast Guard vessels, and the Alaska State Ferry ship *Columbia.* No injuries were reported among either passengers or crew, but *Empress* was out of commission for nearly 2 months while repairs were affected.

PASSENGER PROFILE

Passengers are almost exclusively American, in their mid-sixties and up, and many return every year. Expect to see some families on the modern stern-wheelers from May to August and during the holidays, including kids traveling with their grandparents. The old *Delta Queen* has no kids' program and generally attracts an older crowd.

Passengers should note that no doctors sail aboard. In an emergency, the boats simply pull up along the riverbank to await medical help.

DINING

Compared to some of the smaller, more adventurous lines, the food aboard Majestic America is decidedly more varied and complex, with menus running toward Middle American, Southern, Cajun, and Pacific Northwestern, depending on the sailing region. In the South, expect local specialties, including an **alligator** appetizer, Mississippi Mud Pie, and praline and pecan cheesecake. In the Pacific Northwest and Alaska, expect salmon, seafood chowder, Alaska king crab, and "Mount St. Helens chocolate lava cake." Meals are served in traditional style, with passengers assigned to a set table for dinner.

In 2007, the line began working with Northwest chef and consultant Kathy Casey to create a menu of signature American dishes emphasizing local, seasonal ingredients.

SNACKS & EXTRAS   It doesn't sound like much, but freshly popped **popcorn** is a staple on all the stern-wheelers. Grab a bag and a chair on deck, and watch the river go by. It doesn't get any better than that—unless, perhaps, you dig into the bottomless basket of **fresh chocolate-chip** and **peanut butter cookies.** Each ship except *Contessa* offers casual lunch and other quick foods in one lounge.

Majestic America Fleet Itineraries

Ship	Itinerary
American Queen	**Mississippi/Ohio/Cumberland Rivers:** 7 nights, round-trip from New Orleans, LA (Jan–Apr & Nov–Dec); north- or southbound between New Orleans and Memphis, TN (Apr–June & Nov); Memphis to St. Louis (June); north- or southbound between St. Louis and St. Paul, MN (July–Oct); St. Louis to Memphis (Oct).
Columbia Queen	**Columbia River/Pacific Northwest:** 7 nights, round-trip from Portland, OR (May–Oct).
Contessa	**Baja/Sea of Cortez:** 7 nights, round-trip from La Paz (Jan–Apr & Oct–Dec). **Alaska:** 7-night Inside Passage, north- or Southbound between Ketchikan and Sitka, AK (May–Sept).
Delta Queen	**Mississippi/Ohio/Cumberland Rivers:** 14 nights, New Orleans, LA, to Cincinnati, OH (Apr). 3-night Kentucky Derby, round-trip from Cincinnati (Apr). 5 nights, Cincinnati to Pittsburgh, PA (May). 10 & 11 nights, north- or southbound between Pittsburgh and Nashville, TN (May–July & Sept–Oct). 7 nights, north- or southbound between Nashville and Cincinnati (May–June, Aug & Oct); Nashville to Memphis (July); Memphis to St. Louis, MO (July); St. Louis to Nashville (July–Aug); Memphis to New Orleans (Oct). 10 nights, Cincinnati to Memphis (Oct).
Empress of the North	**Columbia River/Pacific Northwest:** 7 nights, round-trip from Portland, OR (Mar–Apr & Oct–Dec). **Alaska:** 7-night Inside Passage, round-trip from Juneau, AK (May–Aug). 12-night Inside Passage, north- or southbound between Seattle, WA, and Juneau, AK (Apr & Sept).
Mississippi Queen	**Mississippi/Ohio/Cumberland Rivers:** 7 nights, round-trip from New Orleans, LA (Mar–Apr & Nov–Dec); Memphis, TN, to Louisville, KY (Apr); north- or southbound between Louisville and Pittsburgh, PA (Apr–June); Louisville to St. Louis (June); north- or southbound between St. Louis, MO, and St. Paul, MN (July–Aug); St. Louis to Cincinnati (Sept); north- or southbound between Cincinnati and Nashville, TN (Sept–Oct); north- or southbound between Cincinnati and Chattanooga, TN (Sept–Oct); Cincinnati to Memphis (Oct); Memphis to New Orleans (Nov).
Queen of the West	**Columbia River/Pacific Northwest:** 7 nights, round-trip from Portland, OR (Mar–Nov).

ACTIVITIES

You know how you sometimes feel you need a vacation to recover from your vacation? Not so on Majestic America, where the boat's pace usually averages about 6 mph—and yours does too. Learning about the river is the focus of most days, with an **onboard historian or naturalist** describing passing areas, showing you where you are on a chart, or weaving facts and stories about the area into daily talks. Some talks given during breakfast discuss the local history and culture, while talks at night might explain technical details like river-navigation lights.

Other activities include **films** (both historical and current), a lecture from a Mark Twain impersonator on Mississippi itineraries, and **calliope concerts.** On the former Delta Queen ships, the most popular sport is **kite flying.** After putting together your own kite from a kit, head to the top deck and try to get your bird in the air without getting it tangled with other lines, getting it caught under a passing bridge, or landing it in the Mississippi.

CHILDREN'S PROGRAM

While seniors will always outnumber toddlers on Majestic America, an improved children's program on the former Delta Queen vessels *American Queen* and *Mississippi*

Queen has been drawing increased numbers of families over the past few years. On *Mississippi Queen* summer and holiday "riverventures" cruises, a family activity coordinator encourages kids to unplug from video games and TV, and keeps them occupied instead with kite flying, calliope playing, ice-cream parties, and visits to the pilothouse. While typical children's programs entertain kids separately from their parents, Majestic America encourages activities in which the whole family can participate, including family-oriented shore excursions in which everyone tours Mark Twain's cave, sees reenactments at historic forts, or watches how baseball bats are made or how thoroughbred horses are trained. There's a children's menu for all meals. Up to two children under age 18 travel *free* in some staterooms on the *Mississippi Queen* when sharing a stateroom with two full-fare adults.

ENTERTAINMENT

Entertainment on southern routes features **riverboat-style shows** with vaudeville singers and a heavy emphasis on Dixieland jazz. Dancers also appreciate the nightly **big-band concerts,** and theme nights are popular, with '50s sock hops and country music among the favorites. *American Queen* and *Mississippi Queen* have more elaborate evening shows, mostly because they have an actual stage for performers. In the Pacific Northwest and Alaska, show lounges offer small-scale entertainment, including jazz soloists and small song-and-dance revues. The stern-facing lounge on each vessel is the spot for cocktails, card games, scenery gazing, and watching the bright red paddle wheel churning away.

Note that despite their being riverboats, none of the Majestic America vessels has a **casino** on board.

SERVICE

Service on Majestic America isn't polished in a luxe-cruise way, but it sure is more fun, with the crew managing to be friendly and entertaining as well as efficient.

Room service is available only from a very limited breakfast menu.

Delta Queen

The Verdict

Like your favorite B&B, the 1927-built *Delta Queen* oozes charm, personality, and a welcoming friendliness. She's a classic in a league of her own.

Delta Queen *(photo: Majestic America)*

Specifications

Size (in tons)	3,360	Crew	80
Passengers (double occ.)	174	Passenger/Crew Ratio	2.1 to 1
Passenger/Space Ratio	19.3	Year Launched	1927
Total Cabins/Veranda Cabins	87/0	Last Refurbishment/Upgrade	1998

Frommer's Ratings (Scale of 1–5)   ★★★★

Cabin Comfort & Amenities	3.5	Dining Options	3
Appearance & Upkeep	4	Adventure & Fitness Options	2
Public Comfort/Space	4	Children's Facilities	N/A
Decor	5	Enjoyment Factor	5

When we first caught sight of *Delta Queen* nudged against a riverbank, dripping muddy water from her slowly turning paddle wheel, she looked both perfectly in sync with her surroundings and perfectly out of place. Was she a lonely relic from a long-gone time, or were we intruders on her world, where she'd been carrying on commerce as usual for 100 years? It seemed amazing that such a boat still existed, much less still carried passengers.

Built in 1927, *Delta Queen* is the real deal: Nothing seems contrived or fake (because it isn't) and antiques *are* the decor, not just elements dropped in to add authenticity and homeyness. She came to the Mississippi by a circuitous route, with her hull originally fabricated in Scotland, then shipped to California for final assembly. Costing the then-exorbitant price of $1 million, she was known for her fine interiors as she carried overnight passengers between San Francisco and Sacramento. (Her sister, the *Delta King*, still survives as a restaurant in Sacramento.) During WWII, the government took her over, painted her gray, and used her to ferry troops around San Francisco Bay. In 1947 Captain Tom Greene bought her, literally packed her in a big box, and towed her to New Orleans, making her the first steamboat to transit the Panama Canal. Because her superstructure is built almost entirely of wood, her career has been threatened numerous times by newer fire regulations, and in mid-2007 her luck finally ran out. A Congressional exemption that would have given her a few more years as an overnight vessel failed to pass, so she'll finally be forced into retirement at the end of 2008. Book now.

Cabins & Rates

Cabins	Per Diems From	Sq. Ft.	Fridge	Hair Dryer	Sitting Area	TV
Outside	$250	55–229	no	yes	some	no

CABINS   With their stained-glass windows and acres of wood paneling, the cabins aboard *Delta Queen* couldn't be further from the cookie cutters on today's modern ships. Size ranges from tight upper-and-lower-berth cabins with pipe racks for storage to plush if not overly spacious cabins with queen-size beds. Every cabin is outside (though a few have obstructed views) and many feature windows or doors that can be opened to allow the fresh air in. Charmingly, almost all open up directly onto the Promenade decks, which creates a neighborly feel with chairs and rockers situated just outside. Just as charmingly, there are no telephones or TVs in any of the cabins.

Every cabin has its own personality and history: One cabin on Sun Deck is where President Jimmy Carter (one of three presidents to sail aboard) stayed for a week in 1979. Another cabin is said to be haunted by the ghost of the late owner of the company, Ma Greene. Crewmembers swear up and down that they've interacted with her as she keeps an eye on her beloved boat.

Delta Queen has no wheelchair-accessible cabins, nor is there an elevator on board.

PUBLIC AREAS Beautifully maintained and very comfortable, *Delta Queen* seems more like an upscale southern home or warm B&B than a normal cruise ship, with her rich wood interiors, overstuffed couches, and numerous antiques. The Cabin Lounge is the lower of two forward lounges, graced with fluted columns and potted plants, and is suitable for reading, cards, and tea. The wooden grand staircase with shiny brass steps rises to the Victorian-style Texas Lounge, with its bar, daytime games, singer-pianist, and popcorn machine. The Betty Blake Library is an interior room between the cabins on the Cabin Deck and is full of historical exhibits. It's named after the woman who lobbied Congress for years to secure *Delta Queen*'s continued career. The Orleans Room, serving meals in two seatings, doubles as an old-fashioned music hall featuring ragtime, Dixieland, jazz, and blues. Passengers can even visit the engine room, where you'll see spotless brass fittings and gauges. Watching the slow, heaving Pitman arms turning the thrashing red wooden paddle wheel is hypnotic, and a very far cry indeed from the strictly "off limits" culture of most modern ships.

DINING OPTIONS Forget freestyle dining or 10 different restaurants. On *Delta Queen,* the one dining room on board used to be a freight deck and features tin ceilings and an ironwood floor. The room is typically transformed once per cruise into a "picnic" area, complete with checkered tablecloths, denim-clad waiters bringing drinks in wagons, serving chicken and catfish, and scattering plastic ants across the table while crooning, "It's just like a real picnic, isn't it?"

A light breakfast snack is served in the Cabin Lounge for those not wishing to take a full meal in the Orleans Room.

ADVENTURE & FITNESS OPTIONS *Delta Queen* has no exercise facilities save for an exercise bike and elliptical trainer positioned on the stern by the paddle wheel. Shore excursions tend to be fairly low-key, activitywise.

Mississippi Queen • American Queen • Queen of the West • Columbia Queen • Empress of the North

The Verdict

Match the charm and history of the *Delta Queen* with some of the comforts and amenities of a newer ship, and you'll get these five vessels. While not as cozy, these boats still deliver authentic and spirited American river travel.

American Queen *(photo: Majestic America)*

Specifications

Size (in tons)		Queen of the West	71/25
Mississippi Queen	3,364	Columbia Queen	75/23
American Queen	3,707	Empress of the North	115/108
Queen of the West	1,308	Crew	
Columbia Queen	1,599	Mississippi Queen	157
Empress of the North	3,388	American Queen	160
Passengers (double occ.)		Queen of the West	60
Mississippi Queen	416	Columbia Queen	57
American Queen	436	Empress of the North	84
Queen of the West	136	Passenger/Crew Ratio	
Columbia Queen	150	Mississippi/American	2.6 to 1
Empress of the North	235	Queen of the West	2.7 to 1
Passenger/Space Ratio		Columbia Queen	2.6 to 1
Mississippi Queen	8.1	Empress of the North	2.8 to 1
American Queen	8.5	Year Launched	
Queen of the West	9.6	Mississippi Queen	1976
Columbia Queen	10.7	American Queen	1995
Empress of the North	14.4	Queen of the West	1995
Total Cabins/Veranda Cabins		Columbia Queen	2000
Mississippi Queen	208/100	Empress of the North	2003
American Queen	222/31	Last Refurbishment/Upgrade	2007

Frommer's Ratings (Scale of 1–5)   ★★★★

Cabin Comfort & Amenities	4	Dining Options	4
Appearance & Upkeep	4	Adventure & Fitness Options	3
Public Comfort/Space	4	Children's Facilities	2
Decor	5	Enjoyment Factor	5

Treading the line between modern and old-fashioned, these grand riverboats feel authentic while offering such modern amenities as plunge pools, a gym, and private balconies. Don't expect a regular cruise ship, though. The largest stern-wheeler in history, the *American Queen* is grand and magnificent, a tiered wedding cake of filigree and curlicues crowned with two huge fluted smokestacks. Ornamentation and decoration are everywhere, framing an assortment of vintage period pieces and antiques. Even her engine is a vintage steam plant, rescued and restored from a 1930 U.S. Army Corps dredge (though unlike *Delta* and *Mississippi Queen,* her steam plant and paddle wheel are assisted by a modern propulsion system). She looks so beautiful and authentic that it's hard to imagine she was built in the 1990s—and even harder to imagine how much effort and expense were put into her, at a time when most other companies would have cut corners. *Mississippi Queen* was designed in the 1970s by James Gardner, the marine architect who'd previously designed Cunard's *QE2.* A bit drab for many years, she was extensively refurbished in 1996 and brought up to true Victorian form.

The two former American West ships—*Queen of the West,* built in 1995 and operated in the Columbia and Snake rivers ever since, and *Empress of the North,* launched in 2003, intended for Alaska voyages—are more spacious than you may think when you first see them from shore, with public rooms that evoke a bygone era. Both ships are fitted with bow landing ramps, which let them cozy up to shore so passengers can walk easily on and off the vessel, even in secluded spots that lack docking facilities.

Columbia Queen is a 150-passenger stern-wheeler built in 2000 and most recently operated by Great American River Journeys. She joined the Majestic America fleet in spring 2007, too late to be reviewed for this book.

Cabins & Rates

Cabins	Per Diems From	Sq. Ft.	Fridge	Hair Dryer	Sitting Area	TV
Inside	$164	68–140	no	yes	no	yes
Outside	$193	87–353	some	yes	some	yes

CABINS Cabins on the *American Queen,* like almost every other part of the ship, are elaborately decorated, complete with Tiffany-style lamps and plenty of storage space. Decorative moldings and trim surround each cabin door and ceiling, and most cabins feature a large bathroom and tub, as well as a huge sink and a tiled floor. As aboard *Delta Queen,* many cabins open up to the common decks via French doors, creating a neighborly feel. Other cabins have a large bay window or private balconies, and some suites feature extraspacious balconies with views that rival those from the pilothouse. Cabins that open to the deck have a small stained-glass transom window to let fresh air in.

Mississippi Queen's cabins are a bit more standard and are small when compared to those of modern cruise ships, though approximately half offer private balconies. (Given that the *MQ* was built in 1976, this design was way ahead of its time.) The privacy is a trade-off, however, meaning a loss of some of the friendly community feel found on the other boats. It also means the only common Promenade Deck is located at the very top of the boat near the pool area. While it seems a small detail to some, it does create a different feel on board. The same goes for *Queen of the West* and especially *Empress of the North,* a majority of whose cabins have private balconies and open to interior public corridors, as on larger cruise ships. Only one deck on each vessel has cabins opening onto outside promenades. All cabins on both ships are decorated like cozy bedrooms, with dark-wood tones, flowery bedspreads, and lace curtains.

American Queen has a number of cabins designed for solo passengers. *American Queen* has nine wheelchair-accessible cabins, *Mississippi Queen* has one, and *Empress of the North* and *Queen of the West* each have two.

PUBLIC AREAS *American Queen*'s decor is one of the most impressive afloat, with details so numerous you could spend a week just exploring the public rooms. The Ladies' Parlor welcomes anyone to lounge on the swooning couch, facing a fireplace whose wooden mantle is cluttered with black-and-white "ancestral" photographs and flanking vases. Floor lamps with linen shades, silver tea sets, a rosewood pump organ, and floral wallpaper all add to the lovely room—a cozy spot to read or simply gaze out at the river through the room's French doors and pretty curtained bay window. Across the passageway is the Gentlemen's Card Room, a masculine, clubby lounge complete with a stuffed bear. Just aft, the Mark Twain Gallery is a museum space and lounge full of antique furniture, a model of the *Delta Queen,* and views down onto the J. M. White Dining Room below. Further aft on Cabin Deck, the Grand Saloon is an impressive showroom, modeled after grand opera houses of the 1800s and featuring cozy private boxes perfect for watching the shows. The liveliest spot is all the way aft at the Engine Room Bar, where banjo playing, ragtime, and jazz go on late into the night while moody, rhythmic light flickers off the spinning paddle wheel outside the windows. At the Observation Deck's Chart Room, passengers can peruse books about the river, or pretend to drive via the large mounted steering wheel, or enlist the Riverlorian's help in charting the boat's progress. For such a relatively small vessel, *American Queen* has an astonishing variety of spaces.

Most of the *Mississippi Queen*'s public rooms are located on the Observation Deck, with cabins both above and below. The abundance of private balconies detracts somewhat from the boat, as there are not the numerous Promenade decks that are found on the *Delta* and *Mississippi Queen*. Linking the boat's seven decks is a Grand Staircase, crowned by a *trompe l'oeil* ceiling. At the very front of the Observation Deck is the Wheel House, which (like the *AQ*'s Chart Room) acts as home to the Riverlorian, with charts by which passengers can track their progress on the river. Aft is the Grand Saloon, used for most activities during the day and as a showroom at night. Overlooking the boat's 36-foot-wide paddle wheel is the appropriately named Paddlewheel Lounge, offering commanding views of the river from the two-story windows that line three of its sides. Other public areas include the Golden Antlers Bar, the Forward Lounge, the open-air Calliope Bar, a movie theater, a library, and even a salon. The Engine Room is open to passengers on both boats.

Interior decor is similar aboard *Empress of the North* and *Queen of the West*, with pressed-metal ceilings, chandeliers, balloon-back chairs, and other touches lending a period feel. Our favorite room aboard both ships is definitely the Paddlewheel Lounge, where you can sip a cocktail to the thrum of the huge propulsion wheel, visible through the room-wide window at the back. Snacks (and of course drinks) are served here before dinner, and there's entertainment at night. Each ship also has an old-fashioned, one-level show lounge with a dance floor and a small bandstand/stage.

DINING OPTIONS   Breakfast, lunch, and dinner are all served in the ship's main dining rooms, of which the *American Queen*'s J. M. White Dining Room is spectacular and memorable. Recalling the main cabin lounge aboard its late-19th-century namesake steamboat, it has a pair of soaring two-deck sections decorated with white filigree woodwork, colorful tapestries, and two huge, gilded antique mirrors. *Delta, Mississippi,* and *American Queen* also offer buffet breakfast and lunch served in the Front Porch of America, aptly named for its sweeping views over the bow and furnishings of white wicker chairs and painted rockers. Light and casual, the room offers a constant stream of soft ice cream, lemonade, and baskets of freshly baked cookies. Grab some and head out to the porch swings and rocking chairs. Aboard *Queen of the West* and *Empress of the North,* continental breakfast; lunch fare such as burgers, hot dogs, sandwiches, and homemade chili and soup; and snacks of the latte, cappuccino, yogurt sundae, and popcorn variety are available in the Calliope Bar & Grill, a bright, indoor/outdoor space that resembles an old-time ice-cream parlor.

ADVENTURE & FITNESS OPTIONS   *Delta, Mississippi,* and *American Queen* each have a small gym and pool, but you're out of luck if you want those options on *Empress* and *Queen.*

Contessa

The Verdict

Completely unlike all the other Majestic America ships, *Contessa* is an extremely fast, cozily comfortable catamaran. Though lacking the period feel of Majestic America's other vessels, she does offer an intimate cruise experience and the ability to visit tiny ports.

Contessa *(photo: Majestic America)*

Specifications

Size (in tons)	93*	Crew	18
Passengers (double occ.)	49	Passenger/Crew Ratio	2.7 to 1
Passenger/Space Ratio	N/A*	Year Launched	1986
Total Cabins/Veranda Cabins	24	Last Refurbishment/Upgrade	2007

* See note on p. 324 regarding small-ship tonnage and passenger/space measurements.

Frommer's Ratings (Scale of 1–5)   ★★★½

Cabin Comfort & Amenities	3	Dining Options	3
Appearance & Upkeep	4	Adventure & Fitness Options	2
Public Comfort/Space	3	Children's Facilities	N/A
Decor	3	Enjoyment Factor	4

Formerly known as *Executive Explorer* (of the late, lamented Glacier Bay Cruiseline), *Contessa* looks a bit like a wedge of cheese from the outside, but she's actually a comfortable and surprisingly fast little three-deck catamaran. A few years back we arrived in Ketchikan on another vessel just as *Contessa* was getting ready to depart. Her passengers got on board, the captain started the engines, and zoom!—she took off like a sports car and zipped out of sight. She's one speedy little boat.

Cabins & Rates

Cabins	Per Diems From	Sq. Ft.	Fridge	Hair Dryer	Sitting Area	TV
Outside	$385	120	no	no	no	no
Suite	$599	140	yes	no	yes	yes

CABINS   All cabins have large viewing windows, twin beds that can be converted to a double, and considerable closet space. Bathrooms are head-style, with the toilet essentially in the shower stall and sinks out in the main part of the cabin. On Upper Deck, two President's Staterooms face forward over the bow, just below the bridge, providing exceptional views, with two full walls of windows. Much larger than the other cabins on board, they're furnished with a TV/DVD, minifridge, queen-size bed, and larger closets. No cabins are wheelchair accessible.

PUBLIC AREAS   Like most small ships, *Contessa* has only two public rooms: one comfortable main lounge right in the bow, with large windows all around, and one dining room. The lounge has a bar, a small library, and a TV. An open top deck and a covered area on the middle deck are the best spots for wildlife viewing.

DINING OPTIONS   The single, simple dining room is able to serve all passengers comfortably.

ADVENTURE & FITNESS OPTIONS   *Contessa* carries no fitness equipment, and due to her shape there are no wraparound outdoor decks on which to do laps.

8 Mini-Review: RiverBarge Excursions

201 Opelousas Ave., New Orleans, LA 70114. ✆ **888/462-2743**. www.riverbarge.com.

THE LINE IN A NUTSHELL   Barging vacations have grown in popularity over the past 3 decades, especially in England and Continental Europe, and now the concept is available in the U.S. through RiverBarge Excursions, a company created by New Orleans towboat and barge owner Eddie Conrad. Sailing year-round, the company's 198-passenger *River Explorer* navigates the waterways of the Midwest and the South, visiting riverfront cities such as Memphis, St. Louis, Cincinnati, and New Orleans. Itineraries are both cheaper and more inclusive than those of their main competitor, Majestic America Line. In 2005, *River Explorer* was the first vessel to resume New Orleans service following the Hurricane Katrina disaster. **Sails to:** U.S. river cruises.

THE EXPERIENCE   Built in 1998, ***River Explorer*** ★★★½ is actually three different vessels lashed together like train cars. A towboat (the *Miss Nari*) is the rig's engine, with two three-deck hotel barges behind: the *DeSoto* for the cabin accommodations and the *LaSalle* housing the public spaces. The complete vessel has a length of 730 feet and a width of 54 feet, sized to fit into the locks of the Intracoastal Waterway. The interior design is spacious, modern in decor, and features huge windows for viewing the passing riverscape. The favorite perch is the Guest Pilot House, a forward-facing observation lounge with charts to study and communications between river pilots to listen to. The *River Explorer*'s actual navigating pilot is one deck above, and visitors are welcome to drop in, but only when the barge is tied up. The Lobby, aft of the Guest Pilot House, provides lounge and banquette seating. Etched glass panels decorate the seat backs, depicting river bridges. A midships lounge known as the Governor Galvez Room has books and videos for passenger use, and board games and cards to enjoy at three octagonal tables. The Sprague, the two-level show lounge, is the setting for storytelling, local entertainment, and bingo.

The Galley, a huge light-filled space on the lowest passenger deck, serves all meals. Breakfast is a buffet, with omelets to order, and the buffet lunch (called "dinner" here) offers hot and cold selections, with dishes such as catfish and shrimp reflecting the cruising region. Dinner ("supper") has traditional table service and includes an appetizer, soup, salad, choice of two or three entrees, and freshly baked cakes and pies. Preparation is consistently good, and regular menu items are typical Middle American.

Cabins are named after states and arranged in order of their entry into the Union. The square footage is generous, and while all have the same layout, the upper deck rooms have narrow balconies. Large picture windows slide open, and amenities include twin or queen-size beds, TV/VCR, fridge, desk, two chairs, and decent hanging and drawer space. All bathrooms have full tubs and showers.

RiverBarge Excursions Fleet Itineraries

Ship	Itineraries
River Explorer	**"Route of Jean Lafitte":** 7-night Intracoastal Waterway, east- or westbound between Galveston and Port Isabel, TX, and east- or westbound between New Orleans, LA, and Galveston, TX (Jan–Feb). **Mississippi/Ohio/Cumberland Rivers:** 7 nights, round-trip from New Orleans (Feb–May); north- or southbound between New Orleans and Memphis, TN (Mar–May); north- or southbound between Memphis and St. Louis, MO (May–June); north- or southbound between St. Louis and New Orleans (May); round-trip from St. Louis (June); east- or westbound between St. Louis and Cincinnati, OH (June); round-trip from Cincinnati (June); north- or southbound between Cincinnati and Nashville, TN (June–July); north- or southbound between Nashville and St. Louis (July); round-trip from Nashville (July).

Covered and open outdoor deck space stretches nearly the complete length of the top deck. There's bar service up here, and hot and cold hors d'oeuvres are served before dinner.

Weeklong itineraries tend to start around $360 per person, give or take $100 to $300, depending on season.

9 Mini-Review: Sea Cloud Cruises

32–40 N. Dean St., Englewood, NJ 07631. ℂ **888/732-2568** or 201/227-9404. Fax 201/227-9424. www.seacloud.com.

THE LINE IN A NUTSHELL Germany-based Sea Cloud Cruises caters to a well-traveled clientele looking for a deliciously exotic five-star sailing adventure, and an international one too: Typical Caribbean cruises draw about 30% American passengers, 30% German, 20% British, and the rest from elsewhere in Europe. A trip aboard one of the line's sailing ships—the 2,532-ton, 64-passenger *Sea Cloud* ★★★★★ or the 3,849-ton, 94-passenger replica *Sea Cloud II* ★★★★★—will spoil small-ship lovers forever. **Sails to:** Caribbean (plus Europe).

THE EXPERIENCE In 1931, Wall Street tycoon **E. F. Hutton** commissioned construction of the four-masted sailing ship *Hussar* from the Krupp family shipyard in Kiel, Germany. Outfitting of her interior was left to Hutton's wife, heiress and businesswoman **Marjorie Merriweather Post,** who spent 2 years on the task, eventually drafting a full-scale diagram showing every detail of her design, down to the placement of antiques. After the couple's divorce, Post renamed the vessel *Sea Cloud* and sailed her to Leningrad, where second husband Joseph E. Davies was serving as U.S. ambassador. World War II saw the vessel commissioned to the U.S. Navy, which removed her masts and used her as a floating weather station. After the war the vessel went though numerous hands: first back to Post, then to Dominican dictator Rafael Leonidas Trujillo Montinas, then to a number of American owners before she was finally purchased by German economist and seaman Hartmut Paschberg. A lover of great ships, Paschberg and a group of Hamburg investors put up the money for an 8-month overhaul that restored *Sea Cloud's* original grandeur, full of marble, gold, and mahogany detailing. Today the ship offers cabins for 64 passengers, the luckiest (and richest) of whom can stay in Post's own museum-like suite, with its Louis XIV–style bed and nightstands, marble fireplace and bathroom, chandeliers, and

Sea Cloud Fleet Itineraries

Ship	Itineraries
Sea Cloud	**Caribbean:** 7-night eastern/southern, Montego Bay, Jamaica, to Antigua (Jan); round-trip from Antigua (Jan–Mar); north- or southbound between Antigua and Barbados (Feb–Mar); Barbados to Curaçao (Dec); Curaçao to Puerto Limon, Costa Rica (Dec); Puerto Limon to Havana, Cuba (Dec).
Sea Cloud II	**Caribbean:** 10-night eastern/southern, Barbados to Antigua (Mar). 7-night eastern, round-trip from Antigua (Mar).

intricate moldings. The other original suites are similarly if less sumptuously furnished. Standard cabins are comfortable but lack the suites' time-machine quality. Still, everyone aboard gets to enjoy a taste of the past in the main restaurant, with its dark-wood paneling, brass trimmings, and nautical paintings.

The larger, three-masted *Sea Cloud II* is a modern reinterpretation of the classics, built in 2001. Her elegant lounge has rich mahogany woodwork, ornate ceiling moldings, leather club couches, and overstuffed bucket chairs, and she offers several opulent suites, one with burled wood paneling and a canopy bed. On both ships, standard cabins are very comfortable and designed with true yachting elegance. Those on *II* have small sitting areas, and all cabins have TV/VCRs, telephones, safes, hair dryers, bathrobes, and bathrooms with showers and marble sinks.

The dining room on each ship accommodates all guests in a single, open seating, and fine wines and beer are complimentary at lunch and dinner. Breakfast and some lunches are offered buffet-style, while the more formal dinners are served on elegant candlelit tables set with white linens, china, and silver. Most men wear jackets nightly, though the 2 formal nights on each cruise are not black-tie affairs—jackets and ties work just fine. Most cruises also feature a barbecue night out on deck.

These being small sailing ships, organized activities are few; it's the ships themselves that entertain, and watching the crew work the riggings, plus visits to less-touristed ports such as Les Saintes, Dominica, Bequia, Tobago, and St. Barts. Only 1 day of each cruise is spent at sea. Outside decks of both ships are covered with lines, winches, cleats, brass compasses, wooden deck chairs, and other shippy accouterments, providing a wonderfully nostalgic and nautical setting. **Sailing lectures** are offered on every cruise, though passengers are not allowed to handle the sails. *Cloud II* also has a library, a small gym, a sauna, and a swimming platform. Evenings may include piano music and mingling over cocktails. Other occasional activities may include talks by resident guest lecturers; local musicians who come aboard for a few hours; and **"open houses,"** during which guests enjoy champagne and caviar on the Main Deck before touring each other's cabins (with the residents' permission, of course).

Weeklong *Sea Cloud* cruises in the Caribbean run from $4,160 to $8,590. Sailings aboard *Sea Cloud II* run from $4,000 to $12,000. Sea Cloud sometimes charters its ships to other entities, notably Lindblad Expeditions, which has used *Sea Cloud II* in both the Caribbean and Europe recently.

10 Star Clippers

4101 Salzedo Ave., Coral Gables, FL 33146. ℭ **800/442-0551** or 305/442-0550. Fax 305/442-1611. www.star clippers.com.

THE LINE IN A NUTSHELL It's easy to fall in love with the Star Clippers experience—it's simply intoxicating. With the sails and rigging of a classic clipper ship and some of the cushy amenities of modern megas, a cruise on this beauty spells adventure and comfort. **Sails to:** Caribbean (plus Asia, South Pacific, and Europe).

THE EXPERIENCE The more ships we've sailed on, the more Star Clippers stock goes up. Few other lines offer the best of two worlds in such an appealing package. On the one hand, the ships offer comfortable, almost cushy public rooms and cabins. On the other, they espouse an unstructured, let-your-hair-down, hands-on ethic—you can climb the masts (with a harness, of course), help raise the sails, crawl into the bow netting, or chat with the captain on the open-air bridge.

On board, ducking under booms, stepping over coils of rope, leaning against railings just feet above the sea, and watching sailors work the winches are constant reminders that you're on a real working ship. Furthermore, listening to the captain's daily talk about the next port of call, the history of sailing, or some other nautical subject, you'll feel like you're exploring some of the Caribbean's more remote stretches in a ship that really belongs there—an exotic ship for an exotic locale. In a sea of look-alike megaships, *Royal Clipper* stands out, recalling a romantic, swashbuckling era of ship travel.

Pros

- **Hands-on experience:** You never have to lift a finger if you don't want to, but if you do, you're free to help out.
- **Comfortable amenities:** Pools, a piano bar and deck bar, a bright and pleasant dining room serving tasty food, and a clubby, wood-paneled library balance out the swashbuckling spirit. *Bonus:* There's also a gym, a small spa, and marble bathrooms.
- **Rich in atmosphere:** On this ship, the ambience is a real treat.
- **Offbeat itineraries:** Itineraries take passengers to remote places such as the Grenadines and French West Indies.

Cons

- **We're still trying to think of something. . . .**

Compared with the other small-ship lines, here's how Star Clippers rates:

	Poor	Fair	Good	Excellent	Outstanding
Enjoyment Factor					✓
Dining			✓		
Activities			✓		
Children's Program	N/A				
Entertainment		✓			
Service				✓	
Worth the Money					✓

STAR CLIPPERS: COMFY ADVENTURE

Clipper ships—full-sailed, built for speed, and undeniably romantic—reigned for only a brief time on the high seas before being driven out by steam engines and iron (and then steel) hulls. During their heyday, however, these vessels, including famous names such as *Cutty Sark, Ariel,* and *Flying Cloud,* engendered more romantic myths than any before or since, and helped open the Pacific coast of California during the gold rush of 1849, carrying much-needed supplies around the tip of South America from Boston and New York.

By the early 1990s, despite the nostalgia and sense of reverence that had surrounded every aspect of the clippers' maritime history, nothing that could be technically classi-fied as a clipper ship had been built since *Cutty Sark* in 1869. Enter Mikael Krafft, a Swedish-born industrialist and real estate developer with a passion for ship design and deep, deep pockets, who invested vast amounts of personal energy and more than $80 million to build *Star Flyer* and *Star Clipper* at a Belgian shipyard in 1991 and 1992.

To construct these 170-passenger twins, Krafft procured the original drawings and specifications of Scottish-born Donald McKay, a leading naval architect of 19th-cen-tury clipper-ship technology, and employed his own team of naval architects to solve such engineering problems as adapting the square-rigged, four-masted clipper design to modern materials and construction. In mid-2000, Krafft went a step further, launching the 227-passenger *Royal Clipper,* a five-masted, fully rigged sailing ship inspired by the famed *Preussen,* a German clipper built in 1902. *Royal Clipper* now claims the title of the largest clipper ship in the world, and she's a stunning sight.

When compared with Windjammer Barefoot Cruises, which operates original (if modernized) sailing ships, and Windstar Cruises, which operates less authentic elec-tronically controlled sailing ships, Star Clippers is smack dab in the middle—more luxurious and a bit more expensive than the bare-boned, no-frills Windjammer, and less formal and expensive than Windstar (though the posh *Royal Clipper* gets pretty close to Windstar level). Overall, the experience is quite casual, and salty enough to make you feel like a fisherman keeling off the coast of Maine, without the physical hardship of actually being one. As Krafft put it on one sailing, "If you want a typical cruise, you're in the wrong place."

All the Star Clippers vessels are at once traditional and radical. They're the tallest and among the fastest clipper ships ever built, and are so beautiful that even at full stop they seem to soar. As opposed to ships such as Windstar's *Wind Surf,* a bulkier cruise vessel that just happens to have sails, Star Clippers' ships do generally rely on sails alone about 25% to 35% of the time; the rest of the time, the sails are used with the engines. Each ship performs superlatively—*Royal Clipper* was designed to make up to 20 knots under sail (14 max under engine alone), and on a recent cruise, she easily hit 15 knots one afternoon. During most cruises, however, the crew tries to keep pas-sengers comfortable and decks relatively horizontal, so the vessels are kept to speeds of 9 to 14 knots with a combination of sail and engine power.

For 2007 and 2008, *Star Clipper* and *Star Flyer* are scheduled to stay in the Far East, South Pacific, and Mediterranean year-round, and so are not reviewed in this edition.

PASSENGER PROFILE

With no more than 227 passengers aboard, each Star Clippers cruise seems like a tri-umph of individuality and intimacy. The line's unusual niche appeals to passengers who might recoil at the lethargy and/or sometimes forced enthusiasm of cruises aboard larger, more typical vessels. Overall, the company reports that a whopping 60% of passengers on average are repeaters back for another Star Clippers cruise.

While you're likely to find a handful of late-20-something honeymoon-type couples and an extended-family group or two, the majority of passengers are well-traveled couples in their 40s to 60s, all active and intellectually curious professionals (such as executives, lawyers, and doctors) who appreciate a casual yet sophisticated ambience and enjoy mixing with fellow passengers. During the day, polo shirts, shorts, and topsiders are standard issue; and for dinner, many passengers simply change into cleaner and better-pressed versions of the same, with perhaps a switch from shorts to slacks for most men. However, men in jackets and women in stylish dresses aren't uncommon on the night of the captain's cocktail party.

With a nearly even mix of North Americans and Europeans (most often from Germany, Austria, Switzerland, France, and the U.K.) on a typical Caribbean cruise, the international onboard flavor is as intriguing as the ship itself. Announcements are made in English, German, and French.

DINING

Although the quality can still be inconsistent, Star Clippers' cuisine has evolved and improved over the years as the line has poured more time and effort into it, with an enhanced menu that includes four well-presented entree choices at each evening meal. All meals are open seating, with tables for four, six, and eight in the restaurant; the dress code is always casual (though some guests don jackets on the night of the captain's cocktail party). Breakfast and lunch are served buffet-style and are the best meals of the day. The continental cuisine reflects the line's large European clientele and is dominated at breakfast and lunch by cheeses (such as brie, French goat cheese, and smoked Gouda), as well as marinated fish and meats. Breakfasts also include a hot-and-cold buffet spread and an omelet station, where a staff member will make your eggs the way you like them. Late-afternoon snacks served at the Tropical Bar include such munchies as crudités, cheeses, and chicken wings.

Dinners consist of appetizers, soup, salad, dessert, and a choice of five entrees: seafood (such as lobster and shrimp with rice pilaf), meat (beef curry, for example), vegetarian, a chef's special, and a light dish. Dinner choices such as fusilli in a tomato sauce, grilled Norwegian salmon, and herb-crusted rack of lamb are tasty, but tend toward the bland side. Most dinners are sit-down (as opposed to the occasional buffet spread up on deck), and service can feel a bit rushed and frenetic during the dinner

---

Built for Speed

Every other week, when *Royal Clipper* and *Star Clipper* itineraries overlap off the coast of Dominica and the wind is favorable, the ships engage in a race under sail alone. It's great fun (and a great photo op) to watch the captain running energetically around the bridge, barking orders to the staff. A small but really loud minicannon is fired to start the race, and then each ship blasts her horn three times, whipping passengers into a competitive frenzy. Not to handicap the race too much, but the larger and more powerful *Royal Clipper* usually ends up the winner—on a recent cruise, she hit 14.5 knots while doing so.

rush. Breakfast and lunch don't get as crowded because passengers tend to eat at staggered times. Waiters and bartenders are efficient and friendly, and, depending on the cruise director, often dress in costume for several theme nights each week.

A worthwhile selection of wines is available on board, with a heavy emphasis on medium-priced French, German, and California selections.

SNACKS & EXTRAS Coffee and tea are available from a 24-hour coffee station in the piano bar. Passengers staying in the 14 suites and Owner's Suites get 24-hour room service.

ACTIVITIES

If you want action, shopping, and dozens of organized tours, you won't find much of what you're looking for on these ships and itineraries—in fact, their absence is a big part of the line's allure. For the most part, enjoying the experience of being on a sailing ship and socializing with fellow passengers and crewmembers is the main activity, as it is on most any ship this size. Plus, the ships are in port every single day, so boredom is not an issue.

The friendliness starts at the get-go, with smiling waitstaff offering guests complimentary fruit drinks as they board. Throughout the cruise, the captain gives **informal talks** on maritime themes, and, at least once a day, the cruise director speaks about the upcoming ports and shipboard events (though port info may not be as in-depth as you'd expect; on a recent *Royal Clipper* cruise, the cruise director provided only very scant information). Within reason, passengers can lend a hand with deck duties, observe the mechanics of navigation, **climb the masts** (at designated times and with a safety harness), and have a token try at handling the wheel when circumstances and calm weather permit. Each ship maintains an **open-bridge policy,** allowing passengers to wander up to the humble-looking navigation center at any hour of the day or night (you may have to ask to actually go into the chart room, though).

Other activities may include a brief engine-room tour, morning exercise classes on deck, excursions via tender to photograph the ship under sail, in-cabin movies, and hanging out by one of the three pools. Of course, sunbathing is a sport in itself. Best spot for it? In the bowsprit netting, hanging out over the water. It's sunny, it's a thrill in itself, and it's the perfect place from which to spot dolphins in the sea just feet below you, dancing in the bow's wake. Massages are available, too, at a reasonable $65 an hour: There's a dedicated massage room, divided into two areas by a curtain, and also a small gym.

Port activities are a big part of these cruises. Sailing from one island to another and often arriving at the day's port of call sometime after 9am (but usually before 11am, and usually after a brisk early-morning sail), the ship either docks alongside the shore right in town or anchors offshore and shuttles passengers back and forth by tender. On many landings, you'll have to walk a few feet in shallow water between the tender and the beach.

Activities in port revolve around beaches and watersports, and all are complimentary. That's partly because owner Mikael Krafft is an avid scuba diver and partly because itineraries focus on waters that teem with marine life; each ship offers (for an extra charge) the option of PADI-approved **scuba diving.** Certified divers will find all the equipment they'll need on board. Even uncertified/inexperienced divers can pay a fee for scuba lessons that will grant them resort certification and allow them to make a number of relatively simple dives (on every sailing there's a certified diver on the

Star Clippers Fleet Itineraries

Ship	Itineraries
Royal Clipper	**Caribbean:** 7-night eastern/southern, round-trip from Barbados (Jan–Apr).

watersports staff). There's also snorkeling (complimentary equipment is distributed at the start of the cruise), water-skiing, windsurfing, sailing, and banana-boat rides offered by the ship's watersports team in all ports. The ship carries along Zodiac motorboats for this purpose, and *Royal Clipper* has a retractable marina at its stern for easy access to the water. Because there are few passengers on board and everything is so laid-back, no sign-up sheets are needed for these activities; guests merely hang out by the gangway or on the beach until it's their turn.

The ship tends to depart from its ports early so that it can be under full sail during sunset. Trust us on this one: Position yourself at the ship's rail or dawdle over a drink at the deck bar to watch the sun melt into the horizon behind the silhouetted ships' masts and ropes. It's something you won't forget.

CHILDREN'S PROGRAM

An experience aboard a sailing ship can be a wonderfully educational and adventurous experience, especially for self-reliant children who are at least 10 years old. That said, this is not generally a line for young kids (though the line has no age restrictions, there are no supervised activities and no babysitting unless a well-intentioned crewmember agrees to volunteer his or her off-duty hours). The exception is during holiday seasons such as Christmas, when families are accommodated and some children's activities are organized by the watersports staff, including treasure hunts, beach games, and arts and crafts.

ENTERTAINMENT

Some sort of featured entertainment takes place each night after dinner by the Tropical Bar, which is the main hub of activity. There's a crew talent show one night that's always a big hit with passengers; other nights may offer a trivia contest, dance games, or a performance by local entertainers (such as a steel-drum band) who come on board for the evening. A keyboard player is on hand to sing pop songs before and after dinner, but the twangy renditions of tunes such as "Chattanooga Choo Choo" and "Day-O" don't really fit in with the ships' otherwise rustic ambience. Most nights, disco music is put on the sound system and a section of the deck serves as an impromptu dance floor, with the action usually quieting down by about 1am.

You can borrow DVDs from the library or watch the movies that are shown each day on cabin TVs in English, German, and French if you feel like vegging. Besides that, it's just you, the sea, and conversation with your fellow passengers.

SERVICE

Service is congenial, low-key, unpretentious, cheerful, and reasonably attentive. During busy times, expect efficient but sometimes distracted service in the dining rooms; and during your time on deck, realize that you'll have to fetch your own bar drinks and whatever else you may need. *Royal Clipper* has a second bar on the top deck adjacent to the pools, so you're never more than a 30-second walk from a cool drink.

The crew is international, hailing from Poland, Switzerland, Russia, Germany, Romania, Indonesia, the Philippines, and elsewhere, and their presence creates a wonderful international flavor on board. Crewmembers are friendly and usually good-natured about passengers who want to help with the sails, tie knots, and keep the deck shipshape. Because English is not the mother language of some crewmembers, though, certain details may get lost in the translation.

Officers, the cruise director, and the watersports team may dine with passengers during the week, and if you'd like to have dinner with the captain, just go up to the bridge one day and ask; he may oblige you (it depends on the captain). Unlike a lot of other small-ship lines, Star Clippers has a nurse aboard all sailings. **Laundry service** is available and so is dry cleaning.

Royal Clipper

The Verdict

This stunning, fully rigged, five-masted, square-sail clipper is a sight to behold, and the interior amenities, from marble bathrooms to an Edwardian-style three-level dining room, are the company's most plush.

Royal Clipper *(photo: Star Clippers)*

Specifications

Size (in tons)	5,000	Crew	106
Passengers (double occ.)	227	Passenger/Crew Ratio	2.2 to 1
Passenger/Space Ratio	22	Year Launched	2000
Total Cabins/Veranda Cabins	114/14	Last Refurbishment/Upgrade	N/A

Frommer's Ratings (Scale of 1–5)

★★★★

Cabin Comfort & Amenities	4	Dining Options	4.5
Appearance & Upkeep	5	Adventure & Fitness Options	4
Public Comfort/Space	4	Children's Facilities	N/A
Decor	3	Enjoyment Factor	5

Clipper's biggest and poshest ship to date—and at 439 feet in length, one of the largest sailing ships ever built—the 5,000-ton, 227-passenger *Royal Clipper* boasts more luxurious amenities than the line's older ships, including marble bathrooms, roomier cabins, a small gym and spa, and three pools. In fact, the ship definitely gives the somewhat-tired-looking, 15-plus-year-old Windstar ships a run for their money in the amenities department, while still offering a more rustic ambience. With five masts flying 42 sails that together stretch to 56,000 square feet, *Royal Clipper* is powerful too, able to achieve 20 knots under sail power only, and 14 knots under engine power. (Still, as on *Star Clipper*, the sails are more for show, and typically the engines are also in use 60%–80% of the time, especially at night.) Engines or not, for true sailors and wannabes, the web of ropes and cables stretched between *Royal Clipper's* sails, masts, and deck—along with the winches, *Titanic*-style ventilators, brass bells, wooden barrels, and chunky anchor chains cluttering the deck—are constant and beautiful reminders that you're on a real ship. So are the creaking, rolling, and pitching.

The bottom line: This ship is a big winner for those who like the good life, but in a gloriously different way than any mainstream megaship could ever offer.

Cabins & Rates

Cabins	Per Diems From	Sq. Ft.	Fridge	Hair Dryer	Sitting Area	TV
Inside	$277	113	no	yes	no	yes
Outside	$291	148	no	yes	no	yes
Suite	$566	255–320	yes	yes	no	yes

CABINS The ship's 114 cabins are gorgeous and roomy, done up in a nautical motif with navy blue and gold fabrics and dark-wood paneling. All but six are outsides with portholes and measure some 20 to 30 feet larger than cabins aboard *Star Clipper;* they're equivalent in size to the standard cabins on many Royal Caribbean and Norwegian Cruise Line ships, though they're about 40 square feet smaller than Windstar cabins. (On the other hand, they're about 50 sq. ft. larger than the typical cabins on Windjammer's ships.) Bathrooms are marble in all but the six inside cabins, and all cabins have brass and chrome fittings and plenty of elbowroom, as well as brass lighting fixtures, vanity/desks, hair dryers, safes, telephones, and TVs with DVD players. One problem: There are no full-length closets in the cabins—but then again, who's bringing an evening gown?

Some 22 cabins on the Main and Clipper decks have a pull-down third berth, but unfortunately it's only about 2 feet above the beds, so even when folded up, it juts out enough so that you can't sit up in bed without bumping your head.

Six tight 113-square-foot inside cabins on the Clipper Deck (category 6) and four outside cabins in the narrow forward section of the bow on the Commodore Deck (category 5) tend to be the best cabin bargains, if you're looking to save a buck. (See chapter 2, "Booking Your Cruise & Getting the Best Price," for more information about cabin categories.)

The 14 Deluxe Suites located forward on the Main Deck are exquisite, with private balconies, sitting areas, minibars, and whirlpool tubs. The Main Deck also has two Owner's Suites measuring 355 square feet; they're connectable, so you could conceivably book them together to create a 710-square-foot suite. Each boasts a pair of double beds, a sitting area, a minibar, and—count 'em—two marble bathrooms. Neither suite has a balcony. Suite guests get 24-hour butler service.

There are no connecting cabins, nor any wheelchair-accessible cabins.

PUBLIC AREAS *Royal Clipper* is like no other small sailing ship we've ever set foot on, with a three-level atrium and frilly multilevel dining room that are more like what you'd find on a much larger ship. Like the cabins, the decor of the ship's main lounge, library, and corridors follows a strong nautical thread, with navy blue and gold upholstery and carpeting complementing dark-wood paneling.

The open-air Tropical Bar, with its long marble and wood bar, is the hub of evening entertainment and pre-dinner hors d'oeuvres and drinks, while the more elegant piano lounge just inside hosts the weekly captain's cocktail party. (The ceiling of the piano bar is the glass bottom of the main swimming pool, so shave those legs, girls!) A clubby library is adjacent to the Tropical Bar aft on the Main Deck, and far forward on this deck is an observation lounge where you'll find two computers with e-mail and Internet capability (don't expect to see many people here—everyone's out on deck).

On the lowest deck, under the waterline and adjacent to the gym, is a little lounge called Captain Nemos, where an underwater spotlight allows you to see fishy creatures swim past the portholes while at anchor (though we never saw anyone using it when we were on the ship).

DINING OPTIONS The dining room is plush in its deep-red velveteen upholstery and dark paneling, and is spread out over three levels. With its brilliant blue sea-scene murals, white moldings and fluted columns, frilly ironwork railings and staircase, and dark-red upholstery, it's vaguely reminiscent of a room on an early-20th-century ocean liner—and somewhat out of place on an otherwise rustic ship. The buffet table is in the center on the lowest level, with seating fanning out and up. Breakfast and lunch are buffet-style and dinner is sit-down. You may notice that the low overhang from the staircase makes maneuvering around the buffet table in the dining room a bit tricky.

ADVENTURE & FITNESS OPTIONS Considering her size, *Royal Clipper* offers amazing recreation facilities, with three pools, a gym, and a small spa. The spa boils down to one massage room divided by only a curtain into two treatment areas. Leave your American inhibitions behind because not only do you get no modesty towel with these European-style rubs, but the room is so small that you can hear the muffled whispers and massage strokes of the masseuse on the other side of the curtain. Still, the treatments are expertly doled out at a reasonable $65 an hour.

The ship also has a retractable watersports marina at its stern for easy access to kayaking, sailing, and swimming.

11 Windjammer Barefoot Cruises

1759 Bay Rd., Miami Beach, FL 33139 (P.O. Box 190-120, Miami Beach, FL 33119). © **800/327-2601** or 305/672-6453. Fax 305/674-1219. www.windjammer.com.

THE LINE IN A NUTSHELL Ultracasual and delightfully carefree, this eclectic fleet of cozy, rebuilt sailing ships (powered by both sails and engines) lures passengers into a fantasy world of pirates-and-rum-punch adventure.

THE EXPERIENCE Wonderfully different from just about every other cruise experience out there, if you're the romantic and adventurous type, it's hard not to fall in love with the Windjammer way of life. When you see that the captain is wearing shorts and shades and is barefoot like the rest of the laid-back crew, it's clear these aren't your typical cruise ships. Their yards of sails, pointy bowsprits, chunky portholes, and generous use of wood create a swashbuckling, storybook look; and while passengers don't have to fish for dinner or swab the decks, they are invited to help haul the sails, take a turn at the wheel, sleep out on deck whenever they please, and (with the captain's permission) crawl into the bow net. With few rules and lots of freedom, this is the closest thing you'll get to a real old-fashioned Caribbean adventure, visiting off-the-beaten-track Caribbean ports of call. The ships are ultrainformal, and hokey yet endearing rituals make the trip feel like summer camp for adults. Add in the line's tremendous number of repeat passengers (and a few of its signature rum swizzle drinks) and you have an experience that's ultracasual, ultrafun, and downright chummy.

Pros

- **Informal and carefree:** You can wear shorts and T-shirts (and go barefoot) all day—even to dinner and to the bar.
- **Friendly and down-to-earth:** Crew and passengers mix and mingle, and in no time the ships feel like one big happy family at sea.
- **Adventurous:** With the sails flapping and wooden decks surrounding you, it's no great leap of faith to feel like a pirate on the bounding main.
- **Cheap:** Windjammer's rates are lower than those of Star Clippers and significantly lower than those of Windstar Cruises, and bar drinks are a steal.

Cons

- **Tiny cabins:** No polite way to say it: Cabins are cramped.
- **Loose port schedule:** Sailings usually follow the routes described in the brochures, but one destination may be substituted for another if a particularly adverse wind is blowing, or if there's a storm.

WINDJAMMER: LETTING IT ALL HANG OUT

In a class by itself, Windjammer promises a wind-in-your-hair barefoot adventure with zero pretense. These classic tall ships ooze with character and are almost as real and rustic as they come—except maybe for those sound-alike folks up north, the Maine Windjammer Association.

In this age of homogenous, cookie-cutter megaships that barrel their way through the Caribbean headed to crowded ports, the line's four tiny, eclectic, and appealingly imperfect tall ships are a breath of fresh, rustic air. Sure, Windjammer's ships use their engines as much or more than their sails, because it's just not practical to rely on the wind if you hope to maintain any kind of schedule, but whenever possible, the captain will navigate under sail alone for at least a short while. Except for sailing purists who might be disappointed with the use of engines, the Windjammer experience is hard to beat.

From an inspired if unintentional beginning, Windjammer has grown into one of the major lines for people who want a down-to-earth cruise alternative. The famous and now-semiretired Captain Mike Burke—Cap'n Mike, as he's been known for the past half century—founded the company in 1947 with one ship, and for years ran down-and-dirty party cruises popular with singles, purchasing sailing ships rich in history but otherwise destined for the scrap yard and transforming them into one-of-a-kind vessels.

Compared with the other small-ship lines, here's how Windjammer rates:

	Poor	Fair	Good	Excellent	Outstanding
Enjoyment Factor				✓	
Dining			✓		
Activities			✓		
Children's Program			✓*		
Entertainment			✓		
Service			✓		
Worth the Money					✓

* Children's program is available on Legacy and Polynesia only.

Legend has it that Burke, released from navy submarine duty in 1947, headed for Miami with $600 in back pay, intending to paint the town red. He succeeded. The next morning, he awoke with a blinding headache and no money, on the deck of a 19-foot sloop moored somewhere in The Bahamas. Mike Burke had apparently bought himself a boat. Using a mostly empty bottle of Scotch, he christened the boat *Hangover*, and the rest is history. He lived aboard to save money, and then started ferrying friends out for weekends of sailing and fishing. Demand escalated, and Burke quit his full-time job to become a one-man cruise line. In later years, his six children (including company president Michael David Burke) have assisted him in his ventures, renovating the vessels at the line's shipyard in Trinidad.

Though the wild-and-crazy Windjammer that used to advertise in *Hustler*, and promised its passengers they'd get a "bang" out of their vacation, has mellowed through the years, the line still offers just about the most adventurous laid-back way to island-hop in the Caribbean. No cruise can be all bad when it includes complimentary bloody marys in the morning and rum swizzles at sunset. There are no keys for the cabins, rum punch is served in paper cups, daily announcements are written in magic marker on a bulletin board, chances are the purser doubles as the nurse and gift-shop manager, and itineraries are only partially finalized before a ship's departure and may vary based on wind and tides.

Who needs swimming pools and shuffleboard? That stuff's for those other cruise ships; Windjammer offers the basic ingredients for a let-your-hair-down T-shirts-and-shorts adventure with some of the Caribbean's more offbeat islands as the incredible backdrop. That isn't to say Windjammer hasn't rolled with the times like any other cruise line. Through the years, since Mike Burke's children have taken over control of the company, a few more "mainstream" features have been added, such as an activities mate (aka cruise director) to organize more activities for passengers, improved food quality, and a summertime kids' program on *Legacy* and *Polynesia*.

Though you can't climb the masts anymore—the line dislikes being sued by passengers who've had one too many rum swizzles and fallen off—many captains will allow you to sit out in the bow rigging, as a bunch of us did one memorable night a few years back, after much, much champagne. Despite any changes, though, the rum still flows freely and the wind still blows through the rigging, and what more could a wannabe pirate really want? Yo-ho-ho, y'all.

Note: At press time, the dowdy 92-passenger *Amazing Grace*, which had been the fleet's one engine-only vessel and the closest thing to a banana boat in the cruise industry, was laid up indefinitely.

PASSENGER PROFILE

Can we say nutty, quirky, nonconformist? That's why Windjammer is so appealing: It's different—a rare concept in today's mostly homogenous megaship cruise world. Unlike some "all things to all people" lines, Windjammer is for a particular kind of informal, fun-loving, down-to-earth passenger, and though some compare the experience to a continuous frat party, we wouldn't go that far. In fact, the passenger and age mix gives lie to that description. From honeymooning couples in their 20s to grandparents in their 70s, the line attracts a broad range of adventurers who like to have fun and don't want anything resembling a highly regimented vacation. Passengers are pretty evenly divided between men and women, and 15% to 20% overall are single.

Many passengers love the Windjammer experience so much that they return again and again. Last time we checked, the record was still held by the late "Pappy" Gomez of Cleveland, Ohio, who sailed with Windjammer more than 160 times, but many, many others have sailed with the line 30 to 50 times. The line's supply officer told us he never steps aboard one of the ships without seeing passengers he's sailed with before. There's even a reunion of sorts called the Jammerfest that has Windjammer die-hards flocking to Miami for a weekend blitz: Windjammer throws one of the parties and the groupies pick up their hotel, airfare, and everything else. Shows you just how far a Windjammer fan will go to keep the party alive.

Young children should probably not go (in fact, the line doesn't accept passengers under 6), nor should anyone prone to seasickness (there's quite a bit of that the first days out) or anyone wanting to be pampered (there's none of that during any day out). These ships are not for people with disabilities, either.

DINING

When it comes to dining, "slide over and pass me the breadbasket" about sums it up. Family-style and informal, there's nothing gourmet about the food, which ranges from mediocre to quite tasty. All breads and pastries are homemade, and at dinner, after soup and salad are served, passengers can choose from two main entrees, such as curried shrimp and roast pork with garlic sauce. Don't be surprised if the waiters ask for a show of hands to see who wants what. Tasty breakfasts include all the usual, plus items such as eggs Benedict, and lunches include items such as lobster pizza and apple salad. Both of these meals are served buffet-style. At certain islands, the crew lugs ashore a picnic lunch for an afternoon beach party, and each sailing usually includes an on-deck barbecue one evening. There are two open seatings for dinner, marked by the clang of a loud barnyard-style bell, usually around 6:30 and 8pm. Many dishes overall are rooted in Caribbean tradition. The chef will accommodate **special diets,** including vegetarian and low-salt. And don't be shy if it's your birthday: The chef will make you a free cake and serve it at dinner. House wines are free—drink up!

SNACKS & EXTRAS Bloody marys are free at breakfast, and each evening at about 5pm, gallons of complimentary **rum swizzles** are dispensed along with hors d'oeuvres that may include homemade plantain chips and salsa, spicy meatballs, chicken fingers, and cheese and crackers. Guests gather on deck, often still in their sarongs and shorts, mingling in the fresh sea air as island music plays in the background. On one of our trips, a woman sang a silly song she wrote about the cruise and the people she had met, as the line's supply officer accompanied her on his flute.

ACTIVITIES

Windjammer deliberately deemphasizes the activities that dominate life aboard larger vessels, although it may occasionally host an on-deck crab race, knot-tying demonstration, or talk on astronomy or some aspect of sailing. Otherwise, your entertainment is up to you. If the weather's fine and you want to help trim the sails, you may be allowed to lend a hand. If conditions are right and the captain is amenable, passengers can jump overboard, literally, and go for a swim when the ships are anchored offshore.

Just about every day is spent in port somewhere. Generally at least once per cruise, on one of the ships' beach visits—to Jost Van Dyke, perhaps—the activities mate organizes **team games** reminiscent of mid-1960s cocktail-party movies (think Cary Grant and Audrey Hepburn in the nightclub scene in *Charade*). It's the usual embarrassing stuff: Passengers twirl hula hoops while dressed in snorkel gear; pass cucumbers to each other, clasping them only with their thighs; or flop onto slippery foam mats and try to swim to and around a landmark. Silliness, in other words—but it does make for instant camaraderie. After all, after someone's seen you act this dumb, they've seen it all. In other ports, there may also be **organized hikes.**

Snorkeling gear (mask, fins, snorkel, and carrying bag) rents for $25 per week. Certified PADI dive instructors now sail aboard *Legacy, Polynesia,* and *Mandalay* during the summer and teach passengers of all skill levels, including beginners and kids.

There are a handful of **theme cruises** every year, including about six for singles only, plus typically a photography theme sailing and a few focusing on astronomy and even pirates (the latter being Windjammer's wacky pirate's week cruises, described by a company source like this: "We get a bunch of insane Windjammer types together to enjoy a lot of pirate-theme crap," from costume parties to pirate trivia, boat building, treasure hunts, and lots of rum swigging). Sounds fun to us!

CHILDREN'S PROGRAM

Though this is not a children-oriented line in any traditional sense of the word—there are no video arcades, movies, and teen discos—two of Windjammer's ships do offer kids' programs during the summer for families looking for a little adventure. The *Legacy* and *Polynesia* have a "Junior Jammers" kids' program for ages 6 to 17 that can draw as many as 40 kids a cruise in the summer—a full third of the passenger total (pretty much guaranteed to cramp an old salt's party). Both ships offer counselors for two main age groups (6–11 and 12–17) who supervise a roster of summer-camp-style activities between 9am and 9pm daily (they do many activities in empty cabins on the *Poly* and in unused public rooms on the *Legacy*). Programs for younger kids focus on activities such as arts and crafts, face painting, hair braiding, building sand castles, knot tying, hoisting the sails, and visits to the bridge, while teens can do stuff such as sailing, snorkeling, navigating, and kayaking. There are also introductory scuba classes for 8- to 10-year-olds and 11- to 16-year-olds. Do keep in mind, cabins are small and slippery decks aren't sympathetic to running children.

We would not recommend bringing young kids aboard the line's other ships, which don't have any programs or babysitting. For teens, if they can go a week without e-mail and Game Boys, and can divert themselves the same way adults do, with conversation, shore excursions, reading, and watching the wide blue sea, then a week on a tall ship would be a memorable experience for them.

No children under 6 are allowed aboard any ship in the Windjammer fleet. Unlike most megaship lines, which require passengers to be at least 21 years old unless accompanied by parents, Windjammer's minimum unaccompanied age is 17.

Children 6 to 12 sharing a cabin with two adults pay 50% of the adult fare. In June, July, and August on *Legacy* and *Polynesia,* children 6 to 12 are free.

ENTERTAINMENT

Part entertainment, part education, the **Captain's "Story Time"** held each morning out on deck is the first event of the average day on a Windjammer ship. It's a short talk that's 20% ship business; 40% information about the day's port call, activities, or sailing route; and 40% pure humor (on one trip we took, a joke about a cat and a certain part of a woman's anatomy was par for the course). At these morning meetings, the captain will come out and shout "Good morning, everybody!" and the passengers—many of whom have taken these trips before and know the drill—bark back in chorus, "Good morning, Captain SIR!"

Windjammer Fleet Itineraries*

Ship	Itineraries
Legacy	**Caribbean:** 6-night Costa Rica/Panama: Round-trip from Herradura, Costa Rica (Jan–May).
Mandalay	**Caribbean:** 6-night eastern, north- or southbound between Antigua and St. Maarten (Jan–May).
Polynesia	**Caribbean:** 6-night eastern, north- or southbound between St Maarten and Tortola, BVI (Jan–May).
Yankee Clipper	**Caribbean:** 6-night southern, round-trip from Grenada (Jan–May).

* At press time, Windjammer itineraries were only available through May 2008—which is no great surprise since nobody, not even Windjammer's staff, seems to know exactly where the line's ships go, at least not very far ahead of time. But really, it doesn't matter: The islands are always small and beautiful, and the ambience is always wacky. We were aboard for a week once and couldn't remember where we'd been when we got home. We still aren't sure, but we do know we had a great time. A company spokeswoman told us this is fairly common.

The Windjammer crowd loves every minute of it. In fact, the line's accessible and down-to-earth captains are often a part of the entertainment themselves—passengers love them and are like groupies at a rock concert, whether fawning over quiet, charming, fleet hottie Captain Matt, who is often at the helm of *Legacy* these days, or chatting with the more fatherly Captain John, who, as a senior captain, rotates among all the ships of the fleet.

In general, social interaction is centered on the bars and top Sun Deck. There's typically a passenger talent show one night; a local pop band is brought on board for a few hours of dancing once or twice a week; and there's a weekly **barbecue buffet dinner and costume party**—a Windjammer tradition that has passengers (and crew) decked out as cross-dressers, pirates, and other characters (Captain Matt looked mighty dashing as Captain Hook on a cruise a few years ago). Bring your own get-up or rummage through the pile of shabby costumes the crew hauls out before the party. Either way, it's a ball! Otherwise, there's almost no organized nightlife.

After dinner, head up to the on-deck bar (a Bud's $4 and it's $6 for a piña colada) or grab a chair or mat and hit the deck. Generally, the ships stay late in one or two ports so that passengers can head ashore to an island watering hole.

SERVICE

Windjammer tends to attract a staff that shares founder Mike Burke's appreciation for the wide-open sea and barely concealed scorn for corporate agendas and workaday priorities. Many are from the same Caribbean islands the line's ships visit. Service is friendly and efficient but not doting, matter-of-fact and straightforward rather than obsequious. Unlike more upscale cruise lines, with Windjammer there's no master/servant relationship between passengers and staff—the crewmembers just happen to steer the ship or serve dinner or drinks, and will chat like regular folks when they're not. They're a good bunch.

Windjammer's wacky tall ships offer a quaint version of the computerized account system the big lines use to keep track of passengers' onboard purchases. The bar operates on a **doubloon system,** which is a kind of debit card for drinks that amounts to a round paper card passengers purchase and the bartender punches holes in.

Windjammer also offers wedding packages these days, just like the big-ship guys do. Could be pretty neat to tie the knot under the riggings of one of the line's tall ships. Do it on deck or on a beach shore side in Antigua, Aruba, Grenada, Tortola, Nevis, St. Thomas, and other places. You can get married Saturday or Sunday before the cruise, or on Monday morning before the ship's departure; ceremonies officiated by Windjammer captains (not legally binding though, so get the license first) can take place on Monday or Tuesday during your cruise. The line has a wedding consultant to help with the details, including all the legal stuff. Packages range from $750 to $1,100 per couple, with the top-end option including the services of a local wedding coordinator and a nondenominational local officiant, photographer, topical bouquet, boutonniere, wedding cake, champagne toast, dinner with the captain, and more. The line also offers vow-renewal ceremonies officiated by the captain and complimentary honeymoon gift baskets that include a bottle of bubbly and special T-shirts.

Legacy

The Verdict

The brightest, newest, and most spacious of Windjammer's ships, *Legacy* is a real winner in our book, with comfortable cabins, good-size private bathrooms, a cheerful dining saloon with large round booths, and a sprawling expanse of outdoor deck space. Even when full, the ship doesn't feel crowded.

Legacy (photo: Windjammer)

Specifications

Size (in tons)	1,165	Crew	43
Passengers (double occ.)	122	Passenger/Crew Ratio	2.8 to 1
Passenger/Space Ratio	9.7	Year Launched	1959
Total Cabins/Veranda Cabins	61/0	Last Refurbishment/Upgrade	1997

Frommer's Ratings (Scale of 1–5)   ★★★½

Cabin Comfort & Amenities	2	Dining Options	3
Appearance & Upkeep	4	Adventure & Fitness Options	N/A
Public Comfort/Space	4	Children's Facilities	N/A*
Decor	3	Enjoyment Factor	5

* *Legacy has a children's program but no dedicated facilities.*

Rebuilt and relaunched in 1997 as the line's largest and most modern ship, *Legacy* was originally built in 1959 as a motored research vessel for the French government, designed with a deep keel that gave her additional balance during North Atlantic and North Sea storms. At the time, she was one of several government-owned ships sending weather reports to a central agency in Paris, which used them to predict storm patterns on the French mainland. The advent of global satellites made the vessel obsolete, and she was bought in 1988 by Windjammer, which over the course of a decade poured over $10 million into a massive reconfiguration at the family-managed Windjammer shipyard in Trinidad. Four steel masts and 11 sails were added, plus accouterments the vessel needed for barefoot jaunts through the Caribbean. Although still tiny compared to a megaship, at 1,165 tons she's larger than any other vessel in the Windjammer fleet, and is the only one that offers some itineraries from the mainland U.S.

Some hard-core Windjammer veterans consider *Legacy* a wimpy addition to the venerated rough-and-tumble fleet, feeling that it's just not a real yo-ho-ho pirate adventure without their cramped, bare-bones lifestyle. When the vessel was launched, stalwart Windjammer fans wondered whether her comfort level and (gasp!) children's program meant the old days were gone forever. It was like seeing a group of 30- or 40-somethings returning to their favorite college-era dive bar and finding it newly sheathed in wood paneling, with brass lamps in place of the neon lights, and light jazz on the jukebox instead of "Born to Run."

Well, here's the scoop: Though she is indeed the most comfortable of the Windjammer lot, she still embraces that irreverent Windjammer spirit. It takes only a glance at the carved wooden figurehead on the ship's prow—an image of line founder Cap'n Mike Burke in a tropical-print shirt, beer in one hand and a ship's wheel in the other—to see that this is still very much a laid-back, partying vessel. She's just a slightly cushier one.

Cabins & Rates

Cabins	Per Diems From	Sq. Ft.	Fridge	Hair Dryer	Sitting Area	TV
Outside	$169	85	no	no	no	no
Suite	$219	160	no	no	yes	yes

CABINS Cabins aboard *Legacy* are a little larger and more comfortable than those aboard the line's older ships, but if you're used to sailing aboard typical large cruise ships, they'll probably seem cramped. Berths are either doubles or bunk beds, and if you're in the upper portion of the latter, watch your head: More than one passenger has woken up and knocked himself silly on the metal porthole cover, which projects from the wall when open. You'd do well to sleep with your feet toward it.

Suites—both the Admiral Suites and Burke's Berth, which is the best in the house—offer windows instead of portholes, plus space for a third occupant. There are a handful of single cabins, plus triple- and quad-berth options in the Commodore-class cabins, though this affords a minimum of personal space. Burke's Berth is the only cabin aboard that has an entertainment center, a bar, and a vanity.

Storage in all cabins is perfectly adequate for this type of T-shirt-and-shorts cruise, with each containing a small closet/drawer unit and having additional space under the bed. Bathrooms offer enough maneuvering space, but it's a crapshoot on the small, curtained showers—some have a raised lip that contains the runoff and some don't, making for a perpetually wet bathroom floor. Lip or no, small and spartan or not (compared to those offered on larger and glitzier ships), these facilities are still far better than the head-style facilities aboard the other Windjammer sailing ships.

There are no connecting cabins, and like all the other Windjammer ships, *Legacy* has no wheelchair-accessible cabins, and is not a good option for people with disabilities.

PUBLIC AREAS The top deck, with a large canopied area at its center, is the social focus of the cruise, the space where the rum swizzles are dispensed at sunset, where visiting bands perform at night, and where the captain conducts his daily morning "Story Time" session. The ship's bar is also located on this deck, as is the requisite barrel of rum—a real barrel, from which the bartender siphons off what he needs every day.

The Poop Deck offers the best sunbathing space, although shade from the raised sails could force you to move often. Passengers lounge on patio-style white plastic recliners or on the blue cushions strewn about, which many passengers also use to sleep out on deck under the stars, something the line fully encourages.

Navigation of the ship is often from a ship's wheel mounted out in open air near the bow. When seas are calm and sailing is easy, the crew offers passengers a chance to steer. Unlike the practice on most larger cruise ships, *Legacy's* bow is generally open to passengers, allowing you (if the captain approves) to do your Leonardo DiCaprio "king of the world" bit, or, even better, to climb out on the netting that projects to the tip of the bowsprit and lounge there while the blue Caribbean Sea splashes and sprays below you. Don't miss this opportunity if it's offered—trust us.

The only other interior public room is a small and not terribly appealing lounge that offers a TV/video arrangement and a smattering of books and board games. In an entire week aboard, the only person we saw using this room was a 10-year-old boy watching movies. Everyone else was outside, playing.

DINING OPTIONS All meals are served in the comfortable aft dining room, fitted with large circular booths (a bummer if you're stuck in the middle, three or four people from freedom) and decorated with faux tropical plants. Evening hors d'oeuvres are served out on deck.

ADVENTURE & FITNESS OPTIONS As aboard the rest of the line's ships, there are none. No pool, no spa, no gym, no jogging track. Aboard ship, the most exercise you're likely to get is if you volunteer to help hoist the sails. In port, however, you'll have such options as snorkeling, scuba diving, sea kayaking (the ship carries its own kayaks aboard), and hiking to help you work off dessert.

Mandalay • Yankee Clipper • Polynesia

The Verdict

Bound by wood and sails, these oddball little ships have led fascinating and long lives, and today promise adventure, good times, and offbeat ports at a bargain price.

Yankee Clipper *(photo: Windjammer)*

Specifications

Size (in tons)		Crew	
Mandalay	420	*Mandalay*	28
Yankee Clipper	327	*Yankee Clipper*	29
Polynesia	430	*Polynesia*	45
Passengers (double occ.)		Passenger/Crew Ratio	
Mandalay	72	*Mandalay*	2.6 to 1
Yankee Clipper	64	*Yankee Clipper*	2.2 to 1
Polynesia	112	*Polynesia*	2.5 to 1
Passenger/Space Ratio		Year Launched	
Mandalay	5.8	*Mandalay*	1923
Yankee Clipper	5.1	*Yankee Clipper*	1927
Polynesia	3.4	*Polynesia*	1938
Total Cabins/Veranda Cabins		Last Refurbishment/Upgrade	
Mandalay	36/0	*Mandalay*	1982
Yankee Clipper	32/0	*Yankee Clipper*	1984
Polynesia	50/0	*Polynesia*	2002

Frommer's Ratings (Scale of 1–5)   ★★★

Cabin Comfort & Amenities	2	Dining Options	3
Appearance & Upkeep	3	Adventure & Fitness Options	N/A
Public Comfort/Space	3	Children's Facilities	N/A*
Decor	3	Enjoyment Factor	5

* Polynesia *has a children's program but no dedicated facilities.*

Despite different origins and subtle differences in the way they react to the wind and weather, all of these sailing ships share many traits, so we've opted to cluster them into one all-encompassing review. All are roughly equivalent in amenities, activities, and onboard atmosphere; and because each has been extensively refurbished, they have more or less equivalent interior decors. As for their capabilities as sailing ships, Captain Stuart Larcombe, who has served aboard them all, told us that the award goes to *Mandalay* (now that *Flying Cloud,* once a spy ship for the Allied navy in World War II, was retired in 2002). For adventure and interesting ports of call, though, they're all absolutely top-notch, and we advise selecting your ship based on itinerary rather than the ships' minor physical differences.

What make the ships most unique are their histories. *Mandalay* was once the *Hussar IV,* the fourth in a line of same-name yachts built for financier E. F. Hutton, and was, by some accounts, the most sumptuous private yacht in the world. Later, she was commissioned as a research vessel by Columbia University, which sailed her for 1.25 million miles trying to develop theories about continental drift, which have since been proven correct. It's estimated that by the early 1980s, half the knowledge of the world's ocean floor was gathered by instruments aboard this ship.

Yankee Clipper, once the only armor-plated sailing yacht in the world, was built in 1927 by German industrial and munitions giant Krupp-Werft. Allegedly, Hitler once stepped aboard to award the Iron Cross to one of his U-boat commanders. Seized by the United States as booty after World War II, the ship eventually became George Vanderbilt's private yacht and the fastest two-masted vessel sailing off the California coast, once managing 22 knots under full sail. Burke bought the ship just before it was due to be broken down for scrap, then gutted, redesigned, and rebuilt it, stripping off the armor in the process. Renovations in 1984 added a third mast, additional deck space, and cabin modifications. Although not as streamlined as she was originally, she's still a fast and very exciting ship.

Polynesia, built in Holland in 1938, was originally known as *Argus,* and served as a fishing schooner in the Portuguese Grand Banks fleet. Windjammer bought her in 1975, gave her a good scrubbing to wash out the fish smell, and performed a complete reconfiguration of the cabins and interior spaces, adding lots of varnished wood. Less stylish-looking than many of her thoroughbred siblings, she nonetheless remains one of Windjammer's most consistently popular ships, on the one hand due to her handful of annual singles cruises, on the other because she's one of only two Windjammer ships (along with *Legacy*) that offers a children's program.

Cabins & Rates

Cabins	Per Diems From	Sq. Ft.	Fridge	Hair Dryer	Sitting Area	TV
Inside	$200	40–70	no	no	no	no
Outside	$250	40–70	no	no	no	no
Suite	$300	95	some	no	yes	some

CABINS There's no getting around it: Cabins are cramped, just as they would have been on a true 19th-century clipper ship. Few retain any glamorous vestiges of their original owners, and most are about as functional as they come, though wood paneling in *Mandalay* and *Yankee Clipper*'s cabins gives a pleasantly rustic feel. They're all adequate enough, however, and it's the adventurous thrill of sailing on one of these ships that you come for, not luxurious accommodations.

Each cabin has a minuscule bathroom with a shower, many of which function with a push button—for every push you get about 10 seconds' worth of water—that you'll wind up keeping your finger on the whole time while trying to wash with the other. On many vessels, hot water is available only during certain hours of the day, whenever the ships' galleys and laundries aren't using it. Be prepared for toilets that don't always function properly, and retain your sense of humor as they're repaired.

Storage space is limited, but this isn't a serious problem because few passengers bring much with them. Many cabins have upper and lower berths, some have lower-level twins, and a few have doubles (so much for romance). Some standard cabins on *Polynesia* don't have portholes; the rest all do. On *Mandalay* aft deck cabins share a bathroom but are kind of nifty because they have a skylight and a little balcony. They're good for families, couples sailing together, and people who are willing to balance the lack of a private bathroom against double beds and some extra amenities, such as a minifridge. *Polynesia* offers three windowless cabins that sleep four people.

Some vessels have a limited number of suites with minifridges that, although not spacious by the standards of larger ships, seem to be of generous proportions when contrasted with the standard cabins. *Polynesia*'s refit a few years back included the creation of 10 windowed suites on Deck A (the highest cabin deck), with twin beds that can be converted to doubles.

Other than a pair of cabins connecting on *Mandalay*, there are no connecting cabins on these ships. There are no wheelchair-accessible cabins on any of these ships.

PUBLIC AREAS   What glamour may have been associated with these ships in the past is long gone, lost to the years or in the gutting and refitting they required before entering Windjammer service. There's still a lot of rosewood, mahogany, and other woods left; but today it mixes with more practical steel rather than gilt, and makes an appropriate backdrop for passengers so laid-back that few bother to ever change out of their bathing suits and T-shirts. The ships' teak decks are the most popular areas on these ships, and many passengers adopt some preferred corner as a place to hang out.

DINING OPTIONS   Dining rooms are cozy, and paneled to a greater or lesser extent in wood, though overall they've been designed for efficiency. All are air-conditioned except aboard *Mandalay*, whose dining room is open-air, kept cool by evening breezes. *Polynesia*'s recent and extensive refit redecorated her dining saloon and bar with an appropriately Polynesian look, incorporating bamboo and Tiki masks.

ADVENTURE & FITNESS OPTIONS   These ships are too small to offer health clubs, saunas, or the fitness regimens so heavily promoted aboard larger ships, and none has a swimming pool. You'll get an adequate amount of exercise, however, during hikes; snorkeling; diving and swimming off the side of the ships; and scuba sessions conducted at the ports of call.

12 Windstar Cruises

300 Elliott Ave. W., Seattle, WA 98119. ✆ **800/258-7245** or 206/281-3535. Fax 206/281-0627. www.windstar cruises.com.

THE LINE IN A NUTSHELL   Windstar walks a tightrope between luxury line and sailing-ship line, with an always-casual onboard vibe, beyond-the-norm itineraries, and first-class service and cuisine.

THE EXPERIENCE   You say you want a cruise that visits interesting ports; offers superfriendly yet efficient, on-the-nose service; serves excellent cuisine; offers active options like watersports from a retractable platform in the stern; has sails for a romantic vibe; and still doesn't cost an arm and a leg? You pretty much only have one option: Windstar.

This is no barefoot, rigging-pulling, paper-plates-in-lap, sleep-on-the-deck kind of cruise, but a refined yet down-to-earth, yachtlike experience for a sophisticated, well-traveled crowd that wouldn't be comfortable on a big ship with throngs of tourists. On board, stained teak, brass details, and lots of navy blue fabrics and carpeting lend a traditional nautical ambience, and though the ships' tall masts and white sails cut a traditional profile, they're also state-of-the-art, controlled by a computer so that they can be furled or unfurled at the touch of a button. Despite the ships' relatively large size (*Wind Surf* is one of the world's largest sailing ships, if not the largest), they're able to travel at upward of 12 knots under sail power alone, though more usually the sails are up as a fuel-saving aid to the diesel engines.

Pros

- **Sails:** While you won't get a full-on sailing experience here like you do with the Maine Windjammer ships, you do get the ambience, plus the karmic fillip of knowing the sails help save fuel.
- **Service:** Windstar employs mostly Indonesian and Filipino staff, many of whom stay aboard for years. They're extremely professional and friendly as all get-out.
- **Cuisine:** Few small ships can match Windstar for the quality and ambience of their dining experience, with cuisine served in open-seating restaurants where guests can usually get a table for two.
- **Informal and unregimented days:** Beyond "don't wear shorts in the dining rooms," there's no real dress code here, and most men don't even bother with sport jackets at dinner. Similarly, there are zero rah-rah activities, keeping days loose and languid: Explore ashore (the itineraries visit a port almost every day) or kick back and relax aboard ship without a lot of distraction.

Cons

- **Limited activities and entertainment:** This is intentional, but if you need lots of organized hoopla to keep you happy, you won't find much here.
- **No verandas:** If they're important to you, you're out of luck.

WINDSTAR: CASUAL ELEGANCE UNDER SAIL

Thank goodness there's a company like Windstar in the frequently homogenous cruise industry. It's an individual. It's got personality. Its operations are friendly and almost old-fashioned, small-scale and full of employees who've been with the line for years. Reportedly, many repeat passengers check to make sure their favorite cabin steward, waiter, captain, or host/hostess will be aboard before they'll book a particular sailing.

The line got its start in 1984, founded by a consortium of two ship owners and Jean Claude Potier, a former U.S. head of the legendary French Line. From the start, it was all about the sails—and specifically about a new cruise ship design by the Finnish shipbuilding company Wartsila. Dubbed the "Windcruiser," the concept combined 19th-century sailing-ship technology with modern engineering to create a kind of vessel never seen before in the cruise ship world: huge by sailing-ship standards, with at least 21,489 square feet of computer-controlled staysails that furl and unfurl at the touch of a button and can work on their own or in concert with a diesel-electric engine. The concept worked then, and it works now: As you see a Windstar ship

Compared with the other adventure lines, here's how Windstar rates:

	Poor	Fair	Good	Excellent	Outstanding
Enjoyment Factor					✓
Dining				✓	
Activities		✓			
Children's Program	N/A*				
Entertainment		✓			
Service					✓
Worth the Money				✓	

* Windstar has no children's program.

approaching port, with its long, graceful hull and masts the height of 20-story buildings, you'll forget all about the giant megaships moored nearby and think, "Now that's a ship."

In the spirit of keeping up appearances, in late 2006, the *Wind Surf* had a multi-million-dollar face-lift. Dubbed the Degrees of Difference enhancements, public spaces and staterooms were updated, plus a pair of new luxury suites was added on the Bridge Deck, bringing the ship's capacity to 312 passengers. At press time, *Wind Spirit* and *Wind Star* were scheduled to undergo similar enhancements before the end of 2007.

Ownership trivia: In 2007, Ambassadors International—the company that bought Delta Queen and American West Steamboat Company in 2006 and merged them into Majestic America Line—bought Windstar from longtime parent company Holland America.

PASSENGER PROFILE

People who expect high-caliber service and very high-quality cuisine but dislike the formality of the other high-end ships (as well as the mass-mentality of the megaships) are thrilled with Windstar. Most passengers are couples in their late 30s to early 60s, with the average around 51. Overall, an amazing 60% to 70% of passengers are repeaters, back for their annual or semiannual dose of Windstar. There are also usually a handful of honeymoon couples aboard any given sailing—a good choice on their part, as Windstar ranks high on our list of most romantic cruise lines. The line gets very few families with young kids—rarely more than 6 or 7 on any sailing, and those usually in the 10-plus age range, and only during school holiday periods.

Overall, Windstar's sophisticated and well-traveled passengers are more down-to-earth than guests on the luxury lines, but not as focused on nature and learning as guests on most of the other small-ship lines. Most want something different from the regular cruise experience, eschew the "bigger is better" philosophy of conventional cruising, and want their vacation to focus more on the ports than on onboard activities. These cruises are for those seeking a romantic escape and who like to visit islands and ports not often touched by regular cruise ships.

Windstar caters to corporate groups, too, with about 25% of its annual cruises booked as full charters or hosting affinity groups.

DINING

Windstar's cuisine is tops in the small-ship category and is a high point of the cruise, served in two or three always-casual restaurants.

Windstar Fleet Itineraries

Ship	Itineraries
Wind Spirit	**Caribbean:** 7-night eastern, round-trip from St. Thomas (Jan–Mar & Dec).
Wind Star	**Caribbean:** 7-night Costa Rica/Nicaragua, round-trip from Caldera, Costa Rica (Jan–Mar & Dec). **Panama Canal/Caribbean:** 14 nights, east- or westbound between Caldera, Costa Rica, and Barbados (Apr & Nov).
Wind Surf	**Caribbean:** 7-night eastern/southern, round-trip from Barbados (Jan–Mar & Nov–Dec).

TRADITIONAL   Dinner is served primarily in each ship's spacious, nautically appointed main restaurant, though the vibe here is less formal and regimented than aboard most larger ships. At dinner, the line's **no-jackets-required** policy for men means guests do the "casual elegance" thing—pants or casual dresses for women and trousers and nice collared shirts for men—and its open-seating policy means you can show up when you want (within a 2-hr. window) and dine with whomever you want. Restaurants aboard all three ships are set up with an unusual number of tables for two (proving that Windstar is serious about its romantic image), and there's rarely a wait.

The cuisine here was created by chef/restaurateur **Joachim Splichal,** *Bon Appétit's* "Restaurateur of the Year" for 2002. Think straightforward dishes incorporating regional touches and surprising twists. Appetizers may include golden fried Brie served with cranberry sauce and crispy parsley, or a sweet shrimp and crab salad. Among the main courses, you may see a grilled local fish served with a roast corn salsa and sweet plantains, sautéed jumbo prawns served with garlic spinach and spaghetti, or an herb-and-peppercorn-coated prime rib of beef. Desserts such as an apple tart with raspberry coulis and chocolate crème brûlée are beyond tempting. As part of the line's recent "Degrees of Difference" upgrades, in mid-2005 Splichal created 100 new dishes for the line's restaurants. Other additions include a new **wine list** featuring more boutique labels, many from California, Australia, New Zealand, Spain, France, and South Africa; a selection of exotic fine cheeses (many bought fresh in local markets) served table-side from a cheese cart, and petits fours served with coffee after dinner.

Vegetarian dishes and **healthy "Sail Light" choices** designed by light-cooking expert Jeanne Jones are available for breakfast, lunch, and dinner; fat and calorie content is listed on the menu. The light choices may feature Atlantic salmon with couscous and fresh vegetables, or a Thai country-style chicken with veggies and Asian rice. The vegetarian options may feature a fresh garden stew or a savory polenta with Italian salsa.

ALTERNATIVE   Windstar's largest ship, the *Wind Surf,* offers alternative dining at the casual, 128-seat Degrees, an intimate space with an understated fantasy-garden motif and a menu that rotates between steakhouse, Italian, French, and Indonesian dishes. Reservations are required, but there's no additional fee.

CASUAL   Breakfast and lunch are available at the buffet-style Veranda Cafe, which offers a generous spread as well as a specialty omelet station at breakfast and a grill option at lunch. Waiters will bring the latter to your table, so there's no waiting. You can also opt for a simple continental breakfast at the sternside Compass Rose bar.

The once-a-week evening **barbecues** on the pool decks of the *Star* and *Spirit* are wonderful parties under the stars, with an ample and beautifully designed buffet spread, tables set with linens, and (often) a Caribbean-style band adding ambience. On the *Wind Surf,* there's a gala buffet dinner once per cruise in the main lounge, which is transformed into a third dining room for the evening, with a culinary theme matching your cruise region. All three ships also offer weekly barbecue lunches on deck.

SNACKS & EXTRAS Snacks, including pizza and hot dogs, are available from the pool bar in the afternoons. Speedy **room service** offers continental breakfast; a menu of about a dozen sandwiches, salads, seafood, and steaks from 11am to 10pm; and a dozen more snack items (from popcorn and chips and salsa to a cheese platter or beef consommé) 24 hours a day. During restaurant hours you can have items from the restaurant's menu served course by course in your cabin, speedy and hot.

ACTIVITIES

Because Windstar's itineraries emphasize days in port over days at sea (in the Caribbean, most cruises either hit a port every day or spend just 1 day at sea per week), its ships offer few organized activities, leaving days relaxed and unregimented—the way guests prefer it. The handful of scheduled diversions that are available usually include casino gaming lessons, walk-a-mile and stretch classes on deck, and an occasional vegetable-carving or food-decorating demonstration. At ports where the ships anchor offshore (most of them, in the Caribbean), passengers can enjoy complimentary kayaking, sailing, water-skiing, snorkeling, windsurfing, and ski tubing from a **watersports platform** that's lowered from the stern, weather and sea conditions permitting. You can also swim off of the platform on *Wind Spirit* and *Star,* though not on the larger *Wind Surf* due to safety concerns. Up top, the pool deck offers a small pool and hot tub, deck chairs, and an open-air bar. Other open areas, especially on the larger *Wind Surf,* offer quiet spots for reading. There's also a SCUBA diving program for novices and experienced divers.

In port, the company's shore excursions tend to be more creative than usual, and the onboard hosts or hostesses (aka cruise directors, who sometimes double as shore excursions managers and jacks-of-all-trades) are usually very knowledgeable about the ports and are able to point passengers toward good spots for bird-watching, snorkeling, or a nice meal. Brief orientation talks are held before port visits.

The ships all maintain an open-bridge policy, so at most times you're free to walk right in to chat with the captain and officers on duty. There's an extensive DVD and CD collection from which passengers can borrow for use in their cabins. Guests may also check out fully loaded **Apple iPod Nanos** free of charge from the reception desk, using them either with headphones or in conjunction with the Bose SoundDock speakers in each cabin. There are also docking stations and headphones in the Surf's new Yacht Club Internet cafe-cum-lounge. All three ships have some level of Internet connectivity—*Wind Surf* has eight computers in the Yacht Club, and *Star* and *Spirit* have two computers in their libraries, which offer e-mail access only. All three vessels are now rigged for **bow-to-stern Wi-Fi Internet service;** wireless laptops will be rentable at the front desk if you don't want to lug your own.

CHILDREN'S PROGRAM

Because children sail infrequently with Windstar, no activities are planned for them. The kids who do appear on board are generally ages 10 and up, but there are rarely more than six or seven on any sailing, and those only during school breaks. The ships' DVD libraries stock some children's films. The minimum age for children to sail is 2 years.

ENTERTAINMENT

For the most part, passengers entertain themselves, though each ship does carry a number of musicians who provide tunes for evening dancing and background. Most evenings, passengers either retire to their cabins; head for the modest **casino** with its slots, blackjack, roulette, and Caribbean stud poker; or go up to the Compass Rose Bar (and also the indoor/outdoor Terrace Bar on the *Surf*) for a nightcap under the stars. Sometimes after 10 or 11pm, disco/pop music is played in the lounge if guests are in a dancing mood, and once per cruise a **crew show** allows the ship's Indonesian and Filipino crewmembers to strut their stuff to traditional and contemporary music and dance. It's always a crowd pleaser.

SERVICE

Windstar is a class operation, as reflected in its thoughtful service personnel. The staff smiles hello and often learns passengers' names within the first hours of sailing. Dining staff is efficient and first-rate as well, but not in that ultraprofessional, military-esque, five-star-hotel, Seaborn kind of way. That's not what Windstar is all about. As for **tipping,** Windstar automatically adds gratuities of $11 per person per day to the onboard accounts.

Wind Surf

The Verdict

The big boy. An enlarged version of Wind-star's 148-passenger ships, the 312-passenger *Wind Surf* is a sleek, sexy, supersmooth sailing ship offering an extensive spa and lots of suites along with an intimate yacht-like ambience.

Wind Surf *(photo: Windstar Cruises)*

Specifications

Size (in tons)	14,745	Crew	190
Passengers (double occ.)	312	Passenger/Crew Ratio	1.6 to 1
Passenger/Space Ratio	47.9	Year Launched	1990
Total Cabins/Veranda Cabins	154/0	Last Refurbishment/Upgrade	2006

Frommer's Ratings (Scale of 1–5)   ★★★★

Cabin Comfort & Amenities	4	Dining Options	3.5
Appearance & Upkeep	3.5	Gym, Spa & Sports Facilities	5
Public Comfort/Space	4	Children's Facilities	N/A
Decor	4	Enjoyment Factor	4.5

Wind Surf is the pumped-up big sister of Windstar's smaller original vessels, the *Wind Star* and *Wind Spirit.* Built at French shipyard Societe Nouvelle des Ateliers et Chantiers du Havre, she originally sailed for Club Med Cruises (as *Club Med I*), until purchased by Windstar in 1997.

Despite a passenger capacity more than double that of her sister ships (312 vs. 148), *Wind Surf* maintains the feel of a private yacht, but also something more: Unlike almost any ship today, she mimics the size and flavor of some older, more intimate ocean liners, with a real seagoing feel that's rare among today's breed of cruise ships. It's this ambience, too, that sets her off from all the other "small" ships in this chapter, with amenities and an onboard vibe closer to a very high-end mainstream ship or a casual-luxe vessel. In essence, *Wind Surf* is in a class by herself, offering one of the few cruise experiences that really bridges the gap between casual-luxe and adventure, at prices often as low as $1,650 per week.

Cabins & Rates

Cabins	Per Diems From	Sq. Ft.	Fridge	Hair Dryer	Sitting Area	TV
Outside	$250	188	yes	yes	no	yes
Suite	$421	376	yes	yes	yes	yes

CABINS   Decor is nearly identical in all cabins and suites, with shippy white walls, varnished wood detailing, patterned upholstery and bedding, and understated carpets. Amenities include flatscreen TVs, DVD/CD players, Bose SoundDocks (usable with preloaded Apple iPod Nanos that you can check out from the reception desk), minibars, terry-cloth bathrobes, large desks with new granite tops, and full-length mirrors. At 188 square feet, the standard cabins are as large as some of the largest mainstream megaship cabins, and storage space is adequate, though not overly generous. During a late 2006 dry dock, every single stateroom and suite bathroom was redone. Sporting a more contemporary look, the well-designed bathrooms have updated cabinetry with open glass shelves, granite countertops, white porcelain sinks, new custom shower heads, new shower curtains, and an illuminated magnifying mirror. Fortunately, the lovely teak bathroom floors remain intact.

Thirty suites on Deck 3 (which are the combination of two regular staterooms) have a single large space divided into a comfortable sitting area and a bedroom (with a thick curtain to separate them as needed), plus his-and-hers bathrooms, each with shower and toilet, and two flat-panel TVs and DVD players. No cabins or suites have balconies or even picture windows. Instead, chunky portholes add to the ship's nautical ambience. Go with it. We loved 'em.

Most notable, the ship now has two brand-new 500-square-foot plush suites on the bridge deck, carved out of the old conference room and Internet cafe. Each has a living and dining area, separate bedroom, walk-in closet, and marble bathroom with a tub and separate shower. Posh perks for these suites include unpacking service, invitation to dine with the captain, laundry and pressing, evening appetizers, complimentary bottled water in the suite, chilled champagne upon arrival, and extra L'Occitane bath amenities.

Wind Surf has two elevators (unlike the other Windstar ships, which have none), but no cabins tailored for wheelchairs. The vessel is not recommended for people with serious mobility problems.

PUBLIC AREAS   All around, *Wind Surf* is the roomiest of the three Windstar ships, with an airy layout and a passenger-space ratio that matches that of the luxe Seabourn ships.

The vessel's main public room is its nautically decorated main lounge, a bright and airy space with well-spaced tables for four spread around a decent-size dance floor and bandstand. Passengers gather here in the evening for cocktails, music, and port talks, as well as gambling in the adjoining casino. Aft, the Compass Rose bar is the most popular spot aboard, with indoor/outdoor seating, a view over the wake, and music in the evenings. A second small stern lounge, the tiny, adorable Terrace Bar, is the venue for evening "Cigars Under the Stars" sessions, with classic wood paneling, thick leather couches and bar stools, and more seating and tables just outside, on deck.

Midships on Main Deck, just aft of the Lounge, the former library has been transformed into The Yacht Club, the ship's new social hub and Internet cafe. There's an espresso bar and eight computers with Internet access; personal laptops may also connect to wireless Internet. A large flatscreen TV anchors a cluster of comfy couches and chairs. There's a library of books, CDs, and DVDs available for checkout. Nearby are four card tables and the ship's one shop, next to the main reception desk.

DINING OPTIONS *Wind Surf* offers three dining venues: the Restaurant on Main Deck, a casual alternative venue on Star Deck, and the buffet-style Veranda restaurant, also on Star Deck. The Restaurant has 34 tables for two, making it easy for couples to get a romantic dinner alone. Dinners are open seating, served in a 2-hour window between 7:30 and 9:30pm. Dinner in the cozy alternative venue, recently renamed Degrees, is by reservation only and features a Joachim Splichal–inspired steakhouse menu 4 nights a week, and rotating menus from Northern Italy, France, and Indonesia the other nights.

As on the other Windstar ships, a combo buffet and a la carte breakfast and lunch are served in the glass-enclosed Veranda, which also has outdoor seating. Guests can also get grilled lobster, shrimp, ribs, hamburgers, hot dogs, sausages, veggie burgers, and vegetables from the Grill, right outside the Veranda's doors.

POOL, FITNESS, SPA & SPORT FACILITIES *Wind Surf* has the most elaborate fitness and spa facilities in the Windstar fleet, outclassing most facilities on other similar-size ships. At the spa, therapists dole out a variety of massages and other treatments in rooms that may look suspiciously familiar: They were created out of regular cabins when Windstar expanded the spa. Various spa packages geared to both men and women can be purchased in advance through your travel agent, with appointment times made once you're on board.

The ship's glass-walled gym is located on the top deck and is surprisingly well stocked for a vessel this size, with four treadmills, four bikes, several step machines and elliptical trainers, a full Cybex weight circuit, dumbbells, a ballet bar, and a rowing machine with water resistance. Up on deck, you'll find a schedule of yoga, Pilates, "Body Blitz," and self-defense classes for $11 a pop, plus free aerobics, stretching, Fitball, and abs classes.

There are two pools on board: one on the top deck, beneath the sails, and another in the stern, alongside two hot tubs. Adjacent to the pools are brand-new Balinese sun beds. For joggers, a full-circuit teak promenade wraps around the Bridge Deck. Two-person hammocks were recently installed on the flying bridge, providing a prime relaxation opportunity under the ship's billowing sails.

Wind Spirit • Wind Star

The Verdict

Two of the most romantic, cozy-yet-roomy small ships out there, these vessels look chic and offer just the right combination of creature comforts and first-class cuisine, along with a casual, laid-back, unstructured ethic.

Wind Spirit *(photo: Windstar Cruises)*

Specifications

Size (in tons)	5,350	Passenger/Crew Ratio	1.6 to 1
Passengers (double occ.)	148	Year Launched	
Passenger/Space Ratio	36.1	*Wind Spirit*	1988
Total Cabins/Veranda Cabins	74/0	*Wind Star*	1986
Crew	90	Last Refurbishment/Upgrade	2007

Frommer's Ratings (Scale of 1–5)   ★★★½

Cabin Comfort & Amenities	4	Dining Options	3.5
Appearance & Upkeep	3.5	Gym, Spa & Sports Facilities	2
Public Comfort/Space	4	Children's Facilities	N/A
Decor	4	Enjoyment Factor	4.5

These are great ships, combining high-tech design with the lines of a gracious private yacht, from their soaring masts to their needle-shaped bowsprits. They're the kind of lived-in, well-sailed vessels that a certain kind of passenger latches onto forever, and keeps coming back to year after year. To keep these 20-something ships looking fresh, at press time both were about to spruce up their public rooms and cabins.

Cabins & Rates

Cabins	Per Diems From	Sq. Ft.	Fridge	Hair Dryer	Sitting Area	TV
Outside	$264	188	yes	yes	no	yes
Suite	$407	220	yes	yes	yes	yes

CABINS   All cabins are nearly identical, with a burgundy and navy color scheme, a flatscreen TV, a DVD/CD player, Bose SoundDocks (usable with Apple iPod Nanos that you can check out from the reception desk), a minibar, a pair of large round portholes with brass fittings, a compact closet, bathrobes, and fresh fruit. Like the ships' main public rooms, cabins have wood accents and trim, and are attractive and well constructed, with a square footage exceeding those of most small ships and matching the size of the largest standard cabins on the mainstream ships. Teak-decked bathrooms, largish for ships this size, are better laid out than those aboard many luxury vessels, and contain a hair dryer, plenty of towels, and compact but adequate storage space. Another hair dryer (one with enough power to actually dry hair) is stowed out in the main cabin. Both ships have one Owner's Cabin that gives a little more breathing room, at 220 square feet.

Although all the cabins are comfortable, cabins amidships are more stable in rough seas—a rule of thumb aboard all ships. Note that the ships' engines, when running at full speed, can be a bit noisy.

This line is not recommended for passengers with serious disabilities or those who are wheelchair bound. There are no elevators on board, access to port is often by tender, and there are many raised doorsills.

PUBLIC AREAS   There aren't a lot of public areas on these small ships, but they're more than adequate as passengers spend most of their time in port. The four main rooms include two restaurants, a library, and a vaguely nautical-looking bar/lounge with cozy, partitioned-off nooks and clusters of comfy caramel-colored leather chairs surrounding a wooden dance floor. This is where passengers congregate for port talks, pre- and post-dinner drinks, dancing, and performances by local musicians and dancers. A second bar is out on the pool deck, and also attracts passengers before and after dinner for drinks and sometimes cigar smoking under the stars.

The small wood-paneled library manages to be both nautical and collegiate at the same time. Guests can read, play cards, or check out one of the hundreds of DVDs and CDs. You can surf the Internet and e-mail via two computers in the library; there is also wireless access for laptop users.

DINING OPTIONS   The yachtishly elegant, dimly lit main restaurant is styled with teak trim and paneling, rope-wrapped pillars, navy blue carpeting and fabrics, and other nautical touches. It's the sole dinner venue, and occasionally serves lunch as well. The Veranda breakfast and lunch restaurant is a sunny, window-lined room whose tables extend outdoors onto a covered deck. Unfortunately, you have to go outside on deck to enter the restaurant, so if it's raining, you'll get wet.

POOL, FITNESS, SPA & SPORTS FACILITIES   Each ship has a tiny swimming pool and an adjacent hot tub in the stern. Deck chairs around the pool can get filled during sunny days, but there's always space available on the crescent-shaped slice of deck above, outside the Veranda restaurant, and in a nice patch of deck forward of the bridge. Two-person hammocks were recently installed on the flying bridge of both ships, providing a prime relaxation opportunity under the billowing sails.

The ships' small gyms offer elliptical trainers, recumbent bikes, a ballet bar, free weights, and a flatscreen TV. Not bad for ships this size. Deck 4 offers an unobstructed wraparound deck for walkers. Massages, facials, and a few other treatments are available out of a single massage room next to the hair salon on Deck 1. Don't fault it just on size, though: One of the best massages we've ever had at sea was aboard *Wind Spirit*.

Part 3

The Ports

With guides to the 21 big U.S. and Canadian ports of embarkation, overviews of the major river cruise routes, and advice on things to see and do—on your own and via organized shore excursions—in 58 ports of call.

The Ports of Embarkation

Time was, cruises from the U.S. left only from the corners of the country—from Florida to the Caribbean, from New York and Boston to Canada's Maritimes and Bermuda, to Alaska from Vancouver (not in the U.S., but damn close), and to the Mexican Riviera from L.A. and San Diego. That's already a lot of options, but the question remained: Why stop there? Both coasts are full of cities with excellent port facilities, and cruise ships are, after all, ships, not trains on rails. They can sail from anywhere, as long as the water's deep enough.

That realization began dawning on the cruise industry around the turn of the millennium, then grew into a full-blown self-preservation policy after 9/11, when the public's avoidance of air travel threatened to leave ships empty. Once the worst of the jitters wore off, the efficacy of the alternative-home-porting trend had been proven, and there was no going back. Today, cities like Baltimore, Philadelphia, Galveston, Houston, Seattle, Norfolk, and even Bayonne, New Jersey, host cruise ships for all or part of each year.

In this chapter, we'll provide some information on what there is to see and do in each of the 19 major U.S. and Canadian embarkation ports. Cruise lines generally offer **pre- and post-cruise hotel packages** for passengers wanting to extend their vacation or add in some decompression time between boat and home, but in case you want to make your own arrangements, we've also included

some distinctive hotel and restaurant choices. **Hotel prices** listed here are standard rack rates for double rooms unless stated otherwise, and may be lower or higher, depending on what season you visit. For more extensive information on any of these cities, check the relevant Frommer's city, state, or regional guide.

PORTS NOT COVERED IN THIS CHAPTER While **San Juan (Puerto Rico)** and **Honolulu (Hawaii)** are both major ports of embarkation, they're also major ports of call for ships sailing through, and therefore appear in chapters 10 and 14, respectively. Two other ports, **Jacksonville, Florida,** and **Mobile, Alabama,** are currently hosting only one ship apiece (Carnival's *Celebration* in Jacksonville and Carnival's *Holiday* from Mobile), so they are not covered in this book. **Québec City** occasionally acts as a home port for Canada/New England cruises, but since it's more often a port of call, it's discussed in chapter 15.

DRIVING TO THE PORT All the ports in this chapter offer **secure parking** for passengers who drive to the ship. We've included basic driving directions and parking prices in all the reviews. Your cruise line and/or travel agent will also provide info.

FLYING TO THE PORT If you're flying to your port of embarkation, you can take a taxi or purchase transfers from the cruise line to get you from the airport to the cruise port. We've included **taxi**

Choosing a Chain

In addition to the hotels listed in this chapter, the following big motel and hotel chains are represented in most of the port cities.

- **Best Western,** ✆ 800/780-7234; www.bestwestern.com
- **Clarion,** ✆ 877/424-6423; www.clarioninn.com
- **Comfort Inn,** ✆ 800/424-6423; www.comfortinn.com
- **Comfort Suites,** ✆ 800/424-6423; www.comfortsuites.com
- **Courtyard by Marriott,** ✆ 800/321-2211; www.courtyard.com
- **Days Inn,** ✆ 800/329-7466; www.daysinn.com
- **Doubletree,** ✆ 800/222-8733; www.doubletree.com
- **Econo Lodge,** ✆ 800/424-6423; www.econolodge.com
- **Holiday Inn,** ✆ 800/465-4329; www.holiday-inn.com
- **Howard Johnson,** ✆ 800/466-4656; www.hojo.com
- **Motel 6,** ✆ 800/466-8356; www.motel6.com
- **Quality Inn,** ✆ 800/424-6423; www.qualityinn.com
- **Red Roof Inns,** ✆ 800/733-7663; www.redroof.com

prices in all these reviews, so compare them against your cruise line's **transfer prices** to see which you prefer. While cruise line transfers allow you to fall into the cruise line's warm, let-'em-take-care-of-everything embrace immediately (and meet some of your fellow passengers before you board), you'll often have to wait a while for the bus to load up and go. A taxi is speedier.

1 Anchorage, Alaska

Anchorage, which started as a tent camp for workers building the Alaska Railroad in 1914, stands between the Chugach Mountains and the waters of upper Cook Inlet. It was a sleepy railroad town until World War II, when the opening of a couple of military bases livened things up a bit. Even so, Anchorage did not start becoming a city in earnest until the 1950s, when the Cold War (and Alaska's proximity to the ol' "Evil Empire") spurred a huge investment in infrastructure.

Today, Anchorage enjoys the distinction of being incorrectly perceived as the state capital by pretty much everybody in the Lower 48, simply because it seems so obvious that it should be. (Trivial Pursuit answer: Juneau is the real capital; see chapter 11.) It also boasts good restaurants, worthwhile museums, shops, a few small historic attractions, and the must-do **Tony Knowles Coastal Trail** in and around its walkable if not thrillingly attractive 8-by-20-block downtown. Outside town, the world-class **Alaska Native Heritage Center** is a 26-acre celebration of Alaska's five major Native groups. And always, of course, there is wilderness—so close that moose regularly annoy the city's gardeners, and bears sometimes amble though town.

Plan to spend at least a half or full day here. If you have time, plan another half day at the Native Heritage Center or a day trip about 50 miles south along the incredibly scenic inlet known as **Turnagain Arm.**

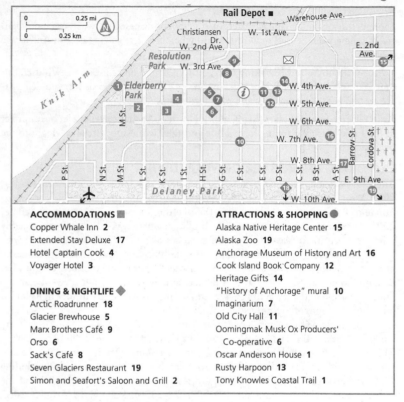

ACCOMMODATIONS ■
Copper Whale Inn **2**
Extended Stay Deluxe **17**
Hotel Captain Cook **4**
Voyager Hotel **3**

DINING & NIGHTLIFE ◆
Arctic Roadrunner **18**
Glacier Brewhouse **5**
Marx Brothers Café **9**
Orso **6**
Sack's Café **8**
Seven Glaciers Restaurant **19**
Simon and Seafort's Saloon and Grill **2**

ATTRACTIONS & SHOPPING ●
Alaska Native Heritage Center **15**
Alaska Zoo **19**
Anchorage Museum of History and Art **16**
Cook Island Book Company **12**
Heritage Gifts **14**
"History of Anchorage" mural **10**
Imaginarium **7**
Old City Hall **11**
Oomingmak Musk Ox Producers'
   Co-operative **6**
Oscar Anderson House **1**
Rusty Harpoon **13**
Tony Knowles Coastal Trail **1**

GETTING TO ANCHORAGE & THE PORT

If you're arriving by plane before your cruise, you'll land at the **Ted Stevens Anchorage International Airport** (© 907/266-2526; www.dot.state.ak.us/anc), located within the city limits, a 10- to 15-minute drive from downtown. **Taxis** run about $25 for the trip. By car, there is only one road into Anchorage from the rest of the world: the Glenn Highway. The other road into town, the Seward Highway, leads up from the Kenai Peninsula.

If you're ending your trip in Anchorage, you'll probably arrive via the port towns of **Seward** or **Whittier.** The reason is speed: From the south, cruising around the Kenai Peninsula to get to Anchorage would add another day to itineraries, so the vast majority of ships dock instead in southerly Seward (about 125 miles from Anchorage, on the southeast coast of the Kenai) or Whittier (in the northwestern waters of Prince William Sound, about 60 miles southeast of Anchorage) and then shuttle passengers to the city by bus or train.

GETTING AROUND   Most **car-rental** companies operate at the airport. A midsize car costs about $75 a day, with unlimited mileage. **Taxis** are available in town at a rate of $2 per mile plus a $2 initial fee. Anchorage's $1.75-per-ride People Mover **bus system** is an effective way of getting to and from the top attractions and activities.

BEST CRUISE LINE SHORE EXCURSIONS

Shore excursions in Anchorage often carry restrictions based on whether (and when) you're sailing from Seward or Whittier and whether you're staying over in Anchorage proper.

Prince William Sound Kayaking ($99, 3 hr.): Offered on cruises from Whittier, this tour takes you to one of Prince William Sound's deep-water fjords for a guided paddle around gorgeous waterfalls and rock formations.

Knik Glacier Jetboat Safari ($159, 4 hr.): North of Anchorage, ride a jet boat upriver to the Knik Glacier, scanning for wildlife and then witnessing glacial calving into the river waters.

EXPLORING ANCHORAGE ON YOUR OWN

Anchorage's downtown area is pleasant, but don't expect an old-fashioned Alaskan town: Most of its buildings were leveled in the big 1964 earthquake, which at a magnitude of 9.2 was more powerful than the one that hit Southeast Asia in December 2004, generating the deadly tsunami. Today, downtown Anchorage is thoroughly modern, albeit in an Alaskan way, with stretches of touristy shops interspersed with government buildings, shops for locals, a few seedy sections, and occasional dashes of homespun public art: Check out Bob Patterson's **"History of Anchorage" mural** at Seventh Avenue and F Street, which depicts exactly that. At Fourth Avenue and E Street, the 1936 **Old City Hall** offers an interesting display of city history in its lobby, including dioramas of the early streetscape.

Our pick for number-one downtown activity is taking a walk along the **Tony Knowles Coastal Trail,** which offers gorgeous views out over the waters of Knik Arm. The trail runs through downtown and the arm for about 11 miles, from the western end of Second Avenue to Kincaid Park. You can hop on at several points, including via **Elderberry Park,** at the western end of Fifth Avenue, where you'll also find the **Oscar Anderson House** museum (© **907/274-2336**). Built in 1915 for Swedish butcher Anderson and his family, it's a quaint dwelling surrounded by a lovely little garden, with a tour that provides a glimpse into the city's short history. Furnishings include a working 1909 player piano. Admission is $3.

The **Anchorage Museum of History and Art,** 121 W. Seventh Ave., between A and C streets (© **907/343-4326;** www.anchoragemuseum.org), is the state's largest museum. Most visitors tour the large Alaska Gallery, an informative and enjoyable walk through the history and some of the anthropology of the state and its Native peoples. The art galleries present Alaskan works from yesterday and today, along with photos of prequake Anchorage and Alaskan pop-culture artifacts. The museum gets Alaska's best touring and temporary exhibits, and its restaurant, operated by the excellent Marx Brothers Café (see below), serves some of the best lunches to be had downtown. Admission costs $6.50. A $21 combo ticket will get you admission and a free shuttle to . . .

. . . the 26-acre **Alaska Native Heritage Center,** 8800 Heritage Center Dr. (© **800/315-6608;** www.alaskanative.net), located about 15 minutes from downtown Anchorage. Opened in 1999, the center introduces visitors to the lives and cultures of the state's five major Alaska Native groupings: the southeast's Tlingit, Eyak, Haida, and Tsimshian tribes; the Athabascans of the interior; the Inupiat and St. Lawrence Island Yupiks of the far north; the Aleuts and Alutiiqs of the Aleutian Islands; and the Yup'ik and Cup'ik tribes of the extreme west. A central "Welcome House" holds a small museum displaying some remarkable Native carvings and masks;

a workshop where Native craftspeople demonstrate their techniques; a theater presenting a rotating series of films on Native culture; and a rotunda where storytelling,
dance, and music performances are presented throughout the day. Outside, spaced
along a walking trail around a small lake, are five traditional dwellings representing the
five Native cultures and regions. Native staffers are on hand at each to provide information about the dwellings. Though the center is offered as a shore excursion by most
ships, it's worth going on your own if you're interested in Native culture, since the
tours don't give you enough time to experience all the place has to offer. Admission is
$24. A free shuttle leaves regularly from the Anchorage Museum, the Anchorage Visi-
tor Center at Fourth Avenue and F Street, the center's downtown gift shop on Fourth
Avenue (see "Shopping," below), and several other sites. Times are posted at all pickup
points, or call © **907/330-8000.**

If you're traveling with children, Anchorage offers a few kid-centric options, including the **Imaginarium,** 737 W. Fifth Ave., between G and H streets, Suite 140
(© **907/276-3179;** www.imaginarium.org), and a science museum with a strong
Alaska theme to many of the displays, including a saltwater touch tank. Admission is
$5.50 adults, $5 kids. The **Alaska Zoo,** 4731 O'Malley Rd., about 8 miles from
downtown (© **907/346-2133;** www.alaskazoo.org), is another option, with gravel
paths meandering through the woods past natural flora and local wildlife such as polar
and brown bears, seals and otters, musk oxen, Dall sheep, moose, caribou, and water-
fowl—most of which you may see on your cruise, but not this close up. There are also
elephants, Siberian tigers, yaks, and Bactrian camels, which you won't see from the
ship unless you're having flashbacks. Admission is $10 adults, $6 kids. To get here,
take either the old or the new Seward Highway south to O'Malley Road, turn left, and
travel for about 1½ miles.

ATTRACTIONS IN SEWARD & WHITTIER

Most people pass through Seward and Whittier without a second glance on their way
to Anchorage, but if you have time, there are a few interesting sights to see in these
two port towns. In Seward, the spectacular **Alaska SeaLife Center,** right on the waterfront at Mile 0 of the Seward Highway (© **800/224-2525;** www.alaskasealife.org),
allows scientists and visitors (the latter through windows) to study the sea lions, porpoises, sea otters, harbor seals, fish, and other forms of marine life that abound in the
area, as well as the umpteen species of local seabirds. Admission costs $15.

As for Whittier, the most amazing thing about the town is that almost the entire
population lives in a single 14-story concrete building known as **Begich Towers.** It
was built during the 1940s, when Whittier's strategic location on the Alaska Railroad
and at the head of a deep Prince William Sound fjord made it a key port in the defense
of Alaska, and after a while everybody just migrated here to make things easier. Eventually, businesses opened here as well—a grocery store on the first floor, a medical
clinic on the third, and even a B&B (**June's Whittier Bed & Breakfast Condo
Suites;** © **888/472-2396** or 907/472-2396; www.breadnbuttercharters.com) on the
top two floors. Kids don't even have to go outside to get to school in winter—a tunnel leads right from the tower to the school building.

SHOPPING

The **Cook Inlet Book Company,** 415 W. Fifth Ave. (© **800/240-4148;** www.cook
inlet.com), sits amid a block of gift shops and seems unpromising from the outside,
but inside is an absolutely huge stock of Alaska-oriented books organized by subject:

Native culture, history, art, fishing, out-of-print, and so on. The shop also stocks fiction and other general topics. Definitely worth a stop.

Many stores in Anchorage carry Native-looking arts and crafts, but most are just touristy knockoffs. Give 'em your back and head for the good stuff instead. The **Oomingmak Musk Ox Producers' Co-operative,** 604 H St., at Sixth Avenue (© **888/360-9665** or 907/272-9225; www.qiviut.com), is a co-op owned by 250 Alaska Native women in villages across the state. All of their products are knitted from qiviut (*kiv*-ee-oot), the light, warm, silky underhair of the musk ox, which is collected from shedding animals. Each village has its own knitting pattern. Items are expensive—adult caps start at $170, scarves at $245—but considering the rarity and beauty of the work, they're really a bargain. The website has a "letters" page with notes sent by the knitters, discussing their work. The **Rusty Harpoon,** 411 W. Fourth Ave. (© **907/278-9011;** www.rustyharpoongifts.com), also has authentic Native items and less expensive crafts, and the longtime proprietors only buy direct from Native artists they know. The Alaska Native Heritage Center's **Heritage Gifts,** 333 W. Fourth Ave. (© **907/272-5048**), also has a good selection of art, books, and music.

WHERE TO STAY

Rooms can be hard to come by in Anchorage in the summer, so be sure to arrange lodging as far in advance of your trip as possible, whether through your cruise line or on your own. Here are some good options:

The **Hotel Captain Cook,** Fourth Avenue and K Street (© **800/843-1950;** www.captaincook.com), is Alaska's great, grand hotel, where royalty and rock stars stay. Rates: from $260. Right across the street from the Anchorage Museum, the fairly stylish **Extended Stay Deluxe Anchorage,** 108 E. Eighth Ave. (© **866/GUEST4U;** www.aspenhotelsak.com/anchorage.htm), offers rooms appointed with just about everything, with amenities such as fully equipped kitchens, DVD players, on-site guest laundry, fitness center, and wireless Internet access. Rates: from $185. The small, unpretentious, and centrally located **Voyager Hotel,** 501 K St. (© **800/247-9070;** www.voyagerhotel.com), has large, light rooms with kitchens, and gets consistent raves from travelers. Rates: from $179. The casual **Copper Whale Inn,** 440 L St. (© **907/258-7999;** www.copperwhale.com), takes up a pair of clapboard houses overlooking Elderberry Park right on the coastal trail downtown, with charming rooms of every shape and size. Rates: from $175 (rooms with shared bathroom from $159).

DINING & NIGHTLIFE

Though hardly a culinary or nightlife capital, Anchorage does have a few good restaurants if you want an evening out before or after your cruise. For a fun, casual experience, the **Glacier Brewhouse,** 737 W. Fifth Ave. (© **907/274-BREW;** www.glacierbrewhouse.com), offers a tasty, eclectic, and ever-changing menu served in a large dining room with lodge decor, where the scent of the wood-fired grill hangs in the air. They brew their own hearty beers behind a glass wall. If it's crowded (and it often is), head for the large bar area, where you can just hover like a vulture till a table opens up. Main courses: $10 to $37. The **Marx Brothers Café,** 627 W. Third Ave. (© **907/278-2133;** www.marxcafe.com), began as a hobby among three friends and has become a standard of excellence in the state. The cuisine is varied and creative, ranging from Asian to Italian, but everyone orders the Caesar salad made at the table. The decor and style are studied casual elegance. Main courses: $32 to $36.

Sack's Café, 328 G St. (© **907/274-4022;** www.sackscafe.com), is the most fashionable restaurant in Anchorage, and one of the best, with an ever-changing menu that mixes Alaskan seafood with Italian influences and eclectic touches. Main courses: $18 to $34. **Orso,** 737 W. Fifth Ave. (© **907/222-3232;** www.orsoalaska.com), offers superb wood-grilled steaks and locally caught seafood as well as excellent pastas, all in an ornate dining room. Main courses: $18 to $37. **Simon and Seafort's Saloon and Grill,** 420 L St. (© **907/274-3502;** www.simonandseaforts.com), is one of Anchorage's great dinner houses with a turn-of-the-20th-century decor, a cheerful atmosphere, and fabulous sunset views of Cook Inlet. Prime rib and seafood are the specialties. Main courses: $16 to $35. Lighter meals are served at the bar. For the best, most original takeout burgers in town, head for **Arctic Roadrunner,** with locations at 2477 Arctic Blvd., at Fireweed Lane (© **907/279-7311**), and 5300 Old Seward Hwy., at International Airport Road (© **907/561-1245**). Try the Kodiak Islander, which has peppers, ham, onion rings, and who knows what else on top.

For a memorable dining experience out of town, the Mount Alyeska Resort's **Seven Glaciers Restaurant** (© **800/880-3880;** www.alyeskaresort.com) offers views that match its name. Located 2,300 feet up a tramway on the mountainside, the restaurant serves trendy and beautifully presented dinners in a sumptuous dining room floating above the clouds. Notable menu selections include the cold smoked and grilled Alaskan salmon and the Alaskan king crab. Main courses: $28 to $64. The resort is on Arlberg Avenue in Girdwood, a funky little town 37 miles south of Anchorage along Turnagain Arm.

2 Baltimore, Maryland

"Charm City" has welcomed visitors since 1729. Founded as a shipping and shipbuilding town and later transformed into a manufacturing center, the city rode the new-economy wave of the '90s with more service industries and nonprofits. Today, tourism plays an ever-increasing role in the local economy, with a combination of historical sights, museums, a revitalized harbor area, and friendly people drawing visitors—and now cruise lines, too.

GETTING TO BALTIMORE & THE PORT

All cruise vessels depart from the Port of Baltimore's **South Locust Point Marine Terminal,** 2001 E. McComas St., about 5 miles from the Inner Harbor, where many of the best attractions and hotels are located. If you're arriving by plane, you'll likely fly into **Baltimore/Washington International Thurgood Marshall Airport** (© **800/I-FLY-BWI;** www.bwiairport.com), located 10 miles south of downtown Baltimore, off I-295 (the Baltimore-Washington Pkwy.). To get to Baltimore, follow I-195 west to Route 295 north, which will take you into downtown. **Taxis** to the port or downtown hotels run about $20. **SuperShuttle** (© **800/258-3826;** www.supershuttle.com) also operates vans every half-hour between the airport and all major downtown hotels for about $12 per person one-way, $18 round-trip.

If you're driving to the port from I-95 north or south, take Keith Avenue/exit 56. Turn left on Keith Avenue until it merges into Broening Highway, and take this 1 mile to the Seagirt Marine Terminal. Use the terminal entrance. Parking costs $7 per day.

GETTING AROUND   If you plan to stay near the Inner Harbor, it's easiest to walk or take **Ed Kane's Water Taxi** (© **800/658-8497;** www.thewatertaxi.com), which charges $8 for an all-day pass. There's also regular metered taxi service to get you to the port. On foot, you only have to know a few streets to get your bearings. The **promenade** around the Inner Harbor will take you to Federal Hill and the American Visionary Art Museum, the Maryland Science Center, Harborplace, the USS *Constellation,* and the National Aquarium. The promenade extends along the water through the Harbor East neighborhood and will eventually extend to Fells Point and Canton. It makes for a pretty walk. **Pratt** and **Lombard streets** are the two major east–west arteries just above the Inner Harbor. **Charles Street** is Baltimore's main route north and home to some good restaurants. **St. Paul Street** is the major route south. If you're driving around, expect things to be fairly easy. The streets are on a straight grid, and many are one-way. All the major **car-rental** companies have offices at the airport.

BEST CRUISE LINE SHORE EXCURSIONS

Baltimore City Tour ($39, 2½ hr.): Take in Baltimore's historic sights, visiting the Harborplace, Babe Ruth's birthplace, Johns Hopkins University, Baltimore's Washington Monument, Fort McHenry, and the historic ships berthed at the seaport.

EXPLORING BALTIMORE ON YOUR OWN

Baltimore's **Inner Harbor** is the starting point for most visitors. Once a major seaport, the freight business ground to a halt in the 1960s, but it's been a destination for pleasure boaters and tall ships since the city began revitalizing the area in the late '70s. In addition to **restaurants** and extensive **shopping** (see below), there are a number of historic attractions in the neighborhood.

The **USS *Constellation,*** moored at 301 E. Pratt St. (© **410/539-1797;** www. constellation.org), is a stunning triple-masted sloop-of-war originally launched in 1854. It's the last Civil War–era vessel afloat. Tour her gun decks, visit the wardrooms, see a cannon demonstration, and learn about the life of an old-time sailor. Admission is $8.75. More seagoing history is to be had at the **Baltimore Maritime Museum** (© **410/396-3453;** www.baltomaritimemuseum.org). Located at Piers 3 and 5, it's really four museums in one. The Coast Guard Cutter *Taney* survived the bombing of Pearl Harbor, the submarine USS *Torsk* sank the last two Japanese merchant ships of World War II, and the lightship *Chesapeake* spent 40 years anchored near the mouth of the Chesapeake Bay. The "screwpile"-style Seven-Foot Knoll Lighthouse looks more like a New England UFO than a traditional lighthouse. Built in 1856, it marked the entrance to Baltimore's harbor for 133 years before being moved to its current location. Admission to all four is $8 adults, $4 kids. Tickets are available at Pier 3, in front of the National Aquarium, and at the USS *Constellation* Building on Pier 1.

At the nearby **National Aquarium,** 501 E. Pratt St. (© **410/576-3800;** www.aqua. org), visitors can walk into a room surrounded by patrolling sharks, wander among the coral reefs, follow the yearly migration of fish, and visit a rainforest on the roof at one of the best aquariums in the country. Though you walk in front of most of the exhibits, you get to actually walk *inside* the doughnut-shaped Coral Reef and the Open Ocean shark tanks. There's also a Marine Mammal Pavilion that's home to a family of dolphins and a new exhibit re-creating an Australian river gorge. Admission costs $22 adults, $13 kids.

Oh, say, can you see by the dawn's early light? Apparently Francis Scott Key could, back in 1814, when the British attacked star-shaped **Fort McHenry,** which sits on a point in the harbor at the end of East Fort Avenue (© **410/962-4290;** www.nps. gov/fomc). It was the sight of the fort's enormous 15-star flag that showed that the fort's

CRUISE TERMINAL 20 ●

ATTRACTIONS & SHOPPING ●
American Visionary Art
  Museum **13**
Baltimore Maritime Museum **10**
Broadway Market **17**
Fort McHenry **18**
Harborplace **11**
Lexington Market **2**
National Aquarium **12**
Oriole Park at Camden Yards **4**
USS Constellation **10**
Walters Art Museum **1**

ACCOMMODATIONS ■
Admiral Fell Inn **8**
Hyatt Regency Baltimore **7**
Intercontinental Harbor Court **9**
Radisson Plaza Lord Baltimore **3**
Renaissance Harborplace Hotel **5**

DINING & NIGHTLIFE ◆
Bertha's **18**
Black Olive **19**
Cat's Eye Pub **18**
Nick's Fish House **20**
Obrycki's **15**
Phillip's Harborplace **11**
Pisces **6**
Vaccaro's **16**

1,000 defenders had held their ground, halting the British offensive and inspiring the U.S. national anthem. After that day, the fort never again came under attack, but it remained an active fort on and off for the next hundred years. Today, it's both a National Park and a National Historic Shrine and still flies its huge flag, which takes about 20 people to manage when it's raised and lowered daily. Stop by at 9:30am or 4:30pm (7:30pm June–Aug) to join in. The fort's buildings display historical and military memorabilia, and you can tour the restored barracks, commander's quarters, guardhouse, and powder magazine. Admission is $7 for adults, free for kids under 16.

The **Walters Art Museum,** 600 N. Charles St. (© 410/547-9000; www.the walters.org), with its collections of ancient art, medieval armor, and French 19th-century painting, has always been one of Baltimore's great attractions, telling the story of Western civilization through its permanent collection, which covers some 55 centuries. Admission is free; closed Monday and Tuesday.

For something different, visit the **American Visionary Art Museum,** 800 Key Hwy., at the base of historic Federal Hill on the south side of the Inner Harbor (© 410/244-1900; www.avam.org). You can't miss it: Just look for the multicolored, 55-foot wind-powered sculpture out front. As defined by the museum, visionary art is "art produced by self-taught individuals, usually without formal training, whose works arise from an innate personal vision that revels foremost in the creative act itself." This can range from narrative embroideries by Holocaust survivors to the 10-foot model of the *Lusitania* that dominates a first-floor gallery—made from 193,000 matchsticks. All in all, it's some of the more interesting art you'll ever see. Admission costs $12; closed Monday.

Baseball fans will want to try to catch a game at **Oriole Park at Camden Yards,** 333 W. Camden St. (© 410/685-9800; www.theorioles.com). If there's a home game during your visit, do whatever it takes to get a ticket: It's a real Baltimore experience. Games are usually held at 1:35 or 7:35pm, with tickets going for about $9 to $65.

SHOPPING

The Inner Harbor is Baltimore's prime shopping district, with malls and hundreds of shops. **Harborplace** (© 410/332-0060; www.harborplace.com) is actually three separate locations with more than 160 stores. Between them, they sell everything from onion rings to diamond rings. The **Light Street Pavilion** has the most food stalls and restaurants, with some souvenir shops. The **Pratt Street Pavilion** offers specialty stores, clothing and jewelry shops, and more restaurants. The **Gallery,** a mall connected to the Renaissance Harborplace Hotel, has three floors of shops and a food court on the fourth.

For a more classic taste of the city, head to one of its centuries-old markets. The 200-year-old **Broadway Market,** on South Broadway between Fleet and Lancaster streets in Fells Point, has two large covered buildings staffed by local vendors selling fresh produce, flowers, crafts, and an assortment of ethnic and raw-bar foods, ideal for snacking, a quick lunch, or a picnic. You'll even find an old-fashioned Baltimore tradition: "sweet potatoes," soft white candies powdered with cinnamon. The **Lexington Market,** 400 W. Lexington St. (© 410/685-6169; www.lexingtonmarket.com), claims to be the oldest continuously operating market in the United States, having opened for business in 1782. This Baltimore landmark on downtown's west side houses more than 140 merchants, selling prepared ethnic foods (for eat-in or take-away), fresh seafood, produce, meats, baked goods, sweets, and even freshly grated coconut. It's worth a visit for the aromas, flavors, sounds, and sights, as well as good shopping. Bring cash, as credit cards are not accepted. Closed Sunday.

WHERE TO STAY

A number of hotels are located in the Inner Harbor and Fells Point neighborhoods, the latter Baltimore's original seaport and home to the first shipyards. Both are located a maximum of 7 miles from the cruise terminal.

The **Hyatt Regency Baltimore,** 300 Light St. (© 800/233-1234; www.hyatt. com), was the Inner Harbor's first hotel 20 years ago and still has its best location, just a few steps from everything. Rooms have breathtaking harbor views; the amenities are terrific. Rates: from $199.

The **Inter-Continental Harbor Court Hotel,** 550 Light St. (© 800/824-0076; www.harborcourt.com), strives for quiet dignity, refinement, and graciousness, with exquisitely furnished rooms. Rates: from $280.

The **Renaissance Harborplace Hotel,** 202 E. Pratt St. (© 800/468-3571; www. renaissancehotels.com), is also located right in the middle of everything, across the street from Harborplace and the Inner Harbor. Rooms are very large, and many have great views. Rates: from $179.

The French Renaissance–style **Radisson Plaza Lord Baltimore,** 20 W. Baltimore St. (© 800/333-3333; www.radisson.com), opened in 1928, so if you love grand old hotels with modern conveniences, this is the one for you. The entrance features marble columns, hand-carved artwork, brass fixtures, and chandeliers, and the Inner Harbor is only 5 blocks away. Rates: from $169.

In Fells Point (southeast of the Inner Harbor), the **Admiral Fell Inn,** 888 S. Broadway (© 866/583-4162; www.harbormagic.com), is composed of seven buildings built between 1790 and 1920, and blends Victorian and Federal-style architecture. Originally a boardinghouse for sailors, later a YMCA, and then a vinegar bottling plant, the inn now includes an antiques-filled lobby and library and guest rooms individually decorated with Federal period furnishings. Rates: from $141.

DINING & NIGHTLIFE

Baltimore used to be very quiet after dark, but not anymore. We suggest heading to the Inner Harbor or Fells Point for some of the town's legendary seafood and an evening out.

Fells Point, the neighborhood where Baltimore began, is one of the city's best areas for seafood, and the benchmark of all the eateries here is **Obrycki's,** 1727 E. Pratt St. (© 410/732-6399; www.baltimorecrabhouse.com). This is the quintessential crab house, where you can crack open steamed crabs in their shells and feast on the tender, succulent meat. There's crab soup, crab cocktail, crab balls, crab cakes, crab imperial, and soft-shell crabs, and the rest of the menu is just as tempting. Main courses: $15 to $30. It's closed November through mid-March. At the **Black Olive,** 814 S. Bond St. (© 410/276-7141; www.theblackolive.com), a Greek taverna located just beyond the busier streets of Fells Point, the combination of Greek fare and the freshest seafood is magic. Choose the catch of the day and trust the chef to make it wonderful. Main courses: $24 to $34. Reservations required.

In a city where lots of restaurants have good views, the view from **Pisces,** 300 Light St., in the Inner Harbor's Hyatt Regency (© 410/528-1234), tops them all, overlooking the Inner Harbor, Camden Yards, and the downtown skyline. The interior is sleek and modern and the menu small but intriguing, stressing seafood. Main courses: $15 to $32. Of more than a dozen restaurants and sidewalk cafes in the festive Harborplace development, **Phillips Harborplace,** on level 1 of Light Street Pavilion (© **800/648-7067**), is a longtime reasonably priced favorite featuring crab in many forms—soft-shell, crab and lobster sauté, crab cakes, crab imperial, and all-you-can-eat portions of steamed crabs. Phillips also offers takeout in the Light Street Pavilion. Main courses: $15 to $30. If you're geographically adventurous, an even better seafood choice is **Nick's Fish House,** 2600 Insulator Dr. (© **410/347-4123;** www.nicksfish house.com). It's located in a very industrial area on the Patapsco River, about 2½ miles south of the Inner Harbor, but the crab cakes are delicious and a good value, the service is friendly and efficient, and the atmosphere is Baltimore–meets–Eastern Shore casual. It's worth going out of the way for.

To top off a perfect day, drop by **Vaccaro's,** 222 Albemarle St. in Little Italy, near Fells Point (© **410/685-4905;** www.vaccarospastry.com), for Italian desserts, coffee, and cappuccino. There's also a location at the Light Street Pavilion in Harborplace. For something more sudsy and musical, head to Fells Point, where the **Cat's Eye Pub,** 1730 Thames St. (© **410/276-9085;** www.catseyepub.com), has live music every night, from Irish folk to zydeco. **Bertha's,** 734 S. Broadway (© **410/327-5795;** www. berthas.com), has live jazz or blues every night, as well as a large menu heavy on seafood and pub grub.

3 Boston, Massachusetts

Founded in 1630, Boston is a port of call on many itineraries that sail from New York and is an embarkation port for a handful of New England/Canada cruises, many of them terminating in Montréal. Of all the New England ports, it has perhaps the richest history, dating from the earliest days of America's settlement through the Revolution and beyond. Wend your way through the city's many important historical sights via the Freedom Trail walking tour, hitting sites from the USS *Constitution* (aka "Old Ironsides") to the **Paul Revere House.** In other neighborhoods, stroll past the beautiful Victorian-era town houses in the stylish Back Bay area, take in the Federal architecture of Beacon Hill, or head across the Charles River to Cambridge for a romp around the classic ivied campus of **Harvard University,** founded nearly 400 years ago. Then again, you can skip the past and focus on pure fun, whether it's shopping (perhaps at **Faneuil Hall Marketplace**) or pub hopping—the beloved *Cheers* bar (at least the exterior used in the opening credits) is on Beacon Street, while a replica of the interior is in Faneuil Hall Marketplace.

GETTING TO BOSTON & THE PORT

Ships dock at the **Black Falcon Cruise Terminal** (© **617/330-1500;** www.massport. com/ports/cruis.html), located at 1 Black Falcon Ave., in the Boston Marine Industrial Park on the South Boston Waterfront, sometimes called the Seaport District. There's nothing at the industrial park but ships and sheds, but the heart of Boston is only a couple of miles away, and tour buses and taxis line up to meet cruise passengers. By air, you'll arrive at Boston's **Logan International Airport** (© **800/23-LOGAN;** www.massport.com/logan), located in East Boston, 3 miles across the harbor from downtown. A **taxi** to the port costs about $20 for two passengers; the drive through the Ted Williams Tunnel takes about 10 to 15 minutes, depending on traffic.

If you're coming by car from the Massachusetts Turnpike traveling east, go past the I-90/I-93 interchange and enter the tunnel eastbound. In the tunnel, take exit

Boston

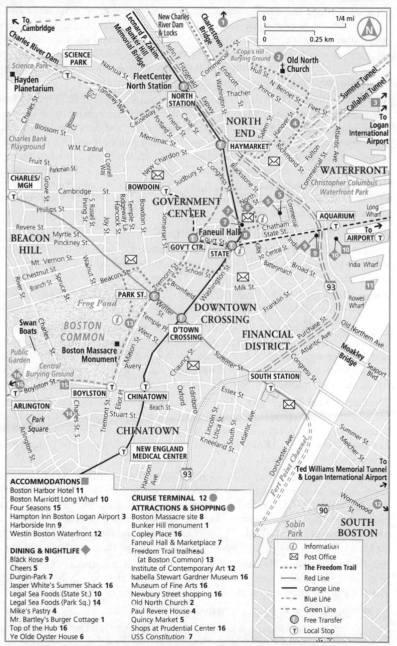

0   1/4 mi
0   0.25 km

ACCOMMODATIONS ■
Boston Harbor Hotel **11**
Boston Marriott Long Wharf **10**
Four Seasons **15**
Hampton Inn Boston Logan Airport **3**
Harborside Inn **9**
Westin Boston Waterfront **12**

DINING & NIGHTLIFE ◆
Black Rose **9**
Cheers **5**
Durgin-Park **7**
Jasper White's Summer Shack **16**
Legal Sea Foods (State St.) **10**
Legal Sea Foods (Park Sq.) **14**
Mike's Pastry **4**
Mr. Bartley's Burger Cottage **1**
Top of the Hub **16**
Ye Olde Oyster House **6**

CRUISE TERMINAL 12 ●
ATTRACTIONS & SHOPPING ●
Boston Massacre site **8**
Bunker Hill monument **1**
Copley Place **16**
Faneuil Hall & Marketplace **7**
Freedom Trail trailhead
(at Boston Common) **13**
Institute of Contemporary Art **12**
Isabella Stewart Gardner Museum **16**
Museum of Fine Arts **16**
Newbury Street shopping **16**
Old North Church **2**
Paul Revere House **4**
Quincy Market **5**
Shops at Prudential Center **16**
USS *Constitution* **7**

ⓘ Information
✉ Post Office
···· **The Freedom Trail**
—— Red Line
—— Orange Line
– – Blue Line
– – – Green Line
Ⓒ Free Transfer
Ⓣ Local Stop

25/South Boston. At the traffic lights, you'll be at Congress Street. Continue forward onto B Street. At the next signal, turn right onto Seaport Boulevard. Continue straight onto Northern Avenue and proceed into the Marine Industrial Park. Continue to the end, turn right onto Tide Street, and make an immediate left onto Drydock Avenue. Follow Drydock Avenue as it turns right at the end of the Boston Design Center. Turn right again onto Black Falcon Avenue. Parking costs $14 per day.

GETTING AROUND   The best way to see the historic heart of Boston is on foot. Alternatively, you can sign up for one of your ship's organized tours, hop on the shuttle bus some cruise lines provide, or grab a taxi at the pier and drop about $15 for the 3-plus-mile ride to Boston Common, a good starting point for walking tours. Once in town, spend the day walking, join a hop-on/hop-off trolley tour, or take advantage of Boston's efficient subway system, the **"T"** (short for MBTA; © **800/392-6100** or 617/222-3200; www.mbta.com), which has stops all over the city. Subway fares are $1.70 to $2, bus fares are $1.25 to $1.50, or you can pay $9 for a 1-day pass that allows unlimited travel on both.

BEST CRUISE LINE SHORE EXCURSIONS

Freedom Trail Walking Tour ($38, 4 hr.): While you can easily do this well-marked walk on your own, if you'd like a guide to explain the highlights, this excursion is a good choice.

Biking Along the Charles River ($89, 3 hr.): A guided ride from Boston Common along the Charles River Esplanade, into Cambridge, and back.

Beacon Hill Walking Tour ($54, 3 hr.): A guided walking tour from the Back Bay neighborhood past Trinity Church, along Newbury Street with its boutiques and cafes, and through the lush Public Garden, with a stop for a quick beer at the *Cheers* pub, inspiration for the classic TV show. Move on to Boston Common, the narrow streets and brick sidewalks of Beacon Hill, and finally to Quincy Market.

The Path of Paul Revere ($52, 4 hr.): This bus ride follows the route of Paul Revere's famous ride to Lexington. In Concord, drive along "Author's Row" for views of the homes of Nathaniel Hawthorne, Ralph Waldo Emerson, and Louisa May Alcott. In Lexington, see where 77 Minutemen faced 700 British soldiers in the first engagement of the American Revolution.

Lexington & Concord Tour ($99, 7½ hr.): Outside Boston, the towns of Lexington and Concord witnessed the first battles of the Revolutionary War. The tour includes the Old North Church; Lexington Green, where the first skirmish of the war took place; and the North Bridge, where the American militia met the British forces. Most tours also stop at Harvard Yard, the USS *Constitution,* and for lunch at Ye Olde Oyster House, America's oldest continuously operating restaurant.

Mayflower **& Plimoth Plantation Tour** ($109, 7 hr.): Step aboard a full-scale replica of the *Mayflower,* take a gander at Plymouth Rock, and then have a lobster lunch at Plimoth Plantation, a living museum where actors re-create 17th-century life.

EXPLORING BOSTON ON YOUR OWN

Boston's cruise port is located in an industrial section of town. The new Institute of Contemporary Art museum (see below) is within easy walking distance, but downtown and most of the city's attractions lie a short distance away by taxi or public transit.

Visitors in town for just a day will probably want to concentrate on the city's famed **Freedom Trail,** a 2½-mile route that links 16 historic sites, many of them associated with the American Revolution and the country's early days. The route begins at **Boston Common,** the country's oldest public park (dating to 1640), and cuts across downtown, passing through the busy shopping area around Downtown Crossing, the Financial District, and the North End, on the way to Charlestown. A line of red paint or red brick on the sidewalk marks the route, markers identify the stops, and plaques point the way from one to the next. The free *Where Boston* magazine (available at the cruise terminal) contains a route map.

Many of the stops along the route will be familiar to anyone who studied American history in school. At State Street and Devonshire Street, a ring of cobblestones on a traffic island marks the spot where, on March 5, 1770, colonists threw snowballs, garbage, rocks, and other debris at a group of redcoats, who responded by firing into the crowd and killing five men. That incident, which became known as the **Boston Massacre,** helped consolidate the spirit of rebellion in the colonies. At Dock Square (Congress St. and North St.), **Faneuil Hall** was built in 1742 and was a site for speeches by orators such as Samuel Adams (whose statue stands outside) in the years leading to the Revolution. In later years, abolitionists, temperance advocates, and suffragists also used the hall as a pulpit. The **Paul Revere House,** 19 North Sq. (© 617/ 523-2338; www.paulreverehouse.org), is the very home from which Revere set off on April 18, 1775, riding to Lexington to warn Samuel Adams and John Hancock that British troops were coming to arrest them. The 2½-story wood structure is the oldest house in downtown Boston, built around 1680 and bought by Revere in 1770. Inside, 17th- and 18th-century furnishings and artifacts—including the famous Revere silver—re-create the period. Admission is $3. A few blocks to the north, the **Old North Church,** 193 Salem St. (www.oldnorth.com), is the place where sexton Robert Newman hung two lanterns from the steeple on the night of Revere's ride, as a signal that British troops were setting out for Lexington in boats, rather than on foot ("One if by land, and two if by sea"). The original steeple fell in hurricanes in 1804 and 1954; the current version is an exact copy. Admission is $3.

At the Charlestown Navy Yard, the **USS *Constitution*** (© 617/242-7511; www.oldironsides.com) is one of the U.S. Navy's six original frigates, constructed between 1794 and 1797 using bolts, spikes, and other fittings from Paul Revere's foundry. As the new nation built its naval and military reputation, the *Constitution* played a key role, battling French privateers and Barbary pirates, repelling the British fleet during the War of 1812, participating in 40 engagements, and capturing 20 vessels. The frigate earned its nickname, "Old Ironsides," during a battle on August 19, 1812, when shots from HMS *Guerrière* bounced off its thick oak hull as if it were iron. The ship is still a commissioned vessel of the U.S. Navy, and the active-duty sailors who lead tours wear 1812 dress uniforms. A museum (**www.ussconstitutionmuseum.org**) is adjacent.

At the end of the Freedom Trail, in Charlestown, the 221-foot **Bunker Hill Monument** (www.nps.gov/bost) honors the memory of the colonists who died in the Battle of Bunker Hill on June 17, 1775. The rebels lost the battle, but not before killing or wounding nearly half the British troops, a loss that contributed to the redcoats' decision to abandon Boston 9 months later.

If you're not psyched about walking the whole route, you can hop on the **Beantown Trolley** (© 781/986-6100; www.beantowntrolley.com), which offers 1½-hour tours on vintage-style red trolleys, visiting sites on the Freedom Trail as well as other parts of the city. You can hop on and off all day long for $29 per adult (which includes a harbor cruise May–Oct), $7 for kids 5 to 11. Tickets are available at Faneuil Hall Marketplace and several other locations.

Beyond Revolutionary sites, Boston offers several wonderful museums. Its **Museum of Fine Arts,** 465 Huntington Ave. (© **617/267-9300;** www.mfa.org), is one of the nation's best, known for its collections of Impressionist paintings (including one of the largest collections of Monets outside of Paris), Asian and Old Kingdom Egyptian collections, classical art, Buddhist temple art, and medieval sculpture and tapestries. Admission is $15 for adults, $6.50 for kids 7 to 17. The **Isabella Stewart Gardner Museum,** 280 The Fenway (© **617/566-1401;** www.gardnermuseum.org), was created by its namesake, who designed her home in the style of a 15th-century Venetian palace and filled it with European, American, and Asian painting and sculpture, including works by Titian, Botticelli, Raphael, Rembrandt, Matisse, James McNeill Whistler, and John Singer Sargent. Admission is $12 for adults, free for kids. The **Institute of Contemporary Art/Boston,** 100 Northern Ave. (© **617/478-3101;** www.icaboston.org), which recently moved into a dramatic waterfront home near the cruise terminal, mounts rotating exhibits of 20th- and 21st-century painting, sculpture, photography, and video and performance art.

SHOPPING

The top shopping area is Boston's **Back Bay,** where dozens of classy galleries, shops, and boutiques make **Newbury Street** a world-famous destination. Nearby, the **Shops at Prudential Center** and **Copley Place** (linked by an enclosed walkway across Huntington Ave.) bookend a giant retail complex that includes the posh department stores **Neiman Marcus** and **Saks Fifth Avenue.** The adjacent **South End,** though less commercially dense, boasts a number of art galleries and quirky shops. Another popular spot is **Faneuil Hall Marketplace,** bounded by North, Congress, and State streets and Atlantic Avenue (© **617/523-1300;** www.faneuilhallmarketplace.com). The shops, boutiques, and pushcarts at Boston's busiest attraction sell everything from cosmetics to costume jewelry, sweaters to souvenirs.

WHERE TO STAY

You've got a lot of choice in Boston's many appealing neighborhoods, from B&Bs to boutique hotels and major chains—but don't expect bargains. Rates are generally on the high side during spring and summer, and are at their steepest during fall foliage season.

The closest hotel to the cruise port is the **Westin Boston Waterfront,** 435 Summer St. (© **800/WESTIN-1;** www.westin.com), at the Boston Convention and Exhibition Center. It opened in 2006 and offers the usual abundant Westin amenities—including their "Heavenly Beds"—and lovely water views. Rates: from $209.

The **Boston Harbor Hotel,** 70 Rowes Wharf, at the waterfront and Faneuil Hall Marketplace (© **800/752-7077;** www.bhh.com), is one of the finest and prettiest choices in town, a 16-story brick building that's within walking distance of downtown and the waterfront attractions. It prides itself on top-notch service. Rooms have wonderful harbor and skyline views. Rates: from $385.

The chief appeal of the **Boston Marriott Long Wharf,** 296 State St. (© **800/228-9290;** www.marriottlongwharf.com), is its easy access to downtown and waterfront attractions. The terraced brick exterior of the seven-story, 389-room hotel is one of the most recognizable sights on the harbor. Rates: from $249.

You get a lot for your money at the **Harborside Inn**, 185 State St. (© **888/723-7565;** www.harborsideinnboston.com), a renovated 1858 warehouse across the street from Faneuil Hall Marketplace and the harbor. The nicely appointed rooms have queen-size beds, hardwood floors, Oriental rugs, and Victorian-style furniture. Rates: from $179.

You can't beat the **Four Seasons**, 200 Boylston St. (© **800/819-5053;** www.four seasons.com), for exquisite service, a beautiful location, elegant guest rooms and public areas, a terrific health club, and wonderful restaurants. If you can afford it, this is unquestionably the place to stay. Each room in the 16-story brick-and-glass building has a great view. Rates: from $425.

The **Hampton Inn Boston Logan Airport,** 2300 Lee Burbank Hwy., Revere (© **800/426-7866;** www.hamptoninn.com), is on an ugly commercial-industrial strip, but it's just 1½ miles from the airport and 3 miles from downtown Boston. A free 24-hour shuttle bus serves the 227-room hotel, transporting guests to and from the airport and nearby restaurants. The hotel also has a pool, and the rates include continental breakfast. Rates: from $139.

DINING & NIGHTLIFE

Downtown, people have poured into **Durgin-Park,** 340 Faneuil Hall Marketplace (© **617/227-2038;** www.durgin-park.com), since 1827 for huge portions of delicious food, famously cranky waitresses, and a rowdy atmosphere where CEOs share tables with students. Feast on prime rib the size of a hubcap, lamb chops, fried seafood, and roast turkey. Fresh seafood arrives twice daily. Main courses: $10 to $30. If you want to check out America's oldest restaurant (which also happens to be Boston's best raw bar), visit **Ye Olde Union Oyster House,** 41 Union St. (© **617/227-2750;** www. unionoysterhouse.com). The place opened in 1826 and looks much the same as it did then, with a menu of traditional New England seafood. Daniel Webster and John Kennedy were regulars. Main courses: $17 to $30.

In Cambridge, **Jasper White's Summer Shack,** 149 Alewife Brook Pkwy. (© **617/520-9500;** www.summershackrestaurant.com), is a one-of-a-kind 300-seat place with picnic-table-style seating and baby blue leather booths. It serves the chef's signature pan-roasted lobster, plus all kinds of seafood, from clam rolls to steamers (not to mention corn dogs). Go for the food and the experience. Main courses: $6 to $29. (Jasper White's also has a location in the Back Bay, at 50 Dalton St.; © **617/867-9955.**) For more mainstream dining, there's **Legal Sea Foods** (www.legalseafoods.com), a local family-run chain known for its top-quality seafood. There are 10 locations around Boston and Cambridge, including 255 State St., on the waterfront (© **617/227-3115**); 36 Park Sq., between Columbus Avenue and Stuart Street (© **617/426-4444**); and Copley Place, 2nd level (© **617/266-7775**). Main courses: $8 to $35. **Legal Test Kitchen,** 225 Northern Ave. (© **617/330-7430**), not far from the cruise port, is a spinoff that serves an eclectic international menu. In Harvard Square, go to **Mr. Bartley's Burger Cottage,** 1246 Massachusetts Ave. (© **617/354-6559**), famous for its burgers, onion rings, and down-to-earth atmosphere. Most items are under $10.

Boston's Italian-American enclave, the North End, has dozens of restaurants; many are tiny and don't serve dessert or coffee. To satisfy those cravings, hit the *caffès* for coffee and fresh pastry in an atmosphere where lingering is welcome. Check out

Mike's Pastry, 300 Hanover St. (© **617/742-3050;** www.mikespastry.com), a bakery that's famous for its bustling takeout business and its cannoli.

Boston's bar scene was the inspiration for the TV show *Cheers.* The Bull & Finch Pub, the original bar that inspired the show, is now known as **Cheers Beacon Hill,** 84 Beacon St. (© **617/227-9605;** www.cheersboston.com). Another Cheers, at Quincy Market in Faneuil Hall Marketplace (© **617/227-0150;** www.cheersboston.com), has an interior modeled after the show's. Nearby, the jampacked **Black Rose,** 160 State St. (© **617/742-2286;** www.irishconnection.com), books live Irish music. The breathtaking 52nd-floor view makes the lounge at **Top of the Hub,** in the Prudential Tower, 800 Boylston St. (© **617/536-1775;** www.topofthehub.net), a favorite destination for dessert, drinks, and live jazz.

Nightlife listings can be found in the city's two main newspapers, the *Boston Globe* and *Boston Herald,* or in free publications (available at newspaper boxes around town) such as the weekly *Boston Phoenix* and the biweekly *Improper Bostonian* and *Stuff@Night.*

4 Cape Canaveral & Cocoa Beach, Florida

Known as the "Space Coast" because of nearby **Kennedy Space Center,** the Cape Canaveral/Cocoa Beach/Melbourne area boasts 72 miles of beaches, plus fishing, golfing, and surfing. The area is only about an hour west of Orlando's theme parks, which explains why long-underutilized Port Canaveral is now busier than ever before, offering many 3- and 4-night cruise options (often sold as packages with pre- or post-cruise visits to the Orlando resorts) as well as weeklong itineraries. It also serves as a port of call for some ships sailing southbound from New York, offering day-trip access to the Orlando parks.

Outside the port area, Cape Canaveral is . . . well, it's no Miami. Highways, strip malls, chain stores, and tracts of suburban homes predominate from the port area south into Cocoa Beach, where most of the hotels, restaurants, and beaches discussed here are located. The central areas of Cocoa Beach are mildly more interesting, with some great '50s and '60s condo and hotel architecture, but stylish they're not. In the other direction, much of the land around NASA is now set aside as the **Canaveral National Seashore** and the **Merritt Island National Wildlife Refuge** (www.nbbd.com/godo/minwr), a prime destination for nature lovers.

GETTING TO CAPE CANAVERAL & THE PORT

Port Canaveral is located at the eastern end of the Bennett Causeway, just off State Road 528 (the Bee Line Expwy.), the direct route from Orlando. From the port, 528 turns sharply south and becomes State Road A1A, portions of which are known as Astronaut Boulevard and North Atlantic Avenue. For information about the port, contact the **Canaveral Port Authority** (© **888/767-8226** or 321/783-7831; www. portcanaveral.org). Those flying in will probably land at the **Orlando International Airport** (© **407/825-2001;** www.orlandoairports.net), a 45-mile drive from Port Canaveral via S.R. 528, or **Melbourne International Airport** (www.mlbair.com), a straight drive from I-95 to S.R. 528. If you've booked air and/or transfers through your cruise line, a representative will meet you. Otherwise, **Cocoa Beach Shuttle** (© **888/784-4144** or 321/631-4144; www.cbshuttle.com) offers shuttle service between Orlando's airport and Port Canaveral; a one-way trip costs $30 per person or

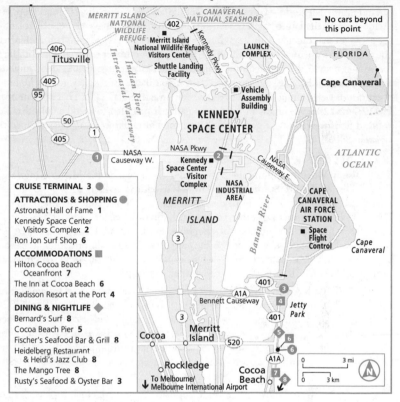

No cars beyond this point

MERRITT ISLAND NATIONAL WILDLIFE REFUGE

CANAVERAL NATIONAL SEASHORE

402

Merritt Island National Wildlife Refuge Visitors Center

LAUNCH COMPLEX

406

Titusville

Shuttle Landing Facility

405

95

50

405

1

Kennedy Pkwy

Indian River

Intracoastal Waterway

Vehicle Assembly Building

KENNEDY SPACE CENTER

NASA Pkwy

NASA Causeway W.

1

Kennedy Space Center Visitor Complex

2

NASA INDUSTRIAL AREA

NASA Causeway E.

ATLANTIC OCEAN

FLORIDA

Cape Canaveral

MERRITT

ISLAND

3

Banana River

CAPE CANAVERAL AIR FORCE STATION

Space Flight Control

Cape Canaveral

CRUISE TERMINAL 3 ●

ATTRACTIONS & SHOPPING ●
Astronaut Hall of Fame 1
Kennedy Space Center Visitors Complex 2
Ron Jon Surf Shop 6

ACCOMMODATIONS ■
Hilton Cocoa Beach Oceanfront 7
The Inn at Cocoa Beach 6
Radisson Resort at the Port 4

DINING & NIGHTLIFE ◆
Bernard's Surf 8
Cocoa Beach Pier 5
Fischer's Seafood Bar & Grill 8
Heidelberg Restaurant & Heidi's Jazz Club 8
The Mango Tree 8
Rusty's Seafood & Oyster Bar 3

401

A1A

Bennett Causeway

3

Cocoa

Merritt Island

520

401

Jetty Park

3

4

5

6

A1A

7

8

Rockledge

To Melbourne/
Melbourne International Airport

Cocoa Beach

0   3 mi
0   3 km

$55 for two people. By car, Port Canaveral and Cocoa Beach are accessible from virtually every interstate highway along the East Coast. Most visitors arrive via Route 1, Interstate 95, or S.R. 528. Parking at the port costs $12 a day.

GETTING AROUND   Having a car is vital here. Most **car-rental** companies operate at the Orlando airport, as do several **taxi** services. The fare to Port Canaveral is a hefty $100-plus; but taxis charge the same rate for up to nine passengers, so if you're traveling with a group, this might be a good option.

BEST CRUISE LINE SHORE EXCURSIONS
The cruise lines offer excursions to **Kennedy Space Center** ($72, 6 hr.) and combo transportation/ticket packages to either **Universal Studios** or **Islands of Adventure** ($64 per park, full day), as well as pre- and post-cruise stays in Orlando and at local beach resorts. Disney Cruise Line (of course) is the leader in linking cruisers to Orlando, with *Disney Wonder*'s 3- and 4-night itineraries specifically designed to integrate 3- and 4-night stays at the Disney resorts.

THE ORLANDO THEME PARKS
All it took was a sprinkle of pixie dust in the 1970s to begin the almost-magical transformation of Orlando from a swath of swampland into the most visited tourist destination in the world. Today, it's home to three giants—Walt Disney World, Universal

Orlando, and SeaWorld—whose local offerings include 7 of the 10 most popular theme parks in the United States. Many cruises from Port Canaveral are sold as land-sea packages that include park stays, but if you decide to visit Orlando before or after your cruise, it's essential to plan ahead. Otherwise, the number of attractions begging for your time and the hypercommercial atmosphere can put a serious dent in your psyche, your wallet, and your stamina. Even if you had 2 weeks, it wouldn't be long enough to hit everything, so don't even try. Stay selective, stay sane. That's our motto. Here's some basic info on each of the main parks. If you plan to spend a considerable amount of time here, we suggest picking up a copy of *Frommer's Walt Disney World & Orlando 2008.*

WALT DISNEY WORLD

Walt Disney World is the umbrella above four theme parks: the **Magic Kingdom, Epcot, Disney–MGM Studios,** and **Animal Kingdom,** which drew a combined attendance of almost 43 million paying customers in 2006. Besides its theme parks, Disney has an assortment of other venues, including two water parks, several entertainment venues, and a number of shopping spots. It's all located southwest of Orlando off Interstate 4, west of the Florida Turnpike. For information, vacation brochures, and videos, contact the Walt Disney World Co. (© **407/934-7639;** www. disneyworld.com) at least 6 weeks in advance of your trip.

TICKET PRICES & HOURS   At press time, 1-day, one-park tickets for any one of the four parks were a whopping $67 for adults, $56 for children 3 to 9 (plus tax). Discounted multiday, multipark tickets are available; many land-sea cruise packages include these passes. Park hours vary, so call ahead or go to **www.disneyworld.com** to check. Generally, expect hours to be from 9am to 8pm (until 6pm for Animal Kingdom), though the parks may open earlier and close later depending on special events and the economy. Epcot is usually open from 10am to 9pm.

THE MAGIC KINGDOM   The most popular theme park on the planet offers some 40 attractions, plus restaurants and shops, in a 107-acre package. Its symbol, **Cinderella Castle,** forms the hub of a wheel whose spokes reach to seven "lands" simulating everything from an Amazonian jungle to Colonial America. If you're traveling with little kids, this is the place to go.

EPCOT   This 260-acre park (the acronym stands for Experimental Prototype Community of Tomorrow) has two sections. **Future World** is centered on Epcot's icon, a giant geosphere that looks like a big golf ball. Major corporations sponsor the park's 10 themed areas, and the focus is on discovery, scientific achievements, and tomorrow's technologies in areas running from energy to undersea exploration. The **World Showcase** is a community of 11 miniaturized nations surrounding a 40-acre lagoon. All of these "countries" have indigenous architecture, landscaping, restaurants, and shops; cultural facets are explored in art exhibits, dance or other live performances, and innovative films. This park definitely appeals more to adults than children, but it has few thrill rides. If that's a requirement, go elsewhere. *Note:* Hiking through this park will often exhaust even the fittest person—some folks say Epcot really stands for "Every Person Comes Out Tired"—so we recommend splitting your visit over 2 days if possible.

DISNEY–MGM STUDIOS   You'll probably spy the **Earrfel Tower**—a water tower outfitted with gigantic mouse ears—before you enter this 110-acre park, which Disney bills as "the Hollywood that never was and always will be." You'll find pulse-quickening rides such as the Aerosmith-themed **Rock 'n' Roller Coaster** and the **Twilight Zone of Terror,** movie- and TV-themed shows such as **Jim Henson's Muppet*Vision 3D,** and some wonderful street performers. Adults and kids both love it. Best of all, it can be done comfortably in a day.

ANIMAL KINGDOM   This 500-acre park combines animals, elaborate landscapes, and a handful of rides. It's a conservation venue as much as an attraction, though, so it's easy for most of the animals to escape your eyes here (unlike at Tampa's Busch Gardens, the state's other major animal park). The thrill rides are better at Busch (though the new Expedition Everest attraction will get your adrenaline pumping), but Animal Kingdom has much better shows, such as *Festival of the Lion King* and *Finding Nemo—the Musical.* The park is good for both adults and children and can be done in a single outing, but if you come on a hot summer day, arrive early or it's unlikely you'll see many of the primo animals, which are smart enough to seek shade.

UNIVERSAL ORLANDO

Universal Orlando (© 800/224-4233 or 407/363-8000; www.universalorlando. com) is Disney's number-one competitor in the ongoing "anything you can do, we can do better" theme-park brawl. Although it's a distant second in terms of attendance, it's unquestionably the champion at entertaining teenagers and the older members of the thrill-ride crowd, with two major parks—**Universal Studios Florida** and **Islands of Adventure**—plus an entertainment district and several resorts. It's located at Universal Boulevard, off Interstate 4.

TICKET PRICES & HOURS   A 1-day, one-park ticket costs $67 for adults, $56 for children 3 to 9 (plus 6.5% tax); a 3-day, two-park Unlimited-Access Pass is $123 for adults, $113 for kids. The parks are open 365 days a year, generally from 9am to 6pm, though often later, especially in summer and around holidays. Call to confirm hours before you go.

UNIVERSAL STUDIOS FLORIDA   Even with fast-paced, grown-up rides such as **Revenge of the Mummy, Terminator** (should they change it to Governator?), and **Men in Black Alien Attack,** Universal Studios Florida is fun for kids. And as a plus, it's a working motion picture and TV studio, so filming is occasionally done at its sound stages. A talented group of actors portraying a range of characters from Universal films usually roams the park. You can do the park in a day, although you'll be a bit breathless when you get to the finish line.

ISLANDS OF ADVENTURE   This 110-acre theme park is, bar none, *the* Orlando theme park for thrill-ride junkies. With areas themed on Dr. Seuss, Jurassic Park, and Marvel comics, the park successfully combines nostalgia with state-of-the-art technology. Roller coasters roar above pedestrian walkways; water rides slice through the park. The **Amazing Adventures of Spider-Man** is a 3-D track ride that is arguably the best all-around attraction in Orlando; the **Jurassic Park River Adventure** has a 70-foot drop that scared creator Steven Spielberg into jumping ship before going over; and both the **Incredible Hulk Coaster** and **Dueling Dragons** draw huge raves from coaster crazies. Unless it's the height of high season, the park can be done in a day. It is not, however, a park for families with young kids: 9 of the park's 14 major rides have height restrictions. If, however, you have teens, or are an adrenaline junkie, this is definitely the place for you.

SEAWORLD

A 200-acre marine-life park, **SeaWorld** (℗ **407/351-3600;** www.seaworld.com) explores the deep in a format that combines conservation awareness with entertainment—pretty much what Disney is attempting at Animal Kingdom, but SeaWorld got here first, and its message is subtler and a more integrated part of the experience. The park is fun for everyone from small children to adults (who doesn't like dolphins and whales?) and is easily toured in a single day. The pace is much more laid-back than at Universal or Disney, so it makes for a nice break if you're in the area for several days. SeaWorld has a handful of high-tech roller coasters such as **Journey to Atlantis** and **Kraken,** but, all in all, the park can't compete in this category with Disney and Universal. On the other hand, those parks don't let you discover the crushed-velvet texture of a stingray or the song of a sea lion, not to mention the killer whale **Shamu,** the park's star attraction, and the other resident orcas. The park entrance is at the intersection of Interstate 4 and State Road 528 (Bee Line Expwy.).

TICKET PRICES & HOURS A 1-day ticket costs $65 for ages 10 and over, $54 for children 3 to 9 (plus 6.5% tax). The park is usually open from 9am to 6pm, later during summer and holidays.

Tip: At press time, SeaWorld had announced plans to open a water-slide theme park called **Aquatica** in spring 2008; details are currently sketchy, so check SeaWorld's website for up-to-date information.

EXPLORING CAPE CANAVERAL & COCOA BEACH ON YOUR OWN

Port Canaveral probably wouldn't be on the cruise industry's radar if it weren't so close to Orlando, and most passengers shuttle directly from theme park to pier rather than spending any significant time here. Nevertheless, anyone interested in the space program and its history should plan to arrive a day early (or stay a day after) to check out Kennedy Space Center and the Astronaut Hall of Fame. There are also a number of attractive beaches.

KENNEDY SPACE CENTER & THE ASTRONAUT HALL OF FAME

Set amid 150,000 acres of marshy wetlands favored by birds, reptiles, and amphibians, the **Kennedy Space Center** (℗ **321/449-4444;** www.kennedyspacecenter.com) has been at the center of America's space program since 1969, when astronauts took off from here to the moon. Even if you've never really considered yourself a science or space buff, you can't help but be impressed by the achievements the place represents. The only public access to the center (Hwy. 405) leads directly to the **Kennedy Space Center Visitor Complex,** which has real NASA rockets, the actual Mercury Mission Control Room from the 1960s, and numerous exhibits and films that look at space exploration from the '50s to today. There's a rocket garden displaying now-obsolete Redstone, Atlas, Saturn, and Titan rockets; a daily "Encounter" with a real astronaut; several pricey dining venues; and an obligatory gift shop selling a variety of space memorabilia and souvenirs. Two space-related IMAX movies (one in 3-D) shown on five-and-a-half-story-high screens are informative and entertaining.

While you could spend your entire day at the visitor complex, you must take the included **KSC Tour** or an optional, extra-cost tour to see the actual space center, where rockets and shuttles are prepared and launched. Buses for the included tour operate continuously, leaving every 15 minutes and making stops at the **LC-39 Observation Gantry,** with a dramatic 360-degree view over launchpads where space shuttles blast off, and the impressive **Apollo/Saturn V Center,** which includes artifacts, photos, interactive exhibits, and the 363-foot **Saturn V,** the most powerful rocket ever launched by the United States. At each stop you can get off, look around, and then take the next bus that comes along. Plan to take the tour early in your visit and be sure to hit the restrooms before boarding—there's only one out on the tour. Several **optional, extra-cost tours** get you closer to sights like the Space Shuttle launchpads, the massive Vehicle Assembly Building, and the original launch sites of the Mercury, Gemini, and Apollo programs. Optional tours frequently sell out in advance, so call ahead for reservations.

At the Visitor Complex, don't miss the **Astronaut Memorial,** a moving black-granite monument that has the names of the U.S. astronauts who have died on missions or while in training. The 60-ton structure rotates on a track that follows the movement of the sun, causing the names to stand out above a brilliant reflection of the sky.

Near the intersection of Routes 1 and 405, across the Indian River to the west of KSC, the **U.S. Astronaut Hall of Fame** features displays, exhibits, and tributes to the heroes of the Mercury, Gemini, and Apollo space programs. Film presentations introduce visitors to the origins of rocketry and to the sheer power of the rockets themselves, while displays of personal memorabilia offer insight into the astronauts' lives. Displays of NASA memorabilia include actual Mission Control terminals (at which you can sit to access interactive information) and, most mind-blowing of all, the actual Apollo 14 command module *Kitty Hawk,* whose plaque bears the inscription "This spacecraft flew to the moon and back January 31 February 9, 1971." Nuff said.

But let's get down to brass tacks. The Astronaut Hall of Fame offers one main thing the rest of the KSC Visitor Complex doesn't: the chance to pretend you're an astronaut through various simulations, including a **G-force simulator** that spins at high speed to simulate four times the force of gravity; a **Mission to Mars** rover simulation that sends you bumping over the surface of the red planet (this one's skippable if you're short on time); and a **Walk on the Moon** weightlessness simulation, using harnesses and counterweights. Now the warnings: Simulators are off-limits to folks under 48 inches, and if you tend to suffer from motion sickness, you'll probably want to avoid everything except the weightlessness simulation. Also, be sure to allow at least a few minutes between simulations, even if you've got a cast-iron constitution. Trust us on this one.

Kennedy Space Center is accessible via State Road 405, just off U.S. 1. The Visitor Complex, including the Astronaut Hall of Fame, is open daily, except Christmas and certain launch days, from 9am to 5:30pm. The last bus tour departs at 2:15pm from the Visitor Complex. Regular admission (including all exhibits, Astronaut Encounter, IMAX space films, the KSC tour, and the Astronaut Hall of Fame) is $38 for adults, $28 for kids 3 to 11. Parking at the Visitor Complex and Hall of Fame is free, but there is no shuttle between the two. Be sure to pick up maps as you enter each branch, and expect to spend most of the day here to get the full experience: You'll need at least 2 hours to see the Visitor Complex (plus another couple to see the IMAX films), another 2 hours to see the highlights of the included tour (plus another 2 or 3 hr. if you linger at the tour stops or take one of the guided tours), and at least another 2 hours to see the Astronaut Hall of Fame.

BEACHES

Though the Cape Canaveral/Cocoa Beach area doesn't have the spectacular beach culture of Miami, it doesn't lack for pleasant coastline, much of which is famous for surfing. The following beaches (or "parks" in the local lingo) are located within an easy drive of the port area. Closest to the cruise ship port and actually part of the larger port complex, the clean, nicely landscaped 4½-acre **Jetty Park,** 400 E. Jetty Rd. (② 321/783-7111; www.portcanaveral.org/recreation/beaches.php#jetty), is the most elaborate of the local beaches, perched at a point from which the whole expanse of the Cape Canaveral/Cocoa Beach coastline stretches away to the south. A snack bar, bathrooms, showers, picnic facilities, a children's playground, and fishing are available. Parking costs $5 per car. Follow the signs after entering the port area, near where State Road 528 and the A1A intersect. A series of beaches are accessible (and generally sign-posted) off the A1A heading south from the port. The **Cocoa Beach Pier,** on Meade Avenue east of A1A (② 321/783-7549; www.cocoabeachpier.com), is a great surfing spot with an open-air bar, volleyball, and a party atmosphere. **Lori Wilson Park,** far-ther south at 1500 N. Atlantic Ave. (② 321/868-1123; www.brevardparks.com/nature/loriwilson.htm), is another nicely landscaped area on the order of Jetty Park, with bathrooms and showers; a rustic boardwalk with some shaded picnic areas and benches; a nature center; and the Hammock, a .25-mile boardwalk nature trail that winds through ferns, twisted trees, and other *Jurassic Park*–like foliage, while butter-flies flutter by and spiders eye them from their webs. Parking is free.

SHOPPING

Let's be unkind: You could shop here, but why bother? The offerings in Cape Canaveral and Cocoa Beach are mostly the kind of national mall chains that you've probably got at home, so save your energy and dollars for the Caribbean. An excep-tion—as much for the experience as for the goods—is the **Ron Jon Surf Shop,** 4151 N. Atlantic Ave./A1A (② 321/799-8888; www.ronjons.com). Inside the blue-and-yellow, South Beach–looking Art Deco building is enough au courant beachwear to transform you and a good-size army into surfer dudes. The store also rents beach bikes, body boards, surfboards, kayaks, beach chairs, and other equipment by the hour, day, or week. It's open 24 hours a day, 365 days a year.

WHERE TO STAY

While the area has a wealth of cheap beach hotels, few are really notable, so we'll con-centrate on the ones that are.

The **Radisson Resort at the Port,** 8701 Astronaut Blvd./A1A (② 800/333-3333; www.radisson.com/capecanaveralfl), is only a 5-minute drive from the port and offers comfortable rooms. Even more comfy are the two-room suites that are a great option for families, featuring a bedroom with a Jacuzzi and a living room with a sofa bed. Cruise passengers arriving by car can leave their vehicles free in the hotel's lot during their cruise and take the free Radisson shuttle to and from the port. Rates: from $139.

At the other end of the spectrum, the **Inn at Cocoa Beach,** 4300 Ocean Beach Blvd., just off the A1A behind the Ron Jon Surf Shop (② 800/343-5307; www.theinn atcocoabeach.com), is almost entirely couples-oriented, presenting itself as more of a personalized inn than a traditional hotel. Almost all of its 50 romantic B&B-style rooms face the ocean and have rocking chairs on their balconies. Two parrots and two dogs are members of the hotel "staff," and guests are treated to daily breakfast, after-noon tea, and evening wine-and-cheese socials. Rates: from $135.

The six-story **Hilton Cocoa Beach Oceanfront,** 2080 N. Atlantic Ave. (② 800/445-8667 or 321/799-0003; www.hilton.com), is one of the few upscale beachfront properties here, with rooms that are spacious and comfortable but weirdly lacking in balconies. Rates: from $139.

DINING & NIGHTLIFE

Bernard's Surf, 2 S. Atlantic Ave., Cocoa Beach (© 321/783-2401), was opened by Bernard Fischer in 1948, and its photos testify to the many astronauts who've celebrated their safe return to Earth with the restaurant's steak and seafood. The latter is provided by the Fischer family's own boats. At the same address, **Fischer's Seafood Bar & Grill** is a *Cheers*-like lounge popular with the locals, serving fried combo platters, shrimp and crab-claw meat, and the like. Another casual option in this complex is **Rusty's Seafood & Oyster Bar,** with spicy seafood gumbo, raw or steamed oysters, burgers and sandwiches, pasta, and so on. The **Rusty's** location at 628 Glen Cheek Dr., Port Canaveral (© 321/783-2033; www.rustysseafood.com), on the south side of Port Canaveral harbor, serves the same menu but with views of the fishing boats and cruise ships heading in and out of the port. Bernard's main courses are $14 to $55; at the others, everything's about $5 to $22.

The **Mango Tree,** 118 N. Atlantic Ave./A1A, between North First and North Second streets (© 321/799-0513; www.themangotreerestaurant.com), is the most beautiful and sophisticated restaurant in Cocoa Beach, serving gourmet seafood, pasta, chicken, and Continental dishes in a plantation-home atmosphere, amid grounds lush with tropical foliage. Main courses: $16 to $40.

In downtown Cocoa Beach, the **Heidelberg Restaurant,** 7 N. Orlando Ave./A1A, at the Minuteman Causeway (© 321/783-6806), serves German and Continental dinner cuisine such as beef stroganoff, goulash, roast duck, sauerbraten, and grilled loin pork chops. Main courses: $15 to $23. The adjoining **Heidi's Jazz Club** (© 321/783-4559; www.heidisjazzclub.com) has music nightly except Mondays, with a jam session Sundays from 7 to 11pm. See the website for a schedule of performances.

The **Cocoa Beach Pier,** 401 Meade Ave., off the A1A, and ½ mile north of State Road 520 (© 321/783-7549; www.cocoabeachpier.com), juts out 800 feet over the Atlantic, offering a casual beer-and-fruity-drinks atmosphere, an open-air tiki bar with live music most nights, an ice-cream shop, sit-down seafood restaurants, and an arcade, plus beach-equipment rentals and volleyball right next door on the sand.

5 Charleston, South Carolina

In the closing pages of *Gone With the Wind,* Rhett tells Scarlett that he's going back home to Charleston, where he can find "the calm dignity life can have when it's lived by gentle folks, the genial grace of days that are gone." In spite of all the changes and upheavals over the years, Rhett's endorsement of Charleston still holds true, sans slavery and petticoats. Near-fanatical preservationists have assured that, architecturally at least, the Old South lives on here, and they've even managed to hold on to some of that famous graciousness, too. It's one of the best-preserved cities in the South, boasting 73 pre-Revolutionary buildings and more than 600 built before the 1840s. With its cobblestone streets and horse-drawn carriages, jasmine and wisteria fragrances, and stately old homes, it's a nice little time machine of a place, totally conscious of its history but gratifyingly averse to turning itself into an Old South theme park.

GETTING TO CHARLESTON & THE PORT

The **Port of Charleston's** cruise ship terminal (© 843/958-8298; www.port-of-charleston.com) is located at 196 Concord St., at the foot of Market Street, smack in the heart of the historic district. You can easily walk anywhere you need to go. People arrive by plane at **Charleston International Airport** (© 843/767-7009; www. chs-airport.com), located in North Charleston, 12 miles from the terminal. If you've made arrangements for transfers through your cruise line, a representative will meet your arriving flight and direct you to shuttle buses. **Taxis** are available to downtown for about $27.

For those arriving by car, take I-95 north or south, then I-26 (SE) toward Charleston. Exit at East Bay Street, and turn left onto Market Street, then right on Washington. The entrance to the terminal will be on your left. Parking lots are located near the terminal, with a shuttle service to take you to the pier. Parking is $15 per day.

GETTING AROUND   You can easily walk around the historic district right from the cruise docks. Narrated horse-drawn **carriage tours** are available at Market Street from several operators. **Palmetto Carriage Tours** (© 843/723-8145; www.carriage tour.com) uses mule teams and takes off from the red barn behind the Rainbow Market. Tickets are available at 40 N. Market St. From there, exit out back and through the parking lot to the barn. A 1-hour tour costs $20 for adults.

BEST CRUISE LINE SHORE EXCURSIONS

Historic Charleston Carriage Tour ($34, 1¼ hr.): As hokey as carriage tours may seem, this is actually a nice way to see historic Charleston. The leisurely ride just seems to match the pace of the place. You'll pass carefully restored 18th- and 19th-century homes and buildings as your guide gives some historical perspective.

Boone Hall Plantation ($64, 2½ hr.): See the historic Boone Hall Plantation, with its *Gone With the Wind* ambience. You can tour the lovely Georgian plantation house as well as the slave quarters, built from brick made on the plantation in the 1800s.

Historic Homes Walking Tour ($54, 2½ hr.): A narrated walking tour of Charleston's historic district, visiting the Nathaniel Russell House and the Edmondston-Alston House (see below) and passing the Old Exchange Building, St. Michael's Episcopal Church, Rainbow Row (the longest set of contiguous Georgian facades in the entire country), Catfish Row (a setting in *Porgy and Bess*), and the Calhoun Mansion.

Historic Charleston & Middleton Plantation ($139, 6 hr.): Middleton Plantation was established in 1741 and was once home to Arthur Middleton, a signer of the Declaration of Independence. Its formal gardens are the oldest in the United States. Tour includes a buffet lunch and a narrated drive through historic Charleston.

EXPLORING CHARLESTON ON YOUR OWN

Charleston's streets are laid out in an easy-to-follow grid. The main north–south thoroughfares are King, Meeting, and East Bay streets. Tradd, Broad, Queen, and Calhoun streets cross the city from east to west. South of Broad Street, East Bay becomes East Battery. The cruise terminal is located in the **Downtown** neighborhood, which extends north from Broad Street to Marion Square at the intersection of Calhoun and Meeting streets. You can't miss the **Old City Market** here (see "Shopping," below), since it shoots straight at the terminal like an arrow. Meeting Street, Church Street, and all the other streets east to the waterfront are full of gorgeous homes and shady gardens, plus many of the historical attractions.

Not far from the City Market, the **Old Exchange & Provost Dungeon,** 122 E. Bay St. (© 843/727-2165; www.oldexchange.com), served as a prison during the American Revolution, then in 1873 became Charleston's City Hall. Its large collection of

Charleston

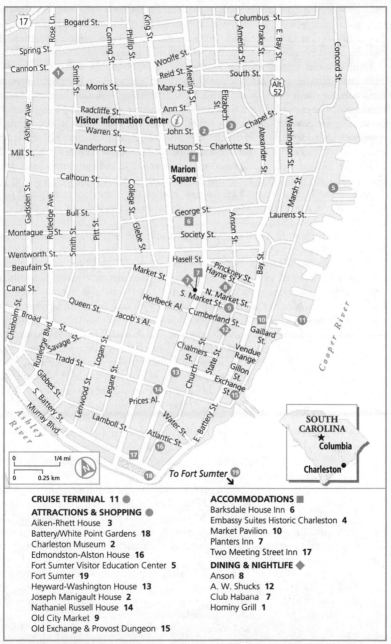

CRUISE TERMINAL 11 ●

ATTRACTIONS & SHOPPING ●
Aiken-Rhett House **3**
Battery/White Point Gardens **18**
Charleston Museum **2**
Edmondston-Alston House **16**
Fort Sumter Visitor Education Center **5**
Fort Sumter **19**
Heyward-Washington House **13**
Joseph Manigault House **2**
Nathaniel Russell House **14**
Old City Market **9**
Old Exchange & Provost Dungeon **15**

ACCOMMODATIONS ■
Barksdale House Inn **6**
Embassy Suites Historic Charleston **4**
Market Pavilion **10**
Planters Inn **7**
Two Meeting Street Inn **17**

DINING & NIGHTLIFE ◆
Anson **8**
A. W. Shucks **12**
Club Habana **7**
Hominy Grill **1**

antique chairs was donated in 1921 by the local Daughters of the American Revolution, and its dungeon (which you tour with a costumed docent) displays the only visible chunk of Charleston's original city wall, the Half-Moon Bastion. We could do without its hokey animatronic displays, though. Admission is $7.

The **Nathaniel Russell House,** 51 Meeting St. (© **843/724-8481;** www.historic charleston.org/experience/nrh), is one of the finest examples of Federal architecture you'll ever see. Built in 1808, it's noted for a "free flying" staircase, spiraling unsupported for three floors. The staircase's elliptical shape is repeated throughout the house. The interiors are ornate with period furnishings, especially the elegant music room with its golden harp and neoclassical-style sofa. Admission runs $10. For a $16 combo ticket, you can also visit the **Aiken-Rhett House,** 48 Elizabeth St. (© **843/ 723-1159;** www.historiccharleston.org/experience/arh), built by merchant John Robinson in 1818 and then expanded by Governor and Mrs. William Aiken in the 1830s and 1850s. Like other Charlestonians of their time, the Aikens furnished their home with crystal and bronze chandeliers, classical sculpture, and paintings purchased on trips to Europe. Today, many of those objects are still in the rooms for which the Aikens bought them. Original outbuildings include the kitchens, slave quarters, stables, privies, and cattle sheds.

The **Charleston Museum,** 360 Meeting St. (© **843/722-2996;** www.charleston museum.org), was founded in 1773, making it the first and oldest museum in America. The collections preserve and interpret the social and natural history of Charleston and the South Carolina coastal region, with early crafts, historic relics, and a series of hands-on exhibits for children. Admission is $10 adults, $5 kids. A $16 combination ticket also gets you admission to the **Joseph Manigault House,** 350 Meeting St. (across from the museum), a three-story Federal-style town house built in 1803 for its namesake, a French Huguenot plantation owner and politician. Many rooms have been restored to their original colors, with period furniture. Outbuildings such as the kitchen, slave quarters, stable, and privy are part of the experience. A $21 combo ticket also includes the museum's **Heyward-Washington House,** 87 Church St., built in 1772 by Daniel Heyward, the "rice king" of Charleston. It was also the home of Thomas Heyward, Jr., a signer of the Declaration of Independence. President George Washington bedded down here in 1791. Many of the fine period pieces in the house are the work of Thomas Elfe, one of America's most famous cabinetmakers. Admission to either house alone is $10.

At the southernmost point of the historic area stands the **Battery** (aka the White Point Gardens), where the Cooper and Ashley rivers converge. It has a landscaped park shaded by palmettos and live oaks, with walkways lined with monuments and other war relics. Virtually every home around here is of historic or architectural interest, including the **Edmondston-Alston House,** 21 E. Battery (© **843/722-7171;** www. middletonplace.org/default.asp?catID=4515), an 1825 house originally built in Federal style and later modified to a Greek Revival style. Inside are heirloom furnishings, silver, and paintings. Robert E. Lee once found refuge here when his hotel uptown caught fire. Admission is $10. The house is a property of the Middleton Place Foundation, which also operates the Middleton Place estate, 14 miles northwest of town.

Head back toward the cruise terminal along the seawall on East Battery and Murray Boulevard to absorb Charleston's riverfront ambience and catch the distant view of **Fort Sumter,** where the first shot of the Civil War was fired on April 12, 1861. Confederate forces launched a 34-hour bombardment of the fort, leading Union forces to surrender and the government in Washington to declare war. Amazingly, Confederate troops held onto Sumter for nearly 4 years, by the end of which time continual Northern bombardment had reduced it to a heap of rubble. You can visit the fort with **Fort Sumter Tours/SpiritLine Cruises** (© **800/789-3678**; www.spirit linecruises.com), which runs ferries across Charleston Harbor from town to the fort. You can buy tickets at Liberty Square's Fort Sumter Visitor Education Center, near the foot of Calhoun Street. The 2¼-hour tour consists of approximately 1 hour at Fort Sumter plus a 30-minute harbor cruise in each direction. Park rangers are on hand at the fort to answer questions, and you can explore gun emplacements and visit a small museum filled with artifacts related to the siege. Ferry tickets cost $14; tours are offered two or three times a day, usually at 9:30am, noon, and 2:30pm, though there are seasonal variations. Call or check the website to confirm times.

SHOPPING

Located within sight of the cruise ship docks, the **Old City Market** comprises four open-sided buildings that run from East Bay Street up to Meeting Street. The market originally sold foodstuffs, including meat, fish, and local produce, but today it's packed with vendors hawking local art, food, books, clothing, and souvenirs. One standout item here: **sea-grass baskets** woven by Gullah women, descendents of coastal slaves who maintain a distinct culture on South Carolina's islands.

King Street is known for its shopping, with antiques at the south end of the street, clothes and jewelry along the main stretch, and housewares and interior decor along North King (aka Upper King).

If you fall for the period furniture you see in the historic houses, you can buy reproductions online from the **Historic Charleston Foundation** (www.historiccharleston. org), which operates the Nathaniel Russell House, the Aiken-Rhett House, and several other historic properties.

WHERE TO STAY

There are quite a few distinctive accommodations in Charleston located within spitting distance of the cruise pier.

The **Embassy Suites Historic Charleston,** 337 Meeting St. (© **843/723-6900**; www.embassysuites.com), is located close to the visitor center, on Marrion Square in the original home of the 19th-century Citadel Military College. It's listed on the National Register of Historic Places and features British West Indies colonial plantation decor and two-room suites. Rates: from $210.

Close to the dock, the **Market Pavilion,** 225 E. Bay St. (© **877/440-2250**; www. marketpavilion.com), offers opulent old-Charleston-style guest rooms with old-world decor, plaster crown moldings, mahogany touches, and four-poster beds. There's also the wonderful rooftop Pavilion Bar and the excellent Grill 225 restaurant. Rates: from $229.

Barksdale House Inn, 27 George St. (© **888/577-4980**; www.barksdalehouse. com), is a neat, tidy, and well-proportioned Italianate building about ¼ mile north of the City Market, constructed as an inn in 1778 and later altered and enlarged. Many bedrooms have four-poster beds and working fireplaces—as if you need more heat in often-sweltering Charleston. Rates: from $129.

The **Planters Inn,** 112 N. Market St. (© **800/845-7082**; www.plantersinn.com), next to the City Market, is an opulent yet tasteful and cozy enclave of Colonial charm, and one of the finest small luxury hotels in the South. The spacious rooms have hardwood floors, marble bathrooms, and 18th-century decor. Afternoon tea is served in the lobby. The Peninsula Grill's setting has a 19th-century charm unlike any other restaurant in Charleston. The menu changes frequently, with main courses in the $26-to-$35 range. Rates: from $250.

Two Meeting Street Inn, 2 Meeting St. (© 843/723-7322; www.twomeeting street.com), has the most enviable location in the city, right across from the Battery, looking over the confluence of the Charles and Ashley rivers. The house was built in 1892 as a wedding gift from a prosperous father to his daughter. Inside, the proportions are as lavish and gracious as the Gilded Age could provide. Rates: from $219.

DINING & NIGHTLIFE

Foodies flock to Charleston for refined Low Country cookery as well as an array of French and international specialties. Among the best is **Anson,** 12 Anson St., in the City Market area (© 843/577-0551; www.ansonrestaurant.com), which blends the grace notes of a big New York restaurant with Low Country charm and cuisine. The setting is a century-old, brick-sided ice warehouse, and the decor is full of Corinthian pilasters salvaged from demolished Colonial houses, with enough Victorian rococo for anyone's taste. Main courses: $18 to $36.

A. W. Shucks, 70 State St. (© 843/723-1151; www.a-w-shucks.com), is a hearty, casual oyster bar in a restored warehouse located next to City Market, around the corner from East Bay Street. Menu highlights are oysters and clams on the half shell, tasty seafood chowders, deviled crab, and a wide beer selection. Main courses: $16 to $20.

Farther from the market area, **Hominy Grill,** 207 Rutledge Ave. (© 843/937-0930; www.hominygrill.com), features simply and beautifully prepared dishes inspired by the kitchens of the Low Country. It has gained a devoted family following, which comes here to feast on such specialties as oven-fried chicken with spicy peach gravy. From the market, head north on Meeting Street, turn left on Calhoun, and walk 7 blocks west to Rutledge. Main courses: $10 to $15.

For a heady after-dinner experience, head to **Club Habana,** 177 Meeting St. (© 843/853-3720; www.clubhabana.com). With the ambience of a private club, this martini-and-wine bar, located on the second floor of a 200-year-old building, lets you relax in any of three Gilded Age salons. The club specializes in exotic cigars and martinis; it also serves appetizers, desserts, fruit and cheese plates, and even some miniature beef Wellingtons. It's above the Tinder Box Internationale, which sells new and vintage pipes, pipe tobacco, and cigars.

6 Fort Lauderdale, Florida

Broward County's Port Everglades is the second-busiest cruise port in the world, drawing more than 3.5 million cruise passengers a year. It boasts the deepest harbor on the eastern seaboard south of Norfolk, 12 ultramodern cruise ship terminals, and an easy access route to the Fort Lauderdale–Hollywood International Airport, less than a 10-minute drive away.

GETTING TO FORT LAUDERDALE & THE PORT

Port Everglades (© 954/523-3404; www.broward.org/port) is located about 23 miles north of Miami within the city boundaries of Fort Lauderdale, Hollywood, and Dania Beach. Interstate 595 will take you right onto the grounds. If you're coming by air, you'll land at the **Fort Lauderdale–Hollywood International Airport** (© 954/359-6100), located less than 2 miles from Port Everglades (5 min. by bus or taxi),

Fort Lauderdale

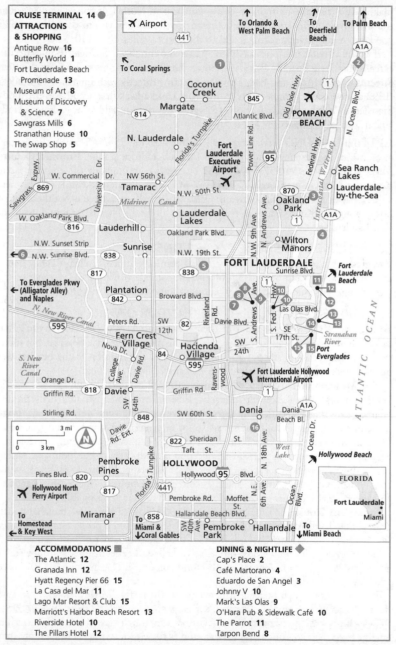

CRUISE TERMINAL 14 ●

ATTRACTIONS & SHOPPING

Antique Row **16**
Butterfly World **1**
Fort Lauderdale Beach
  Promenade **13**
Museum of Art **8**
Museum of Discovery
  & Science **7**
Sawgrass Mills **6**
Stranathan House **10**
The Swap Shop **5**

✈ Airport

441

↖ To Coral Springs

To Orlando &
West Palm Beach ↑

To Deerfield
Beach ↑

To Palm Beach ↑

A1A

2

1

Coconut
Creek

845

Margate

814

Atlantic Blvd.

Old Dixie Hwy.

✈

POMPANO
BEACH

N. Ocean Blvd.

N. Lauderdale

Florida's Turnpike

Fort
Lauderdale
Executive
Airport

Power Line Rd.

95

Federal Hwy.

Intracoastal Waterway

Sawgrass Expwy.

869

W. Commercial Dr.

NW 56th St.

Tamarac

N.W. 50th St.

✈

870

Oakland
Park

Sea Ranch
Lakes

Lauderdale-
by-the-Sea

A1A

University Dr.

Midriver Canal

Lauderdale
Lakes

N.W. 9th Ave.

N. Andrews Ave.

3

1

W. Oakland Park Blvd.

816

Lauderhill

Oakland Park Blvd.

Wilton
Manors

4

N.W. Sunset Strip

← 6 N.W. Sunrise Blvd.

838

Sunrise

N.W. 19th St.

FORT LAUDERDALE

Sunrise Blvd.

Fort
Lauderdale
Beach

817

838

5

11

12

To Everglades Pkwy
← (Alligator Alley)
and Naples

Plantation
842

Broward Blvd.

8
8 9
7

Federal Hwy.

S. Andrews Ave.

10

Las Olas Blvd.

1

12

13

ATLANTIC OCEAN

N. New River Canal

595

Peters Rd.

SW
12th

82

Riverland Rd.

Davie Blvd.

S. Fed. Hwy.

SE
17th St.

14

15

13

Stranahan
River

Fern Crest
Village

Nova Dr.

84

Hacienda
Village
595

SW
24th

Ravenswood

15 Port
Everglades

S. New
River
Canal

College Ave.

Davie Rd.

Orange Dr.

Griffin Rd.

818

Davie

Griffin Rd.

✈ Fort Lauderdale Hollywood
International Airport

Stirling Rd.

SW
64th

848

SW 60th St.

1

Dania

Dania
Beach Bl.

A1A

Ocean Dr.

0   3 mi

0   3 km

N

Davie
Rd. Ext.

822

Sheridan   St.

Taft   St.

N. 18th Ave.

West
Lake

↗ Hollywood Beach

Pembroke
Pines

Florida's Turnpike

HOLLYWOOD

Hollywood 95 Blvd.

N.E.
6th Ave.

Ocean Blvd.

FLORIDA

Pines Blvd.

820

✈ Hollywood North
Perry Airport

817

441

Pembroke Rd.

Moffet
St.

Fort Lauderdale
• Miami

To
Homestead
← & Key West

Miramar

To 858
Miami &
↓Coral Gables

SW 40th Ave.

Hallandale Beach Blvd.

Pembroke
Park

Hallandale

To
↓Miami Beach

ACCOMMODATIONS ■

The Atlantic **12**
Granada Inn **12**
Hyatt Regency Pier 66 **15**
La Casa del Mar **11**
Lago Mar Resort & Club **15**
Marriott's Harbor Beach Resort **13**
Riverside Hotel **10**
The Pillars Hotel **12**

DINING & NIGHTLIFE ◆

Cap's Place **2**
Café Martorano **4**
Eduardo de San Angel **3**
Johnny V **10**
Mark's Las Olas **9**
O'Hara Pub & Sidewalk Café **10**
The Parrot **11**
Tarpon Bend **8**

making this the easiest airport-to-cruise-port trip in Florida. If you've booked air or transfers through the cruise line, a representative will show you to your shuttle after you land. If you haven't, taking a **taxi** to the port costs less than $10.

If you're driving, the port has three passenger entrances: Spangler Boulevard, an extension of State Road 84 East; Eisenhower Boulevard, running south from the 17th Street Causeway/A1A; and Eller Drive, connecting directly with Interstate 595. I-595 runs east–west, with connections to the Fort Lauderdale–Hollywood Airport, I-95, State Road 7 (441), Florida Turnpike, Sawgrass Expressway, and I-75. Parking is available in two large garages for $12 a day.

GETTING AROUND   For a taxi, call **Yellow Cab** (© **954/565-5400**). Rates start at $4.50 for the first mile and are $2.40 for each additional mile. **Broward County Mass Transit** (© **954/357-8400**) runs bus service throughout the county; 1-day passes are $2.50. **Water Taxi** (© **954/467-6677;** www.watertaxi.com), which offers all-day passes for $10, sails between Oakland Park Boulevard and Southeast 17th Street along the Intracoastal Waterway, and west along the New River into downtown Fort Lauderdale.

BEST CRUISE LINE SHORE EXCURSIONS

Everglades Airboat Ride ($52, 4½ hr.): The Seminole Indians called it Pahay Okee, the "grassy water," and on this 30-minute airboat ride you'll get to see some of the area's indigenous wildlife, including water birds and American alligators.

EXPLORING FORT LAUDERDALE ON YOUR OWN

Fort Lauderdale Beach, a 5-mile strip along State Road A1A, gained fame in the 1950s as a spring-break playground, popularized by the movie *Where the Boys Are,* but today the scene is a lot more affluent and family-oriented. In addition to the beaches (see below), there are a few other attractions that might float your boat.

The **Museum of Discovery & Science,** 401 SW Second St. (© **954/467-6637;** www.mods.org), is an excellent interactive science museum with an IMAX theater. "Florida Ecoscapes" is particularly interesting, with a living coral reef, bees, bats, frogs, turtles, and alligators. Admission costs $15 for both the IMAX and the museum. The **Museum of Art,** 1 E. Las Olas Blvd. (© **954/525-5500;** www.moafl.org), is a truly terrific small museum whose permanent collection of 20th-century European and American art includes works by Picasso, Calder, Warhol, Mapplethorpe, Dalí, Frank Stella, and William Glackens. African, South Pacific, pre-Columbian, Native American, and Cuban art are also on display. Admission is about $10, but varies by exhibition.

Stranahan House, 335 SE Sixth Ave. (© **954/524-4736;** www.stranahanhouse. org), is Fort Lauderdale's very oldest standing structure and a prime example of classic "Florida Frontier" architecture. Built in 1901 by the "father of Fort Lauderdale," Frank Stranahan, it's been a post office, town hall, and general store, and now serves as a worthwhile little museum of South Florida pioneer life. Admission is $10; closed Monday and Tuesday.

In the walk-through, screened-in aviary at **Butterfly World,** Tradewinds Park South, 3600 W. Sample Rd., Coconut Creek, west of the Florida Turnpike (© **954/ 977-4400;** www.butterflyworld.com), visitors can watch newly hatched butterflies emerge from their cocoons and flutter around as they learn to fly. There are more than 150 species in residence. Admission is $20.

BEACHES

Backed by an endless row of hotels and popular with visitors and locals alike, the **Fort Lauderdale Beach Promenade** is located along A1A, also known as Fort Lauderdale Beach Boulevard, between SE 17th Street and Sunrise Boulevard. The fabled strip from *Where the Boys Are* is Ocean Boulevard, between Las Olas and Sunrise boulevards. On weekends, parking at the oceanside meters is difficult to find. **Fort Lauderdale Beach** at the Howard Johnson is another perennial local favorite. A jetty bounds the beach on the south side, making it rather private, although the water gets a little choppy. High-school and college students share this area with an older crowd. One of the main beach entrances is at 4660 N. Ocean Dr. in Lauderdale-by-the-Sea.

SHOPPING

If you're looking for unusual boutiques and art galleries, head to quaint **Las Olas Boulevard,** located west of A1A and a block east of Federal Highway/U.S. 1 (off SE 8th St.), where hundreds of shops offer alluring window decorations like kitchen utensils posing as modern-art sculptures. **Las Olas Riverfront,** at SW First Avenue and Las Olas Boulevard (© **954/522-6556;** www.riverfrontfl.com), is a huge retail complex with restaurants, clothing stores, arcades, and a multiplex movie theater.

The **Swap Shop,** 3291 W. Sunrise Blvd. (© **954/791-SWAP;** www.floridaswap shop.com), is one of the world's largest flea markets. In addition to endless acres of vendors, there's a mini–amusement park and a 15-screen drive-in movie theater. It's open daily. About 10 miles outside town, **Sawgrass Mills,** 12801 W. Sunrise Blvd., at Flamingo Road (© **954/846-2300;** www.sawgrassmillsmall.com), is one of the premier outlet malls in the country, with more than 300 shops, kiosks, a 24-screen movie theater, and many restaurants and bars, including a Hard Rock Cafe.

WHERE TO STAY

Fort Lauderdale Beach has a hotel or motel on nearly every block, and the selection ranges from run-down to luxurious.

The **Hyatt Regency Pier 66,** located very close to the port at 2301 SE 17th St. Causeway (© **800/233-1234** or 954/525-6666; www.pier66.hyatt.com), is a circular landmark whose large rooms are decorated with a retro modern look. Its famous revolving rooftop bar, the Piertop Lounge, is often filled with cruise ship patrons. Rates: from $159. The **Harbor Beach Marriott Resort,** just south of Fort Lauderdale's strip at 3030 Holiday Dr. (© **800/222-6543** or 954/525-4000; www.marriott harborbeach.com), is set on 16 acres of beachfront property. All units open onto private balconies overlooking either the ocean or the Intracoastal Waterway. Facilities include two excellent restaurants and a 24,000-square-foot European spa. Rates: from $269. Open since 1936, the **Riverside Hotel,** 620 E. Las Olas Blvd. (© **800/325-3280;** www.riversidehotel.com), is a charming six-story lodging located on the sleepy and scenic New River, capturing the essence of Old Florida. Guest rooms, outfitted in Mexican tile and wicker furnishings, are spacious and well maintained. Try for one of the ground-floor units, which have higher ceilings and more space. Rates: from $139.

Located on its own little island between Lake Mayan and the Atlantic, the **Lago Mar Resort and Club,** 1700 S. Ocean Lane (© **800/524-6627** or 954/523-6511; www.lagomar.com), is an utterly inviting, casually elegant yet family-friendly slice of Old Florida. Rooms and suites have Mediterranean or Key West influences, and guests have access to the broadest and best strip of beach in the entire city, not to mention a wonderful bougainvillea-lined, 9,000-square-foot swimming lagoon. Rates: from

$175. The **Pillars Hotel,** 111 N. Birch Rd. (© **800/800-7666;** www.pillarshotel.
com), is the quintessential Fort Lauderdale retreat, its two-story, 23-room structure
done up in British colonial/Caribbean style, with luxurious rooms, lush landscaping,
and white-tablecloth room service. This is the best hotel of its size in the region. Rates:
from $169. For something modern, try the **Atlantic,** 601 N. Fort Lauderdale Beach
Blvd. (© **800/325-3589** or 954/567-8020; www.starwoodhotels.com), a Starwood
Luxury Collection property that sits on a stunning white-sand beach. Decor is a study
in minimal modernity—soothing, comfortable, and stylish. Rates: from $299.

DINING & NIGHTLIFE

Las Olas Boulevard is the hub for restaurants in Fort Lauderdale. Look here for **Mark's
Las Olas,** 1032 E. Las Olas Blvd. (© **954/463-1000**), the showcase of Miami restaurant mogul Mark Militello. The Continental gourmet menu changes daily and may
include white duck with sweet-potato/vanilla-bean purée or a superb sushi-quality
tuna. Main courses: $14 to $46. Also on Las Olas, **Johnny V,** 625 E. Las Olas Blvd.
(© **954/761-7920;** www.johnnyvlasolas.com), is the domain of chef Johnny
Vinczenz, who cooks up Caribbean-influenced new-Floridian cuisine (think smoked-
pheasant nachos or sage-grilled Florida dolphin with lobster pan gravy served atop
rock-shrimp plantain stuffing with cranberry-mango chutney) for the famous and
not-so-famous. Main courses: $19 to $32. **O'Hara Pub & Sidewalk Café,** 722 E. Las
Olas Blvd. (© **954/524-1764**), is often packed with a trendy crowd that comes for
the live R & B, pop, blues, and jazz. Call the cafe's jazz hot line (© **954/524-2801**)
to hear the lineup.

For something more classic, **Cap's Place,** 2765 NE 28th Court (© **954/941-0418;**
www.capsplace.com), is a famous old-time seafood joint, offering good food at reasonable prices. The restaurant is on a peninsula; you get a ferry ride over (see its website for
directions). Mahimahi and snapper are popular and, like the other meat and pasta dishes
here, can be prepared any way you want. Main courses: $13 to $30. **Tarpon Bend,** 200
SW Second St. (© **954/523-3233**), is one of the few places where the fishermen still
bring the fish to the back door. The oysters from the raw bar are shucked to order, and
the steamed clambake (with half a Maine lobster, clams, potatoes, mussels, and corn on
the cob) is scrumptious and served in its own pot. Main courses: $9 to $17.

Head north for ethnic. **Café Martorano,** 3343 E. Oakland Park Blvd. (© **954/
561-2554;** www.cafemartorano.com), is like a big, fat, Italian wedding, where eating,
drinking, and dancing are paramount. The menu changes daily, and since reservations
aren't accepted, the wait can be up to 2 hours for a table. Main courses: $13 to $40.
A little farther north, **Eduardo De San Angel,** 2822 E. Commercial Blvd. (© **954/
772-4731;** www.eduardodesanangel.com), serves gourmet Mexican cuisine in a room
that resembles an intimate hacienda, adorned with fresh flowers and candlelight. Main
courses: $24 to $32. Closed Sunday.

For pre-cruise imbibing, the **Parrot,** 911 Sunrise Lane (© **954/563-1493;** www.
parrotlounge.com), is Fort Lauderdale's most famous dive bar, a local's and out-of-
towner's choice for an evening of beer (16 kinds on tap) and bonding.

7 Galveston, Texas

Some 50 miles south of Houston, Galveston is located on a 30-mile-long barrier island
that averages only 2 miles wide. Ships departing from here can reach the open sea in
about 30 minutes, compared to several hours of lag time from the Port of Houston.

Galveston

The city's main attractions are the downtown historic district; the Strand, with its Victorian commercial buildings and houses; and the beaches, which draw crowds of Houstonians and other Texans during the summer.

At the end of the 19th century, Galveston was the largest city in Texas and the third-busiest port in the country. But then, on September 8, 1900, a massive storm came ashore, carrying with it 140-mph winds and a 20-foot surge that washed completely over the island. Houses were smashed into matchwood, and more than 6,000 islanders—a sixth of the island's population—were drowned. Those who remained went to work to prevent a recurrence of the disaster, raising the city's ground level by up to 17 feet and erecting a stout seawall that now stretches along 10 miles of shoreline, with several jetties of large granite blocks projecting out into the water. Today, Galveston is a vibrant port city and a hub for cruises to the western Caribbean.

GETTING TO GALVESTON & THE PORT

The **Texas Cruise Ship Terminal** at the Port of Galveston (© **409/766-6113;** www.portofgalveston.com) is at Harborside Drive and 25th Street, on Galveston Island. It's reached via I-45 south from Houston. If you're flying in, you'll land at one of two Houston airports: **William P. Hobby Airport** (south of downtown Houston, and about 31 miles, or a 45-min. drive, from the terminal) or the larger **George Bush**

Intercontinental Airport (just north of downtown Houston, and about 54 miles, or an 80-min. drive, from the terminal). Information on both is available at **www.fly2 houston.com.** Because it's a long way from both airports to the cruise ship terminal (and since taxi prices are correspondingly high), it's a good idea to arrange transfers through your cruise line. You can also call **Galveston Limousine Service** (© **800/ 640-4826** or 409/744-5466), which charges $35 per person for its shuttle from Hobby to Galveston and $40 from Bush.

If you're driving to the port, I-45 is the main artery for those arriving from the north. To get to the terminal, follow I-45 south to exit 1C (at Harborside Dr./Hwy. 275); it's the first exit after the causeway. Turn left (east) onto Harborside Drive and continue for about 5 miles to the cruise terminal. Long-term parking at the port is available. The lots are ½ mile from the cruise ship terminal; shuttle buses transport passengers between the lots and the terminal, where porters are available to carry luggage. Parking costs about $10 per day for an uncovered lot and about $12 per day for a covered lot.

GETTING AROUND Within walking distance of the port's two terminals is the historic **Strand District,** Galveston's revitalized downtown, with shops, art galleries, museums, and eateries lining its quaint brick streets. Most of Galveston's hotels, motels, and restaurants are located along the seawall from where Broadway meets the shore all the way west past 60th Street. If you're on the seawall around 25th Street (near the visitor center), you can take the **Galveston Island Rail Trolley** (© **409/ 797-3900;** www.islandtransit.net) to the Strand District for $1.25.

BEST CRUISE LINE SHORE EXCURSIONS

City Tour ($47, 3½ hr.): For guests with late-departing flights, this bus tour passes through Galveston's scenic and historic Strand District. It then travels to Houston, touring the downtown theater and museum districts; Hermann Park, home to the Houston Zoo; and River Oaks, Houston's most prestigious residential neighborhood, before ending at Bush airport.

Space Center Houston ($69, 6 hr.): Space Center Houston is the official visitor center of Johnson Space Center, the center of design, development, and operations for the U.S. space program. Visits include a 1¼-hour narrated tram tour of the center's sprawling grounds and a visit to historic Mission Control (from which all U.S. space missions were controlled until 1996). You can even touch a moon rock! The tour concludes at both Bush and Hobby airports.

EXPLORING GALVESTON ON YOUR OWN

If you've got only a few hours before you have to board your cruise, focus on the Strand National Historic Landmark District, the heart of Galveston in the late 1800s and early 1900s, and the East End Historic District, both located north of Broadway.

The **Strand District** is the restored commercial district that runs from 19th and 25th streets between Church Street and the harbor piers. When cotton was king, the Strand was dubbed the "Wall Street of the Southwest." Today, its three- and four-story Victorian iron-fronts (so called because of their ironwork facades) are full of shopping and dining options. Near the cruise dock, at Pier 21, the **Texas Seaport Museum** (© **409/763-1877;** www.tsm-elissa.org) is centered around the three-masted, iron-hulled sailing ship *Elissa,* built in 1877 in Aberdeen, Scotland, and still fully functional today. You can also browse a computer database listing the names of 133,000 immigrants who first entered the U.S. through Galveston in the 19th and early 20th centuries. Admission is $8.

The **East End Historic District** is the old silk-stocking neighborhood that runs from 9th to 19th streets between Broadway and Church Street. It has many lovely houses that have been completely restored. The **Galveston Historical Foundation** (www.galvestonhistory.org) offers regular tours of several properties, including the **1859 Ashton Villa,** 2328 Broadway (© **409/762-3933**), the first of Galveston's great Broadway mansions. Other mansions-turned-museums include the ornate Victorian **Bishop's Palace,** 1402 Broadway (© **409/762-2475**), Galveston's grandest and best-known historic building, built between 1887 and 1893; and the **Moody Mansion,** 2618 Broadway (© **409/762-7668;** www.moodymansion.org), whose ornately furnished rooms depict the home life of the wealthy Moody family, who built the house in 1895. Admission to each of the historic homes is $6 for adults.

Elsewhere in town, Postoffice Street is a restored historic district with more than 25 buildings, including the **Grand 1894 Opera House,** still in operation, and the **U.S. Customs House,** now home of the Galveston Historical Foundation.

BEACHES

The beaches are another of Galveston's most popular attractions, with light-tan sand and warm waters much of the year. **East Beach** and **Stewart Beach,** operated by the city, have pavilions with dressing rooms, showers, and restrooms, ideal for day-trippers. Stewart Beach is located at the end of Broadway, while East Beach is about a mile farther east. All of the beaches are free. Another activity popular with visitors and locals alike is walking, skating, or riding a bike atop the **seawall,** which extends 10 miles along the shoreline.

SHOPPING

Galveston has more than 20 art galleries on the Strand, Pier 21, and in the Postoffice Street Entertainment District. The Strand is also known for its quaint antiques, art, and memorabilia shops.

WHERE TO STAY

The **Tremont House,** 2300 Ship's Mechanic Row (© **800/WYNDHAM** or 409/763-0300; www.wyndham.com), is a 117-room gem located in the heart of the Strand neighborhood. A replica of the original 1839-built hotel, which stood nearby, this Tremont occupies the 1879-built Leon & H. Blum Building, and has been designed to re-create the atmosphere of its 19th-century namesake. Rates: from $121.

Harbor House at Pier 21, No. 28–Pier 21 (© **800/874-3721** or 409/763-3321; www.harborhousepier21.com), is a 42-unit hotel built on a pier and overlooking the harbor. It has very modern styling and is very close to the Strand District and many restaurants. Rates: from $109.

Hotel Galvez, 2024 Seawall Blvd. (© **800/WYNDHAM** or 409/765-7721; www.wyndham.com), Galveston's historic grand hotel, is located on the shore facing the seawall and one of the municipal beaches. It has 231 rooms and is on the trolley line leading to the Strand District. Rates: from $140.

Other properties on Seawall Boulevard include the 149-unit **Hilton Galveston Island Resort,** 5400 Seawall Blvd. (© **800/HILTONS** or 409/744-5000; www.hilton.com; rates: from $149); and the 100-unit **Comfort Inn & Suites,** 6302 Seawall Blvd. (© **800/221-2222;** www.comfortinn.com; rates: from $110).

DINING & NIGHTLIFE

Seafood is what people come to Galveston for, and there's quite a variety. **Gaidos,** 3800 Seawall Blvd. (© **409/762-9625;** www.gaidosofgalveston.com), is a Galveston favorite that's been owned and operated by the Gaido family for four generations, offering fresh seafood and attentive service. The soups and side dishes are mostly traditional Southern and Gulf Coast recipes that are comfort food for longtime customers. The stuffed snapper is the best we've had. Main courses: $14 to $35. **Saltwater Grill,** 2017 Postoffice St. (© **409/762-3474**), located in an old building near the Strand, prints a daily menu that usually includes some inventive seafood pastas, a fish dish with an Asian bent, gumbo or bouillabaisse, and a few nonseafood options. Main courses: $14 to $29.

There are enough bars and restaurants along the seawall and in the historic Strand and Postoffice Street districts to pleasantly while away an evening. For concerts, musicals, and plays, check out the 200-seat **Strand Theatre,** 2317 Ship's Mechanic Row (© **877/787-2639;** www.strandtheatregalveston.org), in the heart of the historic district, or the elegant **Grand 1894 Opera House,** 2020 Postoffice St. (© **800/821-1894;** www.thegrand.com), for Broadway productions, orchestral performances, country music, and more.

8 Los Angeles, California

L.A. isn't a city or even a county; it's a whole planet unto itself, its nation-states linked by dozens of superhighways that turn into slow-mo performance art at rush hour. The place is just as sunny, smoggy, rich, poor, sybaritic, hard-boiled, movie-happy, New-Agey, and unreal as the movies make it seem, and so obsessively catalogued by those same movies that you'll be experiencing déjà vu every other minute of your visit, spotting places you've seen on the silver screen. We had an argument with a friend once about which U.S. city would be most recognizable to anybody, anywhere in the world. We said New York, she said L.A., and while we still stick with our opinion, we have to admit she had a point.

Now here's the downside to L.A.'s abundance: Unless you stay for several weeks, you won't have a hope in hell of getting a real handle on the place. It's just too big, too diverse, and takes a much bigger guidebook to cover—one like *Frommer's Los Angeles,* for instance. Hint, hint.

GETTING TO L.A. & THE PORT

There are two major cruise centers in L.A.: the **World Cruise Center,** off Harbor Boulevard in San Pedro (© **310/SEA-PORT;** www.portoflosangeles.org), and Carnival Corporation's **Long Beach Cruise Terminal,** 10 miles west at 231 Windsor Way, Long Beach (www.sanpedro.com/spcom/crusshp2.htm). The World Cruise Center is the busier of the two, hosting Carnival, Celebrity, Crystal, Cunard, HAL, NCL, Princess, Radisson, Royal Caribbean, and Silversea. The Long Beach terminal is pretty much all Carnival, all the time, though Princess also docks here on occasion.

Most visitors fly into **Los Angeles International Airport** (© **310/646-5252;** www.lawa.org/lax), better known as LAX. This behemoth is situated oceanside, between Marina del Rey and Manhattan Beach, about 18 miles north of the World Cruise Center. You may also opt to fly into **Long Beach Municipal Airport,** 4100 Donald Douglas Dr. (© **562/570-2600;** www.lgb.org), if you're heading right to the

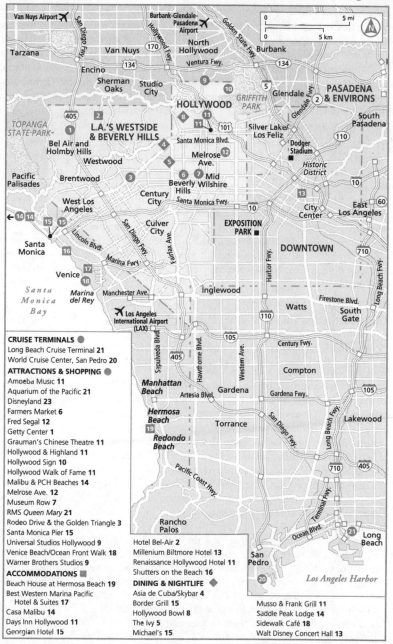

Los Angeles

0 — 5 mi
0 — 5 km

N

Van Nuys Airport ✈

Burbank-Glendale-
Pasadena
Airport ✈

Golden State Fwy.

San Diego Fwy.

Hollywood Fwy.

170

North
Hollywood

Burbank

134

Tarzana

Van Nuys

Ventura Fwy.

134

Encino

Sherman
Oaks

Studio
City

9

5

Glendale

**PASADENA
& ENVIRONS**

TOPANGA
STATE PARK

405

2

1

HOLLYWOOD

GRIFFITH
PARK

Glendale Fwy.

2

South
Pasadena

**L.A.'S WESTSIDE
& BEVERLY HILLS**

8

11

11

Silver Lake/
Los Feliz

110

Bel Air and
Holmby Hills

Santa Monica Blvd.

Dodger
Stadium

Historic
District

Westwood

4

Melrose
Ave.

12

Pacific
Palisades

Brentwood

3

5

6 **7** Mid
Beverly Wilshire
Hills

Santa Monica Fwy.

13

10

West Los
Angeles

Century
City

10

City
Center

East
Los Angeles

60

← **14** **14**

15 **15**

Lincoln Blvd.

San Diego Fwy.

Fairfax Ave.

Culver
City

**EXPOSITION
PARK** ■

Harbor Fwy.

DOWNTOWN

710

Santa
Monica

16

Marina Fwy.

17

18

Venice

Inglewood

Firestone Blvd.

Long Beach Fwy.

Santa
Monica
Bay

Marina
del Rey

Manchester Ave.

Watts

South
Gate

✈ Los Angeles
International Airport
(LAX)

Spulveda Blvd.

Hawthorne Blvd.

105

110

Century Fwy.

405

CRUISE TERMINALS ●
Long Beach Cruise Terminal **21**
World Cruise Center, San Pedro **20**

ATTRACTIONS & SHOPPING ●
Amoeba Music **11**
Aquarium of the Pacific **21**
Disneyland **23**
Farmers Market **6**
Fred Segal **12**
Getty Center **1**
Grauman's Chinese Theatre **11**
Hollywood & Highland **11**
Hollywood Sign **10**
Hollywood Walk of Fame **11**
Malibu & PCH Beaches **14**
Melrose Ave. **12**
Museum Row **7**
RMS *Queen Mary* **21**
Rodeo Drive & the Golden Triangle **3**
Santa Monica Pier **15**
Universal Studios Hollywood **9**
Venice Beach/Ocean Front Walk **18**
Warner Brothers Studios **9**

ACCOMMODATIONS ■
Beach House at Hermosa Beach **19**
Best Western Marina Pacific
    Hotel & Suites **17**
Casa Malibu **14**
Days Inn Hollywood **11**
Georgian Hotel **15**

**Manhattan
Beach**

Western Ave.

Gardena

Artesia Blvd.

Compton

105

**Hermosa
Beach**

19

**Redondo
Beach**

Torrance

San Diego Fwy.

Lakewood

Long Beach Fwy.

710

405

Pacific Coast Hwy.

*Rancho
Palos*

Hotel Bel-Air **2**
Millenium Biltmore Hotel **13**
Renaissance Hollywood Hotel **11**
Shutters on the Beach **16**

DINING & NIGHTLIFE ◆
Asia de Cuba/Skybar **4**
Border Grill **15**
Hollywood Bowl **8**
The Ivy **5**
Michael's **15**

San
Pedro

Terminal Fwy.

Ocean Blvd.

21

Long
Beach

20

Los Angeles Harbor

Musso & Frank Grill **11**
Saddle Peak Lodge **14**
Sidewalk Café **18**
Walt Disney Concert Hall **13**

441

port and don't intend to stay on after. (JetBlue offers excellent fares to Long Beach.) To get to the World Cruise Center from LAX, drive south on I-405, then south on I-110. Exit at Harbor Boulevard, go straight through the intersection, and right into the World Cruise Center. To get to the Long Beach Terminal, take I-405 south to the 710 south and continue till you see signs for the *Queen Mary* (that's the old, original *Queen Mary*—see "Exploring L.A. on Your Own," below). At the *Queen Mary* entrance, stay to the far right of the parking ticket taker and follow the signs. Parking is $12 per day at both terminals.

GETTING AROUND Even though L.A. has been steadily building its public-transportation infrastructure, getting around without a car is still like trying to see Mars without a spacesuit. All the major **car-rental** companies are represented at the airports, but if you want to look like a star on the freeways, you can rent a Porsche, BMW, Mercedes, Lexus, or Hummer at **Budget Beverly Hills Car Collection,** 9815 Wilshire Blvd. (© **800/227-7117** or 310/881-2335; www.budgetbeverlyhills.com). For even more spiff, **Beverly Hills Rent-A-Car,** 9732 Little Santa Monica Blvd., Beverly Hills (© **800/479-5996** or 310/337-1400; www.bhrentacar.com), offers cars from Lamborghini, Maserati, Ferrari, Rolls, and Bentley, plus classic Caddies from the '50s, '60s, and '70s, as well as three different hybrids (for those with a heavy conscience). Both companies offer airport pickup service and complimentary delivery to local hotels.

BEST CRUISE LINE SHORE EXCURSIONS

Universal Studios Tour ($80, 7 hr.): A bus ride takes you to huge Universal Studios, where you board the "Glamour Tram" for a backstage look at the movie biz (see description under "Exploring L.A. on Your Own," below).

EXPLORING L.A. ON YOUR OWN

Los Angeles is a very confusing city in that its "downtown" isn't considered the center of the city. In fact, there really *is* no center—just a whole bunch of neighborhoods and independently incorporated communities that run into one another and spread out as far as the eye can see. The best way to grasp the geography is to break it into six regions, roughly west to east: **Santa Monica** and the beach communities, **L.A.'s Westside** and **Beverly Hills, Hollywood** and **West Hollywood, downtown,** the **San Fernando Valley,** and **Pasadena** and environs. You'll probably concentrate your visit in the city's western districts, since that's where the majority of tourist attractions, restaurants, and shops are. Despite the opening of the Disney Concert Hall and the Staples Center (a major sports and entertainment arena), most short-stay visitors never make it as far east as downtown.

There are so many things to see and do in this town that most *residents* never see and do them all, so in this section we'll be concentrating on the quintessential L.A. experience of taking a big swan dive into pop culture and swimming around.

Begin your adventure on Hollywood Boulevard at the **Hollywood Walk of Fame,** between Gower and La Brea (and also Vine St. between Yucca and Sunset Blvd.). Currently more than 2,200 past and present celebrities have bronze medallions on the world's most famous sidewalk, each one set in the center of a terrazzo star. You'll need a history book for some of them (who's Blanche Thebom again?), but you'll be surprised by how many will pop your brain buttons. A complete list of stars and their addresses is available online at **www.hollywoodchamber.net**. This part of Hollywood is a funky mix of touristy shops and businesses catering to the local rocker and biker culture. And then, of course, there are the **Scientologists,** who own a lot of the local real estate.

At the corner of Hollywood Boulevard and Highland Street, the massive 8¾-acre **Hollywood & Highland** entertainment complex (© 323/467-6412; www. hollywoodandhighland.com) has all the top-end merchants as well as studio broadcast facilities, restaurants, nightclubs, cinemas, the Lucky Strike Lanes "upscale bowling alley/lounge," a hotel (see "Where to Stay," below), and the **Kodak Theatre,** home of the Academy Awards. The mall's other centerpiece is the open-air **Babylon Court,** designed after a set from the 1916 film *Intolerance,* with giant elephant-topped pillars and a colossal arch that frames the **Hollywood sign** in the distance, up on Mount Lee. (Trivia: The sign started as an advertisement for the "Hollywoodland" housing development. It was only later that it lost the "land" and was adopted as the symbol of the movie industry.)

Between Highland and La Brea Avenue is the famed **Grauman's Chinese Theatre,** 6925 Hollywood Blvd. (© 323/464-8111; www.manntheatres.com/chinese), one of the world's great movie palaces, opened in 1927 by impresario Sid Grauman. Visitors by the millions flock to the theater for its famous entry court, where stars such as Gary Cooper, Elizabeth Taylor, Ginger Rogers, and more than 160 others set their signatures and hand-/footprints in concrete.

From Hollywood, you're in an ideal position to set off on a drive along **Sunset Boulevard**—the street, the myth, the legend. This is a must for first-time visitors because you'll see a cross section of everything that is L.A.: legendary clubs, studios, hotels, and zip codes that you'll instantly recognize from movies and television. The 45-minute drive takes you from Hollywood's seedy/starry streets to flamboyant **West Hollywood,** past glittering **Beverly Hills,** through **Brentwood** (O.J.'s old neighborhood), into the secluded enclave of **Pacific Palisades,** and finally to the sea. From there, you can head north to Malibu's fabled beaches (land of *Baywatch*) or head south along the coast to the funkier beach town of **Santa Monica.** Park at the **Santa Monica Pier** and head south on foot toward **Venice Beach** along the carnival-like **Ocean Front Walk.** You haven't visited L.A. properly until you've toured the area on the right kind of wheels (in-line skates), taken in the human carnival around you, noshed on boardwalk food, watched a few street performers, and bought some cheap sunglasses or ethnic garb—all while enjoying the blue sea, the wide beach, and the world's vainest weight lifters, who pump themselves up at an outdoor gym right in the heart of things.

Venice is street theater, but if you want to see some of the big-budget kind, you'll want to tour one of the movie studios. **Warner Brothers Studios,** 3400 Riverside Dr., Burbank (© 818/972-TOUR; www.wbstudiotour.com), offers the most comprehensive tour, taking visitors on a 2¼-hour drive-and-walk around the studio's faux streets. After a brief introductory film, you'll pile into glorified golf carts and cruise past parking spaces marked with stars' names, then walk through active film and television sets, where you'll get a glimpse of how the biz really works. Sometimes you can also visit working sets to watch actors filming. Reservations are required, and children under 8 are not admitted. Bring valid photo ID. Tours are $42 per person, departing every 30 minutes on weekdays (9am–4pm, with extended hours in spring and summer).

The "other" studio tour is at **Universal Studios Hollywood,** Hollywood Freeway (Universal Center Dr. or Lankershim Blvd. exits), Universal City, in the San Fernando Valley (© 800/UNIVERSAL or 818/622-3801; www.universalstudioshollywood. com), but this isn't just a working studio; it's also one of the world's largest amusement

Culture? You Want Culture?

If you have any energy left after being a shameless L.A. tourist, pay a visit to the **Getty Center,** 1200 Getty Center Dr. ((C) **310/440-7300;** www.getty.edu), the Richard Meier–designed cultural cornerstone that displays J. Paul Getty's enormous collection of art, ranging from antiquities to Impressionist painters, contemporary photography, and graphic arts. Admission is free, but you have to pay and make a reservation to park your car, which is *so* L.A. For more culture, there's also **Museum Row,** a stretch of Wilshire Boulevard just east of Beverly Hills that's home to about a dozen different institutions, from the **Los Angeles County Museum of Art,** 5905 Wilshire ((C) **323/857-6000;** www.lacma.org), to the **La Brea Tar Pits** and **George C. Page Museum of La Brea Discoveries,** 5801 Wilshire ((C) **323/934-PAGE;** www.tarpits.org).

parks. The main attraction continues to be the Studio Tour, a 1-hour guided tram ride around the company's 420 acres, passing stars' dressing rooms and visiting famous back-lot sets. The rest of the experience is thrill rides themed on blockbusters such as *Back to the Future, Jurassic Park,* and *Shrek.* Admission is $61. Open daily, from 10am to 6pm on weekdays, from 9am to 7 or 8pm on weekends.

Just outside the gate is **Universal CityWalk** ((C) **818/622-4455;** www.citywalk hollywood.com), a 3-block-long pedestrian promenade crammed with flashy name-brand stores, themed nightclubs, theme restaurants (the Hard Rock Cafe and others), a 3-D IMAX theater, an 18-screen cinema, NASCAR virtual racing, and more, More, MORE! Getting in is free, but after that you're on your own. It's open from 11am to 9pm Sunday through Thursday, 11am to 11pm Friday and Saturday.

Now, lest we forget, **Disneyland** is also not so far away, at 1313 Harbor Blvd. in Anaheim, an hour south of downtown L.A. on the I-5 ((C) **714/781-4565;** www.disneyland.com). The complex is divided into several themed "lands," ranging from the archetypal Main Street U.S.A. to Adventureland, inspired by Asia, Africa, and South America. For our money, no ride in the park (or in its Florida cousin, for that matter) has ever topped **It's a Small World,** a slow-moving indoor river ride in which creepy dolls of all the world's children sing their saccharine song through hinged mouths. When it was built in the '50s, could Walt have known that he was creating a preview of every bad acid trip that happened in the '60s? It's a classic. Admission to the park costs $63 for ages 10 and up, $53 for ages 3 to 9. Multiday passes are also available, as are resort accommodations.

For cruise travelers with a sense of history, one of the most vital attractions in all L.A. has to be the **RMS *Queen Mary,*** 1126 Queen's Hwy. in Long Beach, at the end of I-710 ((C) **562/435-3511;** www.queenmary.com). One of the greatest ocean liners ever, she's now moored permanently in Long Beach, in the same complex that holds Carnival's Long Beach terminal. Though many of her original furnishings are long gone, she's still the only surviving example of this particular kind of 20th-century elegance, from her staterooms' tropical-hardwood paneling to the incredible Deco artwork and miles of Bakelite handrails. Stroll the teakwood decks and, with just a little imagination, you're back in 1936. Admission is $23 adults, $12 kids; open daily. The *Queen Mary* also functions as a hotel, with rates starting at $119. Several onboard restaurants offer brunches and dinners at various rates, and packages are available that include special exhibits, guided tours, and the Soviet submarine moored next door.

Just across the harbor is the huge **Aquarium of the Pacific,** 100 Aquarium Way, off Shoreline Drive (ⓒ **562/590-3100;** www.aquariumofpacific.org), featuring re-creations of three Pacific habitats, from the warm tropics to the frigid Bering Sea. More than 12,000 creatures inhabit its three-story tanks, from sharks and sea lions to delicate sea horses and moon jellies. Admission is $20 adults, $12 kids 3 to 11. Open daily.

BEACHES

Los Angeles County's 72-mile coastline sports more than 30 miles of beaches, most of which are operated by the **Department of Beaches & Harbors,** 13837 Fiji Way, Marina del Rey (ⓒ **310/305-9503;** www.beaches.co.la.ca.us). Parking costs between $2 and $14. For recorded **surf conditions** and coastal weather forecast, call ⓒ **310/ 457-9701.** The following are the best beaches in L.A., listed from north to south.

Jampacked on warm weekends, **Zuma Beach County Park** is L.A. County's largest beach park, located off the Pacific Coast Highway, a mile past Kanan Dume Road. Although it can't claim to be the most scenic beach in the Southland, Zuma has the most comprehensive facilities: plenty of restrooms, lifeguards, playgrounds, volleyball courts, and snack bars. The southern stretch, toward Point Dume, is **Westward Beach,** separated from the noisy highway by sandstone cliffs.

Not just a pretty white-sand beach but an estuary and wetlands area as well, **Malibu Lagoon State Beach** is the historic home of the Chumash Indians. The entrance is on the Pacific Coast Highway south of Cross Creek Road. Marine life and shore-birds teem where the creek empties into the sea, and the waves are always mild.

Highway noise prevents solitude at short, narrow **Topanga State Park,** located where Topanga Canyon Boulevard emerges from the mountains. Why go? Ask the surfers who wait in line to catch Topanga's excellent right point breaks. There are rest-rooms and lifeguard services here, and across the street you'll find one of the best fresh-fish restaurants around. The popular **Will Rogers State Beach,** comprising 3 miles along the Pacific Coast Highway, between Sunset Boulevard and the Santa Monica border, has friendly waves, competitive volleyball games, restrooms, lifeguards, and a snack hut in season.

Santa Monica State Beach, on either side of the Santa Monica Pier, is popular for its white sands and accessibility. A paved path runs along here, allowing you to walk, bike, or skate to Venice. To the south, the wide and friendly **Manhattan Beach** was once a hangout for the Beach Boys. Today, it's lined with beautiful oceanview homes and has some of the best surfing around, plus restrooms, lifeguards, and volleyball courts. Not far away are the wide **Hermosa Beach** and **Redondo Beach.**

SHOPPING

Rodeo Drive and the Golden Triangle, between Santa Monica Boulevard, Wilshire Boulevard, and Canon Drive in Beverly Hills, is the city's (and one of the world's) most famous shopping districts, and so chichi and pricey that it's almost like a theme park, with the theme being *money.* Couture shops from high fashion's old guard are located along these hallowed blocks, along with plenty of newer high-end labels. Come and gawk. Crossing Wilshire a ways east of Rodeo, the blocks of **La Brea Avenue** north of Wilshire are L.A.'s artiest shopping strip, home to lots of great urban antiques stores dealing in Art Deco, Arts and Crafts, 1950s moderne, and the like.

You'll also find vintage clothiers, furniture galleries, and other warehouse-size stores, as well as some of the city's hippest restaurants.

In Hollywood, scruffy but fun **Melrose Avenue** is the city's funkiest shopping district, with many secondhand and avant-garde clothing shops as well as good restaurants and almost-guaranteed celebrity sightings. The original **Fred Segal** complex—breezy, ultrahip boutiques linked like departments of a single-story fashion maze—is at 8100 Melrose (© **323/655-3734**). Shops include the latest apparel for men, women, and toddlers, plus lingerie, shoes, hats, luggage, cosmetics, workout/loungewear, and a cafe. Fred Segal also offers major star-spotting potential. A few blocks to the north, **Amoeba Music,** 6400 Sunset Blvd. (© **323/245-6400;** www.amoebamusic.com), was described to us by a noted L.A. music critic as "the best record store in the *world,*" and after way too many visits, we have to agree. It carries everything, with a huge selection of used CDs and vinyl as well as new disks and videos. A few blocks to the south, **West Third Street** between Fairfax and Robertson is a trendy strip that features some Melrose Avenue émigrés, along with terrific up-and-comers, cafes, and the like. *Fun* is more the catchword here than *funky,* and the shops are a bit more refined than those along Melrose. It's all anchored on the east end by the **Farmers' Market,** 6333 W. Third St. (© **323/933-9211;** www.farmersmarket la.com), a sprawling marketplace with food and produce stalls, a gourmet market, and a wine bar. The original market was just a bunch of Depression-era farmers setting up stands to sell produce, but eventually permanent buildings grew up, including the trademark shingled 10-story clock tower. **The Grove,** 189 The Grove Dr. (© **888/315-8883** or 323/900-8080; www.thegrovela.com), is a huge retail complex at the market's eastern end, with all the usual high-end mall stores and architectural styles ranging from Art Deco to Italian Renaissance.

Santa Monica, location of several of our recommended hotels, is also a great place for shopping. **Main Street,** stretching from Pico Boulevard to Rose Avenue, between Fourth Street and Neilson Way, is an excellent area for strolling, crammed with a combination of mall standards and upscale, left-of-center boutiques. You can also find plenty of casually hip cafes and restaurants. The primary strip connecting Santa Monica and Venice, Main Street has a relaxed, beach-community vibe that sets it apart from similar strips. The **Third Street Promenade,** a pedestrian-only stretch of Third between Broadway and Wilshire Boulevard, is packed with chain stores and boutiques as well as dozens of restaurants and three multiscreen cinemas. It's one of the most popular shopping areas in the city, bustling well into the evening.

WHERE TO STAY

If surf and sand compose the So Cal image in your mind's eye, book a hotel along Santa Monica Bay, on the city's west side, stretching from Redondo Beach in the south to Malibu in the northwest. The more southerly properties are an easy drive to or from the cruise terminals, and all of them are a fairly easy drive to Beverly Hills shopping and the Hollywood attractions.

The **Beach House at Hermosa Beach,** 1300 The Strand, Hermosa Beach (© **888/895-4559;** www.beach-house.com), sports a Cape Cod style that suits the on-the-sand location. It's luxurious and romantic, with 96 beautifully designed and outfitted split-level studio suites. Rates: from $235.

Best Western Marina Pacific Hotel & Suites, 1697 Pacific Ave., Venice (© **800/421-8151;** www.mphotel.com), is a haven of smart value just off the Venice boardwalk. The spacious rooms are brightened with beachy colors, the one-bedroom suites (with kitchens and balconies) are terrific for families, and many units have at least partial ocean views. Rates: from $109.

Shutters on the Beach, 1 Pico Blvd., Santa Monica (© **800/334-9000;** www. shuttersonthebeach.com), is a Cape Cod–style luxury hotel that sits directly on the beach, a block from Santa Monica Pier. Each unit has a beachview balcony. Try to get one of the beach-cottage rooms overlooking the sand—these are more desirable and no more expensive than those in the hotel's towers. Rates: from $480.

The eight-story, Art Deco **Georgian Hotel,** 1415 Ocean Ave. (© **800/538-8147;** www.georgianhotel.com), boasts luxury, loads of historic charm, and a terrific oceanview location, just across from Santa Monica's beach and pier. Established in 1933, the place was popular among Hollywood's golden-age elite, who enjoyed its veranda lounge and beautifully designed guest rooms. Rates: from $235.

Casa Malibu, sitting on its own private beach at 22752 Pacific Coast Hwy., Malibu (© **800/831-0858**), is a leftover jewel from Malibu's golden age that doesn't try to play the sleek resort game. Instead, the modest, low-rise inn sports a traditional California-beach-cottage look that's cozy and timeless, with 21 comfortable, charming rooms. More than half have ocean views, but even those facing the courtyard are quiet and offer easy beach access via wooden stairs. Rates: from $129.

If you don't care to stay by the beach, here are some choices for different personality/family types:

Nestled in the Bel-Air Estates, inland toward Beverly Hills, the **Hotel Bel-Air,** 701 Stone Canyon Rd. (© **800/648-4097;** www.hotelbelair.com), is a stunning Mission-style hotel spread over 12 luxuriant garden acres. All in all, it's one of the most beautiful, romantic, and impressive high-end hotels in the entire state. Expect the best of everything. Rates: from $485. For Oscar-winner wannabes, the **Renaissance Hollywood Hotel,** 1755 N. Highland Ave. (© **800/HOTELS-1;** www.renaissance hollywood.com), is part of the Hollywood & Highland complex (see "Exploring L.A. on Your Own," earlier in this chapter). On Oscar night, it's the headquarters for a frenzy of participants and paparazzi, but the rest of the year it's just a centrally located hotel with a nice respect for its location—think guest rooms outfitted like swinging '50s bachelor pads, with wood-paneled headboards and Technicolor furniture. Rates: from $279.

While it's east of the prime Sunset Strip action, the **Days Inn Hollywood,** 7023 Sunset Blvd., between Highland and La Brea (© **800/329-7466;** www.daysinn.com), is safe and convenient, and extras such as free underground parking and continental breakfast make it an especially good value for travelers on a budget. Some rooms have microwaves, fridges, and coffeemakers. Rates: from $120.

In downtown L.A., the historic **Millennium Biltmore Hotel,** 506 S. Grand Ave. (© **800/245-8673;** www.thebiltmore.com), opened in 1923 and has hosted presidents, kings, and Hollywood celebrities, all of them drawn by its old-world charm, its grand lobby, and its warmly elegant rooms. The Gallery Bar and Cognac Room is one of the best places in town to have a cocktail, and Sai Sai is among the best Japanese restaurants in downtown L.A. Rates: from $189.

DINING & NIGHTLIFE

For a dinner that channels the ghost of Old Hollywood, head to **Musso & Frank Grill,** 6667 Hollywood Blvd., Hollywood (© **323/467-7788**). This comfortable, dark-paneled room, virtually unchanged since 1919, begs you to order up one of

L.A.'s best martinis and some chops or the legendary chicken potpie, then listen to the longtime waitstaff wax nostalgic about the days when Orson Welles held court and Faulkner, Fitzgerald, and Hemingway all popped in for a drink between writing screenplays. Main courses: $13 to $32. You'll always find living celebrities, on the other hand, frequenting the Sunset Strip hot spots, the most sizzling of which is the Mondrian hotel and its chic Chino-Latin restaurant, **Asia de Cuba,** 8440 Sunset Blvd., West Hollywood (© **323/848-6000;** www.mondrianhotel.com). Main courses: $23 to $45. Celebrity dieters can be glimpsed bypassing the eats for the A-list-only **Skybar** on the other side of the pool. The **Ivy,** 113 N. Robertson Blvd., West Hollywood (© **310/274-8303**), a perennial power-spot, attracts L.A.'s more conservative celebs. Main courses: $23 to $38.

Many great restaurants are clustered around the Santa Monica area. For some of the best California cuisine in town, head to chef/owner Michael McCarty's eponymous **Michael's,** 1147 Third St., Santa Monica (© **310/451-0843;** www.michaelssanta monica.com). Main courses: $28 to $39. The **Border Grill,** 1445 Fourth St., Santa Monica (© **310/451-1655;** www.bordergrill.com), fills the ticket if you're craving a taste from south of that border. Main courses: $13 to $25. From here, you can head to Venice's Ocean Front Walk for some primo people-watching. The **Sidewalk Café,** 1401 Ocean Front Walk, Venice (© **310/399-5547;** www.thesidewalkcafe.com), offers unobstructed views of parading skaters, bikers, skateboarders, musclemen, break dancers, street performers, sword swallowers, and other participants in the daily carnival. You can also get your dinner here, if you think you won't be distracted. Main courses: $8 to $18. Farther to the north, the **Saddle Peak Lodge,** 419 Cold Canyon Rd., Calabasas (© **818/222-3888;** www.saddlepeaklodge.com), is a converted hunting lodge in the hills above Malibu. Candlelit tables, a crackling fireplace, and a *Wine Spectator* award-winning wine list make it a romantic favorite. Main courses: $24 to $39.

Bar none, the most classic L.A. thing you can do after the sun goes down is take a picnic dinner to the **Hollywood Bowl,** 2301 N. Highland Ave., Hollywood (© **323/ 850-2000;** www.hollywoodbowl.org). In addition to being the summer home of the Los Angeles Philharmonic, the Bowl hosts visiting performers ranging from chamber-music quartets to jazz greats to folk humorists. The imposing white band shell always elicits appreciative gasps from first-time Bowl-goers. Don't forget your bottle of wine. If you prefer your entertainment with a roof, the **Walt Disney Concert Hall,** at First Street and Grand Avenue, downtown (© **213/972-7211;** www.disneyhall.com/ wdch), should fit the bill. The strikingly beautiful hall, designed by Frank Gehry, has a dazzling 2,273-seat auditorium, plus a cafe, bookstore, gift shop, and Joachim Splichal's flagship restaurant, **Patina** (© **213/972-3331;** www.patinagroup.com/ patina; main courses: $31–$40). The concert hall is open to the public for viewing, but to witness it in its full glory, attend a concert by the world-class Philharmonic.

9 Miami, Florida

It's the most Latin city in the U.S., with a hot-hot-hot club scene, sparkling beaches, crystal-clear waters, and more palm fronds, glittering hotels, and red sports cars than you'll find anywhere outside Monte Carlo and Rio. On top of all that, Miami is also the undisputed cruise capital of the world, with more than four million passengers passing through yearly, and more supersize ships berthing here than anywhere else.

Miami

CRUISE TERMINAL 7 ●

ATTRACTIONS & SHOPPING ●
Bal Harbour Shops **1**
Bass Museum of Art **4**
Bayside Marketplace **9**
CocoWalk **12**
Espanola Way **5**
Lincoln Road shopping **5**
Miami Seaquarium **13**
Miracle Mile **10**
South Beach Art Deco district **5**

ACCOMMODATIONS ■
The Beach House Bal Harbour **2**
Best Western South Beach **5**
Biltmore Hotel **11**
Biscayne Bay Marriott **8**
Catalina Hotel & Beach Club **5**
Crest Hotel Suites **5**

Eden Roc Renaissance Resort **3**
The Hotel **5**
Hotel Astor **5**
Hotel Inter-Continental Miami **9**
Indian Creek Hotel **4**

DINING & NIGHTLIFE ◆
Barton G. **5**
The Forge **3**
Joe's Stone Crab **6**
Larios on the Beach **5**
Lincoln Road pedestrian mall **5**
Nobu **4**
Pacific Time **5**
Prime One Twelve **6**
Skybar **5**
Spris **5**
Sushi Samba **5**
Van Dyke Café **5**

GETTING TO MIAMI & THE PORT

The **Port of Miami** is at 1015 N. America Way on Dodge Island (© **305/371-7678;** www.miamidade.gov/portofmiami), reached via a four-lane bridge from Miami's downtown district. **Miami International Airport** (© **305/876-7000;** www.miami-airport.com) is about 8 miles west of downtown Miami and the port (about a 15-min. drive). If you've arranged air transportation and/or transfers through your cruise line, a representative will meet you and direct you to shuttle buses to the port. **Taxis** are also available; the fare is about $24. Blue taxis serve only the immediate area around the airport; yellow taxis serve all other destinations, including the port. **SuperShuttle** (© **305/871-2000;** www.supershuttle.com) charges $14 per person (with two pieces of luggage) to the port.

If you're arriving by car from the north, take I-95 to I-395 and head east on I-395, exiting at Biscayne Boulevard. Make a right and go south to Port Boulevard. Make a left and go over the Port Bridge. Arriving from the northwest, take I-75 to State Road 826 (Palmetto Expwy.) south to State Road 836 east. Exit at Biscayne Boulevard. Make a right and go south to Port Boulevard. Make a left and go over the Port Bridge. Parking lots right at street level face the cruise terminals. Parking runs $15 per day.

GETTING AROUND   **Taxis** start at $2.50 for the first ¼ mile and cost $2.40 for each additional mile. Fares to some frequently traveled routes are standardized. Almost two dozen taxi companies serve Miami–Dade County, including **Yellow Cab** (© **305/444-4444**) and, on Miami Beach, **Central** (© **305/532-5555**). There's also the **Metromover** (© **305/770-3131**), a 4⅓-mile elevated line that circles downtown, stopping near important attractions and shopping (including Bayfront Park and Bayside Marketplace). It's fun if you've got time to kill. It runs daily from about 5am to midnight; there are 21 stations spaced about 2 blocks apart each; and service is free.

BEST CRUISE LINE SHORE EXCURSIONS

Parrot Jungle Island ($52, 4½ hr.): Parrot Jungle Island is actually a botanical garden, wildlife habitat, and bird sanctuary all rolled into one. It features parrot shows, ape and monkey experiences, and open aviaries.

Everglades Airboat Ride ($54, 4 hr.): The Seminole Indians called the Everglades Pahay Okee, the "grassy water," and on this 40-minute airboat ride you'll get to see some of the area's indigenous wildlife, including water birds and American alligators.

EXPLORING MIAMI ON YOUR OWN

A sizzling, multicultural mecca, Miami offers the best in cutting-edge restaurants, unusual attractions, entertainment, shopping, beaches, and the whole range of hotels, from luxury to boutique, kitschy to charming. Miami's best attraction is actually a neighborhood, the **South Beach Art Deco District,** located at the southern end of Miami Beach below 20th Street. It's filled with outrageous and fanciful 1920s and 1930s architecture, plus outrageous and fanciful 21st-century people. This treasure-trove, usually just called "the Beach" or "SoBe," features more than 900 pastel-painted buildings in the Art Deco, streamline moderne, and Spanish Mediterranean Revival styles. The district stretches from 6th to 23rd streets, and from the Atlantic Ocean to Lennox Court. Ocean Drive boasts many of the premier Art Deco hotels.

Also in South Beach, the **Bass Museum of Art,** 2121 Park Ave. (© **305/673-7530;** www.bassmuseum.org), is Miami's most progressive art museum, with an expanded building designed by Arata Isozakii; a permanent collection of European paintings from the 15th through the early 20th century (including Dutch and Flemish old masters); and collections of textiles, period furnishings, objets d'art, ecclesiastical artifacts, and sculpture. Rotating exhibits include pop art, fashion, and photography. Admission is $8 for adults, $6 for seniors and students.

The adjoining **Coral Gables** and **Coconut Grove** neighborhoods are fun to visit for both their architecture and their ambience. In Coral Gables, the Old World meets the New as curving boulevards, sidewalks, plazas, fountains, and arched entrances evoke Seville. Today, the area is an Epicurean's Eden, boasting some of Miami's most renowned eateries as well as the University of Miami and the ½-mile-long Miracle Mile, a 5-block retail mecca (see "Shopping," below). Coconut Grove, South Florida's oldest settlement, remains a village surrounded by the urban sprawl of Miami. It dates back to the early 1800s, when Bahamian seamen first sought to salvage treasure from the wrecked vessels stranded along the Florida Reef. Mostly people come here to shop, drink, dine, or simply walk around and explore.

Just minutes from the Port of Miami in Key Biscayne, the **Miami Seaquarium,** 4400 Rickenbacker Causeway (© **305/361-5705;** www.miamiseaquarium.com), is a delight. Dolphins such as Flipper, TV's greatest sea mammal, perform along with Lolita the Killer Whale. You can also see endangered manatees, sea lions, tropical-theme aquariums, and the gruesome shark feeding. Admission is $30 adults, $23 kids.

BEACHES

A 300-foot-wide sand beach runs for about 10 miles from south of **Miami Beach** to **Haulover Beach Park** in the north. (For those of you who like to get an all-over tan, Haulover is a nude beach.) Although most of this stretch is lined with a solid wall of hotels, beach access is plentiful, and you are free to frolic along the entire strip. A wooden boardwalk runs along the hotel side from 21st to 46th streets—about 1½ miles. You'll find lots of public beaches here, wide and well maintained, with lifeguards, toilet facilities, concession stands, and metered parking (bring lots of quarters). Lifeguard-protected public beaches include **21st Street,** at the beginning of the boardwalk; **35th Street,** popular with an older crowd; **46th Street,** next to the Fontainebleau Hilton; **53rd Street,** a narrower, more sedate beach; **64th Street,** one of the quietest strips around; and **72nd Street,** a local old-timers' spot. On the southern tip of the beach is family-favorite **South Pointe Park,** where you can watch the cruise ships. **Lummus Park,** in the center of the Art Deco District, is the best place for people-watching and model-spotting. The stretch between 11th and 13th streets is a gay beach. The area from 1st to 15th streets is popular with seniors.

In Key Biscayne, **Crandon Park,** 4000 Crandon Blvd. (© **305/361-5421**), is one of metropolitan Miami's finest white-sand beaches, stretching for some 3½ miles. There are lifeguards here, and you can rent a cabana with a shower and chairs for $22 per day. On Saturday and Sunday, the beach can be especially crowded.

SHOPPING

Most cruise ship passengers shop right near the Port of Miami at **Bayside Marketplace,** 401 Biscayne Blvd. (© **305/577-3344;** www.baysidemarketplace.com), a mall with 150 specialty shops, street performers, live music, and some 30 eateries, including a Hard Rock Cafe and others serving everything from Cuban to crepes. Many restaurants have outdoor seating right along the bay for picturesque views of the yachts harbored here. The mall can be reached via regular shuttle service from the port or by walking over the Port Bridge.

Bal Harbour Shops, 9700 Collins Ave. (© **305/866-0311;** www.balharbourshops. com), is one of the most prestigious fashion meccas in the country, with big-name stores including Chanel, Prada, Armani, Neiman Marcus, Saks Fifth Avenue, and dozens of others.

In South Beach, **Lincoln Road,** an 8-block pedestrian mall, runs between Washington Avenue and Alton Road, near the northern tier of the Art Deco District. It's filled with popular chains such as Victoria's Secret and Banana Republic, interior-design stores, art galleries, and clothing boutiques, as well as coffeehouses, restaurants, and cafes. Despite the recent influx of commercial anchor stores, Lincoln Road still manages to maintain its funky, arty flair, attracting an eclectic, colorful crowd. Or try **Espanola Way,** a small pedestrian road with a European feel that starts at 15th Street and Collins.

Coconut Grove, centered on the intersection of Main Highway and Grand Avenue, is the heart of the city's boutique district and features two open-air shopping-and-entertainment complexes, **CocoWalk,** 3015 Grand Ave. (© **305/444-0777;** www.coco walk.net), and the **Streets of Mayfair,** 2911 Grand Ave. (© **305/448-1700**).

In Coral Gables, **Miracle Mile,** actually a ½-mile stretch of SW 22nd Street between Douglas and Le Jeune roads (aka 37th and 42nd aves.), features more than 150 shops.

WHERE TO STAY

Two hotels—the 34-story **Hotel Inter-Continental Miami,** 100 Chopin Plaza (© **800/327-3005;** www.intercontinental.com/miami; rates: from $199), and the **Biscayne Bay Marriott,** 1633 N. Bayshore (© **800/228-9290;** www.marriott.com/ miami; rates: from $149)—are located right across the bay from the cruise ship piers, near Bayside Marketplace. Thanks to Miami's good highway network, though, you can stay virtually anywhere in Greater Miami and still be within 10 to 20 minutes of your ship.

SOUTH BEACH   Two blocks from the beach, the Art Deco, comfy-chic **Hotel Astor,** 956 Washington Ave. (© **800/270-4981;** www.hotelastor.com), was originally built in 1936. It has opened a new restaurant, Johnny V South Beach, and made significant renovations to its guest rooms and public areas. Rates: from $125.

The **Catalina Hotel & Beach Club,** 1732 Collins Ave. (© **305/674-1160;** www. catalinahotel.com), is one of the newer boutique hotels on South Beach, with a retro *Mod Squad* decor, rooms glazed in white with hints of bright colors, and a happening bar and lounge scene with a decidedly European jet-set vibe. You can get poolside manicures and pedicures at the splashy beach club. Rates: from $95.

The **Hotel,** 801 Collins Ave., at Eighth Street (© **305/531-2222;** www.thehotelof southbeach.com), is a Deco gem with a stylishly whimsical interior designed by haute couturier Todd Oldham. Rates: from $225.

It's hard to find a hotel on South Beach with both good value and excellent service, but the **Crest Hotel Suites,** 1670 James Ave. (© **800/531-3880;** www.cresthotel. com), delivers. It's one of Miami's best bargains and coolest hotels, retaining its original 1939 Art Deco architecture but with a thoroughly modern interior. Rates: from $155. If you're on a budget but want a cozy Deco feel, try the **Best Western South Beach,** 1050 Washington Ave. (© **888/343-1930;** www.bestwestern.com). Rates: from $72.

MIAMI BEACH   At the **Indian Creek Hotel,** 2727 Indian Creek Dr., at 28th Street (© **800/491-2772;** www.indiancreekhotel.com), each room has hardwoo floors and modern decor. Rates: from $95. The **Beach House Bal Harbour,** 9449 Collins Ave., in Surfside (© **305/535-8600;** www.thebeachhousehotel.com), brings a taste of Nantucket to Miami with soothing hues, comfortable furniture, oceanfront views, and a Ralph Lauren–decorated interior. Rates: from $179. The **Eden Roc Renaissance Resort and Spa,** 4525 Collins Ave. (© **800/327-8337** or 305/531-0000; www.edenrocresort.com), is a popular, modernized 1950s resort evoking the bygone Rat Pack era. Rates: from $259.

CORAL GABLES   The famous **Biltmore Hotel,** 1200 Anastasia Ave. (© **305/445-1926;** www.biltmorehotel.com), opened its doors in 1926 and has hosted the likes of Al Capone and the duke and duchess of Windsor. The place is a national landmark, with the largest hotel pool in the continental United States as well as a 300-foot bell tower modeled after the Cathedral of Seville. Rates: from $279. Even if you're not staying here, you can take a free tour on Sundays at 1:30, 2:30, and 3:30pm, conducted by the Dade Heritage Trust.

DINING & NIGHTLIFE

Count on **South Beach** as your dining and nightlife spot, with dozens of first-rate restaurants and cafes. With very few exceptions, the places on **Ocean Drive** are crowded with tourists and priced accordingly. You'll do better to venture a little farther into the pedestrian-friendly streets just west. The **Lincoln Road** pedestrian-mall area is so packed with places offering great food and atmosphere that it would take a full guidebook to list them all. We recommend strolling and browsing. A couple of standout outdoor cafes are **Spris,** a pizzeria at 731 Lincoln Rd. (© **305/673-2020;** www.spris.cc; main courses: $5–$14), and the **Van Dyke Cafe,** 846 Lincoln Rd. (© **305/534-3600;** main courses: $10–$20). For a culinary trendsetter, try **Pacific Time,** 915 Lincoln Rd. (© **305/534-5979;** www.pacifictime.biz), where you can enjoy a taste of the Pacific Rim with a deliciously modern South Beach twist. Main courses: $29 to $40. **Sushi Samba,** 600 Lincoln Rd. (© **305/673-5337**), features a fusion of Brazilian, Peruvian, and Japanese cuisine (main courses $19–$39; sushi priced by the piece), while **Nobu,** at the Shore Club, 1901 Collins Ave. (© **305/695-3232**), is, of course, legendary for its nouvelle Japanese cuisine (main courses: $21–$80; *omakase* "chef's choice" menu from $70).

Even if Gloria Estefan weren't co-owner of **Larios on the Beach,** 820 Ocean Dr. (© **305/532-9577**), the crowds would still flock to this bistro, which serves old-fashioned Cuban dishes such as *masitas de puerco* (fried pork chunks). Main courses: $13 to $19. For a steakhouse vibe, try **Prime One Twelve,** at the Browns Hotel, 112 Ocean Dr., South Beach (© **305/532-8112;** www.prime112.com), which offers a sleek ambience, a bustling bar, and arguably the best beef in the entire city. A powerhouse crowd gathers here for lunch and dinner, and reservations are more rare than the yellowfin tuna tartare appetizer. Main courses: $20 to $88.

At the legendary **Joe's Stone Crab,** 11 Washington Ave., Miami Beach, between South Point Drive and First Street (© **305/673-0365**), about a ton of stone crab claws are served daily during stone crab season from October to May (usually closed May 15–Oct 15). Because the place doesn't take reservations, the wait for a table can be up to 2 hours. Crab prices vary depending on the market rate, but figure about $25 per order.

After dark, look for the klieg lights to direct you to the hot spots of South Beach. While the blocks of Washington Avenue, Collins Avenue, and Ocean Drive are the main nightlife thoroughfares, you'll have better luck spotting a celebrity in a more off-the-beaten-path eatery such as **Barton G. The Restaurant,** 1427 W. Ave., Miami Beach (ⓒ **305/672-8881;** www.bartong.com/restaurant; main courses: $10–$50), or the **Forge,** 432 41st St., Miami Beach (ⓒ **305/538-8533;** www.theforge.com; main courses: $26–$60), an ornately decorated rococo-style venue with a fine wine selection. Also popular are the hotel bars, such as the Shore Club's hot, hauter-than-thou celeb magnet **Skybar,** 1901 Collins Ave. (ⓒ **786/276-6772;** www.shoreclub.com).

For a change of pace from the fast-paced glitz of South Beach or the serene luxury of Coral Gables, head for **Little Havana,** where pre-Castro Cubans commingle with young artists who have begun to set up performance spaces in the area. It's located just west of downtown Miami on SW Eighth Street. In addition to authentic Cuban cuisine, the cafe Cubano culture is alive and well.

10 Montréal, Québec

A good number of New England/Canada cruises start or end in the beautiful city of Montréal, an island set deep into the St. Lawrence River southwest of Québec City. Many ships sail between Montréal and Boston or New York, so unless you stay on an extra night or two in a local hotel, you won't have time to do the city justice.

Canada's second-largest city, Montréal has a strong French heritage dating from the 16th century, when explorer Jacques Cartier arrived here in 1535, believing the wide St. Lawrence River was the ocean and the way to the Orient. Oh well. Cartier's settlement was nothing more than an outpost until 1642, when the colony of Ville-Marie was founded by the soldiers of Paul de Chomedey, Sieur de Maisonneuve. Like Québec City, the fur and timber trade put Montréal on the map. When the British captured Québec City in 1759, for a short time Montréal was the capital of New France—until, that is, it was also taken by the English. Today, the legacies of both the French and the English survive in force. French speakers, known as Francophones, make up about 70% of the city's population.

History aside, Montréal is a very cosmopolitan city that continually wins good press for its charming neighborhoods and thriving restaurants. It's even good-looking below ground: The city's mazelike Underground Pedestrian Network was born in the 1960s with the idea of keeping Montréalers warm during the frigid winters. It's still growing today. Head down and you'll find a controlled climate where it's eternally spring, with more than 1,700 shops, 40 banks, 360 restaurants and food courts, 10 Métro stations, and about 30 cinemas—not to mention waterfalls, fountains, and trees with hanging vines.

Note: All prices in this section were calculated at the rate of US$0.87 = C$1, or US$1 = C$1.15. However, foreign currency rates fluctuate, so prices may not be exactly the same when you arrive in port.

GETTING TO MONTRÉAL & THE PORT
Cruise ships call at the **Iberville Cruise Terminal** at the Port of Montréal on de la Commune Street in Old Montréal (Vieux-Montréal in French). For more information, contact the **Montréal Port Authority** (ⓒ 514/283-7011; www.port-montreal. com). If you're flying in, you'll come through **Montréal-Trudeau Airport** (ⓒ 800/ 465-1213 or 514/394-7377; www.admtl.com). The **taxi** ride between downtown Montréal and the airport is priced at a flat rate of US$30 (C$35) plus tip and takes less than 30 minutes if traffic isn't tangled.

Montréal

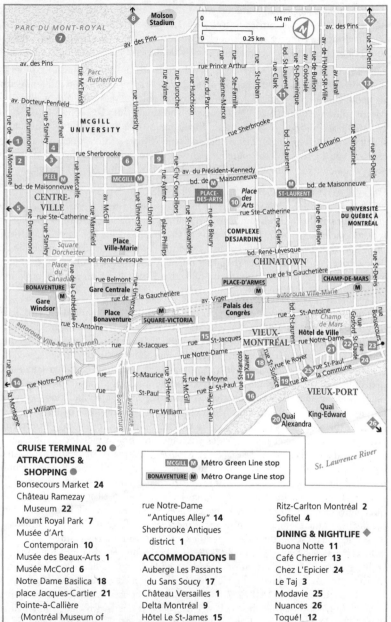

CRUISE TERMINAL 20 ●

ATTRACTIONS &
   SHOPPING ●

Bonsecours Market **24**
Château Ramezay
   Museum **22**
Mount Royal Park **7**
Musée d'Art
   Contemporain **10**
Musée des Beaux-Arts **1**
Musée McCord **6**
Notre Dame Basilica **18**
place Jacques-Cartier **21**
Pointe-à-Callière
   (Montréal Museum of
   Archaeology and History) **16**

rue Notre-Dame
   "Antiques Alley" **14**
Sherbrooke Antiques
   district **1**

ACCOMMODATIONS ■

Auberge Les Passants
   du Sans Soucy **17**
Château Versailles **1**
Delta Montréal **9**
Hôtel Le St-James **15**
Hôtel Nelligan **19**

Ritz-Carlton Montréal **2**
Sofitel **4**

DINING & NIGHTLIFE ◆

Buona Notte **11**
Café Cherrier **13**
Chez L'Epicier **24**
Le Taj **3**
Modavie **25**
Nuances **26**
Toqué! **12**

MCGILL Ⓜ Métro Green Line stop
BONAVENTURE Ⓜ Métro Orange Line stop

Interstates 87, 89, and 93 link up with Canada's Autoroute 15 at the U.S./Canada border and flow right into Montréal. The Trans-Canada Highway, which connects both ends of the country, runs through Montréal. Once in Montréal, follow the signs to Old Montréal. The street that runs alongside the Old Port is rue de la Commune.

GETTING AROUND   Ships dock in Vieux-Montréal, so it's easiest to explore this multidimensional city's old treasures on foot. For a city of nearly two million, getting to know and getting around Montréal is remarkably easy. Aside from walking, the **Métro** (subway) system is fast and efficient, and single rides cost US$2.15 (C$2.50). Note that accessibility is sometimes difficult for people with mobility problems, as many stops require the use of escalators and stairs. Plenty of **taxis** queue up at the terminal if you'd rather go that route for sightseeing; note, however, that drivers do not serve as guides. Rates are metered, with an initial US$2.75 (C$3.15) charge.

BEST CRUISE LINE SHORE EXCURSIONS

Montréal Highlights (US$49, 2½ hr.): Because Montréal is generally a port of embarkation only, the cruise lines generally offer just a basic city tour on the day passengers disembark, and it typically ends at the airport. This bus tour of Montréal's most famed attractions includes a visit to Mont Royal, which towers above the city, plus a drive through the major shopping districts, and finally to Old Montréal to get a look at the remarkable concentration of 17th-, 18th-, and 19th-century buildings.

EXPLORING MONTRÉAL ON YOUR OWN

If you have only a few hours before your cruise departs, a stroll around the **Old Town,** or Vieux-Montréal, is a must. The city was born here in 1642, down by the river at Pointe-à-Callière. Today, especially in summer, activity centers around **place Jacques-Cartier,** where cafe tables line narrow terraces and sun worshipers, flower sellers, itinerant artists, street performers, and strolling locals and tourists congregate—it's a perfect locale for some good old-fashioned people-watching. The area is larger than it might seem at first, bounded on the north by rue St-Antoine and close to rue St-Jacques, once the "Wall Street" of Montréal and still home to some banks, and on the south by the Vieux-Port (Old Port), a linear park bordering rue de la Commune that gives access to the river and provides welcome breathing room for cyclists, in-line skaters, and picnickers. To the east, Vieux-Montréal is bordered by rue Berri, and to the west by rue McGill. Several small but intriguing museums are housed in historic buildings, and the architectural heritage of the district has been substantially preserved. The restored 18th- and 19th-century buildings have been adapted for use as shops, boutique hotels, studios, galleries, cafes, bars, offices, and apartments. Take a walk through the district in the evening, when many of the finer buildings are illuminated.

Among the most worthwhile sites is the Gothic-Revival **Notre-Dame Basilica,** 110 Notre-Dame St. Ouest (© 514/842-2925; www.basiliquenddm.org), built in 1829, with a stunning interior of sculpted wood, gold leaf, and stained glass. Admission is US$3.50 (C$4) for adults. The tin-plated, silver-domed **Bonsecours Market,** 350 Saint-Paul St. Est (© 514/872-7730; www.marchebonsecours.qc.ca), a lively place built in 1847 overlooking the St. Lawrence River, is lined with cafes and small galleries. The 18th-century **Château Ramezay Museum,** 280 Notre-Dame St. Est (© 514/861-3708; www.chateauramezay.qc.ca), is another must. Formerly the governor's home, it's now a history museum with exhibits on Montréal and Québec. Admission is US$6.50 (C$7.50) for adults, US$3.50 (C$4) for kids.

Another worthwhile pursuit is a stroll through the **Mount Royal Park** (Parc du Mont-Royal), where a small village of Iroquois were living when French explorer Cartier first arrived in the 16th century. Montréal is named for it—the "Royal Mountain"—and it's a soothing urban pleasure to drive, walk, or take a horse-drawn carriage, or calèche as they're also known, to the top for a view of the city, the island, and the St. Lawrence River, especially at dusk. The great landscape architect Frederick Law Olmsted, creator of New York's Central Park, designed the oasis. It opened in 1876.

If you're in town for a few days, you may have time to explore Montréal's other neighborhoods. **Chinatown,** just north of Vieux-Montréal, is mostly a neighborhood of restaurants. The **downtown** area is where you'll find the city's office buildings, important museums, and luxury hotels. Other notable 'hoods include **Rue St-Denis,** which stretches from rue Ste-Catherine Est to avenue du Mont-Royal. It's the thumping central artery of Francophone Montréal, running from the Latin Quarter downtown and continuing north into the Plateau Mont-Royal district. Thick with cafes, bistros, offbeat shops, and lively nightspots, it is to Montréal what boulevard St-Germain is to Paris; if you want to know what the students and youth of Montréal are all about, spend an evening here.

SHOPPING

Rue Sherbrooke is a major shopping street for international and domestic designers, luxury items such as furs and jewelry, art galleries, and the Holts department store. **Boulevard St-Laurent** covers everything from budget practicalities to off-the-wall handmade fashions. Look along **avenue Laurier** between St-Laurent and de l'Epée for French boutiques, home accessories, and young Québécois designers. **Rue St-Paul** in Vieux-Montréal has a growing number of art galleries, a few jewelry shops, and T-shirt and souvenir stands. **Antiques** can be found along rue Sherbrooke near the Musée des Beaux-Arts and on the little side streets near the museum. More antiques and collectibles, in more than 50 tempting shops one after another, can be found along the lengthening "Antiques Alley" of **rue Notre-Dame,** especially concentrated between Guy and Atwater. **Rue St-Denis** north of Sherbrooke has strings of shops filled with fun, funky items.

Some of the best shops in Montréal are found in city museums. Tops among them are those in **Pointe-è-Callière** (the Montréal Museum of Archaeology and History), in Vieux-Montréal; the **Musée des Beaux-Arts** and the **Musée McCord,** both on rue Sherbrooke in the center of the city; and the **Musée d'Art Contemporain,** in the Place-des-Arts. **Rue Ste-Catherine** is home to the city's four top department stores and myriad satellite shops, while **rue Peel** is known for its men's fashions. Montréal's long history as a center for the fur trade buttresses the many wholesale and retail furriers, with outlets downtown and in Plateau Mont-Royal, but nowhere more concentrated than on the "Fur Row" of **rue Mayor,** between rue de Bleury and rue City Councillors.

WHERE TO STAY

Accommodations in Montréal range from soaring glass skyscraper lodgings to grand boulevard hotels to converted row houses. Stylish inns and boutique hotels are appearing in increasing numbers, especially in Vieux-Montréal. Except at bed-and-breakfasts, visitors can almost always count on discounts and package deals, especially on weekends, when the hotels' business clients have packed their bags and gone home. Here's a sampling:

If you're looking for some history, the restored **Ritz-Carlton Montréal,** 1228 rue Sherbrooke Ouest (© 800/363-0366 or 514/842-4212; www.ritzmontreal.com), has been around since 1912, giving it a half-century lead on the closest competition. Rates: from US$139 (C$160). The first Canadian branch of a French chain, the **Sofitel Montréal,** 1155 rue Sherbrooke Ouest (© 877/285-9001 or 514/285-9000; www.sofitel.com), matches its luxury rivals in every detail. Rates: from US$165 (C$190). **Château Versailles,** 1659 rue Sherbrooke Ouest (© 888/933-811 or 514/933-811; www.versailleshotels.com), with 65 rooms in navy-and-gold appointments and just a short walk from the Musée des Beaux-Arts, offers a fine buffet breakfast in the main living room, where you can sit at a small table for two or in an easy chair in front of a fireplace. Rates: from US$112 (C$129).

In Vieux-Montréal, **Hôtel Le St-James,** 355 rue St-Jacques (© 866/841-3111 or 514/841-3111; www.hotellestjames.com), raised the boutique bar to an almost impossibly high level with a superbly sybaritic spa, high-tech in-room amenities, and a gorgeous grand hall. Rates: from US$348 (C$400). The **Hôtel Nelligan,** 106 rue St-Paul Ouest (© 877/788-2040 or 514/788-2040; www.hotelnelligan.com), opened in 2002, counters with a great full-service restaurant (Versa), goose-down duvets on the beds, and a rooftop terrace. Rates: from US$187 (C$215). Set in a 1723 former fur warehouse in Vieux-Montréal, **Auberge Les Passants du Sans Soucy,** 171 rue St-Paul Ouest (© 514/842-2634; www.lesanssoucy.com), is a more upscale and stylish B&B than most of its peers, and it's located near the top restaurants and clubs in the old town. Rates: from US$100 (C$115).

For families, the **Delta Montréal,** 475 av. du President-Kennedy (© 877/286-1986 or 514/286-1986; www.deltahotels.com), keeps kids blissfully waterlogged with *two* pools—one inside, one outside—and also has a play center and huge guest rooms. Rates: from US$149 (C$171) for a family package for two adults and two children.

DINING & NIGHTLIFE

Rue Crescent, one of Montréal's major dining and nightlife districts, lies in the western shadow of the downtown skyscrapers. Here you'll find hundreds of restaurants, bars, and clubs of all styles between Sherbrooke and René-Lévesque, centering on rue Crescent and spilling over onto neighboring streets.

Any of a dozen cafes along **St-Denis** will fit the bill if you're looking for food and people-watching ops, especially on weekends, when the **Plateau Mont-Royal** area comes alive. Try the *poutine,* french fries doused with gravy and cheese curds—a Québécois favorite. **Café Cherrier,** 3635 rue St-Denis, at rue Cherrier (© 514/843-4308), might be the most fun, if you can find a seat on the wraparound terrace. Brunch is popular here. Main courses: US$6.95 to US$15 (C$8–C$17). At the gracious, festive **Nuances,** 1 av. du Casino on the Ile Ste-Hélène (© 514/392-2708), set on the top floor of a casino, you'll enjoy superb French and Belgian cuisine and spectacular views of the skyline. Main courses: US$34 to US$42 (C$39–C$48). If great French food is your main goal, then get a reservation at **Toqué!,** 900 Place Jean-Paul-Riopelle in Old Montréal (© 514/499-2084), which is in a league of its own. Main courses: US$26 to US$39 (C$30–C$45). Also in Old Montréal, **Chez l'Epicier,** 331 rue St-Paul Est (© 514/878-2232), is a crisp little eatery that features both high-end delicatessen food to go and a fashionable restaurant with Asian ingredients. Main courses: US$24 to US$34 (C$28–C$39).

Of course, French isn't your only choice. For Italian, check out superchic **Buona Notte,** 3518 bd. St-Laurent, near rue Sherbrooke (© 514/848-0644), where the pastas focaccias, and risottos rival the occasional celebrity sightings. Main courses: US$10 to US$42 (C$12–C$48). The Mediterranean **Modavie,** 1 rue St-Paul Ouest, at rue St-Laurent (© **514/287-9582**), has live jazz in the summer and lamb as its specialty. Main courses: US$14 to US$30 (C$16–C$35). And if price is as appetizing to you as the trendiness quotient, try the all-you-can-eat Indian lunch buffet at **Le Taj,** 2077 rue Stanley, near rue Sherbrooke (© **514/845-9015**). Main courses: US$6.95 to US$22 (C$8–C$25).

11 New Orleans, Louisiana

New Orleans has had a few really bad years.

As anyone not living under a rock knows, floodwaters caused by Hurricane Katrina poured into the city in the last days of August 2005, inundating whole neighborhoods, causing massive destruction and loss of life, and forcing tens of thousands from their homes. It was the largest natural disaster to ever strike a major American city, and its effects will be felt for years to come. Nevertheless, time marches on. Within weeks of the storm, New Orleans's businesses were reopening their doors, working back toward normalcy one step at a time. In late February 2006, the city held Mardi Gras right on time and it was just as grand and fun as ever, if slightly truncated.

To the visitor—and yes, there are visitors—the central parts of town, the most frequently touristed parts, look relatively normal. The **French Quarter,** the oldest and most historic part of the city, saw no flooding and survived almost completely intact, minus a few details. Ditto for the **Garden District,** that area to the southwest full of beautiful ornate homes. Things get worse, though, out beyond the tourist areas. The hard-hit Lower Ninth Ward, for instance, still looks like Hiroshima after the bomb, with block after block of unlivable ruins that were once peoples' homes. It's things like this that remind us everything's not hunky-dory, no matter how normal things look in the French Quarter's busy bars and restaurants. A very bad thing happened here. The city will probably get over it eventually, but it will take time and patience and grit and a helluva lot of hard work. And some federal funding would be nice, too.

GETTING TO NEW ORLEANS & THE PORT

For information, contact the **Port of New Orleans** (© **504/522-2551;** www.portno. com), which operates the **Julia Street Wharf** and the new **Erato Street Cruise Terminal,** located adjacent to each other on the east bank of the Mississippi, south of the French Quarter. The port is also planning construction of an additional cruise terminal on the **Poland Avenue Wharf,** in the Bywater area just east of the French Quarter. If you're flying in, you'll probably land at **Louis Armstrong International Airport** (© **504/464-0831;** www.flymsy.com), about 17 miles from the cruise terminal. A **taxi** costs $29 for two people to the terminal or downtown.

If you're driving, take I-10 east to New Orleans and follow the signs to the New Orleans Business District, U.S. 90 West, Crescent City Connection to the West Bank. Take the last exit before crossing the Mississippi River (exit 11C, Tchoupitoulas and South Peters sts.). Take the down ramp to ground level, go to the second stoplight (Tchoupitoulas St.), and turn right. Go to the next stoplight (Henderson St.) and turn left. Go 2 blocks, pass over the railroad tracks, and turn left. The cruise terminals are directly ahead of you. Parking is available for $14 per day.

GETTING AROUND Taxis are plentiful. If you're not near a taxi stand, call **United Cabs** (© **504/522-9771;** www.unitedcabs.com) and a car will come in

10 minutes. Rates are $2.50 to start, plus $1.60 per mile (20¢ per ⅛ mile) thereafter, with a $1 surcharge for additional passengers. At press time, the famous **St. Charles streetcar** from the French Quarter to the Garden District was still not in service, though it's expected to be up and running again in November 2007. Other streetcar lines are running on schedule.

From Jackson Square (at Decatur St.), you can take a 2¼-mile, 30-minute horse-drawn carriage ride through the French Quarter. **Royal Carriage Tour Co. (© 504/ 943-8820)** offers private rides for up to four passengers in a Cinderella carriage for $60 a pop, daily from 9am to midnight.

BEST CRUISE LINE SHORE EXCURSIONS

City Tour ($40, 5 hr.): Offered post-cruise, this bus tour takes in St. Charles Avenue, the Superdome, the Loyola and Tulane University campuses, Audubon Park and City Park, the Garden District, and the French Quarter, where you get 2 hours to poke around before transferring to the airport.

EXPLORING NEW ORLEANS ON YOUR OWN

Made up of about 90 square blocks, the **French Quarter** (also known as the *Vieux Carré,* or "Old Square") was laid out by the French engineer Adrien de Pauger in 1718, and a strict preservation policy pre-Katrina (and high ground and good luck during and after the storm) has kept it looking much the way it always has. Its major public area is **Jackson Square** (bounded by Chartres, Decatur, St. Peter, and St. Ann sts.), where musicians, artists, fortunetellers, jugglers, and those peculiar "living statue" guys gather to sell their wares or entertain for change. The main drag, however, is **Bourbon Street,** which is basically Sodom and Gomorrah, though in a good way. Many of the Quarter's best attractions are covered under "Dining & Nightlife," below, but here are some of its more historic highlights.

Incorporating seven historic buildings connected by a brick courtyard, the **Historic New Orleans Collection,** 533 Royal St., between St. Louis and Toulouse streets (© 504/523-4662; www.hnoc.org), evokes the New Orleans of 200 years ago. The oldest building in the complex escaped the tragic fire of 1794. The others hold exhibitions about Louisiana's culture and history. All are open from 9:30am to 4:30pm Tuesday through Saturday. Admission is free.

Founded in 1950, the **New Orleans Pharmacy Museum,** 514 Chartres St., at St. Louis Street (© 504/565-8027; www.pharmacymuseum.org), is just what the name implies. In 1823, the first licensed pharmacist in the United States, Louis J. Dufilho, Jr., opened an apothecary shop here. Today you'll find old apothecary bottles, voodoo potions, pill tiles, and suppository molds, as well as the old glass cosmetics counter and a jar of leeches, in case you feel the need to be bled. Admission is $5. Closed Sundays and Mondays.

Constructed from 1795 through 1799 as the Spanish government seat in New Orleans, the **Cabildo,** 701 Chartres St., at Jackson Square (© 800/568-6968 or 504/ 568-6968; http://lsm.crt.state.la.us/cabex.htm), was the site of the signing of the Louisiana Purchase transfer. The building is now the center of the Louisiana State Museum's facilities in the French Quarter, with an exhibition that traces the history of Louisiana from exploration through Reconstruction, covering all aspects of life, including antebellum music, mourning and burial customs, immigrants, and the changing roles of women in the South. Admission is $6 for adults. Closed Mondays.

New Orleans: The French Quarter

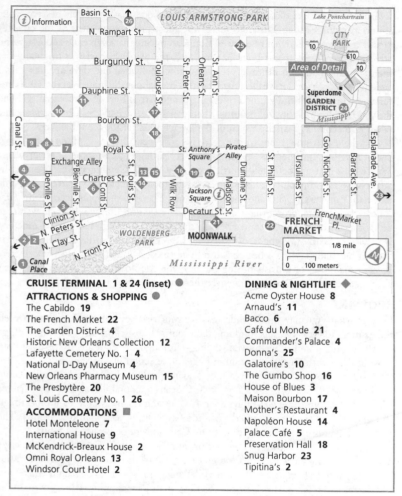

CRUISE TERMINAL 1 & 24 (inset) ●

ATTRACTIONS & SHOPPING ●
The Cabildo **19**
The French Market **22**
The Garden District **4**
Historic New Orleans Collection **12**
Lafayette Cemetery No. 1 **4**
National D-Day Museum **4**
New Orleans Pharmacy Museum **15**
The Presbytère **20**
St. Louis Cemetery No. 1 **26**

ACCOMMODATIONS ■
Hotel Monteleone **7**
International House **9**
McKendrick-Breaux House **2**
Omni Royal Orleans **13**
Windsor Court Hotel **2**

DINING & NIGHTLIFE ◆
Acme Oyster House **8**
Arnaud's **11**
Bacco **6**
Café du Monde **21**
Commander's Palace **4**
Donna's **25**
Galatoire's **10**
The Gumbo Shop **16**
House of Blues **3**
Maison Bourbon **17**
Mother's Restaurant **4**
Napoléon House **14**
Palace Café **5**
Preservation Hall **18**
Snug Harbor **23**
Tipitina's **2**

Also on Jackson Square, the **Presbytère,** 751 Chartres St. (© **800/568-6968** or 504/568-6968; http://lsm.crt.state.la.us/presbex.htm), was planned as housing for clergy but is now a Mardi Gras museum that traces the history of the annual event, with everything from elaborate Mardi Gras Indian costumes to Rex Queen jewelry from the turn of the 20th century on display. A re-creation of a float allows you to pretend you're throwing beads to a crowd on a screen in front of you. Admission is $6 for adults. The museum is currently closed Monday through Thursday.

In the Warehouse District, just west of the Quarter, the **National D-Day Museum,** 945 Magazine St. (© **504/527-6012;** www.ddaymuseum.org), was the creation of historian Stephen Ambrose, telling the story of all U.S. amphibious assaults world-wide on that fateful day. Many of the artifacts on display emphasize personal stories, including audio exhibits that tell the experiences of soldiers and civilians alike. Admission is $14. Closed Mondays.

Aside from the Quarter, the one other neighborhood that absolutely deserves your attention is the **Garden District,** one of the most picturesque areas of the city. It's mostly residential, but what residences! Bounded by St. Charles Avenue and Magazine Street between Jackson and Louisiana avenues, the whole district was originally the site of a plantation, and the land was eventually subdivided and developed as a residential neighborhood for wealthy Americans. Throughout the middle of the 19th century, developers built the Victorian, Italianate, and Greek Revival homes that still line the streets. If it's back up and running when you arrive, take the **St. Charles streetcar** (www.norta.com/st_charles.php) from the French Quarter for the full effect.

And then, of course, there are the dead: Because New Orleans is prone to flooding, bodies have been interred aboveground since its earliest days, in sometimes very elaborate tombs that are definitely worth a visit. **St. Louis Cemetery No. 1,** on Basin Street between Conti and St. Louis streets, at the top of the French Quarter, is the oldest extant cemetery (1789) and the most iconic. The acid-dropping scene from *Easy Rider* was shot here, prompting the city to declare that no film would ever, ever, ever be shot again in one of its cemeteries. In the Garden District, **Lafayette Cemetery No. 1,** 1427 Sixth St., right across the street from Commander's Palace Restaurant, is another old cemetery that's been beautifully restored. Though both of these cemeteries are usually full of tourists during the day, you should still exercise caution when visiting, as they've seen some crime over the years.

SHOPPING

Despite what you may think while making your first walk down **Bourbon Street,** there's more to New Orleans shopping than tourist traps selling cheap T-shirts, alligator snow globes, and other souvenir items—although there are plenty of those too, most of them with an absolutely mind-boggling selection of **hot sauces.**

On Decatur Street across from Jackson Square, the **French Market** has shops selling candy, cookware, fashion, crafts, toys, New Orleans memorabilia, and candles. There's a lot of kitsch, but some good buys are mixed in; and it's always fun to stroll through and grab a few beignets at **Café du Monde** (see "Dining & Nightlife," below). The French Market is open from 10am to 6pm; Café du Monde is open 24 hours.

From Camp Street down to the river on Julia Street, you'll find many of the city's best **contemporary art galleries.** Of course, some of the works are a bit pricey, but there are good deals to be had if you're collecting, and fine art to be seen if you're not.

Magazine Street is the Garden District's premier shopping street, with many antiques stores, art galleries, boutiques, and crafts shops among the 19th-century brick storefronts and cottages.

WHERE TO STAY

In the Garden District, the **McKendrick-Breaux House,** 1474 Magazine St. (© **888/ 570-1700** or 504/586-1700; www.mckendrick-breaux.com), was built at the end of the Civil War by a wealthy plumber and Scottish immigrant. Today, it's one of the best guesthouses for value. It's been completely restored to its original charming state, and each room is furnished with antiques, family collectibles, and fresh flowers. Rates: from $155.

In the Central Business District, just outside the French Quarter and close to the cruise ship terminal, the **International House,** 221 Camp St., just west of Canal (© **800/633-5770** or 504/553-9550; www.ihhotel.com), is a modern, minimalist hotel housed in an old Beaux Arts bank building. Rooms are simple, with high ceilings, ceiling fans, modern bathrooms, dataports, wireless Internet access, CD players with CDs, and photos and knickknacks that remind you that you're in New Orleans. It's all corridors and dark and chic. Rates: from $149.

Also in the Central Business District, the **Windsor Court Hotel,** 300 Gravier St. (© **800/262-2662** or 504/523-6000; www.windsorcourthotel.com), was named "Best Hotel in North America" by *Condé Nast Traveler,* so feel free to hold it to a high standard. Accommodations are exceptionally spacious and classy, with large bay windows or a private balcony overlooking the river or the city. Downstairs, two corridors display original 17th-, 18th-, and 19th-century art. A plush reading area with international newspapers is on the second floor. Rates: from $195.

About 7 blocks from the cruise ship terminal is the atmospheric **Hotel Monteleone,** 214 Royal St., between Iberville and Bienville streets (© **800/535-9595** or 504/523-3341; www.hotelmonteleone.com), the oldest hotel in the city and also the largest hotel in the French Quarter—because of its size you can almost always get a reservation here, even when other places are booked. Everyone who stays here loves it, probably because its staff is among the most helpful in town. Decor and floor layouts are slightly different in each of the rooms, so ask to see a few different ones. Rates: from $199.

The **Omni Royal Orleans,** 621 St. Louis St., between Royal and Chartres streets (© **800/843-6664** or 504/529-5333; www.omnihotels.com), is an elegant hotel located smack in the center of the French Quarter. The lobby is a small sea of marble, and the rooms are sizable and elegant, full of muted tones and plush furniture, with windows that let you gaze out over the Quarter. Service varies, but can be exceptional. Rates: from $169.

DINING & NIGHTLIFE

Restaurants were among the first businesses to bounce back from Katrina, since even rescue workers have to eat. Same logic goes for the bars. At press time, all of the best-loved restaurants and most of the nightspots we listed in previous editions of this book were back up and running. Little wonder, because New Orleans has always essentially been one giant restaurant and nightlife spot. In 1997, a U.S. survey named it "the fattest city in the country," which makes sense once you've tasted the food. After dinner, be sure to head out to the clubs—this is, after all, the city that gave birth to jazz. Many of the best restaurants and clubs are in the French Quarter.

For oysters, head to the **Acme Oyster House,** 724 Iberville St. (© **504/525-1157;** www.acmeoyster.com). It's the Quarter's oldest oyster bar, a noisy, crowded place where you can shoot your freshly shucked half-shell oysters at the bar or order them in a po' boy sandwich. A dozen will cost you $8; po' boys are $5.50 to $7.50.

In business since 1918 and still mighty fine, the legendary **Arnaud's,** 813 Bienville St. (© **504/523-2847;** www.arnauds.com), is set in three interconnected, once-private houses from the 1700s. The restaurant's three Belle Epoque dining rooms are lush with Edwardian embellishments. Especially delicious menu items include snapper or trout topped with crabmeat, filet mignon, oysters stewed in cream, roasted duck in blueberry sauce, and a classic bananas Foster. Dinner main courses: $21 to $36.

Bacco, 310 Chartres St., between Bienville and Conti streets (© **504/522-2426;** www.bacco.com), a great New Orleans bistro, has an elegant setting of pink faux-marble floors and Venetian chandeliers. You can feast on wood-fired pizzas, regional seafood, and such specialties as black-truffle fettuccine and lobster ravioli. Dinner main courses: $18 to $31.

Galatoire's, 209 Bourbon St., at Iberville Street (© **504/525-2021**), feels like a bistro in turn-of-the-20th-century Paris, and is one of the city's most legendary places—it's one of the spots that locals go to for a good meal. Menu items include trout (meunière or amandine), rémoulade of shrimp, oysters en brochette, a savory Creole-style bouillabaisse, and eggplant stuffed with a purée of seafood. Dinner main courses: $14 to $27.

The **Gumbo Shop,** 630 St. Peter St., at Royal Street (© **504/525-1486**), is a cheap and convenient place to get solid, classic Creole food. The menu reads like a textbook list of traditional local fare: red beans and rice, shrimp Creole, crawfish étouffée. The seafood gumbo with okra is a meal in itself, and do try the jambalaya. Dinner main courses: $7 to $19.

Not far outside the Quarter, **Mother's Restaurant,** 401 Poydras St., at Tchoupitoulas Street (© **504/523-9656**), has long lines and zero atmosphere, but damn, those po' boys. Customers have been flocking here since 1938 for homemade biscuits and red-bean omelets at breakfast, po' boys at lunch, and soft-shell crabs and jambalaya at dinner. Everything's between $5 and $21.

Napoleon House, 500 Chartres St., at St. Louis Street (© **504/524-9752;** www. napoleonhouse.com), would have been the home of the lieutenant himself if some locals' wild plan to bring him here to live out his exile had panned out. Instead, it's now a restaurant and bar. At press time, its food service was still limited to lunch; the bar is open until midnight. Sandwiches: $6 to $7. Closed Thursdays.

Right on the border of the French Quarter, the open kitchen at **Palace Café,** 605 Canal St., between Royal and Chartres streets (© **504/523-1661**), serves contemporary Creole food with a big emphasis on seafood: catfish pecan meunière, andouille-crusted fish of the day, and lots more. Don't miss the white-chocolate bread pudding. Dinner main courses: $19 to $28.

Outside the Quarter, at the corner of Washington Avenue and Coliseum Street in the Garden District, **Commander's Palace,** 1403 Washington Ave. (© **504/899-8221**), sustained serious Katrina damage that required a major renovation, but it still reigns as one of the finest dining choices not only in New Orleans, but in the whole United States—the James Beard Foundation voted it the country's best restaurant in 1996. The cuisine is haute Creole. Try anything with Gulf fish, or the Mississippi quail, or . . . oh hell, just try anything. Dinner main courses: $26 to $42.

For a snack any time of the day or night, visit **Café du Monde,** 800 Decatur St., right on the river (© **504/581-2914**). It's basically a 24-hour coffee shop that specializes in beignets, a square, really yummy doughnut-type thing, served hot and covered in powdered sugar. It's a great spot for people-watching, but if you don't want to wait for a table, you can always get a bag of beignets to go. Grab lots of napkins. Moist towelettes would be a good idea too, or maybe just a big wet towel.

Life in the "Big Easy" has always been conducive to all manner of nighttime entertainment, usually raucous, and that spirit is still more or less intact post-Katrina. Do what most people do: Start at one end of **Bourbon Street** (say, around Iberville St.), walk down to the other end, and then turn around and do it again. Along the way, you'll hear R & B, blues, and jazz pouring out of dozens of bars, be beckoned by touts from the numerous strip clubs, and see one tiny little storefront stall after another sporting hand-lettered signs that say OUR BEER IS CHEAPER THAN NEXT DOOR. It's a scene. Bacchanalian? Yes. Will you spend time in purgatory for it? Maybe, but it's loads of fun. Grab yourself a big cheap beer or one of the famous rum-based Hurricanes and join the party.

Most of the places in this section have a cover charge that varies depending on who's performing; some are free.

The famous **Preservation Hall,** 726 St. Peter St., just off Bourbon (© **888/946-JAZZ;** www.preservationhall.com), is a deliberately shabby little hall with very few places to sit and no air-conditioning. Still, crowds show up nearly every night to hear older and younger jazz men and women playing classic jazz the way it was intended, amplified by nothing but passion.

Close by, **Maison Bourbon,** 641 Bourbon St. (© **504/522-8818**), presents authentic and often fantastic Dixieland and traditional jazz. Stepping into the brick-walled room, or even just peering in from the street, takes you away from the mayhem outside. There's a one-drink minimum.

If you're looking to get away from the Bourbon scene and hear some real brass-band jazz, head up to **Donna's,** 800 N. Rampart St., at the top of St. Ann Street (© **504/596-6914;** www.donnasbarandgrill.com). There's no better place to hear the authentic sounds that made New Orleans famous. The cover varies, but is always reasonable.

One block beyond Esplanade, on the periphery of the French Quarter, the jazz bistro **Snug Harbor,** 626 Frenchman St. (© **504/949-0696;** www.snugjazz.com), is a classic spot to hear modern jazz in a cozy setting. Sometimes R & B combos and blues are added to the program. There's a full dinner menu in the restaurant, but only appetizers are served in the club.

Other nightlife options include the nostalgia-laden bar and concert hall **Tipitina's,** way out in Uptown at 501 Napoleon Ave. (© **504/891-8477;** www.tipitinas.com), where jazz, blues, and Dixieland pour out the doors nightly; and **House of Blues,** 225 Decatur St. (© **504/529-2583**), one of the city's largest live-music venues, with several bars and a restaurant on-site.

12 New York City, New York

What can you say about the capital of the world that hasn't already been said? New York is just *it:* the biggest, loudest, and most historic city in the U.S., with a population that encompasses people from every country, race, religion, and social predilection on the face of the earth. It's the melting pot done up in concrete, steel, and glass, with a few patches of green that stand out like moss on a chessboard. And it even looks like a chessboard: From the near-perfect grid of Manhattan's streets and the vertical lines of the skyscrapers to its direct, no-nonsense speaking style, New York is a city of straight lines. And why not? A straight line is, after all, the fastest way to get to the point.

GETTING TO NEW YORK CITY & THE PORT

New York is served by three different cruise ports: one in Manhattan, one in Brooklyn, and another in Bayonne, New Jersey, just across the Hudson.

Manhattan's historic (if a bit ugly) **New York Cruise Terminal** (© **212/246-5450;** www.nycruiseterminal.com) is stretched out along the Hudson River between 46th and 54th streets. It's reached via a vehicle ramp located at 55th Street off the West Side Highway. It's frequently congested on turnaround days, though improvements in the works promise to reduce roadway congestion and improve passenger circulation. Parking is available for $24 a day. One block away, near the corner of 46th Street and 12th

New York City

UPPER WEST SIDE

CENTRA

W. 65th St.
W. 64th St.
W. 63rd St.
W. 62nd St.
W. 61st St.
W. 60th St.
W. 59th St.
W. 58th St.
W. 57th St.
W. 56th St.
W. 55th St.
W. 54th St.
W. 53rd St.
W. 52nd St.
W. 51st St.
W. 50th St.
W. 49th St.
W. 48th St.
W. 47th St.
W. 46th St.
W. 45th St.
W. 44th St.
W. 43rd St.
W. 42nd St.
W. 41st St.
W. 40th St.
W. 39th St.
W. 38th St.
W. 37th St.
W. 36th St.
W. 35th St.
W. 34th St.
W. 33rd St.
W 32nd St.
W. 31st St.
W. 30th St.
W. 29th St.
W. 28th St.
W. 27th St.
W. 26th St.
W. 25th St.
W. 24th St.
W. 23rd St.
W. 22nd St.
W. 21st St.
W. 20th St.
W. 19th St.
W. 18th St.
W. 17th St.
W. 16th St.
W. 15th St.

65th S
Central Park W.
West Drive
Columbus Circle
Central Park S.
Broadway

West End Ave.
Amsterdam Ave.
Columbus Ave.
Tenth Ave.
Ninth Ave.
Eighth Ave.
Seventh Ave.
Eleventh Ave.
Twelfth Ave.
West Side Hwy.

DeWitt Clinton Park

THEATER DISTRICT

MIDTOWN WEST

TIMES SQUARE

Port Authority

Lincoln Tunnel
← To New Jersey

Javits Convention Center

GARMEN DISTRICT

Intrepid Sea-Air-Space Museum

Penn Station/ Madison Square Garden
W 32nd

Tunnel Entrance

Chelsea Park

W. 27th St.

CHELSEA

Chelsea Piers Sports & Entertainment Complex

Hudson River

Chelsea Piers

MEAT-PACKING DISTRICT

Avenue, **H&H Bagels** (www.handhbagel.com) sells the best bagels in New York, hands down, while a block further inland, at 11th Avenue and 46th Street, is the **Landmark Tavern** (© 212/247-2562; www.thelandmarktavern.org), one of the most beautiful and historic bars in New York. When it opened in 1868, it was on the waterfront, meaning everything between it and your ship is landfill created in the last century or so.

Down in the old blue-collar neighborhood of Red Hook, the **Brooklyn Cruise Terminal** (© 718/246-2794; www.nycruiseterminal.com) is located just across New York Harbor from Lower Manhattan and Governors Island, former site of the country's largest U.S. Coast Guard base. The port is easily accessible to locals driving by car, as well as to visitors flying into Kennedy, LaGuardia, and Newark airports. While Red Hook itself is industrial and gritty (if rapidly gentrifying), it's just minutes from picturesque Colonial-era Brooklyn Heights and the great expanse of the **Brooklyn Bridge.** The Brooklyn terminal's most high-profile ship is the *Queen Mary 2,* which homeports here on the western end of her transatlantic crossings. From wherever you're driving, get onto the Brooklyn–Queens Expressway and exit at Hamilton Avenue (exit 26) onto the service road. Stay to the left and make a left U-turn at the intersection of Hamilton with Clinton Street/Ninth Street, then continue west along the westbound Hamilton Avenue service road. Take the service road to its end at Van Brunt Street. Turn left, travel 2 blocks, and then turn right onto Bowne Street to enter the terminal. Parking is $20 per day.

In Bayonne, New Jersey, the **Cape Liberty Cruise Port** (© 201/823-3737; www.cruiseliberty.com) opened in 2004 as a home port for Royal Caribbean and Celebrity vessels. We know: Sailing from Bayonne doesn't sound as romantic as sailing from Manhattan, but Cape Liberty does have the advantage of being less congested. And where else can you get a view of the Statue of Liberty's butt? Located just off the New Jersey Turnpike and I-278, and approximately 15 minutes from the Newark airport, it's easily accessible to those coming from New Jersey, Long Island, and the New York boroughs of Brooklyn and Staten Island. From the New Jersey Turnpike, take exit 14A and follow signs for Route 440 South. Follow 440 to Cape Liberty Terminal Boulevard, which will be on your left. Parking is $15 per day.

If you're coming in by plane, you'll fly into one of three New York–area airports. **John F. Kennedy International Airport (JFK)** is in Queens, about 15 miles southeast of Midtown Manhattan. **LaGuardia Airport (LGA)** is also in Queens, about 8 miles northeast of Midtown Manhattan. **Newark Liberty International Airport (EWR)** is in Essex and Union counties, New Jersey, about 16 miles southwest of Midtown Manhattan. For information on all three, go to the Port Authority of New York & New Jersey website at **www.panynj.gov**. Kennedy and Newark are the larger airports and accommodate both domestic and international flights. If you've arranged air transportation and/or transfers through your cruise line, a representative will direct you to shuttle buses that take you to whichever port your ship is sailing from. Yellow **taxis** are usually lined up in great numbers at the airports and can take you to any of the ports or your hotel, though the fare will be stiff. From JFK to Manhattan, yellow taxis charge a flat fee of $45 per carload, plus tolls and tip. From Newark to Manhattan, flat fees vary from $40 to $60, depending on where you're going. There is no flat fee from LaGuardia—you pay the standard metered rate: $2.50 just to get going, then 40¢ for every ⅕ mile (about 4 blocks) thereafter, with additional surcharges for peak hours (4–8pm Mon–Fri) and after 8pm. **Super Shuttle** (© 212/258-3826;

www.supershuttle.com) is a cheaper alternative, with fares ranging from $13 to $22 per person for the van ride to Manhattan. Twenty-four-hour advance reservations are recommended.

GETTING AROUND   The beauty of New York City is that it's so walkable and so relatively compact, with the island of Manhattan measuring only about 2 miles wide by 13 miles long—and most visitors remain in its bottom half anyway. Most of its streets (north of Greenwich Village, at least) follow a simple grid pattern, so it's next to impossible to lose your way. The Manhattan cruise terminal is close to the heart of Midtown, about a mile from Times Square.

If you don't care to walk everywhere, don't hesitate to take the **subway** or **bus.** Fares for both are just $2 a ride no matter how far you go. You can buy a **MetroCard** pass in any denomination at any subway station. If you'll be riding a lot, you can also get a 1-day $7 Fun Pass that's good for unlimited rides from first use until 3am the following day. Most subway lines in Manhattan run north-to-south, though some veer off at unexpected angles. Be sure to pick up a free map from a station attendant so you can be sure the subway you're on really goes where you think it does. Buses run both north–south and east–west, with routes marked (usually) at each bus stop. They're generally not fast, but they do offer something the subways don't: a view. Buses accept both MetroCards and coins (but not paper money); most have free bus maps available somewhere aboard. Info on routes, schedules, and fares can be found at **www.mta.info**.

You can also hail one of the city's ubiquitous **yellow cabs.** The meter starts at $2.50 and increases 40¢ every ⅕ mile or 90 seconds, whichever comes first. For an overview of town, you can join one of the red double-decker **Gray Line/New York Sightseeing tour buses** (© **800/669-0051** or 212/445-0848; www.coachusa.com/newyork sightseeing) at the Circle Line terminal, just a few steps south of the Manhattan cruise ship piers. A 48-hour hop-on/hop-off pass is $49 for adults, $39 for kids. If you buy tickets online, you get a $10 price break.

BEST CRUISE LINE SHORE EXCURSIONS

Because New York is mostly a port of embarkation, the cruise lines generally offer only a few tour choices, including several **bus tours** ($59–$109, 4–8 hr.). If you've got a day or two in town, though, don't bother: You can see more (and better) on your own.

EXPLORING NEW YORK CITY ON YOUR OWN

There's much more to see and do in New York than we have space for here, so we'll concentrate on some highlights—some big touristy ones, as well as some unexpected ones.

MIDTOWN   Let's triangulate from **Times Square.** Once the center of New York's entertainment industry, the whole area around 42nd Street and Broadway fell into deep, dark, sleazy blight starting in the 1960s and running right up to the early '90s. Time was, you couldn't walk through without being offered heroin, switchblades, or porn. Now, it's a corporate America theme park, overseen by the eight-story **NASDAQ** video screen (the world's largest) at 43rd Street and Broadway, nested in among acres of other high-tech signage. You won't see this much neon anywhere else except maybe Vegas. Even at midnight, the whole area is bright as noon and packed with visitors, musicians, and street artists—but not very many New Yorkers. The fact is, it's a total tourist trap, but it sure is a sight.

At 44th Street, ABC's *Good Morning America* has set up a street-facing studio, while **MTV** has done the same across Broadway at 45th Street, drawing busloads of fans. A couple of blocks away, the former porn-peddler's paradise of **42nd Street** between Seventh and Eighth avenues has been rebuilt into a family-oriented entertainment mecca. In addition to a spate of beautifully renovated theaters—including the **New Victory,** the **New Amsterdam,** and the Selwyn (aka the **American Airlines Theatre**)—the neon-bright block is chock-full with retail and amusements, including two 20-plus-screen movie complexes and **Madame Tussaud's New York,** 234 W. 42nd St. (© **800/246-8872;** www.nycwax.com), a six-floor fully interactive new-world version of London's famous wax museum. Admission is $29 adults, $23 kids.

Just a few blocks east, running from 48th to 50th streets between Fifth and Sixth avenues, the Art Deco buildings of **Rockefeller Center** make you feel like you're standing in a classic 1930s movie. For a dramatic approach, start at Fifth Avenue between 49th and 50th streets, where a promenade leads to the Lower Plaza, home to the famous ice-skating rink in winter and alfresco dining in summer. All around, the flags of the United Nations member countries flap in the breeze. In December and early January, this is also the site of the city's official Christmas tree. **St. Patrick's Cathedral** is on the other side of Fifth Avenue, at 50th Street. Three blocks away, the **Museum of Modern Art,** 11 W. 53rd St., between Fifth and Sixth avenues (© **212/708-9400;** www.moma.org), is one of the world's great modern art museums. Admission is $20; closed Tuesdays.

Now that we've dispensed with the obvious Midtown attractions, you have two main choices: Head uptown or head downtown.

UPTOWN　To the north, starting at 59th Street, is **Central Park.** Laid out between 1859 and 1870 on a design by Frederick Law Olmsted and Calvert Vaux, the park's 843 acres are, just by virtue of their continued existence amid some of the world's priciest real estate, New York's greatest marvel. Highlights include the Wollman Memorial Ice Rink, the Bethesda Fountain, the Sheep Meadow (a huge sunbathing spot in summer), and the old carousel with its 58 hand-carved horses. West of the park, the **Upper West Side** is one of the city's most beautiful residential neighborhoods, its most scenic stretch running from 59th Street north to about 89th. On the park's eastern edge, along Fifth Avenue between 82nd and 104th streets, is **Museum Mile,** home to the **Metropolitan Museum of Art,** at 82nd Street (© **212/535-7710;** www.metmuseum.org), and eight other museums. The Met is one of the country's largest and best museums, with a collection of more than two million works spanning the globe and the ages. "Recommended" admission is $20; closed Mondays. Other museums in the area include the **Solomon R. Guggenheim Museum,** at Fifth Avenue and 88th Street (© **212/423-3500;** www.guggenheim.org), with its landmark seashell design by Frank Lloyd Wright and its collection spanning the period from the late 19th century to the present.

DOWNTOWN & BROOKLYN　Heading downtown from the Times Square area will take you eventually to New York's most historic districts, where the original colony of New Amsterdam got its start. From the corner of Broadway and 42nd Street, look east. That tall building with the gleaming stainless-steel spire is the **Chrysler Building**—the most beautiful skyscraper in the city (sez us and most other New Yorkers). Walk toward it, stopping when you get to Fifth Avenue. Look south from here and start walking toward that other big spire ahead of you, the **Empire State Building,** on the corner of 34th Street (www.esbnyc.com), which is once again the tallest building in Manhattan since the destruction of the World Trade Center. Lines to get up to the 86th-floor observatory can be horrible at the concourse-level ticket booth, so be prepared to wait—or consider purchasing advance tickets online. Admission is $20 adults, $14 to $18 kids. At the observatory, you can walk out on the windy deck and look through coin-operated viewers (bring quarters) over what, on a clear day, can be as much as an 80-mile visible radius.

Once outside, head downtown on Fifth Avenue. Where it crosses Broadway at 23rd Street, you'll see the famous **Flatiron Building** from 1902, looking like the prow of a ship. Walk south along Broadway past **Union Square,** site of protest rallies from the 1870s through today. At Broadway and 10th, **Grace Church** was designed by James Renwick, Jr., who later designed St. Patrick's. At Waverly Place, turn right and go 1 block to **Washington Square Park,** a **Greenwich Village** landmark typically full of musicians and other street performers. Meander through (and maybe take a side trip west into the warren of narrow, cozy streets that make up the Village), then walk south on La Guardia Place past Houston Street and into **SoHo.** Once the city's main arts neighborhood, it's now a center for fashion and design. Give your credit cards to a designated driver.

Après shopping, walk east to Broadway and catch the downtown R train at either Prince or Canal Street. Get off at Court Street/Borough Hall and exit at the rear of the platform. Ta da! You're in **Brooklyn,** the Borough of Kings. Walk west on Montague Street. This is the heart of **Brooklyn Heights,** a Colonial-era village that's now a protected historic district. Wander off on some of the tree-lined side streets to see beautiful 19th-century homes. At the end of Montague, the **Brooklyn Heights Promenade** lets you onto the most spectacular Manhattan view there is, bar none. To the right, that gorgeous span between the two islands is the **Brooklyn Bridge,** completed in 1883. When built, it was the largest suspension bridge in the world, its two stone towers dwarfing every other structure in the city. To New Yorkers, it's as much a marvel now as then, because even though there are larger bridges, there are few as graceful and beautiful.

The best way to see the bridge is to walk it, and that's what you're going to do next. Walk to the end of the Promenade, up the ramp, past Cranberry Street and the playground, and go through the alley to Middagh Street. Take that to the corner of Cadman Plaza Park, where hand-lettered signs direct you to the **Brooklyn Bridge footpath.** The bridge is about 1¼ miles long, with historical plaques on its two towers and the magnificence of New York all around. Prepare to be amazed.

Back in Manhattan, the bridge lets you off facing **City Hall** and its surrounding park. On the far side, the 1910 **Woolworth Building** was the tallest building in the world until the Chrysler beat it out in 1929, and it remains one of New York's most beautiful. Farther down Broadway, at Fulton Street, **St. Paul's Chapel** is New York's oldest, built in 1766. George Washington prayed here on inauguration day 1789, and in 2001 it served as a refuge for 9/11 rescue workers. Thousands of small memorials left by mourners are preserved inside, along with other displays. The **World Trade Center site,** with its constant bustle of rebuilding, is just behind the church's graveyard.

Walk south to narrow little **Wall Street.** On the corner, **Trinity Church** was founded in 1697, with the present structure dating from 1846. Its small cemetery holds the graves of Alexander Hamilton and other great New Yorkers. One block down Wall is the unprepossessing entrance to the **New York Stock Exchange.** Go to the corner on Broad Street for the more ceremonial view. Next door, a statue of George Washington marks the entrance to **Federal Hall,** a reminder that the first seat of U.S. government sat at this location, from 1789 to 1790. In true New York fashion, it was demolished in 1812 to make room for something new.

At the very tip of Manhattan, **Battery Park** and the streets around were where the Dutch first settled "New Amsterdam" in 1625. The park's centerpiece, **Castle Clinton,** began as a fort during the War of 1812 and later served as New York's immigration facility, welcoming eight million new Americans between 1855 and 1890. You can see its more famous successor, **Ellis Island,** from the waterside, adjacent to the **Statue of Liberty.** Ferries sail to both between 9:30am and 3:30pm, with tickets costing $12 for adults, $4.50 for kids 4 to 12, but you'll have to get here early and be prepared to wait in line. You can also buy ferry tickets in advance at www.circlelinedowntown.com.

SHOPPING

Almost every block in New York City has some interesting shop on it, from up-up-upmarket boutiques to funky little joints. Here's a quick read: The fish and herbal markets along Canal, Mott, Mulberry, and Elizabeth streets in **Chinatown** are fun for their bustle and exotica. Dispersed among them—especially along **Canal Street**—you'll find a mind-boggling collection of knockoff sunglasses and watches, cheap backpacks, discount leather goods, and exotic souvenirs. A definite highlight is the **Pearl River** Chinese emporium, a few blocks north of Canal at 477 Broadway. Going north, **SoHo,** stretching from Broadway east to Sullivan Street, and from Houston down to Broome, is still the epicenter of cutting-edge fashion. Going up even farther, **East Ninth Street** between First and Second avenues is lined with an increasingly smart collection of boutiques that sell excellent-quality original fashions for women.

At Herald Square (where 34th St., Sixth Ave., and Broadway converge), you'll find **Macy's,** the self-proclaimed world's biggest department store. Go in if only to see the classic wooden escalators, which have been running since 1902. At **Times Square,** you can step into Richard Branson's rollicking **Virgin Megastore** and the giant **Toys "R" Us** flagship on Broadway and 44th Street, complete with a 60-foot Ferris wheel. West 47th Street between Fifth and Sixth avenues is the city's famous **Diamond District,** with more than 2,600 retail and wholesale diamond and jewelry businesses. **Tiffany & Co.** reigns supreme at Fifth Avenue and 57th Street, with other big-name, big-ticket designers radiating out from the crossroads, including **Versace, Chanel, Dior,** and **Cartier.** You'll also find big-name jewelers in the area, as well as chichi department stores such as **Bergdorf Goodman, Henri Bendel,** and **Saks Fifth Avenue,** all of which help this stretch of Fifth Avenue maintain its classy cachet.

WHERE TO STAY

There are tons of choices all over town, with rates rarely going below $150 a night, and easily running more than $300, $400, or $500—and we're not even getting into the realm of suites and penthouses. That said, there are often special promotions offered on weekends, when the business travelers have all left town. Here's a sampling of the best hotels at a variety of price points.

If the sky's the limit, try the **Mandarin Oriental New York,** 80 Columbus Circle, at 60th Street (© 212/805-8800; www.mandarinoriental.com). Residing high up in the shiny two-towered Time Warner Center, near the southwest corner of Central Park, it boasts great views from all rooms, plus an elegant decor that marries Asia and urban New York. Rates: from $745. A more classic ultraexpensive choice is the grand dame **St. Regis,** 2 E. 55th St. (© 212/753-4500; www.stregis.com). The Beaux Arts beauty celebrated its 100th anniversary in 2004 and still offers impeccable service and unrivaled luxury, full of Louis XVI furniture, crystal chandeliers, and silk wall coverings. Rates:

from $895. A more affordable classic is the **Waldorf=Astoria,** 301 Park Ave. (© **800/ WALDORF;** www.waldorfastoria.com), with rates from $230.

Le Parker Meridien, 118 W. 57th St. (© **800/543-4300;** www.parkermeridien. com), the perfect blending of style, service, and amenities, is a hotel that delivers on every front. It's the best choice if you want a little of everything: luxury, high-tech, comfort, a family-friendly atmosphere, and a great central location. Rates: from $420.

Ritz-Carlton New York, Central Park, 50 Central Park S. (© **212/308-9100;** www.ritzcarlton.com), offers the upscale chain's typically excellent Ritz service, spacious rooms, understated luxury, and an incredible location overlooking Central Park. Rates: from $650. With artistic interiors and great service, the **Muse,** 130 W. 46th St. (© **877/692-6873** or 212/485-2400; www.themusehotel.com), is the hidden jewel of the Theater District, offering beautiful contemporary decor, good-size rooms with featherbeds, and sumptuous bathrooms. Rates: from $229.

The **Kimberly,** 145 E. 50th St. (© **800/683-0400;** www.kimberlyhotel.com), has great suite deals, with full-fledged one- and two-bedroom apartments—complete with full kitchens—for the same price as most standard Midtown hotels. Free access to a fabulous full-service health club and complimentary sunset cruises in summer add to the incredible value. Rates: from $259. The **Hotel Metro,** 45 W. 35th St. (© **800/ 356-3870;** www.hotelmetronyc.com), is a Midtown gem that offers a surprisingly good deal. Rates: from $175.

For a boutique-hotel experience downtown, the 12-room **Inn at Irving Place,** 56 Irving Place, at East 17th Street (© **800/685-1447** or 212/533-4600; www.innatirving. com), is a jewel, created from two joined brownstone town houses built in 1834. Outside, only the address on the door gives away its location; inside, it's all 19th century, from the period furnishings and Persian rugs to the old-style New York grace, dignity, and charm. Rates: from $415.

DINING & NIGHTLIFE

You can get any type of cuisine imaginable in this foodie city, from steakhouse and seafood to Indian, Thai, Ethiopian, Chinese, Japanese, Korean, Portuguese, Argentinean, German, French . . . you get the picture.

In the lobby of the ornate, Art Deco MetLife building, **Eleven Madison Park,** 11 Madison Ave. (© **212/889-0905;** www.elevenmadisonpark.com), serves hearty French-infused country cuisine in a magnificent, high-ceilinged setting. Main courses: $27 to $36. To get even Frencher, visit **La Grenouille,** 3 E. 52nd St. (© **212/752- 1495;** www.la-grenouille.com), which serves the classics with elegant perfection. Three-course prix-fixe dinner: $95. **Aix,** 2398 Broadway (© **212/874-7400;** www.aix nyc.com), is a trilevel restaurant where chef Didier Virot has put smiles on the faces of West Siders with his novel spin on the cuisine of Provence. Main courses: $25 to $34. In the "best views" category, **Asiate,** 80 Columbus Circle, at 60th Street (© **212/ 805-8881;** www.mandarinoriental.com), in the Mandarin Oriental Hotel, might steal the show at some 34 floors above Central Park. The Japanese/French fare is divine, too. Three-course prix-fixe dinner: $75. If it's Italian you're craving, go downtown to **Babbo,** 110 Waverly Place (© **212/777-0303;** www.babbonyc.com), where Food Network chef Mario Batali has created the ideal setting for his exciting northern Italian cooking. Main courses: $23 to $29. For top Japanese, hands down it's **Nobu,** 105 Hudson St., in TriBeCa (© **212/219-0500;** www.myriadrestaurantgroup.com/nobu), which also happens to have a hand in the menus on Crystal Cruise Lines' three ships. Main courses: $28 to $32.

New York's Best Pizza

Is there anything more New York than pizza? Apparently not, because a Google search for the term nets you about 415,000 hits, whereas "New York bagel" scores only some 60,000 and "New York hot dog" gets a measly 33,000. So, there you have it.

Though there are roughly a zillion pizzerias in the naked city (some 47 of them named Ray's, amazingly enough), four stand head and shoulders above the rest. Up at 116th Street in Spanish Harlem, **Patsy's Pizzeria**, 2287 First Ave. (© **212/534-9783**), has been crafting coal-oven pizza since 1933. Its pies—with a slightly sweet sauce, thin and perfectly baked crust, and fresh mozzarella melted evenly across the top—were a longtime favorite of Frank Sinatra, who reportedly had them flown to out-of-town movie locations and nightclubs when he felt a craving. Down in Brooklyn, **Grimaldi's**, 19 Old Fulton St. (© **718/858-4300**; www.grimaldis.com), was founded by Patsy's nephew in 1990, right in the shadow of the Brooklyn Bridge. Its pizza is probably the best in town, with a thin, smoky crust; pools of fresh, warm mozzarella; chunky yet delicate and savory tomato sauce; fresh basil; and prime-quality toppings like roasted red peppers and sausage. You'll probably have to wait on the sidewalk to get in, but it's worth it. Back in Manhattan, **John's of Bleecker Street**, 278 Bleecker St. (© **212/243-1680**; www.johnsofbleeckerstreet.com), is known for its great crust—not too chewy, not too crispy—with full-spread mozzarella, fresh sauce, and generous toppings. Its interior is woody and lived-in, with a tiled floor, muraled walls, and booths and tables covered with decades of carved initials. Finally, down in what remains of once-vibrant Little Italy, **Lombardi's**, 32 Spring St. (© **212/941-7994**; www.lombardispizza.com), was founded by Gennaro Lombardi, the immigrant grocer from Naples who allegedly invented the American pizza pie in 1905. Today it's a bit touristy, but its pizzas are still fine, their smoky crusts slightly blackened and then daubed with warm blobs of fresh mozzarella, tomato sauce, basil, and miscellaneous toppings.

A large pie at any of these places will run you between $11 and $16, without extra toppings. Eat up: It gets no better than this.

In the Theater District, pre-theater diners can't go wrong with **Aquavit**, 65 E. 55th St. (© **212/307-7311**; www.aquavit.org), which offers a three-course pre-theater menu for $55 (otherwise, it's $80). The light Scandinavian cuisine won't weigh you down in your theater seat. After the show, **Joe Allen**, 326 W. 46th St. (© **212/581-6464**; www.joeallenrestaurant.com), is the ultimate Broadway pub—and the meatloaf is marvelous. Main courses: $17 to $29.

Heading downtown, the **Union Square Cafe**, 21 E. 16th St. (© **212/243-4020**; www.unionsquarecafe.com), is a perennial favorite, serving new American cuisine in a cheerful setting. Main courses: $23 to $34. If it's home cooking you want, go to **Home**, 20 Cornelia St. (© **212/243-9579**), where the cumin-crusted pork chop comes with homemade barbecue sauce that's better than Dad used to make, and even

Mom would tip her hat to the silky-smooth chocolate pudding. Main courses: $18 to $22. Holding the torch for the old Jewish Lower East Side, **Katz's Delicatessen,** 205 E. Houston St. (© **212/254-2246;** www.katzdeli.com), is the choice among those who know their kreplach, knishes, and pastramis. The all-beef wieners are the best in a town known for its dogs. For those keeping score, this is the place Meg Ryan had her fake orgasm in *When Harry Met Sally.* Main courses: $5 to $19.

For Indian food, Sixth Street between First and Second avenues is an entire block of inexpensive Indian eats and over-the-top decor. For something a little fancier, head up to **Pongal,** 110 Lexington Ave. (© **212/696-9458**), one of the mainstays of the Little India section of Murray Hill. Main courses: $8 to $11. For very fancy, try **Tamarind,** 41–43 E. 22nd St. (© **212/674-7400;** www.tamarinde22.com), one of the best Indian restaurants in Manhattan, offering innovative and flavorful variations on the old standards. Main courses: $16 to $33.

When it comes to nightlife in NYC, where to start? There's **Broadway** for world-class shows (and the **TKTS** booth in Times Square for cheap-ish last-minute seats: www.tdf.org/tkts); **Carnegie Hall** and **Lincoln Center** for symphonies, opera, and ballet; **Radio City** for concerts and shows; and the **Blue Note,** at 131 W. Third St., for jazz. The list goes on. Or you could just barhop. Assuming you have only a day or two to sample the Big Apple, downtown has the most interesting options, from tren-doid **TriBeCa** and **SoHo** lounges, where a cosmo goes for the price of a small car, to old-time **Greenwich Village** pubs such as the **Corner Bistro** on Jane Street and **Chumley's** on Bedford Street. If you want a more Woody Allen experience, Second and Third avenues between 72nd and 96th streets have no shortage of bars and restaurants where comfortably well-off uptown intellectuals might feel at home, including **Elaine's,** at 88th Street and Second Avenue.

For listings of currents shows, plays, and live music, check out local publications such as *Time Out New York* (www.timeoutny.com), the *Village Voice* (www.villagevoice.com), the *New Yorker* (www.newyorker.com), and *New York* magazine (www.nymag.com).

13 Norfolk, Virginia

Founded in 1682 on two peninsulas formed by the Chesapeake Bay and the Elizabeth and Lafayette rivers, Norfolk is a major seaport and naval base that's replaced its old sailor bars with a modern, spotless downtown of high-rise offices, condos, and all the marinas, shops, and museums that go with them. Interspersed are reminders of the city's past, such as historic houses and the old City Hall, now a museum and memorial to World War II hero Gen. Douglas MacArthur (who was actually born in Little Rock, Arkansas, but chose to be buried in Norfolk because his mother's ancestors lived here). **Downtown** is on the southern side of the city, on the north bank of the Elizabeth River. Bordering downtown to the northwest, **Freemason** is Norfolk's oldest residential neighborhood, with most of its 18th- and 19th-century town houses restored as private homes, businesses, and restaurants. You'll still find a few cobblestone streets here. Northwest of Freemason, across a semicircular inlet known as the Hague, **Ghent** was the city's first subdivision (most houses in "old" Ghent, near the Hague and the Chrysler Museum of Art, were built between 1892 and 1912) and is now its trendiest enclave. Norfolk is one of the newer alternative home ports, with ships sailing to the Caribbean, The Bahamas, and Bermuda.

GETTING TO NORFOLK & THE PORT

Norfolk is located 190 miles southeast of Washington, D.C., and close to the North Carolina border, making it a convenient port for cruisers in the Mid-Atlantic states. Ships dock at the new **Half Moone Cruise and Celebration Center,** 111 Waterside Dr., at Main Street (© **800/664-1080** or 757/664-1000; www.halfmoone.org), named for a fort built on the site "in the form of a half moone" in the late 17th century. It's just steps from the heart of the city and next door to Nauticus, the National Maritime Center (see "Exploring Norfolk on Your Own," below). If you happen to be flying, you'll land at **Norfolk International Airport,** on Norview Avenue, 1½ miles north of I-64 (© **757/857-3351;** www.norfolkairport.com). The port is about 7 miles away, and you can get there in 10 minutes via **taxi** ($20 one-way). There are also shuttle services and car rentals available at the airport.

By car, take I-64, exit onto 264 West toward downtown Norfolk, and take the Waterside Drive exit (exit 9). The terminal is four lights down on the left. There are two different parking areas, both close to the dock, serving different ships. Parking is $10 per day. For more information, check **www.cruisenorfolk.org**.

GETTING AROUND   A car is the easiest way to get around this spread-out area, though you can walk the downtown area around the port. You'll find **car-rental** agencies at the airport. For a taxi, call **Yellow Cab** (© **757/857-8888**). Rates start at $2.75, with another $1.75 for each mile thereafter.

BEST CRUISE LINE SHORE EXCURSIONS

Norfolk & Virginia Beach Highlights ($42, 3 hr.): There's nothing particularly special about this bus tour, but it's a good bet if you want an overview of the city. You visit the MacArthur Memorial, historic lighthouses, and the First Landing Cross at Cape Henry, where English colonists first came ashore in 1607.

EXPLORING NORFOLK ON YOUR OWN

Right at the port, the large gray building is **Nauticus, the National Maritime Center,** 1 Waterside Dr., at Boush Street (© **800/664-1080;** www.nauticus.org), a museum dedicated to U.S. naval sea power. The star attraction is the 888-foot USS *Wisconsin,* berthed alongside on the Elizabeth River. A real live battleship, it was built in 1943 and saw duty during World War II, the Korean War, and the 1991 Gulf War. It's once again on inactive reserve status, but because it has to be ready to go within 3 months if it's called up, the whole ship is hermetically sealed—meaning you can't go inside. You can, however, walk on board and stare up at the enormous 16-inch guns overhanging its teak main deck. When you leave the *Wisconsin,* you'll walk into the **Hampton Roads Naval Museum** (© **757/444-8921;** www.hrnm.navy.mil), with exhibits describing the Civil War battle between the ironclads *Monitor* and *Merrimac* out on Hampton Roads, as well as more info on the U.S. Navy's Norfolk history. On the other side of the building, the **Tugboat Museum** (© **757/627-4884**) is actually the *Huntington,* a tug built in 1933 and used by the Navy to dock its ships for more than 50 years. The **"Nauticus"** part of the complex is a children's museum on the building's third and fourth floors, with hands-on interactive exhibits and theaters. Admission to the naval museum and battleship is free; to the Tugboat Museum, $2 adults, $1 children; to Nauticus, $9.95 adults, $7 children.

Nearby, the **Waterside** (see "Dining & Nightlife," below) is a general entertainment/shopping/dining area that was one of the first pegs in downtown's revitalization.

Norfolk

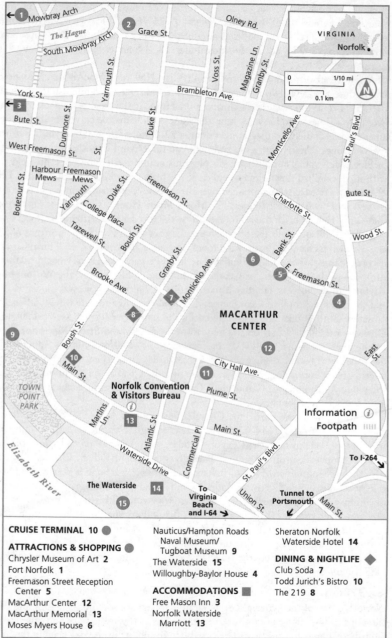

VIRGINIA
Norfolk

0   1/10 mi
0   0.1 km

Mowbray Arch **1**
The Hague
South Mowbray Arch
Grace St. **2**
Olney Rd.
York St.
Bute St. **3**
West Freemason St.
Dunmore St.
Yarmouth St.
Voss St.
Magazine Ln.
Granby St.
Brambleton Ave.
Duke St.
Monticello Ave.
St. Paul's Blvd.
Harbour Mews
Freemason Mews
Botetourt St.
Yarmouth St.
College Place
Duke St.
Freemason St.
Charlotte St.
Bute St.
Wood St.
Tazewell St.
Boush St.
Granby St.
Bank St.
Brooke Ave.
Monticello Ave.
E. Freemason St. **5**
6
7
4
Boush St.
8
9
TOWN POINT PARK
10
Main St.
MACARTHUR CENTER
12
City Hall Ave.
11
Norfolk Convention & Visitors Bureau
Plume St.
East St.
Martins Ln.
13
Atlantic St.
Commercial Pl.
Main St.
St. Paul's Blvd.
Information ⓘ
Footpath ▯▯▯
Elizabeth River
Waterside Drive
The Waterside **14**
15
To Virginia Beach and I-64 →
Union St.
Tunnel to Portsmouth ↓
Main St.
To I-264 ↘

CRUISE TERMINAL 10 ●

ATTRACTIONS & SHOPPING ●
Chrysler Museum of Art **2**
Fort Norfolk **1**
Freemason Street Reception Center **5**
MacArthur Center **12**
MacArthur Memorial **13**
Moses Myers House **6**

Nauticus/Hampton Roads Naval Museum/ Tugboat Museum **9**
The Waterside **15**
Willoughby-Baylor House **4**

ACCOMMODATIONS ■
Free Mason Inn **3**
Norfolk Waterside Marriott **13**

Sheraton Norfolk Waterside Hotel **14**

DINING & NIGHTLIFE ◆
Club Soda **7**
Todd Jurich's Bistro **10**
The 219 **8**

Boats leave from both Nauticus and Waterside for cruises of the harbor. The most charming of these is the ***American Rover*** (© 757/627-7245; www.americanrover. com), a graceful schooner modeled after 19th-century Chesapeake Bay ships. Two-hour cruises cost $12 adults, $8 kids under 12; 3-hour cruises are $16 and $10, respectively.

A few blocks inland, in Norfolk's old City Hall, the **MacArthur Memorial,** MacArthur Square between City Hall Avenue and Plume Street, at Bank Street (© 757/441-2965; www.macarthurmemorial.org), is the final resting place of the World War II hero and his wife, Jean, their side-by-side marble crypts resting beneath an enormous dome. In a theater next door, a 22-minute film will give you a perspective on Douglas MacArthur's life and help you understand the other exhibits, which include MacArthur's famous corncob pipe, his omnipresent sunglasses, his field cap with its sides rolled down, and a replica of the plaque marking the spot on the USS *Missouri* where MacArthur presided over the surrender of Japan. Admission is free.

Nearby are two historic homes: The **Moses Myers House,** 331 Bank St., is a handsome early-Federal brick town house built by the first Jews to settle in Norfolk. They arrived in 1787 and built their home 5 years later. Two Gilbert Stuart portraits of Mr. and Mrs. Myers hang in the drawing room, and some 70% of the overall furniture and decorative arts displayed are original. The fireplace has unusual carvings depicting a sun god—with the features of George Washington. A block away, the **Willoughby-Baylor House/Norfolk History Museum,** 601 E. Freemason St., was built in 1794, and the classic example of Georgian- and Federal-style architecture is now officially a museum. Both houses are administered by the Chrysler Museum (see below), and tours covering both depart on the hour from the **Freemason Street Reception Center,** between the houses at 401 E. Freemason St. (© 800/368-3097). Admission is free; open year-round Wednesday through Saturday from 10am to 4pm, with tours offered on the hour until 3pm. You can also pick up a map at the reception center that will guide you around the **Cannonball Trail,** a walk-it-yourself heritage trail that connects historic sites downtown.

About a mile to the north, the **Chrysler Museum of Art,** 425 W. Olney Rd., at Mowbray Arch (© 757/644-6200; www.chrysler.org), is Virginia's finest art museum, spanning periods from ancient Egypt to today, with outstanding collections of glass and Art Nouveau furniture, as well as exhibits of ancient Indian, Islamic, Oriental, African, pre-Columbian, French, Italian, and American art and a permanent photo gallery. Admission is $7; closed Monday and Tuesday. While you're in this part of town, drop in to **Fort Norfolk,** Front Street (**www.norfolkhistorical.org/fort**; make sure you bring proper ID to do a tour). It's the only survivor of 19 harborfront forts authorized by President George Washington in 1794, and it helped protect Norfolk during the War of 1812. During the Civil War, Confederate forces seized the fort and used its magazine to supply the ironclad *Merrimac* during its famous battle with the USS *Monitor*.

SHOPPING

Norfolk is one of the better places in Virginia to search for antiques, with more than 30 shops selling a range of furniture, decorative arts, glassware, jewelry, and other items, from both home and overseas. The best place to look is in the old neighborhood of **Ghent** (north of the Chrysler Museum), which over the years has transformed from farmland to wealthy residential enclave to bad neighborhood to bohemian center and now to trendy hipville. A number of shops sit along West 21st Street between Colonial Avenue and Granby Street, which also has its own slate of shops.

Downtown Norfolk's centerpiece is the **MacArthur Center,** a $300-million shopping mall built in 1998 and covering the 9 square blocks bordered by Monticello and City Hall avenues, Freemason Street, and St. Paul's Boulevard (© **757/627-6000;** www.shop macarthur.com). The main entry is on Monticello Avenue at Market Street. Anchored by Nordstrom and the largest Dillard's department store in existence, it has most of the mall regulars, an 18-screen cinema, a food court, and full-service restaurants.

WHERE TO STAY

The **Sheraton Norfolk Waterside Hotel,** 777 Waterside Dr. (© **888/625-5144** or 757/622-6664; www.sheraton.com), sits next door to the Waterside, overlooking busy Norfolk Harbor. A contemporary 10-story hotel, it offers spacious rooms furnished with dark-wood furniture, about a third of them with small balconies facing the river. Rates: from $159.

The **Norfolk Waterside Marriott,** 235 E. Main St. (© **800/228-9290;** www. marriott.com), is an elegant 24-story high-rise connected to the Waterside via covered skywalk. It's got a mahogany-paneled 18th-century-style lobby and sumptuously furnished guest rooms. The indoor pool opens to a sun deck overlooking the river. Rates: from $170.

In downtown Norfolk, the **Free Mason Inn Bed & Breakfast,** 411 W. York St. (© **866/388-1897;** www.freemasoninn.com), is a wonderfully renovated turn-of-the-20th-century Victorian home. Rooms are decorated in an elegant English motif, with gas fireplaces, poster beds, and luxury linens. Guests enjoy wine and cheese before dinner in the parlor. Rates: from $149.

DINING & NIGHTLIFE

At Boush Street, opposite the port and Nauticus, **Todd Jurich's Bistro,** 150 Main St. (© **757/622-3210;** www.toddjurichsbistro.com), is one of this region's very best restaurants. It offers creative twists on Southern traditions, such as all-lump-meat crab cakes on brioche with lemon mayonnaise. Everything's made with fresh produce, drawn whenever possible from local farms that practice ecologically sound agriculture. Main courses: $24 to $35.

Norfolk's downtown renaissance has turned the 200 block of **Granby Street** into the town's "Restaurant Row," with a number of notable eateries. The **219,** appropriately at 219 Granby St. (© **757/627-2896**), was a pioneer in downtown's renaissance and is still Granby Street's top restaurant. In fact, its crab cakes are among the best in all of Norfolk. Asian flavors crop up here, too, as in the napa snapper—red snapper with napa cabbage in a lemongrass broth. You also can opt for one-person pizzas with usual and unusual toppings. There's always a vegetarian selection such as tofu fried in a spicy chili and garlic sauce. Main courses: $13 to $22.

For a little after-dinner nightlife (or casual dinner, for that matter), try the **Waterside Festival Marketplace** (aka "The Waterside"), between Waterside Drive and the Elizabeth River (© **757/627-3300**). This was the catalyst for downtown Norfolk's revitalization, and though the MacArthur Center has eclipsed it as a shopping mecca, it's still an after-dark dining-and-entertainment destination, with bars, comedy clubs, restaurants, and live music. You may also want to check out **Club Soda,** 111 Tazewell St. (© **757/200-SODA**), an ultrahappening spot along Norfolk's "Restaurant Row."

14 Philadelphia, Pennsylvania

Philadelphia today is an inseparable mix of old and new. Scratch the surface of William Penn's "green countrie towne" and you'll find both a wealth of history and plenty of modern distractions. Philadelphia has the largest surviving district of original Colonial homes and shops in the country, with dozens of treasures in and around Independence National Historical Park. It boasts the most historic square mile in America, the place where the United States was conceived, declared, and ratified—and the city and federal governments are investing heavily to show this area off and teach its lessons. Philadelphia also offers some of the best dining values and several of the finest restaurants in America. The city is a stroller's paradise of restored Georgian and Federal structures integrated with smart shops and contemporary row-house courts to create a working urban environment. It's a center of professional and amateur sports, with more than 9,800 acres of parkland within the city limits. It's a city filled with art, crafts, and music for every taste, with boulevards made for street fairs and parades all year long. From its row-house boutiques to the Second Continental Congress's favorite tavern, from an Ivy League campus to street artists and musicians, from gleaming skyscrapers to the gritty Italian Market, Philadelphia is a city of the unexpected.

GETTING TO PHILADELPHIA & THE PORT

Ships dock at Pier 1 of the **Philadelphia Cruise Terminal,** 5100 S. Broad St. (© **856/ 968-2052,** or 215/462-6790 on the day of your cruise), on the site of the former Philadelphia Naval Base, one of the nation's oldest naval facilities. Though you can't walk to much of anything from the mostly industrial port area, a short **taxi** ride away are a host of treasures. If you're flying in, the **Philadelphia International Airport** (© **215/937-6800** or 215/937-6937; www.phl.org) is about 7 miles from downtown Philadelphia and less than 10 minutes from the Philadelphia Cruise Terminal at Pier 1. The airport is easily accessible from Interstates 76, 95, and 476.

Those driving in from points north or south of the city (especially New Jersey) should take I-95 to exit 17 (Broad St.). If you're arriving from the south, stay to the left and turn left at the first traffic light onto Zinkoff Boulevard. At the next light, make a quick left onto Broad Street South and continue straight toward the entrance to the Naval Yard. You'll then be directed to turn left onto League Island Boulevard, where you'll find signs directing you to the parking and drop-off location. From points north, turn left at the second traffic light onto Broad Street and continue to the terminal. Signs will direct you to the parking and drop-off areas. If you're driving in from the west, take I-76 east to exit 349 (Broad St.). Bear right at the end of the offramp onto Broad Street South; it's 1 mile to the terminal. For more extensive driving directions from other locations, see **www.cruisephilly.org**. The parking facility charges $10 per day, up front. All vehicle passengers must show a photo ID.

GETTING AROUND   There may not be any taxis waiting at the terminal, but you can call one of these companies: **Olde City Cab** (© 215/338-0838), **City Cab Company** (© 215/492-6500), or **Quaker City Cab** (© 215/728-8000). The meter starts at $2.70 and adds $2.10 for each additional mile.

SEPTA (Southeastern Pennsylvania Transportation Authority; © **215/580-7800;** www.septa.org) operates an extensive network of trolleys, buses, commuter trains, and subways. If you have trouble getting a taxi, SEPTA shuttle bus no. 71 runs frequently between the terminal area and the Pattison Avenue subway stop on Broad Street, about 2 miles away. In Center City, the Rapid Transit subway cars speed under Broad Street (called the Broad St. line) and Market Street (called the Market–Frankford El), intersecting under City Hall, while the city's buses go pretty much everywhere tourists want to go. Visitors might find it easiest to get to know the city via the purple **PHLASH buses** (www.phillyphlash.com), which depart and pick up from attractions and key Center City locations every 12 minutes between 10am and 6pm (May 1–Nov 30). PHLASH buses link Independence Park sites, the Delaware waterfront, the Convention Center, Rittenhouse Square shopping, and the Philadelphia Museum of Art. The total loop takes 50 minutes and makes 20 stops. A one-time pass is $1, but get the all-day unlimited-ride pass for $4, or pay $10 for an all-day pass for a family of four. SEPTA also has an all-day $5.50 fare for city buses, but the two systems *do not* accept each other's passes. Children under 6 ride free on both systems. There are also free shuttle trolleys between the Cruise Terminal and parking facilities.

BEST CRUISE LINE SHORE EXCURSIONS

Philly Highlights ($45, 3 hr.): Because Philadelphia is almost exclusively an embarkation port, most lines offer only the standard city highlights tour for those flying out after about 2 or 3pm. Traveling by bus, you'll pass by Franklin Court, the site of Benjamin Franklin's home; Elfreth's Alley, an oasis of early-18th-century houses believed to be the nation's oldest continuously inhabited street; seamstress Betsy Ross's tiny home on Arch Street, with the Stars and Stripes waving outside; and the impressive Colonial Christ Church. Your scenic drive will take you past Independence National Historic Park and the famous Liberty Bell, plus Independence Hall, where the Declaration of Independence was adopted, and on to Congress Hall, which housed the U.S. legislature between 1790 and 1800 when Philadelphia was the capital city. You'll make a brief stop at the Park Visitor Center before proceeding to the Benjamin Franklin Parkway, a gracious green diagonal modeled after the Champs-Elysées in Paris, connecting City Hall, the nation's largest municipal building, to the famous Philadelphia Art Museum, which resembles a Greek temple. The tour ends at Philadelphia International Airport.

EXPLORING PHILADELPHIA ON YOUR OWN

Consider Philadelphia's sightseeing possibilities: the most historic square mile in America; more than 90 museums; innumerable Colonial churches, row houses, and mansions; an Ivy League campus; and leafy, distinguished green spaces, including Fairmount Park, the largest park within city limits in the United States. Philadelphia has come a long way since 1876, when a guidebook recommended seeing the new Public Buildings at Broad and Market streets, the Naval Yards, the old YMCA, and the fortresslike prison (which is still a tourist sight as the Eastern State Penitentiary!).

Most of what you'll want to see within the city falls inside a rectangle on the map: between the Delaware and Schuylkill rivers in width, and between South and Vine streets in height. It's easy to organize your days into walking tours of various parts of the city; nothing is that far away. A stroll from City Hall (about 5 miles from the cruise terminal) to the Philadelphia Museum of Art takes about 25 minutes, although the flags and flowers along the Parkway will undoubtedly sidetrack you. A walk down Market or one of the "tree" streets (Chestnut, Spruce, Pine, Locust) to Independence National Historical Park and Society Hill should take a little less time—but it probably won't, as there's so much to entice you on the way. If you'd rather ride, the spiffy PHLASH buses loop past most major attractions about every 12 minutes.

Philadelphia

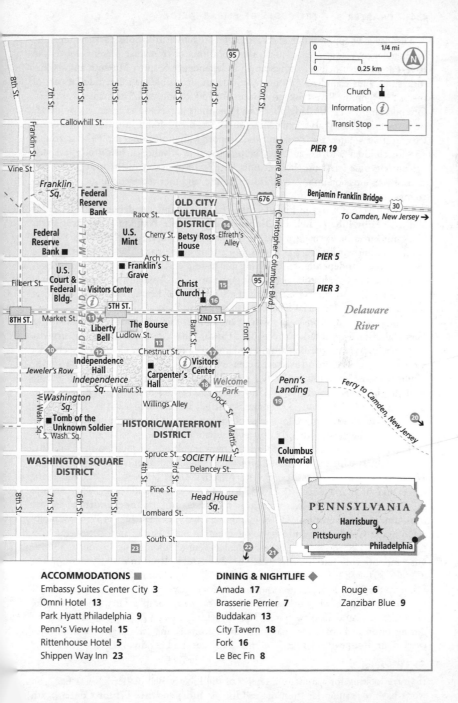

ACCOMMODATIONS ■
Embassy Suites Center City **3**
Omni Hotel **13**
Park Hyatt Philadelphia **9**
Penn's View Hotel **15**
Rittenhouse Hotel **5**
Shippen Way Inn **23**

DINING & NIGHTLIFE ◆
Amada **17**
Brasserie Perrier **7**
Buddakan **13**
City Tavern **18**
Fork **16**
Le Bec Fin **8**

Rouge **6**
Zanzibar Blue **9**

The city is wrapping some of its attractions together in various packages, and the Independence Visitor Center and other locations offer several passes. One is the **RiverPass,** which includes admission to Independence Seaport Museum and its historic ships, plus Camden's Adventure Aquarium, accessible via a free ride (as part of the package) on the RiverLink ferry; prices are $30 for adults, $27 for seniors, and $25 for children 3 to 12. **Philadelphia CityPass** offers admission to seven major attractions, including the Philadelphia Museum of Art, the Franklin Institute, the National Constitution Center, the Zoo, and the Seaport Museum; passes are $47 for adults, $33 for children 3 to 12, and may be purchased in advance at **http://citypass.net/ cgi-bin/citypass** (click on "Philadelphia CityPass") or at any of the included attractions. Passes are good up to 9 days from first use, and they represent about a 50% discount over full admission prices.

If you have just 1 day in Philadelphia, start at the **Independence Visitor Center** and the nearby **Liberty Bell Pavilion** in **Independence National Historical Park,** Chestnut Street between Fifth and Sixth (© 215/965-2305 or 215/297-8787; free admission, but you'll need a ticket to join a tour of the park Mar–Dec), then move south through **Independence Hall** and on to residential **Society Hill,** a neighborhood steeped in U.S. history. See what's going on at the Academy of Music, the Kimmel Center, the Annenberg Center at the University of Pennsylvania, the Wachovia Spectrum, Lincoln Financial Field, or Citizens Bank Park.

If you've got a couple days in town, spend one on this self-guided tour: Starting at **City Hall,** Broad and Market streets (© 215/686-2840; www.phila.gov/property/virtualcityhall), walk up the Benjamin Franklin Parkway to Logan Circle and spend the afternoon at the **Franklin Institute Science Museum,** 222 N. 20th St. (© 215/448-1200; www.fi.edu; admission varies depending on what you want to see), or the **Philadelphia Museum of Art,** at 26th Street (© 215/763-8100; www.philamuseum. org; admission: $10 adults, $7 seniors, students, and children 12–18). Try to circle back to **Rittenhouse Square** for a glass of wine at one of the parkside bistros, or a nibble at any of the neighborhood's dozens of restaurants.

If you're in town for 3 days, spend the morning of one of them in the Old City, viewing **Christ Church,** on Second Street, half a block north of Market (© 215/922-1695; www.christchurchphila.org), and **Elfreth's Alley,** between Second and Front streets and Arch and Race (© 215/574-0560; www.elfrethsalley.org). Then explore the expanding Delaware River waterfront attractions and the **Independence Seaport Museum,** Penn's Landing at 211 S. Columbus Blvd. (© 215/925-5439; www.philly seaport.org). Combined admission to the museum and Historic Ship Zone—the USS *Olympia* and USS *Becuna* are both berthed at Penn's Landing—is $9 adults, $8 seniors, and $6 children. Finally, visit the **Adventure Aquarium,** 1 Aquarium Dr. (© 866/451-2782; www.adventureaquarium.com; admission: $17 adults, $14 kids), formerly the New Jersey State Aquarium and recently renovated to the tune of $40 million, and the newly docked battleship *New Jersey,* both a ferry ride across the Delaware in Camden, New Jersey. The **RiverLink Ferry** (© 215/925-LINK) runs during business hours every day in summer from Penn's Landing, with departures every hour. Round-trip fare is $6 adults, $5 seniors and children.

SHOPPING

If you're looking for a miniature replica of the Liberty Bell or Betsy Ross's flag, you won't have to wander far from the real things: **Independence Visitor Center,** Sixth and Market streets (© 800/537-7676 or 215/965-7676; www.independencevisitor center.com), has a great gift shop—so, for that matter, do the Betsy Ross House and Franklin Court. If it's fashion, home goods, or art you seek, however, your best bets are the shops around **Rittenhouse Square,** 18th and Walnut streets, and **Old City.** Around the former, a mall's worth of upscale chains is peppered with independently owned galleries and boutiques. The latter offers a surprisingly SoHo-like array of stylish shops run by local designers and artists; most Old City shops run along Second and Third streets, from Chestnut Street to Vine Street. For more old-world items, **Antique Row,** along Pine Street from 9th Street to 13th Street, offers a quaint and quirky assortment of shelter stores, antiquaries, and gift shops. A few blocks south, **South Street,** just south of Society Hill, has long been a gathering spot for the younger set who flock here to shop for sneakers, T-shirts, skateboards, hip-hop gear, inexpensive grub—and new mates.

It's useful to note that the outskirts (mainly the north) of Philadelphia contain prime examples of the enormous malls now ubiquitous at the interchanges of American superhighways—the 21st-century version of Colonial village squares. You'll find all the luxury chains, and even some branches of downtown Philly's gems, at the **King of Prussia Mall** (© 610/265-5727; www.kingofprussia.com)—a 400-plus-store behemoth, second only to Minnesota's Mall of America, and about a 30- to 60-minute drive from downtown—and at **Franklin Mills** (© 610/632-1500; www.franklin-mills-mall.com), an outlet mall that draws four times the traffic of the Liberty Bell, and about 25 to 35 minutes away.

WHERE TO STAY

For historic accommodations, the top floor of the **Park Hyatt Philadelphia at the Bellevue,** Broad and Walnut streets (© 800/223-1234; www.parkphiladelphia.hyatt. com), with its occasionally oddly proportioned rooms, carries traces of a century's worth of history (Thomas Edison designed the fixtures). Rates: from $265. They may not have the history, but rooms at the luxurious **Rittenhouse Hotel,** 210 W. Rittenhouse Sq. (© 800/635-1042; www.rittenhousehotel.com), in Center City, offer wonderful views of the Philly landscape, Aveda toiletries in the marble bathrooms, and plush furnishings. Rates: from $310.

Why not wake up to a view of Independence Park through the floral chintz curtains at the **Omni Hotel at Independence Park,** Fourth and Chestnut streets (© 800/843-6664; www.omnihotels.com)? All of this European-style hotel's guest rooms have views of the Greek Revival Second Bank of the U.S. and a half-dozen of America's Georgian jewels. Rates: from $217. The upper floors of the 52-room **Penn's View Hotel,** Front and Market streets (© 800/331-7634; www.pennsviewhotel.com), feel like an exquisite club, with views over the Delaware River. All units are richly decorated with Chippendale-inspired furnishings. Rates: from $120. The oversized and moderately priced lodgings at the **Embassy Suites Center City,** 1776 Benjamin Franklin Pkwy. at Logan Square (© 800/362-2779; www.embassysuites.com), come with cute little open-air balconies (yes, the railings are sturdy). All units are suites with separate bedrooms and living rooms, so parents can have their privacy. Rates: $217.

There are many B&Bs in Philly, but one standout is the **Shippen Way Inn,** 418 Bainbridge St. (© 800/245-4873 or 215/627-7266; www.shippenway.com), a tiny row house in Queen Village built around 1750 and lovingly maintained. Rates: from $105.

DINING & NIGHTLIFE

Philadelphia's restaurants and bars have serious range. Visitors to any section of Center City will have an easy time finding both cozy one-room bistros and sprawling theaters of haute cuisine, chic after-work hangouts and divey corner pubs, romantic candlelit lounges and throbbing temples of cocktail hipness.

Diners who want the latest and greatest in cutting-edge fare would do well to head to **Rittenhouse Square** and **Old City.** Both neighborhoods are dense with dining, with Rittenhouse Square tending toward the buttoned-down business and business-school crowd, and Old City attracting a stylish mix of artsy types and resolute barhoppers. Favorites around Rittenhouse Square include bistro **Rouge,** 205 S. 18th St. (© 215/732-6622), a 1920s-style parlor bistro with an impeccable sidewalk cafe and an even more impeccable crowd (and a splurgy $15 burger). Also nearby: the famed **Le Bec-Fin,** 1523 Walnut St. (© 215/567-1000; www.lebecfin.com; fixed-price dinners: from $135), chef Georges Perrier's five-star homage to the finest of French service and cuisine, along with its younger, less formal sibling, **Brasserie Perrier,** 1619 Walnut St. (© 215/568-3000; www.brasserieperrier.com; main courses: $24–$40), for steak frites and bordeaux.

Old City's most popular eateries include **Buddakan,** 325 Chestnut St. (© 215/574-9440; www.buddakan.com), where a giant gilded Buddha lords over family-style meals of wok-fried lobster and chocolate pagodas. Main courses: $16 to $28. At neighboring **Amada,** 214–216 Chestnut St. (© 215/625-2450; www.amadarestaurant. com), edgy Spanish tapas-style meals come with a side of live flamenco dancing. Tapas dishes: $5 to $32. A romantic escape from showier spots is lovely **Fork,** 306 Market St. (© 215/625-9425; www.forkrestaurant.com), where the worldly menu largely consists of locally produced ingredients. Main courses: $18 to $33. Also in this historic district, the historically correct **City Tavern,** 138 S. Second St., near Walnut Street (© 215/413-1443; www.citytavern.com), is modeled after the same site where Adams, Washington, and the others hammered out our nation over pints of beer. Today, the restaurant replicates a slightly more genteel atmosphere, with 18th-century-recipe potpies and cakes. Main courses: $19 to $29.

Along the Avenue of the Arts (Broad St.) in the very center of town, among the many recognizable chains—Applebee's, Olive Garden, Italian Bistro, McCormick and Schmick's—are a few evening-out gems. Underneath the Park Hyatt at the Bellevue is **Zanzibar Blue,** 200 S. Broad St. (© 215/732-5200; www.zanzibarblue.com), where diners sup on global cuisine and listen to amazing live jazz. Main courses: $19 to $26.

15 San Diego, California

San Diego is best known for its benign climate and fabulous beaches, which combined make the city one big playground on sunny days. With 70 miles of sandy coastline—plus pretty, sheltering Mission Bay—you can choose from a whole slew of watersports, plus biking or skating around splendid Balboa Park, one of the finest urban oases in the country. San Diego was the very first European settlement on the west coast of America, and though it spent a lot of years being looked down on as a conservative, slow-growth Navy town, it's been coming to life over the past decade and a half. Today, the city in the bottom-left corner of the U.S. boasts a diverse population and revitalized neighborhoods, and although its population is 1.3 million and rising, you'll

San Diego

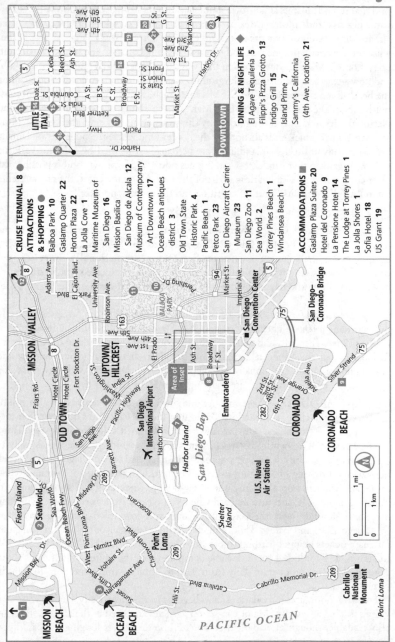

CRUISE TERMINAL 8 ●

ATTRACTIONS & SHOPPING ●

Balboa Park **10**
Gaslamp Quarter **22**
Horton Plaza **22**
La Jolla Cove **1**
Maritime Museum of San Diego **16**
Mission Basilica San Diego de Alcala **12**
Museum of Contemporary Art Downtown **17**
Ocean Beach antiques district **3**
Old Town State Historic Park **4**
Pacific Beach **1**
Petco Park **23**
San Diego Aircraft Carrier Museum **23**
San Diego Zoo **11**
Sea World **2**
Torrey Pines Beach **1**
Windansea Beach **1**

ACCOMMODATIONS ■

Gaslamp Plaza Suites **20**
Hotel del Coronado **9**
La Pensione Hotel **14**
The Lodge at Torrey Pines **1**
La Jolla Shores **1**
Sofia Hotel **18**
US Grant **19**

DINING & NIGHTLIFE ◆

El Agave Tequileria **5**
Filippi's Pizza Grotto **13**
Indigo Grill **15**
Island Prime **7**
Sammy's California (4th Ave. location) **21**

Downtown

LITTLE ITALY

find that it hasn't lost its small-town ambience, nor its strong connection with its Hispanic heritage and culture. (Mexico, remember, is just 16 miles to the south.)

San Diego's **downtown** sits at the edge of San Diego Bay, a large natural harbor with flat Coronado on one side and peninsular Point Loma on the other. North from Point Loma is **Mission Bay,** a lagoon that was carved out of tidal estuary in the 1940s, and now serves as a watersports playground. A series of communities are found along the beach-lined coast: Ocean Beach, Mission Beach, Pacific Beach, La Jolla, and, just outside San Diego's city limits, Del Mar. To the south of downtown you'll find **National City,** which is distinguished by shipyards on its bay side, then Chula Vista, and San Ysidro, which ends abruptly at the border (and where the huge city of Tijuana begins, equally abruptly). Inland areas are perhaps best defined by **Mission Valley,** a mile-wide canyon that runs east–west, 2 miles north of downtown, and is possibly the most congested and least charming part of the city. Along the coast, the city stretches up to **La Jolla,** with its beautiful coastline and filthy-rich populace.

GETTING TO SAN DIEGO & THE PORT

San Diego's **B Street Cruise Ship Terminal** is at 1050 N. Harbor Dr., right in the heart of downtown (© 619/686-6200; www.portofsandiego.org). If you're arriving by air, you'll probably touch down at the **San Diego International Airport** (© 619/231-2100; www.san.org), also called Lindbergh Field. It's located just northwest of downtown, along the bay and close to the piers. Metered **taxis** charge about $8 to the port.

If you're coming by car on the I-5 southbound, take the Front Street exit, stay in the right lane for two lights, turn right at Ash Street, and follow until it dead-ends at Harbor Drive. Turn left, and you'll see the pier on your right. Parking is available for $14 per day at the Lane Field facility on Broadway between Pacific Highway and North Harbor Drive. Additionally, several park-and-ride lots serve both the cruise ship terminal and the airport, with rates ranging from $9 to $24 per day.

GETTING AROUND   Those staying for a short time in the downtown area will be able to cover the close-in attractions (including Balboa Park and Old Town) on foot or by using the city buses. You can also try the narrated **Old Town Trolley Tours** (© 619/298-8687; www.historictours.com/sandiego), which provide an easy way to get an overview of the city and tie together visits to several of San Diego's major attractions without driving or resorting to cabs. The trackless trolleys do a 30-mile circular route, and you can hop off at any one of eight stops (including one at the cruise terminal), explore at leisure, and reboard when you please. Trolleys run every half-hour. Stops include Old Town, the Gaslamp Quarter and downtown area, Coronado, the San Diego Zoo, and Balboa Park. You can begin wherever you want, but you must purchase tickets before boarding (most stops have a ticket kiosk). The tour costs $30 for adults, $15 for kids 4 to 12, for one complete loop; the route by itself takes about 2 hours. The trolleys operate daily from 9am to 4pm in winter and 9am to 5pm in summer.

For attractions, accommodations, and beaches in the greater city, having your own wheels is a big advantage. Major **car-rental** agencies are based at the airport. Taxis are also available, though after dark they don't cruise the streets looking for passengers (except in the Gaslamp Quarter). If you need one, call ahead. Among the local companies are **Orange Cab** (© 619/291-3333), **San Diego Cab** (© 619/226-TAXI), and **Yellow Cab** (© 619/234-6161). The **Coronado Cab Company** (© 935/435-6211) serves Coronado. Rates are $2.20 for the first ¹⁄₁₀ mile and $2.30 for each additional mile.

BEST CRUISE LINE SHORE EXCURSIONS

SeaWorld ($65, 7 hr.): San Diego's SeaWorld Adventure Park is one of the largest and best marine-life parks in the world. While this tour is about $10 to $20 more than the park's admission price, it's a viable option if you don't want to worry about arranging your own transportation.

Coronado Cycling Tour ($35, 3½ hr.): From the ship, you'll take a bus and then ferry over to Coronado, where you'll set off on a ride to visit Glorietta Bay, the world-famous Hotel del Coronado, and Ocean Boulevard with its Victorian mansions and white-sand beaches.

Whale-Watching ($25, 3½ hr.): This fully narrated trip departs right from the pier and heads out in search of Pacific gray whales, which pass San Diego on their 6,000-mile migration from the Arctic to the Baja Coast. This is a seasonal tour that operates from mid-December through the end of March.

EXPLORING SAN DIEGO ON YOUR OWN

Unless you head to the beaches, you'll probably spend most of your time in **downtown** and **Old Town.** The business, shopping, dining, and entertainment heart of the city, the downtown area encompasses the Embarcadero (waterfront), the Gaslamp Quarter, Horton Plaza (see "Shopping," below), the Convention Center, San Diego's Little Italy, and other areas. A **Visitor Information Center** (© 619/236-1212) is located right across the street from the cruise terminal at the corner of Harbor Drive and West Broadway.

Right on the waterfront, just a few blocks north of the cruise terminal, is a flotilla of ships that compose the **Maritime Museum of San Diego,** 1492 N. Harbor Dr. (© 619/234-9153; www.sdmaritime.com). The full-rigged merchant vessel *Star of India* dates from 1863, its impressive masts an integral part of the San Diego cityscape. The gleaming white steam-powered ferry *Berkeley* (1898) once ran the route between San Francisco and Oakland, and worked round-the-clock to carry people to safety following the 1906 San Francisco earthquake. The sleek *Medea* (1904) is one of the world's few remaining large steam yachts. Other vessels include the HMS *Surprise,* the replica 18th-century Royal Navy frigate used in the film *Master and Commander.* You can board and explore each vessel and also check out the collection of maritime artifacts at the museum proper. Admission is $12 adults, $8 kids.

Along the same stretch of the harbor, the **San Diego Aircraft Carrier Museum,** 910 Harbor Dr., at Navy Pier (© 619/544-9600; www.midway.org), is actually the aircraft carrier *Midway,* commissioned in 1945 and a veteran of Vietnam and Gulf War I. In all, more than 225,000 men served aboard the vessel. A self-guided audio tour takes visitors to several levels of the ship, telling the story of life on board. The highlight is climbing up the superstructure to the bridge and gazing down on the 1,001-foot-long flight deck, with various aircraft poised for duty. What really brings the experience to life are the occasional graffiti and other reminders left by the crew. Admission is $15 adults, $10 seniors and veterans, $8 kids 6 to 12. Guided tours are available for an additional cost.

Visitors looking for something less nautical can head across Harbor Drive to the Santa Fe Depot and check out the city's latest cultural landmark, the **Museum of**

Contemporary Art San Diego Downtown, 1100 Kettner Blvd. (© **858/454-3541;** www.mcasd.org). Its gallery spaces were built in 1915 as the baggage building for the historic train station, and now feature permanent, commissioned pieces by artists Richard Serra and Jenny Holzer, along with exhibitions of world-class contemporary art. Admission is $10.

A National Historic District covering 16½ city blocks, San Diego's **Gaslamp Quarter** contains many Victorian-style commercial buildings built between the Civil War and World War I. The center of a massive redevelopment kicked off in the mid-1980s with the opening of the Horton Plaza shopping complex; the once-seedy area is now packed with trendy boutiques, restaurants, and nightspots. Lit by electric versions of old gas lamps, the Gaslamp Quarter lies between Fourth Avenue to the west, Sixth Avenue to the east, Broadway to the north, and L Street and the waterfront to the south. It makes for good walking and shopping during the day, but the real action here is at night. Immediately southeast of the Gaslamp Quarter is the newish **PETCO Park,** home of the San Diego Padres.

At the northeast edge of downtown lies **Balboa Park,** one of San Diego's true treasures, sitting on a 1,200-acre square that contains the San Diego Zoo, more than a dozen museums, a classic carousel, wonderful gardens, and splendid architecture. Stop by the **Balboa Park Visitor Center,** located in the House of Hospitality (© **619/239-0512;** www.balboapark.org), to learn about free walking and museum tours, or to pick up a brochure about the gardens. Balboa was established in 1868 in the heart of the city, fringed by the early communities of Hillcrest and Golden Hill to the north and east. Tree plantings started in the late 19th century, while the initial buildings were created to host the 1915–16 Panama–California International Exposition; another expo in 1935–36 brought additional developments. The park is divided by Highway 163 into two distinct sections. The narrow western wing is largely grassy open areas that parallel Sixth Avenue. It's a good place for picnics, strolling, and sunning. The main portion of the park, east of 163, contains all of the park's 15 museums (many of them in the beautiful Spanish Colonial Revival buildings that line **El Prado,** the park's east–west thoroughfare) and is bordered by Park Boulevard. This is also where you'll find the world-famous **San Diego Zoo,** 2920 Zoo Dr. (© **619/231-1515;** www.sandiegozoo.org), operated by the Zoological Society of San Diego. Founded in 1916 with a handful of animals originally brought here for that same Panama–California Exposition, the zoo now has more than 4,000 creatures in residence, including four giant pandas from the People's Republic of China, wild Przewalski horses from Mongolia, Buerger's tree kangaroos from New Guinea, lowland gorillas from Africa, and giant tortoises from the Galapagos, as well as more than 700,000 plants. The park's Children's Zoo features a nursery with baby animals and a petting area where kids can cuddle up to sheep, goats, and the like. Admission is $23 for adults, $16 for kids 3 to 11. The "best value" package, including a guided bus tour and aerial tram ride, is $33 for adults, $22 for kids.

Northwest of the park, heading toward Mission Bay, is San Diego's **Old Town,** where the first European settlement of California took place. It's the Williamsburg of the West, allowing you to go back to a time of one-room schoolhouses and village greens, when many of the people who lived, worked, and played here spoke Spanish. Even today, life moves more slowly in this part of the city, where the buildings are old or built to look that way. At the **Old Town State Historic Park,** on San Diego Avenue and Twiggs Street (© **619/220-5422;** www.parks.ca.gov), you don't have to look hard or very far to see the past. Dedicated to re-creating the early life of the city from 1821 to 1872, this is where San Diego's Mexican heritage shines brightest. Seven of the park's 20 structures are original, including homes made of adobe; the rest are reconstructed. The park's headquarters is at the **Robinson-Rose House,** 4002 Wallace St., where you can pick up a map and peruse a model of Old Town as it looked in 1872. Among the park's attractions are **La Casa de Estudillo,** which depicts the living conditions of a wealthy family in 1872; and **Seeley Stables,** named after A. L. Seeley, who ran the stagecoach and mail service in these parts from 1867 to 1871. On Wednesdays, costumed park volunteers re-enact life in the 1800s with cooking and crafts demonstrations, a working blacksmith, and parlor singing. Free 1-hour walking tours are available daily from the Robinson-Rose House. The stillness inside the state park is palpable, especially at night, when you can stroll the unpaved streets and look up at the stars. Admission is free.

Not far from Old Town lies the vast suburban sprawl of **Mission Valley.** Until I-8 was built in the 1950s, it was little more than cow pastures with a couple of dirt roads, but shopping malls, motels, a golf course, condos, car dealerships, and a massive sports stadium fill the expanse today, following the San Diego River upstream to the **Mission Basilica San Diego de Alcalá,** 10818 San Diego Mission Rd. (© **619/281-8449;** www.missionsandiego.com). Established in 1769 above Old Town, this was the first link in a chain of 21 missions founded by Spanish missionary Junípero Serra. It was moved to its present location in 1774 for agricultural reasons, and to separate Native American converts from the fortress that included the original building. The mission was burned by Indians a year after it was built, and when Father Serra rebuilt it, he used 5- to 7-foot-thick adobe walls and clay tile roofs—making it less likely to burn again, and in the process inspiring a bevy of 20th-century California architects. It's still an active Catholic parish, and Mass is said daily. Admission is $3.

Head back west toward the water to experience **Mission Bay,** where someone probably took the picture on the postcards you'll send home. Mission Bay is a watery playground perfect for water-skiing, sailing, and windsurfing. The adjacent communities of Ocean Beach, Mission Beach, and Pacific Beach are known for their wide stretches of sand, active nightlife, and casual dining. This is the place to stay if you want to walk barefoot on the sand or are traveling with beach-loving children, and it's also home to **SeaWorld,** 500 Sea World Dr. (© **800/380-3203;** www.seaworld.com), one of the big draws for many visitors to San Diego. Owned by Anheuser-Busch, the 189-acre aquatic theme park features performing dolphins, otters, sea lions, walruses, and seals. Several successive 4-ton black-and-white killer whales have held the role of **Shamu,** the park's mascot, performing in two shows: **"Believe"** and **"Shamu Rocks,"** a new nighttime production that debuted in spring 2007, incorporating concert lighting and contemporary music. There's also a slapstick sea lion show called "Clyde and Seamore's Risky Rescue," a fast-paced dolphin show, and others. Admission costs $56 for adults, $46 for kids 3 to 9. Discount packages that combine SeaWorld with admission to the San Diego Zoo (see above) are available.

BEACHES

San Diego County is blessed with 70 miles of sandy coastline and more than 30 individual beaches that cater equally to surfers, snorkelers, swimmers, sailors, divers, walkers, volleyballers, and sunbathers. Here are some of the best, moving south to north.

Lovely, wide, and sparkling, **Coronado Beach** is conducive to strolling and lingering, especially in the late afternoon. Waves are gentle here, so the beach draws many

Coronado families. South of Mission Bay is **Ocean Beach,** a hot spot for surfers, though the water can be rough for swimming. Above Mission, there's always action at **Pacific Beach,** particularly along Ocean Front Walk, a paved promenade similar to L.A.'s funky Venice Beach promenade. Surfing is popular year-round here, in marked sections, and the beach is well staffed with lifeguards. Just north, **Windansea Beach** is legendary among California's surf elite and remains one of San Diego's prettiest strands. Reached by way of Bonair Street (at Neptune Place), it has no facilities and isn't really ideal for swimming. Come to surf, watch surfers, and soak up the party atmosphere. Up in rich La Jolla, the calm, protected waters of **La Jolla Cove** (part of the San Diego–La Jolla Underwater Park Ecological Reserve) attract snorkelers and scuba divers, along with a fair share of families to its small beach. The park's "look but don't touch" policy protects the colorful garibaldi, California's state fish, plus other marine life, including abalone, octopus, and lobster. The Underwater Park stretches from here to the northern end of Torrey Pines State Reserve, at the southern end of which you'll find **Torrey Pines Beach,** a fabulous underused strand, accessed by a pay parking lot ($6 weekdays, $8 weekends) at the entrance to the park. It's rarely crowded, though be aware that at high tide most of the sand gets a soaking. In almost any weather, it's a great beach for walking.

SHOPPING

Downtown, **Horton Plaza,** 324 Horton Plaza (© **619/239-8180;** www.westfield. com/hortonplaza), is the Disneyland of shopping malls and the heart of the revitalized city center, bounded by G Street, Broadway, and First and Fourth avenues. Covering 6½ city blocks, the multilevel shopping center has more than 180 stores, including major department stores, clothing and shoe stores, art galleries, bookstores, and fun shops for kids, plus a 14-screen cinema and a variety of restaurants and short-order eateries. It's almost as much an attraction as SeaWorld or the San Diego Zoo, transcending its genre with a conglomeration of rambling paths, bridges, towers, piazzas, sculptures, fountains, and live greenery. Performers provide background entertainment throughout the year.

North of downtown, compact **Hillcrest** is the hub of San Diego's gay and lesbian community. As such, swank inspiration and chic housewares rule, with scads of places selling used books, vintage clothing, trinkets, and memorabilia. You'll also see some chain stores, bakeries, cafes, and an array of modestly priced globe-hopping dining options. For antiques, head for the **Ocean Beach Antiques District (www.ocean beachsandiego.com)** along Newport Avenue, just west of Old Town San Diego and a few blocks from the beach.

WHERE TO STAY

The following picks run the gamut of style as well as location, from Coronado and downtown to up beyond La Jolla.

The **Hotel del Coronado,** 1500 Orange Ave., Coronado (© **800/HOTEL-DEL;** www.hoteldel.com), positively reeks of history. Opened in 1888 and the subject of meticulous restoration, this Victorian masterpiece had some of the first electric lights in existence, and its early days are well chronicled in displays throughout the property. Rates: from $295. A more moderate landing is found at the **La Jolla Shores Hotel,** 8110 Camino del Oro (© **866/392-8762;** www.ljshoreshotel.com), where you can walk right onto the wide beach and frolic amid great waves. Lifeguards and the lack of undertow make this a popular choice for families. Though the rooms are plain, the staff is all pro. Rates: from $179.

You don't need to know much about Craftsman-style architecture to appreciate the taste and keen craftsmanship that went into creating the **Lodge at Torrey Pines,** 11480 N. Torrey Pines Rd., La Jolla (© 858/453-4420; www.lodgetorreypines.com). The city's only AAA Five Diamond hotel, it sits next to the Torrey Pines Golf Course, San Diego's top links. You can enjoy a fireplace in your room, sunset ocean views from your balcony, and superb meals at the hotel's A. R. Valentien restaurant. Rates: from $450.

The 11-story **Gaslamp Plaza Suites,** 520 E St. (© 619/232-9500; www.gaslamp plaza.com), is a comfortable landmark (dating from 1913, when it was San Diego's first skyscraper) with superfriendly rates, located smack-dab in the heart of the trendy Gaslamp Quarter. Rates: from $109. In downtown's Little Italy section, **La Pensione Hotel,** 606 W. Date St. (© 800/232-4683; www.lapensionehotel.com), feels like a small European hotel and offers tidy lodgings at bargain prices. There's an abundance of great dining in the surrounding blocks, and you'll be perfectly situated to explore the rest of town by car. Rates: $90.

The gorgeous, Gothic Revival **Sofia Hotel,** 150 W. Broadway (© 619/234-9200; www.thesofiahotel.com), was once one of the city's luxury properties, built in 1926 as the Pickwick. Centrally located on the edge of the Gaslamp Quarter and within walking distance of the Embarcadero, the 212-unit hotel has a comfortably chic design scheme, ultramodern amenities like in-room laptop safes, a 24-hour yoga studio, and an American-style bistro helmed by acclaimed chef Jonathan Pfleuger. Rates: from $195.

The recently renovated **US Grant,** 326 Broadway (© 800/237-5029 or 866/837-4270; www.usgrant.net), is one of San Diego's most historic properties, originally built in 1910 by the son of Ulysses S. Grant. It sits at the northern edge of the Gaslamp Quarter and offers impressive Beaux Arts beauty, 9-foot ceilings, ornate decor, and Native American artwork in the foyer (owing to the fact that it's owned by the Sycuan Band of the Kumeyaay Nation, who were given their sovereignty in 1875 by President Grant). Rates: from $249.

DINING & NIGHTLIFE

You're *sooooo* close to Mexico, might as well have Mexican food, no? The best place in San Diego is, naturally, in Old Town, at **El Agave Tequileria,** 2304 San Diego Ave. (© 619/220-0692; www.elagave.com). Rather than the "combination plate" fare that's common on this side of the border, this place offers a memorable combination of freshly prepared recipes from Veracruz, Chiapas, Puebla, and Mexico City, along with an impressive selection of boutique and artisan tequilas. Main courses: $16 to $32.

If you want to know what San Diego tastes like, you can find out at **Market,** 3702 Via de la Valle (© 858/523-0007; www.marketdelmar.com), where native son Carl Schroeder creates a daily menu from the best ingredients bought from local ranches, farms, and seafood purveyors. Main courses: $27 to $48.

For seafood, try **Island Prime,** 880 Harbor Island Dr. (© 619/298-6802; www. cohnrestaurants.com), which offers over-the-water dining, a patio with fireplace, and a menu by chef Deborah Scott that rivals its spectacular bay and skyline views. Main courses: $22 to $39. Another Scott restaurant, the **Indigo Grill,** 1536 India St., in downtown's Little Italy (© 619/234-6802; www.cohnrestaurants.com), cleverly fuses the flavors of the Pacific Coast from Mexico to Alaska. The results add up to the city's most adventurous menu, and one of its most delicious. Main courses: $18 to $30.

For gourmet pizza from a wood-fired oven, head for **Sammy's California Wood-fired Pizza,** a local institution with several branches, including one at 770 Fourth Ave., in the Gaslamp Quarter (© **619/230-8888;** www.sammyspizza.com). Pizzas: $8.75 to $11. If you want *gigantic* portions (what, that buffet aboard ship wasn't enough for you?), head downtown to **Filippi's Pizza Grotto,** 1747 India St. (© **619/232-5094;** www.realcheesepizza.com), where a salad for one is enough for three, and an order of lasagna must weigh a pound. Filippi's has locations all over, including Pacific Beach, Mission Gorge, and Escondido. Pizzas: $9 to $15.

Wherever you choose to dine, finish your evening in the **Gaslamp Quarter,** which always promises a lively after-dark street scene as well as restaurants, bars, and music venues. Another great option is attending a concert in **Balboa Park.** Free year-round organ concerts are held on Sundays from 2 to 3pm at the **Spreckels Organ Pavilion,** south of El Prado between Park Boulevard and the Cabrillo Freeway (© **619/702-8138;** www.sosorgan.com). The music runs the gamut from classical to contemporary. In summer, the free **Twilight in the Park** series (© **619/239-0512;** www.balboa park.org/twilightpark.html) offers a range of music, from jazz to classical, world and Latin to gospel and even oompah, on Tuesday, Wednesday, and Thursday evenings at the Spreckels Pavilion.

16 San Francisco, California

One of the hallmarks of a world-class city is that it's able to renew itself periodically, getting over economic hard times like a lover recovering from a bad breakup and moving on with life.

Such is the case with San Francisco, which rode the very crest of the New Economy in the late 1990s, then fell with a sickening thud when that fabled dot-com bubble burst. The terrible economic winds that blew over the years that followed didn't help, but today the city has picked itself up, taken a deep breath, and gotten back to business. Not that it was ever really *out* of business, especially as far as travelers were concerned. It's still America's most romantic European-style city, with its stunning bay vistas, Victorian architecture, swank boutiques, clanky cable cars, walkable beaches, staunch liberalism, and hugely influential gay population. Even things that seemed to lose their way in the bad years—the city's storied restaurant scene, for instance—are now back and as happening as ever. San Francisco is open for business.

GETTING TO SAN FRANCISCO & THE PORT

Ships dock at the **Port of San Francisco** piers along the Embarcadero (© **415/274-0400;** www.sfport.com), within walking distance of Fisherman's Wharf. Parking is $12 per day. Union Square, Powell Street, Market Street, and the center of downtown can be reached by **taxi.** If you're driving, find the Embarcadero and watch for the signs.

If you're flying in, you'll land at one of the Bay Area's two major airports. **San Francisco International Airport** (© **650/821-8211;** www.flysfo.com) is 14 miles directly south of downtown on U.S. 101. Travel time to downtown during commuter rush hour is about 40 minutes; at other times, it's about 20 to 25 minutes. **BART (Bay Area Rapid Transit;** © **510/464-6000;** www.bart.gov) runs from the airport to downtown, avoiding gnarly traffic and costing a heck of a lot less than taxis and shuttles—about $5 per person to the Embarcadero. Just jump on the airport's free shuttle bus to the International terminal and the BART station. Trains leave approximately every 20 minutes. A **taxi** from the airport to downtown costs about $35 to $40, plus

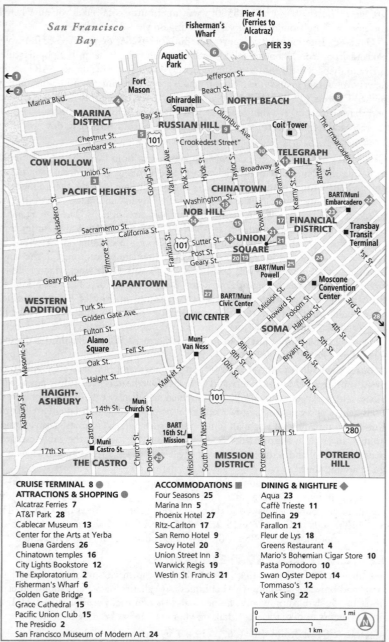

San Francisco

San Francisco Bay

Fisherman's Wharf

Pier 41 (Ferries to Alcatraz)

PIER 39

Aquatic Park

Jefferson St.

Fort Mason

Beach St.

Ghirardelli Square

NORTH BEACH

Marina Blvd.

MARINA DISTRICT

Bay St.

RUSSIAN HILL

Coit Tower

The Embarcadero

Chestnut St.

Lombard St.

101

"Crookedest Street"

Columbus Ave.

TELEGRAPH HILL

COW HOLLOW

Broadway

Union St.

Van Ness Ave.

Gough St.

Polk St.

Hyde St.

Taylor St.

CHINATOWN

Grant Ave.

Kearny St.

Battery St.

PACIFIC HEIGHTS

Washington St.

NOB HILL

Powell St.

BART/Muni Embarcadero

Divisadero St.

Sacramento St.

California St.

FINANCIAL DISTRICT

Transbay Transit Terminal

Fillmore St.

Franklin St.

101

Sutter St.

UNION SQUARE

Post St.

Geary St.

Geary Blvd.

JAPANTOWN

BART/Muni Powell

1st St.

BART/Muni Civic Center

Mission St.

Moscone Convention Center

3rd St.

WESTERN ADDITION

Turk St.

Golden Gate Ave.

CIVIC CENTER

SOMA

Howard St.

Folsom St.

Harrison St.

4th St.

Masonic St.

Fulton St.

Alamo Square

Fell St.

Muni Van Ness

8th St.

9th St.

10th St.

Bryant St.

5th St.

6th St.

7th St.

Oak St.

Haight St.

Market St.

101

HAIGHT-ASHBURY

14th St.

Muni Church St.

BART 16th St./Mission

280

Ashbury St.

Castro St.

Church St.

Dolores St.

17th St.

17th St.

Muni Castro St.

Mission St.

South Van Ness Ave.

MISSION DISTRICT

Potrero Ave.

POTRERO HILL

THE CASTRO

CRUISE TERMINAL 8 ●

ATTRACTIONS & SHOPPING ●
Alcatraz Ferries **7**
AT&T Park **28**
Cablecar Museum **13**
Center for the Arts at Yerba
  Buena Gardens **26**
Chinatown temples **16**
City Lights Bookstore **12**
The Exploratorium **2**
Fisherman's Wharf **6**
Golden Gate Bridge **1**
Grace Cathedral **15**
Pacific Union Club **15**
The Presidio **2**
San Francisco Museum of Modern Art **24**

ACCOMMODATIONS ■
Four Seasons **25**
Marina Inn **5**
Phoenix Hotel **27**
Ritz-Carlton **17**
San Remo Hotel **9**
Savoy Hotel **20**
Union Street Inn **3**
Warwick Regis **19**
Westin St. Francis **21**

DINING & NIGHTLIFE ◆
Aqua **23**
Caffè Trieste **11**
Delfina **29**
Farallon **21**
Fleur de Lys **18**
Greens Restaurant **4**
Mario's Bohemian Cigar Store **10**
Pasta Pomodoro **10**
Swan Oyster Depot **14**
Tommaso's **12**
Yank Sing **22**

0   1 mi
0   1 km

tip. **SuperShuttle** (© 415/558-8500; www.supershuttle.com) takes you anywhere in the city, charging around $15 or so, depending on your destination.

Oakland International Airport (© 800/247-6255 or 510/563-3300; www.oaklandairport.com), about 5 miles south of downtown Oakland, is a popular alternative to flying directly into San Francisco, and is also accessible on the BART system (see above). A **taxi** to downtown San Francisco costs approximately $50, plus tip. **Bayporter Express** (© 877/467-1800 in the Bay Area, or 415/467-1800 elsewhere; www.bayporter.com) is a shuttle service that charges $26 for the first person and $12 for each additional person for the ride from the Oakland Airport to downtown San Francisco.

GETTING AROUND   You can walk to many attractions from the cruise terminal, including the Embarcadero and sights in the Fisherman's Wharf area, such as Ghirardelli Square (once home to the world-famous chocolate factory), the Cannery, the National Maritime Museum, the Museum of the City of San Francisco, and the ferry to Alcatraz. Otherwise, you have lots of transportation options. The San Francisco Municipal Railway, better known as **Muni** (© 415/673-6864; www.sfmuni.com), operates the city's cable cars, buses, and streetcars. Don't miss riding on that classic San Francisco icon, the historic **cable car.** The three lines are concentrated in the downtown area. The most scenic and exciting is the **Powell–Hyde line,** which follows a zigzag route from the corner of Powell and Market streets, over both Nob Hill and Russian Hill, to a turntable at gaslit Victorian Square in front of Aquatic Park (the closet point to the port, near the intersection of Beach and Hyde sts.). The Powell–Mason line starts at the same intersection and climbs Nob Hill before descending to Bay Street, just 3 blocks from Fisherman's Wharf. The third is the California Street line. Rides cost $5.

Buses reach almost every corner of San Francisco and beyond—they even travel over the bridges to Marin County and Oakland. Overhead electric cables power some buses; others use gas engines. All are numbered and display their destinations on the front. Many buses travel along Market Street or pass near Union Square. A bus ride costs $1.50 for adults. If you plan to use public transportation extensively, you might want to invest in a **Muni Street & Transit Map** ($3), sold at the cable car ticket booths at Powell and Market streets and Hyde and Beach streets, as well as in many shops around town.

This isn't New York, so don't expect a **taxi** to appear whenever you need one—or ever, for that matter. You can often find cabs at the major hotels and downtown during rush hour, but otherwise you'd do better calling ahead to **Veteran's Cab** (© 415/552-1300), **Luxor Cabs** (© 415/282-4141), or **Yellow Cab** (© 415/626-2345). Rates are approximately $2.85 for the first mile and 45¢ each ⅕ mile thereafter.

BEST CRUISE LINE SHORE EXCURSIONS

Sausalito & Muir Woods ($49, 4 hr.): After a stop in charming Sausalito for bay views and browsing at the town's boutiques, art galleries, and crafts shops, your bus heads to 550-acre Muir Woods, home to a grove of ancient coastal redwoods. You'll have 1½ hours to hike the area's trails on your own before heading back.

Alcatraz & Sausalito by Bus ($67, 5 hr.): This tour begins with a short drive along the Embarcadero to Fisherman's Wharf, where you board the ferry to Alcatraz Island. When you get to Alcatraz, a park ranger will explain the prison's history before you go inside for a private audio tour—and view cells previously inhabited by prison inmates. Afterward, you travel back to Fisherman's Wharf by ferry and board your bus for a drive over the Golden Gate Bridge. In Sausalito, you're free to walk around town and shop.

EXPLORING SAN FRANCISCO ON YOUR OWN

Just north of the cruise docks, **Fisherman's Wharf** (© 415/674-7503; www.fishermans wharf.org) is almost the definition of "tourist trap," a long coastal shopping mall that stretches from Ghirardelli Square at the west end to Pier 39 at the east. If you like this kind of thing—shops, restaurants, street performers, and the like, few of which have anything intrinsically to do with San Francisco—then linger a bit. If not, stop by for a few minutes to gander at the 600-strong **sea lion colony** that's taken up residence on the west (left) side of Pier 39.

Okay, now leave.

From nearby Pier 41, ferries depart throughout the day bound for **Alcatraz Island** (www.nps.gov/alcatraz), the former military post and maximum-security prison that once housed Al Capone, Machine Gun Kelly, and the famous Birdman, Robert Stroud. Now administered by the National Park Service, "The Rock" offers self-guided tours, ranger-led talks about its famous "escape-proof" prison, and nature trails that lead to spectacular San Francisco views and glimpses of the island's abundant wildlife. Ferries are run by **Hornblower Cruises** (© 415/981-7625; www.alcatraz cruises.com). Tickets are $22 adults, $14 kids, with headset tour. Make your reservation as far in advance as possible, and bring a jacket—it gets cold out there.

Whether traveling to "The Rock" or not, your next stop should be the intersection of Hyde and Beach, where you can hop the **Powell–Hyde cable car.** Sit or stand near the back, on the left-hand side if possible; that way you get the view down snakelike Lombard Street as well as the spectacular bay view from the top of **Nob Hill.** When the cable cars started running in 1873, Nob Hill became the most desirable residential area in the city, chockablock with mansions. Only two survived the earthquake and fire of 1906: the Flood Mansion, which serves today as the **Pacific Union Club,** 1000 California St., at Mason Street, and the **Fairmont Hotel,** 950 Mason St., which was under construction when the earthquake struck and is worth a visit for its spectacular lobby. **Grace Cathedral,** on California Street between Taylor and Jones streets, is notable among other things for its stained-glass windows, depicting Thurgood Marshall, Jane Addams, Robert Frost, John Glenn, and Albert Einstein—representations of divinely inspired human endeavor in law, social work, letters, exploration, and science.

Just northeast of Nob Hill, San Francisco's **Chinatown** gives you a taste of that Asia cruise you couldn't afford this year. The first Chinese immigrants came to San Francisco in the early 1800s to work as servants, and today the city boasts one of the largest Chinese communities in the U.S. Cheesy camera and luggage stores cater to the tourists, but skip those and head for the vegetable and herb markets, restaurants, and shops that draw Chinese shoppers. The gateway at Grant Avenue and Bush Street marks the entry to Chinatown. On Waverly Place, a street where the Chinese celebratory colors of red, yellow, and green are much in evidence, you'll find three **Chinese temples:** Jeng Sen (Buddhist and Taoist) at no. 146, Tien Hou (Buddhist) at no. 125, and Norras (Buddhist) at no. 109. If you enter, do so quietly so that you do not disturb those in prayer. A block west of Grant Avenue, **Stockton Street,** from 1000 to 1200, is the community's main shopping drag, lined with grocers, fishmongers, tea sellers, herbalists, noodle parlors, and restaurants. Here, too, is the **Buddhist Kon Chow Temple,** at no. 855, above the Chinatown post office. About ¼ mile away, the **Cable Car Museum,** 1201 Mason St. (℗ **415/474-1887;** www.cablecarmuseum. org), is the powerhouse, repair shop, and storage place for San Francisco's cable cars. Built in 1887, the building underwent an $18-million reconstruction to restore its original gaslight-era look, install an amazing spectators' gallery, and add a museum of San Francisco transit history. Admission is free.

South of Chinatown and Nob Hill, **Union Square** is the commercial hub of the city, site of most major hotels and department stores. Life is more interesting, though, on the other side of the tracks—or Market Street, as the case may be. There, the neighborhood known as **SoMa** ("South of Market," running between Market, the Embarcadero, and Hwy. 101) was transformed from a district of old warehouses, industrial spaces, and underground clubs into the hub of dot-com-dom in the late '90s, and is now the city's cultural and multimedia center. The **San Francisco Museum of Modern Art,** 151 Third St. (℗ **415/357-4000;** www.sfmoma.org), holds more than 23,000 works, including paintings and sculptures by Henri Matisse, Jackson Pollock, Willem de Kooning, Richard Serra, Diego Rivera, Georgia O'Keeffe, and Paul Klee. Admission is $13; closed Wednesdays. The **Center for the Arts at Yerba Buena Gardens,** 701 Mission St. (℗ **415/978-2700;** www.yerbabuenaarts.org), is San Francisco's official cultural facility, presenting music, theater, dance, and visual arts. Cutting-edge computer art, multimedia shows, traditional exhibitions, and performances occupy the center's high-tech galleries. The 5-acre gardens are a great place to relax in the grass on a sunny day; they feature dramatic outdoor sculpture in memory of Martin Luther King, Jr. Between May and October, the gardens host a series of free concerts, festivals, and community events. Admission to the galleries is $6; closed Mondays. At Third and King streets on SoMa's waterfront, you'll find the home of the **San Francisco Giants** (℗ **415/972-2000;** www.sfgiants.com). Its corporate name has changed three times in the past 6 years because of big-money mergers, and it's now called AT&T Park—a God-awful name for a very pretty ballpark, with its unobstructed bay vistas and bobbing boats beyond the outfield. Tickets are hard to come by, but you can try to track them down through **www.tickets.com.**

Southwest of SoMa, few of San Francisco's neighborhoods are as varied as **Haight-Ashbury,** which gained everlasting fame as a capital of '60s hippie culture. Walk along Haight Street today and you'll encounter a weird mix of aging Deadheads, neo-flowerchildren, homeless people, throngs of tourists, and the kind of clean-cut yuppies who can afford the steep rents of Upper Haight, on the eastern border of **Golden Gate Park.** Funky-trendy shops, clubs, and cafes still line the commercial district, and if someone offers you a bud he's not talking about beer. To the south, **Castro Street,** between Market and 18th streets, is the center of the city's gay community as well as a lovely neighborhood teeming with shops, restaurants, bars, and cafes.

Back up north along San Francisco Bay, the famous **Golden Gate Bridge** connects the City by the Bay with Marin County and the redwoods to the north. Completed in 1937, it's frequently thought of as the world's most beautiful bridge. If at all possible, take a walk across, accessing the walkway from the parking lots on each side of the span.

The bridge is located at the west end of the huge **Presidio** complex; once an Army base, it's now an urban national park full of historic buildings, parkland, and a national cemetery. Near the east end of the park, the **Exploratorium,** 3601 Lyon St.

(© 415/561-0360; www.exploratorium.edu), is a must for families with kids—though be warned that you'll be there most of the day. Designed for hands-on learning, the museum features more than 650 interactive exhibits exploring all facets of science, letting you touch a tornado, shape an electrical current, and finger-paint on a computer. It's located at the gorgeous **Palace of Fine Arts,** the only remaining building from the 1915 Pan-Pacific Exhibition. Admission is $13 adults, $10 kids; closed Mondays.

SHOPPING

San Francisco's most congested and popular shopping mecca is centered on **Union Square** and bordered by Bush, Taylor, Market, and Montgomery streets. Most of the big department stores and many high-end specialty shops are here. Be sure to venture to Grant Avenue, Post and Sutter streets, and Maiden Lane. This area is a hub for public transportation; all Market Street and several other buses run here, as do the Powell–Hyde and Powell–Mason cable car lines. When you pass through the gate to **Chinatown** on Grant Avenue, say goodbye to the world of fashion and hello to a swarm of cheap tourist shops selling everything from linen and jade to plastic toys and $2 slippers. The real gems, however, are tucked away on side streets and in small, one-person shops selling Chinese herbs, art, and jewelry.

Union Street, from Fillmore Street to Van Ness Avenue, caters to the upper-middle-class crowd. It's a great place to stroll, window-shop the plethora of boutiques, try the cafes and restaurants, and watch the beautiful people parade by. Take bus no. 22, 41, or 45. Some of the best shopping in town is packed into the 5 blocks of **Fillmore Street** from Jackson to Sutter in Pacific Heights. It's the perfect place to grab a bite and peruse the high-priced boutiques, crafts shops, and incredible housewares stores.

The shopping in the 6 blocks of **Upper Haight Street** between Central Avenue and Stanyan Street reflects its clientele, offering everything from incense and European and American street styles to furniture and antique clothes. If your shopping tastes run humble, the tourist-oriented malls along Jefferson Street in the **Fisherman's Wharf** area include hundreds of shops, restaurants, and attractions. If your tastes run more literary, head to **City Lights Bookstore,** 261 Columbus Ave., at Broadway on the east edge of Chinatown (© **415/362-8193;** www.citylights.com). Founded by Beat poet Lawrence Ferlinghetti in 1953, the three-level shop specializes in world literature, the arts, and progressive politics.

WHERE TO STAY

Looking like a federal building outside and a mansion within, the **Ritz-Carlton,** 600 Stockton St., in Nob Hill (© **800/241-3333** or 415/296-7465; www.ritzcarlton.com), is the best bet for those with more traditional tastes and a hankering for every possible amenity. Rates: from $455. The **Four Seasons San Francisco,** 757 Market St., SoMa (© **800/819-5053** or 415/633-3000; www.fourseasons.com), opened in 2001 and features understated luxury, great service, and oversized rooms with custom-made mattresses. Rates: from $450. The **Westin St. Francis,** 335 Powell St., Union Square (© **800/WESTIN-1** or 415/397-7000; www.westin.com), is a favorite with VIPs for its luxurious rooms—and with kids because they get complimentary goodies such as coloring books at check-in. Rates: from $209. Also in Union Square are two great boutique hotels, the **Warwick Regis,** 490 Geary St. (© **800/827-3447** or 415/928-7900; warwicksf.com), with rates from $199, and the **Savoy Hotel,** 580 Geary St. (© **800/227-4223** or 415/441-2700; www.thesavoyhotel.com), with rates from $125.

Attention to detail, comfortable rooms, and a location along a prime stretch of Union Street make the tiny, six-unit **Union Street Inn,** 2229 Union St. (© **415/346-0424;** www.unionstreetinn.com), an excellent way to experience true San Francisco–style living. Rates: from $189. The **Phoenix Hotel,** 601 Eddy St. (© **800/248-9466** or 415/776-1380; www.thephoenixhotel.com), is a favorite with the music and movie set (Sinéad O'Connor, David Bowie, and Keanu Reeves have all laid their heads here); it's also one of the only moderately priced hotels in San Francisco with an outdoor pool. Rates: from $159.

At the small, adorable **San Remo Hotel,** 2237 Mason St. (© **800/352-REMO** or 415/776-8688; www.sanremohotel.com), the rooms may be small and the bathrooms shared, but the North Beach location (within walking distance of Fisherman's Wharf), friendly staff, and low prices can't be beat. Rates: from $55. Another top choice for convenient location, room amenities, and budget prices is the **Marina Inn,** 3110 Octavia St., Marina/Pacific Heights (© **800/274-1420** or 415/928-1000; www.marinainn.com). Rates: from $75.

DINING & NIGHTLIFE

Fleur de Lys, 777 Sutter St., Union Square (© **415/673-7779;** www.fleurdelyssf.com), offers formal French cuisine in a romantic dining room. Three-course menu: $70. Whimsical **Farallon,** 450 Post St., Union Square (© **415/956-6969;** www.farallonrestaurant.com), offers high-priced seafood amid an orgy of oceanic artwork, from jellyfish lamps to sea urchin chandeliers. Main courses: $30 to $39. San Francisco's finest seafood restaurant might be **Aqua,** 252 California St. (© **415/956-9662;** www.aqua-sf.com), which dazzles its customers with artfully composed and delicately decadent dishes like Alaskan black cod wrapped in smoked bacon with tomato and date chutney. Main courses: $29 to $39.

For a totally classic San Francisco dining experience, stop by the **Swan Oyster Depot,** 1517 Polk St. (© **415/673-1101**). Opened in 1912, this tiny hole in the wall is little more than a narrow fish market that decided to slap down 20 or so bar stools, all jammed cheek-by-jowl along a long marble bar. The menu is limited to fresh crab, shrimp, oyster, clam cocktails, a few types of smoked fish, Maine lobster, and Boston-style clam chowder, all exceedingly fresh. *Note:* Don't let the lunchtime line dissuade you—it moves fast. Clams and oysters on the half shell: $7.95 per half-dozen. Closed Sundays.

North Beach, San Francisco's Italian quarter, stretches from Montgomery and Jackson to Bay Street. It's one of the best places in the city to grab a coffee, pull up a cafe chair, and do some serious people-watching. Nightlife is equally happening; restaurants, bars, and clubs along Columbus and Grant avenues attract folks from all over the Bay Area, who fight for a parking place and romp through the festive neighborhood. Gourmands and everyday diners alike squeeze into **Tommaso's,** 1042 Kearny St. (© **415/398-9696;** www.tommasosnorthbeach.com), for killer pizza and a no-frills Italian cafe atmosphere. Main courses: $11 to $17; pizzas: $14 to $24. **Pasta Pomodoro,** 655 Union St. (© **415/399-0300;** www.pastapomodoro.com), serves heaping plates of fresh pasta at penny-pinching prices. It has several other locations around town as well. Main courses: $9 to $13. Among the area's coffeehouses, we love the authentic atmosphere at **Mario's Bohemian Cigar Store,** 566 Columbus Ave. (© **415/362-0536;** www.mariosbohemiancigarstore.com), and **Caffè Trieste,** 601 Vallejo St. (© **415/392-6739;** www.caffetrieste.com).

Want a little more atmosphere and more sophisticated Italian cooking? Head to **Delfina,** 3621 18th St., in the Mission District (© 415/552-4055; www.delfinasf. com). Main courses: $13 to $22.

For the best dim sum in the downtown area, go to cavernous **Yank Sing,** 101 Spear St. (© 415/957-9300). Confident, experienced servers take the nervousness out of novices—they're good at guessing your gastric threshold as they stop by your table with shrimp balls, pork buns, *congee* (porridge), spareribs, stuffed crab claws, and other palate pleasers. Most items: $3.65 to $9.30 for two to six pieces.

Greens Restaurant, Building A, Fort Mason Center, Marina/Pacific Heights (© 415/771-6222; www.greensrestaurant.com), serves inventive vegetarian cuisine in an old waterfront warehouse, with a view of the bay and the Golden Gate Bridge. Main courses: $16 to $23.

At night, dozens of piano bars and top-notch lounges augment San Francisco's lively dance-club culture, and skyscraper lounges offer dazzling city views. The city's arts scene is also extraordinary: The opera is justifiably world renowned, the ballet is on its toes, and theaters are high in both quantity and quality. In short, there's always something going on, so get out there. For up-to-date nightlife information, turn to the *San Francisco Weekly* and the *San Francisco Bay Guardian,* both of which run comprehensive listings. They're available free at bars and restaurants and from street-corner boxes all around the city. *Where,* a free tourist-oriented monthly, also lists programs and performance times; it's available in most of the city's finer hotels. As for bars and lounges, there are hundreds of 'em throughout San Francisco. **Chestnut** and **Union Street** bars attract a postcollegiate crowd, **Upper Haight** caters to eclectic neighborhood cocktailers, and **Lower Haight** draws snowboarder types. Tourists mix with theatergoers and thirsty businesspeople in **downtown** pubs, while the **Castro** caters to gay locals and visitors.

17 Seattle, Washington

For 2 decades Seattle has been one of the nation's most talked-about and popular cities, drawing new residents, producing a slew of new money (thank you, Microsoft), and spiffing itself up with new football and baseball stadiums, a new opera house, a new and architecturally avant-garde main library, a new symphony hall, and countless new hotels, restaurants, and shops. It is very much a water-oriented city, set between Puget Sound and Lake Washington, with Lake Union in the center. Practically everywhere you look, the views are of sailboats, cargo ships, ferries, windsurfers, and anglers. The only drawback is the rain, which falls (or threatens to) an average of 226 days a year. But look on the bright side: It's good for your complexion.

After decades in the shadow of Vancouver, British Columbia, Seattle has finally emerged as a major port of embarkation for Alaska-bound ships, which operate throughout the summer, carrying some 735,000 passengers.

GETTING TO SEATTLE & THE PORT

Cruise ships dock at **Pier 66,** the Bell Street Terminal, right in downtown Seattle, or at the **Pier 30** terminal, 2431 E. Marginal Way S., at the south end of Seattle's downtown waterfront, just a few minutes away by car or taxi. See **www.portseattle.org/ seaport/cruise** for maps and other information. If you're arriving by air, you'll fly into the **Seattle-Tacoma International Airport** (© 800/544-1965; www.portseattle.org/ seatac), often referred to as **Sea-Tac,** located about 14 miles south of Seattle and connected to the city by I-5. Generally, allow 30 minutes for the trip between the airport and downtown. A **taxi** downtown will cost you around $33, or you can take the **Seattle Downtown Airporter** (© 800/426-7532; www.graylineofseattle.com) for $10 one-way, $17 round-trip. Another option is **Shuttle Express** (© 425/981-7000; www.shuttleexpress.com), which charges about $28 for two people going downtown or to either of the cruise piers.

If you're arriving by car, you'll likely come in on Interstate 5, which leads right downtown. Alaskan Way runs along the waterfront and past the cruise ship terminal. Parking is $12 per day at Pier 30, $14 per day at Pier 66.

GETTING AROUND   You can walk or take public transportation around downtown Seattle, but if you want a **rental car,** nearly every major company has an outlet at Sea-Tac. **Seattle Metro** (© 206/553-3000; http://transit.metrokc.gov) offers free bus transportation within the downtown area between the hours of 6am and 7pm. The company also operates a waterfront service using old-fashioned streetcars, some of it in the ride-free area, some of it outside. The most it will cost you is $2 one-way. You can also get a 1-day unlimited-ride pass for $5 at various locations (see website for details). Visitors to the Space Needle can use the **Seattle Center Monorail** (© 206/905-2600; www.seattlemonorail.com) from downtown, 1¼ miles away, for $2 one-way.

BEST CRUISE LINE SHORE EXCURSIONS

Shore excursions in Seattle are usually pretty sparse. Often your choices are limited to a **bus tour** ($48; 3½ hr.) that includes the Space Needle, Pioneer Square, and shopping time at Pike Place Market.

EXPLORING SEATTLE ON YOUR OWN

The **Seattle Waterfront,** along Alaskan Way from Yesler Way North to Bay Street and Myrtle Edwards Park, is the city's single most popular attraction, and much like San Francisco's Fisherman's Wharf area, that's both good and bad. Yes, it's very touristy, with tacky gift shops, saltwater taffy, T-shirts galore, and lots of overpriced restaurants, but it's also home to the Seattle Aquarium, the Pike Place Market and its many vendors (see "Shopping," below), and a whole lot of scenery.

Located at Pier 59, the **Seattle Aquarium,** 1483 Alaskan Way (© 206/386-4300; www.seattleaquarium.org), offers well-designed exhibits dealing with the water worlds of the Puget Sound region. The underwater dome is the aquarium's largest and most amazing exhibit, a round undersea room (accessible via a short tunnel) where visitors are surrounded by a fish-filled 400,000-gallon tank. Admission is $13 adults, $8.50 kids, plus extra for special exhibits.

At Pier 57, the **Bay Pavilion** has a vintage carousel and a video arcade to keep the kids busy. At Piers 55 and 56, boats leave for 1½-hour harbor cruises as well as trips to **Tillicum Village,** a faux Northwest Native longhouse built for the 1962 Seattle World's Fair, located at Blake Island State Marine Park, across Puget Sound. It's a beautiful spot. **Tillicum Village Tours** (© 800/426-1205 or 206/933-8600; www.tillicumvillage.com) include a lunch or dinner of alder-smoked salmon and a performance of traditional masked dances. The 4-hour tour costs $79 adults, $30 kids. At Pier 54, you'll find companies offering sea-kayak tours, sport-fishing trips, jet-boat tours, and bicycle rentals.

The **Seattle Art Museum,** 100 University St. (© 206/654-3100; www.seattleart museum.org), is a repository for everything from African masks, old masters, and

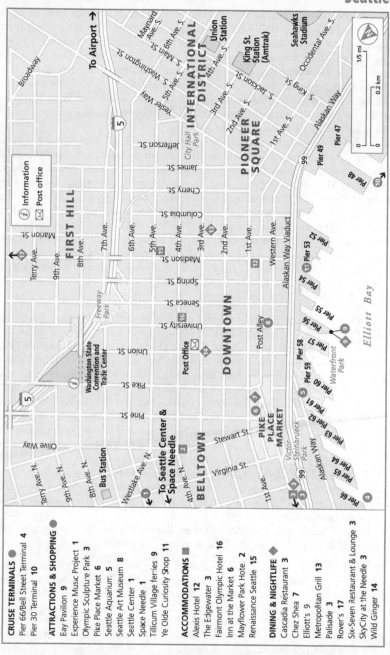

Seattle

CRUISE TERMINALS ●
Pier 66/Bell Street Terminal **4**
Pier 30 Terminal **10**

ATTRACTIONS & SHOPPING ●
Bay Pavilion **9**
Experience Music Project **1**
Olympic Sculpture Park **3**
Pike Place Market **6**
Seattle Aquarium **5**
Seattle Art Museum **8**
Seattle Center **1**
Space Needle **1**
Tillicum Village ferries **9**
Ye Olde Curiosity Shop **11**

ACCOMMODATIONS ■
Alexis Hotel **12**
The Edgewater **3**
Fairmont Olympic Hotel **16**
Inn at the Market **6**
Mayflower Park Hote. **2**
Renaissance Seattle **15**

DINING & NIGHTLIFE ◆
Cascadia Restaurant **3**
Chez Shea **7**
Elliott's **9**
Metropolitan Grill **13**
Palisade **3**
Rover's **17**
Six-Seven Restaurant & Lounge **3**
SkyCity at the Needle **3**
Wild Ginger **14**

Andy Warhol to one of the nation's premier collections of Northwest Coast Indian art. It reopened in summer 2007 after an expansion that added 70% more gallery space. Its entrance is unmistakable, fronted by Jonathan Borofsky's giant, kinetic *Hammering Man* sculpture. Admission is $13 adults, free for kids under 12. One mile northwest along the waterfront, the museum's new **Olympic Sculpture Park,** 2901 Western Ave., at Broad Street, is a 9-acre outdoor site where world-class sculpture (by the likes of Richard Serra, Alexander Calder, Mark Di Suvero, and Tony Smith) sits amid lawns planted with native ground cover, letting onto wide views of the Olympic Mountains and Puget Sound. Admission is free.

To the west, **Seattle Center** was the epicenter of the 1962 World's Fair and is still home to the fair's futuristic **Space Needle,** 203 Sixth Ave. N. (© **206/905-2100;** www.spaceneedle.com), a 607-foot tower that's become the quintessential symbol of Seattle. At 518 feet above ground level, the views from its observation deck are stunning. High-powered telescopes let you zoom in on distant sights, and there's a lounge and two very expensive restaurants inside. Admission is $14 adults, $7 kids. Next door, the **Experience Music Project** (© **877/367-5483;** www.emplive.com) is the Frank Gehry–designed building that looks like it's in the process of melting. Inside, you'll find displays, interactive music rooms, performance spaces, galleries, and research facilities dedicated to all phases of American popular music. Admission is $20 adults, $15 children, free for kids 6 and under.

SHOPPING

Inland from the waterfront, between Pike and Pine streets at First Avenue, the historic **Pike Place Market** (© **206/682-7453;** www.pikeplacemarket.org) was originally a farmers' market and is now a National Historic District, home to more than 200 local craftspeople and artists who sell their creations here throughout the year. It's one of the city's great destinations for both locals and visitors, loaded with excellent restaurants and shops and ornamented by street performers.

To the east, **Ye Olde Curiosity Shop,** 1001 Alaskan Way (© **206/682-5844;** www. yeoldecuriosityshop.com), is a cross between a souvenir store and *Ripley's Believe It or Not.* It's weird! It's tacky! It's always packed! See Siamese-twin calves, a natural mummy, the Lord's Prayer on a grain of rice, a narwhal tusk, shrunken heads, and a 67-pound snail. The collection of oddities was started by Joe Standley in 1899.

The corner of **Pine Street** and **Fifth Avenue** is ground zero for upscale Seattle shopping, home to two major department stores (**Nordstrom** and **Macy's**) and two upscale urban shopping malls (**Westlake Center** and **Pacific Place**). Other boutiques fan out to the east and south.

South of downtown, the historic **Pioneer Square** area has the city's greatest concentration of art galleries, some of which specialize in Native American art.

WHERE TO STAY

Located in an enviable location halfway between Pike Place Market and Pioneer Square and only 2 blocks from the waterfront, the **Alexis Hotel,** 1007 First Ave., at Madison Street (© **800/426-7033;** www.alexishotel.com), part of the Kimpton group of boutique hotels, is a sparkling gem with a pleasant mix of classic styling and a friendly staff. Rates: from $279. The **Fairmont Olympic Hotel,** 411 University St. (© **888/363–5022;** www.fairmont.com/seattle), is one of the bigger, and absolutely one of the most elegant, hotels in Seattle, reminiscent of an Italian Renaissance palace. Rates: from $339.

The **Edgewater,** 2411 Alaskan Way, at Pier 67 (© 800/624-0670; www.edgewater hotel.com), may look like a mountain lodge, but it's actually right on the water, built on Pier 67 over the waters of Elliott Bay, right downtown. Rooms feature rustic lodge-pole-pine furniture; the lobby offers gorgeous sunset views. Rates: from $179.

Renaissance Seattle, 515 Madison St. (© 800/546-9184; www.renaissancehotels. com), offers larger-than-average rooms, many with views of either Puget Sound or the Cascade Range. Rates: from $169. If shopping or sipping martinis is your thing, stay at the **Mayflower Park Hotel,** 405 Olive Way (© 800/426-5100; www.mayflower park.com), built in 1927, connected to the upscale shops of Westlake Center, and flanked by Nordstrom and Macy's. The hotel's Oliver's Lounge also serves Seattle's best martinis. Rates: from $135. The **Inn at the Market,** 86 Pine St. (© 800/446-4484 or 206/443-3600; www.innatthemarket.com), meanwhile, is located right at Pike Place Market, offering an understated European atmosphere, spacious accommodations, proximity to restaurants and shopping, and views of Elliott Bay from its rooftop deck. Rates: from $175.

DINING & NIGHTLIFE

At **Cascadia Restaurant,** 2328 First Ave. (© 206/448-8884; www.cascadia restaurant.com), chef Kerry Sear does wondrous things with local produce and fresh Northwest ingredients. Throw in a variety of tasting menus, martinis made with Douglas-fir sorbet, and a glass front wall that lets in beautiful summer light and you have the quintessential Seattle eatery. Main courses: $25 to $38. In a quiet corner of Pike Place Market, **Chez Shea,** 94 Pike St. (© 206/467-9990; www.chezshea.com), offers candlelit tables, subdued lighting, views of ferries crossing the bay, and superb meals. It all adds up to the perfect combination for a romantic dinner. Main courses: $24 to $35; closed Mondays.

If you're feeling above it all, pick a restaurant to match. **SkyCity at the Needle,** in the Space Needle at 400 Broad St. (© 800/937-9582; www.spaceneedle.com/restaurant), has the best views in Seattle. Simply prepared steaks and seafood make up the bulk of the menu. Main courses: $32 to $52. At **Rover's,** 2808 E. Madison St. (© 206/325-7442; www.rovers-seattle.com), chef Thierry Rautureau combines his love of local ingredients with his classic French training to produce a distinctive take on Northwest cuisine. Main courses: $16 to $22.

For waterfront dining, head to the Edgewater Hotel's **Six-Seven Restaurant & Lounge,** 2411 Alaskan Way, at Pier 67 (© 206/269-4575; www.edgewaterhotel. com), which offers superb food, very cool decor, a great little deck, and one of the best views from any restaurant in the city. Main courses: $24 to $55. Another waterfront option, **Palisade,** Elliott Bay Marina, 2601 W. Marina Place (© 206/285-1000; www.palisaderestaurant.com), offers a 180-degree view that takes in Elliott Bay, downtown, and West Seattle. Never mind that it also has great food and some of the most memorable decor of any Seattle restaurant. Main courses: $23 to $55. For the best selection of oysters, head to **Elliott's,** 1201 Alaskan Way, Pier 56 (© 206/623-4340; www.elliottsoysterhouse.com), where the oyster bar can have as many as 20 varieties available. Main courses: $14 to $40.

Wild Ginger, 1401 Third Ave. (© 206/623-4450; www.wildginger.net), is a long-time Seattle favorite, serving Pan-Asian specialties in a stylish and usually very busy setting. Pull up a comfortable stool around the large satay grill and watch the cooks grill little skewers of anything from chicken to scallops to pork to lamb. Main courses:

$15 to $26. For the best steaks, go to **Metropolitan Grill,** 820 Second Ave. (© **206/ 624-3287;** www.themetropolitangrill.com), which serves corn-fed, aged beef grilled over mesquite charcoal. Main courses: $21 to $65.

Much of Seattle's evening entertainment scene is clustered in the **Seattle Center** and **Pioneer Square** areas, the former hosting theater, opera, and classical-music performances, the latter a bar-and-nightclub district. Seattle Center is home of the Space Needle and several venues used by the Seattle Opera and the Seattle Symphony. Pioneer Square, centered around the corner of First Avenue and Yesler Way, is known for its restored 1890s buildings, tree-lined streets, and cobblestone plazas, plus a plethora of restaurants and bars.

18 Tampa, Florida

Tampa was a sleepy port until Cuban immigrants founded **Ybor City**'s cigar industry in the 1880s. A few years later, Henry B. Plant built a railroad to carry tourists into town and constructed his garish Tampa Bay Hotel (now the Henry B. Plant Museum). During the Spanish-American War, Teddy Roosevelt trained his Rough Riders here and walked the Ybor City streets with Cuban revolutionary José Marti. A land boom in the 1920s gave the city its charming, Victorian-style **Hyde Park** suburb (now a gentrified area, just across the Hillsborough River from downtown), and the go-go 1980s and 1990s brought skyscrapers, a convention center, a performing-arts center, and lots of shopping and dining options to the **downtown** area.

On the western shore of Tampa Bay, **St. Petersburg** is the picturesque and pleasant flip side of Tampa's busy business, industrial, and shipping life. Originally conceived and built primarily for tourists and wintering snowbirds, it's got a nice downtown area, some quality museums, and a few good restaurants.

The Port of Tampa is set amid a complicated network of channels and harbors near historic Ybor City and its deep-water Ybor Channel. Ships sailing from here head primarily to the western Caribbean, the Yucatán, and Central America.

GETTING TO TAMPA & THE PORT

Tampa's cruise terminals are all located along Channelside Drive, close to the heart of the city. They're operated by the **Tampa Port Authority** (© **813/905-7678;** www. tampaport.com). If you're coming by air, you'll probably land at **Tampa International Airport** (© **813/870-8700;** www.tampaairport.com), 5 miles west of downtown Tampa, near the junction of S.R. 60 and Memorial Highway. If you haven't arranged transfers with your cruise line, the port is an easy 30-minute **taxi** ride away; the set fare is $22 per car for up to four people.

By car, Tampa lies 188 miles southwest of Jacksonville, 50 miles north of Sarasota, and 245 miles northwest of Miami. From I-75 and I-4 to Terminals 2 and 6, take I-4 west to exit 1 (Ybor City), go south on 21st Street, turn right on Adamo Drive (Hwy. 60), and then go left on Channelside Drive. For Terminal 7, go south on 21st Street (21st St. merges with 22nd St. after crossing Adamo Dr.), turn right on Maritime Boulevard, and then go left on Guy N. Verger to Hooker's Point. Parking at the port costs $12 per day.

GETTING AROUND   Taxis in Tampa do not normally cruise the streets for fares; instead, they line up at public loading places, such as the airport, cruise terminal, and major hotels. **Yellow Cab** (© **813/253-0121**) and **United Cab** (© **813/253-2424**)

Tampa

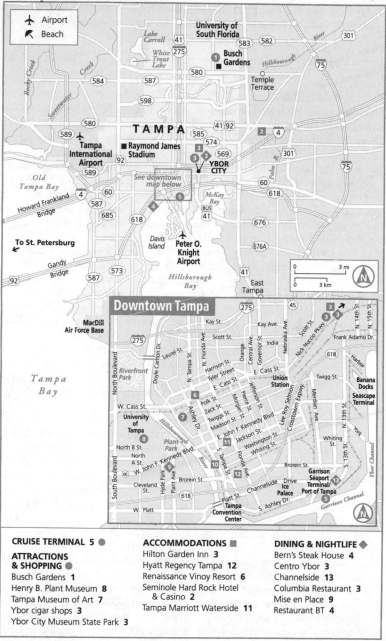

CRUISE TERMINAL 5 ●

ATTRACTIONS & SHOPPING ●
Busch Gardens **1**
Henry B. Plant Museum **8**
Tampa Museum of Art **7**
Ybor cigar shops **3**
Ybor City Museum State Park **3**

ACCOMMODATIONS ■
Hilton Garden Inn **3**
Hyatt Regency Tampa **12**
Renaissance Vinoy Resort **6**
Seminole Hard Rock Hotel & Casino **2**
Tampa Marriott Waterside **11**

DINING & NIGHTLIFE ◆
Bern's Steak House **4**
Centro Ybor **3**
Channelside **13**
Columbia Restaurant **3**
Mise en Place **9**
Restaurant BT **4**

charge $2 at flag fall, plus $2.25 for each mile thereafter. Should you wish to drive your own vehicle, all major **car-rental** companies have counters at the airport.

BEST CRUISE LINE SHORE EXCURSIONS

Tampa City Tour ($38, 4 hr.): This tour visits Ybor City and the Ybor State Museum and passes the University of Tampa and Hyde Park on the way to the airport.

BUSCH GARDENS

Admission prices are high, but **Busch Gardens,** 3000 E. Busch Blvd., at McKinley Drive/North 40th Street (© **888/800-5447;** www.buschgardens.com), remains Tampa Bay's most popular attraction. The 335-acre family entertainment park features thrill rides, animal habitats, live entertainment, shops, restaurants, and games. The park's zoo ranks among the best in the country, with nearly 3,400 animals.

Montu, the world's tallest and longest inverted roller coaster, is part of **Egypt,** the park's ninth themed area, which also includes a replica of King Tutankhamen's tomb and a sand-dig area for kids. **Gwazi** is the largest and fastest double wooden roller coaster in the southeastern U.S., with two coasters starting simultaneously and whizzing within a few feet of each other six times at 50 mph.

At **Stanleyville,** you can hop aboard SheiKra, a heart-stopping dive coaster that reaches speeds of 70 mph. **Timbuktu** is a replica of an ancient desert trading center, complete with African craftspeople at work. It also features a sandstorm ride, a boat-swing ride, a video-game arcade, and the Scorpion, a high-speed number with a 60-foot drop and 360-degree loop. **Morocco,** a walled city with exotic architecture, has Moroccan crafts demonstrations and a sultan's tent with snake charmers. The **Congo** features white-water raft rides; Kumba, the largest steel roller coaster in the southeastern United States; and Claw Island, a display of rare white Bengal tigers in a natural setting. **Rhino Rally** is an off-road adventure in 16-passenger "Ralliers," or Land Rovers, which travel a bumpy course that allows views of Asian elephants, buffalo, antelope, and more. Hang on to your hat when a flash flood whisks away the bridge—and your vehicle.

The **Serengeti Plain** is an open area with more than 500 African animals roaming in herds. This 80-acre natural grassy veldt can be viewed from the tram ride, the Trans-Veldt Railway, or the Skyride. **Nairobi** is home to a natural habitat for various species of gorillas and chimpanzees, a baby-animal nursery, a petting zoo, reptile displays, and Curiosity Caverns, where visitors can observe animals active at night. **Bird Gardens,** the original core of Busch Gardens, offers rich foliage, lagoons, and a free-flight aviary holding hundreds of exotic birds, including golden and American bald eagles, hawks, owls, and falcons. This area also features Land of the Dragons, a children's adventure.

For great views while you eat, **Crown Colony** is a multilevel restaurant overlooking the Serengeti Plain. The Anheuser-Busch hospitality center, near the Bird Gardens, is home to a team of Clydesdale horses. **Akbar's Adventure Tours,** which offers a flight simulator, is also located here.

To get here, take Interstate 275 northeast of downtown to Busch Boulevard (exit 33), and go east 2 miles to the entrance on 40th Street (McKinley Ave.). Admission is $62 for adults and $52 for kids 3 to 9. Parking is $9. Park hours are at least 10am to 6pm; hours are usually extended during summer and on holidays. See the website for exact opening and closing times.

EXPLORING THE REST OF TAMPA ON YOUR OWN

Tampa is best explored by car, as only the commercial district can be covered on foot. If you want to go to the beach, you'll have to head to neighboring St. Petersburg. **Ybor City,** Tampa's historic Latin enclave and one of only three National Historic Districts in Florida, lies only a mile or so from the cruise ship docks. Once known as the cigar capital of the world, Ybor offers a charming slice of the past with its Spanish architecture, antique street lamps, wrought-iron balconies, ornate grillwork, and renovated cigar factories. Stroll along Seventh Avenue, the main artery (closed to traffic at night), where you'll find cigar shops, boutiques, nightclubs, and the famous 100-year-old Columbia Restaurant (see "Dining & Nightlife," below). The **Ybor City Museum State Park,** 1818 Ninth Ave., between 18th and 19th streets (© 813/247-6323; www.ybormuseum.org), is primarily devoted to the area's cigar history, with a collection of cigar labels, cigar memorabilia, and works by local artisans. Admission is $3.

Thirteen silver minarets and distinctive Moorish architecture make the stunning **Henry B. Plant Museum,** 401 W. Kennedy Blvd. (© 813/254-1891; www.plant museum.com), the focal point of the Tampa skyline. This national historic landmark, built in 1891 as the Tampa Bay Hotel, is filled with European and Oriental furnishings and decorative arts from the original hotel collection. Admission is $5; closed Mondays.

The permanent collection of the **Tampa Museum of Art,** 600 N. Ashley Dr. (© 813/274-8732; www.tampamuseum.com), is especially strong in ancient Greek, Etruscan, and Roman artifacts, as well as 20th-century art. The museum grounds, fronting the Hillsborough River, contain a sculpture garden and a decorative fountain. Admission is $8 for adults; closed Mondays.

If you want to see one of the country's largest and busiest ports in action, the **Port Authority of Tampa** (© 813/905-5131) offers a free 1½-hour tour around Tampa Bay. The 45-passenger *SeePort Adventure* catamaran departs from Terminal 2 Monday through Friday at 9:30am. Reservations are suggested at least 2 weeks in advance.

BEACHES

You have to start at **St. Petersburg,** across the bay, for a north-to-south string of interconnected white sandy shores. Most beaches have restrooms, refreshment stands, and picnic areas. You can park either on the street at a meter (usually 25¢ for each half-hour) or at one of the four major parking lots located, from north to south, at **Sand Key Park,** in Clearwater, beside Gulf Boulevard (also known as Rte. 699), just south of the Clearwater Pass Bridge; **Redington Shores Beach Park,** beside Gulf Boulevard at 182nd Street; **Treasure Island Park,** on Gulf Boulevard just north of 108th Avenue; and **St. Pete Beach Park,** beside Gulf Boulevard at 46th Street.

SHOPPING

The most distinctive shopping here is in Ybor City. The area is no longer the major producer of hand-rolled cigars it once was, but you can still watch artisans making stogies at the **Gonzalez y Martinez Cigar Factory/Columbia Cigar Store,** 2103 Seventh Ave., in the Columbia Restaurant building (© 813/247-2469). Rollers are on duty Monday through Saturday. You can also stock up on fine domestic and imported cigars at **El Sol,** 1728 E. Seventh Ave. (© 813/248-5905), the city's oldest cigar store; **King Corona Cigar Factory,** 1523 E. Seventh Ave. (© 813/241-9109); and **Metropolitan Cigars & Wine,** 2014 E. Seventh Ave. (© 813/248-3304).

WHERE TO STAY

All of the hotels listed in this section are in downtown Tampa or Ybor City.

The modern, four-story **Hilton Garden Inn,** 1700 E. Ninth Ave. (© **800/445-8667;** www.hiltongardeninn.com), is primarily oriented to business travelers, but it's located just 2 blocks north of the heart of Ybor City's dining and entertainment district. Rates: from $119. The **Hyatt Regency Tampa,** Two Tampa City Center at 211 N. Tampa St. (© **800/233-1234;** http://tamparegency.hyatt.com), sits in Tampa's commercial center and also caters mostly to the corporate crowd. Rates: from $199. The **Tampa Marriott Waterside,** 700 S. Florida Ave. (© **800/228-9290;** www.marriotthotels.com), offers a lot of rooms with balconies overlooking the bay or city (the best views are high up on the south side). Rates: from $159.

If the slots on the ship aren't enough for you, the new 500-room **Seminole Hard Rock Hotel & Casino,** 5223 Orient Rd. (© **866/502-7529;** www.hardrockhotel casinotampa.com), has a 130,000-square-foot casino plus several other grand features—stay here if you're looking for lots of excitement. Rates: from $140.

For a special experience farther from the cruise docks, the **Renaissance Vinoy Resort,** 501 Fifth Ave. NE, at Beach Drive, St. Petersburg (© **800/HOTELS1;** www.renaissancehotels.com), is the grande dame of the region's hotels. Built as the Vinoy Park in 1925, this elegant Spanish-style establishment reopened in 1992 after a meticulous $93-million restoration. Many rooms offer lovely views of Tampa Bay. Accommodations in the new wing ("The Tower") are slightly larger than those in the hotel's original core. Rates: from $219.

DINING & NIGHTLIFE

Nightfall transforms **Ybor City,** Tampa's century-old Latin Quarter, into a hotbed of ethnic food, music, poetry readings, and after-midnight coffee and dessert. The nearly 100-year-old **Columbia Restaurant,** 2117 Seventh Ave. E. (© **813/248-4961**), occupies an attractive tile-sheathed building that fills an entire city block between 21st and 22nd streets, about a mile from the cruise docks. The aura is pre-Castro Cuba, and the simpler your dish is, the better it's likely to be. Filet mignon; roasted pork; and the black beans, yellow rice, and plantains are flavorful and well prepared. Catch a flamenco show on the dance floor Monday through Saturday. Main courses: $15 to $25. After dinner, all you have to do is stroll along Seventh Avenue East, between 15th and 20th streets, and you'll hear music blaring out of the clubs that change names and characters frequently. Just follow your ears into the one that sounds best to you. With all of the sidewalk seating, it's easy to judge what the clientele is like, too. At **Centro Ybor,** a shopping/entertainment complex between Seventh and Eighth avenues and 15th and 17th streets (© **813/242-4660;** www.centroybor.com), you'll find a multiscreen cineplex, several restaurants, a comedy club, a large open-air bar, a bunch of typical mall-type stores, and **GameWorks,** a high-tech entertainment center designed by Steven Spielberg's DreamWorks and Universal Studios. The Ybor City Chamber of Commerce has its **Cigar Museum & Visitor Center** here, too, on Eighth Avenue next to Centro Español.

Although Ybor City is better known, Tampa's trendiest dining scene is actually along South Howard Avenue, between West Kennedy Boulevard and the bay in affluent Hyde Park. That's where you'll find **Mise en Place,** 442 W. Kennedy Blvd., opposite the University of Tampa (© **813/254-5373;** www.miseonline.com), run by chef Marty Blitz and his wife, Maryann, the culinary darlings of Tampa since 1986. They present the freshest of ingredients on a creative, eclectic menu that changes weekly. Main courses: $15 to $29. Hyde Park is also the home of **Bern's Steak House,** 1208 S. Howard Ave. (© **813/251-2421**), whose steaks are close to perfect. You order according to thickness and weight. Main courses: $27 to $60. Close by, **Restaurant BT,** 1633 W. Snow Ave. (© **813/258-1916;** www.restaurantbt.com), deserves every bit of the massive hype it's received lately, serving French-Vietnamese fare that's as gorgeous as it is delicious—and with a sophisticated, stylish ambience to boot. Main courses: $16 to $24.

Within steps of the cruise ship piers, the shopping, dining, and entertainment complex known as **Channelside,** 615 Channelside Dr., adjacent to the Florida Aquarium (© **813/223-4250;** www.channelsidetampa.com), continues to grow. Worthwhile eateries here include Grill 29, Stumps Supper Club, and Tinatapas.

19 Vancouver, British Columbia

Located in the extreme southwestern corner of British Columbia, Vancouver is probably one of the "newest" cities you'll ever visit, and it's certainly one of the most cosmopolitan, with a skyline of new glass-and-steel high-rises ringing the Inner Harbour and a medley of foreign tongues testifying to its international character. There's a youthfulness, too, a certain Pacific Northwest chic that's equal parts movie-biz buzz (the city's been a setting for so many movies that it's sometimes called "Hollywood North") and pure wonderment over living in such a beautiful, vibrant place. It's everything a small city should be—both majestic and intimate, bustling and laid-back, sophisticated and free-spirited—and ringed with a ridiculous wealth of natural beauty all around, from the wide waters of Burrard Inlet to the deep green of Stanley Park (one of the world's largest urban parks) to the snow-capped mountains in the north. Rich Northwest Coast Native culture, a thriving Asian community, numerous summertime festivals, and a great arts scene fill out the picture. What's more, those Vancouverites are just so blatantly *nice.* Maybe it's all that fresh air. Who knows, but it makes us want to move here every time we visit.

Though Seattle has usurped some of Vancouver's cruise steam over the past several years, Vancouver is still the major southern transit point for Alaska cruises, and is occasionally a port of call as well.

Note: All prices in this section were calculated at the rate of US$0.87 = C$1, or US$1 = C$1.15. However, foreign currency rates fluctuate, so prices may not be exactly the same when you arrive in port.

GETTING TO VANCOUVER & THE PORT

Most cruise ships dock at **Canada Place,** at the end of Burrard Street (© **604/775-7200;** www.canadaplace.ca). The pier terminal is a city landmark, noted for its five-sail structure that reaches into the harbor like a ship setting off. It's located at the edge of the downtown district and is just a quick stroll from the **Gastown** area, with its cafes, art galleries, and souvenir shops (see below), and from **Robson Street,** a destination for trendy fashions. Hotels, restaurants, and shops are all located right near the terminal. Most visitors arrive in Vancouver by plane, touching down at **Vancouver International Airport** (© **604/207-7077;** www.yvr.ca), located 8 miles south of downtown. The average **taxi** fare from the airport to downtown is about US$20 to US$23 (C$23–C$26). The **YVR Airporter** (© **604/946-8866;** www.yvrairporter. com) buses also offer service to the city for about US$11 (C$13) per person one-way.

GETTING AROUND   You can easily walk the downtown area of Vancouver, but if you want transportation, you've got a few options. **Car-rental** agencies with local branches include Avis, Budget, Hertz Canada, and Thrifty, and **taxis** are always found around the major hotels and tourist sights. For public transportation, the **Translink system** (© **604/953-3333;** www.translink.bc.ca) includes electric buses, ferries, and the magnetic-rail SkyTrain. Fares per zone are US$2 (C$2.30). A day pass allowing unlimited rides is also available for US$7 (C$8.05).

BEST CRUISE LINE SHORE EXCURSIONS

Capilano Suspension Bridge & Grouse Mountain Skyride (US$90, 4 hr.): Visit two highlights of Vancouver, heading from sea level to 4,000 feet. Your tour begins as your bus travels across Lions Gate Bridge, which spans Burrard Inlet. Once in North Vancouver, you'll visit the narrow, historic, 450-foot Capilano Suspension Bridge, from whose 230-foot height even the towering evergreens below look tiny. From here, you'll take the Grouse Mountain Skyride to the 4,000-foot summit, where you can hike one of the nature trails or grab lunch.

EXPLORING VANCOUVER ON YOUR OWN

Located within easy walking distance of the pier, **Gastown**—situated between the waterfront and Hastings Street, from Canbie Street to Columbia—is Vancouver's oldest neighborhood, and retains its Victorian flavor of low, shoulder-to-shoulder buildings, ornate streetlights, and cobblestone streets, now leavened by expensive condos and high-end boutiques. The area was named for "Gassy" Jack Deighton, who in 1867 built a saloon in Maple Tree Square (at the intersection of Water, Alexander, and Carrall sts.) to serve the area's loggers and trappers. The Gastown of today offers a touch of bohemia, with street musicians, galleries, boutiques, and antiques and art shops, plus lots of touristy stuff, and even more restaurants, clubs, and cafes. At the corner of Water and Cambie streets, a **steam-powered clock** draws its power from an underground steam system that heats many of downtown's buildings. It hoots the traditional clock tune every 15 minutes as steam vents from its top.

Adjoining Gastown, Vancouver's historic **Chinatown**—bordered by East Pender and Keefer streets between Carrall Street and Gore Avenue—is one of the largest in North America. Even though much of Vancouver's large Asian population has moved out, they return here to shop, keeping the area vital and lively. It's filled with bright-red low-rise buildings, photogenic Chinese gates, food, and open-air markets selling Chinese wares. Chinatown's biggest draw is the **Dr. Sun Yat-Sen Garden,** 578 Carrall St. (© **604/689-7133;** www.vancouverchinesegarden.com), a perfectly traditional Chinese garden based on the yin-yang principle, in which harmony is achieved by placing contrasting elements in juxtaposition: soft moving water against solid stone, smooth swaying bamboo around gnarled immovable rocks, dark pebbles against light pebbles, and so on. It's one of only two classical Chinese gardens in North America (along with the one in Portland, Oregon), and was created by master artisans from Suzhou, the garden city of China. Admission is US$7.60 (C$8.75) adults, free for kids under 5. Immediately next door, separated from the garden by only a classical footbridge and koi pond, the public **Dr. Sun Yat-Sen Park** is less meditative but beautiful in its own right, with walking paths winding among Chinese trees and foliage. Admission to the park is free.

Downtown, the **Vancouver Art Gallery,** 750 Hornby St. (© **604/662-4719;** www. vanartgallery.bc.ca), is housed in a grand neoclassical building originally used as a

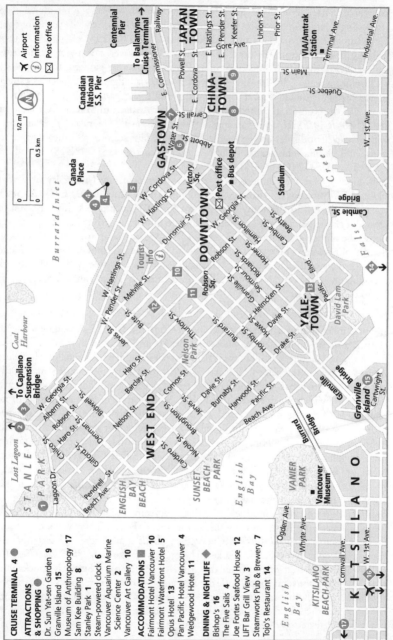

Vancouver

Legend:
- ✈ Airport
- ⓘ Information
- ⊠ Post office

Scale: 0 — 1/2 mi / 0 — 0.5 km

CRUISE TERMINAL 4 ●

ATTRACTIONS & SHOPPING ●
Dr. Sun Yat-sen Garden 9
Granville Island 15
Museum of Anthropology 17
Sam Kee Building 8
Stanley Park 1
Steam-powered clock 6
Vancouver Aquarium Marine Science Center 2
Vancouver Art Gallery 10

ACCOMMODATIONS ■
Fairmont Hotel Vancouver 10
Fairmont Waterfront Hotel 5
Opus Hotel 13
Pan Pacific Hotel Vancouver 4
Wedgewood Hotel 11

DINING & NIGHTLIFE ◆
Bishop's 16
The Five Sails 4
Joe Fortes Seafood House 12
LIFT Bar Grill View 3
Steamworks Pub & Brewery 7
Tojo's Restaurant 14

Map labels:
Burrard Inlet
Coal Harbour
Lost Loon
STANLEY PARK
Lagoon Dr.
Pendrell St.
Beach Ave.
Gilford St.
Chilco St.
Denman St.
Bidwell St.
Cardero St.
Nicola St.
Broughton St.
Jervis St.
Bute St.
Thurlow St.
Burrard St.
Hornby St.
Howe St.
Granville St.
Seymour St.
Richards St.
Homer St.
Hamilton St.
Cambie St.
Beatty St.
Haro St.
Barclay St.
Comox St.
Davie St.
Burnaby St.
Harwood St.
Pacific St.
Beach Ave.
Nelson St.
Helmcken St.
Drake St.
Davie St.
Pacific Blvd.
WEST END
SUNSET BEACH PARK
ENGLISH BAY BEACH
English Bay
Nelson Park
W. Georgia St.
Alberni St.
Robson St.
W. Pender St.
W. Hastings St.
Melville St.
W. Cordova St.
W. Hastings St.
Dunsmuir St.
W. Georgia St.
Robson St.
Robson Sq.
Victory Sq.
Tourist Info ⓘ
Post office ⊠
Bus depot ■
DOWNTOWN
YALE-TOWN
David Lam Park
GASTOWN
Water St.
Abbott St.
Carrall St.
CHINA-TOWN
JAPAN TOWN
E. Cordova St.
E. Hastings St.
E. Gore Ave.
E. Pender St.
E. Keefer St.
Union St.
Prior St.
Powell St.
E. Commissioner
Railway
To Ballantyne Cruise Terminal →
Centennial Pier
Canadian National S.S. Pier
Canada Place
Main St.
Quebec St.
Terminal Ave.
Industrial Ave.
VIA/Amtrak Station
Stadium
Creek
False Creek
Cambie St. Bridge
Granville Bridge
Burrard Bridge
VANIER PARK
Vancouver Museum
Ogden Ave.
Whyte Ave.
Cornwall Ave.
W. 1st Ave.
KITSILANO
KITSILANO BEACH PARK
English Bay
Granville Island
Cartwright St.
To Capilano Suspension Bridge

513

courthouse. Its collection of more than 8,000 works is heavy on regional work (including a large collection by B.C. native Emily Carr) and related works by other Canadian and international artists. Admission is US$13 (C$15).

Just a few miles from the heart of downtown Vancouver, northwest of the cruise ship terminal, the 1,000 acres of **Stanley Park** contain rose gardens, totem poles, a yacht club, a water park for kids, miles of wooded hiking trails, and great vantage points for views of Lions Gate Bridge. Simply put, the park is one of Vancouver's gems. On the grounds, the outstanding **Vancouver Aquarium Marine Science Center** (© **604/659-FISH;** www.vanaqua.org) is one of North America's largest and best, with an excellent display on the Pacific Northwest, plus sea otters, beluga whales, sea lions, and Pacific white-sided dolphins. Admission is US$16 (C$18) for adults, US$9.50 to US$12 (C$11–C$14) for kids.

If you're up for a 20-minute drive west of downtown, the **University of British Columbia's Museum of Anthropology,** 6393 NW Marine Dr. (© **604/822-3825;** www.moa.ubc.ca), isn't just any old museum. In 1976, architect Arthur Erickson recreated a classic Native post-and-beam structure out of modern concrete and glass to house one of the world's finest collections of West Coast Native art. You enter through doors that resemble a huge, carved, bent-cedar box. Artifacts from potlatch ceremonies flank the ramp leading to the Great Hall's collection of totem poles and Haida artwork, including masterpieces by sculptor Bill Reid. Admission is US$7.80 (C$8.95) adults, US$6 (C$6.90) kids.

SHOPPING

About 2 miles southwest of the cruise docks, **Granville Island** (www.granvilleisland. com) is a former industrial site whose warehouses and factories now house galleries, museums, restaurants, a small brewery, theaters, shops, and a few remaining industrial businesses to keep the place real. It has so much to offer that even a day may not be enough to experience it all, but you can certainly give it a good shot. Browse for crafts, grab picnic fixin's from the incredible **Public Market** (one of the best gourmet food markets we've ever seen, anywhere), watch a comedy show or attend a theater performance, stroll along the waterfront, enjoy a great dinner, or simply run through the elaborate sprinklers on a hot summer day. If you have a few thousand bucks to drop (or are willing to pretend you do), stop in to **Eagle Spirit Gallery,** 1803 Maritime Mews (© **604/801-5205;** www.eaglespiritgallery.com), which specializes in original, museum-quality Northwest Coast Native and Inuit art, including hand-carved masks, argillite stone carvings, and paintings. To get to Granville Island, walk or take a taxi south on Burrard street from the cruise docks. At some point, make a left 1 block to Hornby Street and then continue south all the way to the end. There you'll find a dock for the **Aquabus** (© **604/689-5858;** www.theaquabus.com), a cute little ferry that will deposit you right by the Public Market. The one-way fare is only US$2.20 (C$2.50).

Downtown, not far inland from the cruise docks, **Robson Street** is chockablock with boutiques, souvenir shops, coffeehouses, and bistros. Look for high-end fashions, with a focus on clothes for the younger set. In Gastown, **Water Street** may be a little too heavy on the knickknack shops, but it also boasts galleries of First Nations art, funky basement retro boutiques, and antiques shops.

WHERE TO STAY

Virtually all of Vancouver's downtown hotels are within walking distance of shops, restaurants, and attractions.

The **Fairmont Hotel Vancouver,** 900 W. Georgia St. (© **800/257-7544** or 604/684-3131; www.fairmont.com), is the grande dame of Vancouver's hotels. Designed on a generous scale, with a copper roof, marble interiors, and massive proportions, the hotel is all luxury and spaciousness, with marble bathrooms and mahogany furnishings in the guest rooms. Rates: from US$243 (C$279).

The **Fairmont Waterfront Hotel,** 900 Canada Place Way (© **866/540-4510** or 604/691-1991; www.fairmont.com), is an ultramodern, 23-story building right on the harbor, offering spectacular waterfront and mountain views from 70% of the rooms. A concourse links the hotel to the rest of Waterfront Centre, Canada Place, and the cruise ship terminal. Rates: from US$234 (C$269).

The **Pan Pacific Hotel Vancouver,** 300–999 Canada Place (© **800/937-1515;** www.panpacific.com), sits right atop Canada Place, home of the cruise terminal and a convention center. All of the guest rooms are modern, spacious, and comfortably furnished. Try to book a harborside room so you can enjoy the view. Rates: from US$416 (C$478).

Among boutique hotels, the **Wedgewood Hotel,** 845 Hornby St. (© **800/663-0666** or 604/689-7777; www.wedgewoodhotel.com), has racked up numerous honors thanks to its luxurious accommodations, stellar service, and elegant bar. It's the only boutique hotel in the downtown area, and the shops of Robson Street are less than a block away. Rates: from US$164 (C$189).

Right at the western end of the Robson Street shopping and restaurant strip, the **Listel Vancouver,** 1300 Robson St. (© **800/663-5491;** www.listel-vancouver.com), offers subtly luxurious rooms and public areas adorned with quality contemporary art. In the evenings, you can hear live jazz at O'Doul's, the hotel's street-level restaurant and bar. Rates: from US$190 (C$219). In trendy Yaletown, near Granville Island, the 96-unit **Opus Hotel,** 322 Davie St. (© **866/642-6787** or 604/642-6787; www.opushotel.com), has rooms furnished according to one of five "personalities" (ranging from modern minimalist to eclectic), with superb beds, bright color schemes, and a contemporary aesthetic. Rates: from US$199 (C$229).

DINING & NIGHTLIFE

The **Five Sails,** in the Pan Pacific Hotel, 999 Canada Place Way (© **604/891-2892;** www.dinepanpacific.com/fivesails.php), combines truly top-notch food and a killer view of Coal Harbour, the Lions Gate Bridge, and the mountains. Cuisine is an eclectic mix of Thai, Mongolian, Japanese, Vietnamese, and nouvelle influences. Main courses: US$23 to US$45 (C$26–C$52).

For something a little different, **LIFT Bar Grill View,** 333 Menchions Mews (© **604/689-5438;** www.liftbarandgrill.com), not only has awesome views of Coal Harbour, Stanley Park, and the North Shore mountains, but also features small dishes, called "whet plates," to be shared. Sample fare such as venison with a chocolate-cherry demi-glace, jumbo wild prawns with seared foie gras, and Thai curry duck confit. Main courses: US$20 to US$29 (C$23–C$33); whet plates: US$9.60 to US$17 (C$11–C$20).

Joe Fortes Seafood House, 777 Thurlow St. (© **604/669-1940;** www.joefortes. ca), is a two-story, dark-wood restaurant with an immensely popular bar. The roof garden is pure Vancouver, and pan-roasted oysters are a menu staple. Main courses: US$23 to US$39 (C$26–C$45).

At **Bishop's,** 2183 W. Fourth Ave. (© **604/738-2025;** www.bishopsonline.com), owner John Bishop makes every customer feel special, and the candlelight, white linen, and soft jazz don't hurt, either. The food is even better: a mix of "contemporary home cooking" like roasted duck breast with sun-dried Okanagan Valley fruits and candied ginger glace. Main courses: US$30 to US$35 (C$35–C$40); reservations required.

For Japanese food, head to **Tojo's Restaurant,** located above an A&W burger joint at 1133 W. Broadway (© **604/872-8050;** www.tojos.com). Hidekazu Tojo's sushi is Vancouver's best, attracting Japanese businessmen, Hollywood celebrities, and anyone else who's willing to pay. Tell Tojo how much you want to spend, and he'll prepare an incredible meal to fit your budget. Main courses: US$14 to US$26 (C$16–C$30); closed Sunday; reservations required for the sushi bar.

After dinner, take a walk through Gastown's cobbled streets (avoiding the panhandlers when you can), and drop in to bars such as the **Steamworks Pub & Brewery,** 375 Water St. (© **604/689-2739;** www.steamworks.com), home to a dozen in-house beers and multiple rooms with different moods, from classy old pub to hot London bar to Bavarian beer hall, complete with long benches and enormous copper kettles.

The Caribbean, The Bahamas & the Panama Canal

The Caribbean is the classic cruise destination, tailored to people who want nice white-sand beaches, tiki bars serving tropical drinks, some hot island music, and sun, sun, sun—plus throngs of other cruise passengers enjoying it all with you. Culture and history also have their place. In general, western Caribbean itineraries offer opportunities for visiting the ruins of Maya cities and temple sites on the mainland, while eastern Caribbean itineraries are more likely to offer reminders of British, French, Spanish, and Dutch colonial history. Panama Canal itineraries mix the lore of that massive construction effort with rich Central American culture. And, of course, there's all that gorgeous scenery, from the lush jungles of Dominica to the arid moonscape of Aruba.

Here's the good news: There are hardly any lousy Caribbean islands, though depending on your likes and dislikes, you'll appreciate some more than others. Some—especially St. Thomas and Nassau—are much more touristy and commercial than others, but they'll appeal to shoppers with their large variety of bustling stores. Others—Virgin Gorda, St. John, and Jost Van Dyke, for instance—are quieter and more natural and will appeal to those who'd rather walk along a calm beach or take a drive along a lonely, winding road amid lush tropical foliage. Ports such as St. Barts and Bequia offer a low-key yachting-port atmosphere, while ports such as Key West and

Cozumel are all about whooping it up. In general, all the Caribbean islands are getting more business by bigger and bigger ships, and more of them. It's harder than ever to find the unspoiled, uncrowded corners of the Caribbean, though they're there if you know where to look.

HOME PORTS FOR THIS REGION Though the majority of Caribbean cruises still leave from the traditional Florida ports of **Miami, Fort Lauderdale, Port Canaveral,** and to a lesser extent **Tampa,** you can also sail from Galveston and Houston, Texas; New Orleans; Charleston, South Carolina; Norfolk, Virginia; Jacksonville, Florida; and even New York, Baltimore, and Philadelphia. Some Caribbean islands also commonly serve as home ports, especially Puerto Rico's capital, **San Juan,** but also St. Thomas, Barbados, and others. The upside to these is that you'll start your cruise in the midst of the islands, and probably be able to visit more ports over the course of your trip. The downside is that except for San Juan, it can be more complicated and expensive to fly to these ports than to one of the mainland embarkation points.

LANGUAGE & CURRENCY Both vary by island, though English is spoken widely in all the port towns and the U.S. dollar is commonly accepted everywhere. All prices in this chapter are quoted in U.S. dollars, though we've included information on local currency in the individual reviews.

CALLING FROM THE U.S. & CANADA Most of the islands in this chapter are part of the North American Numbering Plan, meaning you call them just as you would another state or territory on the mainland, adding a "1" before the area code and local number. Where that is not the case (as with Mexico, Belize, the French islands, and so forth), we've included dialing information in the port review.

SHOPPING TIPS You'll find it all here, from cheesy tourist souvenirs to jewelry (lots and lots of jewelry), perfume (ditto), and electronics, with some quality indigenous arts available, too, if you look hard enough. Prices vary by port. Some—such as the U.S. Virgin Islands, St. Barts, St. Martin, and Aruba—are pretty pricey, while Cozumel and the ports of Jamaica and the Grenadines are cheaper. **Duty-free merchandise** can save you as little as 5% to as much as 50%, so if you have particular goods you're thinking of buying, it pays to check prices at your local discount retailer before you leave home so you'll know whether you're really getting a bargain. Many ports offer particularly good deals on **liquor,** though keep in mind you'll pay tax when coming back into the U.S. if you buy more than your legal limit (see the section on U.S. Customs in chapter 3 for more info).

When shopping, be aware that some items you see offered may not be allowed by U.S. Customs. You might be eyeing that gorgeous piece of **black-coral jewelry,** for instance, but laws prohibiting the trade in endangered species make it illegal to bring many products made from coral and other marine animals back to the United States. (Remember, corals aren't rocks, they're living animals—a single branch of coral contains thousands of tiny marine invertebrates called polyps.) **Sea turtles,** too, are highly endangered, and sea horses, while not yet protected by law, are currently threatened with extinction. The shopkeeper selling items made from these creatures probably won't tell you they're questionable from a Customs standpoint, but the Customs agent sure will, and may fine you or, at the very least, confiscate the item if he catches you with it. Better to buy a cheap underwater camera and take pictures of these beauties on a snorkeling expedition—you get the memories, the evidence, a little exercise, and good karma to boot.

Cuban cigars are also prohibited by U.S. Customs. You'll see them all over the islands, but be aware that, *legally* speaking, you have to smoke 'em before you head for home.

1 The Cruise Lines' Private Islands

Ideally, a Caribbean cruise should be like acting out a Jimmy Buffett song—lots of eating, drinking, and hanging out on deserted beaches. If only it were that easy. As ships get bigger and cruise line fleets grow, some Caribbean ports feel a lot like being at home in your SUV: all pimped up and no place to go. Recent experiences in St. Thomas, San Juan, Cozumel, and Nassau were more about traffic jams and crowded shopping malls than frosty margaritas on windswept beaches. With easily 15,000-plus passengers pouring off as many as 8 to 10 ships on an average day, it's goodbye relaxing beach paradise, and hello queues, crowds, gridlock, and pushy touts.

The antithesis to all of this Caribbean madness, of course, is the cruise line private island, where only one ship at a time (or two, tops) stops for the day. It would seem they were invented solely to preserve the sanity of the cruise passenger. The mission is simple: provide passengers with a sane, surefire, hassle-free means to enjoy a classic day of sun and fun. All the mainstream lines (except Carnival) have private islands (or parts of islands) that are included as a port of call on many of their Caribbean and Bahamas itineraries. While few offer any kind of true Caribbean culture, they do offer cruisers a guaranteed beach day with all the trimmings and a more private experience than you'll get at most ports' public beaches. Note that aside from Disney's Castaway Cay, none of the islands has a large dock, so passengers are ferried ashore by tender.

CELEBRITY CRUISES   See "Royal Caribbean & Celebrity Cruises," below.

COSTA CRUISES   Passengers on Costa's eastern Caribbean itineraries spend 1 day at **Catalina Island,** off the coast of the Dominican Republic. This relaxing patch of paradise offers a long beach fringed by palm trees, with activities such as volleyball, beach Olympics, and snorkeling. The area adjacent to the tender dock is the busiest spot, as is to be expected, but if you walk down the beach a bit you'll get a quieter, more private experience (though the coastline gets a little rocky when you get farther out from the dock). Costa provides cruisers with floating beach mats free of charge (most lines charge for them), so you can find your quiet nirvana by paddling out to sea. A local island vendor rents jet skis and offers banana-boat rides, the ship's spa staff sets up a cabana to do massages on the beach, and locals often roam around offering them, too. (For a fraction of what the ship charges, a local woman gave Heidi a great foot and shoulder massage.) Locals also sell coconuts for a couple of bucks apiece, hacking the end off and plunking in a straw or two so you can get at the milk. After you're finished, take it back and they'll whack the thing to pieces with a machete and scrape out the tender coconut meat for you. Music and barbecues round out the day, and there's also a strip of shops hawking jewelry, beachwear, and other souvenirs. *Note:* On some itineraries, passengers must pay to hang out here for the day.

DISNEY CRUISE LINE   A port of call on all *Disney Magic* and *Disney Wonder* cruises, 1,000-acre, 3×2-mile **Castaway Cay** is rimmed with idyllically clear Bahamian water and fine sandy beaches. Disney has developed less than 10% of the island, but in that 10% guests can swim and snorkel, rent bikes and boats, get their hair braided, shop, send postcards, have a massage, or just lounge in a hammock or on the beach. Barbecue burgers, ribs, fish, and chicken are available at Cookie's Bar-B-Q, and several bars are scattered around near the beaches. Recent enhancements include the barnacle-encrusted 175-foot *Flying Dutchman* ghost ship anchored just offshore. An actual prop from Disney's *Pirates of the Caribbean: Dead Man's Chest,* which was filmed in Freeport, it's a whimsical backdrop for photos.

The island's best quality is its accessibility. Unlike the other private islands, which require ships to anchor offshore and shuttle passengers back and forth on tenders, Castaway Cay's dock allows guests of *Magic* and *Wonder* to just step right off the ship and walk or take a shuttle tram to the island's attractions. Families can head to their own beach, lined with lounge chairs and pastel-colored umbrellas, where they can swim, explore a 12-acre snorkeling course, climb around on the offshore water-play structures, or rent a kayak, paddle boat, banana boat, sailboat, or other beach equipment. Teens have a beach of their own, where they can play volleyball, soccer, or tetherball; go on a "Wild Side" bike, snorkel, and kayak adventure; or design, build, and race their own boats. Parents who want some quiet time can drop preteens at Scuttle's Cove, a supervised children's activity center for ages 3 to 12 where activities include rts and crafts, music and theater, and scavenger hunts. An excavation site here allows

The Gulf of Mexico & the Caribbean

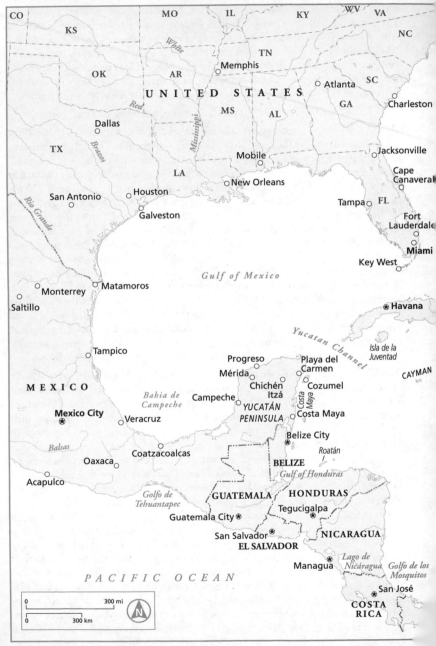

CO
KS
OK
TX
San Antonio
Dallas
MO
IL
KY
WV
VA
NC
TN
Memphis
UNITED STATES
AR
MS
AL
GA
Atlanta
SC
Charleston
Red
White
Mississippi
Brazos
Rio Grande
LA
Mobile
New Orleans
Houston
Galveston
Jacksonville
Cape Canaveral
Tampa
FL
Fort Lauderdale
Miami
Key West
Gulf of Mexico
Monterrey
Matamoros
Saltillo
Havana
Isla de la Juventad
CAYMAN
Yucatan Channel
Tampico
MEXICO
Bahia de Campeche
Progreso
Mérida
Chichén Itzá
Playa del Carmen
Cozumel
Campeche
YUCATÁN PENINSULA
Costa Maya
Costa Maya
Mexico City
Veracruz
Belize City
Oaxaca
Coatzacoalcas
BELIZE
Roatán
Gulf of Honduras
Acapulco
Balsas
Golfo de Tehuantepec
GUATEMALA
HONDURAS
Tegucigalpa
Guatemala City
San Salvador
EL SALVADOR
NICARAGUA
Managua
Lago de Nicáragua
Golfo de los Mosquitos
San José
COSTA RICA
PACIFIC OCEAN
0   300 mi
0   300 km
N

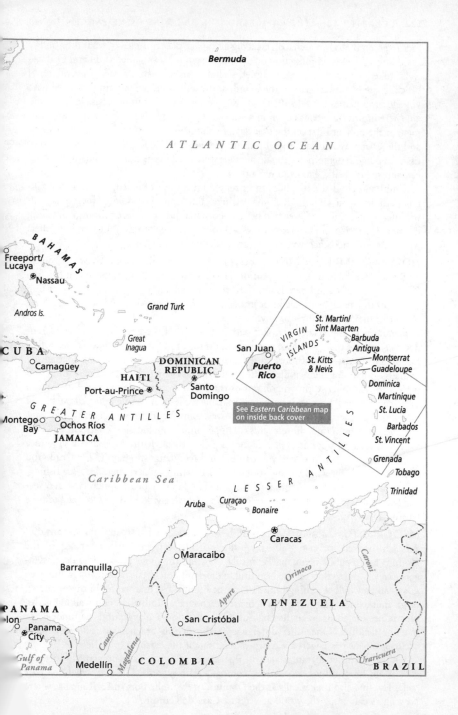

Bermuda

ATLANTIC OCEAN

BAHAMAS

Freeport/
Lucaya

⊛Nassau

Andros Is.

Grand Turk

CUBA

Camagüey

Great
Inagua

VIRGIN
ISLANDS

St. Martin/
Sint Maarten

San Juan

Barbuda

Antigua

DOMINICAN
REPUBLIC

HAITI

Puerto
Rico

St. Kitts
& Nevis

Montserrat

Guadeloupe

Port-au-Prince ⊛

⊛
Santo
Domingo

Dominica

See Eastern Caribbean map
on inside back cover

Martinique

GREATER ANTILLES

St. Lucia

Montego
Bay

Ochos Ríos

Barbados

St. Vincent

JAMAICA

LESSER ANTILLES

Grenada

Caribbean Sea

Tobago

Trinidad

Aruba

Curaçao

Bonaire

⊛
Caracas

Maracaibo

Caroni

Barranquilla

Orinoco

PANAMA

lon

Apure

VENEZUELA

Panama
City

San Cristóbal

Gulf of
Panama

Cauca

Magdalena

COLOMBIA

Uraricuera

BRAZIL

Medellín

kids to go on their own archaeological dig and make plaster molds of what they find—including a 35-foot reproduction of a whale skeleton. Meanwhile, Mom and Dad can walk, bike, or hop the shuttle to quiet, secluded Serenity Bay, a mile-long stretch of beach in the northwest part of the island, at the end of an old airstrip decorated with vintage prop planes for a 1940s feel. Twenty-five- and 50-minute massages are available here in private cabanas open to a sea view on one side (sign up for your appointment at the onboard spa on the first day of your cruise to ensure that you get a spot), and the Castaway Air Bar serves up drinks. Heidi sampled a piña colada and a deep-tissue massage at Serenity Bay while her kids were back in the nursery aboard the *Wonder,* and she gives it a giant thumbs up.

Adult- and child-size bicycles can be rented for $6. A newly lengthened bike/walking path lets you stretch those hamstrings, but don't go looking for scenery or wildlife—at best, all you'll see will be the occasional bird or leaping lizard. Parasailing is available for $75 (45 min., airborne 7–9 min.; over age 8 only). All-terrain strollers with canopies and beach wheelchairs are available free of charge.

HOLLAND AMERICA LINE   Located on the Bahamian island of San Salvador, 2,500-acre **Half Moon Cay** is a port of call on most of HAL's Caribbean and Panama Canal cruises. The sand here is ultrasoft, so go ahead and lie right down in it or flop on one of the many beach chairs or under a blue canvas sun shade (though you'll have to rent it; they're in limited supply).

Families will appreciate the water park at one end of the beach (closest to the tender pier), where there are three water slides on the sand for young children, as well as a couple for teens. Just offshore in the shallow turquoise sea, a cluster of floating toy animals—including a crocodile, shark, and octopus—are tethered to the seafloor and perfect for climbing. Other highlights of the beach area include massage huts as well as air-conditioned, beachfront cabanas available for rent. A couple hundred bucks will buy you butler service and an open bar. Away from the main beach area and accessible via a short tram ride, shore-excursion opportunities include horseback riding ($79; 1½ hr., including a scenic trail ride and a gallop through the surf) and a visit to a 150×75-foot water pen where you can pet and feed tame stingrays ($29; 1 hr.). You can also sign up for windsurfing, snorkeling, kayaking, scuba diving, deep-sea fishing, parasailing, sailboarding, or aqua-cycling. Half Moon Cay boasts lunch facilities, several bars, a playground, and even nature trails through a wild bird preserve at a remote part of the island.

MSC CRUISES   Most of MSC's Caribbean cruises spend a day in **Cayo Levantado,** a beach-rimmed, palm-tree-lined rainforest island off the northeast coast of the Dominican Republic's Samana Peninsula. As at all the other private islands, passengers may choose to flop on the beautiful white-sand beach, take a tour (including jeep safaris and a whale-watching cruise to see the humpbacks that winter in these waters), or go snorkeling or swimming. There are beach chairs, umbrellas, and walking paths, plus tables for an open-air lunch. But you won't find a playground, hammocks, or massage facilities. One other difference: A day at this beach is considered a shore excursion, thus passengers are charged a flat rate if they want to play here.

Unlike the other private islands in this section, Cayo Levantado actually isn't private at all: It's run by a Dominican company with whom MSC has scheduled port calls. The line also makes calls at the Dominican Republic port of La Romana, where passengers can enjoy the 7,000-acre resort **Casa de Campo.**

NORWEGIAN CRUISE LINE   NCL's private island, **Great Stirrup Cay**, is a stretch of palm-studded beachfront in the southern Bahamas, and was the very first private resort developed by a cruise line in the Caribbean. It's also the most cramped of the cruise line private islands, and part of the shoreline is very rocky. Still, after a piña colada—or two—you probably won't notice its flaws. Rest assured, the bar, lunch, and watersports facilities are hopping, as the sleepy beach turns into an instant party whenever one of the NCL vessels is in port. Music is either broadcast or performed live, barbecues are fired up, hammocks are strung between palms, and there's a definite beach buzz that takes over. Passengers can ride paddle boats, sail Sunfish, go snorkeling or parasailing, hop on a banana boat, join a game of volleyball on the three deep-sand courts, get a massage at one of the beachside stations (though they're not very private or quiet), or do nothing more than sunbathe all day long. For kids, organized activities include volleyball tournaments and sand-castle building, though there is no playground here.

PRINCESS CRUISES   Most of Princess's eastern and western Caribbean itineraries offer a stop at **Princess Cays**, a 40-acre beachfront strip off the southwestern coast of Eleuthera in The Bahamas, pretty much cut off from the rest of the island. The half-mile of shoreline allows passengers to swim, snorkel, and make use of Princess's fleet of Hobie Cats, Sunfish, banana boats, kayaks, and pedal boats. (If you want to rent watersports equipment, be sure to book while aboard ship or even online, before your cruise, to ensure that you get what you want.) There's also a beach barbecue—though don't look for live music or massage facilities, as there aren't any. Anyone who wants to get away from it all can head for the several dozen tree-shaded hammocks at the far end of the beach. For kids, there's a supervised play area with a sandbox and a pirate-ship-themed playground. The Princess shop sells T-shirts and other clothing, plus souvenirs of the mug-and-key-chain variety, and local vendors set up stands around the island to hawk conch shells, shell anklets, straw bags, and other crafts, as well as to offer hair braiding.

ROYAL CARIBBEAN & CELEBRITY CRUISES   Many ships of sister lines Royal Caribbean and Celebrity stop for a day at one or another of the line's two private beach resorts, CocoCay and Labadee. At both, organized children's activities include beach parties, volleyball, seashell collecting, and sand-castle building.

At **CocoCay** (aka Little Stirrup Cay), an otherwise uninhabited 140-acre landfall in The Bahamas' Berry Islands, you'll find lots of beach, hammocks, food, drink, and watersports, plus such activities as limbo contests, water-balloon tosses, relay races, and volleyball tournaments. Kids big and small will like the aqua park that includes a floating trampoline, water slides, and a sunken airplane and schooner for snorkelers. The newest gimmick: Kids 3 to 8 can now hop in battery-operated mini race cars for what the line's billing as a "special driving adventure" on the Fisher-Price Power Wheels Track. For something quieter, head for Wanderer's Beach; it's a longer walk from the tender pier than the other beaches, so it tends to be less crowded and quieter. Its calm surf and ultrasoft sand make it perfect for families with young children.

Labadee, an isolated, sun-flooded, 270-acre peninsula along Haiti's north coast, is so completely tourist-oriented that you'd never know it was attached to the rest of poverty-stricken Haiti. Labadee is a rarity among the cruise lines' private islands in that it gives you a real glimpse of island culture. At the straightforwardly named "Folkloric Show," a large, colorfully costumed troupe performs Haiti's distinctly African brand of dancing, drumming, and song, while bands at the various bars and restaurants play the kind of acoustic guitar, banjo, and percussion "mento" music that was a precursor to reggae and other Caribbean styles. Five beaches spread around the peninsula are progressively less crowded the farther you walk from the dock, where enormous tenders make the short ride to and from the ship. For children, there's the pirate-themed "Splash Bash" area with water sprinklers, fountains, and spilling buckets. There are also floating trampolines, inflatable iceberg-shaped slides, and water seesaws. Kayaking and parasailing are offered from a dock nearby. The latest rage is a new 2,800-foot-long zipline called Dragons Breath that takes you over the water of Dragons Tail Beach. At the center of the peninsula, the Haitian Market and Artisans' Market are the port's low points, full of cheesy Africanesque statues and carvings, with touts trying to lure you in with "Sir, let me just show you something over here." Steer clear unless you're desperate for a souvenir. When we were here last, a painter near the dock had much more interesting work for sale.

2 Antigua

Though it's the largest of the British Leeward Islands, Antigua (pronounced An-*tee*-gah) is still only 23km (14 miles) long and 18km (11 miles) wide, and offers a much more laid-back experience than you'll get at some of the glitzier Caribbean islands. Nice, relaxing beaches are close to port, and **St. John's,** the island's capital and main town, is sleepy and undemanding, full of cobblestone sidewalks and weather-beaten wooden houses. Close to port, you can shop lazily in historic, restored warehouses, while away from St. John's, the rolling, rustic island boasts important historic sites. **Nelson's Dockyard,** for example, was once Britain's main naval station in the Lesser Antilles, and is now a well-maintained national park.

COMING ASHORE Most cruise ships dock at **Heritage Quay** (pronounced *Key*) or the **Nevis Pier,** or, if both are occupied, the commercial pier at **Deepwater Harbour.** All are in St. John's, the island's only town of any size, located on Antigua's western coast. The three piers have a total capacity of six ships. From the piers, you can either walk or take a short taxi ride into town. A handful of smaller vessels drop anchor at **Falmouth Harbour,** on the English Harbour main road in Falmouth, on the south side of the island. This anchorage is also used for overflow if the St. John's piers are all occupied. Heritage Quay was upgraded in December 2006, and renovations are planned for the Deepwater Harbour pier in late 2007. The modern cruise terminals host bars, restaurants, shopping, Internet cafes, and casinos. Plans are in place for a new cruise facility to handle the latest supermegaships.

GETTING AROUND Most of the major attractions here are beyond walking distance. **Taxis** meet every cruise ship. Although meters are nonexistent, rates are fixed by the government and are posted at the taxi stand at the end of Heritage Quay's pedestrian mall. Drivers often double as tour guides for about $20 per hour for up to four people, with a 2-hour minimum. Tip between 10% and 15% for all rides. **Water taxis** are also available, usually prearranged by the cruise lines or tour operators. Privately operated **buses** are cheaper (little more than $1 to almost anywhere on the island), but service is erratic. Avis, Budget, Hertz, and National all offer **rental cars** on the island, but driving is on the left, signage is inadequate, and you have to buy a $20 temporary driving permit.

LANGUAGE & CURRENCY The language is **English,** often spoken with a musical West Indian lilt. The **Eastern Caribbean dollar** (EC$2.70 = US$1; EC$1 = US37¢) is Antigua's official currency, but the U.S. dollar is readily accepted.

BEST CRUISE LINE SHORE EXCURSIONS

Nelson's Dockyard National Park Tour ($49, 3 hr.): The tour begins with a drive through the capital of St. John's and stops at Antigua's national park before heading to Nelson's Dockyard for a guided tour of the admiral's house, sailmaker's loft, officers' quarters, and an 18th-century inn. A short drive brings you to the Blockhouse Ruins, Indian Creek, and the St. James Club and Shirley Heights—the latter sitting atop a rugged cliff offering spectacular views.

Helicopter to Montserrat Volcano ($254, 2 hr.): In December 1997, the Soufrière Hills Volcano on the neighboring island of Montserrat blew its top, spewing lava and ash over a huge area and burying large swaths of the island, including the former capital, Plymouth. This trip takes you over both the volcano and the charbroiled highlights of Montserrat's exclusion zone, the area declared off-limits to ground transportation.

Off-Road 4x4 Jeep Safari Adventure ($59, 3 hr.): Tour the island's only remaining rainforest via a four-wheel-drive vehicle, and stop at the ruins of forts, sugar mills, and plantation houses. The excursion includes beach time.

Hiking Safari Adventure ($49, 3 hr.): This 4-mile uphill/downhill hike takes you through Antigua's rainforest, offering a panoramic view from one of the island's highest peaks (360m/1,181 ft.).

Bird Island Catamaran Sail ($82, 5 hr.): Sail along the reef-protected north coast of Antigua into the sheltered bay of Bird Island, a designated national park that is perfect for the beginning snorkeler. If you want some exercise, venture up the trail for a fantastic view of the Atlantic from 100-foot cliffs.

ON YOUR OWN: WITHIN WALKING DISTANCE

In addition to shopping (see below), St. John's has a few attractions that can be easily reached on foot. The **Museum of Antigua and Barbuda,** at the intersection of Market Street and Long Street (© **268/462-1469**), traces the history of the nation from its geological birth to the present day. Housed in a neoclassic former courthouse, built in 1750, its exhibits include pre-Columbian tools and artifacts, a replica of an Arawak wattle-and-daub hut, African-Caribbean pottery, and sections dedicated to the island's naval, sugar, and slavery eras. It's open Monday through Friday from 8:30am to 4pm, Saturday from 10am to 2pm. Tickets are $3. A couple of blocks uphill from the museum, bordered by Church, Long, and Newgate streets, **St. John's Anglican Cathedral** dominates St. John's skyline with its 21m (69-ft.) aluminum-capped twin spires. The original St. John's, a simple wooden structure built in 1681, was replaced in 1720 by a brick building, which was destroyed during an 1843 earthquake. Upon its completion in 1847, the present baroque structure was not universally appreciated: Ecclesiastical architects criticized it as being like "a pagan temple with two dumpy pepper-pot towers." The cavernous interior is entirely encased in pitch pine, a construction method intended to secure the building from hurricanes and earthquakes.

ON YOUR OWN: BEYOND THE PORT AREA

One of the major historical attractions of the eastern Caribbean, **Nelson's Dockyard National Park** (© **268/481-5021;** www.antiguamuseums.org/nelsonsdockyard.htm) lies 18km (11 miles) southeast of St. John's, alongside one of the world's best-protected natural harbors. English ships used the site as a refuge from hurricanes as early as 1671, and the dockyard played a major role during the 18th century, an era of privateers, pirates, and great sea battles. Admiral Nelson's headquarters from 1784 to 1787, the restored dockyard today remains the only Georgian naval base still in use. At its heart, the **Dockyard Museum,** housed in a former naval officers' house built in 1855, traces the history of the site from its beginning as a British Navy stronghold to its development as a national park and yachting center. Nautical memorabilia make up much of the display. Uphill and east of the Dockyard, the **Dow's Hill Interpretation Center** (✆ 268/481-5045) features an entertaining 15-minute multimedia overview of Antiguan history and an observation platform that affords a 360-degree view of the park. Farther uphill, Palladian arches mark the **Blockhouse,** a military fortification built in 1787 that included officers' quarters and a powder magazine. For an eagle's-eye view of English Harbour, continue to the hill's summit, to the **Shirley Heights Lookout.** Fortified to defend the precious cargo in the harbor below, Fort Shirley's barracks, arched walkways, batteries, and powder magazines are scattered around the hilltop. The Lookout, with its view of the French island of Guadeloupe, was the main signal station used to warn of approaching hostile ships.

The grounds of the national park, which represent 10% of Antigua's total land area, are well worth exploring. Bordered on one side by sandy beaches, the park is blanketed in cactus, tamarind, cinnamon, and turpentine trees, as well as mangroves that shelter African cattle egrets. An array of **nature trails,** which take anywhere from 30 minutes to 5 hours to walk, meander through the vegetation and offer vistas of the coast. One trail climbs to **Fort Berkeley,** built in 1704 to protect the harbor's entrance. Admission, which is $5 for adults and free for children under 12, covers the Dockyard, the Dockyard Museum, Dow's Hill Interpretation Center, the Blockhouse, Shirley Heights, and the rest of the park. The complex is open daily from 9am to 5pm. It's within walking distance of cruise ships that dock at English Harbour. Free guided tours of the dockyard last 15 to 20 minutes; tipping is discretionary.

If you've worked up an appetite, the Dockyard's rustic **Admiral's Inn** (✆ 268/460-1027) offers lunches that usually include pumpkin soup and main courses such as local red snapper, grilled steak, and lobster. Built in 1788, the restored brick building originally stored barrels of pitch, turpentine, and lead used to repair ships. Lunch prices start at $12.

To see what's billed as the only operational 18th-century sugar mill in the Caribbean, visit **Betty's Hope,** not far from Pares village on the island's east side (✆ 268/462-1469). On-site are twin mills, the remnants of a boiling house, and a small visitor center, which opens its doors Monday through Friday from 8:30am to 4pm and Saturday from 10am to 2pm. Gardeners should be able to spot golden seal bushes, neem trees, and wild tamarinds on the rolling hills. Serene cows saunter lazily on the grounds.

Not far from Betty's Hope, on the extreme eastern tip of the island, **Devil's Bridge** is one of Antigua's most picturesque natural wonders. Over the centuries, powerful Atlantic breakers, gathering strength over the course of their 4,830km (3,000-mile) run from Africa, have carved out a natural arch in the limestone coastline and created blowholes through which the surf spurts skyward at high tide.

Another option for nature lovers is **Wallings Conservation Area,** Antigua's largest remaining tract of tropical rainforest. Located in the southwest, this lush wilderness area features three hiking trails and numerous opportunities to spot wildlife (including many Caribbean birds) and rich vegetation. If you've spent your day at Nelson's

Dockyard, pass through the area on the way back to your ship via the circular Fig Tree Drive. Although plagued with potholes, this is the island's most scenic drive. It winds through the tropical forest, passing fishing villages, frisky goats, and old sugar mills along the way.

BEACHES

Antiguans claim that the island is home to 365 beaches, one for each day of the year. True or not, all of them are public, and quite a few are spectacular. Closest to St. John's, **Fort James Beach,** located 5 minutes and a $7 cab fare from the cruise dock, is popular with both locals and tourists. There's volleyball and cricket pretty much daily, plus umbrellas and beach chairs available for rent. For a change of pace, hike up the hill to explore the authentically derelict ruins of Fort James, which once protected St. John's harbor. A bit farther north, a $10 cab ride from the dock, the half-mile beach at **Dickenson Bay** is the island's most bustling, with numerous hotels, restaurants, and watersports vendors. The water is calm, and chairs and umbrellas are available for rent. If you crave complete peace and quiet, head to Antigua's most beautiful beach, at **Half Moon Bay,** isolated at the island's southeast extreme. Waves at the beach's center are great for bodysurfing, while the quieter eastern side is better for children and snorkeling. A restaurant and bar are near the parking lot.

Antigua's **dive sites** include reefs, wall drops, caves, and shipwrecks. To arrange a dive, contact **Dive Antigua,** at the north end of Dickenson Bay (© **268/462-3483**). A two-tank dive costs $85. Reef snorkeling is $30.

SHOPPING

To your right as you leave the docks, **Redcliffe Quay** is Antigua's most interesting shopping complex. Most of the sugar, coffee, and tobacco produced on the island in years past was stored in the warehouses here, and slave auctions were common before the island abolished slavery in 1834. Today, the restored buildings house an array of boutiques and restaurants. For more local color, turn right (south) once you've reached Market Street and walk 5 blocks to the **Public Market,** which is a good place to sample locally produced fruits and vegetables or to pick up some Antiguan pottery or baskets. Other shopping districts include **Heritage Quay,** right at the dock (home to some 40 duty-free shops), and **St. Mary's Street.**

3 Aruba

Located only 32km (20 miles) north of Venezuela, arid Aruba has unwaveringly sunny skies, warm temperatures, and cooling breezes, along with some of the best beaches in the Caribbean, scuba diving, snorkeling, windsurfing, and all the other watersports you'd expect. Away from the beach, Aruba is full of cactus, iguanas, and strange boulder formations. Contrasting sharply with the southern shoreline's beaches, the north coast features craggy limestone cliffs, sand dunes, and crashing breakers. Focused on shopping? The concentration of stores and malls in **Oranjestad,** the island's capital, is as impressive as any in the Caribbean. In between purchases, try your luck at one of the island's dozen casinos; two are just steps away from your ship. Aruba's still part of the Netherlands, so there's a Dutch influence, which adds a nice European flavor. Though it has a few small museums, and some centuries-old indigenous rock glyphs and paintings, nobody comes to Aruba for culture or history.

COMING ASHORE   Cruise ships arrive at the **Port of Oranjestad.** The three recently renovated terminals host tourist information booths, phones, ATMs, and plenty of shops. The terminals can accommodate three megaships and two smaller ships; one of the three terminals is a container berth a short walk from the main terminal. From the pier it's a 5-minute walk to the shopping districts of downtown Oranjestad and a 10-minute drive to the beaches.

GETTING AROUND   You'll need transportation to get to most of the beaches. **Taxis** line up at the dock to take you wherever you want to go. Fares are fixed, and every driver has a copy of the official rate schedule (it's generally $8–$10 to the beach resorts). Excellent roads connect major tourist attractions, and all the major **car-rental** companies accept valid U.S. or Canadian driver's licenses. Avis, Budget, Dollar, Hertz, and National all have offices here. There's also good daily **bus service** offering round-trip $2 trips between the beach hotels and Oranjestad. The bus terminal is across the street from the cruise terminal on L. G. Smith Boulevard. Have exact change ready.

LANGUAGE & CURRENCY   The official language is **Dutch,** but nearly everybody speaks **English.** Spanish and Papiamento are also widely spoken. The **Aruba florin** (AFl) is the official currency (1.77 AFl = US$1; 1 AFl = US56¢), but U.S. dollars are as widely accepted.

BEST CRUISE LINE SHORE EXCURSIONS

In addition to the tours described here, cruise lines typically offer about a dozen snorkeling, diving, sailing, and other water-oriented tours.

Island Bike Adventure ($58, 3½ hr.): Explore Aruba's wild northeast coast by mountain bike, pedaling 16km (10 miles) and visiting the Baby Natural Bridge (cut by the sea and wind), the Bushiribana Gold Mine, the Alto Vista Chapel, and the California Lighthouse.

Arikok National Park Hike & Beach ($49, 3½ hr.): Travel about 30 minutes by bus to Aruba's east end, where a park ranger will lead you on a hike though the desertlike environment, full of divi-divi trees, iguanas, cacti, and (if you can spot 'em) wild donkeys. Posthike, you can cool off with a swim or go snorkeling at Baby Beach.

Off-Road Land Rover Adventure ($98, 4½ hr.): Take off into Aruba's backcountry in an SUV, with you behind the wheel and in radio contact with your guide. You'll visit attractions such as the Baby Natural Bridge, an ostrich farm, and the Bushiribana Gold Mine.

Atlantis Submarine Adventure ($89, 1½ hr.): Cruise 45m (148 ft.) below the sea in a submarine. During the gentle descent, you'll pass by scuba divers, coral reefs, shipwrecks, and hundreds of curious sergeant majors, damselfish, parrotfish, and angelfish.

ON YOUR OWN: WITHIN WALKING DISTANCE

Aruba's capital has a sunny Caribbean demeanor, with Dutch colonial buildings painted in vivid colors. The main thoroughfare, **L. G. Smith Boulevard,** runs along the waterfront and is crowded with marinas, shopping malls, restaurants, and bars. The harbor is packed with fishing boats and schooners docked next to stalls, where vendors hawk fruits, vegetables, and fish. Two casinos—the elegant, 24-hour **Crystal Casino,** at the Aruba Renaissance Beach Resort, L. G. Smith Blvd. 82 (© **297/58-36000**), and the less

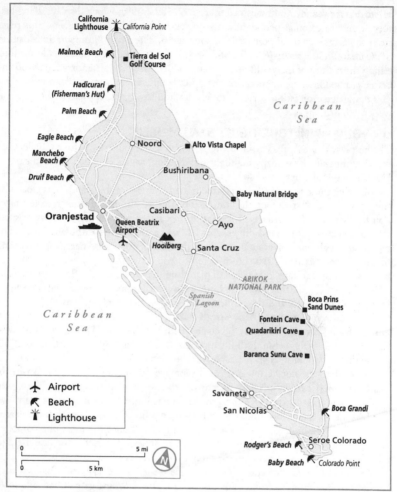

Caribbean Sea

Caribbean Sea

California Lighthouse — California Point
Malmok Beach
Tierra del Sol Golf Course
Hadicurari (Fisherman's Hut)
Palm Beach
Noord
Alto Vista Chapel
Eagle Beach
Bushiribana
Manchebo Beach
Druif Beach
Baby Natural Bridge
Oranjestad
Casibari
Queen Beatrix Airport
Ayo
Hooiberg
Santa Cruz
ARIKOK NATIONAL PARK
Spanish Lagoon
Boca Prins Sand Dunes
Fontein Cave
Quadarikiri Cave
Baranca Sunu Cave
Savaneta
Boca Grandi
San Nicolas
Rodger's Beach
Seroe Colorado
Baby Beach
Colorado Point

✈ Airport
🏄 Beach
🕯 Lighthouse

0   5 mi
0   5 km

assuming **Seaport Casino,** L. G. Smith Blvd. 9 (© **297/58-36000**)—are located steps from the dock.

For a dash of culture, head to one of the town's small museums, which are open on weekdays only. Squeezed between St. Franciscus Roman Catholic Church and the parish rectory is the small **Archaeological Museum of Aruba,** J. E. Irausquinplein 2A (© **297/58-28979**), which was closed at press time, but expected to reopen by late 2007. Exhibits highlight the island's Amerindian heritage, with pottery vessels, shell and stone tools, burial urns, and skulls and bones on display. Admission is free. There is talk of relocating the museum to a historic building closer to the center of town, so call before you plan a visit.

To defend the island against pirates, the Dutch erected **Fort Zoutman** in 1796, and added a tower in 1867. Since 1992, the complex has housed the modest **Museo**

Historico Arubano, Zoutmanstraat 4 (© **297/582-6099**), which displays island history from the colonial period till now, prehistoric Amerindian artifacts, and relics from the Dutch colonial period. Admission is $6. The small **Numismatic Museum of Aruba,** Westraat z/n (© **297/582-8831**), has meticulous, homemade exhibits telling the history of the world through coins. Dedicated numismatists can spend the better part of the morning perusing the 35,000 different specimens from more than 400 countries. Admission is free, though donations are appreciated. Open only on weekday mornings.

ON YOUR OWN: TOURING BY RENTAL JEEP

The best way to see Aruba's desertlike terrain is to rent a four-wheel-drive vehicle. Car-rental companies have maps highlighting the best routes to reach the attractions. Here's one popular option:

Following the system of roads that traces the perimeter of the island, start clockwise from Oranjestad. Drive past the hotel strip, toward the island's northwesternmost point. Here, the **California Lighthouse** affords sweeping 360-degree views of spectacular scenery—gentle sand dunes, rocky coral shoreline, and turbulent waves. The picturesque lighthouse gets its name from the *California,* a passenger ship that sank off the nearby coast in 1916. From here on, your adventure will take you into the island's moonlike terrain, past heaps of giant boulders and barren rocky coastline. The well-maintained road that links the hotel strip with Oranjestad deteriorates abruptly into a band of rubble, and the calm, turquoise sea turns rough and rowdy.

By the time you reach the **Alto Vista Chapel,** about 8km (5 miles) from the lighthouse, chances are you'll already be coated with red dust that'll contrast nicely with the quaint pale-yellow church, built by native Indians and Spanish settlers in 1750, before the island had its own priest. It was the island's first chapel.

Farther along the northern coast, you'll approach the hulking ruins of the **Bushiribana Gold Smelter.** Built in 1872, its massive stone walls are remnants of Aruba's 19th-century gold-mining heritage. Climb the multitiered interior for impressive sea views. Too bad the walls have been marred with artless graffiti. Too bad, too, that the nearby Natural Bridge, a limestone arch above the sea that was once the most photographed attraction in Aruba, collapsed in 2005. You can still see the **Baby Natural Bridge,** though, in the same area, its span carved out by centuries of pounding surf.

Next, head toward the center of the island and the bizarre **Ayó and Casibari rock formations.** Looking like something out of *The Flintstones,* the gargantuan Ayó rocks served Aruba's early inhabitants as a dwelling or religious site. The reddish-brown petroglyphs on the boulders suggest mystical significance.

Farther east, back along the northern coast, **Arikok National Park,** Aruba's showcase ecological preserve, sprawls over roughly 20% of the island. Its premier attractions are a series of caves that punctuate the cliff sides of the area's mesas. The most popular, **Fontein Cave,** has brownish-red drawings left by Amerindians and graffiti etched by early European settlers. Nearby **Quadirikiri Cave** boasts two large chambers with roof openings that allow sunlight in, making flashlights unnecessary. Hundreds of small bats use the 30m-long (98-ft.) tunnel to reach their nests deeper in the cave. You'll need a flashlight (rentable at the entrance; be sure to ask for spare batteries so you're not left in the dark halfway through) to explore the 90m (295-ft.) passageway of **Baranca Sunu,** another cave in the area commonly known as the Tunnel of Love because of its heart-shaped entrance.

Heading southeast toward Aruba's behemoth oil refinery, you'll eventually come to **Baby Beach,** at the island's easternmost point. Like a great big bathtub, this shallow bowl of warm turquoise water is protected by an almost complete circle of rock—it's a great place for a dip after a sweaty day behind the wheel.

BEACHES

All of Aruba's beaches are public, but chairs and shade huts are hotel property. If you use them, expect to be charged. Shade huts located at beaches where there are no hotels are free of charge. **Palm Beach,** home of Aruba's glamorous high-rise hotels, is great for swimming, sunbathing, sailing, people-watching, fishing, and snorkeling. It has two piers and numerous watersports operators, and can get crowded. Separated from Palm Beach by a limestone outcrop, **Eagle Beach** stretches as far as the eye can see. The sugar-white sand and gentle surf are ideal for swimming, and though the nearby hotels offer watersports and beach activities, the ambience is relaxed and quiet. A couple of bars punctuate the expansive strand, and shaded picnic areas are provided for the public. Well-protected **Baby Beach** (see above) is a prime destination for families with young children.

The island's best **snorkeling sites** are around Malmok Beach (also a great **windsurfing** spot) and Boca Catalina, where the water is calm and shallow and marine life is plentiful. **Dive sites** stretch along the entire southern coast, but most divers head for the German freighter *Antilla,* which was scuttled during World War II off the island's northwestern tip, near Palm Beach. The island's largest watersports operators, **Pelican Adventures** (© 297/58-63271) and **Red Sail Sports** (© 297/58-72302), offer sailing, windsurfing, and water-skiing in addition to one- and two-tank dives ($73 and $95, respectively) and snorkeling trips ($43 for 2½ hr., $62 for 4½ hr., champagne brunch sometimes included).

SHOPPING

Because the island is part of the Netherlands, Dutch goods such as Delft porcelain, chocolate, and cheese are especially good buys. Items from Indonesia, another former Dutch colony, are reasonably priced too. Skin- and hair-care products made from locally produced aloe are also popular and practical. If you're looking for big-ticket items, Aruba offers the usual array of watches, cameras, gold and diamond jewelry, Cuban cigars, premium liquor, English and German china, porcelain, French and American fragrances, and crystal, and its 3.3% duty and lack of sales tax make for some decent prices.

Caya G. F. Betico Croes (aka Main St.) is the city's major shopping venue, running roughly parallel to the waterfront several blocks inland. **Renaissance Mall** and **Renaissance Marketplace,** right downtown, feature more than 130 stores, 20 restaurants and cafes, two casinos, and a movie theater. Just down the road, **Royal Plaza Mall** is chock-full of popular restaurants and generally upscale boutiques.

4 The Bahamas: Nassau & Freeport

Nassau and **Freeport** are some of the busiest cruise ports on the Caribbean circuit, even though technically The Bahamas aren't in the Caribbean at all—they're in the Atlantic, north of the Caribbean and less than 161km (100 miles) from Miami. Though holdovers from Great Britain's long colonial occupation linger in some architecture and culture, the vibe here isn't all that much different from parts of Florida, and the ports are totally tourist-oriented, with more shopping than the Mall of America, all surrounded by beaches and casinos.

LANGUAGE & CURRENCY   **English** is the official language of The Bahamas. Its legal tender is the **Bahamian dollar** (B$), whose value is always the same as that of the U.S. dollar. Both currencies are accepted everywhere on the islands.

NASSAU

Nassau is the cultural, social, political, and economic center of The Bahamas. With its beaches, shopping, resorts, casinos, historic landmarks, and water and land activities, it's also the island chain's most visited destination—one million travelers a year make their way to the town, and Nassau is one of the world's busiest cruise ship ports. The Nassau/Paradise Island area comprises two separate islands. Nassau is on the northeastern shore of 34km (21-mile) New Providence Island, while tiny Paradise Island is linked to New Providence by bridges, and protects Nassau harbor for a 5km (3-mile) stretch.

COMING ASHORE   The cruise ship docks at **Prince George Wharf** are in the center of town at Rawson Square, in the middle of Nassau's shopping frenzy. The main docks can accommodate six larger cruise ships and one smaller one on an innermost dock. There are plans in place to widen the entrance channel to better accommodate megaships like the *Queen Mary 2*.

GETTING AROUND   Walk. The major attractions and stores are pretty concentrated, and if you're really fit you can even trek over to Cable Beach or Paradise Island. Otherwise, you'll have no problem finding taxis—they'll find you. There's no good reason to rent a car here.

BEST CRUISE LINE SHORE EXCURSIONS

In addition to the excursions below, cruise lines typically offer a variety of snorkeling, diving, and boat tours. Avoid the city bus tours, which are dull, dull, dull.

Harbor Cruise & Atlantis Resort ($54, 2½ hr.): A tour boat with a local guide shows you the sights (such as they are) from the water. It then drops you at the fanciful Atlantis Resort for a brief tour that includes a visit to Predator Lagoon, home to sharks, barracuda, and other toothy fish.

Thriller Powerboat Tour ($39, 1 hr.): A thrill-seeker's excursion, with high-speed boats roaring around the waters off Nassau, scaring the hell out of the fish. Not our personal favorite way to see . . . well, anything, but it sure is fast. Vroom.

ON YOUR OWN: WITHIN WALKING DISTANCE

As you exit from the cruise ship wharf into the main port area, you'll have no choice but to pass through **Festival Place,** a barnlike hall full of little shops and stalls selling arts and crafts, T-shirts, hot sauces, and other touristy items. Outside, hawkers will encourage you to have your hair braided at the **Hairbraider's Centre.** This government-sponsored open-air pavilion attracts braiding experts from all over the island.

Shopping is *the* thing here, but there are a few other sights of interest. Just across Bay Street from Rawson Square (inland from the wharf) are the flamingo-pink government buildings of **Parliament Square,** constructed in 1815. The House of Assembly, old colonial Secretary's Office, and Supreme Court flank a statue of Queen Victoria, while a bust on the north side of the square honors Sir Milo B. Butler, the first governor-general of The Bahamas. One block inland, the pink, octagonal **Nassau**

Nassau

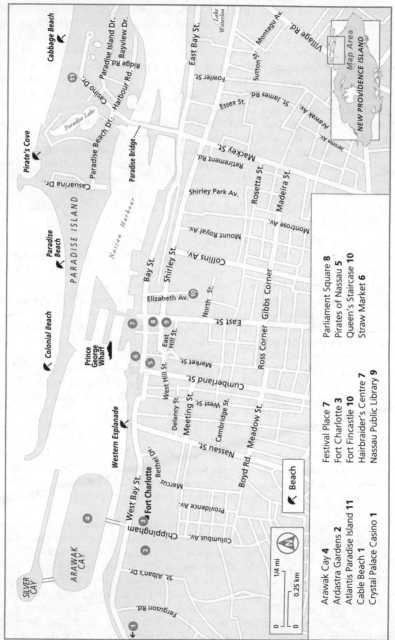

Cabbage Beach

Pirate's Cove

Paradise Beach

Colonial Beach

PARADISE ISLAND

Paradise Lake

Nassau Harbour

Casuarina Dr.

Paradise Beach Dr.

Paradise Bridge

Paradise Island Dr.

Bayview Dr.

Ridge Rd.

Harbour Rd.

Casino Dr.

Lake Waterloo

East Bay St.

Fowler St.

Sutton St.

Montagu Av.

Village Rd.

St. James Rd.

Essex St.

Arawak Av.

Jerome Av.

Map Area

NEW PROVIDENCE ISLAND

Mackey St.

Retirement Rd.

Shirley Park Av.

Rosetta St.

Madeira St.

Montrose Av.

Mount Royal Av.

Collins Av.

Bay St.

Shirley St.

Elizabeth Av.

North St.

East St.

Gibbs Corner

Ross Corner

Western Esplanade

Prince George Wharf

West Hill St.

East Hill St.

Market St.

Cumberland St.

West St.

Meeting St.

Delancy St.

Cambridge St.

Nassau St.

Meadow St.

Boyd Rd.

Providence Av.

Columbus Av.

Marcus

Bethel D'.

West Bay St.

Fort Charlotte

Chippingham

St. Alban's Dr.

Ferguson Rd.

ARAWAK CAY

SILVER CAY

Beach

N

1/4 mi

0.25 km

Arawak Cay **4**
Ardastra Gardens **2**
Atlantis Paradise Island **11**
Cable Beach **1**
Crystal Palace Casino **1**

Festival Place **7**
Fort Charlotte **3**
Fort Fincastle **10**
Hairbraider's Centre **7**
Nassau Public Library **9**

Parliament Square **8**
Pirates of Nassau **5**
Queen's Staircase **10**
Straw Market **6**

Public Library was built as a prison in 1798, and today its collection of books, historical prints, colonial documents, and Arawak Indian artifacts are kept in what were once cells. It's one of the city's oldest buildings.

Slaves carved the **Queen's Staircase** out of a solid limestone cliff in 1793. Originally designed as an escape route for soldiers, each step now represents a year in Queen Victoria's 65-year reign. Lush plants and a waterfall stand guard over the staircase, which is located a few blocks up from the library on East Street and leads to **Fort Fincastle,** on Elizabeth Avenue, built in 1793 by Lord Dunmore, the royal governor. An elevator climbs a 38m-high (125-ft.) water tower, where you can look down on the arrowhead-shaped fort. Walk around on your own or hire a guide.

At the corny **Pirates of Nassau Museum,** at King and George streets (② **242/356-3759;** www.pirates-of-nassau.com), Captain Teach and his fearsome crew guide you through the age of piracy in the lawless Nassau of 1716. Admission is a steep $12 for adults—only worth it if you're with kids, as each adult may bring two children under 12 for free (each additional child pays $6). Hours are Monday through Saturday from 9am to 6pm, Sunday from 9am to 12:30pm.

ON YOUR OWN: BEYOND THE PORT AREA

About a mile west of downtown Nassau, just off West Bay Street, **Fort Charlotte** is the largest fort in The Bahamas, covering more than 41 hilltop hectares (100 acres) and offering impressive views of Paradise Island, Nassau, and the harbor. The complex, constructed in 1788, features a moat, dungeons, underground passageways, and 42 cannons. Nearby, parading pink flamingos are the main attraction at the lush, 2-hectare (5-acre) **Ardastra Gardens, Zoo & Conservation Center,** on Chippingham Road (② **242/323-5806;** www.ardastra.com). The graceful birds obey the drillmaster's orders daily at 10:30am, 2:10pm, and 4:10pm. Other exotic wildlife—parrots, boa constrictors, honey bears, macaws, and capuchin monkeys—are less talented but still fascinating in their own right. Meandering paths show off the garden's exotic fruit trees, coconut palms, ackee and mango trees, bougainvillea, and hibiscus blossoms. Admission is $12 for adults, $6 for children 4 to 12.

If you're in the mood for some conch, head for **Arawak Cay,** a small man-made island across West Bay Street from Ardastra Gardens and Fort Charlotte. Join the locals in sampling conch with hot sauce, and wash it down with a cocktail made from coconut water and gin. Farther to the west, the 3,252-sq.-m (35,000-sq.-ft.) **Crystal Palace Casino,** West Bay Street, Cable Beach (② **800/222-7466** or 242/327-6200), is the only casino on New Providence Island. Slots are open all night long, but tables close at 4am.

On Paradise Island, the towering, fancifully designed megaresort known as **Atlantis Paradise Island** (② **242/363-3000;** www.atlantis.com) is the largest gaming and entertainment complex in the Caribbean, its casino boasting nearly 1,000 slot machines and 78 gaming tables, all tied together with a "Lost City of Atlantis" theme. Though only paying hotel guests can use Atlantis's beaches, water slides, and pools, cruise passengers in for the day can visit the casino, eat at the restaurants, and sign up for the "Discover Atlantis" tour. The guided excursion, which includes round-trip ferry transport between the ship and property, includes a walk through the resort's sprawling 11-million-gallon lagoon system that boasts more than 200 sea species and 50,000 individual creatures. You'll also tour **"The Dig,"** a fantastic world of faux Atlantis ruins flooded by the sea. The interconnected passageways, boulevards, and chambers, now inhabited by piranhas, hammerhead sharks, stingrays, and morays, are visible through huge glass windows. It is purported to be the largest man-made marine habitat in the world. To see this part of the resort, you must sign up for the guided "Discovery Tour." Tickets, available at the resort's guest services desks, cost $29 adults, $21 kids 4 to 12. Another tour, available to Disney and Royal Caribbean guests only, gives access to the resort's beaches and restaurants.

BEACHES

On New Providence Island, sun worshippers make the 8km (5-mile) pilgrimage to 6.5km (4-mile) **Cable Beach,** which offers various watersports and easy access to shops, a casino, bars, and restaurants. Not on the same level but more convenient for cruise ship passengers, the **Western Esplanade** sweeps westward from the Hilton British Colonial hotel, with changing facilities, restrooms, and a snack bar.

Paradise Beach, on Paradise Island, is a ferry ride away from Prince George Wharf. The price of admission ($3 for adults, $1 for children) includes use of a shower and locker. An extra $10 deposit is required for towels. Paradise Island has a number of smaller beaches as well, including **Pirate's Cove Beach** and **Cabbage Beach,** the latter of which often fills up with guests of the nearby resorts.

SHOPPING

In 1992, The Bahamas abolished import duties on 11 luxury-goods categories, including china, crystal, fine linens, jewelry, leather goods, photographic equipment, watches, and fragrances. Even so, you can end up spending more on an item here than you would at home. True bargains are rare.

The principal shopping area is **Bay Street** and the adjacent blocks, which are almost the first things you see when you leave your ship. Here you'll find dozens of duty-free luxury-goods stores, plus hundreds of others selling T-shirts, tourist gimcracks, duty-free booze and cigars, and recordings of Junkanoo music. The crowded aisles of the **Straw Market,** a few blocks west of the docks, display all manner of straw hats, handbags, dolls, place mats, and other items, but be aware that most aren't of the best quality, nor even made locally—much of it has been imported from Asia. Welcome to the global market.

FREEPORT/LUCAYA

Freeport/Lucaya, on Grand Bahama Island, is the second-most-popular destination in The Bahamas. Technically, Freeport is the landlocked section of town, while adjacent Lucaya hugs the waterfront. Originally two separate developments, they've grown together over the years, and though they offer none of Nassau's colonial charm, they do offer plenty of sun, surf, golf, tennis, and watersports. Gambling and shopping were big business here for a while, but three hurricanes in 2 years have quelled the frenzy, leaving the port with a calmer, quieter feel.

COMING ASHORE   Ships dock at **Lucayan Harbor,** a dreary port in the middle of nowhere, with a small straw market, shopping area, and hair braiders camped out in the middle of an industrial zone. The docks can accommodate three larger ships, or several smaller ones. You're better served by taking a $24 taxi ride to the **Port Lucaya Marketplace,** where you'll find most of the action. Closer to the pier, but not as bustling, is the **International Bazaar,** which will cost you $16 in cab fare.

GETTING AROUND   Once you get to Freeport by **taxi,** you can explore the center of town on foot. Taxis can also take you to farther-flung attractions. The government sets taxi rates, which start at $4 and increase 40¢ for each additional .5km (¼ mile; plus $3 extra per passenger).

BEST CRUISE LINE SHORE EXCURSIONS

UNEXSO Dolphin Encounter ($80–$89, 3¼ hr.): Pat a dolphin on the nose! On this excursion you can watch, touch, and photograph Flipper, or at least one of his relatives. Organized by UNEXSO Dolphin Encounter (at Sanctuary Bay).

Kayak Nature Tour ($70–$75, 6 hr.): Visit a protected island creek, kayak through a mangrove forest, explore the island's caves, and take a guided nature walk into Lucayan National Park. The excursion includes lunch and beach time.

ON YOUR OWN: BEYOND THE PORT AREA

Nothing of note is within walking distance of the port. You must take a cab over to Freeport/Lucaya for all attractions.

A couple of miles east of downtown Freeport on East Settlers Way, the 40-hectare (100-acre) **Rand Nature Centre** (© 242/352-5438) serves as the regional headquarters of The Bahamas National Trust. Pineland nature trails meander past native flora and wild birds, including the Bahama parrot. Other highlights include native animal displays (don't miss the boa constrictors), an education center, and a gift shop. Admission is $5; open Monday through Friday from 9am to 4pm.

If you'd like a taste of The Bahamas the way they used to be, head for the **Star Club,** on Bayshore Road, on the island's west end (© 242/346-6207). Built in the 1940s, the Star was Grand Bahama's first hotel, and over the years it's hosted many famous guests. You can order Bahamian chicken in the bag, burgers, fish and chips, "fresh sexy" ceviche conch salad, or cooked conch prepared as chowder and fritters. But don't come for the food; come for the good times and to mix with the locals. Lunch costs $8. Next door, **Austin's Calypso Bar** is a colorful old dive if ever there was one.

BEACHES

Grand Bahama Island has miles of white-sand beaches. **Xanadu Beach,** immediately east of Freeport at the Xanadu Beach Resort, is the closest to the cruise pier, but two of the island's best are **Taíno Beach** and **Lucayan Beach,** both located on the Lucaya oceanfront. Of the two, Lucayan Beach is easiest to reach and closest to the Port Lucaya Marketplace, and offers beach-chair rentals, watersports, and restaurants. A 20-minute ride east of Lucaya, **Gold Rock Beach** may be the island's best if total isolation is your thing. Hidden away in Lucayan National Park, it has barbecue pits, picnic tables, and a spectacular low tide. **Barbary Beach,** slightly closer to Lucaya, is great for seashell hunters, and white spider lilies in the area bloom spectacularly in May and June.

SHOPPING

The **International Bazaar,** at East Mall Drive and East Sunrise Highway, is pure 1960s Bahamian kitsch, and though relentlessly cheerful, it's rather long in the tooth. Each area of the 4-hectare (10-acre), 100-shop complex attempts to capture the ambience of a different region of the globe. Buses marked INTERNATIONAL BAZAAR deliver passengers to the center's much-photographed Torii Gate, a Japanese symbol of welcome.

The **Port Lucaya Marketplace,** on Seahorse Road, across the street from the Lucayan Beach, is a large shopping-and-dining complex that in recent years has eclipsed the International Bazaar. This is definitely where the shopping/dining action

Bahamas Golf Excursions

Our Lucaya Beach & Golf Resort, Royal Palm Way, F-42500, Lucaya (© 242/373-2003; www.ourlucaya.com), offers two 18-hole, par-72 courses. The Lucayan course, designed by Dick Wilson, features well-protected elevated greens, fairways lined with tropical foliage, and doglegs. The links-style Reef course, designed by Robert Trent Jones, Jr., has water traps on 13 of 18 holes. Greens fees are $140 for 18 holes, including cart. Club rentals are $45.

is now. Many of the restaurants and shops overlook a 50-slip marina next to **UNEXSO** (© **242/373-1244;** www.unexso.com), a resource for swimming, snorkeling, and diving gear. A two-tank dive will cost you $70 per person; dolphin encounters start from $75 per adult and $38 for kids. Call ahead for reservations.

Next door to the marketplace, the **Straw Market** features items with a Bahamian touch—baskets, hats, handbags, and place mats. Quality varies, so look around before buying.

5 Barbados

No port of call in the southern Caribbean can compete with Barbados when it comes to natural beauty, attractions, and especially its seemingly endless stretches of pink and white sandy beaches—among the best in the entire Caribbean Basin. Originally operated on a plantation economy that made its British colonial aristocracy rich, the island is the most easterly in the Caribbean, floating in the mid-Atlantic like a great coral reef. Topography varies from rolling hills and savage waves on the eastern (Atlantic) coast to densely populated flatlands, rows of hotels and apartments, and sheltered beaches in the southwest. The people in Barbados are called Bajans, and you'll see this term used everywhere.

COMING ASHORE   Located about a mile from the capital, **Bridgetown,** the island's modern cruise ship terminal offers car rentals, taxi services, sightseeing tours, and a tourist information office, plus shops, bars, restaurants, an Internet cafe, a post office, and scads of vendors. The main terminal has docking capacity for five cruise ships. A sixth can tie up at a nearby commercial pier, a 5-minute shuttle ride from the terminal.

GETTING AROUND   You'll need transportation to get to the beaches, though you can walk into Bridgetown in about 15 minutes via a park that runs along the shoreline between the port and city center. You'll find **taxis** just outside the cruise terminal. They're not metered, but their rates are fixed by the government (settle on the price before getting in). Recently, a **shuttle service** was started that also takes visitors to key attractions.

LANGUAGE & CURRENCY   **English** is spoken with an island lilt. The **Barbados dollar** (BD$) is the official currency (BD$1.98 = US$1; BD$1 = US50¢), but U.S. dollars are commonly accepted.

BEST CRUISE LINE SHORE EXCURSIONS

It's not easy to get around Barbados quickly and conveniently, so a shore excursion is a good idea here.

Kayak & Turtle Encounter ($84, 4 hr.): A boat ride along the west coast brings you to the beach, where you'll clamber into a kayak for a 45-minute paddle along the shore. Once at the snorkel site, you'll be able to swim with and feed sea turtles.

Mount Gay Rum Distillery & Banks Beer Tour ($42, 3½ hr.): Talk about getting in the spirit. This excursion takes you for a tour and tipple at Barbados's number-one rum distillery; then it heads over to the Banks Brewery for the yeasty side of things.

Rainforest Hike & Cave Adventure ($74, 4 hr.): A guide leads your group through one of Barbados's rainforest gullies, then down into a natural cave.

Harrison's Cave & Tropical Rainforest Hike ($79, 4 hr.): Most cruise lines offer a tour to Harrison's Cave in the center of the island (see "On Your Own: Beyond the Port Area," below, for details), coupled with a 45-minute guided hike through the rainforest.

Horseback Riding & Country Drive ($94, 3½ hr.): Horse treks through the heart of the island wind past old plantation houses, sugar cane fields, old sugar factories, small villages, and, if you're lucky, green monkeys scouting for food.

ON YOUR OWN: BEYOND THE PORT AREA

For the purposes of argument, let's consider Bridgetown "beyond walking distance," but, in any case, don't waste too much time here—it's hot, dry, and dusty, and the honking horns of traffic jams only add to its woes. Unless you want to go shopping, you should spend your time exploring all the beauty the island has to offer instead.

All cruise ship excursions visit **Harrison's Cave,** Welchman Hall, St. Thomas (© 246/438-6640), Barbados's top tourist attraction. At press time, the cave was closed for renovations, with plans to reopen by the end of 2007. Here you can see a beautiful underground world from aboard an electric tram and trailer. Admission is $16 for adults and $6 for children. If you'd like to go on your own, the taxi ride takes about 30 minutes and costs at least $20 each way. About 1.6km (1 mile) away is the **Flower Forest,** Richmond Plantation, St. Joseph (© 246/433-8152), a former sugar plantation that's now a junglelike botanical garden, with paths winding among huge tropical flowers and plants. Admission is $10.

Welchman Hall Gully, St. Thomas (Hwy. 2 from Bridgetown), is a lush tropical garden owned by the Barbados National Trust. It's 13km (8 miles) from the port (reachable by bus) and features some plants that were here when the English settlers landed in 1627, plus later imports that include cocoa bushes, exotic orchids, and breadfruit trees that are supposedly descendants of the seedlings brought ashore by Captain Bligh, of *Bounty* fame. Many of the plants are labeled; occasionally you'll spot a wild monkey. Admission is $10.

The **Sunbury Plantation House,** 25 minutes from Bridgetown along Highway 5 (© 246/423-6270), is the only plantation great house on Barbados whose rooms are all open for viewing. The 300-year-old house is steeped in history, featuring mahogany antiques, old prints, and a collection of horse-drawn carriages. Admission is $7.50. Signs along the highway will guide you in, right before Six Cross Roads.

BEACHES

Beaches on the island's western "Gold Coast" are far preferable (and closer) than those on the surf-pounded Atlantic side, which are dangerous for swimming. All Barbados beaches are open to the public, even those in front of the big resort hotels and private homes. You'll need to snag a taxi to get to them.

ON THE GOLD COAST Payne's Bay, with access from the Coach House (© 246/432-1163) or Mannie's Suga Suga restaurant (© 246/419-4511), is a good beach for watersports, especially snorkeling. There's also a parking area here. This beach can get rather crowded, but the beautiful bay makes it worth it. Directly south of Payne's Bay, at Fresh Water Bay, is a trio of fine beaches: **Brighton Beach, Brandon's Beach,** and **Paradise Beach.** Farther north, **Church Point** can get crowded, but it's one of the most scenic bays in Barbados, and the swimming is ideal. Retreat under some shade trees when you've had enough sun. You can also order drinks at the Colony Club Resort's beach terrace.

Snorkelers in particular seek out the glassy blue waters by **Mullins Beach.** There are some shady areas, and you can park on the main road. Just north of here is another good stretch, **Heywoods Beach.**

ON THE SOUTH COAST Just outside Bridgetown, **Carlisle Bay Beach** is popular with locals and is a great snorkeling spot. Farther south, near Rockley, **Accra Beach** is the biggest on the south coast, and very popular with both locals and visitors. **Sandy Beach,** reached from the parking lot on the Worthing main road, has tranquil waters opening onto a lagoon. This is a family favorite, with lots of screaming and yelling, especially on weekends. Food and drink are sold here. Windsurfers are particularly fond of the trade winds that sweep across wide **Casuarina Beach,** even on the hottest summer days. Access is from Maxwell Coast Road, across the property of the Casuarina Beach Hotel. **Silver Sands Beach** is to the east of the town of Oistins, near the very southernmost point of Barbados, directly east of South Point Lighthouse. This white sandy beach is a favorite with many Bajans, who probably want to keep it a secret from as many visitors as possible. (Tough luck, Bajans!) Windsurfing is good here, and you can rent boards at **Club Mistral,** at the Silver Sands Resort (© 246/428-6001; www.clubmistralbarbados.com). Open daily from 8am to 5pm.

ON THE SOUTHEAST COAST The southeast coast is known for its big waves, especially at **Crane Beach,** a white sandy stretch backed by cliffs and palms that often appears in travel-magazine articles about Barbados. The beach offers excellent body-surfing—but this is real ocean swimming, not the calm Caribbean, so be careful. This one will cost you about $20 in taxi fare from the cruise pier, each way.

SHOPPING

The shopping-mall-size cruise terminal contains retail stores, duty-free shops, and a plethora of vendors selling arts and crafts, jewelry, liquor, china, crystal, electronics, perfume, leather goods, and great local hot sauce, as well as yummy Punch de Crème (you can get a free sample before buying), a creamy rum drink. Among Barbados handicrafts, you'll find lots of black-coral jewelry, but beware—because black coral is endangered, it's illegal to bring it back to the United States. We suggest looking, but not buying. Local clay potters turn out some really interesting products, some based on centuries-old designs.

6 Belize

Located on the northeastern tip of Central America, bordering Mexico on the north, Guatemala to the west and south, and the Caribbean to the east, Belize combines Central American and Caribbean cultures, offering both ancient Maya ruins and a 298km (185-mile) coral reef that runs the entire length of the country—it's the largest in the Western Hemisphere and the second-largest in the world, supporting a tremendous number of patch reefs, shoals, and more than 1,000 islands called cayes (pronounced *keys*), the largest and most populous being **Ambergris Caye.** (Both Ambergris Caye and Caye Caulker are popular with visitors, but require a flight from Belize City. However, smaller lines such as Windstar may just skip Belize City completely and anchor offshore from the cayes and other parts of the mainland, such as southern Dangriga and Placencia.) Unlike many other Caribbean countries, Belize is serious in its dedication to conservation: One-fifth of its total landmass is dedicated as nature reserves, and 7,770 sq. km (2,973 sq. miles) of its waters are protected as well.

Belize City is the economic center of the country. Trying to choose which natural or man-made wonder to explore will be the most stress you'll feel in this very laid-back, diverse, stable, and English-speaking nation, whose population comprises Creoles, Garifuna (Black Carib Indians), mestizos (a mix of Spanish and Indian), Spanish, Mayan, English, Lebanese, Chinese, and Eastern Indians. The country has the highest concentration of Maya sites among all Central American nations.

COMING ASHORE   Shallow waters mean ships must anchor offshore and tender passengers in—a 15- to 20-minute trip. You arrive at a multi-million-dollar pier called the **Fort Street Tourism Village,** which has four main terminals with shopping, restaurants, and tourist information. The port can accommodate four cruise ships on a given day; each is assigned to a separate terminal.

GETTING AROUND   Taxis are available at the pier, in town, and in resort areas, and are easily recognized by their green license plates. Although the taxis have no meters, the drivers do charge somewhat standard rates, but it's always important to settle what your fare will be before hiring a taxi. Aside from the local shopping, most other attractions are about an hour away.

LANGUAGE & CURRENCY   **English** is the official language of Belize, although Spanish, Creole, Garifuna, and Mayan are spoken throughout the country as well. The **Belize dollar** (BZ) has a fixed exchange rate of BZ$1.95 = US$1 (BZ$1 = US51¢). Most establishments, as well as taxis and vendors on the street, take U.S. dollars. In especially touristy areas, just be sure to ask if the price quoted is in U.S. or BZ dollars. Unless otherwise specified, prices in this section are given in U.S. dollars.

CALLING FROM THE U.S.   To make a call from the U.S. to Belize, dial the international access code **(011),** the country code **(501),** and then the number of the establishment.

BEST CRUISE LINE SHORE EXCURSIONS

Lamanai ($96, 7½ hr.): Lamanai is one of the largest ceremonial centers in Belize. In the original Mayan language, its name means "submerged crocodile," and you will see various crocodile carvings throughout the site. After a 45-minute drive up the Northern Highway to Tower Hill, you'll board a riverboat and head up the New River. Along the way, through the mangroves, your guide will point out crocodiles basking in the sun, a variety of birds (including jaçanas and hawks), delicate waterlilies, and other exotic flowers such as black orchids. You'll pass local fisherman and, surprisingly, Mennonite farms—Mennonites from Canada and Mexico began arriving in Belize in 1958 in search of land and a more isolated and simple life, and today their community numbers around 7,000. Landing at the Lamanai grounds, you'll have lunch and then tour the series of temples. There are more than 700 structures, most of them still buried beneath mounds of earth. For a view above the thick jungle, you can climb some of the temples—look in the trees for toucans and spider monkeys playing or napping. You won't mistake the roar of the howler monkey. Your guide may tell you about the red gumbo-limbo tree, whose bark becomes a shade of red and then peels off—it's jokingly referred to as the tourist tree. A small archaeological museum is on the site, as well as a few stands that sell souvenirs.

Xunantunich ($89, 7½ hr.): This site, also called Maiden of the Rock, is located near the Guatemalan border overlooking the Mopan River; it was a major ceremonial center during the classic Maya period. After crossing the river by hand-cranked ferry, you can explore six major plazas surrounded by more than 25 temples and palaces, including El Castillo (the castle), the largest of the temples. Be sure to climb to the top—it's well worth it for the amazing panoramic view. There's also a new visitor center with old excavation photos, a scale model, and a few exhibits and souvenir shops. Afterward, you'll head to San Ignacio to eat lunch and enjoy a marimba band.

Hol Chan Marine Reserve & Shark Ray Alley ($99, 7½ hr.): You'll head north for an hour-long speedboat ride to Hol Chan (Mayan for "little channel"), 6.4km (4 miles) southeast of San Pedro on Ambergris Caye; snorkel the reef for about an hour; and then head off to the Shark Ray Alley dive site, about 5 minutes away, where you'll see and pet dozens of southern stingrays and nurse sharks.

Jungle Survival Trek ($99, 4½ hr.): After an hour's drive to Peccary Park, you'll hike down a jungle trail. Along the way, a survival expert will explain how to build natural shelters, find water, start fires, hunt for food, and perform other skills. At the top of a steep incline, you'll rappel down a part of the hill or take the trail down.

Cave Tubing & Jungle Trek ($98, 6¼ hr.): On arriving at Jaguar Paw, you take a 45-minute hike down a jungle trail where your guide will point out various plants and trees used by the ancient Maya for medicinal purposes. When you get to the cave, your guide will hand out flashlights and inner tubes and set you afloat, propelled by the current, through the cave system. On several occasions, you'll emerge into the sunlight before entering another cave. The float lasts about 2 hours, after which you'll have lunch. Bring a change of clothes. Minimum age: 12 years.

Two-Tank Scuba Dive at Turneffe Atoll ($159, 6 hr.): After a 50-minute boat ride, you arrive at Turneffe Atoll for dives at two different sites (with depths of 50–70 ft.) among reef fish and growths of sponge and coral.

ON YOUR OWN: WITHIN WALKING DISTANCE

Belize City is the hub of the country, but doesn't boast the country's major attractions. The historic **harbor district** right around the pier is small and quaint. You'll find a few restaurants here, and the **Baron Bliss Park and Lighthouse** is just a short stroll away. After sailing from Portugal, the eponymous baron arrived sick with food poisoning and remained aboard his yacht for 2 months while local fisherman and administrators treated him kindly and taught him about Belize. He died soon after, but not before changing his will and leaving $2 million to Belize in a trust fund. That money made possible the building of the Bliss Institute Library and Museum and a number of health clinics and markets around the country, as well as helping with the Belize City water system. The baron is considered Belize's greatest benefactor, and Baron Bliss Day, a national holiday, is celebrated on March 9.

Outside the immediate port area, much of the rest of the city is run-down and poor, with narrow, crowded streets and many old colonial structures that are in need of repair. However, since tourism is an important industry in Belize, the country is making an effort to spruce up the city and reduce crime, instituting a squad of tourism police to patrol popular tourist areas. Its officers are dressed in brown uniforms.

ON YOUR OWN: BEYOND THE PORT AREA

See "Best Cruise Line Shore Excursions," above, for a discussion of the Maya ruins. Animal enthusiasts might want to visit the **Community Baboon Sanctuary,** located about 48km (30 miles) west of Belize City off the Northern Highway in the Belize District (© **501/220-2181;** www.howlermonkeys.org), which offers a guided tour through forest trails. Through a grass-roots effort, the villagers and landowners have committed to preserving the habitat necessary to ensure a healthy population of black howler monkeys (known locally as baboons). Those more interested in birding can tour the **Crooked Tree Wildlife Sanctuary,** about 8km (5 miles) farther up the Northern Highway (© **501/614-5658**). The sanctuary provides a habitat for more than 360 species of birds. A visit to the **Belize Zoo,** along the Western Highway (© **501/220-8004;** www.belizezoo.org), is a worthwhile venture. First created as a haven for injured animals that couldn't be returned to the wild, the zoo now houses an impressive array of large cats, primates, reptiles, and birds in large, airy enclosures. Admission is $8 for adults, $4 for children

Back in Belize City, if you want to do some gambling, the small **Princess Hotel-Casino** is located 2km (1¼ miles) from the cruise pier on Newtown Barricks Road (© **501/223-2670**); it's about 10 minutes and $5 by taxi from the pier.

BEACHES

Compared to many other parts of the Caribbean, the beaches of Belize are neither the biggest nor the widest, but they are relaxing, with very clear water. Areas that offer the best beach sunbathing are in the cayes, including Ambergris Caye, Caye Caulker, Tobacco Caye, and on the mainland to the south in Dangriga and Placencia. There are no beaches near Belize City.

SHOPPING

In general, the best buys in Belize are wooden and slate carvings, Maya calendars, pottery, ceramics, and furniture made by the Mennonites. At the pier, the new **Tourism Village** offers shops specializing in local souvenirs such as mahogany bowls, jewelry, clothes, assorted carvings, and artwork. A local favorite is **Marie Sharp's hot sauces and jams.** They're served everywhere and can be purchased to take home.

7 British Virgin Islands: Tortola & Virgin Gorda

With small bays and hidden coves that were once havens for pirates (Norman Island is said to have been the prototype for Robert Louis Stevenson's *Treasure Island*), the British Virgin Islands (BVIs) are among the world's loveliest cruising regions. Among its 60-some islands, only **Tortola, Virgin Gorda,** and **Jost Van Dyke** (plus Anegada, 16 miles to the north) are of significant size. The English officially annexed the islands in 1672, and today they're a British territory, with their own elected government and a population of about 21,000. Tortola attracts the megaships, while Virgin Gorda and Jost Van Dyke attract the small ships of the Seabourn, SeaDream, Windstar, Star Clippers, and Windjammer Barefoot fleets.

LANGUAGE & CURRENCY   **English** is spoken here, and the **U.S. dollar** is the legal currency (much to the surprise of arriving Brits).

TORTOLA

Located on the island's south shore, the once-sleepy village and colonial capital of **Road Town** became a bustling center after the 70-acre Wickhams Cay marina brought in a massive yacht-chartering business. The rest of the southern coast is characterized by rugged mountain peaks. On the northern coast are beautiful bays with white sandy beaches, banana trees, mangoes, and clusters of palms.

If your ship isn't scheduled to visit Virgin Gorda but you want to, you can catch a boat, ferry, or launch here and be on the island in no time, since it's only a 12-mile trip.

COMING ASHORE   Many ships dock right in **Road Town Harbour** or anchor offshore and tender in passengers. Two megaships can tie up at the **Cruise Pier,** while smaller ships or tenders may dock at nearby **Road Town Jetty** or the **West End** ferry terminal. **Soper's Hole** is a popular tender destination as well.

GETTING AROUND   You can walk around Road Town. Open-air and sedan-style **taxis** meet every arriving cruise ship to carry passengers to the beaches and other attractions. Fares are set, so ask what you'll be paying before you get in.

BEST CRUISE LINE SHORE EXCURSIONS

Town & Country Excursion ($34, 3½ hr.): Tour the island in an open-air minibus, visiting the Botanic Gardens, Cane Garden Bay, Bomba's Surfside Shack at Cappoon's Bay, and Soper's Hole.

Tortola Snorkeling Adventure ($54, 3 hr.): Cross the Sir Frances Drake Channel by boat to Norman Island, one of the BVI's prime snorkel sites, full of coral formations, colorful fish, and a group of caves at Treasure Point, where pirate treasure is reputed to have been hidden.

Forest Walk & Beach Tour ($46, 4½ hr.): Safari buses take you to Tortola's interior for a 1-mile hike through the Sage Mountain rainforest to the highest point in the Virgin Islands, then head down the Ridge Road for a brief stop at the Botanic Gardens. Minimum age: 12 years.

Wreck of the *Rhone* Two-Tank Certified Dive ($129, 4 hr.): A guided dive takes you to a British ship sunk in an 1867 hurricane, her bow lying almost fully intact in 80 feet of water. All divers must be certified and have dived within the past 2 years.

The Baths at Virgin Gorda ($59, 4 hr.): If your ship doesn't stop in Virgin Gorda, you can still go from Tortola, taking a 45-minute cruise across the Drake Channel and then spending a couple hours swimming around at the Baths, a veritable bouquet of seaside boulders formed by volcanic activity (see description under Virgin Gorda, below).

ON YOUR OWN: WITHIN WALKING DISTANCE

Besides the handful of shops on Main and Upper Main streets in Road Town, there's also the **Botanic Gardens** (✆ **284/494-4557**) right in the middle of town, across from the police station. It's open daily from 8am to 4:30pm and features a wide variety of flowers and plants, including a section on medicinal plants. Admission is $1.

ON YOUR OWN: BEYOND THE PORT AREA

You have mainly nature to look at on Tortola. The big attraction is **Sage Mountain National Park** (www.bvinationalparkstrust.org/toparks.html), its peak rising to 1,716

A Slice of Paradise: Jost Van Dyke

Covering only 4 square miles, mountainous Jost Van Dyke is an offbeat treat, visited mostly by private yachts and a few small cruise ships (which all anchor offshore) such as Windjammer Barefoot Cruises, which often throw afternoon beach parties on the sands at White Bay, with the crew lugging ashore a picnic lunch for a leisurely afternoon of eating, drinking, and swimming. If your ship stays late, don't miss a trip to **Foxy's** (© 284/495-9258), a well-known watering hole at the far end of Great Harbour that's popular with the yachting set as well as locals. It's your classic island beach bar, with music pounding and drinks flowing into the wee hours.

feet, the highest point in the BVIs and USVIs. The park was established in 1964 to protect those remnants of Tortola's original forests not burned or cleared during its plantation era. You'll find a lush forest of mango, papaya, breadfruit, coconut, birch berry, mountain guava, and guava berry trees, many labeled for identification. This is a great place to enjoy a picnic while overlooking neighboring islets and cays. Any taxi driver can take you to the mountain. Before going, stop at the Wickhams Cay tourist office, near the pier, and pick up a brochure with a map and an outline of the park's trails. The two main hikes are the Rain Forest Trail and the Mahogany Forest Trail.

BEACHES
Most of the beaches are a 20-minute taxi ride from the cruise dock. Figure on about $15 per person one-way (some will charge less, about $8–$9 per person if you've got a group), but discuss it with the driver before setting out. You can also ask him to pick you up at a designated time.

The finest beach is at **Cane Garden Bay** on the island's northwest coast, across the mountains from Road Town but worth the trip. **Rhymer's** (© 284/495-4639) serves a good if not inexpensive lunch of the conch, whelk, and barbecue-spareribs variety (main courses: $15 and up). Surfers like **Apple Bay,** also on the northwest side, while next-door **Cappoon's Bay** is known more for **Bomba's Surfside Shack** (© 284/495-4148), the oldest, most memorable bar on Tortola, covered with Day-Glo graffiti and laced with wire and rejected odds and ends of plywood, driftwood, and abandoned rubber tires. Lunch is about $10, and beer and Painkillers, that classic Caribbean rum specialty, are dispensed till the cows come home. At the extreme west end of the island, **Smuggler's Cove** is a wide crescent of white sand wrapped around calm, sky-blue water.

SHOPPING
Shopping on Tortola is a minor activity compared to other Caribbean ports. Only British goods are imported without duty, and they are the best buys, especially English china. You'll also find West Indian art, terra-cotta pottery, wicker and rattan home furnishings, Mexican glassware, dhurrie rugs, baskets, and ceramics.

Most stores are on Main Street in Road Town. The **Pusser's Company Store,** Main Street, Road Town (© 284/494-2467; www.pussers.com), offers a selection of classic travel and adventure clothing, along with Pusser's famous (though not terribly good) rum, which was served aboard British Navy ships for over 300 years. A good, cheap gift item is packets of Pusser's coasters, on which is written the recipe for the Painkiller. The adjacent Pusser's Road Town Pub serves lunch and, of course, Painkillers.

VIRGIN GORDA

Instead of visiting Tortola, some small cruise ships put in at lovely Virgin Gorda, famous for its boulder-strewn beach known as the **Baths.** The third-largest island in the colony, it got its name ("Fat Virgin") from Christopher Columbus, who thought the mountain framing it looked like a protruding stomach. Megaships that stop at Tortola usually offer a 4½-hour excursion to Virgin Gorda for about $50.

COMING ASHORE   Virgin Gorda doesn't have a pier to suit any of the large ships. Most vessels anchor in Gorda Sound and tender passengers to a pier at **Spanish Town,** which can accommodate smaller cruise ships. Ferries from Tortola also berth here.

GETTING AROUND   Taxis are available at the pier and will take visitors to the Baths and area beaches for about $8 per person each way. For a tour of the island, contact Andy Flax of the **Virgin Gorda Tours Association** (c/o the Fischers Cove Beach Hotel; © **284/495-5252**). It will run you about $40 per couple, and they'll pick you up at the dock if given at least 24-hour notice.

BEST CRUISE LINE SHORE EXCURSIONS

Island Tour & the Baths ($40–$51, 3½ hr.): Most Virgin Gorda tours are variations on this theme, touring the island by open-air bus, stopping at its highest point for a snapshot, taking in the village of Spanish Town, then stopping at Copper Mine National Park, where Amerindian and later European miners once dug for copper. The ruins you see today are what's left of a British operation from 1860. Tours end at the Baths, where you'll have time for swimming, snorkeling, and exploring among the boulders.

ON YOUR OWN: WITHIN WALKING DISTANCE

The **Virgin Gorda Yacht Harbour** at St. Thomas Bay has several restaurants and shops.

ON YOUR OWN: BEYOND THE PORT AREA

You might consider cabbing up to glamorous **Little Dix Bay Resort** (© **284/495-5555**), established by Laurance Rockefeller in 1965, to enjoy a lunch buffet at an outdoor pavilion that shows off Virgin Gorda's beautiful hills, bays, and sky. Aside from this, most people head for the Baths, which really is spectacular (see "Beaches," below).

BEACHES

The major reason cruise ships come to Virgin Gorda is to visit the **Baths,** where geologists believe ice age eruptions caused house-size boulders to topple onto one another to form the saltwater grottoes we see today. The pools around the Baths are excellent for swimming and snorkeling (equipment can be rented on the beach), and a crawl between and among the boulders, which in places are very cavelike, is more than a little bit fun. A cafe sits just above the beach for a quick snack or a cool drink.

Devil's Bay, a great beach just south of the Baths, is usually less crowded. Just north of the Baths is **Spring Bay,** one of the best of the island's beaches, with white sand, clear water, and good snorkeling. Nearby is the **Crawl,** a natural pool formed by rocks that's great for novice snorkelers; a marked path leads here from Spring Bay. **Trunk**

Bay, just to the north, is a wide sand beach that can be reached via a rough path from Spring Bay.

Devil's Bay National Park can be reached by a trail from the Baths. The walk to the secluded coral-sand beach takes about 15 minutes through a natural setting of boulders and dry coastal vegetation.

SHOPPING

The only shopping of note here is right at the Yacht Harbour complex, where you'll find a few dive shops, boutiques, and handicrafts shops.

8 Cozumel & the Yucatán Peninsula

The island of Cozumel, just off Mexico's Yucatán coast, is one of the busiest cruise ports you'll ever see, with up to 16 ships visiting every day during high season, counting those that anchor offshore and ferry passengers in by tender. All that activity can make the port town of **San Miguel** seem more like Times Square than the sleepy, refreshingly gritty town it once was, and the pace of transformation doesn't seem to be slowing down, despite the major thrashing the island received from Hurricane Wilma in 2005. A superfast cleanup and rebuilding effort had such success that ships began returning to the port only a month after the storm hit, and things have been moving apace ever since. By the time you read this, Wilma's damage should be completely erased.

The bustling shops, bars, and restaurants of San Miguel have their draw, but for us the major allure of Cozumel remains its proximity to the ancient Mayan ruins such as **Tulum** and **Chichén Itzá,** on the mainland of the Yucatán Peninsula. To see the ruins from here, you must take the 45-minute ferry ride between Cozumel and **Playa del Carmen,** on the mainland, though a few cruise ships call directly at Playa, anchoring offshore. Many ships en route to Cozumel pause in Playa del Carmen to drop off passengers who have signed up for ruins tours. After the tours, passengers take a ferry back to the ship in Cozumel (or, if the tour is by plane, get dropped off at the airport in Cozumel, near downtown). If your ship is not stopping at Playa, bear in mind that the ferry ride back and forth from Cozumel will take almost 2 hours total; if you're more interested in just relaxing, you may want to simply hang out on the island.

In recent years, a handful of other Yucatán ports have come onto the scene, including **Calica,** just south of Playa, where there's little more than a pier; **Costa Maya,** about 161km (100 miles) south near the sleepy fishing village of Mahajual; and **Progreso,** on the Gulf coast of the Yucatán, making it the closest to Chichén Itzá, as well as the city of Mérida.

LANGUAGE & CURRENCY **Spanish** is the tongue of the land, although **English** is spoken in most places that cater to tourists. The Mexican currency is the **nuevo peso** (new peso). Its symbol is the "$" sign, but it's hardly the equivalent of the U.S. dollar—the exchange rate is about $11 pesos = US$1 ($1 peso = about US9¢). The main tourist stores gladly accept U.S. dollars.

CALLING FROM THE U.S. You need to dial the international access code **(011)** and the country code **(52)** before the numbers listed below.

MAYA RUINS & OTHER MAINLAND ATTRACTIONS

Because all of the sites listed here are quite far from the cruise piers, most cruise passengers visit them as part of **shore excursions.** Admission to the sites is included in the excursion prices, which typically run from $99 (by bus) to $186 (plus $39 airport tax) by plane for Chichén Itzá, around $87 for a bus to Tulum, and about $99 for a bus to Cobá. Chichén Itzá and Cobá are all-day excursions. Visits to smaller Tulum are often paired with a visit to the Xel-Ha Eco Park, making it a full-day trek ($129). Guests are usually served free and refreshingly coooollllldddd Mexican beer on the bus ride back after exploring the ruins.

CHICHEN ITZA   The largest and most fabled of the Yucatán ruins, Chichén Itzá (meaning "Mouth of the Well of the Itza Family") was founded in A.D. 445 by the Maya and later inhabited by the Toltecs of central Mexico. At its height, the city had about 50,000 residents, but it was mysteriously abandoned only 2 centuries after its founding. After lying dormant for 2 more centuries, the site was resettled and enjoyed prosperity again until the early 13th century, when it was once more relinquished to the surrounding jungle. The area covers 18 sq. km (7 sq. miles), so you can see only a fraction of it on a day trip. These are some of the highlights.

The best known of Chichén Itzá's ruins is the magnificent **El Castillo pyramid** (also called the Pyramid of Kukulkán), which was built with the Maya calendar in mind. The four stairways leading up to the central platform each have 91 steps, making a total of 364; when you add the top central platform you get the 365 days of the solar year. On either side of each stairway are nine terraces, for a total of 18 on each face of the pyramid, equaling the number of months in the Mayan solar calendar. On the facing of these terraces are 52 panels that represent the 52-year cycle when both the solar and religious calendars would become realigned. The pyramid's alignment is such that on the **spring** or **fall equinox,** light striking the pyramid gives the illusion of a snake slithering down the steps to join its gigantic stone head mounted at the base.

Northwest of El Castillo is Chichén's main **Ball Court (Juego de Pelota),** the largest and best preserved such Mayan ruin anywhere. Carved on both walls of the ball court are scenes showing Mayan figures dressed as ball players and decked out in heavy protective padding. The carved scene also shows a headless player kneeling with blood shooting from his neck; another player holding the head looks on. Here's the way it worked: Players on two teams tried to knock a hard rubber ball through one of the two stone rings placed high on either wall, using only their elbows, knees, and hips. According to legend, the losing players paid for defeat with their lives. Some experts, however, say the victors were the only appropriate sacrifices for the gods. Note the lack of bleacher seating: As the games were played as a ritual, for the entertainment of the gods, only a single judge looked on.

Temples are located at both ends of the ball court. The **North Temple** has sculptured pillars and more sculptures inside, as well as badly ruined murals. The acoustics of the ball court are so good that from the North Temple, a person speaking can be heard clearly at the opposite end, about 136m (450 ft.) away. Near the southeastern corner of the main ball court is the **Temple of the Jaguars,** a small temple with serpent columns and carved panels showing warriors and jaguars. Up the steps and inside the temple, a mural chronicles a battle in a Maya village. To the right of the ball court is the **Temple of the Skulls (Tzompantli),** decorated with rows of skulls carved into the stone platform. When a sacrificial victim's head was cut off, it was impaled on a pole and displayed in a tidy row with the others.

Follow the dirt road (actually an ancient *sacbé,* or causeway, made from a white, compacted, claylike soil that made the way visible at night) that heads north from the

Platform of Venus. After about 5 minutes, you'll come to the **Sacred Cenote,** a great natural well that may have given Chichén Itzá its name. This well was used for ceremonial purposes, not for drinking water. According to legend, sacrificial victims adorned with gold and other riches were drowned in this pool to honor the rain god Chaac. In the early 20th century, American consul and Harvard professor Edward Thompson bought the ruins of Chichén Itzá and explored the cenote with dredges and divers, unearthing (and exporting) a fortune in gold and jade.

Due east of El Castillo is one of the most impressive structures at Chichén: the **Temple of the Warriors,** named for the carvings of warriors marching along its walls. It's also called the Group of the Thousand Columns for the rows of broken square pillars that flank it. A figure of Chaac-Mool sits at the top of the temple, surrounded by impressive columns carved in relief to look like enormous feathered serpents. According to scholars, the high priest would tear out a sacrificial victim's heart here and then throw the body down the steps, where another priest would strip off its skin. The high priest would then dress himself in the skin, cross to a nearby platform, and dance. Lovely, huh?

South of the temple is another group of columns (these ones round) that were once an important **market,** controlling the trade in salt on the Yucatán. South of the market, a cluster of interesting ruins include the **Observatory (El Caracol),** a complex building with a circular tower through whose slits astronomers could observe the cardinal directions and the approach of the all-important spring and autumn equinoxes; the **Edifice of the Nuns (Edificio de las Monjas),** which was named for its resemblance to a European convent; and the **Church (La Iglesia),** one of the oldest buildings at Chichén and named for its beautiful decorations. Its ceiling, with a Maya false arch, is a stone replica of the thatched ceiling in a typical Maya home of the period.

TULUM   About 130km (80 miles) south of Cancún and about a 30-minute drive from Playa del Carmen, the small walled city of Tulum is the single-most-visited Maya ruin due to its proximity to the ports. It was the only Mayan city built on the coast and the only one inhabited when the Spanish conquistadors arrived in the 1500s. From its dramatic perch atop seaside cliffs, you can see wonderful panoramic views of the Caribbean. Though nowhere near as large and impressive as Chichén Itzá, Tulum shares a similar prominent feature: a ruin topped with a **temple to Kukulkán,** the primary Maya/Olmec god. Other important structures include the **Temple of the Frescoes,** the **Temple of the Descending God,** the **House of Columns,** and the **House of the Cenote,** which is a well. There's also a sliver of silky beach amid the site, so bring your bathing suit for a quick refreshing dip. New visitor facilities include a well-stocked bookstore and a soon-to-open museum.

COBÁ   A 35-minute drive northwest of Tulum puts you at Cobá, site of one of the most important city-states in the Mayan empire. Cobá flourished from A.D. 300 to 1000, with its population numbering perhaps as many as 40,000. Excavation work began in 1972, but archaeologists estimate that only a small percentage of this dead city has yet been uncovered. The site lies on four lakes. Its 81 primitive acres provide excellent exploration opportunities for hikers. Cobá's pyramid, **Nohoch Mul,** is the tallest in the Yucatán.

XCARET ECOLOGICAL PARK   About 6.5km (4 miles) south of Playa del Carmen on the coast, Xcaret (pronounced Ish-car-*et*) is a 100-hectare (247-acre) ecological theme park with small Maya ruins scattered about the lushly landscaped acres.

Cozumel & the Yucatán Ports

To Progreso

El Cuyo

Holbox

Isla Holbox

Chiquilá

Isla Contoy

RÍO LAGARTOS NATURE RESERVE

Buenaventura

QUINTANA ROO STATE

Punta Sam

Cancún

Isla Mujeres

Puerto Juárez

Isla Cancun

YUCATÁN STATE

180

180 D

180 D

Nuevo Xcan

To Valladolid & Chichén Itzá

180

Chemax

Cobá

Puerto Aventuras

Akumal

Xelha Lagoon National Park

Tancah

Tulum

Chunyaxche

Muyil

Chumpón

Vigia Chíco

Peninsula Vigia Grande

Bahía de la Ascensión

Felipe Carrillo Puerto

SIAN KA'AN BIOSPHERE RESERVE

To Chetumal & Costa Maya

Croco-Cun

Jardín Botanico

Puerto Morelos

307

Punta Bete

Xcaret

Calica

Playa del Carmen

Pamul

Xpuha

Yalku Lagoon

San Gervasio

San Miguel de Cozumel

El Cedral

Chankanaab Nature Park

ISLA DE COZUMEL

Caribbean Sea

Boca Paila

Punta Allen

0		25 mi
0		25 km

✈ Airport

🚢 Cruise Ship Dock

- - - - Ferry Route

||||| Reef

◆◆ Ruins

Visitors can put on life jackets and snorkeling gear and ride the currents through more than a kilometer of well-lit underground caves, or don a Sea-Trek helmet and walk across the ocean floor. (You can also swim with dolphins, though this is not included in the cost of excursions.) The park has a botanical garden, an aquarium, a sea-turtle breeding and release facility, a dive shop, a rotating observation tower, a Mayan village, and two theaters that put on worthwhile cultural shows. Excursions run about $98 and take up a full day from Cozumel.

XEL-HA ECO PARK   Farther south of Xcaret, Xel-Ha (pronounced Shell-*ha*) features a sprawling natural lagoon filled with sparkling blue-green water and surrounded by lush foliage. The use of inner tubes and life vests is included in the admission price, and you can spend a great couple of hours wending your way from one end of the snaking body of calm water to the other, accompanied by schools of tropical fish—or you can just chill on a beach chair and grab lunch from one of the restaurants. Xel-Ha has dolphins, too, and snorkeling gear, snuba, and sea trekking are also available at additional cost. Alternatively, you can take a trail walk with a knowledgeable, eco-minded guide who will identify local plants and take you to sacred cenote sinkholes where ancient Mayans made offerings to the gods.

COZUMEL

The ancient Mayans, who lived here for 12 centuries, would be shocked by the two-million-plus cruise passengers who now visit Cozumel each year, and by the fast-food, raucous-bar, and power-shopping character of San Miguel. Outside town, though, development hasn't squashed the island's natural beauty, and there are still acres of low-lying scrub forest containing protected plant and animal species. Offshore, the government has set aside 32km (20 miles) of coral reefs as an underwater national park, including the stunning **Palancar Reef,** the world's second-largest natural coral formation.

COMING ASHORE   Hurricane Wilma did a number on Cozumel's cruise piers when it hit in October 2005. The **Puerto Maya** pier, about 5km (3 miles) south of tourist hub San Miguel, was completely destroyed, and at press time was still nowhere close to reopening. The busy International Pier (a bit closer to town) and San Miguel's centrally located Punta Langosta cruise pier were also damaged, but are now back in commission. Up to four megaships can dock at these two piers; additional ships arriving on busy days must anchor offshore. Both Puerto Maya and the International Pier lie about a $10 taxi ride from town. The beaches are close to the International Pier.

GETTING AROUND   The town of San Miguel is so small, you can walk anywhere you want to go. For pedestrians, the classic grid layout makes it easy to get around, though note that all odd-numbered streets are on the south side of the pier and all even-numbered streets are heading north. Essentially, there's only one major road on the island—it starts at the northern tip, hugs the western shoreline, then loops around the southern tip and returns through the middle of the island to the capital.

Taxis are available at the piers; the average fare from San Miguel to most major resorts and beaches is about $25. More distant island rides cost $25 and up. It's customary to overcharge cruise ship passengers, so settle on a fare before getting in. **Motor scooters** and **mopeds** are also a popular means of getting around (though be careful!!), and can be rented from (among others) **Auto Rent** (© **987/872-3532**), in the Hotel El Cid La Ceiba, right next to the International Pier. The cost is about $35 per day, including helmet; insurance is an extra $6.

BEST CRUISE LINE SHORE EXCURSIONS

See "Maya Ruins & Other Mainland Attractions," above, for details on the big mainland excursions. In addition to those below, the cruise lines also offer dozens of different snorkeling, party-boat, and underwater excursions in Cozumel.

Tropical 4x4 Safari Tour ($54, 4 hr.): Hop in a four-seat jeep, draw straws to see who gets to drive, and explore the natural side of Cozumel. Much of the roller-coaster-like route is off-road, and the jeeps travel in a convoy, stopping eventually at a lovely secluded beach for swimming, snorkeling, and a picnic lunch.

Mayan Frontier Horseback Riding ($89, 3–4 hr.): Worthwhile horseback-riding tours offer a chance to see Cozumel's landscape, but although they tout visits to Mayan ruins, don't get your hopes up—there's little more than a few refrigerator-size rocks here and there on Cozumel. A bus transports riders to a ranch, where the ride begins.

Segway Tour ($89, 2½ hr.): Mount up on a Segway Human Transporter for a ride along a scenic bike track that parallels the Caribbean, ending with swimming and snorkeling time.

ON YOUR OWN: WITHIN WALKING DISTANCE

Avenida Rafael Melgar, the principal street along the waterfront, traces the western shore of the island, site of the best resorts and beaches. Most of the shops and restaurants are along this street. The things to do here are basically shop and drink, and boy oh boy are there a lot of choices.

Carlos 'n Charlie's, Av. Rafael Melgar 551 (© **987/869-1647;** www.carlosandcharlies.com), is Mexico's equivalent of the Hard Rock Cafe, but much wilder. Though it moved a few years ago from its old beer-slopped digs into a more sterile Houlihan's-style space right across from the Punta Langosta pier, it's still got deafening music and dancing tourists pounding down yard-long glasses of beer. Many a cruise passenger has stumbled back from this place clutching a souvenir glass as though it were the Holy Grail—dubious proof of a visit to Mexico. Other party spots include the **Hard Rock Cozumel** itself, at Av. Rafael Melgar 2A (© **529/872-5273;** www.hardrock.com), and **Fat Tuesday,** at the end of the International Pier (© **987/872-5130**), where 16-ounce margaritas cost $5 a pop and 24-ounce versions a few bucks more.

If that's not your scene, you can drop into the small **Museo de la Isla de Cozumel,** on Rafael Melgar between calles 4 and 6 North (© **987/872-1475**). Once Cozumel's first luxury hotel, it now displays exhibits that take you from pre-Hispanic times and through the colonial era to the present. Admission is $3.

ON YOUR OWN: BEYOND THE PORT AREA

About a $10 taxi ride from the center of San Miguel is the **Chankanaab Nature Park,** Carretera Sur, km 9 (no phone), where a saltwater lagoon, offshore reefs, and underwater caves have been turned into an archaeological park, botanical garden, and wildlife sanctuary. More than 10 countries have contributed seedlings and cuttings. Some 60 species of marine life occupy the lagoon, including sea turtles and captive dolphins (that you can swim with for $155 for 3 hr., ages 6 and up). Reproductions of Mayan dwellings are scattered throughout the park. There's also a wide white-sand beach with thatch umbrellas and a changing area with lockers and showers. Both scuba divers and snorkelers enjoy examining the sunken ship offshore; there are four dive shops here. Admission is $11. The 10-minute taxi ride from the downtown tender and ferry pier (Muelle Fiscal) costs about $15.

The few Mayan ruins on Cozumel—**San Gervasio** (north of San Miguel), once a ceremonial center and capital, and **El Cedral** (to the south), site of a Mayan arch and a few small ruins covered in heavy growth—are very, very minor compared to those on the mainland, and worth visiting only if you happen to be in the neighborhood (visiting Playa San Francisco, say, which lies about 3.2km/2 miles from El Cedral).

BEACHES

Cozumel's best powdery white-sand beach, **Playa San Francisco,** stretches for some 5km (3 miles) along the southwestern shoreline. You can rent equipment for watersports here, or have lunch at one of the many palapa restaurants and bars on the shoreline. There's no admission to the beach, and it's about a $10 taxi ride south of San Miguel's downtown pier. If you land at the International Pier, you're practically at the beach already.

Playa Mia (formerly called Playa del Sol) is a fine beach located about a mile south of Playa del San Francisco, but because it has a big reputation, it's likely to be wall-to-wall with your fellow cruisers. It's also built up with bars, restaurants, watersports rentals, a miniature zoo, and more, and charges a $12 entrance fee.

Playa Bonita (sometimes called Punta Chiqueros) is one of the least crowded beaches; it lies on the east (windward) side of the island and is difficult to reach unless you rent a vehicle or throw yourself on the mercy of a taxi driver. It sits in a moon-shaped cove sheltered from the Caribbean Sea by an offshore reef. Waves are only moderate, the sand is powdery, and the water is clear.

If you don't want to go far, two hotel beaches are a stone's throw north of the International Pier (facing the water, they're on the right). Both welcome day visitors to use their small beach, cabanas, pools, and changing facilities. **El Cid La Ceiba** charges $10 per person for the day, while the **Park Royale** charges $25, which includes all drinks, snacks, and lunch. At press time, both were closed for post-hurricane renovations, so check with the tourism booth at the pier before you head out.

SHOPPING

Wall-to-wall shops along the waterfront in San Miguel, starting right across the street from the Punta Langosta pier and stretching in every direction, sell the usual tourist goods, Mexican crafts, and especially **silver jewelry,** which is big business here. The latter is generally sold by weight. Because of the influx of cruise ship passengers, prices are relatively high, but you can and should bargain. The International Pier and Puerto Maya both had on-pier gift shops before Hurricane Wilma took them out, and presumably will have them again when the piers reopen in 2007.

PLAYA DEL CARMEN

Some cruise ships spend a day at Cozumel and then anchor offshore at Playa del Carmen for another day, but most ferry passengers to Playa from Cozumel for tours to Tulum and Chichén Itzá, then head on to spend the day tied up at Cozumel. The famed white-sand beach was washed away by Hurricane Wilma, but is already back thanks to an aggressive beach-recovery program that plopped tons of sand ashore at a rate of 1km (⅔ mile) per week. Shops, too, have bounced back with a vengeance, and if you can tolerate the crowds, the snorkeling is still excellent over the offshore reefs. Turtle-watching is another popular pastime.

COMING ASHORE   Some cruise ships anchor offshore or at the pier of Cozumel, then send passengers over to Playa del Carmen by tender. Others dock at the **Puerto Calica Cruise Pier** (which doubles as a dock for cement freighters), 13km (8 miles) south of Playa del Carmen. Taxis meet each arriving ship here, and drivers transport visitors into the center of Playa del Carmen—which is a good thing, as there's nothing to do at Calica save for making a phone call or buying a soda.

GETTING AROUND   The ferry dock is right in town, near the beach and most major shops. You probably won't need them, but **taxis** are available to take you anywhere. If you'd like to drive your own vehicle for the day, Avis, Budget, Hertz, and National all have **car-rental** offices right next to the ferry pier.

BEST CRUISE LINE SHORE EXCURSIONS

Most visitors head for the Maya ruins or one of the local water parks the moment they reach shore (see "Best Cruise Line Shore Excursions" in the "Cozumel" section, above).

ON YOUR OWN: WITHIN WALKING DISTANCE

From the ferry docks, you can walk to the center of Playa del Carmen, to the beach, and to the small but ever expanding shopping district, which has some pretty trendy boutiques and hip restaurants. **Señor Frog's,** right at the ferry pier (© **984/873-0930**), is another of those "all the beer and shots you can stomach" places, like **Carlos 'n Charlie's** (© **984/803-3498**), which sits just up the street. For all attractions beyond town, see "Maya Ruins & Other Mainland Attractions," p. 546.

SHOPPING

From the tender pier, you are funneled like cattle in a chute right into the **Paseo del Carmen Shopping Mall.** Most shops are along Avenida 5, which runs parallel to the coast and has a pedestrian-only stretch not far from the dock. The **Rincon del Sol** plaza is a tree-filled courtyard between Calle 4 and Calle 6, built in the colonial Mexican style. It has the best collection of handicrafts shops in the area, some of which offer much better quality items than the junky souvenirs peddled elsewhere.

COSTA MAYA

Costa Maya is located near the sleepy fishing village of Mahajual, just over 161km (100 miles) south of Playa del Carmen and not too far from the Mexico/Belize border. Millions of dollars were invested in a pier that opened here not too many years ago, and in a lavish oceanfront shopping and restaurant complex that caters exclusively to the needs of the cruise ship passengers. Princess, Royal Caribbean, Carnival, and Norwegian are among the lines that visit the port. The Maya ruins of nearby **Kohunlich** and **Chacchoben** are the draw, along with silky white beaches and diving and snorkeling at the **Chincorro,** Mexico's largest coral atoll.

COMING ASHORE   Costa Maya is a self-contained port stop, dropping you right at the purpose-built facilities.

GETTING AROUND   **Taxis** line up just outside the pier, and are the only way of getting to sites beyond walking distance. Because of this, prices are steep and non-negotiable. Visiting the Mayan ruins of Kohunlich will set passengers back $65 per person round-trip, while a round-trip ride to Chacchoben comes in around $45 per person. With prices like these, we recommend you book the shore excursions instead (see below).

BEST CRUISE LINE SHORE EXCURSIONS

Maya Ruins of Kohunlich ($82, 7 hr.): Located in a secluded jungle setting near the border of Belize, this Mayan city was built between A.D. 200 and 900, spanning the early- through late-classical periods. The trail to the ruins is marked by a tree that was uprooted and replanted upside down—a means of marking sites used by the apparently brilliant, though obviously eccentric, Mexican archaeologist who first explored the site. Check out the **Plaza of the Acropolis,** where two temples are aligned with the equinox, and the 6th-century **Temple of the Masks,** where 1.8m (6-ft.) stucco masks of the Mayan sun god are remarkably well preserved.

Mayan Ruins of Chacchoben ($69, 4 hr.): Opened to the public in 1999, this collection of temples dates from A.D. 360, or the middle of the early-classical period, and it played an important role as a trading center for wood, jade, and colorful birds. There are more than two dozen structures; to date, less than 5% of the site has been excavated. The first temple encountered is the **Temple of Venus,** a tribute to fertility. The pyramids are in an excellent state of preservation, and their distinctive curved edges and soft lines are particularly beautiful. Climbing to the first plateau affords an impressive view of the surrounding area.

Bike & Kayak Adventure ($48, 3 hr.): Starting off on a mountain bike, you'll pedal along a dirt road past a small mangrove lagoon with views of the coastline, then through the village of Mahajual (don't blink or you'll miss it), and finally arrive at the beach. After a short refreshment break, trade in your helmet for a paddle and pair up with a partner for a kayak trip out along the nearby reef. The small two-person kayaks are launched from the shore and easy to handle. The bike ride back includes another beach stop.

Coral Reef Sail & Snorkel ($59, 3 hr.): A boat takes you to a nearby coral reef, which you can explore with an expert guide.

Dune Buggy Jungle & Beach Safari ($84, 3½ hr.): This is a drive-yourself convoy excursion in honest-to-God dune buggies (how '60s), leaving from Mahajaul out onto unpaved roads on the way to La Palapa Beach, where you'll have time to swim or use the kayaks and volleyball court.

Jungle Beach Break ($38, no set time): A shuttle operates between the nearby Uvero Beach and the pier every 35 minutes, allowing you to come and go as you please—not that you'll want to leave the snow-white beaches and crystal-blue water, not to mention the chaise longues and umbrellas; open bar; free snorkel gear; paddle boats; and sea kayaks, jet skis, and power boats you can rent. Changing rooms with showers and a snack bar are on-site (food not included). Parasailing is also available.

ON YOUR OWN: WITHIN WALKING DISTANCE

At the one-stop-shop pier complex, a 650-seat amphitheater offers daily **cultural shows,** from pre-Hispanic dances to Mexican folkloric performances. There are also activities throughout the day in and around the pier, from guacamole-making classes to aqua-aerobics, games, and contests, plus sprawling restaurants (one with a balcony, another with outdoor seating and a stage for live music), two saltwater pools, a pool bar, a trampoline, and plenty of shops. Check the daily **entertainment schedule** posted near the restrooms for performance times and activities. Immediately next to the pier is a lovely **private beach club** with umbrellas, chairs, hammock swings, and a small restaurant and bar. There's a small fee for day passes. Enter from the parking lot near the bus departure point.

ON YOUR OWN: BEYOND THE PORT AREA

The only town in the area is the **Mahajual** fishing village, which until quite recently did not even have electricity. A single main road is lined with a short row of rustic, screened-in restaurants and a miniscule grocery; across the street is a long white beach lined with fishing boats and noticeably devoid of beach umbrellas and sunbathers. Unless you're just curious, there's no real reason to go.

SHOPPING

Because the port at Costa Maya was constructed with the sole purpose of serving American and European cruise ship passengers, you can bet your last enchilada that shopping abounds. There are some 70 shops in a mall-like setting, some of them familiar to the seasoned cruiser, others unique. **Ultra Femme** specializes in fragrances and cosmetics cheaper than you'll find at the duty-free. If it's gold and jewels you're after, head over to **Tanzanite International** for a wide selection and friendly staff, or to **Diamond International** for some great bargains. Next door, you can haggle over "art in silver" at **Taxco Factory.** For something different, head over to the two nearby palapas, where local artisans craft their wares as potential buyers look on.

PROGRESO/MERIDA

Visited by a fraction of the ships that call at Cozumel, Progreso has one major advantage over its rival: proximity to **Chichén Itzá** (p. 547), which lies only 2 hours south by motorcoach. This also makes excursions to the ruins considerably cheaper than from Cozumel, averaging about $95 per person. Progreso itself is almost nothing but a port. Ships dock here at the end of a man-made causeway that juts several miles out into the Gulf of Mexico, making it very difficult to visit anything on your own (we recommend taking a tour). Aside from visits to Chichén Itzá and the smaller Maya ruins at **Uxmal** and **Dzibilchaltun,** cruise passengers can take a tour of **Mérida,** the capital of Yucatán state (about 32km/20 miles away), visit the **Celestun Estuary Nature Reserve** to see pink flamingos in their natural habitat, or take an off-road jeep trek to two local haciendas.

9 Curaçao

Welcome to Curaçao (pronounced Coo-ra-*sow*), the largest and most populous of the Netherlands Antilles, just 56km (35 miles) north of the Venezuelan coast. Because much of the island's surface is an arid desert, Dutch settlers in the 17th century developed it into a trading post rather than trying to farm, and a huge oil-processing operation located here in the early 20th century resulted in a large population influx and today's curious mixture of bloodlines, including African, Dutch, Venezuelan, and Pakistani. Today the island still retains a Dutch flavor, especially in **Willemstad,** whose harbor is bordered by rows of picture-postcard, pastel-colored, gabled Dutch colonial houses. While these structures give the town a storybook appearance, the rest of the island looks like the American Southwest, its desertlike landscape dotted with three-pronged cacti, spiny-leafed aloes, and divi-divi trees bent by trade winds.

COMING ASHORE   As you sail into the harbor of Willemstad, be sure to look for the quaint **Queen Emma floating pontoon bridge,** which swings aside to open the narrow channel. It was recently removed for renovations and is now back in service. One large cruise ship at a time can dock at the recently upgraded megapier just beyond the bridge at **Rif Otrobanda,** which leads to the duty-free shopping sector and the famous Floating Market in downtown Willemstad. Adjacent to the megapier, the Rif Fort Renaissance hotel and entertainment development was nearing completion at press time, offering shops, restaurants, and casinos. A second megapier is being planned adjacent to the first, with a targeted completion date of 2010. Three to four smaller cruise ships may dock inside the entrance channel at the **St. Annabay Wharves;** there is no anchorage for passenger ships.

GETTING AROUND   From the pier, it's a 5- to 10-minute walk to the center of town, or you can take a **taxi** from the stand. The town itself is easy to navigate on foot. Most of it can be explored in 2 or 3 hours, leaving plenty of time for beaches or watersports. Taxi drivers waiting at the cruise dock will take you to any of the beaches. To be on the safe side, arrange to have your driver pick you up at a certain time and take you back to the cruise dock. Up to four passengers can share the price of an island tour by taxi, which costs about $30 per hour.

LANGUAGE & CURRENCY   Dutch, Spanish, and English are spoken on Curaçao. The official currency is the **Netherlands Antilles florin** (ANG), also called a guilder (1.78 ANG = US$1; 1 ANG = US56¢). Most places accept U.S. dollars for purchases.

BEST CRUISE LINE SHORE EXCURSIONS

Many excursions aren't really worth the price here—you can easily see the town on your own and hop a taxi to the few attractions on the island outside of Willemstad.

Spanish Water Kayaking & Snorkeling ($69, 3½ hr.): At Jan Sofat, you'll board kayaks for a paddle through the Spanish Water Lagoon, heading for Barbara Beach. Swim and relax before paddling back.

Exploring Curaçao's Jewish Heritage ($52, 3½ hr.): Jews have lived on Curaçao since the mid–17th century. On this tour, participants visit the Mikve Emmanuel Israel synagogue (the Western Hemisphere's oldest) as well as Beth Haim Cemetery (consecrated in 1659) and Landhouse Bloemhof, with its collections of art and artifacts from Curaçao's Jewish past.

ON YOUR OWN: WITHIN WALKING DISTANCE

Willemstad is the major attraction here, and you can see it on foot. After years of restoration, the town's historic center and the island's natural harbor, Schottegat, have been inscribed on UNESCO's World Heritage List. Be sure to watch the **Queen Emma pontoon bridge** in action. It's motorized, and a man actually drives it to the side of the harbor every so often to allow ships and boats to pass through the channel—it's the coolest thing to see. In the **Brionplein** square at the Otrabanda end of the bridge, a statue commemorates Curaçao-born Pedro Luis Brion, who fought for the independence of Venezuela and Colombia as an admiral under Simón Bolívar. **Fort Amsterdam,** site of the Governor's Palace and the 1769 Dutch Reformed church, has the task of guarding the waterfront. The church still has a British cannonball embedded in it. A corner of the fort stands at the intersection of Breedestraat and Handelskade, the starting point for a plunge into the island's major shopping district.

A few minutes' walk from the pontoon bridge, at the north end of Handelskade, is the **Floating Market,** where scores of sailing ships arrive from Venezuela, Colombia, and neighboring West Indian islands, tying up alongside the canal to sell tropical fruits, vegetables, and handicrafts.

Between the I. H. (Sha) Capriles Kade and Fort Amsterdam, at the corner of Columbusstraat and Hanchi di Snoa, is the **Mikve Israel-Emanuel Synagogue.** Dating from 1651, the Jewish congregation here is the oldest in the New World. Next door, the **Jewish Cultural Historical Museum,** Hanchi Snoa 29 (© **599/9-461-1633;** www.snoa.com), is housed in two buildings dating from 1728. They were the rabbi's residence and the mikvah (bath) for religious purification purposes. Entry is through the synagogue; admission is $2.15.

The **Curaçao Museum,** Van Leeuwenhoekstraat (© **599/9-462-3873**), is housed in a restored 1853 building constructed by the Royal Dutch Army as a military hospital. Today, it displays paintings, objets d'art, and antique furniture, as well as a large collection from the Caiquetio tribes. Admission is $3.25.

ON YOUR OWN: BEYOND THE PORT AREA

Cacti, bromeliads, rare orchids, iguanas, donkeys, wild goats, and many species of birds thrive in the **Christoffel National Park** (© **599/9-864-0363**), located about a 30-minute taxi or car ride from the capital near the northwestern tip of Curaçao. The park rises from flat, arid countryside to 369m (1,211-ft.) **St. Christoffelberg,** the tallest point in the Dutch Leewards. Along the way are ancient Arawak paintings and the **Piedra di Monton,** a rock heap piled by African slaves who cleared this former plantation. Legend says slaves could climb to the top of the rock pile, jump off, and fly back home across the Atlantic to Africa. If they had ever tasted a grain of salt, however, they would crash to their deaths. The park has 32km (20 miles) of one-way trail-like roads. The shortest is about 8km (5 miles) long, but takes about 40 minutes to drive because of its rough terrain. One of several hiking trails goes to the top of St. Christoffelberg. It takes about 1½ hours to walk to the summit (come early in the morning before it gets hot; trails open at 7:30am). Admission is $10.

The **Curaçao Sea Aquarium,** off Bhpor Kibra (© **599/9-461-6666;** www.curacao-sea-aquarium.com), displays more than 400 species of fish, crabs, anemones, and other invertebrates, sponges, and coral. Admission is $15. It also offers an "Animal Encounter" experience and various **dolphin swims,** starting at $144 (© **599/9-465-8900;** www.dolphin-academy.com). Nonswimmers can see the underwater life from a 14m (46-ft.) semisubmersible observatory.

Stalactites are mirrored in a mystical underground lake in **Hato Caves,** F. D. Rosseveltweg (© **599/9-868-0379**). Long ago, geological forces uplifted this limestone terrace, which was originally a coral reef. The limestone formations were created over thousands of years by water seeping through the coral. After crossing the lake, you enter two caverns known as the Cathedral and La Ventana ("The Window"), where you'll see samples of ancient Indian petroglyphs. Local guides take visitors through every hour. Admission is $7.

BEACHES

Curaçao has some 38 beaches, but in general they aren't as good as others in the region. The **Curaçao Sea Aquarium** has the island's only full-facility, white-sand, palm-shaded beach, but you'll have to pay the full aquarium admission to get in (see "On Your Own: Beyond the Port Area," above).

The rest of the beaches are public. Southeast of Willemstad, **Santa Barbara Beach** sits on land owned by a mining company between the open sea and the island's primary watersports and recreational area, known as **Spanish Water.** It's got pure-white sand and calm water; a buoy line protects swimmers from boats; and there are restrooms, changing rooms, watersports equipment, and a snack bar available. The beach has access to the **Curaçao Underwater Park** (© **599/9-462-4242**), which stretches from the Breezes Resort to the eastern tip of Curaçao and includes some of the island's finest reefs.

Blauwbaai (Blue Bay), just north of town, is the largest and most frequented beach on Curaçao, with enough white sand for everybody. Along with showers and changing facilities, there are plenty of shady places to retreat from the noonday sun. At the top of the island, **Westpunt** is known for its gigantic cliffs and the Sunday divers who jump from them into the ocean below. **Knip Bay** and **Playa Abao,** just south of West-punt, have beautiful turquoise waters.

SHOPPING

Curaçao is a shopper's paradise, with some 200 stores lining Heerenstraat, Breedestraat, and other streets in the 5-block district called the **Punda.** Many shops occupy the town's old Dutch houses.

The island is famous for its 2.2kg (5-lb.) "wheelers" of Gouda and Edam cheese. Also look for good buys on wooden shoes, French perfumes, Dutch blue Delft sou-venirs, finely woven Italian silks, Japanese and German cameras, jewelry, silver, Swiss watches, linens, leather goods, liquor, and island-made rum and liqueurs, especially Curaçao liqueur, some of which has a distinctive blue color. Some stores also offer good buys on intricate lacework imported from everywhere between Portugal and China. If you're a street shopper and want something colorful, consider a carving or flamboyant painting from Haiti or the Dominican Republic; both are hawked by street vendors at all of the main plazas.

10 Dominica

First things first. It's pronounced Dome-i-*nee*-ka, not Doe-*min*-i-ka. And it has noth-ing to do with the Dominican Republic. The Commonwealth of Dominica is an inde-pendent country, and English, not Spanish, is the official language. The only Spanish commonly understood in Dominica is *mal encaminado a Santo Domingo* ("acciden-tally sent to the Dominican Republic"), the phrase stamped on the many letters that make it to their proper destination only after an erroneous but common detour.

Dominica is the lushest and most mountainous island in the eastern Caribbean, a 47×26km (29×16-mile) swath of crystal-pure rivers, dramatic waterfalls, volcanic lakes, and gargantuan foliage, all accessible via river trips or hikes along undemanding jungle trails. The island's people, primarily descendants of the West African slaves, are another great natural resource. Don't be surprised when you're greeted with a smile and an "okay," the island's equivalent of "hi." Unfortunately, in Roseau, the main city, you may also be greeted by drug dealers offering to sell you some of the local weed—tourism might be a still-developing industry here, but some others are obviously a lit-tle further along. The island is also notable for its population of some 3,000 Caribe Indians, the last remaining descendants of the people who dominated the region when Europeans arrived.

COMING ASHORE   Dominica has three cruise ship ports that can each handle one ship at a time. The most frequented is the cruise ship berth in the heart of

Roseau, the country's capital and largest town. The **Woodbridge Bay** port is about a mile north of Roseau, and the other is the Cabrits cruise berth, near the northwestern town of **Portsmouth,** with a tourist welcome center and quick access to Fort Shirley and Cabrits National Park. Additional cruise ships must anchor offshore and tender passengers to the terminal (which takes about 5 min.). Plans are underway for expanding the Woodbridge Bay cruise port, increasing the docking capacity to three ships and creating a "cruise village" with shops, restaurants, and other amenities.

GETTING AROUND   **Taxis** and **public minivans** are designated by license plates that begin with the letters *H, HA,* or *HB*. Also look for a round decal on the front of the car, which means the driver is a certified tourism operator. Fleets of both await cruise ship passengers at the Roseau and Portsmouth docks. Drivers are generally knowledgeable about attractions and local history, and the standard sightseeing rate averages $25 per site per person. The vehicles are unmetered, so negotiate a price in advance and make sure everyone's talking about the same currency.

LANGUAGE & CURRENCY   **English** is Dominica's official language. The **Eastern Caribbean dollar** (EC$2.70 = US$1; EC$1 = US37¢) is its official currency, but U.S. dollars are accepted almost everywhere.

BEST CRUISE LINE SHORE EXCURSIONS

Trafalgar Falls & Emerald Pool Nature Tour ($52, 4½ hr.): Drive to Morne Bruce for a panoramic view of Roseau and learn about local flora and fauna at the Botanical Gardens. Proceed to a lookout point for a majestic view of Trafalgar Falls. Another drive and a 15-minute walk along a relatively easy trail take you to the Emerald Pool, named for the moss-covered boulders that enclose it. You can splash in the refreshing water if you like, floating on your back to see the thick rainforest canopy, the 15m (50-ft.) waterfall, and the bright blue sky above you.

Carib Indian Territory & Emerald Pool ($59, 5 hr.): The tour stops at the Emerald Pool before heading to a rugged portion of Dominica's northeastern coast, where the 1,327-hectare (3,278-acre) Carib Territory is home to the world's last surviving Carib Indians. The Caribs today live like most other rural islanders—growing bananas and coconuts, fishing, and operating small shops—but their sturdy baskets of dyed and woven larouma reeds and their wooden canoes carved from the trunks of massive gommier trees are evidence of the people's links to the past. Kalinago Barana Aute, the "Carib Cultural Village by the Sea," honors the diversity, history, and heritage of the Kalinago people. There are traditional crafts demonstrations and dance performances, an herbal medicine garden, trails, a food and beverage concession stand, and an arts-and-crafts gallery.

Rain Forest Aerial Tram ($114, 3 hr.): A 1,402m (4,600-ft.) tram offers a scenic 70-minute journey through the treetops, over streams and waterfalls, and across the Breakfast River Gorge.

Layou Gorge River Tubing ($69, 3 hr.): A 40-minute drive takes you into the Layou Valley, where tubing guides will take you down the river, lined with tall, overhanging cliffs and lush vegetation. A longer version of this tour also pays a visit to the Emerald Pool ($82–$99, 4 hr.).

Dominica by Jeep & Swimming at the Titou Gorge ($89, 3½ hr.): A jeep convoy heads up Morne Bruce for a picturesque view, stopping at the Botanical Gardens and the Wotten Waven Sulpher Springs before arriving at the volcanic Titou Gorge, where sheer 20-foot black walls, rock outcrops, caves, and a thundering waterfall provide an exhilarating swimming experience. Scenes from *Pirates of the Caribbean* were filmed here.

ON YOUR OWN: WITHIN WALKING DISTANCE

IN ROSEAU   As you come ashore, you'll see the **Dominica Museum,** which faces the bayfront. Housed in an old market building dating from 1810, the museum's permanent exhibit provides a clear and interesting overview of the island's geology, history, archaeology, economy, and culture. The displays on pre-Columbian peoples, the slave trade, and the Fighting Maroons—slaves who resisted their white slave owners and established their own communities—are particularly informative. Admission is $3. It's usually closed Sundays, but opens when a ship is in port.

It took more than 100 years to build the **Roseau Cathedral of Our Lady of Fair Heaven,** on Virgin Lane. Made of cut volcanic stone in the Gothic-Romanesque Revival style, it was finally completed in 1916. The original funds to build it were raised from levies on French planters; Caribs erected the first wooden ceiling frame, and convicts on Devil's Island built the pulpit.

On the eastern edge of Roseau, the **Botanical Gardens** lie at the base of Morne Bruce, the mountain overlooking the town. The gardens were established at the end of the 19th century to encourage crop diversification and to provide farmers with correctly propagated seedlings. London's Kew Gardens provided exotic plants collected from every corner of the tropical world, and experiments conducted to see what would grow in Dominica revealed that everything does.

IN PORTSMOUTH   The cruise ship dock at Portsmouth leads directly to 104-hectare (260-acre) **Cabrits National Park,** which features stunning mountain scenery, tropical deciduous forest and swampland, volcanic-sand beaches, coral reefs, and the romance of 18th-century **Fort Shirley,** which, along with more than 50 other major structures, composes one of the most impressive and historic military complexes in the West Indies. Admission is $2.

ON YOUR OWN: BEYOND THE PORT AREAS

Approximately 15 to 20 minutes by car from Roseau, **Trafalgar Falls** is actually two separate falls referred to as the mother and the father falls. The cascading white torrents dazzle in the sunlight before pummeling black-lava boulders below. The surrounding foliage comes in innumerable shades of green. To reach the brisk water of the natural pool at the base of the falls, you'll have to step gingerly along slippery rocks, so the nonballetic shouldn't attempt the climb. The constant mist that tingles the entire area beats any spa treatment. The rainbows are perpetual.

Hard-core masochists have an easy choice—the forced march through the **Valley of Desolation** to **Boiling Lake.** Experienced guides say this 6-hour hike is like spending hours on a maximally resistant Stairmaster. So why would any sane person endure this hell? To breathe in the harsh, sulfuric fumes that have killed all but the hardiest vegetation? Because the idea of baking a potato in the steam rising from the earth is irresistible? Maybe to feel the thrill that comes with the risk that you might break through the thin crust that separates you from hot lava? Or could it be the final destination, the wide cauldron of bubbling, slate-blue water of unknown depth? Don't even think about taking a dip in this flooded fumarole: The water temperature is about 190°F (88°C). Can we sign you up?

Other beautiful natural areas of the island are discussed in "Best Cruise Line Shore Excursions," above.

BEACHES

If your sole focus is beaches, you'll likely find Dominica disappointing. Much of the seacoast is rocky, and many beaches have dark, volcanic sand. There are golden-sand beaches as well, but all are located on the northern coast, quite far from Roseau.

SHOPPING

In addition to the usual duty-free items, Dominica offers handicrafts and art not obtainable anywhere else, most notably **Carib Indian baskets** made of dyed larouma reeds and balizier (heliconia) leaves, their designs handed down from generation to generation. More than a souvenir, these baskets are a real link to the pre-Columbian Caribbean, and one of the most "authentic" items you can buy in the whole Caribbean. You can buy Carib crafts directly from the craftspeople in the Carib Territory or at various outlets in Roseau. Prices are ridiculously reasonable.

In Roseau, the cobbled **Old Market Square** is a bustling market located directly behind the Dominica Museum, offering mostly handicrafts and souvenirs. At **Tropicrafts,** at the corner of Queen Mary Street and Turkey Lane, you can watch local women weave grass mats with designs as varied and complex as those you made as a child with your Spirograph. The large store also stocks Carib baskets, locally made soaps and toiletries, rums, jellies, condiments, woodcarvings, and masks made from the trunks of giant fougère ferns.

11 Grand Cayman

Flat, relatively unattractive, and full of scrubland and swamp, Grand Cayman and its sister islands (Cayman Brac and Little Cayman) nevertheless boast more than their share of upscale, expensive private homes and condos, owned by millionaire expatriates from all over who come because of the tiny nation's lenient tax and banking laws. (Enron, the poster child of shady business dealings, reportedly had more than 690 different subsidiaries here to help it avoid paying U.S. taxes.) Grand Cayman is also popular because of its laid-back civility—so civil that ships aren't allowed to visit on Sunday. **George Town** is the colony's capital and its commercial hub, and many hotels line the sands of the nation's most famous sunspot, **Seven Mile Beach.** Scuba divers and snorkelers come for the coral reefs and other formations, some of which lie within swimming distance of the shoreline.

In 2004, Hurricane Ivan tore through Grand Cayman, causing substantial flooding, destroying many homes and businesses, and severely damaging power and sewage networks. Things were such a mess that the island was officially closed to tourists for 2 months. However, with tourism accounting for some 45% of the Caymans' GDP, cleanup was swift, and things are more or less back to normal.

COMING ASHORE   Typically, up to nine cruise ships can anchor off **George Town** and ferry their passengers to a pier at the new $23-million cruise terminal on Harbour Drive, right in the midst of George Town's shopping district. Future plans include berthing for up to four cruise ships, but work has not yet begun. A unique feature of this port is that some tour and dive operators have their own water shuttles that come out to greet the ship and take booked passengers directly to their activity, eliminating the tender ride to shore.

GETTING AROUND Taxis line up at the pier to meet cruise ship passengers. Fares are fixed; typical one-way fares range from $12 to $20. **Motor scooters** and **bicycles** are another way to get around. **Island Scooter Rental** (© 345/949-2046), at Bernard Drive in Industrial Park, offers shuttle service to and from George Town and rents scooters for $30 a day. A public **bus service** has recently started, offering inexpensive service to local attractions for about $1.50 to $2 a person one-way.

LANGUAGE & CURRENCY English is the official language of the islands. The legal tender is the **Cayman Islands dollar** (CI84¢ = US$1; CI$1 = US$1.19), but U.S. dollars are commonly accepted. Be sure to note which currency is referred to on price tags before making a purchase.

BEST CRUISE LINE SHORE EXCURSIONS

Cruise lines typically offer about 30 shore excursions here, most of them of the swimming, snorkeling, sailing, submarine, and glass-bottom-boat variety.

Stingray City ($45–$59, 2–3 hr.): The waters off Grand Cayman are home to Stingray City, one of the world's most unusual underwater attractions. Set in very shallow waters of North Sound, about 2 miles east of the island's northwestern tip, the site was discovered in the mid-1980s when local fishermen noticed that scores of stingrays were showing up to feed on the offal they dumped overboard. Today, anywhere from 30 to 100 relatively tame stingrays swarm around the hundreds of visiting snorkelers like so many aquatic basset hounds, eager for handouts. The guides bring buckets of squid and show you the correct way to feed the stingrays, which sort of suck the food right out of your hand. Stingrays are terribly gentle creatures, and love to have their bellies rubbed, but never try to grab one by the tail—their barbed stingers can inflict a lot of pain. Be sure to bring your waterproof camera for this one.

Atlantis Submarine Expedition ($95, 1½ hr., including 45-min. dive): Board a 48-passenger sub and descend to 100 feet through coral canyons, with an automatic fish feeder drawing swarms of colorful marine creatures.

Cayman Cycling ($69, 3 hr.): Pick up your touring mountain bike at the Spanish Bay Reef Resort and ride along the rugged coastline of Boatswain Bay and the palm-covered country lanes of the Cobalt Coast. On the final leg, participants can visit the Turtle Farm and the post office in Hell before returning to the Spanish Bay.

ON YOUR OWN: WITHIN WALKING DISTANCE

In George Town, the small **Cayman Islands National Museum,** Harbour Drive (© 345/949-8368; www.museum.ky), is housed in a veranda-fronted building that once served as the island's courthouse. Exhibits include Caymanian artifacts collected by Ira Thompson (beginning in the 1930s), and other items relating to the natural, social, and cultural history of the Caymans. Facilities include a gift shop, theater, and cafe. Admission is $4.75 for adults, $2.40 for seniors and students; closed Sundays. At press time, the museum was closed for renovation and is slated to reopen in September 2007.

The **National Gallery of the Cayman Islands,** Harbour Place, South Church Street (© 345/945-8111; www.nationalgallery.org.ky), is an educational nonprofit organization that supports the growth of the Cayman Islands arts scene, offering an average of eight exhibitions of both local and international art per year. Admission is free; closed Sundays.

ON YOUR OWN: BEYOND THE PORT AREA

For years, one of Grand Cayman's most popular attractions has been the **Cayman Turtle Farm** (© 345/949-3894), the only green-sea-turtle farm of its kind in the world. Once a multitude of turtles lived in the waters surrounding the Cayman Islands, but today these creatures are an endangered species. The turtle farm's purpose is twofold: to replenish the waters with hatchlings and yearling turtles and, at the other end of the spectrum, to provide the local market with edible turtle meat. You can peer into about 100 circular concrete tanks containing turtles ranging in size from 6 ounces to 600 pounds, or sample turtle dishes at a snack bar and restaurant. The turtle farm is now part of a 23-acre marine park called **Boatswain's Beach** (pronounced *Boe*-suns; www.boatswainsbeach.ky), which will also include a snorkeling lagoon, a predator tank full of sharks and moray eels, a separate tank for dolphin swims, an aviary, a nature trail, and other mostly marine-oriented displays. Many, but not all, of the exhibits are completed. Admission is $35 for adults and $5 for children, which includes access to the entire facility. Admission for the Turtle Farm only is $13 for adults and $8.25 for kids.

The nearby town of **Hell** is mostly notable for its name (and the T-shirts bearing it), but there are also some unusual rock formations from which the town got its name. If you mail your postcards from here, guess what the postmark says.

BEACHES

Lined with condominiums and plush resorts, **Seven Mile Beach** begins north of George Town, an easy taxi ride from the cruise dock. It has sparkling white sands with a backdrop of casuarina trees, and is known for its array of watersports and its translucent aquamarine waters. The average water temperature is a balmy 80°F (27°C).

SHOPPING

There's duty-free shopping here for silver, china, crystal, Irish linens, and British woolen goods, but we've found most prices to be similar to those in the United States. You'll also find cigar shops and international chains. Don't succumb and purchase turtle or black-coral products. You'll see them everywhere, but it's illegal to bring them back into the United States and most other Western nations.

12 Grand Turk

Welcome to the Caribbean's newest cruise port. Just 11km (6¾ miles) long and about 2km (1¼ miles) wide, with 3,700 residents, Grand Turk has long been known as one of the top five diving destinations in the world, owing to the fact that, just a few hundred yards from shore, the shallow continental shelf suddenly plunges 2,135m (7,000 ft.) straight down, with healthy coral reefs and great visibility making conditions absolutely perfect. The whole western shore of the island is a protected underwater park. Above water, things are practically perfect too, with an average temperature of 83°F (28°C) and an amazing 350 days of sunshine a year. It can reach the 90s (30s Celsius) in the summer, but the surprisingly strong trade winds keep things comfy.

While ships had visited the island in the past, it really wasn't equipped to handle a massive influx of passengers until the Grand Turk Cruise Center opened in February 2006, its deepwater pier able to accommodate even the largest megaships. Carnival was the prime mover behind the project, leasing 15 hectares (37 acres) from the government and developing less than half of them, building a transportation center, restaurant, shopping area, crafts stalls, fountains, and duty-free building. The cruise center will welcome all ships, not just Carnival lines.

About 5km (3 miles) from the pier is charming downtown **Cockburn Town,** a sleepy half-mile stretch that also happens to be the administrative capital of the Turks and Caicos Islands. Along its streets, Bermudan-influenced colonial buildings mix with simple gift shops, guesthouses, and a couple of laid-back bars, plus miles of public powder-white beaches. Islanders describe the ambience here as the way the rest of the Caribbean was 25 years ago. A bit neglected over the years, Grand Turk received a $7-million boost from Carnival for infrastructure improvements, ranging from pedestrian crossings to the creation of ready-made tourist attractions based on the island's substantive history.

So far, Grand Turk retains its air of quaintness, but developers are moving in; and plans call for 370,000 cruise visitors a year by the end of 2007—about 100 times as many people as actually live on the island. This is one port you may want to make a special effort to visit as soon as you can.

COMING ASHORE   Located on the south side of Grand Turk, the **Grand Turk Cruise Center** may seem to arriving passengers like one of the cruise lines' private islands, with its carefully placed landscaping between the dock and the beach. Its advantages, of course, are that (a) it's part of a real country, and (b) passengers don't have to tender ashore because the cruise pier can accommodate the largest ships. However, in the event that there are two ships at the pier, the third must then drift (ships may not anchor) and tender passengers ashore, usually no more than a 10-minute ride. At the cruise center, you can get visitor info, rent a car, eat, drink, shop, or catch a taxi or water taxi into Cockburn Town, about 5km (3 miles) away.

GETTING AROUND   **Taxi** fares from the port to Cockburn Town run about $10 for the first person and $4 for each additional person, but get a quote from the driver before you commit. There's no public transportation on the island, but one shore excursion offered by the cruise lines is a **bus loop** from which you can hop off and on at will (see below). **Car-rental** desks are located at the cruise terminal, but if you want a car, be sure to book ahead, as supplies are limited. Also be prepared to drive on the left side of the road, since the Turks and Caicos are a British colony.

LANGUAGE & CURRENCY   **English** is spoken everywhere. The official currency is the **U.S. dollar,** but there's a local currency called the TCI crown (equivalent in value to the dollar) and a quarter, either of which makes nice souvenirs.

BEST CRUISE LINE SHORE EXCURSIONS

In addition to the excursions listed here, **whale-watching** will be added to ships' offerings on an ad hoc basis. It has to be the right season and the right weather, but Atlantic humpback whales travel down Turk's Passage trench on the western side of the island every year, heading for their breeding grounds south of Grand Turk, where they take care of their calves from January to April. Otherwise, the thing to do in Grand Turk is get underwater.

Scuba Diving ($109–$119, 2½–4 hr.): You won't get better conditions anywhere in the Caribbean than Grand Turk, with its tranquil, crystal-clear waters and protected reef. Experienced divers will be wowed by the manta rays, whale sharks, and sea turtles, and the beautiful colors of the third-largest coral reef in the world. Even a first-timer can get to the reefs via a resort course, with intensive one-on-one instruction followed by a half-hour of diving.

Snorkeling ($49, 2½ hr.): If you're not up for scuba, you can at least go snorkeling to see the beauty of Grand Turk's undersea world. Snorkeling cruises departing from the cruise terminal visit two sites, typically Horseshoe Reef (with depths averaging 1.8–3.7m/6–12 ft.) and a reef off Round Cay, one of Grand Turk's best dive locations.

Grand Turk Helmet Dive ($109, 2 hr.): Yet another way of getting underwater is via a helmet dive, in which a helmet provides a constant air supply as you walk around on the ocean floor.

Grand Turk Semisub ($49, 1 hr.): If you don't want to get your feet wet at all, sign up for this semisubmersible excursion, where you travel 2.4m (8 ft.) below the surface to view sea life and get a glimpse of Grand Turk's famous coral reefs.

Hop-On, Hop-Off Island Tour ($39, duration varies): Air-conditioned buses loop around the island whenever there's a ship in port, letting booked excursioners see things at their leisure. A wristband allows entry to various tourist venues along the route, including Cockburn Town's Millennium Clock Tower and restored 1800s prison; Lighthouse Park, with its namesake light built in 1852 and two nature trails; the Turks and Caicos National Museum, which has some information on John Glenn's splashdown off Grand Turk in 1962; and the Philatelic Bureau. Anyone who's ever collected stamps will know that Turks and Caicos is well known for its beautiful stamps, created almost solely for collectors. Stops are located approximately every half-mile along the route, with many sited close to island attractions. Buses arrive at each stop approximately every 15 minutes.

ON YOUR OWN: WITHIN WALKING DISTANCE

Passengers could easily spend their whole day just hanging out at the cruise center, whose biggest structure by far is the two-story, 1,560-sq.-m (17,000-sq.-ft.) **Margaritaville Cafe,** the largest stand-alone Jimmy Buffett franchise in the Caribbean. Wastin' away again? Behind the restaurant is a giant amoeba-shaped swimming pool with swim-up bar, slide, cabanas, and infinity-edge view. It's open to the public and, because it's only 1m (3¼ ft.) deep, it makes a great place to hang out with the younger kids.

ON YOUR OWN: BEYOND THE PORT AREA

Cockburn Town's **historic district** is centered along Duke and Front streets, where some houses built of wood and limestone stand along the waterfront. Historic government buildings surround a small plaza where cannons and a bronze plaque mark the spot where Christopher Columbus allegedly first set foot in the New World, on October 14, 1492. Columbus's logbook notes landfall at a bean-shaped island, but there's no absolute proof that said bean was Grand Turk.

Also on Front Street is the **Turks and Caicos National Museum** (© **649/946-2160;** www.tcmuseum.org). Housed in 180-year-old Guinep House, the museum includes wreckage from a Spanish caravel that sank in shallow offshore water sometime before 1513, plus exhibits on the island's natural history, salt industries, plantation economy, and pre-Columbian inhabitants. Admission is $5; closed Sundays.

Just behind Cockburn Town's historic waterfront is the town's **saltwater pond,** and out in the middle of that is an island once used to quarantine sick sailors. Today, it's a favorite of birders who come to see some of Grand Turk's 190 bird species, including the flamingos, pelicans, and herons who feed in the pond's shallow waters.

BEACHES

The cruise terminal's powder-white-sand beach is just steps from the pier, and you'll find lounge chairs, hammocks, and bartending staff coming by to take your drink orders. For $19 a day, you can rent a clamshell shade with room for two lounge chairs. You can also get a taste of the underwater view that makes Grand Turk famous by snorkeling, with equipment available for rent or purchase.

On the island's southwest coast, below Cockburn Town, **Governor's Beach** is one of the few blue-flagged beaches in the Caribbean, which means it's passed stringent tests for water quality, cleanliness, and lifeguard availability. It's also reputed to have the best snorkeling on the island. Right next door is **Waterloo,** the governor's mansion, a pretty structure with the curved stucco architecture characteristic of Bermudan buildings.

SHOPPING

Grand Turk isn't particularly known for its arts and crafts, though you will find shops at the cruise center and at the island's various attractions and museums, plus a couple along Duke Street, which borders the western beach in the downtown area.

13 Grenada

Once a British crown colony, the now-independent nation of Grenada (Gre-*nay*-dah) produces more spices than anywhere else in the world, including clove, cinnamon, mace, cocoa, tonka beans, ginger, and a third of the world's nutmeg—thus its nickname, the "Spice Island." **St. George's,** the country's capital, is one of the most colorful ports in the West Indies, nearly landlocked in the deep crater of a long-dead volcano, full of charming Georgian colonial buildings, and flanked by old forts. The island's coast is white and sandy, while its interior is a jungle of palms, oleander, bougainvillea, and other tropical foliage, crisscrossed by roads and trails.

Grenada was one of the hardest hit Caribbean islands during 2004's devastating hurricane season. Almost every building sustained some level of damage, but you can't keep a good island down. Known for its lushness and most extravagant fertility (results of a gentle climate and volcanic soil), Grenada started springing back almost immediately, its coastal greenery growing back rapidly and its rainforests filling out a little more slowly. You should, however, expect to see some construction in process as the island continues to rebuild.

COMING ASHORE   Two ships at a time can dock at the modern **Melville Street Cruise Terminal,** plus one more at the main quay. Up to four vessels can anchor in the picturesque St. George's harbor and send their passengers on a short tender ride to the pier. Passengers exit the cruise terminal through the brand-new Esplanade shopping mall onto the Carenage (St. George's main street).

GETTING AROUND   Taxi fares are set by the government. A one-way taxi to Grand Anse (one of the Caribbean's best beaches) is about $12 to $15 for up to four passengers. You can also tap most taxi drivers as a guide for a day's sightseeing, for about $25 per hour. **Water taxis** also head from the cruise ship welcome center to Grand Anse; the round-trip fare is about $6.

LANGUAGE & CURRENCY   **English** is commonly spoken on this island, and the official currency is the **Eastern Caribbean dollar** (EC$2.70 = US$1; EC$1 = US37¢), though dollars are widely accepted. Always determine which dollars—EC or U.S.—you're talking about when discussing a price.

BEST CRUISE LINE SHORE EXCURSIONS

Because of Grenada's lush landscape, we recommend spending at least a few hours touring its interior, one of the most scenic in the West Indies.

Hike to Seven Sisters Waterfalls ($64, 3½ hr.): After a 40-minute hike along a muddy path in the lush Grand Etang rainforest, passengers are free to take a swim in the natural pools or hop off the edge of the cascading waterfalls. It's gorgeous and lots of fun. Don't forget to wear your bathing suit and maybe a pair of Teva-type sandals.

Island Tour, Grand Etang Lake & Fort Frederick ($44, 4½ hr.): This is a great way to experience Grenada's lush, cool, dripping-wet tropical interior. You travel by bus past the red-tiled roofs of St. George's en route to the bright-blue Grand Etang Lake, within an extinct volcanic crater some 530m (1,740 ft.) above sea level. On the way, you drive through rainforests and stop at a spice estate. Some tours include a visit to Annandale Falls and Fort Frederick.

ON YOUR OWN: WITHIN WALKING DISTANCE

In St. George's, you can visit the **Grenada National Museum,** at the corner of Young and Monckton streets (© **473/440-3725**), set in the foundations of an old French army barracks and prison built in 1704. Small but interesting, it houses ancient petroglyphs and other archaeological finds, a rum still, Joséphine Bonaparte's bathtub from her girlhood in Martinique, and various Grenada memorabilia. Admission is $2.50 for adults and $1 for kids.

If you're up for a good hike, walk around the historic Carenage from the cruise terminal and head up to **Fort George,** built in 1705 by the French and originally called Fort Royal. While the fort ruins and the 200- to 300-year-old cannons are worth a peek, it's the 360-degree panoramic views of the entire harbor area that are most spectacular. You can pick up a rudimentary walking-tour map from the cruise terminal to help you find interesting sights along the way. **Church Street,** which leads right to the fort, has lots of quaint 18th- and 19th-century architecture, as well as several 19th-century cathedrals and the island's Houses of Parliament.

ON YOUR OWN: BEYOND THE PORT AREA

You can take a taxi up Richmond Hill to **Fort Frederick,** which the French began in 1779. The British retook the island in 1783 and completed the fort in 1791. From its battlements you'll have a panoramic view of the harbor and the yacht marina.

Don't miss the mountains northeast of St. George's. If you don't have much time, 15m (49-ft.) **Annandale Falls** is just a 15-minute drive away, on the outskirts of the **Grand Etang Forest Reserve.** The overall beauty is almost Tahitian. You can swim and picnic surrounded by liana vines, elephant ears, and other tropical flora and spices. If you've got more time and want a less crowded spot, the even better **Seven Sisters Waterfalls** are farther into Grand Etang, an approximately 30-minute drive and then a mile hike along a muddy trail. It's well worth the trip—you'll really get a feel for the power and beauty of the tropical forest here. The falls themselves are lovely, and you can climb to the top and jump off into the pool below.

If you have time, head to **Levera National Park,** in the north of the island, for hikes through a mangrove swamp and a bird sanctuary. Just to the south of there, the 1912 **Morne Fendue Plantation House,** at St. Patrick's (© **473/442-9330**), offers a chance to enjoy old-time island recipes while you dine as an upper-class family would have in the 1920s. It serves a fixed-price ($16) lunch Monday through Saturday from 12:30 to 3pm; call for reservations.

BEACHES

Grenada's **Grand Anse Beach,** with its 3km (2 miles) of wide sugar-white sands, is one of the best in the Caribbean, boasting calm waters and a great view of St. George's. There are several restaurants beachside, and you can also join a banana-boat ride or rent a Sunfish sailboat.

SHOPPING

Grenada is no grand Caribbean merchandise mart, so if you're cruising on to such islands as Aruba, St. Martin, or St. Thomas, you might want to postpone serious purchases until then. On the other hand, you can find some fine local handicrafts, gifts, and art here. The best buy is, of course, fresh **spices** and related items. Nutmeg products are especially popular. The Grenadians use every part of the nutmeg: They make the outer fruit into a tasty liqueur and a rich jam, and ground the orange membrane around the nut into a different spice called mace. You'll also see the outer shells used as gravel to cover trails and parking lots.

14 Jamaica

A favorite of North American honeymooners, Jamaica is the third-largest of the Caribbean islands after Cuba and Hispaniola, with dense jungle in its interior, mountains rising as high as 2,220m (7,283 ft.), and many beautiful white-sand beaches along its northern coast, where the cruise ships dock. Most head for **Ocho Rios,** although more and more are opting to call at the city of **Montego Bay** ("Mo Bay"), 108km (67 miles) to the west. These ports offer comparable attractions, shore excursions, and shopping possibilities.

One of the most densely populated nations in the Caribbean, with a vivid sense of its own identity, Jamaica has a history rooted in the plantation economy and some of the most impassioned politics in the Western Hemisphere, all of which leads to a sometimes-turbulent day-to-day reality. You've probably heard, for instance, that the island's vendors and hawkers can be pushy and the locals not always the most welcoming to tourists. While there's some truth to this, we've had nothing but positive experiences, so keep an open mind.

LANGUAGE & CURRENCY   The official language is **English,** but most Jamaicans speak a richly nuanced patois. The unit of currency is the **Jamaican dollar** (J$68 = US$1; J$1 = US2¢). Visitors can pay in U.S. dollars, but always find out if a price is being quoted in Jamaican or U.S. dollars—though it'll probably be obvious by the huge difference.

SHORE EXCURSIONS OFFERED FROM BOTH PORTS

Since there's little besides shopping near the docks at either Ocho Rios or Montego Bay, most passengers sign up for shore excursions. The following are usually offered from both ports.

Dunn's River Falls Tour ($45, 4–4½ hr. from Ocho Rios; $70, 7½ hr. from Mo Bay): These falls cascade 180m (591 ft.) to the beach and are the most visited attraction in Jamaica, which means they're hopelessly overcrowded when a lot of cruise ships are in port. Tourists are allowed to climb the falls, and it's a ball to slip and slide your way up with hundreds of others, forming a human chain of sorts. Wear a bathing suit under your clothes, and don't forget your waterproof camera and your aqua-socks. (If you do forget, most cruise lines will rent you aqua-socks for an extra $5.) The prettiest part of the falls, known as the Laughing Waters, was used in the James Bond classics *Dr. No* and *Live and Let Die*. This tour usually visits other local attractions as well, with time allocated for shopping.

River Tubing Safari ($75, 3½ hr.): This is one of the best excursions we've ever taken. After a scenic van ride deep into the pristine jungles, the group of 20 or so passengers and a couple of guides sit back into big black inner tubes (they have wooden boards covering the bottom so your butt doesn't get scraped on the rocks) and glide a few miles downriver, passing gorgeous, towering bamboo trees and other lush foliage. It's sometimes peaceful and sometimes exhilarating—especially when you hit the rapids! If you're docking in Ocho Rios, this tour is usually on the White River; if in Montego Bay, it's on the Great River. *Note:* We find this trip much more interesting than the popular **Martha Brae River Rafting,** which takes you down the river on two-seat bamboo rafts. The cost is about the same.

Horseback-Riding Excursion ($89, 3–3½ hr.): Riders will love this trip: After a 45-minute ride from the stables through fields, you'll gallop along the beach and take your horse bareback into the surf for a thrilling ride.

OCHO RIOS

Once a small banana and fishing port, Ocho Rios is now Jamaica's cruise ship capital, welcoming a couple of ships every day during high season. Though the area has some of the Caribbean's most fabled resorts, and Dunn's River Falls is just a 5-minute taxi ride away, the town itself is not much to see, despite there being a few outdoor local markets within walking distance. Don't expect to shop in the markets without a lot of hassle and a lot of very pushy hawking of merchandise—some of which is likely to be ganja (the wacky weed). In recent years, an army of blue-uniformed "resort patrol" officers on bikes have been helping to keep order.

COMING ASHORE   Most cruise ships dock at the **Ocho Rios Cruise Terminal,** near Dunn's River Falls and adjacent to Island Village and several shopping and eating options. The normal docking area has space for three ships; megaships occasionally use the adjacent industrial pier, which is a short walk from the terminal. Additional vessels must anchor and tender passengers for the short 15- to 20-minute trip to the terminal.

GETTING AROUND   It's about a 5-minute walk to the shopping area, but otherwise **taxis** are your best means of getting around on your own. They'll be waiting for you at the pier. Those licensed by the government display *JTB* decals, indicating they're official Jamaican Tourist Board taxis. Fixed rates are posted.

BEST CRUISE LINE SHORE EXCURSIONS
In addition to the excursions offered from both Jamaican ports (see "Shore Excursions Offered from Both Ports," above), tours to several nearby attractions are also offered from Ocho Rios.

Prospect Plantation & Dunn's River Falls ($82, 4 hr.): About 5km (3 miles) east of town, Prospect Plantation offers a taste of Jamaica's colonial days (sans slavery), with a tractor-drawn jitney taking you among seasonal crops that include bananas, sugar cane, coffee, pineapple, and papaya. The trip includes a stop at Dunn's River Falls (see above).

Coyaba River Garden & Dunn's River Falls ($59, 3½ hr.): About 1.6km (1 mile) from town, Coyaba River Garden and Museum was built on the grounds of the former Shaw Park plantation. The museum displays artifacts from the Arawak, Spanish, and English settlements in the area, while the gardens are filled with native flora, a cut-stone courtyard, and fountains. Like many of the other tours in Ocho Rios, it hits Dunn's Falls on the way back.

Mountain Biking to Chukka Cove ($69, 4 hr.): A minivan takes you into the mountains above St. Ann, where you hop on your bike for the ride down back roads, through meadows and woodlands, to picturesque Chukka Cove, where you can take a swim.

Dolphin Cove ($34–$89, 2 hr.): Various excursions to this beachfront site allow you to gander at, touch, or swim with the resident dolphins. For about $10 more, you can add on 1½ hours at (you guessed it) Dunn's River Falls.

ON YOUR OWN: WITHING WALKING DISTANCE

Adjacent to the cruise pier, **Island Village** (www.islandjamaica.com) is a 1.6-hectare (4-acre) entertainment-and-shopping complex developed by Island Records' Chris Blackwell. Attractions include the ReggaeXplosion museum, a museum of Jamaican art, a casino, an outdoor concert venue and indoor theater, a beach with watersports, shopping (lots of it), and a branch of Jimmy Buffett's Margaritaville.

ON YOUR OWN: BEYOND THE PORT AREA

South of Ocho Rios, **Fern Gully** was originally a riverbed. Today, the main A3 road winds through a rainforest filled with wild ferns, hardwood trees, and lianas. For the botanist, there are hundreds of varieties of ferns; for the less plant-minded, roadside stands sell fruits and vegetables, carved-wood souvenirs, and basketwork. The road runs for about 6.4km (4 miles).

The 1817 **Brimmer Hall Estate,** Port Maria, St. Mary's (© **876/994-2309**), 34km (21 miles) east of Ocho Rios, is a working plantation where you're driven around in a tractor-drawn jitney to see the tropical fruit trees and coffee plants. Knowledgeable guides tell you about the processes necessary to produce the fine fruits of the island. Afterward, you can relax beside the pool and sample a wide variety of drinks, including an interesting one called "Wow!" The Plantation Tour Eating House offers typical Jamaican dishes for lunch. Tours run daily if there are enough people, so call ahead. Admission is $18. In the same general area, toward the coast, **Firefly,** Grants Pen, above Oracabessa (© **876/725-0920**), was the home of Sir Noël Coward and his longtime companion, Graham Payn, who, as executor of Coward's estate, donated it to the Jamaica National Heritage Trust. The recently restored house is as it was on the day Sir Noël died in 1973. It's open Monday through Thursday and Saturday from 9am to 5pm. Admission is $10.

BEACHES

The **Sunset Jamaica Grande Resort,** on Main Street (© **876/974-2201**), has two beaches, shared by hotel guests and cruise ship passengers. The beaches, located at the North and South Towers, can sometimes get jampacked. You might also want to check out the big **James Bond Beach,** in Oracabessa, about 20 minutes from town. Bond author Ian Fleming's home, Goldeneye, is located nearby.

SHOPPING

Shopping in Ocho Rios is not as good as in Montego Bay and other ports, but if your money's burning a hole in your pocket, you can wander around the **Ocho Rios Craft Park,** opposite the **Ocean Village Shopping Centre** off Main Street. Some 150 stalls stock hats, handbags, place mats, woodcarvings, and paintings, plus the usual T-shirts and jewelry. The **Island Plaza** shopping complex, right in the heart of town, has paintings by local artists, local handmade crafts (be prepared to do some bargaining), carvings, ceramics, and even kitchenware. At all of these places, prepare yourself for aggressive selling and fierce haggling. Every vendor asks too much for an item at first; it gives them the leeway to negotiate the price. (Note that some so-called duty-free prices are indeed lower than stateside, but then the Jamaican government hits you with a 16.5% "General Consumption Tax," so figure that in when shopping.)

MONTEGO BAY

Montego Bay has better beaches, shopping, and restaurants than Ocho Rios, as well as some of the best golf courses in the Caribbean. Like Ocho Rios, Mo Bay also has its crime, traffic, and annoyances, but there's much more to see and do here, at least nearby. (There's little of interest in the town itself except shopping.) Getting from place to place is one of the major difficulties, however. Whatever you want to visit seems to be in yet another direction. Shore excursions and taxis are the way to go.

COMING ASHORE   Montego Bay has a modern, recently expanded cruise dock for three to four ships, with a large terminal offering the usual duty-free stores, refreshments, phones, tourist information, and taxi/bus stands.

GETTING AROUND   If you don't book a shore excursion, **taxis** are the way to get around. They'll be waiting for you at the pier. Those licensed by the government display *JTB* decals, indicating they're official Jamaican Tourist Board taxis. Fixed rates are posted.

BEST CRUISE LINE SHORE EXCURSIONS

In addition to the excursions offered from both Jamaica ports (see "Shore Excursions Offered from Both Ports," above), Mo Bay offers tours to several interesting plantations and great houses.

Rose Hall Great House ($43, 3 hr.): This is the most famous plantation home in Jamaica. Built about 2 centuries ago by John Palmer, it gained notoriety from the doings of "Infamous Annie" Palmer, wife of the builder's grandnephew, who supposedly dabbled in witchcraft and took slaves as lovers, killing them when they bored her. Annie was also said to have murdered several of her husbands while they slept, and eventually suffered the same fate herself. For what it's worth, many Jamaicans insist the house is haunted.

Greenwood Great House & Town Drive ($39, 3½ hr.): More interesting to some than Rose Hall, this Georgian-style building was the residence of Richard Barrett, a first cousin of Elizabeth Barrett Browning. On display are the family's library, portraits, antiques, and period musical instruments.

Croydon Plantation Tour ($64, 6 hr.): A guided tour of this mountain estate includes a .5km (⅓-mile) walk over gently sloping terrain, with a lot of great views. Stops are made for refreshments and seasonal fresh fruits, and at the end you get a traditional Jamaican-style lunch.

ON YOUR OWN: BEYOND THE PORT AREA

There are no real attractions within walking distance. If you're not taking a shore excursion, consider a visit to **Rocklands Wildlife Station,** Anchovy, St. James (© 876/952-2009). Lisa Salmon, known as the "Bird Lady of Anchovy," established

Montego Bay Golf Excursions

Montego Bay offers a number of excellent golf opportunities. Various cruise lines offer organized excursions, but you can also arrange play ahead of time on your own, and then taxi it to the course.

- **Tryall Club** (© 876/956-5660; www.tryallclub.com), 19km (12 miles) from Montego Bay, is an excellent, regal 18-hole, par-72 course that's often been the site of major golf tournaments, including the Jamaica Classic Annual and the Johnnie Walker Tournament. Greens fees are about $125, plus $30 for a cart and $40 for clubs.

- **Rose Hall Resort & Country Club,** at Rose Hall (© 876/953-2650), has a noted 18-hole, par-71 course with an unusual and challenging seaside and mountain layout. The 90m-high (295-ft.) 13th tee offers a rare panoramic view of the sea, and the 15th green is next to a waterfall once featured in a James Bond movie. A fully stocked pro shop, a clubhouse, and a professional staff are among the amenities. Greens fees are about $141, which includes a cart and a caddy.

- **Half Moon,** at Rose Hall (© 876/953-2211; www.halfmoon-resort.com/golf), features an 18-hole, par-72 championship course designed by Robert Trent Jones, Sr. Greens fees are about $169, plus $25 for a mandatory caddy.

- **Ironshore Golf & Country Club,** Ironshore, St. James, Montego Bay (© 876/953-3681), a well-known 18-hole, par-72 course, is privately owned but open to the public. Greens fees are about $50, plus $35 for a cart and $16 for a mandatory caddy (for 18 holes).

this sanctuary, which is perfect for nature lovers and bird-watchers. You can feed small doves and finches from your hand, and with luck you can coax a Jamaican doctor bird to perch on your finger and drink syrup. Rocklands is about 1.2km (¾ mile) outside Anchovy on the road from Montego Bay. Admission is $10.

BEACHES

Doctor's Cave Beach (© 876/952-2566) on Gloucester Avenue across from the Doctor's Cave Beach Hotel (© 876/952-4355; www.doctorscave.com), helped launch Mo Bay as a resort in the 1940s. Dressing rooms, chairs, umbrellas, and rafts are available.

One of the premier beaches of Jamaica, **Aquasol Theme Park** (formerly Walter Fletcher Beach) is in the heart of Mo Bay. It's noted for its tranquil waters, which makes it a particular favorite for families with children. Changing rooms are available, and lifeguards are on duty. Nearby, the **Pork Pit,** 27 Gloucester Ave. (© 876/952-1046), is the best place to go for the famous Jamaican jerk pork and jerk chicken. Many beachgoers come over here for a big lunch. Picnic tables encircle the building, and everything is open-air and informal. Order half a pound of jerk meat with a baked yam or baked potato and a bottle of Red Stripe beer. Prices are very reasonable; lunch will cost $10.

On the main road 18km (11 miles) east of Montego Bay, the .75km (½-mile) **Rose Hall Beach Club** has a secure, secluded, white sandy beach, offering crystal-clear water, a full restaurant, two beach bars, a covered pavilion, an open-air dance area, showers, restrooms, and changing facilities, plus beach volleyball courts, various beach games, live music, and a full watersports activities program.

Note: All of these beaches charge admission, which runs about $8 for adults.

SHOPPING

The main shopping areas are at **Montego Freeport,** within easy walking distance of the pier; **City Centre,** where most of the duty-free shops are located, aside from those at the large hotels; and **Holiday Village Shopping Centre,** across from the Holiday Inn on Rose Hall Road, heading toward Ocho Rios.

The **Old Fort Craft Market,** a shopping complex with nearly 200 vendors licensed by the Jamaica Tourist Board, fronts Howard Cooke Boulevard up from Gloucester Avenue in the heart of Montego Bay, on the site of Fort Montego. With a varied assortment of handicrafts, this is browsing country. You'll see wall hangings, hand-woven straw items, and hand-carved wood sculptures, and you can also get your hair braided. Vendors can be extremely aggressive, so be prepared for some major hassles, as well as some serious negotiation. Persistent bargaining on your part will lead to substantial discounts.

You can find the best selection of handmade Jamaican souvenirs at the **Crafts Market,** near Harbour Street in downtown Montego Bay. Straw hats and bags, wooden platters, straw baskets, musical instruments, beads, carved objects, and toys are all available here. That "jipijapa" hat will come in handy if you're going to be out in the island sun.

15 Key West

Located at the very end of the Florida Keys, Key West is America's southernmost city and has a vibe that mixes colorful Caribbean outpost with a dash of New Orleans high life. It's a fun-loving, heavy-drinking town with a lot of history, more than a little touristy goofiness, a thousand Hemingway look-alikes, and a large gay community. It's a regular melting pot. It's also, as many tour guides like to point out, the Pulitzer Prize–winner capital of the U.S., with more winners per capita than anywhere else in the country. The proximity of most attractions to the cruise docks means there's little sense in taking an excursion here unless you have mobility problems. Wander around touristy Mallory Square and Duval Street, check out some of the theme bars, and then take a walk down some of the quieter side streets, maybe visiting Truman's Little White House or the Hemingway Home & Museum. Or, you might want to spend your day playing golf, diving, or snorkeling. Several "raw bars" near the dock area offer seafood, including oysters and clams, although the king here is conch—served grilled, ground into burgers, made into chowder, fried in batter as fritters, or served raw in a conch salad (though beware, some of the quickie conch vendors near the docks are pretty skimpy with the conch . . . can we say dough balls?). If you've got more of a sweet tooth than anything else, be sure to sample the decadent frozen, chocolate-dipped, Key lime pie on a stick that you can pick up from several places in town.

COMING ASHORE Medium-sized ships dock at **Mallory Square** (Old Town's tourist central), while larger ships pull alongside at the nearby Westin Resort's **Pier B** and at the U.S. Navy base's **"Outer Mole" pier.** All are on the Gulf side of the island

Deep-Sea Fishing in Key West

As Hemingway, an avid fisherman, would attest, the waters off the Florida Keys are some of the world's finest fishing grounds. You can follow in Papa's wake aboard the 40-foot *Linda D IV* and *Linda D V* (© 800/299-9798 or 305/296-9798; www.charterboatlindad.com), which offer the best deep-sea fishing here. Full-day charters for up to six people cost $900; a half-day charter is $600. Full-day shared charters are $200 per person; a half-day goes for $150. Make arrangements as far in advance as possible.

and all can accommodate one ship at a time. Passengers arriving at the Navy pier must take an official shuttle bus the short distance to and from Mallory Square, as individuals are not permitted to transit the base on their own. Additional ships can anchor for the short tender ride to shore.

GETTING AROUND   The island is only 4 miles long and 2 miles wide, so getting around is easy. The most popular attractions are within walking distance of Mallory Square. The farthest is Hemingway Home, about a mile down Duval. Many passengers opt for one of the island's tram tours, which are sold as shore excursions but are also available on a walk-up basis. The **Conch Tour Train** (© 305/294-5161; www.conchtourtrain.com) is a narrated 90-minute tour that offers commentary on 100 local sites. The depot is located at Mallory Square, and trains depart every 30 minutes ($25 adults, $12 children 4–12). The trip has only one stop where passengers can get on and off (at the Historic Seaport). If you want more flexibility, try the **Old Town Trolley** (© 305/296-6688; www.trolleytours.com), which allows you to hop on and off its trains to explore on your own. Prices are the same as the Conch Train, and pickup stops are signposted around town. If you want wheels of your own, **bicycles** and **motor scooters** are a good bet here and are widely available, with daily rates hovering around $14 and $30, respectively.

LANGUAGE & CURRENCY   The official language is **English.** The unit of currency is the **U.S. dollar.**

BEST CRUISE LINE SHORE EXCURSIONS

In addition to the Conch Tour Train described above, most cruise lines offer walking tours and sometimes bike tours for those who like the services of a guide. But this is really a port to explore on your own.

Key West Catamaran Sail & Snorkel Tour ($48, 3–3½ hr.): The popular Fury catamarans take passengers to a reef for some snorkeling and then finish the trip back to shore with music, booze, and a good time.

ON YOUR OWN: WITHIN WALKING DISTANCE

All attractions in Key West are within walking distance, though the Hemingway Home and Nancy Forrester's Secret Garden are at least 20 minutes from Mallory Square.

Bars—large, packed theme bars, usually with someone playing guitar and singing the hits in one corner—are a big draw in Key West. **Captain Tony's Saloon,** 428 Greene St. (© 305/294-1838), is the oldest active bar in Florida, and is both heavily patronized by cruise ship passengers and tacky as hell. The 1851 building was the original Sloppy Joe's, a rough-and-tumble fishermen's saloon. Hemingway drank here from

Key West

Audubon House and Tropical Garden **5**
Captain Tony's Saloon **3**
Harry S Truman Little White House **6**
Hemingway Home **9**
Heritage House Museum/
  Robert Frost Cottage **5**
Hog's Breath Saloon **1**

Jimmy Buffett's Margaritaville **7**
Key West Aquarium **2**
Mallory Square **1**
Mel Fisher Maritime Heritage Society
  Museum **5**
Nancy Forrester's Secret Garden **8**
Sloppy Joe's **4**

1933 to 1937; Jimmy Buffett got his start here before opening his own bar and going on to fame and fortune. The current **Sloppy Joe's,** 201 Duval St. (© 305/294-5717), is the most touristy bar in Key West, visited by almost all cruise ship passengers—even those who don't normally go to bars. It aggressively plays up its association with Hemingway, with pictures of Hemingway look-alike contest winners plastered all over the walls. **Jimmy Buffett's Margaritaville,** 500 Duval St. (© 305/296-3070), is kind of a refugee from Branson, Missouri, but if you've got a hankering for a cheeseburger from paradise or want to waste away again on margaritas, this is your place. Much less commercial is the open-air **Hog's Breath Saloon,** 400 Front St. (© 305/296-4222), near the cruise docks. Raucous and loud, it's populated by visiting fishermen and bikers alike, all of them with a drink in hand. Wherever you end up, try some of the favorite local beer, Hog's Breath, or some of the favorite local rum, Key West Gold (even though it's a cheat—it isn't actually made on the island). Most places recommended offer fast food to go with their drinks.

There's a bar at the **Harry S Truman Little White House,** 111 Front St. (© 305/294-9911; www.trumanlittlewhitehouse.com), too, back in the back room where Truman and his friends played poker—though visitors can't drink there. The house, formerly the home of the Navy base commander, served as Truman's vacation home during his presidency and today remains just as he left it, decorated in late 1940s style.

By the time the guides get through their well-organized 1-hour tour, you'll feel as if you've gone back in time. Admission is $11 for adults, $4 for kids; tours run daily every 15 minutes from 9:30am till 4pm.

The **Hemingway Home,** 907 Whitehead St. (© **305/294-1136;** www.hemingway home.com), provides a similar if less formal look back at the island's old days. "Papa" lived here with his second wife, Pauline, completing *For Whom the Bell Tolls* and *A Farewell to Arms* in the studio annex out back. Hemingway had some 60 polydactyl (many-toed) cats, whose descendants still live on the grounds. Admission costs $11.

The **Audubon House and Tropical Garden,** 205 Whitehead St., at Greene Street (© **877/281-2470** or 305/294-2116; www.audubonhouse.com), is dedicated to the 1832 Key West sojourn of the famous naturalist John James Audubon. The ornithologist didn't live in this three-story building, but it's filled with his engravings. The main reason to visit is to see how wealthy sailors lived in Key West in the 19th century, and to admire the lush tropical gardens surrounding the house. Admission is $10.

The **Key West Heritage House Museum and Robert Frost Cottage,** 410 Caroline St. (© **305/296-3573;** www.heritagehousemuseum.org), was the home of Jessie Porter Newton, the grande dame of Key West, and today it's filled with mementos of the illustrious guests who partook of her hospitality, including Tennessee Williams, Gloria Swanson, and Robert Frost, who stayed in a cottage out back. Closed Sundays.

On the waterfront at Mallory Square, the **Key West Aquarium,** 1 Whitehead St. (© **305/296-2051;** www.keywestaquarium.com), in operation since 1932, was the first tourist attraction built in the Florida Keys. The aquarium's special feature is a touch tank where you can feel a sea urchin, a sea star, or a conch, the town's mascot and symbol. Admission is $10 for adults, $5 for kids.

Near the docks, the **Mel Fisher Maritime Heritage Museum,** 200 Greene St. (© **305/294-2633;** www.melfisher.org), contains some of the more than $400 million in gold jewelry, doubloons, and other artifacts the late treasure hunter Mel Fisher plucked from the Spanish galleon *Nuestra Señora de Atocha,* which sunk off the Keys in 1622. Educational exhibits explain salvage operations and the history of the Spanish and piracy in the islands. Admission is $11.

Nancy Forrester's Secret Garden, 1 Free School Lane, off Simonton between Southard and Fleming streets (© **305/294-0015;** www.nfsgarden.com), is the most lavish and verdant garden in town, with some 150 species of palms and thousands of orchids, climbing vines, and ground covers. Admission is $6.

BEACHES

Beaches are not too compelling here, but the best and closest to the cruise docks is **Fort Zachary Taylor State Beach** (© **305/292-6713**), a 12-minute walk away. To get here, go through the gates leading into the Truman Annex (site of the Little White House).

SHOPPING

Within a 12-block radius of **Mallory Square,** you'll see mostly tawdry, overpriced tourist merchandise, but if you're in the market for some Key West kitsch, you'll find flamingo snow globes, floppy straw hats, seashell ashtrays, and the like. At Mallory itself, shops sell seashells from the seashore—actually, from around the world, including some you'd hardly believe are real. They also sell wine-bottle holders shaped like lobsters, but what the hell. As you move farther along **Duval Street** from Mallory, you'll notice that the shops get more and more stylish. Could it be a coincidence that this part of town is the center of Key West's gay community? We don't think so.

16 Martinique

Fairy-tale romance and horrific disaster: Who could resist such an enticing combination? As if being the birthplace and childhood home of Empress Joséphine, sweetheart and wife of Napoleon, weren't enough, Martinique mesmerizes with the epic tragedy that befell St. Pierre one fair day in 1902: bustling cosmopolitan capital one minute, devastated volcanic graveyard of 30,000 souls the next. Love and death make quite a one-two punch, but they're just the hook. Look a bit deeper to appreciate Martinique's subtler attractions—quaint seaside villages, colonial ruins dating from when France and England vied for the island, and captivatingly beautiful rainforests and beaches. In 1946, Martinique became an overseas department of France, which it remains today.

COMING ASHORE   Most cruise ships dock in the heart of Fort-de-France, at the **Pointe Simon Cruise Dock,** which has quays for two mid- to large-sized vessels. Because Martinique is a popular port of call, one megaship, or two smaller vessels, may also wind up docking at the **Tourelles Passenger Terminal** at the main harbor, a 5-minute cab ride from Fort-de-France. Expansion of the Pointe Simon area is underway, including new hotels, restaurants, and construction to allow additional berthing for the megaships. When all cruise piers are full, additional ships can dock across from the Tourelles terminal at a commercial pier, about a 5-minute shuttle ride from Tourelles.

GETTING AROUND   Travel by **taxi** is convenient but expensive. Most cabs are metered; you'll find them waiting at the cruise pier. To cross the bay to La Pagerie (Empress Joséphine's birthplace) and the resort area of Pointe du Bout, take one of the blue **ferries** that sail from east of the cruise dock in Fort-de-France at least once per hour. Round-trip tickets cost about $6 per person. Avis, Budget, and Hertz all offer **rental cars,** too.

LANGUAGE & CURRENCY   **French** is Martinique's official language, but you can get by with **English** at most restaurants and tourist sights. Martinique is an overseas region of France, so the **euro** (€) is the official currency (.76€ = US$1; 1€ = US$1.31). U.S. dollars are commonly accepted in tourist areas.

CALLING FROM THE U.S.   When calling Martinique from the U.S., dial the international access code **(011)** and the country code **(596)** before the numbers listed in this section. The numbers listed here already begin with 596, but an effort by the French telephone authorities to standardize procedures requires that you dial those three digits twice.

BEST CRUISE LINE SHORE EXCURSIONS

Rainforest & Plantations 4WD Safari ($99, 4–5 hr.): Take your off-road vehicle through tropical forests and sugar cane plantations (stopping to sample the crop) to a banana plantation and a distillery, where you'll do short tours.

Martinique Snorkeling ($59, 3 hr.): Across the bay from Fort-de-France, the reef at Anse Dufour offers excellent snorkeling for experts and novices. The reef is filled with marine animals, including French grunts, blackbar soldierfish, and silversides. Snorkeling equipment is provided, as are professional instruction, supervision, and transportation.

ON YOUR OWN: WITHIN WALKING DISTANCE

Fort-de-France is a bustling town of 100,000 residents, full of ochre buildings, ornate wrought-iron balconies, cascading flowers, and tall palm trees. The town's narrow streets, cluttered with boutiques and cafes, climb from the bowl of the sea to the surrounding hills, forming a great urban amphitheater. There's plenty here to keep you busy.

At the eastern end of downtown, **La Savane** is a broad formal park with palms, mangoes, and manicured lawns, perfect for a promenade or rest in the shade. Its most famous feature is the **Statue of Empress Joséphine,** carved in 1858 by Vital Dubray. Expect her to be headless: Napoleon's Little Creole was unceremoniously decapitated in 1995 in commemoration of her role in reinstating slavery on the island in the early 1800s. Across the street, **Bibliothèque Schoelcher** (Schoelcher Library; © 596/70-26-67) is one of Fort-de-France's great Belle Epoque buildings. Named in honor of Victor Schoelcher, one of France's most influential abolitionists, this elaborate structure, designed by French architect Henri Pick, was first displayed at the 1889 Paris Exposition. Four years later it was dismantled and shipped across the Atlantic. Today, it houses Schoelcher's books as well as an impressive archive of colonization, slavery, and emancipation documents. Admission is free; closed Sundays.

Another Henri Pick masterpiece, **St. Louis Cathedral,** on rue Victor Schoelcher at rue Blénac, was built in 1895. A contemporary of Gustave Eiffel (of Eiffel Tower fame), Pick used massive iron beams to support the walls, ceiling, and spire. A grand example of Industrial Revolution architecture, it's been likened to a Catholic railway station. The organ, stained-glass windows, and ornamented interior walls are well worth a look and can be viewed every morning except Saturday.

Built in 1640, **Fort St. Louis,** boulevard Alfassa, dominates the rocky promontory east of La Savane. A noteworthy example of 17th- and 18th-century military architecture, it first was used to defend Fort-de-France in 1674 against Dutch invaders. Today, the bastion remains the French navy's headquarters in the Caribbean and as such is open to visitors only on special occasions.

The best of Fort-de-France's many museums, the **Musée Départemental d'Archéologie Précolombienne Préhistoire,** 9 rue de la Liberté (© 596/71-57-05), traces 2,000 years of Martinique's pre-Columbian past with more than a thousand relics from the Arawak and Carib cultures. Admission is $4 for adults; closed Sundays.

You can expect to find great food all over town if you want to stop for lunch. More than any other island in the French West Indies, Martinique gives French and Creole cuisine equal billing.

ON YOUR OWN: BEYOND THE PORT AREA

Martinique is much too large to tackle in a single day. You'll have to make some tough choices about which of its many museums, plantations, floral parks, and natural wonders to visit. Here are two suggested itineraries for the day.

NORTH OF FORT-DE-FRANCE   Martinique's Carib name, Madiana, means "island of flowers." To see what the Caribs were talking about, stroll through the **Jardin de Balata** (© 596/64-48-73). Located about 8km (5 miles) north of town, this lush, Edenic garden showcases 200 species of plants, trees, and tropical flowers, as well as resident hummingbirds, frogs, and lizards. Admission is about $9.

Yes, it's hot outside, but things could be worse. One of Martinique's must-see attractions, the village of **St. Pierre** on the northwest coast, was the cultural and economic capital of the island until 8am on May 8, 1902, when the **Mount Pelée** volcano exploded in fire and lava. Three minutes later, all but two of St. Pierre's 30,000 inhabitants had been incinerated, buried in ash and lava, or asphyxiated by poisonous gas. The town once hailed as the "Paris of the Antilles" became the "Pompeii of the Caribbean," and today it's no more than a sleepy fishing village, home to fewer than 5,000 souls. Ruins of a church, theater, and other buildings punctuate the town, memorials to St. Pierre's former glory. The one-room **Musée Volcanologique,** rue Victor Hugo (© **596/78-15-16**), traces the story of the cataclysm through pictures and relics excavated from the debris. Admission is about $4. In lieu of walking from one ruin to another, you can hop on the Cyparis Express trolley from here for an hourlong tour (tickets about $11). The trolley is named in honor of Cyparis, a prisoner locked behind thick cell walls, who was one of the survivors of the eruption. He later toured with P. T. Barnum's circus, showing off his burn scars.

Part sugar-plantation ruins, part tropical paradise, **Habitation Céron** (© **596/52-94-53**) is the most evocative of Martinique's historical agricultural sites. This sprawling 17th-century estate, 15 minutes north of St. Pierre, is almost as wild and tranquil as the surrounding rainforest, but its verdigris cisterns, moss-covered stone buildings, and archaic, still functioning water mill are all haunted with the ghosts of a time when sugar was king, slaves toiled in the heat, and French colonists lived in languid comfort. Admission costs $9.

A few miles south of St. Pierre, **Le Carbet** is where Columbus landed in 1502, the first French settlers arrived in 1635, and the French painter Paul Gauguin lived for 5 months in 1887. The unassuming **Musée Paul Gauguin,** Anse Turin (© **596/78-22-66**), sits not far from the hut the painter once occupied. It has no original paintings, but you will see biographical texts and whiny, self-pitying letters he wrote to his wife back in France. Admission is about $5.

SOUTH OF FORT-DE-FRANCE Marie Josèphe Rose Tascher de la Pagerie was born in 1763 in the quaint little village of **Trois Ilets,** across the bay from Fort-de-France. As Joséphine, she became the wife of Napoleon Bonaparte in 1796 and Empress of France in 1804. A small museum, the **Musée de la Pagerie** (© **596/68-33-06**), sits in the former estate kitchen building, where Joséphine gossiped with her slaves. Displays include the bed that she slept in until she departed for France at age 16; portraits of her and of Napoleon; invitations to Parisian balls; and several letters, including a passionate missive from lovelorn Napoleon. Admission costs about $7; closed Mondays.

You'll have passed through a number of quaint coastal villages by this time, but none sweeter than **Ste. Luce.** Absurdly picturesque with its blindingly white stucco walls, red-tile roofs, turquoise sea, and multicolored fishing boats, this town is pure sun-drenched maritime serenity. Swim or snorkel off the small, pleasant beach; meditate on horizon-dominating Diamond Rock (a former British citadel); or check out the village boutiques and cafes. For an unhurried taste of French island life, this is as good a place as any to spend the day.

BEACHES

Serious beach bunnies hop south of Fort-de-France to **Grand Anse des Salines,** widely regarded as Martinique's nicest strand. At the island's extreme southern tip, about an hour from the capital by car, it features coconut palm trees, views of Diamond Rock, and white sand that seems to go on for miles. Beachside stands offer refreshment. To get to the island's main **gay beach,** turn right at the entrance to Grand Anse des Salines and drive to the far end of the parking lot, near the sign for Petite Anse des Salines. Follow the path through the woods and then veer left till you find the quiet section with the good-looking guys.

Martinique Golf Excursions

When Robert Trent Jones, Sr., designed **Golf de la Martinique** (ⓒ **596/68-32-81**) in 1976, he chose a picturesque, historic site: the seaside hills neighboring La Pagerie, the birthplace of Empress Joséphine. Thirty-two kilometers (20 miles) from Fort-de-France, this good, tough, 18-hole, 6,640-yard, par-71 course features emerald hills, swaying palms, constant vistas of the turquoise sea, and, thankfully, year-round trade winds that help keep things cool. The par-5 12th, with a dogleg to the right, is the most difficult hole. The fairway here is narrow, the green is long, and the wind, especially between December and April, is tricky. The 15th and 16th require shots over sea inlets. Facilities include a pro shop, a golf academy, a bar, a restaurant, and tennis courts. English-speaking pros are at your service. Greens fees and cart rental run about $130 for 18 holes, about $85 for 9 holes. A set of clubs is another $46. Some cruise lines offer an organized excursion to the club.

Conveniently located across the bay from Fort-de-France, **Pointe du Bout** is Martinique's most lavish resort area. Aside from a marina and a variety of watersports, the area has some modest man-made, white-sand beaches. The sandy, natural beaches at nearby **Anse Mitan** and **Anses d'Arlet** are popular with both swimmers and snorkelers.

Beaches north of Fort-de-France have mostly gray (they like to call it silver) volcanic sand. The best of the bunch is **Anse Turin,** just to the side of the main Caribbean coastal road, between St. Pierre and Le Carbet. Extremely popular with locals and shaded by palms, it's where Gauguin swam when he called the island home.

Martinique has no legal nudist beaches, but toplessness is as common here as anywhere in France. As a rule, public beaches lack changing cabins or showers, but hotel lockers and changing cabanas can be used by nonguests for a charge.

SHOPPING

Martinique offers a good selection of French luxury items—perfumes, fashionable clothing, luggage, crystal, and dinnerware—at prices that can be as much as 30% to 40% lower than those in the States. Unfortunately, because some luxury goods, including jewelry, are subject to a hefty value-added tax, the savings are ultimately less compelling. Paying in dollar-denominated traveler's checks or credit cards is sometimes good for a 20% discount.

The main shopping district in Fort-de-France is bound by rue Ernest Deproge (on the waterfront), La Savane, rue Lamartine, and rue de la République, with **rue Victor Hugo** being the single-most-important stretch. Martinican goods, such as the excellent island rum, Creole jewelry, madras fabric, folk paintings, and hand-woven baskets, are good buys and more representative of the island. The **open-air market** in La Savane, at rue de la Liberté and rue Ernest Deproge, has the best selection of these items.

17 Nevis

Off the beaten tourist track, south of St. Martin and north of Guadeloupe, Nevis is the junior partner in the combined Federation of St. Kitts and Nevis, which gained self-government from Britain in 1967 and became a totally independent nation in 1983. Though smaller than St. Kitts and lacking a major historical site like that island's Brimstone Hill Fortress, Nevis is nevertheless the more appealing and upbeat of the two islands. Columbus first sighted the island in 1493, naming it Las Nieves, Spanish for "snows," because its 970m (3,182-ft.) mountain reminded him of the Pyrenees. Settled by the British in 1628, Nevis became a prosperous sugar-growing island as well as the most popular spa island of the 18th century, when people flocked in from other West Indian islands to visit its hot mineral springs. Nevis's two most famous historical residents were Admiral Horatio Nelson, who married a local woman here in 1787, and Alexander Hamilton, who was born here and went on to find fame as a drafter of the American Federalist Papers, as George Washington's treasury secretary, and as Aaron Burr's unfortunate dueling partner. Today, the island's capital city, **Charlestown,** has a lovely mixture of port-town exuberance and small-town charm, and the popular **Pinney's Beach** is just a knockout.

COMING ASHORE   Only small ships can dock at the **Charlestown Port,** right in the center of Charlestown. Larger vessels must anchor off the coast of **Pinney's Beach.** The small cruise terminal has restrooms and a bar, but the main street is just a few steps away and is where you'll find eats, shops, and taxis.

GETTING AROUND   The entirety of Charlestown is accessible on foot, but if you want to visit Pinney's Beach or elsewhere on the island, you can get a **taxi** from Charlestown. Rates range from $5 up to about $17, which will get you to the island's farthest point. Taxis also offer island tours; just negotiate a price with your driver.

LANGUAGE & CURRENCY   **English** is the language of both St. Kitts and Nevis. The local currency is the **Eastern Caribbean dollar** (EC$2.70 = US$1; EC$1 = US37¢), though most shops and restaurants quote prices in U.S. dollars. Always determine which currency locals are talking about before making a purchase.

BEST CRUISE LINE SHORE EXCURSIONS

Some of the small-ship lines offer a day at Pinney's Beach as part of their regular visit, and might also offer hiking and snorkeling options, but Nevis is so small and easy to negotiate on your own that excursions are neither necessary nor advised.

ON YOUR OWN: WITHIN WALKING DISTANCE

If your ship docks in Charlestown, you're at dead center of a perfect walking-tour opportunity. Charlestown is a lovely little place, laid back in somewhat the same manner as St. John, but with some of the really rural character of sister island St. Kitts.

If you head left from the docks and walk a little ways (around .4km/¼-mile) along Main Street, you'll come to the **Alexander Hamilton Birthplace** (© **869/469-5786;** www.nevis-nhcs.org/nevishistory.html), where the road curves just before the turnoff to Island Road. It's a rustic little two-level house set right on the coastline. On the first floor is the small **Museum of Nevis History** and gift shop (admission $5; closes at noon Sat; closed all day Sun).

Backtracking along Main Street, you'll pass several serviceable if unremarkable shops. Keep walking through the center of town, saying hi to the occasional mama goat and kids you'll pass, and then turn left onto Government Road. One block up on the left, you'll find the **Jews' Burial Ground,** with graves from 1684 to 1768. When we were there, the dead were being entertained with reggae music drifting over from a shop across the street, while a breeze stirred the few trees on the property. All in all, not a bad resting spot.

Head back to Main Street, turn left, and continue on past the Grove Park Cricket Ground, bearing left when the road forks. Head up the hill (where you'll see several buildings standing alone on the hill to your right) and then turn at the first right, which will bring you back behind those buildings, the first of which is the inaccessible Government House and the second of which is the **Nelson Museum** (© 869/469-5786; www.nevis-nhcs.org/nelsonmuseum.html). A very small, very homemade, and very appealing kind of place, it traces the history of Admiral Horatio Nelson's career enforcing England's Navigation Acts in the Caribbean, and also houses artifacts from Nevis's Carib, Arawak, and Aceramic peoples. The timeline of Nelson's Caribbean career includes ship models, ceramic and bronze Nelson figures, paintings of his battles and other scenes, a scrap from the Union Jack under which the admiral was standing when he was shot, and more memorabilia. Admission is $5. The museum closes at noon on Saturday and is closed all day Sunday.

Once back outside, amble slowly off in the same direction you were going (right from the gate). Keep bearing right and you'll eventually be back on Main Street, in plenty of time to do a little shopping or stop into one of the local bars or restaurants.

ON YOUR OWN: BEYOND THE PORT AREA

The 3.2-hectare (8-acre) **Botanical Garden of Nevis** (© 869/469-3399) is located 5km (3 miles) south of Charlestown on the Montpelier Estate. There are several gardens, including a tropical rainforest conservatory, a rose and vine garden, a cactus garden, a tropical fruit garden, and an orchid garden. Fountains, ponds, and re-creations of Maya sculptures dot the grounds. Admission costs $10; closed on weekends.

BEACHES

The name to know on Nevis is **Pinney's Beach,** located north of Charlestown. It's a lovely spot for swimming, snorkeling, beachcombing, or just sitting back and watching the pelicans dive-bomb into the surf. It's home to the gorgeous Four Seasons resort and, as a counterpoint to conspicuous luxury, the rickety **Sunshine's Bar and Grill** (© 869/469-5817), which bills itself as "Home of the Killer Bee." Sunshine's sits right on the beach and offers beer and other refreshments along with the aforementioned Bee, a "killer" rum drink.

SHOPPING

Nevis is no shopping hub. A few uninteresting gift shops dot Main Street. The **Nevis Philatelic Bureau,** at the Head Post Office, on Market Street next to the public market, 1 block south and 1 block east of the docks (© 869/469-5535), has a range of Nevis stamps for collectors.

18 The Panama Canal

The Panama Canal is an awesome feat of engineering and human effort. Construction began in 1880 and wasn't completed until 1914, at the expense of thousands of lives, and the vast majority of the original structure and equipment is still in use. Transiting the canal, which links the Atlantic Ocean with the Pacific, is a thrill for anyone even vaguely interested in engineering or history.

Passing completely through the canal takes about 8 hours from start to finish, and is a fascinating procedure—the route is about 80km (50 miles) long and includes passage through three main locks, which, through gravity alone, raise ships over Central America and down again on the other side. Between the locks, ships pass through artificially created lakes such as the massive Gatun Lake, 26m (85 ft.) above sea level. It often costs ships about $100,000 to pass through, with fees based on each ship's weight. Your ship will line up in the morning, mostly with cargo ships, to await its turn through the canal. While you're transiting, there will be a running narration of history and facts about the canal by an expert who's brought on board for the day. The canal is so vital to the cruise industry that it's spawned its own word, *panamax*, meaning the maximum size a ship can be and still make it through. Panamax ships, it should be noted, make for a tight fit: Sometimes there's only a couple feet between their hull and the sides of the lock. Sitting in a lower-deck lounge and watching the walls go by less than an arm's length out the windows is a really, really disorienting experience. That tight-fit experience may soon be a thing of the past, though. In late 2006, Panamanian voters approved a plan to widen and modernize the Panama Canal, digging a new, 60% wider channel that will parallel the existing canal along its narrowest sections on either side of Gatun Lake. Once complete (somewhere around 2014), it will effectively double the canal's capacity and give cruise lines much greater flexibility in planning the deployment and itineraries of their largest, post-Panamax ships.

Cruises that include a **canal crossing** are generally 10 to 14 nights long, with popular routes running between Florida and Acapulco, visiting a handful of Caribbean and Mexican ports and a few ports in Central America along the way, including Panama's San Blas Islands, Costa Rica's Puerto Caldera, and Guatemala's Puerto Quetzal. Many ships also do a **partial crossing** of the canal, sailing into Gatun Lake from the Caribbean side, docking to let passengers off for excursions, then sailing back out again.

COLON

In compliance with a treaty signed between the United States and Panama in 1977, canal operations passed from U.S. to Panamanian hands at the stroke of midnight on December 31, 1999. Not only did the transition go smoothly, but the canal changeover spurred government agencies and private developers in Panama to expand the canal zone's tourism infrastructure—not simply trying to attract as many ships as possible, but also developing new attractions at the canal's Atlantic entrance to lure cruise passengers off their ships and into Panama's interior on shore excursions and for pre- and post-cruise stays. Even ships not transiting the canal are being wooed, with a long-term goal of making the city of Colón a home port for cruise ships sailing to the southern Caribbean.

The linchpin project in the new canal-area developments is **Colón 2000,** a $45-million private port development that opened in October 2000 in Colón, near the canal's Caribbean entrance, and that is capable of handling any size cruise vessel—even the 100,000-plus-ton ships that are too large to pass through the canal. Colón 2000's developer, Corporación de Costas Tropicales, has created a tour company, **Adventuras 2000** (www.colon2000.com), which offers a series of shore excursions highlighting Panama's history, culture, and diverse natural attractions (see "Best Cruise Line Shore Excursions," below). The project has opened many new jobs to locals, who are being trained as bilingual tour guides, drivers, and so on.

Colón 2000's glass-and-marble terminal building has a large lounge, an Internet cafe, a huge duty-free shopping mall (part of the Colón Free Zone, the second-largest tax-free zone in the world), restaurants, and crafts shops. Unfortunately, the town surrounding the splashy new development remains depressed, so there's no question passengers calling here should book an organized tour.

Another new development in Colón, the **Cristobal Cruise Terminal (Pier 6)**, offers piers for two ships of any size and has a duty-free shopping area, restaurants, and telephones.

BEST CRUISE LINE SHORE EXCURSIONS

The following excursions represent a sampling of those offered from Colón.

Emberá Indian Village Tour ($75, 3 hr.): Today, Panama's Emberá Indians live much as they did in the early 16th century, when their first tourist—Vasco Nunez de Balboa, who "discovered" the Pacific Ocean—came through. You'll travel by dugout canoe up the Chagres River, visit the Emberá village, witness a performance of traditional dance, and (surprise, surprise) have an opportunity to purchase handicrafts.

Kayak in the Panama Canal ($132, 9 hr.): From Colón, you'll travel to Sol Melina, where you'll spend about an hour kayaking amid the plant life, mammals, and birds. You'll then head by bus to the Gatun Locks for a look at the canal's workings.

Panama City Tour ($89, 5½ hr.): Visit the ruins of Old Panama, founded in 1519 by Pedro Arias Davila and destroyed in 1671 by the pirate Sir Henry Morgan; head to colonial Panama, built to replace the original capital; and then visit the Miraflores Locks for a look at the canal.

Monkey Watch ($84, 5½ hr.): After a 30-minute ride at high speed through the heart of the Panama Canal, the boat will slow down and enter the labyrinth of jungle-covered islands of Gatun Lake. Wildlife is plentiful in this protected area: You are likely to encounter capuchin monkeys, three-toed sloths, howler monkeys, toucans, turtles, butterflies, crocodiles, and more.

PORTS ALONG THE CANAL ROUTE

The **San Blas Islands** are a beautiful archipelago and home to the Kuna Indians, whose women are well known for their colorful, hand-embroidered stitching. If you get a chance to go ashore, the tiny women, dressed in their traditional molas (bright, intricately appliquéd blouses), sell all manner of this textile art in square blocks and strips, all of which are known as molas and make great pillow covers or wall hangings. They cost about $10 each, but don't try to bargain too much—these gals will only go so low before standing firm. When your ship anchors offshore at the islands, be prepared for throngs of Kunas to emerge from the far-off distance, paddling (or, in a few cases, motoring) their dugout canoes up to the ship, where they will spend the entire day calling for money or anything else ship passengers toss overboard. The Kuna seem to enjoy diving overboard to retrieve coins thrown to them, but, of course, it's a sad sight, too, watching entire families so needy. Makes you feel damn guilty for rolling in on that fancy cruise ship of yours.

In Costa Rica, many ships call at **Puerto Caldera,** on the Pacific side, or **Puerto Limón,** on the Atlantic side. While there's nothing to see from either cargo port, both are great jumping-off points for tours that all visiting ships offer of the country's lush, beautiful rainforests, which are alive with some 850 species of birds, 200 species of mammals, 9,000 species of flowering plants, and about 35,000 species of insects. After a scenic bus ride, tours will take you on a nature walk through the jungle or a mild white-water rafting trip.

In Guatemala, most Panama Canal–bound ships call at **Puerto Quetzal,** on the Pacific coast; a few may call at **Santo Tomas,** on the Caribbean side. Both are used as gateways to Guatemala's spectacular Maya ruins at Tikal. They're the country's most famous attractions, and are considered the most spectacular yet discovered, with more than 3,000 temples, pyramids, and other buildings of the ancient civilization—some of them dating as far back as A.D. 300—nestled in a thick, surreal jungle setting. Excursions here are neither cheap nor easy—a 10-hour tour involves buses, walking, and a 1-hour flight, and costs about $500—but the journey is well worth the effort. Excursions to the less-spectacular Mayan sites in Honduras are also offered from Puerto Quetzal, as are several overland tours of Guatemala's interior.

19 Puerto Rico

San Juan, the capital of Puerto Rico, has the busiest ocean terminal in the West Indies and is one of the cruise trade's most important ports. While cruise groups, by their sheer size, can overwhelm many ports of call, San Juan absorbs them with ease. The San Juan metropolitan area, home to about a third of Puerto Rico's 3.8 million people, is one of the largest and most sophisticated urban centers in the Caribbean, offering all the amenities of a modern major city: great shopping, interesting neighborhoods, beautiful people, excellent restaurants, glamorous bars and nightclubs, and fine museums. **Old San Juan** is the prime haunt for cruise passengers both because it's the most beautiful, historic part of town and because the docks are right at its foot. The neighborhood's hilly cobblestone streets are lined with brightly painted colonial town houses, colonial churches, intimate parks, and sun-drenched plazas. Like the pyramids of Egypt and the Great Wall of China, Old San Juan's Spanish colonial forts and city walls are United Nations World Heritage Sites, and our top pick for spending your day here.

COMING ASHORE   Almost all cruise ships dock at historic **Old San Juan,** but during periods of heavy volume, you may get stuck at one of the much less convenient cargo piers across the water from the Old Town, requiring a taxi ride.

GETTING AROUND   Old San Juan is eminently walkable, if hilly. **Taxis** operated by the Tourist Transportation Division will be available at the piers. They're metered in San Juan, but the fare structure between major tourism zones is standardized. The set rates from the cruise ship piers are $6 to Old San Juan, $10 to Condado, and $16 to Isla Verde. The minimum fare is $3. After 10pm, there's a night charge (add $1 to the meter reading). Call **Metro Taxi** (© 787/725-2878) or **Taxi Association** (© 787/795-5286) for a cab.

LANGUAGE & CURRENCY   **Spanish** is the native tongue, but most people on the island also speak **English** (both are official languages here). The farther you venture from San Juan, the more likely it is you'll have to practice your Spanish. Because Puerto Rico is part of the United States, the **U.S. dollar** is the coin of the realm.

BEST CRUISE LINE SHORE EXCURSIONS

Unless you want a guide to offer historical perspective ($33, 2½ hr.), don't bother with organized tours of Old San Juan—it's easy enough to get around on your own. On the other hand, if you explore somewhere farther afield, an organized tour is a good idea.

San Juan as a Port of Embarkation

Puerto Rico is the number-one port of embarkation in the Caribbean, with more than 1.2 million visitors embarking on 700 cruises every year from here. Most cruise lines sell pre- and post-cruise packages that include hotel stays.

GETTING TO SAN JUAN & THE PORT   Luis Muñoz Marín International Airport (© 787/791-1014) is on the city's east side, about 7½ miles from the port. Taxi fares from the airport are fixed at $10 to Isla Verde, $15 to Condado and Ocean Park, and $20 to Old San Juan and the cruise ships. The ride to the port takes at least 30 minutes—longer if traffic is heavy, and it often is.

ACCOMMODATIONS   Following are some of the hotels commonly packaged by the cruise lines, plus a couple other options. Rates are per room based on double occupancy.

- **Sheraton Old San Juan Hotel & Casino,** 100 Brumbaugh St. (© 800/325-3535 or 787/721-5100; www.sheratonoldsanjuan.com), on the waterfront across the street from the cruise ship docks. Rates: $235 to $735.
- **Hotel El Convento,** 100 Calle del Cristo (© 800/468-2779 or 787/723-9020; www.elconvento.com), a former Carmelite convent, with large rooms, many with views of the Old Town. Rates: $365 to $420 winter; $235 to $295 summer.
- **El Condado Plaza Hotel & Casino,** 999 Ashford Ave. (© 800/468-8588 or 787/721-1000; www.luxuryresorts.com), in Condado, the original high-rise, high-glamour section of modern San Juan, to the east of Old Town. Rates: $119 to $260.
- **San Juan Marriott Resort & Stellaris Casino,** 1309 Ashford Ave., also in Condado (© 800/981-8546 or 787/722-7000; www.marriott.com). Rates: $240 to $390.

El Yunque Rainforest ($35, 4–5 hr.): Get acquainted with one of Puerto Rico's premier natural wonders. After arriving at Baño Grande, a natural swimming hole, hike half an hour along the Camimitillo trail and see parrot nests, giant ferns, orchids, and palms. Listen for the song of Puerto Rico's national symbol, the tiny coqui tree frog. After a short stop at an interpretive station, proceed to Yohakú observation tower and Coca waterfall.

Rainforest Horseback Adventure ($89, 3½ hr.): Once you get to the ranch, you'll meet your horse, briefly learn the ropes, and then ride down a beautiful beach. Take a quick swim during the refreshment stop.

City Tour & Bacardi Rum Distillery ($30, 4 hr.): After a tour of the old city, with a stop at the San Cristobal fort, you'll travel to the Bacardi distillery to learn about the Puerto Rican sugar and rum industries, watch giant fermenting tanks transform sugar cane into rum, learn how to pronounce the product's name (Baa-carrrr-*di!*), and then get a taste for yourself.

WALKING TOUR | OLD SAN JUAN

The streets are narrow and teeming with traffic, but strolling through Old San Juan is like walking through 5 centuries of history. More than 400 Spanish colonial buildings from the 16th and 17th centuries, many featuring intricate wrought-iron balconies with lush hanging plants, have been lovingly restored here. The streets' blue paving stones were originally used as ballast by ships crossing the ocean from Spain. Although Old San Juan is a National Historic Zone, it's as vibrant today as it ever has been. Block after block, you'll find shops, cafes, museums, plazas, people, and pigeons. The crowds thin out by late afternoon, so linger around to experience Old San Juan's more sedate charms.

Begin your adventure near the post office, amid the taxis, buses, and urban hubbub of:

❶ Plaza de la Marina

The plaza is a small park that overlooks San Juan Bay, which was one of the New World's most important harbors for trading and for military protection. Walking west from the plaza, you'll come to San Juan's showcase promenade, El Paseo de Princesa. This renovated 19th-century walkway traces the ancient city walls past heroic statues, gurgling fountains, and landscaped gardens.

Proceed along the Paseo to:

❷ La Princesa

This gray-and-white building on the right served as one of the Caribbean's most notorious prisons for centuries. Today, it houses contemporary Puerto Rican art exhibits and the offices of the Puerto Rico Tourism Company.

Continue walking westward to the fountain near the sea's edge. Turn right and follow the promenade as it skirts the base of the:

❸ City Wall (La Muralla)

The wall was completed in the 1700s and once formed part of the New World's most impregnable defenses against enemy invaders and pirates. Marvel at the immensity, antiquity, and engineering genius of the wall, which on average is 40 feet high and 20 feet thick.

Follow the promenade until you reach the:

❹ San Juan Gate

The gate stands at Calle San Juan and Recinto del Oeste. Turn right through the portal. The gate was built in 1635 and served as the main entrance into San Juan. Today, it's the only remaining passage through the wall into the city.

Turn right at the first street and walk uphill along Calle Recinto del Oeste to the wrought-iron gates of:

❺ La Fortaleza

Also known as Santa Catalina Palace, La Fortaleza is the residence of Puerto Rico's governor. Although it initially served military purposes, it's now the oldest executive mansion in continuous use in the Western Hemisphere (built in 1540). English-language tours are given on weekdays, every hour from 9am to 3pm.

Now retrace your steps along Calle Recinto del Oeste, downhill to Caleta de San Juan. The colonial house at no. 51, on the northeast corner, is the:

❻ Felisa Rincón de Gautier Museum

This is the former home of one of San Juan's most popular mayors. An organizer of the city's women and other dispossessed people, Fela, as her many admirers called her, swept into power in 1946 and led the city for 22 years.

Walking back to Calle Recinto del Oeste, turn right and proceed 1 block to Caleta de las Monjas. Fork left to a panoramic view and a modern statue marking the center of:

❼ Plazuela de la Rogativa

According to local legend, the British, while besieging San Juan in 1797, misidentified the flaming torches of a *rogativa,* or religious procession, as Spanish reinforcements. Frightened by the display, the would-be invaders hastily retreated. Statues in this plaza memorialize the event.

Continue west, parallel to the city wall, passing through a pair of urn-topped gateposts. The road will fork. Bear to the right and continue climbing the steep cobblestone-covered ramp to its top. Walk west across the field toward the neoclassical gateway leading to the:

❽ Castillo San Felipe del Morro ("El Morro")

The big draw in Old San Juan, this castle's strategic position was the envy of the Caribbean for several centuries. It's where Spanish Puerto Rico defended itself against the navies of Great Britain, France, and Holland, as well as hundreds of pirate ships. First built in 1539, and substantially enhanced in 1787, the fortress was part of a comprehensive defense network. The six-level complex rises 140 feet above the sea on a rocky promontory. You can spend the better part of the morning exploring its labyrinth of dungeons, barracks, towers, ramps, and tunnels on your own. Check out the small, air-conditioned military museum and the gift shop. Both El Morro and San Cristóbal (see no. 19, below) are managed by the U.S. National Park Service, which provides continuous video presentations and guided tours in English (admission $3; San Cristobal open daily 9am–6pm, El Morro daily 9am–5pm).

Retrace your steps through the treeless field to Calle del Morro; then walk uphill to the small plaza at the top of the street. On the right is:

❾ Casa Blanca

Though it was his family home, Juan Ponce de León, the conquistador and Puerto Rico's first governor, never actually lived here: While the structure was being built, he was off looking for the Fountain of Youth, ironically dying from battle wounds along the way, in 1521. The city's oldest fort, Casa Blanca, was San Juan's only defense against attacks until La Fortaleza was completed in 1533. Today, it features a small museum (1 Calle de San Sebastián; ✆ 787/725-1454; admission $3; closed Sun) illustrating Indian life and 16th- and 17th-century colonial family life. The garden and fountains in back are a tranquil respite from the streets.

Exit through the front entrance and walk downhill, retracing your steps for a half block; then head toward the massive tangerine-colored building on your right, the:

❿ Cuartel de Ballajá

These former military barracks once housed 1,000 Spanish soldiers and their families. Built between 1854 and 1864, the complex is the last and largest military building erected by Spain in the Western Hemisphere. Today, the building's second floor is home to the **Museo de las Américas** (Museum of the Americas; Cuartel de Ballajá; ✆ 787/724-5052; admission $5; closed Mon), which showcases Caribbean as well as North, Central, and South American cultures. The popular art exhibits focus on housing and furniture styles, handicrafts, tools, musical instruments, toys, clothing, and religious objects. The carved wooden saints *(santos)* are especially interesting.

Exit through the barracks' eastern door, where you'll immediately spot the dramatic and modern:

⓫ Plaza del Quinto Centenario (Quincentennial Plaza)

This plaza is dominated by a large, totem-pole-like column that commemorates the 500th anniversary of Columbus's arrival.

Old San Juan Walking Tour

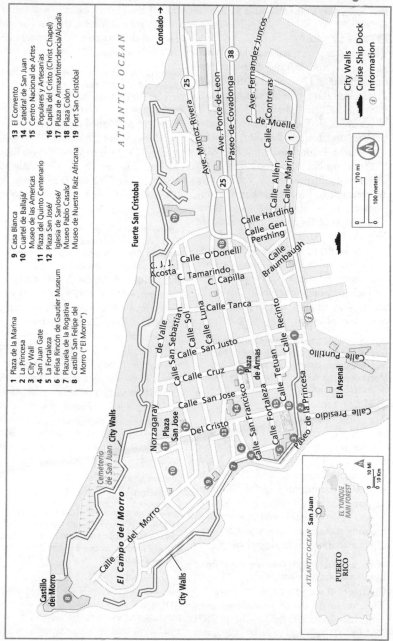

1 Plaza de la Marina
2 La Princesa
3 City Wall
4 San Juan Gate
5 La Fortaleza
6 Felisa Rincón de Gautier Museum
7 Plazuela de la Rogativa
8 Castillo San Felipe del Morro ("El Morro")
9 Casa Blanca
10 Cuartel de Ballajá/ Museo de las Americas
11 Plaza del Quinto Centenario
12 Plaza San José/ Iglesia de SanJosé/ Museo Pablo Casals/ Museo de Nuestra Raíz Africana
13 El Convento
14 Catedral de San Juan
15 Centro Nacional de Artes Populares y Artesanías
16 Capilla del Cristo (Christ Chapel)
17 Plaza de Armas/Intendencia/Alcadía
18 Plaza Colón
19 Fort San Cristóbal

City Walls
Cruise Ship Dock
ⓘ **Information**

1/10 mi
100 meters

Condado →

ATLANTIC OCEAN

Castillo del Morro

El Campo del Morro

Cementerio de San Juan

City Walls

Fuerte San Cristóbal

Calle del Morro

Ave. Muñoz Rivera
Ave. Ponce de Leon
Paseo de Covadonga
C. Ave. Fernandez Juncos
Calle Contreras
C. de Muelle
Calle Marina
Calle Allen
Calle Harding
Calle Gen. Pershing
Calle Braumbaugh
Calle O'Donell
C. J. J. Acosta
C. Tamarindo
C. Capilla
Calle Tanca
Calle Recinto
de Valle
Calle San Sebastian
Calle Sol
Calle Luna
Calle San Justo
Calle Cruz
Calle Tetuan
Calle San Jose
Plaza de Armas
Calle San Francisco
Calle Fortaleza
Del Cristo
Plaza San Jose
Norzagaray
Paseo de la Princesa
Calle Puntillo
El Arsenal
Calle Presidio

38
25
25
1
18
1

ⓘ

ATLANTIC OCEAN
San Juan
EL YUNQUE RAIN FOREST
PUERTO RICO
10 MI
10 Km

589

Now walk a short block southeast to the borders of:

⑫ Plaza San José

This plaza features a statue of Juan Ponce de León cast from an English cannon captured during a 1797 naval battle. Three sites around this square are worth visiting. Built in 1532, the **Iglesia de San José** is where Ponce de León's descendants worshipped, and features beautiful artwork. The **Museo Pablo Casals** (© 787/723-9185; admission $1; closed Sun–Mon) honors the Spanish-born cellist who adopted Puerto Rico as his home; it displays his cello, his piano, and original manuscripts of his music. The **Museo de Nuestra Raíz Africana** (Museum of Our African Roots; © 787/724-4294; admission $2; closed Sun–Mon) traces the slave experience and focuses on African contributions to local music, dance, clothing, art, cuisine, religion, and language. Placards are in Spanish.

Exiting from the plaza's southwestern corner, walk downhill along one of the capital's oldest and best-known streets, Calle del Cristo. Two blocks down, on the north side of shady Plaza de las Monjas, look for:

⑬ El Convento

The New World's first Carmelite convent, El Convento opened in 1651 with 30-foot-thick walls designed to withstand hurricanes and enemy attacks. The building remained a convent for 250 years, but fell on hard times early in the 20th century and served as a dance hall and flophouse. Today, the beautifully restored building is the Hotel El Convento, possibly Puerto Rico's most elegant hotel.

Across the street from El Convento stands the island's most famous church, the:

⑭ Catedral de San Juan

The original thatch-roofed wooden cathedral (153 Calle del Cristo; © 787/722-0861), built in the early 1520s, was destroyed by a hurricane in 1529. Reconstruction in 1540 added a circular staircase and vaulted Gothic ceilings, but most of the current church was built in the 1800s. Look for the tomb of Ponce de León and the wax-encased mummy of St. Pio, a Roman martyr.

Now walk 2 blocks south along Calle del Cristo, through one of the Caribbean's most attractive shopping districts. After passing Calle La Fortaleza, look on your left for the:

⑮ Centro Nacional de Artes Populares y Artesanías

Operated by the Institute of Puerto Rican Culture, this center, at 253 Calle del Cristo (© 787/722-0621; admission $3; closed Sun), displays a collection of the island's folk arts and crafts.

Continue to the southernmost tip of Calle del Cristo (just a few steps away) to the wrought-iron gates that surround a chapel no bigger than a newspaper kiosk, the:

⑯ Capilla del Cristo (Christ Chapel)

Legend has it that in 1753, a young rider lost control of his horse in a race down Calle del Cristo during the feast of St. John the Baptist and plunged over the steep precipice at the street's end. A witness to the tragedy promised to build a chapel if the young man's life was saved. Records maintain that the horseman died, but lore contends otherwise. In another version of the story, the horseman, after himself praying to God while falling over the cliff, survived to build the chapel. The delicate silver altar here can be seen through glass doors (free admission; open Mon, Wed, and Fri).

Retrace your steps about a block north along the Calle del Cristo; then turn right on Calle Fortaleza. A block later, take a left onto Calle San José and proceed another block to the capital's liveliest square, the:

⑰ Plaza de Armas

This broad, open plaza has lots of pigeons, several old men playing dominos, office workers and shoppers basking in the sun, and a 19th-century statue representing the four seasons. Originally used for military drills, the plaza now hosts folk dances and concerts on weekends. The neoclassical

Intendencia (which houses offices of the U.S. State Department) and the **Alcadía** (San Juan's city hall) flank the square.

Walk east along the plaza's northern border, Calle San Francisco, for 4 blocks until you reach another square:

⑱ Plaza Colón

This park is notable for its **statue of Cristóbal Colón (Christopher Columbus).** Bronze plaques at the monument's base commemorate episodes in the explorer's life.

Finally, walk to the plaza's northeast corner, where Calle San Francisco meets Boulevard del Valle. Turn left and follow the signs to:

⑲ Fort San Cristóbal

Built in 1634 (and expanded in the 1770s), this fortress rises more than 150 feet above the sea. A complex maze of tunnels and moats connects the central fort with wave after wave of outlying posts. Don't miss the Garita del Diablo (Devil's Sentry Box), a lonely post at the edge of the sea where, legend has it, the devil himself snatched away solitary sentinels. (The Fort is uphill from Plaza Colón on Calle Norzagaray; © **787/729-6960;** admission $3; ticket stubs from El Morro are good for admission here, too.)

CASINOS

Most large hotels have casinos, which are one of San Juan's biggest draws. They're generally open daily from noon to 4am, but some never close. The **Casino at the Ritz-Carlton,** Avenue of the Governors, Isla Verde (© **800/241-3333** or 787/253-1700), is the largest in Puerto Rico. Combining elegant 1940s decor with tropical fabrics and patterns, it's one of the plushest entertainment complexes in the Caribbean. The **Inter-Continental San Juan,** 5961 Isla Verde Ave. (© **800/303-1758** or 787/791-6100), is another elegant place to rendezvous. One of its Murano glass chandeliers is, they say, "longer than a bowling alley." Most convenient for cruise ship passengers, the **Sheraton Old San Juan Hotel & Casino,** 100 Brumbaugh St. (© **800/325-3535** or 787/721-5100), is directly across from Pier 3 and often bustling.

BEACHES

Puerto Rico is ringed by hundreds of miles of sandy beaches, and you won't have to leave San Juan to play in the surf. Perhaps the most famous beach in the Caribbean, **Condado Beach,** at the western end of Ashford Avenue, is the backyard playground of Condado's resort hotels. A favorite of families, it can get pretty crowded in winter. The beaches of **Isla Verde,** behind the hotels and condominiums along Isla Verde Avenue, are less rocky and are excellent for people-watching. Both have white sand, palm trees, ocean breezes, beautiful bodies, and ample eating and drinking options. Snorkeling gear and other watersports equipment are available to rent.

SHOPPING

San Juan has some great bargains—prices here are often even lower than those in St. Thomas—and U.S. citizens pay no duty on items bought in Puerto Rico. The streets of the Old Town, especially **Calle San Francisco** and **Calle del Cristo,** are a major shopping venue. Local handicrafts can be good buys, including *santos* (hand-carved wooden religious figures), needlework, straw work, hammocks, loose-fitting guayabera shirts, papier-mâché masks, and paintings and sculptures by local artists.

Puerto Rico Golf Excursions

Puerto Rico is a golfer's dream, but you'll need to sign up for a ship excursion or rent a car to reach the major courses from San Juan.

- **Hyatt Dorado Beach Resort & Country Club** (© 787/796-8916; www. hyatt.com) offers the greatest concentration of golf in the Caribbean, with 72 holes. All four 18-hole courses at the Hyatt's Regency Cerromar and Dorado Beach properties here were designed by Robert Trent Jones, Sr. Jack Nicklaus ranks the 4th hole at the Dorado Beach East course as one of the 10 best-designed holes in the world. Greens fees, including cart, are $195 for play before 1pm and $105 after 1:30pm. Club rentals are $55.

- **Doral Resort at Palmas del Mar** (© 787/285-2256; www.palmascountry club.com), 45 miles east of San Juan, has two courses: the par-71 Palm course, designed by Gary Player, and the newer 18-hole Flamboyan course, designed by Rees Jones. Greens fees at the Palm or the Flamboyan are $107 for 18 holes, including cart, plus $40 for clubs.

- **Westin Rio Mar Golf Resort & Spa** (© 787/888-6000; www.westinriomar. com), 20 miles from San Juan in Rio Grande, also has two 18-hole courses, one designed by Tom and George Fazio, the other by Greg Norman. Greens fees, including cart, are $190 (or $130 for play after 2pm).

20 St. Barts

Chic, sophisticated St. Barts (or, technically, St. Barthélemy, a name no one ever uses) is internationally renowned as one of the ritziest refuges in the Caribbean, rivaled only by Mustique as the preferred island retreat of the rich and famous. Yet despite all the hoopla, St. Barts retains its charm, serenity, natural beauty, and incredibly French flavor—in contrast to most Caribbean islands, where descendants of African slaves form the majority, St. Barts's 7,000 year-round residents are primarily of French ancestry. **Gustavia,** the main port (whose name harks back to the 19th c., when Sweden controlled the island), is full of French restaurants and semichic, semiboho nightspots. Many of the small luxe ships that call here stay into the evening so passengers can get a night out. Away from town, the island is full of dramatic hills and pristine white-sand beaches.

COMING ASHORE   Cruise ships anchor off **Gustavia,** the main town, and ferry passengers to the dollhouse-size harbor and town via tenders.

GETTING AROUND   Taxis congregate at Gustavia's harbor to take cruise passengers to the beaches. For **car rentals,** Budget, Avis, Hertz, and National all have offices here. If you want some stylin' Euro-fun, rent a bright orange or red Smart Car, the hippest toys on the island, for a ride up and down the picturesque, hilly local roads.

LANGUAGE & CURRENCY   **French** is the official language, but virtually everyone speaks **English** as well. St. Barts is part of the French overseas region of Guadeloupe, so the **euro** (€) is the official currency (.76€ = US$1; 1€ = US$1.31). U.S. dollars are commonly accepted.

CALLING FROM THE U.S.   When calling St. Barts from the United States, dial the international access code **(011)** and the country code **(590)** before the numbers listed here, which also begin with 590. That's right: If you want to make a connection, you have to dial 590 twice. It's just one of those oddities that makes the world go round.

BEST CRUISE LINE SHORE EXCURSIONS

Jet-Set Boat & Beach Excursion ($200–$400, 4 hr.): Circumnavigate St. Barts in a 40-foot cruiser; then tender ashore at St. Jean Beach for a swim, snorkel, and drinks from the open bar.

St. Barts on Horseback ($55, 2 hr.): Travel to northern St. Barts for a relaxed guided ride through the island's outback.

ON YOUR OWN: WITHIN WALKING DISTANCE

For a taste of the island's celeb vibe, make a beeline to **Le Select,** rue de la France at rue du Général de Gaulle (© **590/27-86-87**), the epicenter of Gustavia's social life for more than 50 years. This cafe's tables rest in a tree-shaded garden a block from the harbor. A full bar is available, along with simple meals. The classic, funky ambience inspired Jimmy Buffett's "Cheeseburger in Paradise," and a mix of salty locals, celebrities, and chic tourists typically make up the clientele.

Aside from hanging out, shopping, and eating, cruisers sticking close to port can also visit Gustavia's modest points of interest. **St. Bartholomew's Church,** on rue Samuel Fahlberg, dates from the 1850s and features limestone and volcanic stone walls, as well as imported pitch-pine pews. Across from the dock, the **Municipal Museum,** on rue Duquesne (© **590/29-71-55**), is an unfocused but respectable introduction to the history, sociology, ethnology, economy, and ecology of the island. The most interesting items include Amerindian artifacts, rustic farm furnishings, and clothing used by early French settlers. Admission costs about $2; closed Wednesday afternoon, Saturday afternoon, and Sunday.

ON YOUR OWN: BEYOND THE PORT AREA

Visiting the tiny fishing village of **Corossol** is a vibrant way to experience the St. Barts of the past. About 10 minutes by taxi from the dock, this quaint, totally unchic hamlet is home to traditional folk who still live off the sea. It's your best bet for spotting women in traditional 17th-century bonnets and for watching roadside vendors weave items from palm fronds.

On the town's waterfront, just to the left of the road from Gustavia, the **Inter Oceans Museum** (© **590/27-62-97**) catalogs thousands of shells, corals, sand dollars, sea horses, sea urchins, and fish from around the world, all displayed in endearingly homemade style (literally homemade—the museum is an extension of the owner's house). Don't miss the collection of sand from beaches around the world: A cocktail umbrella is planted in each specimen. Admission is about $3. Stop by **Le Regal** (© **590/27-85-26**) afterward and have a beer or a bite with the locals.

BEACHES

The 22 beaches of St. Barts are first-rate. Few are ever crowded, even during the peak season, and all are public, free, and easily accessible by taxi from the cruise pier (make arrangements with your driver to be picked up at a specific time). As St. Barts is a French island, toplessness is common at all beaches.

Shell Beach, just a short walk from the harbor in Gustavia, is the most convenient place to soak up the sun if your time is limited. The water is calm, and **Do Brazil** (© 590/29-06-66), a lively fusion restaurant right on the beach, is an ideal spot for lunch or for watching the sunset. You can also grab a sandwich to go at **Zen Beach Bar** (© 590/27-19-39).

If you're looking for an active beach strand, with restaurants and watersports, **Grand Cul de Sac** fits the bill, with waters that are shallow, warm, and protected. An even busier and equally social beach, **St. Jean** is actually two beaches divided by a rock promontory. Protected by a coral reef, the calm waters here attract families and watersports enthusiasts, including windsurfers, and there are numerous eating, drinking, shopping, and people-watching opportunities.

Gouverneur, on the south-central coast, is quiet and relatively remote. Its idyllic setting and unspoiled beauty make it a favorite with locals. Farther east, in a wild and rustic area that was once the site of salt ponds, **Saline** is reached by a 3-minute hike over a sand dune. Most famous for its adult environment and nude bathers, it also boasts great bodysurfing waves.

SHOPPING

A duty-free port, St. Barts is a good place to buy liquor, perfume, and other French luxury items. Good buys on apparel, crystal, porcelain, and watches can also be found, especially during April, the biggest sale month. Moisturizer mavens can stock up on the island's own cosmetic line, Ligne St. Barth.

Shops are concentrated in Gustavia and St. Jean, where the quality-to-schlock ratio is as high as anywhere in the Caribbean. Most shops and offices close for a long lunch, usually from noon to 2pm.

21 St. Kitts

Somewhat off the beaten tourist track, south of St. Martin and north of Guadeloupe, St. Kitts forms the larger half of the combined Federation of St. Kitts and Nevis, two islands separated by only about 3.2km (2 miles) of ocean. St. Kitts—or St. Christopher, a name hardly anyone uses—is by far the more populous of the two islands, with some 35,000 people. St. Kitts is almost ridiculously lush and fertile, dotted with rainforests and waterfalls and boasting some lovely beaches along its southeast coastline, but it's also extremely poor, still dependent on the same sugar cane crop that brought its English plantation owners riches (and its slaves hot misery) back in colonial days. Cane fields climb the slopes of its volcanic mountain range, and you'll see ruins of old mills and plantation houses as you drive around the island. **Basseterre,** the capital city, is full of old-time colonial architecture, but it's a small-scale place with little to offer visitors beyond a pleasant walk around. The island's most impressive landmark, **Brimstone Hill Fortress,** is about 15km (9⅓ miles) west of town.

COMING ASHORE   The newly dedicated cruise pier at **Port Zante** can accommodate two megaships. Shopping, restaurants, and a welcome center are close by. Additional vessels may dock at nearby commercial **Birdrock Deepwater Port,** about 3km (2 miles) from downtown Basseterre.

GETTING AROUND   You can walk around Basseterre, but you'll need **taxis** to get anywhere else. They greet cruise passengers (loudly) at the docks and also around the Circus, a public square near the docks at the intersection of Bank and Fort streets. Taxis aren't metered, so you must agree on the price before heading out. Fares range from $10 to $20 for one to four passengers, depending on destination. Always ask if the rates quoted are in U.S. dollars or Eastern Caribbean dollars.

LANGUAGE & CURRENCY   **English** is the language of both St. Kitts and Nevis. The local currency is the **Eastern Caribbean dollar** (EC$2.70 = US$1; EC$1 = US37¢). Many shops and restaurants quote prices in U.S. dollars; always determine which currency locals are talking about before making a purchase.

BEST CRUISE LINE SHORE EXCURSIONS

Brimstone Hill Fortress & Gardens ($46, 3 hr.): Among the largest and best-preserved forts in the Caribbean, **Brimstone Hill** (www.brimstonehillfortress.org) dates from 1690, when the British fortified the hill to help recapture Fort Charles, located below, from the French. Today, it's the centerpiece of a national park crisscrossed by nature trails, with a population of green vervet monkeys to keep things lively. Perched on the upper slopes of a tall, steep hill, it's a photographer's paradise, with views of mountains, fields, and the Caribbean Sea. Tours typically include a visit to the beautiful **Romney Gardens,** located amid the ruins of a sugar estate between Basseterre and the fort. You can check out the lush hillside gardens or shop at **Caribelle Batik** (© 869/465-6253), one of the island's most popular boutiques, where artisans demonstrate their Indonesian-style hand-printing amid rack after rack of brightly colored clothes.

Mount Liamuiga Volcano Hike ($109, 7 hr.): This dormant volcano, in the northwest area of the island, has long been known as "Mount Misery." On this excursion, you'll hike about 241m (792 ft.) to the summit, traveling along narrow trails and through the island's rainforest. It takes about 3 hours to reach the top. Two lookout points offer views of the crater and lake below. Refreshments are offered before the hike back down. This is a great trip if you're in shape.

Mountain Biking & Beach Tour ($78, 4 hr.): From the pier, you'll ride through Basseterre and then out through sugar cane fields and up 450m (1,476-ft.) Olivees Mountain for views and refreshments. After the ride down, you'll stop at Friar's Bay for a swim and snack. It's a nice way to see this lush island.

Rainforest & Gardens Hiking Safari ($59, 4 hr.): Departing from Romney Gardens, you'll hike along a loop of trails through lush rainforest. With luck, you'll catch sight of some of the island's resident monkeys.

Sail & Snorkel Catamaran Trip ($59, 3½ hr.): A sailing catamaran takes you to secluded Smitten's Bay for snorkeling among diverse reef fish and coral formations. Complimentary drinks and snacks are served aboard the boat on your return trip.

ON YOUR OWN: WITHIN WALKING DISTANCE

The capital city of Basseterre, where the docks are located, has typical British colonial architecture and some quaint buildings, a few shops, and a market where locals display fruits and flowers—but even this description might be giving you the wrong idea about this place. The truth is, it's a very poor town, with few attractions aimed at visitors. When we were last here, there were chickens walking around in front of the government buildings. **St. George's Anglican Church,** on Cayon Street (walk straight up Church St. or Fort St. from the dock), is the oldest church in town and is worth a look. **Independence Square,** a stone's throw from the docks along Bank Street, is pretty, with its central fountain and old church, but there's no good reason to linger unless it's to sit in the shade and toss back a bottle of Ting, the local grapefruit-based soda.

ON YOUR OWN: BEYOND THE PORT AREA

All of the good out-of-town sites on St. Kitts are covered under "Best Cruise Line Shore Excursions," above.

BEACHES

The narrow peninsula in the southeast contains the island's salt ponds and also boasts the best white-sand beaches (approach via the winding, hilly road for a dramatic and gorgeous view). You'll find the best swimming at **Conaree Beach,** 5km (3 miles) from Basseterre; **Frigate Bay,** with its talcum-powder-fine sand; and the twin beaches of **Banana Bay** and **Cockleshell Bay,** at the southeast corner of the island. Most popular is **Turtle Beach,** where you just might be greeted by the resident pig, Wilbur. If you're lucky, the green vervet monkeys may come down from the hillside behind the beach to say hello as well. Food and drink are available. (*Beware:* The monkeys have been known to steal drinks from unsuspecting tourists.) All beaches, even those that border hotels, are free and open to the public. You must, however, usually pay a fee to use a hotel's beach facilities.

SHOPPING

Basseterre is not a shopping town, despite handout maps that show a listing of shops that would put St. Thomas to shame. Look closer and you'll see entries such as "R. Gumbs Electrical," "TDC/Finco Finance Co.," and "Horsford Furniture Store." Turns out they just listed every business on every street in town, no matter whether it's of interest to visitors or not. Strength in numbers, we suppose. The port complex does offer shopping. The most popular shop with visitors is probably **Caribelle Batik,** which is a stop on many shore excursions (see above).

22 St. Lucia

With a turbulent history shared by many of its Caribbean neighbors, St. Lucia (pronounced *Loo*-sha) changed hands often during the colonial period, being British seven times and French seven times. Today, though, it's an independent state that's become one of the most popular destinations in the Caribbean, with some of the finest resorts. The heaviest development is concentrated in the northwest, between the capital of Castries and the northern end of the island, where there's a string of white-sand beaches. The interior boasts relatively unspoiled green-mantled mountains and gentle valleys, as well as the volcanic **Mount Soufrière.** Two dramatic peaks—the **Pitons**—rise along the southwest coast.

Castries, the capital, has grown up around an extinct volcanic crater that's now a large harbor surrounded by hills. Because of fires that devastated many of its older structures, the town today has touches of modernity, with glass-and-concrete buildings, although there's still an old-fashioned Saturday-morning market on Jeremie Street. The country women dress in traditional cotton headdresses to sell their luscious fruits and vegetables, while weather-beaten men sit close by playing *warrie* (a fast game played with pebbles on a carved board) or dominoes using tiles the color of cherries.

COMING ASHORE Most cruise ships arrive at the fairly new pier at **Pointe Seraphine,** within walking distance of the center of Castries and boasting St. Lucia's best shopping right on-site. Two mid- to large-sized cruise ships can be handled. With the rapid increase in cruise tourism, the limited capacity at Pointe Seraphine may necessitate docking at **Port Castries,** an industrial terminal on the other side of the colorful harbor. There's a shopping terminal here called La Place Carenage. Some smaller lines, such as Star Clippers, Seabourn, and Clipper, visit other sites around the island, anchoring off **Rodney Bay** to the north or **Soufrière** to the south and carrying passengers ashore by tender.

GETTING AROUND There is an official **taxi** association servicing both Pointe Seraphine and La Place Carenage, with standard fares posted. You can hire a taxi to go to Soufrière, too. Many taxi drivers offer 3- to 4-hour tours, with a stop at the beach, for $120 for four people. Be sure to find out whether you're talking U.S. or EC dollars before agreeing on a price.

LANGUAGE & CURRENCY **English** is the official language. The official currency is the **Eastern Caribbean dollar** (EC$2.70 = US$1; EC$1 = US37¢), though shops and restaurants commonly take the U.S. dollar as well. Be sure you know which currency locals are talking about before making a purchase.

BEST CRUISE LINE SHORE EXCURSIONS

Because of the difficult terrain, shore excursions are the best means of seeing this beautiful island in a day or less. In addition to the sampling below, most ships typically offer bus tours (many visiting the island's banana plantations) and snorkeling cruises.

Pigeon Island Sea Kayaking ($65–$70, 3 hr.): After transferring to Rodney Bay, you'll make the roughly 30-minute paddle out to the island, where you'll have time to swim, kayak some more, or make the steep climb up to Fort Rodney. From the summit, you'll have great views of the Pitons; sometimes you'll even be able to see Martinique.

Rainforest Bicycle Tour ($49, 4½ hr.): After being dropped off by bus in the middle of the forest, you'll ride past banana plantations and the Errard Falls waterfall, stopping to sample various fruits that grow along the roadside. Some time for swimming at the falls is usually included. A different tour called **Jungle Biking** ($104, 4½ hr.) takes you by boat to the Jungle Biking facility, located on an 18th-century sugar plantation. Here, you can explore 16km (10 miles) of trails at your own pace. Beach time is included at the end.

Soody Nature Hike & Mineral Waterfall ($55, 7 hr.): Drive along the west coast through fishing villages, banana plantations, and the edge of the rainforest before arriving at Soufrière, location of the Pitons and the Diamond Botanical Gardens. A guided 1-hour hike through the volcanic forest introduces you to the island's flora and fauna, ending up at a therapeutic sulfuric waterfall where you can take a dip to cure what ails ya. Lunch at a Creole restaurant is included.

Beach Snorkel ($64, 3½ hr.): Snorkeling is spectacular around St. Lucia. This trip departs the Castries harbor by boat, traveling an hour en route to the island's marine reserve, which has an area set aside especially for snorkeling. There's also a supersize 7-hour ($93) version of this trip that includes a buffet lunch.

ON YOUR OWN: WITHIN WALKING DISTANCE

The principal streets of Castries are **William Peter Boulevard** and **Bridge Street.** Don't miss a walk through town: People are very friendly, and **Jeremie Street** is chockablock with variety stores of the most authentic local kind, selling everything from spices to housewares. A Roman Catholic cathedral stands on **Columbus Square,** which has a few restored buildings. Take a gander at the enormous 400-year-old "rain" tree, also called a "no-name" tree, that grows in the square. The nearby **Government House** is a late-Victorian structure.

Beyond Government House lies **Morne Fortune,** which means "Hill of Good Luck." Actually, no one's had much luck here, certainly not the French and British soldiers who battled for **Fort Charlotte.** The fort switched between the two sides many times. You can visit the 18th-century barracks, complete with a military cemetery, a small museum, the Old Powder Magazine, and the "Four Apostles Battery"—four grim muzzle-loading cannons. The view of the harbor of Castries is panoramic from this point. You can also see north to Pigeon Island or south to the Pitons. To reach Morne Fortune, head east on Bridge Street.

Castries has a very colorful **Central Market,** right near the dock, that's also worth a visit. The airplane-hangar-size emporium sells local food, trinkets, and produce. Buy some banana ketchup or local cinnamon sticks to take home.

ON YOUR OWN: BEYOND THE PORT AREA

St. Lucia's first national park, the 18-hectare (44-acre) **Pigeon Island National Landmark** (© 758/450-0603), was originally an island but is now joined to the northwest shore of the mainland by a very environmentally unfriendly causeway. It's about 30 minutes by taxi from Castries. The park, an ideal spot for picnics and nature walks, is covered with lemongrass, which spread from original plantings made by British light opera singer Josset, who leased the island for 30 years and grew the grass to provide thatch for her cottage's roof. The island's **Interpretation Centre** contains artifacts and a multimedia display of local history, covering everything from the Amerindian settlers of A.D. 1000 to 1782's Battle of Saints, when Admiral Rodney's fleet set out from Pigeon Island and defeated the French admiral De Grasse. Right below the interpretation center is the cozy **Captain's Cellar Pub,** located in what was formerly a soldiers' mess. From the tables outside, you get amazing scenes of the crashing surf on the Atlantic coast, just a few steps away. From here, you can walk up the winding and moderately steep path to a **lookout,** from which you get a wonderful view that stretches all the way to Martinique. Two white-sand beaches lie on the island's west coast. Island admission is $13.

La Soufrière, a fishing port and St. Lucia's second-largest settlement, is dominated by Petit Piton and Gros Piton, collectively known as the **Pitons,** two of the dramatic pointed peaks that rise right from the sea to 738m and 786m (2,421 ft. and 2,579 ft.), respectively. Formed by lava and once actively volcanic, these mountains are now cloaked in green vegetation, with waves crashing around their bases. Their sheer rise from the water makes them such visible landmarks that they've become the very symbol of St. Lucia. Near the town lies the famous "drive-in" volcano, **La Soufrière,** a rocky lunar landscape of bubbling mud and craters seething with fuming sulfur. You can literally drive into an old crater and walk between the sulfur springs and pools of hissing steam. The fumes are said to have medicinal properties. A local guide is usually waiting nearby; if you do hire a guide, agree—and then doubly agree—on what the fee will be. Nearby are the **Diamond Mineral Baths.** They were originally constructed in 1784 by order of Louis XVI, whose doctors told him that these waters were similar in mineral content to the waters at Aix-les-Bains. The baths were built to help French soldiers who had been fighting in the West Indies recuperate from wounds and disease.

BEACHES

If you don't take a shore excursion, you might want to spend your time on one of St. Lucia's famous beaches, all of which are open to the public, even those at hotel properties (though you must pay to use a hotel's beach equipment). Taxis can take you to any of the island's beaches, but we recommend that you stick to the calmer shores along the western coast, since the rough surf on the windward Atlantic side makes swimming potentially dangerous.

Leading beaches include **Pigeon Island,** off the northern shore, with white sand and picnic facilities; **Vigie Beach,** north of the Castries harbor, with fine sand; **Marigot Beach,** south of the Castries harbor, framed on three sides by steep emerald hills and skirted by palm trees; and **Reduit Beach,** between Choc Bay and Pigeon Point, with fine brown sand. Just north of Soufrière is a beach connoisseur's delight, **Anse Chastanet** (© 758/459-7000), boasting an expanse of white sand at the foothills of lush mountains. This is a fantastic spot for snorkeling, with spectacular coral reefs starting only a little way offshore, providing shelter for thousands of fish and other sea creatures.

SHOPPING

You'll find some good but not remarkable buys on bone china, jewelry, perfume, watches, liquor, and crystal. Souvenir items include designer bags and mats, local pottery, and straw hats—again, nothing remarkable. *A tip:* If your cruise is also calling in St. Thomas, let the local vendors know; it may make them more amenable to bargaining.

Built for cruise ship passengers, **Pointe Seraphine** has the best collection of shops on the island. You must present your cruise pass when making purchases here. If you're in Soufrière, you might want to make a detour to the southwest, just past the small village of Choiseul, to the **Choiseul Craft Centre,** La Fargue (© 758/459-3226), a government-funded retail outlet and training school that perpetuates the tradition of handmade Amerindian pottery and basketware. Some of the best basket weaving on the island is done here, using techniques practiced only in St. Lucia, St. Vincent, and Dominica. Look for place mats, handbags, woodcarvings (including bas-reliefs crafted from screw pine), and pottery. It's open weekdays only.

23 St. Martin/Sint Maarten

Who can resist a two-for-one sale? That's what you get on St. Martin, a 96-sq.-km (37-sq.-mile) island that's been shared by France (with 52 sq. km/20 sq. miles of it) and the Netherlands (with 44 sq. km/17 sq. miles) for more than 350 years. Although the border between the two sides is virtually imperceptible—a monument along the road marks the change in administration—each side retains elements of its own heritage. The French side, with some of the best beaches and restaurants in the Caribbean, emphasizes quiet elegance. French fashions and luxury items fill the shops, and the fragrance of croissants mixes with the spicy aromas of West Indian cooking. The Dutch side, officially known as Sint Maarten, reflects Holland's anything-goes philosophy: Development is much more widespread, flashy casinos pepper the landscape, and strip malls make the larger towns look as much like Anaheim as Amsterdam. The 100% duty-free shopping has turned both sides of the island into a bargain hunter's paradise.

COMING ASHORE Cruise ships usually dock on the Dutch side, at **Dr. A. C. Wathey Pier,** about 1.6km (1 mile) southeast of Philipsburg. The majority of passengers are then tendered to the smaller Captain Hodge Pier at the center of town, but others choose to walk the distance on a newly developed boardwalk or take taxis. The pier can accommodate up to four vessels; any more than that may anchor in **Great Bay,** a superquick tender from the Captain Hodge Pier, where a terminal has shops, food outlets, ATMs, and an Internet cafe. Smaller vessels sometimes dock on the French side of the island, at **Marina Port la Royale,** adjacent to the heart of Marigot.

GETTING AROUND   Taxis on both sides of the island are unmetered. Agree on a rate and currency before getting in. Dutch law requires that drivers list government-regulated fares based on two passengers. Privately owned and operated **minivans,** with signs to indicate their destination, can be hailed anywhere on the street. Fares are usually about $1.50. **Rental cars** are a great way to see both sides of the island. Avis, Budget, and Hertz all have offices here. **Water taxis** are also a popular way to get around.

LANGUAGE & CURRENCY   Surprise, surprise: The official language on the Dutch side is **Dutch,** and the official language on the French side is **French.** Most people on both sides also speak **English.** The legal tender in Dutch Sint Maarten is the **Netherlands Antilles florin,** also called a guilder (1.78 ANG = US$1; 1 ANG = US56¢), and the official currency on the French side is the **euro** (.76€ = US$1; 1€ = US$1.31). Most prices are also quoted in U.S. dollars, which are widely accepted on both sides.

CALLING FROM THE U.S.   When calling Dutch Sint Maarten from the United States, simply dial the international access number **(011)** before the numbers listed here. Calling French St. Martin requires more of an effort: Dial **011** and then **590** before the numbers listed. Yes, 590 already appears in the numbers in this section, but those three digits must be dialed twice to make a connection.

BEST CRUISE LINE SHORE EXCURSIONS

America's Cup Sailing Regatta ($89, 2½ hr.): Get a taste of nautical exhilaration by competing in a race aboard an America's Cup–winning sailboat. This extremely popular hands-on excursion lets you grind winches, trim sails, and duck under booms—after you've been trained by professionals, of course. Alternatively, sit back and watch others do all the work.

Pinel Island Shore Snorkel & Beach Tour ($39, 3½ hr.): After a scenic bus ride to the French town of Cul de Sac, along the northeast coast, hop on a tender to the small offshore island of Ilet Pinel for some of St. Martin's best snorkeling.

Hidden Forest Hike ($84, 5 hr.): Take a 45-minute drive to Loterie Farm, where you'll do a 2-hour hike through the tropical forest, eventually emerging at Pic Paradise, the island's highest point. Along the way, your guide will point out a secret freshwater spring and the island's famous guava berry trees. Return to the farm for a complimentary rum or fruit punch and a typical Caribbean farmhouse lunch.

Butterfly Farm & Marigot ($39, 3½ hr.): After a scenic drive through both the French and Dutch sides of the island, walk through a surrealistic enclosed garden that features pools, waterfalls, and hundreds of exquisitely beautiful and exotic butterflies from around the world. Amusing guides identify species, describe courtship and mating rituals, and give tips on attracting butterflies to your garden at home. Afterward, absorb the Creole charm and French atmosphere of Marigot.

ON YOUR OWN: WITHIN WALKING DISTANCE

Shopping, sunbathing, and gambling are the pastimes that interest most cruisers who hit this island, but folks with a taste for culture and history can make a day of it here as well.

ON THE DUTCH SIDE   Directly in front of the Philipsburg town pier, on Wathey Square, the **Courthouse** combines northern European sobriety with Caribbean brightness. Originally built in 1793 of freestone and wood, this venerable old building has suffered numerous hurricanes, but has been restored after each tempest and continues to house government offices. East of the Courthouse, down a little shopping alley, the tiny **Sint Maarten Museum,** 7 Front St. (✆ 599/542-4917), features modest, cluttered exhibits that focus on the island's history and geology. The second-floor gallery is open weekdays, but closed Saturday and Sunday. Admission is free.

Fort Amsterdam is the Dutch side's most important historic colonial site. Since 1631, it has looked out over Great Bay from the hill west of Philipsburg. The fort was the Netherlands' first military outpost in the Caribbean. The Spanish captured it 2 years later, making it their most significant bastion east of Puerto Rico. Peter Stuyvesant, who later became governor of New Amsterdam (now New York), lost his leg to a cannonball while trying to reclaim the fort for Holland. The site provides grand views of the bay, but ruins of the walls and a couple of rusty cannons are all that remain of the original fort.

Gambling is also big here, with several casinos clustered along Front Street in the heart of Philipsburg. All of them open early enough to snag cruisers.

ON THE FRENCH SIDE   **Fort St. Louis** is Marigot's answer to Fort Amsterdam. Built in 1767 to protect the waterfront warehouses that stored the French colony's agricultural riches, the cannons of this bastion frequently fired on hostile British raiders from Anguilla. After restorations and modification in the 19th century, the fort was eventually abandoned. In addition to the fort's cannons, crumbling walls, and French tricolor flag flapping in the breeze, the short climb up the hill flanking Marigot Bay's north end affords splendid vistas. As a respite from the sun, duck into Marigot's **Museum of Saint Martin** (✆ 590/29-22-84), next to the tourism office and adjacent to the marina. Much more thorough and scholarly than its Philipsburg counterpart, this institution boasts a first-rate collection of Ciboney, Arawak, and Carib artifacts excavated from the island's Amerindian sites, plus a reproduction of a 1,500-year-old burial mound. Another display details the history of the plantation and slavery era, while early-20th-century photographs trace the island's modern development. Admission costs about $5; closed Sundays.

BEACHES

St. Martin has more than 30 beautiful white-sand beaches—some social, some serene. The busier ones boast bars, restaurants, watersports, and hotels, where changing

---

St. Martin Golf Excursions

The **Mullet Bay Golf Course** (✆ 599/545-2850), on the Dutch side, has an 18-hole course designed by Joseph Lee that's considered one of the more challenging in the Caribbean, especially the back 9. Mullet Pond and Simpson Bay lagoon provide both beauty and hazards. Greens fees, including cart, are $120 for 18 holes, $65 for 9 holes. Club rental is an additional $30 for 18 holes, $25 for 9. The course opens daily at 7am.

facilities are usually available for a small fee. Toplessness is ubiquitous; nudism is common on the French side, and increasingly evident on the Dutch side as well.

ON THE DUTCH SIDE **Great Bay Beach** is your best bet if you want to stay in Philipsburg. This mile-long stretch is convenient and has calm water, but it lacks the tranquility and cleanliness of the more remote beaches.

Just west of the airport, on the west side of the island, **Maho Beach** boasts a casino, shade palms, and a popular beachside bar and grill. It's a good snorkeling spot, too. Farther west, **Mullet Beach** borders the island's golf course. Shaded by palm trees and crowded on weekends, it's popular with swimmers and snorkelers. On-site vendors rent an array of watersports equipment. **Dawn Beach,** on the east coast, is the best snorkeling site on the island. Rent equipment from Busby's Beach Bar, which is right on the sand.

ON THE FRENCH SIDE Far and away the island's most visited strand, **Orient Beach,** on the northeast coast, fancies itself the St. Tropez of the Caribbean. Hedonism is the name of the game here: plenty of food, drink, music, and flesh (a naturist resort occupies the beach's southern tip, but nudism isn't confined to any one area). Watersports abound. South of Orient Beach, the waveless waters of **Coconut Grove** or **Galion Beach** are shallow up to 30m (98 ft.) offshore. Protected by a coral reef, this area is popular with kids and windsurfers.

On the island's west coast, just north of the Dutch border, **Long Bay** is the island's longest beach and another refuge for adults seeking peace and quiet. There are no facilities here, but this wild beach bordering some of the island's grandest mansions is popular with the rich and (sometimes) famous. The water and sand here are silky. **Friars Beach,** just outside of Marigot, is a quiet sheltered cove at the end of a bumpy road, offering gorgeous views of the neighboring island Anguilla on clear days. Beach chairs, umbrellas, and food are available on the beach.

SHOPPING

St. Martin is a true free port—no duties are paid on any item coming in or going out—and neither side of the island has a sales tax. Shops on the much busier Dutch side are concentrated in Philipsburg, along **Front Street** and the numerous alleys radiating from it. The district is largely nondescript, but you'll find all the usual jewelry/gift/luxury-item shops, as well as some quirky local boutiques. In general, prices in the major stores are nonnegotiable, but at small, family-run shops, you can try your luck with a little polite bargaining. The T-shirt and souvenir epicenter is in the open-air market behind the Courthouse in front of the town pier. **Guavaberry Emporium,** 8–10 Front St., sells Guavaberry "island folk liqueur," an aged rum with a distinctive fruity, woody, almost bittersweet flavor; it's available only on St. Martin.

On the French side, Marigot features a much calmer, more charming, and sophisticated ambience, with waterfront cafes where you can rest your weary over-shopped feet. Many shops here close their doors for a 2-hour lunch break starting at noon. The wide selection of European merchandise is skewed toward an upscale audience, but French crystal, perfume, liqueur, jewelry, and fashion can be up to 50% less expensive than in the States.

24 U.S. Virgin Islands: St. Thomas & St. John

Ever since Columbus discovered the Virgin Islands during his second voyage to the New World in 1493, they have proven irresistible to foreign powers seeking territory, at one time or another being governed by Denmark, Spain, France, England, Holland, and, since 1917, the United States.

Vacationers discovered **St. Thomas** right after World War II and have been flocking here ever since. Tourism and U.S. government programs have raised the standard of living to one of the highest in the Caribbean, and today the island is one of the busiest and most developed cruise ports in the Caribbean, often hosting more than six ships a day during the peak winter season. **Charlotte Amalie** (pronounced Ah-*mahl*-yah), named in 1691 in honor of the wife of Denmark's King Christian V, is the island's capital and has become the Caribbean's major shopping center.

The most tranquil and unspoiled of the U.S. Virgins is **St. John,** the smallest of the lot, more than half of which is preserved as the gorgeous **Virgin Islands National Park.** A rocky coastline, forming crescent-shaped bays and white-sand beaches, rings the whole island, whose miles of serpentine hiking trails lead past the ruins of 18th-century Danish plantations and let onto panoramic ocean views. A few ships anchor directly off St. John, but those that dock in St. Thomas usually offer excursions here as well, via ferry.

LANGUAGE & CURRENCY   English is spoken on all three islands, and the **U.S. dollar** is the official currency. Americans get a break on shopping in the U.S. Virgins, since they can bring home $1,600 worth of merchandise without paying duty, as opposed to $400 from most other Caribbean ports. You can also bring back more liquor from here. See p. 71 for more **Customs** information.

ST. THOMAS

With a population of more than 50,000 and a large number of American expatriates and temporary sun-seekers in residence, tiny St. Thomas isn't exactly a tranquil tropical retreat. You won't have any beaches to yourself. Shops, bars, and restaurants (including a lot of fast-food joints) abound here, and most of the locals make their living off the tourist trade.

COMING ASHORE   Most cruise ships anchor at **West Indian Dock/Havensight Mall.** Located along the southern end of Charlotte Amalie Harbor, 2½ miles from the town center, it's got its own restaurants, bookstores, banks, postal van, and lots of duty-free shops. The dock can accommodate three to four large ships, or one to two megaships. If Havensight is clogged with cruise ships, you'll dock at the **Crown Bay Cruise Ship Terminal,** to the west of Charlotte Amalie. The two piers can accommodate three ships of varying size, although unlike Havensight, they cannot dock the megaships. If both options are at capacity, ships anchor in **Charlotte Amalie Harbor.** From the terminals, some people make the long, hot, 30-minute-plus walk into Charlotte Amalie, but it's not terribly picturesque. A taxi ride into town costs about $5; keep in mind there are often traffic jams, so it could take as much as 30 minutes or longer to get into town on the busiest days.

GETTING AROUND   Taxis are the chief means of transport here. They're unmetered, but a guide of point-to-point fares around the island is included in most tourist magazines. Fares range from $10 to $15 per person to the popular destinations.

Less formal, privately owned **taxi vans** make unscheduled stops along major traffic arteries, charging less than a dollar for most rides. If you look like you want to go somewhere, one will likely stop for you. They may or may not have their final destinations written on a cardboard sign displayed on the windshield.

BEST CRUISE LINE SHORE EXCURSIONS

In addition to the excursions below, a bajillion booze cruises, island tours, and beach/snorkeling tours are offered here. The waters off these islands are rated among the most beautiful in the world.

Coral World & Island Drive ($39–$42, 3 hr.): Coral World Underwater Observatory and Marine Park is St. Thomas's number-one attraction. The 3½-acre complex features a three-story underwater observation tower 100 feet offshore, plunging into the depths to provide views of tropical fish, coral formations, sharks, and other sea beasts. In the Marine Gardens Aquarium, saltwater tanks display everything from sea horses to sea urchins, and a Touch Pool lets you fondle some of them. Another tank is devoted to sea predators, including circling sharks.

Kayaking the Marine Sanctuary ($72, 3½ hr.): Kayak from the mouth of the marine sanctuary at Holmberg's Marina and spend nearly an hour paddling among the mangroves while a naturalist explains the ecosystem. This trip includes a free half-hour to snorkel or walk along the coral beach at Bovoni Point.

St. John Ecohike ($55, 4 hr.): Take the ferry to St. John for a walkabout through Virgin Islands National Park. The Lind Point Trail ascends about 250 feet to the Lind Point Overlook for views of St. John, St. Thomas, and the surrounding islands. An expert guide discusses the park's ecosystem and St. John's cultural history while you walk to Honeymoon Beach for a little swimming.

Atlantis Submarine Expedition ($89, 2 hr.): Descend about 100 feet into the ocean in this air-conditioned submarine for views of exotic fish and sea life.

Water Island Bike Trip & Beach Adventure ($79, 3½ hr.): After a ferry ride to Water Island, a 5-minute bus ride brings you to the island's highest point, from which you get a nice downhill ride. Your guide will point out various historic sights and wildlife en route to Honeymoon Beach, where you can swim and enjoy a drink.

ON YOUR OWN: WITHIN WALKING DISTANCE

In days of yore, seafarers from all over the globe flocked to the old Danish town of Charlotte Amalie, including pirates and, during the Civil War, Confederate sailors. The old warehouses that once held pirates' loot still stand and, for the most part, house shops, shops, and more shops. The main streets (called *gades* here in honor of their Danish heritage) are a veritable shopping mall, especially close to the waterfront. Stray farther landward and you'll find pockets of 19th-century houses and the truly charming, brick-and-stone **St. Thomas Synagogue,** built in 1833 by Sephardic Jews high on steep, sloping Crystal Gade. There's a great view from here as well.

Dating from 1672, **Fort Christian,** 32 Raadets Gade, rises from the harbor to dominate the center of town. Named after Danish King Christian V, the structure has been everything from a governor's residence to a jail. Many pirates were hanged in its courtyard. Some of the cells have been turned into the rather minor **American-Caribbean Historical Museum,** displaying Indian artifacts of only the most passing interest. Admission is $3; closed weekends.

The U.S. & British Virgin Islands

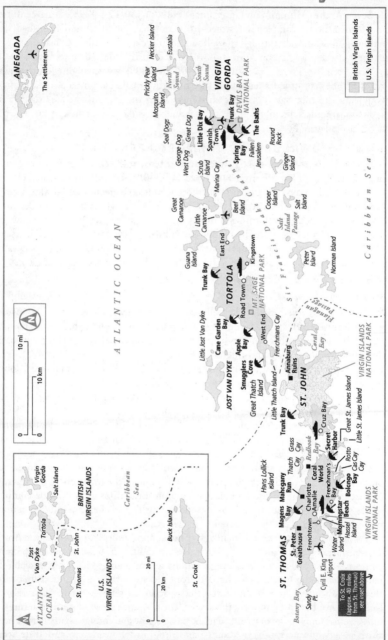

Seven Arches Museum, on Government Hill (© **340/774-9295**), is a 2-centuries-old Danish house completely restored to its original condition and furnished with antiques. You can walk through the yellow ballast arches and visit the great room with its view of the busy harbor. Admission is $5; open daily from 10am to 4pm.

The **Paradise Point Tramway** (© **340/774-9809;** www.paradisepointtramway.com) affords visitors a dramatic view of Charlotte Amalie Harbor at a peak height of 697 feet. The tramway transports customers from the Havensight area to Paradise Point, where riders disembark to visit shops and a popular restaurant and bar. The cost is $18 round-trip.

ON YOUR OWN: BEYOND THE PORT AREA

The lush **St. Peter Greathouse Estate and Gardens,** at the corner of St. Peter Mountain Road (Rte. 40) and Barrett Hill Road (© **340/774-4999**), ornaments 11 acres on the volcanic peaks of the island's northern rim. It's the creation of Howard Lawson DeWolfe, a *Mayflower* descendant who, with his wife, Sylvie, bought the estate in 1987 and set about transforming it into a tropical paradise. It's filled with some 200 varieties of plants and trees, including an umbrella plant from Madagascar. There's also a rainforest, an orchid jungle, waterfalls, and reflecting ponds. From a panoramic deck you can see some 20 of the Virgin Islands. The house itself is worth a visit, its interior filled with local art. Admission is $12.

BEACHES

St. Thomas has some good beaches, all of which are easily reached by taxi. Arrange for your driver to return and pick you up at a designated time. All the beaches in the U.S. Virgin Islands are public, but some still charge a fee. Mind your belongings, as St. Thomas has pickpockets and thieves who target visitors. If you're going to St. John, you may want to do your sunning there instead (see "Beaches" under "St. John," below), as the beach options there are generally nicer.

Located 3 miles north of Charlotte Amalie, across the mountains on the north side of the island, **Magens Bay Beach** was once hailed as one of the world's most beautiful, but it isn't as well maintained as it should be and is often overcrowded, especially when many cruise ships are in port. Admission is $3. Changing facilities, bathrooms, a snack bar, snorkel gear, and float rentals are available. In the northeast, near Coral World, **Coki Beach** is another good but often crowded spot. Snorkelers come here often. Also on the north side, **Sapphire Beach** is one of the finest on St. Thomas, set against the backdrop of the Doubletree Sapphire Beach Resort & Marina complex, where you can lunch or order drinks. Windsurfers like this beach a lot; you can also rent snorkeling gear and lounge chairs.

On the island's south side, **Morningstar** lies about 2 miles east of Charlotte Amalie at Marriott's Frenchman's Reef Beach Resort. You can wear your most daring swimwear here. Sailboats, snorkeling equipment, and lounge chairs are available for rent. To reach the beach, take the cliff-front elevator at the Marriott. **Bluebeard's Beach Club,** just a little to the east, offers a secluded setting. Farther east still, the **Bolongo Bay Beach Club** lures those who love a serene spread of sand. You can feed hibiscus blossoms to iguanas and rent snorkeling gear and lounge chairs here. There's also a variety of watersports, including parasailing. At the far eastern end, little **Secret Harbor** sits near a collection of condos. With its white sand and coconut palms, it's a veritable cliché of Caribbean charm.

SHOPPING

Shopping is the number-one activity in Charlotte Amalie, and you'll sometimes find well-known brand names at savings of up to 40% off prices in the States—but you have to plow through a lot of junk to find the bargains. The main goodies are jewelry, watches, cameras, china, and leather, plus the local Cruzan Rum, which is so ridiculously cheap you'll think it's mismarked.

Many cruise ship passengers shop at the **Havensight Mall,** where the ships dock, but the major shopping goes on along the harbor of Charlotte Amalie. **Main Street** (or Dronningens Gade, its old Danish name) is the prime shopping area, with nearby **Back Street,** or Vimmelskaft, not too far behind. Many shops are also spread along the **Waterfront Highway** (also called Kyst Vejen) and along the side streets. All the usual Caribbean mega-tourist-shops sell all the usual jewelry, watches, perfume, gift items, and so on, but you'll also find some more singular boutiques and gift shops mixed in. At the **Vendors Plaza,** on the corner of Veterans Drive and Tolbod Gade, hundreds of street vendors ply their trade beneath oversize parasols. Food vendors set up on sidewalks outside.

ST. JOHN

A tiny gem, lush St. John lies about 3 miles east of St. Thomas across Pillsbury Sound. It's the smallest and least populated of the U.S. Virgins, only about 7 miles long and 3 miles wide, with a total land area of some 19 square miles. The island was slated for big development under Danish control, but a slave rebellion and the decline of the sugar cane plantations ended that idea. Since 1956, more than half of St. John's landmass, as well as its shoreline waters, have been set aside as the **Virgin Islands National Park,** and today the island leads the Caribbean in eco- (or "sustainable") tourism. Miles of winding hiking trails lead to panoramic views and the ruins of 18th-century Danish plantations. Mysterious geometric petroglyphs incised into boulders and cliffs can be seen all over the island (ask a guide to point them out if you can't find them). These figures, of unknown age and origin, have never been deciphered. Since St. John is easy to reach from St. Thomas and the beaches are spectacular, many cruise ship passengers spend their entire day here.

COMING ASHORE   Cruise ships cannot dock at either of the piers in St. John. Instead, they moor off the coast at **Cruz Bay,** sending in tenders to the National Park Service Dock, the larger of the two piers. Most cruise ships docking at St. Thomas offer shore excursions to St. John's pristine interior and beaches.

GETTING AROUND   You'll find shopping, bars, and restaurants right by the docks. Otherwise, the most popular way to get around the island is by **surrey-style taxi.** Typical fares from Cruz Bay are $8 to Trunk Bay, $9 to Cinnamon Bay, and $13 to Maho Bay. Taxis wait at the pier. You can also rent open-sided **jeeps;** Avis and Hertz both have offices here. Just remember to drive on the left, even though steering wheels are on the left, too. Go figure.

BEST CRUISE LINE SHORE EXCURSIONS

St. John Island Tour ($45, 4½ hr.): Because most ships tie up in St. Thomas, tours of St. John first require a ferry or tender ride to Cruz Bay in St. John. Then you board open-air safari buses for a tour that includes a stop at the ruins of a working plantation (the Annaberg Ruins), as well as a pause at Trunk Bay or one of the other beaches. The island and sea views from the coastal road are spectacular.

ON YOUR OWN: WITHIN WALKING DISTANCE

Most cruise passengers dart through **Cruz Bay,** a cute little West Indian village with interesting bars, restaurants, boutiques, and pastel-painted houses. **Wharfside Village,** near the dock, is a complex of courtyards, alleys, and shady patios with a mishmash of boutiques, restaurants, fast-food joints, and bars. Located at the public library, the **Elaine Ione Sprauve Museum** (© 340/776-6359) isn't big, but it does have some local artifacts, and will teach you about some of the history of the island. Admission is free; closed weekends.

ON YOUR OWN: BEYOND THE PORT AREA

In November 1954, the wealthy Rockefeller family began acquiring large tracts of land on St. John. They then donated more than 5,000 acres to the Department of the Interior for the creation of **Virgin Islands National Park,** which Congress voted into existence on August 2, 1956. Over the years, the size of the park has grown steadily; it now totals 12,624 acres, including over two-thirds of St. John's landmass plus submerged land and water adjacent to the island. Stop off first at the **visitor center** (© 340/776-6201) right on the dock at St. Cruz, where you'll find some exhibits and learn more about what you can see and do in the park. You can explore the more than 20 miles of biking trails; rent your own car, jeep, or Mini-Moke; or hike. If you decide to hike, stop at the visitor center first to pick up maps and instructions. The starting points of some trails are within walking distance, while others can be reached by taxi for about $5 to $20. Within the park, try to see the **Annaberg Ruins,** on Leinster Bay Road, where the Danes founded thriving plantations and a sugar mill in 1718. They're located off North Shore Road, east of Trunk Bay on the north shore.

BEACHES

For a true beach lover, missing the great white sweep of Trunk Bay would be like touring Europe and skipping Paris. That said, it's usually overcrowded. The beach has lifeguards and rents snorkeling gear to those wanting to explore the underwater trail near the shore. Snorkelers find good reefs at Cinnamon Bay and Maho Bay, also a great place to spot turtles and schools of parrotfish. Changing rooms and showers are available.

SHOPPING

Compared to St. Thomas, St. John is a minor shopping destination, but the boutiques and shops at Cruz Bay make up in interest and quality what they lack in number. Most of them are clustered at **Mongoose Junction** (www.usvi.net/shopping/mongoose), in a woodsy area beside the roadway, about a 5-minute walk from the ferry dock in Cruz Bay.

11

Alaska & British Columbia

Alaska brings to mind a series of images: Two black bears padding along the shoreline of Dundas Bay, eyeing us curiously as we drift just yards away in a kayak. Walking along the Totem Trail at Sitka's National Historic Park, struck by the intense artistry of Southeast's Native cultures. Plucking a 1945 edition of John Steinbeck's *Cannery Row* off the shelf of a used bookstore in Juneau, then chatting with the 70-something proprietor about the ups and downs of the author's reputation. Watching Metlakatla's traditional Killer Whale Dancers perform at the town's clan house, and hearing one young member sound as enthusiastic as a hip-hop producer as he talked about a new beat he'd created that week. Seeing a humpback whale breach for the first time, hurling its tanker trunk body gracefully into the air, then letting it fall back to water with the goofy joy of a beer drinker in a belly-flop contest. Standing on deck at midnight, looking up at the Northern Lights for the first time and wondering if people ever get used to skies like that. Flying over Juneau's Mendenhall Glacier in a helicopter and realizing the immensity of the thing for the first time, then landing for an hour's visit and stooping to drink from the cold meltwater on its surface.

It's practically impossible not to be amazed by Alaska. Much of its coastline is wilderness, with snowcapped mountain peaks, enormous glaciers, dense rainforests, deep fjords, and the cycles of geologic time visible all around. Visit the towns, and you'll find people who retain the spirit of frontier independence that brought them here in the first place. Add Alaska's history and heritage, with its rich Native culture, its European influences, and its gold-rush and oil-pipeline chutzpah, and you have a destination that is utterly and endlessly fascinating.

The fact that some 750,000 cruise passengers arrive annually has had its impact, of course, turning some towns into veritable tourist malls populated by seasonal vendors hawking imported souvenirs and jewelry—lots and lots of jewelry. Even in the most touristy towns, though, it's easy to get out and experience the real thing. In Skagway, walk up one of the trails to the east of town and in 10 minutes you'd never know there are 6,000 other cruisers shopping behind you. In Ketchikan, walk in either direction out of the dockside tourist zone and you're suddenly in residential Alaska, where the real people live. Throughout the regions, you'll also find the influence of the region's great **Native peoples,** the Tlingit (pronounced Klink-*get*), Haida, and Tsimshian, who continue to make their presence felt in business, art, and politics.

Cruises in Alaska concentrate mostly on the **Inside Passage,** a series of connecting waterways threaded between the thousands of forested islands that make up the panhandle commonly known as Southeast Alaska or just **Southeast.** The passage actually begins in British Columbia, though ships tend to buzz through here without stopping en route to Alaskan waters, which begin just south of Ketchikan. From here, the region is home to scattered fishing towns, a number of larger towns and cities (including state capital Juneau), and many of the natural wonders visited by most ships, including Glacier Bay National Park, Tracy Arm fjord, and (mostly for small ships) Misty Fjords National Monument. The area teems with wildlife, including large populations of whale, bear, eagle, sea lion, sea otter, and mountain sheep. North of Southeast, ships sailing one-way itineraries also visit attractions such as Hubbard Glacier and College Fjord along the **Gulf of Alaska,** which starts just above Glacier Bay.

HOME PORTS FOR THIS REGION Vancouver, British Columbia, and **Seattle,** Washington, are the main southern termini for Alaska cruises, with ships either sailing round-trip or doing alternating north- and southbound departures between here and either Seward or Whittier, the two main port towns for **Anchorage.** Some lines also offer Alaska cruises that sail round-trip from **San Francisco.** Most of the small ships sail from one or another of the ports in Southeast (primarily **Juneau,** but also Ketchikan and Sitka), though some also operate out of Anchorage and Seattle.

LANGUAGE & CURRENCY English and dollars. You may want to get some Canadian dollars if you're sailing from Vancouver or visiting Victoria, but even that's not really necessary, as most businesses will accept U.S. currency.

SHOPPING TIPS Shops throughout Alaska are chock-full of knockoff "Native Alaskan" art shipped in from Asia. So, when shopping for the real thing, ask the dealer for details about the artist, and also look for the **Silver Hand sticker,** a state certification that guarantees the item was, in fact, crafted in Alaska by a Native artist. The other thing that'll usually identify real pieces? Sky-high prices. You get what you pay for.

1 Cruising Alaska's Natural Wonders

Most Alaska cruises spend at least 3 days cruising the natural areas of the state's coast, including areas protected as national parks and national monuments. Regulations control access to some of them (most notably Glacier Bay, where only two large cruise ships and several smaller ones are permitted on any given day), while geography controls access to others: Misty Fjords, for instance, gets very narrow just where it gets most interesting, so only small ships can enter.

GLACIER BAY

There are about 5,000 glaciers in Alaska, but **Glacier Bay (www.nps.gov/glba)** definitely has The Big Mo, with the kind of name recognition the other glaciers can only dream about. Mostly, this is due to the fact that, in little more than 200 years, the area has gone from being a solid wall of ice up to 4,000 feet thick to being a 65-mile bay ecosystem full of wildlife, whales, and slowly returning vegetation, with glaciers extending up from its cold waters like fingers.

When first noted by Western man in 1794, Glacier Bay was just an indentation in the shoreline of Icy Strait, plugged by a glacial cork. A mere 105 years later, the ice had receded some 35 miles, allowing naturalist **John Muir** to penetrate a landscape he described as "a solitude of ice and snow and newborn rocks," the latter not yet smoothed by the elements, and still retaining the heavy scratches left by the retreating glaciers. Today, that ice has retreated even farther, leaving behind a series of inlets headed by 11 tidewater glaciers. Among them, the **Johns Hopkins, Reid, Lamplugh,**

Margerie, and **Grand Pacific** are all in the bay's western arm, and are regularly approached by cruise ships. Calving activity from these glaciers is the big draw (Johns Hopkins calves so much that ships can seldom approach closer than 2 miles, though it feels a lot closer), but don't forget to look at the land, which is a kind of living time-lapse photograph of earth's life cycles. Trees grow thick near the bay's head, but as you penetrate farther and farther you'll see less and less vegetation, and finally none at all. It just hasn't had time to grow back yet.

Glacier Bay was named a national park in 1925, and today each ship that enters takes aboard a park ranger to provide information about glaciers and wildlife (which includes mountain goats, brown bears, and minke, orca, and humpback whales) and the history of Native peoples and white men in the bay. On large ships, the ranger will speak over the PA and may also give a presentation about conservation in the show lounge; on small ships, he or she will often be on deck throughout the day, speaking over the PA and/or just talking with the passengers and answering questions.

TRACY ARM & ENDICOTT ARM

Located about 50 miles due south of Juneau, these long, deep fjords reach back from the Stephens Passage stretch of the Inside Passage into the Coastal Mountain Range, their steep-sided waterways ending in active glaciers—the **North Sawyer** and **South Sawyer Glaciers** in Tracy Arm and **Dawes Glacier** in Endicott. All of them calve constantly, filling the waters with miles of brash ice and bergs that ping and thunk off your ship's hull as you approach the ice faces. The show can be pretty spectacular. Two years ago, we saw South Sawyer calve off a sheet of ice as big as our ship. Granted, we were on one of Cruise West's small 100-passenger vessels, but still . . .

The passage through either fjord is incredibly dramatic, the sheer mountain walls rising literally a mile high straight from the water, cut by cascading waterfalls and tree-covered, snow-topped mountain valleys. Wildlife here might include Sitka black-tailed deer, bald eagles, mountain goats, and harbor seals (which often haul themselves out on ice floes to get some sun). You may also see the odd black bear. In 2003 we looked all day without luck, then, at dinner, our friend Cindy looked up from her salmon and spotted one on shore, eating a salmon of its own.

MISTY FJORDS NATIONAL MONUMENT

The 2.3-million-acre, Connecticut-size area of Misty Fjords starts at the Canadian border in the south and runs on the eastern side of the Behm Canal, which has Revillagigedo Island on the other side. (Ketchikan is on the western coast of Revillagigedo.) It is topography, not wildlife, that makes a visit here worthwhile, with volcanic cliffs rising up to 3,150 feet and plunging farther hundreds of feet below the waterline, reminding you you're sailing in a flooded cleft between mountains. Peace and serenity are the stock in trade of the place, with its namesake mists imparting a storybook, *Lord of the Rings* kind of atmosphere, abetted by dense hemlock and spruce forests, high ridges covered in alpine grass, and the occasional petrified lava flow reaching toward the shoreline.

Only passengers on small ships will see Misty Fjords close up, as its waterway is too narrow in most places for big ships. The bigger ships pass the southern tip of the area and then veer away northwest to dock at Ketchikan, where shore excursions can take you back into the area by **floatplane.** Some fly in, do a water landing, and then fly out again. Others fly you to an excursion boat for exploration of the monument, then make the short cruise back to Ketchikan.

Alaska

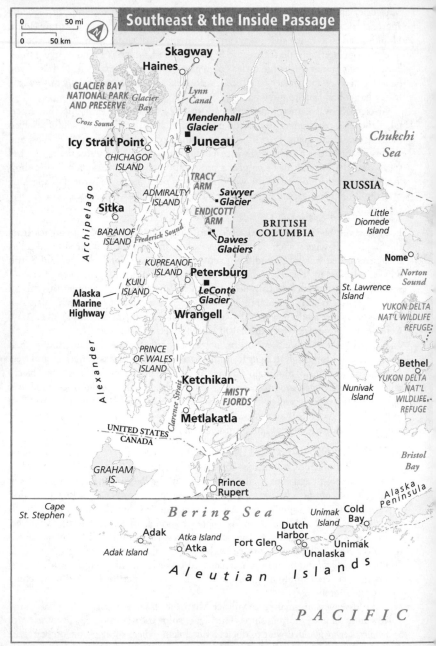

Southeast & the Inside Passage

0   50 mi
0   50 km

Skagway
Haines

GLACIER BAY
NATIONAL PARK
AND PRESERVE
Glacier
Bay

Lynn
Canal

Cross Sound

Mendenhall
Glacier

Icy Strait Point

Juneau

CHICHAGOF
ISLAND

TRACY
ARM

Sawyer
Glacier

ADMIRALTY
ISLAND

ENDICOTT
ARM

BRITISH
COLUMBIA

Sitka

BARANOF
ISLAND

Frederick Sound

Dawes
Glaciers

Archipelago

KUPREANOF
ISLAND

Petersburg

KUIU
ISLAND

LeConte
Glacier

Alaska
Marine
Highway

Wrangell

PRINCE
OF WALES
ISLAND

Alexander

Ketchikan

MISTY
FJORDS

Clarence Strait

Metlakatla

UNITED STATES
CANADA

GRAHAM
IS.

Prince
Rupert

Chukchi
Sea

RUSSIA

Little
Diomede
Island

Nome

Norton
Sound

St. Lawrence
Island

YUKON DELTA
NAT'L WILDLIFE
REFUGE

Bethel

YUKON DELTA
NAT'L
WILDLIFE
REFUGE

Nunivak
Island

Bristol
Bay

Alaska Peninsula

Cape
St. Stephen

Bering Sea

Unimak
Island

Cold
Bay

Adak

Atka Island

Atka

Fort Glen

Dutch
Harbor

Unalaska

Unimak

Adak Island

Aleutian Islands

PACIFIC

612

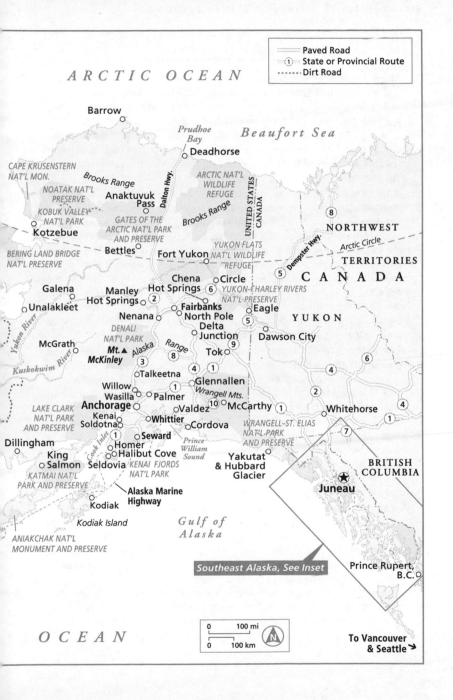

ARCTIC OCEAN

Barrow

Prudhoe Bay

Beaufort Sea

Deadhorse

CAPE KRUSENSTERN NAT'L MON.

Brooks Range

ARCTIC NAT'L WILDLIFE REFUGE

NOATAK NAT'L PRESERVE

Anaktuvuk Pass

Dalton Hwy.

Brooks Range

UNITED STATES

CANADA

KOBUK VALLEY NAT'L PARK

Kotzebue

GATES OF THE ARCTIC NAT'L PARK AND PRESERVE

NORTHWEST

⑧

Arctic Circle

BERING LAND BRIDGE NAT'L PRESERVE

Bettles

Fort Yukon

YUKON FLATS NAT'L WILDLIFE REFUGE

Dempster Hwy.

⑤

TERRITORIES

CANADA

Galena

Manley Hot Springs

Chena Hot Springs ⑥

Circle

YUKON-CHARLEY RIVERS NAT'L PRESERVE

Unalakleet

Hot Springs ②

Fairbanks

Eagle

YUKON

Nenana

North Pole

McGrath

DENALI NAT'L PARK

Mt. ▲ McKinley

Alaska Range

Delta Junction ⑤

Tok ⑨

Dawson City

⑥

④

③

⑧

④ ①

Talkeetna

Willow

Glennallen

Wrangell Mts.

②

④

Wasilla Palmer

⑩ McCarthy ①

Anchorage

Valdez

Whitehorse

①

Kenai Soldotna

Whittier

Cordova

WRANGELL–ST. ELIAS NAT'L PARK AND PRESERVE

⑦

BRITISH COLUMBIA

Dillingham

① Seward

King Salmon

Homer Halibut Cove

Seldovia

Prince William Sound

KENAI FJORDS NAT'L PARK

Yakutat & Hubbard Glacier

★ Juneau

KATMAI NAT'L PARK AND PRESERVE

Kodiak

Alaska Marine Highway

Gulf of Alaska

ANIAKCHAK NAT'L MONUMENT AND PRESERVE

Kodiak Island

Southeast Alaska, See Inset

Prince Rupert, B.C.

OCEAN

| Paved Road |
| ① State or Provincial Route |
| Dirt Road |

0   100 mi

0   100 km

N

To Vancouver & Seattle →

Yukon River

Kuskokwim River

Cook Inlet

LAKE CLARK NAT'L PARK AND PRESERVE

Glaciers: An Intro to the Ice

Along with whales, glaciers are the big drawing card on Alaska cruises, and with good reason: They're truly awesome. To see one spread between the bulk of massive mountains, flowing down into the sea, is to quite literally see how our world came to be. As the naturalist John Muir wrote while standing near an Alaskan glacier in the late 19th century, "Standing here with facts so fresh and telling and held up so vividly before us . . . one learns that the world, though made, is yet being made; that this is still the morning of creation."

HOW GLACIERS FORM Glaciers form when snow accumulates over time at high altitudes. Successive snowfalls add more and more weight, compacting the snow underneath into extremely dense **glacial ice.** As the accumulation assumes mass, forming what is known as an **ice field,** gravity takes over and the ice field begins to flow very slowly downhill through the lowest, easiest passage. The glacier's enormous mass sculpts the landscape as it goes, grinding the shale and other rock and pushing rubble and silt ahead and to the sides. This sediment is known as **moraine.** *Terminal moraine* is the accumulation of rubble at the front of a glacier; *lateral moraine* lines the sides of glaciers. A dark area in a glacier's center—seen when two glaciers flow together, pushing their ice and crushed rubble together—is *median moraine.*

TYPES OF GLACIERS Glaciers come in several different varieties. **Tidewater glaciers** are the kind most often seen on postcards; they spill down out of the mountains and run all the way to the sea. **Piedmont glaciers** are two glaciers that have run together into one. When seen from above, piedmonts resemble a highway interchange, edged by road slush, with the median moraine looking like lane dividers. There are also mountain or **alpine glaciers,** which are confined by surrounding mountain terrain and unable to flow. Other types—such as *hanging glaciers* that spill over rounded hillsides, *valley glaciers* that are confined by valley walls, and *cirque glaciers* that sit in basins and are usually circular (as opposed to river-shaped)—are essentially variants on these three main varieties.

GLACIAL BEHAVIOR Glaciers are essentially rivers of ice that flow continually downhill. When they reach the sea, the effects of water and gravity cause **calving,** a phenomenon where large chunks of their ice face break off from the mass and crash into the sea, producing a sound like two 1,000-foot bowling balls colliding. The ice that's calved off floats away as an **iceberg.** Calvings are always a high point on a cruise.

Depending on temperature and the rate of precipitation, glaciers may either **advance** or **retreat.** Think of glaciers as human bodies and snowfall as calories—when the accumulation of snowfall (and resultant glacial ice) is greater than the amount of ice lost to melting and calving, the glacier grows, which is known as *advancing*. When the opposite occurs—when melting and calving outpace new buildup of ice—the glacier is said to be *retreating*. Glaciers can also be in a state of equilibrium, where the amount of snowfall roughly equals the amount of melt-off. Even where this is the case, the glacier is still a slow-moving river, always flowing downhill—it's just that its total length remains the same, with new ice replacing old at a more or less constant rate.

In recent years, **global warming** has begun to have a noticeable effect on Alaska's glaciers. All over the state—and in other northern lands such as Greenland and the Canadian Arctic—temperatures have risen three to five times more than the global average, causing glaciers, sea ice, and permafrost to melt. Juneau's popular Mendenhall Glacier, for instance, lost 656 feet of its ice in 2004 and another 269 feet in 2005, and scientists project that it will recede away from Mendenhall Lake in little more than 10 years, retreating farther and farther into the mountains. Without action on climate change, the great glaciers could disappear forever.

AN ICEBERG BY ANY OTHER NAME When a glacier calves, the icebergs it forms are classified differently depending on their size, a system that allows one ship's captain to warn another of the relative ice hazard. Very large chunks are officially called **icebergs**; pieces of moderate size (usually 7–15 ft. across) are known as **bergy bits; growlers** are slightly smaller still, at less than 7 feet across, with less than 3 feet showing above water; and **brash ice** consists of any random smaller chunks. And remember the adage: What you're seeing is only the tip—most of the berg is below the water.

By the way, glacial ice isn't blue. It may look blue—and a startling, electric blue at that—but it's really a trick of the light. The ice absorbs all colors of the spectrum *except* blue, which is then reflected away, making the ice itself appear to be blue.

THE VIEW FROM ABOVE While glaciers are impressive enough from the water, it takes a **glacier flightseeing trip** to really drive home how completely stupendous they are, stretching away into the mountains as far as the eye can see. It's literally like getting a glimpse back into the ice age. The trips are expensive, yes, but definitely worth it. On many trips, your helicopter flightseeing will be combined with time spent down on the glacial ice, where you'll have a chance to walk around on the surface. It's like being on Mars.

If you want to explore glaciers further, the National Snow and Ice Data Center has a great glacier website, with many photos, a glossary, and other data, at **http://nsidc.org/glaciers**.

Cruisetours—'Cause All Alaska Ain't on Water

Most folks who go to the trouble of getting to a place as far off the beaten path as Alaska try to stick around for a while once they're there. Knowing this, the cruise lines have set themselves up in the land-tour business as well, offering a number of land-based extensions that can be tacked on to your cruise experience, either before you sail or after.

ANCHORAGE-DENALI-FAIRBANKS The most popular cruisetour, a typical Anchorage-Denali-Fairbanks package might include a 7-night Vancouver-Anchorage cruise, followed by 2 nights in Anchorage and a scenic ride in a private railcar into **Denali National Park** for 2 more nights at one or another of the cruise line's lodges. A full day in the park allows guests to view the staggeringly beautiful wilderness expanse and its wildlife. If you're lucky, the cloud gods will part to give you a look at **Mount McKinley,** North America's highest peak at 20,320 feet. From there, you'll go by train to **Fairbanks,** spending 2 more days. Fairbanks itself isn't much to look at, but the activities available in outlying areas are fantastic, and include paddle-wheel day cruises on the Chena and Tanana rivers, jet-boat rides, and excursions to gold mines and dredges. Passengers typically fly home from Fairbanks. A shorter variation of that itinerary might skip Fairbanks and return to Anchorage for departure. Princess's cruisetours bypass Anchorage on the way north, giving more time in the interior.

YUKON TERRITORY Tours into Canada's Yukon Territory typically combine a 3- or 4-day cruise between Vancouver and Juneau/Skagway with a land program into the Klondike. En route, passengers travel by rail, riverboat, motorcoach, and possibly air. Tours typically include overnight stops in

HUBBARD GLACIER

Hubbard lies at the northern end of **Yakutat Bay** and has two claims to fame: It's the largest tidewater glacier on the North American continent (with Alaska's widest ice face, at about 6 miles across), and it's one of the fastest moving glaciers in Alaska. In the mid-1980s it moved so fast it created a wall across the mouth of **Russell Fjord,** one of the inlets lining Yakutat Bay. That effectively turned the fjord into a lake and trapped hundreds of migratory marine creatures inside. After causing such a hubbub, it receded to its original position again several months later. It's still an active mother, calving off a substantial amount of ice.

PRINCE WILLIAM SOUND & COLLEGE FJORD

Located directly south of Anchorage on the bottom side of the Kenai Peninsula, Prince William Sound suffered mightily following the *Exxon Valdez* oil spill in 1989, which killed innumerable marine creatures and birds. Today, following decades of cleanup, the area is on the rebound, with whales, harbor seals, eagles, sea lions, sea otters, puffins, and fish all returned to its waters. It's truly one of Alaska's most appealing wilderness areas, surrounded on three sides by the Chugach Mountains and only sparsely populated by humans, most of them congregated in a few isolated towns such as Valdez, Whittier, Cordova, and the Native villages of Tatitlek and Chenega.

Whitehorse, the territorial capital, and **Dawson City,** a remote, picture-perfect gold rush town, then cross the Alaska border near Beaver Creek, travel to Fairbanks, and from there go through Denali to Anchorage. The tour can be taken in either direction.

CANADIAN ROCKIES A Canadian Rockies cruisetour offers some of the finest mountain scenery on earth. It's not just that the glacier-carved mountains are astonishingly dramatic and beautiful; it's also that there are hundreds and hundreds of miles of this wonderful wilderness high country. Between them, **Banff National Park** and **Jasper National Park** preserve much of this mountain beauty. Other national and provincial parks make accessible other vast and equally spectacular regions of the Rockies, as well as portions of the nearby Columbia and Selkirk mountain ranges. The beautiful **Lake Louise,** colored deep green from its mineral content, is located 35 miles north of Banff.

KENAI PENINSULA The Kenai Peninsula, located just across a narrow channel from Anchorage, has long been known as the city's natural playground, packed with opportunities for fishing, hiking, sightseeing, kayaking, and wildlife watching. Cruisetours that include the areas are typically 2-night add-ons to a regular Denali-Fairbanks route, though Holland America (one of the leaders in the cruisetour market) offers a dedicated 13-night Kenai-centric trip, with nights spent in Homer, Cooper Landing, and Anchorage either before or after your 7-night cruise.

Other cruisetour options include an add-on to **Wrangell–St. Elias National Park,** east of Anchorage.

College Fjord is in the northern sector of Prince William Sound, roughly midway between Whittier and Valdez. It's not one of the more spectacular Alaska glacier areas, being very much overshadowed by Glacier Bay, Yakutat Bay (for Hubbard Glacier), and others, but it's scenic enough to merit a place on a lot of cruise itineraries, mostly for **Harvard Glacier,** which sits at its head. The fjord was named by members of the 1899 Harriman Expedition, which saddled the glaciers lining College Fjord and neighboring Harriman Fjord with the names of prominent eastern schools—hence Harvard, Vassar, Williams, Yale, and so on. Perhaps the most spectacular of the sound's ice faces is **Columbia Glacier,** whose surface spreads over more than 400 square miles and whose tidewater frontage is nearly 6 miles across. Columbia is receding faster than most of its Alaska counterparts. Scientists reckon it will retreat more than 20 miles in the next 20 to 50 years, adding yet another deep fjord to Prince William Sound's collection.

2 Haines

Sitting near the northern end of the Lynn Canal, Haines (pop. 2,500) is a small, laid-back Alaska town, without the kind of self-referential tourist gloss that's so evident in neighboring Skagway, about 15 miles farther upwater. Despite a dramatic setting amid the peaks of the Fairweather Mountain Range, few ships come here, partly because of a shortage of large, deepwater docks, partly because of a shortage of large, obvious attractions. If you're sailing on a ship that does, you'll be experiencing a town that maintains its local vibe well.

Haines was established in 1879 by Presbyterian missionary S. Hall Young and naturalist John Muir as a place to convert the Chilkoot and Chilkat Tlingit tribes to Christianity. They named it for Mrs. F. E. Haines, secretary of the Presbyterian National Committee, who had raised the funds for their exploration. The Tlingits called the place *Dei-Shu,* or "end of the trail," while traders knew it as Chilkoot. The U.S. military arrived in the early part of the 20th century and constructed **Fort William H. Seward,** a very 19th-century-looking group of white clapboard structures arranged around a rectangular parade ground. The fort was decommissioned after World War II, and today its structures have been turned into private homes, B&Bs, and arts and performances spaces, some of them devoted to Native culture (see below). A re-created Tlingit tribal house sits at the center of the parade ground.

Ships that don't stop in Haines regularly offer excursions to the town from Skagway, traveling by boat. Some are simple tours of town attractions (cost: $85–$99); others combine a quick tour of town with a float or jet-boat ride through the **Chilkat Bald Eagle Preserve** (see below; the cost of these trips from Skagway is typically $165–$175) or **kayaking** in the waters around town ($165).

COMING ASHORE Ships tie up to the **Port Chilkoot Dock,** directly opposite Fort Seward and ½ mile from downtown. Visitor information is available at the dock.

GETTING AROUND It's easy to explore Fort Seward and the town on foot, or you can rent a bike at **Sockeye Cycle,** 24 Portage St. in Fort Seward, just uphill from the dock (© **877/292-4154** or 907/766-2869; www.cyclealaska.com). Rentals cost $14 for 2 hours, $25 for 4 hours, or $35 for 8 hours, helmet and lock included. They also offer bike tours of the area.

BEST CRUISE LINE SHORE EXCURSIONS

Chilkat Bald Eagle Preserve Float Trip ($99, 4 hr.): Head out to the Chilkat Preserve (see below) by bus, then suit up in boots and a life vest for a gentle float by rubber raft down the Chilkat River. An expert guide both rows and provides commentary on the area's natural environment, steering the raft close to shore to spot animal tracks and keeping an eye out for moose, bears, eagles, and wolves. A **jet-boat trip** ($99, 4 hr.) is also available on a different section of the river, and the trips generally report wildlife sightings.

Chilkoot Lake Bicycle Adventure ($87, 3 hr.): After driving to your start point, you'll ride 8 miles along the shore of Lutak Inlet, where the river meets the sea. Highlights include some amazing views of the lake, glaciers, waterfalls, and mountains, and a chance at spotting eagles and bears.

Offbeat Haines ($30, 2 hr.): Where else but Haines can you take a tour that includes the world's one and only hammer museum (see below), a visit to an artists' studio out in Mud Bay, and a stop at a set created for the Disney film *White Fang.* Includes a 10-mile drive along the Chilkat River.

Valley of the Eagles Golf ($79, 3½ hr.): Outside town, along the banks of the Chilkat River, the 9-hole, par-36 Valley of the Eagles Golf Links give you the rare opportunity of being able to say you golfed in Alaska. The course meanders through typical Alaskan landscape and offers beautiful views of the Chilkat Mountains.

Taste of Haines Tour ($59, 2 hr.): Visit the Haines Brewing Company, the smallest brewery in Alaska, for a sample and a talk with the brewmaster, then head to a local smoked-salmon shop to sample and learn how the stuff is prepared.

Best of Haines by Classic Car ($54, 1 hr.): Explore Haines in style in a 1930s or 1940s vintage automobile. The entertaining guides share the history of the area, and you'll get an insight into how Hainesians live and make their livings.

ON YOUR OWN: WITHIN WALKING DISTANCE

The **Alaska Indian Arts Cultural Center,** located in the old fort hospital on the south side of the Fort Seward parade grounds (© **907/766-2160;** www.alaskaindianarts.com), has a small gallery selling traditional artwork and prints, plus a carvers' workshop where you may be able to see totem carving in progress. Between the fort and the town center, the **American Bald Eagle Foundation and Natural History Museum,** Haines Highway at 2nd Avenue (© **907/766-3094;** www.baldeagles.org), is essentially a huge diorama representing 48,000 acres of the Chilkat Bald Eagle Preserve, with more than 180 stuffed eagles and other animals. Admission is $3. The place has a real folk-art quality that's entirely appropriate for Haines. Ditto for Dave and Carol Pahl's quirkily remarkable **Hammer Museum** on Main Street (© **907/766-2374;** www.hammermuseum. org), which displays more than 1,500 completely different hammers from all over the world, including whale-blubber hammers, bookbinders' hammers, little hammers used by 1920s nightclub patrons to applaud performers, and Tlingit ceremonial hammers. Some are displayed in action, wielded by life-sized mannequins donated by the Smithsonian Institution. Admission costs $3. Also on Main Street, down near the small-boat harbor, the small **Sheldon Museum and Cultural Center** (© **907/766-2366;** www. sheldonmuseum.org) was established by local shopkeepers Steve and Bess Sheldon around 1925. It has a great collection of Hainesiana: Tlingit artifacts, gold-rush-era weaponry, military memorabilia, and more. Admission is $3.

ON YOUR OWN: BEYOND THE PORT AREA

Haines is probably the best place on earth to see bald eagles. About 20 miles outside town, the **Chilkat Bald Eagle Preserve** protects 48,000 acres of river bottom along the Chilkat River. Summer cruisers will miss the biggest eagle season (Oct to mid-Dec, when up to 3,000 eagles gather in the cottonwood trees, waiting to swoop down on late-spawning salmon), but a healthy 200 to 400 are in residence the rest of the year. You'll really need to take a float-trip shore excursion to see the place in the limited time you have here. The water is gentle, so much so that if your raft gets stuck, the guide will just hop out and push. Eagle sightings are practically guaranteed, and occasionally you might spot a moose along the shoreline too.

SHOPPING

More than a dozen galleries and shops are located around Fort Seward (mostly concentrating on Native arts) and the downtown area.

3 Icy Strait Point

Located on Chichagof Island about 50 miles west of Juneau and 22 miles southeast of Glacier Bay, **Icy Strait Point** (www.icystraitpoint.com) is a stop on some Holland America, Princess, Celebrity, and Royal Caribbean cruises. Unlike all the other ports in this chapter, though, it's not a town; rather, it's a self-contained destination owned and managed by Tlingit Indians from the nearby village of Hoonah and designed specifically for cruise passengers. Opened to ships in 2004, the site is centered around a restored 1930s salmon cannery that now houses a museum, a 1930s cannery display, a restaurant, and shops. Principally, though, Icy Strait Point is a destination for shore excursions.

BEST CRUISE LINE SHORE EXCURSIONS

Tribal Dance & Cultural Legends ($36, 1 hr.): At the Native Heritage Center Theater, near the cannery, a group of Huna Tlingit performs traditional song, dance, and storytelling.

Whale & Marine Mammals Cruise ($125, 2½ hr.): Sail aboard a sightseeing boat through Icy Strait to Point Adolphus, one of Alaska's best whale-watching sites. An onboard naturalist discusses marine life as you scan for humpbacks and orcas, Stellar sea lions, and harbor seals.

Remote Bush Exploration & Brown Bear Search ($104, 2½ hr.): Head toward the Spasski River Valley by bus, then take a short hike on gravel and boardwalk paths to viewing platforms that provide opportunities for viewing bald eagles, land otters, Sitka black-tail deer, and Alaska coastal brown bears—aka Grizzlies.

Glacier Bay Flightseeing ($299, 1¾ hr.): Take off in a fixed-wing plane from Hoonah Airport and spend an hour flying above Glacier Bay, including the glaciers, waterfalls, deep crevasses, and new forests of the park, as well as the humpback whale feeding grounds of Point Adolphus.

Saltwater Salmon Fishing ($199, 3 hr.): Board a cabin cruiser for a fishing excursion in Icy Strait, where five species of salmon make for some great angling. (*Note:* A $20 fishing license and $10 king-salmon tag are extra. For an additional charge, your catch can be packed and shipped to your home.)

Halibut Fishing ($239, 3⅓ hr.): Head out into Icy Strait for a little halibut fishing. See above for licensing requirements and fees.

Hoonah Bike Tour ($65, 2 hr.): Take an 8-mile ride through Alaska's largest Tlingit village, home to about 900 residents. Along the way, your guide will discuss the town's history and present-day life.

4 Juneau

Juneau's a great town. Fronted by the busy Gastineau Channel and backed by 3,819-foot Mount Juneau and 3,576-foot Mount Roberts, its location is beyond picture-perfect. But it's the city's quirks we appreciate, like the fact that it's the capital of the state but is completely surrounded by water, forest, and the massive Juneau Icefield, and is therefore unreachable by land. Or the fact that the whole town lies at the base of a landslide zone, and has numerous treeless hillsides to prove it. Or that at one time a bull terrier named Patsy Ann was the official town greeter, trotting down to the docks whenever a ship came in. (Long dead now, she's memorialized with a bronze statue in Marine Park, where the cruise ships dock.) We even appreciate the love-hate relationship the town has with the cruise industry, with many lamenting the fact that downtown and the Egan Expressway are completely overrun by visitors and tour buses from late May through September. Democracy thrives on debate, and we can't argue with the locals' concerns: On any given day, four or five cruise ships may be in port, rang-ing from megaships to microships. That means about 6,000 people are added daily to a population that numbers only 31,000 total—and those are spread out across the greater town's 3,255-square-mile area. It makes for a bit of chaos.

Tourism woes aside, modern Juneau is a product of Alaska's golden past. It was no more than a fishing outpost for local Tlingit Indians until 1880, when gold was dis-covered in a creek off the Gastineau Channel by Chief Kowee of the Auk Tlingit clan. Kowee passed the information on to German engineer George Pilz in return for 100 warm blankets and a promise of work for his tribe, and agreed to lead prospectors Joe Juneau and Richard Harris to the find. Mines quickly sprang up on both sides of the channel, including the **Alaska-Juneau Mine,** known locally simply as the A-J, which produced a whopping 3.5 million ounces of gold before it closed in 1944. You can still see its remains up on the slope of Mount Roberts.

Outside of town, the big attraction is **Mendenhall Glacier.** Twelve miles long and 1½ miles wide, it's the most visited glacier in the world.

COMING ASHORE   Both large and small ships dock right in the downtown area, along Marine Way. Occasionally, overcrowding might mean a ship has to anchor in the channel and tender people to shore. A visitor information center is located in a green building right on the dock, near the base of the Mount Roberts Tram. The Patsy Ann statue is on the dock at Marine Park. Pat her head and consider yourself greeted.

GETTING AROUND   Most of the in-town sites are within walking distance of the pier, though some of it is tough going due to hills. The **Juneau Trolley Car Company** (© **907/789-4342;** www.juneautrolley.com) also provides narrated tours of the downtown area. You can get off and on as you like at various marked sites. Fares are $14 adults, $11 kids. Visits to the Mendenhall Glacier and other sights along the Egan Expressway will require an excursion or a taxi. You'll find the latter waiting at the pier.

BEST CRUISE LINE SHORE EXCURSIONS

The number of excursions typically offered in Juneau is fairly stupefying, but that's because a lot of mixing and matching is going on: a glacier visit paired with a salmon bake or a horseback trek, a salmon bake paired with a flightseeing adventure, or a half-dozen different helicopter/glacier options. Here are some of the best.

Glacier Helicopter Tour ($265–$399, 2½–6½ hr.): This is one of the very best shore excursions we've ever taken. After transferring to the airport by bus, guests board heli-copters for a flight that follows the flowing ice of Mendenhall Glacier high into the mountains. While glaciers are impressive enough from the water, this trip gives you an idea of how magnificent they really are. After about 20 minutes of flightseeing, your helicopter will touch down on the glacial ice, where (outfitted in special boots pro-vided by the helicopter company) you'll have a chance to walk around on the surface. Different packages give you more or less time on the glacier, with some options adding in additional activities, such as the **Glacier Dog-Sled Expedition** that combines a flight over the Juneau Icefield with a landing on either the Norris or the Mendenhall glacier, where you'll board dog sleds with an Iditarod veteran ($499, 3½ hr.). The **Helicopter Glacier Trek** ($399, 4¼ hr.) and **Extended Helicopter Glacier Trek** ($499, 6½ hr.) involve a flight onto the Juneau Icefield followed by either 2 or 3 hours of hiking and climbing in rugged terrain, descending ice walls, and exploring glacial pools and ice caves along the way. It's one of the most amazing shore excursions we've ever done.

Mendenhall Glacier & Salmon Bake ($70, 4 hr.): Three for the price of one: a visit to the Macaulay Salmon Hatchery to learn about rearing or raising salmon; a visit to Mendenhall, where you can stick to the interpretive center or get closer to the ice on one of several different trails; and an all-you-can-eat salmon bake in a rustic setting, with folk-music entertainment, the ruins of an old mine to explore, and lush rainforest all around. A less expensive option ($40, 3 hr.) visits only the hatchery and glacier, while a more expensive one ($85, 4 hr.) replaces the salmon bake with a bus tour of the city.

Bike & Brew Tour ($89, 4½ hr.): This bicycle tour sets off outside town along Fritz Cove Road, offering views of picturesque Auke Bay and the Mendenhall Glacier. The 11-mile ride ends at the Alaska Brewing Company for a tour and sampling of the wares.

Mendenhall Glacier Float Trip ($115, 4 hr.): On the shore of Mendenhall Lake you'll board 10-person rafts. An experienced oarsman will guide you from there out past icebergs and into the Mendenhall River, where you'll encounter moderate rapids and stunning views. Expect a snack of smoked salmon and reindeer sausage somewhere along the way.

Mendenhall Lake Canoe Adventure ($130, 3½ hr.): Board 12-person Native canoes, paddling out onto the lake's water while a guide shares natural history and Native stories about the surrounding scenery and wildlife. You'll pull into shore near roaring Nugget Falls, just a few yards from the glacier face.

Alaska-Gastineau Gold Mine Tour ($65, 3½ hr.): Located just south of town, the Alaska-Gastineau mine was once one of the world's richest. Today, you can don a hard hat and venture down a 360-foot mine tunnel, where experienced miners demonstrate hard-rock mining techniques and explain mine operations. Dress warm: It's cold down there.

ON YOUR OWN: WITHIN WALKING DISTANCE

Juneau's town center is compact and fun to walk around, but if you want to escape the crowd or get an overview (literally), take the **Mount Roberts Tramway** (© **888/461-8726** or 907/463-3412; www.goldbelttours.com) from the docks up to the clear air and overwhelming views at the 1,760-foot tree line. The ride takes only 6 minutes, but it's like entering another world. At the top there's a reception center with a restaurant/bar, a gift shop (of course), and a theater showing a pretty good film about Tlingit culture, but try not to linger here too long. Instead, head outside to the network of paths that let on to really incredible views as you pass through a fascinating alpine ecosystem. If you're energetic, you can start a 6-mile round-trip to the Mount Roberts summit (at 3,819 ft.), though there are also several shorter loops. Watch your footing up here, especially if the trails are wet or covered in snow—a possibility in the shoulder seasons. Tickets are $25 adults, $14 children 12 and under, and allow unlimited rides. Most ships offer the tram as an excursion for the same price, but we suggest waiting till you get to town and buying a ticket on your own, as it's not worth the ride if you arrive on an overcast day.

Heading into town, the faux-notorious and realistically touristy **Red Dog Saloon,** 278 S. Franklin St. (© **907/463-3658;** www.reddogsaloon.cc), stands right at the intersection where Egan Drive heads left toward Mendenhall Glacier and Franklin Street continues up into town. Through its swinging doors you'll find a slightly contrived but still infectious frontier atmosphere, with a sawdust-covered floor, live music, and walls covered with memorabilia and messages from previous visitors. You'll also find current visitors—lots of them. Locals and less touristy tourists are more apt to hang out up the street at **The Alaskan Bar,** 167 S. Franklin St. (© **907/586-1000**), a two-story Victorian barroom in an authentic gold rush hotel. Down Egan, **The Hangar,** 2 Marine Way (© **907/586-5018**), also serves a good brew, as well as decent pizza.

Continue down Egan, and make a right at Whittier to get to the **Alaska State Museum** (© **907/465-2901;** www.museums.state.ak.us) and its large collection of art and artifacts. Opened as a territorial museum in 1900, it has a wildlife exhibit, reminders of the city's mining and fisheries heritage, and a first-class collection of artifacts reflecting the state's Russian history and Native cultures. A clan house in the Alaska Native Gallery contains the kinds of art you'd find in the real thing during a memorial potlatch. Admission is $5. Not far off, at the intersection of Main and Fourth streets, the fun little **Juneau-Douglas City Museum** (© **907/586-3572;** www.juneau.lib.ak.us/parksrec/museum) displays artifacts and photographs from the city's pioneer and mining history and Tlingit culture, with special exhibits changing annually. The plaza in front is where the 49-star U.S. flag was first raised in 1959, when Alaska got its statehood before Hawaii. Admission is $4. About 3 blocks away, at Fifth and Gold, the tiny, octagonal **St. Nicholas Russian Orthodox Church** was built in 1893 by local Tlingits who, under pressure to convert to Christianity, chose the only faith that allowed them to keep their own language.

ON YOUR OWN: BEYOND THE PORT AREA

About 13 miles from downtown, at the head of Mendenhall Valley, the **Mendenhall Glacier** (© **907/789-0097;** www.fs.fed.us/r10/tongass/districts/mendenhall) glows bluish white, looming above the suburbs like an ice age monster that missed the general extinction. Mendenhall is a truly impressive sight, with its ice face dipping down into Mendenhall Lake and calving off truck-size bergs, but it's also the most easily accessible glacier in Alaska, with great views from the parking lot across the lake to the glacier's face, and a wheelchair-accessible trail that leads to the water's edge. The land near the parking lot shows the signs of the glacier's recent passage: little topsoil, stunted vegetation, and, in many places, bare rock that shows the scratch marks of the glacier's movement. It's still moving, too, and fast: Scientists predict that, due to global warming, the glacier will recede from the lake in little more than 10 years. Trails of various lengths depart from the Forest Service visitor center, the easiest being a half-mile nature trail, the longest being two fairly steep, 3.5-mile hikes that approach each side of the glacier. The visitor center itself contains a glacier museum with excellent explanatory models, computerized displays, and ranger talks. Admission is $3.

Along the Egan Expressway about 3 miles from downtown, the **Macaulay Salmon Hatchery,** 2697 Channel Dr. (© **877/463-2486** or 907/463-5114; www.dipac.net), has a visitor center where you can watch the whole process of harvesting and fertilizing salmon eggs. The resultant offspring are later released back into the wild. If that doesn't float your boat, try the nearby **Alaskan Brewing Company** (© **907/780-5866;** www.alaskanbeer.com). Located off Egan at Vanderbilt Hill Road (then right on Anka St. and right again on Shaune Dr.), they offer low-key tours with a sampling of beer at the end, and their logo-wear is also pretty hip. The brewery started small in 1986 when Geoff and Marcy Larson had the idea of bringing a local gold-rush-era brew back to life. It worked, and now Alaskan Amber and several other brews are found everywhere in Alaska, and are mighty tasty too.

SHOPPING

The shops near the dock are mostly aimed at tourists, with cheap souvenir stores mixed in with jewelry shops, but there are some good picks among the litter, including **The Raven's Journey,** 435 S. Franklin St. (© **907/463-4686**), selling Tlingit and other Northwest Indian art; the **Decker Gallery,** 233 S. Franklin St. (© **907/463-5536**), selling the works of local artist Rie Muñoz; and **Galligaskins,** 219 S. Franklin St. (© **800/586-5861**), selling clothing with Alaska-theme designs. If you're in need of reading material, this is probably the best port to buy a book, with several decent shops located downtown. If you're in need of smoked salmon (and who ain't?), **Taku Smokeries,** 550 S. Franklin St. (© **800/582-5122;** www.takusmokeries.com), will ship it anywhere in the U.S.

5 Ketchikan

Ketchikan sits just north of the Canadian border, and like many border towns it wears its mercantile heart on its sleeve. They call it "Alaska's first city" because it's the first port visited on most northbound cruises, but the way people throng the port area's gift shops, you'd think it was the last chance they had to use their credit cards before Judgment Day. Here's our advice: Walk down the gangway, take three deep breaths, and say to yourself, "I do not need to shop." Instead, walk right past the shops and head for one of the town's several **totem-pole** parks or take an excursion to **Misty Fjords.** When you get back you can spend some time poking around the galleries and shops on Creek Street.

Shopping aside, the town's port area is interesting in that much of it is either landfill or sitting on stilts above the water. The town is also notable for being one of the soggiest in Alaska: The average annual rainfall is about 160 inches (more than 13 ft.), and has topped 200 inches in its most intense years.

COMING ASHORE   Ships dock right at the pier in downtown Ketchikan.

GETTING AROUND   Ketchikan's downtown port area is completely flat and walkable. Taxis are available at the pier if you want to go out to Totem Bight Park on your own.

BEST CRUISE LINE SHORE EXCURSIONS

Misty Fjords Flightseeing ($240–$319, 2–4½ hr.): Everyone gets a window seat aboard the floatplanes that run these flightseeing jaunts over mysterious, primordial Misty Fjords National Monument (see "Cruising Alaska's Natural Wonders," on p. 610). The less expensive options tool around, make a water landing so you can step out onto the pontoon, and then return to Ketchikan by air. The more expensive (and better) option transfers you to a tour boat after landing at the monument, allowing you to see more of it from sea level. The boat takes you back to Ketchikan at the end.

Saxman Native Village Tour ($55, 2½ hr.): This Native village, situated about 2½ miles outside Ketchikan, is home to hundreds of Tlingit, Tsimshian, and Haida, and is a center for the revival of Native arts and culture. The tour includes a storytelling session and a performance by the Cape Fox Dancers at the Beaver Clan House, as well as a guided walk through the grounds to see the totem poles and learn their stories. Craftspeople are sometimes on hand in the working sheds to demonstrate totem-pole carving. A short bus tour of Ketchikan is usually appended to the end of the trip.

Rainforest Wildlife Sanctuary ($80, 2½ hr.): After an 8-mile coastal drive you'll do a half-mile hike with a naturalist guide, trying to spot eagles, bears, seals, and various birdlife. After, you'll have an opportunity to feed Alaskan reindeer, watch a totem-pole carver at work, and take a tour of a historic sawmill.

Sport-Fishing ($189, 5 hr.): If catching salmon is your goal, Ketchikan is a good spot to do it. Chartered fishing boats come with tackle, bait, fishing gear, and crew to help you strike king and coho around the end of June, or pink, chum, and silver from July to mid-September. *Note:* A $20 fishing license and $10 king-salmon tag are extra.

Tatoosh Island Sea Kayaking ($140, 4½ hr.): There are typically two kayaking excursions offered in Ketchikan: this one (which requires you to take a van and motorized boat to the islands before starting your 90-min. paddle) and a trip that starts from right beside the cruise ship docks. Of the two, this one is far more enjoyable, getting you out into a wilder area rather than just sticking to the busy port waters. The scenery is incredible, and you have a good chance of spotting bald eagles, leaping salmon, and seals, which may be swimming around your boat or just basking on the rocks.

Totem Bight Historical Park & City Tour ($39, 2½ hr.): This tour takes you by bus around Ketchikan and through the Tongass National Forest to see a historic Native fish camp where a ceremonial clan house and totem poles sit amid the rainforest. A fair amount of walking is involved.

The Great Alaskan Lumberjack Show ($34, 1½ hr.): Touristy fun: Watch lumberjacks compete in logrolling, speed climbing, tree topping, chainsaw carving, and all of the other skills every lumberjack needs. The amphitheater, located behind Salmon Landing, just a few hundred yards from the pier, has covered grandstands to keep you from getting soggy. If you don't book this as an excursion, you can still buy tickets at the door for the same price.

ON YOUR OWN: WITHIN WALKING DISTANCE

Near the pier, the **Southeast Alaska Discovery Center,** 50 Main St. (© **907/228-6220;** www.fs.fed.us/r10/tongass/districts/discoverycenter), houses the best museum in the region for illustrating the interaction of the region's ecology and human society, both Native and white. An auditorium shows a high-tech slide show, and there are also information desks and a good bookstore. Admission to the exhibits is $5.

The centerpiece of downtown Ketchikan is **Creek Street,** a row of quaint wooden houses built on pilings above a busy salmon stream. Today, the narrow, boardwalked street is filled mainly with boutiques, funky restaurants, and galleries specializing in offbeat pieces by local artists, but back in the day it was Ketchikan's notorious and semicondoned red-light district, with more than 30 brothels lining the waterway. That all came to an end in the mid-1950s, and today all that's left of it is the touristy **Dolly's House museum,** 24 Creek St. (© **907/225-6329**), once the establishment of a madam who worked under the name Dolly Arthur. Like the house's old clientele, you have to pay to get inside. We don't know what the old patrons had to shell out, but today it'll cost you $5. At the end of Creek Street, a **funicular** takes you uphill to the Westmark Cape Fox Lodge, which offers nice views. Walk through the lobby and follow the signs to the **Married Men's Trail,** allegedly a route taken by local men to reach the "spawning grounds" below. It makes for a nice little hike back into town.

Near its bottom, the Married Men's Trail branches off, left to Creek Street and right to Park Avenue. At Park, an observation deck above the artificial **salmon ladder** lets you watch the determined fish battle the current to their spawning grounds at the top of Ketchikan Creek. Walk about ⅓ mile up Park Avenue and make a right at Herring Way to reach the indoor **Totem Heritage Center,** 601 Deermount St. (© **907/225-5900;** www.city.ketchikan.ak.us/departments/museums/totem.html), built by the city in 1976 to house a fine collection of 33 original totem poles from the 19th century, retrieved from the Tlingit Indian villages of Tongass and Village Islands and the Haida village of Old Kasaan. The Tsimshian people are also represented in some exhibits. The poles have not been restored, and are displayed mostly unpainted, many with the grass and moss still attached from when they were rescued from the elements. Totem poles were never meant to be maintained or repainted—they generally disintegrate after about 70 years, and were constantly replaced—but these were preserved to help keep the culture alive. A high ceiling and muted lighting highlight the spirituality of the art. Well-trained guides are on hand to explain what you're looking at, and there are good interpretive signs, as well as authentic Native crafts for sale. Admission is $5. Across the creek, the **Deer Mountain Tribal Hatchery and Eagle Center,** 1158 Salmon Rd. (© **907/228-5530;** www.kictribe.org/Hatchery/Hatchery.htm), raises and releases young salmon to supplement the natural runs. You can view them in holding pools and learn about their lifecycle, then wander over to the huge outdoor cages, home to injured eagles that were nursed back to health and are unable to return to the wild. Admission is $9, free for kids 12 and under.

Okay, now you can go shopping.

ON YOUR OWN: BEYOND THE PORT AREA

About 10 miles outside town, **Totem Bight State Historical Park,** 9883 N. Tongass Hwy. (© **907/247-8574;** www.dnr.state.ak.us/parks/units/totembgh.htm), presents poles and a clan house carved beginning in 1938. Working under the New Deal's Civilian Conservation Corps, Native craftsmen used traditional tools to copy fragments of historic poles that had mostly rotted away, thereby helping to preserve an aspect of Tlingit and Haida culture that had essentially been outlawed until that time. The setting, purportedly the site of a traditional fishing camp, is a peaceful spot at the end of a short walk through the woods. Admission is free. Closer to town (about 2½ miles south of the pier on the Tongass Hwy.), **Saxman Indian Village** (© **907/225-4846;** www.capefoxtours.com) has artifacts similar to those at Totem Bight Park, but with an added resource: You can see carvers work in the building to the right of the park. The place is set up more for people on excursions (see above), but you can also visit the studio and the poles without joining a tour, using a pamphlet that costs $1.50. Note, however, that interpretive materials are scant compared to those at Totem Bight.

SHOPPING

You'll wonder whether the town should be renamed Kitschikan if you spend much time in the many souvenir stores that line Front Street and the rest of the port area, but there are a few decent shops among them. Our favorites are all on **Creek Street,** which has galleries, kitchenware shops (with moose-shaped cookie molds), bookshops, and other appealing places to drop some change.

6 Sitka

Geographically speaking, Sitka's not on the Inside Passage at all, but rather on the Pacific coast of Baranof Island, sheltered by a fringe of islands at the head of Sitka Sound. Its name, in fact, comes from the Tlingit *Shee Atika,* which means "people on the outside of Shee." Small ships can thread in through narrow Peril Strait, which separates Baranof

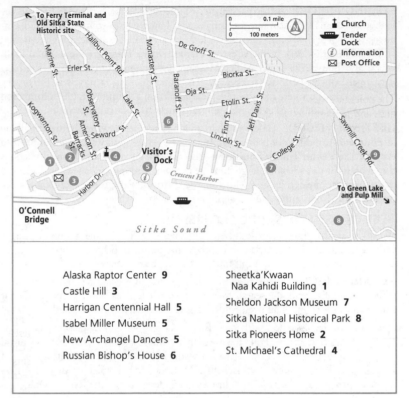

To Ferry Terminal and Old Sitka State Historic site

Church
Tender Dock
Information
Post Office

Marine St.
Erler St.
Halibut Point Rd.
Monastery St.
De Groff St.
Biorka St.
Baranoff St.
Oja St.
Etolin St.
Kogwanton St.
Observatory St.
American St.
Barracks St.
Lake St.
Seward St.
Finn St.
Jeff Davis St.
Lincoln St.
College St.
Sawmill Creek Rd.

Visitor's Dock

Crescent Harbor

Harbor Dr.

To Green Lake and Pulp Mill

O'Connell Bridge

Sitka Sound

Alaska Raptor Center **9**
Castle Hill **3**
Harrigan Centennial Hall **5**
Isabel Miller Museum **5**
New Archangel Dancers **5**
Russian Bishop's House **6**

Sheetka'Kwaan
Naa Kahidi Building **1**
Sheldon Jackson Museum **7**
Sitka National Historical Park **8**
Sitka Pioneers Home **2**
St. Michael's Cathedral **4**

and Chichagof islands, but the big cruise ships have to sail around Baranof into the open Pacific. This minor inconvenience—and the fact that Sitka lacks docking facilities for megaships, which must send passengers ashore in tenders—means the town sees a lot fewer cruise ship visits than Juneau, Ketchikan, and Skagway. Because of this, it retains a more residential feel than similar-sized towns in Southeast, and its combination of location, multicultural heritage, a mixed economy, and sheer local pride keep it just plain beautiful to look at, and remarkably little has changed since the old days: Historic photographs bear a remarkable resemblance to today's city.

Sitka's history is by far Alaska's richest. The powerful and sophisticated Kiksadi Tlingit clan called this part of Baranof Island home for centuries. In 1799, however, they came face to face with European power when Alexander Baranof, manager of the fur-trading Russian-American Company, established a new fort here in order to expand their sea otter hunting operations and territorial claims. Faced with the prospect of subjugation, the Tlingit attacked the Russian's redoubt in 1802 and killed almost everyone inside. Two years later Baranof returned with reinforcements, forcing the tribe to make way for the new colonial city of Novoarkhangelsk (New Archangel). Today, Sitka preserves the Russian buildings of Alaska's earliest white settlement and, more deeply, the story of the cultural conflict between Alaska Natives and the invaders, and their resistance and ultimate accommodation to the new ways.

COMING ASHORE   Most passengers will arrive in Sitka by tender because the harbor is too small to accommodate large ships. Tenders drop you right in the downtown area, where small ships can also dock. Maps are available at the volunteer-staffed visitor information desk in the Crescent Harbor Dock's **Harrigan Centennial Hall,** which also houses the Isabel Miller Museum and the auditorium where the New Archangel Dancers perform (see below). The other docking facility is at the nearby O'Connell Bridge, where maps can be picked up from a volunteer at the information kiosk (mornings only). Map boards are located near both docking facilities.

GETTING AROUND   Unless you have mobility problems, we recommend walking in this town. You can hoof it to everything there is to see, and it's a beautiful place to explore. The **Visitor Transit Shuttle bus** also makes a circuit of the town's attractions throughout the day whenever large ships are in town, meeting arrivals at the docks and stopping at the Sheldon Jackson Museum, the Historical Park, the Alaska Raptor Center, the Tribal Community House, and downtown. An all-day pass costs $7.

BEST CRUISE LINE SHORE EXCURSIONS

We advise against shore excursions here. The town is lovely enough by itself, and the various attractions have very good interpretive programs. If, however, you want something organized or want to get out in the wilds, here are a few options.

Sea Otter and Wildlife Quest ($114, 3 hr.): Cruise in a water-jet-driven tour boat while a naturalist leads the search for sea otters, whales, sea lions, porpoise, harbor seals, brown bears, blacktail deer, bald eagles, and a variety of marine birds.

Russian America Tour ($46, 2½ hr.): Tour Sitka on foot and by coach, visiting the Russian Cemetery, Castle Hill, the Russian Blockhouse, Sitka National Historical Park, and St. Michael's Russian Orthodox Cathedral. Later, take in a performance of Russian folk dances by the New Archangel Dancers (see below). The **Russian America & Raptor Center Tour** ($56, 4 hr.) also includes a visit to the Raptor Rehabilitation Center.

Sitka Bike & Hike ($76, 3 hr.): After transferring to Sawmill Creek, you'll ride 4 miles and then hike approximately 1 mile in the Tongass National Forest before being brought back to the docking area. The **Advanced Bike Adventure** ($105, 4 hr.) is designed for experienced riders, covering 22 miles along the coast, with an elevation gain of 1,000 feet. It includes a visit to the Medvejie Fish Hatchery or a ½-mile hike to Beaver Lake. Lunch is included.

Sport-Fishing ($199, 4 hr.): An experienced captain will guide your fully equipped boat to a good spot for halibut and salmon; the rest is up to you. Your catch can be frozen or smoked and, if you wish, shipped to your home. *Note:* A $20 fishing license and a $10 king-salmon tag are extra.

ON YOUR OWN: WITHIN WALKING DISTANCE

Essentially, everything in Sitka is within walking distance, though the farthest attraction, the Alaska Raptor Center (see below) might prove too much of a hike for some.

　　St. Michael's Cathedral, with its striking onion-shaped dome and its ornate gilt interior, is located on Lincoln Street, at the focal point of the downtown thoroughfare. One of the 49th state's most striking and photogenic structures, the current church is actually a replica of the original 1840s church, which burned to the ground one night in 1966. So revered was the cathedral that Sitkans, whether Russian Orthodox or not, formed a human chain and carried many of the cathedral's precious icons, paintings, vestments, and jeweled crowns from the flames. Later, with contributions of cash and labor from throughout the land, St. Michael's was lovingly re-created on the same site and rededicated in 1976. It still houses those religious symbols that the citizens worked so hard to rescue from the inferno, and is the official seat of the Russian Orthodox Church in Alaska. The vast majority of the church's congregation is made up of Alaska Native peoples, who were evangelized by the original cathedral's designer, Bishop Innocent Veniaminov, in the 19th century. Admission is $2.

Innocent's 1842 home, straightforwardly called **The Russian Bishop's House** (© **907/747-6281;** www.nps.gov/sitk), is a fascinating place a few blocks east at Lincoln and Monastery streets. It is now operated by the National Park Service, which provides surprisingly enjoyable and informative tours of the bishop's furnished quarters and an impressive chapel. Born in 1797 in a remote Siberian village, Innocent first traveled to Alaska as a missionary in 1824, and was named the territory's first resident bishop in 1840. A giant for his time at 6 feet 3 inches, he was also something of a Renaissance man, accomplished in architecture, carpentry (he built several of the pieces on display), ethnography, clockmaking, and linguistics. During his service, he became fluent in Tlingit and Aleut, and translated liturgical texts and his own spiritual treatises into these languages by adapting the Russian Cyrillic alphabet. Exhibits downstairs trace Sitka's history. Admission costs $4.

A little farther down Lincoln you'll see the campus of Sheldon Jackson College, founded by its namesake Presbyterian missionary in 1878 as a vocational school for young Tlingits. The **Sheldon Jackson Museum** (© **907/747-8981;** www.museums. state.ak.us), located on the grounds, contains a fine collection of Native artifacts, including Tlingit, Aleut, Athabascan, Haida, and Tsimshian peoples, as well as the Native peoples of the Arctic. The core of the collection was assembled by Jackson himself on his travels around the territory. Admission is $4.

Continue down Lincoln until you come to the **Sitka National Historical Park** (© **907/747-6281;** www.nps.gov/sitk). This is where the Tlingit made their stand against Russia in 1804, holding off imperial gunboats and Aleut mercenaries for 6 days before finally melting away one night after taking heavy losses. The land was officially protected starting in 1890, and in 1910 the site was designated a National Historic Park, emphasizing the Native perspective. In the visitor center, exhibits explain the history and the art of totem carving, with 19th-century poles displayed in one hall and new ones created in the on-site Southeast Alaska Indian Cultural Center, which also has windowed workshops devoted to traditional crafts of metal, wood, beads, textiles, and woven grass. Outside, a **rainforest trail** winds along the coast of the 113-acre park past a collection of towering totems nestled among the spruce and hemlock. The **battle site**—just a grassy area now—is also along the trail, but among the trees and totems, with the sound of the lapping sea and raven's call, you can feel deep down what the Tlingits were fighting for. Admission costs $4.

Beyond here, just across Indian River, the **Alaska Raptor Center,** 1101 Sawmill Creek Rd. (© **907/747-8662;** www.alaskaraptor.org), is just on the border between "within walking distance" and not. A nonprofit venture supported by tour companies, cruise lines, and public donations, the center was opened in 1980 to treat sick or injured birds of prey (primarily eagles), and to provide an educational experience for visitors. Birds that cannot be returned to the wild are sent to zoos or housed here permanently, providing guests the rare experience of standing just a few feet from a huge, unblinking eagle. The flight center offers an exciting view of the eagles training just prior to release. Admission costs $12 adults, $6 kids under 12.

Back in the center of town are several worthwhile sites. **Castle Hill,** up the stairs near the intersection of Lincoln and Katlian streets, was where the first U.S. flag was raised on Alaskan soil, after the U.S. and Russia held a transfer ceremony here in 1867. You get a great panoramic view of town from the top. Across the street, the beautiful building behind the big bronze statue is the **Sitka Pioneers Home,** a state retirement home. Next to the Pioneers Home, the **Sheetka'Kwaan Naa Kahidi Building,** 200 Katlian St. (© 888/270-8687; www.sitkatribal.com), is a modern version of a traditional Tlingit tribal house. It hosts regular performances of traditional Tlingit dance, often coinciding with cruise ship visits. Show times are posted here and at the Centennial Hall. Behind the stage is the largest hand-carved wooden screen in Southeast Alaska, depicting Eagle and Raven, the two principle clans of the Tlingit people.

Next to the Crescent Harbor Dock, the **Isabel Miller Museum** at the Harrigan Centennial Hall (© 907/747-6455; www.sitka.org/historicalmuseum) outlines the city's history with art, artifacts, and a large diorama of Sitka as it was in 1867. Admission is free, though donations are welcome. Centennial Hall is also the home of the **New Archangel Dancers** (© 907/747-5516; www.newarchangeldancers.com), an all-woman company that gives 30-minute performances of Russian and Ukrainian traditional dance on most days that cruise ships are in port. Admission is $7, and tickets must be purchased at least a half-hour before the show. The schedule is posted at the hall.

SHOPPING
There are some good shops and galleries in Sitka, mostly on Lincoln and Harbor streets, with several shops selling **Russian crafts** clustered in the neighborhood of St. Michael's Cathedral. The gift shop at the **Sheldon Jackson Museum** is an excellent place to buy authentic Alaska Native arts and crafts.

7 Skagway

Located at the end of the picturesque Lynn Canal, Skagway served as the jumping-off point for the tidal wave of prospectors who arrived in 1897 for the short but intense **Yukon Gold Rush.** Greed is a great motivator, but not many of these fellas realized the hardships they'd have to endure before they could get close to the stuff, hiking some 3,000 vertical feet over 20 miles along either the **White Pass** or the **Chilkoot Pass** through the coastal mountain range to the Canadian border. By itself, that might not have been too bad, but by order of Canada's North West Mounted Police, they had to have at least a year's supply of provisions with them before they could enter the country. Numbed by wind and temperatures that fell at times to 50 below zero—Skagway's Tlingit name, *Skagua*, means "home of the North Wind"—most inched their way up, carrying some of their supplies midway then returning for more. The process often required as many as 20 trips.

The town, such as it was then, was entirely a product of the rush, having been established as a dock and lumber mill by former steamboat captain William Moore and his son in the 1890s, after they realized the nearby pass would be a good entry to Canada if gold were ever discovered there. They were right, but rather than enriching the Moores as intended, the rush simply brought total anarchy to Skagway, with a swarm of opportunists arriving with the prospectors to either service or swindle them—usually both. The most notorious of the Skagway bad men was Jefferson Randolph

"Soapy" Smith, a con man and thug who knew an open town when he saw it, and effectively took the place over before getting himself shot in a now-mythic gunfight with city surveyor Frank Reid. Reid died in the fight too, and both were buried in the town's Gold Rush Cemetery—Reid inside, under a granite marker that reads "He gave his life for the honor of Skagway," Smith under a simple marker in unconsecrated ground. As is the way of things, it's Smith whose name is all over today's Skagway, part of the town's totally Disneyesque "wild and wonton frontier town" image—about which you'll hear a lot.

Remember the actor Walter Brennan, who played the old coot in every other Hollywood Western from the '30s through the '50s? Well, every single person in Skagway seems to have gone to his acting school. Yes, people do live here (862 of them year-round, according to the 2000 census), but most of the folks you see in the summer are seasonal workers, brought in essentially as actors to man the set. It's some set, with the wide main drag, Broadway, lined end-to-end with gold-rush-era buildings and protected as a National Historic District. A few that look like real businesses turn out to be displays showing how it was back in frontier days, but most house gift shops—lots and lots of gift shops.

Pieces of history are preserved all around town, from cute touches such as the huge watch painted on the mountainside, advertising long-gone Kirmse's watch repair, to the monumental **White Pass and Yukon Route Railroad,** which opened in 1900 to carry late stampeders into Canada and bring gold out. It's one of the first things you'll see when coming in from the cruise ship piers. The round-trip to the summit of the pass, following a route carved out of the side of the mountain by an American/Canadian engineering team, takes 3 hours from the depot, located right at the foot of town.

COMING ASHORE   Ships dock at the cruise pier, at the foot of Broadway or off Congress or Terminal Way. Though the docks are in sight of downtown, it's about a 20-minute walk, so take one of the frequent shuttle buses if you don't feel a need to stretch your legs.

GETTING AROUND   Skagway is almost hermetically self-contained, like a theme park. The only street you really need to know about is **Broadway,** which runs through the center of town and off which everything branches. **Walking maps** describing the historic buildings and **trail maps** of the surrounding area are both available at the Arctic Brotherhood Hall on Broadway between 2nd and 3rd and at the National Historic Park visitors center, located at the railroad depot. Hikes range from 1 to 10 miles, and most involve some good hill-walking. The Skagway Streetcar Company also offers tours via historic period limos (see below).

BEST CRUISE LINE SHORE EXCURSIONS

White Pass & Yukon Route Railway ($107, 3½ hr.): The sturdy engines and vintage parlor cars of this famous narrow-gauge railway take you from the town past waterfalls and still-visible parts of the famous "Trail of '98" to the White Pass Summit, the boundary between Canada and the United States. On a clear day, you'll be able to see all the way down to the harbor, and you might see the occasional hoary marmot or other critter fleeing from the train's racket. A couple variations are offered, one an up-and-back trip to the summit, one a bus ride to the village of Carcross near Lake Bennett, Yukon Territory, where you have lunch at the Caribou Trading Post before boarding the train for the ride back to Skagway. Now the caveat to the whole experience: On an overcast day, you won't see a damn thing. If you're on the fence, consider waiting to buy your tickets at the depot when you arrive, if there are seats available. Schedule info is available at **www.wpyr.com**. The **White Pass Lake Bennett Adventure** ($269, 8½ hr.) adds a walking tour of this gold-rush-era town; a "prospector's meal" of gold miner's stew, nugget baked beans, sourdough bread, and apple pie; and a motorcoach trip back to Skagway via the Klondike Highway.

Dyea Rainforest Bicycle Tour ($85, 3 hr.): The ghost town of Dyea, about 9 miles west, was established around the same time as Skagway but was abandoned completely after the gold rush. On this tour, you'll start in Dyea and ride 6 miles back to Skagway through the rainforest, whose coastal tidal flats are home to eagles, salmon, and wildflowers.

Dyea on Horseback ($165, 3½ hr.): A van takes you to Dyea, where you tour the town aboard an even-tempered mount while your guide spins some history.

Sled Dog Musher's Camp ($109, 2¾ hr.): An introduction to the sled-dog life, with a tour of a musher's camp, a 20-minute ride through the forest aboard a wheeled sled, and a chance to cuddle husky pups.

Chilkoot Trail Hike & Float Trip ($99, 4½ hr.): From the pier, travel to the historic Dyea ghost town and hike the first 2 miles of the Chilkoot Trail through the rainforest. At the shore of the Taiya River you'll board 18-foot rafts for a float back to Dyea.

Klondike Bicycle Tour ($85, 2½ hr.): After vanning it to the White Pass summit, you'll ride down the Klondike Highway, 15 miles from peak to sea, pausing along the way for photos.

Yukon Golf Odyssey ($179, 8 hr.): After a ride across the White Pass, you'll head into the Yukon to the town of Carcross and its 9-hole, par-36 Meadow Lakes Golf & Country Club course, with four sets of tees on each hole and lengths ranging from 1,800 yards to 2,800 yards. Golfing in the Yukon! There's something to tell your regular partners.

Skagway by Streetcar ($40, 2 hr.): As much performance art as historical tour, guides in period costume relate tales of the boomtown days as you tour the sights both in and outside of town in a 1920s limo. Though theatrical, it's all done in a homey style, as if you're getting a tour from your cousin. The guide is as likely to point out funky oddities as major historical sights. After seeing the Historic District, the Lookout, the Gold Rush Cemetery, and other sights, guests see a little song-and-dance and film presentation about Skagway, and become honorary members of the Arctic Brotherhood. This last part is very, very hokey.

ON YOUR OWN: WITHIN WALKING DISTANCE

Though Skagway's historic district includes some three dozen buildings from the 1890s and early 1900s, most are either privately owned or leased by the Park Service for use as businesses. Be sure to pick up the "Skagway Walking Tour" map mentioned above in "Getting Around," and consult it as you wander around town. A little knowledge could transform that souvenir shop back into a dry goods store. Everything here is within walking distance, though the Gold Rush Cemetery (see below) might be a bit far for some. If so, skip it; it's not that interesting by itself.

As you're coming into town from the docks, you'll be greeted by a few interesting sights. To the right, that fiendish-looking machine near the tracks is a **rotary snowplow** that was used by the railroad whenever the White Pass tracks got snowed in. The two buildings just behind it, on the corner of 2nd and Broadway, house the offices of the **National Park Service,** with the **White Pass and Yukon Route** depot right next door.

The NPS buildings are worth a stop for information and historical ambience (they once housed the original railroad depot and offices), while the latter merits a stop for its gift shop, which has some nifty railroad souvenirs.

Across the street, at the corner of 2nd Avenue, bartenders at the **Red Onion Saloon** (© **907/983-2222**) still serve drinks over the same mahogany bar as did their predecessors back in gold rush days. Waitresses wear busty dance-hall outfits, as do the double-entendre-flinging docents, who lure visitors to the former bordello upstairs for a $5 tour. If you have less time, you can even get a "quickie" tour for less. It's actually interesting, with rooms re-created to look as they would in the 1890s, and a decent presentation by the guides too.

On the same block, the **Arctic Brotherhood Hall** is mostly notable for its facade, covered in thousands of pieces of driftwood.

At the other end of town, at 7th Avenue and Spring Street, the 1899 McCabe College building houses the **Skagway Museum** (© **907/983-2420;** www.skagway museum.org), a very professional display offering a look at Skagway's history through artifacts, photographs, and historical records. Items on display include a Tlingit canoe and Bering Sea kayaks, as well as a collection of gold rush supplies and tools and Native American items including baskets and beadwork. Admission is $2. If you'd like to get out of town a while, continue walking about a mile and a half up State Street to the old **Gold Rush Cemetery,** where Frank Reid and Soapy Smith are buried.

Back on Broadway, at 6th Avenue, the *Days of '98 Show* has been playing at the Fraternal Order of Eagles Hall No. 25 (© **907/983-2545**) since 1927, which tells you how long Skagway has been relying on tourism. A melodrama of the Gay '90s featuring dancing girls, ragtime music, a recitation of Robert Service poetry, and (naturally) actors playing Smith and Reid in their historic shootout, the show is almost always offered as part of a shore excursion, but you can also buy tickets at the door for $14. Walk down Sixth from the theater and make a right to see the historic **Moore Cabin,** built in 1887 by Skagway founder William Moore.

SHOPPING

Skagway is all about shopping, but we try to avoid it. Most of the shops sell either cheap tourist gimcracks or jewelry. The most characteristic items from town are probably railroad souvenirs from the **White Pass and Yukon Route,** available at the depot.

8 Victoria, British Columbia

Cruises that start in Seattle or San Francisco typically visit Victoria on the way up to Alaska. Located on Vancouver Island, this lovely little city is the capital of British Columbia, and appropriately so as it's almost more British than Britain, with gorgeous Victorian architecture and lovely gardens among its main attractions. Take a tour around the island and you'll see beautiful homes, stately government buildings, and views that include the snowcapped mountains of Washington State.

COMING ASHORE   Cruise ships dock at the Ogden Point cruise ship terminal on the Strait of Juan de Fuca, about a mile southwest of the **Inner Harbour** and the **Downtown/Old Town** area, where most attractions are located.

GETTING AROUND   Cruise lines offer a shuttle to the Inner Harbour, where flower baskets, milling crowds, and street performers liven the scene around the grand Fairmont Empress hotel, famed setting for English-style high tea.

Note: All prices in this section were calculated at the rate of US$0.87 = C$1 or US$1 = C$1.15. Foreign currency rates fluctuate, so prices may not be exactly the same when you arrive in port.

BEST CRUISE LINE SHORE EXCURSIONS

Butchart Gardens (US$65, 3½ hr.): The world-renowned Butchart Gardens are set in a former quarry (see details below). Expanded trips include high tea at the gardens (US$109, 4 hr.), or combine a visit to Craigdarroch Castle (see below) with a visit and gourmet picnic at the gardens ($165, 5 hr.).

Victoria Pub Crawl (US$75, 3½ hr.): Visit three of the city's finest pubs and sample its best local brews, all without having to choose a designated driver.

Orca & Wildlife Watching Adventure (US$114, 3½ hr.): A catamaran takes you out on the waters off southern Vancouver Island, home to killer whales, seals, porpoises, and myriad birds.

Horse-Drawn Trolley Tour (US$45, 1 hr.): A fully narrated tour that takes you past James Bay, Beacon Hill Park, and Victoria's Old Town, which includes the Legislative Buildings and the Fairmont Empress.

ON YOUR OWN: WITHIN WALKING DISTANCE

It's about a mile from the docks to the central attractions around the Inner Harbour, but let's call that walking distance, for argument's sake. Once you're there, the big attraction is the ivy-covered, grandly Edwardian **Fairmont Empress,** 721 Government St. (© **250/384-8111;** www.fairmont.com/empress). Built in 1908, the hotel has a grand lobby and is *the* place to go for British-style high tea. Many shore excursions include tea here; but if you plan to go on your own, call 2 weeks before your cruise for reservations, and be sure to follow the dress code: no sleeveless shirts, tank tops, short-shorts, or cutoffs. To the side of the hotel, you'll find the **Miniature World** museum (© **250/385-9731;** www.miniatureworld.com), with quirky displays that include big dollhouses, the world's smallest working sawmill, and a model of London in 1670. Admission is US$7.85 (C$9) adults, US$6 (C$7) kids 4 to 12. Nearby, British Columbia's **Legislative Buildings,** 501 Belleville St. (© **250/387-3046**), exude typical British government gravitas, their stony bulk surrounded by vast lawns and headed by a statue of the city's namesake, Queen Victoria. Tours of the interior are offered every 20 to 30 minutes in summer.

Just to the east sits the **Royal British Columbia Museum,** 675 Belleville St. (© **888/ 447-7977;** www.royalbcmuseum.bc.ca), its entrance graced by towering totem poles and other large sculptural works by Northwest First Nations' artists. Inside, exhibits highlight the natural history of the province and Victoria's recent past, and another demonstrates how archaeologists study ancient cultures, using artifacts from numerous local tribes. Admission is US$12 (C$14) adults, US$8.25 (C$9.50) kids 6 to 18. The museum's **National Geographic IMAX Theatre** shows movies on various scientific themes and exotic locations. Adjacent to the museum is **Thunderbird Park,** with Native totem poles and a ceremonial house.

ON YOUR OWN: BEYOND THE PORT AREA

Some 13 miles north of downtown Victoria on the Saanich Peninsula, the 130-acre **Butchart Gardens,** 800 Benevenuto Ave., in Brentwood Bay (© **866/652-4422** or 250/652-5256; www.butchartgardens.com), started as a beautification project by the

CRUISE TERMINAL 7 ●
ATTRACTIONS ●
Butchart Gardens 1
Craigdarroch Castle 8
Fairmont Empress Hotel 3
Miniature World 2
Legislative Buildings 4
Royal British Columbia
   Museum 5
Thunderbird Park 6

wife of a quarry owner, and today features world-renowned English, Italian, and Japanese gardens; water gardens; and rose gardens. There are also restaurants and a gift shop on-site. Admission is US$22 (C$25) adults, US$11 (C$13) kids 13 to 17, US$2.60 (C$3) kids 5 to 12. Most cruise passengers visit as part of a shore excursion. Ditto for the Highland-style **Craigdarroch Castle,** 1050 Joan Crescent (© **250/592-5323;** www.craigdarrochcastle.com), which was built in the 1880s as the home of millionaire Scottish coal magnate Robert Dunsmuir. Four stories high and 39 rooms strong, it's topped with stone turrets and furnished in opulent Victorian splendor. Admission is US$10 (C$12) adults, US$3.25 (C$3.75) kids 6 to 18. Those wishing to visit on their own can make the 40-minute walk up Fort Street from the Inner Harbor, or grab a taxi.

SHOPPING

At the Inner Harbor, the **Government Street promenade** is a 5-block stretch of souvenir shops sprinkled with the occasional treasure, including shops selling thick Cowichan Indian sweaters. On the eastern edge of downtown, a 3-block stretch on Fort Street between Blanshard and Cook streets is known as **Antique Row,** renowned for quality British collectibles.

12

The Mexican Riviera & Baja

The so-called Mexican Riviera—the stretch of port cities and resorts extending from Mazatlán in the north to Acapulco in the south—is one of the classic cruise destinations, and not just because it's where *The Love Boat* used to sail every week. Blessed with miles of beaches backed by picturesque mountains, and with a climate that practically guarantees perfect beach weather any day of the year, this is the Caribbean for folks who live on the West Coast.

Spanish conquistadors and missionaries came to this coast in the 16th and 17th centuries to find riches, convert the heathen (frequently at sword point), and establish ports for sailing to the Far East. But it wasn't until the mid–20th century that other travelers discovered that the region was almost tailor-made for relaxation. Hollywood arrived first, heading south for anonymity and great sport-fishing. Later the spring-break crowd followed, seeking a place to get lewd and goofy on $1 beers. Today, the region still offers a bit of both, plus plenty of family-oriented relaxation, a dash of history, and a dash of culture, including lots of traditional and modern art.

In addition to the Riviera ports, many cruises on these itineraries also stop at **Cabo San Lucas,** at the tip of the Baja Peninsula, a great town that's all about beaches and bars, but is also growing to accommodate some amazing golf courses and adventure-travel excursions.

HOME PORTS FOR THIS REGION Cruises to this region sail from **San Diego, Los Angeles,** and **San Francisco.**

LANGUAGE & CURRENCY **Spanish** is the tongue of the land, although **English** is spoken in most places that cater to tourists. The Mexican currency is the **nuevo peso** (new peso). Its symbol is the "$" sign, but it's hardly the equivalent of the U.S. dollar—the exchange rate is about $11 pesos to US$1 ($1 peso = about US9¢). Most tourist stores gladly accept U.S. dollars. *Note:* All prices in this chapter are given in U.S. dollars.

CALLING FROM THE U.S. & CANADA You need to dial the international access code **(011)** and country code **(52)** before the numbers listed in this chapter.

1 Acapulco

Why is it we think of Ricardo Montalban every time we think of Acapulco? Some kind of mixed 1970s TV series metaphor, we suppose, but it still works: The city is like Ricardo—you know he's not the bronzed TV star he once was, but he's still so charming that you go along with the act anyway. The town's temptations are hard to resist. Where else do men dive from cliffs into the sea at sunset, and where else does the sun shine 360 days a year? Though most beach resorts are made for relaxing, Acapulco has nonstop 24-hour energy, and its perfectly sculpted bay is an adult playground filled

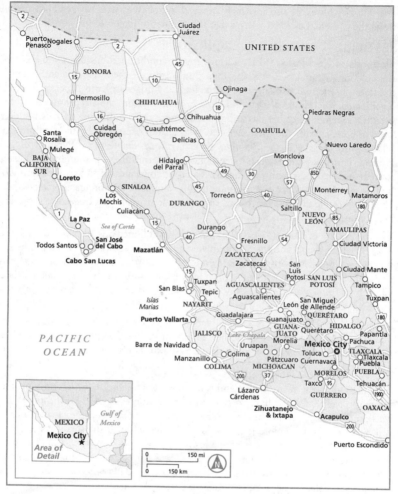

with water-skiers and studs on WaveRunners. Back in the days when there was a jet set, this was their town, and it's not hard to understand why: The view of Acapulco Bay, framed by mountains and beaches, is just breathtaking.

COMING ASHORE Cruise ships dock west of the Golden Zone hotel strip, a 5-minute walk from Old Acapulco's main plaza, the *zócalo*, right on the Costera (aka Avenida Costera Miguel Aleman), the main avenue through the tourist zone, lined with hotels, restaurants, shopping centers, and open-air beach bars. Fort San Diego is just above the docks.

GETTING AROUND **Taxis** are more plentiful than tacos in Acapulco—and practically as inexpensive (only a few dollars) if you're traveling in the downtown area only. Just remember that you should always establish the price with the driver before starting out. The city **buses** are also amazingly easy and inexpensive, with covered bus stops all along the Costera, posted with maps that show routes to major sights.

BEST CRUISE LINE SHORE EXCURSIONS

Pyramids of Xochicalco ($149, 12 hr.): An air-conditioned bus takes you through the mile-long Acapulco Tunnel and then climbs into the Sierra Nevada and through the state of Guerrero, crossing one of the highest bridges in Latin America to reach **Xochicalco,** the "House of Beautiful Flowers." Dating from the 8th century B.C., this beautiful ceremonial center has artifacts and inscriptions indicating that its builders were in contact with the Mixtec, Aztec, Maya, and Zapotec. The most impressive building on the site is the *Pirámide de la Serpiente Emplumada* (Pyramid of the Plumed Serpent), with its magnificent reliefs. Underneath the pyramid is a series of tunnels and chambers with wall murals. The tour continues on to **San Jose de Vista Hermosa,** a former sugar cane plantation built originally by conquistador Hernando Cortés, where you'll have lunch and time to look around. The drive to Xochicalco takes about 3½ hours each way.

The Silver City of Taxco ($139, 12 hr.): An air-conditioned bus takes you though the Acapulco Tunnel and into the Sierra, traveling to Taxco. Founded in 1528 by the silver- and gold-obsessed Spanish, the town is still an important producer of silver jewelry and other handicrafts. The tour also includes a visit to the baroque **Santa Prisca Church** and lunch at San Jose de Vista Hermosa (see above). The drive to Taxco is approximately 3½ hours each way.

Acapulco City Highlights & Cliff Divers ($42, 4 hr.): A bus tour that travels from one end of Acapulco Bay to the other, taking in the beaches, resort hotels, and **La Quebrada,** where the world-famous divers leap into the Pacific.

ON YOUR OWN: WITHIN WALKING DISTANCE

Acapulco's all about great beaches and watersports (and nightlife, which early-departing cruise passengers will have to put out of their minds), and as with most of the Mexican Riviera ports, the thing to do here is take in the surf and the seaside cafes. If you have an urge to explore the traditional downtown area, the shady *zócalo* (also called Plaza Alvarez) is worth a trip, allowing you a glimpse of local life and color. Inexpensive cafes and shops border the plaza, which is shaded by huge mango and rubber trees. At its far north end is the **Nuestra Señora de la Soledad** cathedral with its blue, onion-shaped domes and Byzantine towers. Though reminiscent of a Russian Orthodox church, it was actually built as a movie set, then later adapted into a house of worship. From the church, turn east along the side street going off at a right angle (Calle Carranza) to find an arcade with newsstands and more shops. The hill behind the cathedral provides a fantastic view of the town. Just follow the signs for **El Mirador** (lookout point), or take a taxi if it looks like too much of a walk for you.

Near the cruise docks, star-shaped **Fort San Diego** was built in 1616 to defend the bay, and was later rebuilt after a 1776 earthquake leveled the original structure. After years of baking in the Acapulco sun, it was finally refurbished and turned into a museum directed by Mexico's department of archaeological and historic preservation. Today, the fort houses the **Acapulco Historical Museum** (© 744/482-3828), whose displays illuminate Acapulco's past, from precolonial times though the conquistador era to the silver trade between Acapulco and China, the Mexican War of Independence, and beyond. A glass floor in several rooms allows visitors to see the remains of the original fort. Admission costs $3; closed Mondays.

Located just above downtown, on the other side of the narrow Peninsula de las Playas, **La Quebrada** is probably the most recognized Acapulco icon. It's from here that high-divers leap each day at 1pm from a ledge on the cliff, plunging into the roaring surf of an inlet that's just 20 feet wide and 12 feet deep—but 130 feet down. Many shore excursions include the show as part of a larger city tour, but you can also go on your own, starting behind the cathedral and walking 4 blocks along La Quebrada Street. Admission is $2.50.

All out-of-town activities are covered under "Best Cruise Line Shore Excursions," above.

BEACHES

In the old days, the downtown beaches—Manzanillo, Honda, Caleta, and Caletilla—were the focal point of Acapulco. The latter two remain popular with both visitors and locals, but today beaches and resort developments also stretch all along the 4-mile length of the bay's shore. Here's a rundown, going from west to east around the bay.

Playa la Angosta is a small, sheltered, often-deserted cove just around the bend from **La Quebrada,** where the cliff divers perform. About 10 minutes south of downtown by taxi, on the Peninsula de las Playas, **Caleta** and **Caletilla** beaches have calm waters and thatched-roofed restaurants, with watersports equipment, beach chairs, and umbrellas for rent. From here, brightly painted boats ferry passengers to **Roqueta Island,** a good place to snorkel, sunbathe, hike to a lighthouse, visit a small zoo, or have lunch. The ride across costs about $5 round-trip.

East of the *zócalo,* the major beaches are **Hornos** (near Papagayo Park), **Hornitos, Paraíso, Condesa,** and **Icacos,** followed by the naval base (**La Base**) and **Punta del Guitarrón.** From here, the road climbs to the legendary Las Brisas hotel, then continues to the small, clean bay of **Puerto Marqués,** followed by **Punta Diamante,** about 12 miles from the *zócalo,* fronting the open Pacific and dominated by several resort hotels.

SHOPPING

Acapulco is not among the best places to buy Mexican crafts, but it does have a few interesting shops. The best are at the **Mercado Parazal** (often called the Mercado de Artesanías), on Calle Velázquez de León near Cinco de Mayo in the downtown *zócalo* area. When you see Sanborn's department store/drugstore, turn right and walk behind it for several blocks, asking directions if necessary. Here you'll find stalls of curios from around the country, including silver, embroidered cotton clothing, rugs, pottery, and papier-mâché, as well as on-site artists painting ceramics with village scenes. The shopkeepers aren't pushy, but they'll test your bargaining mettle. Before buying silver, examine it carefully and look for ".925" stamped on the back. This supposedly signifies that the silver is 92.5% pure, though the less expensive silver called *alpaca* may also bear this stamp.

For resort wear, head to the boutiques crowding the **Costera,** where you'll find prices generally lower than what you'd pay in the United States.

2 Cabo San Lucas

Cabo San Lucas, the rowdier half of the conjoined towns commonly referred to as Los Cabos, is one big bar-and-beach scene perched at the very tip of the Baja Peninsula, with the Pacific Ocean on one side and the mouth of the Sea of Cortez on the other. (Its quieter twin, San Jose del Cabo, is about 21 miles away, down a corridor lined with resorts.) Cabo made hardly a blip on the world's radar until after World War II, when Hollywood celebs and yachters started traveling here for sport-fishing. In 1973, the completion of the Transpeninsular Highway finally linked the town to the rest of North America. By the early 1980s, the Mexican government had realized the area's growth potential and began investing in new highways, a larger airport, golf courses, and modern marine facilities. Today, the town is a playground seemingly built entirely for vacationers' gratification, full of beaches, beach bars, bar bars, crafts shopping, restaurants, and did we mention bars? There's almost nothing of cultural or historic significance here (unless you're big on pop sociology), so your choices are to throw yourself into the hedonism or sign up for a nature- or adventure-oriented excursion.

COMING ASHORE   Cabo San Lucas lacks pier facilities for anything but small ships (in the 100-passenger range), so large cruise ships must anchor just offshore and ferry passengers in by tender. You step ashore in the **Cabo San Lucas Marina** (in the Cabo San Lucas Bay harbor), which is chockablock with tour operators, information stands, shops, and transportation options.

GETTING AROUND   The tender dock at the Marina is a pleasant 10- to 15-minute walk from the town center, around the rim of the Y-shaped harbor. Essentially, everything in town is within a few blocks of the harbor rim. If you keep walking all the way around (at least a 30-min. walk, just because of the harbor's twists and turns), you'll reach the start of the beaches, but the fastest way to access them is by **water taxi,** which costs about $3 per person. You can also catch a regular **car taxi** (about $5 per carload) or a **bicycle taxi** (for which you'll have to negotiate a rate). All are in vast supply right at the dock. Taxis can also take you to the golf courses on the corridor between Cabo San Lucas and San Jose del Cabo; expect to pay between $15 and $25 each way.

BEST CRUISE LINE SHORE EXCURSIONS

In addition to the excursions listed here, the cruise lines typically offer nearly two dozen other snorkeling, scuba, sailing, and bus tours.

Cabo San Lucas Sport-Fishing ($159, 5 hr.): Superb sport-fishing put Cabo San Lucas on the map. After boarding your sport-fishing vessel, you'll take a brief cruise to the fishing grounds, then spend a few hours trolling for marlin and sailfish. The good news: Beer is included. The bad news: Because the cruise ships can't store your catch, fishing for trophy fish is catch-and-release. Nontrophy fish are kept by the crew. A $10 fishing license is required.

Cabo Zodiac Whale-Watch ($65, 2½ hr.): Every year from January to March, Cabo San Lucas is visited by humpback, gray, and blue whales, and the best, most intimate, and action-packed way to see them is aboard one of these inflatable craft, which seat only 15 people.

Horseback Ride on the Beach ($71, 3 hr.): Mount up for an hour-long ride along Cabo's cactus-lined beaches, followed by a cool drink at a beach hotel and another hour free to swim and work on your tan.

ON YOUR OWN: WITHIN WALKING DISTANCE

Cabo is small and manageable, spreading out north and west of the harbor and edged by foothills, dramatically jagged rocks, and desert mountains. A wide **walkway** wraps most of the way around the harbor, lined with bars, restaurants, and shopping. On the

Small-Ship Cruises in Baja's Sea of Cortez

The Baja Peninsula, stretching some 800 miles from the U.S. border to Cabo San Lucas, is almost like a sunbaked version of southeast Alaska, a long, thin strip of mainland and islands, sparsely inhabited in places and often breathtakingly gorgeous. So, it's no wonder some of the same small-ship lines that sail Alaska in the summer move their ships here in winter to offer cruises on the Sea of Cortez side of the peninsula, concentrating on nature, whale-watching, and visits to the region's historic ports. Usually sailing from **La Paz** (the capital city of Baja California Sur) or **Cabo San Lucas,** these small vessels spend time sailing among the sparsely inhabited **coastal islands,** where guests can hike the arid landscape and go tide-pooling along the rocky coast.

There are also visits to historic towns such as **Loreto,** site of the first permanent Spanish settlement on the peninsula, with its manicured fig trees, cobblestone streets, and lovely colonial architecture. Arts-and-crafts shops line the streets, and a museum at the historic mission—the first in the Californias, founded in 1697—offers a glimpse into Baja's past.

Most small-ship cruises also include an excursion by bus to **Bahía Magdalena** on the Pacific coast, where guides take you out in small *panga* boats to one of the world's best whale-watching grounds. Gray whales winter here, birthing their calves and getting ready for their trip back to the Arctic and Bering seas. When we went, a 40-foot mother gray and her calf swam right toward our small boat, ducking under on one side and coming up on the other. That's some close interaction, but not as close as some others get: Occasionally, a gray will pop up right next to the boats to see what's going on, and allow people to pat it on the head. Talk about up-close and personal. **American Safari Cruises, Cruise West,** and **Lindblad Expeditions** all offer winter Baja sailings (see chapter 8 for more on these lines).

other side of those bars and restaurants, about 650 feet from the water's edge, **Boulevard Marina** is the main artery that curves around the harbor—it essentially *is* the town, at least from a short-term visitor's standpoint. Bars and Mexican restaurants featuring fresh seafood crowd one another for space, so pick the one that seems to say "you." The most famous of the bunch is the **Cabo Wabo Cantina** (© 624/143-1188; www.cabowabo.com), partly owned by former Van Halen frontman Sammy Hagar. It's right in the center of town, with a big sign on Marina and the main entrance around back on Vicente Guerrero at Cárdenas. Expect a rock-theme-bar atmosphere, with Van Halen videos and music playing on TV monitors. Unfortunately for cruise passengers, the place doesn't get happening till the evening, after your ship has sailed. Nearby, **El Squid Roe,** on Marina opposite Plaza Bonita (© 624/147-5127; www. elsquidroe.com), is another "Spring Break for Life" kind of bar of the Señor Frog and Carlos 'n Charlies variety. For an antidote to big bars, drop into **Slim's Elbow Room,** "The World's Smallest Bar," on Marina just in front of the building that houses Cabo Wabo. It's just a little bit bigger than a pool table. That's our kind of place.

ON YOUR OWN: BEYOND THE PORT AREA

Cruise ship passengers in town for just a few hours should stick to downtown Cabo and the beaches unless they're on a shore excursion and/or want to play **golf,** a sport with which Los Cabos is increasingly associated. Most of the courses are along the Corridor between the two towns.

- The 18-hole, 7,100-yard, Nicklaus-designed Ocean Course at the Corridor's **Cabo del Sol Resort** (© **800/386-2465;** www.cabodelsol.com) is known for its challenging three finishing holes. Tom Weiskopf designed the newer 18-hole Desert Course. Greens fees for both are $125 to $350 (including cart), depending on time and season.
- The 18-hole, 6,945-yard course at **Cabo Real,** by the Meliá Cabo Real Hotel in the Corridor (© **624/144-0232;** www.caboreal.com), was designed by Robert Trent Jones, Jr., and features holes that sit high on mesas overlooking the Sea of Cortez. Greens fees are $180 to $280, including cart.
- The 18-hole course at **Cabo San Lucas Country Club/Raven Golf Club,** designed by Roy Dye (© **624/143-4653;** www.golfincabo.com), overlooks the juncture of the Pacific Ocean and Sea of Cortez, including the famous Land's End rocks. It includes the longest hole in Mexico, a 607-yard par-5. Greens fees are $79 to $169.

BEACHES

When your ship anchors offshore, you'll see the long, curving sweep of **Medano Beach** stretching into the distance to the right of town (on the east side of the bay). It looks to be about a 5-minute walk from the docks, but looks can be deceiving: The Marina's two main arms stand between the tender dock and the sand, so you either have to walk all the way around (about a 30-min. trek) or hop a water taxi or regular taxi (see "Getting Around," above). At practically any point along the stretch, you'll be able to rent WaveRunners, kayaks, windsurfing boards, and snorkeling gear. Restaurant/bars line the sand at intervals, with some quiet stretches in between.

As your ship comes into the bay, you may see a small beach off your port bow, nestled amid the rugged rocks that separate the bay from the Pacific. This is **Lovers Beach,** the most beautiful beach spot in town. It's accessible only by water taxi from the docks, and there are no facilities to speak of (just the occasional local selling drinks); but it's totally dreamy, with a real *From Here to Eternity* kind of vibe. At low tide, you can cross through the famous arch that connects the two seas here. Swimming is generally safe only on the Sea of Cortez side, facing the bay. Farther north, along the Pacific Coast, Playa Solmar (at the Solmar and Playa Grande resorts) is a magnificent stretch of sand, but don't bother going unless you just want a great view: There's a bad riptide, and swimming is prohibited.

SHOPPING

You'll find no shortage of shopping opportunities in Cabo, but few surprises either. Just beyond the tender dock at the harbor, a large, covered **handicrafts market** has scores of vendors selling pretty much the same merchandise you'll find in town: a mixture of T-shirts, crafts, blankets, trinkets, and tequila. In town, Cabo Wabo (see above) sells its own brand, **Tequila Cabo Wabo,** at its gift shop, while other shops stock every other brand in existence. Shops and crafts marts alternate with jewelry stores and high-end (if not too inspiring) art galleries along Boulevard Marina.

3 Ixtapa/Zihuatanejo

Located side by side about 158 miles northwest of Acapulco, Ixtapa and Zihuatanejo are the odd couple of twin beach resorts. Ixtapa (Eex-*tah*-pah) is a model of modern infrastructure, services, and luxury resorts, while Zihuatanejo (See-wah-tah-*neh*-hoh, or just "Zihua"), only 4 miles to the south, is the quintessential rustic Mexican beach village—and, oddly, the place where cruise ships pull in. The area, with a backdrop of the Sierra Madre mountains and a foreground of Pacific Ocean waters, provides opportunities for beaching, scuba diving, deep-sea fishing, and golf.

Zihuatanejo spreads out around a beautiful bay, with the downtown area to the north and a beautiful long beach and the Sierra foothills to the east. The heart of town is the Paseo del Pescador, a brick waterfront walkway bordering the Municipal Beach and boasting many shops and calm, casual restaurants. A good highway connects Zihua to **Ixtapa,** where tall hotels line the wide Playa Palmar beach, with lush palm groves and mountains as their backdrop. The main street, Boulevard Ixtapa, is full of small shopping plazas and restaurants, with the Marina Ixtapa at the north end of the beach from the hotel zone boasting excellent restaurants, private yacht slips, and an 18-hole golf course. Unless you want to play golf or explore Ixtapa's more resortish style, we recommend settling back for a quiet day in Zihua.

COMING ASHORE   Ships anchor in sheltered **Zihuatanejo Bay** and tender passengers to the town's municipal pier. The brick-paved Paseo del Pescador adjoins, with shops and restaurants within easy walking distance.

GETTING AROUND   You can walk around Zihuatanejo. **Taxi** fares between Ixtapa and Zihuatanejo run about $5, while fares within either town hover in the $3-to-$6 range.

BEST CRUISE LINE SHORE EXCURSIONS

Zihuatanejo Sail & Snorkel ($67, 3 hr.): Climb aboard a trimaran and sail to Manzanillo Beach, one of the best snorkeling spots on the bay, where you'll drop anchor for direct access to the water.

Countryside Tour ($54, 3½ hr.): Leave Zihuatanejo by bus and head into the countryside, where you'll tour a fruit plantation that raises papaya, mango, grapefruit, and coconut; then visit an open-air factory to see bricks and floor tiles made using traditional methods. At Barra de Potosi lagoon, you can stroll the beach and watch local fishermen cast their nets.

Island Getaway ($44, 4½ hr.): Travel to Ixtapa and board a *panga* boat for the 5-minute ride to Isla Ixtapa, which is half nature reserve and half tourist area, with restaurants and beaches.

ON YOUR OWN: WITHIN WALKING DISTANCE

In Zihuatanejo, here's what you do: Step off the tender, take a big breath, then let it out and order a beer or margarita. That's about it. **Paseo del Pescador** is full of nice little bars, shops, and seafood restaurants, and occasionally a musician will stroll by. For a little history, the **Museo de Arqueología de la Costa Grande,** near Guerrero at the east end of Paseo del Pescador, traces the history of the Acapulco-to-Ixtapa/Zihuatanejo "Costa Grande" region starting in pre-Hispanic times (when it was known as Cihuatlán) through the colonial era. Most of the museum's pottery and stone artifacts give evidence of extensive trade with far-off cultures and regions, including the Toltec and Teotihuacán near Mexico City, the Olmec on the Pacific and Gulf coasts, and areas known today as the states of Nayarit, Michoacán, and San Luis Potosí. Local indigenous groups gave the Aztec tribute items, including cotton *tilmas* (capes) and *cacao* (chocolate), representations of which can be seen here. Signs are in Spanish, but an accompanying brochure is available in English. Admission is $1; closed Mondays.

Beyond the port area, there's only Ixtapa, and for cruise visitors, Ixtapa is mostly about . . .

BEACHES

IXTAPA   Ixtapa's main beach, **Playa Palmar,** is a lovely white-sand arc on the edge of the hotel zone, with dramatic rock formations silhouetted in the sea. The surf can be rough; use caution, and don't swim when a red flag is posted. Lovely **Playa Vista Hermosa,** located just south of Ixtapa, fronting the Hotel Las Brisas Ixtapa, is framed by striking rock formations and is very attractive for sunbathing—but has heavy surf and strong undertow (use caution if you swim here). **Playa Linda,** about 8 miles north of Ixtapa, is the primary out-of-town beach, with watersports equipment and horse rentals available.

ZIHUATANEJO   At Zihuatanejo's town beach, **Playa Municipal,** the local fishermen pull their colorful boats up onto the sand, making for a fine photo op. The small shops and restaurants lining the waterfront are great for people-watching and absorbing the flavor of daily village life. A cement-and-sand walkway runs from the *malecón* east along the water to **Playa Madera (Wood Beach),** which is good for bodysurfing. To the south is Zihuatanejo's largest and most beautiful beach, **Playa La Ropa,** a mile-long sweep of sand with calm waters and a great view of the sunset. Palm groves edge the shoreline, and some lovely small hotels and restaurants nestle in the hills. A taxi from town costs about $3. The beach's name stems from the sinking of a galleon that was carrying silk clothing *(ropa)* back from the Philippines. When the ship went down, its cargo washed ashore here. **Playa Las Gatas (Cats Beach),** across the bay from Playa La Ropa and Zihuatanejo, has exceptionally clear waters and a man-made reef that makes for calm swimming (good for kids) and good snorkeling. A little dive shop on the beach rents gear; there are also a number of open-air seafood restaurants. Water taxis from the Zihuatanejo town pier can get you here for about $3 round-trip.

SHOPPING

IXTAPA   Shopping in Ixtapa is not especially memorable: mostly T-shirts and Mexican crafts, plus brand-name sportswear. All of the shops are in the same area on Boulevard Ixtapa, across from the beachside hotels.

ZIHUATANEJO   Zihuatanejo has its share of T-shirt and souvenir shops, but it's also a decent place to buy crafts, folk art, and jewelry. The **artisans' market** on Calle Cinco de Mayo is a good place to start browsing before moving on to specialty shops that spread inland from the waterfront. For a taste of local commerce, visit the **municipal market,** which sprawls over several blocks off Avenida Benito Juárez (about 5 blocks inland from the waterfront). Here, produce, fish, and nut vendors mix with stands selling huarache sandals, hammocks, and baskets.

4 Mazatlán

Almost straight across the Sea of Cortez from Cabo San Lucas, Mazatlán—"The Land of the Deer" in the old Nahuatl language—dates from the beginning of the 19th century, when German immigrants developed it as a shipping port. After a lull of about 160 years, it gained new fame as a sport-fishing capital, then as a destination for American college kids on spring break. Today, families and mature vacationers are flocking here as well, taking advantage of the low prices and 10-plus miles of beaches. For cruise travelers, the points of interest form a huge barbell shape, with the historic **downtown** area at the south end (near where your ship docks), the tourist-oriented **Zona Dorada** (Golden Zone) about 4 miles to the north, and the long, uninteresting curve of Avenida del Mar between.

COMING ASHORE   Ships dock on the south side of town along a navigational channel, in the midst of substantial commercial shipping. Disembarking passengers must take a short tram from the ship to the welcome terminal, where they run a veritable gauntlet of gift and craft shops before popping out into air again on the far side.

GETTING AROUND   The port is about a 15- or 20-minute walk from the center of the old downtown, but you can also take a **taxi**. In fact, we challenge you *not* to—there are so many of them on hand at the pier that you might find yourself sitting in one without ever having intended to. In addition to the green-and-white, fixed-rate **Eco-Taxis,** you'll also see hundreds of open-sided **Pulmonía** cars, which look like a cross between a jeep and a golf cart. Apparently the name (which literally means pneumonia) stems from an old belief that riding in an open-air car can make you sick. Fares between the port (or Old Mazatlán) and the Zona Dorada average $4 to $7 for either kind of taxi.

BEST CRUISE LINE SHORE EXCURSIONS

In addition to the tours listed here, cruise lines offer a lot of "mix-and-match" Mazatlán bus tours, taking in highlights of downtown and almost always heading through the Golden Zone for shopping.

Old Mazatlán Walking Tour ($33, 4 hr.): Start at the shore-side Cerro de Neveria, where divers plunge off a cliff into the sea. Then amble through Old Mazatlán's narrow, shady streets, visiting the Teatro Angela Peralta (see "On Your Own," below), stopping at a cafe for refreshment and Nidart Gallery (see "Shopping," below) for some shopping, and then heading to the main plaza and the cathedral. It's not a bad way to get oriented, and you can continue walking on your own around the old market and then (if you like) around the coast or out to the Golden Zone.

Sierra Madre Tour ($65, 7½ hr.): Travel by bus into the foothills of the Sierra Madre to the town of Concordia, founded in 1550 and famed for its furniture, handmade pottery, and baroque church. Continue to Copala, a former gold-mining town founded in 1565, where you can wander the narrow, cobbled streets and see the old colonial houses and 16th-century stone church. The tour includes a traditional Mexican lunch and a shopping stop in the Zona Dorada.

Sport-Fishing Tournament ($139, 7 hr.): Everyone competes on this tour, in which passengers sail on 40-foot fishing boats and troll for marlin and sailfish. Beer is provided, and the winner gets a plaque. Now the bad news: Because the cruise ships can't store your catch, fishing for trophy fish is catch-and-release. Nontrophy fish are kept by the crew.

Pacifico Brewery Tour ($45, 2½ hr.): Founded in 1900, Pacifico brews one of Mexico's most popular beers. Tour the brewery, have a taste or three, and take in the incredible view of Mazatlán from the rooftop bar/hospitality room.

ON YOUR OWN: WITHIN WALKING DISTANCE

Though most people will probably take a taxi the short distance to downtown, we're going to consider it "walking distance" both for argument's sake (we walked it easily) and to distinguish it from the distant Golden Zone.

Downtown Mazatlán is centered around the palm-shaded **Plaza Principal,** also called Plaza Revolución and filled with vendors, pigeons, shoeshine men under blue Pacifico beer umbrellas, and old gentlemen sitting in the shade. A Victorian-style wrought-iron bandstand sits at its center and the **Cathedral of the Immaculate Conception** hovers over one end. Built in the 1800s, the cathedral has twin, yellow-tiled steeples, while its interior has a vaulted ceiling and more than a dozen chandeliers. It's worth a quick peek. One block behind the cathedral is the covered **Mercado Municipal** (aka Mercado Pino Suarez, or just "the municipal market"). Taking up the whole city block between Juarez and Serdan, it's got its share of tourist shops but is more a place for locals, with stands selling fresh produce, meat, clothing, herbal remedies, and religious mementos. It's a vibrant slice of life, as are all the streets around it.

Backtrack along Juarez a few blocks to reach Mazatlán's **historic district,** a 20-square-block area centered around the pretty little **Plazuela Machado,** which boasts a few sidewalk restaurants and sometimes hosts local events. It's bordered by Frías, Constitución, Carnaval, and Sixto Osuna. On one corner of the square stands the Italian-style **Teatro Angela Peralta** (© **669/982-4447;** www.culturamazatlan.com/tap-en.php), built between 1869 and 1881. A center of Mazatlán arts and culture for its first 40 years, the theater fell into disrepair following the Mexican revolution of 1910 and began a period of decay that lasted until the late 1980s, when a group of concerned citizens spearheaded its renewal. Today, the 841-seat theater is a national historic monument and regularly hosts folkloric ballets, contemporary dance, symphony concerts, opera, and jazz performances. Its sumptuous, jewel-box-like interior, with three levels of dark, woody balconies, has been restored to its 19th-century glory. It costs $1 to tour the building. The blocks around the theater and Plazuela abound with beautiful old buildings and colorful town houses trimmed with wrought iron and carved stone. Many buildings were restored as part of a downtown beautification program, and small galleries are beginning to move into the area as the neighborhood becomes the center of Mazatlán's artistic community. Half a block to the right of the theater's entrance is the **Nidart Gallery** (see "Shopping," below). Check out the **town houses** on Libertad between Domínguez and Carnaval and the two lavish **mansions** on Ocampo at Domínguez and at Carnaval. For a rest stop, try the **Café Pacífico** (decorated with historic pictures of Mazatlán) or one of the other cafes on the Plazuela. Those with an interest in Mexican history can walk a couple blocks down Sixto Osuna to Venustiano Carranza, where you'll find the small **Museo Arqueológico de Mazatlán,** Sixto Osuna 76 (© **669/981-1455**), which displays both pre-Hispanic artifacts and contemporary art. Admission is free; closed Mondays.

If you feel like taking a good, tiring walk, head west down Constitución toward the ocean; then turn left and walk along the oceanside walkway on Paseo Clausen. Passing the beach at Olas Altas (the original Mazatlán beach strip), you'll see signs for **Cerro del Vigía** (Lookout Hill). Follow these up the steep hill at the edge of town, bending

Mazatlán Golf Excursions

Mazatlán offers probably the best golf value in Mexico, with two notable courses open to the public.

- The 27-hole course at the **El Cid** resorts, just east of the Zona Dorada (© **669/913-3333;** www.elcid.com), has 9 holes designed by Lee Trevino as well as 18 designed by Robert Trent Jones, Jr. It's open to the public, though preference is given to hotel guests, and tee times book up quickly. Greens fees are $75 for 18 holes, plus $17 for the caddy.
- The **Estrella del Mar Golf Club,** across the channel from downtown, on Isla de la Piedra (© **669/982-3300;** www.estrelladelmar.com), is an 18-hole, 7,004-yard course, also designed by Robert Trent Jones, Jr. Greens fees, including cart, run $75 to $110 depending on the season.

around the school and then hugging the coast. Below, accessible via several sets of stairs, is **Playa del Centenario,** a lovely stretch of pounding surf with views of the offshore Sea Lion rocks, the El Faro lighthouse (the second-highest in the world, after Gibraltar), and Deer and Wolf islands, just off the Zona Dorada. Frigate birds and pelicans soar overhead, and down below are sea-carved arches and patches of bright-green vegetation. You'd be pounded to death on the rocks if you tried to swim here, but it's a romantic picnic spot. At the point of the lookout, a stair-path leads out to a viewing platform that resembles the prow of a ship and lets onto some wonderful vistas. From here, continue following the coast road right around and back to the cruise docks.

ON YOUR OWN: BEYOND THE PORT AREA

Four miles from downtown, the **Zona Dorada (Golden Zone)** begins where Avenida del Mar intersects Avenida Rafael Buelna and becomes Avenida Camarón Sábalo, which leads north through the tourist zone. While shops, restaurants, and bars are much more abundant here than downtown, it's very, very, very touristy, and worth the drive only if you're in a beach-party mood.

BEACHES

Much as we're not nuts about the Golden Zone, it is the better spot for beaches. At the beginning of the Zone, you'll find **Playa Gaviotas** and several other beaches backed by resort hotels. Remember that all beaches in Mexico are public property, so all of these are accessible to visitors. Farther north, **Playa Sábalo** is perhaps the best beach in Mazatlán. The next point jutting into the water is Punta Sábalo, beyond which you'll find a bridge over a channel that flows in and out of a lagoon. Beyond the marina, more beaches stretch all the way to Los Cerritos.

In the downtown area, **Playa Olas Altas** (at the western edge of town) is a thin strip of curving beach backed by several low-key sidewalk bars. It's the closest beach to the docks, but lacks any amenities or any kind of "scene." Around a rocky promontory north of Olas Altas is **Playa Norte,** which offers several miles of good sand beach with numerous *palapa* bars, but busy Avenida del Mar is right there behind you, taking something away from the experience.

SHOPPING

La Zona Dorada is the biggest area for shopping, with hundreds of shops and stalls selling the usual for this part of Mexico: jewelry, shell-covered art, T-shirts, and lots of other touristy souvenirs, with a smattering of folk art mixed in, most of it of dubious quality. **Downtown** is more oriented toward locals, but is much more authentic. Small galleries and shops are beginning to appear in the historic district around the Teatro Angela Peralta, among them the wonderful **Nidart Galería,** Av. Libertad 45 at Carnaval (© **669/985-5991;** www.nidart.com), an exhibition space selling works created by local artists on-site, as well as works from around Mexico. This is quality stuff, including clay and leather sculptures and masks, paintings, woodwork, jewelry, and other items, priced much lower than you'd expect. Many city tours offered by the cruise lines include a stop here.

5 Puerto Vallarta

Looking at the vibrant, bustling Puerto Vallarta of today, it's hard to imagine that only 50 years ago the only tourists who stopped here landed on a dirt airstrip outside town. Established in the 1850s as a port for processing silver from the Sierra Madre mountains, the place took off as a resort destination only when Hollywood stars began arriving 110 years later. In 1963, John Huston brought stars Ava Gardner and Richard Burton here to film the Tennessee Williams play *Night of the Iguana,* and Burton's new love, Elizabeth Taylor, came along even though both were married to other people at the time. Paparazzi arrived hot on their heels, and Puerto Vallarta was established as a tropical cauldron of sin and sun.

Downtown, a seaside promenade (or *malecón*) runs north–south beside Paseo Díaz Ordaz, adorned with public art and stretching the length of El Central—the center of town. From the waterfront, cobblestone streets reach a mere half-dozen blocks back into the hills. The areas bordering the **Río Cuale** are the oldest parts of town, and a lovely island in midstream, **Isla Cuale,** is full of shops and lush foliage. Three bridges link the two sections of downtown, the most pleasant being a footbridge that hugs the shoreline. Isla Cuale can be accessed from any of them. The area north of the river is the main tourist zone, while the area immediately to the south is home to a growing number of sidewalk cafes and fine restaurants, plus the town's better beaches.

Many excursions here will take you outside town and up into the foothills of the **Sierra Madre.** Farther up, the Huichol Indians still live in relative isolation, simultaneously protecting their culture from outside influences and making a living off their distinctive beaded artwork, which you'll see around town.

COMING ASHORE Cruise ships dock at the **Puerto Vallarta Marina,** about 3 miles north of downtown along the busy Avenida Francisco Medina Ascencio. A plethora of crafts and T-shirt shops, along with several small bars and restaurants, are clustered right in the port area; but it's not a destination in itself, so plan to take a taxi into town if you're not doing an excursion. Marina Vallarta, a resort and yacht harbor, is located just north of the terminal.

GETTING AROUND Technically, you can walk into town. We did it, just to see if it's worth doing, and here's the scoop: It's not. Instead, take a shore excursion to get back into the hills, or grab one of the **taxis** that greet ships at the dock, charging about $5. Once you're in the center of town, nearly everything is within walking distance both north and south of the river. And don't worry about getting back to the ship from here; the cabbies will find you.

BEST CRUISE LINE SHORE EXCURSIONS

Jungle Canopy Adventure ($99, 5 hr.): Ever wanted to be George of the Jungle? At a private reserve in the Sierra Madre, professional guides help you master the techniques of using horizontal traverse cables to travel through the jungle canopy, high up in the trees. Observation platforms give you a breather and a chance to observe the flora and fauna. At the end of your adventure, you rappel down a tree to the forest floor.

Deluxe Puerto Vallarta, Bullfight Demonstration & Show ($52, 4 hr.): A bus ride shows you some highlights of Vallarta (including Burton's and Taylor's old homes) before arriving at the central plaza for a little shopping, then on to the Plaza Del Toros, where a Mexican-style rodeo precedes a nonlethal demonstration of the art of the *corrida*—no bulls are injured.

Sierra Madre Hiking Expedition ($38, 4 hr.): Head by bus to Rancho Sierra Madre, where a local naturalist leads your 5-mile hike through the forest to a volcanic hot spring, where you can take a dip. Back at the ranch, you're free to wander around to check out the operation or just relax with a drink.

Hideaway at Las Caletas ($82, 7½ hr.): Las Caletas was Oscar-winning director John Huston's hideaway, so basically on this tour you get to live like a celeb, traveling to the cove by motor launch, relaxing on its palm-lined beaches and drinking in its bar, taking a nature hike, or going kayaking or snorkeling. Some of Huston's possessions are still on display.

San Sebastian/Sierra Madre Flightseeing ($169, 5 hr.): A 15-minute flight drops you off in the heart of the Sierra Madre, 4,200 feet above sea level, for a visit to the 17th-century silver-mining town of San Sebastian. Set in a mountain valley, it's full of colonial architecture and cobbled streets. The trip includes a walking tour of town, a visit to local homes to watch coffee being roasted, and lunch at a local restaurant.

Swimming with Dolphins ($159, 2–3 hr.): At the Dolphin Adventure Center, you get a half-hour in a saltwater pool with two Pacific bottlenose dolphins. Do we really have to say more? A longer excursion, **Dolphin Trainer for a Day** ($275, 7 hr.), lets you work with dolphin trainers in the water and out.

Swimming with Sea Lions ($92, 2½ hr.): At the Dolphin Adventure Center, you'll get an orientation about sea lion physiology and behavior before entering the water to swim with the big goofballs.

ON YOUR OWN: BEYOND THE PORT AREA

Assuming you don't want to make the hot, sometimes dusty 3-mile walk into town, let's call everything here beyond walking distance. Once you do make it to town, though, Puerto Vallarta's cobblestone streets are a pleasure to explore on foot: filled with small shops, rows of windows edged with curling wrought iron, and vistas of red-tile roofs and the sea. Start with a walk up and down the *malecón*, taking in the fine collection of public art that stretches from end to end. Across from Carlos O'Brien's restaurant on the north end is Ramiz Barquett's *Nostalgia,* depicting a couple sharing a romantic moment while gazing out to the bay. Farther south is an array of fanciful, almost Dr. Seuss–like chairs by renowned Mexican artist Alejandro Colunga, one topped with a large octopus head, another with giant ears for backrests. Farther south is Sergio Bustamante's *Ladder to Heaven,* depicting children climbing a ladder to nowhere. Closer to the main square, you'll find *Boy on the Seahorse,* which has become a Puerto Vallarta icon.

Near here, the main square is headed by the **Parish of Nuestra Señora de Guadalupe church,** topped with a curious crown held in place by angels. It's a replica of the one worn by Empress Carlota during her brief time in Mexico as Emperor Maximilian's wife. On its steps, women sell religious mementos; across the narrow street, stalls sell native herbs for curing common ailments. Stretching along the north end of the square, the municipal building has a large, folkloric **Manuel Lepe mural** inside in its stairwell.

Three blocks south of the church, head east on Libertad, lined with small shops and pretty upper windows, to the **Río Cuale municipal market** by the river (see "Shopping," below); then cross the bridge to **Isla Cuale.** Near the sea end of the island, the small **Museo Río Cuale** has a permanent exhibit of pre-Columbian ceramics, jewelry, and statuary (free admission).

Retrace your steps to the market and Libertad, and follow Calle Miramar to the set of rough stone steps. Follow these past the cute little blue-and-white **Graffity** cafe then take the steep, narrow, pastel steps up to Calle Zaragoza, pausing on the stairs to catch your breath and also for a nice view of the sea. Once on Zaragoza, go right 1 block to the famous **arched pink bridge** that connected Richard Burton's and Elizabeth Taylor's houses.

BEACHES

For years, beaches were Puerto Vallarta's main attraction. Unfortunately, those near the cruise terminal are the worst in the area, with darker sand and seasonal inflows of stones. Stretching south to town, the **hotel zone** is known for broad, smooth beaches, open to the public and accessible primarily through hotel lobbies. Just south of town, the easiest beach to reach is **Playa Los Muertos** (aka Playa Olas Altas or Playa del Sol), just off Calle Olas Altas, south of the Río Cuale. The water can be rough, but the wide beach is home to several *palapa* restaurants that offer food, beverage, and beach-chair service. About 6 miles south of town along Highway 200, **Playa Mismaloya,** where *Night of the Iguana* was filmed, boasts clear waters. Entrance to the public beach is just to the left of the Jolla de Mismaloya Resort. There's an *Iguana*-themed restaurant and bar on-site.

SHOPPING

Puerto Vallarta is one big shopping opportunity, with hundreds of small stores selling everything from fine folk art and modern art to tacky T-shirts, plus tremendous amounts of silver jewelry and sculpture depicting everything from Aztec calendars to Mickey Mouse. The **municipal market** is just north of the Río Cuale, where Calle Libertad and Calle Rodríguez meet. The *mercado* sells clothes, jewelry, serapes, shawls, leather accessories and suitcases, papier-mâché parrots, stuffed frogs and armadillos, and, of course, T-shirts. Be sure to comparison-shop, and definitely bargain before buying. Upstairs, a sort of low-key food court serves inexpensive Mexican meals, giving adventurous visitors a cheap, authentic dining experience. Exit the market by the corner of Encino and Maramoros and walk across the suspended plank-and-rope bridge to **Río Cuale Island,** where outdoor stalls sell crafts, gifts, folk art, and clothing.

Back in El Centro, head for the corner of Calle Galeana and Calle Morelos (right across from the *Boy on the Seahorse* statue) to find the **Huichol Collection Museum**

Gallery (© 322/223-2141), the best place in town for authentic Huichol Indian art. Descendants of the Aztec, the Huichol live in the high sierra north and east of Vallarta. They produce remarkable beadwork and "yarn painting" inspired by visions they experience during hallucinogenic peyote ceremonies. The colors explode from wall hangings, masks, bowls, and animal forms, the latter three made from carved wooden shapes to which incredibly intricate beadwork is added, eventually covering the entire surface. A Huichol artist is often at work in the back of the shop, and explanations in English tell you what you're looking at. Prices can be high for large pieces, but it's worth it for the quality.

Some of the more attractive shops are a block or two inland from the *malecón*, centered roughly around the intersection of Calle Corona and Calle Morelos. One block north, near the corner of Calle Aldama, **La Casa del Tequila** (© 322/222-2000) offers a tasting room where you can sample a selection of fine tequilas, plus a hacienda-style taco bar with swirling ceiling fans and cane seating.

13

Bermuda

This neat and tidy oasis in the middle of the Atlantic is edged in pink-sand beaches and rocky cliffs—and crawling with Brits in shorts. And not just any shorts, but shorts colored in perky tones of pink, green, or yellow, and paired with sports jackets, ties, and knee-highs. To the casual visitor, Bermuda is a pleasant paradox of sorts, mixing sane and proper with a healthy dose of silly (back to those shorts again). But what really matters to the cruise passenger is that Bermuda is an orderly, beautiful, easy place to visit. Aside from the Caribbean, the island nation of Bermuda, sitting out in the Atlantic roughly parallel to South Carolina (or Casablanca, if you're measuring from the east), is the other major cruise destination from the U.S. Eastern Seaboard.

Although the Spanish stumbled upon Bermuda in the early 16th century, it was the British who first settled here in 1609, when the ship *Sea Venture,* en route to Virginia's Jamestown colony, was wrecked on the island's reefs. No lives were lost, and the crew and passengers built two new ships and continued on to Virginia; but three crewmembers stayed behind and became the island's first permanent settlers. Bermuda became a crown colony in 1620 and remains one today, retaining a very British character—the island is divided up into parishes, driving is on the left, and horse-drawn carriages trot about—but the sun and the ubiquitous Bermuda shorts serve as proof you're in the islands.

That's not to say things aren't bustling when the ships are in town at Hamilton and St. George's, Bermuda's two main port towns, but a calm and controlled atmosphere reigns as visitors fan out across the island. There are many powdery-soft beaches easily accessible by taxi or motor scooter, and Bermuda has more golf courses per square mile than any other place in the world. For shoppers, Front and Queen streets in Hamilton offer dozens of shops and department stores, most specializing in English items, while the interest of history buffs is piqued by the nearly 300-year-old St. Peter's Church, museums, and other sites within walking distance of the pier in St. George's. There are also impressive exhibits at the Maritime Museum, which is built into the ruins of Bermuda's oldest fort at the Royal Naval Dockyard, the island's third, and least used, port at the West End.

Cruise ships have been sailing to Bermuda for over a century, making it one of the earliest cruise destinations. The Quebec Steamship Company, which eventually evolved into the Furness Bermuda Line, began service from New York to Bermuda in 1874 with the small steamers *Canima* and *Bermuda* and then added the *Orinoco* in 1881, the *Trinidad* in 1893, and the liner *Pretoria,* acquired from the Union Line, in 1897.

Unlike most Caribbean itineraries, on which ships visit ports for a day at most, the majority of Bermuda-bound ships

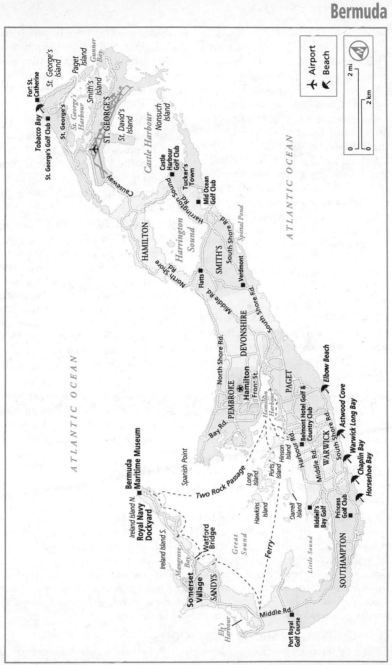

Bermuda

Airport ✈
Beach 🏄

2 mi
2 km

ATLANTIC OCEAN

ATLANTIC OCEAN

Fort St. Catherine
Tobacco Bay
St. George's Golf Club
St. George's
St. George's Island
Paget Island
Gunner Bay
Smith's Island
St. George's Harbour
ST. GEORGE'S
St. David's Island
Nonsuch Island
Castle Harbour
Castle Harbour Golf Club
Tucker's Town
Mid Ocean Golf Club
Causeway
Harrington Sound
Harrington Sound Rd.
Spital Pond
HAMILTON
South Shore
Verdmont
SMITH'S
Flatts
North Shore Rd.
Middle Rd.
South Shore Rd.
DEVONSHIRE
North Shore Rd.
PEMBROKE
Hamilton
Front St.
Hamilton Harbour
PAGET
Elbow Beach
Bay Rd.
Belmont Hotel Golf & Country Club
Astwood Cove
Warwick Long Bay
Spanish Point
Bermuda Maritime Museum
Harbour Rd.
Middle Rd.
South Shore Rd.
WARWICK
Chaplin Bay
Horseshoe Bay
Two Rock Passage
Long Island
Ports Island
Hinson Island
Riddell's Bay Golf
Princess Golf Club
Ireland Island N.
Royal Navy Dockyard
Hawkins Island
Darrell Island
Little Sound
SOUTHAMPTON
Ireland Island S.
Watford Bridge
Great Sound
Ferry
Mangrove Bay
Somerset Village
SANDYS
Ely's Harbour
Middle Rd.
Port Royal Golf Course

653

spend several whole days at the island. To protect its hotel trade and to maintain a semblance of order and keep the island from getting overrun by too many tourists, the government of Bermuda limits the number of ships that can visit the island on a regular basis during its season, late April through October, when the temperatures hover between 75°F and 85°F (24°C and 29°C) and extended rainfall is rare. Currently, no more than five ships are permitted on weekdays (and no more than 8,500 passengers on any one day), though the overall number of cruise ship visits has been increasing over the past few years. So has the size of ships. In the old days, 50,000 tonners were about as big as the Island chain got. Now, supermegas, such as the 142,000-ton *Explorer of the Seas,* are regulars.

HOME PORTS FOR THIS REGION **New York, New Jersey,** and **Boston** are the main hubs for Bermuda cruises, with ships sailing round-trip on mostly 7-night itineraries. A few ships also sail to Bermuda round-trip from **Baltimore** and **Philadelphia.** Still a few more itineraries include Bermuda on **transatlantic crossings** in spring and fall, or visit the island as part of longer itineraries that also include Caribbean ports.

LANGUAGE & CURRENCY The official language is **English.** The currency is the **Bermuda dollar** (BD$), which is pegged to the U.S. dollar on an equal basis—BD$1 equals US$1. There's no need to exchange any U.S. money for Bermudian.

SHOPPING TIPS While St. George's and the Royal Naval Dockyard both have their souvenir shops, Hamilton is the center of Bermuda's shopping universe. Here, it's all about English (and some Irish) goodies such as porcelain, crystal, wool clothing, cashmere sweaters, and linens, and it's all within walking distance, right outside of the terminal. Don't expect great deals, though—prices in Bermuda are generally on the high side.

1 Hamilton

Hamilton was once known as the "Show Window of the British Empire." It has been the capital of Bermuda since 1815, when it replaced St. George's. Today, it's the economic hub of the island.

COMING ASHORE Cruise ships tie up at docks smack-dab in the middle of town. The terminal funnels passengers right into the main shopping drag on Front Street.

GETTING AROUND You can walk to all of the shops and department stores in town, or take a walking tour for a more historic perspective. Walking-tour maps are available in the terminal. If you're beach-bound or heading for a day of golf or some other attraction, there are **taxis** lined up outside the terminal (they're metered and expensive, starting at $4.80 and going up $1.70 for each additional mile). Roads are well maintained, but narrow and winding. The **bus** and **ferry** systems are also userfriendly. There are **horse-drawn carriages** at the terminal, and many folks go the **scooter** or **moped** route; rentals are available near the terminal.

BEST CRUISE LINE SHORE EXCURSIONS

Though there's much you can do independently, from beach hopping to shopping and walking tours, if you crave a guide to narrate the highlights, or want to do something active such as snorkel or bike ride, the ships' organized tours are your best bet. The sampling below is generally offered from both Hamilton and St. George's.

Guided Walking Tour of St. George's ($52, 2 hr.): Learn about Bermuda's history, including its churches, art galleries, libraries, and private gardens.

Railway Trail Cruise & Bike Tour ($72, 3 hr.): Take a scenic coastal cruise to the rural West End, where you'll hop on a 21-speed bike. Pedal along the path where the original Bermuda Railway once ran on narrow-gauge tracks. The tracks are gone, but a trail remains behind; and this excursion is a great opportunity to get views of the ocean and the island's lush gardens and bird life. The flat route covers 8km to 13km (5–8 miles).

Snorkeling Trip ($60, 3 hr.): From Hamilton, board a boat and motor out to a snorkeling spot near the West End as the captain talks to passengers about Bermuda history and customs. Then, after an hour or so of snorkeling, the fun begins: The music is turned on, the dancing starts, and the bar opens as the boat heads back to port.

Coral Reef Glass-Bottom Boat Cruise ($38, 1½ hr.): See the coral reefs and colorful fish living in Bermuda's waters; then view one of Bermuda's famous shipwrecks and enjoy a rum swizzle from a fully stocked bar.

Golf Excursion ($55–$225, half-day): Excursions include tee times for 18 holes at challenging courses such as Mid Ocean Golf Club, among the best in the world; Riddells Bay Golf & Country Club, a veritable golfing institution built in 1922; Port Royal Golf Course; and St. George's Golf Club, designed by Robert Trent Jones. A taxi to and from the courses may be extra and club rental is about $30 extra, but carts are included. The golf excursions are often sold directly through an onboard golf pro who organizes lessons on the ship, too.

ON YOUR OWN: WITHIN WALKING DISTANCE

A walking tour is a great option. Pick up a map in the cruise terminal and you're on your leisurely way to visiting sights that range from the 200-year-old post office to the exhibits in the Bermuda Historical Society Museum. If a relaxing lunch on the waterfront appeals to your sense of adventure, stroll on over to the waterside **Poinciana Terrace at the Waterloo House,** on Pitts Bay Road (© **441/295-4480;** www.waterloo. com), an elegant property within walking distance of the ship docks. Lunch is served on the outdoor patio overlooking the colorful and idyllic harbor, and many snazzy-looking businesspeople dine here. If it's on the menu, the fish chowder, laced with rum and sherry peppers, is a local favorite and a great choice. Lunch costs around $30.

Consider a visit to the **Bermuda Underwater Exploration Institute** (© **441/292-7219;** www.buei.bm); it's adjacent to the Hamilton docks near the roundabout on East Broadway. There are two floors of interactive exhibits about the ocean, plus the highlight: a capsule that simulates a 3,600m (11,800-ft.) dive below the ocean's surface (it accommodates 21 people at a time). Open 9am to 5pm Monday through Friday, 10am to 5pm Saturday and Sunday (last admission is 3pm); admission is $13 for adults and $6 for kids 6 to 16.

The **Bermuda Railway Trail** offers about 29km (18 miles) of trails divided into easy-to-explore sections. It was created along the course of the old Bermuda Railway, which stretched a total of 34km (21 miles) and served the island from 1931 to 1948, until the automobile was introduced. Armed with a copy of the *Bermuda Railway Trail Guide,* available at the various visitor centers located in and right outside the cruise terminals, you can set out on your own expedition via foot or bicycle (most of the moped/scooter rental agencies have bicycles as well). Most of the trail winds along a car-free route, and there is a section of trail in St. George's and near Hamilton.

ON YOUR OWN: BEYOND THE PORT AREA

The throngs head to the beaches, and for good reason. Many are powdery soft and some even pinkish (from crushed shells, corals, and other sea life), they're easily accessible by taxi or motor scooter from Hamilton and St. George's, and most (including Horseshoe Bay) are free. **Horseshoe Bay,** in Southampton Parish, is our top pick. Though you certainly won't have it to yourself because it's so popular with lots of other tourists, the horseshoe-shaped beach has scenic rocky cliffs at its edges and a vast soft plane of sand in the middle. It's perfect for little kids, as the sand is so silky smooth, it won't irritate delicate little faces. Horseshoe is free and has a snack bar, bathrooms, and showers.

Other beach options include **Elbow Beach** (in Paget Parish), **Astwood Cove** (Warwick Parish), **Chaplin Bay** (Warwick and Southampton parishes), **Warwick Long Bay** (Warwick Parish), and **Tobacco Bay Beach** (St. George's Parish), where the water is very calm and the beach is tiny.

The more adventurous can hop on a scooter and beach-hop among the many unnamed slivers of silky sand tucked into the jagged coastline. If you're itching to see more than Hamilton, and beaches aren't your bag, another great option is hopping on a local ferry (the terminal is next to the cruise docks). For just a few bucks, either ride just for the view of Bermuda's colorful harbors and coastline, or head to the Royal Naval Dockyard on the island's far west end, where you can tour the historic fortress ruins and excellent museums.

2 St. George's

Quaint and historic, St. George's was the second English town established in the New World, after Jamestown in Virginia. King's Square, also called Market Square or the King's Parade, is the center of life here, and it's just steps from where the cruise ships dock.

COMING ASHORE   Cruise ships tie up at the docks smack-dab in the middle of town.

GETTING AROUND   Same deal as Hamilton, above: You can walk to a handful of historic attractions (see below), or if you're beach-bound or heading off for a day of golf, there are **taxis** lined up steps from the ships in King's Square (they're metered and expensive, starting at $4.80 and going up $1.70 for each additional mile). The island's **bus** and **ferry** systems are also user-friendly (though you have to get to Hamilton or the Royal Naval Dockyard to catch a ferry), and many fearless folks go the **scooter** or **moped** route; rentals are available near the terminal for about $50 to $60 per day. Try **Oleander Cycles** (© 441/295-0919), **Smatt's Cycle Livery** (© 441/295-1180), or **Wheels Cycles** (© 441/292-2245).

BEST CRUISE LINE SHORE EXCURSIONS

See "Best Cruise Line Shore Excursions" under "Hamilton," above.

ON YOUR OWN: WITHIN WALKING DISTANCE

As in Hamilton, a great option is grabbing a free walking-tour map from the tourism office in King's Square, just steps from your ship. Sights on the 17-stop tour include **Ordnance Island,** a tiny piece of land that juts into the harbor just in front of the dock, where a replica of *Deliverance*—the vessel that carried the shipwrecked *Sea Venture* passengers on to Virginia—stands. Don't miss a quick stop at **St. Peter's Church,** on Duke of York Street, believed to be the oldest Anglican place of worship in the Western Hemisphere; some headstones in the cemetery date back 300 years, and the present church was built in 1713. The oldest stone building in Bermuda, the **Old State House,** built about 1620, sits at the top of King Street and was once the home of the Bermuda Parliament. At the intersection of Featherbed Alley and Duke of Kent Street is **St. George's Historical Society Museum,** which houses a collection of Bermudian historic artifacts and cedar furniture.

ON YOUR OWN: BEYOND THE PORT AREA

A mile or so from King's Square in St. George's (you could actually walk it without too much effort if you like a hardy trek), overlooking the beach where the shipwrecked crew of the *Sea Venture* came ashore in 1609, is **Fort St. Catherine,** which you'll want to see. Completed in 1614, and reconstructed several times after, it was named for the patron saint of wheelwrights and carpenters. The fortress houses a museum, with several worthwhile exhibits. Admission costs $5.

In **Flatts Village,** about halfway between Hamilton and St. George's, is the **Bermuda Aquarium, Museum & Zoo** (📞 441/293-2727; www.bamz.org). There are interactive displays, huge aquariums, and seal feedings throughout the day. Open daily from 9am to 5pm (last admission at 4pm); admission is $10 for adults and $5 for seniors and children 6 to 12.

You can also opt for the same beaches, golf courses, and other attractions mentioned in the "Hamilton" section, above. St. George's and Hamilton are about a 20- to 30-minute taxi ride apart (depending on traffic).

3 Royal Naval Dockyard

A few ships, usually the largest ones, dock at the Royal Naval Dockyard, sometimes called King's Wharf, on the West End; you can walk to the sprawling complex there. Constructed by convict labor, this 19th-century fortress was used by the British Navy until 1951 as a strategic dockyard. Today, it's a major tourist attraction whose centerpiece is the **Bermuda Maritime Museum** (📞 441/234-1418; www.bmm.bm), the most important and extensive museum on the island. Exhibits are housed in six large halls within the complex, and the displays all relate to Bermuda's long connection with the sea, from Spanish exploration to 20th-century ocean liners. You can have a look at maps, ship models, and such artifacts as gold bars, pottery, jewelry, and silver coins recovered from 16th- and 17th-century shipwrecks such as the *Sea Venture*. Open daily from 9:30am to 5pm (last admission at 4pm); admission is $10 adults, $5 kids. There are a handful of restaurants in the complex, as well as shops. Taxis are also readily available.

14

Hawaii

Honeymooners flock here for a reason: The place is gorgeous and culturally vibrant. Even *The Brady Bunch* schlepped Alice and the six kids to Hawaii (you didn't see them going to Disney World, did you?). But it's not all about surfer boys and hula girls. The diverse landscape on this cluster of islands in the Pacific ranges from fuming volcanoes to crashing surf, serene beaches, and lush jungles. In a place where the weather really is perfect all the time, it's no surprise that the locals are so mellow. Learn to surf, go to a luau, snooze on the sand, enjoy the local coffee, or check out the native Hawaiian culture, which the locals are fiercely proud of. The past survives alongside the modern world in a vibrant arts scene, which includes traditional Polynesian dance and music, as well as painting, sculpture, and crafts. You'll also likely get a glimpse of age-old customs such as outrigger canoe races, the most popular sport in all of Hawaii, and, of course, the ubiquitous ukulele playing.

Norwegian Cruise Line (NCL) rules the roost here, with three ships doing year-round cruises among the islands round-trip from Honolulu (and a fourth, part of the year). Thanks to some intense lobbying in Congress (because the vessels were all either partially or completely built abroad), NCL's three Hawaii vessels sail under the U.S. flag, which means the ships can concentrate solely on the islands and don't have to throw in a call to a foreign port (a requirement for foreign-flagged vessels). In isolated Hawaii, this is a real advantage that no competing line is currently able to offer (see NCL review on p. 199 for details).

Aside from NCL's cruises, ships typically stop in the islands in April, May, September, and October. The four main ports here are **Oahu,** where you'll find the famous Waikiki Beach; **Maui,** home of the historic town of Lahaina; **Kauai,** the most natural and undeveloped of the four; and the **Big Island,** home of the state's famous volcanoes, including Mauna Kea and the still-active Kilauea.

HOME PORTS FOR THIS REGION Honolulu, on Oahu, is the main hub for interisland cruises. Foreign-flagged vessels generally sail from the mainland—from ports such as **Ensenada** (Mexico), **San Diego, Seattle,** and/or **Vancouver**—hitting the Hawaiian Islands as they cruise between seasons in the Caribbean and Alaska.

LANGUAGE & CURRENCY While **English** is the official language, it is infused with a few native **Hawaiian** words, including the customary greeting, *aloha.* (Contrary to what you may believe, "Book 'em, Danno" is not actually a native phrase.) The **U.S. dollar** is the official currency.

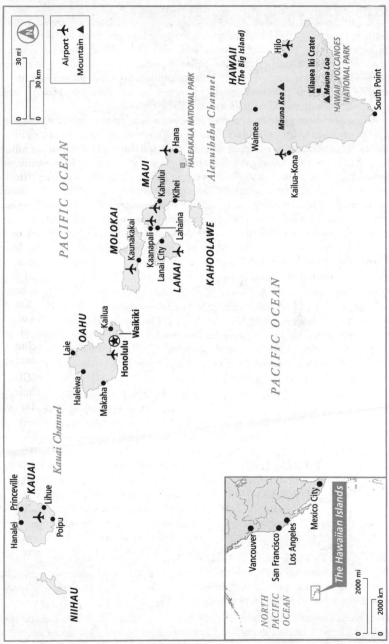

The Hawaiian Islands

Airport ✈
Mountain ▲

30 mi
30 km

PACIFIC OCEAN

NIIHAU

Kauai Channel

KAUAI
Hanalei
Princeville
Lihue
Poipu

OAHU
Laie
Haleiwa
Makaha
Kailua
Honolulu
Waikiki

MOLOKAI
Kaunakakai

LANAI
Lanai City

MAUI
Kaanapali
Lahaina
Kahului
Kihei
Hana
HALEAKALA NATIONAL PARK

KAHOOLAWE

Alenuihaha Channel

HAWAII
(The Big Island)
Hilo
Waimea
Kailua-Kona
Kilauea Iki Crater
Mauna Kea ▲
▲*Mauna Loa*
HAWAII VOLCANOES
NATIONAL PARK
South Point

PACIFIC OCEAN

NORTH PACIFIC OCEAN
Vancouver
San Francisco
Los Angeles
Mexico City

The Hawaiian Islands

2000 mi
2000 km

1 Oahu

Oahu is a relatively small island, measuring 26 miles long and some 44 miles across at its widest, totaling 597 square miles of land, with 112 miles of coastline. Everyone ventures to Oahu seeking a different experience. Some talk about wanting to find the "real" Hawaii, some are looking for heart-pounding adventure, some yearn for the relaxing and healing powers of the islands, and others are drawn by Hawaii's aloha spirit, where kindness and friendliness prevail.

All kinds of memorable experiences can be yours here. Imagine yourself sitting in a kayak watching the brilliant colors of dawn etch themselves across the sky, sipping a mai tai while you take in sweeping views of the south shore and the Waianae Mountains, battling a magnificent game fish on a high-tech sport-fishing boat, or listening to melodic voices chant the stories of a proud people and a proud culture that was overthrown little more than a century ago. By far the most social of the islands, Oahu has some of the best shopping and most fashionable promenade strips, as well as beautiful beaches with all the classic ingredients: tall palms, white sand, gentle surf, and plenty of sunshine. **Waikiki Beach** offers the best of both worlds. Its trendy eateries, high-end hotels, and ritzy shops collide with a stunning beachfront. It's like Rodeo Drive meets South Beach, only better.

COMING ASHORE   Ships dock at the Port of Honolulu, Pier 10, alongside the festive, well-appointed **Aloha Tower Marketplace** in Honolulu. Half shopping center, half cruise pier and promenade, this waterfront two-level mall centers around a five-story tower built in the 1920s. It's a landmark focal point that can easily be spotted around town. The pier can accommodate two ships. At press time, a new $25-million cruise terminal was expected to open shortly at the former industrial Pier 2 nearby. This pier will accommodate an additional cruise ship, bringing the total capacity in Honolulu to three.

GETTING AROUND   Aloha Tower is a convenient jumping-off point for walking tours of the downtown historic sights, and it's just a short taxi ride to nearby beaches, shopping, and museums. **Taxis** queue up at the information booth near the adjacent parking area; a ride to Ala Moana Beach costs about $10 for up to five people. If you miss out, call **City Taxi** (© **808/524-2121**) or hop on the San Francisco–style open-air trolley called **Waikiki Trolley** (© **800/824-8804** or 808/593-2822; www.waikiki trolley.com), which runs to Ala Moana shopping center, Ala Moana Beach, and downtown. **TheBus** (© **808/848-5555;** www.thebus.org) leaves every 30 minutes or so from in front of the Maritime Center and stops at several locations. You can also pick up a **rental car** at the nearby airport, but with so many other transportation options, it's unnecessary (and the one-way road system can be confusing).

BEST CRUISE LINE SHORE EXCURSIONS

Pearl Harbor and USS *Missouri* ($75, 6½ hr.): For those old enough to remember World War II and those who can't forget 9/11, a tour of Pearl Harbor and the USS *Missouri* is a deeply moving experience.

Historic & Cultural Honolulu ($55, 4½ hr.): A good sampler, this tour makes stops at Pearl Harbor, 'Iolani Palace, and Chinatown in downtown Honolulu, as well as Punchbowl National Cemetery. See "On Your Own: Within Walking Distance," below, for descriptions of these locations.

Grand Circle Island Tour ($89, 7 hr.): Given the island's immense natural beauty, a drive around Oahu is time well spent (make sure to bring your camera with you on the bus!). Views from inside Diamond Head Crater, an extinct volcano, rival those of the breathtaking carved shoreline at Hanauma Bay or the sweeping coastal vistas from Pali Lookout. Lunch is included.

ON YOUR OWN: WITHIN WALKING DISTANCE

Right next to the pier is the **Hawaii Maritime Center** (© 808/523-6151; www.holo holo.org/maritime), where you can learn about Hawaii's maritime history and view artifacts from the days of sailing, whaling, yachting, and Matson Line cruising. Admission is $7.50 for adults, $4.50 for children, and free for kids 5 and under. You can also visit a sailing ship, the *Falls of Clyde,* as well as a replica of an ancient Polynesian canoe.

A short walk up Richards Street, across Nimitz Highway, brings you into downtown Honolulu. If you go right on South King Street, you'll come to a statue of **King Kamehameha I,** the famed Hawaiian ruler. Across the street, at the corner of South King and Richards streets, stands **'Iolani Palace** (© 808/522-0832; www.iolani palace.org), America's only royal residence, where Hawaii's last monarch ruled until 1893. The building of this Italian Renaissance palace, which had electricity before both the White House and Buckingham Palace, nearly bankrupted the kingdom. Admission is $20 adults, $5 children (kids under 5 admitted only in the gallery); open Tuesday through Saturday. One block farther up King Street, **Kawaiahao Church,** 957 Punchbowl St. (© 808/522-1333), was the first stone church built on Oahu and is home to a royal burial ground. Admission is free. Next door is the **Mission House Museum,** 553 S. King St. (© 808/531-0481; www.missionhouses.org), a cute old mission house open for tours Tuesday through Saturday. Admission is $10 adults, $6 kids; tickets must be purchased in advance.

Walking 5 blocks west from the museum along South King Street brings you to America's oldest **Chinatown.** Selling everything from flower leis to exotic fruits and vegetables, this crowded market area is a haggler's dream.

ON YOUR OWN: BEYOND THE PORT AREA

Just north of Lunalilo Freeway at the end of Puowaina Drive is **Punchbowl Crater,** which houses the **National Memorial Cemetery of the Pacific** (© 808/532-3720; www.interment.net/data/us/hi/oahu/natmem/index.htm). This natural landscape feature, called "hill of sacrifice" by early Hawaiians, now serves as a burial ground for 3,500 victims of war. Admission is free. To really learn about the history of Hawaii and its people, drop in at the **Bishop Museum,** 1525 Bernice St. (© 808/847-3511; www.bishopmuseum.org). Created in 1889, and now the State Museum of Natural and Cultural History, this Victorian building houses an extensive collection of artifacts from ancient Polynesians, Hawaiian royalty, turn-of-the-20th-century immigrants, and more. Daily cultural shows and tours enrich the experience. Admission is $16 adults, $13 kids.

At **Pearl Harbor** (© 808/422-0561), you can't miss the *Arizona* **Memorial** (© 808/422-2771; www.nps.gov/usar), built right above the shallow water where the ship was sunk on December 7, 1941, or the battleship **USS** *Missouri* (© 808/423-2263; www.ussmissouri.com), on the decks of which peace was declared. Admission to the *Arizona* is free. Tickets for the *Missouri* are $16 for adults, $8 for children under 12, plus additional fees for guided tours. What you may not notice, and should, is the

If You're Embarking in Honolulu . . .

WHERE TO STAY

In the minds of many, Oahu and its most famous city, Honolulu, are synonymous. Honolulu's best-known neighborhood, Waikiki, is actually pretty small, but its spectacular beach and array of resort hotels are the attractions that originally put Hawaii on the tourist map. The choices for accommodations are nearly limitless, ranging from budget to ultraluxury.

For families watching their wallet, there are nearly a dozen **Ohana Hotels** that offer clean and affordable lodging in convenient downtown locations. Try the **Ohana Waikiki West,** 2330 Kuhio Ave. (© **808/922-5022;** www.ohana hotels.com), 2 blocks from Waikiki Beach. Downside? It's on a very busy part of Kuhio Avenue. But rooms can go to as low as $99 per night in the off season. To escape the hustle and bustle, head over to the **Hawaiiana Hotel,** 260 Beachwalk (© **808/923-3811;** www.hawaiianahotelatwaikiki.com), or next door to the **Breakers,** 250 Beachwalk (© **808/923-3181**). Both properties offer spacious motel-style rooms that surround a tranquil pool and garden; rates start at about $125 double.

Trendy visitors should check into the **Resort Quest Waikiki Beach Hotel,** 2570 Kalakaua Ave. (© **800/922-7866;** www.resortquesthawaii.com), where New York City chic meets Miami cool. Check out the surfboards adorning the walls of the lobby. Rates for a standard room start as low as $150 double. If it's a Victorian setting you crave, don't miss the **Sheraton Moana Surfrider,** 2365 Kalakaua Ave. (© **808/922-3111;** www.sheraton-hawaii. com). Lovingly referred to as the first lady of Waikiki, this grand hotel debuted in 1901 as the first true resort on the island and still retains the

---

USS *Bowfin* **Submarine Museum and Park** (© 808/423-1341; www.bowfin.org). This National Historic Landmark offers a rare glimpse into the thrill and danger of life aboard a submarine. The self-guided audio tour is narrated by the vessel's last captain, who takes you through the cramped quarters where men slept nose-to-nose with torpedoes, bathed in miniscule showers, and took turns eating in the tiny galley. This tour is not recommended for people with claustrophobia or those who may have difficulty going up or down ladders. Admission is $10 adults, $3 kids 4 to 12.

BEACHES

Nearby **Ala Moana Beach Park,** on Ala Moana Park Drive, has white sand and calm warm water—it's perfect for families. Like most beaches in Hawaii, it's free and uncrowded, especially on weekdays. It has a paved walkway and grassy areas where you can lounge or picnic under a tree. A taxi here costs about $10 from the port, or you can catch a bus from the Maritime Center for $2.

A few miles farther south is the famous **Waikiki Beach.** One-way taxi fare will run about $15. This beach is popular with locals, who will often occupy the cement picnic tables under open-air shelters and play chess or just watch the action. While surprisingly small, it is favored for surfing, suntanning, or just people-watching. Restrooms, showers, and beach rentals are all to be had at the far end near Kapiolani Park.

same elegance and charm it started with 100 years ago. Rates for a standard city-view room start at $310 double.

WHERE TO DINE

On the second floor of the Resort Quest Waikiki Beach Hotel, **Tiki's Grill and Bar,** 2570 Kalakaua Ave. (© 808/923-TIKI; www.tikisgrill.com), is a restaurant and open-air tiki bar that overlooks the promenade and beach. The live music plays second fiddle to the sunset views and trendy crowd. The pig quesadilla is loaded with tender pork, plenty of cheese, and topped with fresh corn salsa. Main courses run $12 to $30.

Surprisingly popular is the **Cheesecake Factory,** near the Royal Hawaiian Shopping Center (© 808/924-5001). Serving its standard plethora of trendy dishes in heaping portions, the alfresco dining and central location mean there's usually a wait for a table. Main courses cost $15 to $30.

With an equally long wait, but lower price tag, **Cheeseburger in Paradise,** 2500 Kalakaua Ave. (© 808/923-3731), delivers exactly that. Served in a basket, with a side of fries, the burgers come in nearly every incarnation, including chili, guacamole, bacon, and Island Style, with a slice of grilled Maui pineapple. There are also tasty salads and veggie or tofu burgers, with or without cheese. Main courses average $9 to $13.

For a serene outdoor dining experience, try dinner on the **Banyan Veranda,** at the Sheraton Moana Surfrider (see "Where to Stay," above). Its prix-fixe dinner menu is available nightly from 5:30 to 9pm. Afternoon tea is served Monday through Saturday from 1 to 4pm and Sunday from 3 to 4pm.

Sandy Beach, on the eastern tip of the island, is a favorite spot for boogie boarding. While the white crashing surf may look appealing, take a moment to read the numerous warning signs, and exercise great care—lifeguards do more beach rescues here than anywhere else. If a red flag is flying, it means the surf is too dangerous to enter. A taxi will cost between $50 and $70 each way; keep in mind that many taxis can accommodate six or eight passengers, so the fare can be shared.

Another popular beach is **Hanauma Bay,** nestled in a volcanic crater just before Sandy Beach. You approach the beach from above and pass through the Marine Education Center, which also provides a motorized tram that will take you down the steep road to the beach and back for $1 round-trip. There's a $5 entrance fee; the beach is closed every Tuesday. There is also a shuttle ($2 each way) from Waikiki to Hanauma Bay that runs every half-hour between 9am and 1pm, with stops at city bus stops and several hotels. For more info, call **TheBus** (© 808/848-5555; www.thebus.org).

SHOPPING

The majority of stores in **Aloha Tower** cater to tourists, selling uniquely Hawaiian wares. Some fine carved wood and bark cloth can be found at a few shops on the second level. For those who like to indulge in serious window-shopping, head to **Kalakaua Avenue** at Waikiki Beach, where you can find everything from Coach bags to board shorts, all on a bustling strip complete with statues, reflecting pools, street performers, and, at dusk, flaming tiki torches and alfresco dining. To see some of the island's handmade artwork, drop into the **Nohea Gallery,** in the lobby of the Sheraton Moana Surfrider, 2365 Kalakaua Ave. (© **808/922-3111;** www.moana-surfrider.com).

2 Kauai

Kauai ranks right up there with Bora Bora, Huahine, and Rarotonga on any list of the world's most spectacular islands. All the elements are here: moody rainforests, majestic cliffs, jagged peaks, emerald valleys, palm trees swaying in the breeze, daily rainbows, and some of the most spectacular beaches you'll find anywhere. Soft tropical air, sunrise bird song, essences of ginger and plumeria, golden sunsets, sparkling waterfalls—you don't just go to Kauai, you absorb it with all of your senses. It may get more than its fair share of tropical downpours, but that's what makes it so lush and green—and creates an abundance of rainbows.

Kauai is essentially a single large shield volcano that rises 3 miles above the sea floor. The island lies 90 miles across the open ocean from Oahu, but it seems at least a half-century removed in time. It's often called "the separate kingdom" because it stood alone and resisted King Kamehameha's efforts to unite Hawaii. In the end, a royal kidnapping was required to take the Garden Isle: After King Kamehameha died, his son, Liholiho, ascended the throne. He gained control of Kauai by luring Kauai's king, Kaumualii, aboard the royal yacht and sailing to Oahu; once there, Kaumualii was forced to marry Kaahumanu, Kamehameha's widow, thereby uniting the islands.

A Kauai rule is that no building may exceed the height of a coconut tree—between three and four stories. As a result, the island itself, not its palatial beach hotels, is the attention-grabber. There are no opulent shopping malls here, but what Kauai lacks in glitz, it more than makes up for in sheer natural splendor, with verdant jungle, the endless succession of spectacular beaches, the grandeur of Waimea Canyon, and the drama of the Napali Coast. Many Hollywood movies were filmed here, including *Raiders of the Lost Ark; Six Days, Seven Nights;* and parts of all three *Jurassic Park* films.

COMING ASHORE About the only fun thing to do at **Nawiliwili Harbor** is pronounce the name (*Nah*-willy-willy). The port can accommodate two ships at a time: one at a pier, and one anchored with a short tender ride. Some of the small local malls offer free shuttle buses, but the real attraction is the phenomenal beach that is tucked quietly behind the Anchor Cove shopping mall, less than a mile from the pier.

GETTING AROUND Taxis from the **Kauai Taxi Company** (© **808/246-9554**) and other companies typically meet cruise ships at the pier. Rates are $2.50 for the first ⅛ mile, plus $2.40 for each additional mile.

BEST CRUISE LINE SHORE EXCURSIONS

Jungle Mountain Trek, Wagon & Zip Line Adventure ($149, 7 hr.): Paddle a kayak through a mangrove forest, soar across a jungle stream on a high-wire zipline, swing from a rope swing, leap off a waterfall, and more on this action-packed all-day adventure. This excursion takes you along jungle trails to some of the most scenic waterfalls and ponds in the area. The beauty of the surrounding mountains is sublime, and it's impossible not to enjoy the guides' colorful retelling of ancient folklore while bouncing through a green valley in a tractor-pulled wagon surrounded by ridges and peaks that served as the inspiration of the folklore. Be sure to wear comfortable walking shoes; bring a swimsuit and a towel, too. Lunch is served on a treehouse platform near a waterfall.

Waimea River & Fern Grotto ($55, 4 hr.): This excursion takes you to some of the most breathtaking and contrasting natural wonders of Kauai. First, visit the jagged red-earth cliffs and canyons of Waimea, the "Grand Canyon of the Pacific," whose depth measures 2,587 feet. Once you've had appropriate time to marvel at the view (don't forget a camera!), you're off via riverboat to explore the verdant green valley of Fern Grotto. Break in your shoes before you take this excursion. Lunch is included.

Tubing the Ditch ($120, 3 hr.): Travel to a former sugar cane plantation in Kauai's interior and the headwaters of the Hanamaulu Ditch system, a series of open ditches, tunnels, and flumes that once provided irrigation for the farmlands. There you'll get an inner tube, be outfitted with helmet lamps, and begin your float trip through the tunnels. Not for the claustrophobic!

ON YOUR OWN: WITHIN WALKING DISTANCE

A few shopping malls are a short walk from the pier (see "Shopping," below) and a sunny beach is even closer still (see "Beaches," below). Otherwise, you'll need wheels of some sort or another.

ON YOUR OWN: BEYOND THE PORT AREA

To understand life in a small town built around a sugar plantation, head to **Old Koloa Town.** This tiny collection of small wooden buildings, now turned into shops and restaurants, was the new home for waves of immigrants who came to work on the sugar plantations. In the center of town is a small history center that houses a few artifacts from the turn of the 20th century. Plaques on each building describe the original purpose and history. It's about an hour's drive from the harbor, so this is a good bet only for those who've rented wheels.

A visit to the **McBryde Garden** of the **National Tropical Botanical Garden,** Lawai Road, across the street from Spouting Horn, Poipu (© **808/742-2623;** www.ntbg.org), will leave you breathless as you wander amid the intoxicating array of tropical flowers and fragrances. Take a self-guided ethnobotanical tour ($20 adults; $10 kids 6–12) to learn about the many useful and culturally significant plants growing in this green oasis. Trams run Monday through Saturday from 9:30am to 2:30pm.

BEACHES

Nestled just behind the Anchor Cove shopping center, less than a mile from the pier, is **Kalapaki Beach.** Used by locals and tourists, this strip of natural beauty seems out of place next to the parking lot and strip mall. Protected by a jetty and patrolled by lifeguards, the beach is safe for swimming and ideal for families with children. Restrooms are available at the nearby restaurants, where you can also change and grab a snack.

Beautiful **Poipu Beach** can be reached by heading south from the port along Highway 50 for about 15 miles. This romantic spot has crystal-blue water, pure white sand, palm trees, and even a patch of grass big enough for a game of Frisbee. At the eastern end is a small beach with lava rocks and moderate surf, while to the west, you'll see a string of small crescent beaches. Watch for rare and endangered Hawaiian monk seals that occasionally haul out and lounge on the sand. While seemingly tame, they are dangerous to approach and protected by law. In addition to lifeguards, there are showers, restrooms, and covered picnic areas. A taxi here costs about $38 each way.

Heading north on Highway 56, up the Coconut Coast, is **Kee Beach,** a favorite mong locals. At the northern tip is a deep but calm swimming area in summer, ough just off to the left (when facing the sea) are some dangerous and very sharp rocks just beyond the surf, so take care before you rush in. There are no lifeguards, so stay in the same swimming area as everyone else. If no one is in the water, it is usually for good reason. A taxi runs about $110 each way; but many cars can carry up to six passengers, so you can share the cost with some of your shipmates.

SHOPPING

At the **Anchor Cove** shopping center, you can purchase some of the most breathtaking pearl jewelry this side of Asia. **South Pacific Gallery** stocks a wide variety of locally crafted jewelry and art. Don't miss **Seven Seas Trading Company,** with Asian and Hawaiian clothing, art, candles, statues, and more. For spectacular artwork made out of glass, go north on Kuhio Highway and stop in at **Kela's Glass Gallery,** 4-1354 Kuhio Hwy., Kapaa (© **888/255-3527** or 808/822-4527). Along the Coconut Coast is the **Yellowfish Trading Company,** in the town of Hanalei (© **808/826-1227**), where kitschy Hawaiiana harks back to the 1950s.

3 Maui

Maui, also called the Valley Isle, is just a small dot in the vast Pacific Ocean, but it has the potential to offer visitors unforgettable experiences: floating weightless through rainbows of tropical fish, standing atop a 10,000-foot volcano watching the sunrise color the sky, listening to the raindrops in a bamboo forest, and sunning on idyllic beaches. The island is also packed with interesting cultural sights and colorful history. Here, you can set foot on the spot where ancient Hawaiian royalty and priests once walked, gathered, and worshiped. Later, at the turn of the 20th century, it became a bustling home to native Hawaiians, immigrants, and missionaries. Cruise ships call on two ports, **Kahului** and **Lahaina.**

KAHULUI

COMING ASHORE   Coming ashore at the **Port of Kahului,** an industrial port that can accommodate one cruise ship at a time, may leave you less than inspired. Don't bother braving the maze of roads that weave around containers and warehouses—all that lies beyond in the immediate vicinity are strip malls and roads. It's best to hop in a taxi to explore the island or sign up for one of the shore excursions.

GETTING AROUND   Taxis, as well as **shuttle buses,** line up in an orderly fashion under large well-marked signs at the pier. If for some reason you don't see one, try **Sunshine Cabs of Maui** (© **800/922-8294** or 808/879-2220) or **Islandwide Taxi and Tours** (© **808/874-TAXI**). Rates are $3.50 for the first ⅛ mile, plus $3 for each additional mile.

BEST CRUISE LINE SHORE EXCURSIONS

Haleakala Crater ($49, 5 hr.): Don't miss this chance to experience the dramatic landscape of a dormant volcano. Haleakala, whose vast crater measures 7½ by 2½ miles and is 3,000 feet deep, last erupted in 1790. As you ascend, the terrain changes from forest to scrub to a seemingly barren wasteland near the top. Surprisingly, it is here among the lava rocks and chilly slopes that some of Hawaii's most rare and endangered species of plants and animals can be found. Bring a sweater, as temps at the top can sink as low as 40°F (4°C).

Maui Ocean Center & Iao Valley ($54, 4 hr.): This tour combines a modern interactive aquarium (see below for more information), which displays Hawaii's indigeno marine life, with Iao Valley, a lush state park and sacred site of religious and cultural significance for ancient Hawaiians.

Maui Whale-Watch ($50, 2 hr.): Some things have to be seen in person, and a breaching whale is one of them. The beauty and grace of these behemoths as they glide between our world and theirs is not to be missed. And, with such abundance here (about a third of all Pacific whales migrate here for the winter), your chances of seeing a whale are good (though not absolute). A guide from the Pacific Whale Foundation shares insights into the animals' behavior as you "listen in" to the mammals' conversation via underwater hydrophones. *Note:* This tour is usually offered from mid-December to April only.

ON YOUR OWN: WITHIN WALKING DISTANCE

The Kahului harbor functions as a working cargo port in addition to serving cruise ships, so there's not much to see in the immediate vicinity. Stick to shore excursions or take a taxi.

ON YOUR OWN: BEYOND THE PORT AREA

To see one of the most vibrant yet historic towns in Hawaii, go to **Lahaina** (see "Lahaina," below, for details).

For a unique eating experience, try some local fare at **Aloha Mixed Plate,** 1285 Front St. (© **808/661-3322**). Nowhere else short of a luau can you try the local favorites such as *kailua* roast pork (a full pig wrapped in palm leaves and cooked in a fire pit with lava rocks for 12 hr.), *lomi lomi* salmon (fresh salmon minced with raw tomatoes and spices), *lau lau* (pork cooked with taro leaves that taste like fresh spinach), and, of course, the Hawaiian staple, *poi* (a locally beloved but flavorless goo made from taro root). The cultural experience is well worth the short taxi ride from nearby Lahaina. Main courses average $6 to $14.

The **Maui Ocean Center,** 192 Ma'alaea Rd. (© **808/270-7000;** www.mauiocean center.com), invites you to explore Hawaii's native marine life in a safe and enjoyable setting. This modern family-friendly facility is the largest tropical reef aquarium in the Western Hemisphere. It has both indoor and outdoor exhibits where you can go nose to nose with an octopus, watch a turtle swim, and even touch a squishy sea cucumber. Admission costs $23 for adults, $16 for children 3 to 12.

To learn everything you ever wanted to know about whaling, head to the **Whaling Museum** in **Whalers Village,** 2435 Kaanapali Pkwy. (© **808/661-5992;** www. whalersvillage.com). This compact museum houses a prized collection of scrimshaw and lets you step into the world of whaling through an innovative self-guided audio tour. Admission is free; open daily from 9am to 10pm.

BEACHES

About 2 miles from the pier is the long and wide **Kanaha Beach Park.** Because there are no lifeguards here, swimming is at your own risk, though the white sand and sweeping vista make lounging on the sand and dabbling your toes in the water more than enough of a reward. Kanaha has restrooms, showers, a picnic area, picnic tables, a campsite, and parking. Head up to **Hookipa Beach** to relax and watch windsurfers from around the world work the waves. While not always safe for swimming, this is the best free windsurf stunt show in town. The beach has bathrooms, showers, picnic tables, barbecues, and parking.

SHOPPING

Your shopping options are to either head over to **Lahaina** and **Whalers Village,** 2435 Kaanapali Pkwy. (© **808/661-4567;** www.whalersvillage.com), or drive south to the **Shops at Wailea,** 3750 Wailea Alanui Dr. (© **808/891-6770;** www.shopsatwailea. com). Both shopping centers feature upscale classics (Louis Vuitton, Tiffany & Co.), as well as more affordable standards a la Tommy Bahama. They are also home to a number of restaurants.

LAHAINA

COMING ASHORE   One ship at a time can anchor offshore at the **Port of Lahaina.** A 10-minute tender ride takes passengers across the small harbor and alongside a pier right in the middle of town.

GETTING AROUND   Pretty much everything you could want to do—from sightseeing to shopping, beaching, and diving—can be done within walking distance of the pier. If you want to venture farther, **taxis** are usually waiting at the pier; if not, call **Alii Taxi** (© **808/661-3688**) or **Sunshine Cabs of Maui** (© **800/922-8294** or 808/ 879-2220). Rates are $3.50 a mile.

BEST CRUISE LINE SHORE EXCURSIONS

Atlantis Submarine Adventure ($105, 2 hr.): If you don't scuba dive, this 65-foot, air-conditioned submarine is the perfect way to view the spectacle of marine life nearly 150 feet below the surface.

Catch a Wave! ($89, 5 hr.): If you've ever wanted to surf the big kahuna, this is your chance. The gentle surf and excellent instructors nearly guarantee that anyone, young and old, can master the ancient Hawaiian art of surfing, even if it's only to stand up long enough for a souvenir snapshot ($10 for a CD of all photos taken of all participants). While not strenuous, this is not for the devout couch potato, since you do have to paddle back to shore after you catch a wave.

ON YOUR OWN: WITHIN WALKING DISTANCE

Lahaina (© **808/667-9193;** www.visitlahaina.com) is one of the most vibrant yet historic towns in Hawaii. It's rich in history, plus loaded with great shopping, watersports, and restaurants. Stop by the centrally located **Courthouse** to browse the two art galleries, grab a self-guided walking-tour pamphlet, or check out the historical exhibits at the newly opened (and free) **Lahaina Heritage Museum** (© **808/661-1959**), on the second floor. Just outside the Courthouse, artists are camped under a great banyan tree, the largest you're ever likely to see.

As you meander among the shops and sights, clearly numbered plaques correspond to the walking tour. Head for the two-story **Pioneer Inn,** 658 Wharf St. (© **808/661-3636**), which was Maui's first hotel; the bar remains a favorite watering hole. Then check out the nearby **Baldwin House Museum,** 120 Dickenson St. (© **808/661-3262;** www.lahainarestoration.org), where a local missionary and medical doctor, Dwight Baldwin, single-handedly vaccinated and thereby saved nearly the entire town from a deadly smallpox outbreak in the mid–19th century. Admission is $3. Stroll farther down Front Street, heading west, and drop in at the **Wo Hing Museum** (© **808/ 661-5553**), once an ancient Chinese fraternal society. Admission is $1. While the museum merits only a quick tour, don't miss the film loop playing in the adjacent cookhouse—you can view footage of Hawaii shot by Thomas Edison nearly 100 years ago

ON YOUR OWN: BEYOND THE PORT AREA

See "On Your Own: Beyond the Port Area" in the "Kahului" section, above.

BEACHES

The beach at **Lahaina** is calm, clean, and a great place to watch surfers take their first lessons on the baby waves. Located between a stone breakwater and the shops at 505 Front St., this beach is known by locals as either 505 or the break wall. There are restrooms, shops, and restaurants nearby. **Kaanapali Beach,** directly behind **Whalers Village** (see above), is a safe and popular beach stretching about a mile past several resorts. Beach chairs, umbrellas, kayaks, boogie boards, and other rentals are available at **Beach Activities of Maui** (© 808/661-5552; www.mauiwatersports.com), located nearby next to the Westin Hotel. Restrooms and showers are both available.

SHOPPING

Front Street in Lahaina is a shopper's mecca, with clothing boutiques full of aloha (aka Hawaiian) shirts, jewelry stores selling pearls and tourmaline, and the usual assortment of galleries. The best art can be found at the **Lahaina Arts Society** galleries inside the Courthouse, 648 Wharf St. (© 808/661-0111). Also check out the **Village Gallery in Lahaina,** 120 Dickenson St. (© 808/661-4402; www.villagegallerymaui. com). Not far away on Honoapi'ilani Highway is the **Lahaina Cannery Mall** (© 808/661-5304; www.lahainacannery.com), which used to be a huge pineapple cannery; it now houses lots of shops carrying locally made handicrafts. For information on Whalers Village, see "Shopping" in the "Kahului" section, above.

4 The Big Island

Big surprise, the Big Island is the largest island in the Hawaiian chain (4,028 sq. miles—about the size of Connecticut), the youngest (800,000 years), and the least populated (with 30 people per sq. mile), and has an unmatched diversity of terrain and climate: fiery volcanoes and sparkling waterfalls, black-lava deserts and snow-capped mountain peaks, tropical rainforests and alpine meadows, a glacial lake, and miles of golden, black, and green (!) sand beaches. A 50-mile drive will take you from snowy winter to sultry summer, passing through spring or fall along the way. The island looks like the inside of a barbecue pit on one side, and a lush jungle on the other. In a word, it's bizarre, and takes some people aback because it doesn't fit the tropical stereotype.

Five volcanoes—one still erupting—have created this island, which is growing bigger every day. At its heart is snowcapped **Mauna Kea,** the world's tallest mountain (measured from the ocean floor), complete with its own glacial lake. Mauna Kea's nearest neighbor is **Mauna Loa** ("Long Mountain"), creator of one-sixth of the island; it's the largest volcano on earth, rising 30,000 feet out of the ocean floor (of course, you can see only the 13,677 ft. that are above sea level). Erupting **Kilauea** makes the Big Island bigger every day—and, if you're lucky and your timing is good, you can stand just a few feet away and watch it do its work. In just a week, the Kilauea volcano can produce enough lava to fill the Astrodome.

HILO

COMING ASHORE Up to two cruise ships can pull alongside the docks at the **Port of Hilo,** which is not much more than an industrial port, so don't plan on walking into town. An organized shore excursion is your best bet here.

GETTING AROUND   In the unlikely event there are no **taxis** waiting at the pier, you can call **Ace-1** (© **808/935-8303**). Note that because the island is so big, taxi rides can be quite expensive. Taxis are metered and start at $3; the first mile costs $5.60 and each subsequent ⅛ mile is 30¢.

BEST CRUISE LINE SHORE EXCURSIONS

If the weather's good, you can't go wrong with a scenic helicopter tour over Kilauea volcano; there are also a variety of golf excursions offered on the Big Island. Otherwise, here are some of our favorite options.

Kilauea Volcano ($49–$47, 4½ hr.): Volcanoes National Park is by far Hawaii's premier tourist destination and well worth a visit. On your excursion, you'll get a look at the still-active Kilauea (5,000 ft.), walk the extinct Thurston Lava Tube, and check out the exhibits at the National Volcano Observatory. There's no need to worry about dramatic eruptions; for the most part, Hawaii's volcanoes are quite tame.

Kilauea Lava Viewing Adventure ($110, 6 hr.): Drive 51 miles, climb 4,000 feet up Kilauea, and then descend to sea level to watch lava flowing into the sea. The land here is some of the newest on earth, formed by the cooling lava sometimes only hours before you arrive. It's often so hot it'll melt the soles of your sneakers if you don't keep moving. This is one that's only for the really fit, requiring a 2- to 6-mile hike on rough surfaces. Many folks who start out don't make it and have to head back to the van without seeing what they came to see.

Waipi'o Valley Horseback Ride ($159, 5–5½ hr.): There is no better way to appreciate the natural beauty of this sacred "Valley of the Kings" than from horseback. You'll ride along the rim of the valley until you reach Hiilawe Falls—one of the most spectacular in Hawaii—where you can enjoy a vista of the Pacific. All riders must weigh no more than 230 pounds. Closed-toe shoes are required, and long pants are recommended.

Hawaii Tropical Botanical Garden ($35, 2½ hr.): Even if you aren't a plant enthusiast, you will be awestruck by the sheer beauty of this garden, set in one of the most spectacular locations in Hawaii. The orchids and other exotic plants (2,500 different species in all) are offset by the dramatic cliffs, vistas, and crashing surf below. The tour is self-directed along a mile or so of trails within the gardens. It's a shutterbug's paradise, so don't leave your camera on the ship.

ON YOUR OWN: BEYOND THE PORT AREA

To enjoy the beauty of a formal Japanese garden, head down Banyan Drive to **Queen Liliuokalani Gardens,** right near **Coconut Island.** This picturesque 30-acre park has many bonsai trees as well as carp ponds, pagodas, and an arched bridge. To truly understand the power and fury of the Pacific Ocean, visit the **Pacific Tsunami Museum,** 130 Kamehameha Ave. (© **808/935-0926;** www.tsunami.org). Be sure to speak with the volunteers on hand, many of whom have lived through the "walls of water" that hit Hilo in 1946 and 1960.

To learn more about Hawaii's marine ecosystems, visit the **Mokupapapa Discovery Center,** 308 Kamehameha Ave., Suite 109, in the South Hata Building (© **808/933-8195;** www.hawaiireef.noaa.gov). This education facility opened in 2003 and is run by the National Marine Sanctuaries and the National Oceanic and Atmospheric Administration. Exhibits include a 2,500-gallon saltwater aquarium, a number of photographs and murals, and several interactive research stations. Admission is free open Tuesday through Saturday.

BEACHES

At the start of Banyan Drive (about 2 miles from the cruise dock) is **Reeds Bay Park,** a small beach popular with locals. While there are no lifeguards or facilities here, the shallow water is well protected from waves and jagged rocks, making it ideal for swimming.

Near the other end of Banyan Drive is Moku Ola, or **Coconut Island.** Accessible by a walking bridge, this serene destination is also popular with locals who want to stroll the shady perimeter, bathe in the rocky pools, or swim off the small grassy beaches.

About 3 miles from the pier on Kalanianaole Avenue is **Leleiwi Beach Park.** Not a traditional white-sand beach, this one has black-lava rocks that form small tide pools, ideal for snorkeling. Keep an eye out for endangered sea turtles that are attracted to this spot. There are lifeguards here, and facilities include showers, restrooms, and a small marine police station.

SHOPPING

The best shopping in Hilo can be found along Kamehameha Avenue in the heart of downtown. Stop by **Dreams of Paradise Gallery,** 308 Kamehameha Ave. (© **808/ 935-5670;** www.dreamsofparadisegallery.com), to see impressive examples of local artwork. A wide selection of black-pearl jewelry can be found at the adjacent **Black Pearl Gallery** (© **800/343-2994** or 808/935-8556).

KAILUA-KONA

COMING ASHORE   Two cruise ships anchor offshore here; a 10-minute tender ride takes passengers to the sleepy pier in Kailua-Kona. There's plenty to do within steps of this modest pier, including beach-hopping, shopping, and more. Taxis line up at the dock to whisk you away, but with so much going on at the pier, there is little reason to leave.

GETTING AROUND   As at the other ports in Hawaii, **taxis** await the arrival of cruise ship passengers, in this case lining up in front of the King Kamehameha Hotel. If you need to call for one, try **AAA-1 TAXI** (© **808/325-3818**); keep in mind, though, that because the island is so big, long-distance trips can be very pricey. **DJ's Rentals** (© **808/329-1700;** www.harleys.com) is easily spotted right across from the Kailua Pier. It can hook you up with either a scooter or a Harley Davidson, for full-day ($90–$145) or half-day ($50–$90) rentals. To cruise the waterfront and around town, rent a bike for $15 a day at **Dave's Bike and Triathlon Shop** (© **808/329-4522**), across from the Kailua Pier behind Atlantis Submarine. Or try **Hawaiian Pedals** (© **808/329-2294**), in the Kona Inn Shopping Village about half a mile down on Alii Drive.

BEST CRUISE LINE SHORE EXCURSIONS

Catamaran Sail & Snorkel ($80, 3¾ hr.): Head out on a catamaran to Pawai Bay and enjoy a morning of cruising, music, snacking, and snorkeling. The bay is loaded with multicolored fish, rays, and lava-encrusted coral reefs. In winter, there's a great chance you'll see whales or spinner dolphins breaching and cavorting.

Kona Cloud Forest Botanical Walk ($80, 4 hr.): Knowledgeable naturalists guide you through a lush forest sanctuary on the slopes of the sleeping Hualalai Volcano. A good pick for someone who wants something more active than a bus tour, but less active than a fitness hike, as this covers about 1½ miles at a leisurely pace in cool mountainside weather. If you're into gardening, it's bliss; if you're into coffee, the end-of-tour stop at a Kona coffee farm will net you a free tasting and beans at a low price.

Big Island Helicopter Spectacular ($399, 4½ hr.): There is no better way to see the Big Island's beauty and volcanic fury than from a helicopter. On this journey, you soar over the tropical valleys and waterfalls of the Kohala Mountains, the rainforest of the Hamakua Coast, and the spectacular lava flows of Hawaii Volcanoes National Park.

ON YOUR OWN: WITHIN WALKING DISTANCE

There is plenty to see and do right near the pier. Just head right down the seawall and enjoy the breathtaking view of the ocean on one side, and the endless stream of shops and galleries that line the opposite side of the street. Be sure to stop in at **Hulihee Palace,** 75-5718 Alii Dr. (© **808/329-1877;** www.huliheepalace.org), a two-story New England–style palace. Built in 1838 as a summer residence for Hawaii's royalty, it was, at the time, the largest and most elegant home on the island. Today, it's a well-run and -preserved museum. Admission is $6. Across the street is **Mokuaikaua Church** (© **808/329-1589**), the oldest Christian church in Hawaii (free admission; open daily).

ON YOUR OWN: BEYOND THE PORT AREA

St. Benedict's Catholic Church, on Highway 19 (© **808/328-2227**), is more commonly known as the Painted Church because of the colorful murals and frescoes that cover its walls and ceilings. It was painted by Father John Velge, the church's first priest, in an attempt to enlighten and educate his congregation, who were predominantly illiterate. Admission is free.

Ancient **Hawaiian petroglyphs** can be seen near the **Kings' Shops** at the Waikoloa Beach Resort, just off Waikoloa Beach Drive about 30 miles north on Highway 19 (© **808/886-8811**). Free tours meet at the food court in the Kings' Shops; they depart weekdays at 10:30am and weekends at 8:30am. You can also tour the ancient markings on your own at any time. Follow the signs to the petroglyphs; then take the small path that leads to a craggy trail through a lava field once used by Hawaiian travelers.

Nonguests are welcome to visit **Hilton Waikoloa Village,** 425 Waikoloa Beach Dr. (© **808/886-1234;** www.h-wv.com), and enjoy its spectacularly landscaped grounds and walkways that meander past enormous statues, dramatic waterfalls, sweeping coastal vistas, and $7 million worth of artwork. If you like Atlantis on Paradise Island in The Bahamas, you'll love this resort. Enjoy any of the nine restaurants, all of which can be reached via either air-conditioned tram or open-air mahogany boats that run from one end of the property to the other. For a steep $80, families can use the pools and man-made beach as well (call first to make sure there's availability the day you're in port).

BEACHES

At the Kailua-Kona pier, you're practically standing on the beach at the **King Kamehameha Hotel.** Because all beaches are public in Hawaii, this small and sweet waterfront resort is yours to enjoy. For a fee, you can rent watersports gear, a lounge chair, or an umbrella. For those who prefer to swim without all the trappings, there is a miniscule scrap of beach just on the other side of the parking lot. Here, the calm water makes for great paddling, swimming laps, or just floating your cares away.

The best beach for snorkeling (especially for beginners) is **Kahaluu Beach Park,** located about 2 miles down Alii Drive from the pier. The salt-and-pepper-colored beach is convenient to restrooms, a snack truck, and sheltered picnic tables. While shallow, the water can become rough in the winter.

Beautiful **Hapuna Beach State Park,** past the Hilton Waikoloa Village and Mauna Lani Resort, is about 35 miles up the Kohala Coast from the pier. Follow the highway signs and turn left toward the ocean off Highway 19. You'll be greeted by a large white-sand beach. The area is serene and well maintained, and has a food pavilion, restrooms, and showers.

SHOPPING

There is ample shopping on Alii Drive, which starts at the Kailua Pier and extends southward along a nearly endless strip of small shopping galleries with similar names and equally similar wares. Artist Rapozo displays his colorful and romantic paintings at **Rapozo Images,** at the Seaside Mall (© **808/326-1359;** www.rapozo-studio.com). For something out of the ordinary, stop in at the **Eclectic Craftsman,** in the Kona Marketplace (© **808/334-0562**), to see the beautifully carved wood. Farther down, inside Waterfront Row, marvel at the marine-life sculptures made from wood, stone, and metal at **Wyland Gallery** (© **808/334-0037**).

15

New England & Eastern Canada

Back in the year 1614, the first successful American colony, at Jamestown, Virginia, was only 7 years old, and exploration of North America had only just begun. No one knew yet just how vast the continent was, but Europe's great powers had already begun fighting for its bounty. To the north, the lands known as "Northern Virginia" caught the imagination of Jamestown founder John Smith, who mounted an expedition along the coasts of what are now Massachusetts and Maine. Returning to England with stories of the region's natural wealth, he argued strongly for its colonization and renamed it "New England," a name that King James I made official in 1620. A few years later James's son, Charles I, sent a party of Scots to colonize the land even farther north, in what are now the Canadian Maritimes. And so it came to pass that, just as England has Scotland on her northern border, New England's nearest neighbor is beautiful Nova Scotia—the "New Scotland."

The legacies left by the English, Scottish, French, and other settlers that immigrated to these parts have lent ports along the New England/Canada coast their unique character, whether it's the Puritan ethic of stubborn independence and thriftiness that many New Englanders still cling to, or the French culture and language that thrive in the Providence of Québec. On a cruise, you'll see lots of **historical sites,** from Boston's Paul Revere House to the *Titanic* exhibit at the Maritime Museum in Halifax and Québec City's 17th-century Notre-Dame des Victoires Church. But you'll also get a dose of the region's inimitable character: fishing boats piled with netting, Victorian mansions built by wealthy whalers, lighthouses atop windswept bluffs, and the cold, hard beauty of the north Atlantic sea.

The classic time to cruise here is in autumn, when a brilliant sea of **fall foliage** blankets the region. You can also cruise these waters in the spring and summer, aboard either big 3,000-plus-passenger ships or smaller vessels carrying a tenth of that load. Depending on the size of the ship and the length of the cruise, itineraries may include passing through **Nantucket Sound,** around **Cape Cod,** or into the **Bay of Fundy** or **Gulf of St. Lawrence.** Some ships traverse the St. Lawrence Seaway or the smaller Saguenay River.

HOME PORTS FOR THIS REGION **New York, Boston,** and **Montréal** are the main hubs for these cruises, joined occasionally by **Québec City.**

LANGUAGE & CURRENCY English and dollars. Virtually all businesses in Canadian ports such as Halifax and Saint John accept U.S. dollars, though if you're spending time pre- or post-cruise in Montréal or Québec, you'll want to pick up some Canadian dollars (US$0.87 = C$1 or US$1 = C$1.15).

SHOPPING TIPS You don't go on a New England/Canada cruise for the shopping, though there are a few choice spots. Of course, New York City, Boston, and Montréal, being major cities, offer lots of shopping ops. In Canada, keep in mind that sales tax is added directly to prices rather than being tagged on at checkout

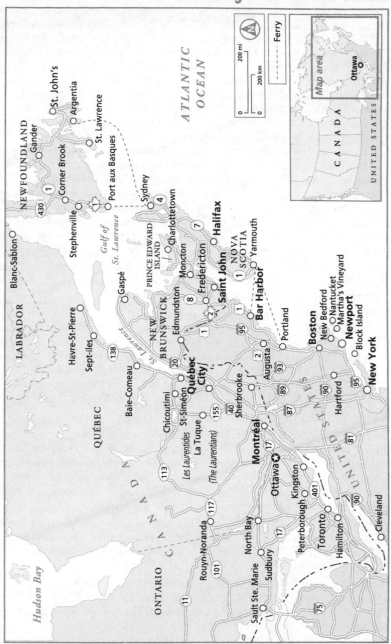

1 Bar Harbor, Maine

Bar Harbor is located on the mid-Maine coast, overlooking Frenchman's Bay from its perch on the eastern shore of Mt. Desert Island—its name an anglicization of Isles des Monts-Deserts ("bare mountains"), the name French explorer Samuel de Champlain gave the island in 1604. In its 19th-century heyday, Bar Harbor was one of the premier resort areas on the East Coast, attracting Astors, Vanderbilts, Rockefellers, and other wealthy families looking for a rustic summer getaway. Today it's a humbler place with no shortage of T-shirt shops and ice-cream parlors, but is no less popular with tourists.

Bar Harbor's biggest pull is its proximity to the lush **Acadia National Park,** which got its start in 1901 when millionaire George B. Dorr formed a preservation group and began buying up land, eventually turning over thousands of acres to the federal government. The park today covers most of the 12-by-16-mile island and a few neighboring islands, totaling some 35,000 acres of lake-dotted fir and spruce forests and surrounded by great whale-watching offshore. Winding amid its acreage is a 57-mile network of carriage roads created by John D. Rockefeller, Jr., as well as 120 miles of hiking trails—all of them motor free, open for walking and bicycling only.

COMING ASHORE   While small ships less than 200 feet long can pull alongside the Town Pier, most ships must anchor offshore and send passengers to the Harbor Place pier via tenders. The ride to the pier takes only about 10 minutes. The two piers are next to each other in the downtown waterfront area.

GETTING AROUND   Once in town, you can walk along the waterfront and to many shops, restaurants, and a few attractions (highlighted below in "Within Walking Distance"), but to see Acadia, your best bet is signing up for one of your ship's shore excursions or renting a bicycle from a local dealer. Try **Bar Harbor Bicycle Shop,** 141 Cottage St. (© 207/288-3886; www.barharborbike.com), or **Acadia Bike,** 48 Cottage St. (© 800/526-8615; www.acadiabike.com). If you want a taxi and there aren't any waiting, try **At Your Service Taxi Cab Co.** (© 207/288-9222); they also offer guided tours of the park.

BEST CRUISE LINE SHORE EXCURSIONS

Best of the Park and the Town ($89, 6 hr.): Traverse the 27-mile Park Loop Road of Acadia National Park via bus, taking in spectacular coastal, mountain, and forest scenery. Tours include a lobster lunch and visits to Seal Harbor (home to the rich and famous), the summit of Cadillac Mountain, and Thunder Hole, where the right tidal conditions can send flumes of ocean spray high into the air.

A Walk in the Park ($38, 3 hr.): A naturalist guide leads a 2-mile hike along Acadia's trails and offers insight into the park's ecosystem, geology, natural history, and legends. The tour also includes a drive to the top of Cadillac Mountain for a 360-degree view of Mount Desert Island.

Acadia Carriage Ride ($59, 3 hr.): Fifteen-person horse-drawn carriages offer a chance to experience John D. Rockefeller's carriage paths the way he expected you to. Approximately 1 hour is spent in the carriage itself. The tour also includes a drive to the top of Cadillac Mountain for the view.

Biking in Acadia ($49, 2½ hr.): Jump on a 24-speed mountain bike and follow the guide through the park's hard-packed gravel carriage trails, which crisscross some of the most scenic areas of the park. The guide makes stops to discuss the island's history and lore.

Frenchman Bay Kayak Adventure ($50, 2½ hr.): This scenic paddle passes ocean-front mansions not visible from the road, gives great views of Cadillac Mountain, and offers opportunities to spot harbor seals, porpoises, and seabirds such as the storm petrel, shearwater, and northern gannet.

Whale Watching ($49, 3½ hr.): This excursion allows visitors to view the humpbacks, finbacks, minkes, and dolphins that gather in the waters off the island between April and October.

ON YOUR OWN: WITHIN WALKING DISTANCE

If for some reason you're allergic to beautiful forests and want to stay in town, close to the ship, you can check out the great views of the area from the foot of Main Street at grassy **Agamont Park,** which overlooks the town pier and Frenchman Bay. From here, set off past the Bar Harbor Inn on the **Shore Path,** a wide, winding trail that follows the shoreline for about half a mile along a public right of way. The pathway offers views of many elegant summer homes (some converted to inns) and of **The Porcupines,** a cluster of spruce-studded islands just offshore. So named because they look like a group of porcupines migrating southward, the islands' distinctive shape—gently sloped facing north, with abrupt cliffs facing south—is the result of ancient pressure from a southward-moving glacier.

For a glimpse of the area's past life, stroll on over to the **Abbe Museum,** 26 Mt. Desert St. (© **207/288-3519;** www.abbemuseum.org), a sprawling 17,000-square-foot gallery housing a top-rate collection of Native American artifacts. Admission is $6. Around the corner is the **Bar Harbor Historical Society,** 33 Ledgelawn Ave. (© **207/288-0000;** www.barharborhistorical.org), located in a handsome 1918 former convent. Its collection encompasses exhibits on old-time Mt. Desert Island hotels and estates, photos of most of the 200 estate homes burned during the great fire of 1947, and a collection of milk bottles from the more than 40 dairy farms that were once active on the island.

Somewhere during your stay, try some fresh **Maine lobster**—served boiled, baked, broiled, in rolls, and any other number of ways—at one of the many restaurants along the waterfront area.

ON YOUR OWN: BEYOND THE PORT AREA

You don't want to come to Bar Harbor without getting a taste of the most famous attraction: **Acadia National Park (www.nps.gov/acad).** Sign up for a guided hike or drive along the 27-mile Park Loop Road, which wends around 1,530-foot-high Cadillac Mountain, the highest point on the Atlantic coast. If you luck out and there's no fog, expect awesome views of spectacular natural sights like Thunder Hole, where ocean surf dramatically crashes against granite cliffs. Perhaps the best way to really experience the nature here is bicycling a stretch of the 55-mile car-free carriage trails that wind through the park (rent a bike in town or sign up for one of your ship's biking excursions). Horse-drawn carriage rides are another popular way to tour. No matter what your transport, there's a great chance you'll spot some wildlife, from the occasional moose to beavers, foxes, eagles, hawks, and peregrine falcons.

SHOPPING   You don't come here for the shopping (unless lobster potholders are your thing), though there are a handful of interesting shops on **Main Street** selling locally made and/or inspired handicrafts and gifts. At **Island Artisans,** 99 Main St. (© 207/288-4214; www.islandartisans.com), you can browse for local handicrafts such as tiles, sweet-grass baskets, pottery, jewelry, and soaps. Down the street is the **Bar Harbor**

Hemporium, 116 Main St. (© **207/288-3014;** www.barharborhemp.com), an interesting store dedicated to promoting clothing, paper, and other products made from hemp, an environmentally friendly fibrous plant that's usually known for other reasons entirely.

2 Halifax, Nova Scotia

Located midway up the Nova Scotia coast, Halifax is the top port of call for big ships on the New England and Eastern Canada circuit, owing to the city's large natural deep-water port and its especially pleasing harborside setting and tree-lined streets. Its history goes back to the days of the Micmac Indians, who called Nova Scotia Chebuctook ("Great Long Harbor"). In 1605, the French staked their claim and renamed it Acadia ("Peaceful Land"). By 1621, the British had a foothold and renamed the land Nova Scotia ("New Scotland"), and in 1749, Edward Cornwallis founded Halifax, naming it for George Montagu Dunk, second earl of Halifax. Residents tend to agree that it was a great stroke of luck that the city avoided the name Dunk. Halifax eventually became a thriving shipbuilding and trading center as well as a military hub for the Royal Army and Navy. Even into the 20th century, it had strong military ties, serving as an important supply and convoy harbor in both World War I and World War II. In recent years, it's evolved into a vital commercial and financial hub, as well as a home to a number of colleges and universities.

COMING ASHORE   All ships dock right in town, with Halifax's attractions just steps away. Typically, two ships are in port at one time, though occasionally as many as four or five ships may be tied up. Be sure you're awake when your ship docks so you can go out on deck to hear the Halifax Town Crier and members of the 78th Highlander Regiment, who greet all ships with an exciting program of bagpipe and drum music.

GETTING AROUND   Halifax is exceedingly walkable (there are free walking-tour maps available at the terminal), but there are also plenty of **taxis** at the docks if you're inclined to head for the hills.

Note: All prices in this section were calculated at the rate of US87¢ = C$1 or US$1 = C$1.15. Foreign currency rates fluctuate, so prices may not be exactly the same when you arrive in port.

BEST CRUISE LINE SHORE EXCURSIONS

Highlander for Half a Day ($199, 3½ hr.): Those who want an up-close-and-personal experience of 19th-century Halifax military life can sign up for this excursion offered at the Halifax Citadel. Participants don the uniform of a soldier in Her Majesty's 78th Highland Regiment and go through a series of training exercises, including learning to load and fire a period rifle.

Treasures of the *Titanic* ($44, 2½ hr.): When the fabled liner *Titanic* sank on April 15, 1912, three ships from Halifax drew the grim job of recovering victims from the icy waters 500 miles southeast. In all, only 335 bodies were found, of which 150 were later laid to rest in three Halifax cemeteries. This tour includes all aspects of Halifax's connection to the tragedy, including the historic pier from which the ships were dispatched to pick up victims; the church where memorial services were held; the temporary morgue sites that housed the bodies of such wealthy victims as John Jacob Astor; the cemeteries where rows upon rows of identical gravestones mark the fin resting place of 150 victims; and the Maritime Museum of the Atlantic, which houses an excellent permanent exhibit on the disaster, featuring the world's largest collection of wooden artifacts—including a post from the famous Grand Staircase and one of the few intact *Titanic* deck chairs in the world.

Pub-Crawl ($45, 2½ hr.): Led by a kilted guide and a bagpiper, this tour visits several of Halifax's favorite old-English-style pubs, with libations and music included.

Peggy's Cove ($42, 3½ hr.): For a glimpse of Nova Scotia's more rugged side, several different shore excursions head about 45 minutes south to the tiny fishing village of Peggy's Cove, propped picturesquely on the eastern shore of St. Margarets Bay. Settled by six families in 1811, the village hasn't grown much since, but what it lacks in population it makes up for in scenic beauty, sitting on solid rock just above the crashing surf. A kilted guide leads a walking tour along the craggy coastline, with its bold glacier-formed outcroppings of granite rubbed smooth by eons of crashing waves, and past the town's impressive lighthouse, one of the most photographed spots in Canada. A longer version of the tour ($94, 6½ hr.) visits the 200-year-old hamlet at Fisherman's Cove and includes a lobster lunch at a local restaurant.

Tidal Bore Rafting Adventure ($199, 5½ hr.): The Bay of Fundy is home to what's probably the world's strongest tidal bore, when 2 billion gallons surge into the bay, creating waves up to 10 feet high. The trip is timed so you can watch the river change direction, creating the surge.

Lunenburg Getaway ($69, 6½ hr.): Just southwest of Halifax, Lunenburg is Nova Scotia's main fishing port, with an Old Town that's been restored to its original colonial character. Tours include a 45-minute walking tour and free time to explore the town's shops and cafes.

ON YOUR OWN: WITHIN WALKING DISTANCE

Right at the cruise docks, **Pier 21** (© **902/425-7770;** www.pier21.ca) was Halifax's version of Ellis Island, where between 1928 and 1971 more than a million immigrants entered Canada. Opened as a museum in 1999, it offers an interactive experience that re-creates 43 years of immigrant experiences through displays, films, and sound clips. Admission is US$7 (C$8).

To the north, **Alexander Keith's Nova Scotia Brewery,** 1496 Lower Water St. (© **902/455-1474;** www.keiths.ca), offers one of the best brewery tours we've ever taken. Unlike the typical walk-through of a modern plant with a few historical exhibits, Keith's has restored significant portions of its plant to the way they looked when Keith established his business in 1820. Costumed actors take you through grain storehouses, historic brewing displays, and residential rooms en route to the 19th-century barroom for a sip (or two, or three) of Keith's brew. It's entertaining and fun, it's historical (Keith's is, after all, the oldest brewery in North America), and there's music to boot. Hour-long tours run every half-hour from late May through early October, 11am until 7 or 8pm (noon–4pm Sun). Admission is US$14 (C$16).

A few blocks farther north, the **Maritime Museum of the Atlantic,** 1675 Lower Water St. (© **902/424-7490;** http://museum.gov.ns.ca/mma), provides a window into the lives of Halifax's sailors and shipbuilders, its galleries displaying some 24,000 artifacts, 20,000 photos, and even whole vessels. Exhibits include an impressive collection of *Titanic* artifacts, and there's also a fascinating exhibit on the incredible explosion that leveled much of the city in 1917 when a French munitions ship collided with a Norwegian steamer. Admission is US$7 (C$8).

The Small Ports of New England & Eastern Canada

Aside from the major ports listed in this chapter, there are a number of smaller ports that small-ship lines such as American Cruise Lines (p. 327), American Canadian Caribbean Line (p. 326), and Cruise West (p. 335) include on their itineraries. Big ships may also visit some of these ports, on occasion.

Block Island, RI (www.blockislandchamber.com): The Nature Conservancy has called Block Island one of the "last great places in the Western Hemisphere," an 11-square-mile Yankee gem where more than 300 freshwater ponds are dotted among rolling green hills that end in dramatic 250-foot bluffs that look like the cliffs of western Ireland. A full third of the island is set aside as a wildlife refuge, accessible via 30-plus miles of hiking trails and cliffside bike paths. Down at the shore, the island is ringed by some 17 miles of beach.

Nantucket, MA (www.nantucketchamber.org): Located 30 miles off the coast of Cape Cod, Nantucket Island is classic New England, and was the world's top whaling hub before New Bedford stole the show. Today it's vastly popular with summer tourists, but still manages to maintain a low-key attitude. Its main town, also named Nantucket, is all cobblestone streets, historic buildings, and yacht-filled harbor, while out around the residential island you'll find tranquil villages, rolling moors, heaths, cranberry bogs, and miles of exquisite public beaches, including Jetties near Nantucket Town and Surfside on the Atlantic coast.

Martha's Vineyard, MA (www.mvy.com): New England's largest island, Martha's Vineyard boasts handsome old towns, lighthouses, white picket fences, and charming ice-cream shops . . . plus lots of summer visitors. You'll find great beaches (though many are private), as well as dramatic cliffs and meadows that make for great long walks and bicycle rides. The most genteel of the island's six towns is **Edgartown,** full of regal sea captains' houses and manicured gardens.

Fall River, MA (www.fallriverchamber.com/tourism.htm): Located in the northern reaches of Narragansett Bay, about 20 miles north of Newport, Fall River offers visitors a chance to visit **Battleship Cove (www.battleship cove.org),** a collection of preserved American warships that includes the

Up at downtown's highest point, about 9 blocks from the waterfront, the star-shaped **Halifax Citadel** (© **902/426-5080;** www.pc.gc.ca/lhn-nhs/ns/halifax/index_e.asp) was built by the British between 1820 and 1856, mostly to guard against attack by the United States. The U.S. never did strike (we picked on Mexico instead), but the ever-vigilant British still maintained a garrison here until 1906, after which it was manned by Canadian forces. Restored now to its mid-19th-century appearance, it's one of the most-visited National Historic sites in Canada, with costumed animators portraying a regiment of Scottish soldiers and their families. Visitors can see displays of weapons and uniforms, view audiovisual presentations and demonstrations by soldiers' wives, take an hour-long guided tour, take in the panoramic views from it battleship USS *Massachusetts,* submarine *Lionfish,* and other veterans of World War II. At the town's Marine Museum, you'll find artifacts from the *Titanic,* while at the Lizzie Borden Museum, you can get the down and dirty details on that famous unsolved murder mystery.

New Bedford, MA (www.newbedford.com): In the 19th century, New Bedford was the whaling capital of the world. Today it remains a major deep-sea fishing port, and boasts a beautifully restored waterfront area. The town's **Whaling Museum (www.whalingmuseum.org)** displays ship replicas, whale skeletons and paintings, glasswork, and scrimshaw, which is carved whalebone or whale ivory.

Portland, ME (www.visitportland.com): Maine's largest city is set on a peninsula in scenic Casco Bay. The top attractions include the Portland Headlight (the oldest American lighthouse in continuous use) and the lovely Old Port neighborhood, a revitalized warehouse district that now boasts boutiques, restaurants, and entertainment along its cobblestone streets. Nearby Freeport is a town-size outlet center anchored by *très* Maine **L.L. Bean (www.llbean.com).**

Sydney, Cape Breton Island, Nova Scotia (www.cbisland.com): Nova Scotia's northernmost landmass, Cape Breton Island was principally settled by Highland Scots, and today that influence remains in the island's Scottish-style folk music. The island's scenic highlight is **Cape Breton Highlands National Park (www.pc.gc.ca/pn-np/ns/cbreton/index_e.asp)** on the northwestern coast, its spectacular highlands, dramatic cliffs, and ocean scenery accessible via the 185-mile roadway known as the Cabot Trail.

Charlottetown, Prince Edward Island (www.visitcharlottetown.com): In Canada's smallest province you can visit historic sites such as the house of Lucy Maud Montgomery, who wrote *Anne of Green Gables* about the innocence and beauty of life on the island at the turn of the 19th century. You can also opt for a drive along one of the island's scenic highways, which wend past sandstone cliffs, rocky coves, lovely beaches, and fishing villages.

ramparts, and watch maneuvers and bagpipe concerts on the central parade ground. At noon each day, one of the fort's cannons is fired ceremoniously. Boom! Admission is US$9.50 (C$12). To get here, head up Carmichael Street from Grand Parade Square/Barrington Street toward the old **Town Clock,** gifted to the city by Edward, Duke of Kent, who commanded a garrison here in 1800. A staircase at the foot of the clock, on Brunswick Street, will take you to the Citadel's main entrance.

South of the Citadel, Halifax's famous 17-acre **Public Gardens (www.halifax publicgardens.ca)** make a beautiful spot to relax after a long walking tour. Created through the merger of the old Nova Scotia Horticultural Society Garden (laid out in 837) and an adjacent public park opened in 1866, they're the oldest formal Victorian gardens in North America, and look much as they have since the 1870s. The best place to enter is via the ornate, Scottish-made wrought-iron gates at the corner of Spring Garden Road and South Park Street. Inside, winding gravel paths meander among the trees and flowerbeds, with exotic plants from around the world, commemorative statuary and fountains, and, at the park's center, a red-roofed gazebo built in 1887 to celebrate Queen Victoria's Golden Jubilee.

ON YOUR OWN: BEYOND THE PORT AREA

For information on **Peggy's Cove,** see "Best Cruise Line Shore Excursions," above. Nearer to Halifax is the **Fairview Cemetery,** where 120 *Titanic* victims were buried in 1912. At least one of your ship's organized excursions will generally include a stop here, with the guide explaining Halifax's role in the ocean disaster.

SHOPPING

Locally made maritime handicrafts such as hooked rugs, pottery, wood items, quilt work, and hand-knit woolens are big in Halifax. With its Scottish roots, you'll also find plenty of tartans and gifts made of pewter. There is no shortage of shops in and around the waterfront, including the **Historic Properties** (© 902/422-3077; www. historicproperties.ca), a group of warehouses from as far back as 1800 that have been converted into a shopping, dining, and entertainment complex. It's located a little north of the Maritime Museum, with cobblestone streets leading between buildings that once held goods seized by privateers who plundered enemy vessels for the British Crown. Outside, street musicians and painters add a touch of the artistic; inside, you'll find fashion, gifts, pubs, and lunch spots.

3 Newport, Rhode Island

Sitting on the southern tip of Aquidneck Island in Narragansett Bay and connected to the mainland by three bridges, Newport is practically synonymous with the term "idle rich." In the late 19th century it was *the* place for America's wealthy aristocrats to summer. From the Vanderbilts to the Astors, all the Gilded Age gazillionaires had summer mansions (or, as they called them, "cottages") here, each grander than the next, with an aesthetic that's half château, half Versailles, and 100% over-the-top opulence.

It's not difficult to understand how this picture-postcard seaside setting drew the elite. During the Colonial period Newport rivaled Boston and New York as a center of New World trade, and during the Civil War it became home to the U.S. Naval Academy. After the war, the town began to draw wealthy industrialists, railroad tycoons, coal magnates, and financiers, who began to establish its reputation as the center of the U.S. sailing universe. In 1854, the New York Yacht Club held its first annual regatta off Newport, and from 1930 to 1983 the club held the great America's Cup race here in "The City by the Sea"—stopping only after the cup was snatched by the Australian sloop *Australia II* after a 132-year American reign. Despite the fact that U.S. boats won the cup back in 1987, 1988, and 1992, the race has never returned to Newport's waters—at least not yet—but the city continues to be a major sailing center, hosting more than 40 races each summer and fall.

Today, Newport offers beautiful sea, rocky coastline, and a bustling town that's all cobblestone streets, shady trees, cute cafes, and historical homes. Much of the hubbub is along the waterfront and its parallel streets: America's Cup Avenue and Thames Street, the latter Americanized from the British *Tems* to *Thaymz* after the Revolution

Though millions visit every year, Newport has managed to retain much of its small-town charm and hasn't been overtaken by T-shirt shops and fast-food outlets.

COMING ASHORE   Ships large and small are calling on Newport these days, all of them anchoring just a short distance offshore and shuttling passengers to the tender pier, located just a block from the Newport Visitors Information Center at 23 America's Cup Avenue. A kiosk is also often set up on the pier. You'll find all of Newport's most popular sights, including its famed mansions, within a short walk or drive of the downtown area.

GETTING AROUND   From the tender pier you can walk around the historic town or hop on the **Yellow Line/Rte. 67 RIPTA trolley** (© 401/781-9400; www.ripta. com/content320.html), which visits the mansions, Bellevue Avenue shopping, the Cliff Walk, Rough Point, and other highlights. It'll cost you $6 for an all-day hop-on/hop-off pass, and it boards at the Visitor Information Center (see above). If you want a taxi to drop you off at the mansions, try **Yellow Cab Service** (© 401/846-1500). Another great way to get around town and out to the mansions is by bicycle. Among several rental shops is **Ten Speed Spokes,** 18 Elm St. (© 401/847-5609; www.tenspeedspokes.com), located a couple blocks inland from the tender pier.

BEST CRUISE LINE SHORE EXCURSIONS

Newport Walking Tour ($24, 1½ hr.): An expert guide takes you through a 10-block area of Colonial Newport, noted for nearly 200 restored 18th- and 19th-century Colonial and Victorian homes and landmarks. You'll walk along the city's quaint and shady streets where no buses are allowed, and hear how tobacco heiress Doris Duke and many other residents led the fight to rescue this once-neglected area. Stroll by the superb 1726 Trinity Church, architect Peter Harrison's Brick Market, the Touro Synagogue (the oldest in the country), the Quaker Meeting House, and the Old Colony House.

Guided Cliff Walk Tour ($29, 1½ hr.): You can walk Newport's famous Cliff Walk (see below) on your own, but this option comes with narration. Your choice . . .

The Vanderbilt's Newport ($62, 3½ hr.): This tour combines visits to two of Newport's grandest mansions, Cornelius Vanderbilt II's The Breakers and William K. Vanderbilt's Marble House. Another mansion tour, typically called **Grand Mansions of Newport** ($45, 3 hr.) visits The Elms or Rosecliff, the latter built in 1902 by architect Stanford White on the model of Versailles' Grand Trianon.

ON YOUR OWN: WITHIN WALKING DISTANCE

This is a place for walking, if there ever was one. If you're reasonably fit, the famed mansions on Bellevue and Ocean avenues are within 1 to 4 miles' walking distance of the tender pier, or you can take the trolley or a taxi (see "Getting Around," above).

Ten of Newport's grandest 19th-century mansions are operated by the **Preservation Society of Newport County** (© 401/847-1000; www.newportmansions.org). The most famous is **The Breakers,** Ochre Point Ave., east of Bellevue Avenue (© 401/847-1000), a 70-room Italian Renaissance–style palace built for Cornelius Vanderbilt II in 1895. Perched above the sea, it was designed by Richard Morris Hunt, the Beaux Arts master who also designed the Metropolitan Museum of Art in New York City. Highlights include the gilded 2,400-square-foot dining room (lit by 12-foot chandeliers) and the great hall, which was designed to resemble an open-air Italian courtyard—right down to the 45-foot sky-blue ceiling. Admission is $15.

While none of the other Newport mansions is quite as grand as The Breakers, several come close. **Marble House** was built between 1888 and 1892 for Cornelius Vanderbilt's younger brother, William, making it the earliest of all the Newport mansions. Some $7 million worth of marble was used in its construction. **The Elms** was built for Pennsylvania coal baron Edward Julius Berwind in 1901, its stately design inspired by the Chateau d'Asnieres, a mid-18th-century home outside Paris. **Rosecliff** was built in 1902 for Nevada silver heiress Theresa Fair Oelrichs, designed by architect Stanford White after the Grand Trianon at Versailles. All the mansions are located off Bellevue Avenue, and tours run throughout the day. Admission is $10 for any one house (except The Breakers), $22 for The Breakers and any one of the other mansions, or $31 for any five mansions—the latter a bit too much to squeeze into your time ashore.

Several other mansions are privately held and open to the public. At the **Astors' Beechwood,** 580 Bellevue Ave. (© **401/846-3772;** www.astorsbeechwood.com), daily tours are led by actors portraying the wealthy Astor family in the year 1891. Admission is $18. The 60-room **Belcourt Castle,** 657 Bellevue Ave. (© **401/846-0669;** www.belcourtcastle.com), was built from the inherited fortunes of August Belmont, the Rothschild Banking representative in America. Its current owners, the Tinney family, still reside here, opening their home daily to tours. Admission is $12.

The 3.5-mile **Cliff Walk** meanders between Newport's rocky coastline and many of the town's Gilded Age estates, providing a better view of them than you get from the street. Traversing its length, high above the crashing surf, is more than a stroll but less than an arduous hike. For the full 3.5-mile length, walk about a mile from the pier to the path's start at the intersection of Memorial Boulevard and Eustis Avenue. For a shorter walk, end at the Forty Steps (an access point between the path and the street), which is at the end of Narragansett Avenue, off Bellevue. If you want to do the entire Cliff Walk, but don't want to walk all the way back to the pier when you've reached the end, consider taking the trolley back. You can grab it on Bellevue, just 1½ blocks from the walk. Keep in mind that there are some mildly rugged sections to negotiate, no facilities, and no phones. A number of mansions, such as the Breakers, Rosecliff, Astors Beechwood, Marble House, and Rough Point, are just on the other side of the walk; others are a few blocks inland from the path.

Just a few blocks from the pier, Newport's **Historic Hill** section contains one of the most impressive concentrations of original 18th- and 19th-century Colonial, Federal, and Victorian houses in America, many of them designated National Historic Sites. Spring Street, the Hill's main drag, is an architectural treasure-trove dominated by the 1725 **Trinity Church,** at the corner of Church Street. Said to have been influenced by the work of the legendary British architect Christopher Wren, it certainly reflects that inspiration in its belfry and distinctive spire, which can be seen from all over downtown. Not far away, **Touro Synagogue,** 85 Touro St. (© **401/847-4794;** www.tourosynagogue.org), is the country's oldest continually operating synagogue, dedicated in 1763. Admission is $5. All around Historic Hill you'll find homes marked with signs that read NRF, denoting that they're among the 83 **18th-century houses** that were restored by tobacco heiress Doris Duke's Newport Restoration Foundation between 1968 and 1984. All are now owned and maintained by the foundation and rented privately. Historic Hill rises from America's Cup Avenue, along the waterfront, and runs inland to Bellevue Avenue. Maps are available at **www.newportrestoration.com.**

Other Newport attractions include the Gothic **St. Mary's Church,** 70 Church St. where John F. Kennedy and Jacqueline Bouvier married, and the **Internation**-

Tennis Hall of Fame, 194 Bellevue Ave. (© 800/457-1144; www.tennisfame.org), one of the few places in North America where you can play on a grass court. Museum admission is $8. To play on the grass courts, visitors must call 401/846-0642 and reserve in advance. Prices for play start at $70/hr. for two players.

SHOPPING

Lower Thames Street offers some quirky shopping opportunities, including stores that sell vintage clothing, salvaged architectural components, books, and sailing gear. **Spring Street** is noted for its antiques shops and purveyors of crafts, jewelry, and folk art. Spring intersects with **Franklin Street,** which harbors even more antiques shops in its short length. **Bellevue Avenue** also offers a collection of resort-type boutiques— shopping in the true Newport style.

4 Québec City, Québec

Perched on a cliff top overlooking the St. Lawrence River, Québec City remains the soul of New France, an enormous territory that once included all of eastern Canada, the eastern U.S., the Great Lakes, and Louisiana, stretching from Hudson Bay in the north to Florida in the south. In 1608, the French explorer Samuel de Champlain was the first European to claim Québec City, and soon after established a fur trading post. It was the first significant settlement in Canada, and today it is the capital of Québec, a politically prickly province larger than Alaska. The old city, a tumble of colorful metal-roofed houses clustered around the dominating Château Frontenac, is a haunting evocation of a coastal town in the motherland, as romantic as any on that continent. Because of its history, beauty, and unique stature as the only walled city north of Mexico, the historic district of Québec was named a UNESCO World Heritage Site in 1985—one of only three areas so designated in North America.

The city is split into two sections. The **Lower Town** (or Basse-Ville) is where the port is, while the **Upper Town** (Haute-Ville), the city's oldest section, dates back nearly 400 years and is still surrounded by its old stone walls.

Though some 95% of Québec's 167,000 citizens are French speakers, most people who work in hotels, restaurants, and shops also speak English.

Note: All prices in this section were calculated at the rate of US$0.87 = C$1 or US$1 = C$1.15. Foreign currency rates fluctuate, so prices may not be exactly the same when you arrive in port.

COMING ASHORE

The cruise docks at the **Port of Québec,** which includes a bustling commercial shipping operation, are located within walking distance of the historic **Lower Town,** just outside the walled city. The **Upper Town** can be reached via a steep walk up the hill or the **funicular** (see below).

GETTING AROUND   Virtually no place of interest is beyond walking distance, so your own two feet are definitely the best way to explore. Although there are streets and stairs between the Upper and Lower Towns, there is also a **funicular,** which has long operated along an inclined 210-foot track between the Quartier Petit-Champlain and the Terrasse Dufferin, up top. The upper station is near the front of the Château Frontenac, the majestic hotel that towers over the city, and Place d'Armes, a central square; the lower station is actually inside the Maison Louis-Jolliet, a teeny building on rue du Petit-Champlain. It runs year-round daily and wheelchairs are accommodated. The one-way fare is US$1.30 (C$1.50).

If you aren't up for walking, or if you're going between opposite ends of Lower and Upper Towns, a **taxi** might be the answer. They're everywhere, and your best bet for getting one is by locating a stand—such as the ones on the Place d'Armes and in front of the Hôtel-de-Ville (City Hall). Restaurant managers and hotel bell captains will also summon them if you ask. Fares are somewhat expensive given the short distances of most rides. The starting rate is US$2.75 (C$3.15), and you should tip an additional 10% to 15%. To call a cab, try **Taxi Coop** (© **418/525-5191**) or **Taxi Québec** (© **418/525-8123**).

BEST CRUISE LINE SHORE EXCURSIONS

City Walking Tour ($34, 3 hr.): If you're up for it, the best way to discover Québec's historical side is by walking through the city's narrow cobblestone streets with a knowledgeable guide leading the way. Stroll along the first shopping street in North America, Le Petit Quartier Champlain, in the Lower Town. In the Upper Town, 3 centuries of history come to life in sites such as la Place d'Armes, la Terrasse Dufferin, Place de l'Hôtel de Ville, and le Musée des Ursulines. Finally, stop for tea at the Fairmont Château Frontenac Hotel, Québec City's best-known landmark, for a plate of delicious pastries.

City Highlights by Bus ($39, 2½ hr.): Explore the narrow streets and stately residences that have hardly changed in more than 3 centuries. Enjoy panoramic views of the St. Lawrence River from the oldest part of town, drive through the Grande Allée neighborhood for a peek at the Victorian-era homes, and then on to the Château Frontenac landmark hotel, where there's time to explore. Finally, drive on to the Plain of Abraham, where the battle between the French and British armies eventually sealed the fate of the French colony.

Biking to Montmorency Falls ($59, 4 hr.): Peddle a mountain bike some 8 miles to Montmorency Falls, which plummet down a 272-foot cliff into the St. Lawrence River. Along the way you'll pass the Québec Yacht Harbor and cross the St. Charles River to Domaine Maizerets, then ride along the St. Lawrence for views of Québec's skyline and the Island of Orleans.

ON YOUR OWN: WITHIN WALKING DISTANCE

Spend a day strolling Québec City's hilly cobblestone streets, taking in their 17th- and 18th-century buildings, cafes, shops, and homes. Québec's Lower Town encompasses the restored Quartier Petit-Champlain, including pedestrian-only **rue du Petit-Champlain,** and **Place Royale,** home to the small **Notre-Dame-des-Victoires church,** the city's oldest, dating from 1688. Petit-Champlain is undeniably touristy, but not unpleasantly so, with several agreeable cafes and shops. Restored **Place Royale** is perhaps the most attractive of the city's many squares, upper or lower. Also in Lower Town, the impressive **Museum of Civilization,** 85 rue Dalhousie (© **418/643-2158;** www.mcq.org), is an excellent interactive museum with rotating exhibits representing historical, current, and controversial subjects. Admission is US$7 (C$8).

The highlight of the Upper Town is the gorgeous **Fairmont Château Frontenac hotel,** rue St-Louis (© **800/828-7447** or 418/692-3861; www.fairmont.com/frontenac), a beauty set high above the St. Lawrence River. Colonial governors used to reside on the site of this turreted gem with slanted copper roofs. The actual building was erected in 1883 as a prestigious hotel where the likes of Winston Churchill and Queen Elizabeth II have stayed. Linger for a drink and savor the magical aura. Other popular attractions in the Upper Town include the outdoor **Parc-de-l'Artillerie,** 2 rue d'Auteuil (© **418/648-4205;** www.pc.gc.ca/artillerie), a fortification whose walls were erected by the French in the 17th and 18th centuries (admission US$3.50, C$4), and the **Basilica of Notre-Dame,** 20 rue Buade (© **418/694-0665**), the oldest Christian parish north of Mexico.

On a sloped hill just to the south of the Château is the **Citadel,** 1 Côte de la Citadelle (© **418/694-2815;** www.lacitadelle.qc.ca), a partially star-shaped fortress begun by the French in the 18th century and augmented by the English well into the 19th century. Admission is US$7 (C$8). At the eastern edge of the Citadel, the **Terrasse Dufferin** is a pedestrian promenade that attracts crowds in all seasons for its magnificent views of the river and the land to the south, ferries gliding back and forth, and cruise ships and Great Lakes freighters putting in at the harbor below.

SHOPPING

Côte de la Montagne, which leads from the Upper Town to the Lower Town as an alternative to the funicular, has a few stores with more tourist-geared items and some crafts and folk art. The Lower Town itself, particularly the **Quartier Petit-Champlain,** just off Place Royale and encompassing the tiny streets of rue du Petit-Champlain, boulevard Champlain, and rue Sous-le-Fort (opposite the funicular entrance), offers many possibilities—clothing, souvenirs, gifts, household items, collectibles. On the other side of the old city, a few blocks past Parliament down Grande-Allée, **avenue Cartier** has shops and restaurants of some variety, from clothing and ceramics to housewares and gourmet foods. The 4 or 5 blocks attract crowds of generally youngish locals, and the hubbub revs up on summer nights and weekends. The area remains outside the tourist orbit.

Dealers in **antiques** have gravitated to the cute **rue St-Paul** in the Lower Town, offering everything from brass beds and Québec country furniture to knickknacks, paddywhacks, and post–World War II U.S. kitsch. To get there, follow rue St-Pierre from the Place Royale, and then head west on rue St-Paul.

5 Saint John, New Brunswick

New Brunswick's largest city, Saint John sits along a sizable commercial harbor on the Bay of Fundy, at the mouth of the St. John River. Like Halifax, it was an important shipbuilding hub around the turn of the 20th century, and today its deep-water harbor can accommodate the world's largest liners.

Don't expect a picture-postcard-perfect place overflowing with gardens and neat homes. Instead, Saint John is a predominantly industrial city, with large shipping terminals, oil storage facilities, and paper mills serving as the backdrop to the waterfront area. If you make an effort to look, though, you'll see that downtown's buildings boast some wonderfully elaborate Victorian flourishes, while a handful of impressive mansions lord over the side streets, their interiors a forest of intricate woodcarving—appropriate for the timber barons who built them.

The first Europeans to settle here were the French, when Samuel de Champlain led an exploration party into the Bay of Fundy and founded the first French settlement n North America in 1604. A hundred years later, the British were on the scene, cap-·ring Saint John, which, in 1785, became Canada's first incorporated city.

COMING ASHORE Ships dock right at the **Pugsley Cruise Terminal,** in the industrial heart of the city, just steps from the city's downtown.

GETTING AROUND If you haven't signed up for an organized tour, you can walk right into town or opt for a 1-hour city-highlights tour on the vintage bus-style trolleys or horse-drawn trolleys that meet the ship. If you'd rather travel by **taxi,** they queue up at the docks and work on set rates, depending on where you're going. Taxi tours covering major city sights are about US$35 (C$40) an hour for one to four passengers. If you need to call a taxi, try **Coastal Taxi Limited** (© **506/635-1144**) or **Diamond Taxi** (© **506/648-8888**).

Note: All prices in this section were calculated at the rate of US$0.87 = C$1 or US$1 = C$1.15. Foreign currency rates fluctuate, so prices may not be exactly the same when you arrive in port.

BEST CRUISE LINE SHORE EXCURSIONS

Historical Walking Tour ($29, 2 hr.): See the restored historic district known as Trinity Royal and the bustling City Market that survives from the late 1800s. A bus takes groups to the farthest destination, the Loyalist Burial Ground, where the walk starts. Gravestones there date as far back as 1784. Sights along the way include the beautiful brick town houses along Germain Street; the historic commercial buildings of Prince William Street, whose elaborate facades are decorated with gargoyles, pediments, and Ionic columns; the Market Slip, where thousands of American Colonists who remained loyal to the British Crown landed in 1783; and King's Square, designed in 1848 in the shape of the Union Jack to show loyalty to England.

Reversing Falls Rapids by Jetboat ($109, 3 hr.): Reversing Falls Rapids is a much-photographed spot where the Bay of Fundy meets the St. John River, and strong tidal conditions cause harbor currents to reverse. This large tidal swing means some 2 billion gallons of water surge into the Bay twice a day—that's 2 *billion.* Near Fallsview Park, an underwater ledge 36 feet down causes a boiling series of rapids and whirlpools, and the rising tide slows the river current to a stop for about 20 minutes. The tour begins with an orientation drive through Saint John, stopping at the Old City Market (open since 1876). You then head to Fallsview Park, don life jackets and rain gear, and board your high-speed jet boat for a ride over and around the rapids. You can take the jet-boat ride (referred to as the Thrill Ride) without signing on to a tour by contacting **Reversing Falls Jet Boat Rides** (© **506/634-8987;** www.jetboat rides.com); the 20-minute rides cost US$33 (C$38).

Canadian Beer Tasting & Saint John Highlights Tour ($49, 3 hr.): Heads up, beer lovers: This is your chance to sample Canadian beers and enjoy a famous local Irish pub, O'Leary's. Also included is a drive around the Saint John area, time at the Old City Market, and a visit to the famous Reversing Falls.

ON YOUR OWN: WITHIN WALKING DISTANCE

Start your visit by wandering around near the waterfront, taking note of the gargoyles and sculpted heads that adorn the brick and stone 19th-century buildings. The Saint John visitor information board publishes several **self-guided walking tours** that will give you a great overview of the city. Text and maps are available for download at www. tourismsaintjohn.com/files/fuse.cfm?section=14&screen=228.

Of the handful of museums in Saint John, the important one to visit is the **New Brunswick Museum,** 1 Market Sq. (© **506/643-2300;** www.nbm-mnb.ca

Established in 1842, it's the oldest continuously operating museum in Canada. Exhibits include a marine mammals gallery whose focal point is "Delilah," the full skeletal remains of a 40-foot North Atlantic right whale that beached off Grand Manan in 1992. Other displays include local and Canadian art, the best collection of Loyalist artifacts on the North American continent, and the largest collection of ships' portraiture in Canada. Don't miss a peek at the cool tidal tube in the lobby. It's connected to the harbor, and water in the tube rises and falls with the tide. Admission is US$5.20 (C$6).

If the weather's disagreeable when you arrive, you can head indoors to Saint John's elaborate network of underground and overhead pedestrian walkways, dubbed **The Inside Connection.** Passages link the city's downtown malls and shops, two major hotels, the provincial museum, the city library, the city market, a sports arena, and an aquatics center. Another indoor option is the **Old City Market,** 47 Charlotte St. (© **506/658-2820**), a spacious, bustling marketplace crammed with vendors hawking cheeses, flowers, baked goods, meat, fresh seafood, and fresh produce. The market was built in 1876, and it has been a center of commerce for the city ever since. A number of vendors offer meals to go, and there's a bright seating area in an enclosed terrace on the market's south side.

ON YOUR OWN: BEYOND THE PORT AREA

If you don't sign on to one of the ship's shore excursions, you can walk to the **Reversing Falls Rapids** via the **Harbour Passage,** an interconnected system of walking and biking trails that winds along the waterfront from Market Square to the Reversing Falls, a distance of just under 3 miles. To immerse yourself in an even more natural side of New Brunswick, book an excursion or take a taxi to **Irving Nature Park,** Sand Cove Road (© **506/653-7367**), located along the coast across the Saint John River, less than 3 miles southwest of town. The park consists of 243 hectares (600 acres) of dramatic coastal scenery where as many as 240 species of birds have been spotted. Soft wood-chipped trails and marsh boardwalks provide access to a lovely forest and wild, salty seascapes.

SHOPPING

You'll find art galleries, antiques shops, souvenir shops, and boutiques within a 10-minute walk of the cruise terminal, clustered around **Market Square, Brunswick Square, King Street,** and **Prince William Street.**

16

U.S. River Cruise Routes

In addition to sailing in the Caribbean, Central America, Alaska, Baja's Sea of Cortez, and New England/Canada, many of the small ships reviewed in chapter 8 also offer cruises on America's great rivers, visiting historic towns and sailing through gorgeous countryside. Experiences range from real Americana on the Mississippi and Erie Canal to a totally sybaritic experience sailing between vineyards in California's wine country. As these rivers cover a good chunk of the continental United States, and because each ship makes different stops along the way, we've limited ourselves to giving you a sort of "virtual float" along each river, with a sampling of the highlights seen on many regional cruises.

1 The California Wine Country

San Francisco's Bay Area easily qualifies as one of the world's greatest natural harbors, its shores fringed with national parklands and some of America's most prized residential communities. At the bay's eastern end, the Sacramento River Delta leads to the United States' leading wine-growing region. While a driving holiday is a fine way to explore vineyard and redwood country, a cruise includes behind-the-scenes visits, expert presentations ashore and on board, and, of course, a designated driver. As an added benefit, many of the region's real scenic delights, including the graceful bridges and lovely islands of San Francisco Bay, are at their best when viewed from the water. wine-country cruises draw mostly American passengers in the 30s-to-70s age range, and sail from San Francisco in the fall (generally Sept–Nov).

Many of Napa's and Sonoma's vineyards trace their ancestries from immigrants who realized the soil and climate were perfect for growing European varietals from France, Italy, Germany, and Switzerland. New hybrid vines developed later, resulting in today's booming U.S. wine industry and the proliferation of prosperous wine estates, some of them designed in a modern California-ranch style, others in Spanish Colonial or Spanish Mission, wooden Victorian, or European château style. The sites you'll visit will vary depending on the date you sail, but most departures have a similar routing.

The City by the Bay, **San Francisco** (see chapter 9), is a must-see from the water. Its parallel streets run from the shore steeply up Knob, Russian, and Telegraph hills, with North Beach, Marina, and the Financial District sandwiched in between. The harbor entrance is flanked by dramatic natural headlands and spanned by the graceful **Golden Gate Bridge,** its towers often poking through a tongue of mist sweeping in from the colder Pacific.

The captain usually takes his ship under the span and sails until the ocean swells begin to rock, then makes a 180-degree turn to hug the **Sausalito** waterfront for several miles along the Marin County shore. A walk from the pier reveals Sausalito's varied lifestyles, from ramshackle houseboats to some of the most expensive waterfron property in America, and also lets you explore the city's popular boutique and art gallery district. An organized excursion visits the U.S. Army Corps of Engineers, caretakers of the inland waterways, where a 1½-acre, three-dimensional hydraulic Bay Model lays out the Bay's intricate water control system. From Sausalito, coaches drive north into the **Muir Woods National Monument** (www.nps.gov/muwo) for a stroll among the California Redwoods, the world's tallest trees, set in a canyon beneath Mt. Tamalpais. A pedestrian tunnel has been carved through one trunk of particularly amazing girth.

Sailing from Sausalito, the ship passes Tiburon, an upscale bedroom suburb ranging up the slopes of a peninsula jutting into the bay, then skirts **Alcatraz,** the once-notorious island prison that's now a national historic park. Nearby **Angel Island** (www.angelisland.org), even more impressive in height and size, was once the Ellis Island of the West, admitting thousands of immigrants to the country. It now provides recreational facilities for picnic and hikes. From here, ships usually turn north, sailing past **Berkeley** and under the Richmond–San Rafael Bridge into a widening San Pablo Bay. Some cruises will sail through the narrow Carquinez Strait into the **Sacramento Delta,** an expansive area of marshlands and natural and man-made waterways. Early morning is likely to give rise to tule fog, a heavy mist that rises from the swampy bulrushes, then burns off in the morning sun.

Your ship may dock at **Vallejo** at the mouth of the Napa River or continue sailing for several hours to land closer to the wine-growing region. From here, buses take passengers on full-day trips and then return to the ship in the late afternoon.

The **Napa and Sonoma valleys** (www.napavalley.org; www.sonomacounty.com) run north by northwest between a ridge of low mountains rising not much more than 2,500 feet. The region is a major tourist area, more so in the fall during the harvest season and to a lesser extent in the green spring. While some of the vineyard names may be unfamiliar, you'll recognize the chardonnays, merlots, pinot noirs, and zinfandels they produce. And you'll get plenty of chances to sample them, either via **wine tastings** or by sipping the vintages chosen for dinner. These will include both table- and premium-quality varieties, including sparkling wines created using the champagne method.

A tour of **Benziger Vineyards** (www.benziger.com) includes a tractor-pulled tram tour into the Sonoma Hills for terrific views of the surrounding vineyard landscape, a blanket of color in the autumn. The **Markham Vineyards** (www.markhamvineyards. com) dates from 1874, when French immigrant Jean Laurent started his Laurent Winery on the site. Some visits include lunch in the 1879 stone cellar barrel room, which houses aging red wine.

St. Supéry (www.stsupery.com) is owned by third-generation French winemakers and is noted for its cabernet sauvignon and sauvignon blanc. Its 1880 Victorian house is on the National Register of Historic Places and includes an art gallery. **Schramsberg** (www.schramsberg.com) has a garden setting and produces well-regarded sparkling wine using the champagne method. Fermenting takes place along thousands of feet of tunnels dug by Chinese laborers brought in to work during the 19th century. Robert Louis Stevenson called Schramsberg's wine "bottled poetry."

The Chinese also helped to build the rail line used by the **Napa Valley Wine Train** (www.winetrain.com) for its 30-mile town-and-country route. Some cruise departures include a ride in the wine-red lounge cars and full dinners while the train travels the Napa Valley.

If you're up early enough, your arrival back in San Francisco at the end of your cruise will probably coincide with dawn breaking over one of the world's most beautiful cities. With luck, you've planned to stay on for a few days rather than rushing off to the airport. You can choose a location near Fisherman's Wharf, Ghirardelli Square, and Pier 39 or a more central one near Union Square. Both areas are close to those little cable cars that rise halfway to the stars. See chapter 9 for some great hotel picks in town.

LINES SAILING THESE ROUTES   Cruise West (p. 335) is currently the only line offering wine-country cruises. They run 3 and 4 nights, throughout September and October.

2 The Columbia & Snake Rivers, Pacific Northwest

The Columbia–Snake system is one of America's most important river systems, second only to the Mississippi–Missouri in the size of the area it drains. The Columbia River flows 1,200 miles from the Canadian Rockies in southeast British Columbia into Washington, and then forms the border with Oregon on its way to the Pacific. The 1,000-mile Snake River starts in Yellowstone National Park and flows through Idaho into eastern Washington, where it meets the Columbia.

The two rivers have historically served as the primary artery for east–west travel in the Pacific Northwest, used first by the Nez Perce Indians and later by western explorers, fur traders, settlers, military expeditions, and missionaries. Settlers came in increasing numbers in the few years prior to the 1846 Oregon Treaty, and in 1859 Oregon became the 33rd state. Washington, once part of Oregon, was organized as a separate territory in 1853, but did not become the 42nd state until 1889.

Today, the Columbia–Snake corridor provides a fascinating trip into more varied landscapes than one will find along any North American river. Beginning at the Pacific Ocean breakers, the river mouth near Astoria begins as a broad bay, narrows upriver to a more natural stream, and then squeezes dramatically through the deep **Columbia Gorge** (www.fs.fed.us/r6/columbia/forest). Thickly forested slopes rise to flanking high cliffs while melting snow cascades into pencil-thin waterfalls. The river's surface is turbulent and the winds are strong, but a series of dams built beginning in the Great Depression tames the flow into a series of separate pools. **Navigation locks** lift boats and barges while parallel fish ladders provide a bypass for salmon heading upstream to spawn, as well as for the young heading in the other direction, toward the Pacific.

Beyond the gorge, the land becomes drier, and with the right soil and an ideal climate, **vineyards** have burgeoned in both Washington and Oregon to create the country's second-largest wine-producing region in the U.S. after California's. **Wildlife** is abundant here, as hundreds of thousands of birds come to roost and nest, especially in the **Umatilla Wildlife Refuge** (http://midcolumbiariver.fws.gov/Umatillapage.htm). By the time your ship reaches the Snake River, the land on either side shows few signs of habitation, instead rising from the waterline in layers of basalt laid down millions of years ago, forming multicolored buttes and mesas.

Portland, Oregon, a city of just over a half-million (with another 1.5 million in its metropolitan area), is the embarkation city for nearly all Columbia–Snake cruises. The city has kept its human scale better than most, maintained a vibrant downtown and much of its traditional architecture, and prevented major expressways from slicing through its heart. Known as the Rose City, Portland boasts 250 parks, gardens, and greenways, and since 1907 has celebrated the annual Portland Rose Festival for several weeks each June with an extravagant floral parade, music, car and boat races, and visits by U.S. Navy ships.

The city's core is **Pioneer Courthouse Square,** with a prosperous late-19th-century feel and street life generated by stores, offices, restaurants, and traditional-style hotels. Less than a mile northeast, in the Old Town/Chinatown neighborhood, the weekend **Saturday Market** (www.saturdaymarket.org) is a huge draw for its open-air handicraft, clothing, and jewelry stalls. Nearby, the **Portland Classical Chinese Garden** (www.portlandchinesegarden.org) is one of only two in North America (along with the one in Vancouver, British Columbia), taking up an entire walled block. Stepping through the gate feels like walking into an entirely different world, with pavilions, bridges, walkways, hundreds of native Chinese plant species, and a teahouse arranged around a central reflecting pond. About a half-mile west, **Powell's Books** (www.powells. com) is the world's largest independent bookstore, with new and used books shelved together in a warren of rooms spread over three floors and a whole city block.

Up in the hills about 3 miles west of downtown, Washington Park's terraced **International Rose Test Garden** (www.rosegardenstore.org) displays some 560 varieties of roses, usually at their blooming peak during June and July and again in September and October. Just up the hill, the park's 5½-acre **Japanese Garden** (www.japanesegarden. com) is one of the finest of its type outside Japan, with walking paths leading among streams, ponds, Japanese flora, and five distinct gardens representing classical Japanese styles. The views of **Mount Hood** from the Japanese and Rose gardens are spectacular.

Upon leaving Portland, cruises sail overnight downriver to where the widening Columbia meets the Pacific Ocean and call at **Astoria,** Oregon, tying up at a pier adjacent to the Columbia Bar lightship *Columbia* and Coast Guard cutter *Steadfast,* both of which are open for visitors. The **Columbia River Maritime Museum** (www. crmm.org) is part of the pier complex, exhibiting the history of Columbia River trade in ship models, drawings, and photographs. Don't miss the 20-minute walk up Coxcomb Hill to the 125-foot **Astoria Column,** which dominates the landscape from its 600-foot elevation. Erected in 1926 to mark the location of the first permanent American settlement west of the Rockies, it was designed by New York architect Electus D. Litchfield after the Trajan Column in Rome. Italian artist Attilio Pusterla created a bas-relief mural that scrolls around the column to depict the history of the town. The views here are extraordinary, both from the top of the column and from the property around it.

Organized excursions head downriver to **Fort Clatsop** (www.nps.gov/lewi/planyour visit/fortclatsop.htm), where Lewis and Clark spent four wet winter months in 1805–06. A historically accurate re-creation of their fort is on-site. Another stop, the seaside resort of **Cannon Beach,** is a big draw for its wooden weathered-cedar shopping district with typical craft-type boutiques.

Longview, Washington, gives access to **Mount St. Helens** (www.fs.fed.us/gpnf/ mshnvm), the site of the May 18, 1980, volcanic eruption that in minutes reduced the mountain's height by about 1,000 feet. The drive uphill winds through increasingly scarred hillsides covered in lava, ash, mud, and 150 square miles of destroyed forest to an interpretive center overlooking the cloud-enshrouded mountaintop and deep into a valley wasteland.

Bonneville Dam (www.nwp.usace.army.mil/op/b), dedicated by President Franklin Delano Roosevelt in 1937, signaled the first major WPA undertaking by the U.S.

Army Corps of Engineers to create a safe passage through the Cascade Rapids. The dam created 48-mile-long Lake Bonneville, and its hydroelectric plants generate enough power to light 40,000 homes. The visitors center screens a slide film showing the dam under construction and describing how the salmon fish ladders work.

Farther upriver, the **Columbia Gorge Discovery Center** (www.gorgediscovery.org) exhibits the area's history and geology in a film that reveals how the Columbia Gorge was formed by violent volcanic upheavals and raging floods. Another film shows the building of the Columbia River Scenic Highway, which leads to Multnomah Falls. An exhibit illustrates how Lewis and Clark equipped their expedition.

Six thousand feet up the slopes of 11,245-foot **Mount Hood** stands **Timberline Lodge** (www.timberlinelodge.com), a timber-and-stone hotel hand-built in 1936–37 by unemployed craftsmen hired by the WPA. It was dedicated in September 1937 by Franklin Roosevelt. The view is north to 12,307-foot Mount Adams, part of a line of volcano-formed mountains that include Mount St. Helens and Mount Rainier.

At **The Dalles Lock & Dam,** an excursion crosses the river to **Maryhill Museum of Art** (www.maryhillmuseum.org), located high above the river in Washington. A Midwestern Quaker pacifist named Samuel Hill, son-in-law of James J. Hill of the Great Northern Railroad, established the museum in the late 1920s. It now exhibits Russian Orthodox icons, Rodin sculptures, a collection of 250 chess sets, Queen Marie of Romania's royal regalia, miniature fashion costumes on stage sets, and Native American clothing, baskets, and weapons. Four miles east of the museum, just off Washington Scenic Route 14, is a full-scale **replica of Stonehenge** built by Sam Hill as a monument to Klickitat County soldiers who lost their lives in World War I.

Stops in **Pendleton,** Oregon, may include a visit to the grounds of the annual September **Pendleton Round-Up** (www.pendletonroundup.com) for a presentation of rodeo riding, country music, flintlock rifle firing, and other activities. In town, **Pendleton Underground** (www.pendletonundergroundtours.org) is an odd tour centered around a huge warren of tunnels dug by Chinese laborers in the 19th century. The Chinese lived and ran businesses here entirely underground, while some areas of the complex were used as bars, opium dens, and later Prohibition-era speak-easies. Elsewhere in town, the **Tamastslikt Cultural Institute** (www.tamastslikt.com) presents a variety of Native American traditions, including dancing, drumming, and storytelling. Exhibits include horse regalia, war bonnets, bows, and demonstrations of saddle making. Nearby, the **Fort Walla Walla Museum** (www.fortwallawallamuseum. org) exhibits a collection of carefully restored and re-created historic buildings that include a schoolhouse, doctor's office, railroad station, and houses arranged in a closed compound. Other buildings house farm equipment and a fire engine once drawn by a 33-mule team.

Finally, after passing through four **Snake River locks and dams,** your ship reaches the end of deep-water navigation at the border towns of Lewiston, Idaho, and Clarkston, Washington, 465 miles upriver from the Pacific Ocean. From here, an all-day **jet boat ride** heads into **Hells Canyon,** Idaho (www.hellscanyonvisitor.com). Set aside as a National Recreation Area, the Snake River starts out sluggish but soon becomes a fast-flowing stream of twisting rapids with 20-mph currents. The high bluffs and mountains on either side increase in height, creating a canyon 7,900 feet deep—1,900 feet deeper than the Grand Canyon. Passengers are likely to see bighorn sheep standing still on rocky ledges, mule deer down by the water, eagles and osprey overhead, and Nez Perce Indian petroglyphs inscribed on the flat rock surfaces depicting bighorn sheep.

LINES SAILING THESE ROUTES   **Majestic America Line** (p. 359) operates here almost year-round, minus January. **Cruise West** (p. 335), **Lindblad Expeditions** (p. 345), and **American Safari Cruises** (p. 334) offer cruises here in the spring and/or fall.

3 The Hudson River, Erie Canal & Great Lakes

Inland cruises in the U.S. Northeast sail waterways such as the Hudson River, the Erie Canal, the St. Lawrence Seaway, and the Great Lakes, mixing and matching among these waterways to create itineraries of a week to 12 days. Most ships sail from New York.

UP THE HUDSON

The navigable portion of the **Hudson River** (www.hudsonriver.com) extends through New York for about 150 miles, from Manhattan to Albany and Troy. The river is considered to be an estuary as tidal effects reach the base of the canal locks above Albany, and saltwater content extends about 60 miles northward from Manhattan, and even farther during long periods of dry weather. On a cruise, one gets superb water-level views of the Hudson Valley, the towering New Jersey Palisades, the rugged Hudson Highlands, sprawling country estates, and the mighty fortress at West Point.

Leaving from **Manhattan**'s west side, ships skirt the majestic skyline and pass under the two-level George Washington Bridge. **Palisades Interstate Park** (www.njpalisades. org) rises on the New Jersey side, an especially beautiful scene during fall foliage season. Fishermen will be out in force on weekends, as it's once again safe to eat the catch (though everyday consumption is not recommended). After passing Yonkers, the Hudson widens into the Tappan Zee, passing under the **Tappan Zee Bridge** carrying the New York State Thruway north to Albany and west to Buffalo.

Looking carefully, one may glimpse **Washington Irving's house** in the Hudson Valley town of Sunnyside; Tarrytown's Victorian gothic **Lyndhurst Castle,** owned by the National Trust for Historic Preservation; and **Philipsburg Manor,** a 17th-century Dutch farming complex located in the town of Sleepy Hollow. From the decks you get a long-range view north to the Hudson Highlands, and at Ossining the stone walls of **Sing Sing Prison** parallel the river. Information on all these attractions can be found online at **www.hudsonvalley.org**.

As your ship approaches Bear Mountain State Park on the left and the Bear Mountain Bridge, a flag rises above the trees marking the rustic **Bear Mountain Inn** (www. bearmountaininn.com), built in 1915. The river becomes noticeably narrower, and the channel under the Bear Mountain suspension bridge deepens dramatically to over 300 feet as the surrounding land rises steeply.

On the cliff tops opposite, the grounds of the United States Military Academy at **West Point** (www.usma.edu) begin, marked first by officers' houses, then the Hotel Thayer, and finally the gray-stone fortress-style buildings. At the base of the cliff, a launch docked near the West Shore Line station brings cadets and officers across the Hudson to Garrison station for trains to New York. The colorful cluster of wooden Victorian buildings across the street from the Garrison depot served as the setting for Dolly's return to Yonkers in the film *Hello Dolly.* Most cruises stop at West Point for tours of the academy and historic Hudson Valley homes.

Rising from the river you'll see the grassy grounds and yellow Federal-style buildings of **Boscobel** (www.boscobel.org), a museum of Early American furniture and decorative arts. Nearby, the 18th- and 19th-century river town of **Cold Spring** is full of restaurants (including the **Hudson House Inn;** www.hudsonhouseinn.com), antiques shops, and collectibles stores. If you come back on your own, it also makes a good base for hiking the Hudson Highlands.

North of Cold Spring is **Bannerman's Island** (www.bannermancastle.org), on which you'll find a mock 19th-century Scottish-style castle and estate built by a New York arms and surplus merchant as a munitions warehouse and country retreat. They were destroyed in a huge fire in 1974, leaving behind the stabilized ruins one sees today.

At **Poughkeepsie,** nearby sites include **Franklin Roosevelt's Hyde Park house** (www.nps.gov/hofr/hofrhome.html), with Eleanor's cottage a short distance away; and the **Culinary Institute of America** (www.ciachef.edu), one of the leading U.S. cooking schools.

The Hudson passes numerous **lighthouses** and small river towns en route to Albany, the New York state capital, dominated by Nelson Rockefeller's 98-acre, Internationalist-style **Empire State Plaza,** with its glass-and-marble office towers; reflecting pools; and huge, egg-shaped arts and conference center known as "The Egg" (www.theegg.org). Not all cruises come this far, and those that do (the ACCL ships) simply pass by to begin their trek through the Erie Canal.

INTO THE ERIE CANAL

The Erie's highlights are the **Waterford Flight** of five locks (which lift ships a total of 150 ft.), old factory towns such as Amsterdam and Little Falls, and the 22-mile Oneida Lake crossing. From Syracuse to Buffalo, ships pass through **Montezuma Wildlife Refuge** (www.fws.gov/r5mnwr) for possible sightings of bald eagles and Canada geese, past restored canal towns such as Fairport and Pittsford, and through the original canal's small locks and stone-arched aqueducts. These last structures were built by Frederick Law Olmsted, whose most famous work is New York's Central Park. Turning into the Oswego Canal, the vast expanse of **Lake Ontario** is ahead, and soon one is threading among the beautiful **Thousand Islands** (www.thousandislands.com). Stops are made at Clayton's **Antique Boat Museum** (www.abm.org) and **Upper Canada Village** (www.uppercanadavillage.com), whose houses, churches, and public and farm buildings span 100 years of Canadian architecture and small-town life. Small ships share the **St. Lawrence Seaway** with huge lake carriers and lock through to Montréal for a stop and a landing at Bay of Eternity in the dramatic **Saguenay fjord.** From here, your ship typically returns upriver to disembark at **Québec City** (see chapter 15).

THE GREAT LAKES

Until the mid-1960s, the five **Great Lakes** were popular summer cruising grounds for Canadian- and U.S.-flag ships, some of which dated from before World War I. When these ships went out of service, the industry died until American Canadian Caribbean Line started offering cruises here again in the late 1990s. A great idea, but keep in mind that the lakes are large bodies of water, and small, shallow-draft coastal cruisers like these can get bounced around during summer storms. In the past few years, German line **Hapag-Lloyd** (www.hl-cruises.com) has begun offering cruises aboard the 14,903-ton, 410-passenger *C. Columbus,* a more stable oceangoing cruise ship. While she caters mainly to German-speaking passengers, her Great Lakes cruises, offered in September and October, are bilingual, with announcements, menus, programs, and shore excursions offered in English.

Great Lakes itineraries are varied and may begin in any number of ports, such as Toronto, Windsor/Detroit, or Chicago. The following ports-of-call sampling will give you some idea of what there is to be seen.

Cruises originating at Toronto will pass from Lake Ontario through the **Welland Canal** locks to Lake Erie, and an excursion will run to **Niagara Falls** (www.tourism niagara.com), including a wet boat trip on the *Maid of the Mist* to the base of the falls.

As you pass into Lake Huron, you'll see **Tobermory** (www.tobermory.org), a fishing port settled by Scots in the early 19th century and the center for a resort region in the beautiful island-studded Georgian Bay. Michigan's **Mackinac Island** (www. mackinacisland.org) is entirely car free and a popular summer resort. Its centerpiece, the venerable **Grand Hotel** (www.grandhotel.com), is one of the great hotels of North America, built in the 1890s and still maintaining its high standards. **Sault Ste. Marie,** strategically placed between lakes Huron and Superior, is the site for the **Soo Locks,** transited on some cruises that sail into the largest of the lakes. The scenic **Algoma Central rail excursion** (www.agawacanyontourtrain.com) from the Soo into the North Country's Agawa Canyon is highly recommended.

Large cities featured on all cruises in this region include **Detroit** for the incredible **Henry Ford Museum and Greenfield Village** (www.thehenryford.org); **Milwaukee** for its German heritage and art museum; and **Chicago** for its outstanding architecture, lakefront skyline, museums, neighborhoods, and the Chicago River.

LINES SAILING THESE ROUTES **American Cruise Lines** (p. 327) and **Cruise West** (p. 335) offer Hudson River cruises that sail round-trip from New York. **American Canadian Caribbean Line** (p. 326) uses the Hudson to reach the Erie Canal for the passage across New York State to the Great Lakes and St. Lawrence Valley. It also offers Great Lakes cruises from Chicago. **Hapag-Lloyd** (see above; www.hl-cruises. com) does Great Lakes cruises.

4 The Mississippi River System

The **Mississippi River system** (www.nps.gov/miss) consists of some 50 rivers and tributaries, seven of which—the Atchafalaya, Arkansas, Ohio, Tennessee, Cumberland, Missouri, and Illinois—are navigable for considerable distances. Known as the Western Rivers because they formed part of the original American West, their drainage basin covers an area of 1,245,000 square miles (a full 41% of the contiguous 48 states) and includes all or parts of 31 states and two Canadian provinces. The Lower Mississippi is defined as the 954 miles between the mouth of the river just in from the Gulf of Mexico and the junction with the Ohio River. **New Orleans** (see chapter 9) has historically been the principal embarkation port and terminus for most Lower Mississippi River cruises, though cruises also depart from Memphis, Cincinnati, Pittsburgh, Nashville, St. Louis, St. Paul, and several smaller cities.

THE LOWER MISSISSIPPI

Sailing from New Orleans, the heavily commercial waterway gives way to rural, mostly flat southern Louisiana. The river, however, remains a remarkable commercial artery used by the world's most impressive tow ships. As many as 30 to 40 barges loaded with grain, salt, lime, coal, rocks, petroleum products, and other materials may be strapped together to form a solid flotilla that can equal the carrying capacity of 1,800 to 2,400 tractor-trailers. All along the route, you'll see the kind of levees Hurricane Katrina made infamous, built to prevent high water from flooding the adjoining farmlands and towns—if they work. Some levees are high enough to block the view inland except from the highest decks, though in other places the long-range vistas remain.

It's the **Antebellum South** (or the present-day interpretation of it) that lower-river cruisers come to see. The rural plantation homes and the stately mansions clustered in towns and cities exhibit rich examples of American architecture, some rebuilt after the Civil War, others that have undergone considerable restoration after periods of neglect.

Laura Plantation, Louisiana (www.lauraplantation.com), was originally French owned, but during its most significant period it was owned by a Creole family. The main house, built around 1805, has a raised brick basement story with the upper floors executed in Federal style. Six slave quarters and a collection of outbuildings show the development of the sugar cane industry that lasted into the 20th century.

Oak Alley, Louisiana (www.oakalleyplantation.com), built in 1837–39, features a quintessential double line of live oaks that stretches from the river landing to the main Greek Revival–style house. The 1840 white-pillared Greek Revival **Houmas House** (www.houmashouse.com) lies at the end of a double line of equally old oak trees, and was once the largest slave-holding plantation in the South.

Baton Rouge, Louisiana, offers the nation's tallest state capitol building, a 34-story Art Deco masterpiece constructed on the orders of legendary governor Huey P. Long. Nearby, the most enlightening experience takes place at the Louisiana State University's **Rural Life Museum** (http://rurallife.lsu.edu), arranged as if one had stepped out the back door of the "Big House" to see how the rest of the working antebellum plantation was going about its daily life.

St. Francisville, Louisiana, boasts 140 structures listed on the National Register of Historic Places, including the Georgian Revival courthouse, Romanesque Revival Bank of Commerce & Trust, and French colonial, antebellum, neoclassical, gingerbread Victorian, and "dog trot" houses. The latter get their name from their design, with a long open corridor through which a dog could trot, if he had a mind to.

Natchez, Mississippi, has 200 historic homes among more than 500 antebellum structures, and about three dozen are open to the public. Your ship will probably offer a tour. In **Vicksburg,** Mississippi, the **National Military Park** (www.nps.gov/vick) is the principal destination. An organized tour details the story of the Civil War city, which suffered through a 42-day siege by Union troops. Its surrender to Ulysses S. Grant on July 4, 1863, coupled with the fall of Port Hudson, Louisiana, divided the South and gave the North control of the Mississippi.

Memphis, Tennessee, a city that bills itself as Home of the Blues and Birthplace of Rock 'n' Roll, is usually an embarkation or disembarkation port for river cruises. Small ships dock at Mud Island River Park, a recreation and museum center, and a Main Street trolley gives access to the Beale Street Entertainment District and the **National Civil Rights Museum** (www.civilrightsmuseum.org), where Martin Luther King, Jr., was shot on April 4, 1968. Outside the city, **Graceland** (www.elvis.com), Elvis Presley's jazzed-up Georgian-style home, draws the largest crowds north of New Orleans.

THE UPPER MISSISSIPPI

Some river aficionados consider cruises between St. Louis and St. Paul to be the most interesting because of the combination of flanking high bluffs, pleasant farmlands, locking operations, and the intriguing small Victorian-era towns that the ships visit. In fall, the foliage in Wisconsin rivals that of New England.

The upper Midwest's first inhabitants were the Native Sioux and Algonquin peoples, then came the French fur trappers and traders, prospectors to tap the rich lead deposits, entrepreneurs to invest in lumbering, and pioneering Anglo farmers to clear the land for agriculture. Ensuing manufacturing, trade, and transportation in the stretch between St. Paul and St. Louis created numerous river towns and cities of considerable if relatively short-lived importance, such as Cape Girardeau, Missouri; Burlington, Fort Madison, and Dubuque, Iowa; Galena, Illinois; LaCrosse, Wisconsin; and Winona, Wabasha, and Red Wing, Minnesota.

The Upper Mississippi officially begins at Mile 0, Cairo Point, Illinois (where the Ohio River converges), and ends 839 miles to the north at Minneapolis/St. Paul, Minnesota. Locking through is an interesting procedure, and on a 7-day Upper Mississippi cruise you'll be doing this an average of four times a day. Some locks are set up as tourist attractions, with observation towers and parks alongside. It's like a scene out of a history book, with passengers lining the ship's rails exchanging pleasantries with people on shore while the boat sinks or rises in the chamber.

St. Louis, Missouri, historically "The Gateway to the West," is a major embarking and debarking port and worth a night or two before or after the cruise. Eero Saarinen's 630-foot **Gateway Arch** (www.nps.gov/jeff), completed in 1965, gave the city a much-needed icon as well as a monument of considerable beauty, especially when the stainless steel skin reflects the sun. The **Museum of Westward Expansion,** located below the arch, offers an overview of the Lewis and Clark Expedition. The Romanesque train shed at the venerable **St. Louis Union Station** (www.stlouisunion station.com), about a dozen blocks west of the arch, is now a vast shopping and restaurant mall.

Hannibal, Missouri, opens the world of Mark Twain with a complex of museums and the cave that Tom Sawyer and Becky Thatcher explored.

St. Paul, Minnesota, is the beginning or end of an Upper Mississippi cruise. The city retains a compact center where most of the great civic architecture is located, such as the Beaux Arts–style Minnesota State Capitol Building (1905); the riverfront **Minnesota Museum of American Art** (www.mmaa.org); and the top city attraction, the **James J. Hill House** (www.mnhs.org/places/sites/jjhh), an elaborate Romanesque mansion built in 1891 for the Great Northern Railway baron.

THE OHIO RIVER

Some river aficionados consider the scenic **Ohio** (www.ohioriverfdn.org) to be the most interesting Midwestern waterway because of its variety: its high bluffs, its attractive agricultural landscapes, the way it twists below Pittsburgh, its small rivers towns and rust belt cities with their active and abandoned industries, its wide variety of graceful bridges, the occasional cross-river ferries, and the impressive arrivals and departures at Pittsburgh and Cincinnati. Most cruises do not cover the entire Ohio River in one go, but include substantial portions such as the stretches between Cincinnati and Pittsburgh, or Cincinnati and Louisville to St. Louis or Memphis. Trips that travel the Cumberland and Tennessee rivers also include short stretches of the Lower Ohio en route to or from Memphis or St. Louis.

Most towns where boats call put out a warm welcome, showing visitors how the river affected their roles in the development of Midwestern culture, manufacturing, and transportation.

The Ohio River, Mile 0, begins at the western Pennsylvanian junction of the Monongahela and Allegheny rivers at **Fort Point,** the very tip of the pie that forms downtown Pittsburgh. From here it's 982 twisting river miles to Cairo Point, where the Ohio joins the Mississippi (see above), en route forming the borders of West Virginia, Ohio, Kentucky, Indiana, and Illinois.

The Ohio provides more water than the Upper Mississippi and itself is fed by the two Pittsburgh rivers, and by others such as the Kanawha, Big Sandy, Licking, Kentucky, Green, Wabash, Cumberland, and Tennessee. Eighteen locks and dams provide safe navigation, some replacing others that are now submerged in a constant effort to improve river commerce.

Architecturally rich downtown **Pittsburgh** is known as the Golden Triangle. It's clean and clear, with a compact center that's easy to navigate on foot. There's plenty to do if you're staying over before or after your cruise, including a visit to **Station Square** (www.stationsquare.com), the former Pittsburgh and Lake Erie Station and now a restaurant and shop complex; a ride on the scenic **Monongahela or Duquesne Inclines,** the last 2 of the 19 funicular railways that once connected the town with the residential hills; a visit to the **Carnegie Museum of Art** and the **Carnegie Museum of Natural History;** or a stop at the **Andy Warhol Museum,** just across the 7th Street Bridge from downtown (www.carnegiemuseums.org for all three). The **Frick Art and Historical Center** (www.frickart.org), former home of industrialist Henry Clay Frick, is about 20 minutes east of downtown.

Leaving Pittsburgh, the 172 miles to Marietta, Ohio, are among the loveliest rural stretches of river in the country. High banks define the stream, and where the woods part, farming fields spill right down to the water. **Marietta** is a quintessential Victorian riverfront community that still exudes its historical importance, and boats dock here adjacent to a lovely city park. The **Ohio River Museum** (www.ohiohistory.org/places/ohriver), minutes on foot from the landing, displays steamboat history in models, photographs, an excellent film, and the *W. P. Snyder, Jr.,* the last of the steam-powered stern-wheel towboats.

Maysville, Kentucky, derived its importance from firing bricks and manufacturing wrought-iron fences, gates, and ornamental street furnishings such as clocks, lampposts, benches, and signs. The town's prosperity is revealed in a 24-block, 160-building historic district that is on the National Register of Historic Places, featuring brick streets and Romanesque, Georgian, and Victorian styles, all walkable from the steamboat landing.

The graceful 1931 suspension bridge spanning the river near **Ripley,** Ohio, was the prototype for San Francisco's Golden Gate Bridge. Once an important stop on the Underground Railroad, Ripley also served as the setting for Eliza's escape in Harriet Beecher Stowe's *Uncle Tom's Cabin.*

Arriving at **Cincinnati,** Ohio, boats dock at the Public Landing opposite the Great American Ballpark and just upriver from the **Roebling Suspension Bridge,** once the world's longest suspension bridge and the 1868 prototype for Roebling's masterpiece, New York's Brooklyn Bridge. Just up from the landing, the downtown area is anchored by Fountain Square and the 1931 Art Deco **Carew Tower,** which offers a great view from the 48th floor. **Mt. Adams,** a short taxi ride up one of Cincinnati's seven hills, combines a trendy residential neighborhood, restaurants, a wonderful Ohio River overlook, and leafy Eden Park, where the **Cincinnati Art Museum** is located (www.cincinnatiartmuseum.org).

You'll likely hit several towns and cities below Cincinnati. **Madison,** Indiana, is a repository of 19th-century residential architecture. **Louisville,** Kentucky (www.goto louisville.com), is the home of the **Louisville Slugger Museum** (www.sluggermuseum. org) and the 1914 steamboat *Belle of Louisville* (www.belleoflouisville.org), the city's icon and the oldest river steamer in the U.S. An excursion will take you out to Bluegrass Country and **Churchill Downs** (www.churchilldowns.com), home of the annual Kentucky Derby. **Henderson,** Kentucky (www.hendersonky.org), boasts the WPA-constructed **John James Audubon Museum** (www.parks.ky.gov/stateparks/au/ index.htm), dedicated to the wildlife of the area and housing the largest collection of Audubon memorabilia, including original drawings, paintings, and watercolors, and a complete collection of his publications. Finally, **Paducah,** Kentucky, located at the junction of the Tennessee and Ohio rivers, is a barge and tow repair center and home to the **Museum of the American Quilters' Society** (www.quiltmuseum.org), a non-profit organization dedicated to the art, history, and heritage of hand-sewn and machine-made quilts.

Casting off from Paducah, your boat has just 47 miles to go to the meeting of the waters of the Ohio and Mississippi at Cairo Point. Depending on the itinerary, you'll make a hard right for an upriver sail to St. Louis or go gently left downriver to Memphis.

LINES SAILING THESE ROUTES   **Majestic America Line** (p. 359) is the major player here, along with **RiverBarge Excursions** (p. 369).

Index

5 REASONS WHY YOU SHOULD USE

FOR YOUR NEXT CRUISE VACATION

Planning a cruise today can be confusing and time consuming. Just Cruisin' Plus not only can arrange your cruise and even your transportation to your port city, but also may be able to save you money with our special fares with the cruise lines.

1 **SAVE MONEY!** - Our strong working relationships with the cruise lines and the latest in computer reservations technology enable us to access the most up-to-date information on how to get you the best value. As members of Vacation.com, North America's largest vacation selling network, we have added value amenities on hundreds of cruises.

2 **CRUISE ADVOCATE** – Your best interests are our priority. You will always have a person, not a computer monitor, with whom to communicate whenever you need help.

3 **CONVENIENCE** – We offer one-stop shopping for all of your travel arrangements.

4 **SERVICE** – Our agents are knowledgeable and active in the travel industry. Vacation.com provides education and training for our agents, equipping them with the tools to offer you the highest quality of service.

5 **OUR AGENTS WILL GO THE EXTRA MILE** – We will work for you and will do everything we can to meet your travel needs.

(615) 833-0922 • 1-800-888-0922
Email: info@justcruisinplus.com • Web: www.justcruisinplus.com

FROMMER'S® CRUISE GUIDES

Alaska Cruises & Ports of Call · Cruises & Ports of Call · European Cruises & Ports of Call

FROMMER'S® NATIONAL PARK GUIDES

Algonquin Provincial Park · National Parks of the American West · Yosemite and Sequoia & Kings
Banff & Jasper · Rocky Mountain · Canyon
Grand Canyon · Yellowstone & Grand Teton · Zion & Bryce Canyon

FROMMER'S® MEMORABLE WALKS

London · Paris · San Francisco
New York · Rome

FROMMER'S® WITH KIDS GUIDES

Chicago · National Parks · Toronto
Hawaii · New York City · Walt Disney World® & Orlando
Las Vegas · San Francisco · Washington, D.C.
London

SUZY GERSHMAN'S BORN TO SHOP GUIDES

France · London · Paris
Hong Kong, Shanghai & Beijing · New York · San Francisco
Italy

FROMMER'S® IRREVERENT GUIDES

Amsterdam · London · Rome
Boston · Los Angeles · San Francisco
Chicago · Manhattan · Walt Disney World®
Las Vegas · Paris · Washington, D.C.

FROMMER'S® BEST-LOVED DRIVING TOURS

Austria · Germany · Northern Italy
Britain · Ireland · Scotland
California · Italy · Spain
France · New England · Tuscany & Umbria

THE UNOFFICIAL GUIDES®

Adventure Travel in Alaska · Hawaii · Paris
Beyond Disney · Ireland · San Francisco
California with Kids · Las Vegas · South Florida including Miami &
Central Italy · London · the Keys
Chicago · Maui · Walt Disney World®
Cruises · Mexico's Best Beach Resorts · Walt Disney World® for
Disneyland® · Mini Mickey · Grown-ups
England · New Orleans · Walt Disney World® with Kids
Florida · New York City · Washington, D.C.
Florida with Kids

SPECIAL-INTEREST TITLES

Athens Past & Present · Frommer's Exploring America by RV
Best Places to Raise Your Family · Frommer's NYC Free & Dirt Cheap
Cities Ranked & Rated · Frommer's Road Atlas Europe
500 Places to Take Your Kids Before They Grow Up · Frommer's Road Atlas Ireland
Frommer's Best Day Trips from London · Great Escapes From NYC Without Wheels
Frommer's Best RV & Tent Campgrounds · Retirement Places Rated
  in the U.S.A.

FROMMER'S® PHRASEFINDER DICTIONARY GUIDES

French · Italian · Spanish

I don't speak sign language.

A hotel can close for all kinds of reasons.
Our Guarantee ensures that if your hotel's undergoing construction, we'll let you know in advance. In fact, we cover your entire travel experience. See www.travelocity.com/guarantee for details.

travelocity®
You'll never roam alone.